SABAN'S

MIGHTY MORPHIN
POWER RANGERS™

ARCHIVE

BOOM!
STUDIOS

ROSS RICHIE CEO & Founder
JOY HUFFMAN CFO
MATT GAGNON Editor-in-Chief
FILIP SABLIK President, Publishing & Marketing
STEPHEN CHRISTY President, Development
LANCE KREITER Vice President, Licensing & Merchandising
PHIL BARBARO Vice President, Finance & Human Resources
ARUNE SINGH Vice President, Marketing
BRYCE CARLSON Vice President, Editorial & Creative Strategy
SCOTT NEWMAN Manager, Production Design
KATE HENNING Manager, Operations
SPENCER SIMPSON Manager, Sales
SIERRA HAHN Executive Editor
JEANINE SCHAEFER Executive Editor
DAFNA PLEBAN Senior Editor
SHANNON WATTERS Senior Editor
ERIC HARBURN Senior Editor
WHITNEY LEOPARD Editor
CAMERON CHITTOCK Editor
CHRIS ROSA Editor
MATTHEW LEVINE Editor

SOPHIE PHILIPS-ROBERTS Assistant Editor
GAVIN GRONENTHAL Assistant Editor
MICHAEL MOCCIO Assistant Editor
AMANDA LaFRANCO Executive Assistant
JILLIAN CRAB Design Coordinator
MICHELLE ANKLEY Design Coordinator
KARA LEOPARD Production Designer
MARIE KRUPINA Production Designer
GRACE PARK Production Design Assistant
CHELSEA ROBERTS Production Design Assistant
SAMANTHA KNAPP Production Design Assistant
ELIZABETH LOUGHRIDGE Accounting Coordinator
STEPHANIE HOCUTT Social Media Coordinator
JOSÉ MEZA Event Coordinator
HOLLY AITCHISON Operations Coordinator
MEGAN CHRISTOPHER Operations Assistant
RODRIGO HERNANDEZ Mailroom Assistant
MORGAN PERRY Direct Market Representative
CAT O'GRADY Marketing Assistant
BREANNA SARPY Executive Assistant

MIGHTY MORPHIN POWER RANGERS ARCHIVE Volume Two, January 2019. Published by BOOM! Studios, a division of Boom Entertainment, Inc. ™ and © 2019 SCG Power Rangers LLC and Hasbro. All rights reserved. Used Under Authorization. BOOM! Studios™ and the BOOM! Studios logo are trademarks of Boom Entertainment, Inc., registered in various countries and categories. All characters, events, and institutions depicted herein are fictional. Any similarity between any of the names, characters, persons, events, and/or institutions in this publication to actual names, characters, and persons, whether living or dead, events, and/or institutions is unintended and purely coincidental. BOOM! Studios does not read or accept unsolicited submissions of ideas, stories, or artwork.

BOOM! Studios, 5670 Wilshire Boulevard, Suite 400, Los Angeles, CA 90036-5679. Printed in China. First Printing.

ISBN: 978-1-68415-313-8, eISBN: 978-1-64144-166-7

MIGHTY MORPHIN POWER RANGERS ARCHIVE
VOLUME TWO

Designer
EVAN METCALF

Collection Assistant Editor
MICHAEL MOCCIO

Collection Editor
DAFNA PLEBAN

Senior Vice President, Franchise Development & Production, Power Rangers
BRIAN CASENTINI

Hasbro Publishing Story Team
**MELISSA FLORES, JASON BISCHOFF,
PAUL STRICKLAND, MEGAN RUGGIERO,
ED LANE, and BETH ARTALE**

TABLE OF CONTENTS

PAPERCUTZ

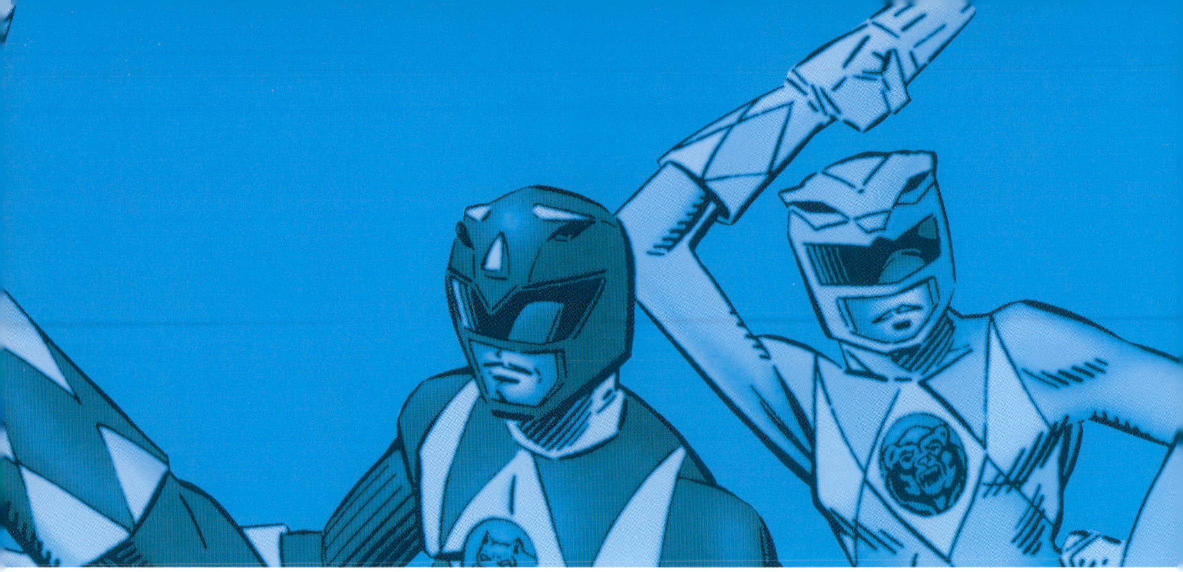

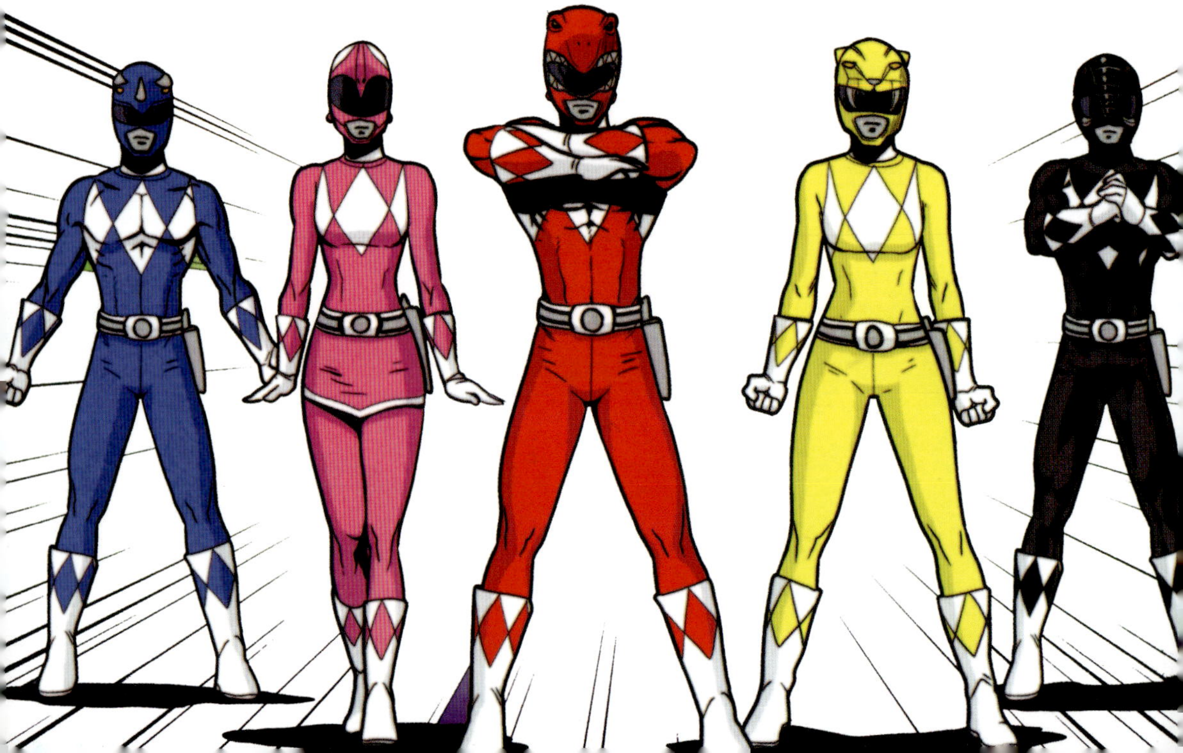

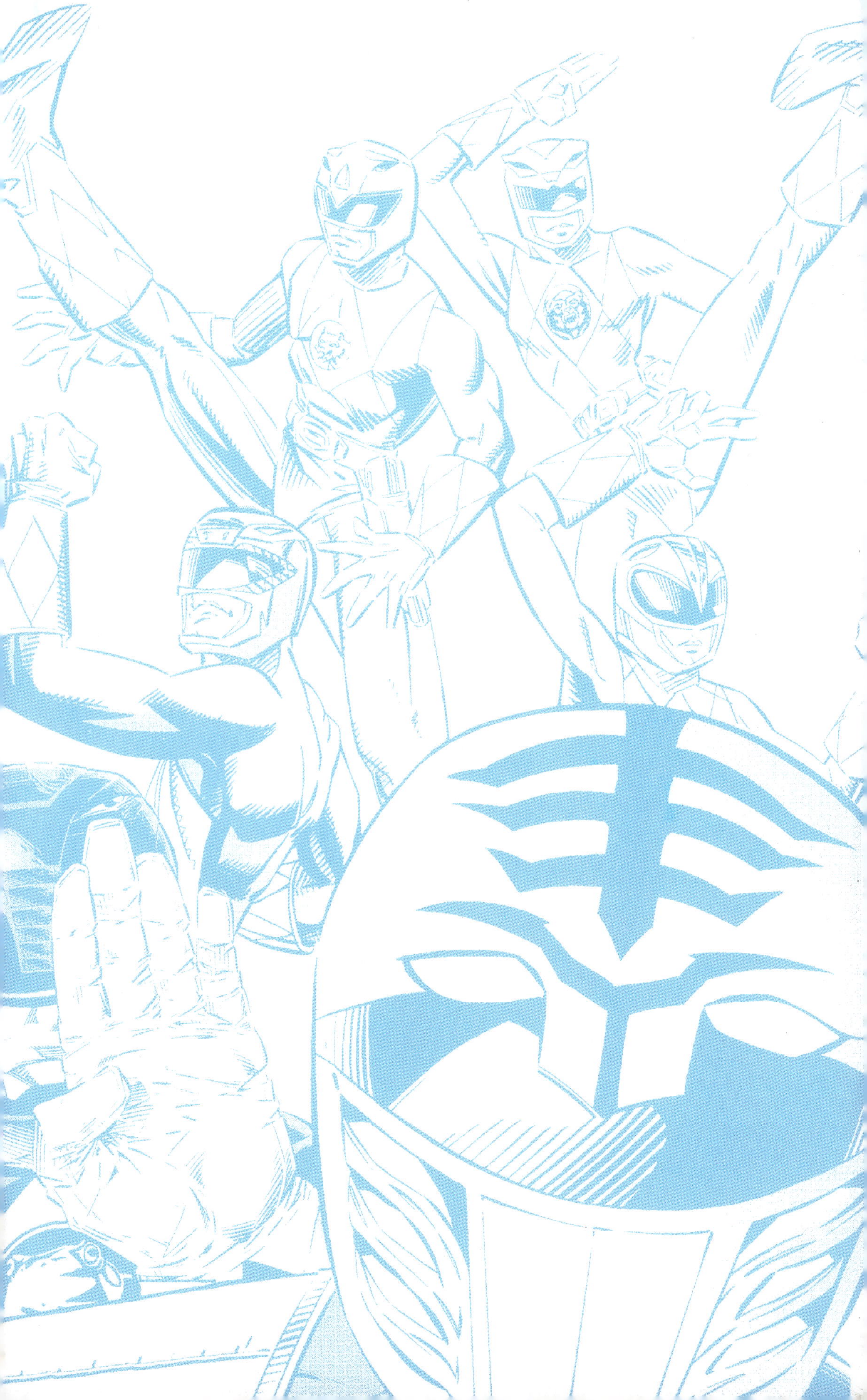

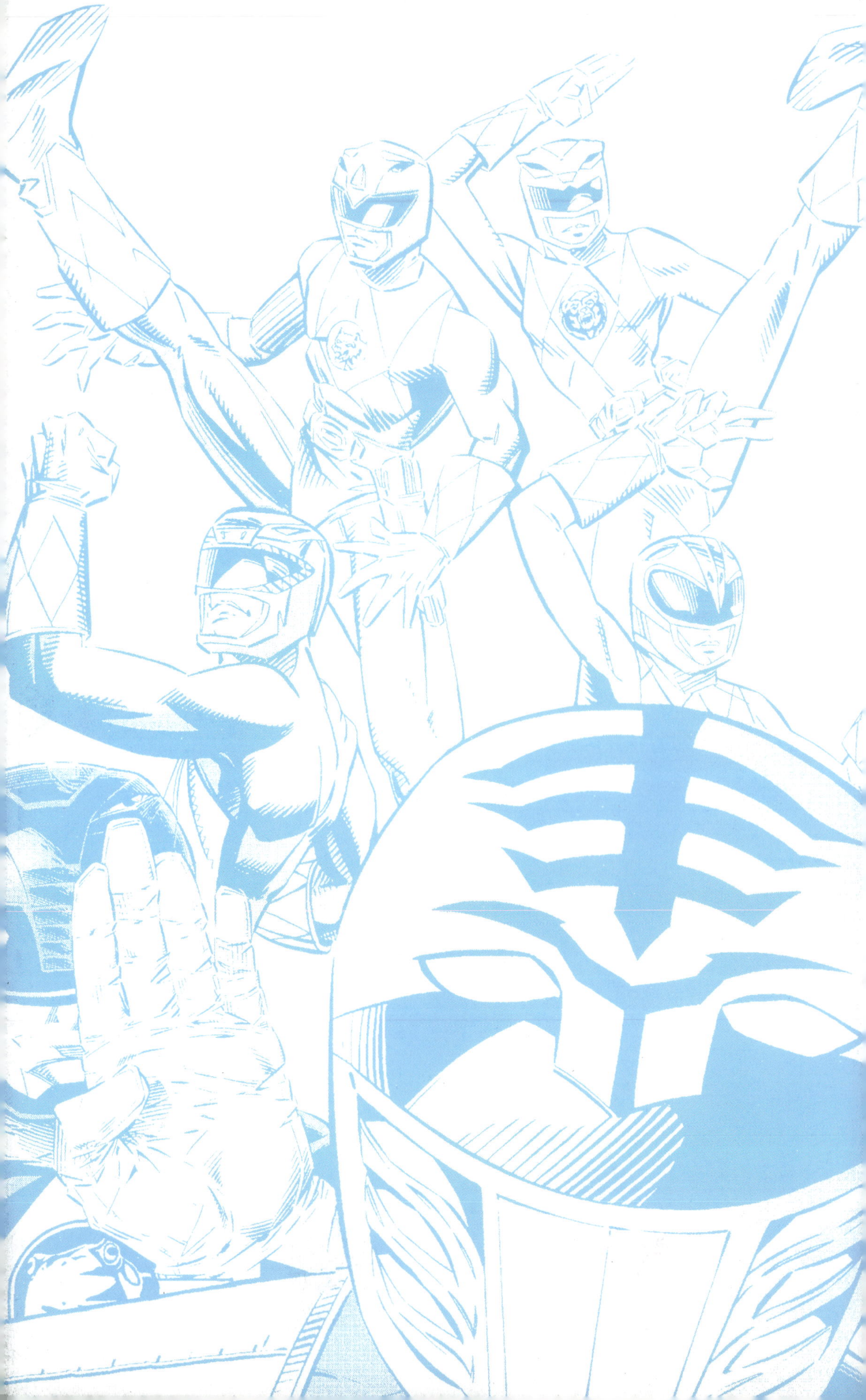

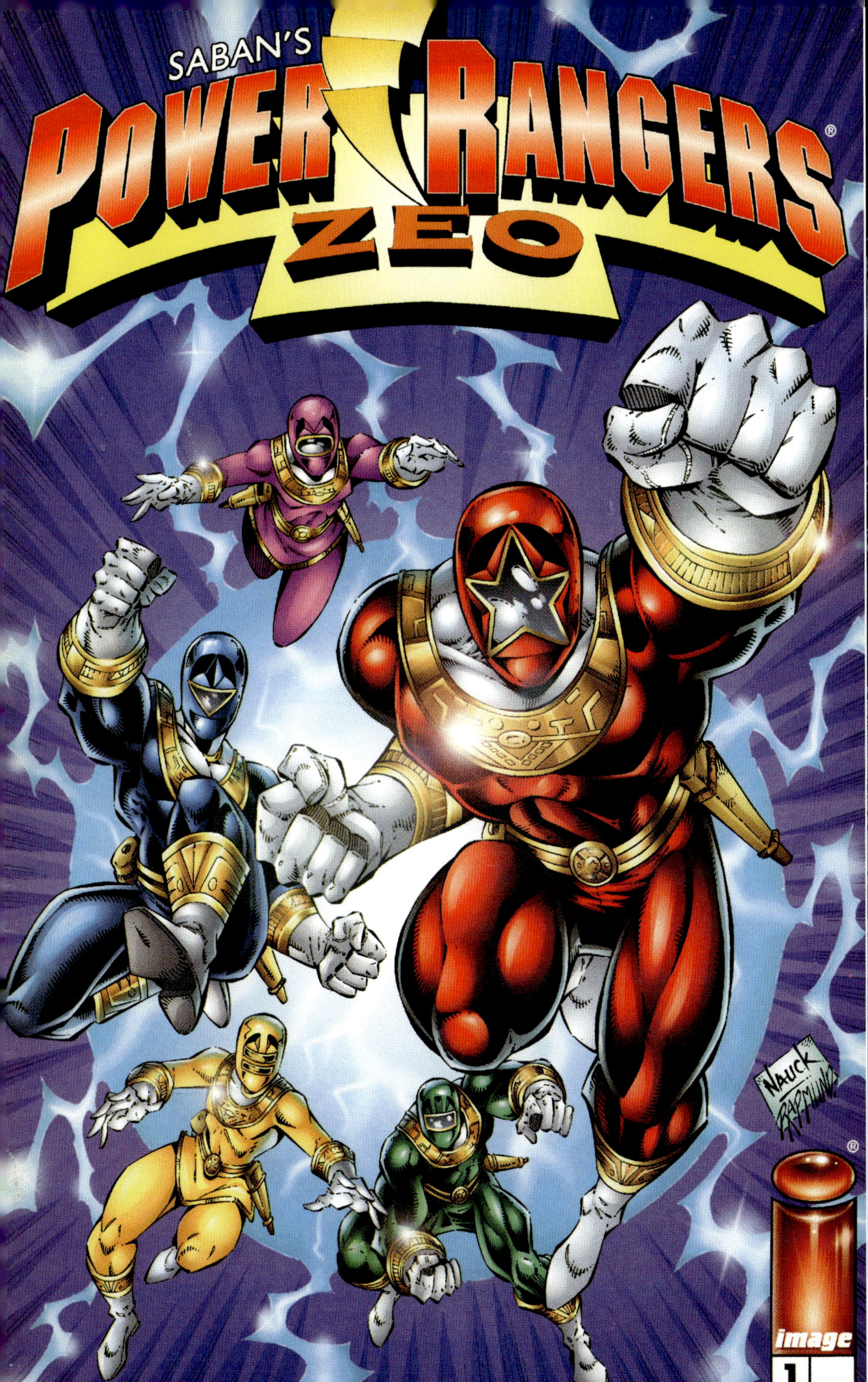
SABAN'S
POWER RANGERS®
ZEO
NAUCK
RAPMUND
image
1

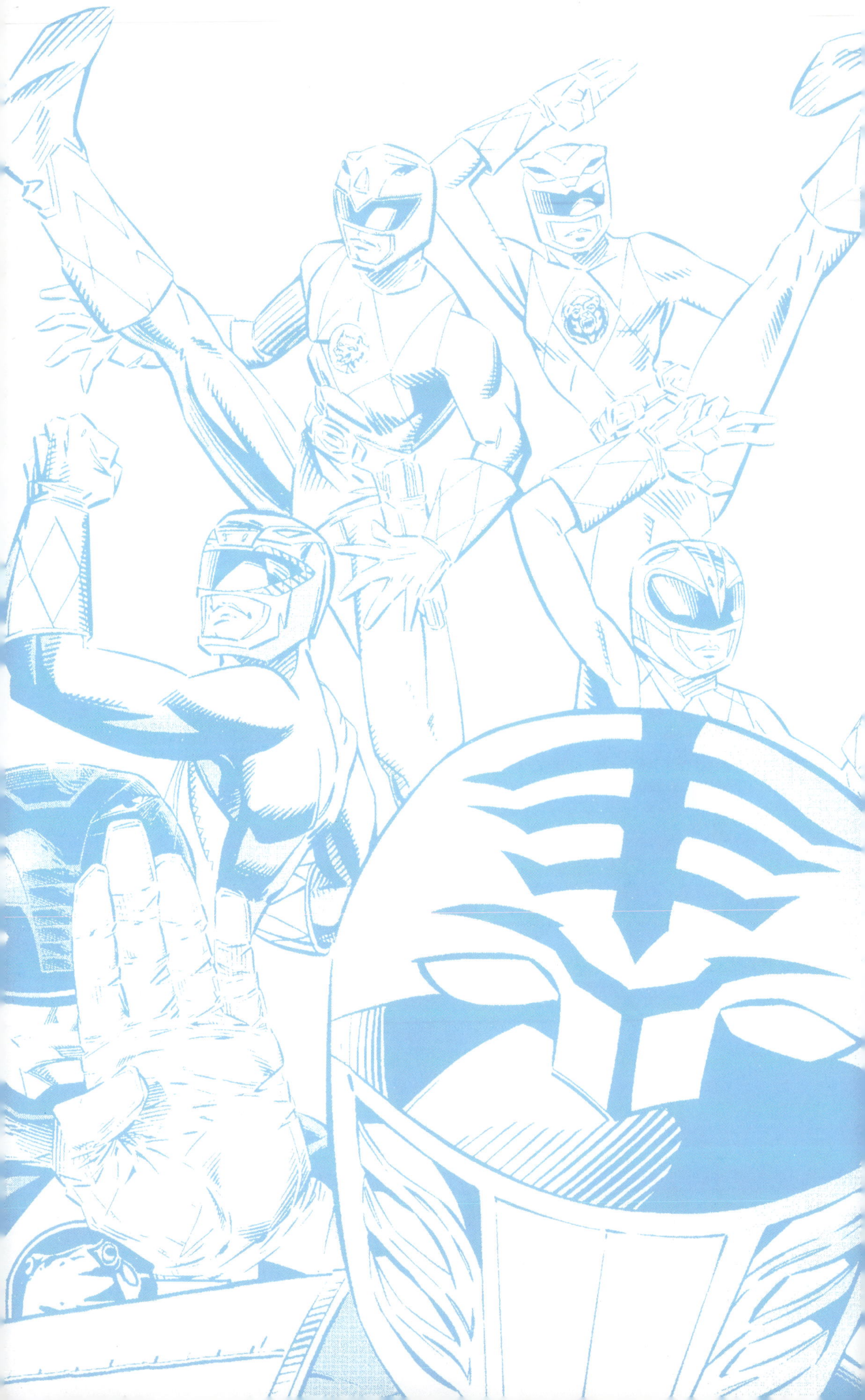

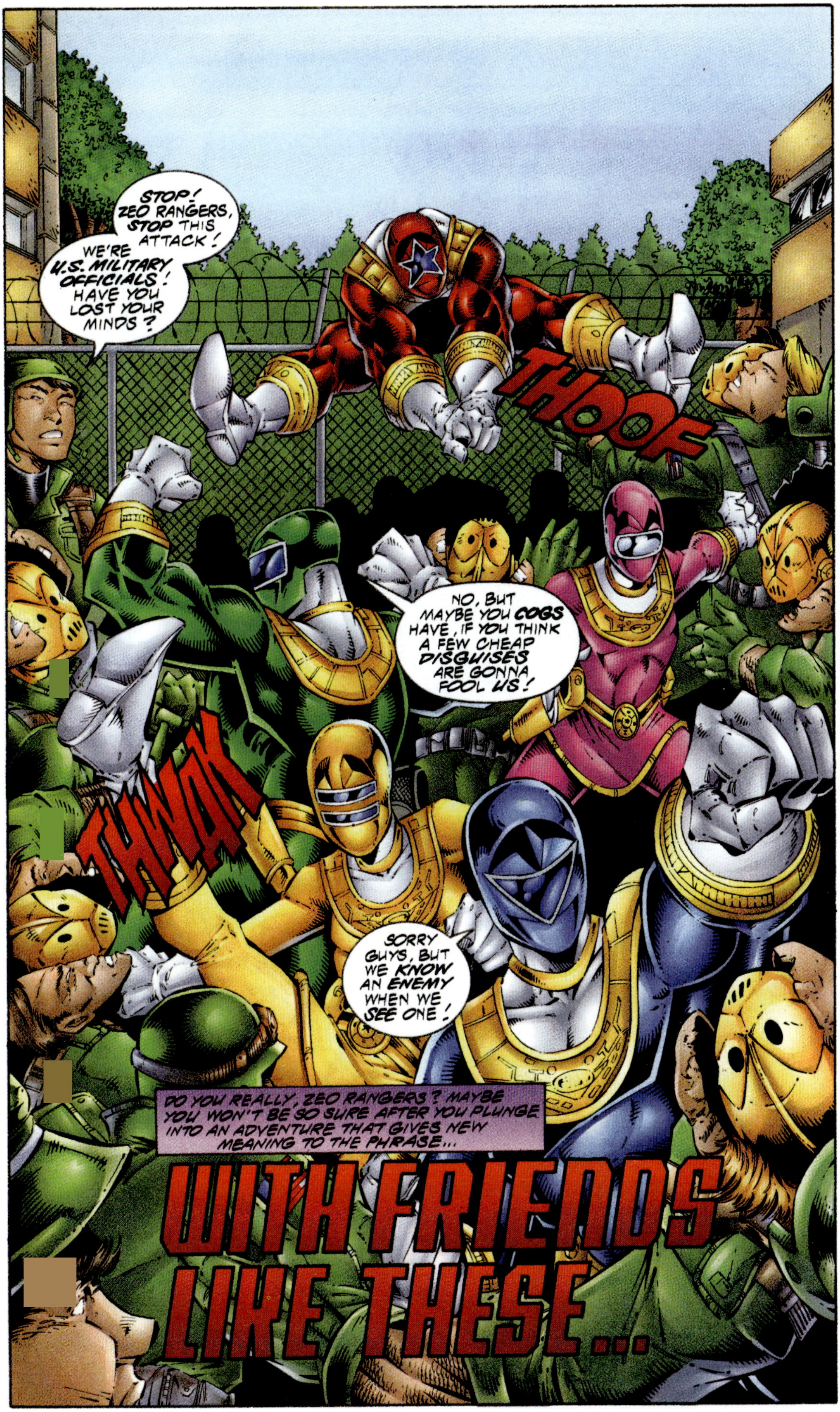
STOP! ZEO RANGERS, STOP THIS ATTACK!
WE'RE U.S. MILITARY OFFICIALS! HAVE YOU LOST YOUR MINDS?
THOOF
NO, BUT MAYBE YOU COGS HAVE, IF YOU THINK A FEW CHEAP DISGUISES ARE GONNA FOOL US!
THWAK
SORRY GUYS, BUT WE KNOW AN ENEMY WHEN WE SEE ONE!
DO YOU REALLY, ZEO RANGERS? MAYBE YOU WON'T BE SO SURE AFTER YOU PLUNGE INTO AN ADVENTURE THAT GIVES NEW MEANING TO THE PHRASE...
WITH FRIENDS LIKE THESE...

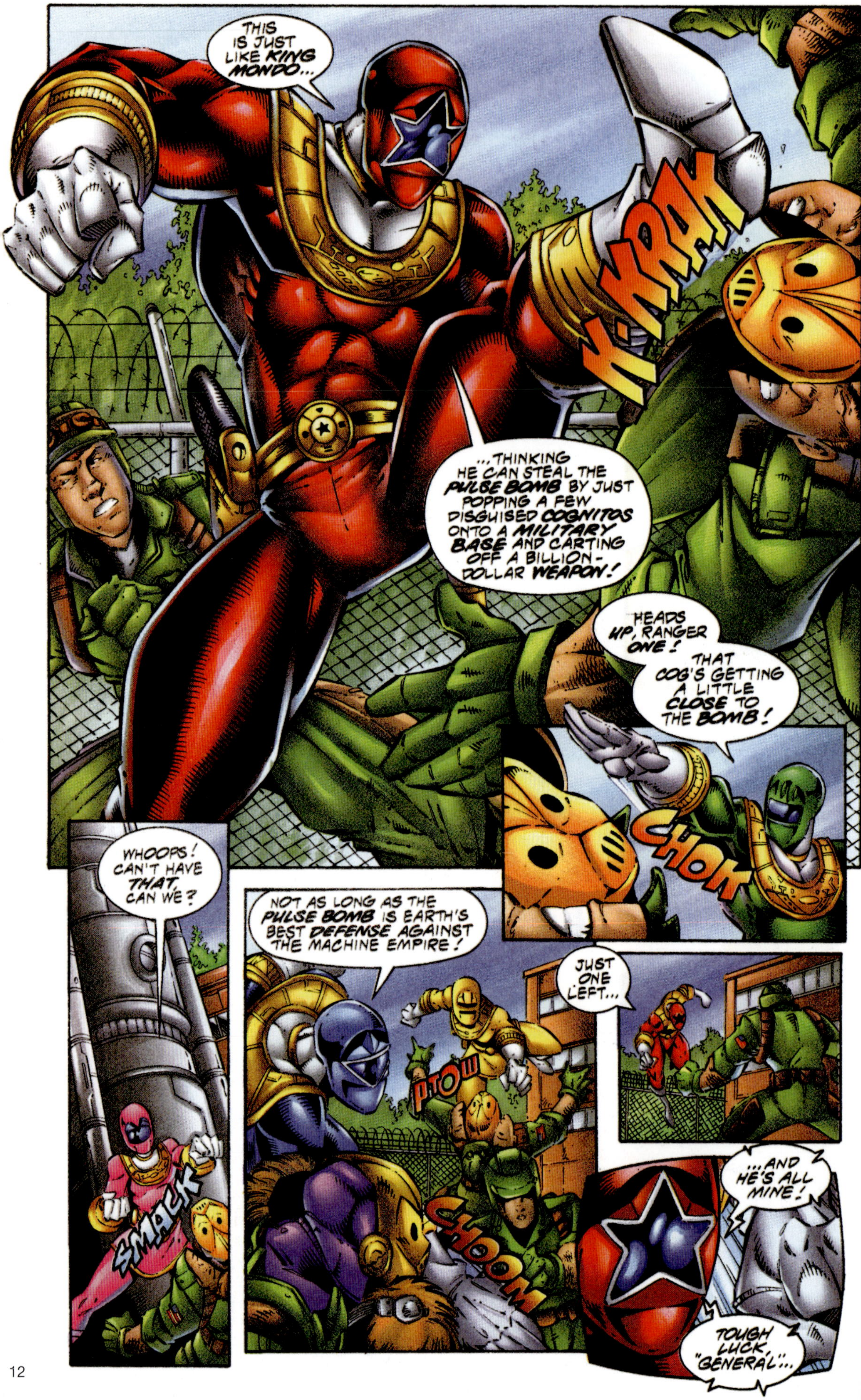
THIS IS JUST LIKE KING MONDO...
KKRAK
...THINKING HE CAN STEAL THE PULSE BOMB BY JUST POPPING A FEW DISGUISED COGNITOS ONTO A MILITARY BASE AND CARTING OFF A BILLION-DOLLAR WEAPON!
HEADS UP, RANGER ONE!
THAT COG'S GETTING A LITTLE CLOSE TO THE BOMB!
CHOK
WHOOPS! CAN'T HAVE THAT, CAN WE?
SMACK
NOT AS LONG AS THE PULSE BOMB IS EARTH'S BEST DEFENSE AGAINST THE MACHINE EMPIRE!
PTOW
CHOOM
JUST ONE LEFT...
...AND HE'S ALL MINE!
TOUGH LUCK, "GENERAL"...

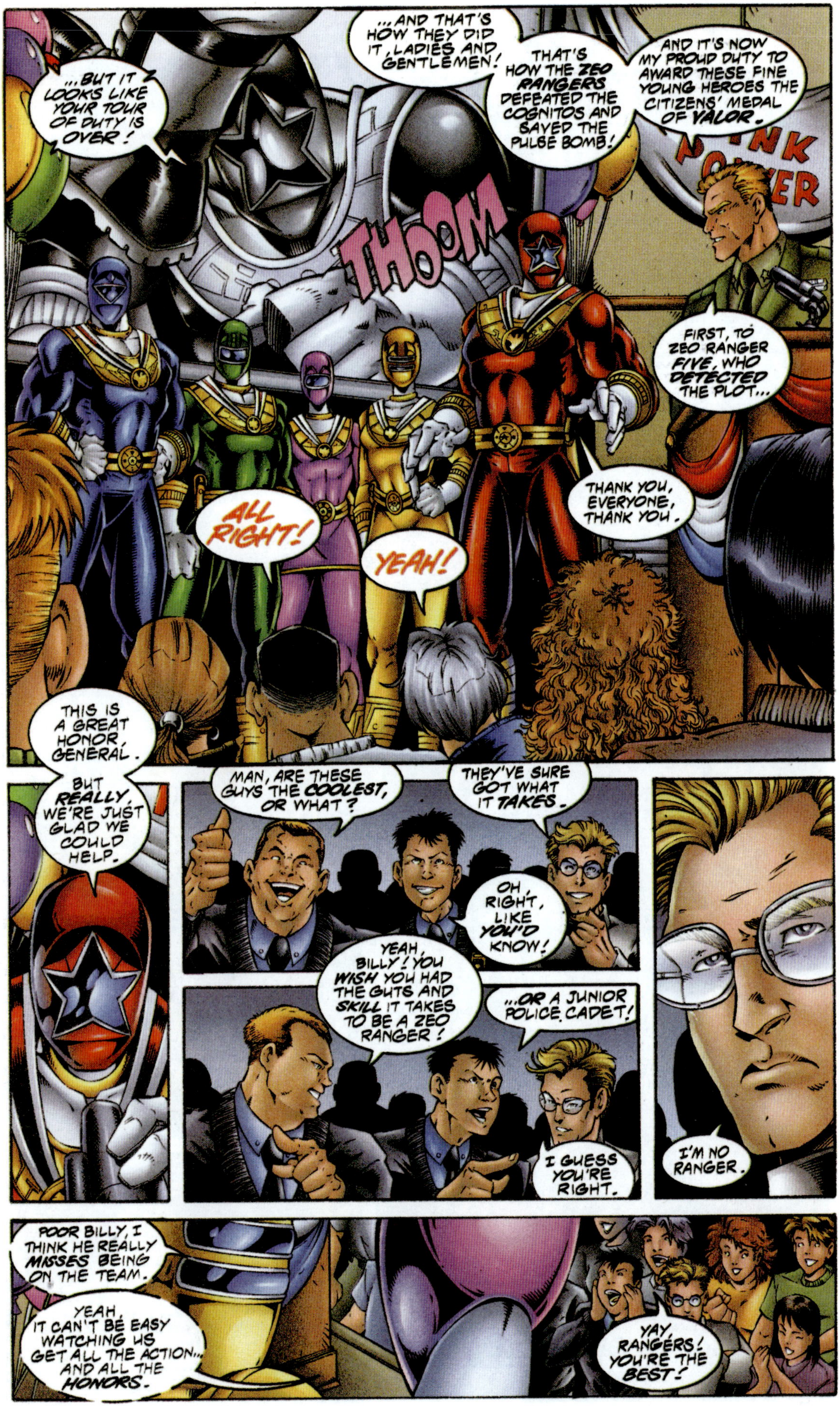
...BUT IT LOOKS LIKE YOUR TOUR OF DUTY IS OVER!
...AND THAT'S HOW THEY DID IT, LADIES AND GENTLEMEN!
THAT'S HOW THE ZEO RANGERS DEFEATED THE COGNITOS AND SAVED THE PULSE BOMB!
AND IT'S NOW MY PROUD DUTY TO AWARD THESE FINE YOUNG HEROES THE CITIZENS' MEDAL OF VALOR.
THOOM
FIRST, TO ZEO RANGER FIVE, WHO DETECTED THE PLOT...
THANK YOU, EVERYONE, THANK YOU.
ALL RIGHT!
YEAH!
THIS IS A GREAT HONOR, GENERAL.
BUT REALLY, WE'RE JUST GLAD WE COULD HELP.
MAN, ARE THESE GUYS THE COOLEST, OR WHAT?
THEY'VE SURE GOT WHAT IT TAKES.
OH, RIGHT, LIKE YOU'D KNOW!
YEAH, BILLY! YOU WISH YOU HAD THE GUTS AND SKILL IT TAKES TO BE A ZEO RANGER!
...OR A JUNIOR POLICE CADET!
I GUESS YOU'RE RIGHT.
I'M NO RANGER.
POOR BILLY, I THINK HE REALLY MISSES BEING ON THE TEAM.
YEAH, IT CAN'T BE EASY WATCHING US GET ALL THE ACTION... AND ALL THE HONORS.
YAY, RANGERS! YOU'RE THE BEST!

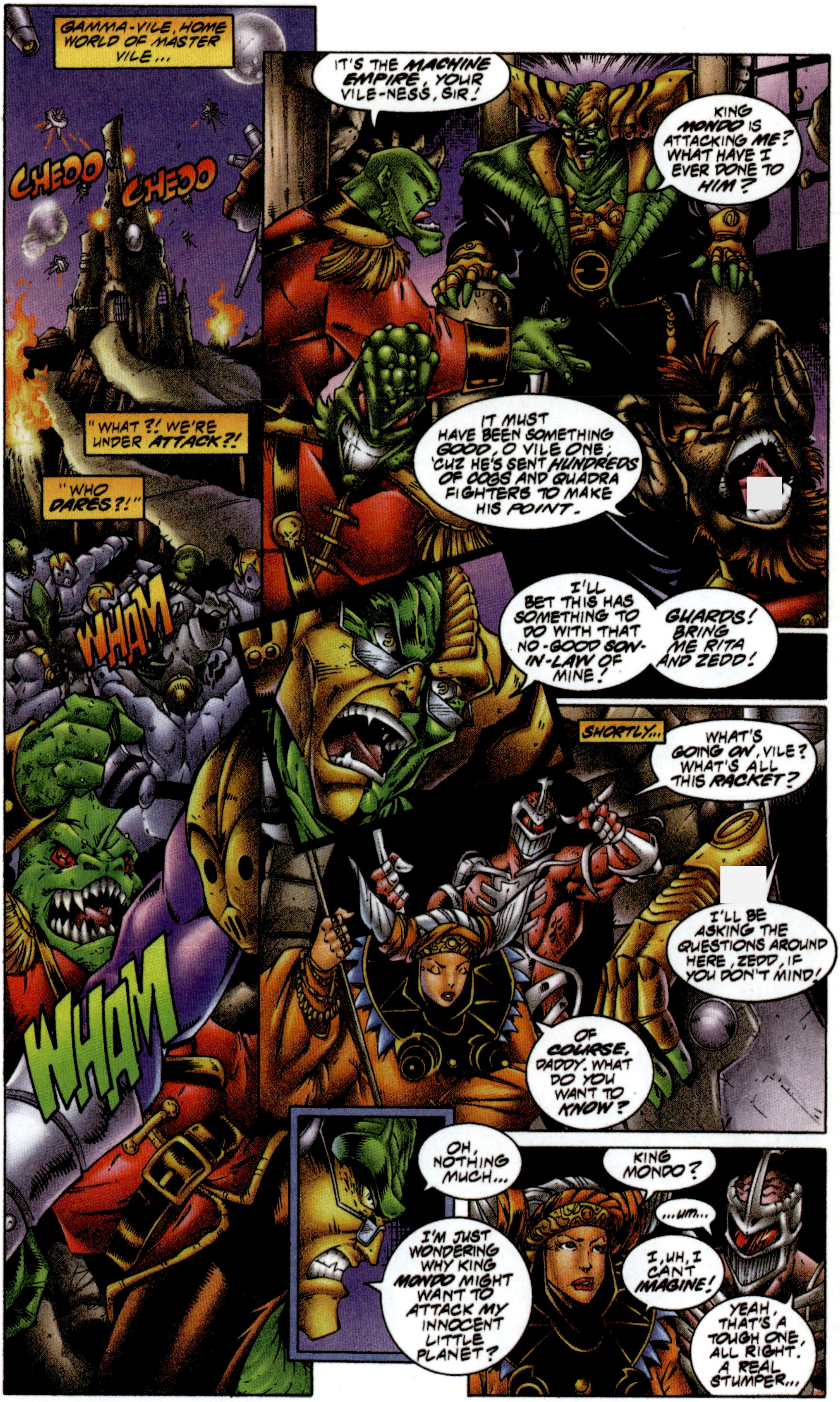
GAMMA-VILE, HOME WORLD OF MASTER VILE...
CHEOO CHEOO
"WHAT ?! WE'RE UNDER ATTACK?!"
"WHO DARES?!"
WHAM
WHAM
IT'S THE MACHINE EMPIRE, YOUR VILE-NESS, SIR!
KING MONDO IS ATTACKING ME? WHAT HAVE I EVER DONE TO HIM?
IT MUST HAVE BEEN SOMETHING GOOD, O VILE ONE; 'CUZ HE'S SENT HUNDREDS OF COGS AND QUADRA FIGHTERS TO MAKE HIS POINT.
I'LL BET THIS HAS SOMETHING TO DO WITH THAT NO-GOOD SON-IN-LAW OF MINE!
GUARDS! BRING ME RITA AND ZEDD!
SHORTLY...
WHAT'S GOING ON, VILE? WHAT'S ALL THIS RACKET?
I'LL BE ASKING THE QUESTIONS AROUND HERE, ZEDD, IF YOU DON'T MIND!
OF COURSE, DADDY. WHAT DO YOU WANT TO KNOW?
OH, NOTHING MUCH...
I'M JUST WONDERING WHY KING MONDO MIGHT WANT TO ATTACK MY INNOCENT LITTLE PLANET?
KING MONDO?
...UM...
I, UH, I CAN'T IMAGINE!
YEAH, THAT'S A TOUGH ONE, ALL RIGHT. A REAL STUMPER...

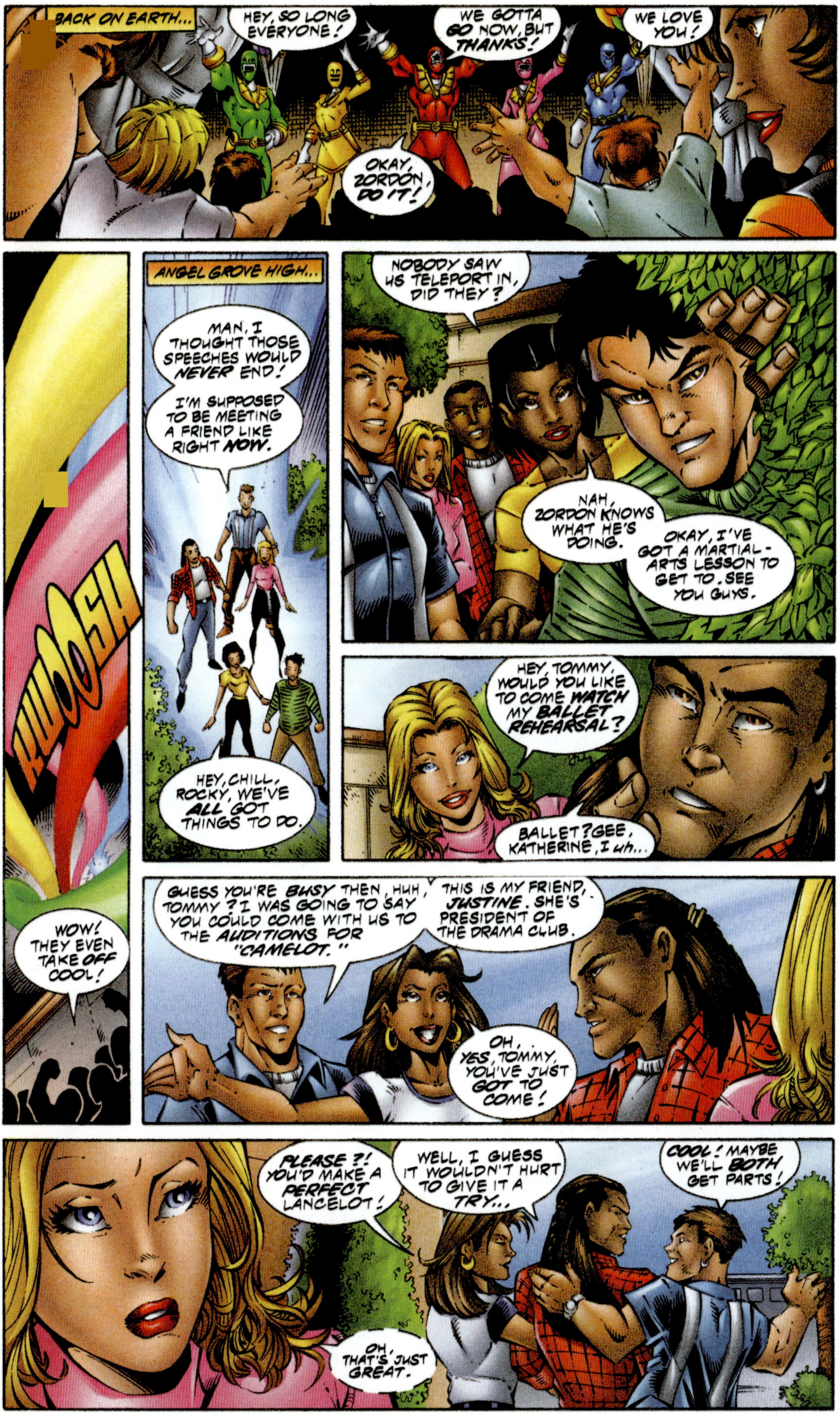
BACK ON EARTH...
HEY, SO LONG EVERYONE!
WE GOTTA GO NOW, BUT THANKS!
WE LOVE YOU!
OKAY, ZORDON, DO IT!
WHOOSH
WOW! THEY EVEN TAKE OFF COOL!
ANGEL GROVE HIGH...
MAN, I THOUGHT THOSE SPEECHES WOULD NEVER END!
I'M SUPPOSED TO BE MEETING A FRIEND LIKE RIGHT NOW.
HEY, CHILL, ROCKY, WE'VE ALL GOT THINGS TO DO.
NOBODY SAW US TELEPORT IN, DID THEY?
NAH, ZORDON KNOWS WHAT HE'S DOING.
OKAY, I'VE GOT A MARTIAL-ARTS LESSON TO GET TO. SEE YOU GUYS.
HEY, TOMMY, WOULD YOU LIKE TO COME WATCH MY BALLET REHEARSAL?
BALLET? GEE, KATHERINE, I uh...
GUESS YOU'RE BUSY THEN, HUH, TOMMY? I WAS GOING TO SAY YOU COULD COME WITH US TO THE AUDITIONS FOR "CAMELOT."
THIS IS MY FRIEND, JUSTINE. SHE'S PRESIDENT OF THE DRAMA CLUB.
OH, YES, TOMMY, YOU'VE JUST GOT TO COME!
PLEASE?! YOU'D MAKE A PERFECT LANCELOT!
WELL, I GUESS IT WOULDN'T HURT TO GIVE IT A TRY...
COOL! MAYBE WE'LL BOTH GET PARTS!
OH, THAT'S JUST GREAT.

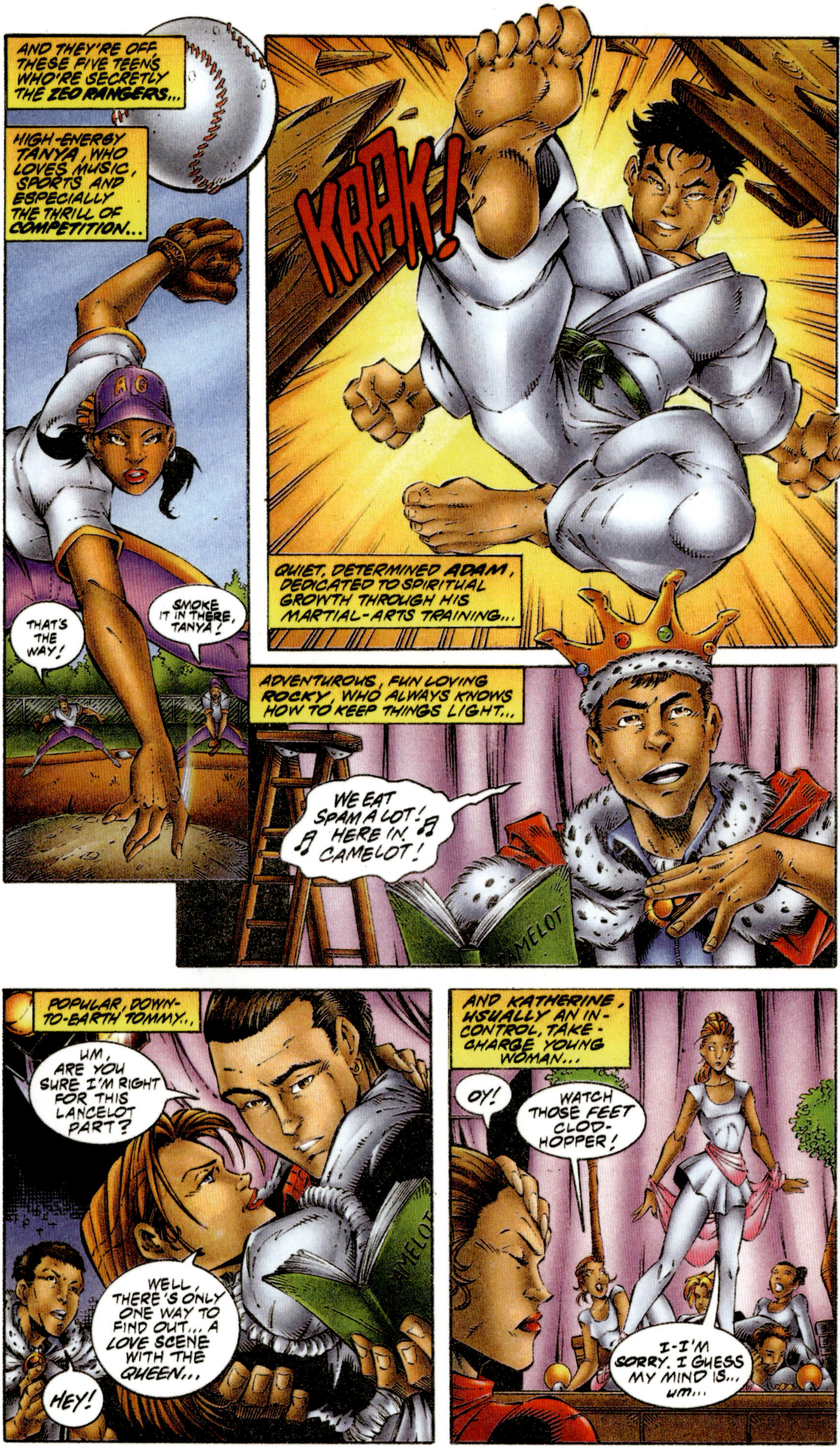
AND THEY'RE OFF. THESE FIVE TEENS WHO'RE SECRETLY THE ZEO RANGERS...
HIGH-ENERGY TANYA, WHO LOVES MUSIC, SPORTS AND ESPECIALLY THE THRILL OF COMPETITION...
THAT'S THE WAY!
SMOKE IT IN THERE, TANYA!
KRAK!
QUIET, DETERMINED ADAM, DEDICATED TO SPIRITUAL GROWTH THROUGH HIS MARTIAL-ARTS TRAINING...
ADVENTUROUS, FUN LOVING ROCKY, WHO ALWAYS KNOWS HOW TO KEEP THINGS LIGHT...
WE EAT SPAM A LOT! HERE IN CAMELOT!
POPULAR, DOWN-TO-EARTH TOMMY...
UM, ARE YOU SURE I'M RIGHT FOR THIS LANCELOT PART?
WELL, THERE'S ONLY ONE WAY TO FIND OUT... A LOVE SCENE WITH THE QUEEN...
HEY!
AND KATHERINE, USUALLY AN IN-CONTROL, TAKE-CHARGE YOUNG WOMAN...
OY!
WATCH THOSE FEET CLOD-HOPPER!
I-I'M SORRY. I GUESS MY MIND IS... UM...

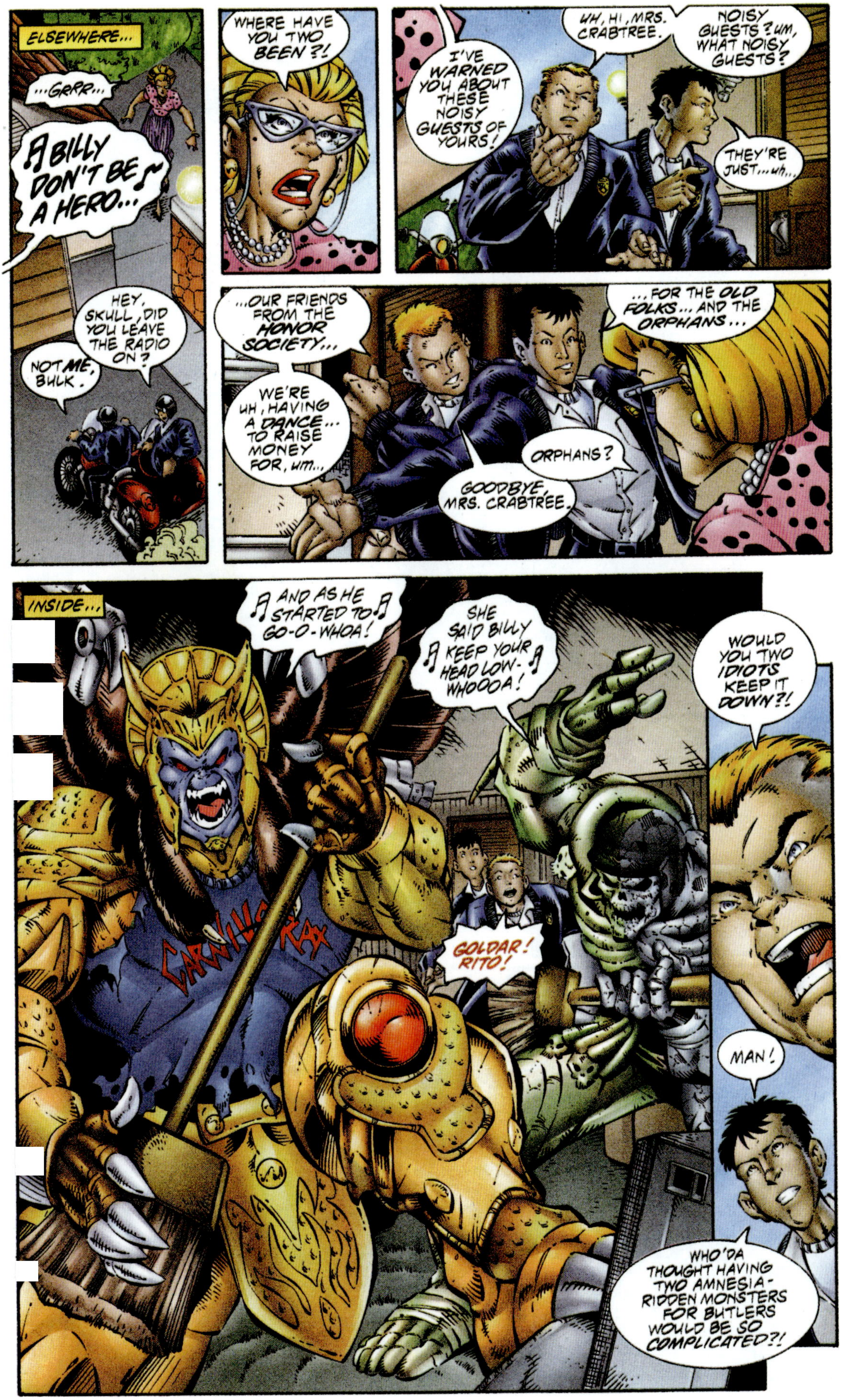
ELSEWHERE...
...GRRR...
BILLY DON'T BE A HERO...
WHERE HAVE YOU TWO BEEN?!
I'VE WARNED YOU ABOUT THESE NOISY GUESTS OF YOURS!
UH, HI, MRS. CRABTREE.
NOISY GUESTS? UM, WHAT NOISY GUESTS?
THEY'RE JUST... UH...
HEY, SKULL, DID YOU LEAVE THE RADIO ON?
NOT ME, BULK.
...OUR FRIENDS FROM THE HONOR SOCIETY...
WE'RE UH, HAVING A DANCE... TO RAISE MONEY FOR, UM...
...FOR THE OLD FOLKS... AND THE ORPHANS...
ORPHANS?
GOODBYE, MRS. CRABTREE.
INSIDE...
AND AS HE STARTED TO GO-O-WHOA!
SHE SAID BILLY KEEP YOUR HEAD LOW-WHOOOA!
WOULD YOU TWO IDIOTS KEEP IT DOWN?!
GOLDAR! RITO!
CARNIVORAX
MAN!
WHO'DA THOUGHT HAVING TWO AMNESIA-RIDDEN MONSTERS FOR BUTLERS WOULD BE SO COMPLICATED?!

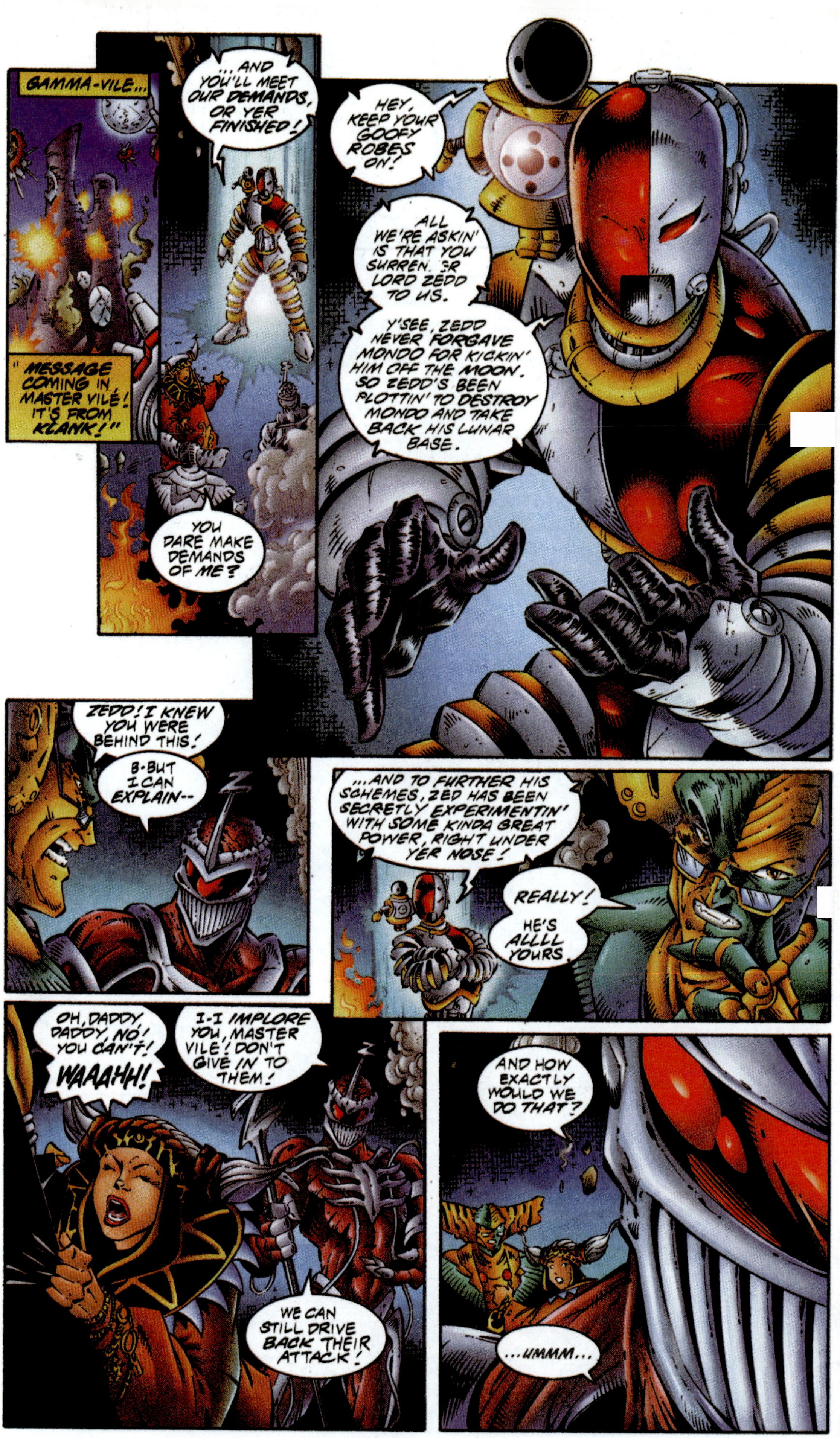

GAMMA-VILE...
...AND YOU'LL MEET OUR DEMANDS, OR YER FINISHED!
"MESSAGE COMING IN MASTER VILÉ! IT'S FROM KLANK!"
YOU DARE MAKE DEMANDS OF ME?
HEY, KEEP YOUR GOOFY ROBES ON!
ALL WE'RE ASKIN' IS THAT YOU SURREN ER LORD ZEDD TO US.
Y'SEE, ZEDD NEVER FORGAVE MONDO FOR KICKIN' HIM OFF THE MOON. SO ZEDD'S BEEN PLOTTIN' TO DESTROY MONDO AND TAKE BACK HIS LUNAR BASE.
ZEDD! I KNEW YOU WERE BEHIND THIS!
B-BUT I CAN EXPLAIN--
...AND TO FURTHER HIS SCHEMES, ZED HAS BEEN SECRETLY EXPERIMENTIN' WITH SOME KINDA GREAT POWER, RIGHT UNDER YER NOSE!
REALLY!
HE'S ALLLL YOURS.
OH, DADDY, DADDY, NO! YOU CAN'T! WAAAHH!
I-I IMPLORE YOU, MASTER VILE! DON'T GIVE IN TO THEM!
WE CAN STILL DRIVE BACK THEIR ATTACK!
AND HOW EXACTLY WOULD WE DO THAT?
...UMMM...

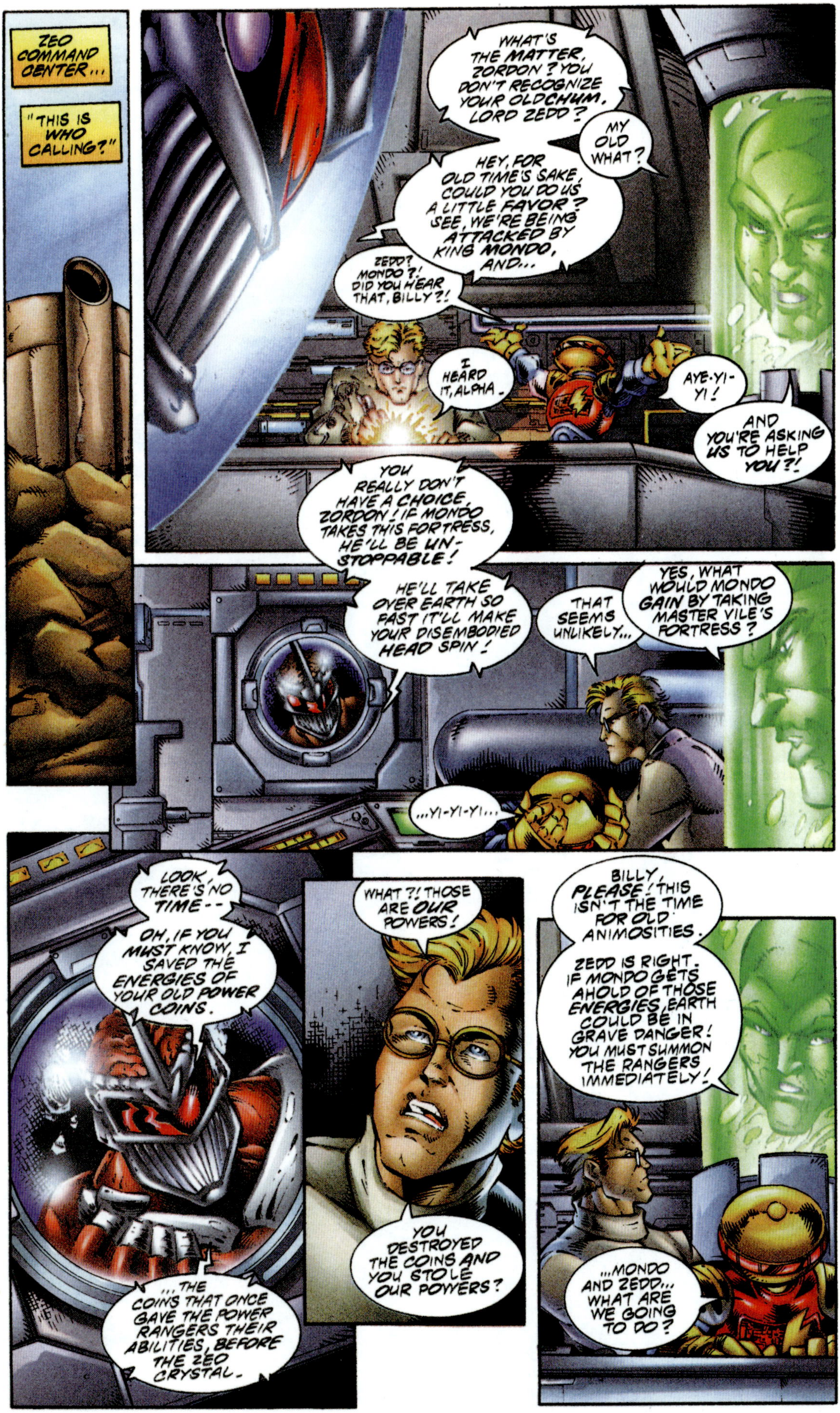

ZEO COMMAND CENTER...
"THIS IS WHO CALLING?"
WHAT'S THE MATTER, ZORDON? YOU DON'T RECOGNIZE YOUR OLD CHUM, LORD ZEDD?
MY OLD WHAT?
HEY, FOR OLD TIME'S SAKE, COULD YOU DO US A LITTLE FAVOR? SEE, WE'RE BEING ATTACKED BY KING MONDO, AND...
ZEDD?! MONDO?! DID YOU HEAR THAT, BILLY?!
I HEARD IT, ALPHA.
AYE-YI-YI!
AND YOU'RE ASKING US TO HELP YOU?!
YOU REALLY DON'T HAVE A CHOICE, ZORDON! IF MONDO TAKES THIS FORTRESS, HE'LL BE UN-STOPPABLE!
HE'LL TAKE OVER EARTH SO FAST IT'LL MAKE YOUR DISEMBODIED HEAD SPIN!
THAT SEEMS UNLIKELY...
YES, WHAT WOULD MONDO GAIN BY TAKING MASTER VILE'S FORTRESS?
...YI-YI-YI...
LOOK, THERE'S NO TIME--
OH, IF YOU MUST KNOW, I SAVED THE ENERGIES OF YOUR OLD POWER COINS.
...THE COINS THAT ONCE GAVE THE POWER RANGERS THEIR ABILITIES, BEFORE THE ZEO CRYSTAL.
WHAT?! THOSE ARE OUR POWERS!
YOU DESTROYED THE COINS AND YOU STOLE OUR POWERS?
BILLY, PLEASE! THIS ISN'T THE TIME FOR OLD ANIMOSITIES.
ZEDD IS RIGHT. IF MONDO GETS AHOLD OF THOSE ENERGIES, EARTH COULD BE IN GRAVE DANGER! YOU MUST SUMMON THE RANGERS IMMEDIATELY!
...MONDO AND ZEDD... WHAT ARE WE GOING TO DO?

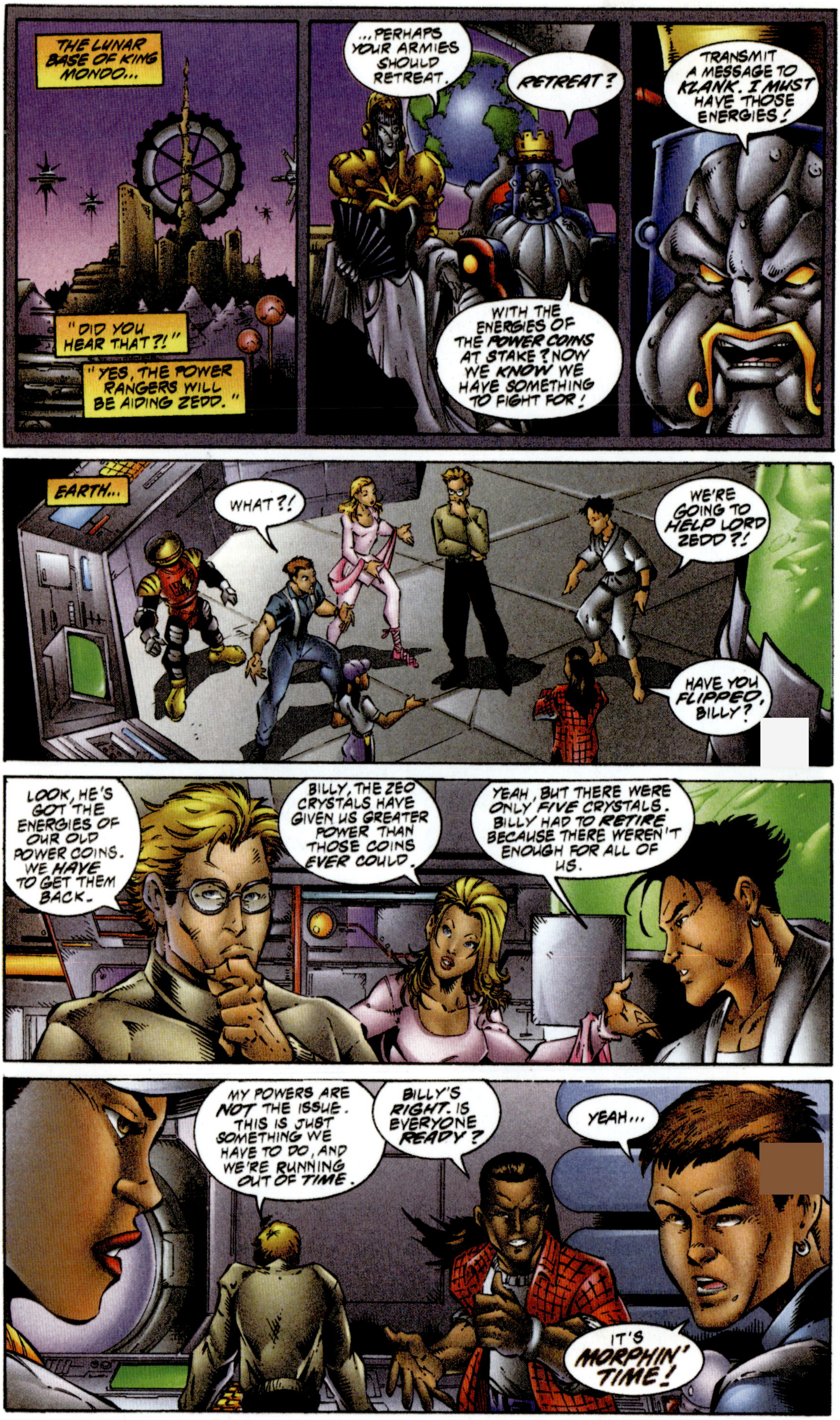
THE LUNAR BASE OF KING MONDO...
"DID YOU HEAR THAT?!"
"YES, THE POWER RANGERS WILL BE AIDING ZEDD."
...PERHAPS YOUR ARMIES SHOULD RETREAT.
RETREAT?
WITH THE ENERGIES OF THE POWER COINS AT STAKE? NOW WE KNOW WE HAVE SOMETHING TO FIGHT FOR!
TRANSMIT A MESSAGE TO KLANK. I MUST HAVE THOSE ENERGIES!
EARTH...
WHAT?!
WE'RE GOING TO HELP LORD ZEDD?!
HAVE YOU FLIPPED, BILLY?
LOOK, HE'S GOT THE ENERGIES OF OUR OLD POWER COINS. WE HAVE TO GET THEM BACK.
BILLY, THE ZEO CRYSTALS HAVE GIVEN US GREATER POWER THAN THOSE COINS EVER COULD.
YEAH, BUT THERE WERE ONLY FIVE CRYSTALS. BILLY HAD TO RETIRE BECAUSE THERE WEREN'T ENOUGH FOR ALL OF US.
MY POWERS ARE NOT THE ISSUE. THIS IS JUST SOMETHING WE HAVE TO DO, AND WE'RE RUNNING OUT OF TIME.
BILLY'S RIGHT. IS EVERYONE READY?
YEAH...
IT'S MORPHIN' TIME!

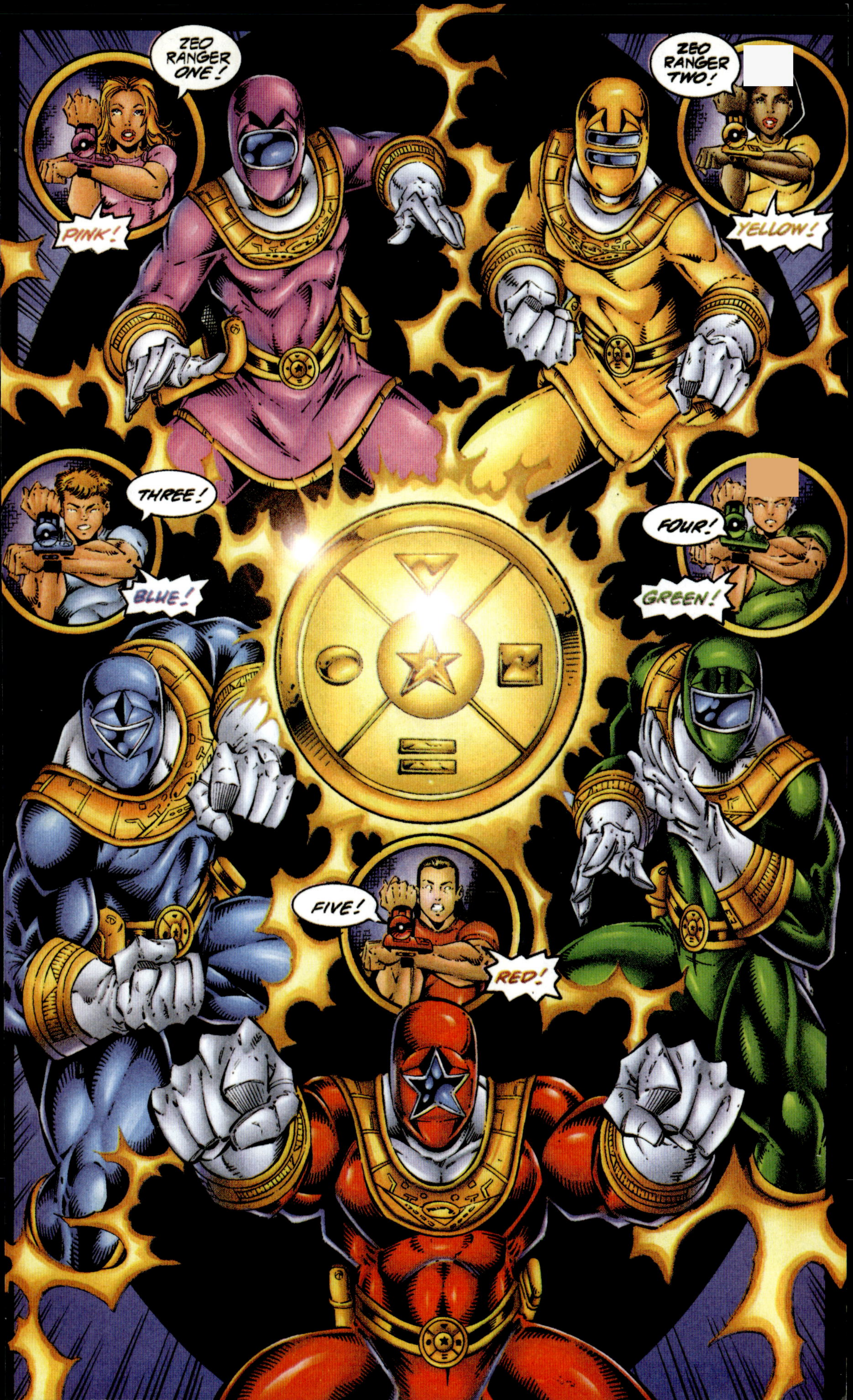
ZEO RANGER ONE!
PINK!
ZEO RANGER TWO!
YELLOW!
THREE!
BLUE!
FOUR!
GREEN!
FIVE!
RED!

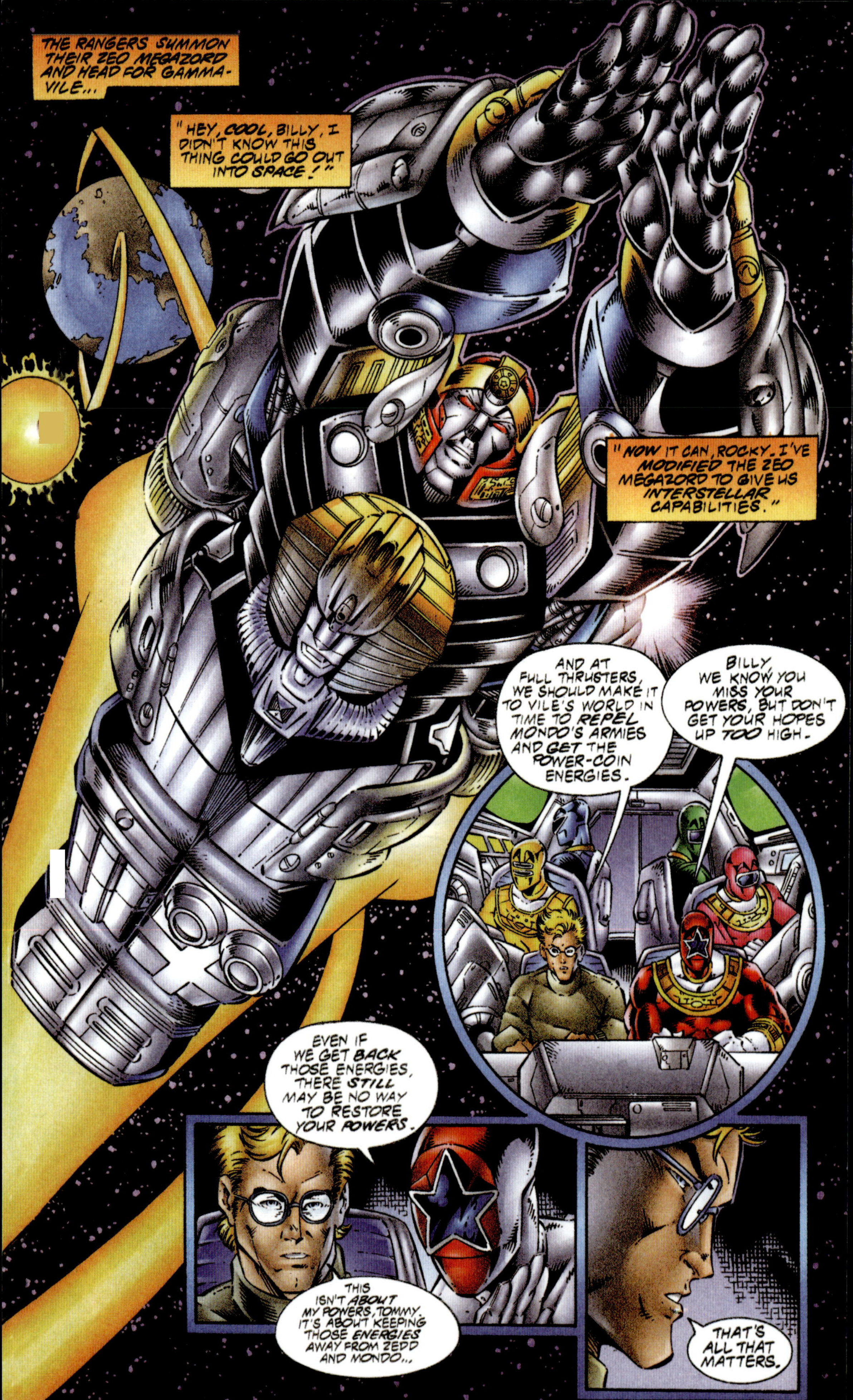
THE RANGERS SUMMON THEIR ZEO MEGAZORD AND HEAD FOR GAMMA-VILE...
"HEY, COOL, BILLY, I DIDN'T KNOW THIS THING COULD GO OUT INTO SPACE!"
"NOW IT CAN, ROCKY. I'VE MODIFIED THE ZEO MEGAZORD TO GIVE US INTERSTELLAR CAPABILITIES."
AND AT FULL THRUSTERS, WE SHOULD MAKE IT TO VILE'S WORLD IN TIME TO REPEL MONDO'S ARMIES AND GET THE POWER-COIN ENERGIES.
BILLY, WE KNOW YOU MISS YOUR POWERS, BUT DON'T GET YOUR HOPES UP TOO HIGH.
EVEN IF WE GET BACK THOSE ENERGIES, THERE STILL MAY BE NO WAY TO RESTORE YOUR POWERS.
THIS ISN'T ABOUT MY POWERS, TOMMY. IT'S ABOUT KEEPING THOSE ENERGIES AWAY FROM ZEDD AND MONDO...
THAT'S ALL THAT MATTERS.

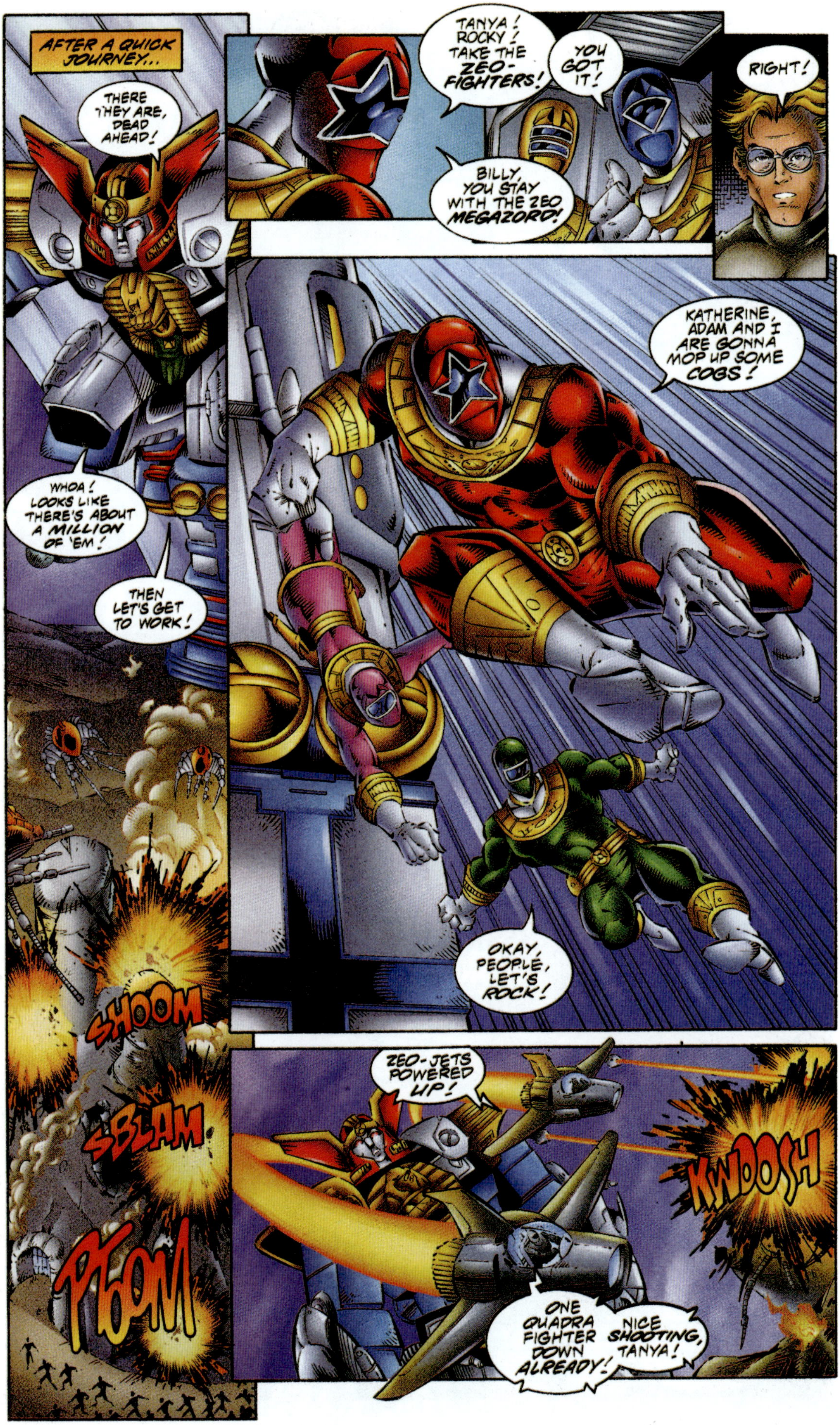

AFTER A QUICK JOURNEY...
THERE THEY ARE, DEAD AHEAD!
TANYA! ROCKY! TAKE THE ZEO-FIGHTERS!
YOU GOT IT!
BILLY, YOU STAY WITH THE ZEO MEGAZORD!
RIGHT!
KATHERINE, ADAM AND I ARE GONNA MOP UP SOME COGS!
WHOA! LOOKS LIKE THERE'S ABOUT A MILLION OF 'EM!
THEN LET'S GET TO WORK!
OKAY, PEOPLE, LET'S ROCK!
SHOOM
SBLAM
PTOOM
ZEO-JETS POWERED UP!
KWOOSH
ONE QUADRA FIGHTER DOWN ALREADY!
NICE SHOOTING, TANYA!

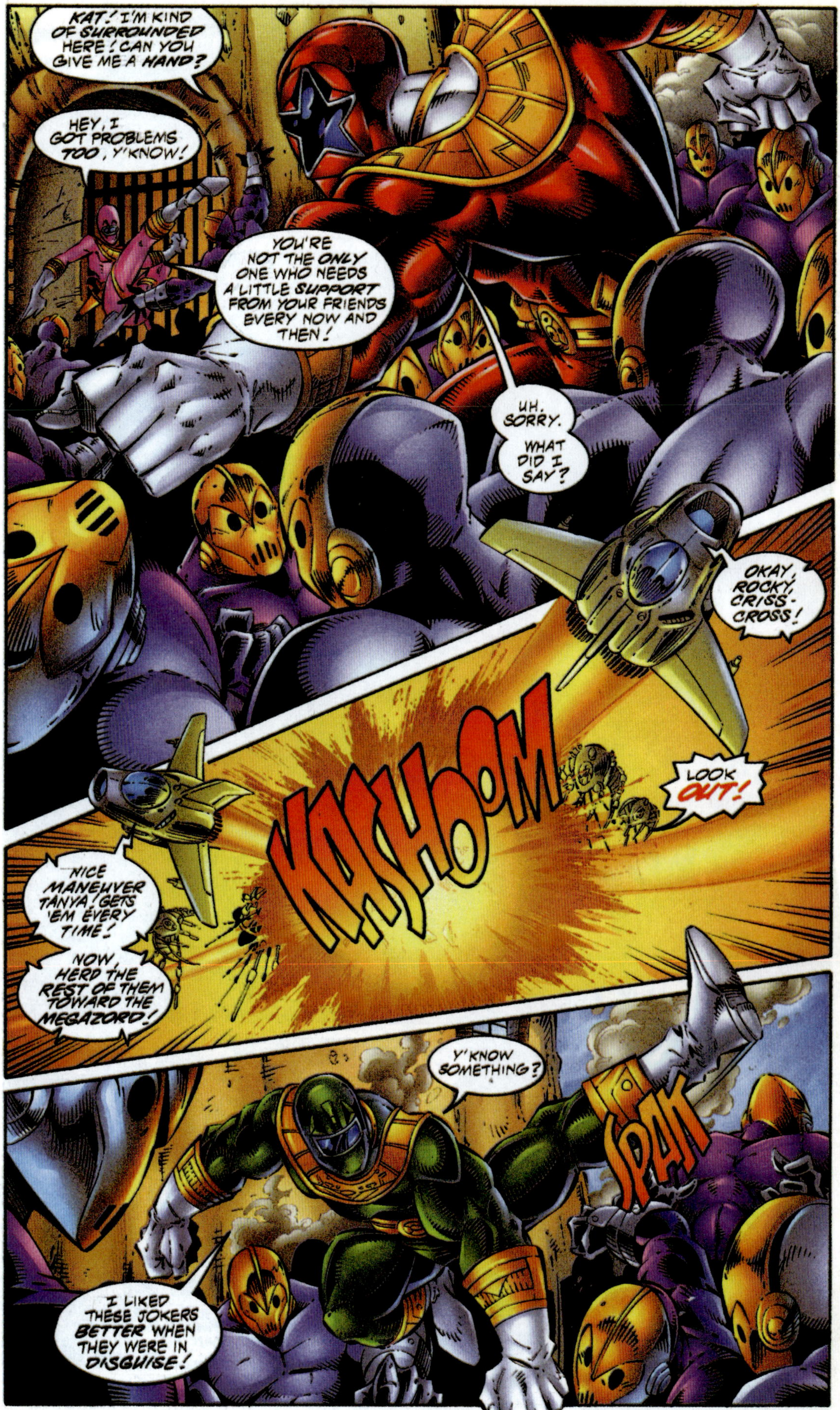
KAT! I'M KIND OF SURROUNDED HERE! CAN YOU GIVE ME A HAND?
HEY, I GOT PROBLEMS TOO, Y'KNOW!
YOU'RE NOT THE ONLY ONE WHO NEEDS A LITTLE SUPPORT FROM YOUR FRIENDS EVERY NOW AND THEN!
UH. SORRY. WHAT DID I SAY?
OKAY, ROCKY, CRISS-CROSS!
KASHOOM
LOOK OUT!
NICE MANEUVER TANYA! GETS 'EM EVERY TIME!
NOW, HERD THE REST OF THEM TOWARD THE MEGAZORD!
Y'KNOW SOMETHING?
SPAK
I LIKED THESE JOKERS BETTER WHEN THEY WERE IN DISGUISE!

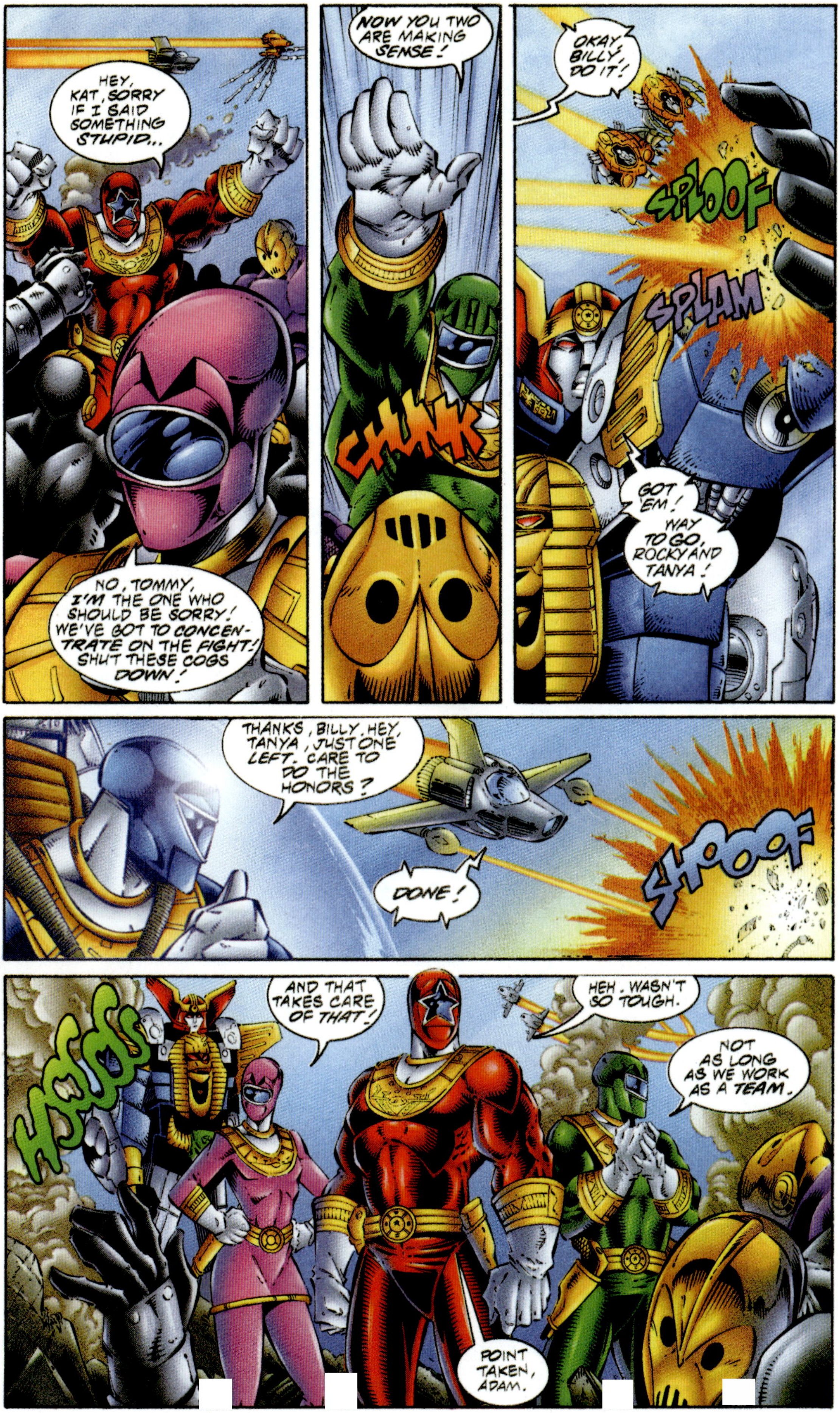
HEY, KAT, SORRY IF I SAID SOMETHING STUPID...
NO, TOMMY, I'M THE ONE WHO SHOULD BE SORRY! WE'VE GOT TO CONCENTRATE ON THE FIGHT! SHUT THESE COGS DOWN!
NOW YOU TWO ARE MAKING SENSE!
CHUNK
OKAY, BILLY, DO IT!
SPLOOF
SPLAM
GOT 'EM! WAY TO GO, ROCKY AND TANYA!
THANKS, BILLY. HEY, TANYA, JUST ONE LEFT. CARE TO DO THE HONORS?
DONE!
SHOOOF
HOOOOSH
AND THAT TAKES CARE OF THAT!
HEH. WASN'T SO TOUGH.
NOT AS LONG AS WE WORK AS A TEAM.
POINT TAKEN, ADAM.

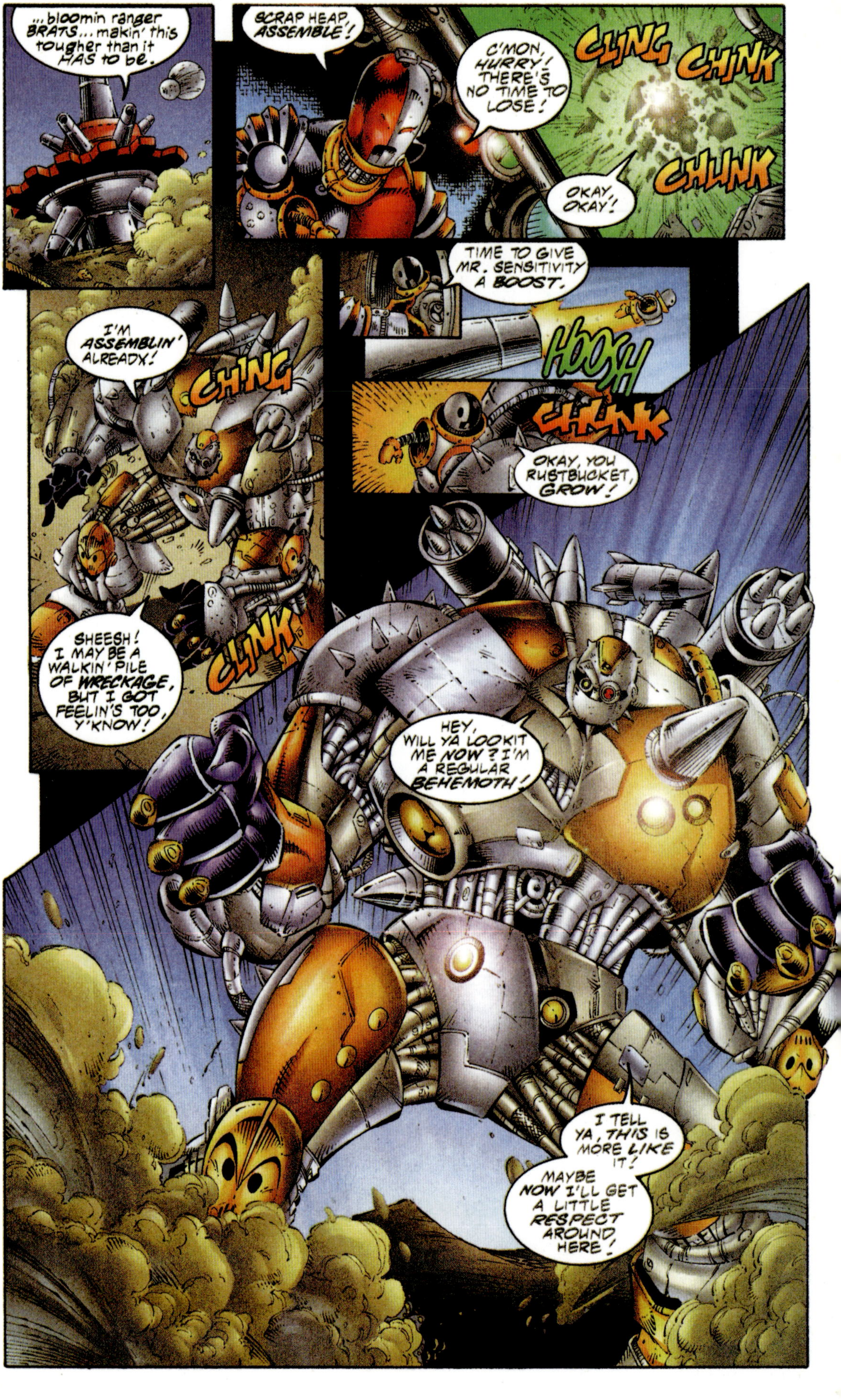
...bloomin ranger BRATS... makin' this tougher than it HAS to be.
SCRAP HEAP, ASSEMBLE!
C'MON, HURRY! THERE'S NO TIME TO LOSE!
CLING CHINK
CHUNK
OKAY, OKAY!
TIME TO GIVE MR. SENSITIVITY A BOOST.
HOOSH
I'M ASSEMBLIN' ALREADY!
CHING
CHUNK
OKAY, YOU RUSTBUCKET, GROW!
CLINK
SHEESH! I MAY BE A WALKIN' PILE OF WRECKAGE, BUT I GOT FEELIN'S TOO, Y'KNOW!
HEY, WILL YA LOOKIT ME NOW? I'M A REGULAR BEHEMOTH!
I TELL YA, THIS IS MORE LIKE IT!
MAYBE NOW I'LL GET A LITTLE RESPECT AROUND HERE!

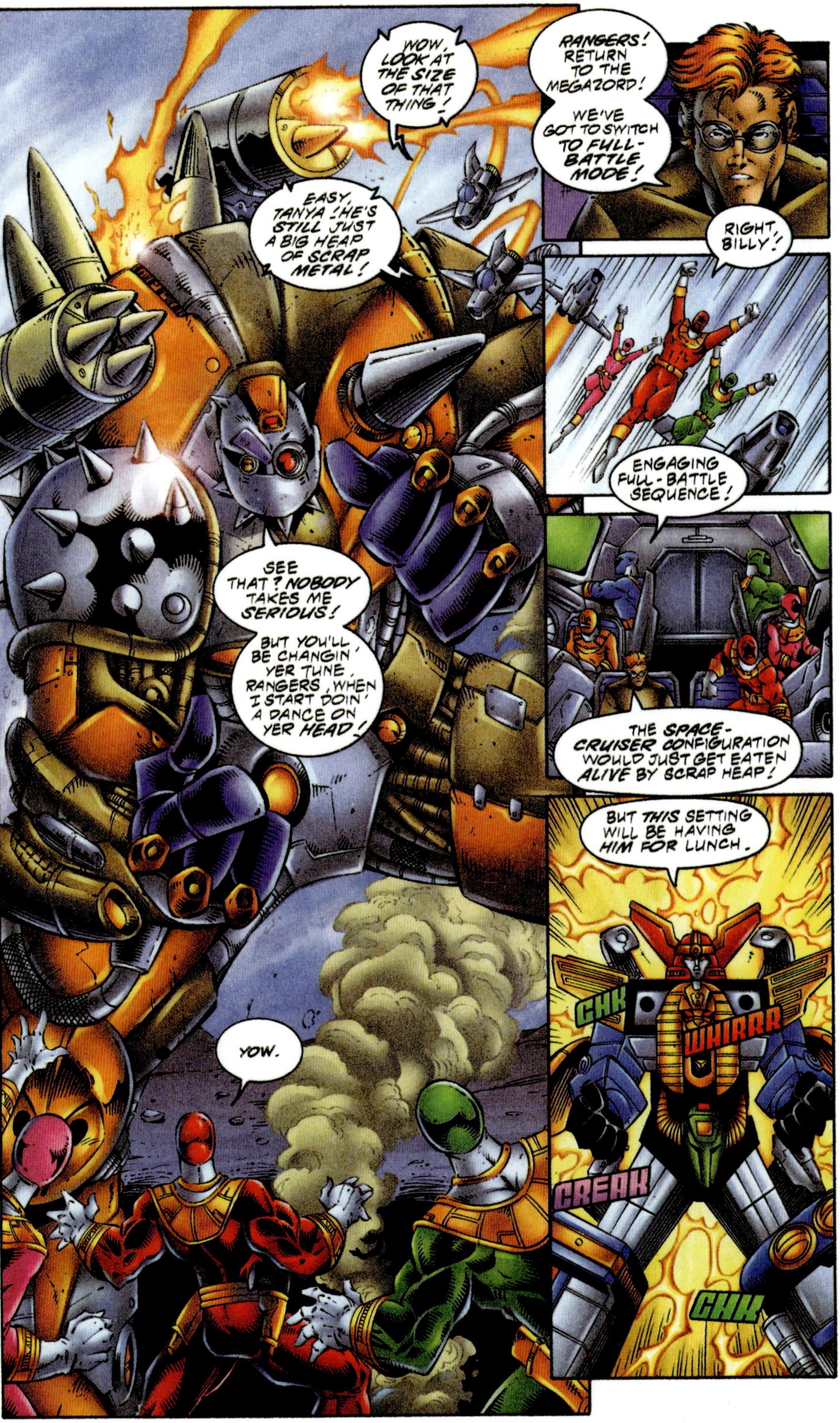
WOW, LOOK AT THE SIZE OF THAT THING!
EASY, TANYA! HE'S STILL JUST A BIG HEAP OF SCRAP METAL!
RANGERS! RETURN TO THE MEGAZORD!
WE'VE GOT TO SWITCH TO FULL-BATTLE MODE!
RIGHT, BILLY!
ENGAGING FULL-BATTLE SEQUENCE!
THE SPACE-CRUISER CONFIGURATION WOULD JUST GET EATEN ALIVE BY SCRAP HEAP!
BUT THIS SETTING WILL BE HAVING HIM FOR LUNCH.
CHK
WHIRRR
CREAK
CHK
SEE THAT? NOBODY TAKES ME SERIOUS!
BUT YOU'LL BE CHANGIN' YER TUNE, RANGERS, WHEN I START DOIN' A DANCE ON YER HEAD!
YOW.

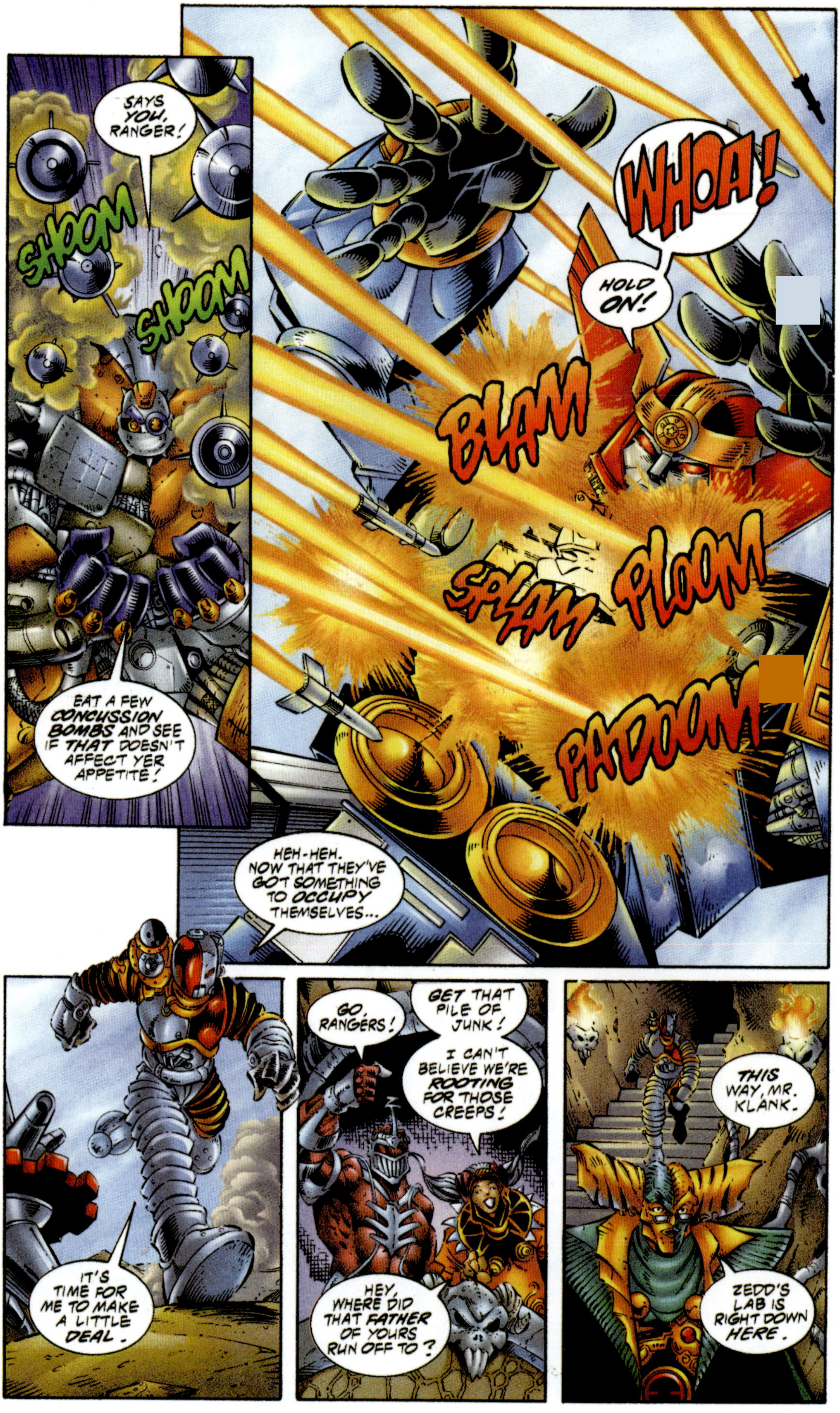
SAYS YOU, RANGER!
SHOOM
SHOOM
EAT A FEW CONCUSSION BOMBS AND SEE IF THAT DOESN'T AFFECT YER APPETITE!
WHOA!
HOLD ON!
BLAM
SPLAM
PLOOM
PADOOM
HEH-HEH. NOW THAT THEY'VE GOT SOMETHING TO OCCUPY THEMSELVES...
IT'S TIME FOR ME TO MAKE A LITTLE DEAL.
GO, RANGERS!
GET THAT PILE OF JUNK!
I CAN'T BELIEVE WE'RE ROOTING FOR THOSE CREEPS!
HEY, WHERE DID THAT FATHER OF YOURS RUN OFF TO?
THIS WAY, MR. KLANK.
ZEDD'S LAB IS RIGHT DOWN HERE.

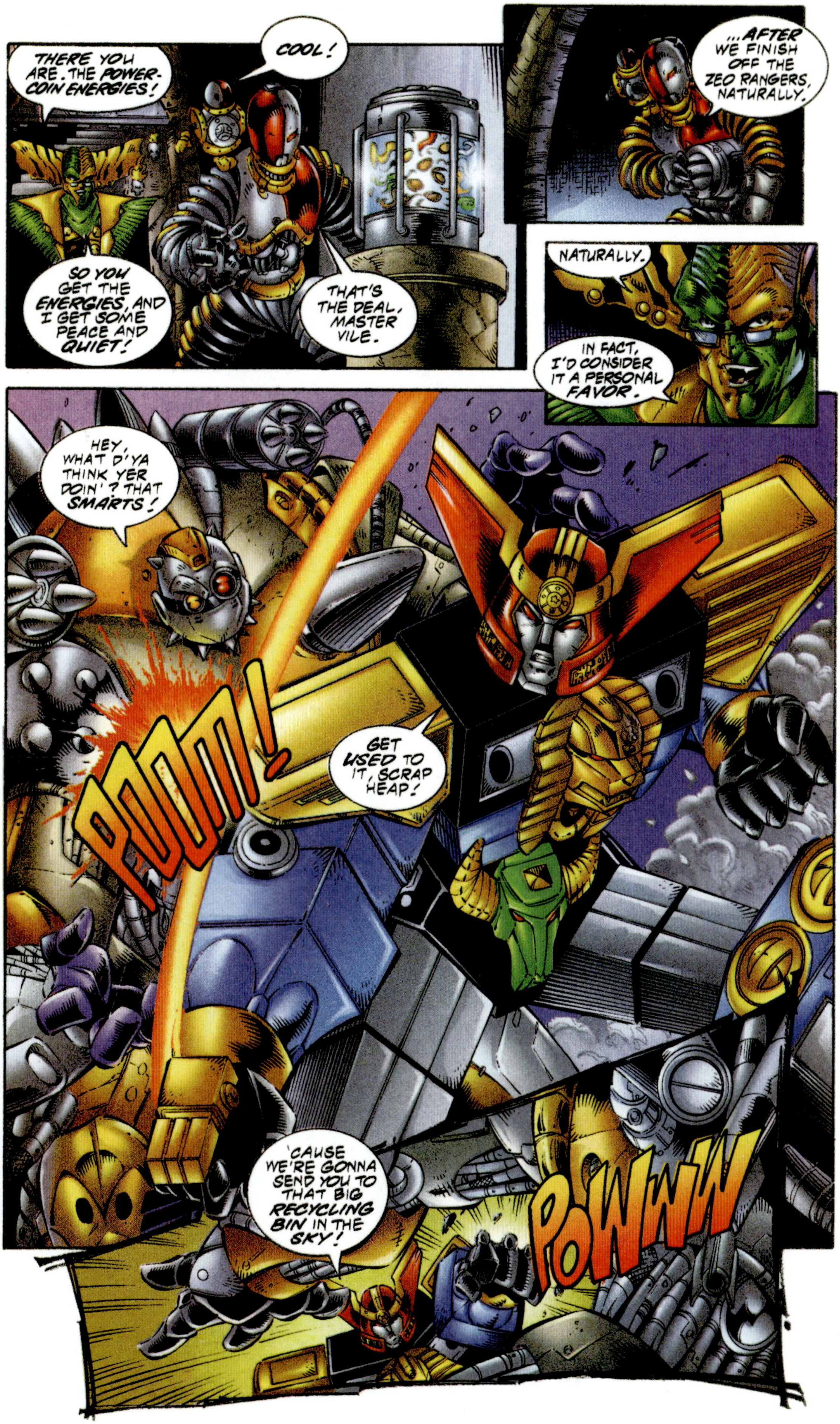
THERE YOU ARE. THE POWER-COIN ENERGIES!
COOL!
SO YOU GET THE ENERGIES, AND I GET SOME PEACE AND QUIET!
THAT'S THE DEAL, MASTER VILE.
...AFTER WE FINISH OFF THE ZEO RANGERS, NATURALLY.
NATURALLY.
IN FACT, I'D CONSIDER IT A PERSONAL FAVOR.
HEY, WHAT D'YA THINK YER DOIN'? THAT SMARTS!
BOOM!
GET USED TO IT, SCRAP HEAP!
'CAUSE WE'RE GONNA SEND YOU TO THAT BIG RECYCLING BIN IN THE SKY!
POWWW

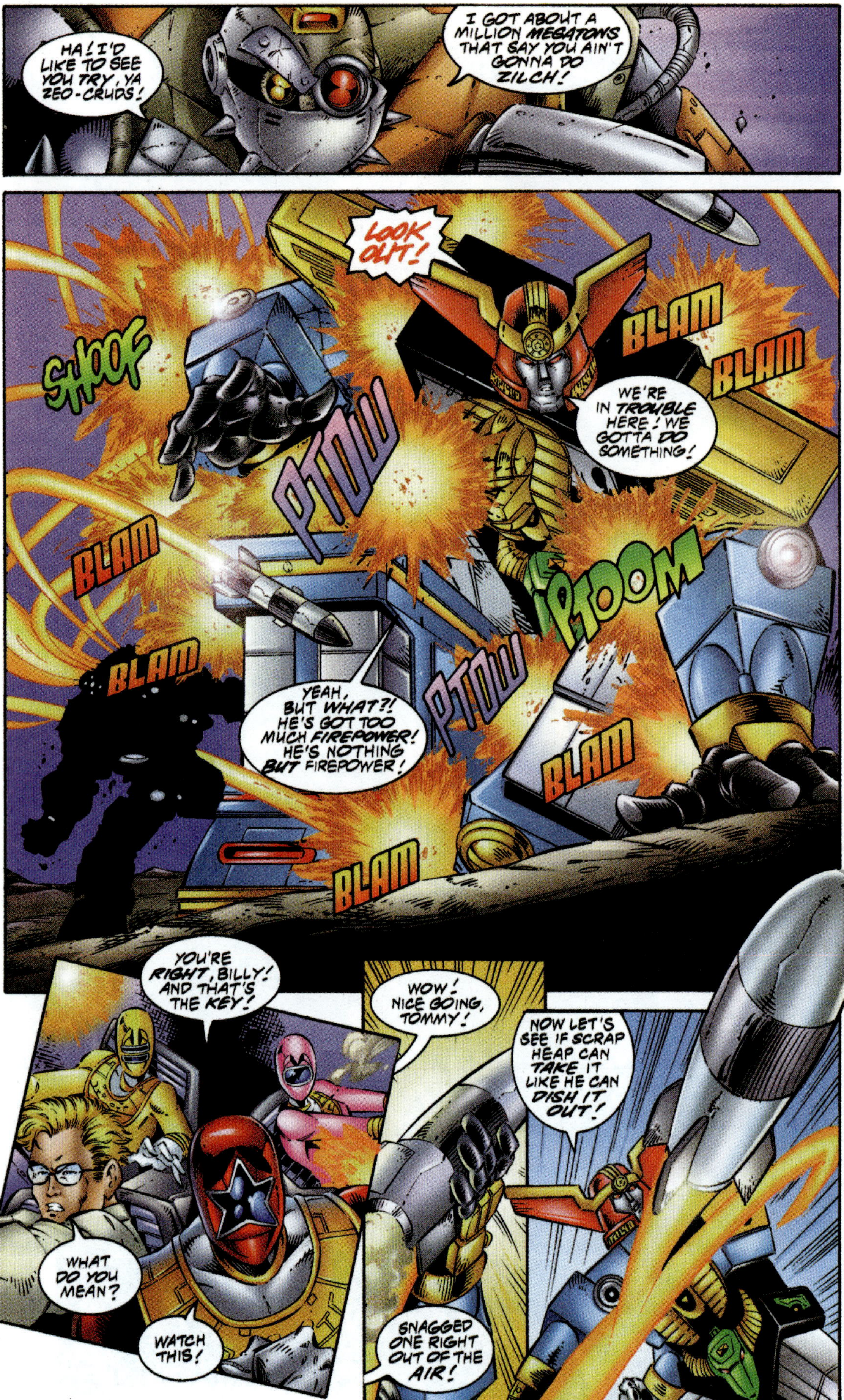
HA! I'D LIKE TO SEE YOU TRY, YA ZEO-CRUDS!
I GOT ABOUT A MILLION MEGATONS THAT SAY YOU AIN'T GONNA DO ZILCH!
LOOK OUT!
SHOOF
BLAM
BLAM
WE'RE IN TROUBLE HERE! WE GOTTA DO SOMETHING!
PTOW
BLAM
PTOOM
BLAM
YEAH, BUT WHAT?! HE'S GOT TOO MUCH FIREPOWER! HE'S NOTHING BUT FIREPOWER!
PTOW
BLAM
BLAM
YOU'RE RIGHT, BILLY! AND THAT'S THE KEY!
WHAT DO YOU MEAN?
WATCH THIS!
WOW! NICE GOING, TOMMY!
NOW LET'S SEE IF SCRAP HEAP CAN TAKE IT LIKE HE CAN DISH IT OUT!
SNAGGED ONE RIGHT OUT OF THE AIR!

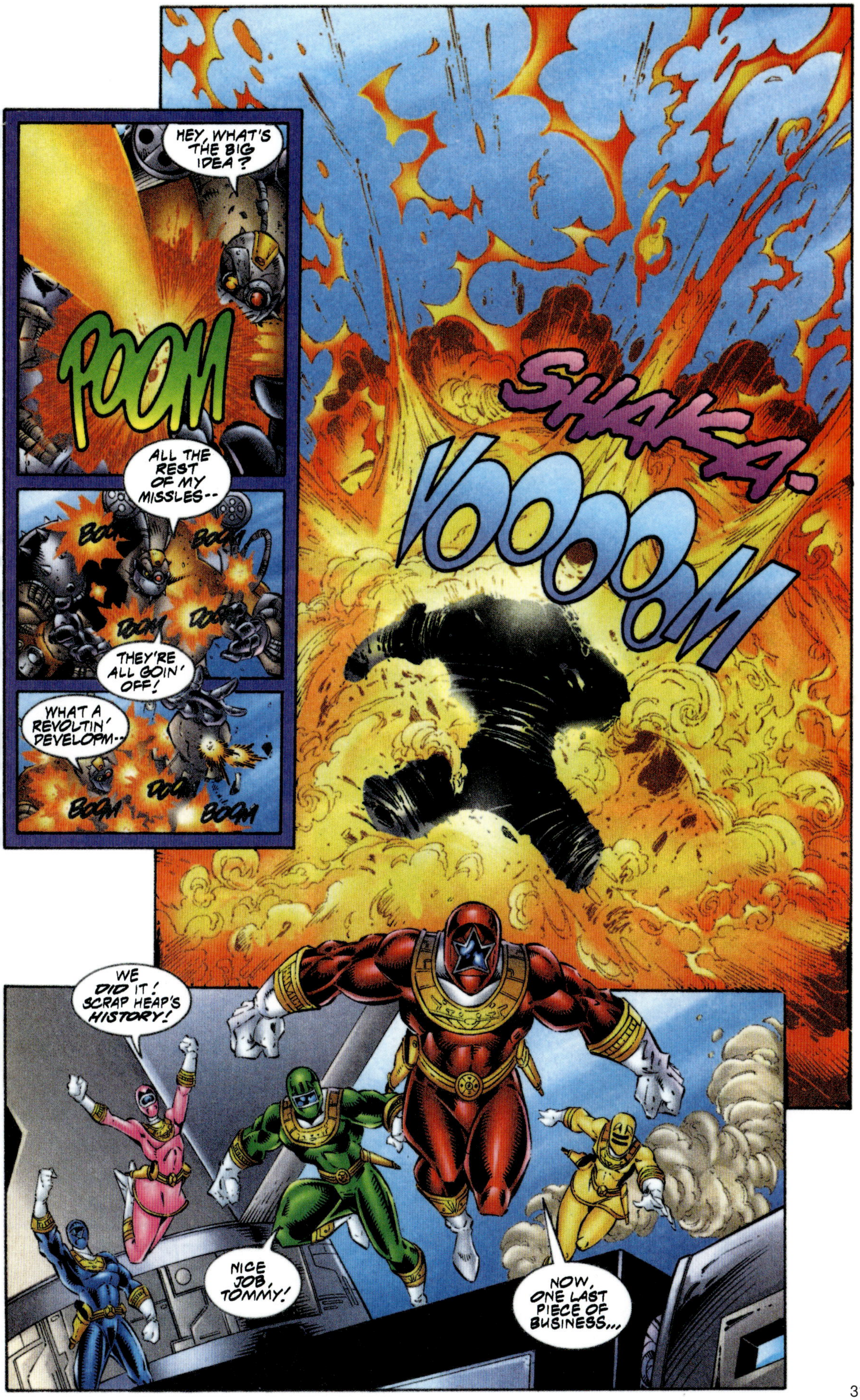
HEY, WHAT'S THE BIG IDEA?
POOM
ALL THE REST OF MY MISSLES--
BOOM
BOOM
POOM
DOOM
THEY'RE ALL GOIN' OFF!
WHAT A REVOLTIN' DEVELOPM--
BOOM
DOOM
BOOM
SHAKA-VOOOOOM
WE DID IT! SCRAP HEAP'S HISTORY!
NICE JOB, TOMMY!
NOW, ONE LAST PIECE OF BUSINESS...

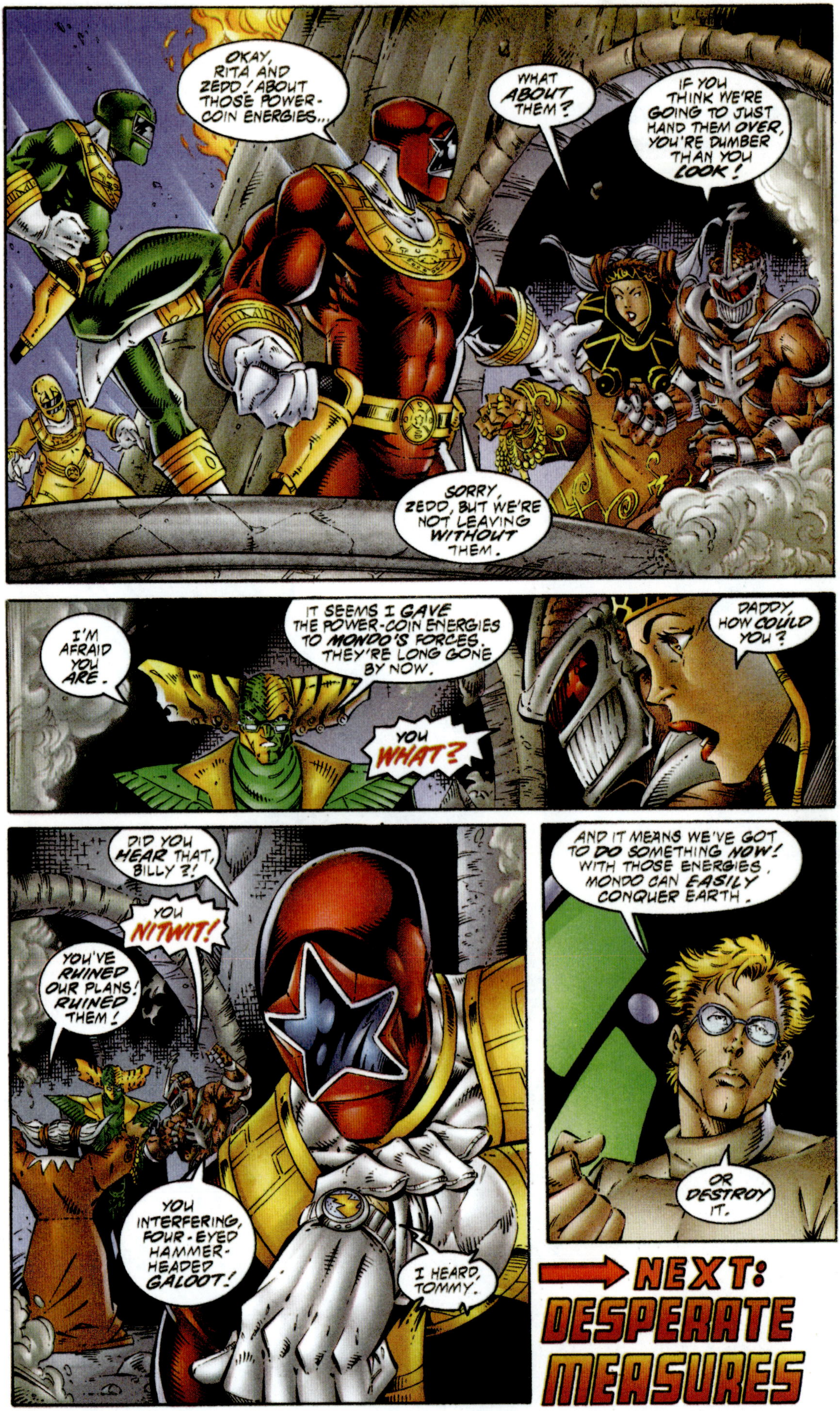
OKAY, RITA AND ZEDD! ABOUT THOSE POWER-COIN ENERGIES...
WHAT ABOUT THEM?
IF YOU THINK WE'RE GOING TO JUST HAND THEM OVER, YOU'RE DUMBER THAN YOU LOOK!
SORRY, ZEDD, BUT WE'RE NOT LEAVING WITHOUT THEM.
I'M AFRAID YOU ARE.
IT SEEMS I GAVE THE POWER-COIN ENERGIES TO MONDO'S FORCES. THEY'RE LONG GONE BY NOW.
YOU WHAT?
DADDY, HOW COULD YOU?
DID YOU HEAR THAT, BILLY?!
YOU NITWIT!
YOU'VE RUINED OUR PLANS! RUINED THEM!
YOU INTERFERING, FOUR-EYED HAMMER-HEADED GALOOT!
I HEARD, TOMMY.
AND IT MEANS WE'VE GOT TO DO SOMETHING NOW! WITH THOSE ENERGIES, MONDO CAN EASILY CONQUER EARTH.
OR DESTROY IT.
NEXT: DESPERATE MEASURES

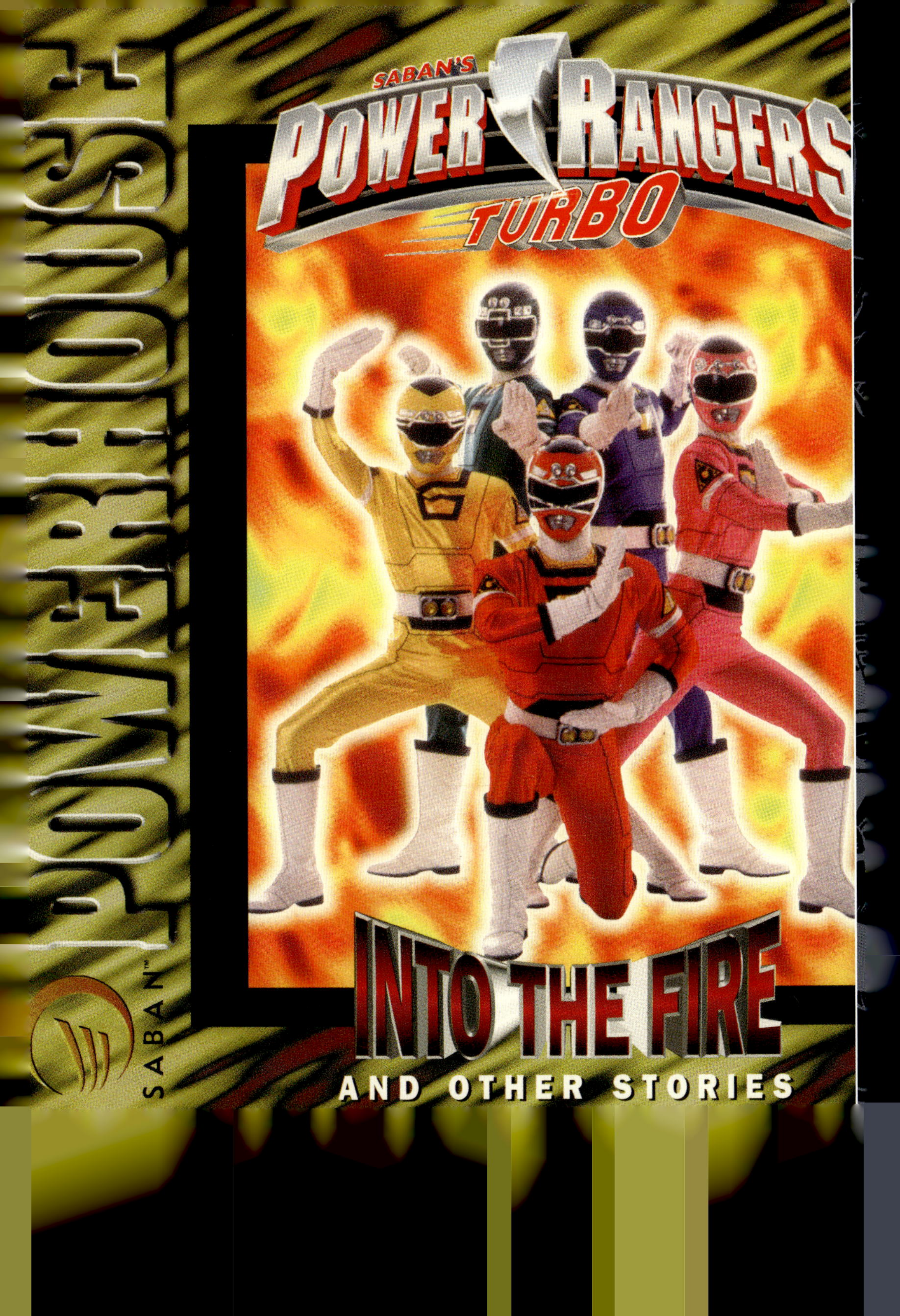
POWERHOUSE
SABAN'S
POWER RANGERS
TURBO
INTO THE FIRE
AND OTHER STORIES
SABAN™

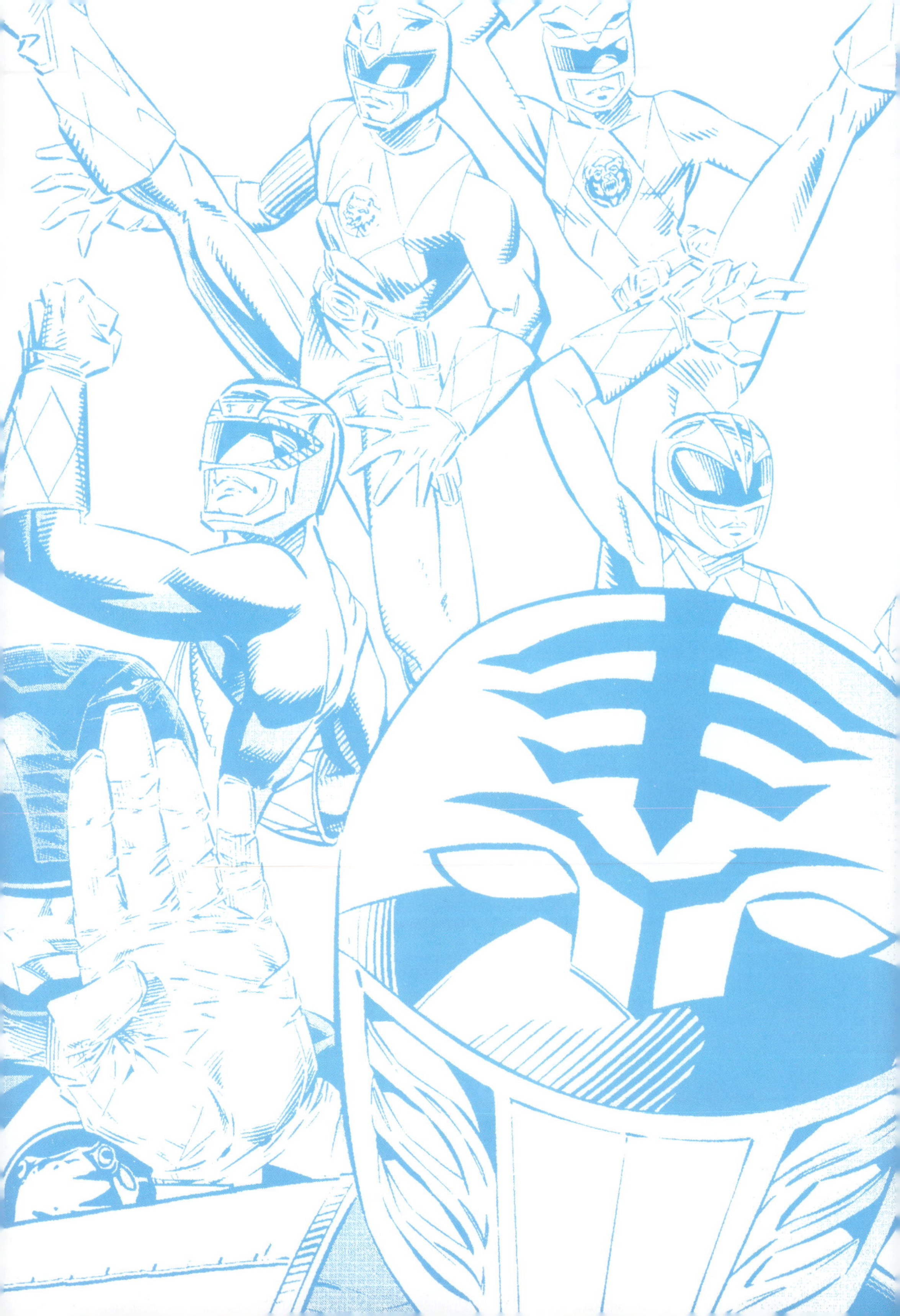

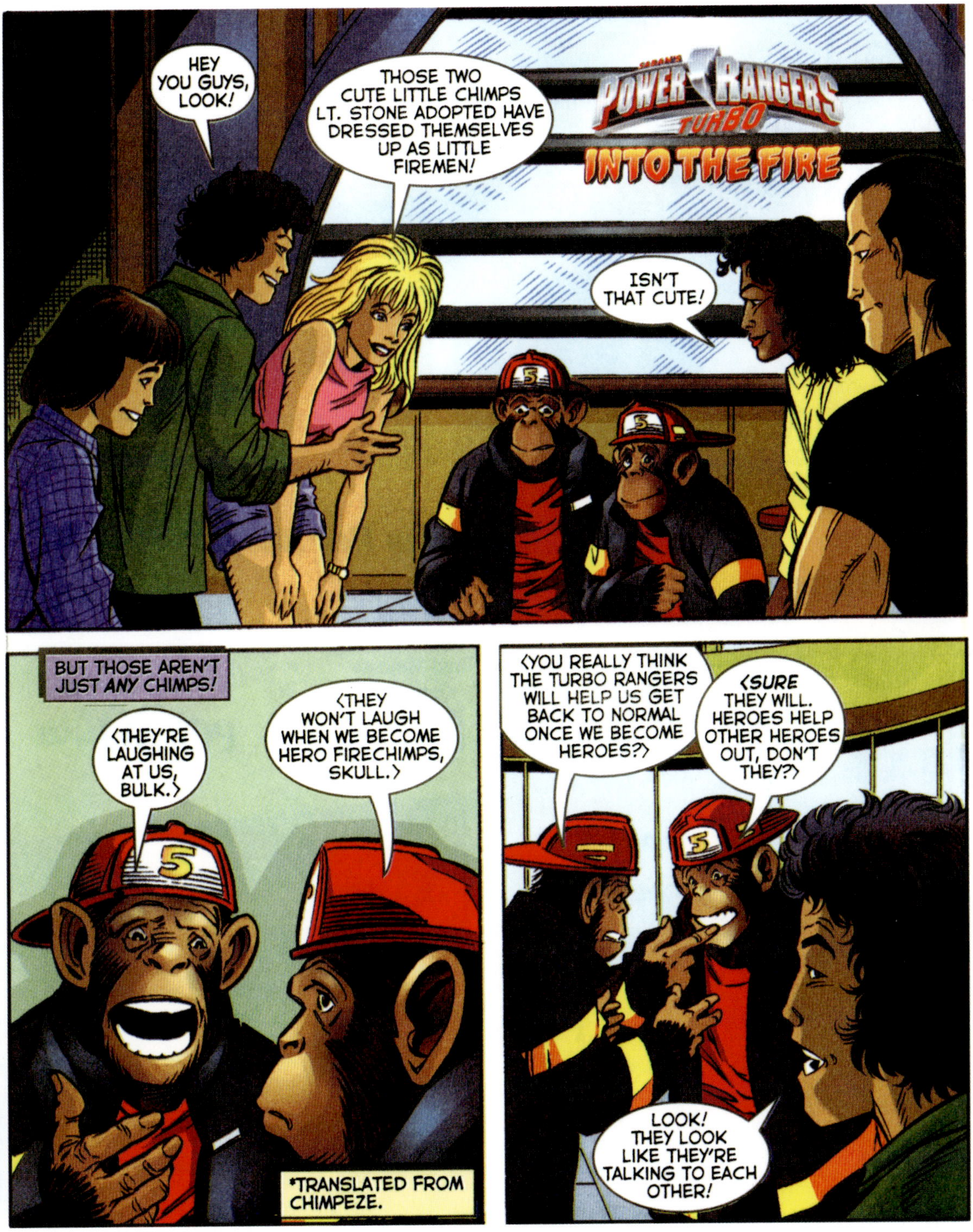
POWER RANGERS TURBO
INTO THE FIRE
HEY YOU GUYS, LOOK!
THOSE TWO CUTE LITTLE CHIMPS LT. STONE ADOPTED HAVE DRESSED THEMSELVES UP AS LITTLE FIREMEN!
ISN'T THAT CUTE!
BUT THOSE AREN'T JUST *ANY* CHIMPS!
<THEY'RE LAUGHING AT US, BULK.>
<THEY WON'T LAUGH WHEN WE BECOME HERO FIRECHIMPS, SKULL.>
*TRANSLATED FROM CHIMPEZE.
<YOU REALLY THINK THE TURBO RANGERS WILL HELP US GET BACK TO NORMAL ONCE WE BECOME HEROES?>
<*SURE* THEY WILL. HEROES HELP OTHER HEROES OUT, DON'T THEY?>
LOOK! THEY LOOK LIKE THEY'RE TALKING TO EACH OTHER!

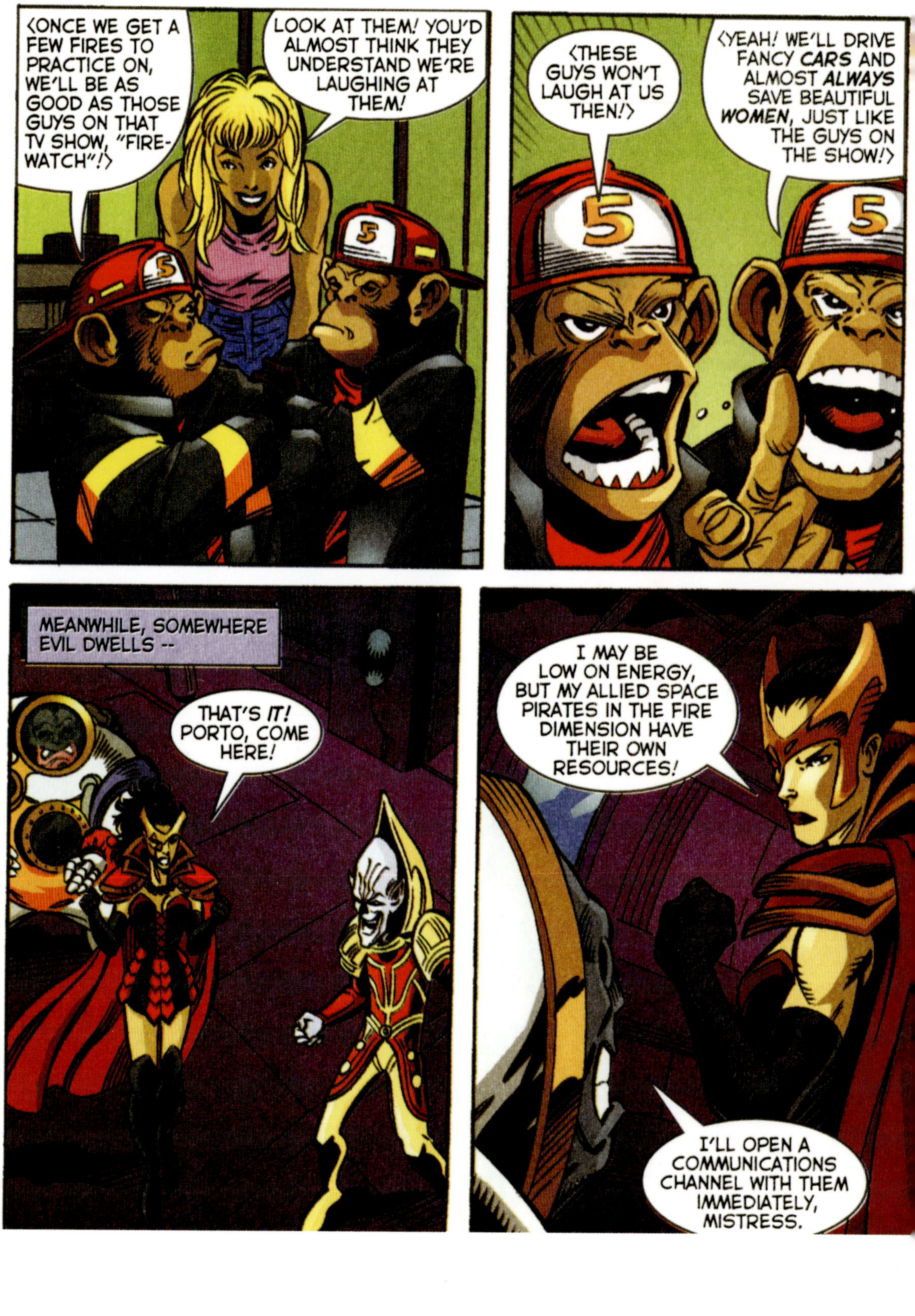

‹ONCE WE GET A FEW FIRES TO PRACTICE ON, WE'LL BE AS GOOD AS THOSE GUYS ON THAT TV SHOW, "FIRE-WATCH"!›
LOOK AT THEM! YOU'D ALMOST THINK THEY UNDERSTAND WE'RE LAUGHING AT THEM!
‹THESE GUYS WON'T LAUGH AT US THEN!›
‹YEAH! WE'LL DRIVE FANCY CARS AND ALMOST ALWAYS SAVE BEAUTIFUL WOMEN, JUST LIKE THE GUYS ON THE SHOW!›
MEANWHILE, SOMEWHERE EVIL DWELLS --
THAT'S IT! PORTO, COME HERE!
I MAY BE LOW ON ENERGY, BUT MY ALLIED SPACE PIRATES IN THE FIRE DIMENSION HAVE THEIR OWN RESOURCES!
I'LL OPEN A COMMUNICATIONS CHANNEL WITH THEM IMMEDIATELY, MISTRESS.

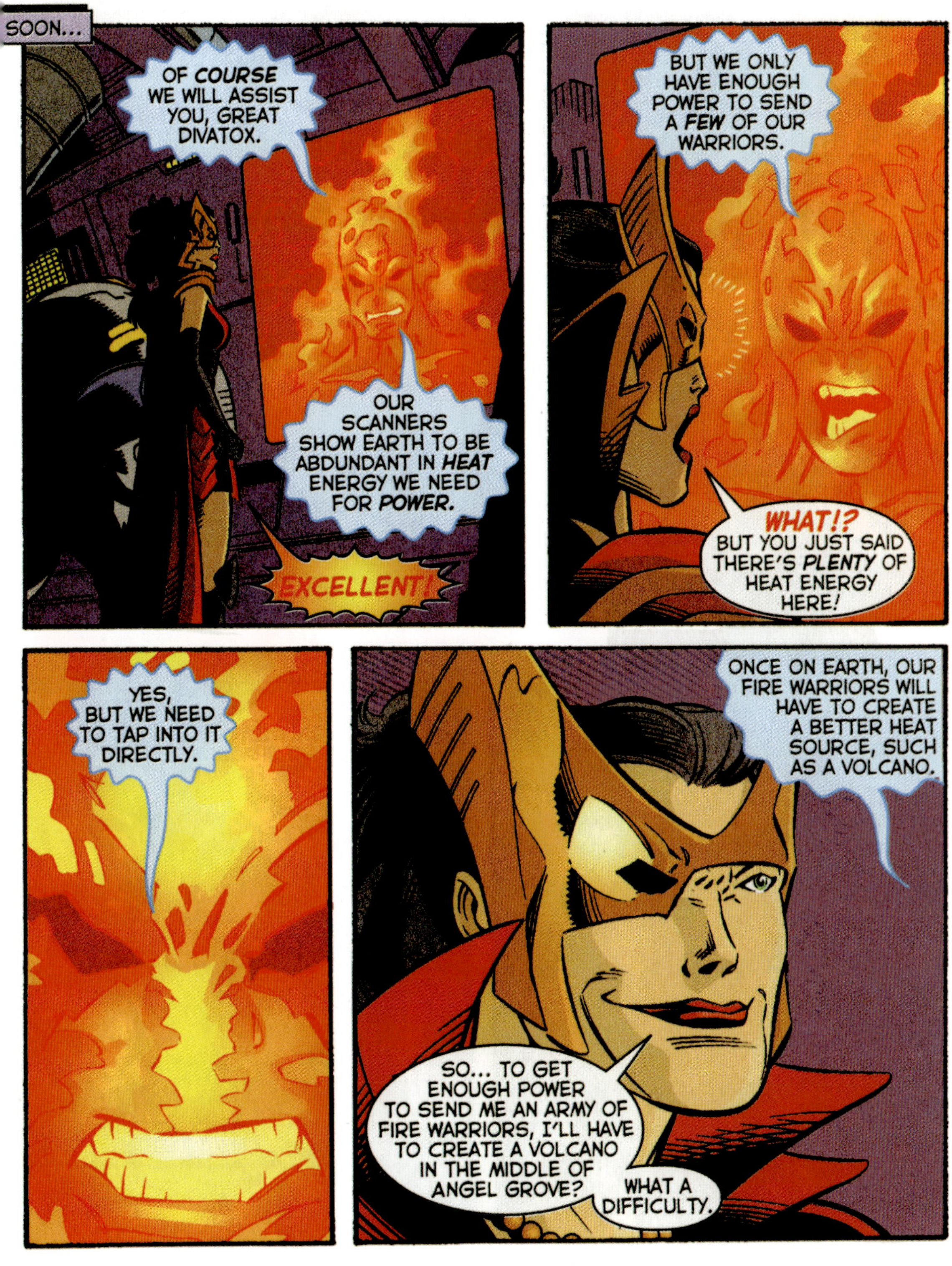
SOON...
OF COURSE WE WILL ASSIST YOU, GREAT DIVATOX.
OUR SCANNERS SHOW EARTH TO BE ABUNDANT IN HEAT ENERGY WE NEED FOR POWER.
EXCELLENT!
BUT WE ONLY HAVE ENOUGH POWER TO SEND A FEW OF OUR WARRIORS.
WHAT!? BUT YOU JUST SAID THERE'S PLENTY OF HEAT ENERGY HERE!
YES, BUT WE NEED TO TAP INTO IT DIRECTLY.
ONCE ON EARTH, OUR FIRE WARRIORS WILL HAVE TO CREATE A BETTER HEAT SOURCE, SUCH AS A VOLCANO.
SO... TO GET ENOUGH POWER TO SEND ME AN ARMY OF FIRE WARRIORS, I'LL HAVE TO CREATE A VOLCANO IN THE MIDDLE OF ANGEL GROVE?
WHAT A DIFFICULTY.

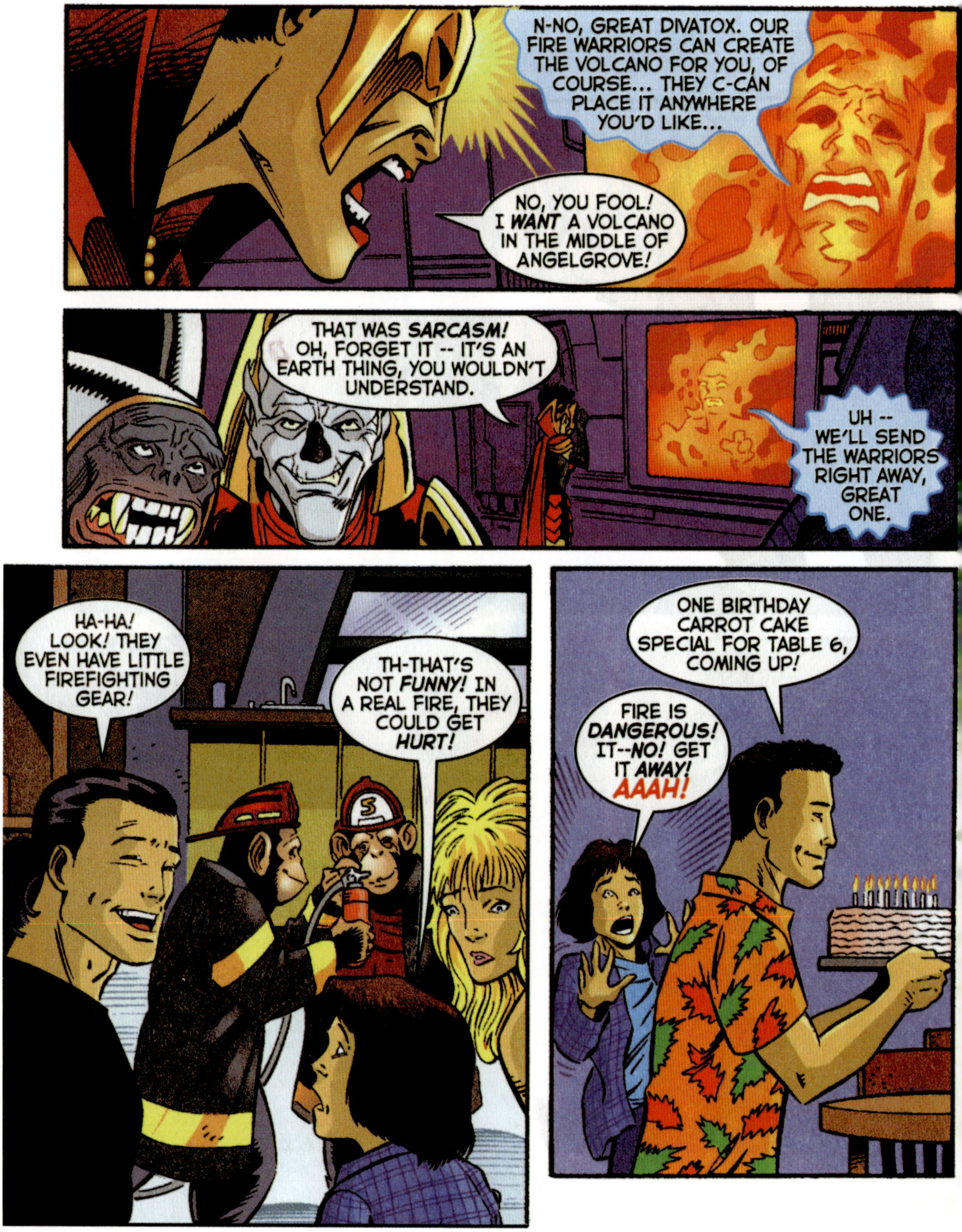
N-NO, GREAT DIVATOX. OUR FIRE WARRIORS CAN CREATE THE VOLCANO FOR YOU, OF COURSE... THEY C-CAN PLACE IT ANYWHERE YOU'D LIKE...
NO, YOU FOOL! I WANT A VOLCANO IN THE MIDDLE OF ANGELGROVE!
THAT WAS SARCASM! OH, FORGET IT -- IT'S AN EARTH THING, YOU WOULDN'T UNDERSTAND.
UH -- WE'LL SEND THE WARRIORS RIGHT AWAY, GREAT ONE.
HA-HA! LOOK! THEY EVEN HAVE LITTLE FIREFIGHTING GEAR!
TH-THAT'S NOT FUNNY! IN A REAL FIRE, THEY COULD GET HURT!
ONE BIRTHDAY CARROT CAKE SPECIAL FOR TABLE 6, COMING UP!
FIRE IS DANGEROUS! IT--NO! GET IT AWAY! AAAH!

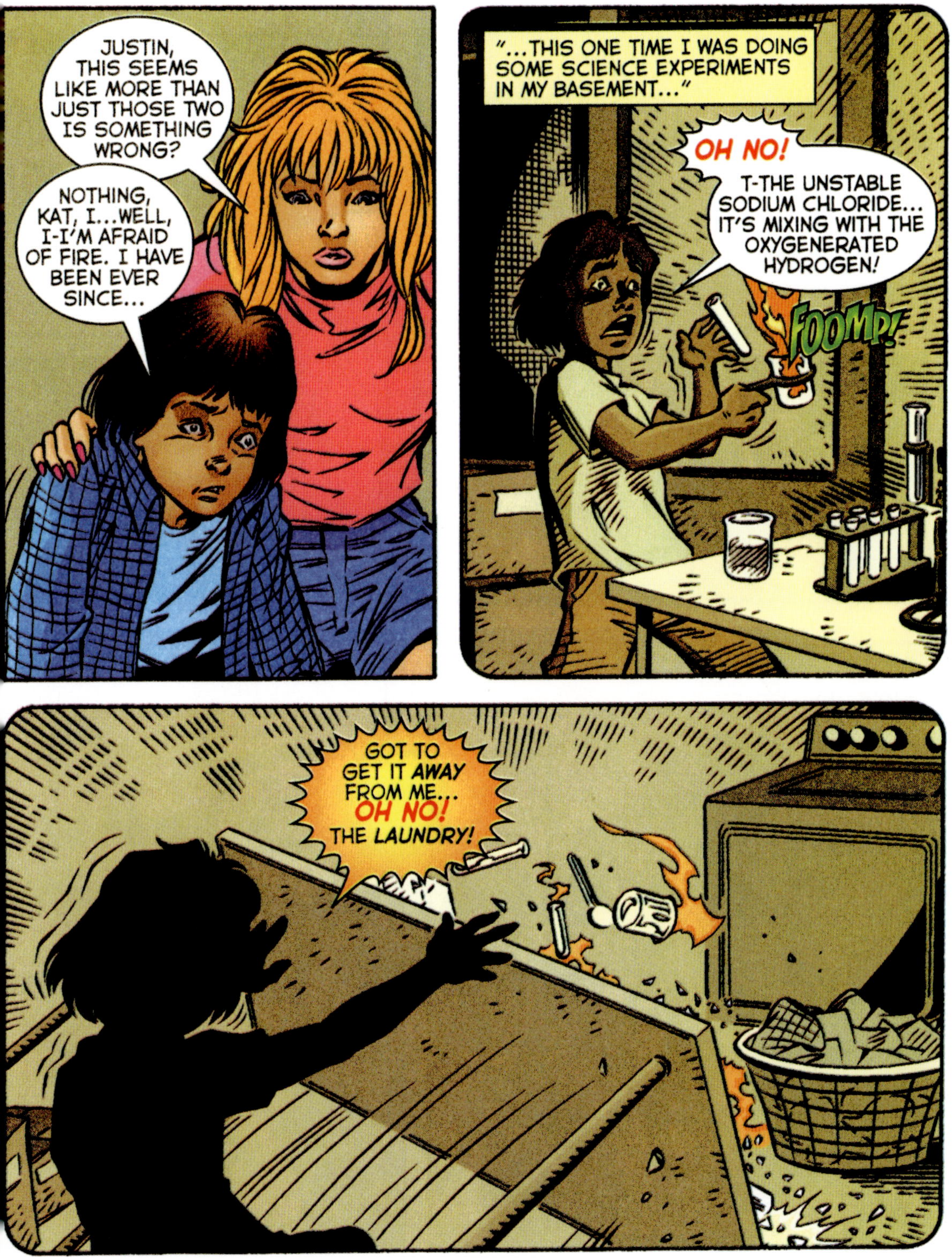

JUSTIN, THIS SEEMS LIKE MORE THAN JUST THOSE TWO IS SOMETHING WRONG?
NOTHING, KAT, I...WELL, I-I'M AFRAID OF FIRE. I HAVE BEEN EVER SINCE...
"...THIS ONE TIME I WAS DOING SOME SCIENCE EXPERIMENTS IN MY BASEMENT..."
OH NO!
T-THE UNSTABLE SODIUM CHLORIDE... IT'S MIXING WITH THE OXYGENERATED HYDROGEN!
FOOMP!
GOT TO GET IT AWAY FROM ME... OH NO! THE LAUNDRY!

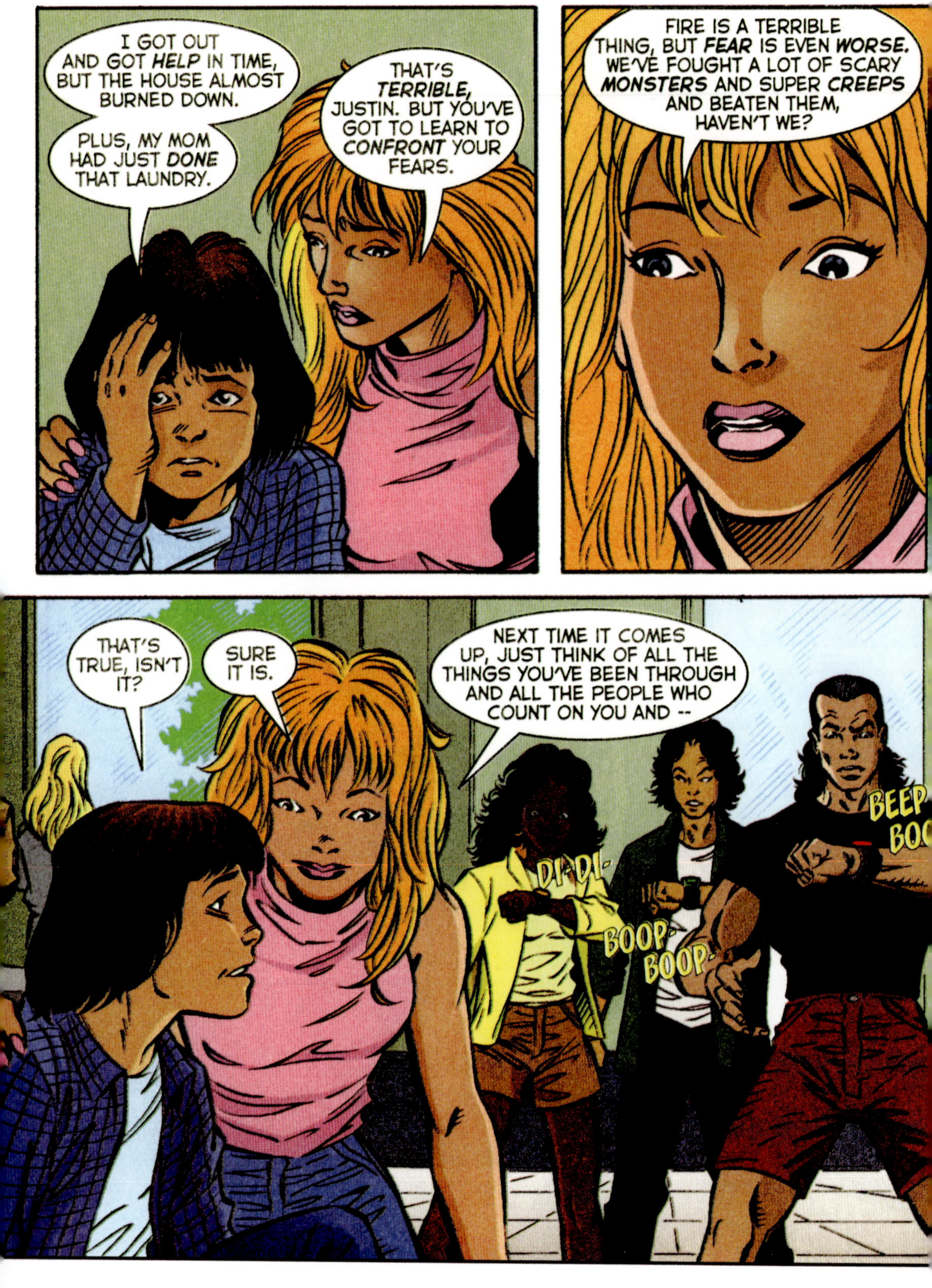

I GOT OUT AND GOT HELP IN TIME, BUT THE HOUSE ALMOST BURNED DOWN.
PLUS, MY MOM HAD JUST DONE THAT LAUNDRY.
THAT'S TERRIBLE, JUSTIN. BUT YOU'VE GOT TO LEARN TO CONFRONT YOUR FEARS.
FIRE IS A TERRIBLE THING, BUT FEAR IS EVEN WORSE. WE'VE FOUGHT A LOT OF SCARY MONSTERS AND SUPER CREEPS AND BEATEN THEM, HAVEN'T WE?
THAT'S TRUE, ISN'T IT?
SURE IT IS.
NEXT TIME IT COMES UP, JUST THINK OF ALL THE THINGS YOU'VE BEEN THROUGH AND ALL THE PEOPLE WHO COUNT ON YOU AND --
DI-DI-
BOOP-BOOP-
BEEP

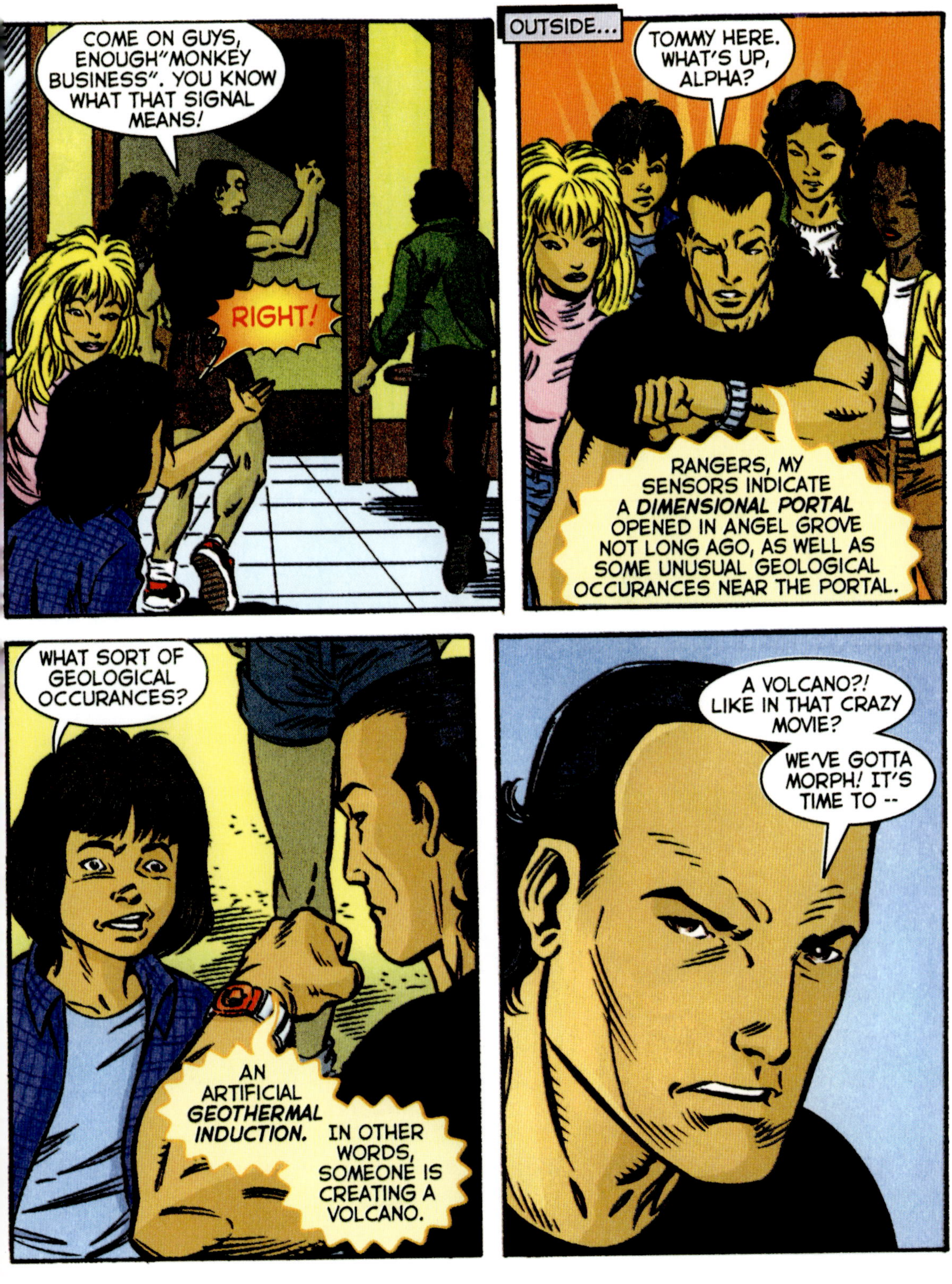

COME ON GUYS, ENOUGH "MONKEY BUSINESS". YOU KNOW WHAT THAT SIGNAL MEANS!
RIGHT!
OUTSIDE...
TOMMY HERE. WHAT'S UP, ALPHA?
RANGERS, MY SENSORS INDICATE A *DIMENSIONAL PORTAL* OPENED IN ANGEL GROVE NOT LONG AGO, AS WELL AS SOME UNUSUAL GEOLOGICAL OCCURANCES NEAR THE PORTAL.
WHAT SORT OF GEOLOGICAL OCCURANCES?
AN ARTIFICIAL *GEOTHERMAL INDUCTION.* IN OTHER WORDS, SOMEONE IS CREATING A VOLCANO.
A VOLCANO?! LIKE IN THAT CRAZY MOVIE?
WE'VE GOTTA MORPH! IT'S TIME TO --

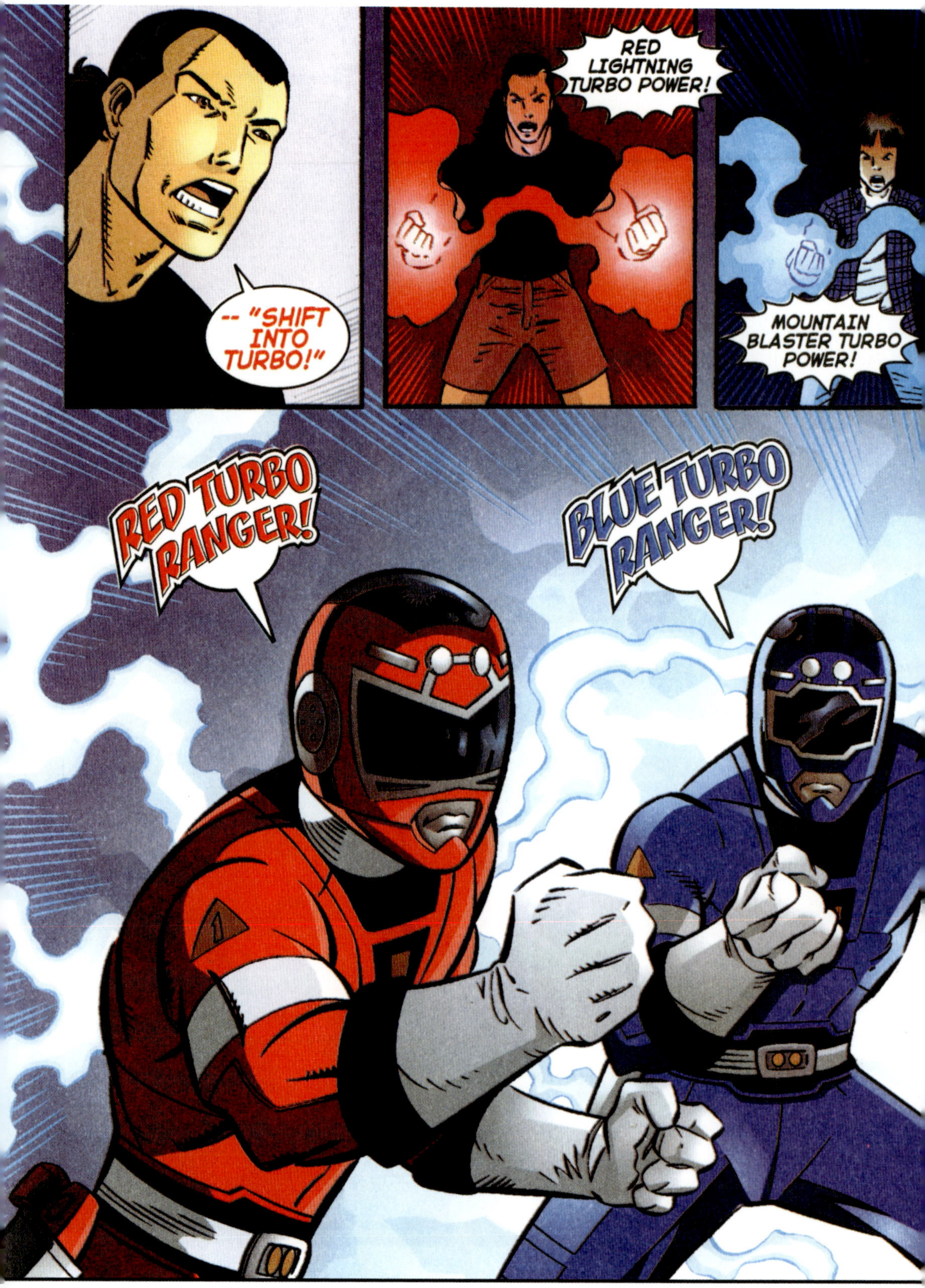
-- "SHIFT INTO TURBO!"
RED LIGHTNING TURBO POWER!
MOUNTAIN BLASTER TURBO POWER!
RED TURBO RANGER!
BLUE TURBO RANGER!

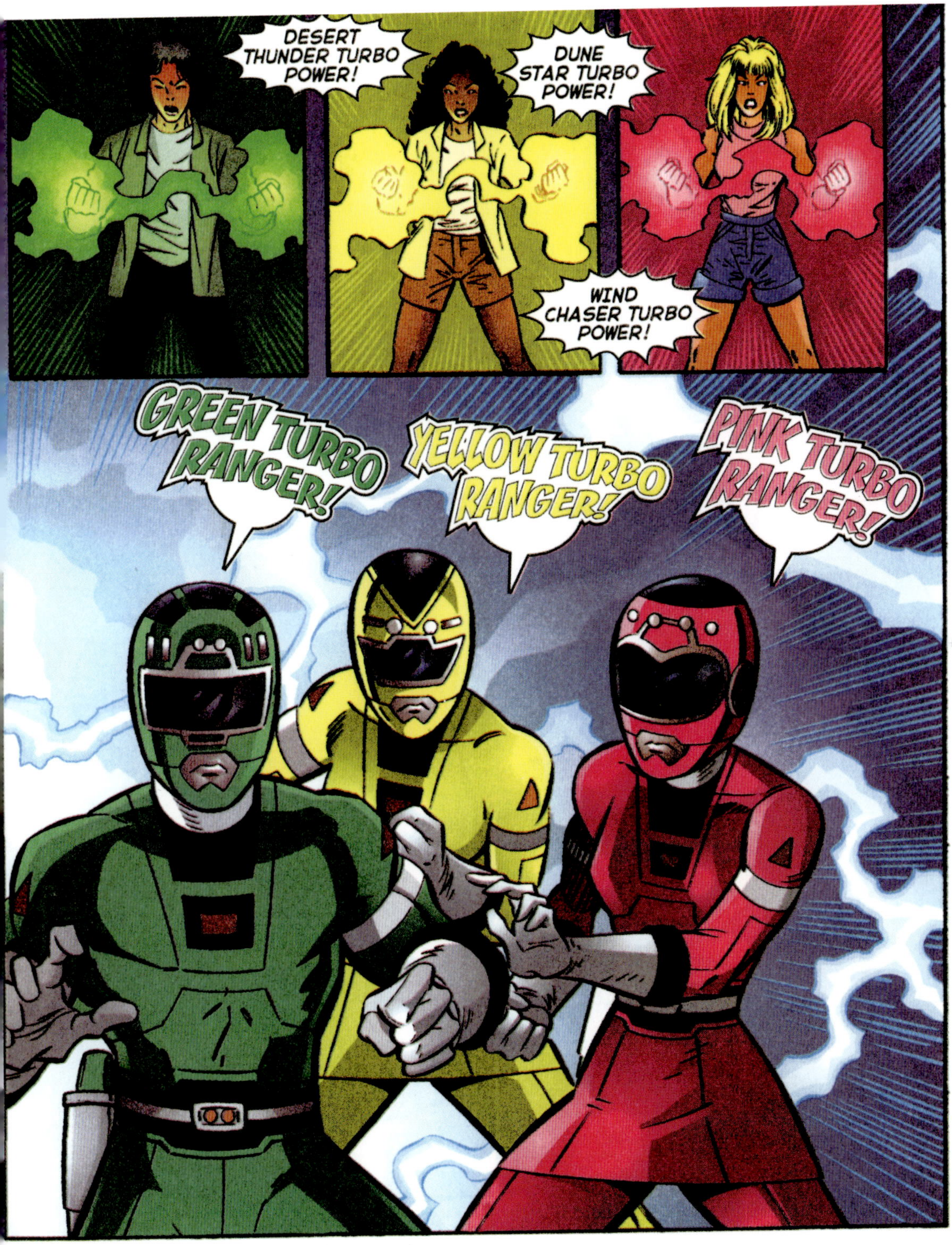
DESERT THUNDER TURBO POWER!
DUNE STAR TURBO POWER!
WIND CHASER TURBO POWER!
GREEN TURBO RANGER!
YELLOW TURBO RANGER!
PINK TURBO RANGER!

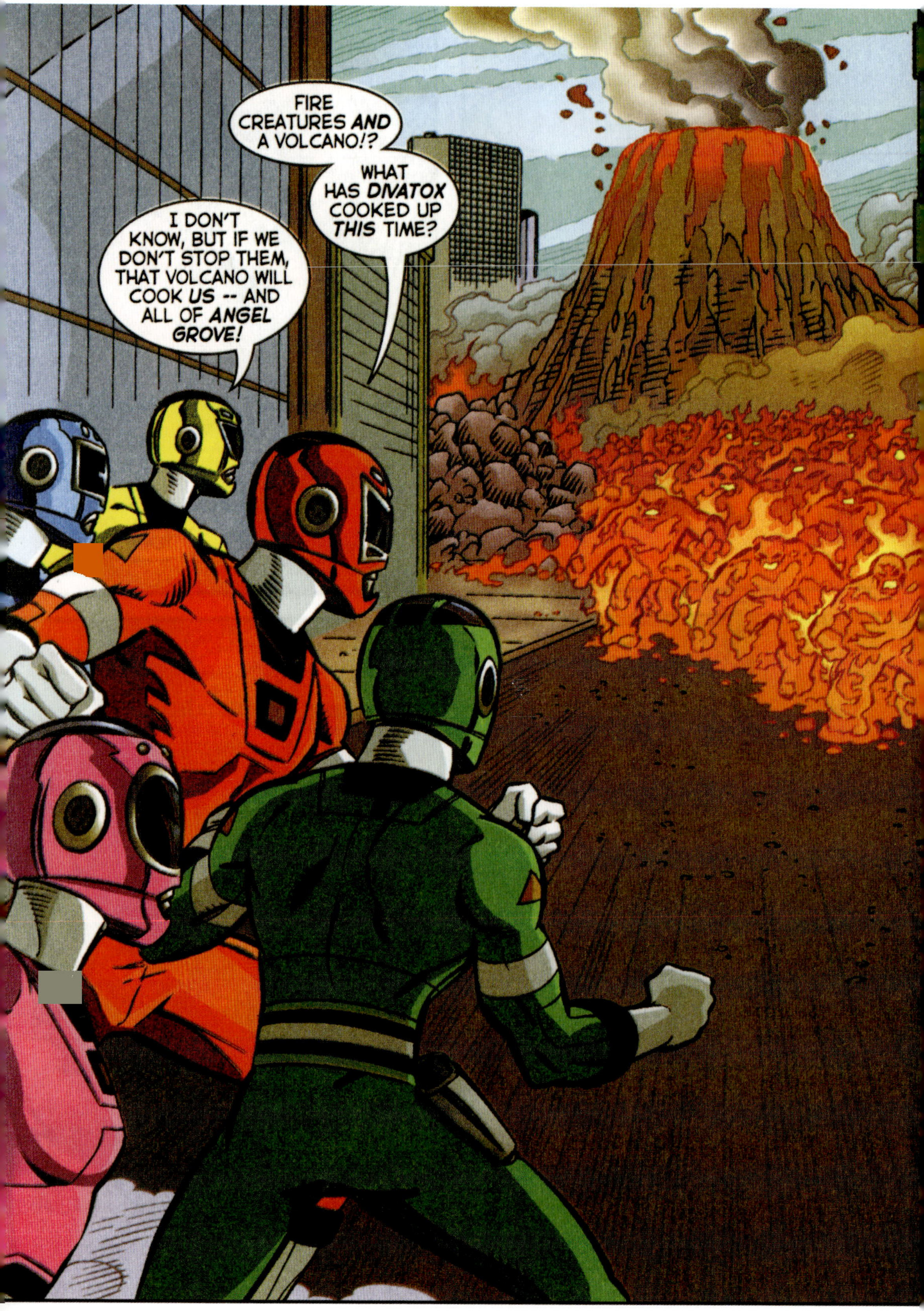
FIRE CREATURES AND A VOLCANO!?
WHAT HAS DIVATOX COOKED UP THIS TIME?
I DON'T KNOW, BUT IF WE DON'T STOP THEM, THAT VOLCANO WILL COOK US -- AND ALL OF ANGEL GROVE!

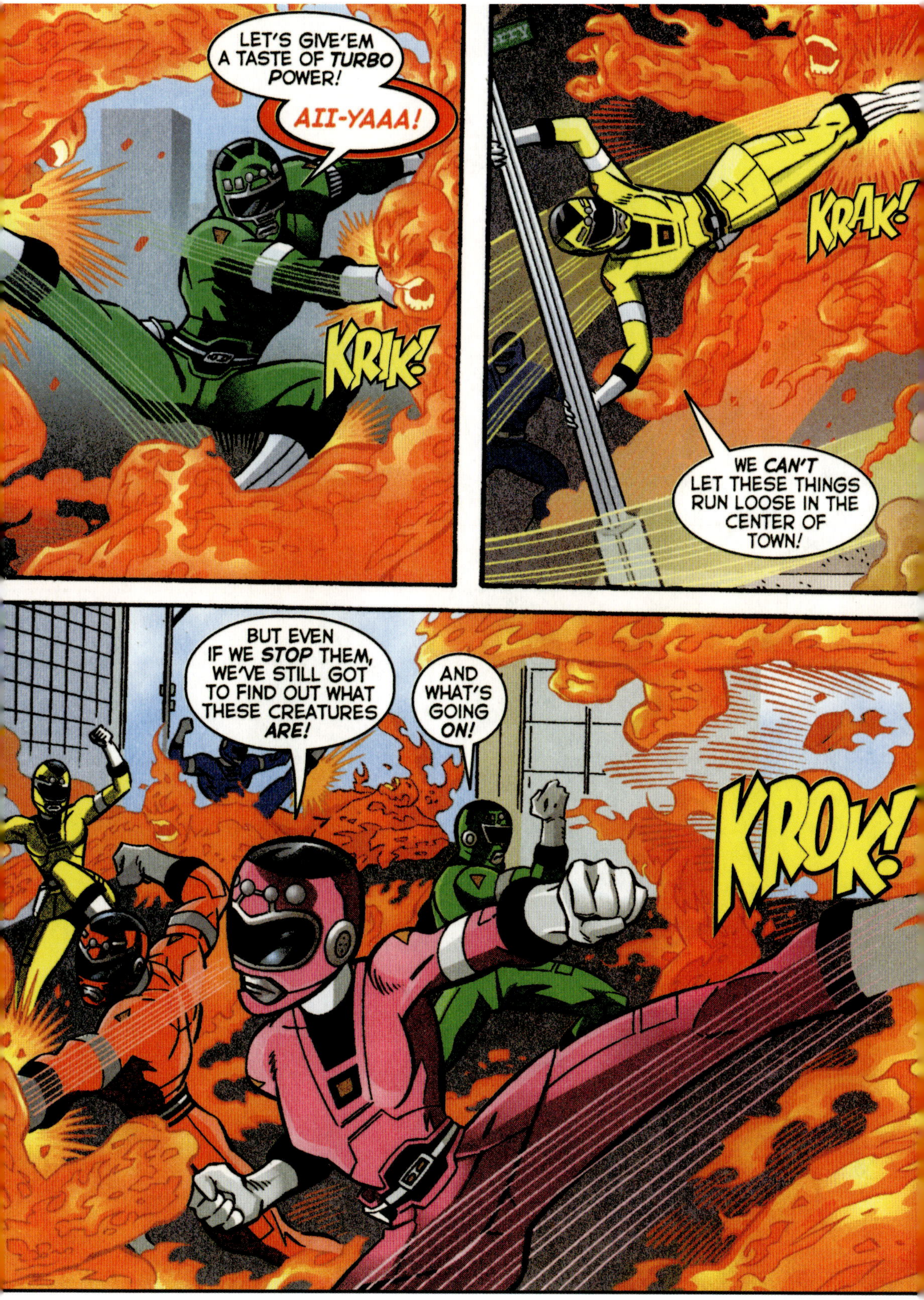
LET'S GIVE'EM A TASTE OF TURBO POWER!
AII-YAAA!
KRIK!
KRAK!
WE CAN'T LET THESE THINGS RUN LOOSE IN THE CENTER OF TOWN!
BUT EVEN IF WE STOP THEM, WE'VE STILL GOT TO FIND OUT WHAT THESE CREATURES ARE!
AND WHAT'S GOING ON!
KROK!

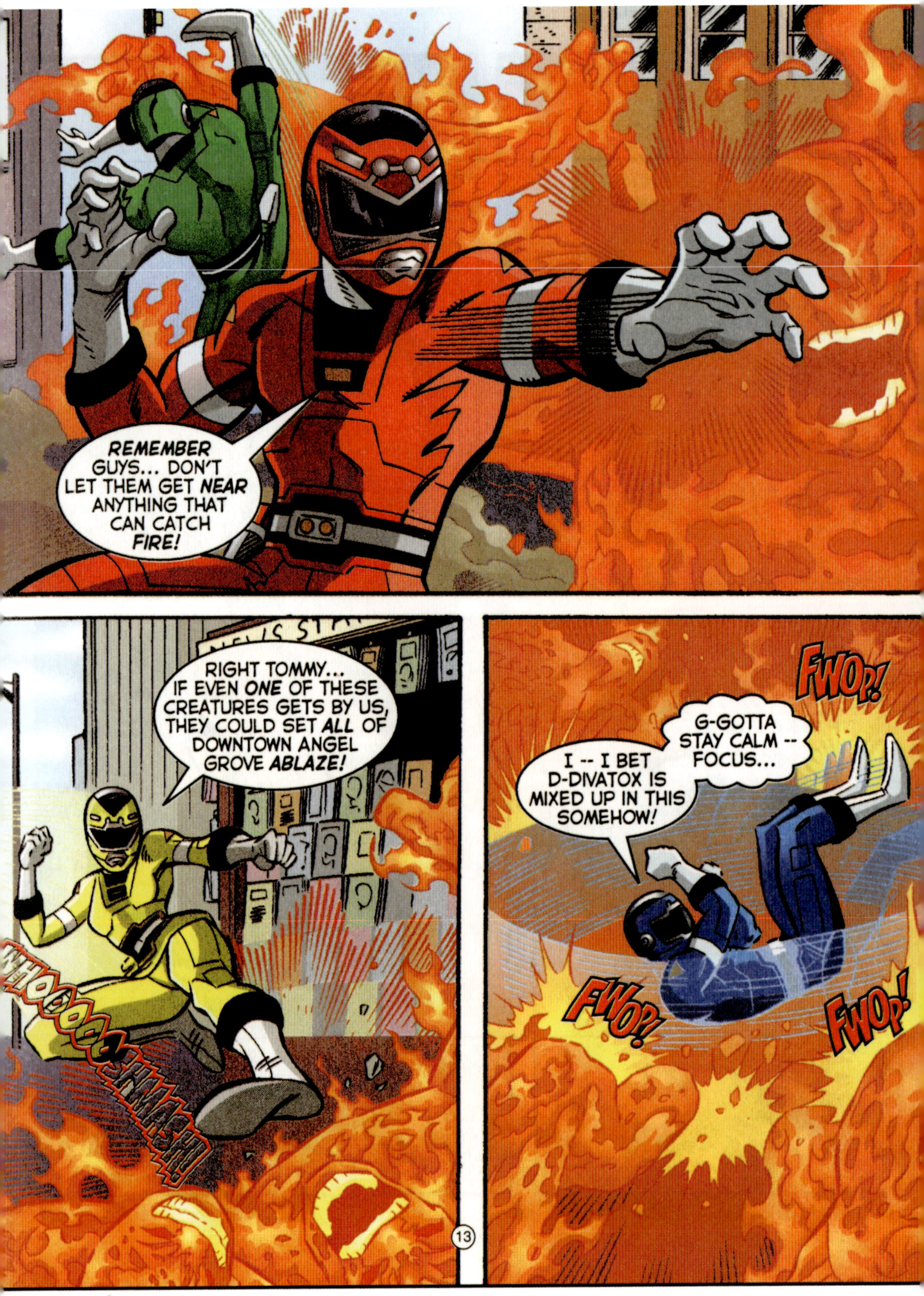
REMEMBER GUYS... DON'T LET THEM GET NEAR ANYTHING THAT CAN CATCH FIRE!
RIGHT TOMMY... IF EVEN ONE OF THESE CREATURES GETS BY US, THEY COULD SET ALL OF DOWNTOWN ANGEL GROVE ABLAZE!
FWOP!
G-GOTTA STAY CALM -- FOCUS...
I -- I BET D-DIVATOX IS MIXED UP IN THIS SOMEHOW!
FWOP!
FWOP!
13

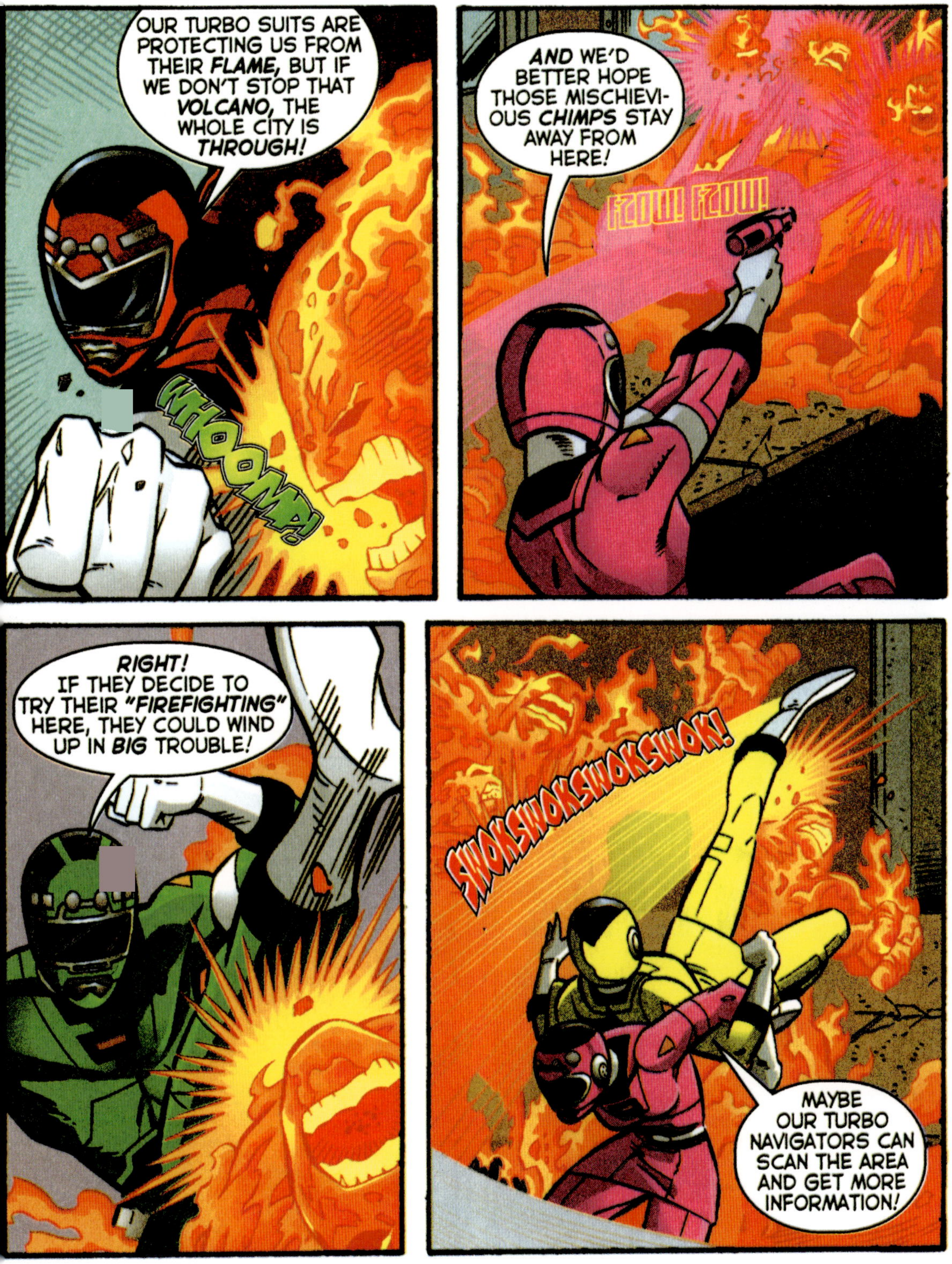
OUR TURBO SUITS ARE PROTECTING US FROM THEIR FLAME, BUT IF WE DON'T STOP THAT VOLCANO, THE WHOLE CITY IS THROUGH!
WHOOOMP!
AND WE'D BETTER HOPE THOSE MISCHIEVI-OUS CHIMPS STAY AWAY FROM HERE!
FZOW! FZOW!
RIGHT! IF THEY DECIDE TO TRY THEIR "FIREFIGHTING" HERE, THEY COULD WIND UP IN BIG TROUBLE!
SWOKSWOKSWOKSWOK!
MAYBE OUR TURBO NAVIGATORS CAN SCAN THE AREA AND GET MORE INFORMATION!

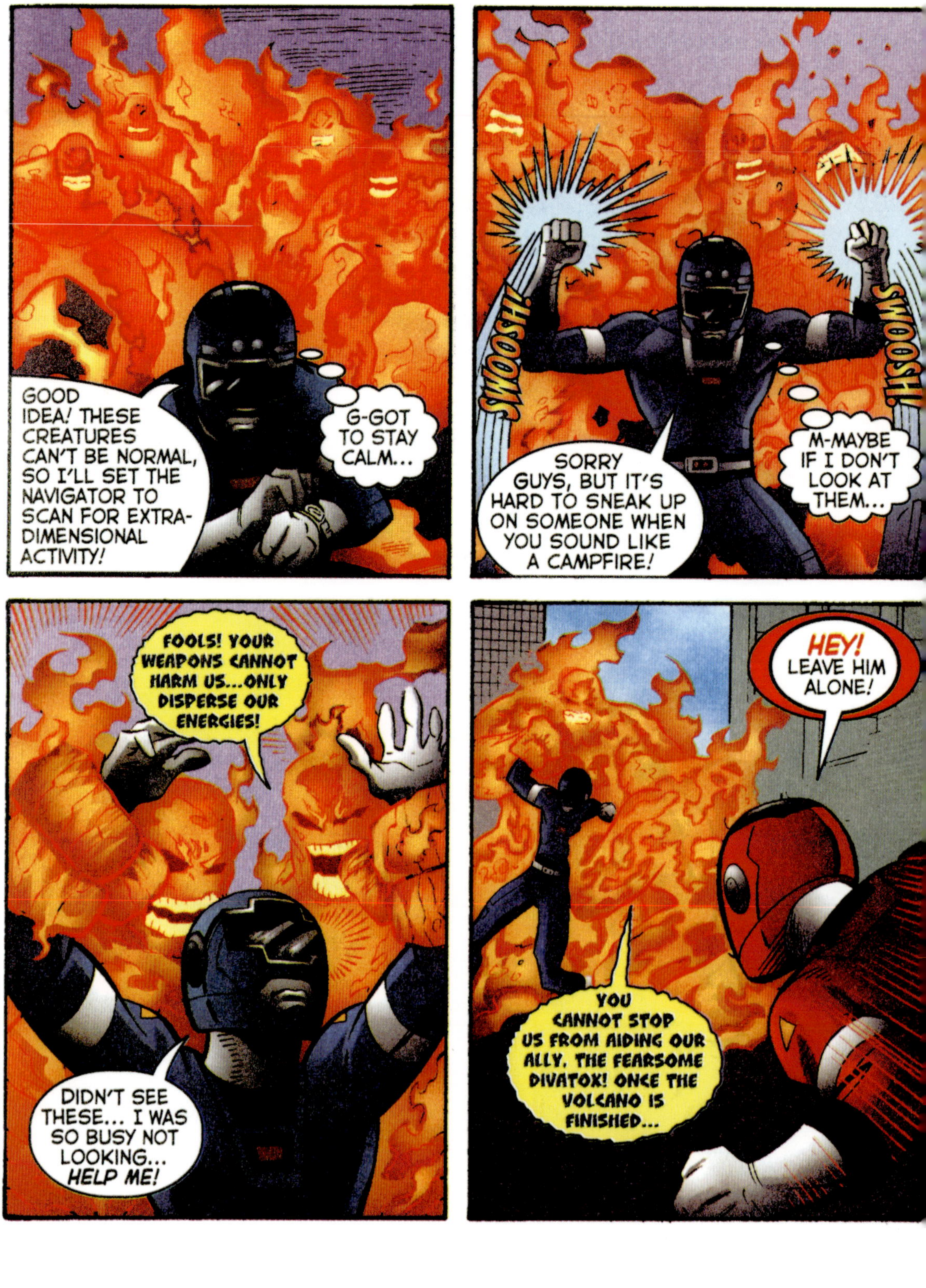
GOOD IDEA! THESE CREATURES CAN'T BE NORMAL, SO I'LL SET THE NAVIGATOR TO SCAN FOR EXTRA-DIMENSIONAL ACTIVITY!
G-GOT TO STAY CALM...
SWOOSH!
SWOOSH!
SORRY GUYS, BUT IT'S HARD TO SNEAK UP ON SOMEONE WHEN YOU SOUND LIKE A CAMPFIRE!
M-MAYBE IF I DON'T LOOK AT THEM...
FOOLS! YOUR WEAPONS CANNOT HARM US...ONLY DISPERSE OUR ENERGIES!
DIDN'T SEE THESE... I WAS SO BUSY NOT LOOKING... HELP ME!
HEY! LEAVE HIM ALONE!
YOU CANNOT STOP US FROM AIDING OUR ALLY, THE FEARSOME DIVATOX! ONCE THE VOLCANO IS FINISHED...

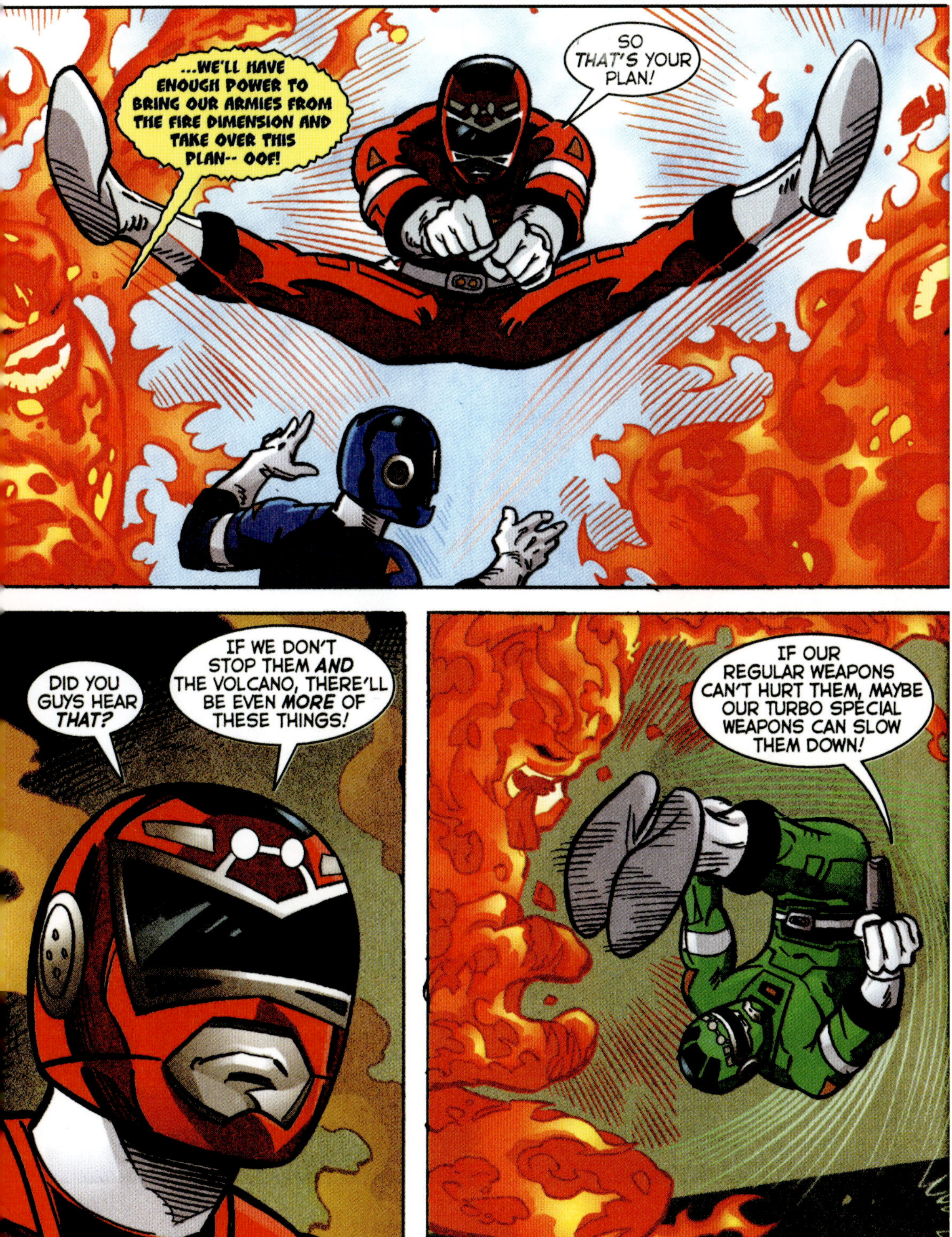
...WE'LL HAVE ENOUGH POWER TO BRING OUR ARMIES FROM THE FIRE DIMENSION AND TAKE OVER THIS PLAN-- OOF!
SO *THAT'S* YOUR PLAN!
DID YOU GUYS HEAR *THAT?*
IF WE DON'T STOP THEM *AND* THE VOLCANO, THERE'LL BE EVEN *MORE* OF THESE THINGS!
IF OUR REGULAR WEAPONS CAN'T HURT THEM, MAYBE OUR TURBO SPECIAL WEAPONS CAN SLOW THEM DOWN!

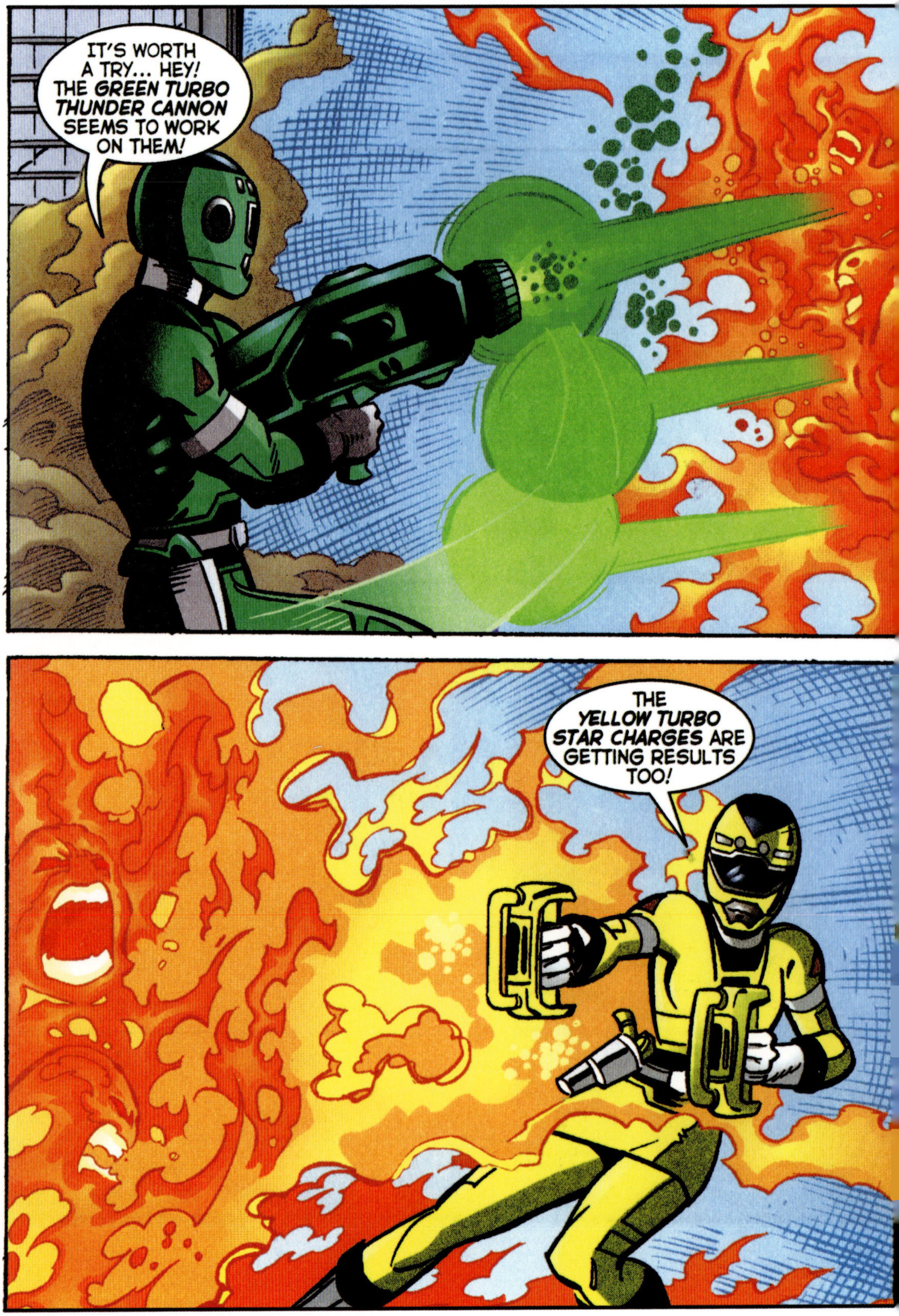
IT'S WORTH A TRY... HEY! THE GREEN TURBO THUNDER CANNON SEEMS TO WORK ON THEM!
THE YELLOW TURBO STAR CHARGES ARE GETTING RESULTS TOO!

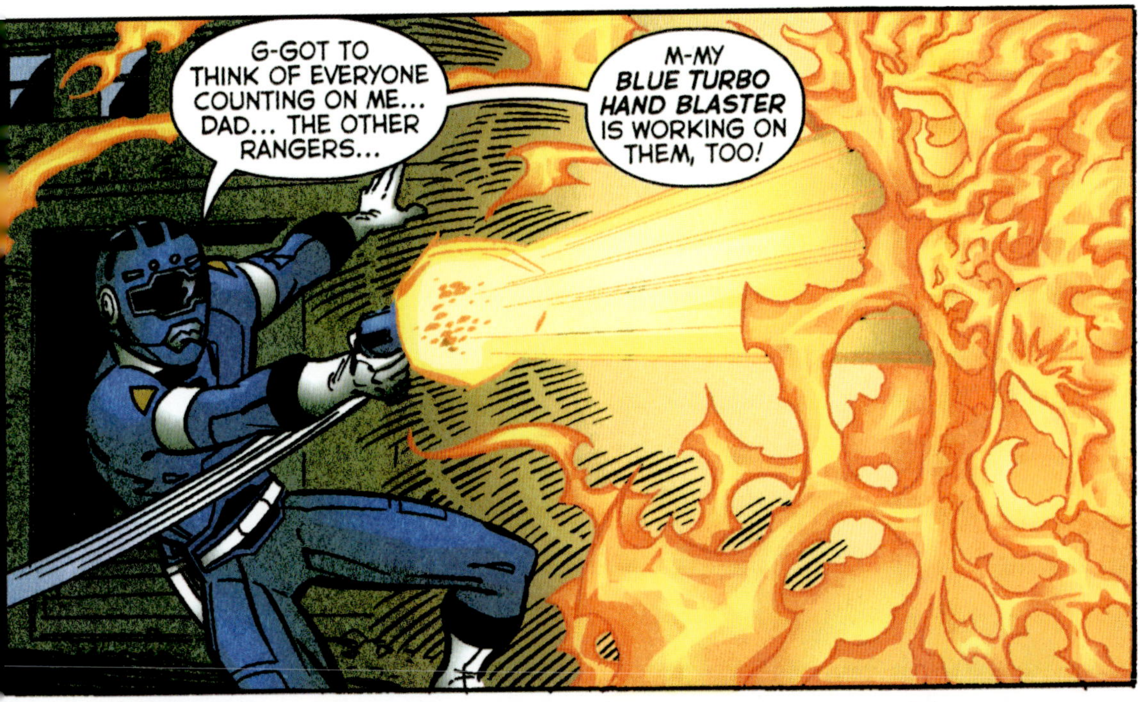
G-GOT TO THINK OF EVERYONE COUNTING ON ME... DAD... THE OTHER RANGERS...
M-MY BLUE TURBO HAND BLASTER IS WORKING ON THEM, TOO!

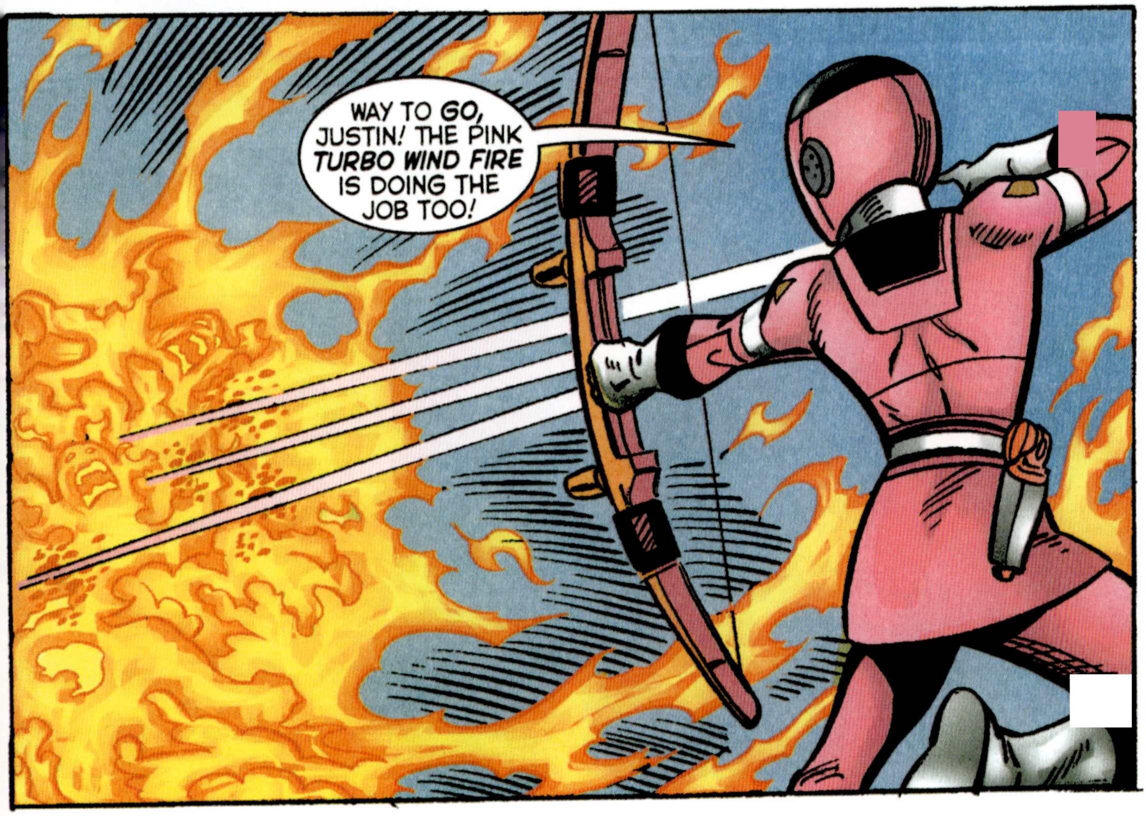
WAY TO GO, JUSTIN! THE PINK TURBO WIND FIRE IS DOING THE JOB TOO!

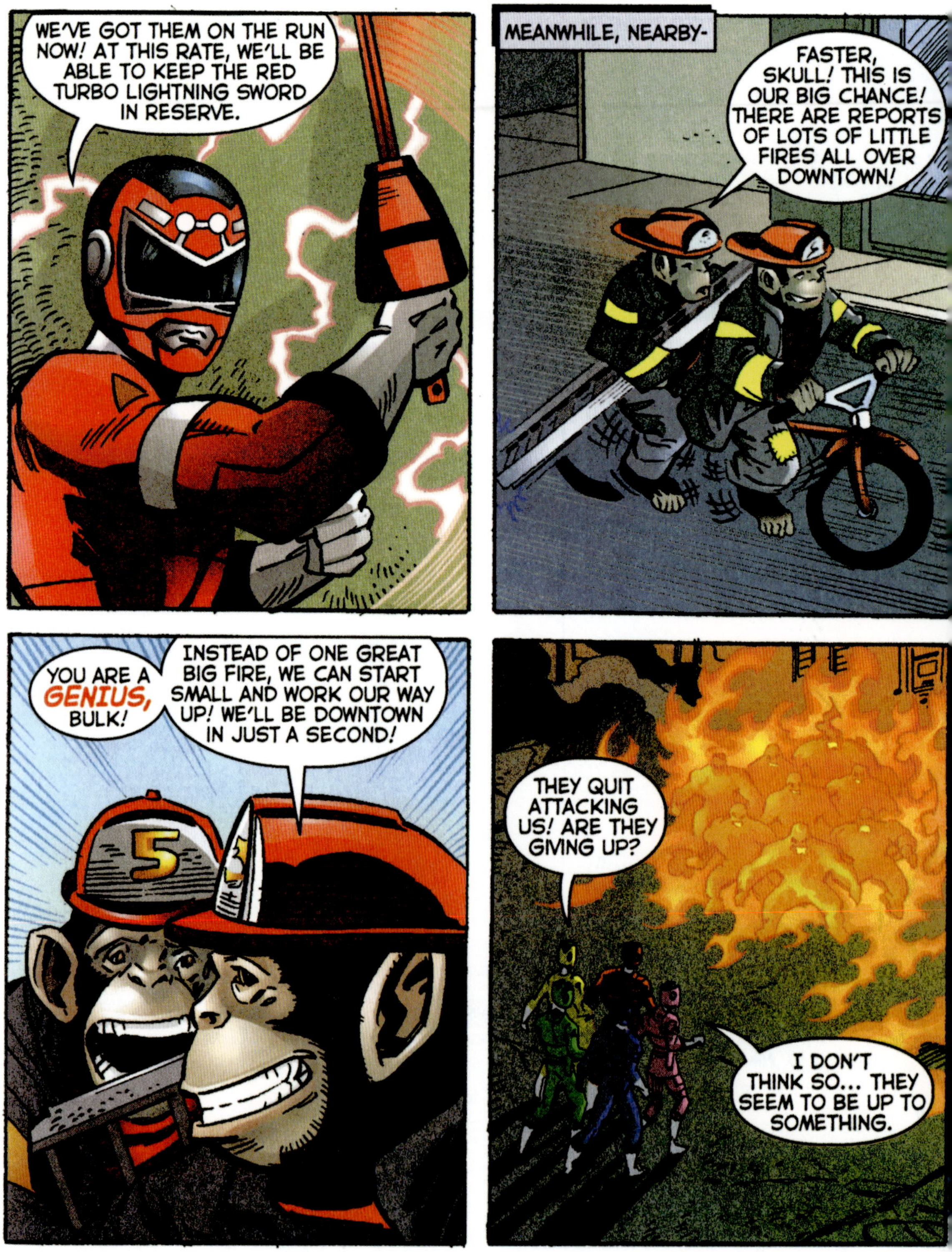
WE'VE GOT THEM ON THE RUN NOW! AT THIS RATE, WE'LL BE ABLE TO KEEP THE RED TURBO LIGHTNING SWORD IN RESERVE.
MEANWHILE, NEARBY-
FASTER, SKULL! THIS IS OUR BIG CHANCE! THERE ARE REPORTS OF LOTS OF LITTLE FIRES ALL OVER DOWNTOWN!
INSTEAD OF ONE GREAT BIG FIRE, WE CAN START SMALL AND WORK OUR WAY UP! WE'LL BE DOWNTOWN IN JUST A SECOND!
YOU ARE A GENIUS, BULK!
THEY QUIT ATTACKING US! ARE THEY GIVING UP?
I DON'T THINK SO... THEY SEEM TO BE UP TO SOMETHING.

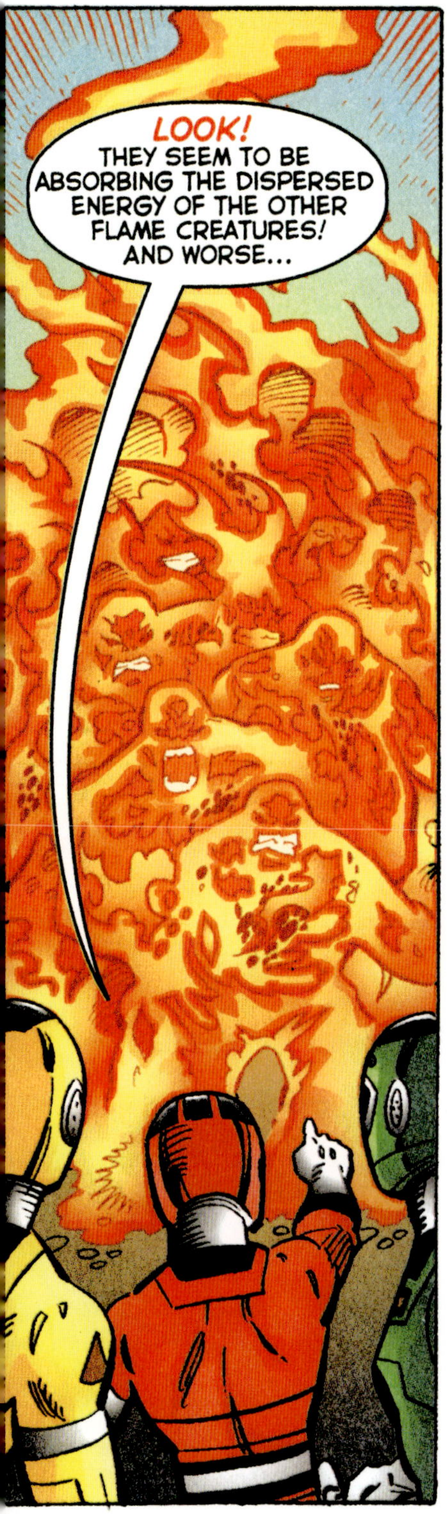
LOOK! THEY SEEM TO BE ABSORBING THE DISPERSED ENERGY OF THE OTHER FLAME CREATURES! AND WORSE...

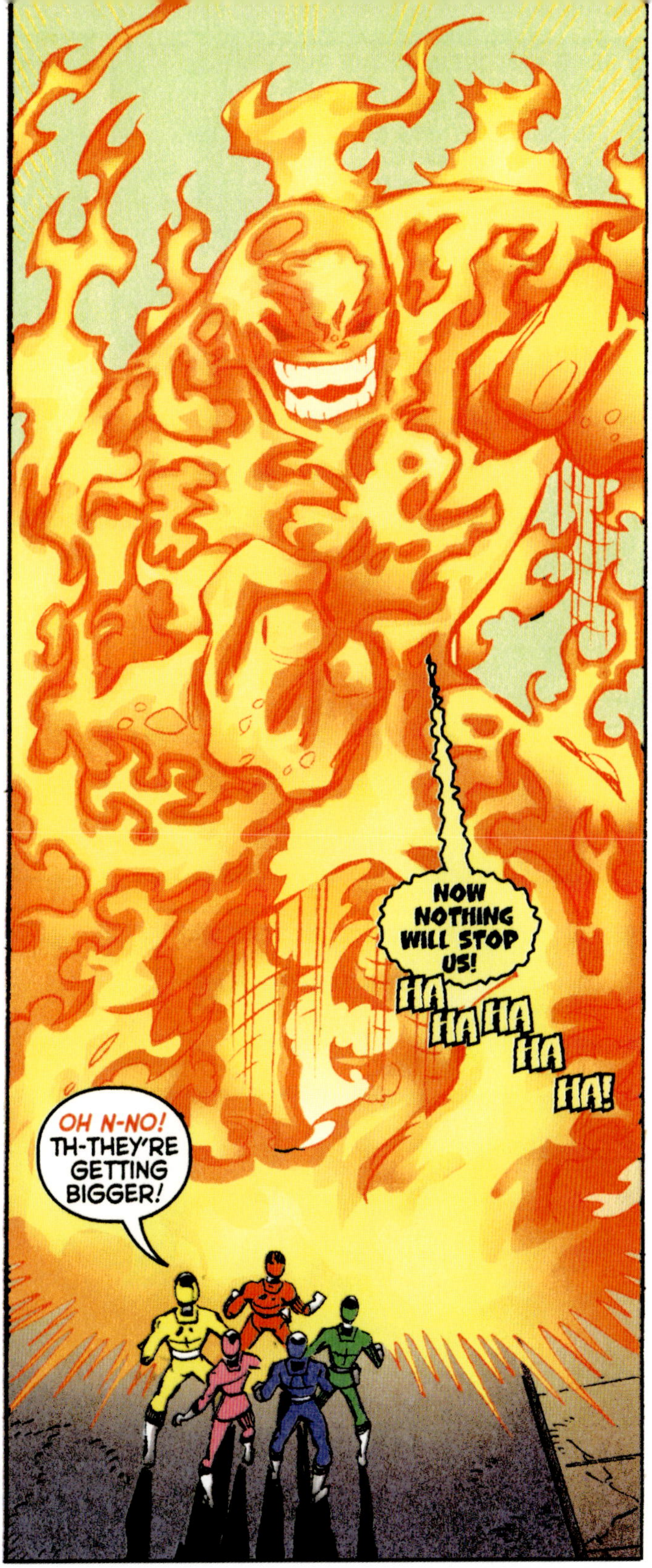
NOW NOTHING WILL STOP US!
HA HA HA HA HA!
OH N-NO! TH-THEY'RE GETTING BIGGER!

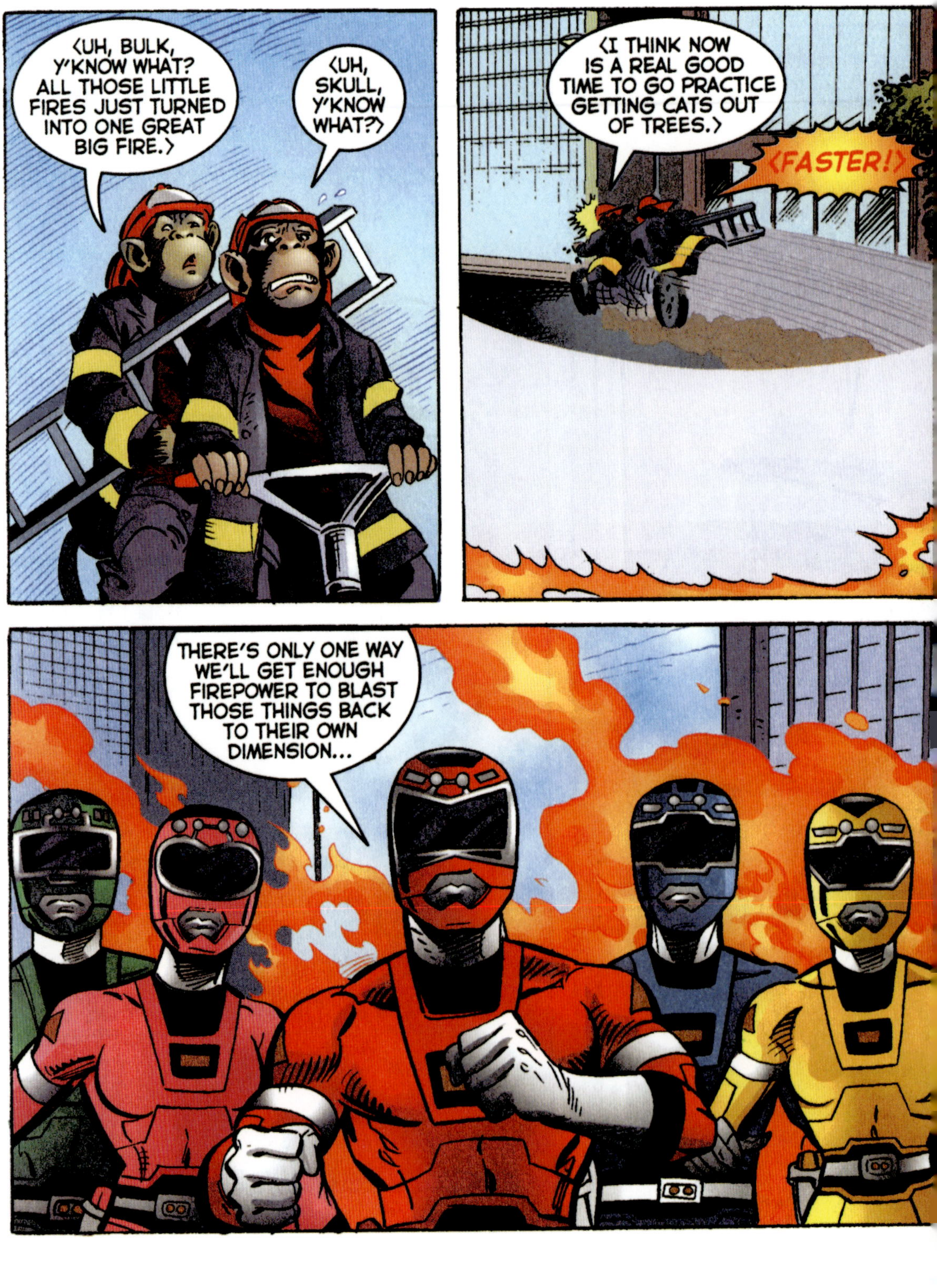

⟨UH, BULK, Y'KNOW WHAT? ALL THOSE LITTLE FIRES JUST TURNED INTO ONE GREAT BIG FIRE.⟩
⟨UH, SKULL, Y'KNOW WHAT?⟩
⟨I THINK NOW IS A REAL GOOD TIME TO GO PRACTICE GETTING CATS OUT OF TREES.⟩
⟨FASTER!⟩
THERE'S ONLY ONE WAY WE'LL GET ENOUGH FIREPOWER TO BLAST THOSE THINGS BACK TO THEIR OWN DIMENSION...

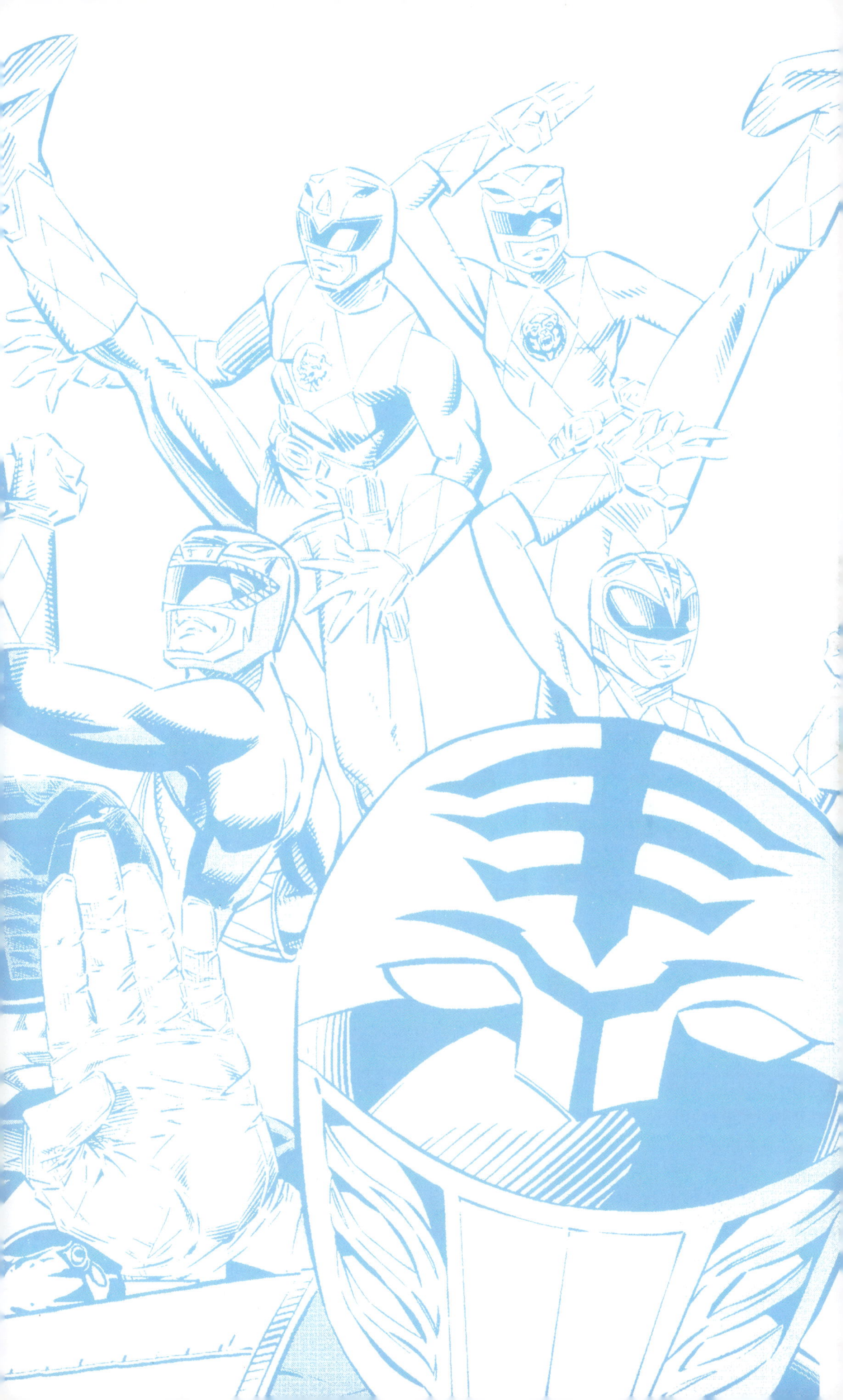

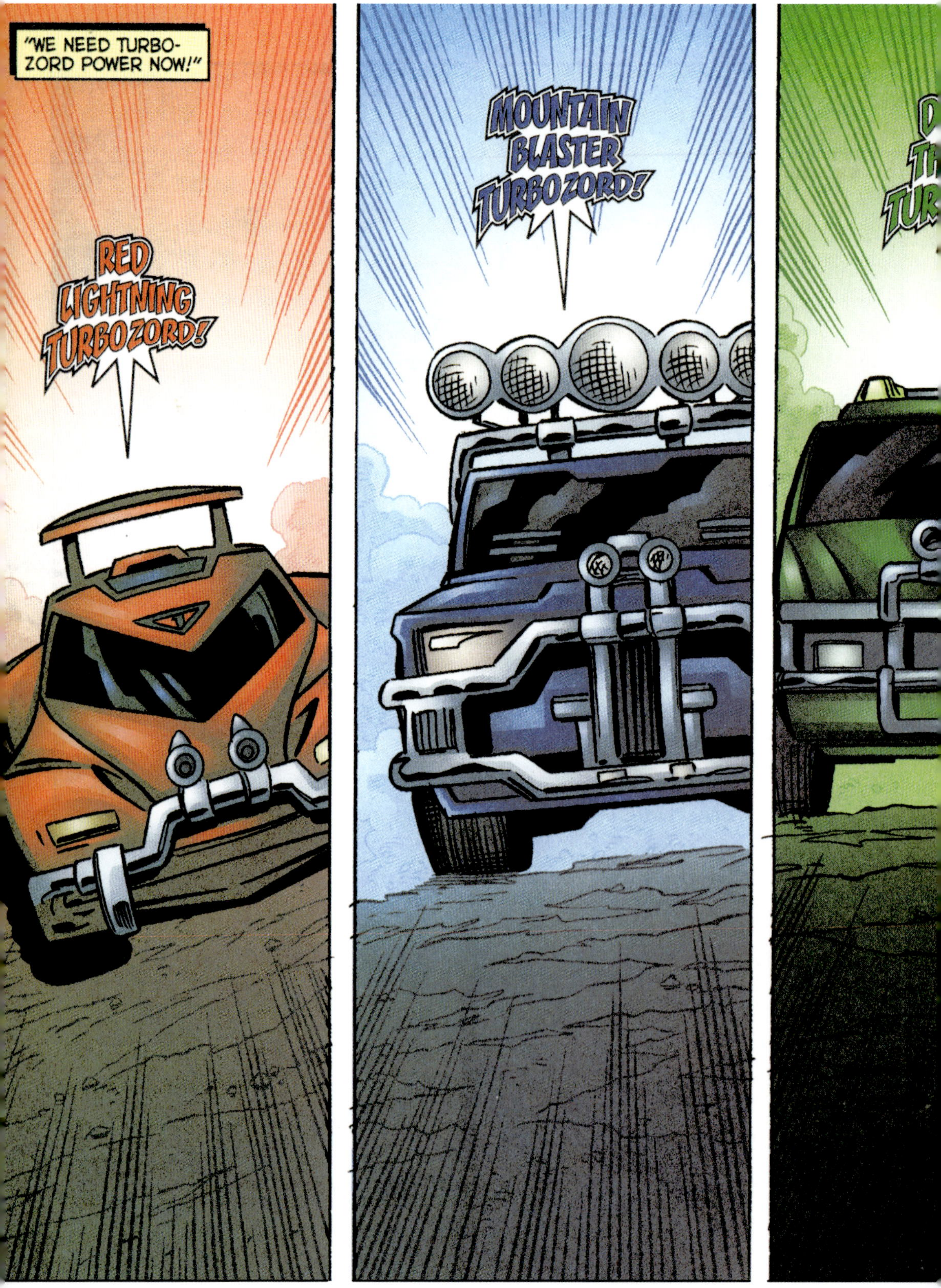
"WE NEED TURBO-ZORD POWER NOW!"
RED LIGHTNING TURBOZORD!
MOUNTAIN BLASTER TURBOZORD!

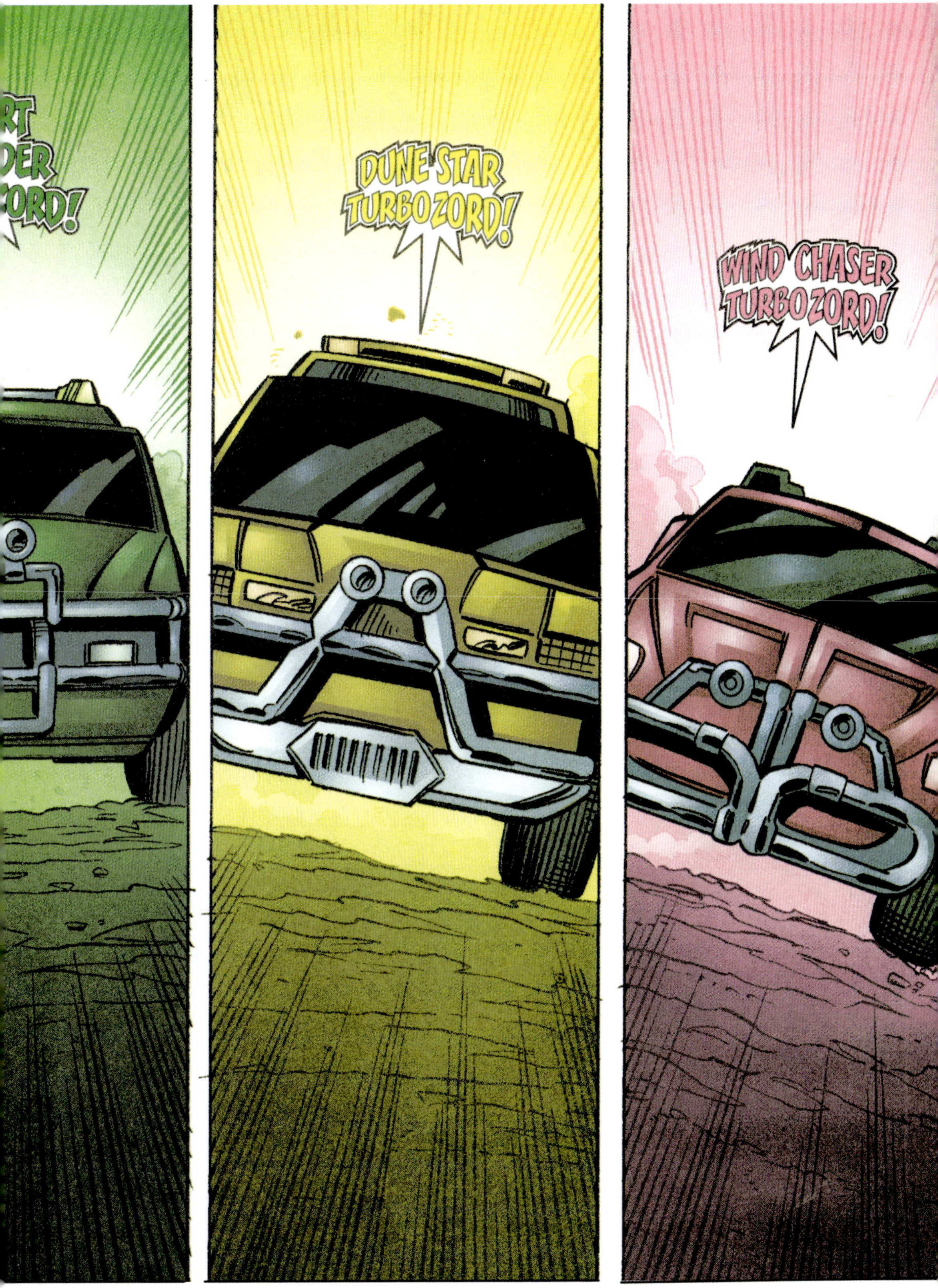
DUNE STAR TURBOZORD!
WIND CHASER TURBOZORD!

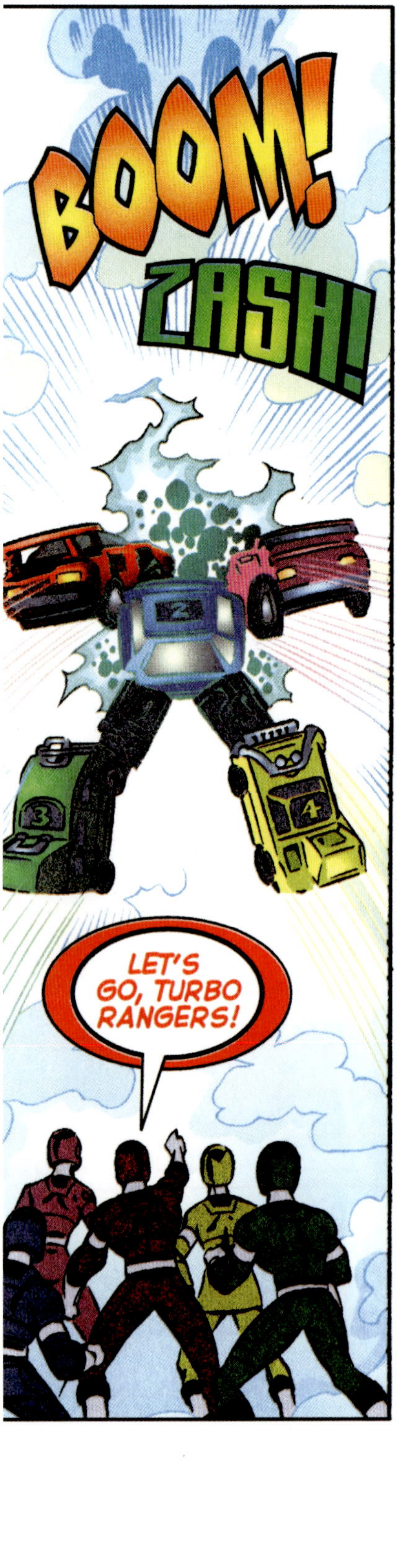
BOOM!
ZASH!
LET'S GO, TURBO RANGERS!
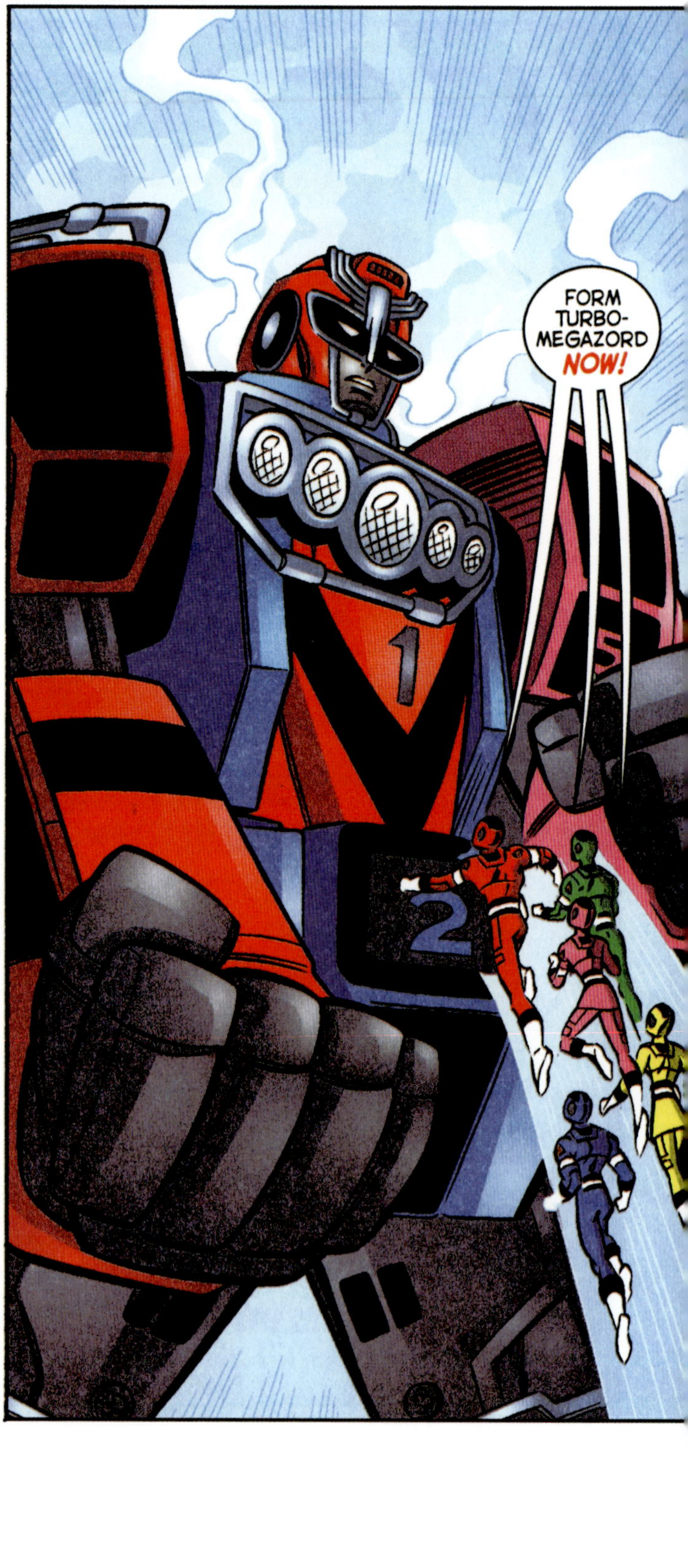
FORM TURBO-MEGAZORD NOW!

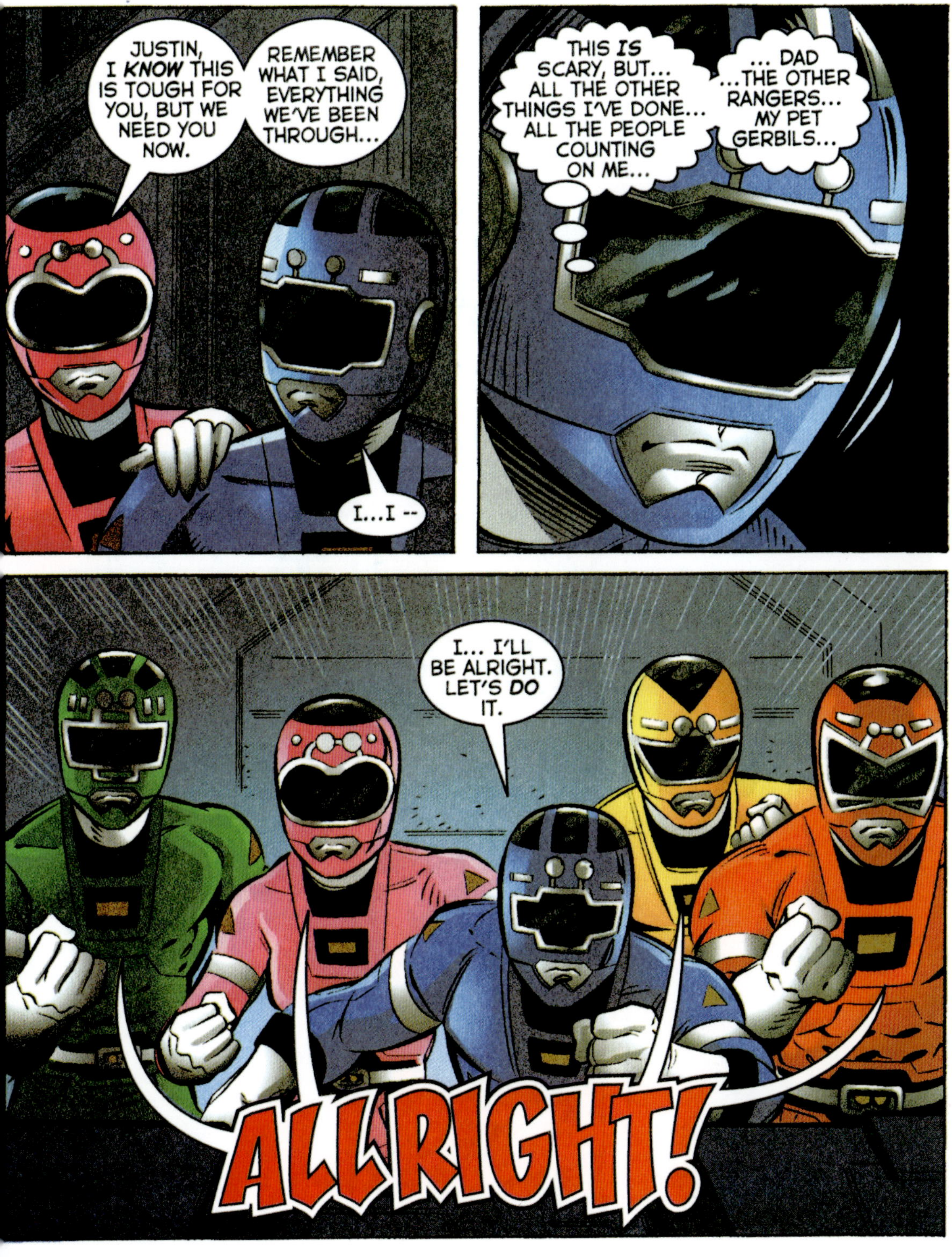
JUSTIN, I KNOW THIS IS TOUGH FOR YOU, BUT WE NEED YOU NOW.
REMEMBER WHAT I SAID, EVERYTHING WE'VE BEEN THROUGH...
I...I --
THIS IS SCARY, BUT... ALL THE OTHER THINGS I'VE DONE... ALL THE PEOPLE COUNTING ON ME...
... DAD ...THE OTHER RANGERS... MY PET GERBILS...
I... I'LL BE ALRIGHT. LET'S DO IT.
ALLRIGHT!

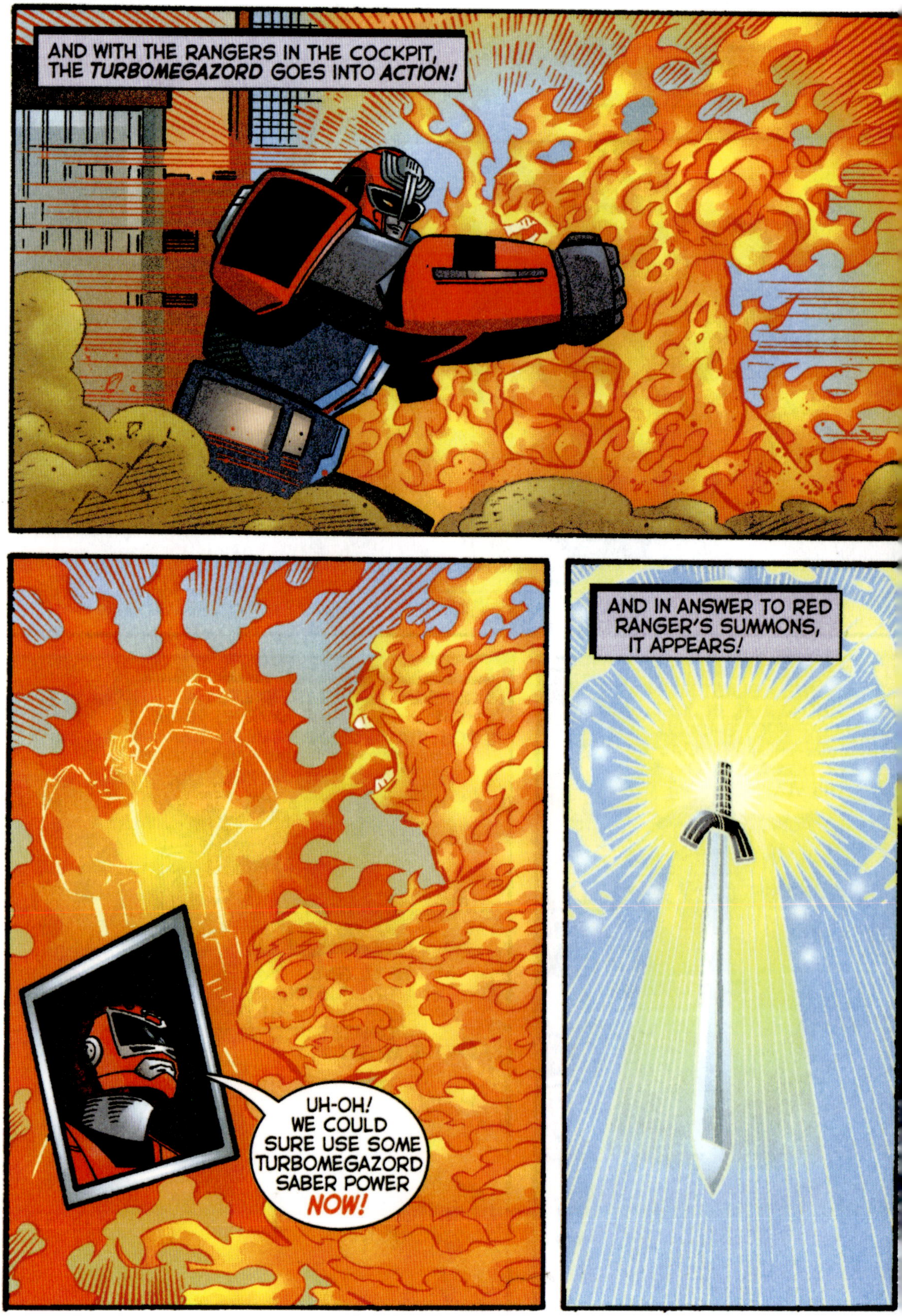
AND WITH THE RANGERS IN THE COCKPIT, THE *TURBOMEGAZORD* GOES INTO *ACTION!*
UH-OH! WE COULD SURE USE SOME TURBOMEGAZORD SABER POWER *NOW!*
AND IN ANSWER TO RED RANGER'S SUMMONS, IT APPEARS!

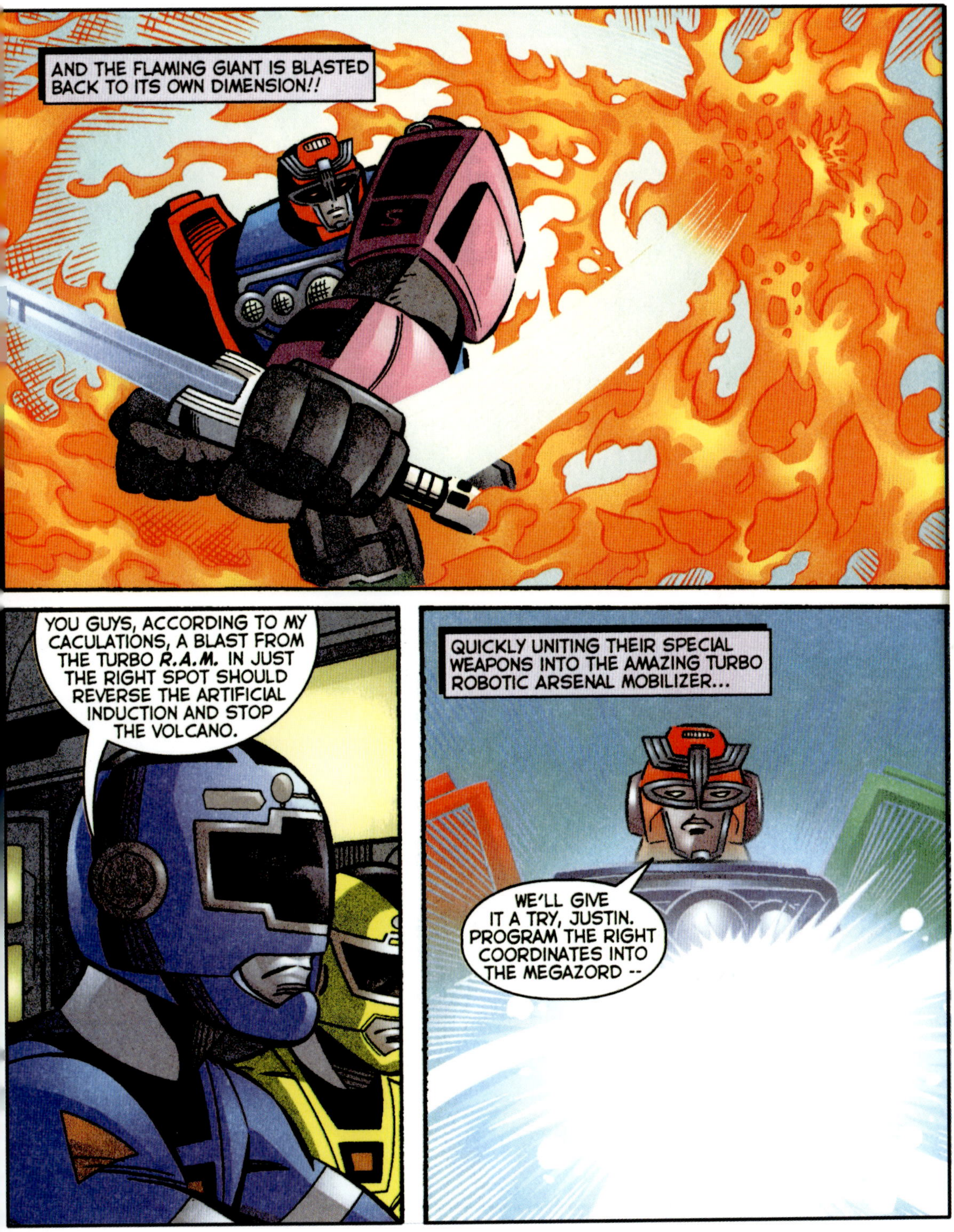
AND THE FLAMING GIANT IS BLASTED BACK TO ITS OWN DIMENSION!!
YOU GUYS, ACCORDING TO MY CACULATIONS, A BLAST FROM THE TURBO *R.A.M.* IN JUST THE RIGHT SPOT SHOULD REVERSE THE ARTIFICIAL INDUCTION AND STOP THE VOLCANO.
QUICKLY UNITING THEIR SPECIAL WEAPONS INTO THE AMAZING TURBO ROBOTIC ARSENAL MOBILIZER...
WE'LL GIVE IT A TRY, JUSTIN. PROGRAM THE RIGHT COORDINATES INTO THE MEGAZORD --

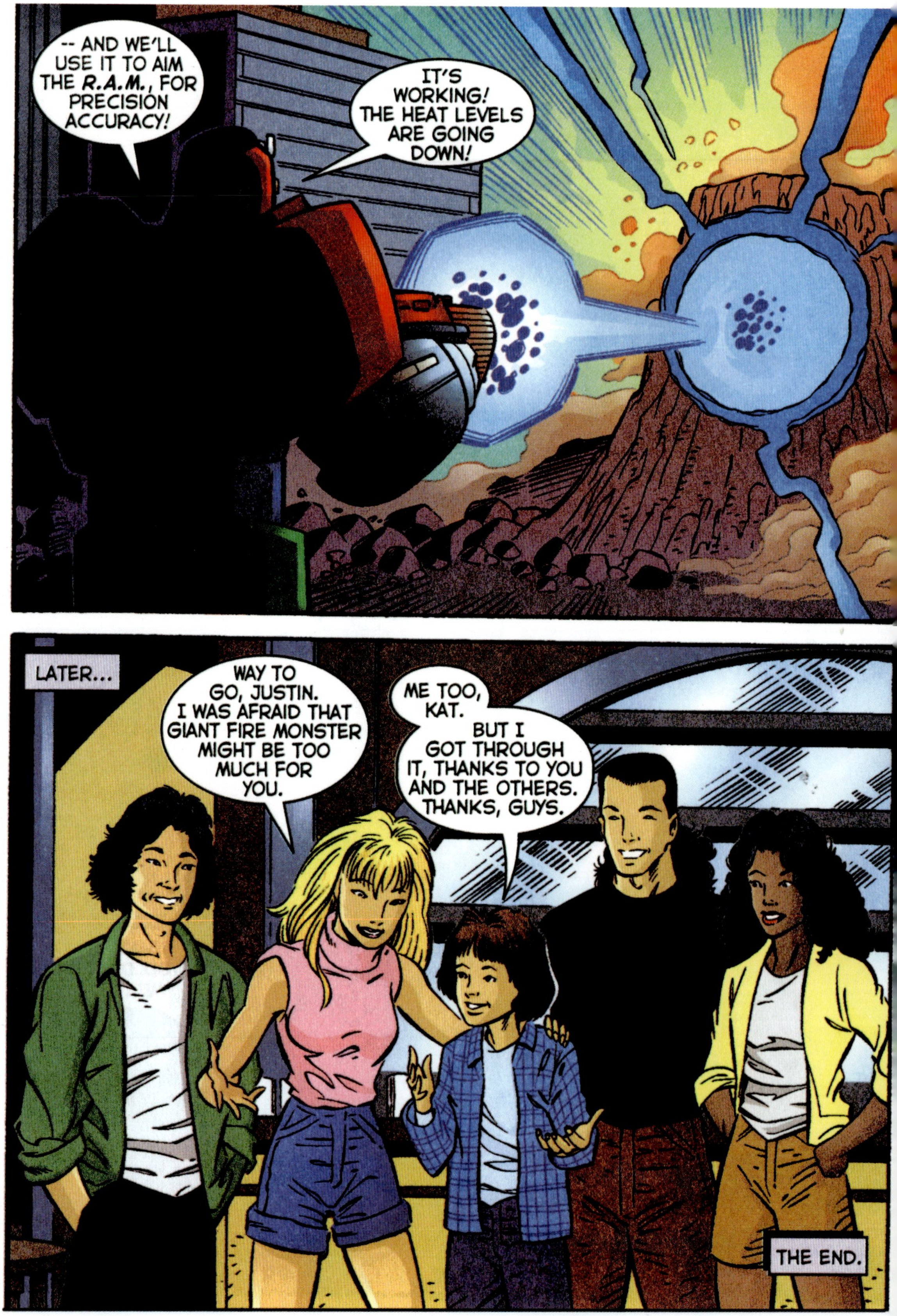
-- AND WE'LL USE IT TO AIM THE *R.A.M.*, FOR PRECISION ACCURACY!
IT'S WORKING! THE HEAT LEVELS ARE GOING DOWN!
LATER...
WAY TO GO, JUSTIN. I WAS AFRAID THAT GIANT FIRE MONSTER MIGHT BE TOO MUCH FOR YOU.
ME TOO, KAT.
BUT I GOT THROUGH IT, THANKS TO YOU AND THE OTHERS. THANKS, GUYS.
THE END.

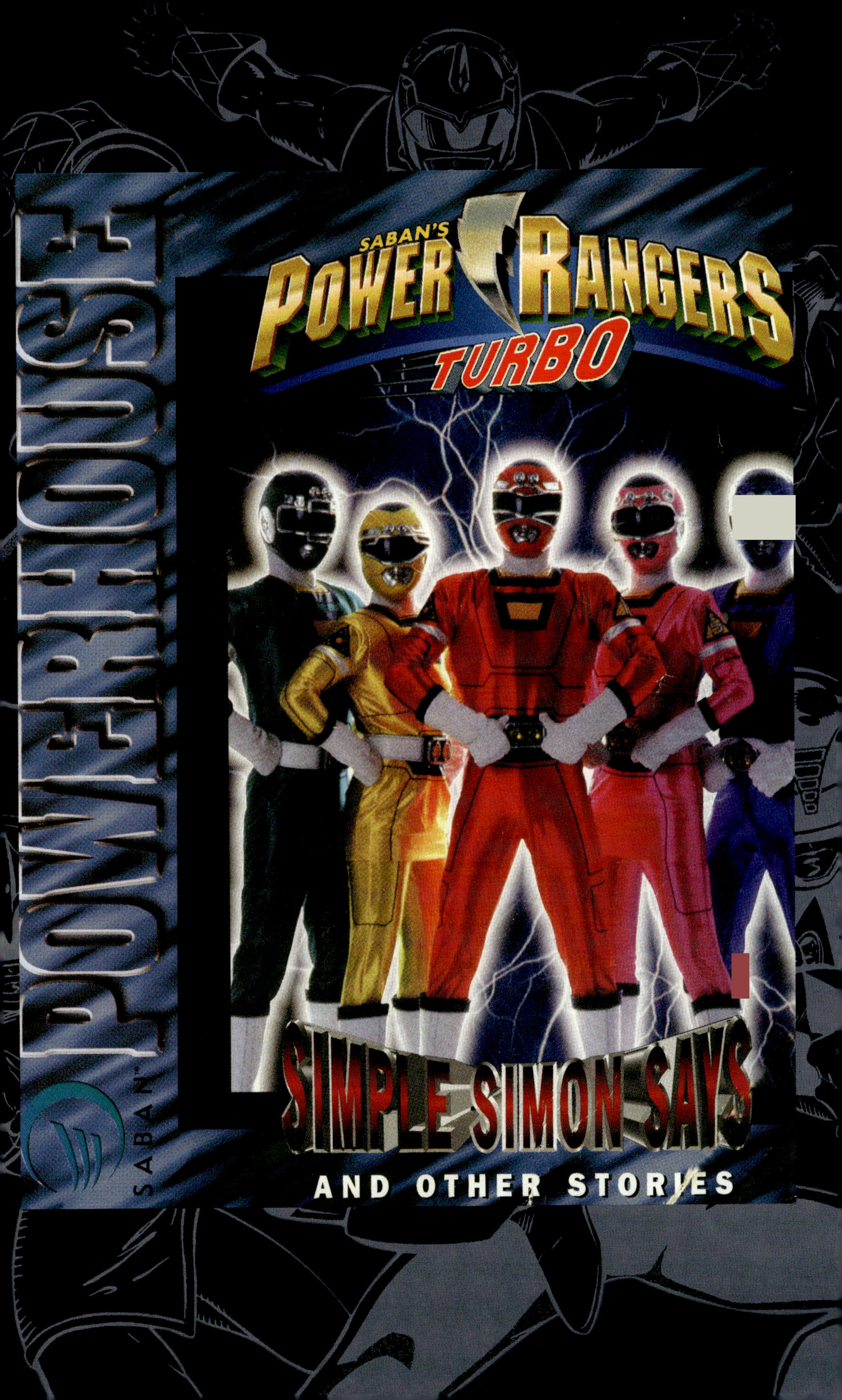
SABAN'S
POWER RANGERS
TURBO
SIMPLE SIMON SAYS
AND OTHER STORIES
POWERHOUSE
SABAN

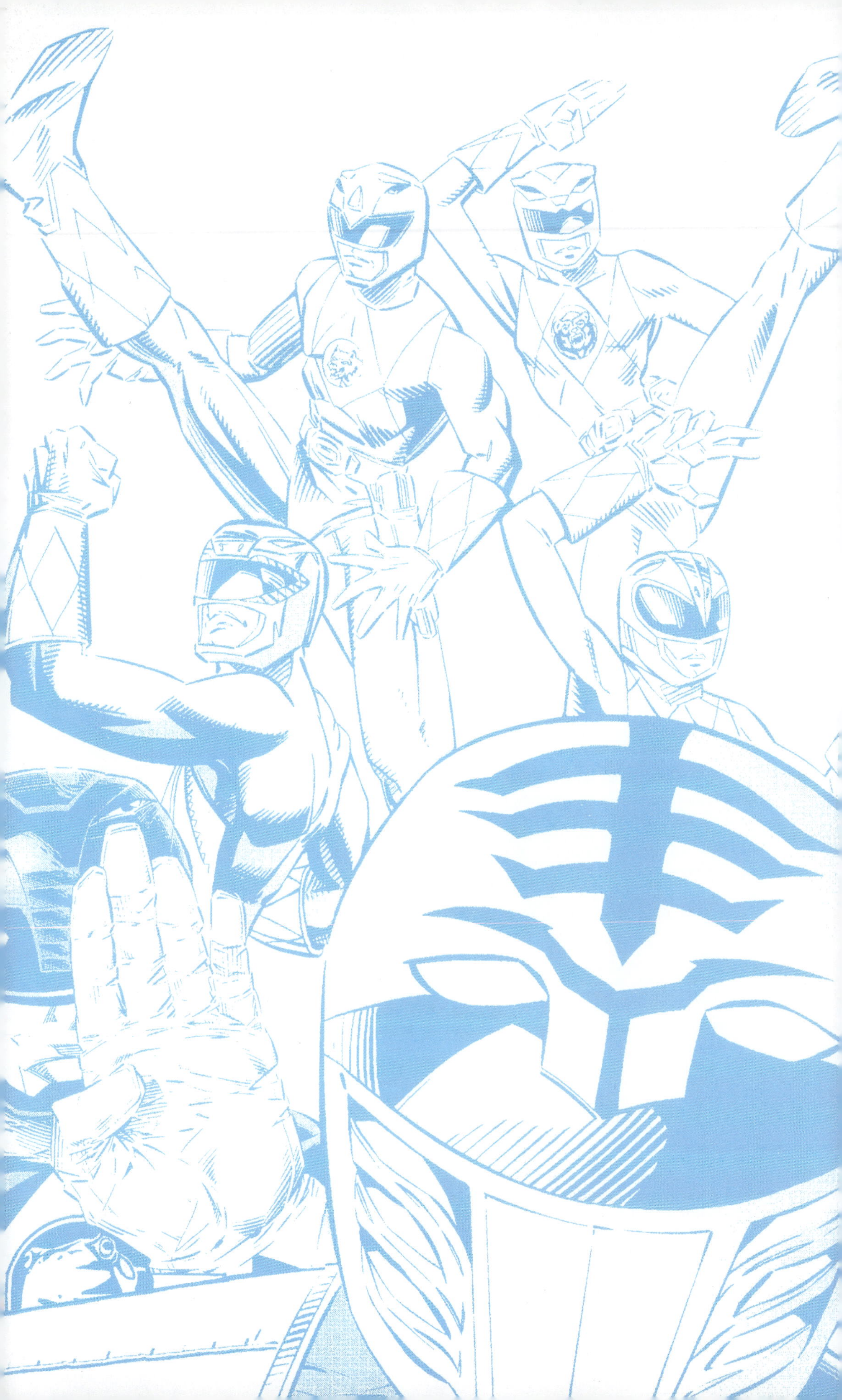

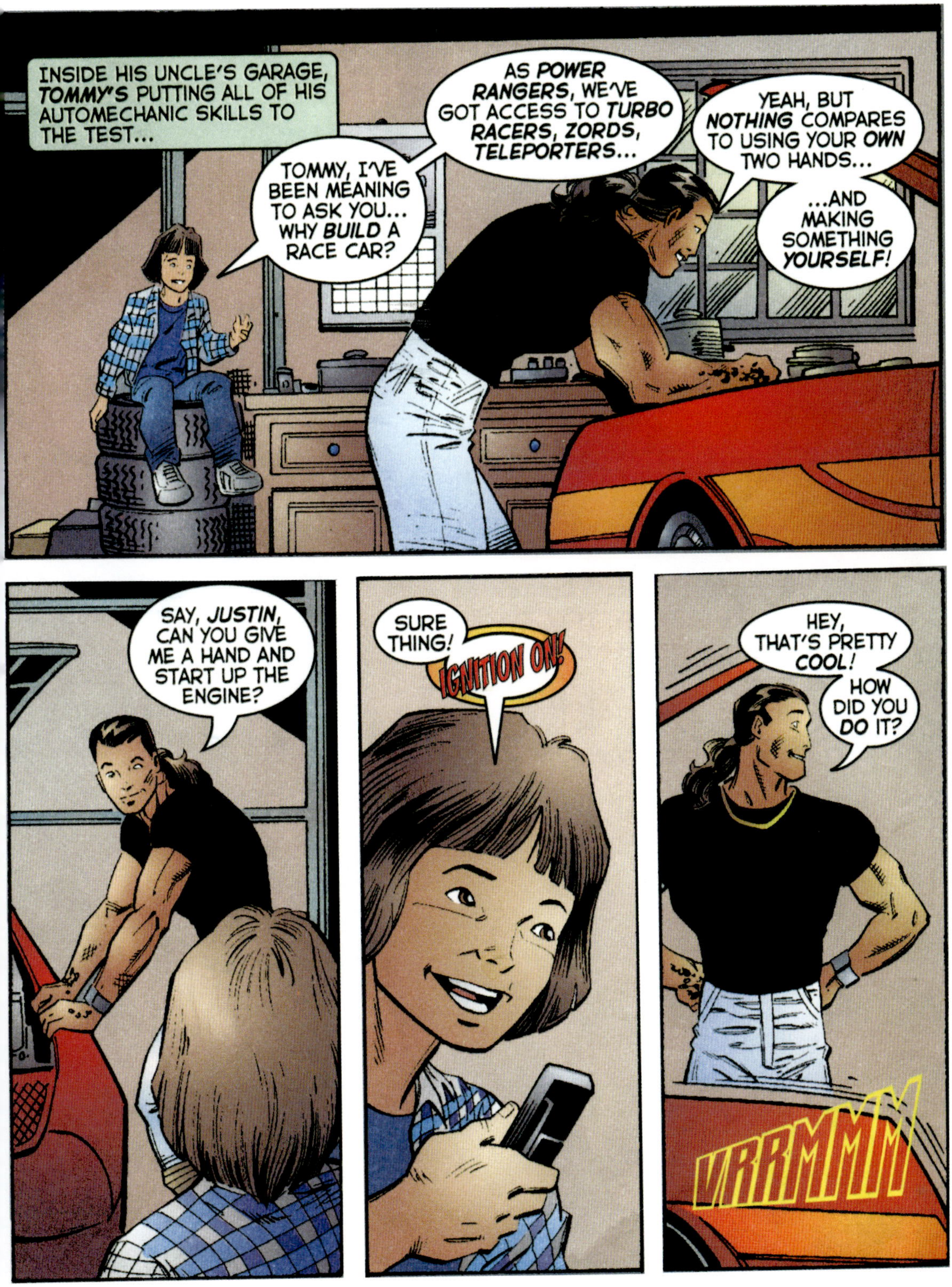
INSIDE HIS UNCLE'S GARAGE, TOMMY'S PUTTING ALL OF HIS AUTOMECHANIC SKILLS TO THE TEST...
TOMMY, I'VE BEEN MEANING TO ASK YOU... WHY BUILD A RACE CAR?
AS POWER RANGERS, WE'VE GOT ACCESS TO TURBO RACERS, ZORDS, TELEPORTERS...
YEAH, BUT NOTHING COMPARES TO USING YOUR OWN TWO HANDS...
...AND MAKING SOMETHING YOURSELF!
SAY, JUSTIN, CAN YOU GIVE ME A HAND AND START UP THE ENGINE?
SURE THING!
IGNITION ON!
HEY, THAT'S PRETTY COOL!
HOW DID YOU DO IT?
VRRMMM

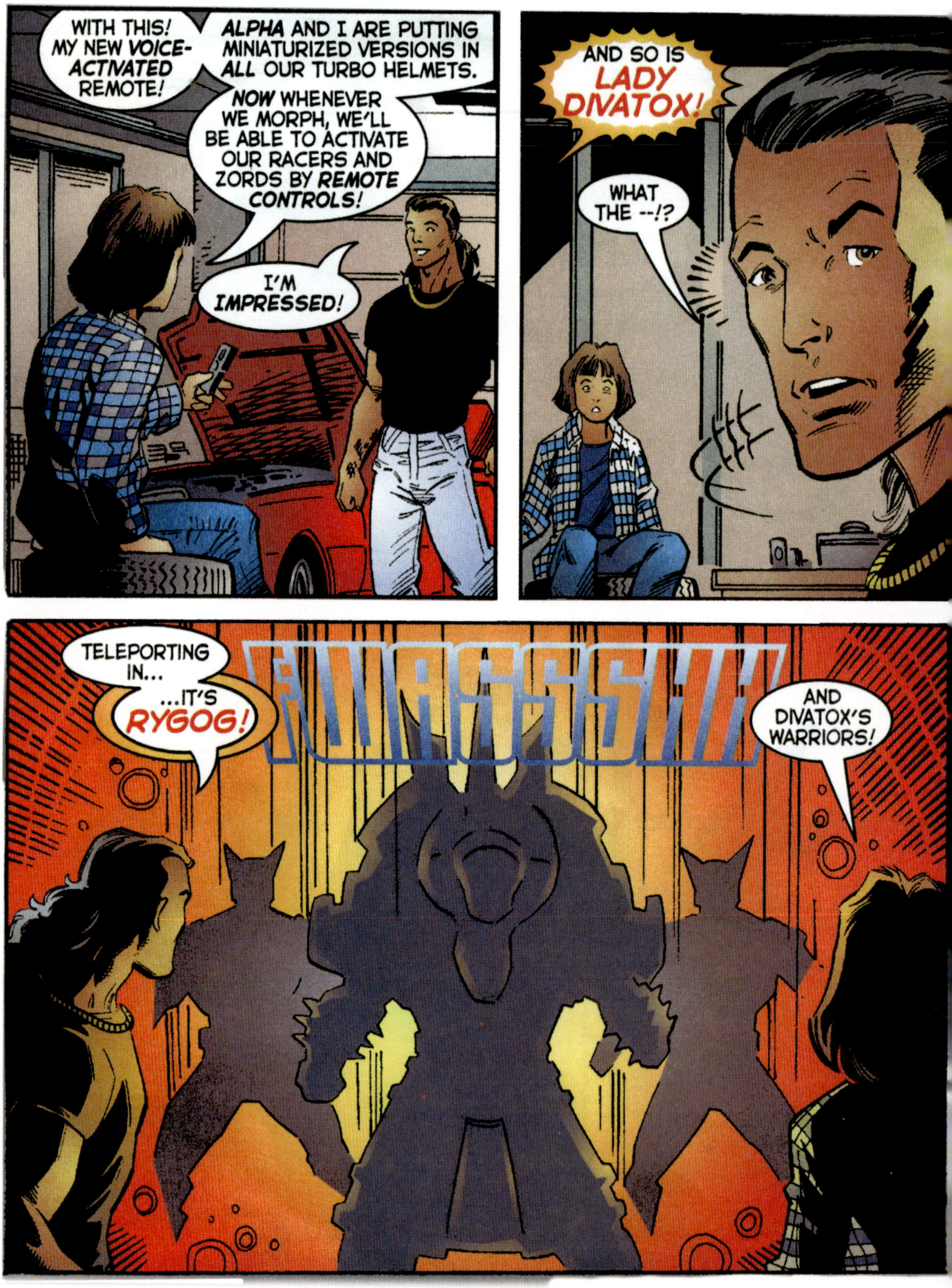

WITH THIS! MY NEW VOICE-ACTIVATED REMOTE!
ALPHA AND I ARE PUTTING MINIATURIZED VERSIONS IN ALL OUR TURBO HELMETS.
NOW WHENEVER WE MORPH, WE'LL BE ABLE TO ACTIVATE OUR RACERS AND ZORDS BY REMOTE CONTROLS!
I'M IMPRESSED!
AND SO IS LADY DIVATOX!
WHAT THE --!?
TELEPORTING IN...
...IT'S RYGOG!
AND DIVATOX'S WARRIORS!

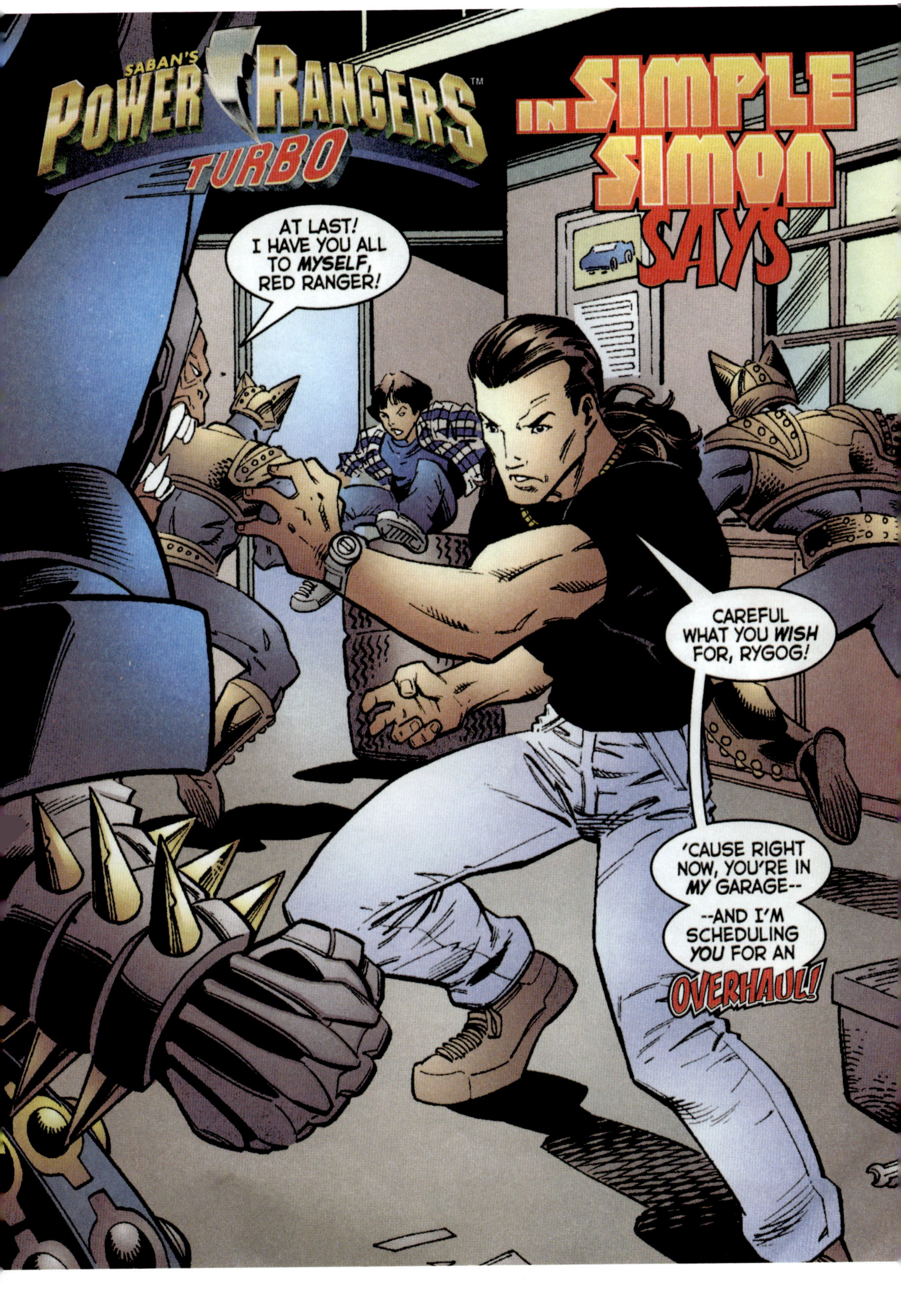
SABAN'S POWER RANGERS TURBO
IN... SIMPLE SIMON SAYS
AT LAST! I HAVE YOU ALL TO MYSELF, RED RANGER!
CAREFUL WHAT YOU WISH FOR, RYGOG!
'CAUSE RIGHT NOW, YOU'RE IN MY GARAGE--
--AND I'M SCHEDULING YOU FOR AN OVERHAUL!

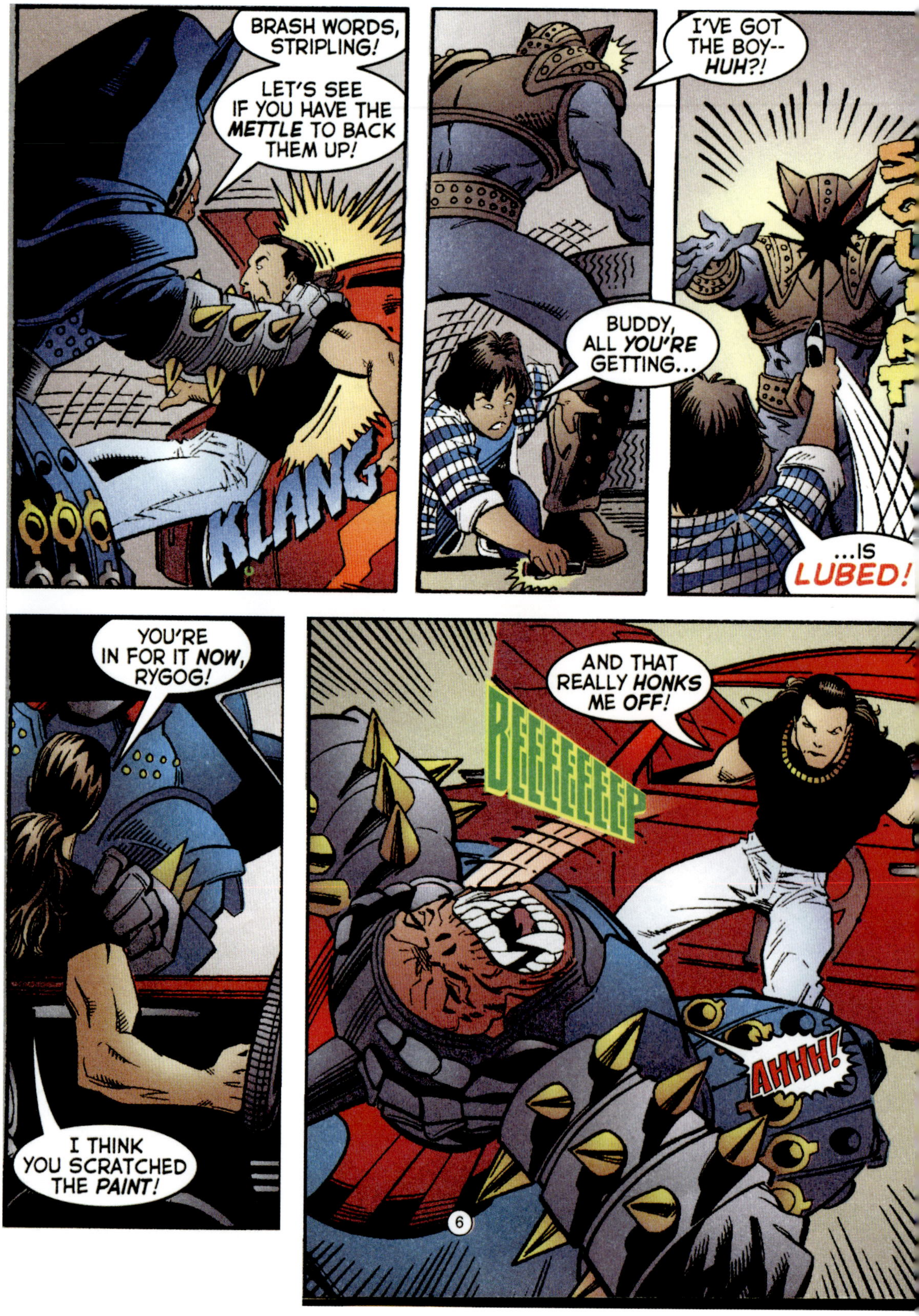
BRASH WORDS, STRIPLING!
LET'S SEE IF YOU HAVE THE METTLE TO BACK THEM UP!
KLANG
I'VE GOT THE BOY-- HUH?!
BUDDY, ALL YOU'RE GETTING...
...IS LUBED!
YOU'RE IN FOR IT NOW, RYGOG!
I THINK YOU SCRATCHED THE PAINT!
AND THAT REALLY HONKS ME OFF!
AHHH!
6

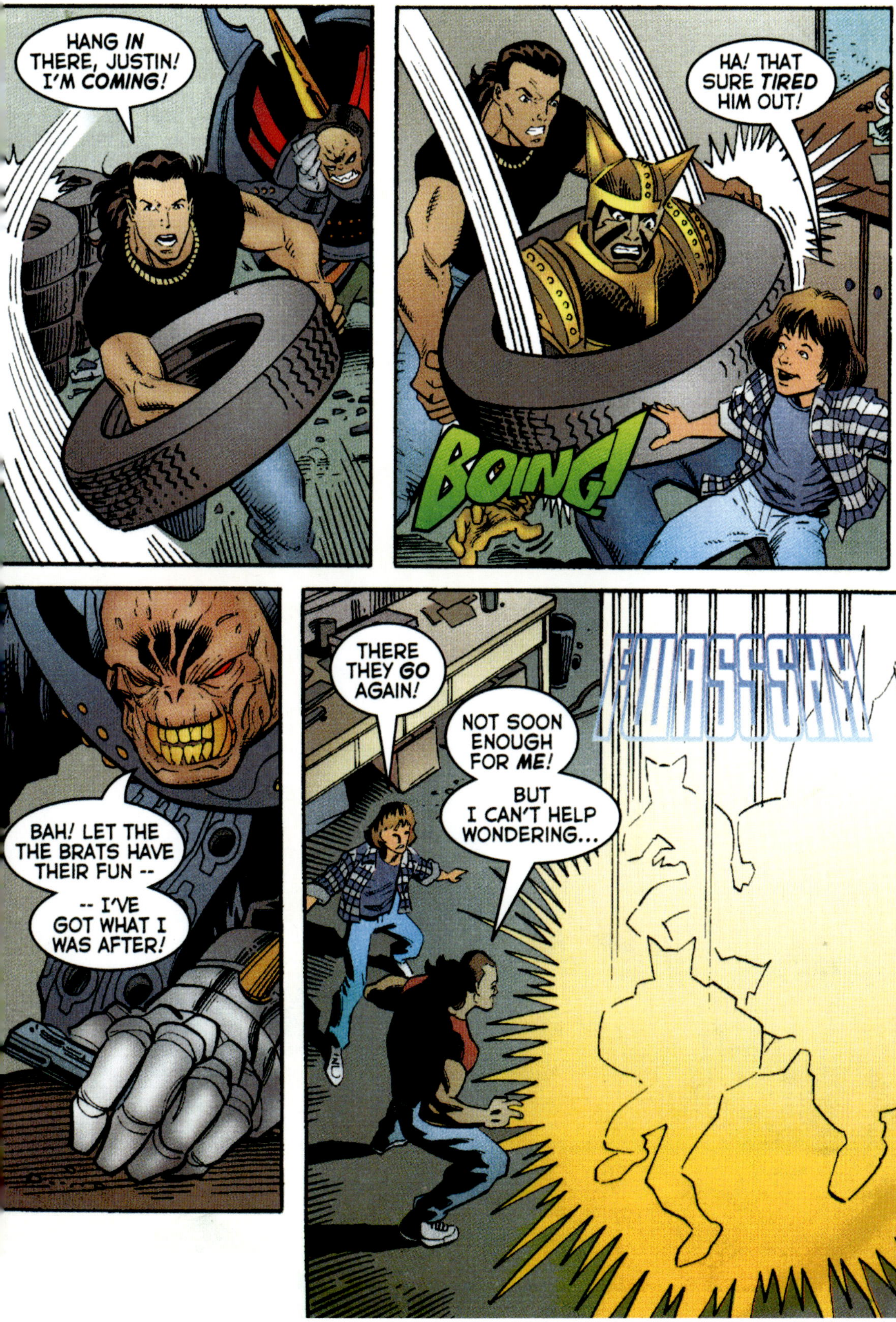
HANG IN THERE, JUSTIN! I'M COMING!
HA! THAT SURE TIRED HIM OUT!
BOING!
BAH! LET THE THE BRATS HAVE THEIR FUN --
-- I'VE GOT WHAT I WAS AFTER!
THERE THEY GO AGAIN!
NOT SOON ENOUGH FOR ME!
BUT I CAN'T HELP WONDERING...

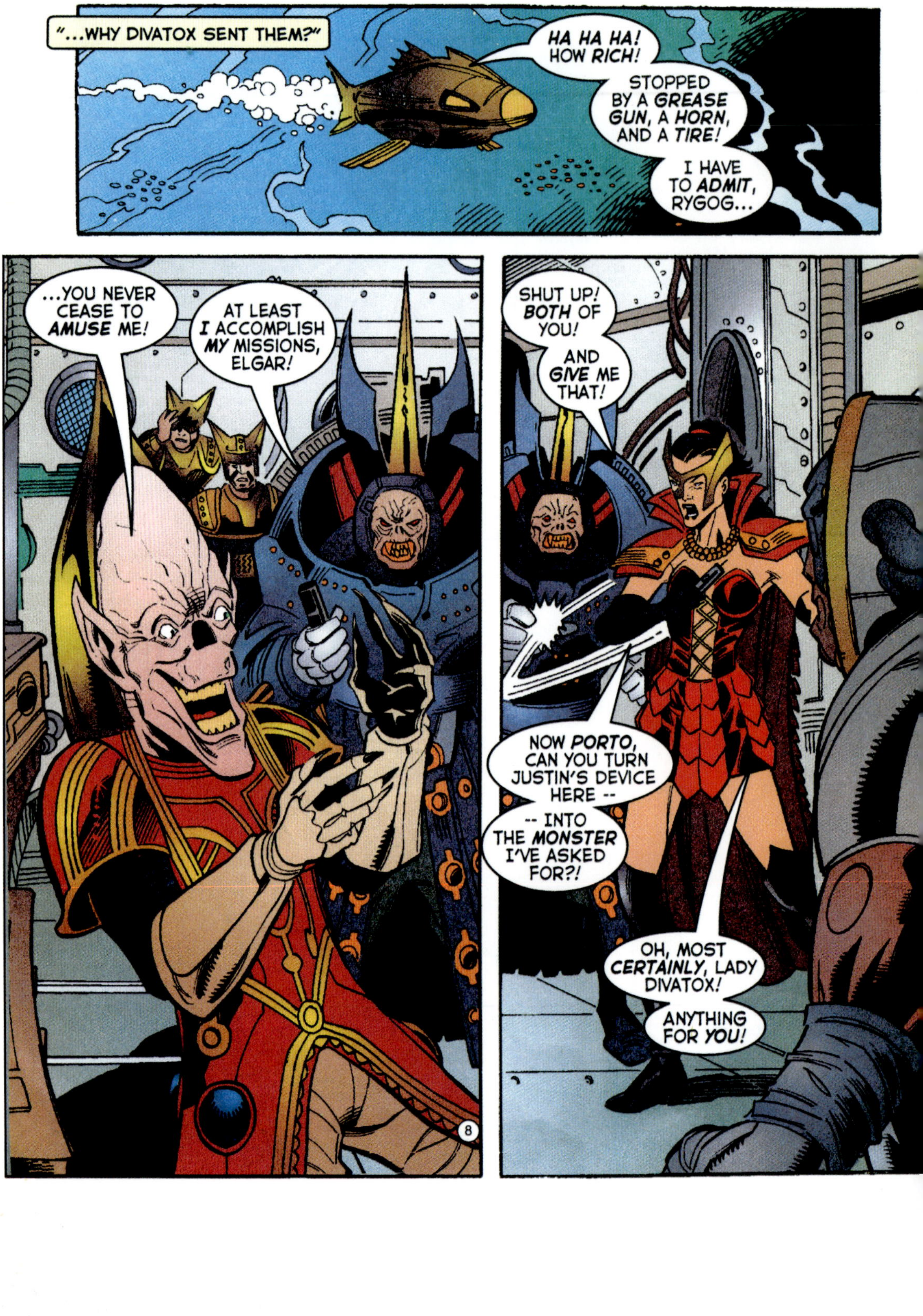
"...WHY DIVATOX SENT THEM?"
HA HA HA! HOW RICH!
STOPPED BY A GREASE GUN, A HORN, AND A TIRE!
I HAVE TO ADMIT, RYGOG...
...YOU NEVER CEASE TO AMUSE ME!
AT LEAST I ACCOMPLISH MY MISSIONS, ELGAR!
8
SHUT UP! BOTH OF YOU!
AND GIVE ME THAT!
NOW PORTO, CAN YOU TURN JUSTIN'S DEVICE HERE --
-- INTO THE MONSTER I'VE ASKED FOR?!
OH, MOST CERTAINLY, LADY DIVATOX!
ANYTHING FOR YOU!

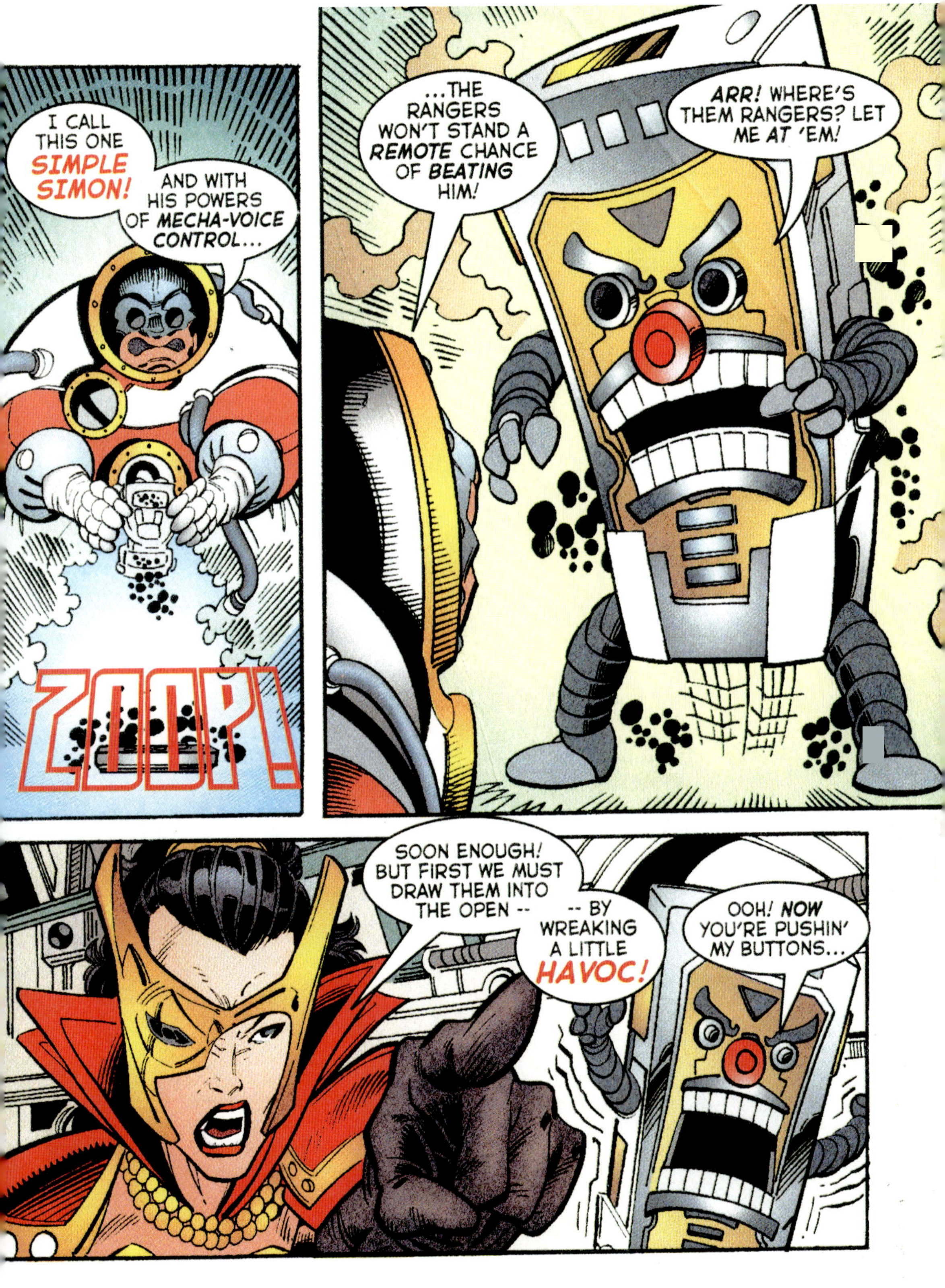
I CALL THIS ONE SIMPLE SIMON!
AND WITH HIS POWERS OF MECHA-VOICE CONTROL...
ZOOP!
...THE RANGERS WON'T STAND A REMOTE CHANCE OF BEATING HIM!
ARR! WHERE'S THEM RANGERS? LET ME AT 'EM!
SOON ENOUGH! BUT FIRST WE MUST DRAW THEM INTO THE OPEN --
-- BY WREAKING A LITTLE HAVOC!
OOH! NOW YOU'RE PUSHIN' MY BUTTONS...

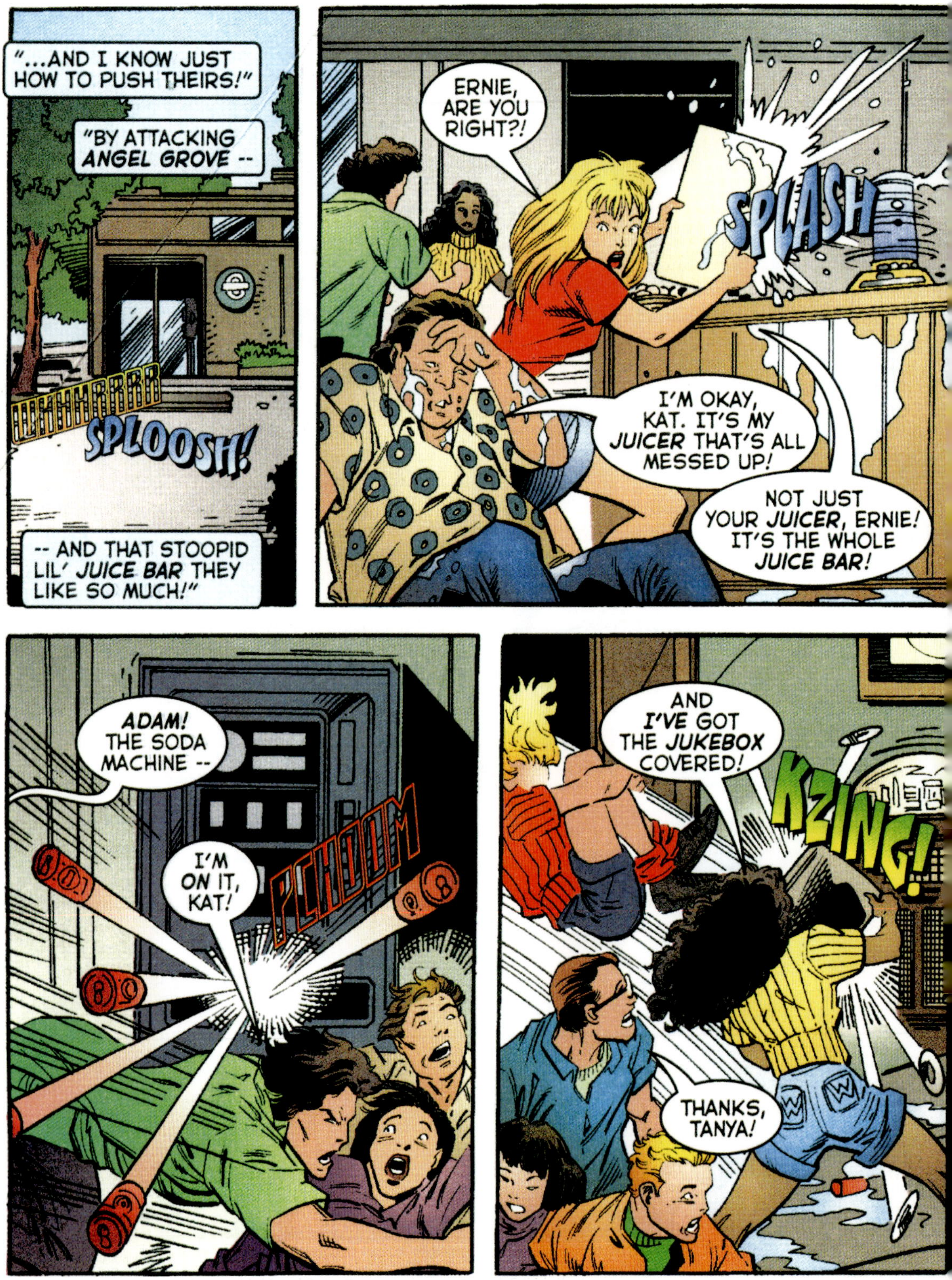
"...AND I KNOW JUST HOW TO PUSH THEIRS!"
"BY ATTACKING ANGEL GROVE --
WHHHRRRR
SPLOOSH!
-- AND THAT STOOPID LIL' JUICE BAR THEY LIKE SO MUCH!"
ERNIE, ARE YOU RIGHT?!
SPLASH
I'M OKAY, KAT. IT'S MY JUICER THAT'S ALL MESSED UP!
NOT JUST YOUR JUICER, ERNIE! IT'S THE WHOLE JUICE BAR!
ADAM! THE SODA MACHINE --
I'M ON IT, KAT!
PCHOOM
AND I'VE GOT THE JUKEBOX COVERED!
KZING!
THANKS, TANYA!

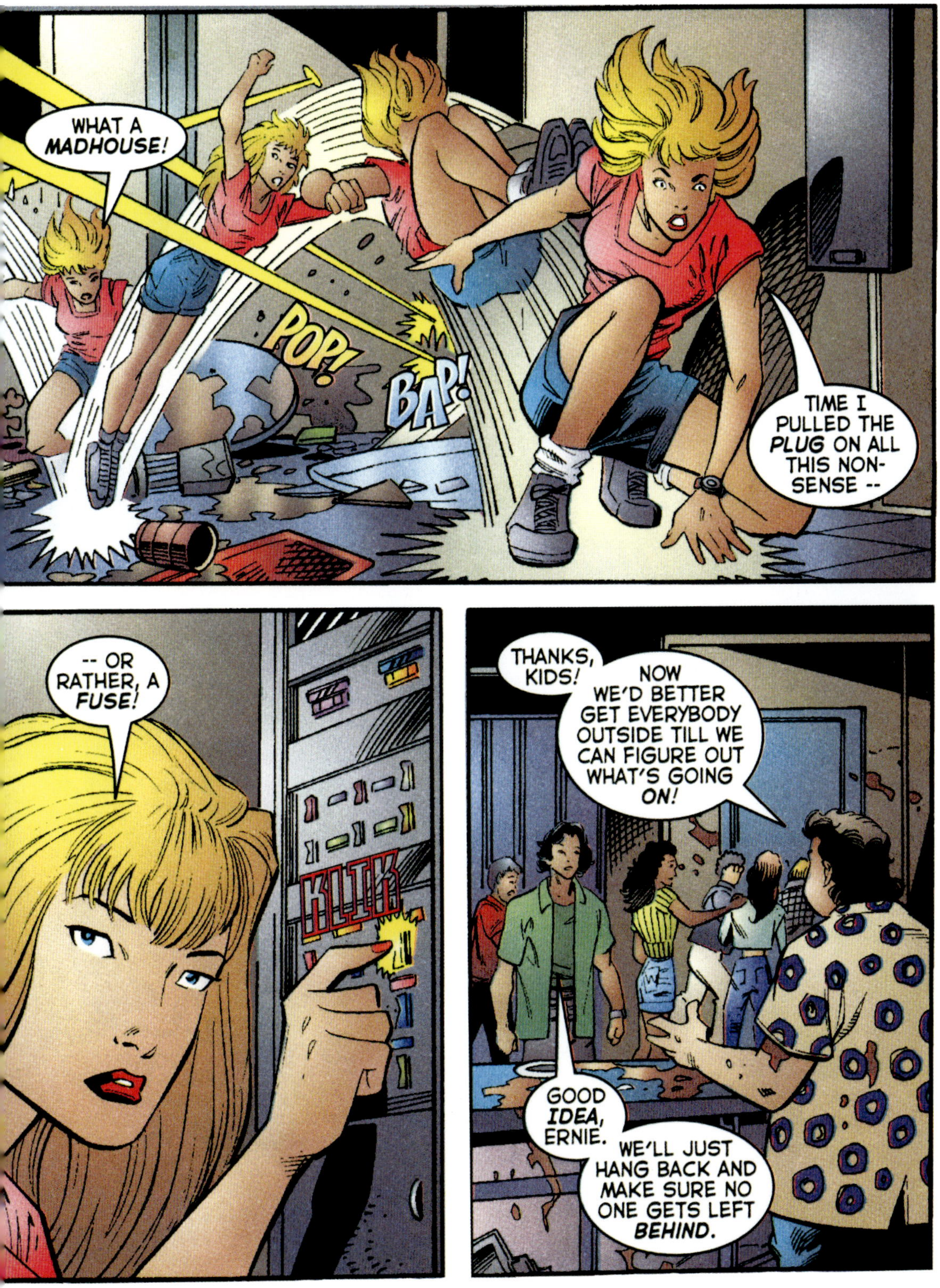

WHAT A MADHOUSE!
POP!
BAP!
TIME I PULLED THE PLUG ON ALL THIS NON-SENSE --
-- OR RATHER, A FUSE!
KLIK
THANKS, KIDS!
NOW WE'D BETTER GET EVERYBODY OUTSIDE TILL WE CAN FIGURE OUT WHAT'S GOING ON!
GOOD IDEA, ERNIE.
WE'LL JUST HANG BACK AND MAKE SURE NO ONE GETS LEFT BEHIND.

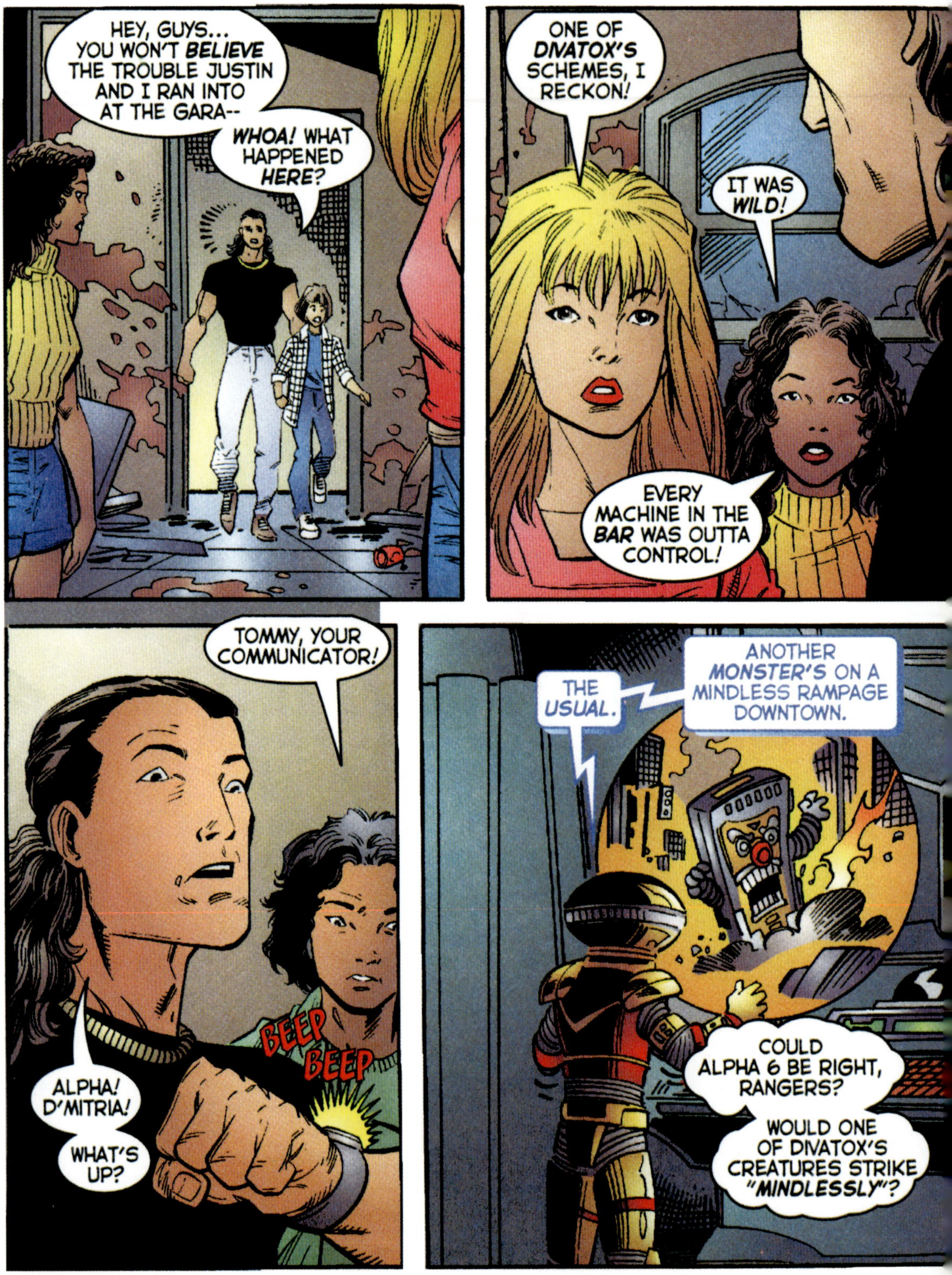
HEY, GUYS... YOU WON'T BELIEVE THE TROUBLE JUSTIN AND I RAN INTO AT THE GARA--
WHOA! WHAT HAPPENED HERE?
ONE OF DIVATOX'S SCHEMES, I RECKON!
IT WAS WILD!
EVERY MACHINE IN THE BAR WAS OUTTA CONTROL!
TOMMY, YOUR COMMUNICATOR!
BEEP BEEP
ALPHA! D'MITRIA!
WHAT'S UP?
THE USUAL.
ANOTHER MONSTER'S ON A MINDLESS RAMPAGE DOWNTOWN.
COULD ALPHA 6 BE RIGHT, RANGERS?
WOULD ONE OF DIVATOX'S CREATURES STRIKE "MINDLESSLY"?

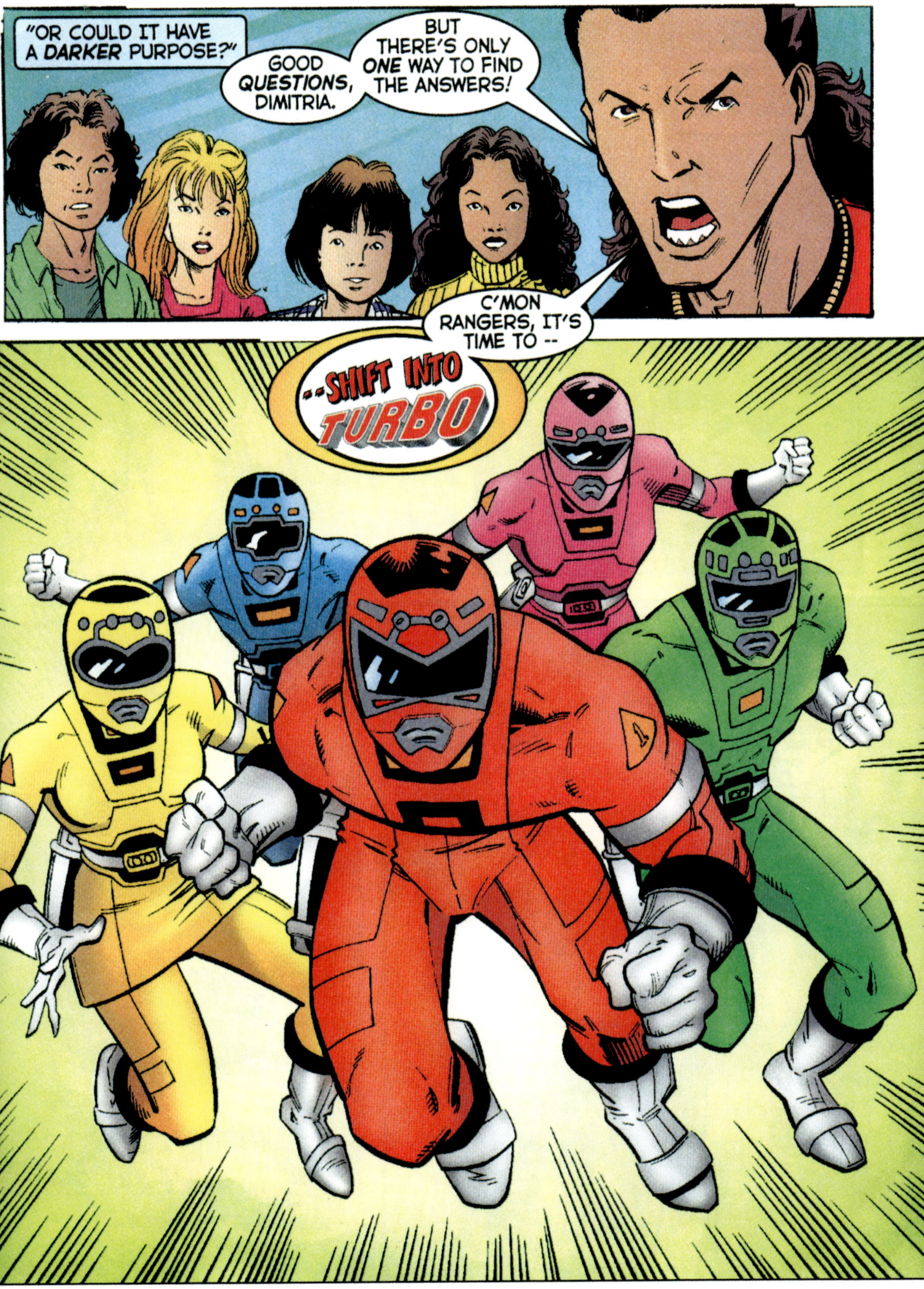
"OR COULD IT HAVE A DARKER PURPOSE?"
GOOD QUESTIONS, DIMITRIA.
BUT THERE'S ONLY ONE WAY TO FIND THE ANSWERS!
C'MON RANGERS, IT'S TIME TO --
--SHIFT INTO TURBO

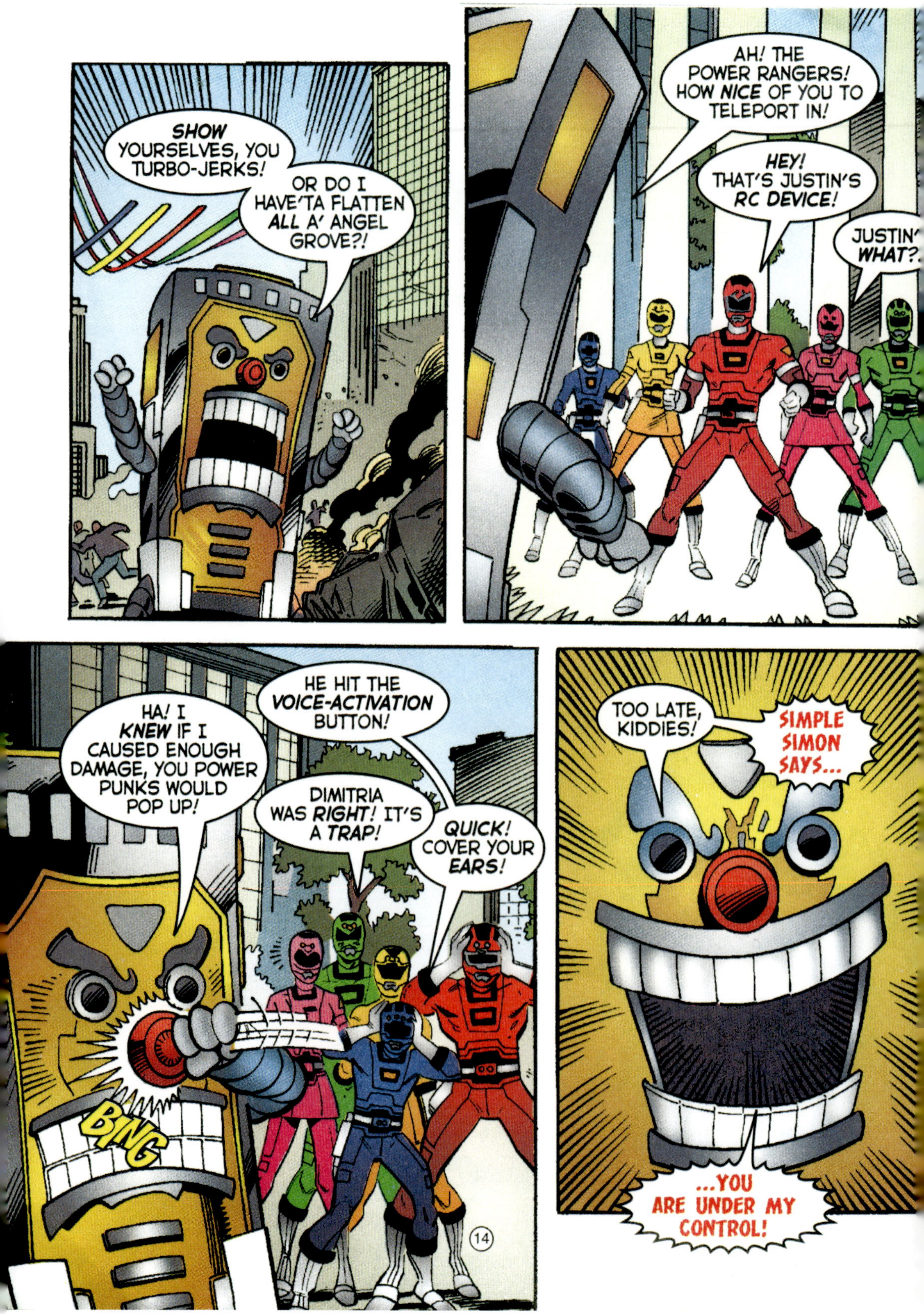

SHOW YOURSELVES, YOU TURBO-JERKS!
OR DO I HAVE'TA FLATTEN ALL A' ANGEL GROVE?!
AH! THE POWER RANGERS! HOW NICE OF YOU TO TELEPORT IN!
HEY! THAT'S JUSTIN'S RC DEVICE!
JUSTIN'S WHAT?
HA! I KNEW IF I CAUSED ENOUGH DAMAGE, YOU POWER PUNKS WOULD POP UP!
HE HIT THE VOICE-ACTIVATION BUTTON!
DIMITRIA WAS RIGHT! IT'S A TRAP!
QUICK! COVER YOUR EARS!
BING
14
TOO LATE, KIDDIES!
SIMPLE SIMON SAYS...
...YOU ARE UNDER MY CONTROL!

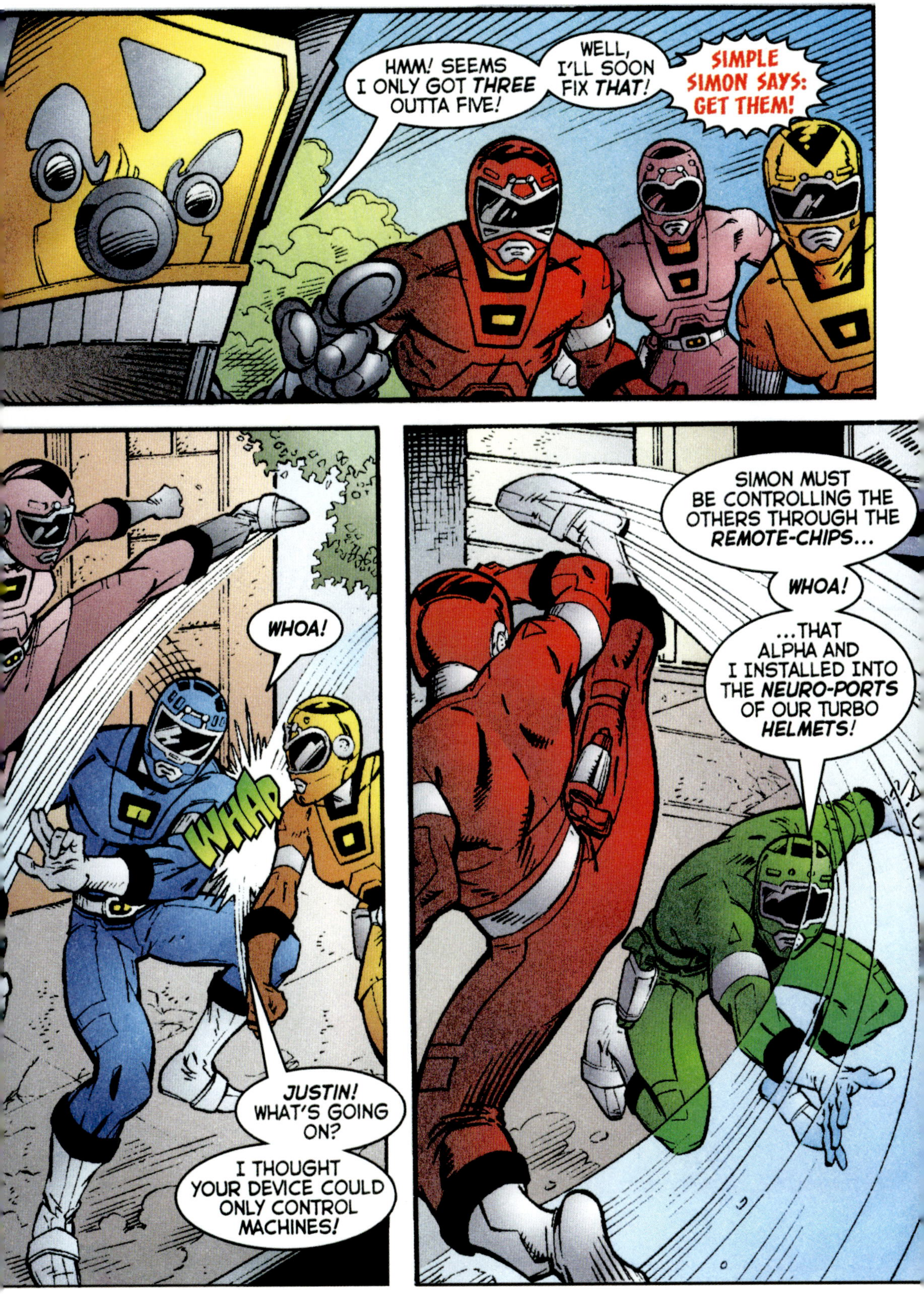
HMM! SEEMS I ONLY GOT THREE OUTTA FIVE!
WELL, I'LL SOON FIX THAT!
SIMPLE SIMON SAYS: GET THEM!
WHOA!
WHAP
JUSTIN! WHAT'S GOING ON?
I THOUGHT YOUR DEVICE COULD ONLY CONTROL MACHINES!
SIMON MUST BE CONTROLLING THE OTHERS THROUGH THE REMOTE-CHIPS...
WHOA!
...THAT ALPHA AND I INSTALLED INTO THE NEURO-PORTS OF OUR TURBO HELMETS!

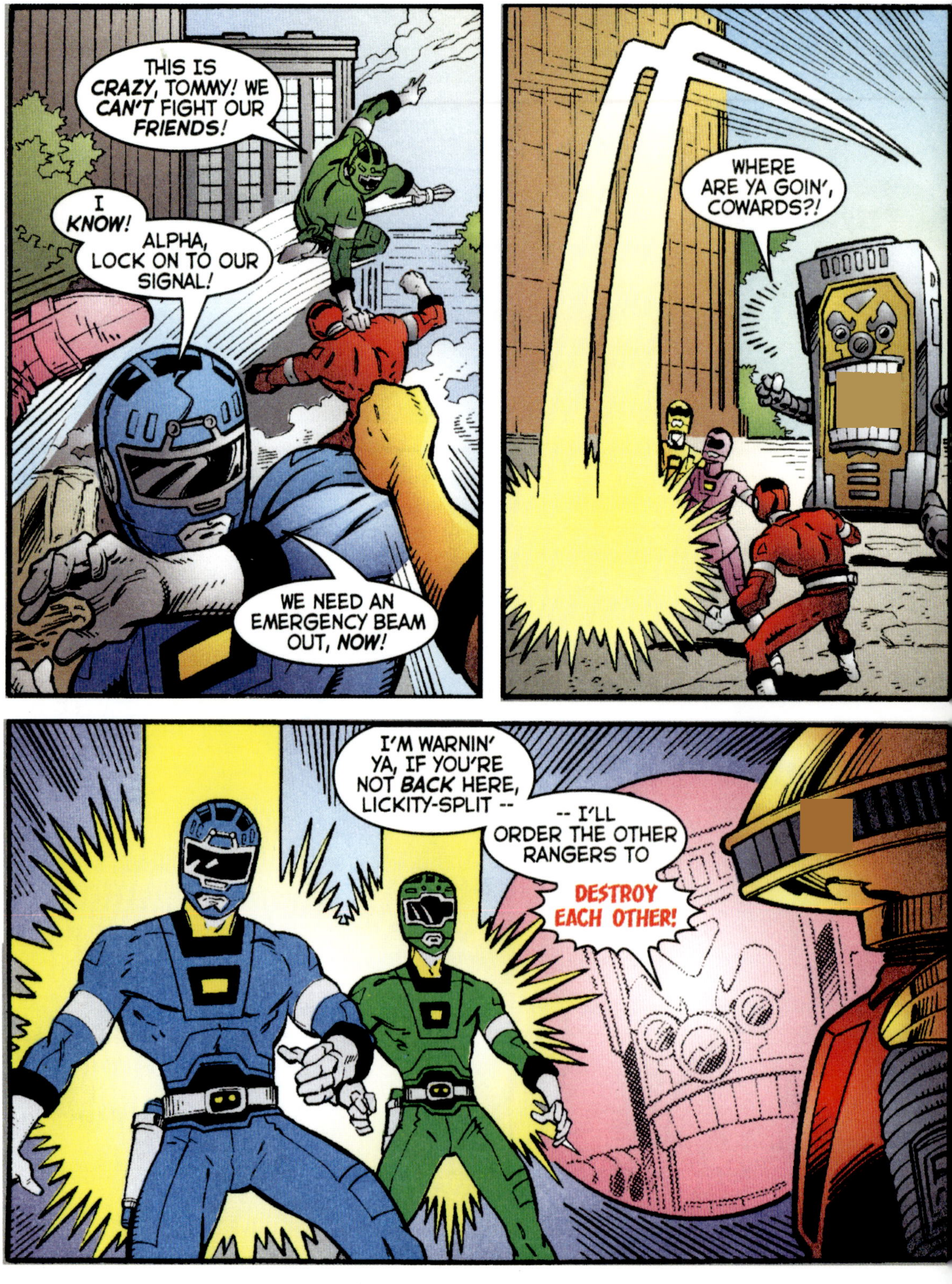
THIS IS CRAZY, TOMMY! WE CAN'T FIGHT OUR FRIENDS!
I KNOW!
ALPHA, LOCK ON TO OUR SIGNAL!
WE NEED AN EMERGENCY BEAM OUT, NOW!
WHERE ARE YA GOIN', COWARDS?!
I'M WARNIN' YA, IF YOU'RE NOT BACK HERE, LICKITY-SPLIT --
-- I'LL ORDER THE OTHER RANGERS TO
DESTROY EACH OTHER!

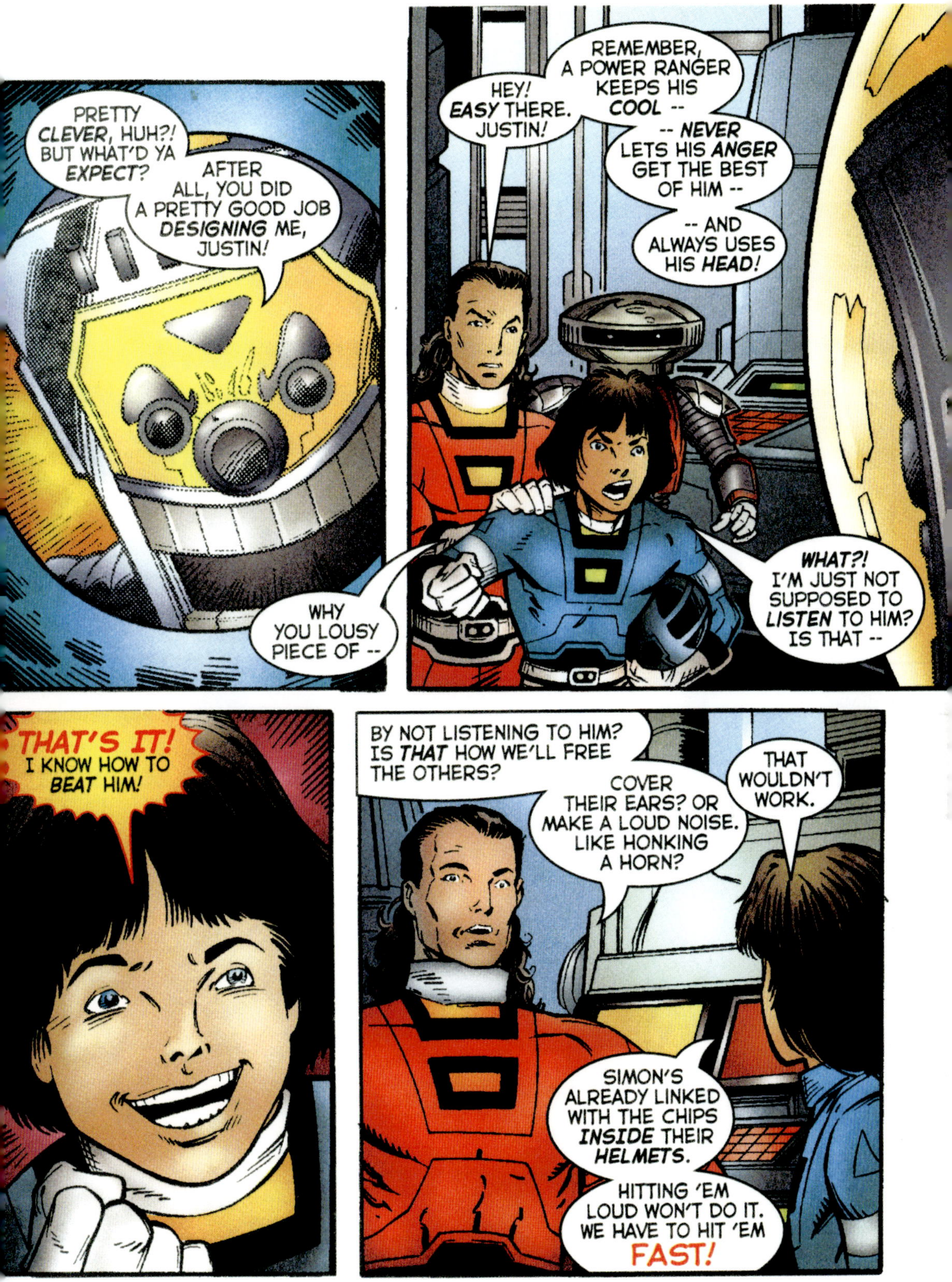
PRETTY CLEVER, HUH?! BUT WHAT'D YA EXPECT?
AFTER ALL, YOU DID A PRETTY GOOD JOB DESIGNING ME, JUSTIN!
WHY YOU LOUSY PIECE OF --
HEY! EASY THERE. JUSTIN!
REMEMBER, A POWER RANGER KEEPS HIS COOL --
-- NEVER LETS HIS ANGER GET THE BEST OF HIM --
-- AND ALWAYS USES HIS HEAD!
WHAT?! I'M JUST NOT SUPPOSED TO LISTEN TO HIM? IS THAT --
THAT'S IT! I KNOW HOW TO BEAT HIM!
BY NOT LISTENING TO HIM? IS THAT HOW WE'LL FREE THE OTHERS?
COVER THEIR EARS? OR MAKE A LOUD NOISE. LIKE HONKING A HORN?
THAT WOULDN'T WORK.
SIMON'S ALREADY LINKED WITH THE CHIPS INSIDE THEIR HELMETS.
HITTING 'EM LOUD WON'T DO IT. WE HAVE TO HIT 'EM FAST!

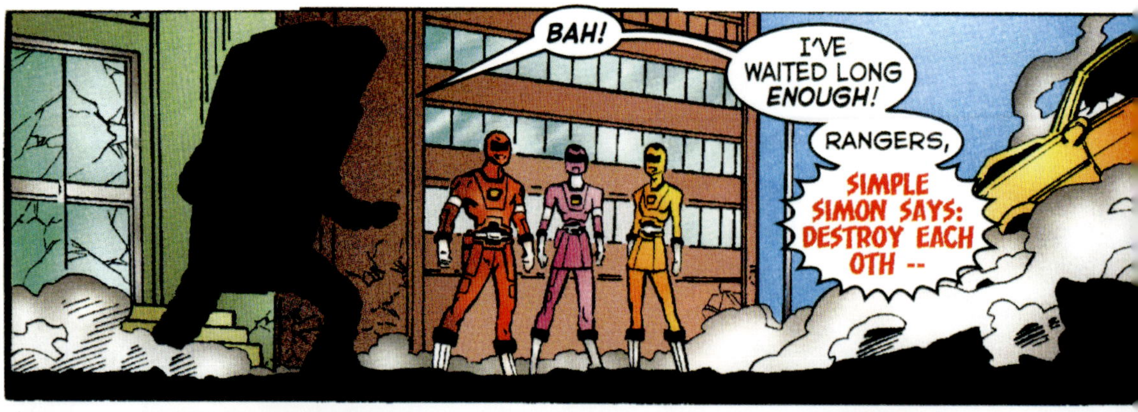
BAH!
I'VE WAITED LONG ENOUGH!
RANGERS,
SIMPLE SIMON SAYS: DESTROY EACH OTH --

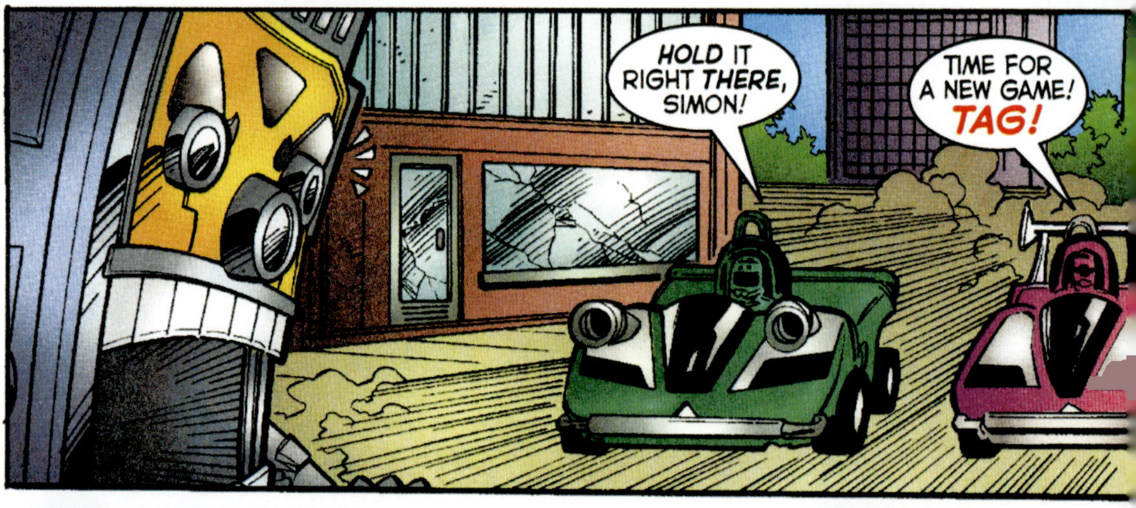
HOLD IT RIGHT THERE, SIMON!
TIME FOR A NEW GAME! TAG!

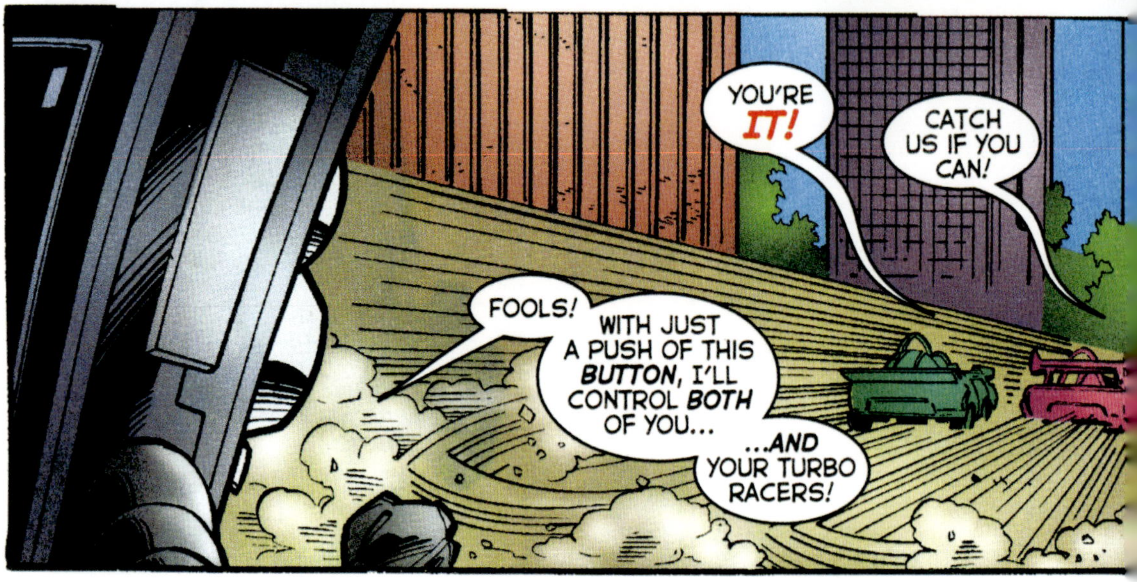
YOU'RE IT!
CATCH US IF YOU CAN!
FOOLS!
WITH JUST A PUSH OF THIS BUTTON, I'LL CONTROL BOTH OF YOU...
...AND YOUR TURBO RACERS!

DARN IT!

I'M TOO LATE! THEY'RE OUT OF MY RANGE!

BING

WELL, WHAT ARE YOU WAITING FOR?!

SIMPLE SIMON SAYS: HUNT THEM DOWN!

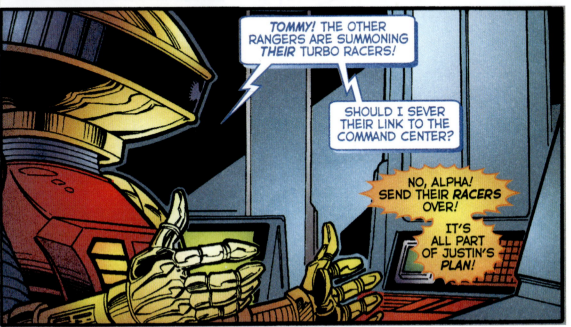

TOMMY! THE OTHER RANGERS ARE SUMMONING THEIR TURBO RACERS!

SHOULD I SEVER THEIR LINK TO THE COMMAND CENTER?

NO, ALPHA! SEND THEIR RACERS OVER!

IT'S ALL PART OF JUSTIN'S PLAN!

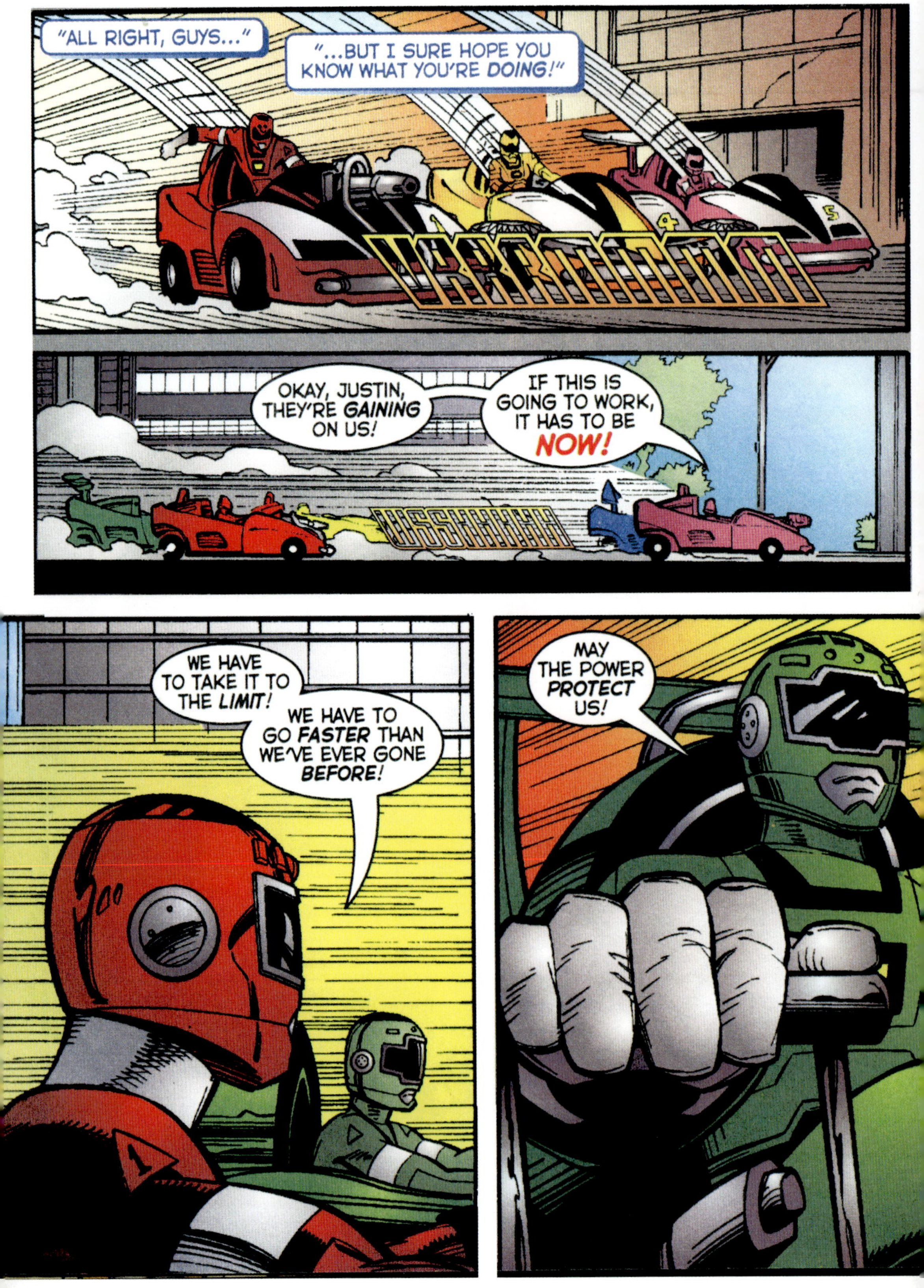
"ALL RIGHT, GUYS..."
"...BUT I SURE HOPE YOU KNOW WHAT YOU'RE DOING!"
OKAY, JUSTIN, THEY'RE GAINING ON US!
IF THIS IS GOING TO WORK, IT HAS TO BE NOW!
WE HAVE TO TAKE IT TO THE LIMIT!
WE HAVE TO GO FASTER THAN WE'VE EVER GONE BEFORE!
MAY THE POWER PROTECT US!

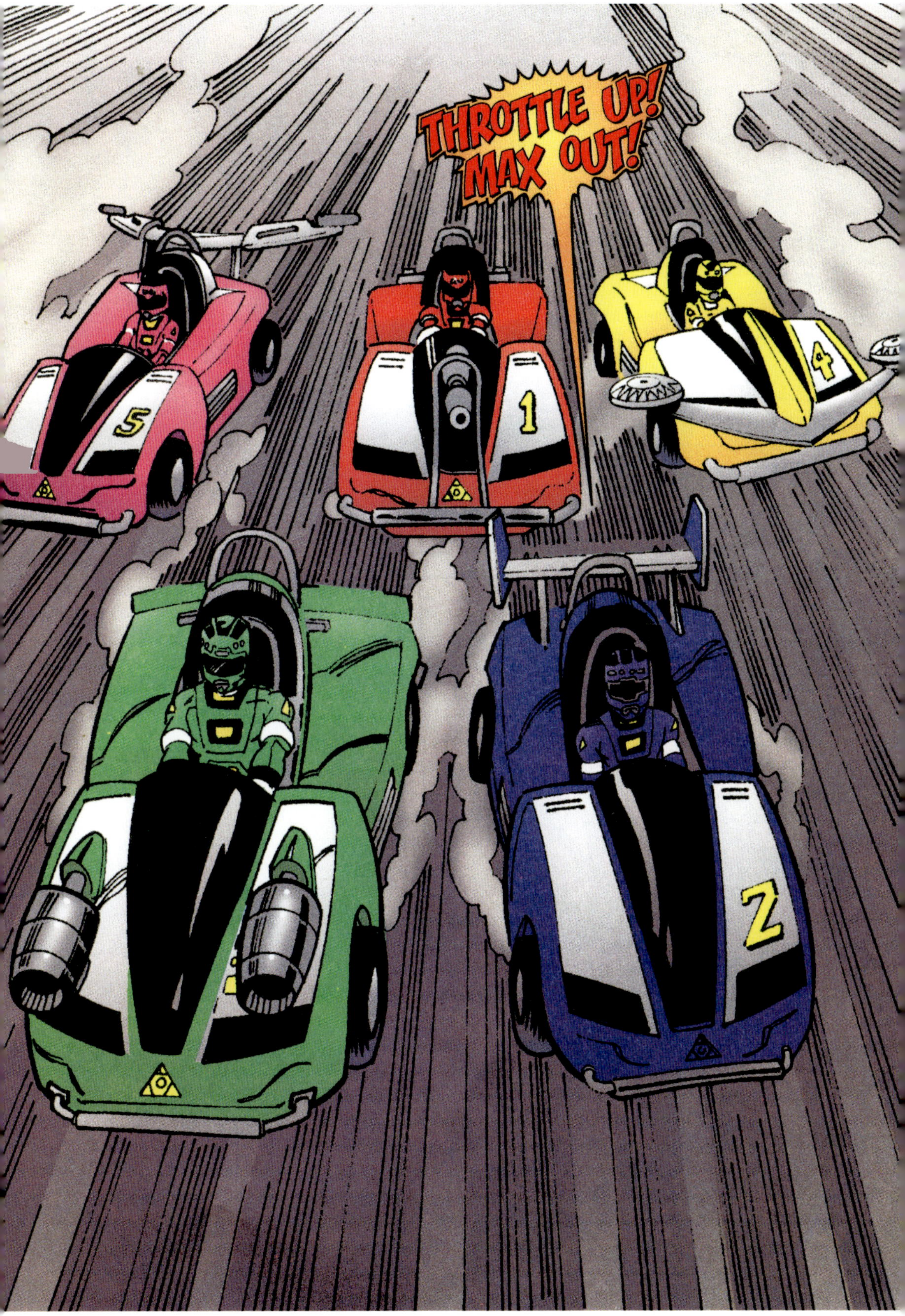
THROTTLE UP! MAX OUT!
5
1
4
2

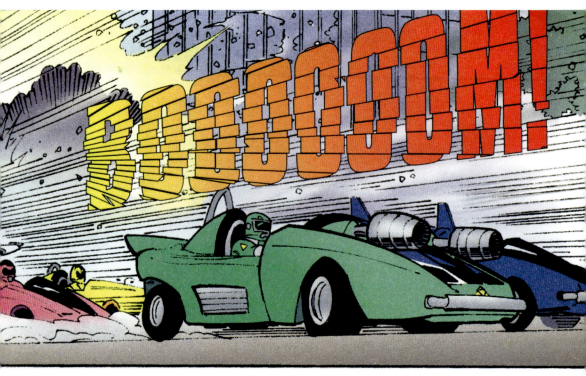

BOOOOOM!

KSHHH

THAT'S IT, MY SLAVES!

SIMPLE SIMON SAYS: OVERTAKE THEM --

-- AND BRING THEM TO ME!

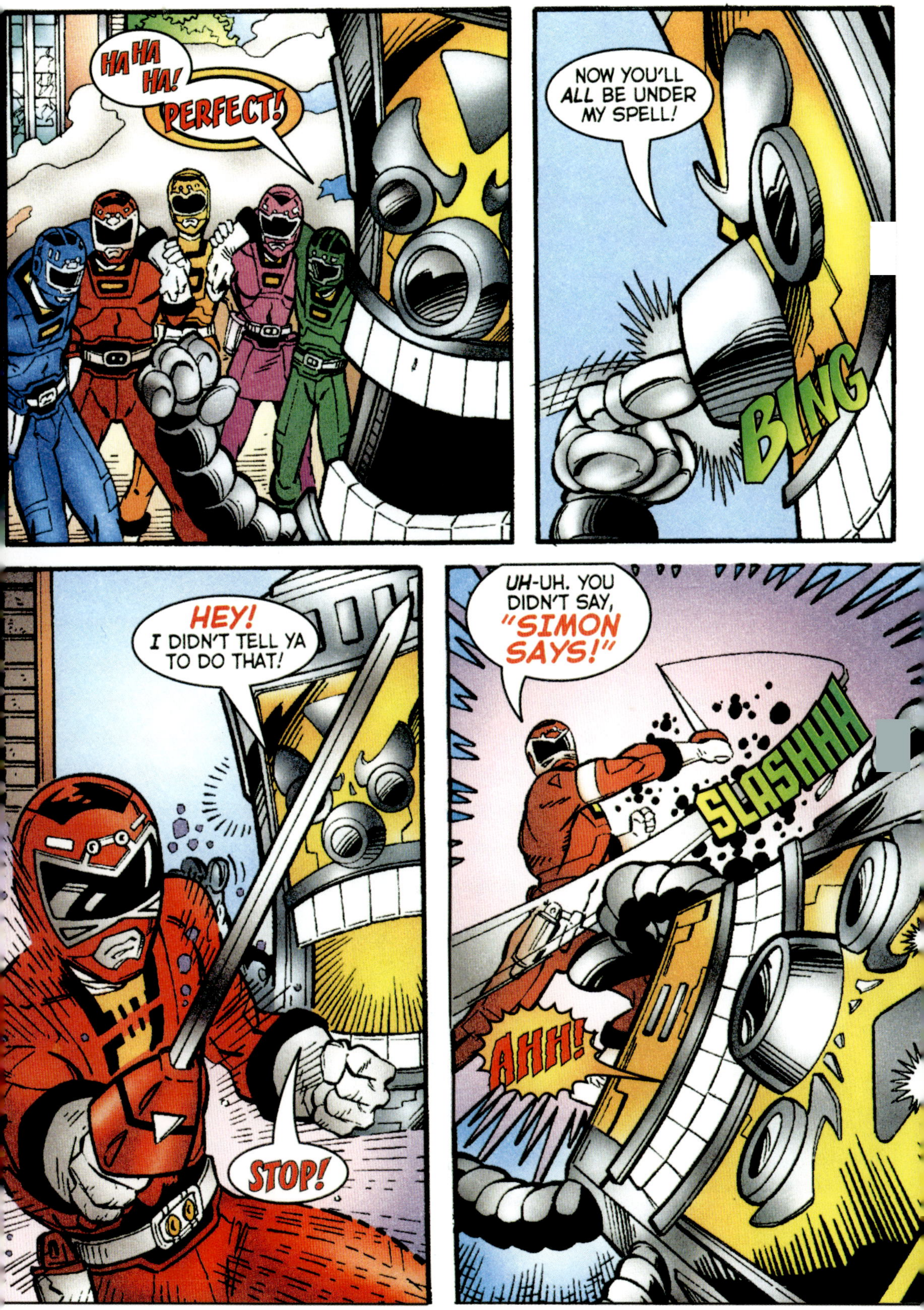
HA HA HA! PERFECT!
NOW YOU'LL ALL BE UNDER MY SPELL!
BING
HEY! I DIDN'T TELL YA TO DO THAT!
STOP!
UH-UH. YOU DIDN'T SAY, "SIMON SAYS!"
SLASHHH
AHH!

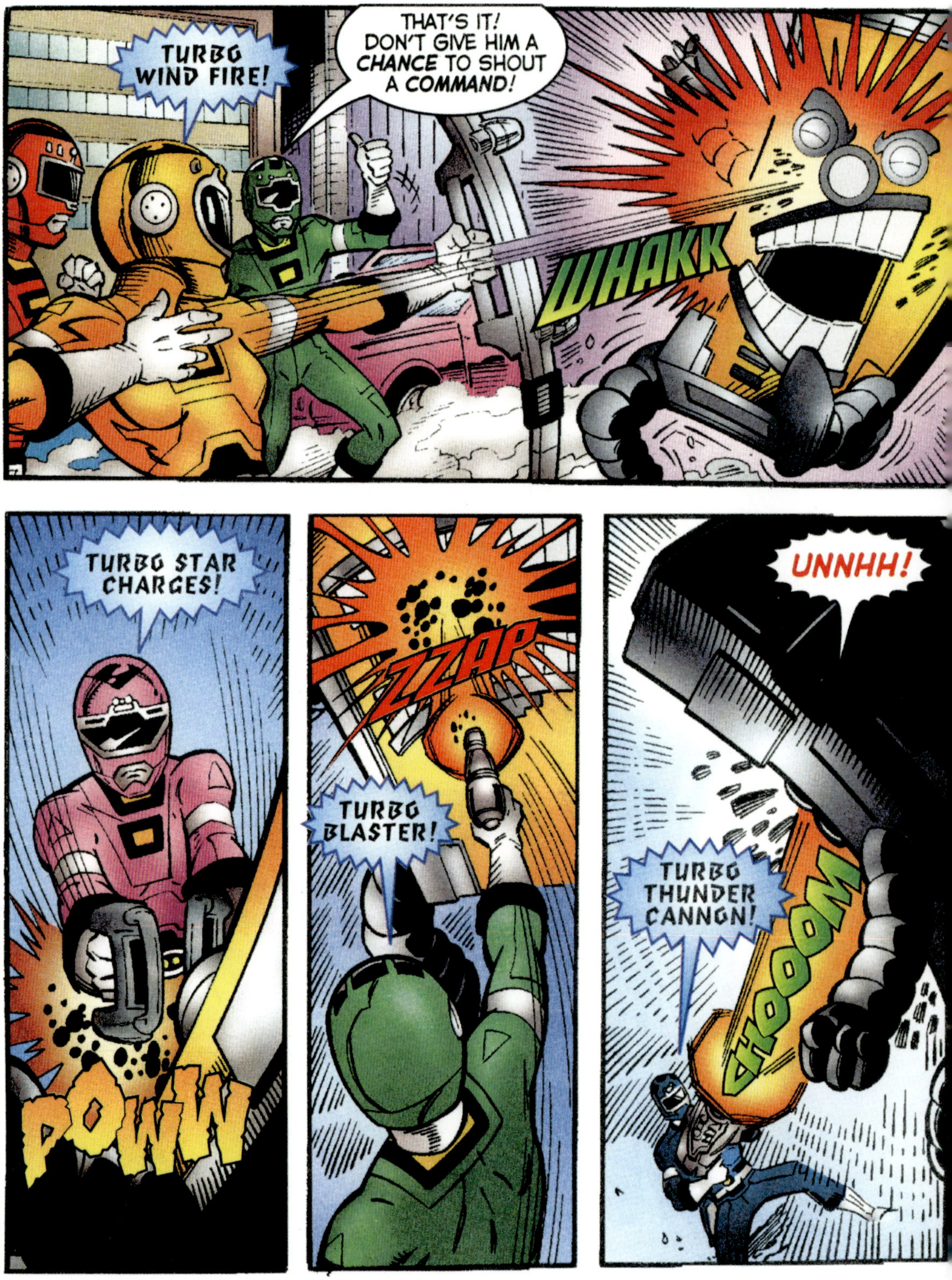
TURBO WIND FIRE!
THAT'S IT! DON'T GIVE HIM A *CHANCE* TO SHOUT A *COMMAND!*
WHAKK
TURBO STAR CHARGES!
POWW
ZZAP
TURBO BLASTER!
UNNHH!
TURBO THUNDER CANNON!
CHOOOOM

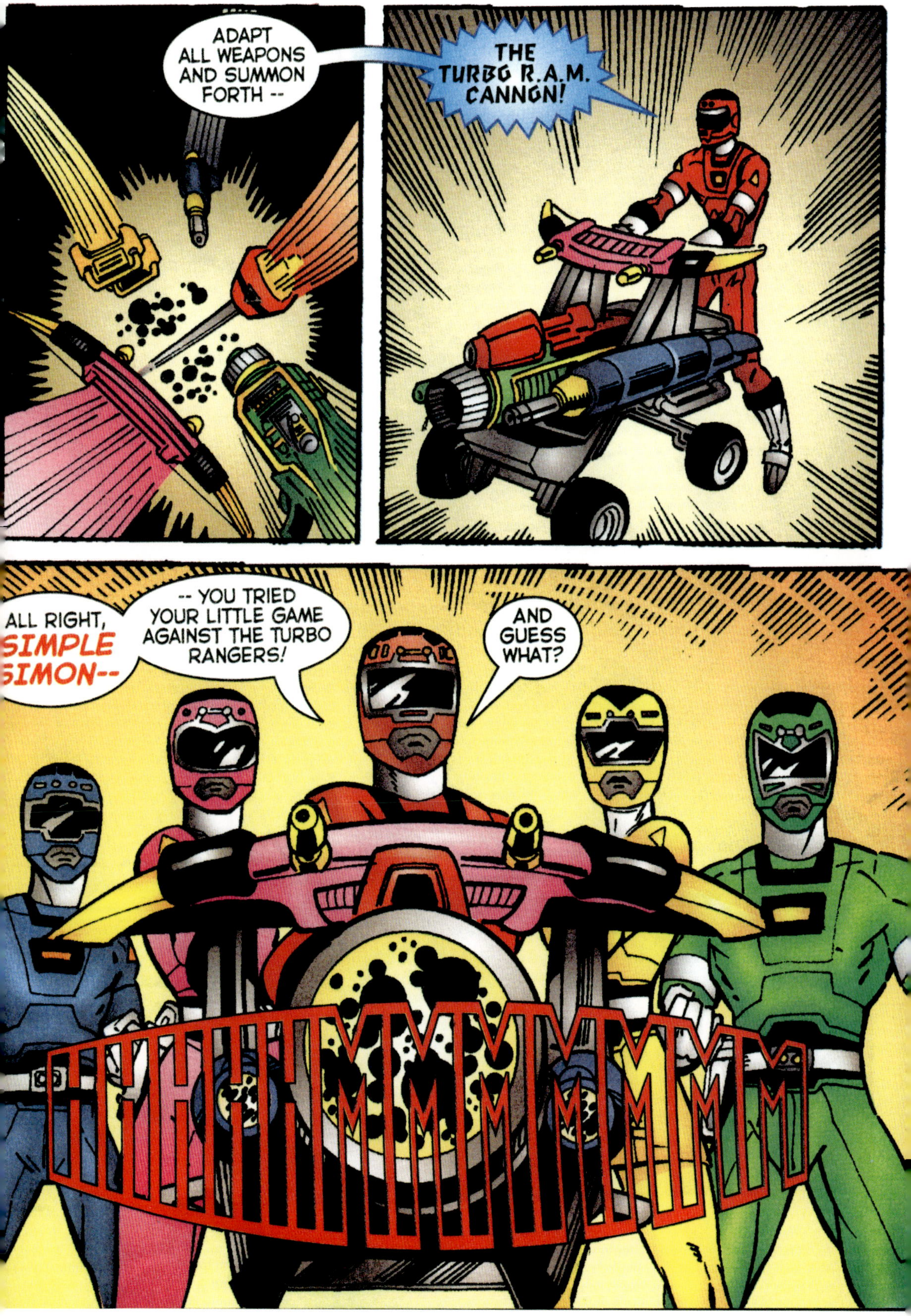
ADAPT ALL WEAPONS AND SUMMON FORTH --
THE TURBO R.A.M. CANNON!
ALL RIGHT, SIMPLE SIMON--
-- YOU TRIED YOUR LITTLE GAME AGAINST THE TURBO RANGERS!
AND GUESS WHAT?
HHHMMMMMMMMM

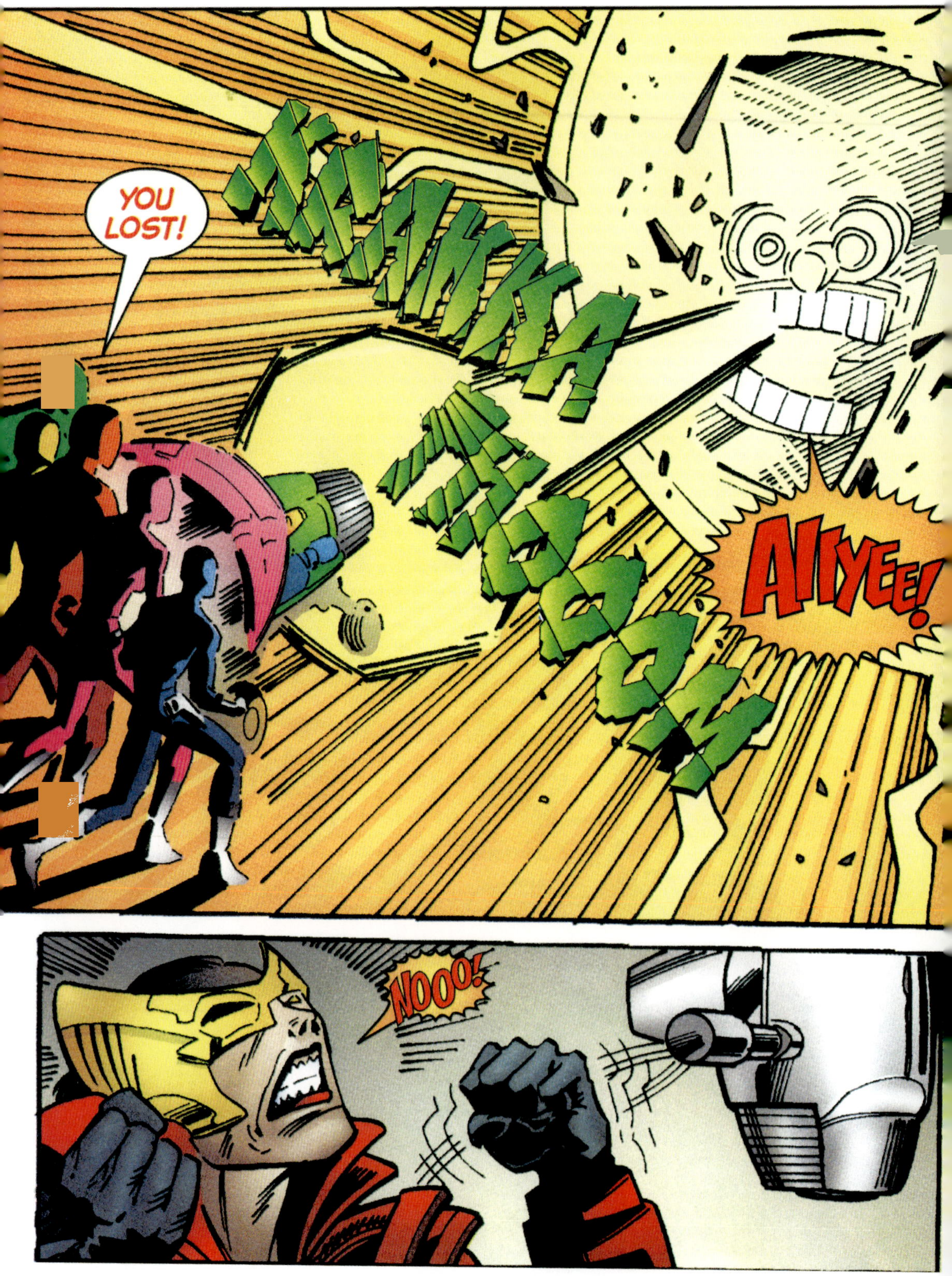
YOU LOST!
THOOOM
AIIYEE!
NOOO!

GRRRRR

AUNTIE DIVATOX *ALMOST* HAD COMPLETE CONTROL OF THE RANGERS...

...BUT *NOW* I DON'T THINK SHE CAN CONTROL *HERSELF!*

MAYBE IT'S A GOOD TIME TO *HIDE!*

FOR *ONCE*, ELGAR, I *AGREE* WITH YOU!

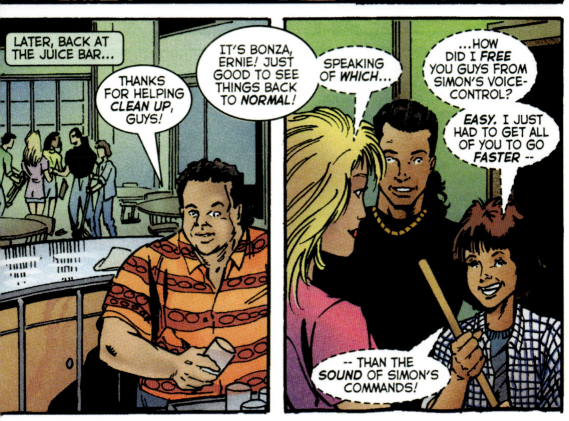

LATER, BACK AT THE JUICE BAR...

THANKS FOR HELPING *CLEAN UP*, GUYS!

IT'S BONZA, ERNIE! JUST GOOD TO SEE THINGS BACK TO *NORMAL!*

SPEAKING OF *WHICH*...

...HOW DID I *FREE* YOU GUYS FROM SIMON'S VOICE-CONTROL?

EASY. I JUST HAD TO GET ALL OF YOU TO GO *FASTER* --

-- THAN THE *SOUND* OF SIMON'S COMMANDS!

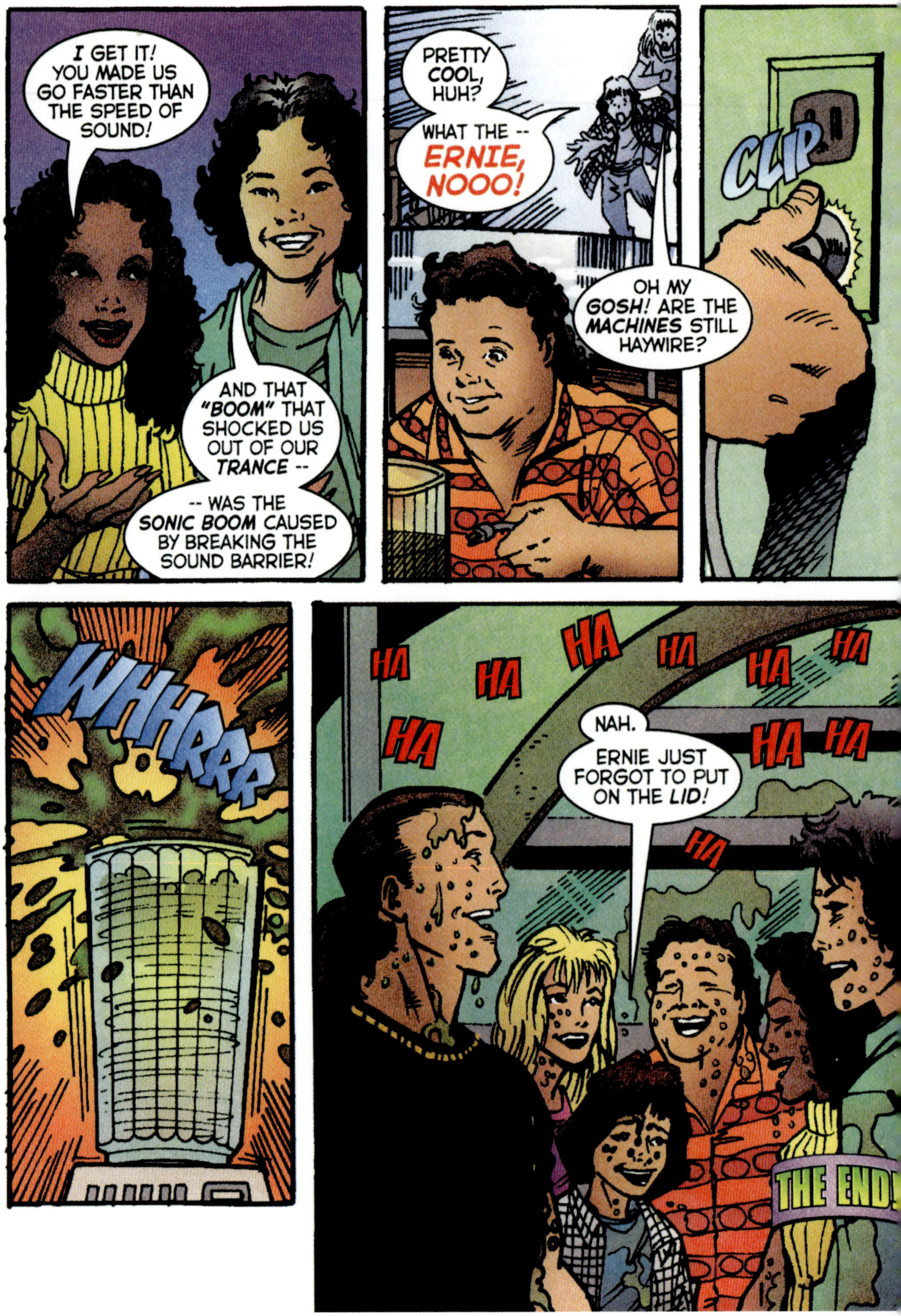
I GET IT! YOU MADE US GO FASTER THAN THE SPEED OF SOUND!
AND THAT "BOOM" THAT SHOCKED US OUT OF OUR TRANCE --
-- WAS THE SONIC BOOM CAUSED BY BREAKING THE SOUND BARRIER!
PRETTY COOL, HUH?
WHAT THE -- ERNIE, NOOO!
OH MY GOSH! ARE THE MACHINES STILL HAYWIRE?
CLIP
WHHRRRR
HA HA HA HA HA HA HA HA HA HA HA
NAH.
ERNIE JUST FORGOT TO PUT ON THE LID!
THE END

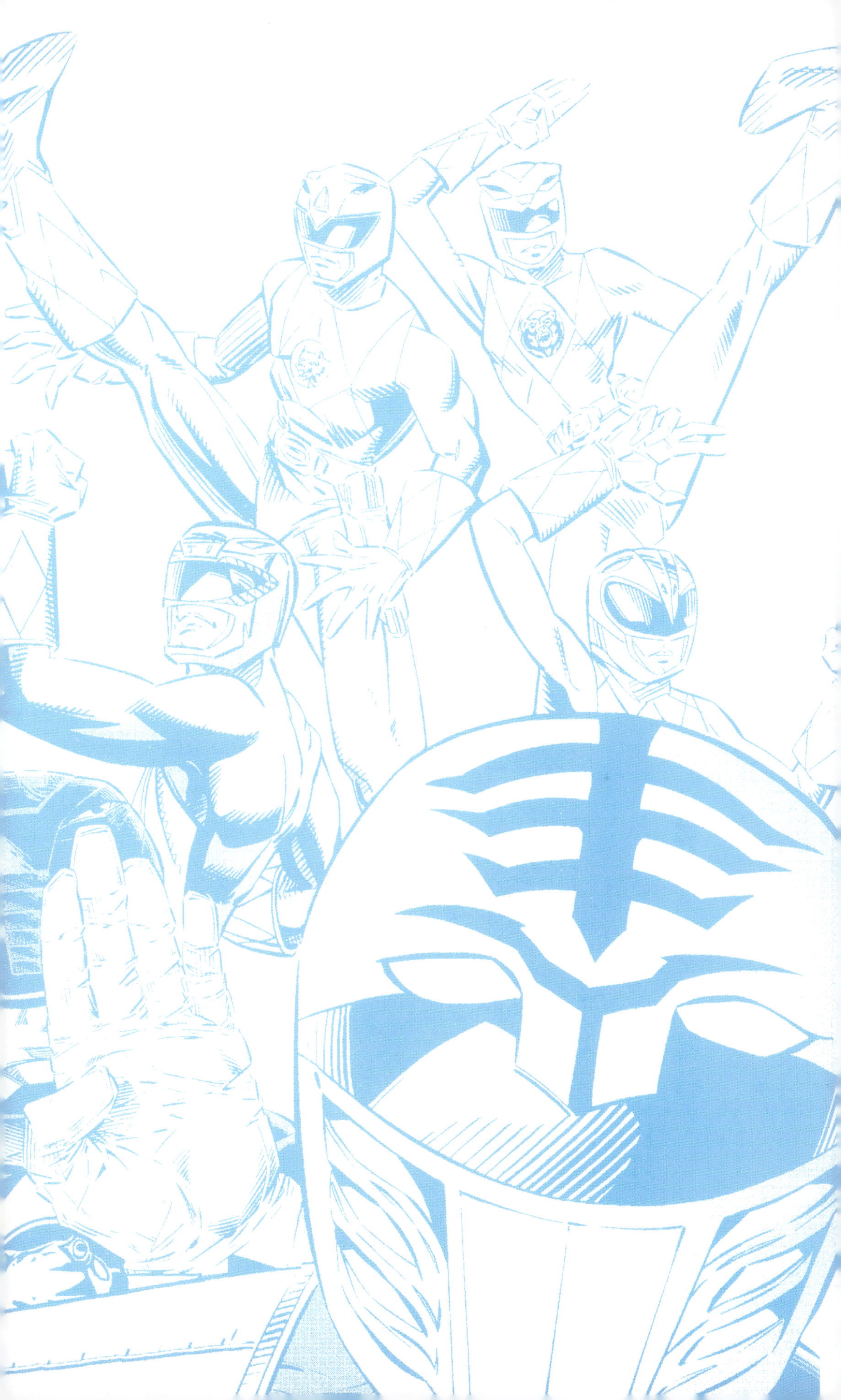

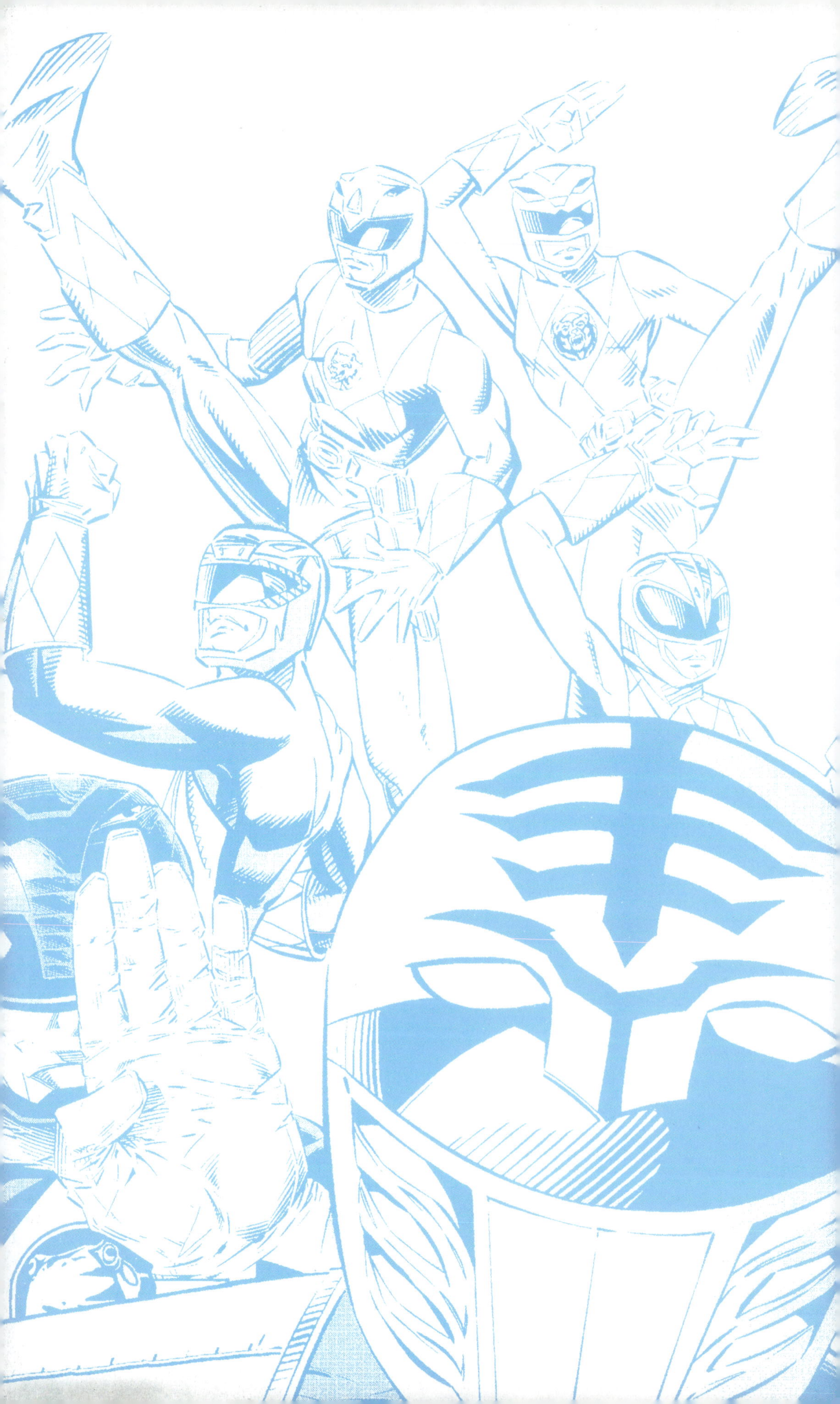

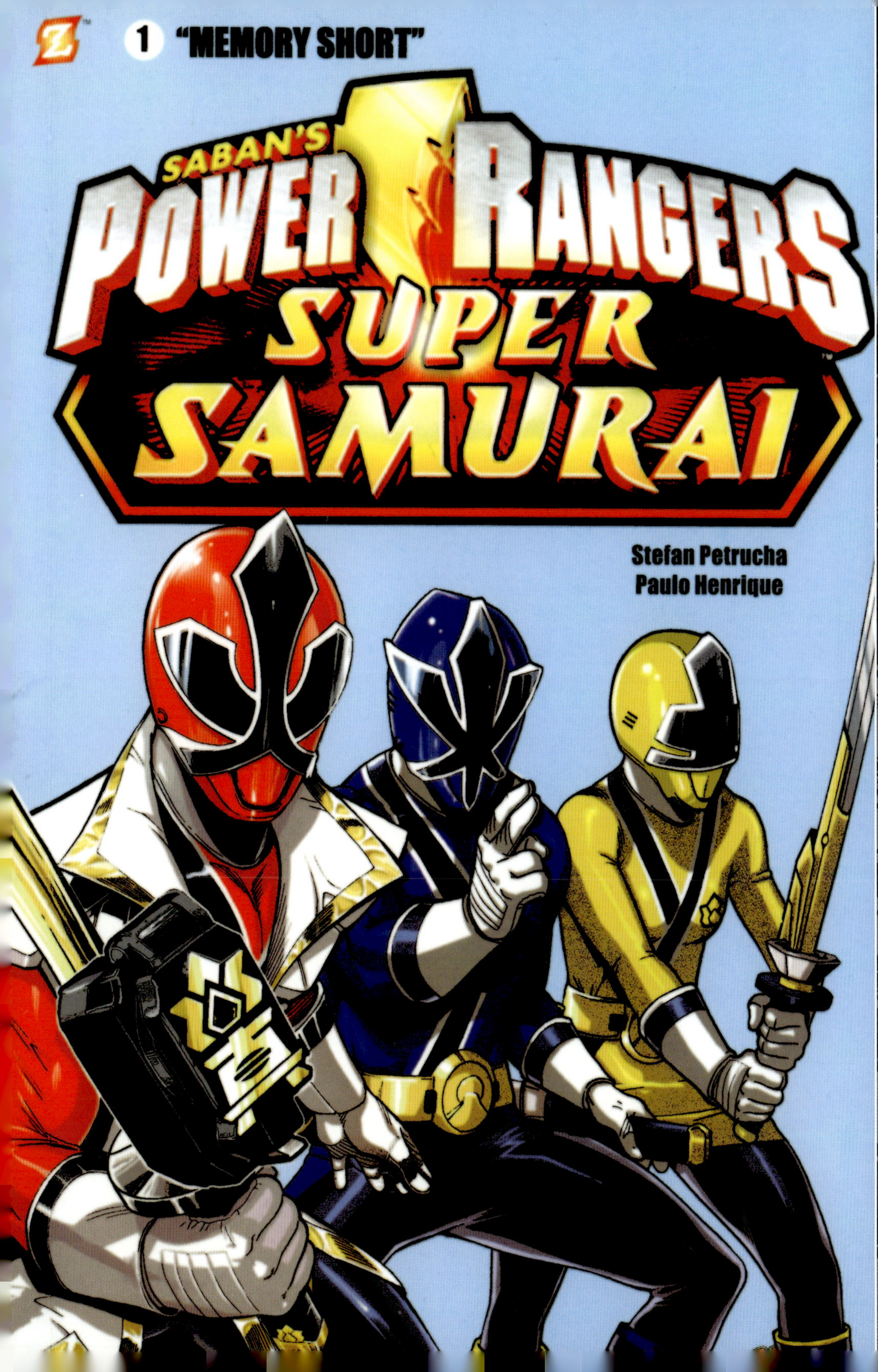
1 “MEMORY SHORT”
SABAN'S
POWER RANGERS
SUPER SAMURAI
Stefan Petrucha
Paulo Henrique

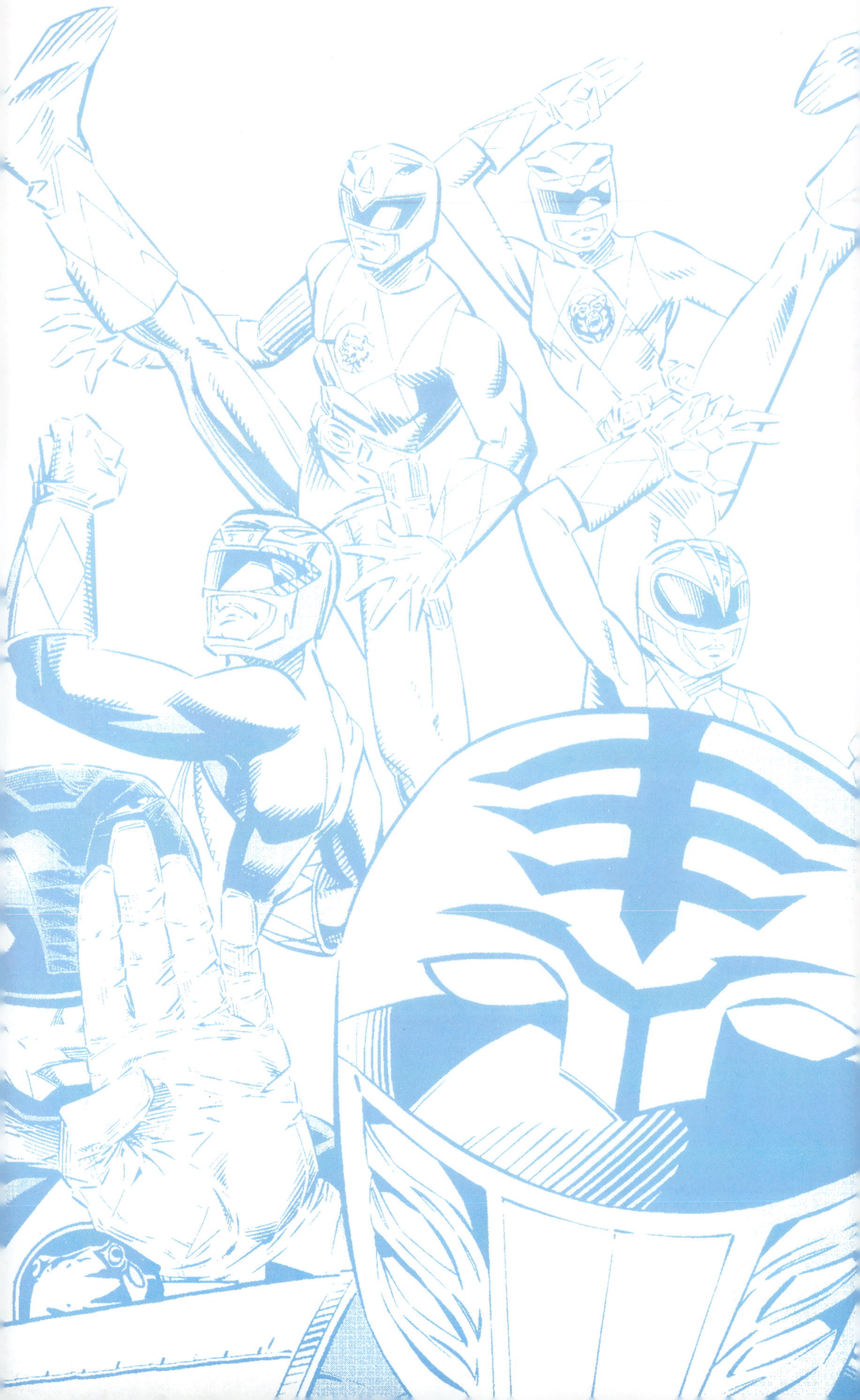

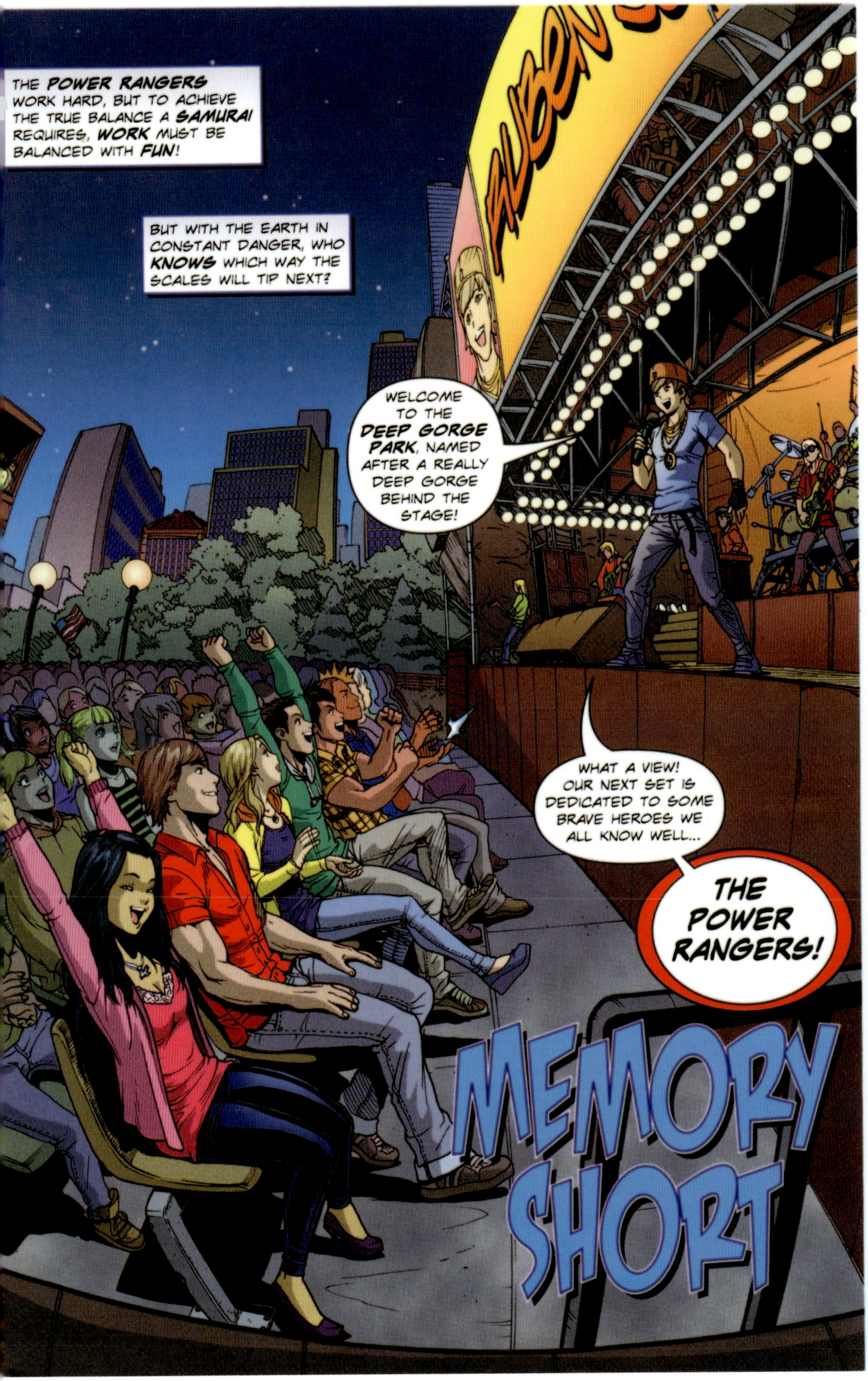
THE POWER RANGERS WORK HARD, BUT TO ACHIEVE THE TRUE BALANCE A SAMURAI REQUIRES, WORK MUST BE BALANCED WITH FUN!
BUT WITH THE EARTH IN CONSTANT DANGER, WHO KNOWS WHICH WAY THE SCALES WILL TIP NEXT?
WELCOME TO THE DEEP GORGE PARK, NAMED AFTER A REALLY DEEP GORGE BEHIND THE STAGE!
WHAT A VIEW! OUR NEXT SET IS DEDICATED TO SOME BRAVE HEROES WE ALL KNOW WELL...
THE POWER RANGERS!
MEMORY SHORT

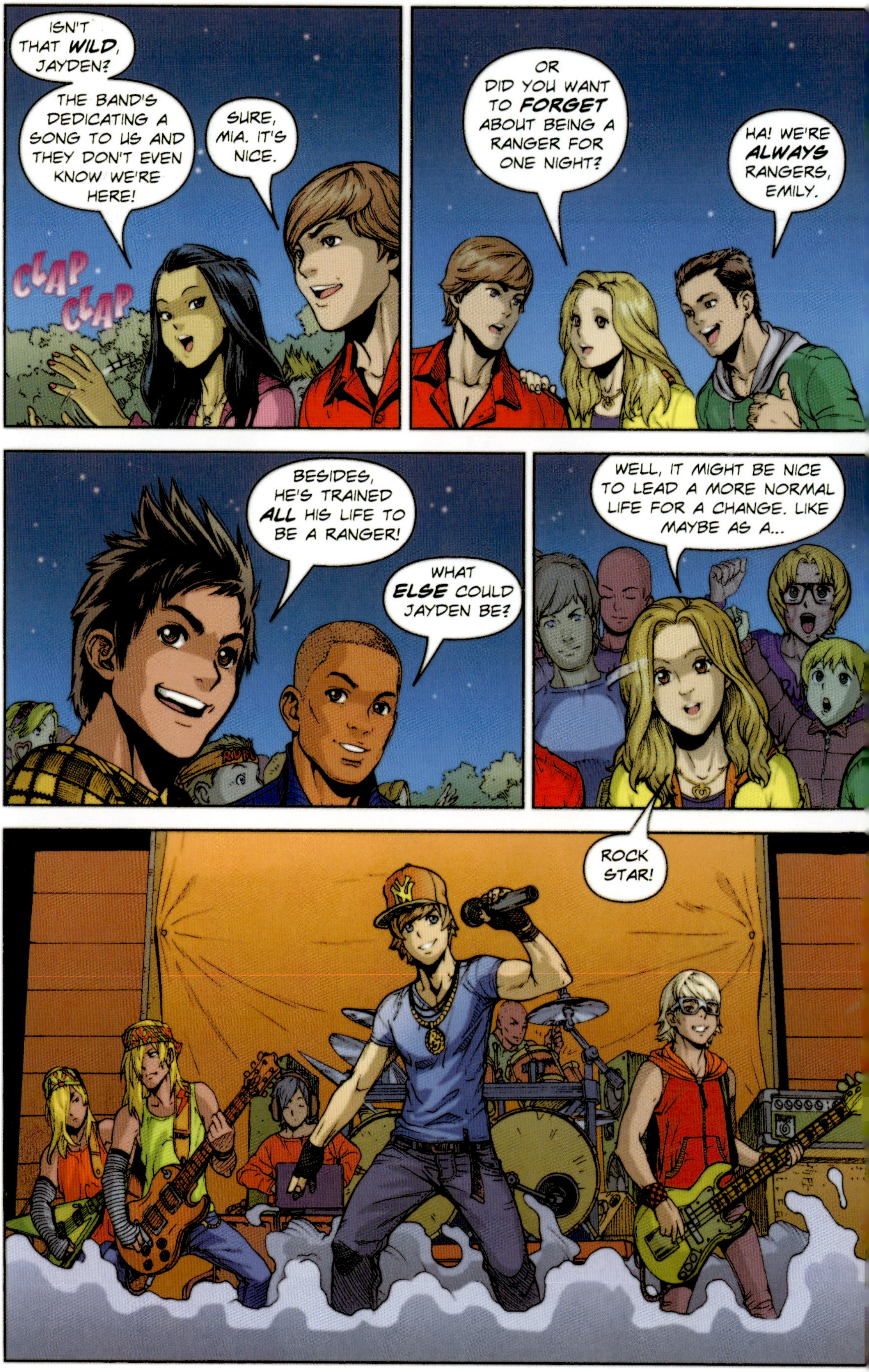
ISN'T THAT **WILD**, JAYDEN?
THE BAND'S DEDICATING A SONG TO US AND THEY DON'T EVEN KNOW WE'RE HERE!
CLAP CLAP
SURE, MIA. IT'S NICE.
OR DID YOU WANT TO **FORGET** ABOUT BEING A RANGER FOR ONE NIGHT?
HA! WE'RE **ALWAYS** RANGERS, EMILY.
BESIDES, HE'S TRAINED **ALL** HIS LIFE TO BE A RANGER!
WHAT **ELSE** COULD JAYDEN BE?
WELL, IT MIGHT BE NICE TO LEAD A MORE NORMAL LIFE FOR A CHANGE. LIKE MAYBE AS A...
ROCK STAR!

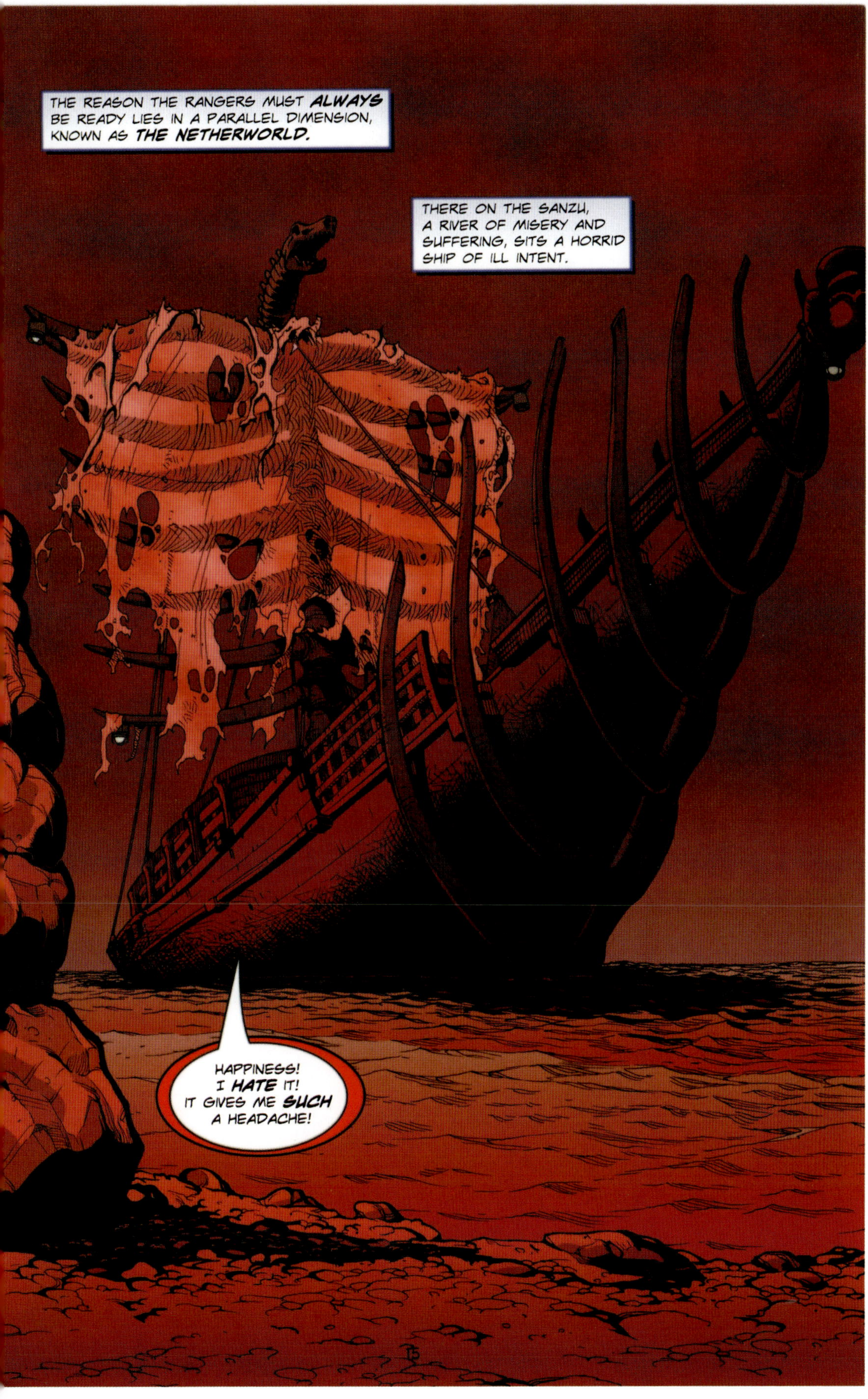
THE REASON THE RANGERS MUST ALWAYS BE READY LIES IN A PARALLEL DIMENSION, KNOWN AS THE NETHERWORLD.
THERE ON THE SANZU, A RIVER OF MISERY AND SUFFERING, SITS A HORRID SHIP OF ILL INTENT.
HAPPINESS! I HATE IT! IT GIVES ME SUCH A HEADACHE!

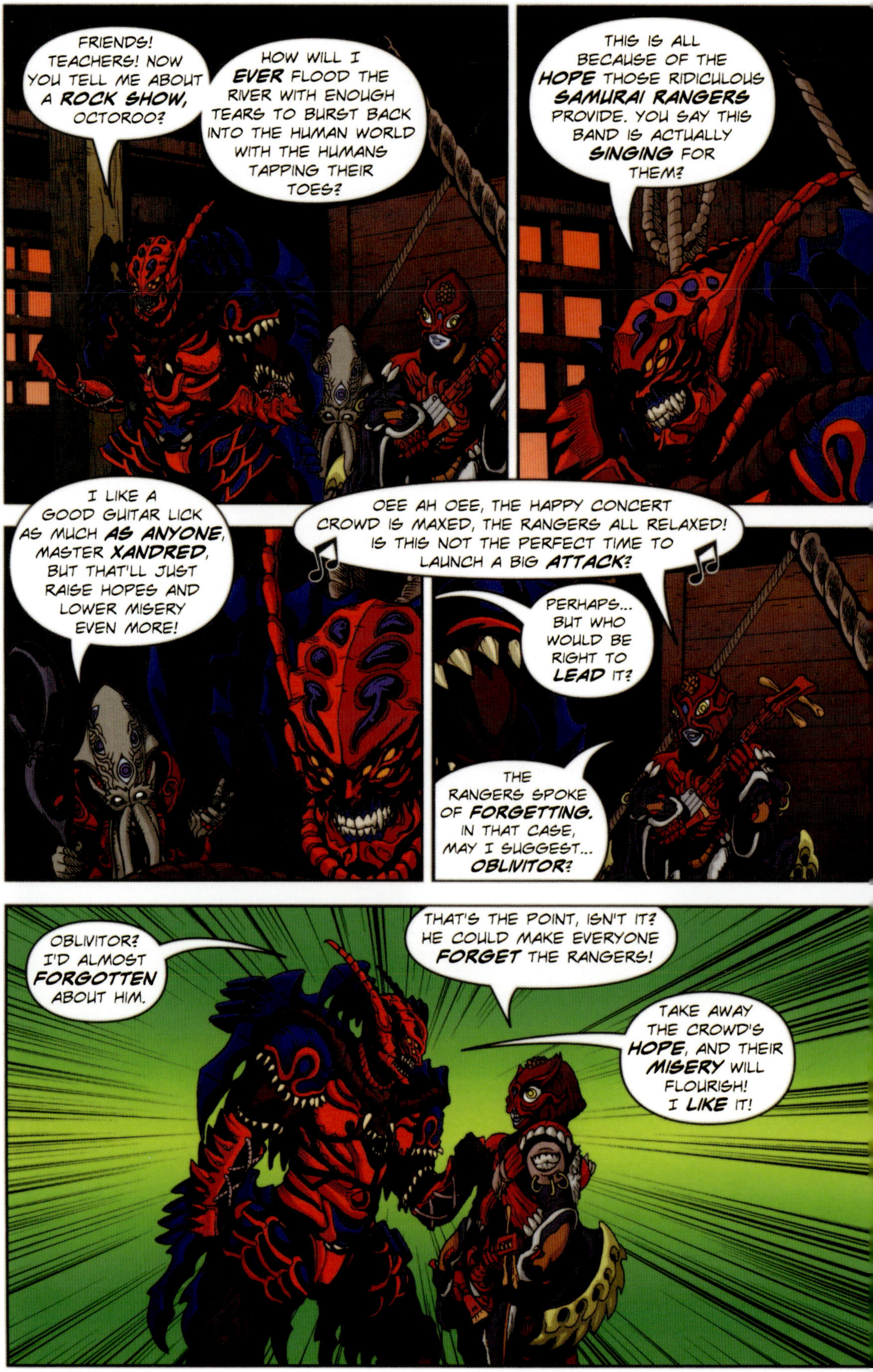
FRIENDS! TEACHERS! NOW YOU TELL ME ABOUT A ROCK SHOW, OCTOROO?
HOW WILL I EVER FLOOD THE RIVER WITH ENOUGH TEARS TO BURST BACK INTO THE HUMAN WORLD WITH THE HUMANS TAPPING THEIR TOES?
THIS IS ALL BECAUSE OF THE HOPE THOSE RIDICULOUS SAMURAI RANGERS PROVIDE. YOU SAY THIS BAND IS ACTUALLY SINGING FOR THEM?
I LIKE A GOOD GUITAR LICK AS MUCH AS ANYONE, MASTER XANDRED, BUT THAT'LL JUST RAISE HOPES AND LOWER MISERY EVEN MORE!
OEE AH OEE, THE HAPPY CONCERT CROWD IS MAXED, THE RANGERS ALL RELAXED! IS THIS NOT THE PERFECT TIME TO LAUNCH A BIG ATTACK?
PERHAPS... BUT WHO WOULD BE RIGHT TO LEAD IT?
THE RANGERS SPOKE OF FORGETTING. IN THAT CASE, MAY I SUGGEST... OBLIVITOR?
OBLIVITOR? I'D ALMOST FORGOTTEN ABOUT HIM.
THAT'S THE POINT, ISN'T IT? HE COULD MAKE EVERYONE FORGET THE RANGERS!
TAKE AWAY THE CROWD'S HOPE, AND THEIR MISERY WILL FLOURISH! I LIKE IT!

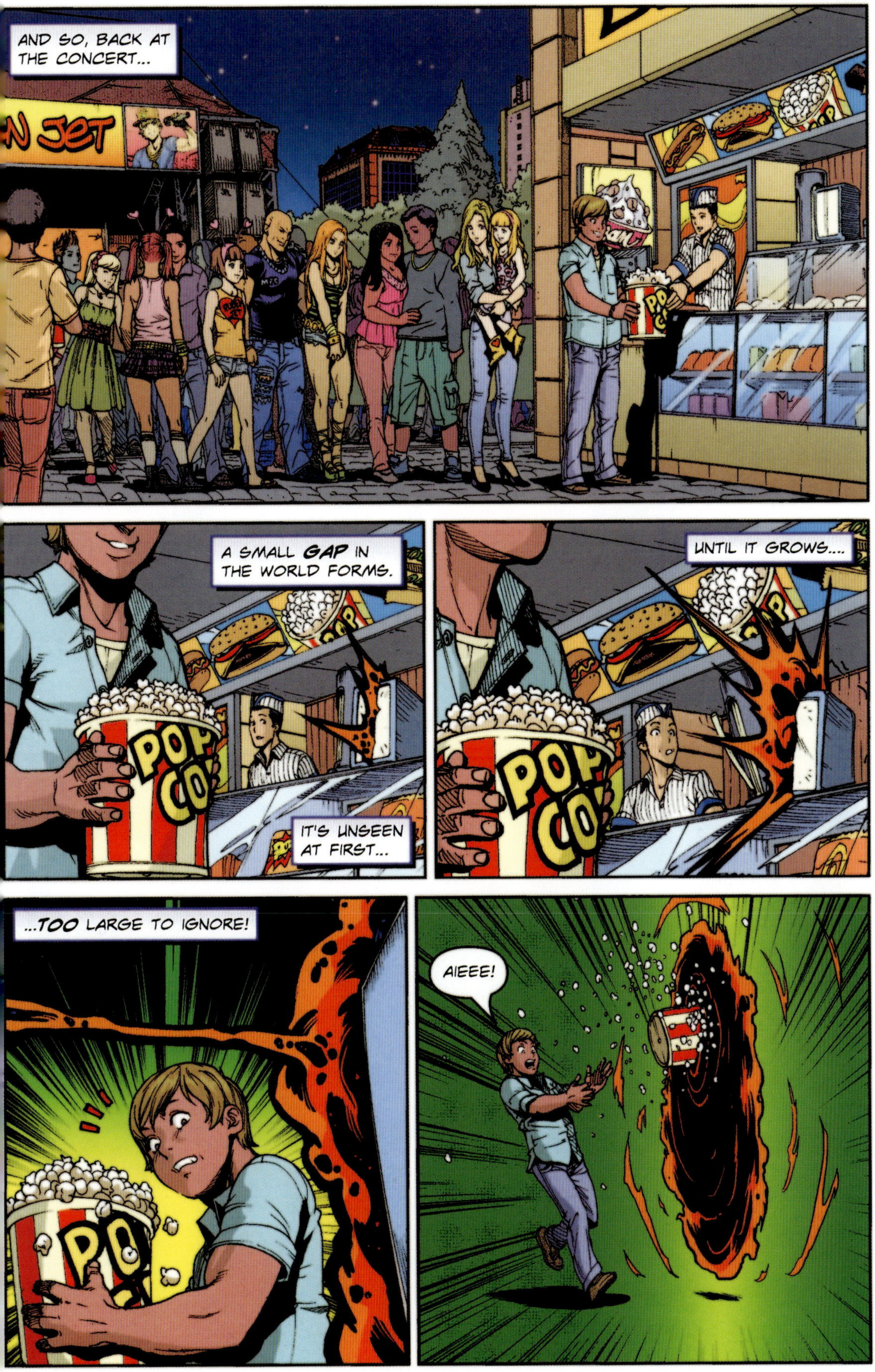
AND SO, BACK AT THE CONCERT...
A SMALL GAP IN THE WORLD FORMS.
IT'S UNSEEN AT FIRST...
UNTIL IT GROWS....
...TOO LARGE TO IGNORE!
AIEEE!

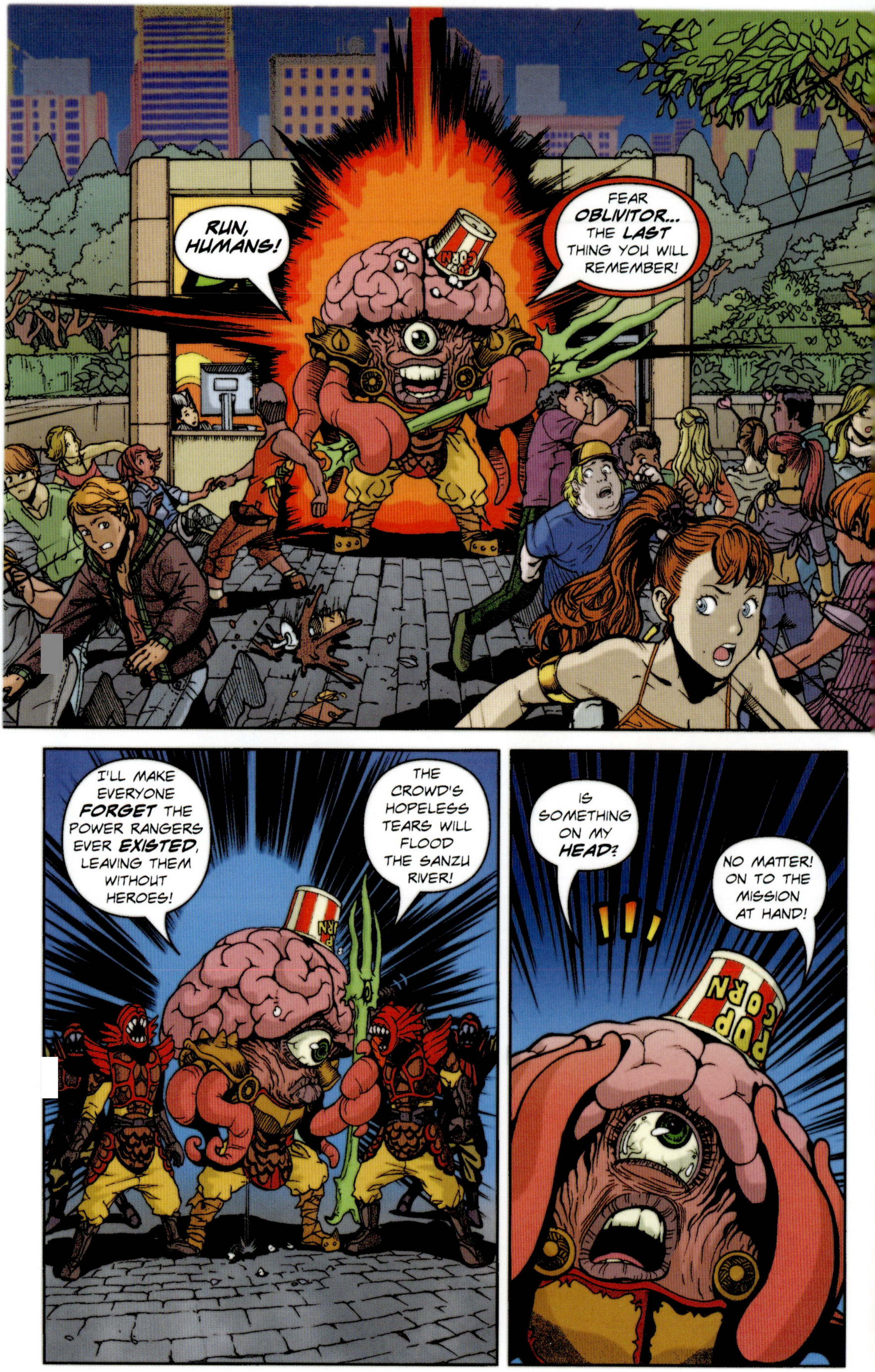
RUN, HUMANS!
FEAR OBLIVITOR... THE LAST THING YOU WILL REMEMBER!
I'LL MAKE EVERYONE FORGET THE POWER RANGERS EVER EXISTED, LEAVING THEM WITHOUT HEROES!
THE CROWD'S HOPELESS TEARS WILL FLOOD THE SANZU RIVER!
IS SOMETHING ON MY HEAD?
NO MATTER! ON TO THE MISSION AT HAND!

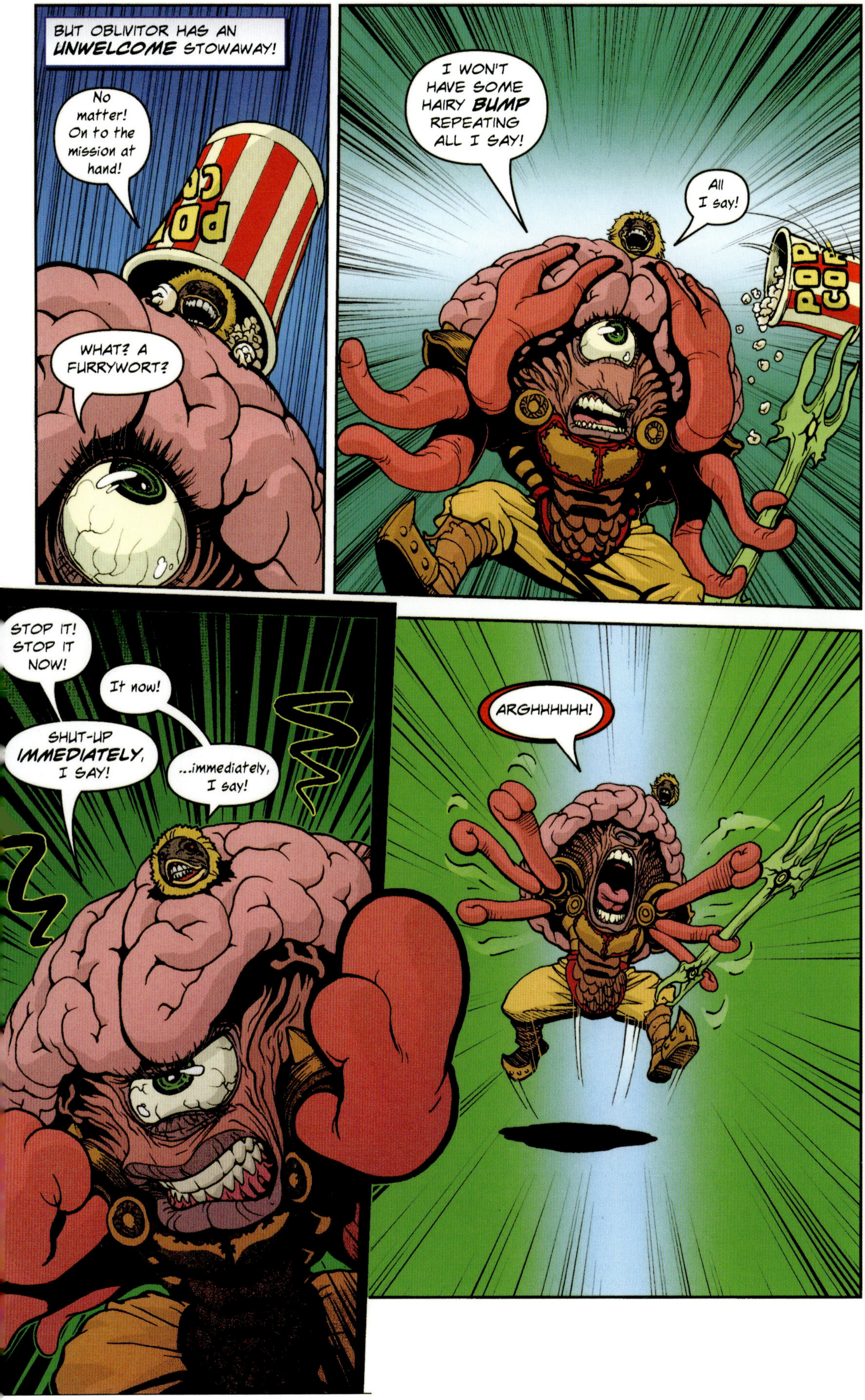

BUT OBLIVITOR HAS AN UNWELCOME STOWAWAY!
No matter! On to the mission at hand!
WHAT? A FURRYWORT?
I WON'T HAVE SOME HAIRY BUMP REPEATING ALL I SAY!
All I say!
STOP IT! STOP IT NOW!
It now!
SHUT-UP IMMEDIATELY, I SAY!
...immediately, I say!
ARGHHHHHH!

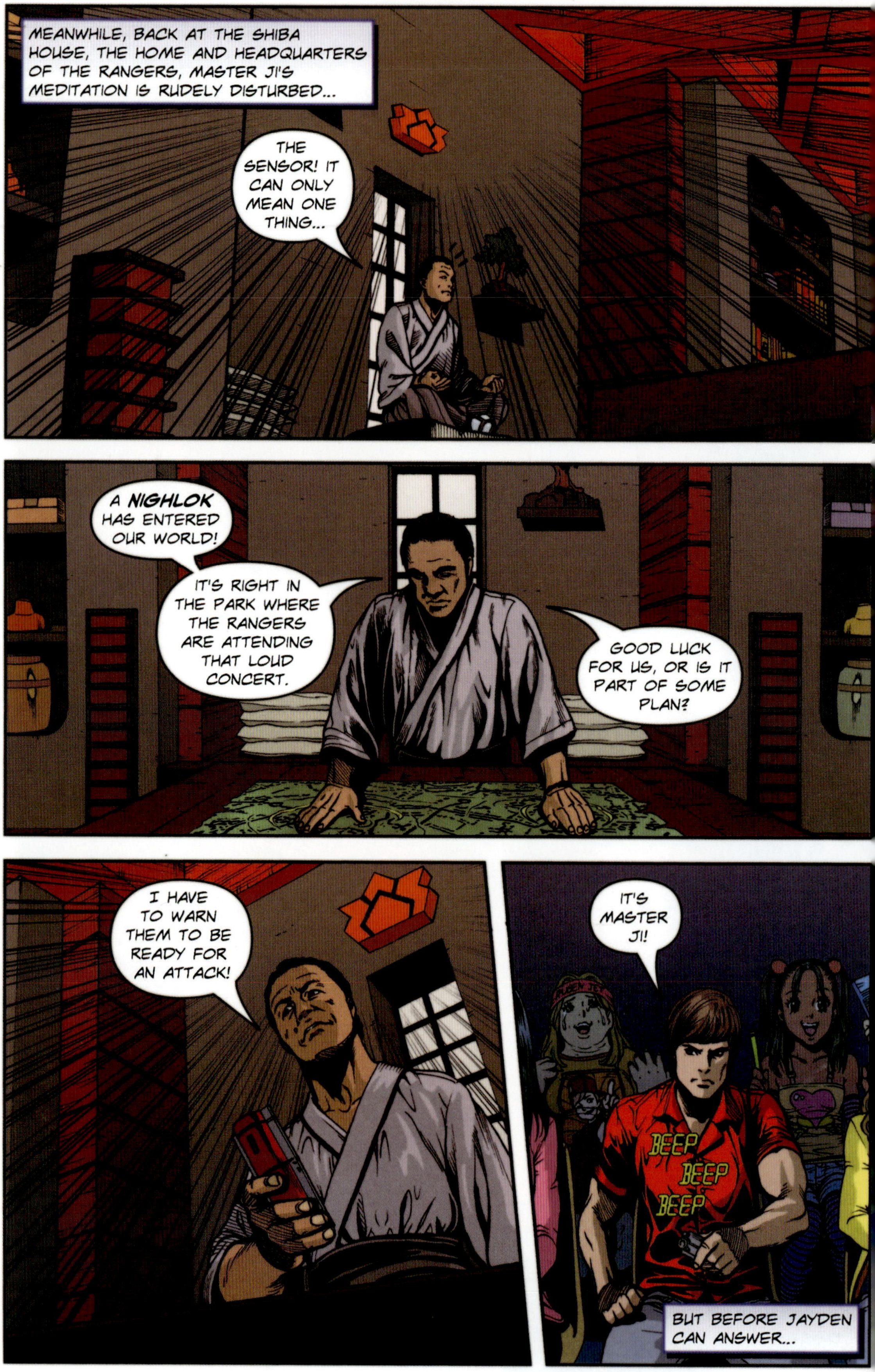
MEANWHILE, BACK AT THE SHIBA HOUSE, THE HOME AND HEADQUARTERS OF THE RANGERS, MASTER JI'S MEDITATION IS RUDELY DISTURBED...
THE SENSOR! IT CAN ONLY MEAN ONE THING...
A NIGHLOK HAS ENTERED OUR WORLD!
IT'S RIGHT IN THE PARK WHERE THE RANGERS ARE ATTENDING THAT LOUD CONCERT.
GOOD LUCK FOR US, OR IS IT PART OF SOME PLAN?
I HAVE TO WARN THEM TO BE READY FOR AN ATTACK!
IT'S MASTER JI!
BEEP
BEEP
BEEP
BUT BEFORE JAYDEN CAN ANSWER...

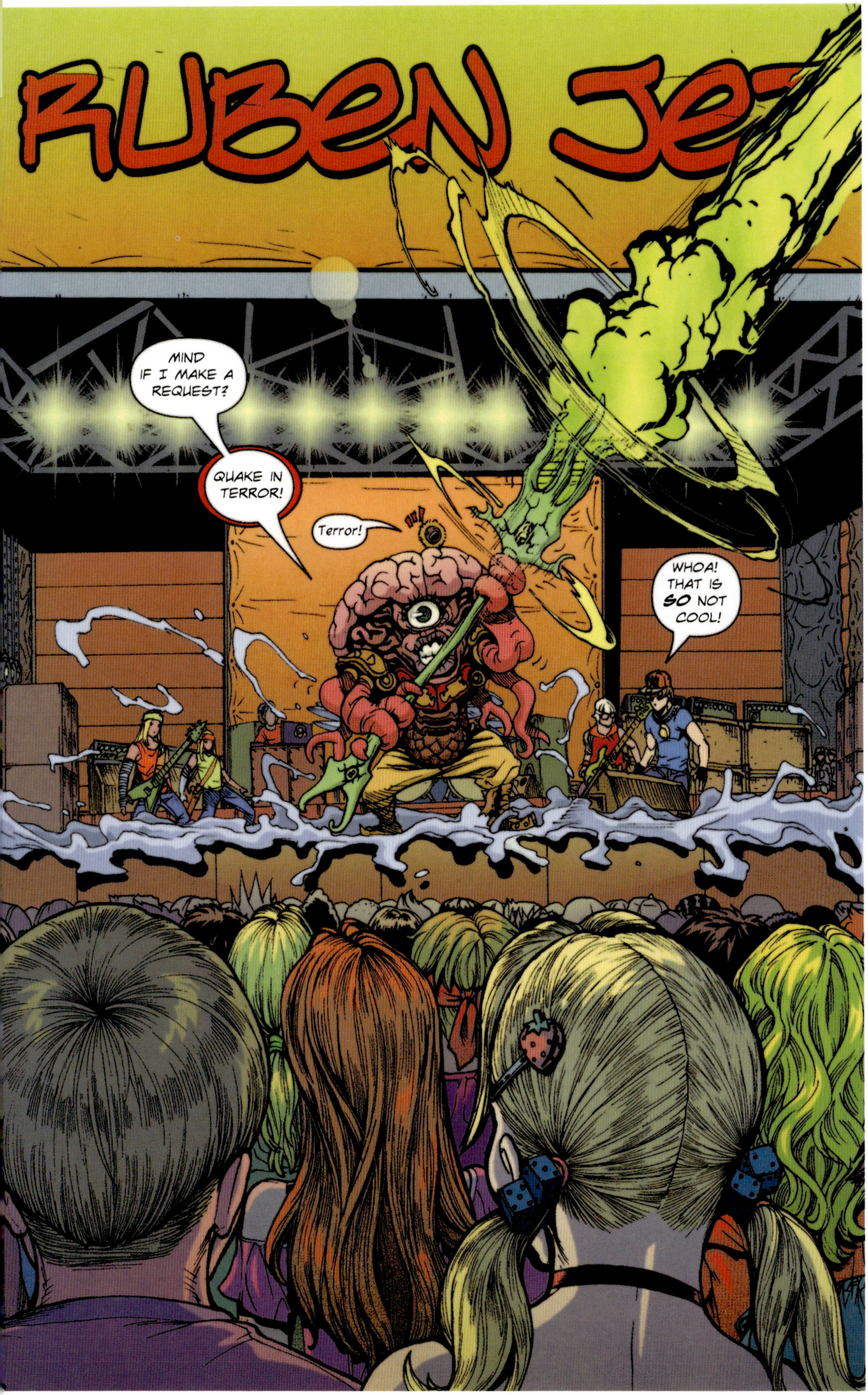
RUBEN JE
MIND IF I MAKE A REQUEST?
QUAKE IN TERROR!
Terror!
WHOA! THAT IS SO NOT COOL!

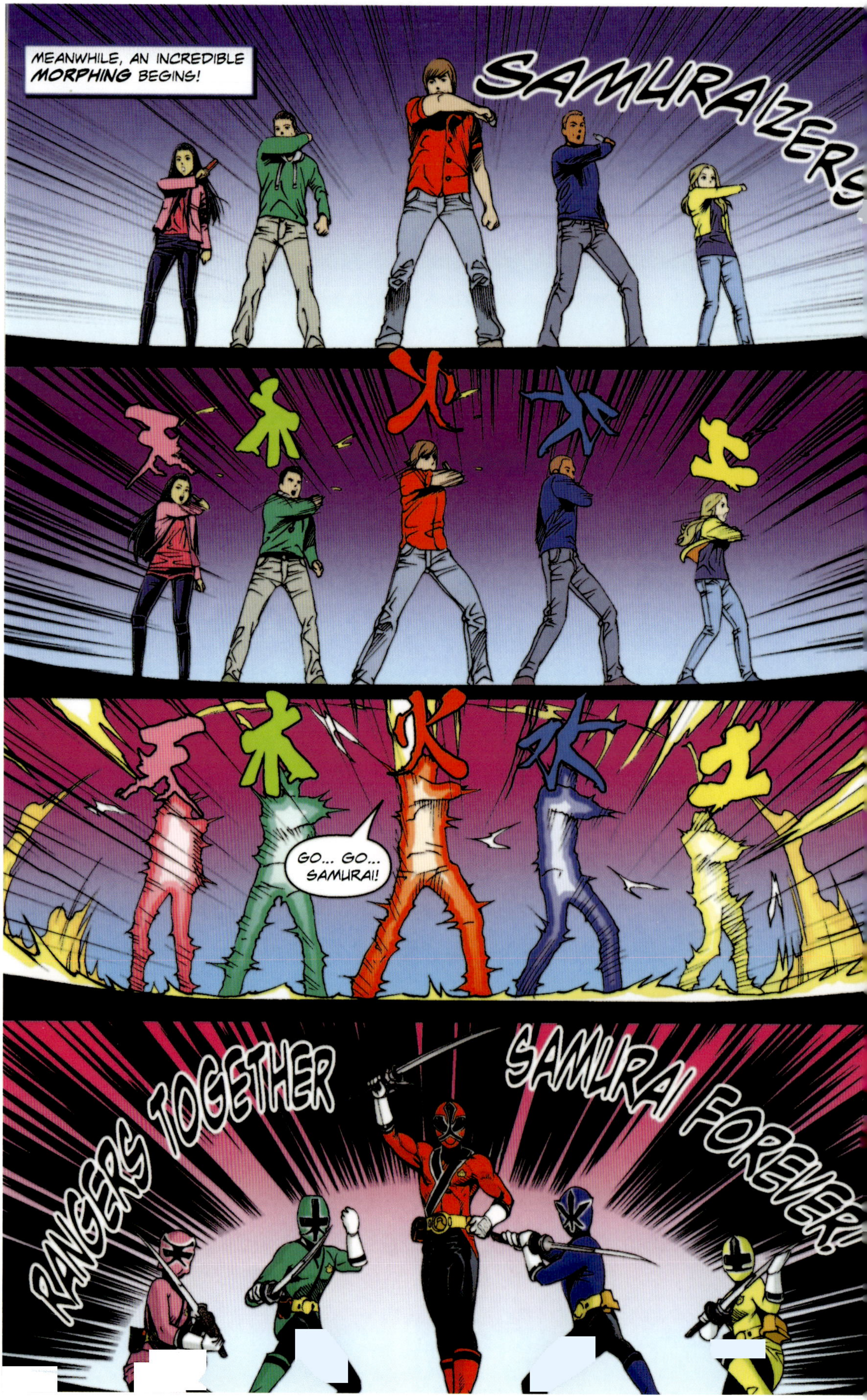

MEANWHILE, AN INCREDIBLE **MORPHING** BEGINS!
SAMURAIZERS
GO... GO... SAMURAI!
RANGERS TOGETHER
SAMURAI FOREVER!

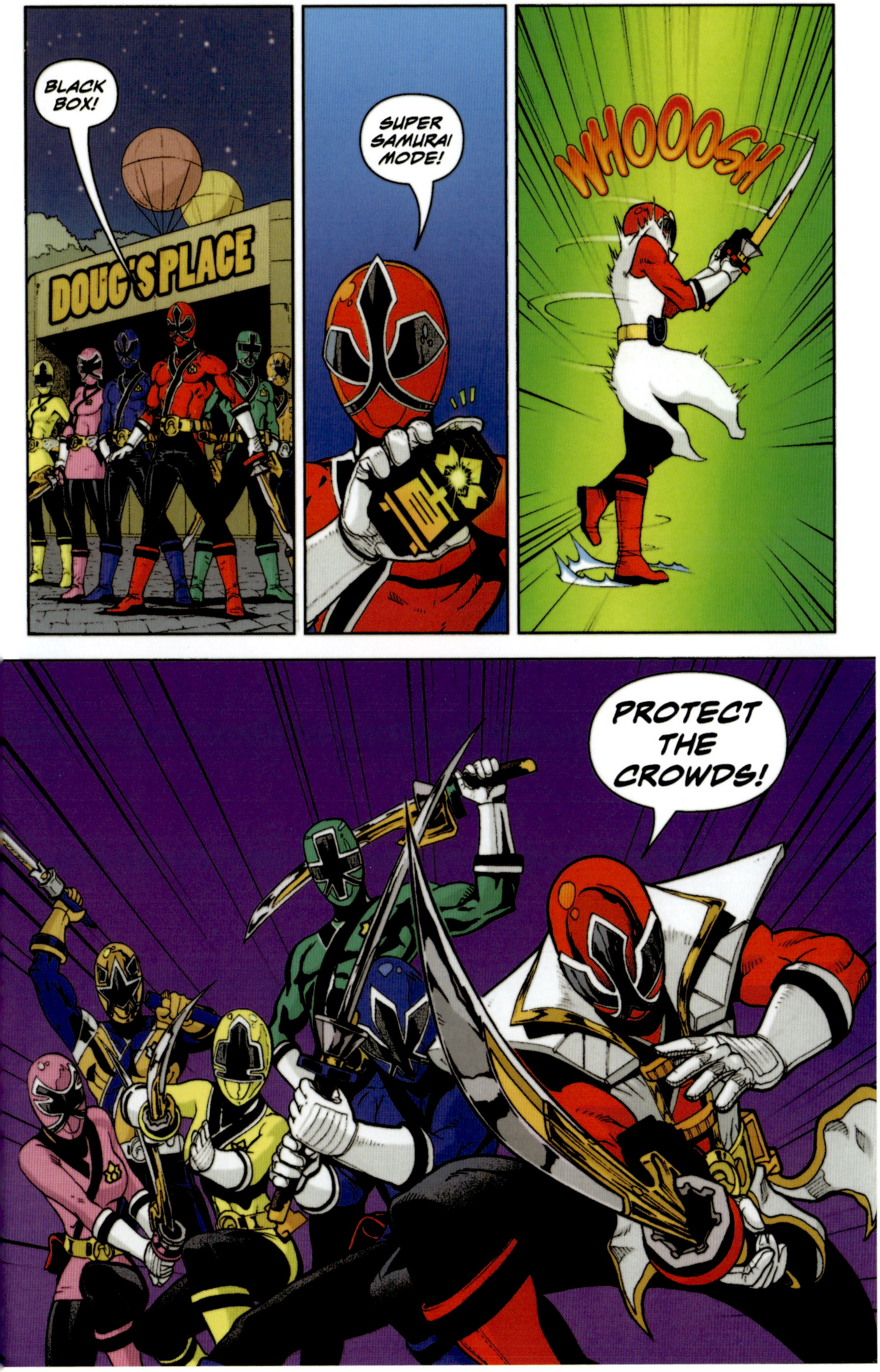
BLACK BOX!
DOUG'S PLACE
SUPER SAMURAI MODE!
WHOOOSH
PROTECT THE CROWDS!

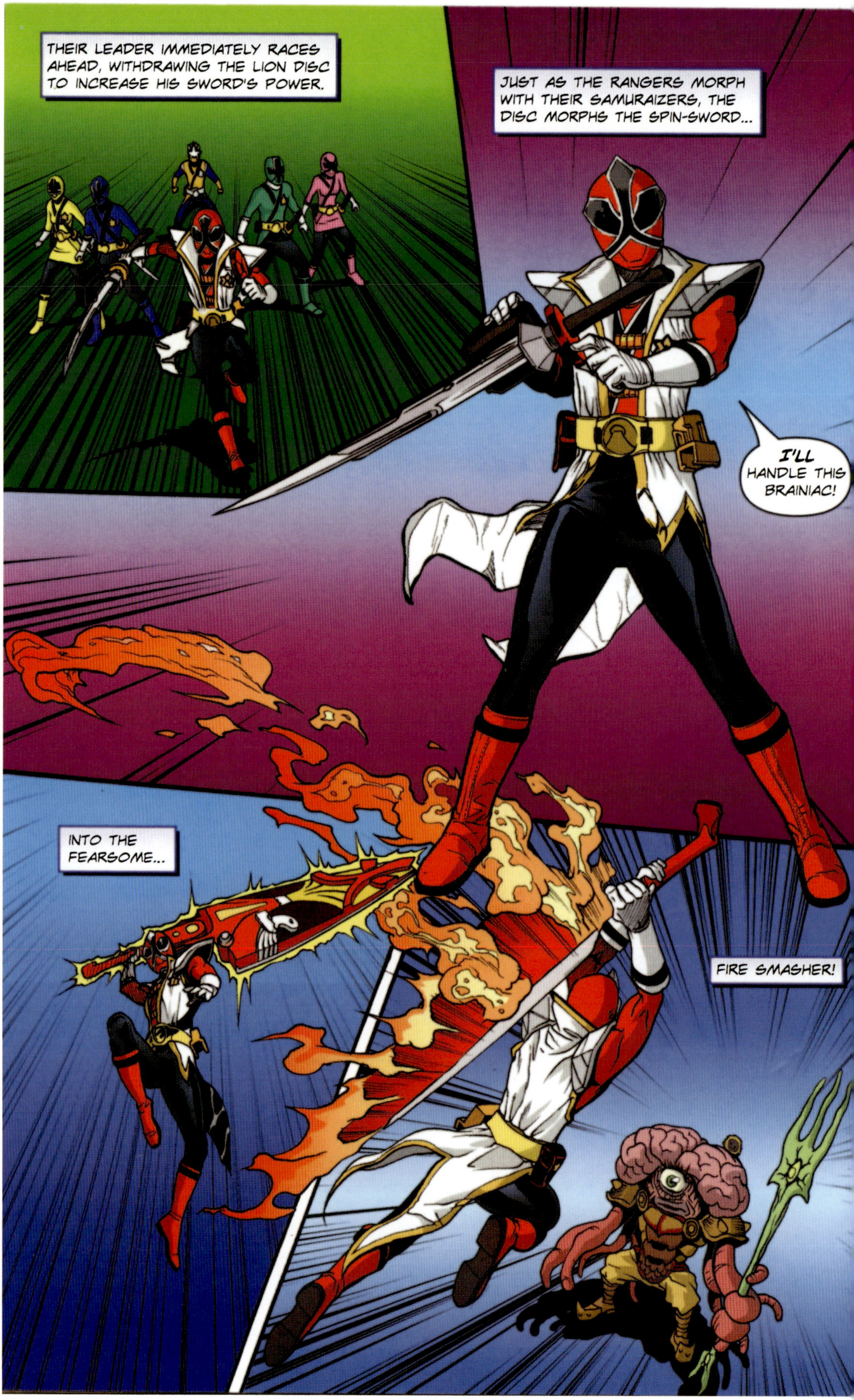
THEIR LEADER IMMEDIATELY RACES AHEAD, WITHDRAWING THE LION DISC TO INCREASE HIS SWORD'S POWER.
JUST AS THE RANGERS MORPH WITH THEIR SAMURAIZERS, THE DISC MORPHS THE SPIN-SWORD...
I'LL HANDLE THIS BRAINIAC!
INTO THE FEARSOME...
FIRE SMASHER!

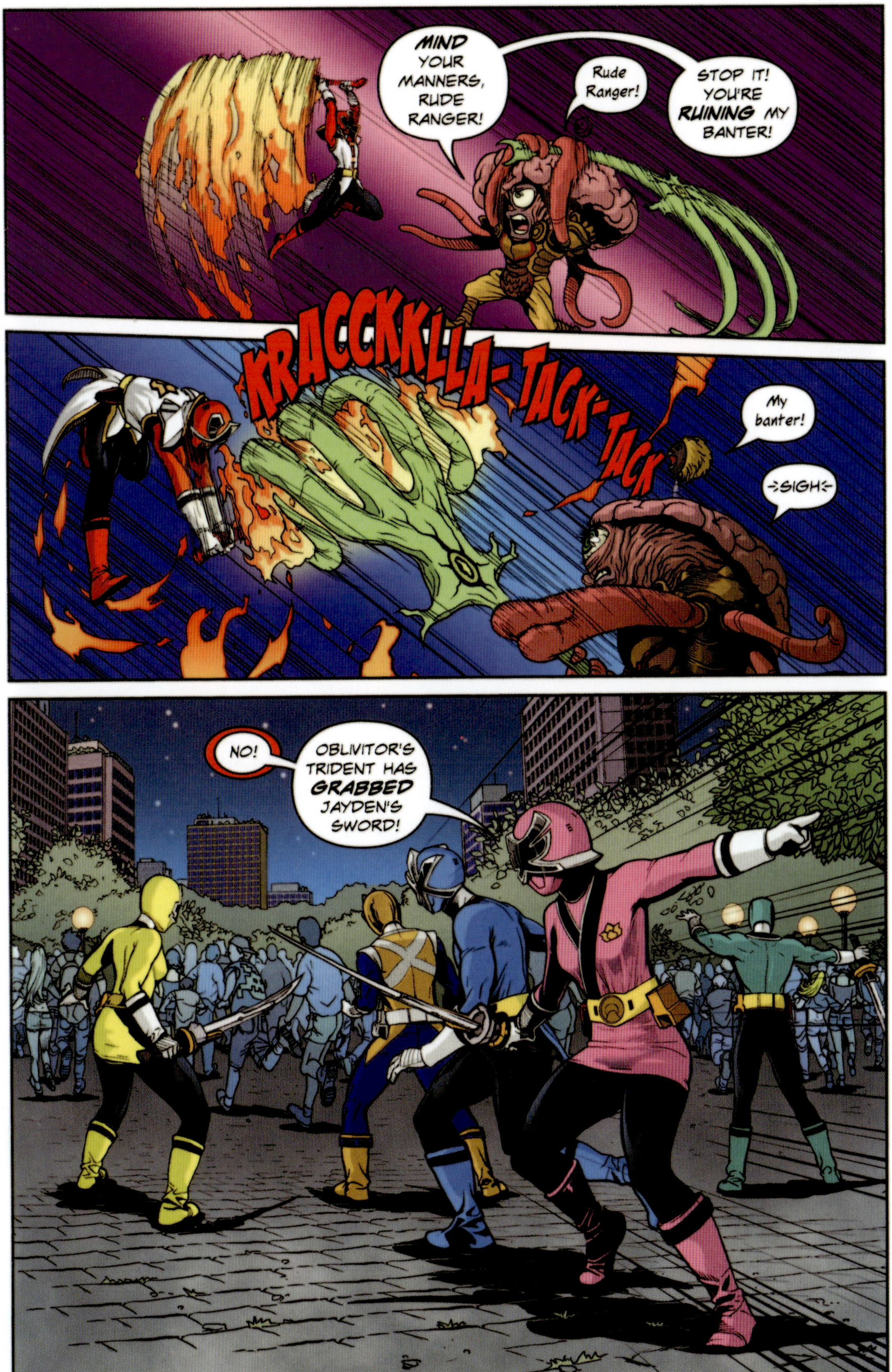
MIND YOUR MANNERS, RUDE RANGER!
Rude Ranger!
STOP IT! YOU'RE RUINING MY BANTER!
KRACCKKLLA-TACK-TACK
My banter!
SIGH
NO!
OBLIVITOR'S TRIDENT HAS GRABBED JAYDEN'S SWORD!

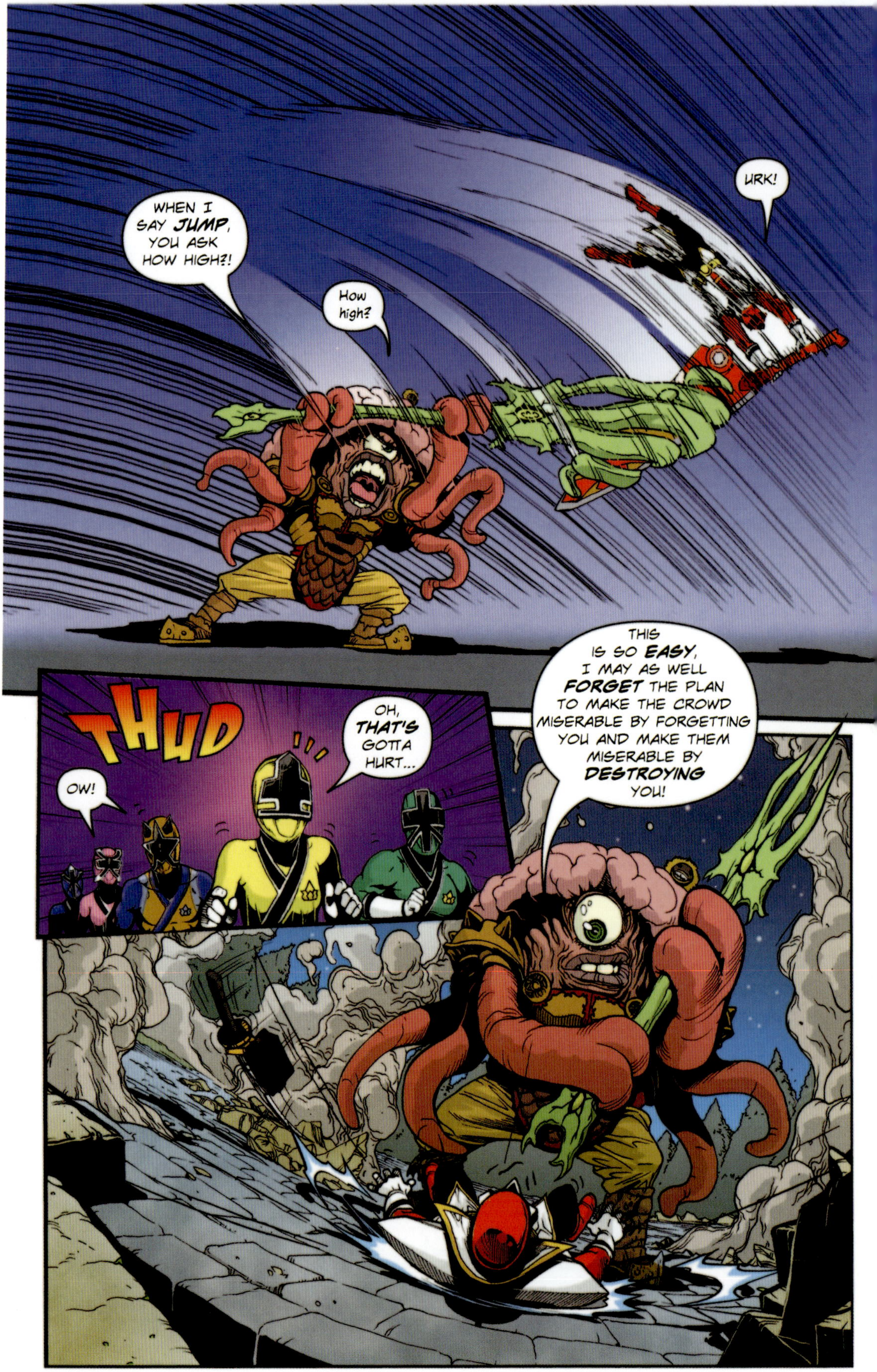
WHEN I SAY JUMP, YOU ASK HOW HIGH?!
How high?
URK!
THUD
OW!
OH, THAT'S GOTTA HURT...
THIS IS SO EASY, I MAY AS WELL FORGET THE PLAN TO MAKE THE CROWD MISERABLE BY FORGETTING YOU AND MAKE THEM MISERABLE BY DESTROYING YOU!

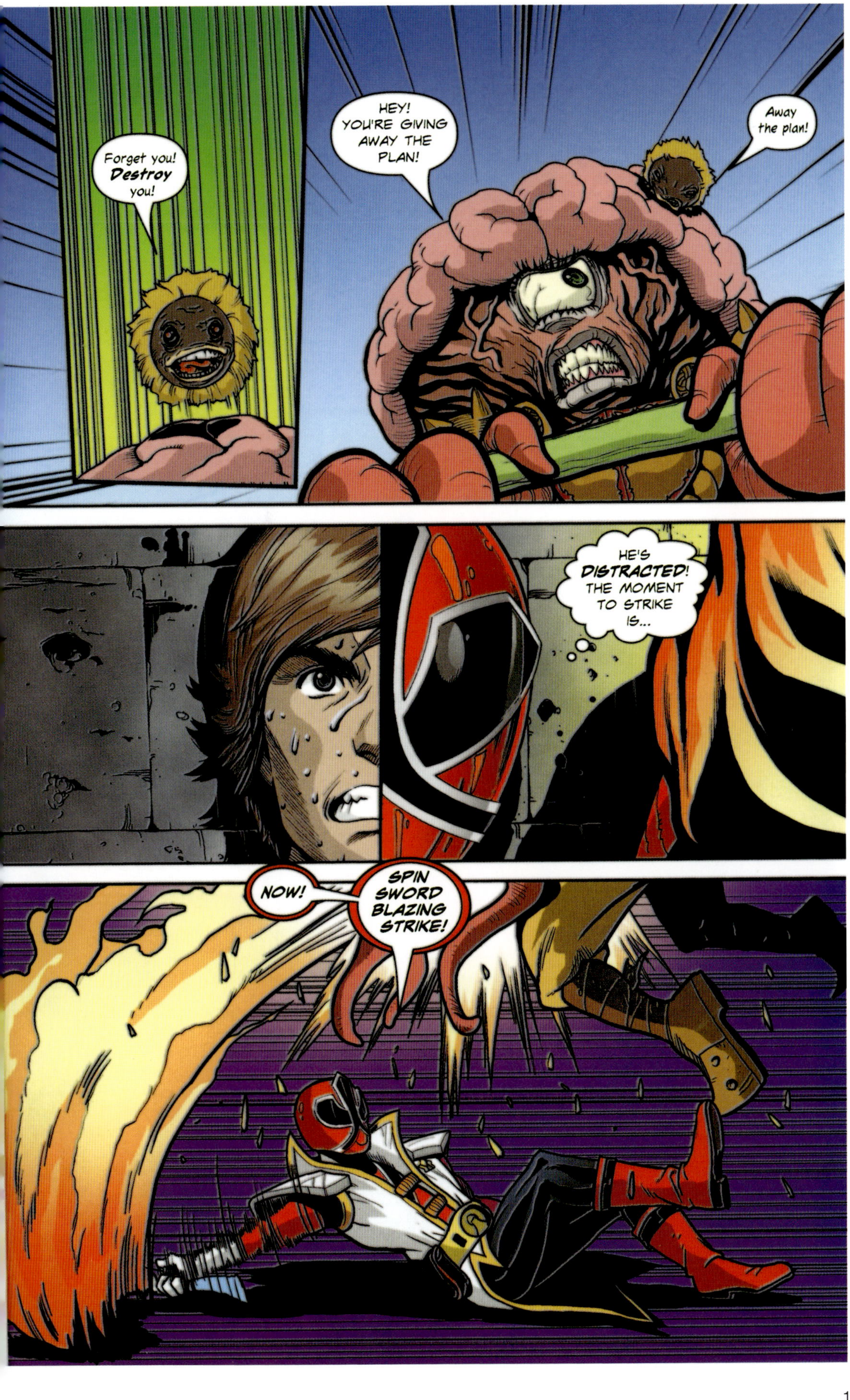
Forget you! **Destroy** you!
HEY! YOU'RE GIVING AWAY THE PLAN!
Away the plan!
HE'S **DISTRACTED**! THE MOMENT TO STRIKE IS...
NOW!
SPIN SWORD BLAZING STRIKE!

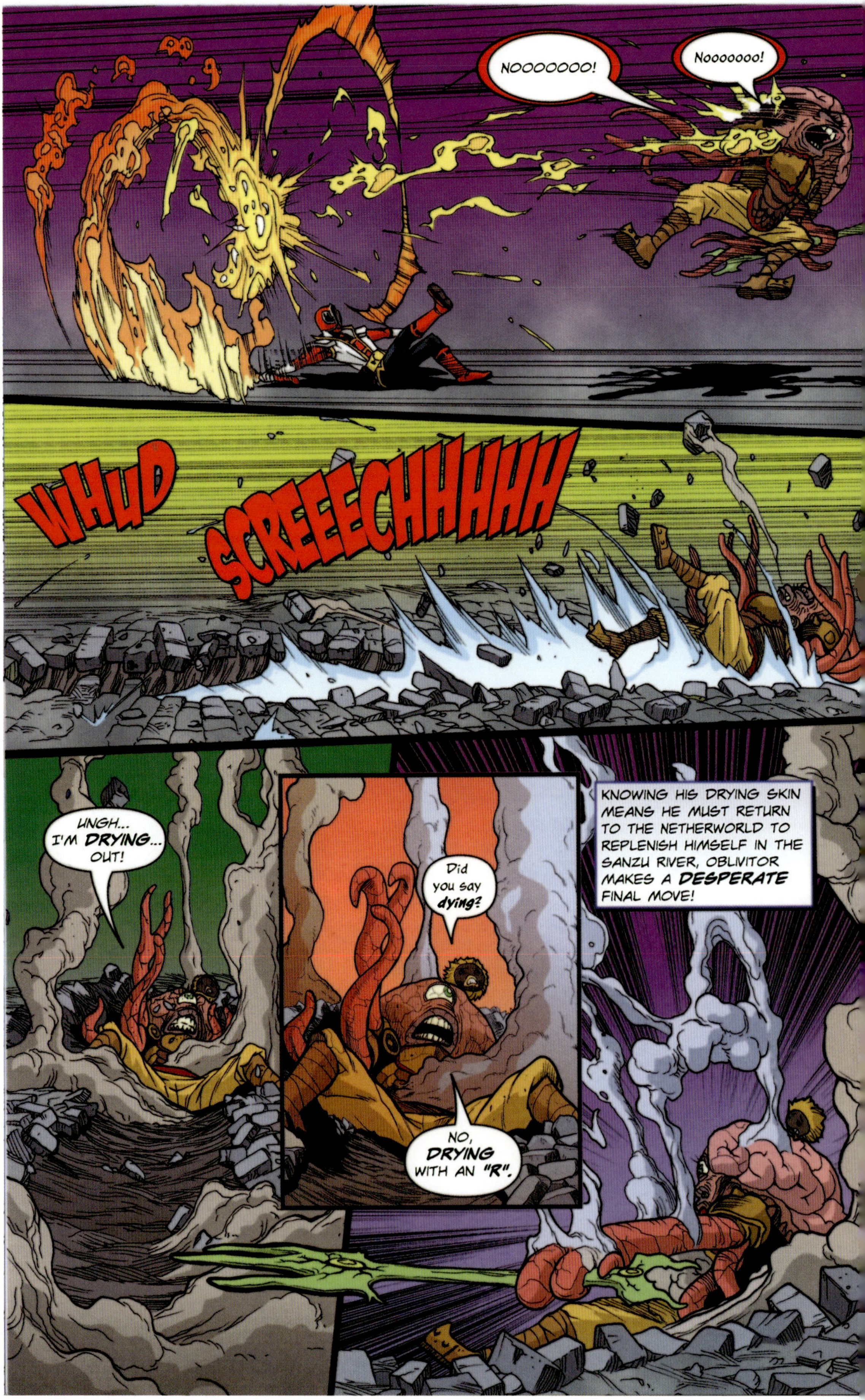

NOOOOOOO!
Nooooooo!
WHUD
SCREEECHHHHH
UNGH... I'M DRYING... OUT!
Did you say dying?
NO, DRYING WITH AN "R".
KNOWING HIS DRYING SKIN MEANS HE MUST RETURN TO THE NETHERWORLD TO REPLENISH HIMSELF IN THE SANZU RIVER, OBLIVITOR MAKES A DESPERATE FINAL MOVE!

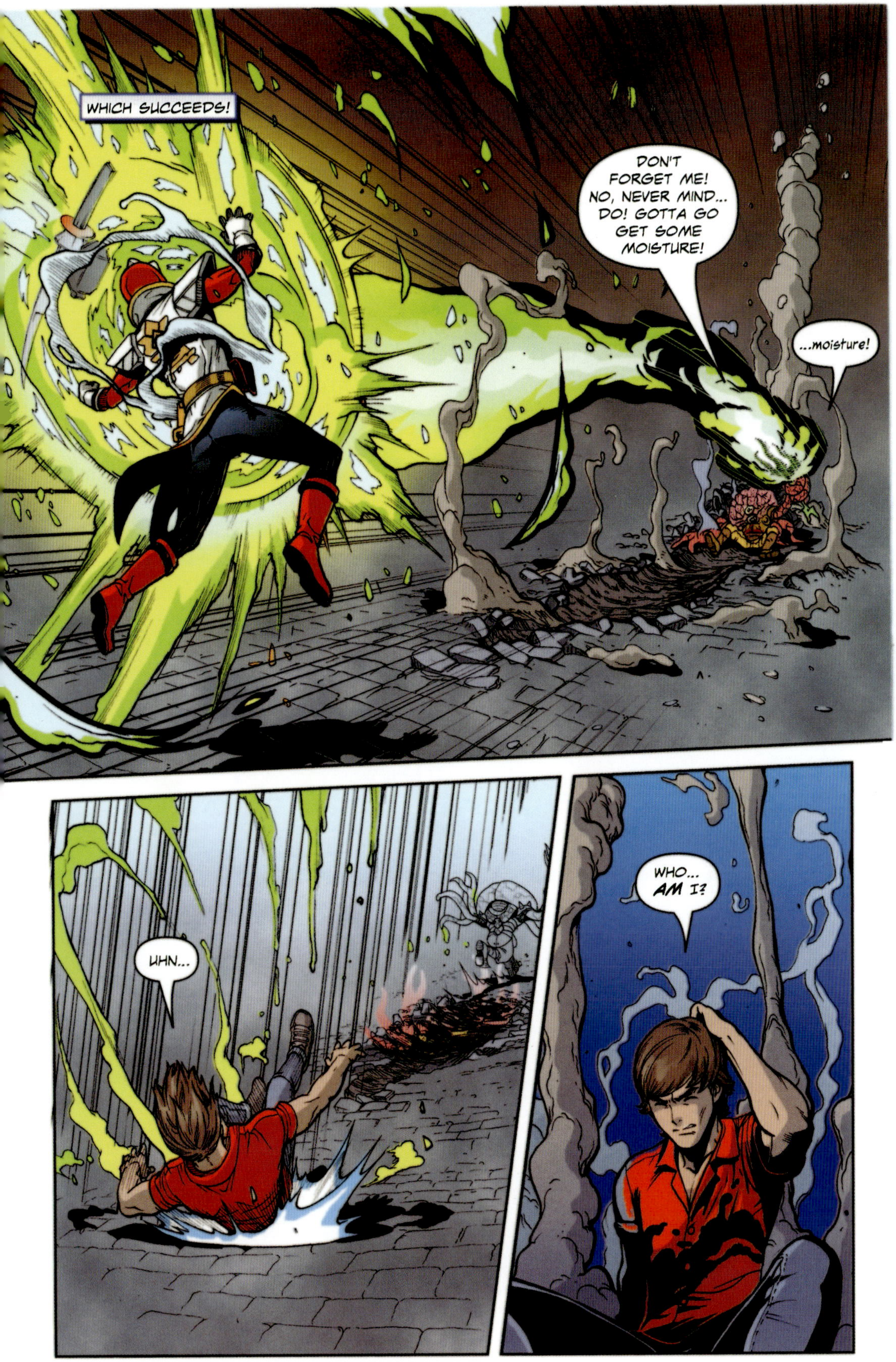
WHICH SUCCEEDS!
DON'T FORGET ME! NO, NEVER MIND... DO! GOTTA GO GET SOME MOISTURE!
...moisture!
UHN...
WHO... AM I?

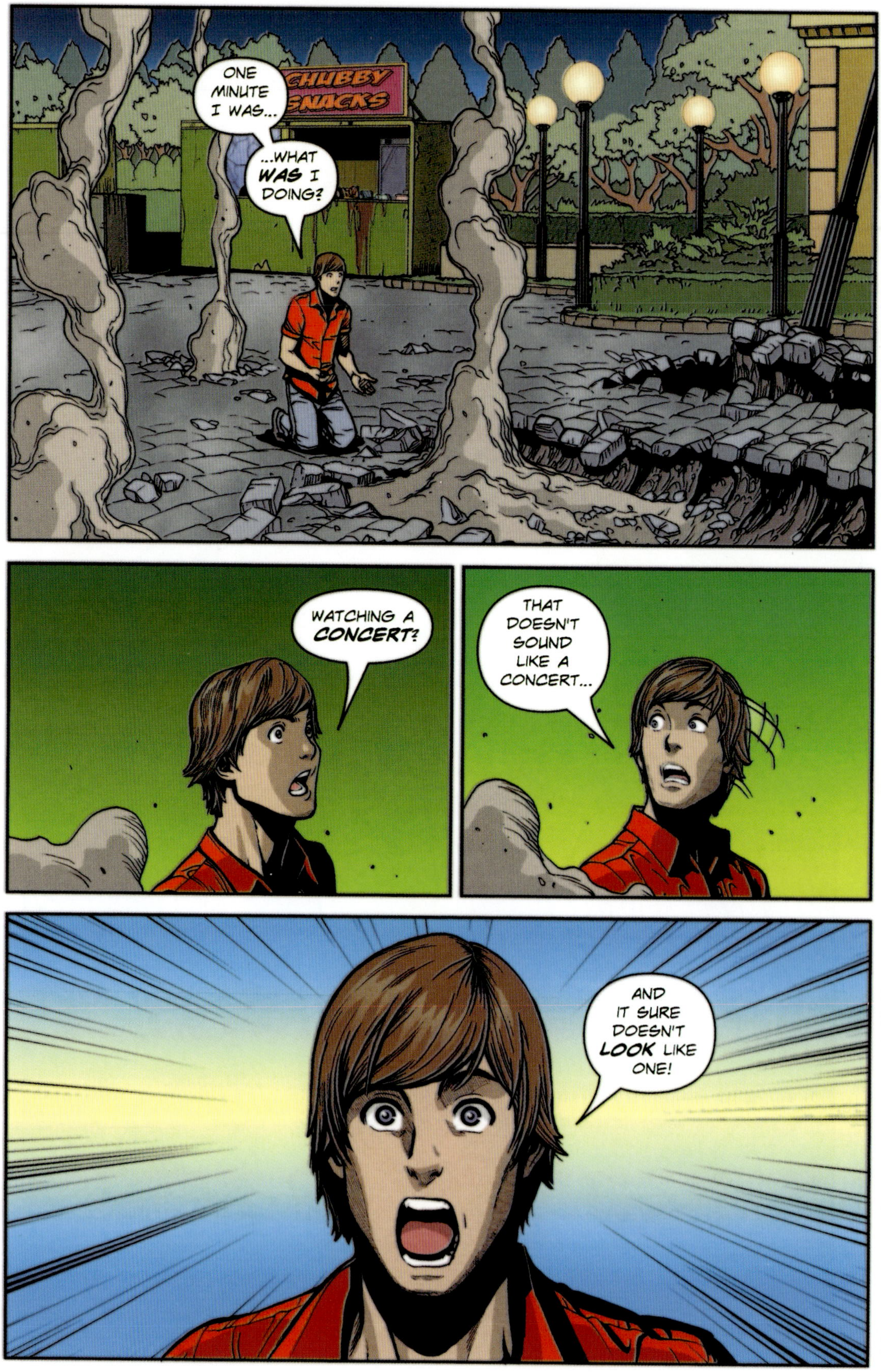
ONE MINUTE I WAS...
CHUBBY SNACKS
...WHAT WAS I DOING?
WATCHING A CONCERT?
THAT DOESN'T SOUND LIKE A CONCERT...
AND IT SURE DOESN'T LOOK LIKE ONE!

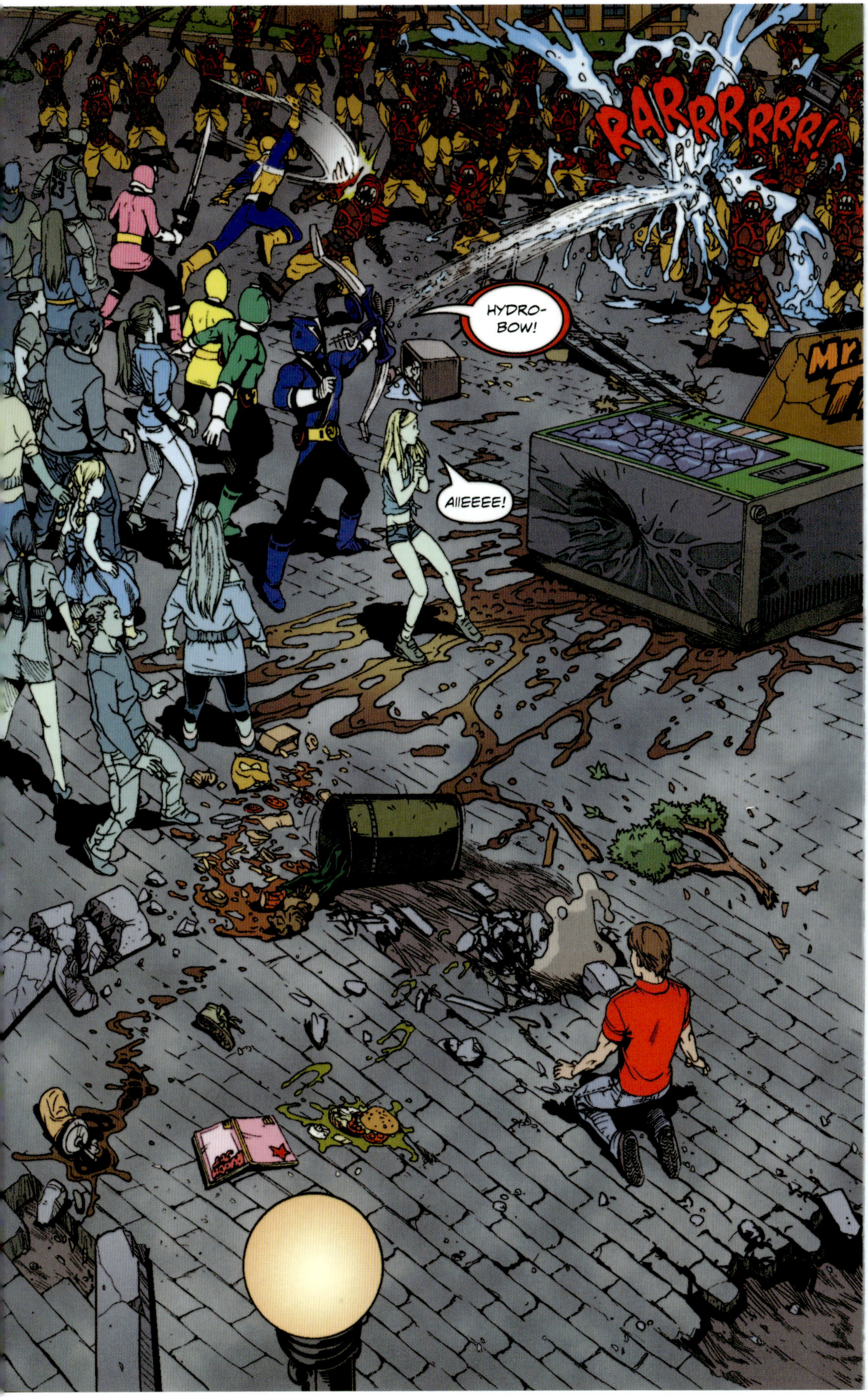
RARRRRRR!
HYDRO-
BOW!
AIIEEEE!

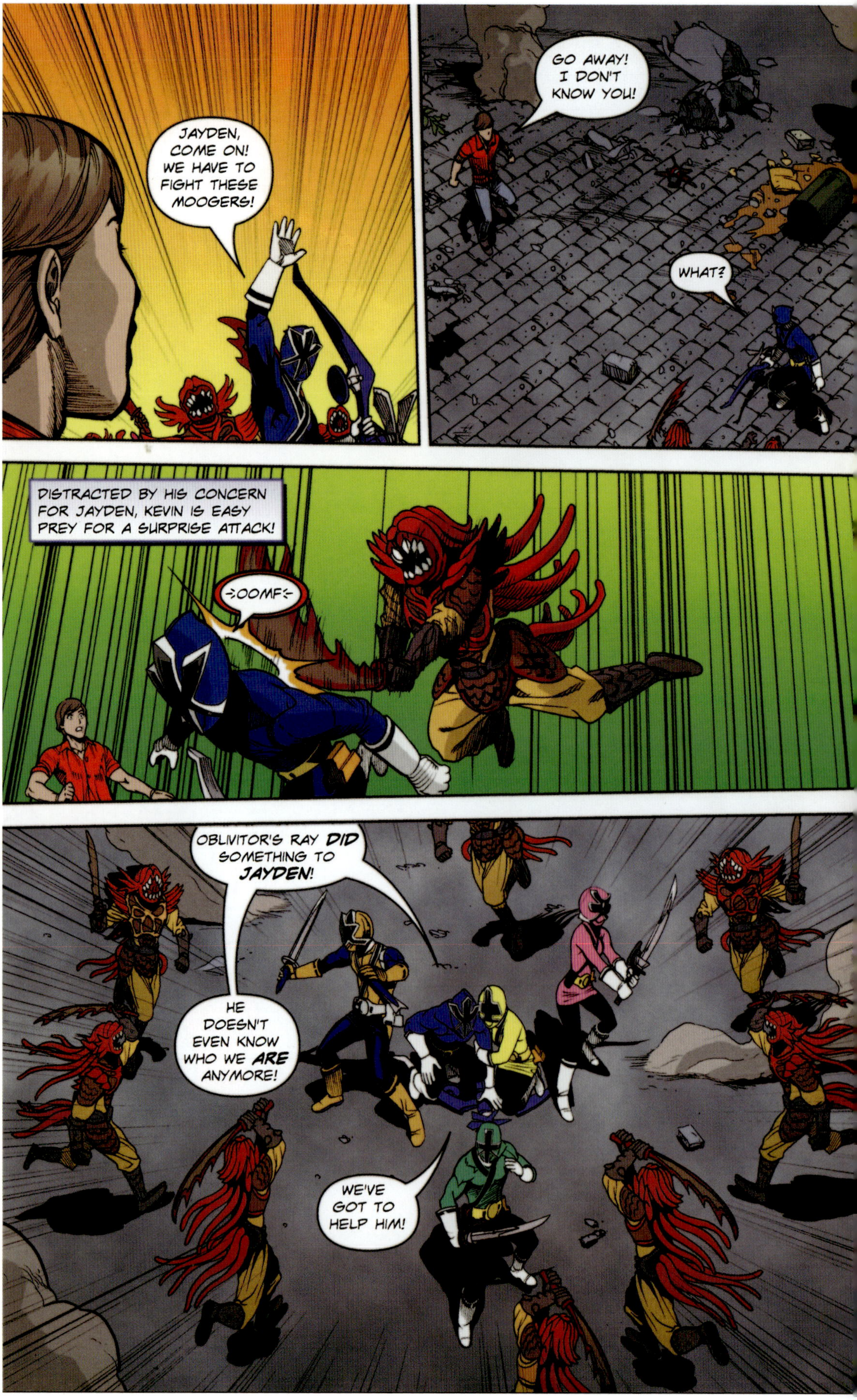
JAYDEN, COME ON! WE HAVE TO FIGHT THESE MOOGERS!
GO AWAY! I DON'T KNOW YOU!
WHAT?
DISTRACTED BY HIS CONCERN FOR JAYDEN, KEVIN IS EASY PREY FOR A SURPRISE ATTACK!
OOMF
OBLIVITOR'S RAY DID SOMETHING TO JAYDEN!
HE DOESN'T EVEN KNOW WHO WE ARE ANYMORE!
WE'VE GOT TO HELP HIM!

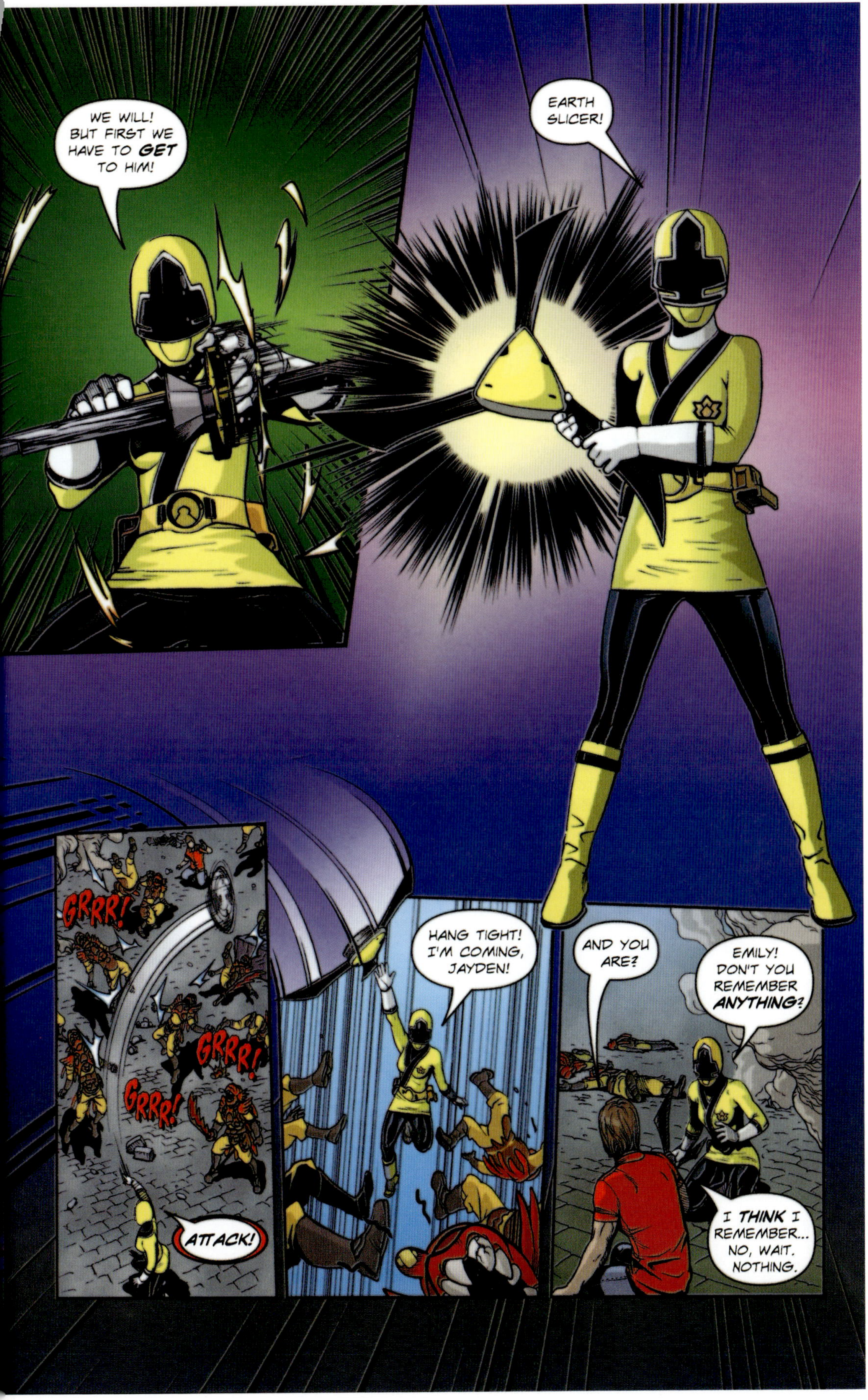
WE WILL! BUT FIRST WE HAVE TO GET TO HIM!
EARTH SLICER!
GRRR!
GRRR!
GRRR!
ATTACK!
HANG TIGHT! I'M COMING, JAYDEN!
AND YOU ARE?
EMILY! DON'T YOU REMEMBER ANYTHING?
I THINK I REMEMBER... NO, WAIT. NOTHING.

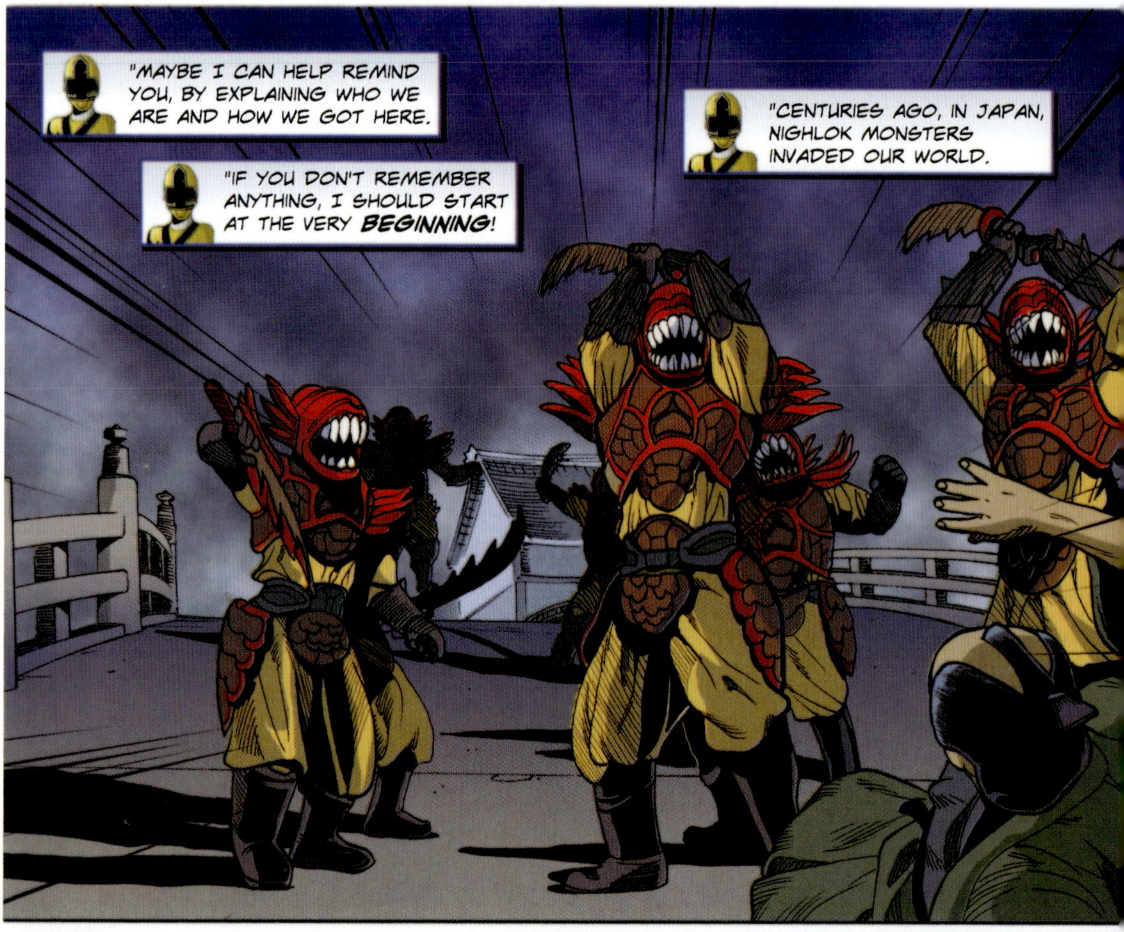
"MAYBE I CAN HELP REMIND YOU, BY EXPLAINING WHO WE ARE AND HOW WE GOT HERE.
"IF YOU DON'T REMEMBER ANYTHING, I SHOULD START AT THE VERY BEGINNING!
"CENTURIES AGO, IN JAPAN, NIGHLOK MONSTERS INVADED OUR WORLD.

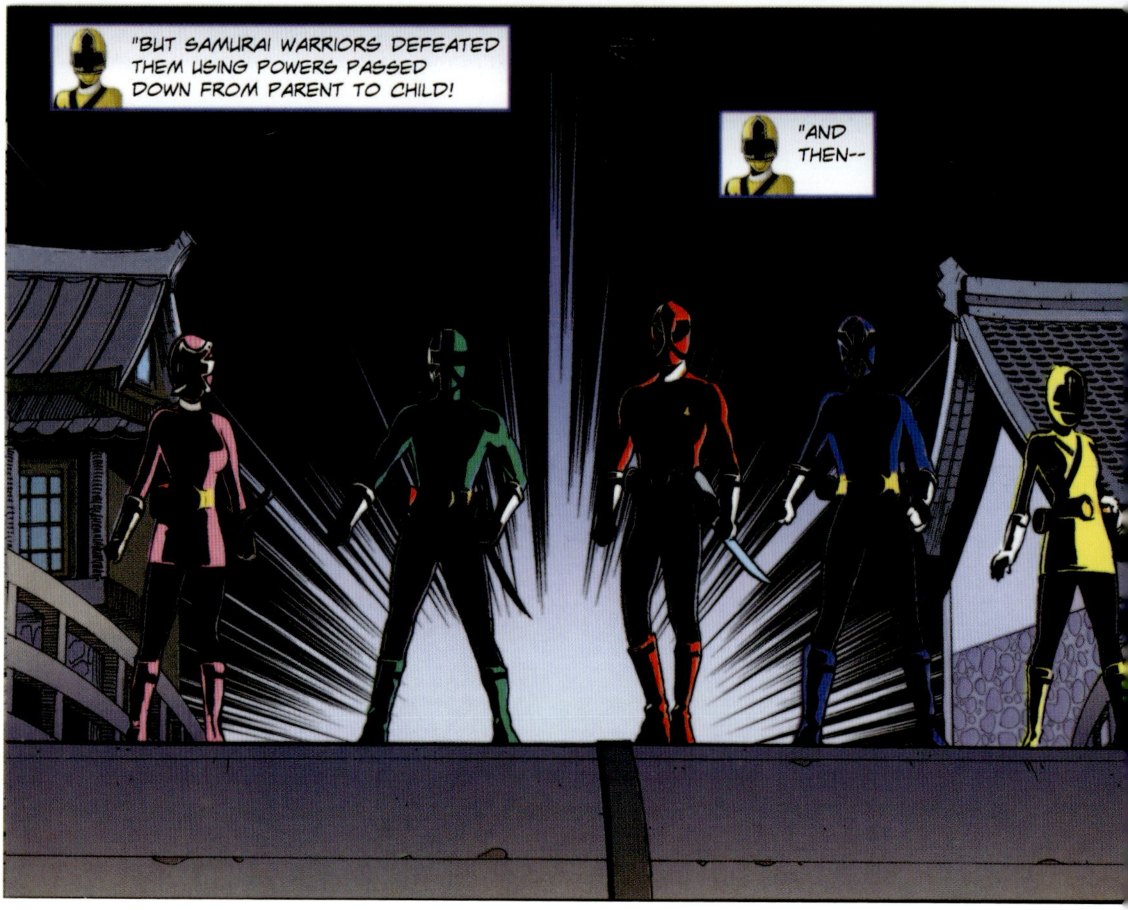
"BUT SAMURAI WARRIORS DEFEATED THEM USING POWERS PASSED DOWN FROM PARENT TO CHILD!
"AND THEN--

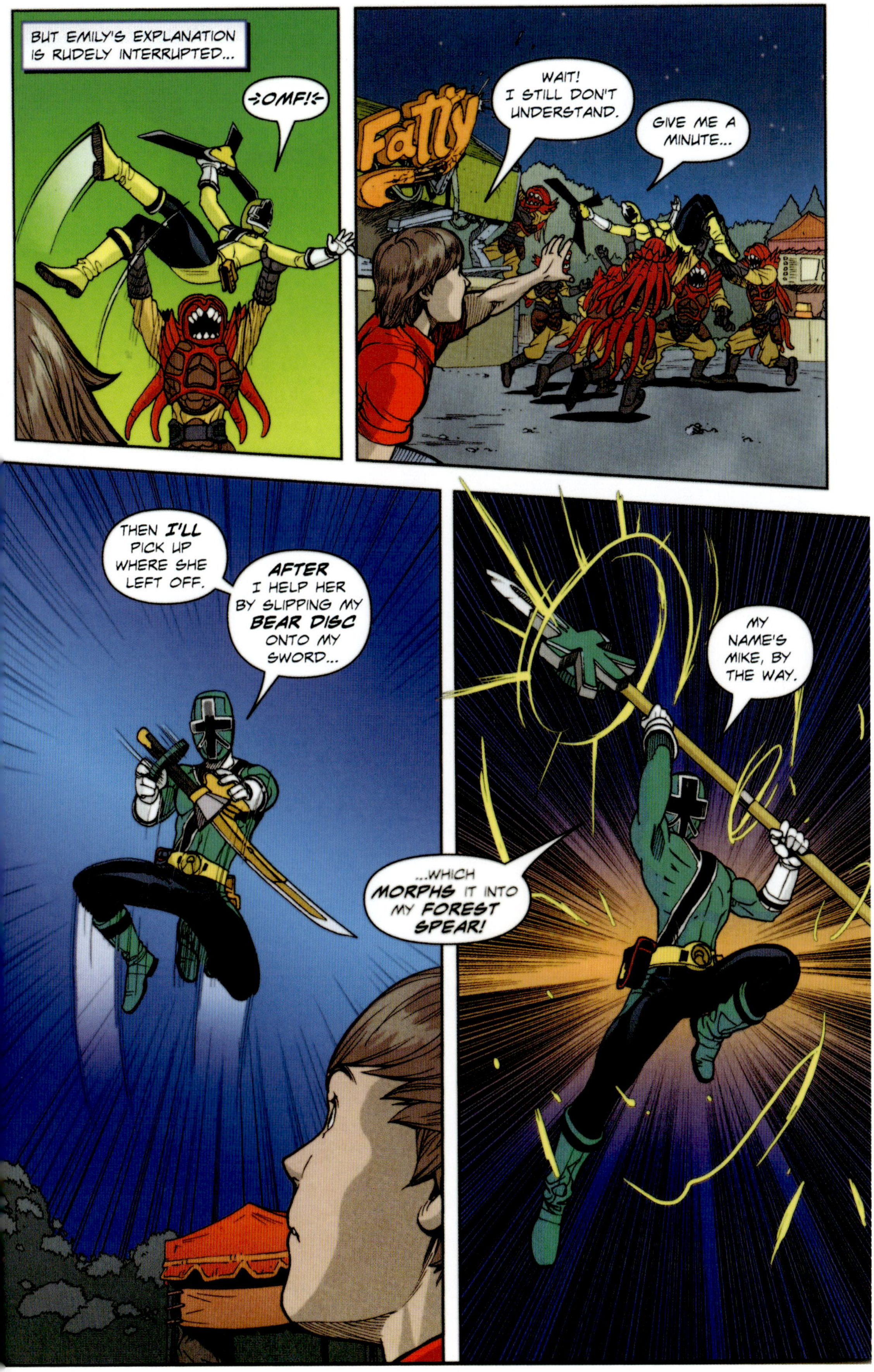
BUT EMILY'S EXPLANATION IS RUDELY INTERRUPTED...
OMF!
WAIT! I STILL DON'T UNDERSTAND.
GIVE ME A MINUTE...
Fatty
THEN I'LL PICK UP WHERE SHE LEFT OFF.
AFTER I HELP HER BY SLIPPING MY BEAR DISC ONTO MY SWORD...
...WHICH MORPHS IT INTO MY FOREST SPEAR!
MY NAME'S MIKE, BY THE WAY.

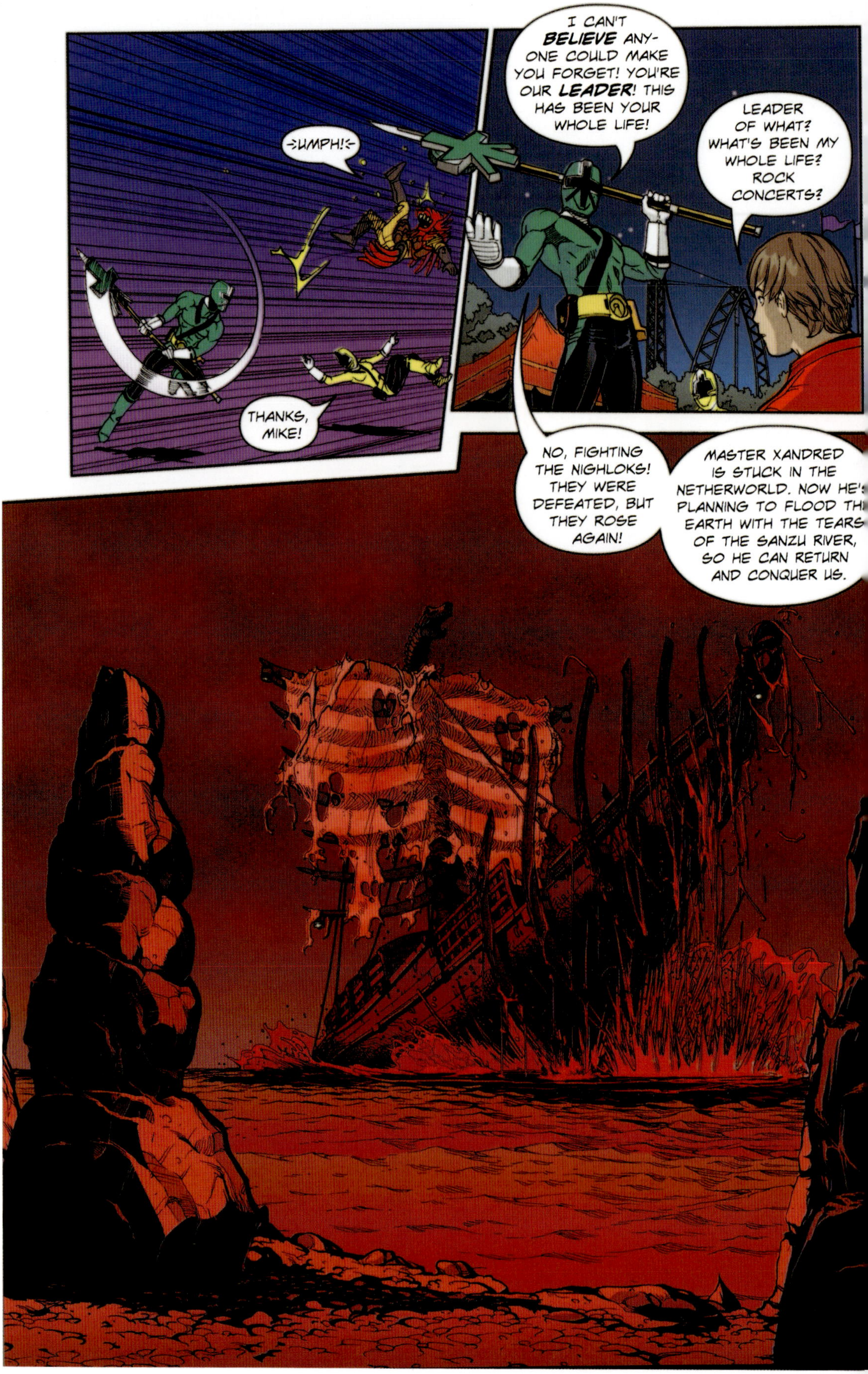

-UMPH!-
THANKS, MIKE!
I CAN'T BELIEVE ANYONE COULD MAKE YOU FORGET! YOU'RE OUR LEADER! THIS HAS BEEN YOUR WHOLE LIFE!
LEADER OF WHAT? WHAT'S BEEN MY WHOLE LIFE? ROCK CONCERTS?
NO, FIGHTING THE NIGHLOKS! THEY WERE DEFEATED, BUT THEY ROSE AGAIN!
MASTER XANDRED IS STUCK IN THE NETHERWORLD. NOW HE'S PLANNING TO FLOOD THE EARTH WITH THE TEARS OF THE SANZU RIVER, SO HE CAN RETURN AND CONQUER US.

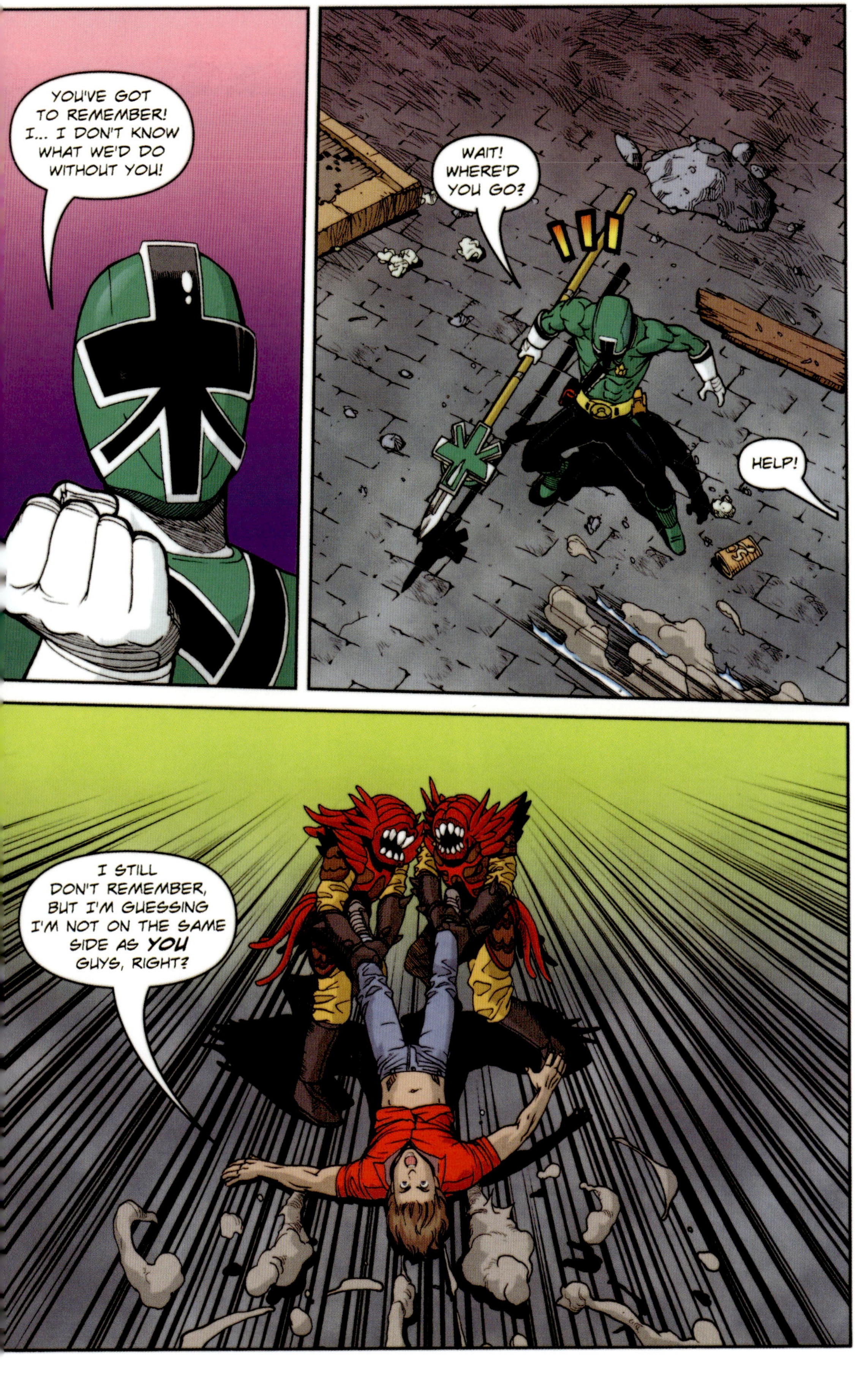
YOU'VE GOT TO REMEMBER! I... I DON'T KNOW WHAT WE'D DO WITHOUT YOU!
WAIT! WHERE'D YOU GO?
HELP!
I STILL DON'T REMEMBER, BUT I'M GUESSING I'M NOT ON THE SAME SIDE AS YOU GUYS, RIGHT?

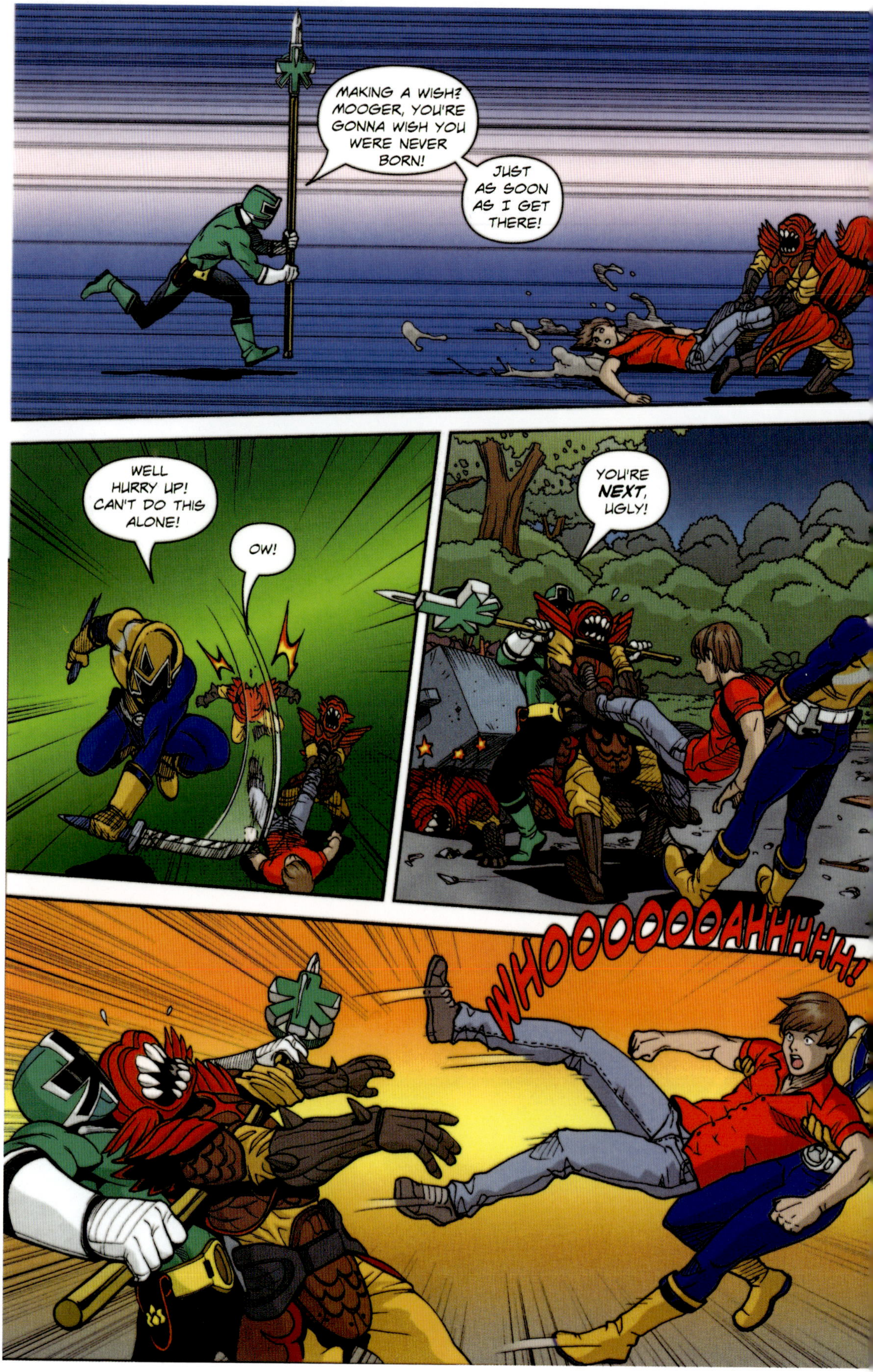
MAKING A WISH? MOOGER, YOU'RE GONNA WISH YOU WERE NEVER BORN!
JUST AS SOON AS I GET THERE!
WELL HURRY UP! CAN'T DO THIS ALONE!
OW!
YOU'RE **NEXT**, UGLY!
WHOOOOOOAHHHHH!

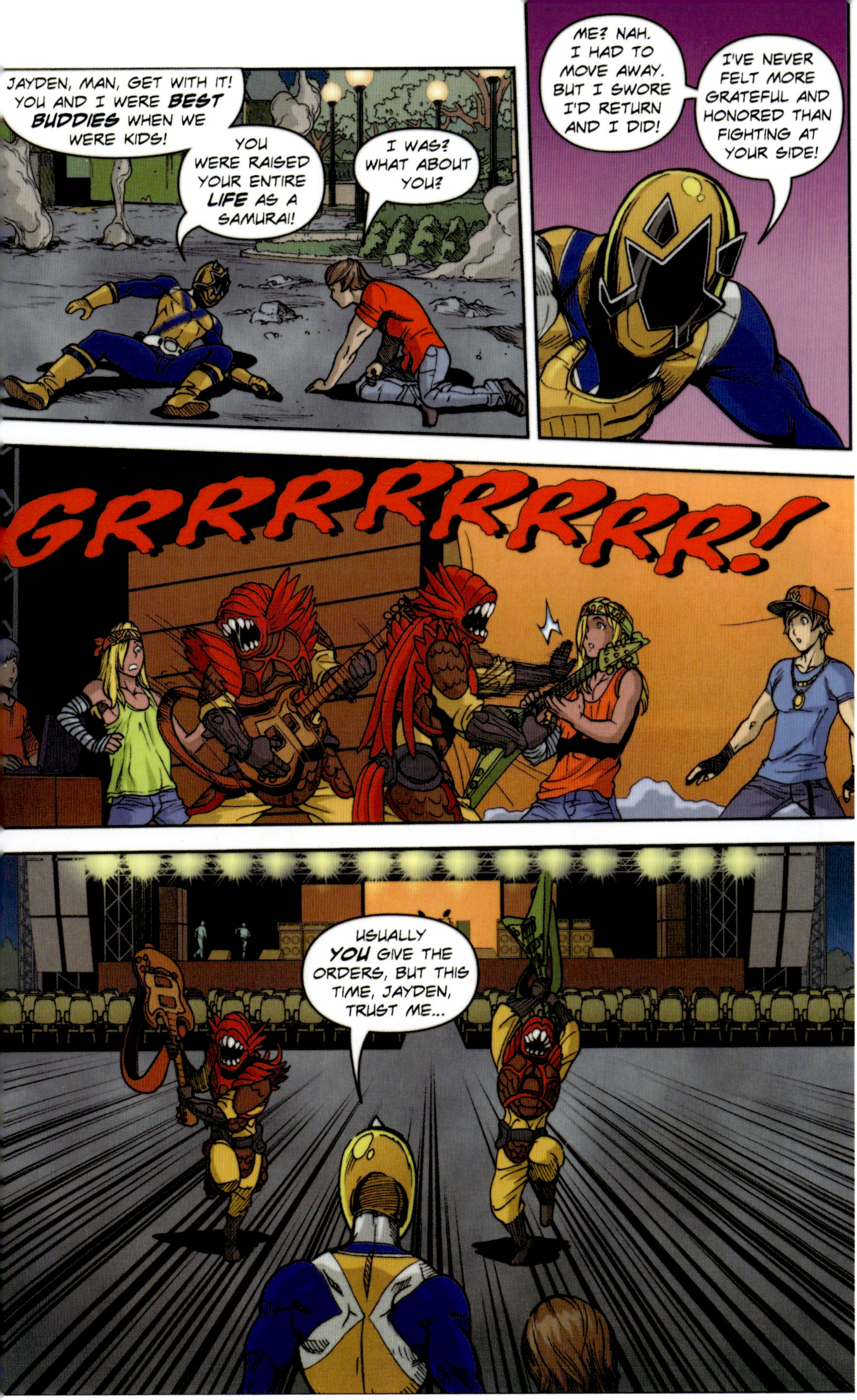

JAYDEN, MAN, GET WITH IT! YOU AND I WERE **BEST BUDDIES** WHEN WE WERE KIDS!
YOU WERE RAISED YOUR ENTIRE **LIFE** AS A SAMURAI!
I WAS? WHAT ABOUT YOU?
ME? NAH. I HAD TO MOVE AWAY. BUT I SWORE I'D RETURN AND I DID!
I'VE NEVER FELT MORE GRATEFUL AND HONORED THAN FIGHTING AT YOUR SIDE!
GRRRRRRRR!
USUALLY **YOU** GIVE THE ORDERS, BUT THIS TIME, JAYDEN, TRUST ME...

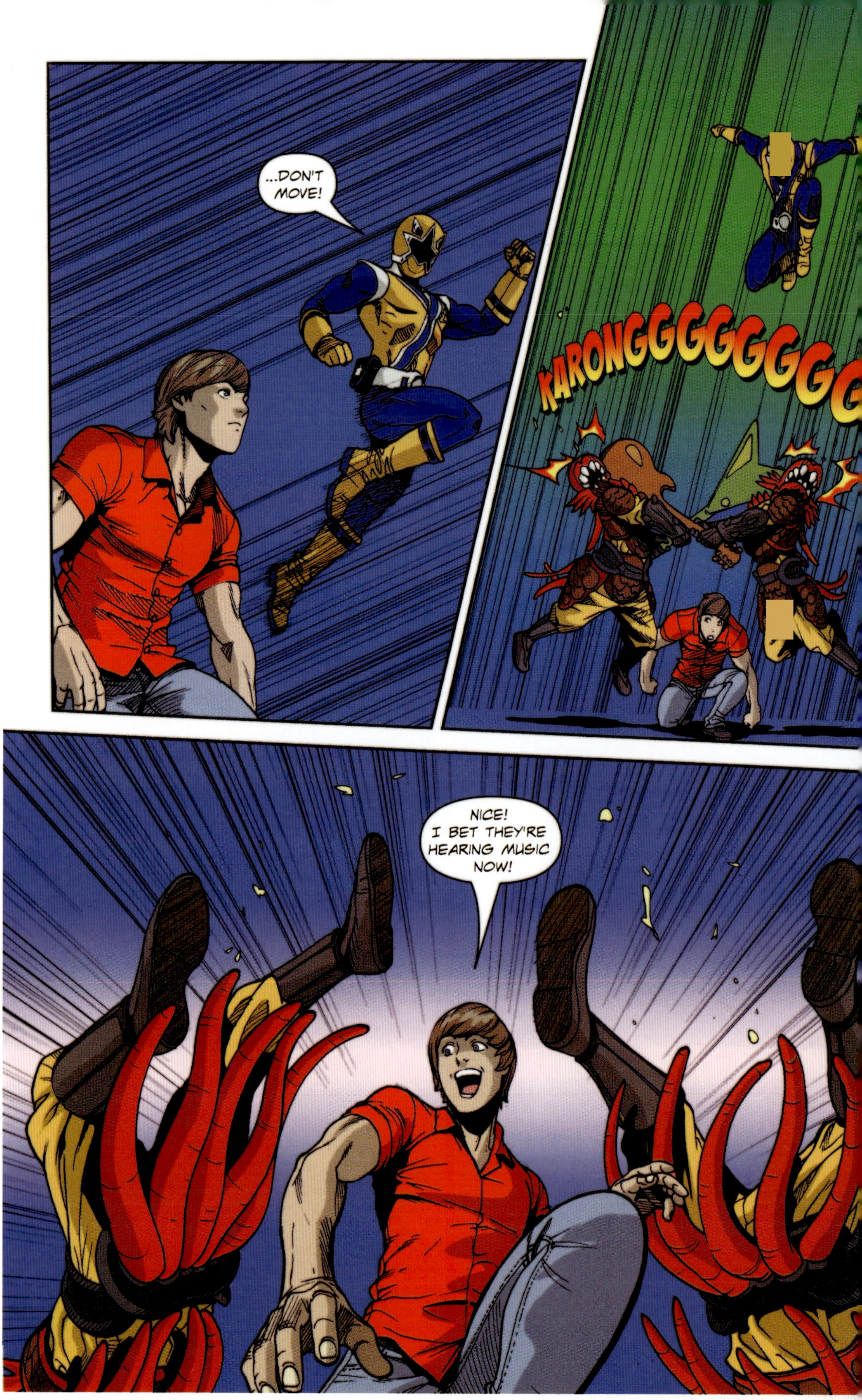
...DON'T MOVE!
KARONGGGGGGGGG
NICE! I BET THEY'RE HEARING MUSIC NOW!

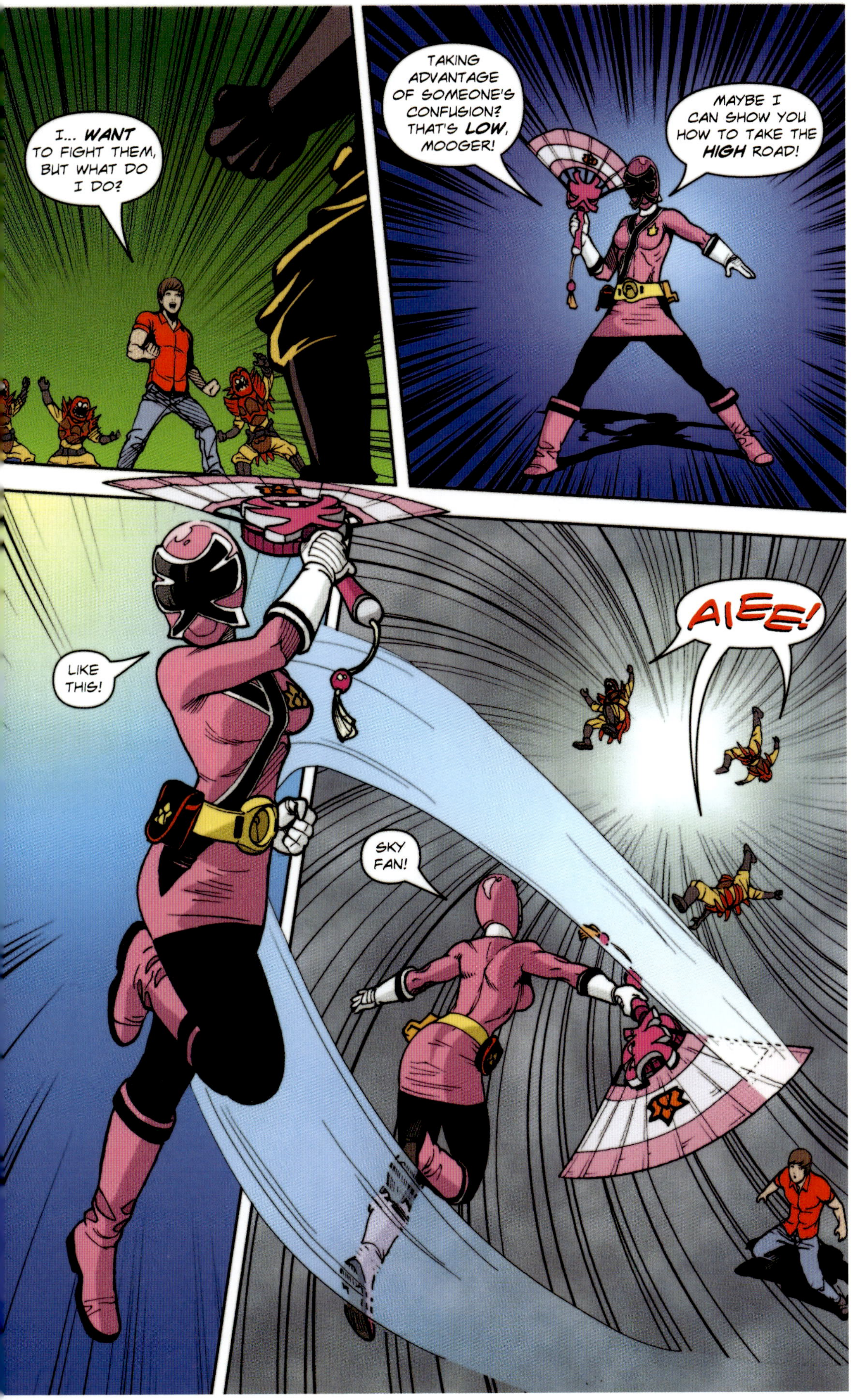
I... WANT TO FIGHT THEM, BUT WHAT DO I DO?
TAKING ADVANTAGE OF SOMEONE'S CONFUSION? THAT'S LOW, MOOGER!
MAYBE I CAN SHOW YOU HOW TO TAKE THE HIGH ROAD!
LIKE THIS!
AIEE!
SKY FAN!

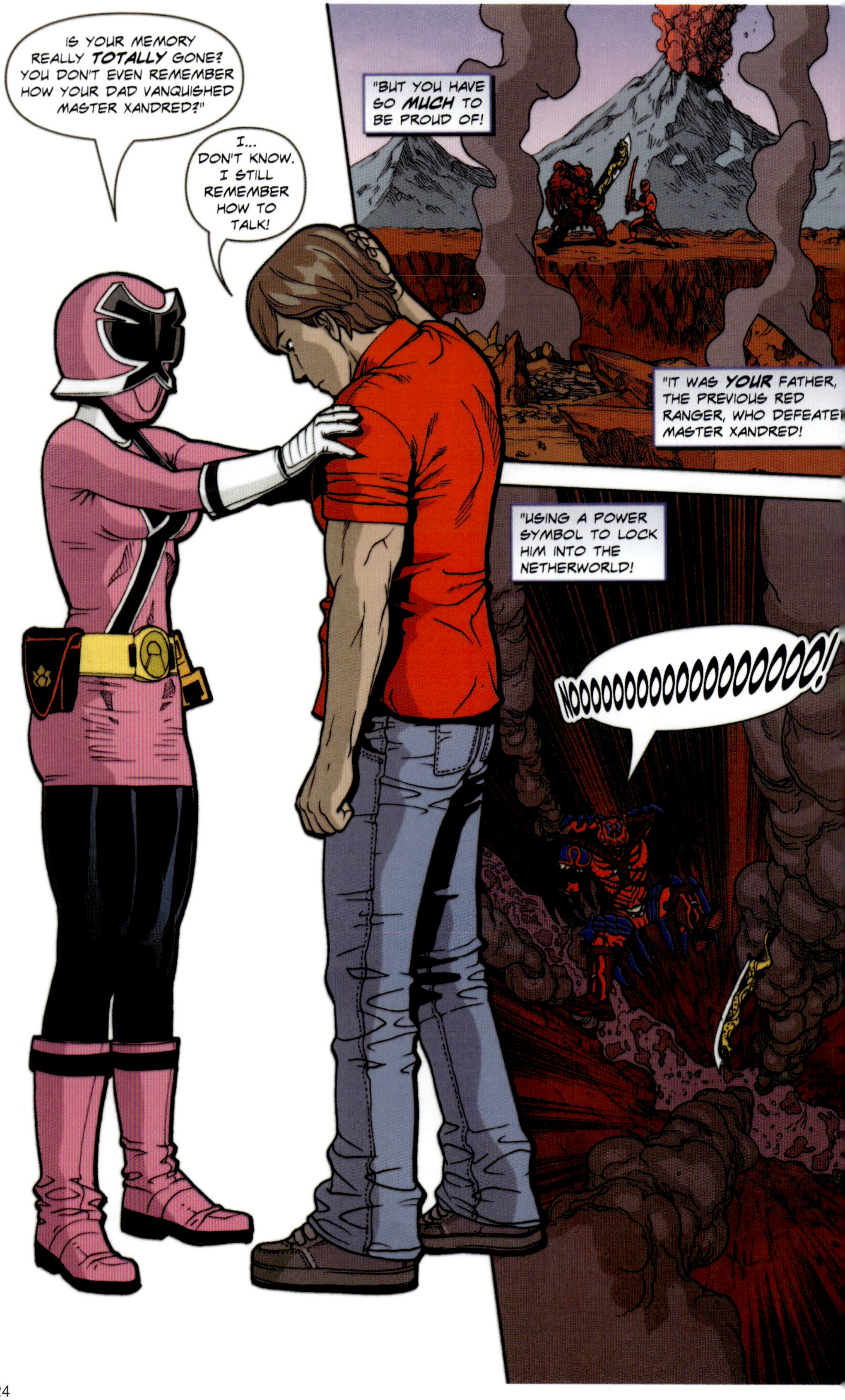

IS YOUR MEMORY REALLY TOTALLY GONE? YOU DON'T EVEN REMEMBER HOW YOUR DAD VANQUISHED MASTER XANDRED?"
I... DON'T KNOW. I STILL REMEMBER HOW TO TALK!
"BUT YOU HAVE SO MUCH TO BE PROUD OF!
"IT WAS YOUR FATHER, THE PREVIOUS RED RANGER, WHO DEFEATE MASTER XANDRED!
"USING A POWER SYMBOL TO LOCK HIM INTO THE NETHERWORLD!
NOOOOOOOOOOOOOOOOOO!

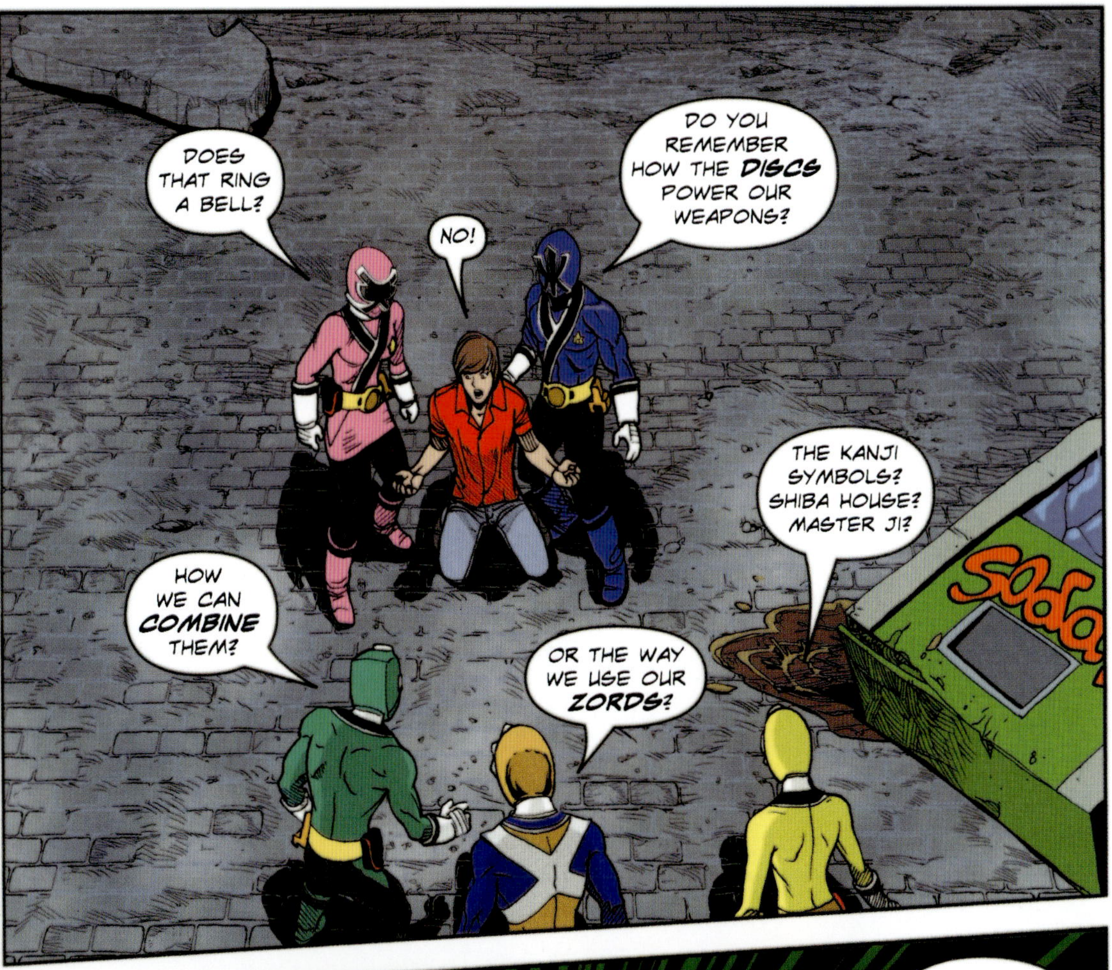
DOES THAT RING A BELL?
NO!
DO YOU REMEMBER HOW THE DISCS POWER OUR WEAPONS?
THE KANJI SYMBOLS? SHIBA HOUSE? MASTER JI?
HOW WE CAN COMBINE THEM?
OR THE WAY WE USE OUR ZORDS?
Soda

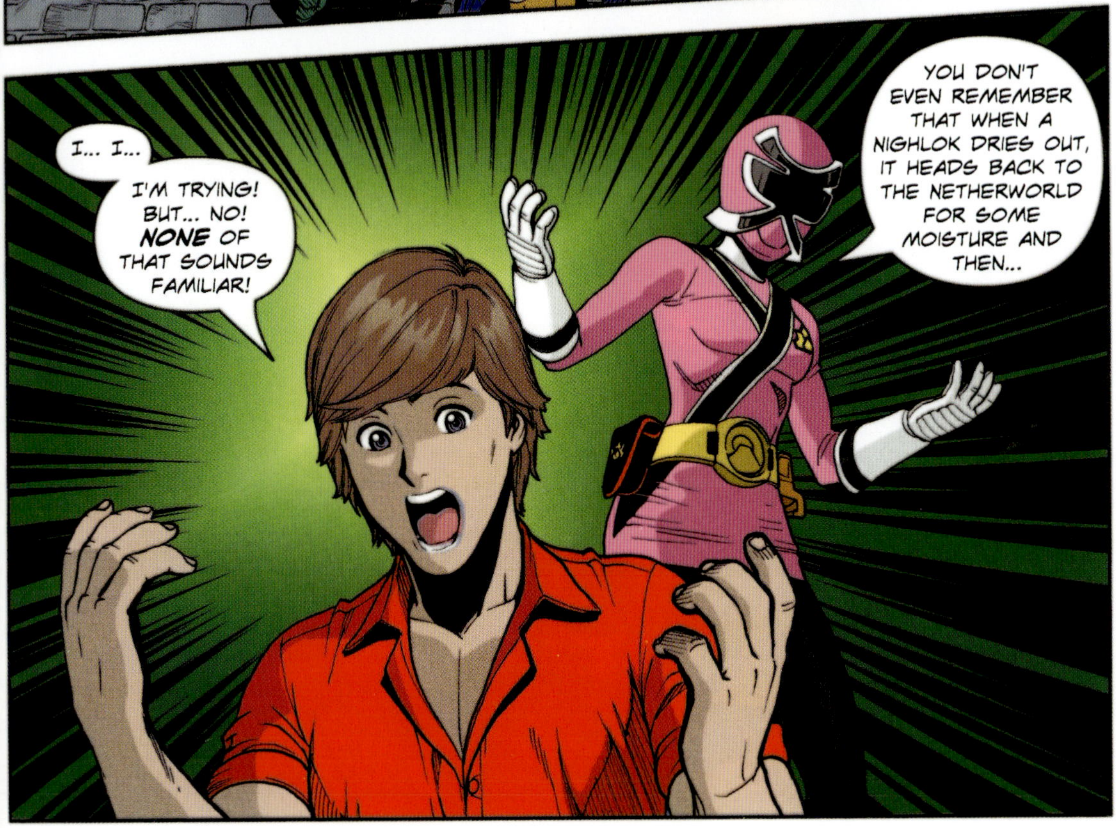
I... I...
I'M TRYING! BUT... NO! NONE OF THAT SOUNDS FAMILIAR!
YOU DON'T EVEN REMEMBER THAT WHEN A NIGHLOK DRIES OUT, IT HEADS BACK TO THE NETHERWORLD FOR SOME MOISTURE AND THEN...

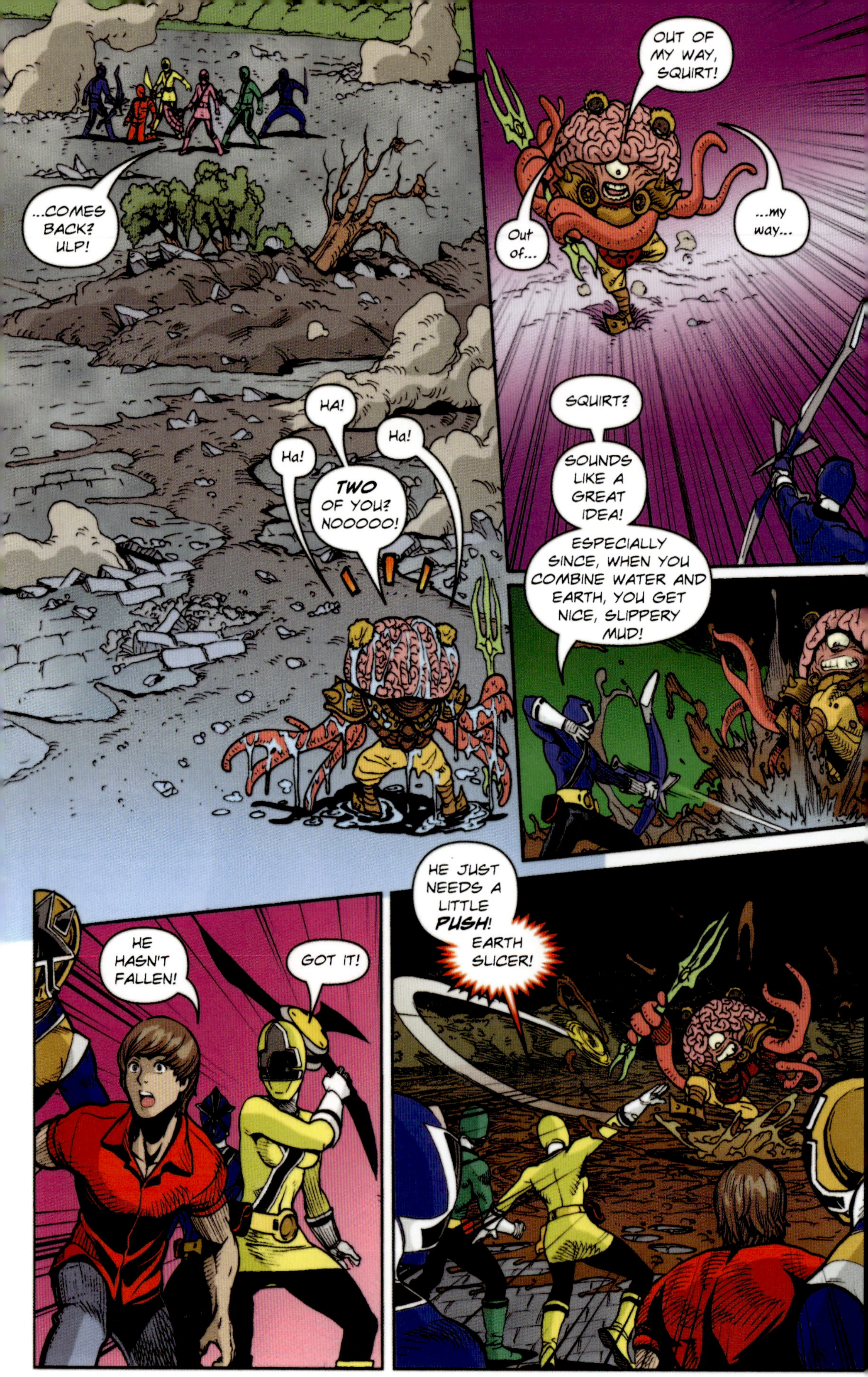
...COMES BACK? ULP!
OUT OF MY WAY, SQUIRT!
Out of...
...my way...
HA!
Ha!
Ha!
TWO OF YOU? NOOOOO!
SQUIRT?
SOUNDS LIKE A GREAT IDEA!
ESPECIALLY SINCE, WHEN YOU COMBINE WATER AND EARTH, YOU GET NICE, SLIPPERY MUD!
HE HASN'T FALLEN!
GOT IT!
HE JUST NEEDS A LITTLE PUSH!
EARTH SLICER!

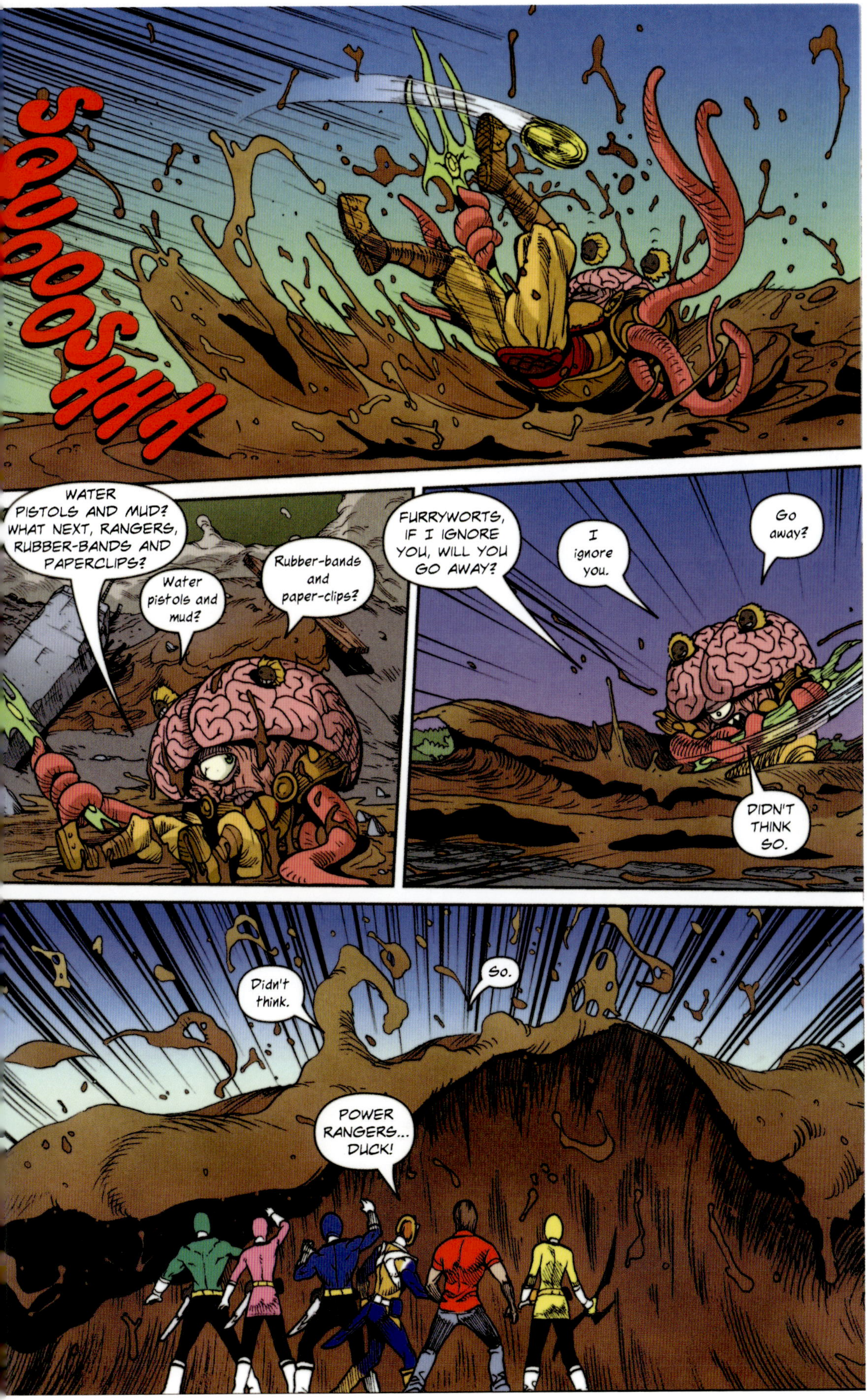
SQUOOOSHHH
WATER PISTOLS AND MUD? WHAT NEXT, RANGERS, RUBBER-BANDS AND PAPERCLIPS?
Water pistols and mud?
Rubber-bands and paper-clips?
FURRYWORTS, IF I IGNORE YOU, WILL YOU GO AWAY?
I ignore you.
Go away?
DIDN'T THINK SO.
Didn't think.
So.
POWER RANGERS... DUCK!

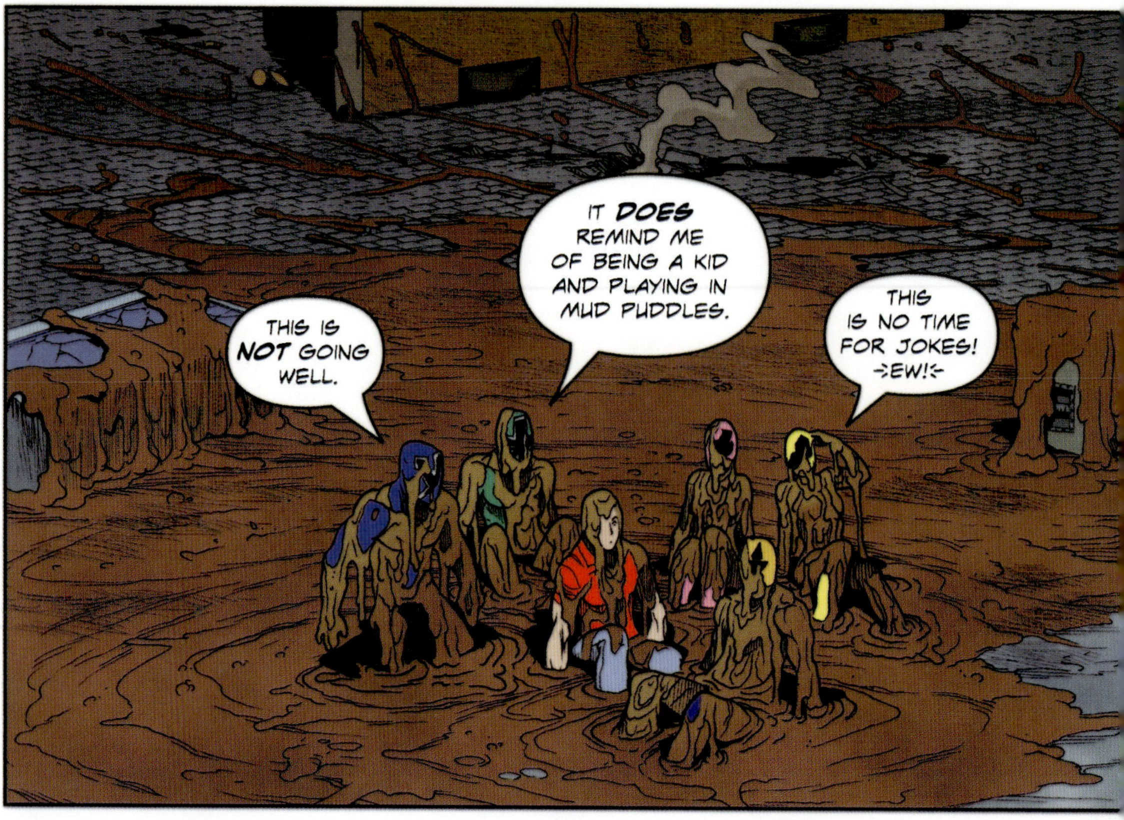
THIS IS NOT GOING WELL.
IT DOES REMIND ME OF BEING A KID AND PLAYING IN MUD PUDDLES.
THIS IS NO TIME FOR JOKES! >EW!<
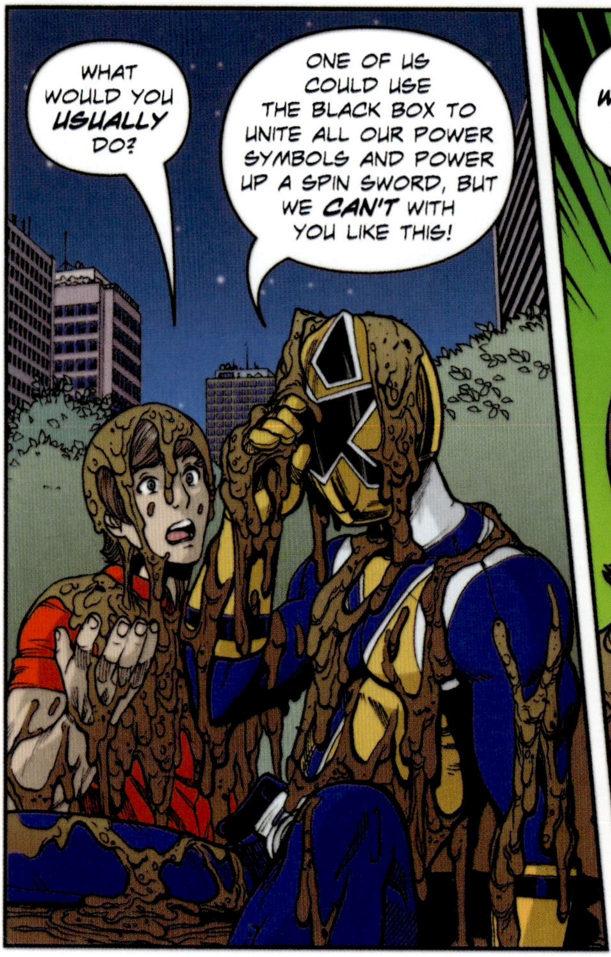
WHAT WOULD YOU USUALLY DO?
ONE OF US COULD USE THE BLACK BOX TO UNITE ALL OUR POWER SYMBOLS AND POWER UP A SPIN SWORD, BUT WE CAN'T WITH YOU LIKE THIS!
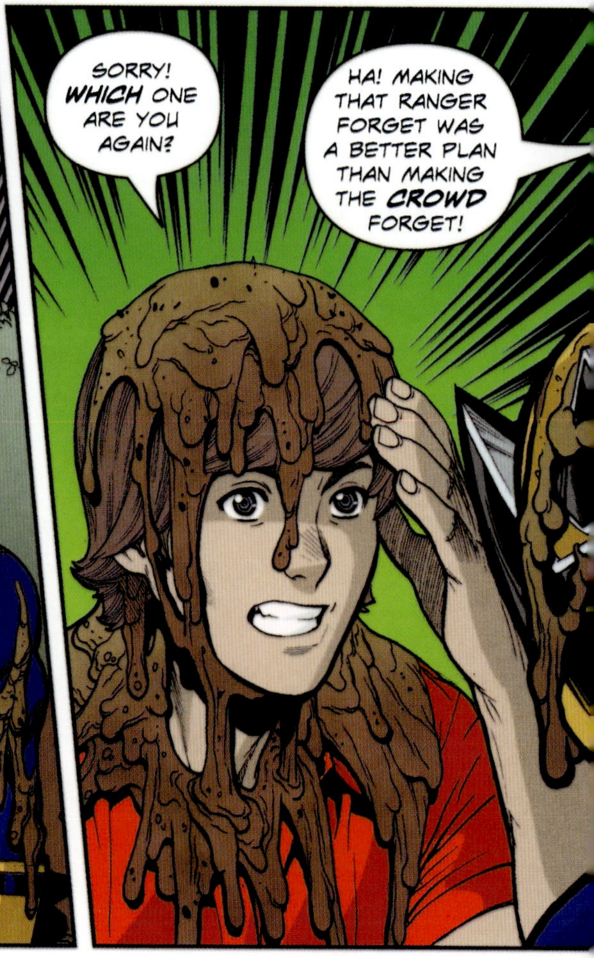
SORRY! WHICH ONE ARE YOU AGAIN?
HA! MAKING THAT RANGER FORGET WAS A BETTER PLAN THAN MAKING THE CROWD FORGET!

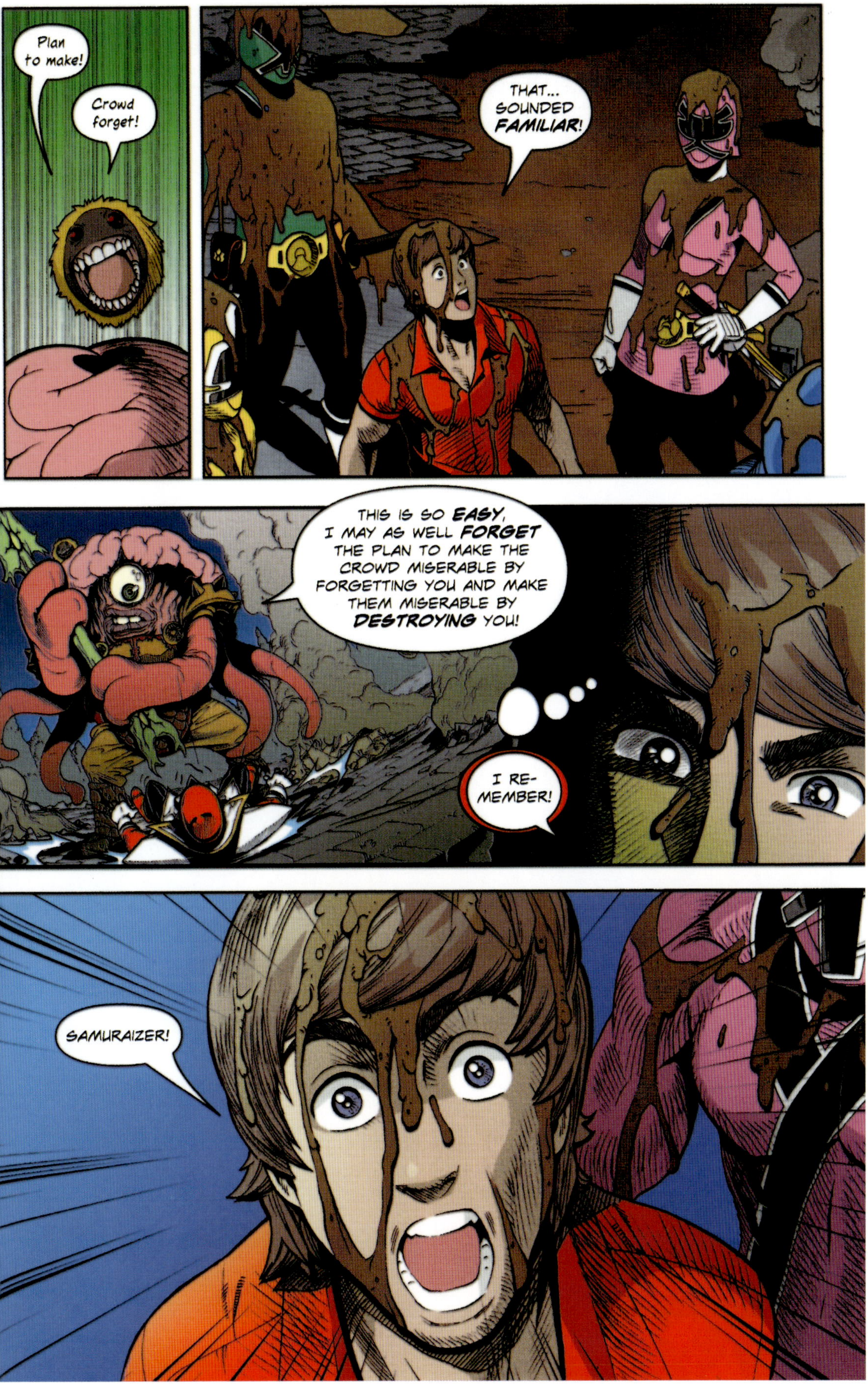
Plan to make!
Crowd forget!
THAT... SOUNDED FAMILIAR!
THIS IS SO EASY, I MAY AS WELL FORGET THE PLAN TO MAKE THE CROWD MISERABLE BY FORGETTING YOU AND MAKE THEM MISERABLE BY DESTROYING YOU!
I RE-MEMBER!
SAMURAIZER!

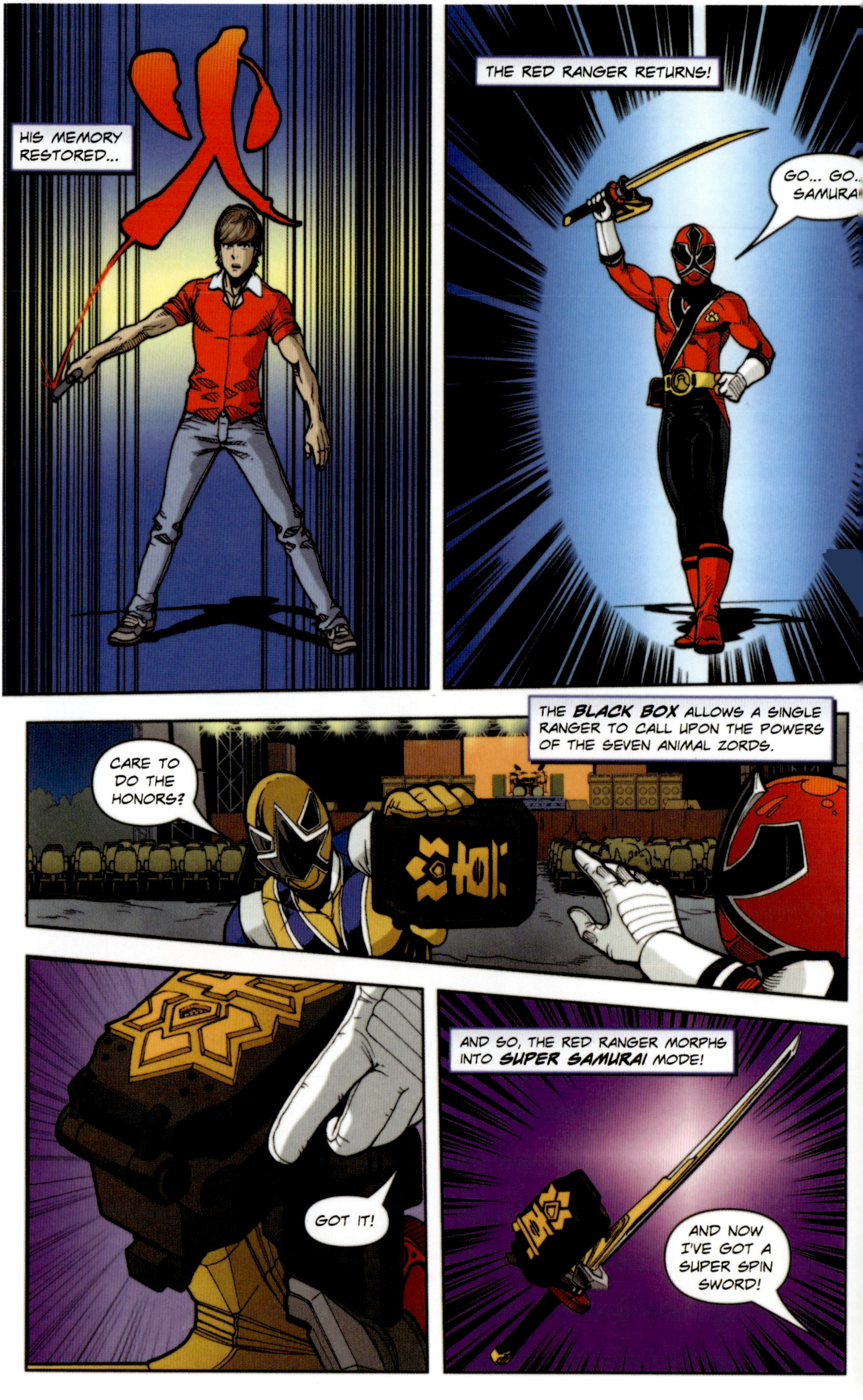
HIS MEMORY RESTORED...
THE RED RANGER RETURNS!
GO... GO... SAMURA
THE BLACK BOX ALLOWS A SINGLE RANGER TO CALL UPON THE POWERS OF THE SEVEN ANIMAL ZORDS.
CARE TO DO THE HONORS?
GOT IT!
AND SO, THE RED RANGER MORPHS INTO SUPER SAMURAI MODE!
AND NOW I'VE GOT A SUPER SPIN SWORD!

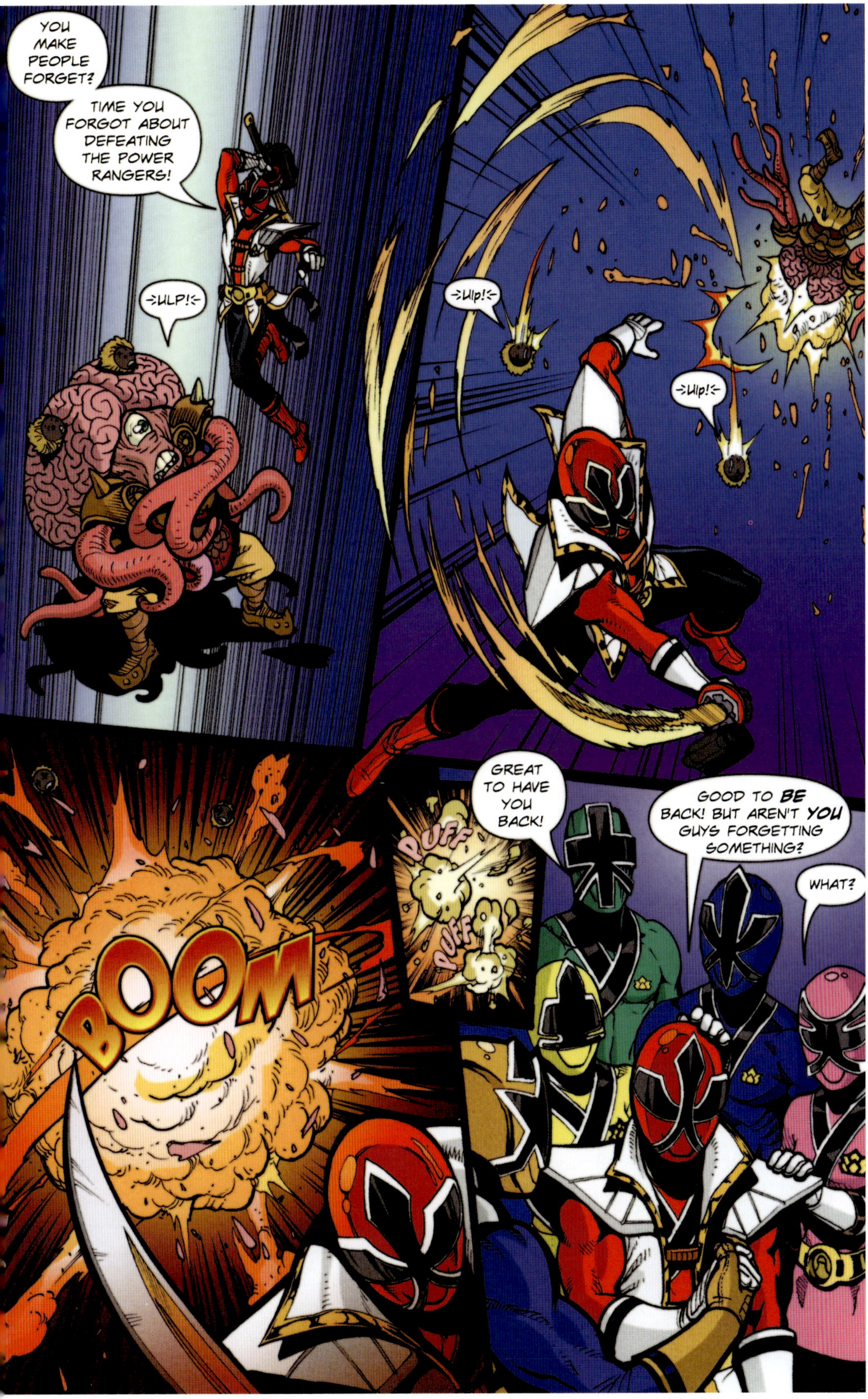
YOU MAKE PEOPLE FORGET?
TIME YOU FORGOT ABOUT DEFEATING THE POWER RANGERS!
ULP!
Ulp!
Ulp!
BOOM
PUFF
PUFF
GREAT TO HAVE YOU BACK!
GOOD TO BE BACK! BUT AREN'T YOU GUYS FORGETTING SOMETHING?
WHAT?

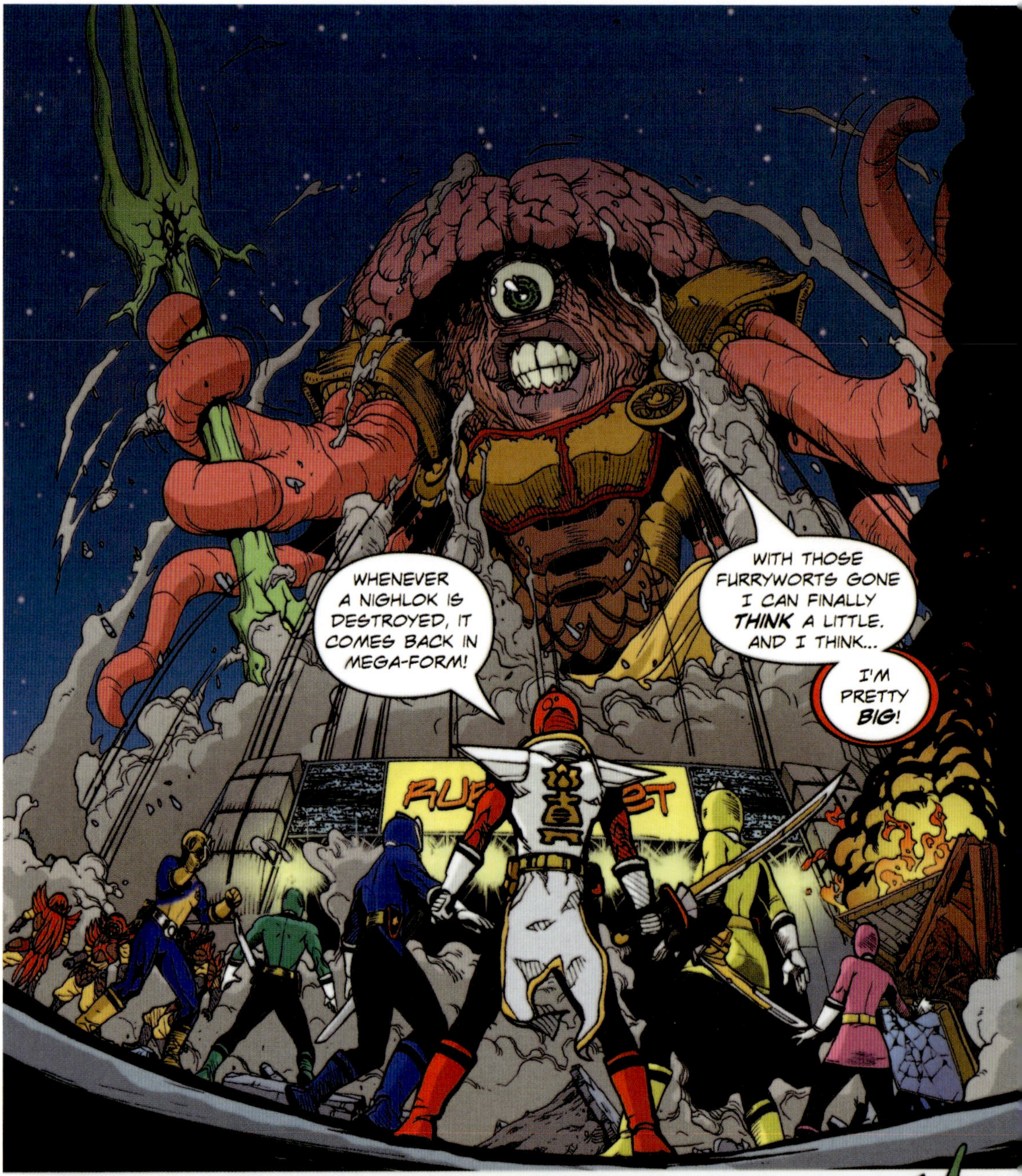
WHENEVER A NIGHLOK IS DESTROYED, IT COMES BACK IN MEGA-FORM!
WITH THOSE FURRYWORTS GONE I CAN FINALLY *THINK* A LITTLE. AND I THINK...
I'M PRETTY *BIG*!
RUBEN JET

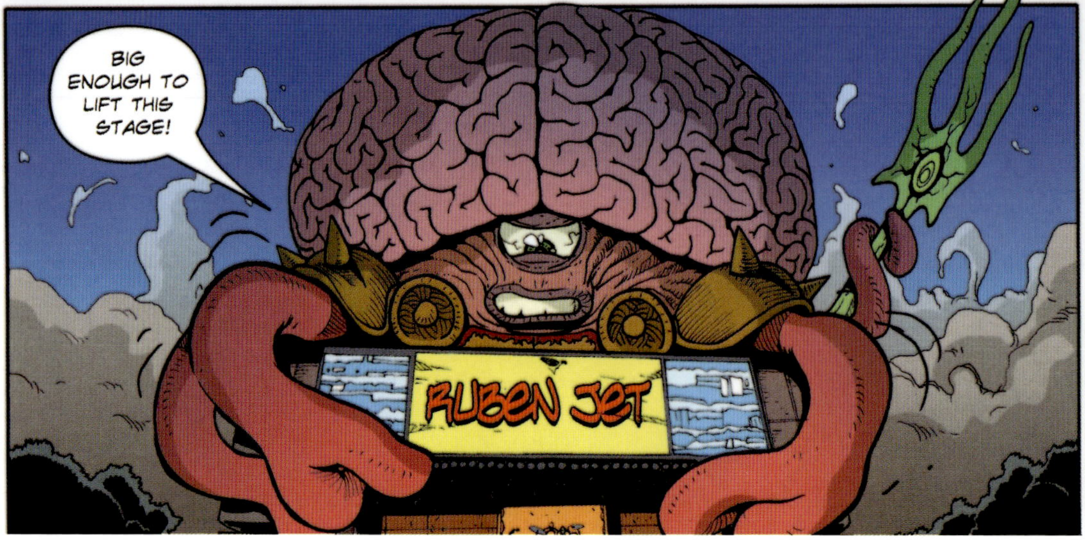
BIG ENOUGH TO LIFT THIS STAGE!
RUBEN JET

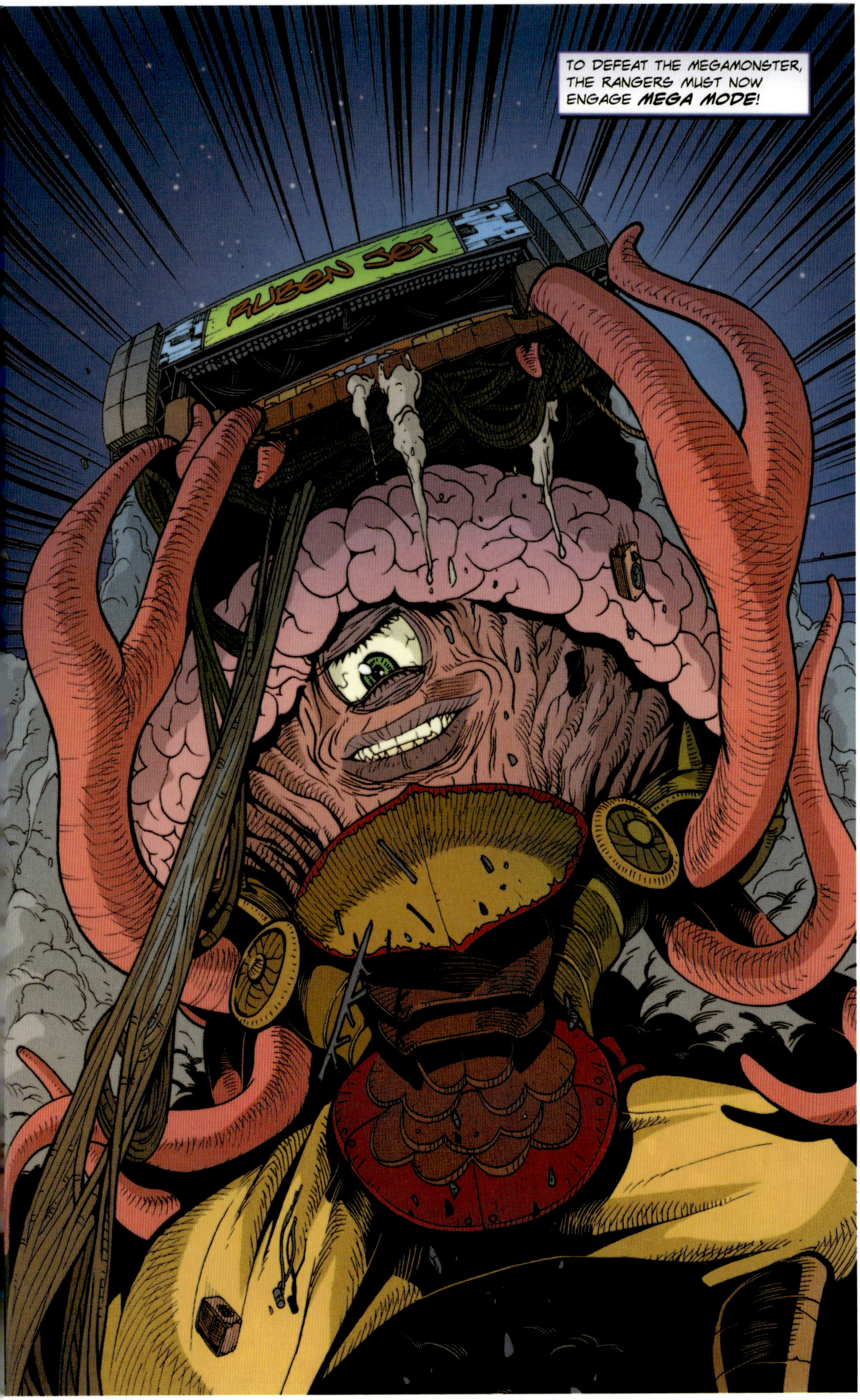
TO DEFEAT THE MEGAMONSTER, THE RANGERS MUST NOW ENGAGE ***MEGA MODE***!
RUBEN JET

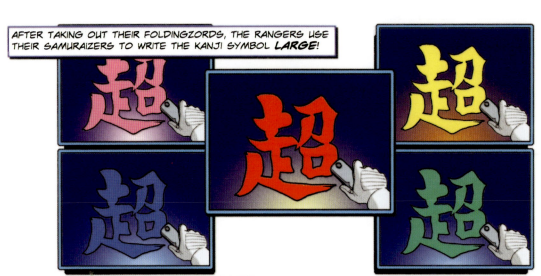

AFTER TAKING OUT THEIR FOLDINGZORDS, THE RANGERS USE THEIR SAMURAIZERS TO WRITE THE KANJI SYMBOL *LARGE!*

ALL SIX RANGERS MORPH INTO MEGA MODE...

AND ENTER THEIR MEGAZORD COCKPIT

ONCE INSIDE, JAYDEN ALSO WRITES THE KANJI SYMBOL *COMBINATION.*

ZORDS *COMBINE!*

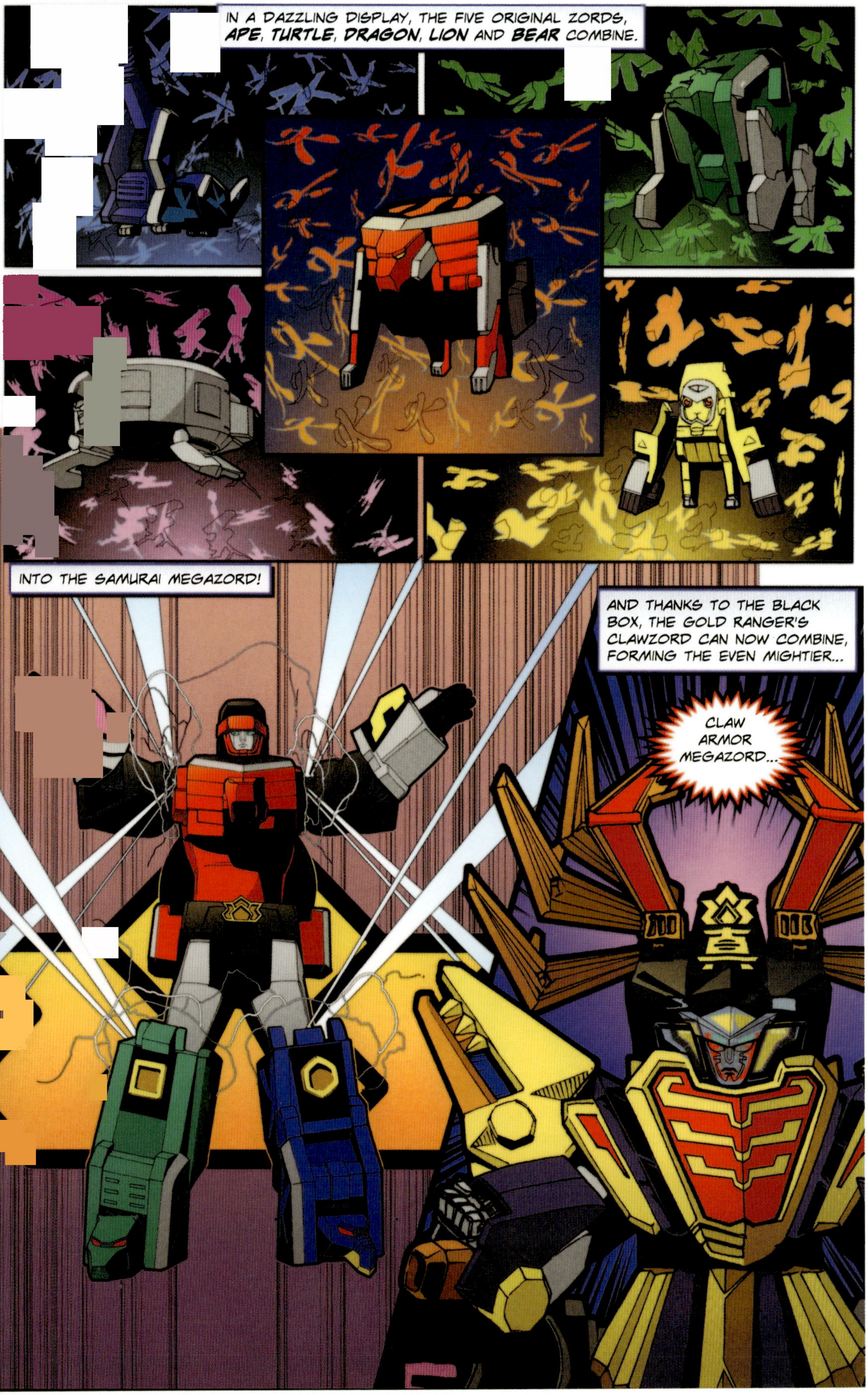
IN A DAZZLING DISPLAY, THE FIVE ORIGINAL ZORDS, **APE**, **TURTLE**, **DRAGON**, **LION** AND **BEAR** COMBINE.
INTO THE SAMURAI MEGAZORD!
AND THANKS TO THE BLACK BOX, THE GOLD RANGER'S CLAWZORD CAN NOW COMBINE, FORMING THE EVEN MIGHTIER...
CLAW ARMOR MEGAZORD...

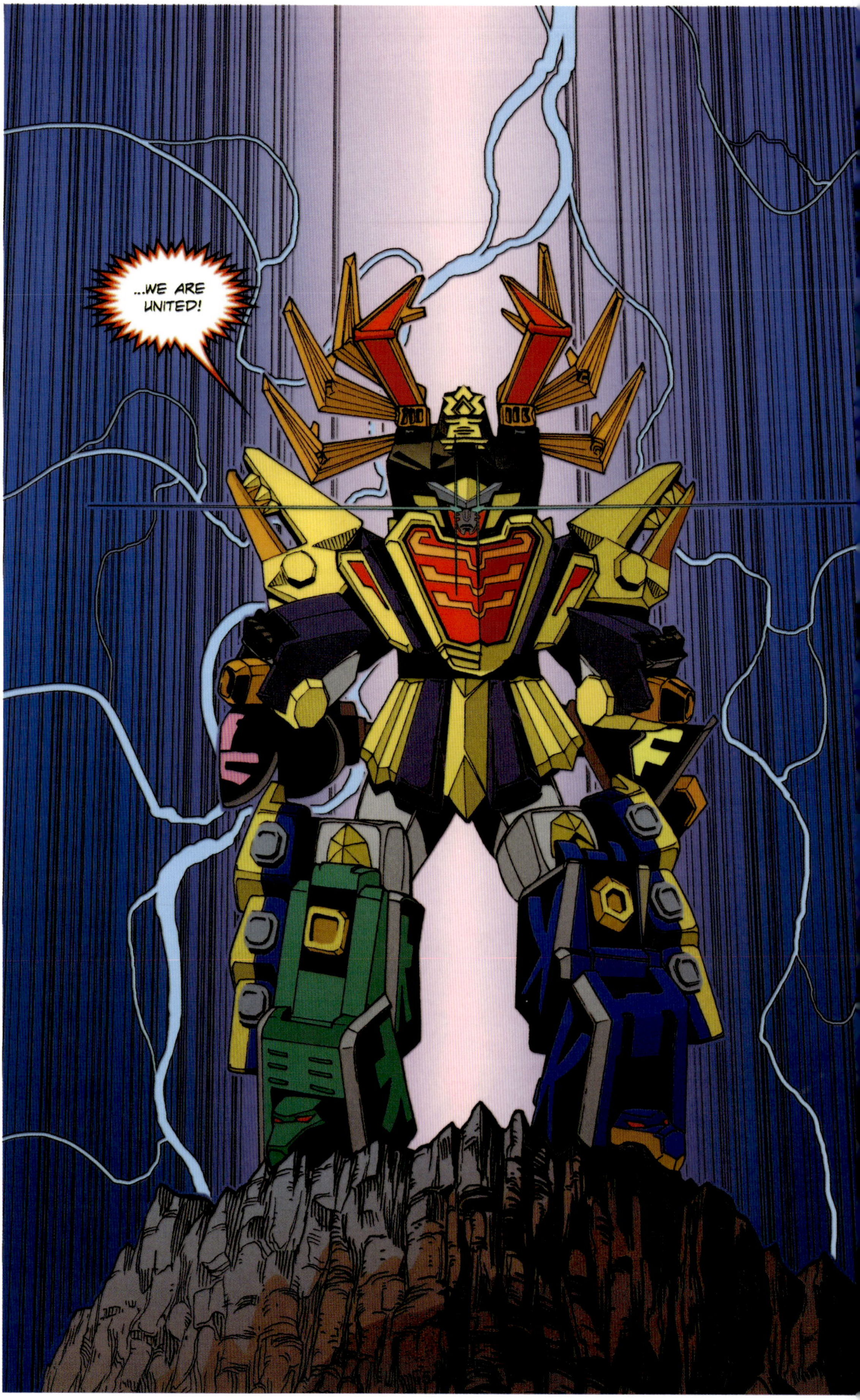
...WE ARE UNITED!

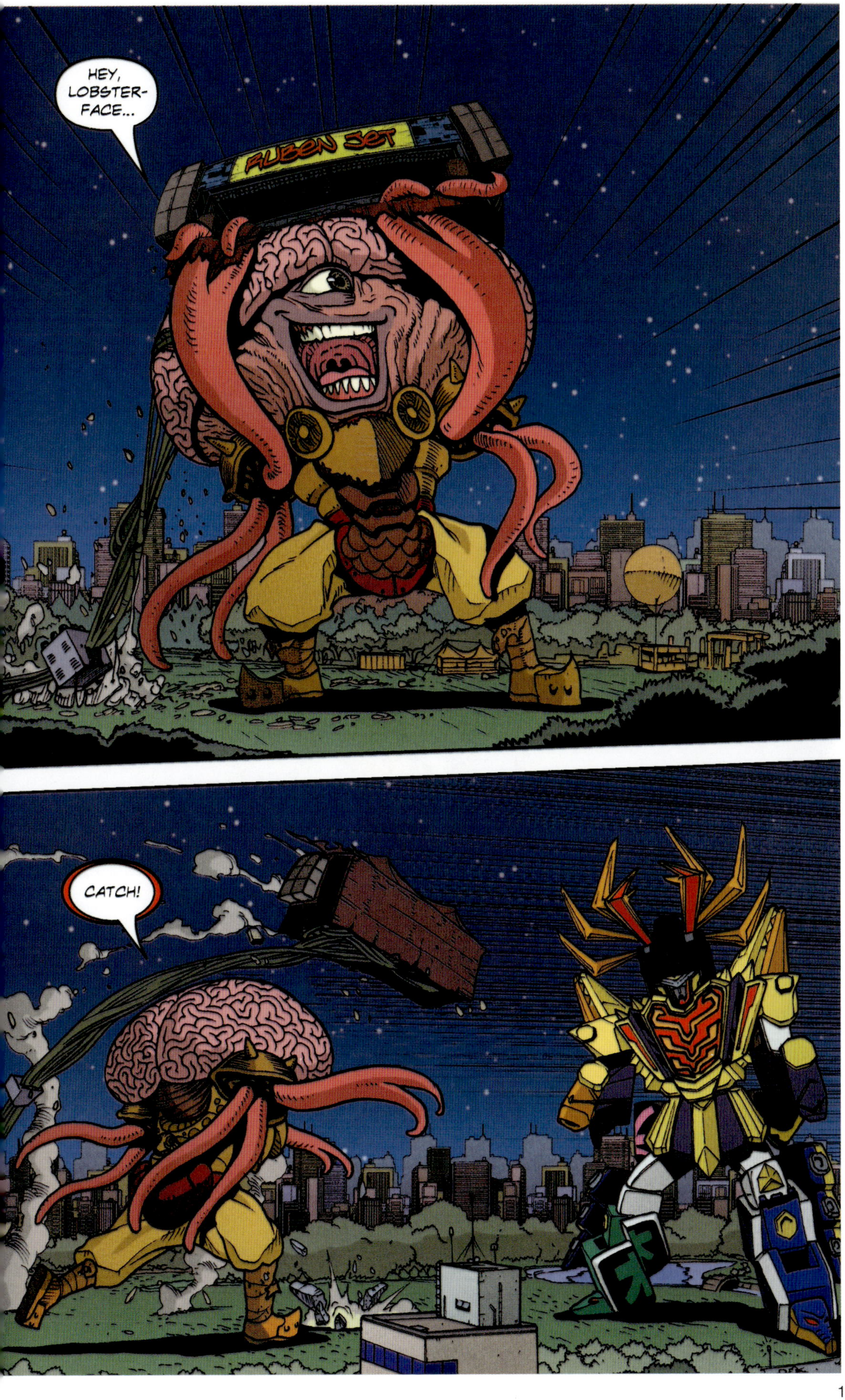
HEY, LOBSTER-FACE...
RUBEN JET
CATCH!

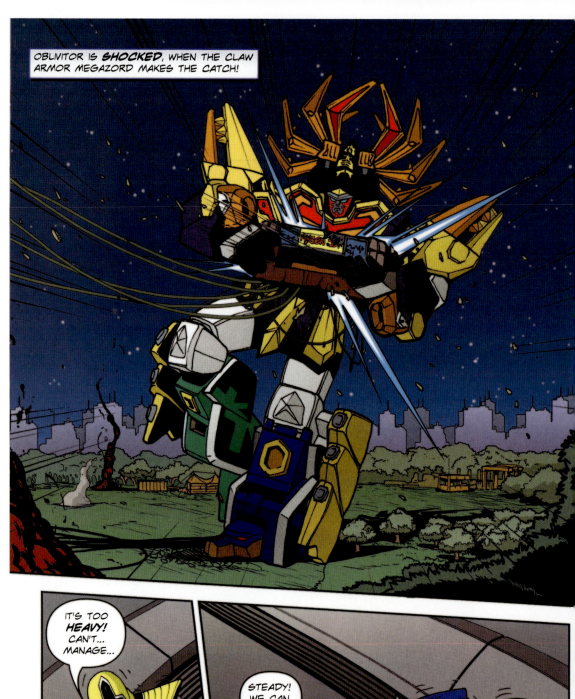

OBLIVITOR IS **SHOCKED**, WHEN THE CLAW ARMOR MEGAZORD MAKES THE CATCH!

IT'S TOO **HEAVY!** CAN'T... MANAGE...

STEADY! WE CAN DO IT!

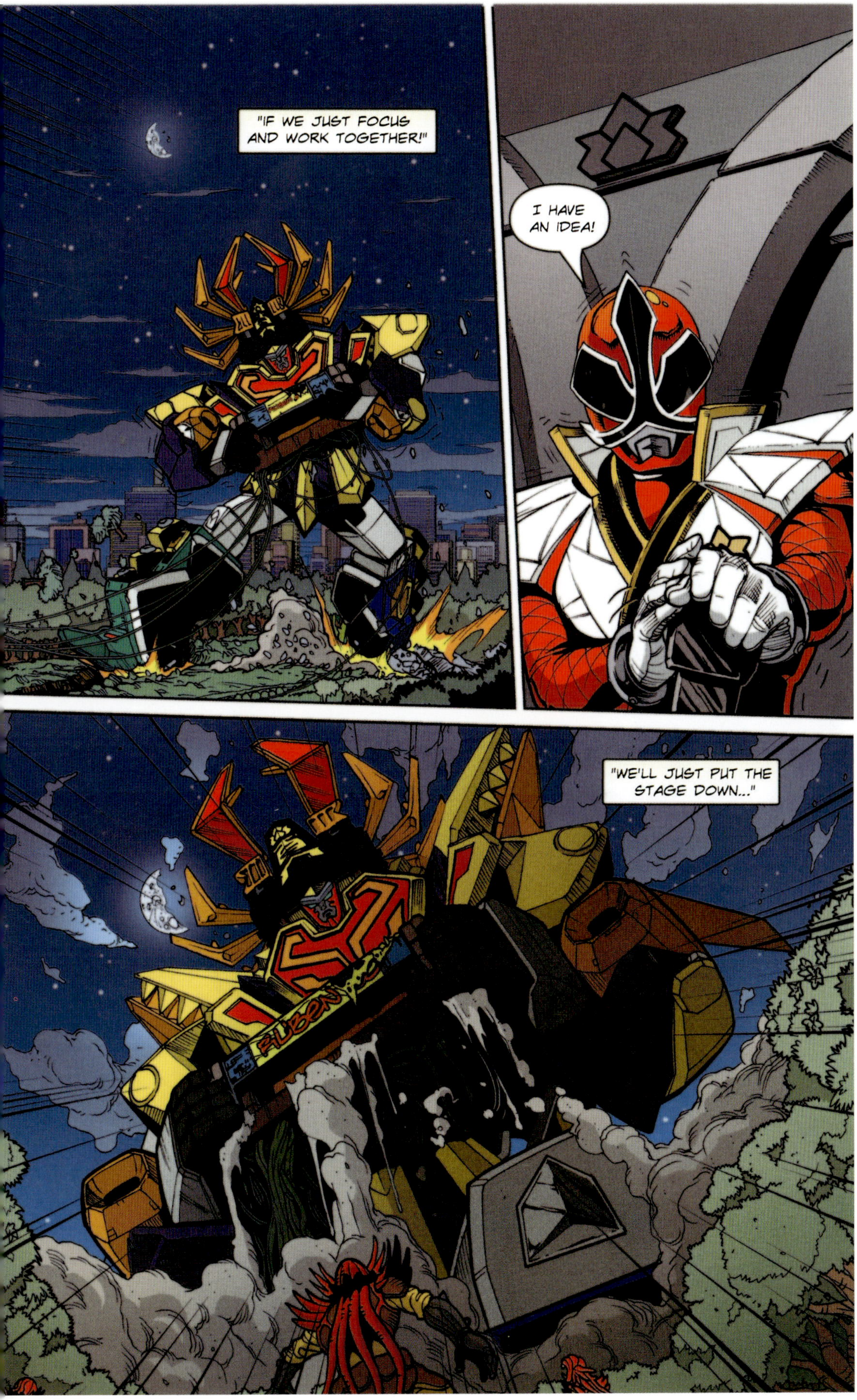
"IF WE JUST FOCUS AND WORK TOGETHER!"
I HAVE AN IDEA!
"WE'LL JUST PUT THE STAGE DOWN..."

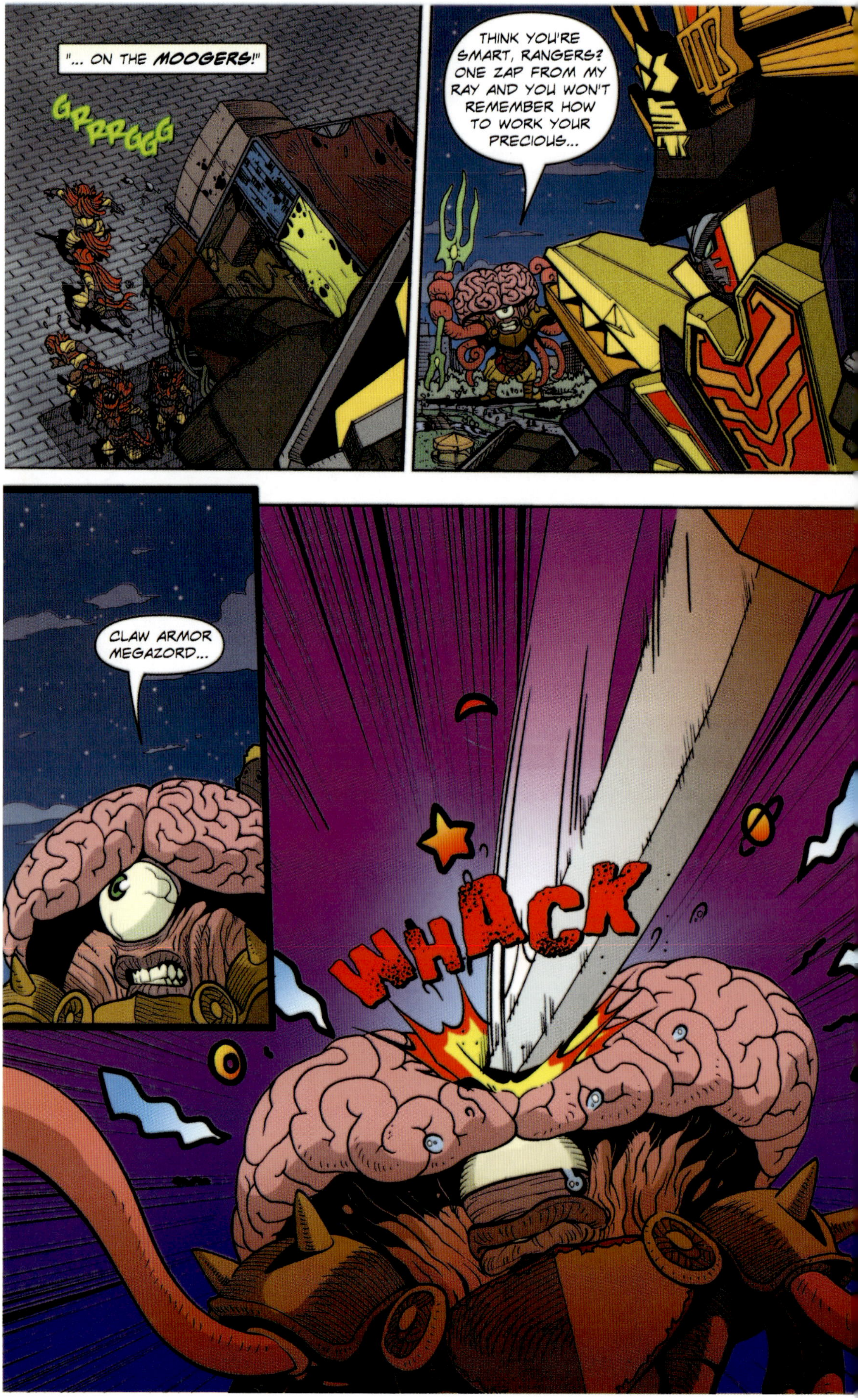
"... ON THE MOOGERS!"
GRRRGGG
THINK YOU'RE SMART, RANGERS? ONE ZAP FROM MY RAY AND YOU WON'T REMEMBER HOW TO WORK YOUR PRECIOUS...
CLAW ARMOR MEGAZORD...
WHACK

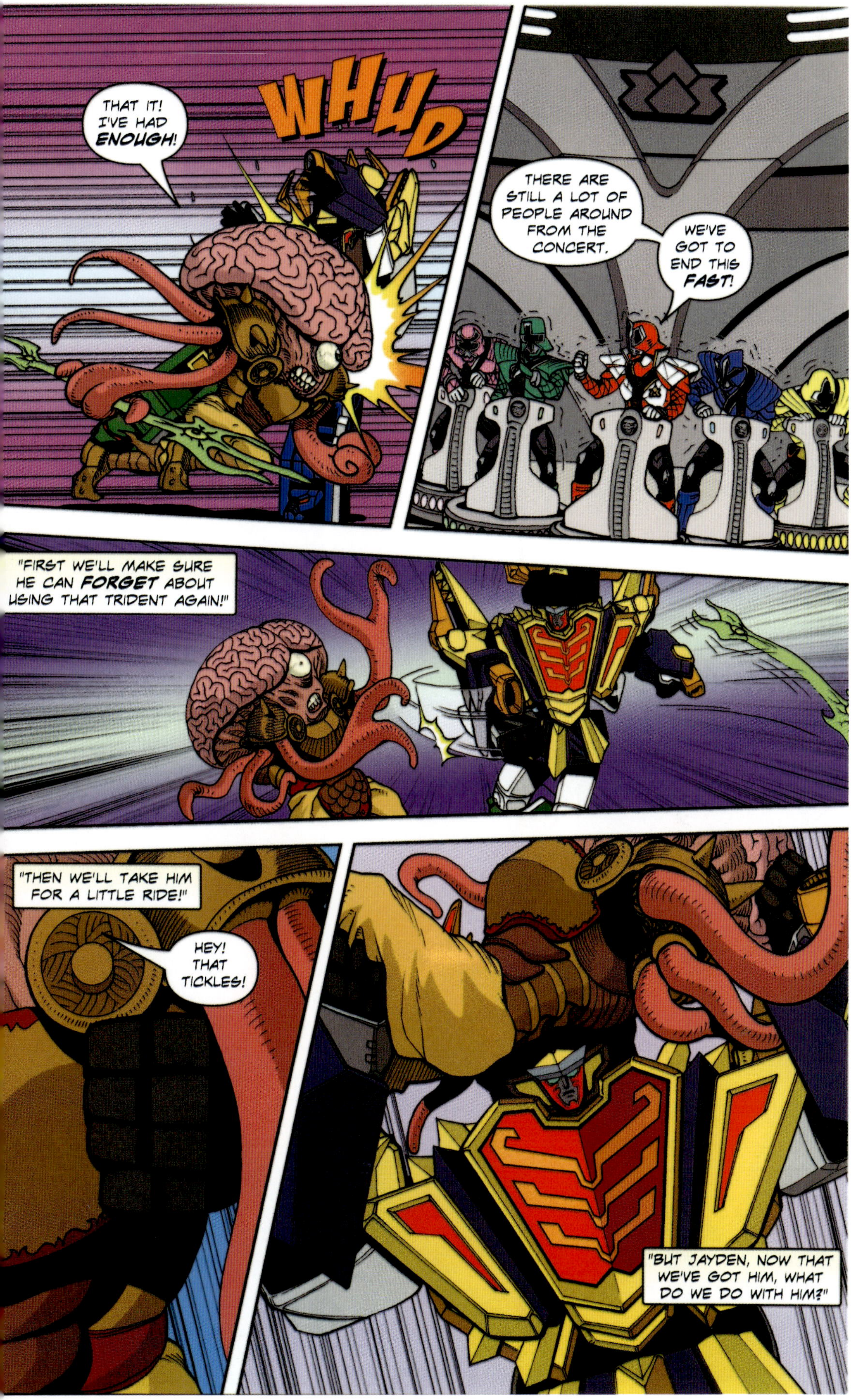
THAT IT! I'VE HAD ENOUGH!
WHUD
THERE ARE STILL A LOT OF PEOPLE AROUND FROM THE CONCERT.
WE'VE GOT TO END THIS FAST!
"FIRST WE'LL MAKE SURE HE CAN FORGET ABOUT USING THAT TRIDENT AGAIN!"
"THEN WE'LL TAKE HIM FOR A LITTLE RIDE!"
HEY! THAT TICKLES!
"BUT JAYDEN, NOW THAT WE'VE GOT HIM, WHAT DO WE DO WITH HIM?"

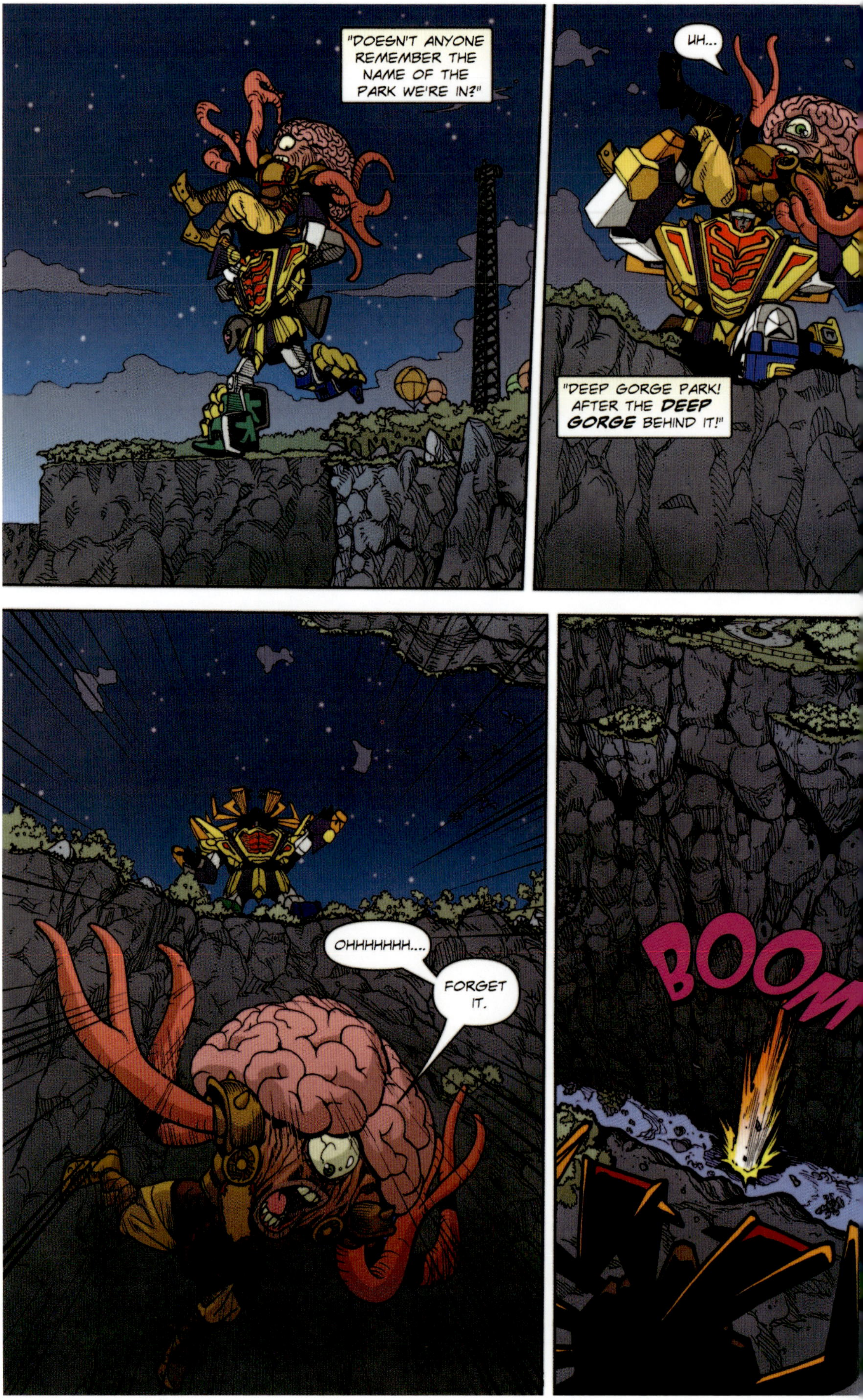
"DOESN'T ANYONE REMEMBER THE NAME OF THE PARK WE'RE IN?"
UH...
"DEEP GORGE PARK! AFTER THE DEEP GORGE BEHIND IT!"
OHHHHHHH....
FORGET IT.
BOOM

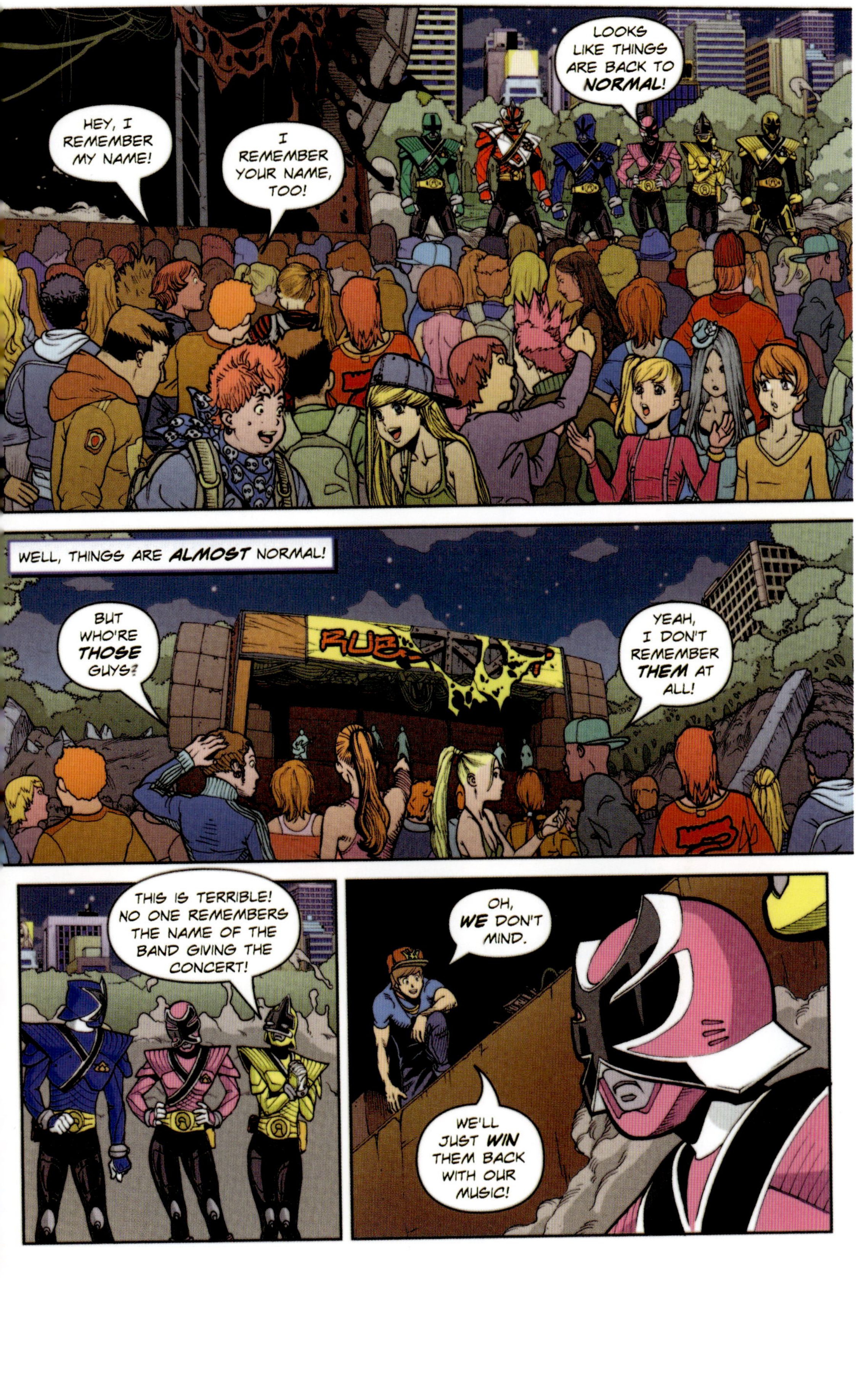

LOOKS LIKE THINGS ARE BACK TO NORMAL!
HEY, I REMEMBER MY NAME!
I REMEMBER YOUR NAME, TOO!
WELL, THINGS ARE ALMOST NORMAL!
BUT WHO'RE THOSE GUYS?
YEAH, I DON'T REMEMBER THEM AT ALL!
THIS IS TERRIBLE! NO ONE REMEMBERS THE NAME OF THE BAND GIVING THE CONCERT!
OH, WE DON'T MIND.
WE'LL JUST WIN THEM BACK WITH OUR MUSIC!

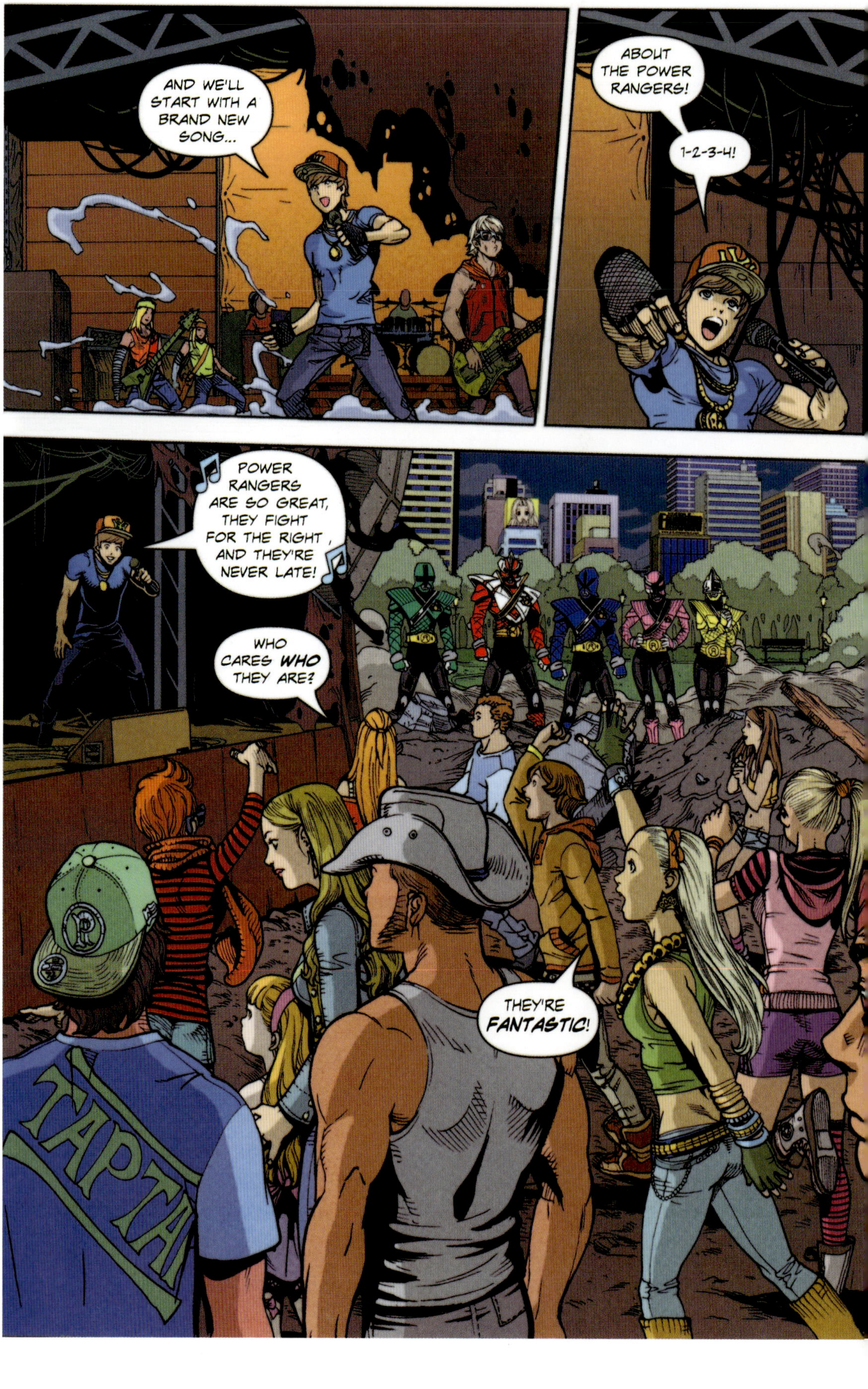
AND WE'LL START WITH A BRAND NEW SONG...
ABOUT THE POWER RANGERS!
1-2-3-4!
POWER RANGERS ARE SO GREAT, THEY FIGHT FOR THE RIGHT, AND THEY'RE NEVER LATE!
WHO CARES WHO THEY ARE?
THEY'RE FANTASTIC!
TAPTAI

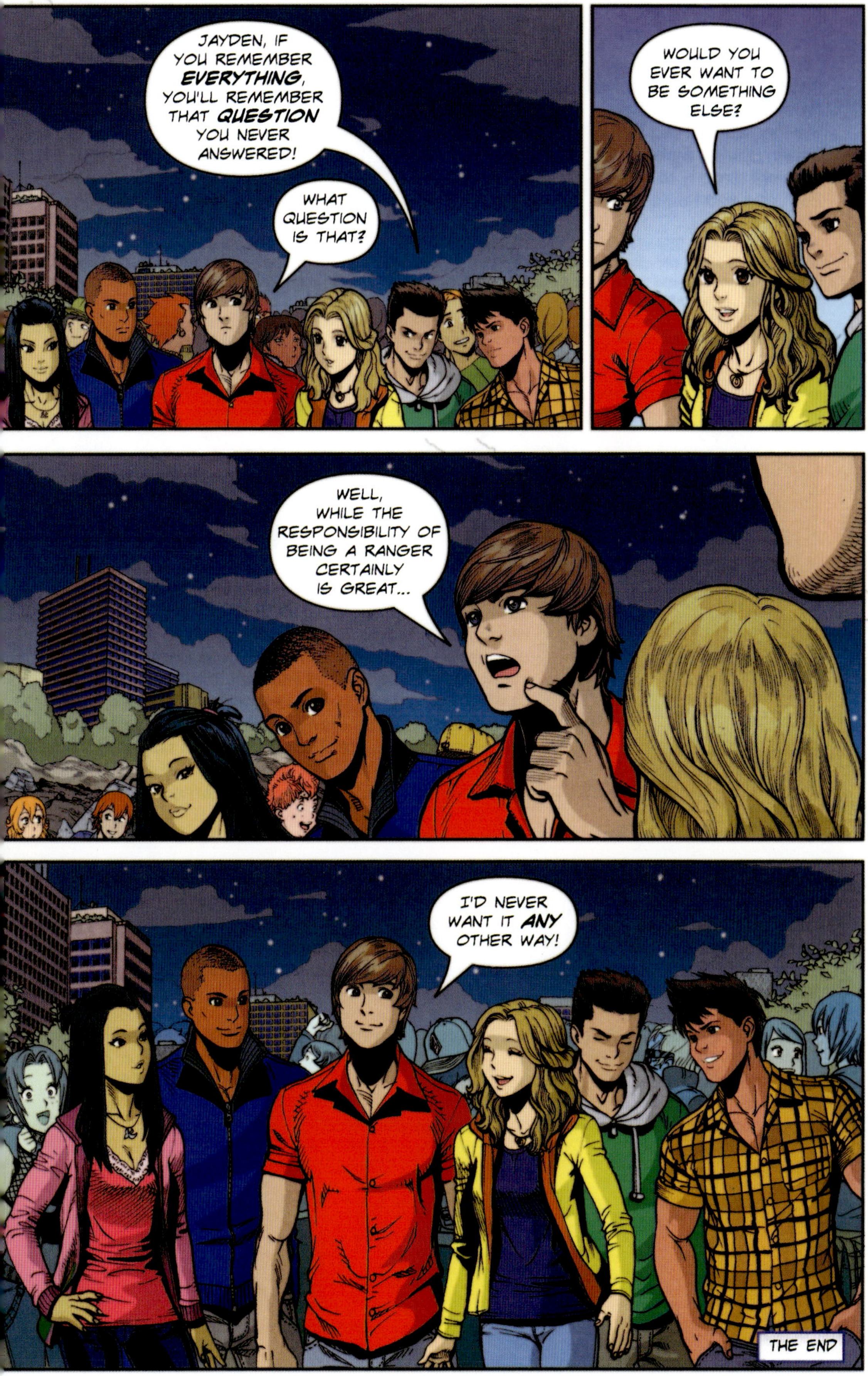
JAYDEN, IF YOU REMEMBER **EVERYTHING**, YOU'LL REMEMBER THAT **QUESTION** YOU NEVER ANSWERED!
WHAT QUESTION IS THAT?
WOULD YOU EVER WANT TO BE SOMETHING ELSE?
WELL, WHILE THE RESPONSIBILITY OF BEING A RANGER CERTAINLY IS GREAT...
I'D NEVER WANT IT **ANY** OTHER WAY!
THE END

2 "TERRIBLE TOYS"

Stefan Petrucha • Paulo Henrique

SABAN'S POWER RANGERS SUPER SAMURAI™

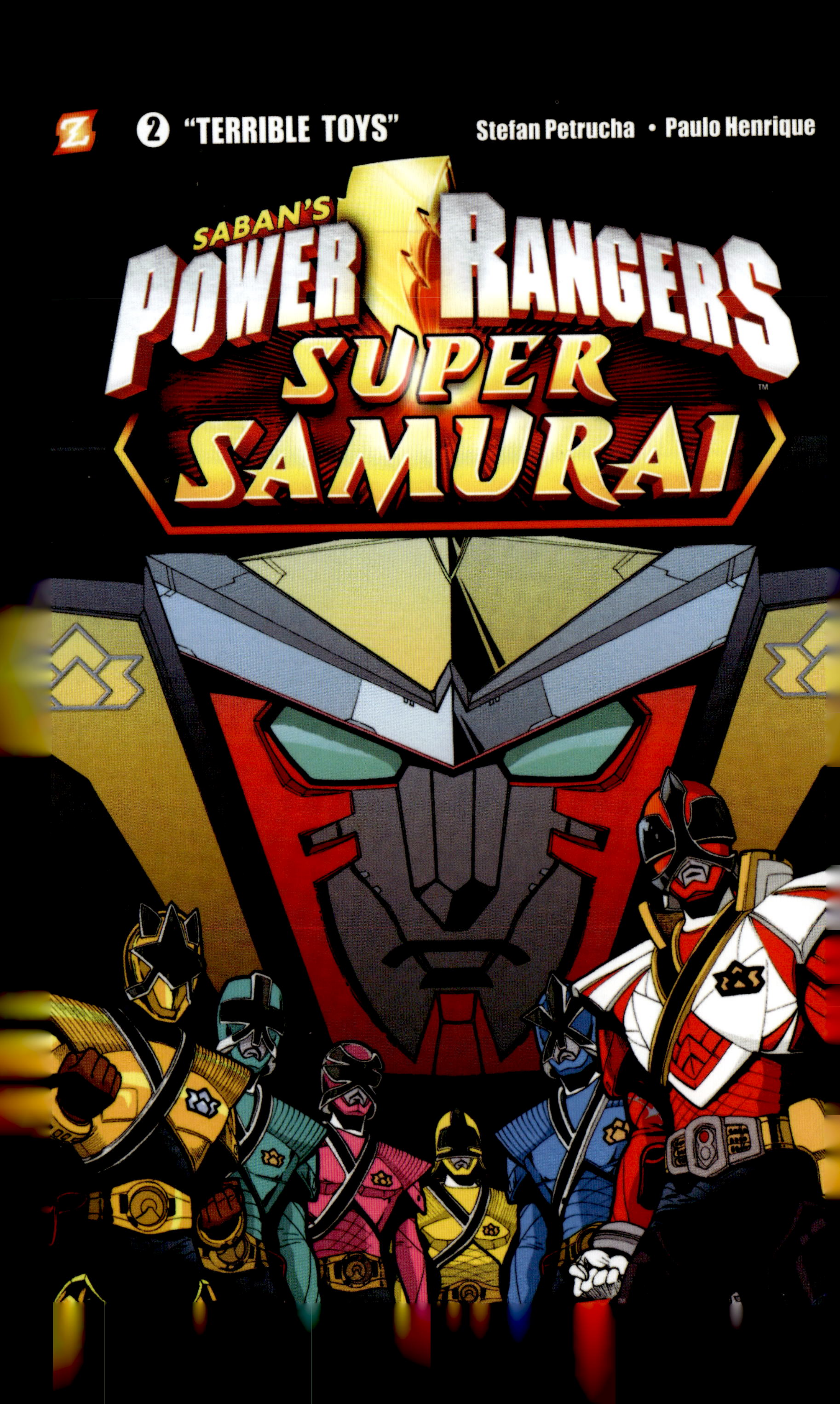

ARE YOU SURE ABOUT THIS, BILL?
DON'T WORRY, HE'LL LOVE IT!
THESE THINGS ARE SELLING LIKE HOT-CAKES ALL OVER TOWN! AND I CAN SEE WHY!
HEY, IT EVEN MOVES! LOOK AT THAT SUCKER GO!
SEE? HE LIKES IT!

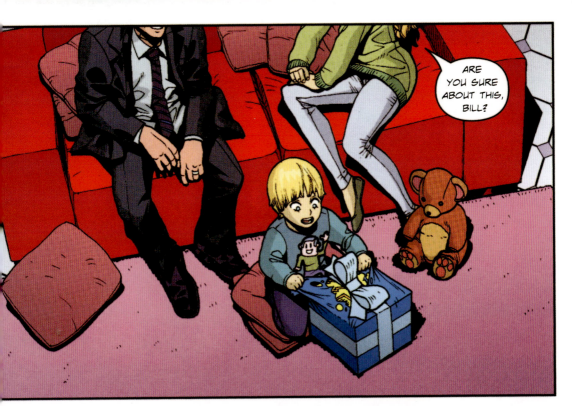

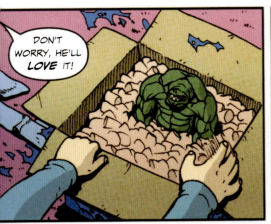

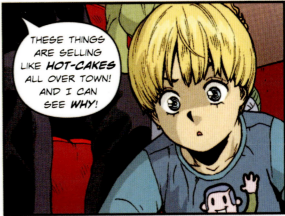

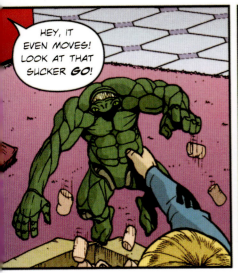

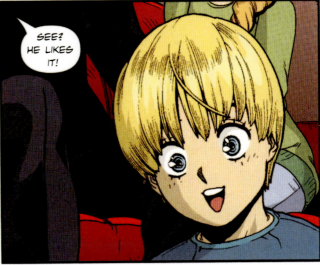

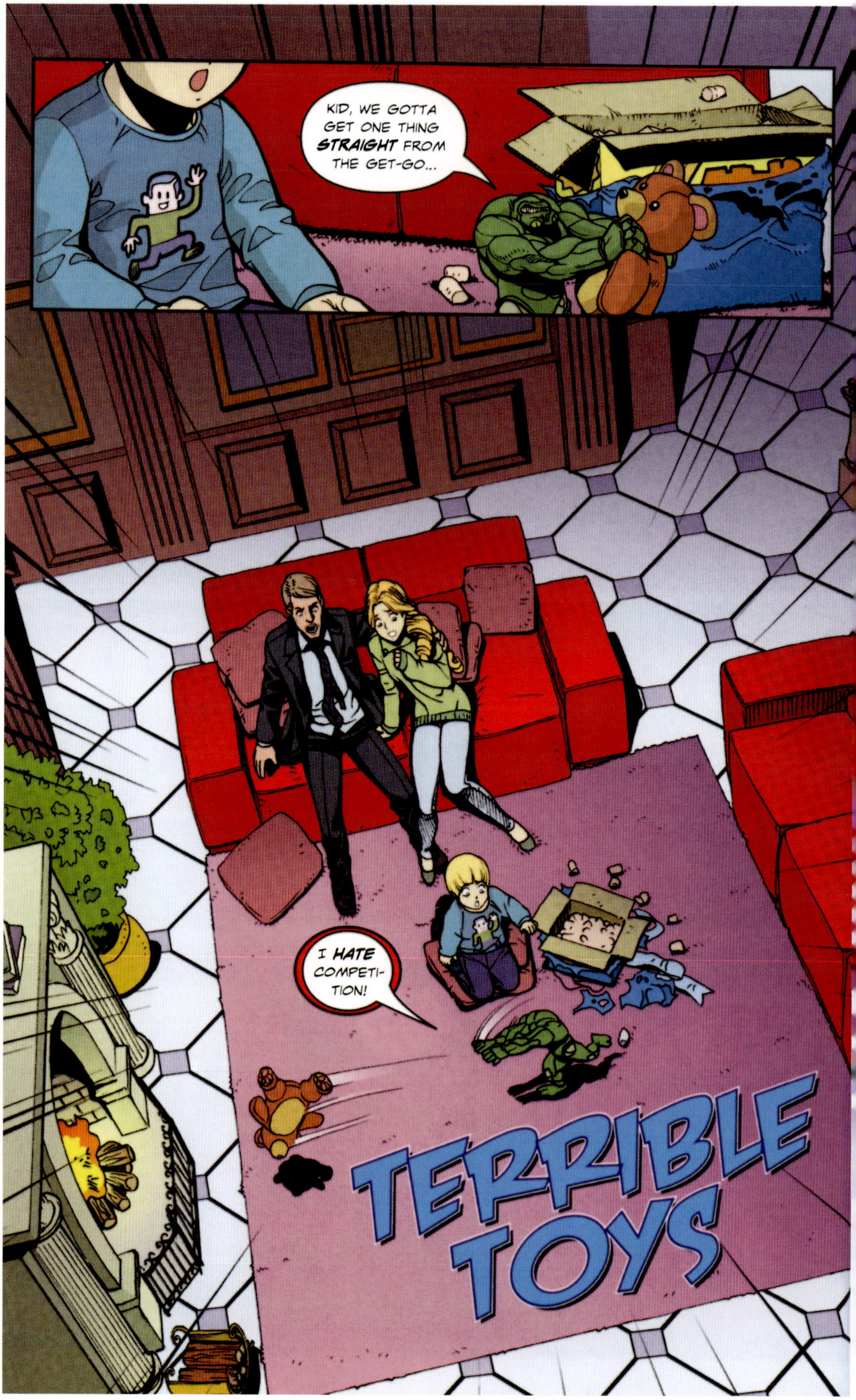
KID, WE GOTTA GET ONE THING STRAIGHT FROM THE GET-GO...
I HATE COMPETITION!
TERRIBLE TOYS

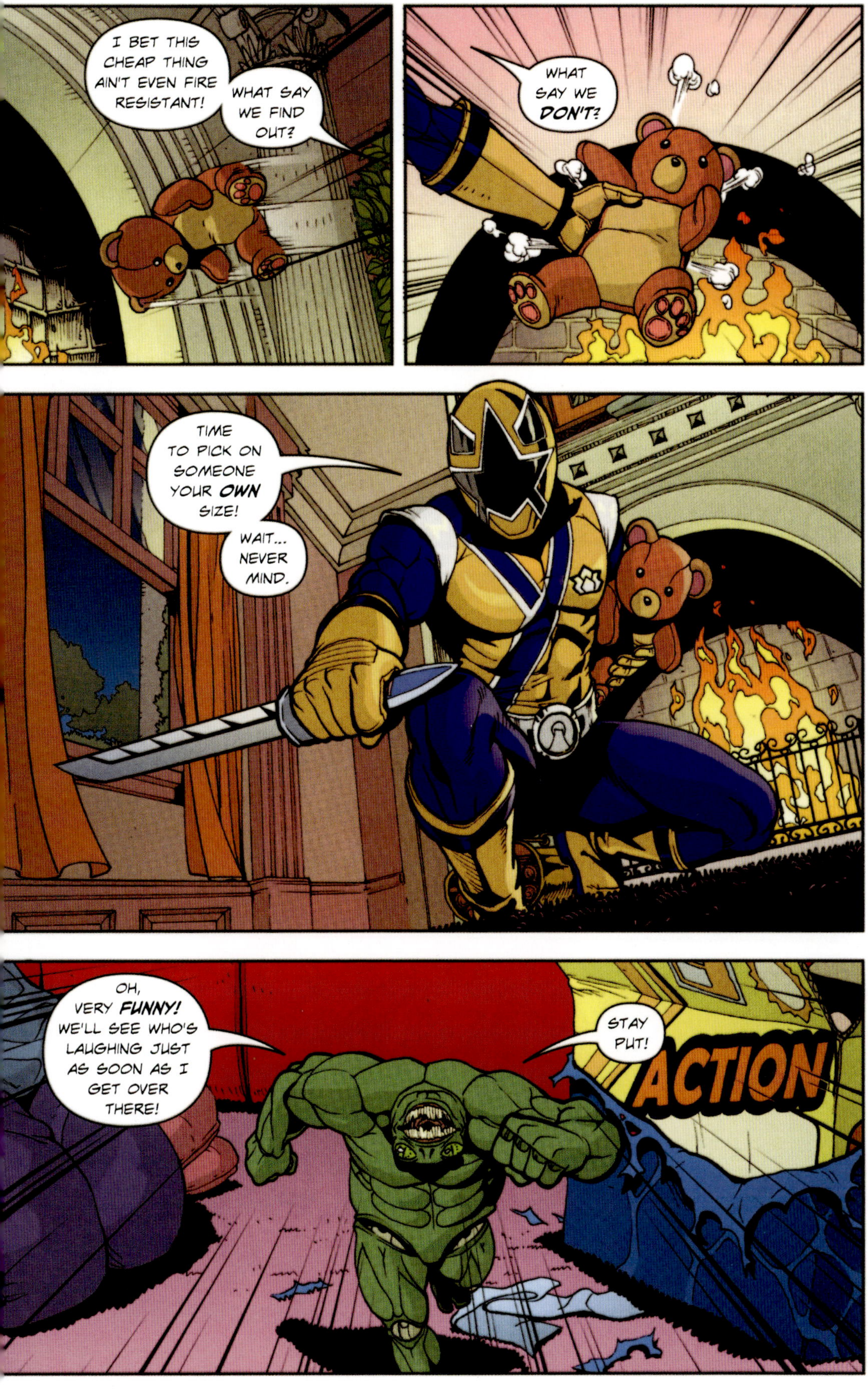
I BET THIS CHEAP THING AIN'T EVEN FIRE RESISTANT!
WHAT SAY WE FIND OUT?
WHAT SAY WE DON'T?
TIME TO PICK ON SOMEONE YOUR OWN SIZE!
WAIT... NEVER MIND.
OH, VERY FUNNY! WE'LL SEE WHO'S LAUGHING JUST AS SOON AS I GET OVER THERE!
STAY PUT!
ACTION

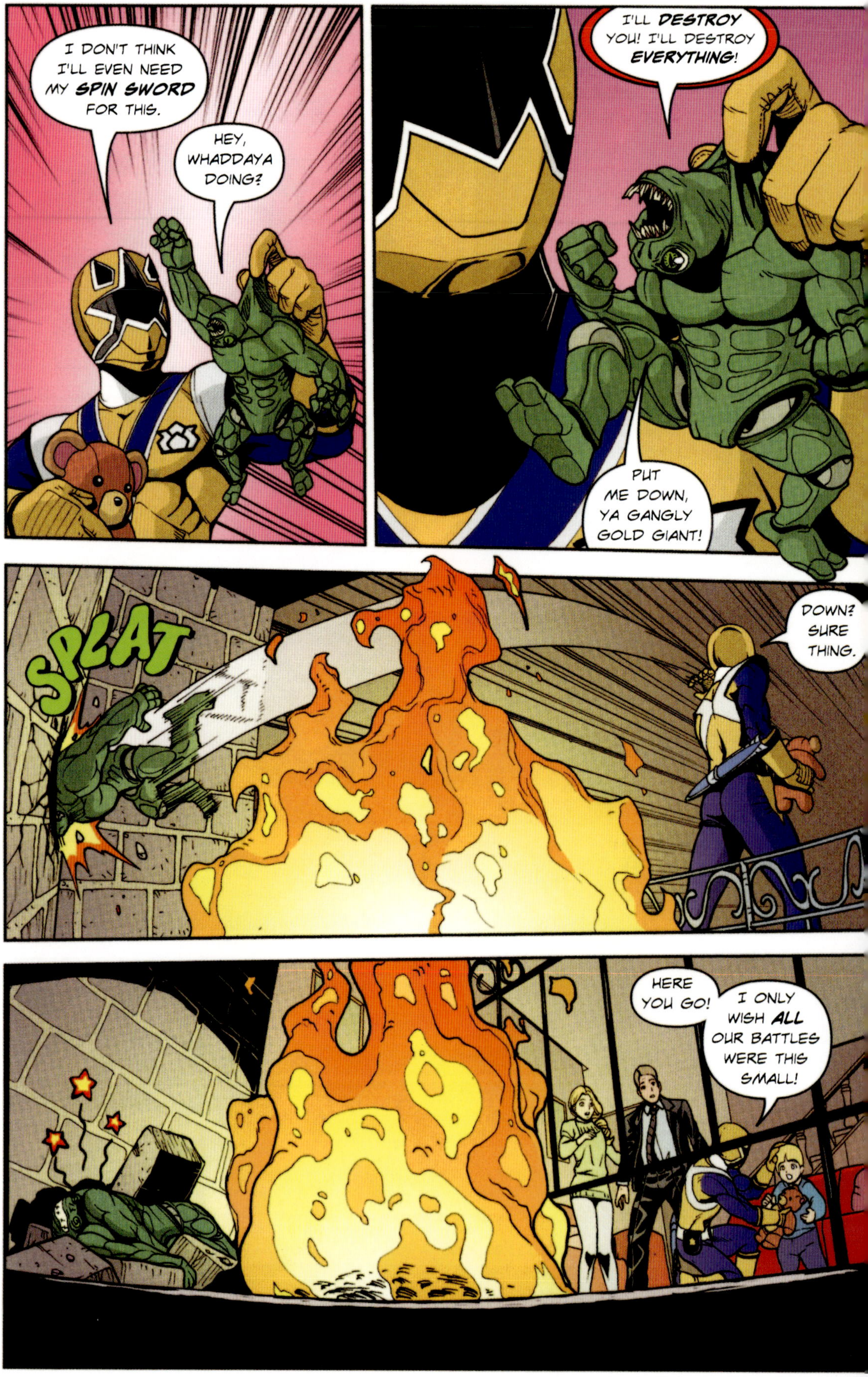
I DON'T THINK I'LL EVEN NEED MY **SPIN SWORD** FOR THIS.
HEY, WHADDAYA DOING?
I'LL **DESTROY** YOU! I'LL DESTROY **EVERYTHING**!
PUT ME DOWN, YA GANGLY GOLD GIANT!
DOWN? SURE THING.
SPLAT
HERE YOU GO!
I ONLY WISH **ALL** OUR BATTLES WERE THIS SMALL!

After returning to Shiba house, Antonio relaxes with Jayden over what seems a simple game.

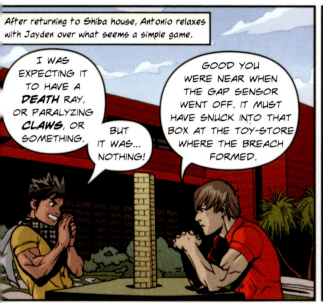

I WAS EXPECTING IT TO HAVE A **DEATH** RAY, OR PARALYZING **CLAWS**, OR SOMETHING.

BUT IT WAS... NOTHING!

GOOD YOU WERE NEAR WHEN THE GAP SENSOR WENT OFF. IT MUST HAVE SNUCK INTO THAT BOX AT THE TOY-STORE WHERE THE BREACH FORMED.

MENTOR'S WORRIED IT ALMOST **WASN'T** DETECTED BECAUSE THE BREACH WAS SO **SMALL**, SO HE'S MAKING ADJUSTMENTS.

WHICH GIVES US A MINUTE TO ACTUALLY PLAY A **GAME** FOR A CHANGE, LIKE THE OLD DAYS.

IT'S NOT JUST A GAME, IT'S A **LESSON**. REMEMBER, THE GOAL IS TO MAKE THE TOWER FALL BY PULLING OUT THE FEWEST PIECES.

I'VE GOT IT! EASIER THAN FIGHTING THAT TINY NIGHLOK.

HEY, IS THIS THING **BROKEN**?

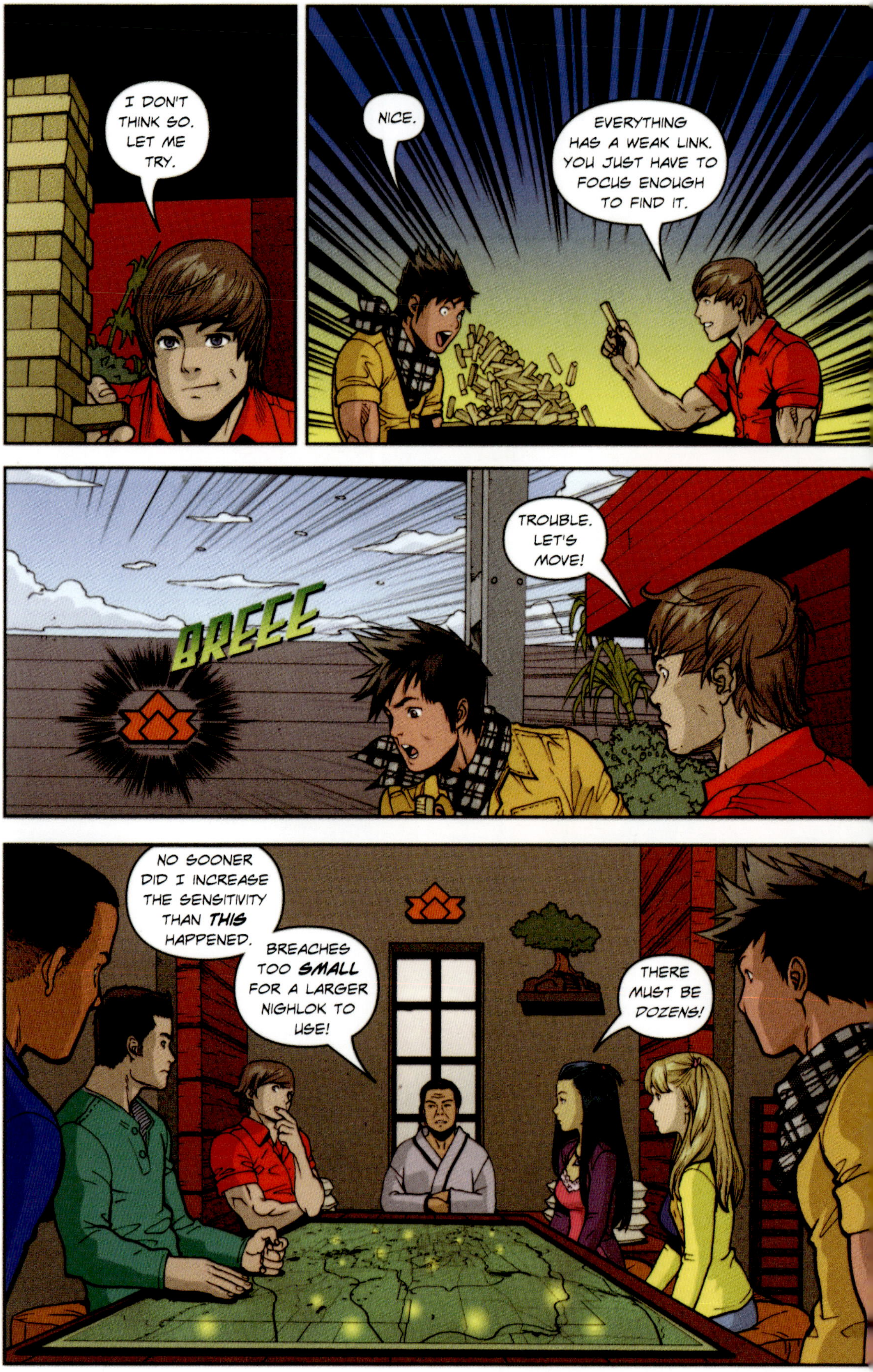
I DON'T THINK SO. LET ME TRY.
NICE.
EVERYTHING HAS A WEAK LINK. YOU JUST HAVE TO FOCUS ENOUGH TO FIND IT.
BREEE
TROUBLE. LET'S MOVE!
NO SOONER DID I INCREASE THE SENSITIVITY THAN THIS HAPPENED.
BREACHES TOO SMALL FOR A LARGER NIGHLOK TO USE!
THERE MUST BE DOZENS!

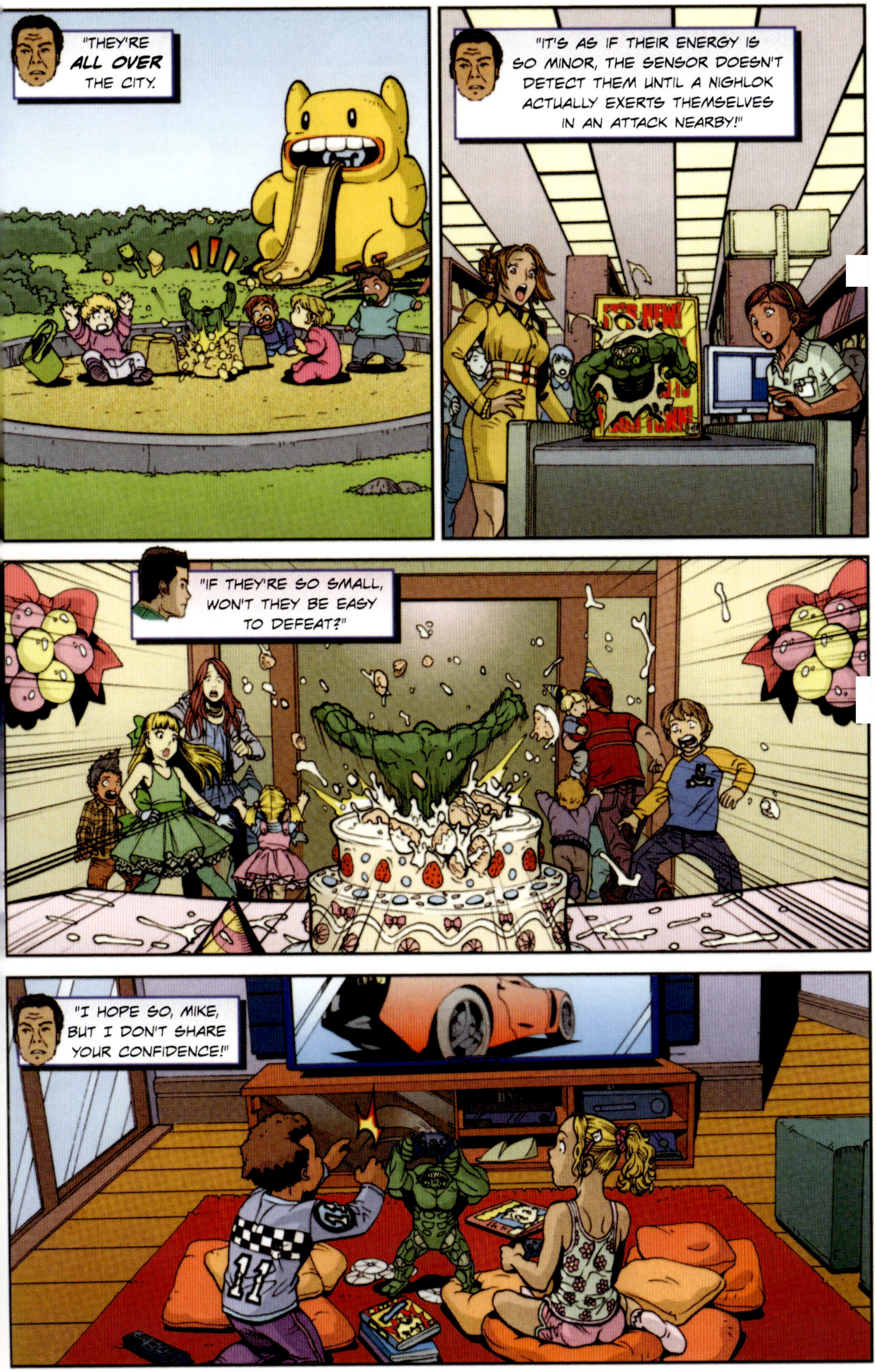
"THEY'RE ALL OVER THE CITY.
"IT'S AS IF THEIR ENERGY IS SO MINOR, THE SENSOR DOESN'T DETECT THEM UNTIL A NIGHLOK ACTUALLY EXERTS THEMSELVES IN AN ATTACK NEARBY!"
IT'S NEW!
"IF THEY'RE SO SMALL, WON'T THEY BE EASY TO DEFEAT?"
"I HOPE SO, MIKE, BUT I DON'T SHARE YOUR CONFIDENCE!"

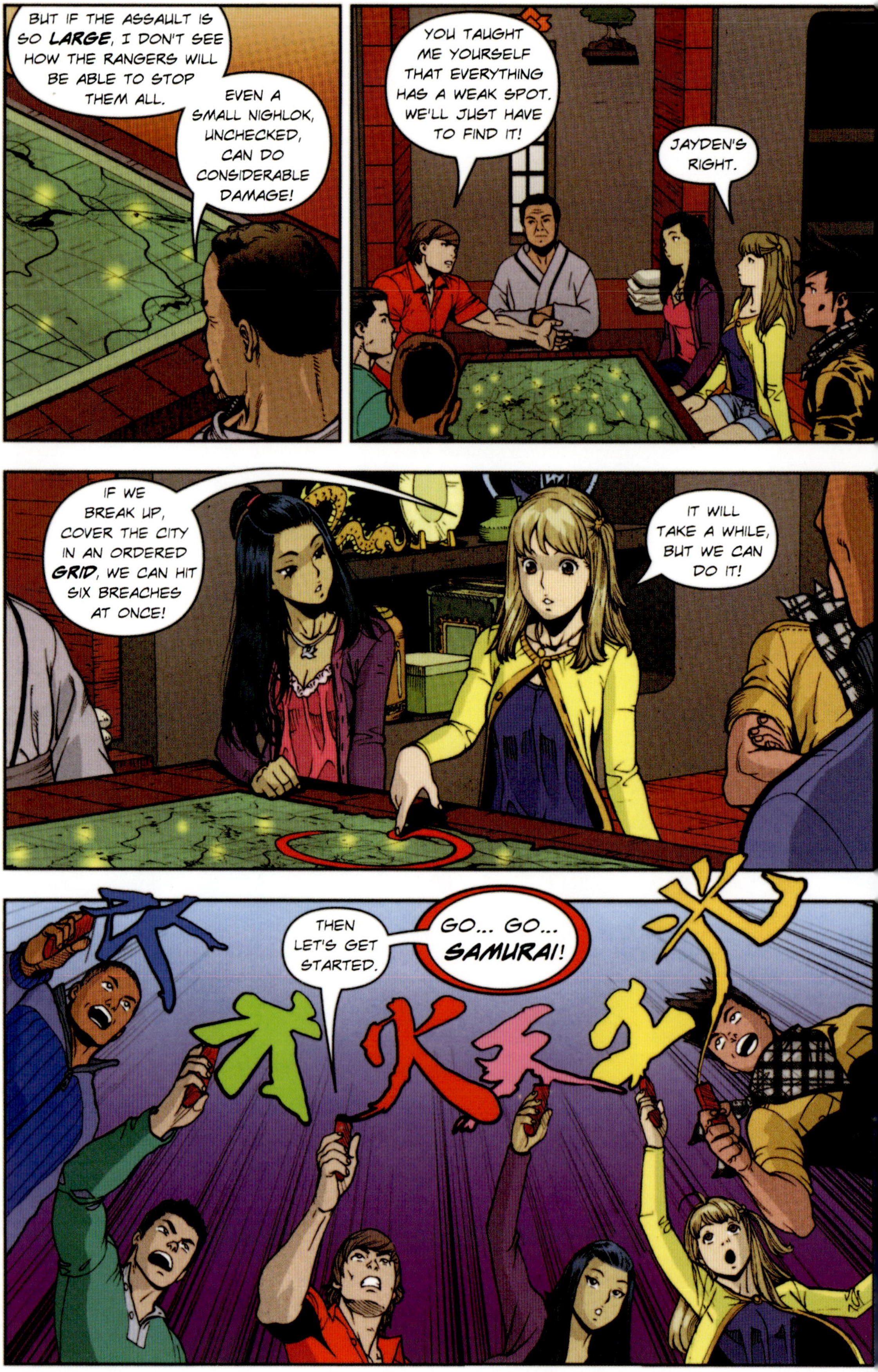
BUT IF THE ASSAULT IS SO **LARGE**, I DON'T SEE HOW THE RANGERS WILL BE ABLE TO STOP THEM ALL.
EVEN A SMALL NIGHLOK, UNCHECKED, CAN DO CONSIDERABLE DAMAGE!
YOU TAUGHT ME YOURSELF THAT EVERYTHING HAS A WEAK SPOT. WE'LL JUST HAVE TO FIND IT!
JAYDEN'S RIGHT.
IF WE BREAK UP, COVER THE CITY IN AN ORDERED **GRID**, WE CAN HIT SIX BREACHES AT ONCE!
IT WILL TAKE A WHILE, BUT WE CAN DO IT!
THEN LET'S GET STARTED.
GO... GO... **SAMURAI!**

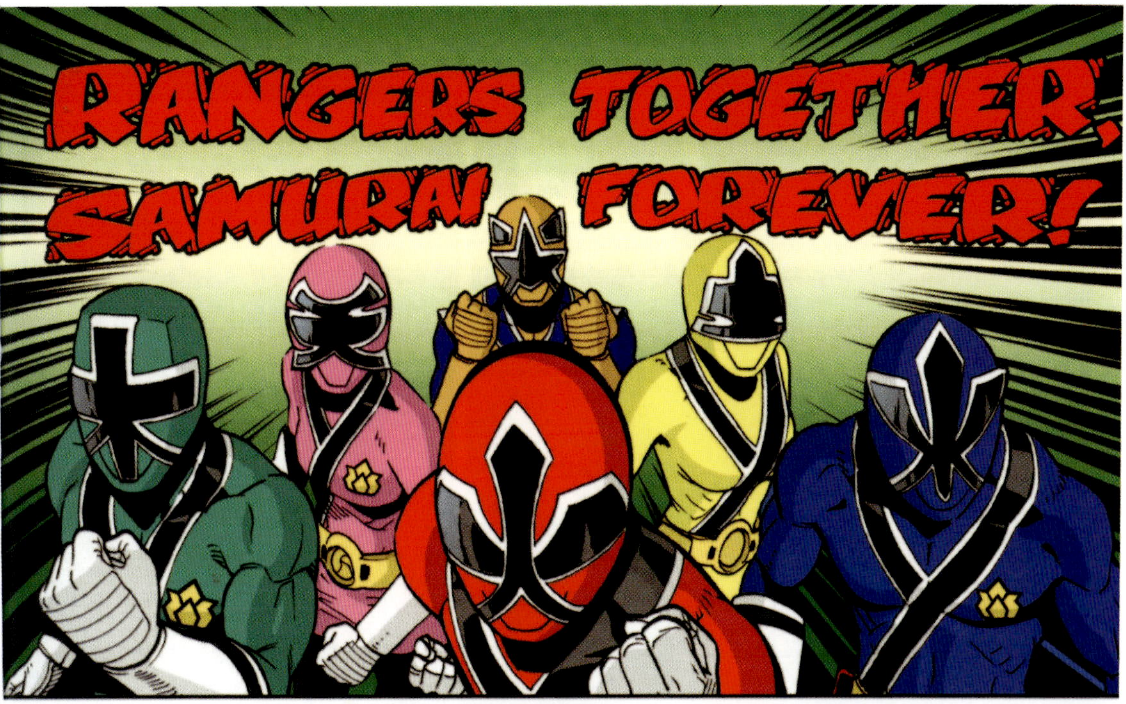
RANGERS TOGETHER, SAMURAI FOREVER!

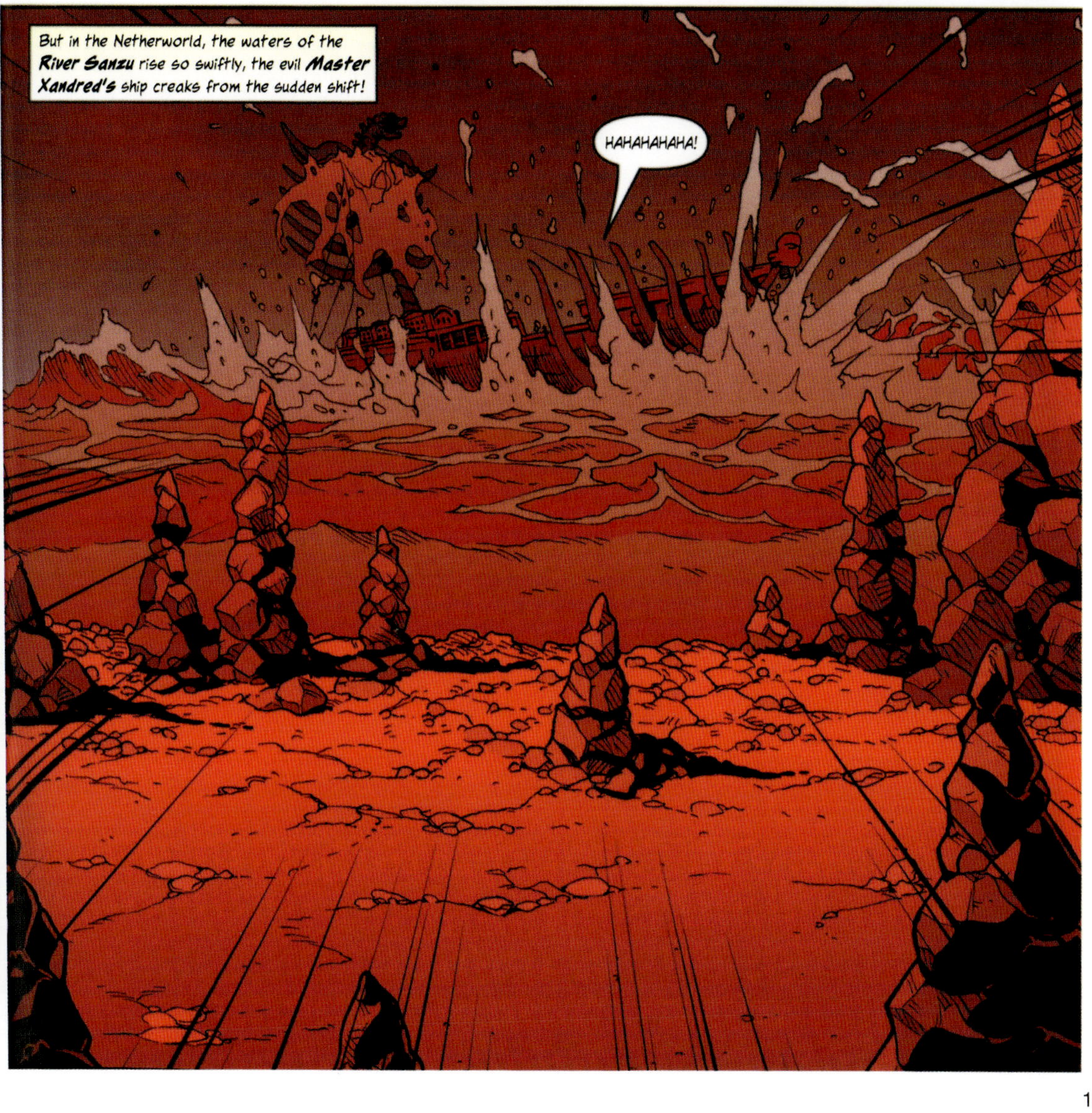
But in the Netherworld, the waters of the River Sanzu rise so swiftly, the evil Master Xandred's ship creaks from the sudden shift!
HAHAHAHAHA!

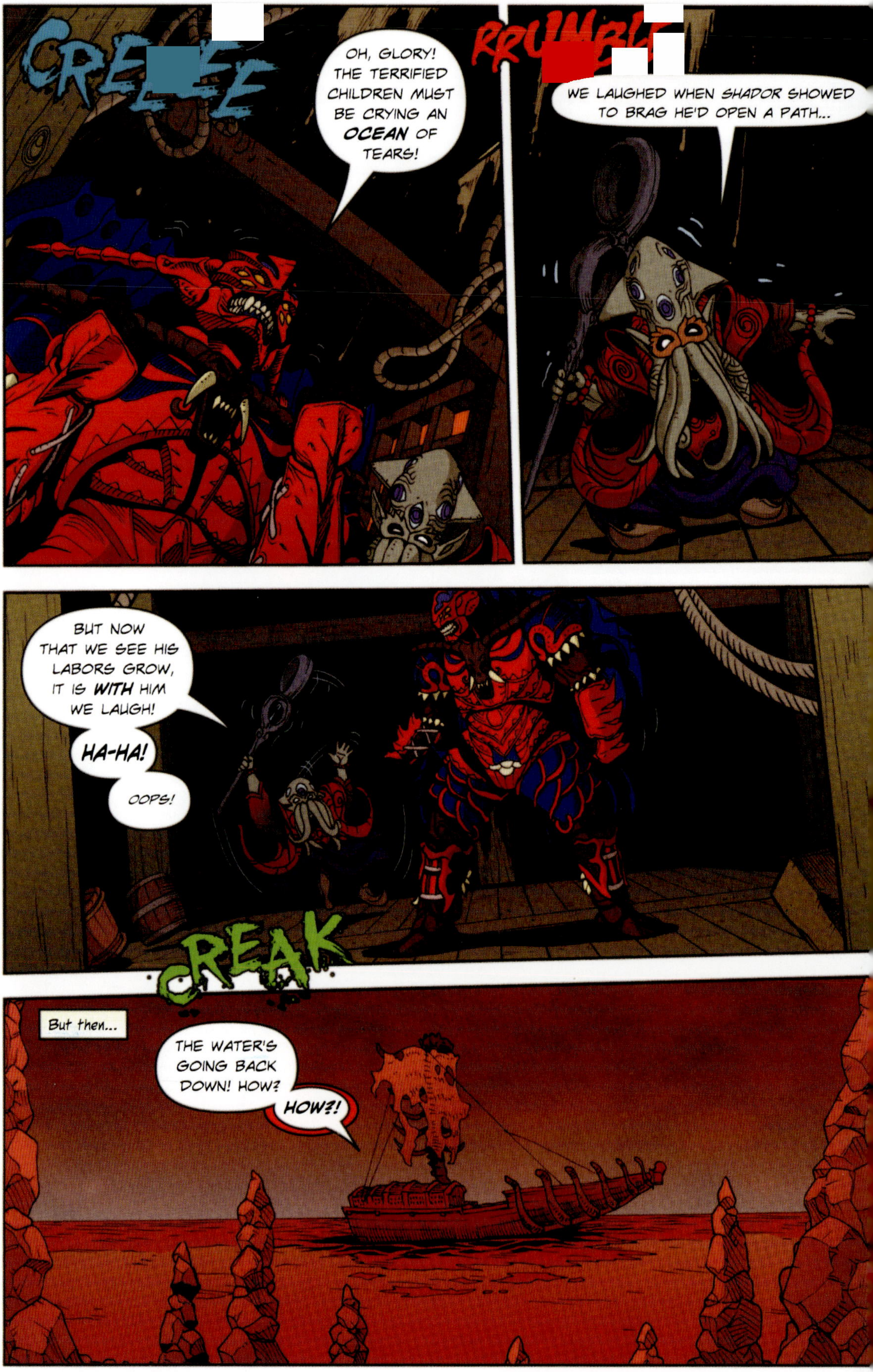
OH, GLORY! THE TERRIFIED CHILDREN MUST BE CRYING AN OCEAN OF TEARS!
WE LAUGHED WHEN SHADOR SHOWED TO BRAG HE'D OPEN A PATH...
BUT NOW THAT WE SEE HIS LABORS GROW, IT IS WITH HIM WE LAUGH!
HA-HA!
OOPS!
CREAK
But then...
THE WATER'S GOING BACK DOWN! HOW?
HOW?!

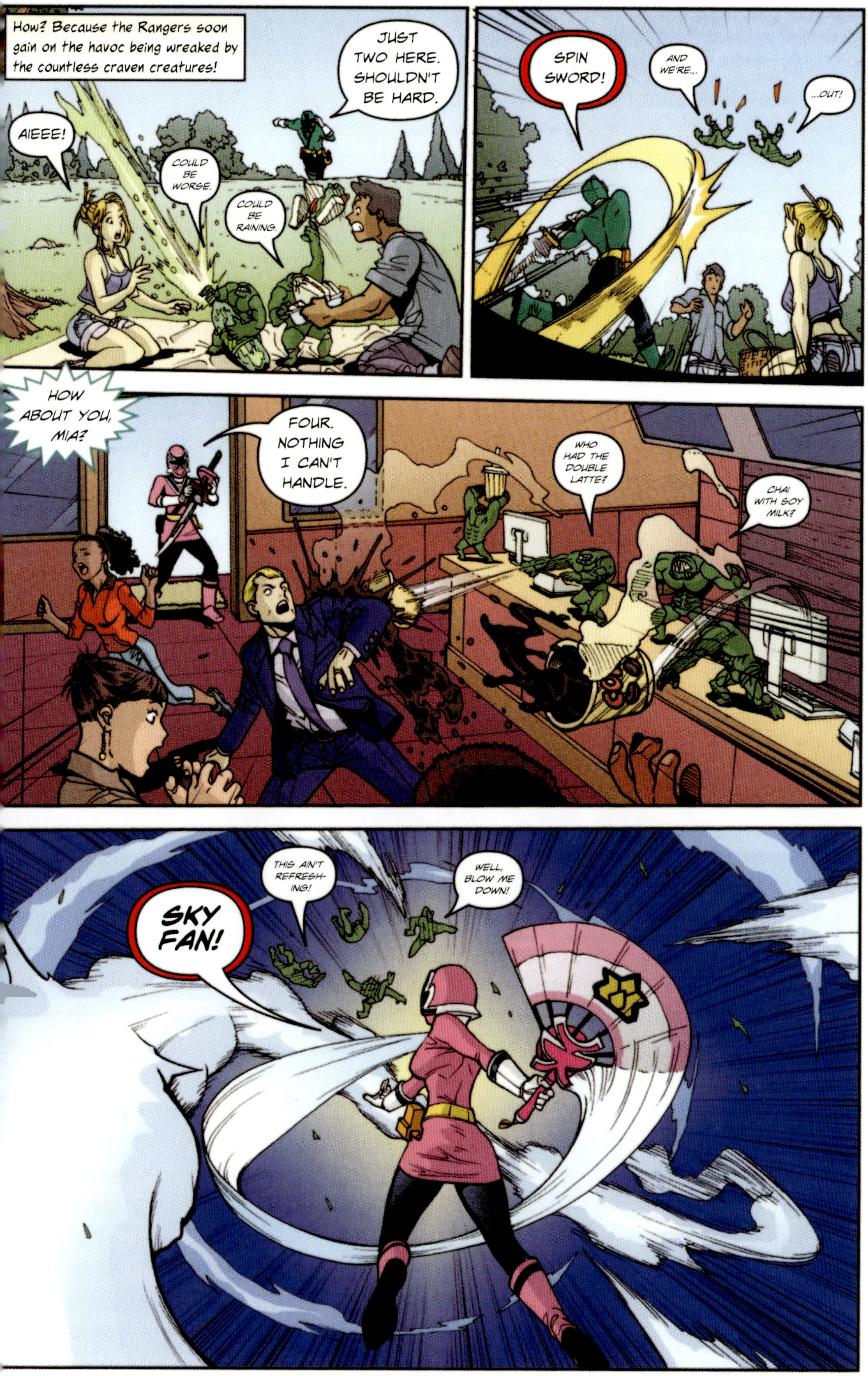
How? Because the Rangers soon gain on the havoc being wreaked by the countless craven creatures!
JUST TWO HERE. SHOULDN'T BE HARD.
AIEEE!
COULD BE WORSE.
COULD BE RAINING.
SPIN SWORD!
AND WE'RE...
...OUT!
HOW ABOUT YOU, MIA?
FOUR. NOTHING I CAN'T HANDLE.
WHO HAD THE DOUBLE LATTE?
CHAI WITH SOY MILK?
SKY FAN!
THIS AIN'T REFRESH-ING!
WELL, BLOW ME DOWN!

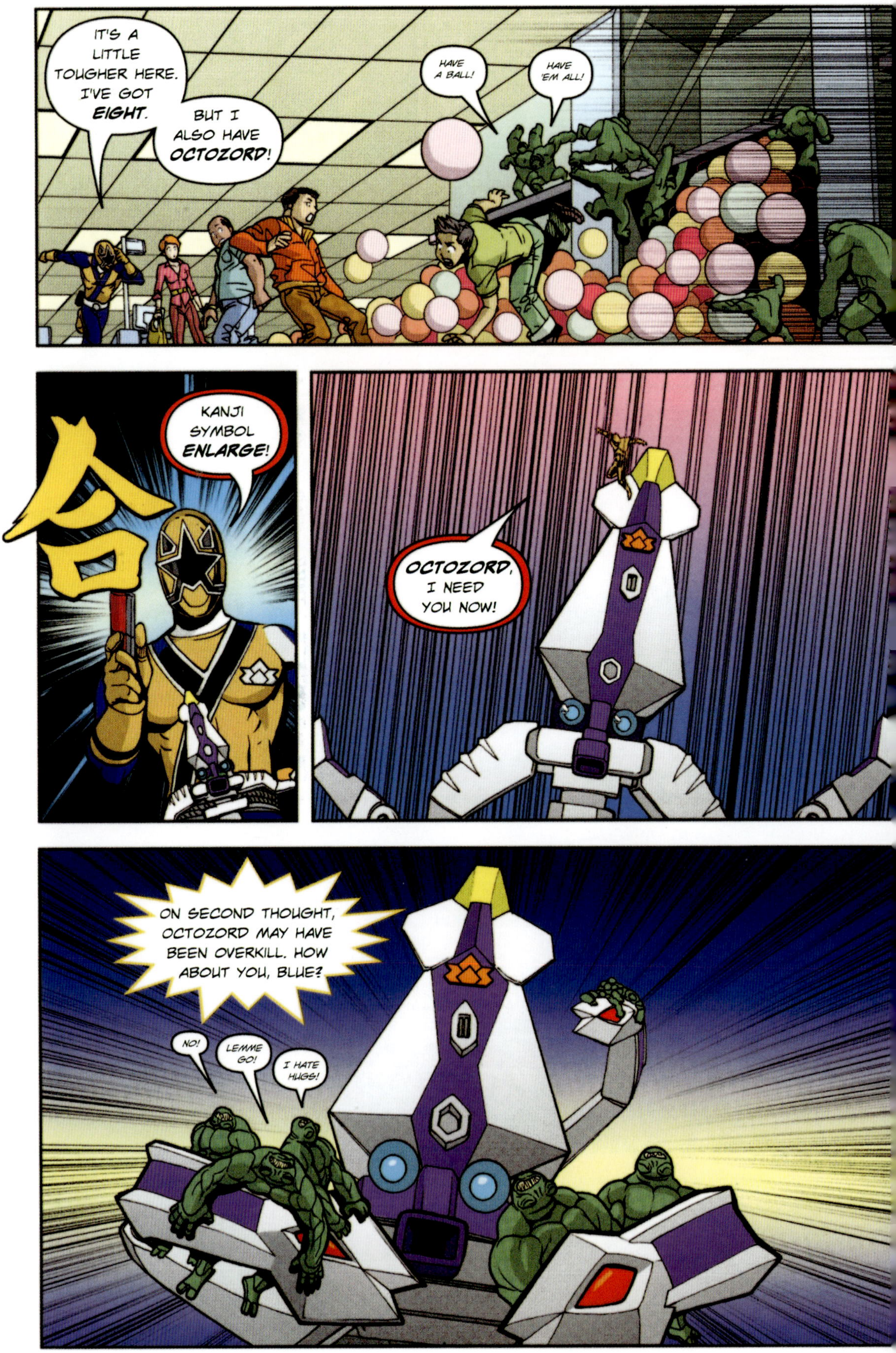

IT'S A LITTLE TOUGHER HERE. I'VE GOT EIGHT.
BUT I ALSO HAVE OCTOZORD!
HAVE A BALL!
HAVE 'EM ALL!
KANJI SYMBOL ENLARGE!
合
OCTOZORD, I NEED YOU NOW!
ON SECOND THOUGHT, OCTOZORD MAY HAVE BEEN OVERKILL. HOW ABOUT YOU, BLUE?
NO!
LEMME GO!
I HATE HUGS!

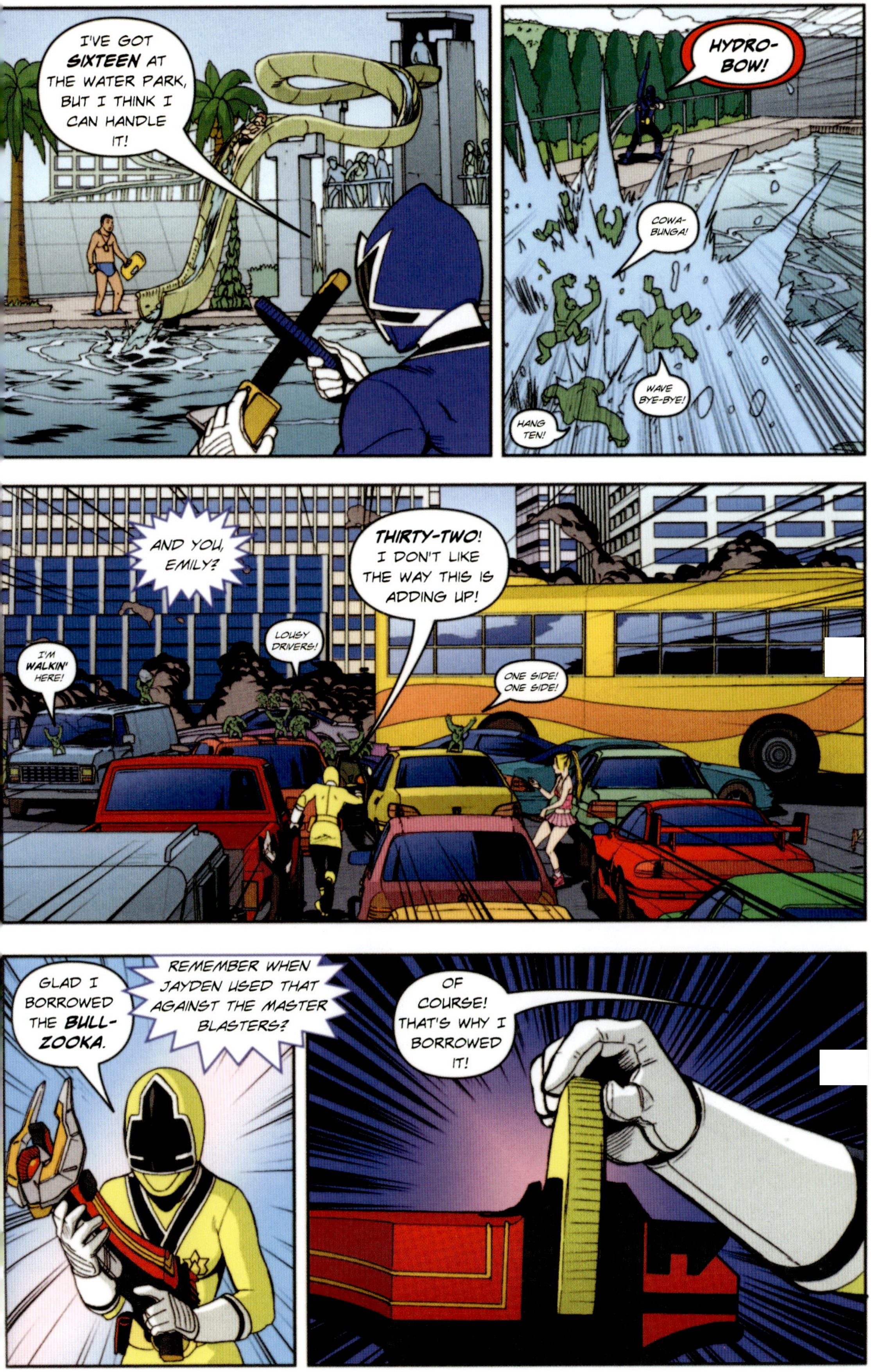
I'VE GOT SIXTEEN AT THE WATER PARK, BUT I THINK I CAN HANDLE IT!
HYDRO-BOW!
COWA-BUNGA!
WAVE BYE-BYE!
HANG TEN!
AND YOU, EMILY?
THIRTY-TWO! I DON'T LIKE THE WAY THIS IS ADDING UP!
LOUSY DRIVERS!
I'M WALKIN' HERE!
ONE SIDE! ONE SIDE!
GLAD I BORROWED THE BULL-ZOOKA.
REMEMBER WHEN JAYDEN USED THAT AGAINST THE MASTER BLASTERS?
OF COURSE! THAT'S WHY I BORROWED IT!

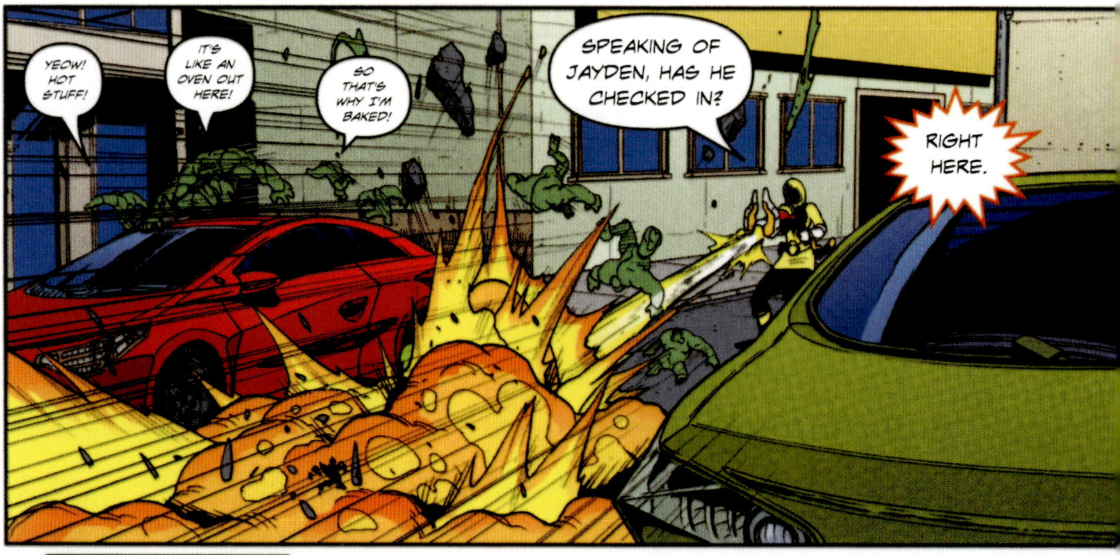
YEOW! HOT STUFF!
IT'S LIKE AN OVEN OUT HERE!
SO THAT'S WHY I'M BAKED!
SPEAKING OF JAYDEN, HAS HE CHECKED IN?
RIGHT HERE.

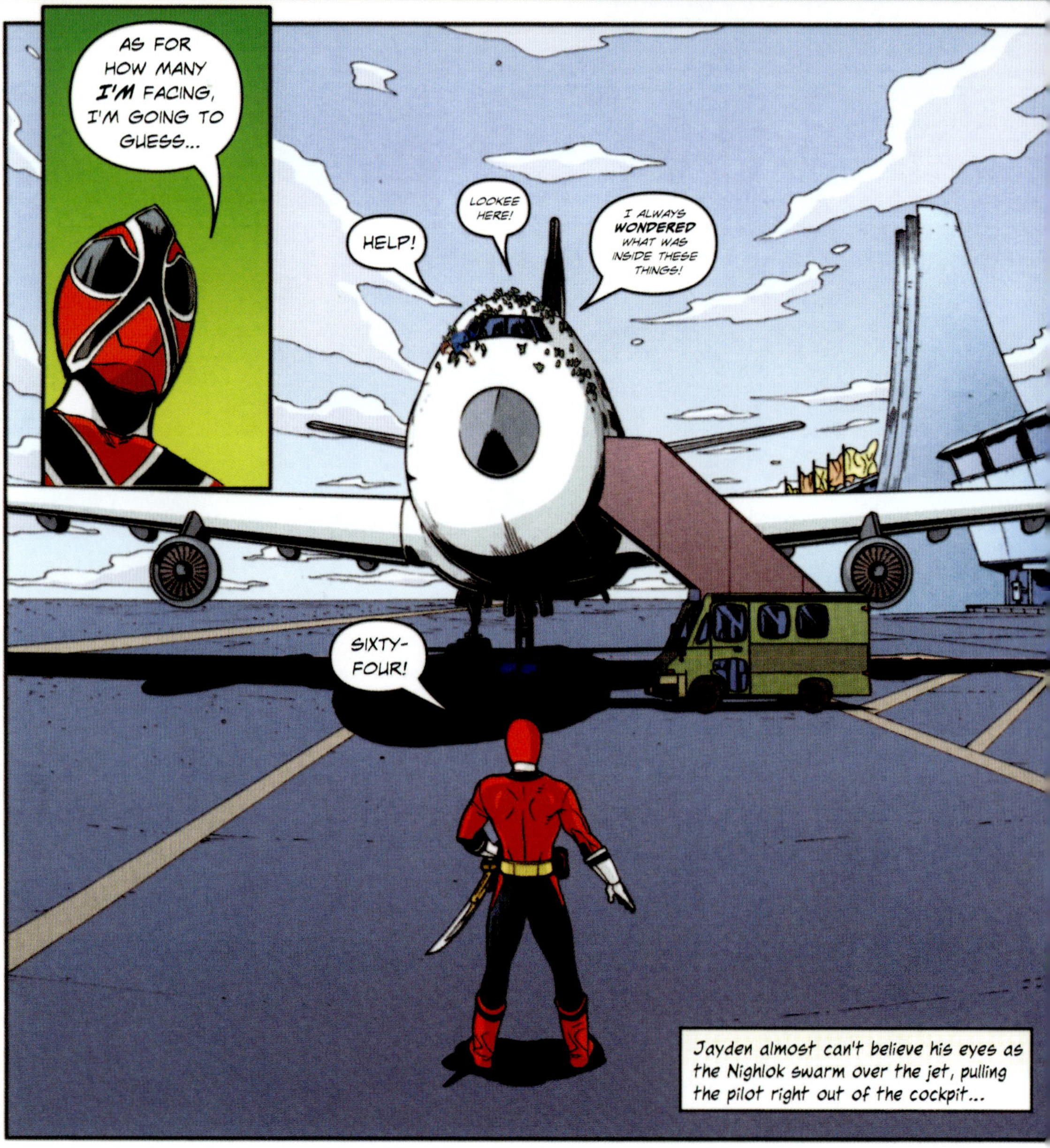
AS FOR HOW MANY I'M FACING, I'M GOING TO GUESS...
HELP!
LOOKEE HERE!
I ALWAYS WONDERED WHAT WAS INSIDE THESE THINGS!
SIXTY-FOUR!
Jayden almost can't believe his eyes as the Nighlok swarm over the jet, pulling the pilot right out of the cockpit...

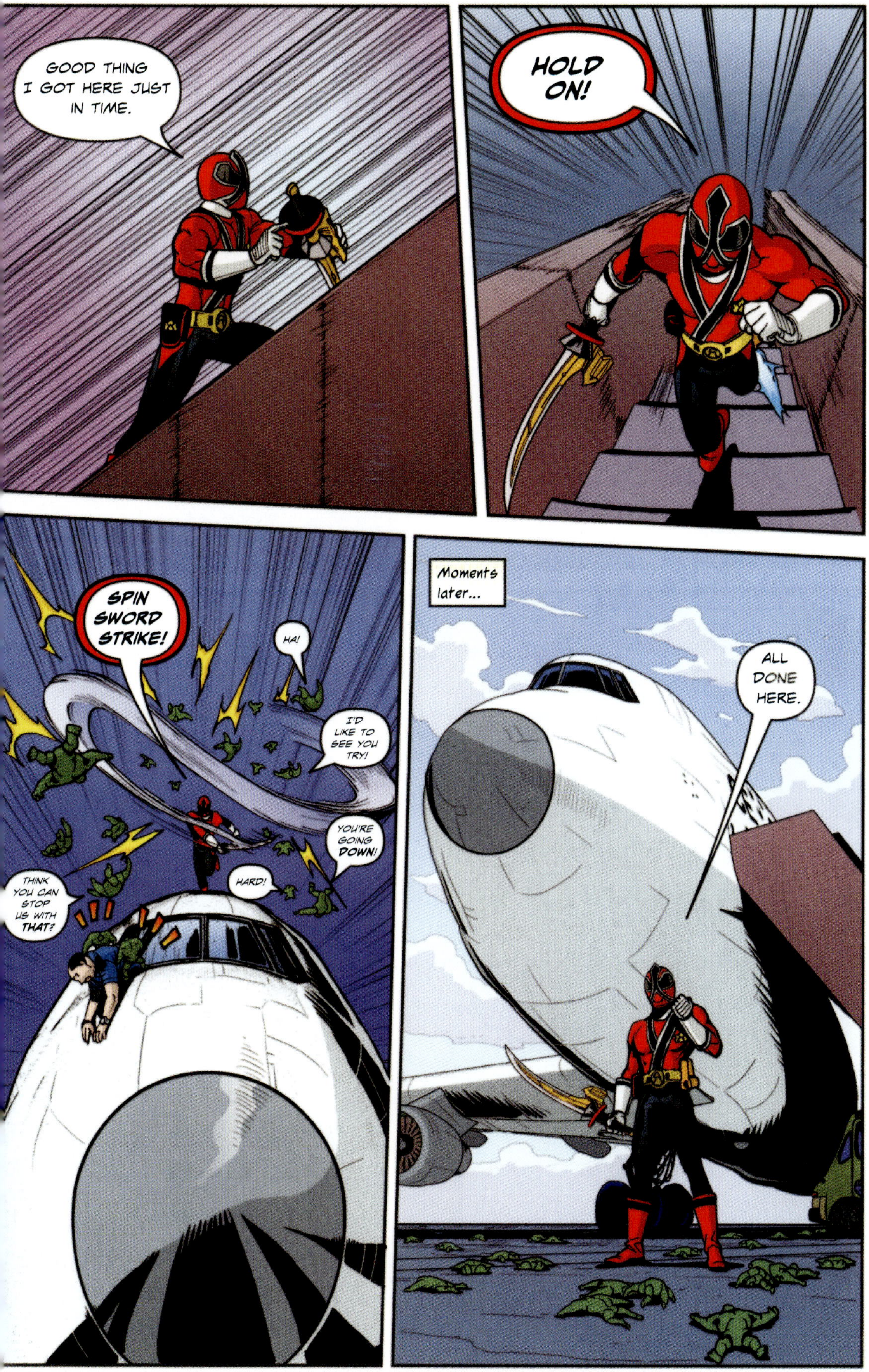
GOOD THING I GOT HERE JUST IN TIME.
HOLD ON!
SPIN SWORD STRIKE!
HA!
I'D LIKE TO SEE YOU TRY!
YOU'RE GOING DOWN!
HARD!
THINK YOU CAN STOP US WITH THAT?
Moments later...
ALL DONE HERE.

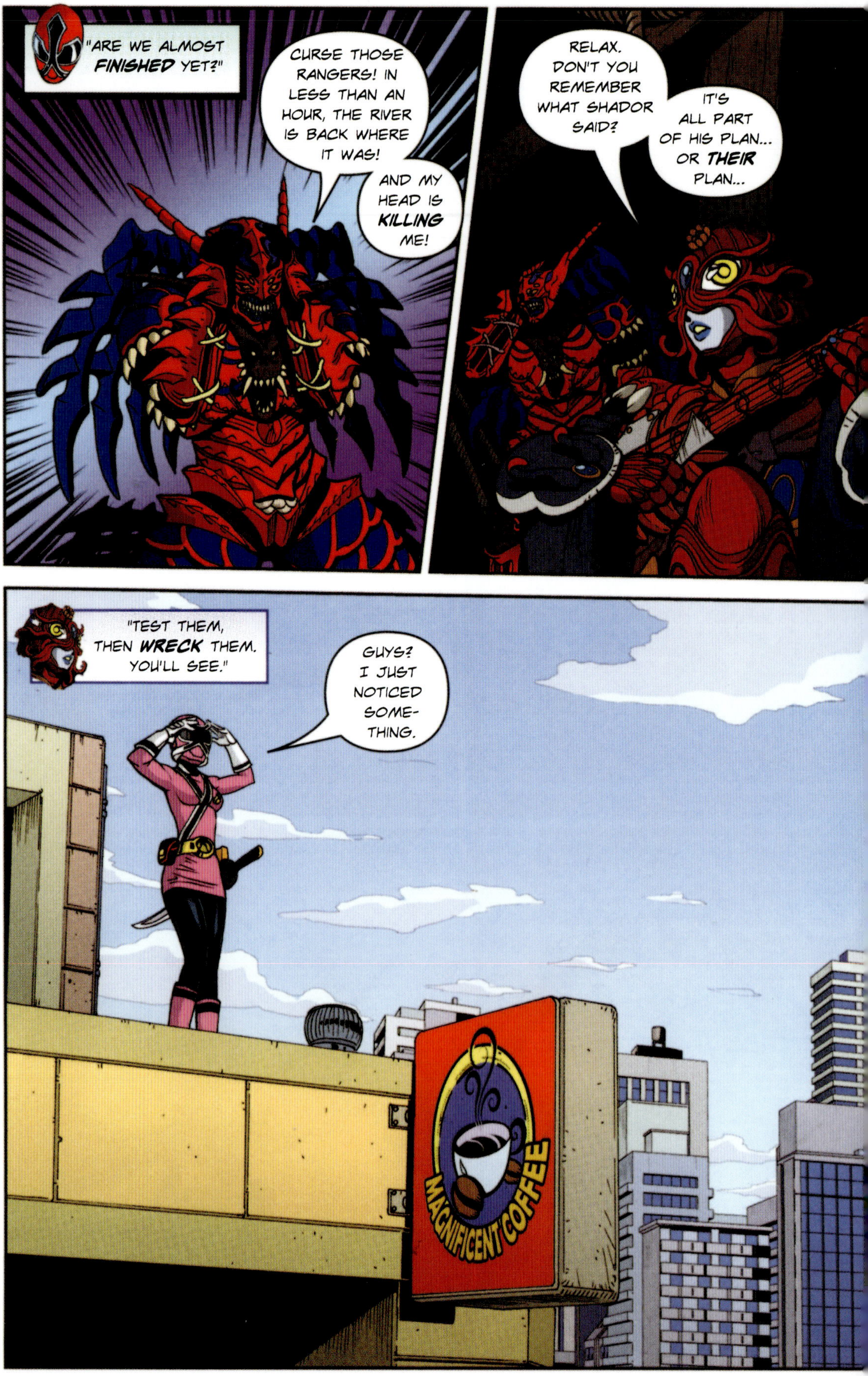
"ARE WE ALMOST FINISHED YET?"
CURSE THOSE RANGERS! IN LESS THAN AN HOUR, THE RIVER IS BACK WHERE IT WAS!
AND MY HEAD IS KILLING ME!
RELAX. DON'T YOU REMEMBER WHAT SHADOR SAID?
IT'S ALL PART OF HIS PLAN... OR THEIR PLAN...
"TEST THEM, THEN WRECK THEM. YOU'LL SEE."
GUYS? I JUST NOTICED SOME-THING.
MAGNIFICENT COFFEE

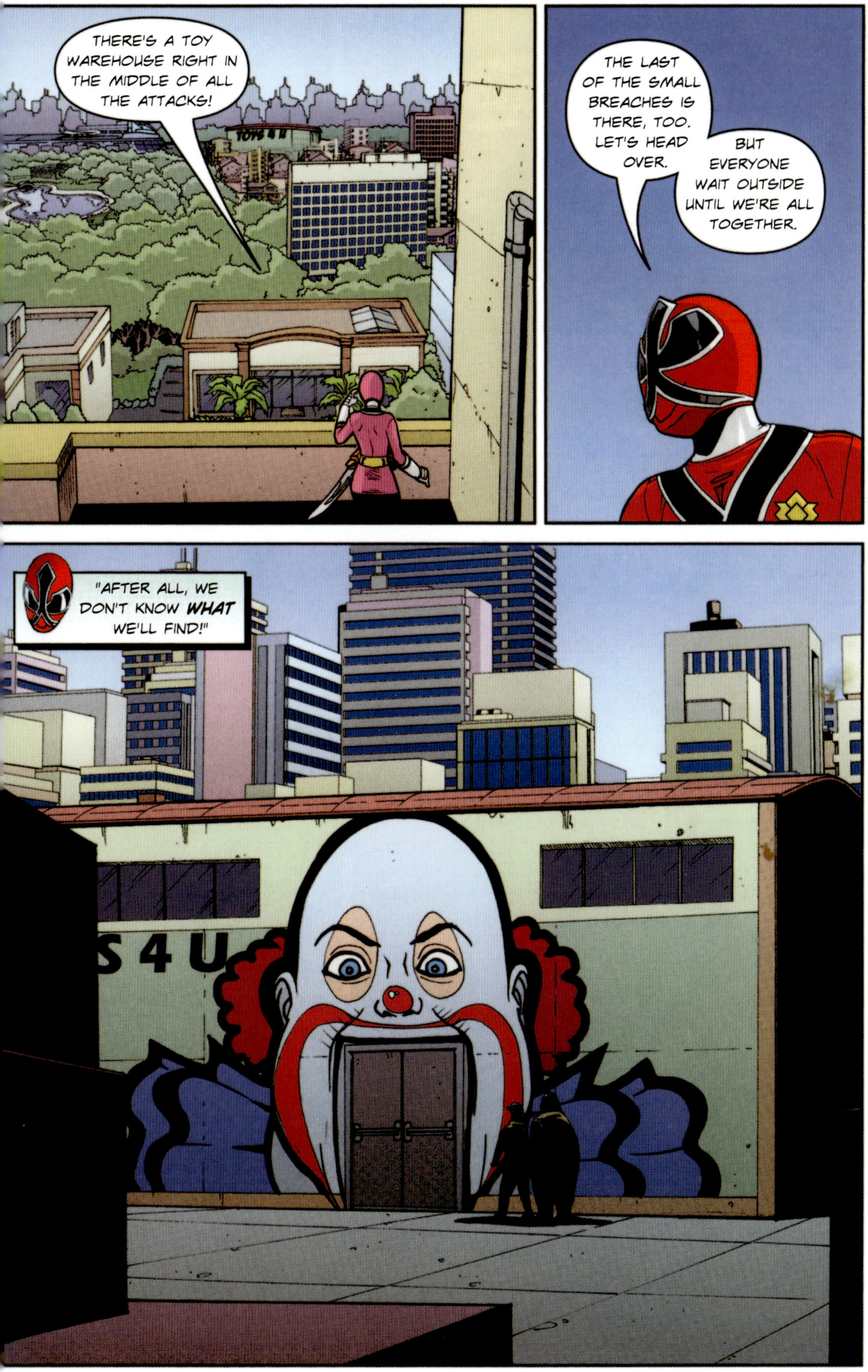
THERE'S A TOY WAREHOUSE RIGHT IN THE MIDDLE OF ALL THE ATTACKS!
THE LAST OF THE SMALL BREACHES IS THERE, TOO. LET'S HEAD OVER.
BUT EVERYONE WAIT OUTSIDE UNTIL WE'RE ALL TOGETHER.
"AFTER ALL, WE DON'T KNOW WHAT WE'LL FIND!"
S 4 U

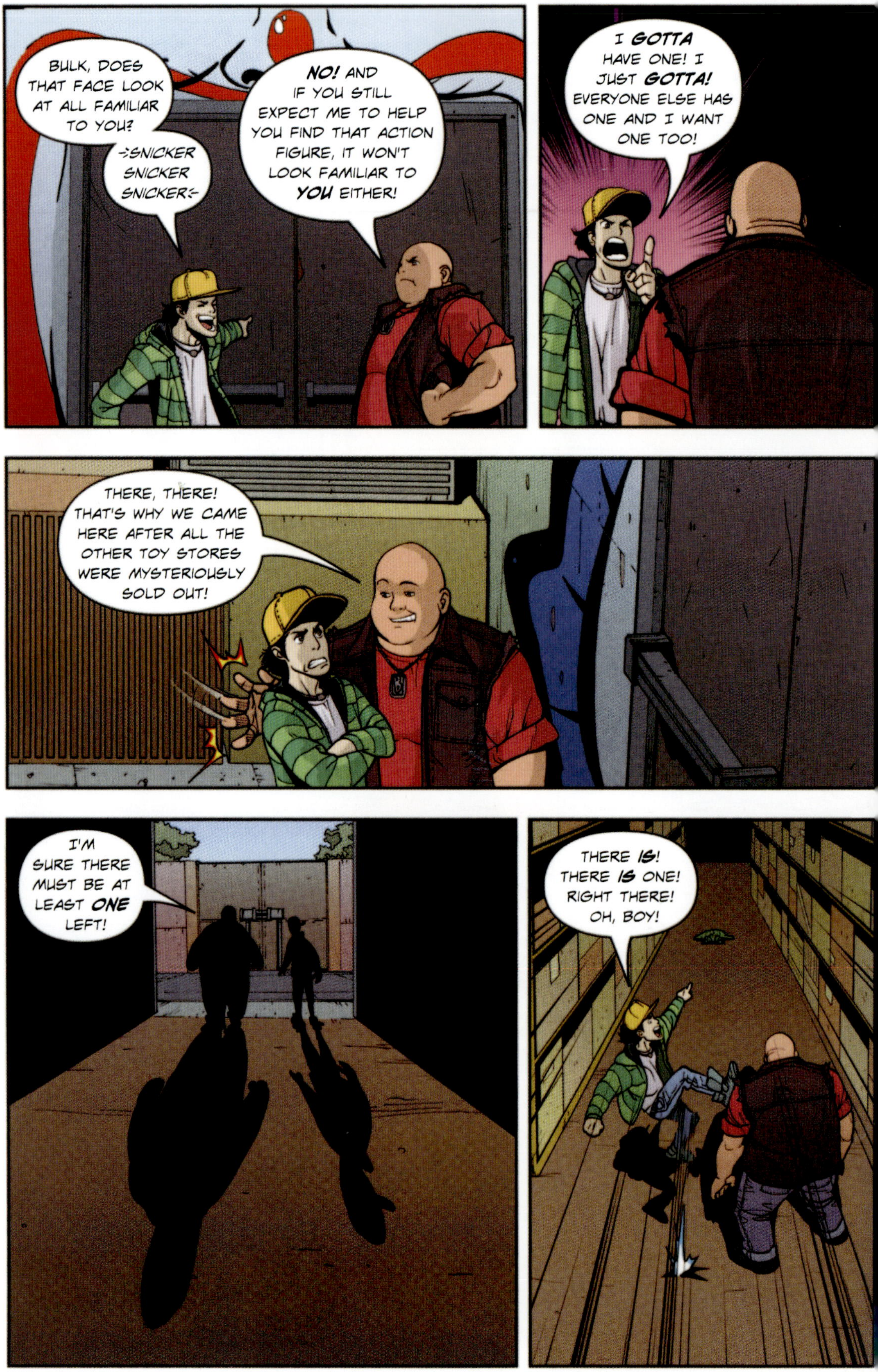
BULK, DOES THAT FACE LOOK AT ALL FAMILIAR TO YOU?
SNICKER SNICKER SNICKER
NO! AND IF YOU STILL EXPECT ME TO HELP YOU FIND THAT ACTION FIGURE, IT WON'T LOOK FAMILIAR TO YOU EITHER!
I GOTTA HAVE ONE! I JUST GOTTA! EVERYONE ELSE HAS ONE AND I WANT ONE TOO!
THERE, THERE! THAT'S WHY WE CAME HERE AFTER ALL THE OTHER TOY STORES WERE MYSTERIOUSLY SOLD OUT!
I'M SURE THERE MUST BE AT LEAST ONE LEFT!
THERE IS! THERE IS ONE! RIGHT THERE! OH, BOY!

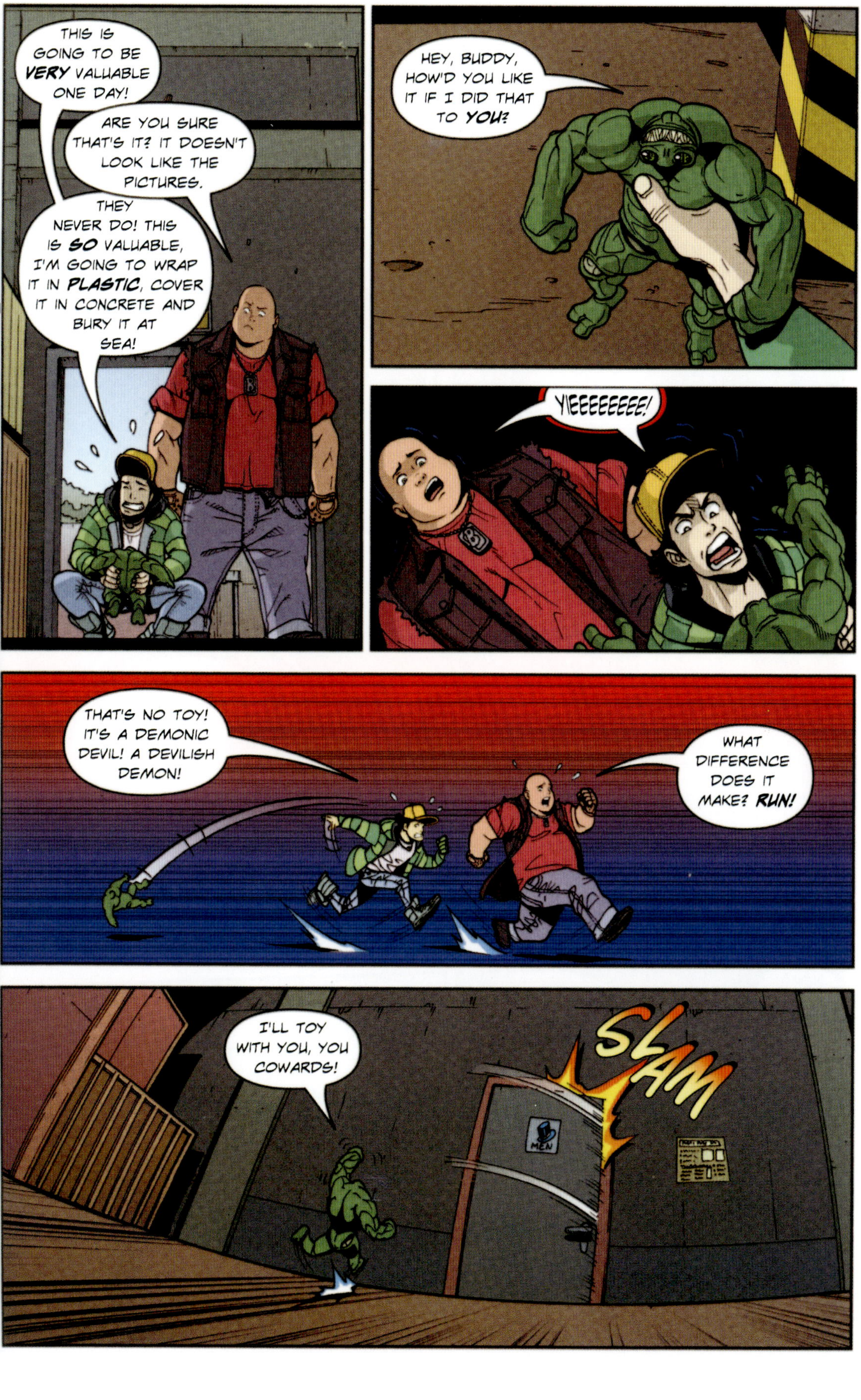
THIS IS GOING TO BE **VERY** VALUABLE ONE DAY!
ARE YOU SURE THAT'S IT? IT DOESN'T LOOK LIKE THE PICTURES.
THEY NEVER DO! THIS IS **SO** VALUABLE, I'M GOING TO WRAP IT IN **PLASTIC**, COVER IT IN CONCRETE AND BURY IT AT SEA!
HEY, BUDDY, HOW'D YOU LIKE IT IF I DID THAT TO **YOU**?
YIEEEEEEEE!
THAT'S NO TOY! IT'S A DEMONIC DEVIL! A DEVILISH DEMON!
WHAT DIFFERENCE DOES IT MAKE? **RUN!**
I'LL TOY WITH YOU, YOU COWARDS!
SLAM
MEN

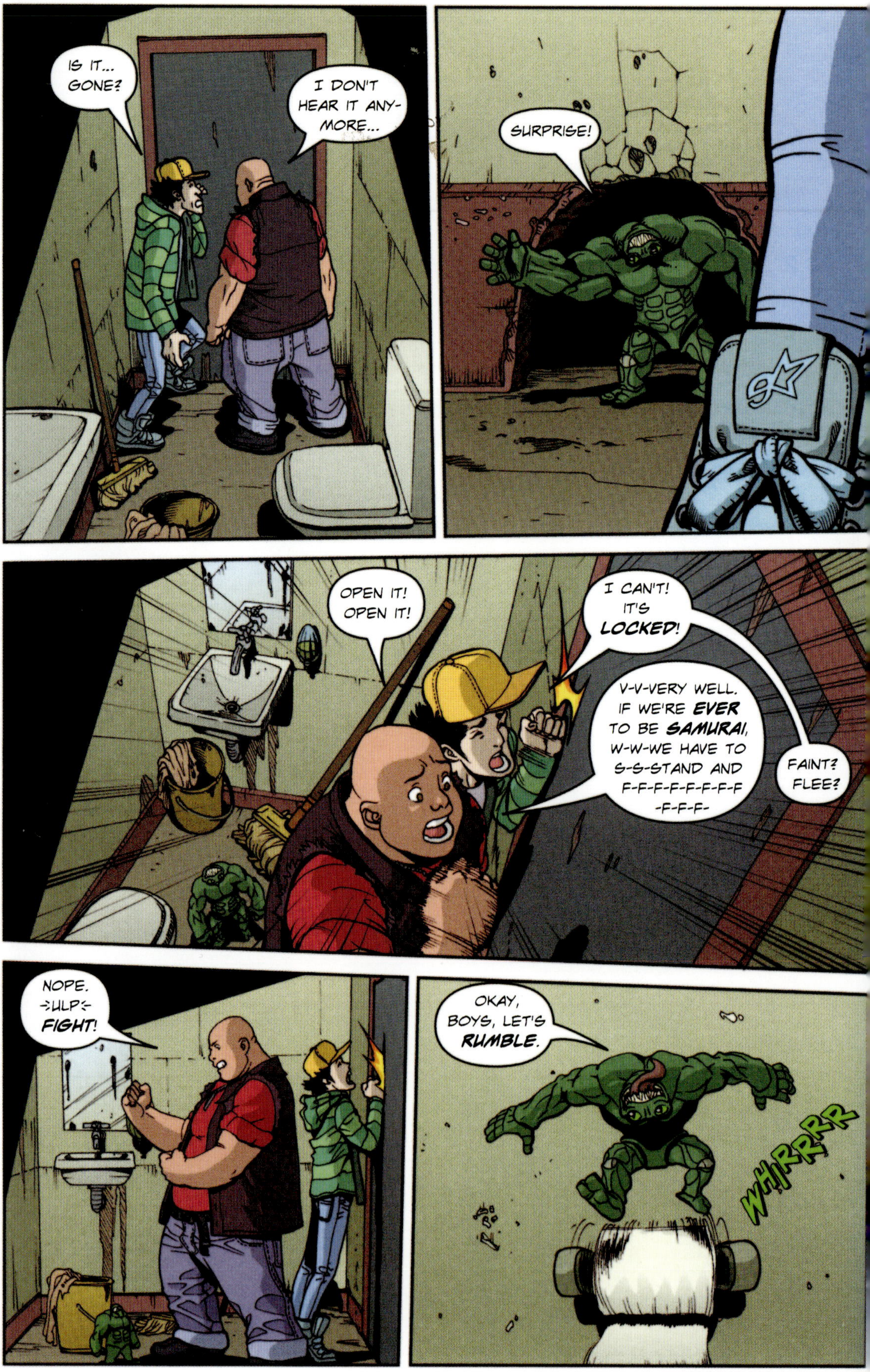

IS IT... GONE?
I DON'T HEAR IT ANY-MORE...
SURPRISE!
OPEN IT! OPEN IT!
I CAN'T! IT'S LOCKED!
V-V-VERY WELL. IF WE'RE EVER TO BE SAMURAI, W-W-WE HAVE TO S-S-STAND AND F-F-F-F-F-F-F-F-F -F-F-F-
FAINT? FLEE?
NOPE. -ULP- FIGHT!
OKAY, BOYS, LET'S RUMBLE.
WHIRRR

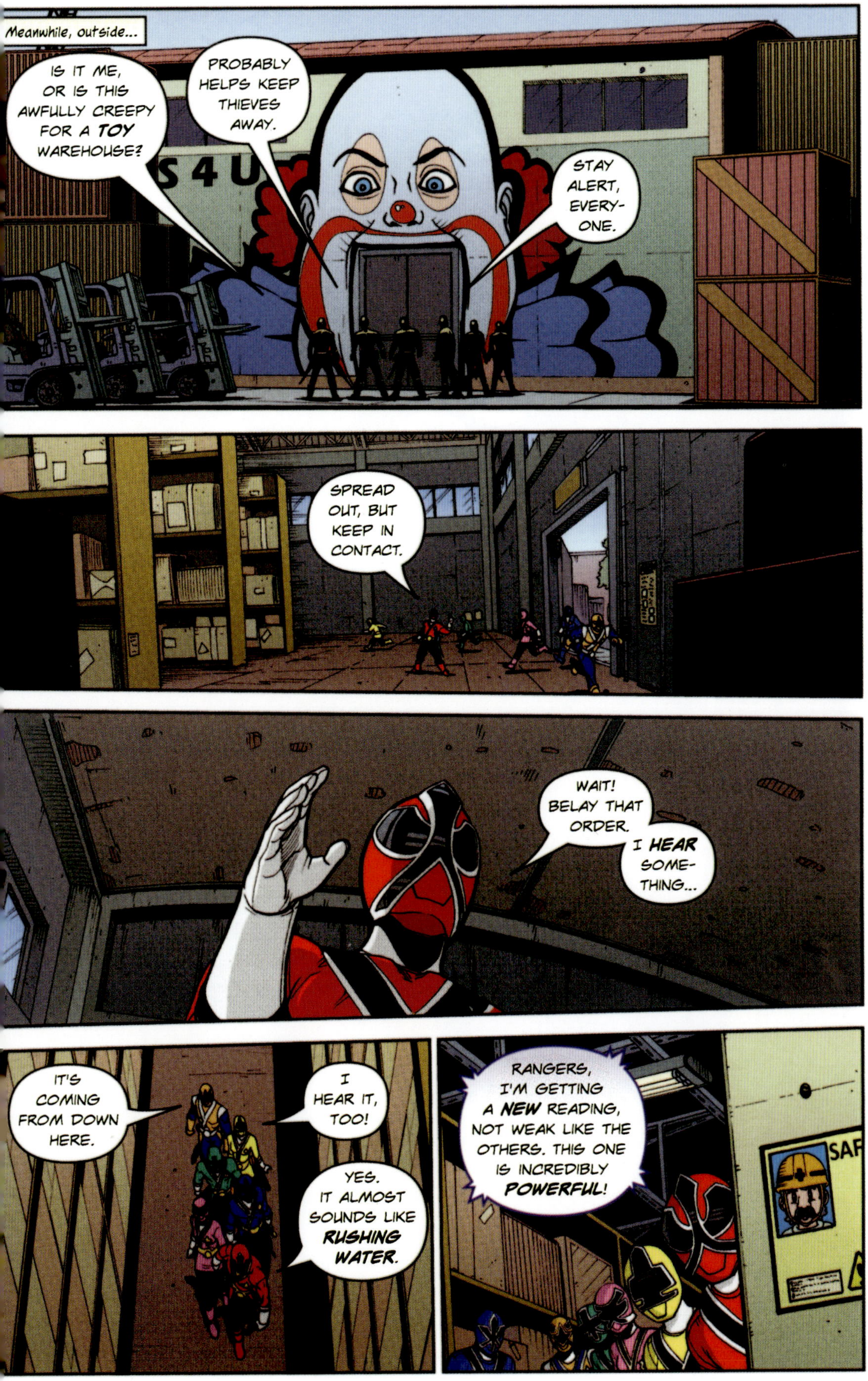
Meanwhile, outside...
IS IT ME, OR IS THIS AWFULLY CREEPY FOR A TOY WAREHOUSE?
PROBABLY HELPS KEEP THIEVES AWAY.
STAY ALERT, EVERY-ONE.
SPREAD OUT, BUT KEEP IN CONTACT.
WAIT! BELAY THAT ORDER.
I HEAR SOME-THING...
IT'S COMING FROM DOWN HERE.
I HEAR IT, TOO!
YES. IT ALMOST SOUNDS LIKE RUSHING WATER.
RANGERS, I'M GETTING A NEW READING, NOT WEAK LIKE THE OTHERS. THIS ONE IS INCREDIBLY POWERFUL!

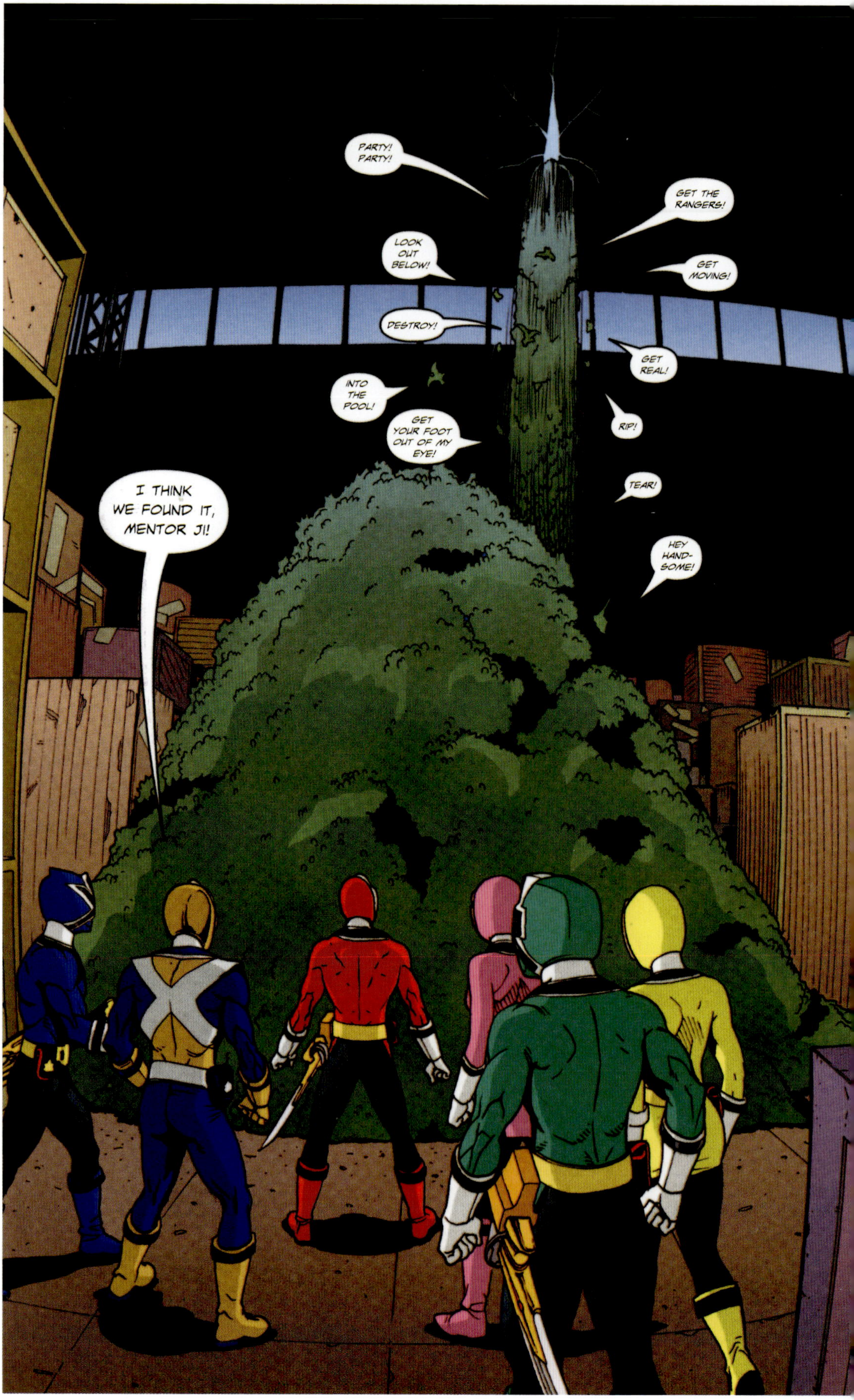
PARTY! PARTY!
GET THE RANGERS!
LOOK OUT BELOW!
GET MOVING!
DESTROY!
GET REAL!
INTO THE POOL!
RIP!
GET YOUR FOOT OUT OF MY EYE!
TEAR!
I THINK WE FOUND IT, MENTOR JI!
HEY HAND-SOME!

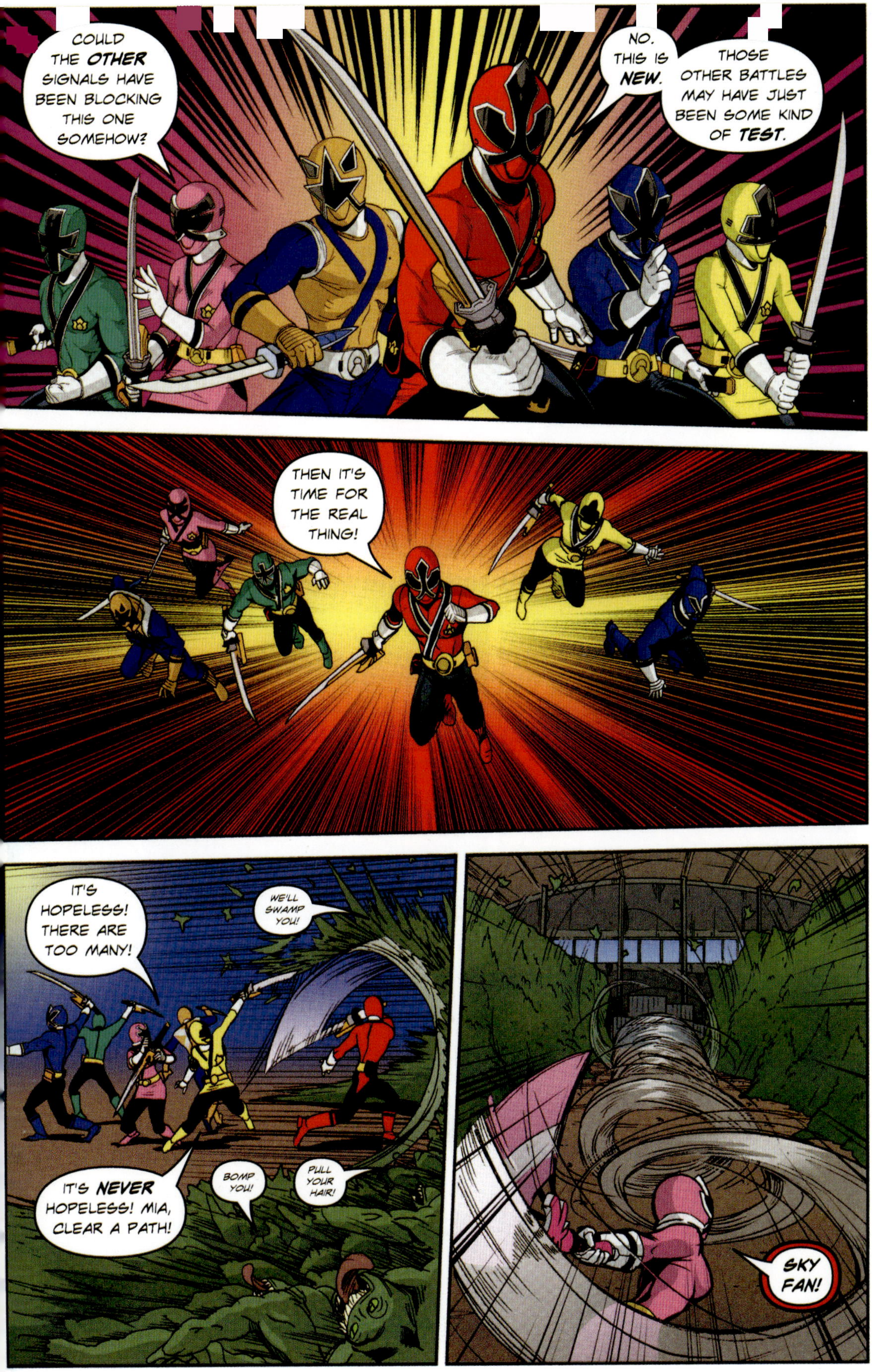
COULD THE OTHER SIGNALS HAVE BEEN BLOCKING THIS ONE SOMEHOW?
NO. THIS IS NEW.
THOSE OTHER BATTLES MAY HAVE JUST BEEN SOME KIND OF TEST.
THEN IT'S TIME FOR THE REAL THING!
IT'S HOPELESS! THERE ARE TOO MANY!
WE'LL SWAMP YOU!
IT'S NEVER HOPELESS! MIA, CLEAR A PATH!
BOMP YOU!
PULL YOUR HAIR!
SKY FAN!

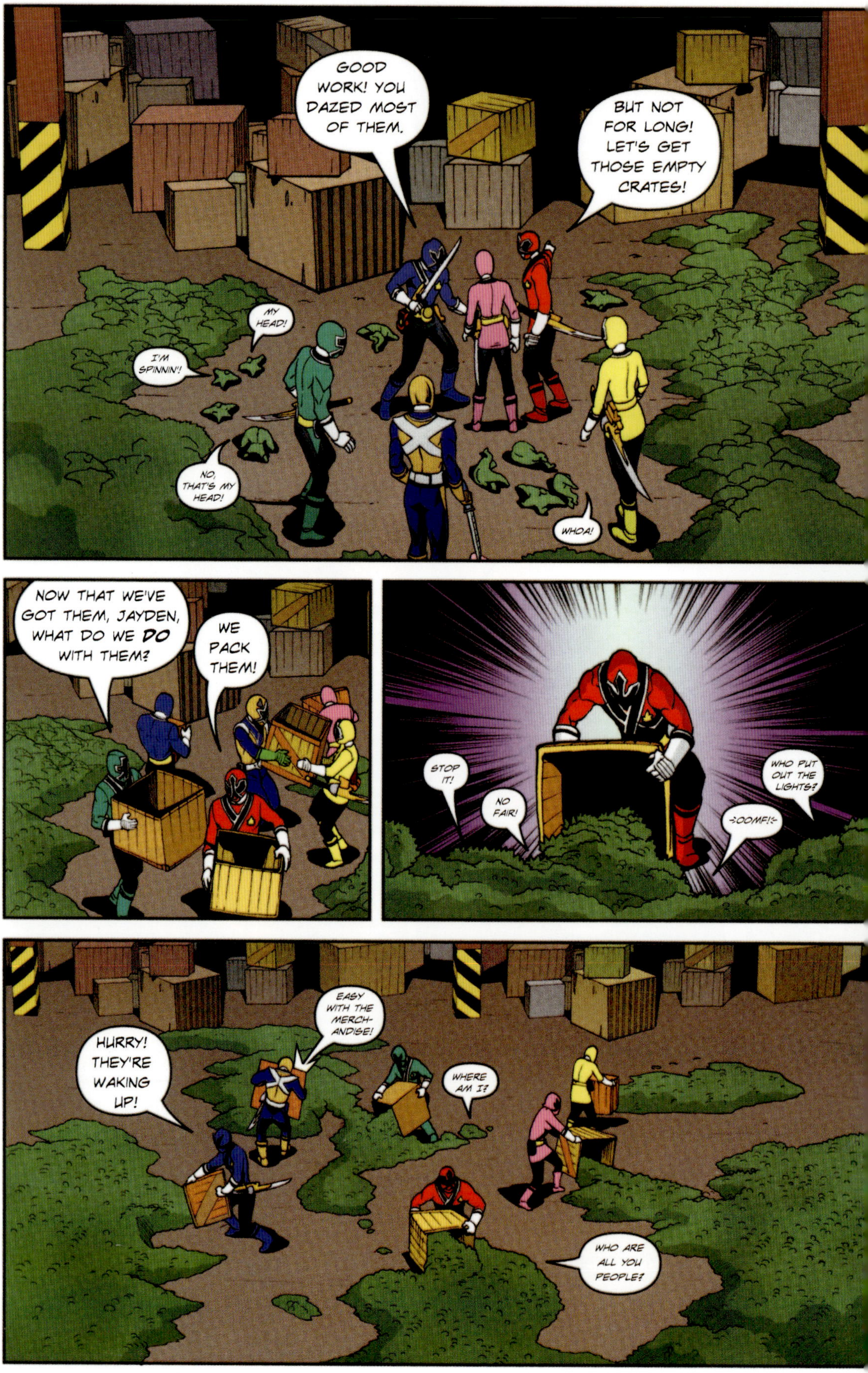

GOOD WORK! YOU DAZED MOST OF THEM.
BUT NOT FOR LONG! LET'S GET THOSE EMPTY CRATES!
MY HEAD!
I'M SPINNIN'!
NO, THAT'S MY HEAD!
WHOA!
NOW THAT WE'VE GOT THEM, JAYDEN, WHAT DO WE **DO** WITH THEM?
WE PACK THEM!
STOP IT!
NO FAIR!
WHO PUT OUT THE LIGHTS?
OOMF!
HURRY! THEY'RE WAKING UP!
EASY WITH THE MERCH-ANDISE!
WHERE AM I?
WHO ARE ALL YOU PEOPLE?

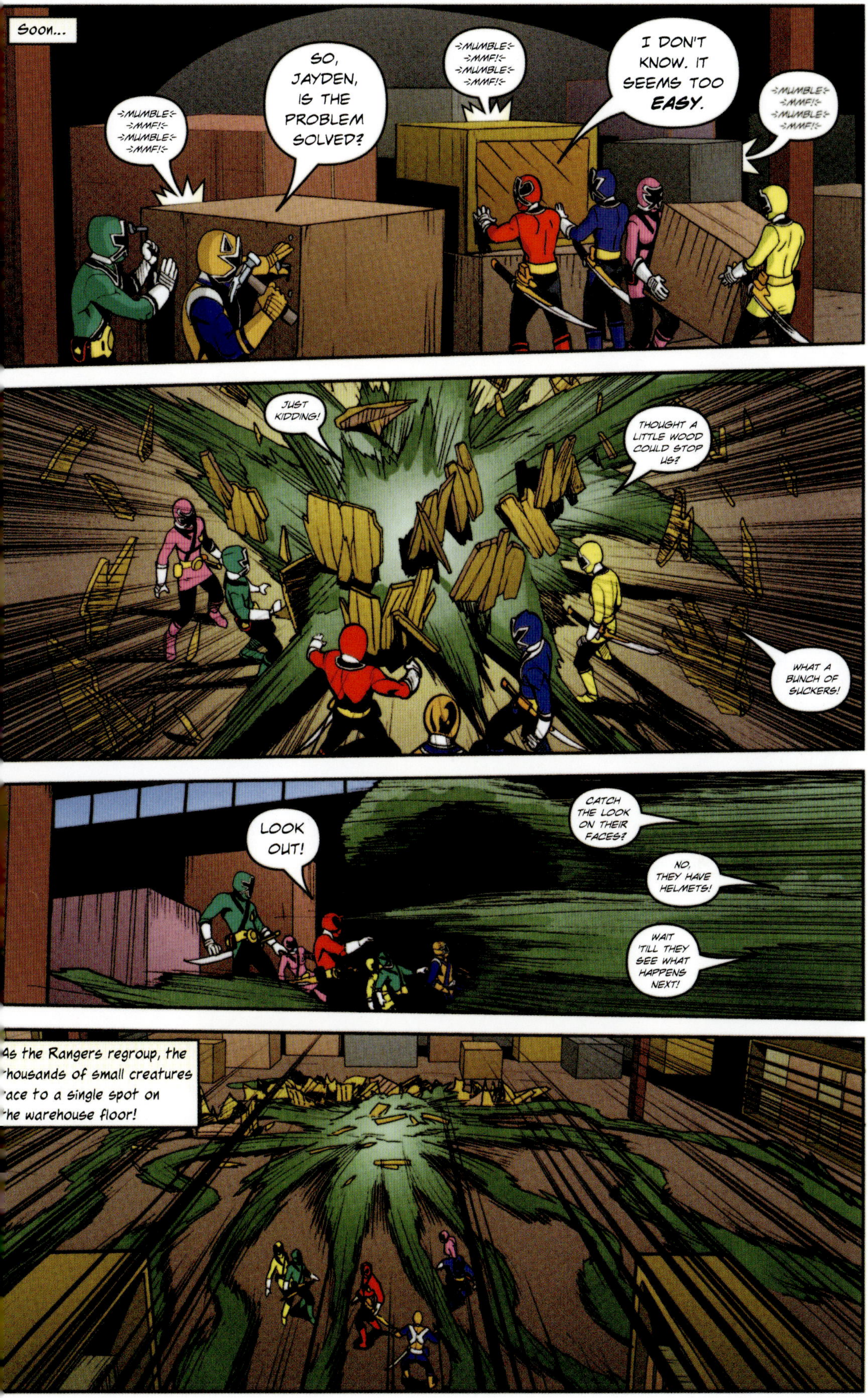
Soon...
⇢MUMBLE⇠ ⇢MMF!⇠ ⇢MUMBLE⇠ ⇢MMF!⇠
SO, JAYDEN, IS THE PROBLEM SOLVED?
⇢MUMBLE⇠ ⇢MMF!⇠ ⇢MUMBLE⇠ ⇢MMF!⇠
I DON'T KNOW. IT SEEMS TOO EASY.
⇢MUMBLE⇠ ⇢MMF!⇠ ⇢MUMBLE⇠ ⇢MMF!⇠
JUST KIDDING!
THOUGHT A LITTLE WOOD COULD STOP US?
WHAT A BUNCH OF SUCKERS!
LOOK OUT!
CATCH THE LOOK ON THEIR FACES?
NO, THEY HAVE HELMETS!
WAIT 'TILL THEY SEE WHAT HAPPENS NEXT!
As the Rangers regroup, the thousands of small creatures race to a single spot on the warehouse floor!

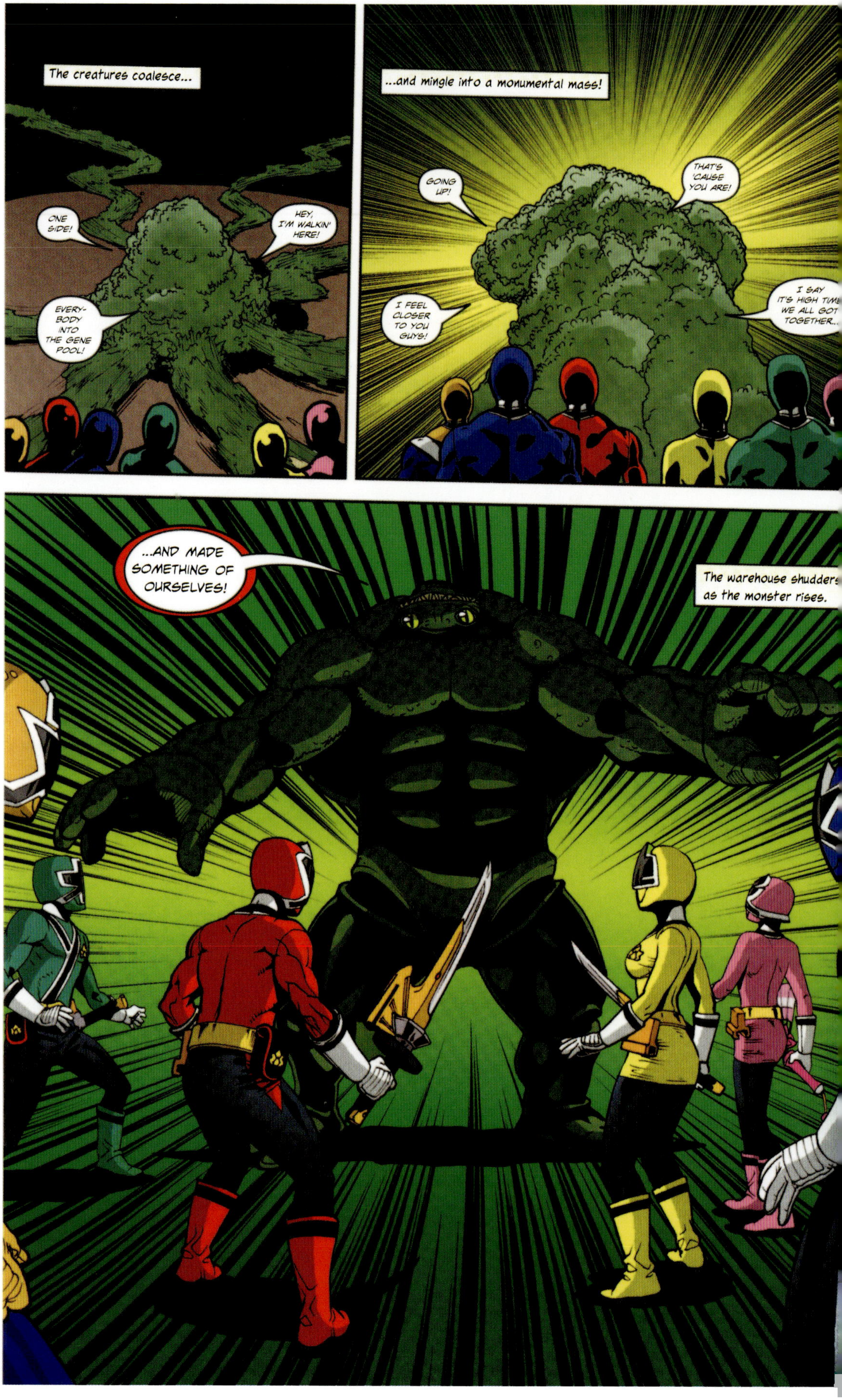
The creatures coalesce...
ONE SIDE!
HEY, I'M WALKIN' HERE!
EVERY-BODY INTO THE GENE POOL!
...and mingle into a monumental mass!
GOING UP!
THAT'S 'CAUSE YOU ARE!
I FEEL CLOSER TO YOU GUYS!
I SAY IT'S HIGH TIME WE ALL GOT TOGETHER...
...AND MADE SOMETHING OF OURSELVES!
The warehouse shudders as the monster rises.

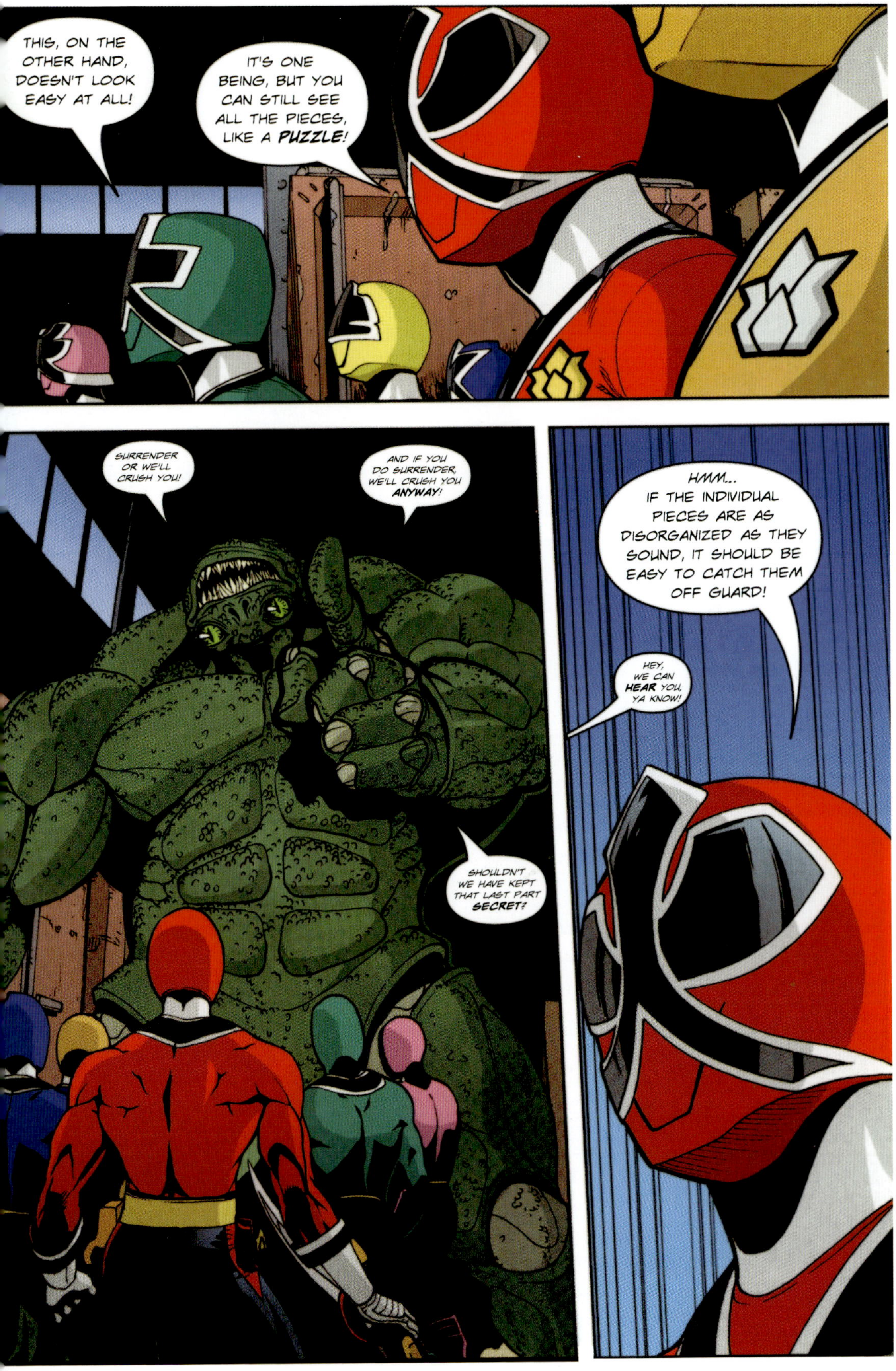
THIS, ON THE OTHER HAND, DOESN'T LOOK EASY AT ALL!
IT'S ONE BEING, BUT YOU CAN STILL SEE ALL THE PIECES, LIKE A PUZZLE!
SURRENDER OR WE'LL CRUSH YOU!
AND IF YOU DO SURRENDER, WE'LL CRUSH YOU ANYWAY!
SHOULDN'T WE HAVE KEPT THAT LAST PART SECRET?
HMM... IF THE INDIVIDUAL PIECES ARE AS DISORGANIZED AS THEY SOUND, IT SHOULD BE EASY TO CATCH THEM OFF GUARD!
HEY, WE CAN HEAR YOU, YA KNOW!

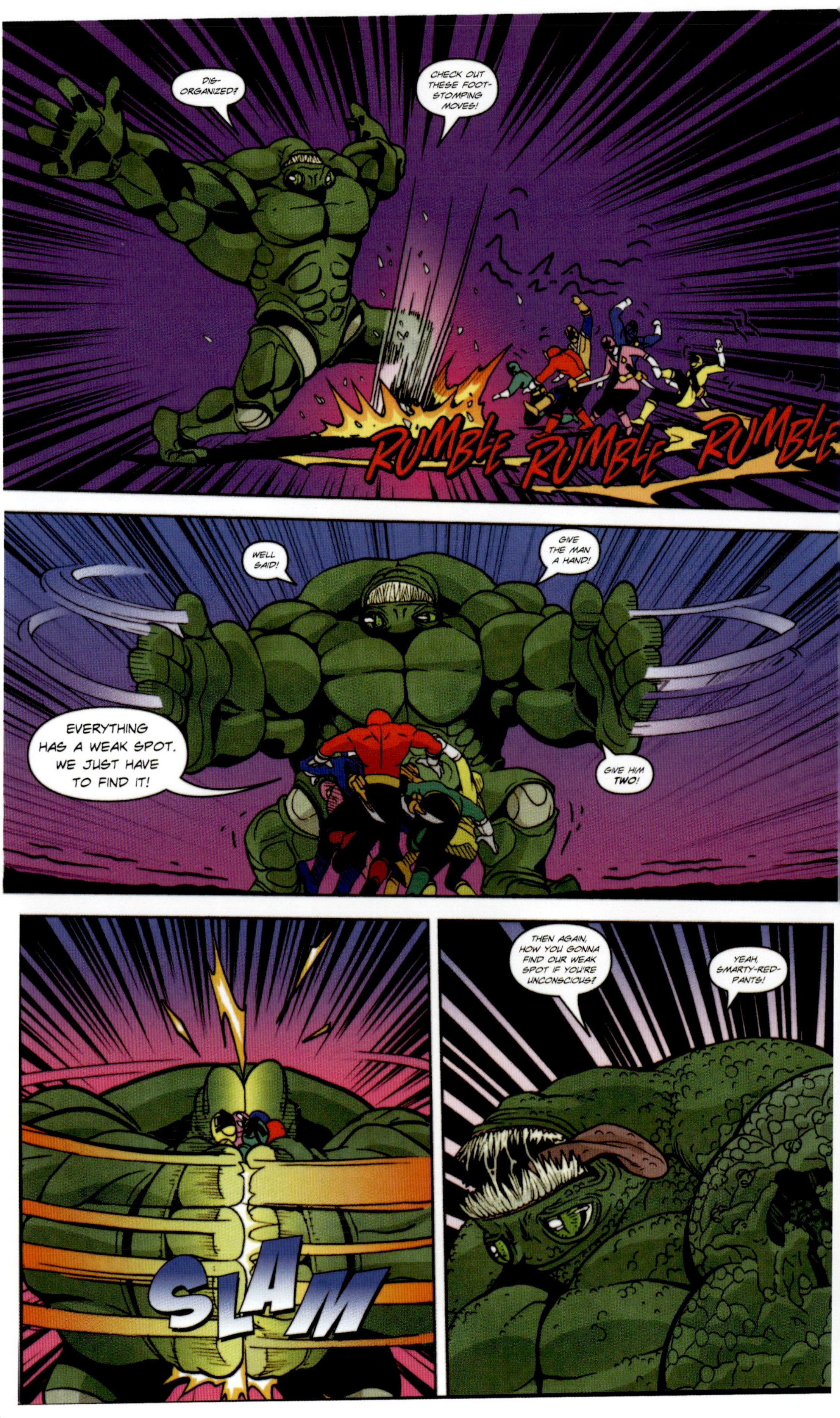
DIS-ORGANIZED?
CHECK OUT THESE FOOT-STOMPING MOVES!
RUMBLE RUMBLE RUMBLE
WELL SAID!
GIVE THE MAN A HAND!
EVERYTHING HAS A WEAK SPOT. WE JUST HAVE TO FIND IT!
GIVE HIM TWO!
SLAM
THEN AGAIN, HOW YOU GONNA FIND OUR WEAK SPOT IF YOU'RE UNCONSCIOUS?
YEAH, SMARTY-RED-PANTS!

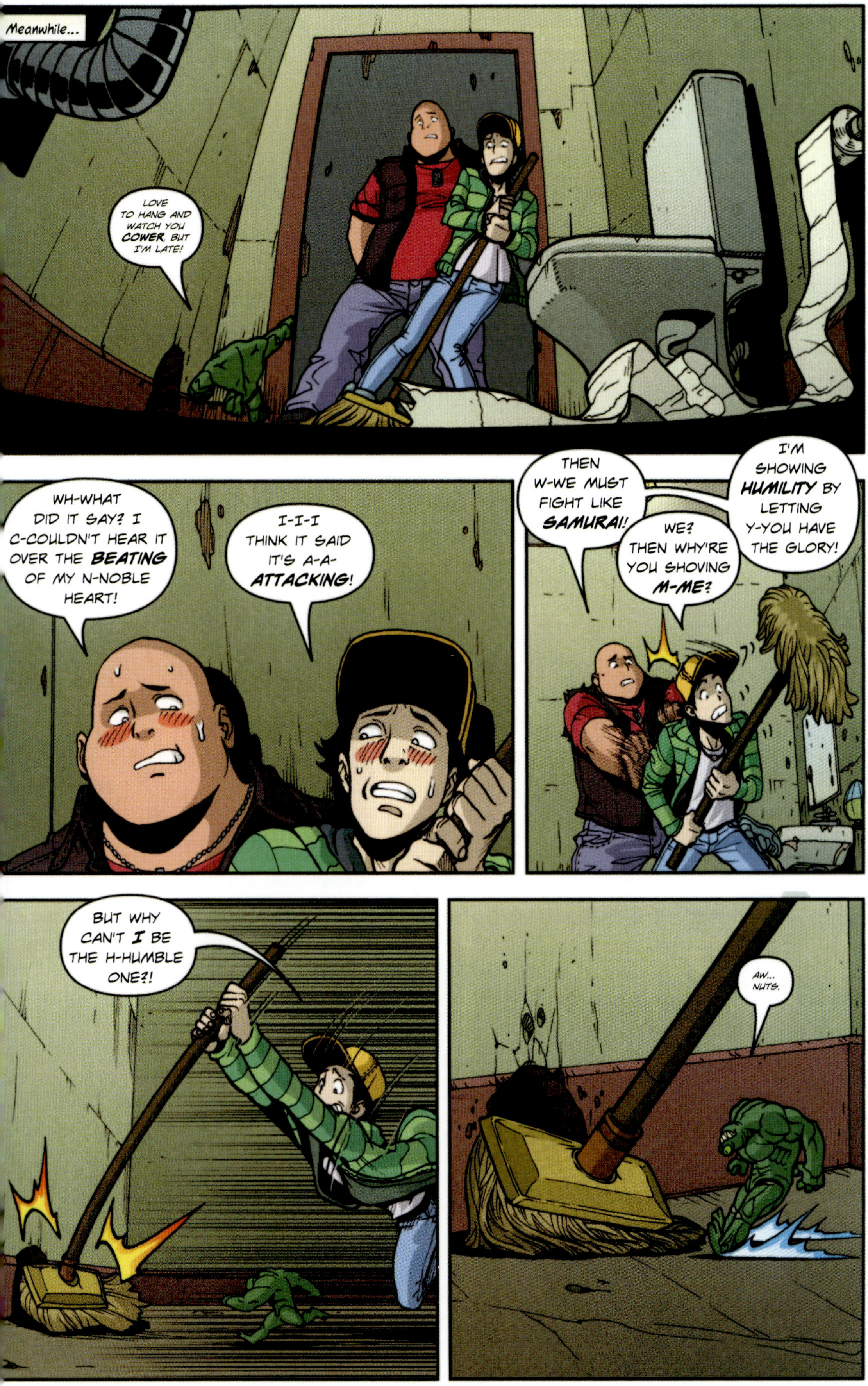
Meanwhile...
LOVE TO HANG AND WATCH YOU COWER, BUT I'M LATE!
WH-WHAT DID IT SAY? I C-COULDN'T HEAR IT OVER THE BEATING OF MY N-NOBLE HEART!
I-I-I THINK IT SAID IT'S A-A-ATTACKING!
THEN W-WE MUST FIGHT LIKE SAMURAI!
WE? THEN WHY'RE YOU SHOVING M-ME?
I'M SHOWING HUMILITY BY LETTING Y-YOU HAVE THE GLORY!
BUT WHY CAN'T I BE THE H-HUMBLE ONE?!
AW... NUTS.

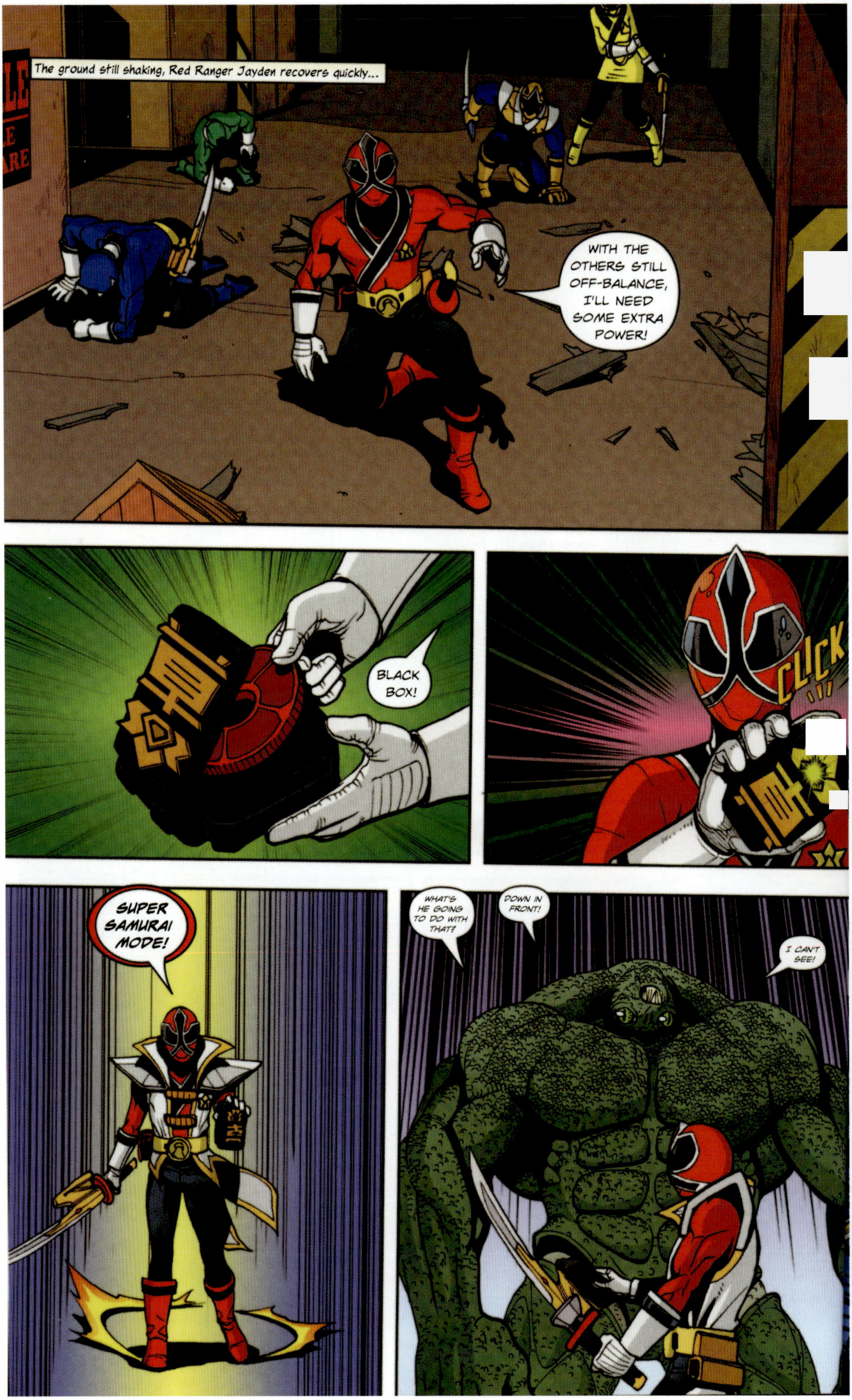
The ground still shaking, Red Ranger Jayden recovers quickly...
WITH THE OTHERS STILL OFF-BALANCE, I'LL NEED SOME EXTRA POWER!
BLACK BOX!
CLICK
SUPER SAMURAI MODE!
WHAT'S HE GOING TO DO WITH THAT?
DOWN IN FRONT!
I CAN'T SEE!

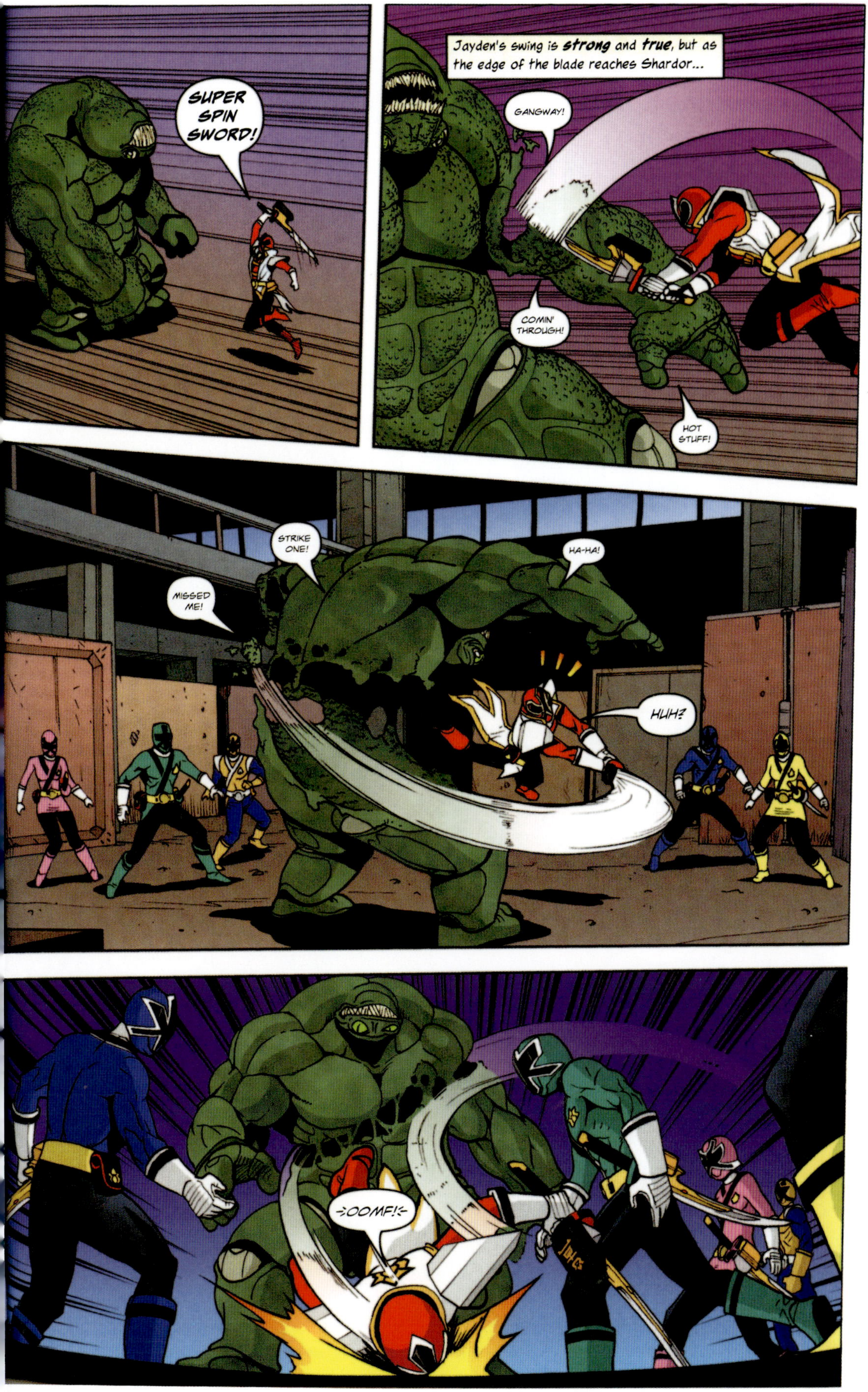
SUPER SPIN SWORD!
Jayden's swing is strong and true, but as the edge of the blade reaches Shardor...
GANGWAY!
COMIN' THROUGH!
HOT STUFF!
STRIKE ONE!
HA-HA!
MISSED ME!
HUH?
OOMF!

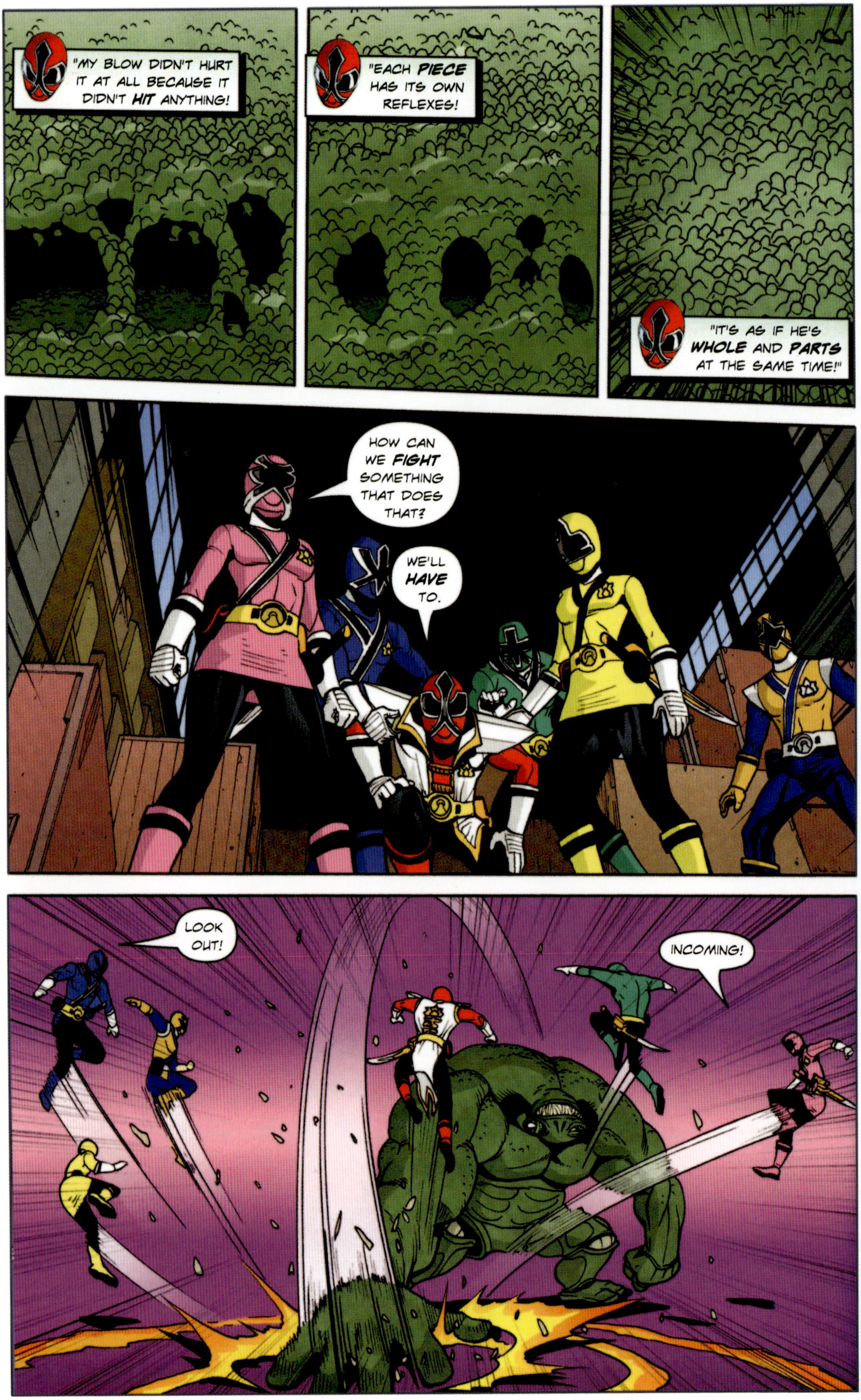
"MY BLOW DIDN'T HURT IT AT ALL BECAUSE IT DIDN'T HIT ANYTHING!
"EACH PIECE HAS ITS OWN REFLEXES!
"IT'S AS IF HE'S WHOLE AND PARTS AT THE SAME TIME!"
HOW CAN WE FIGHT SOMETHING THAT DOES THAT?
WE'LL HAVE TO.
LOOK OUT!
INCOMING!

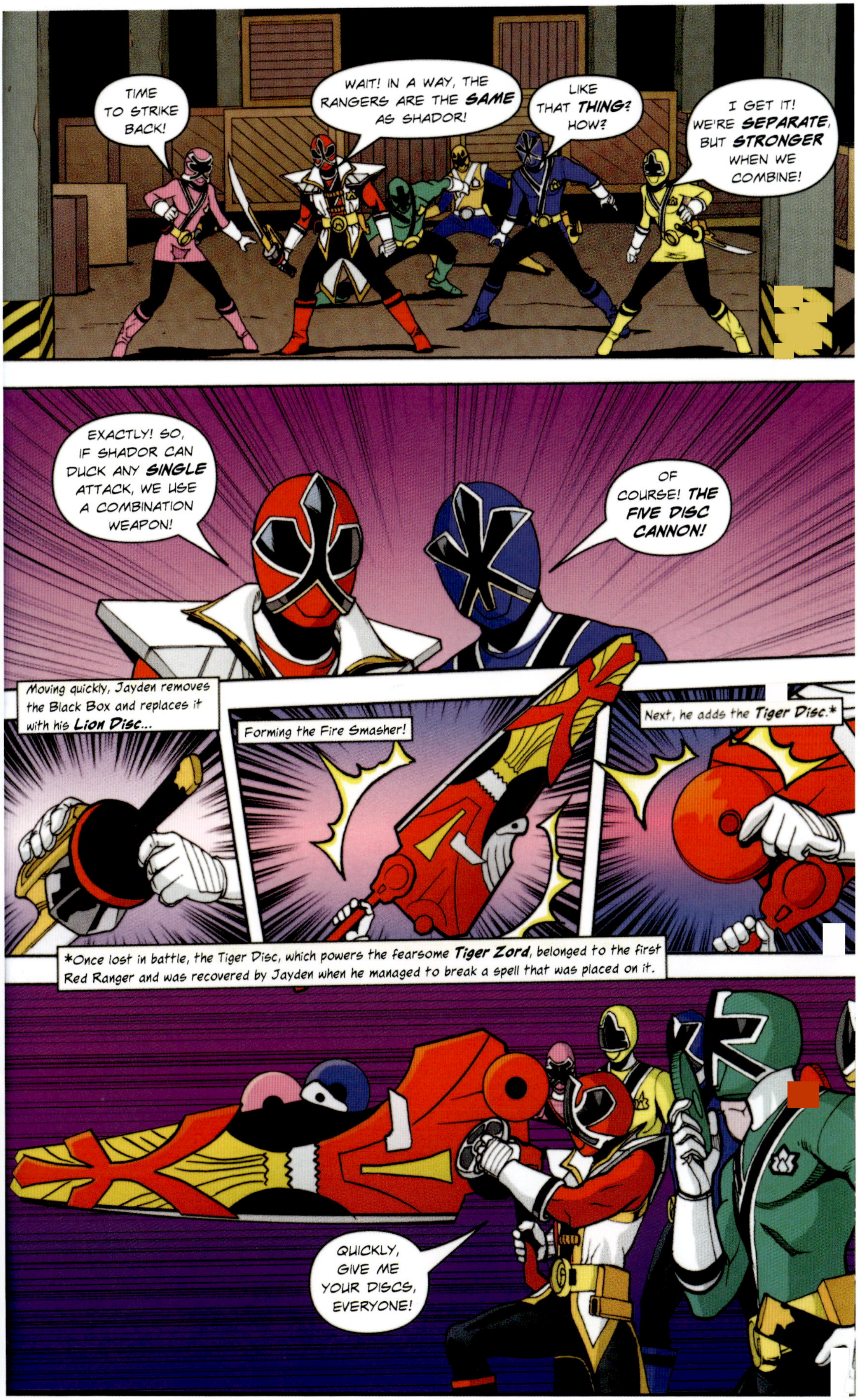
TIME TO STRIKE BACK!
WAIT! IN A WAY, THE RANGERS ARE THE SAME AS SHADOR!
LIKE THAT THING? HOW?
I GET IT! WE'RE SEPARATE, BUT STRONGER WHEN WE COMBINE!
EXACTLY! SO, IF SHADOR CAN DUCK ANY SINGLE ATTACK, WE USE A COMBINATION WEAPON!
OF COURSE! THE FIVE DISC CANNON!
Moving quickly, Jayden removes the Black Box and replaces it with his Lion Disc...
Forming the Fire Smasher!
Next, he adds the Tiger Disc.*
*Once lost in battle, the Tiger Disc, which powers the fearsome Tiger Zord, belonged to the first Red Ranger and was recovered by Jayden when he managed to break a spell that was placed on it.
QUICKLY, GIVE ME YOUR DISCS, EVERYONE!

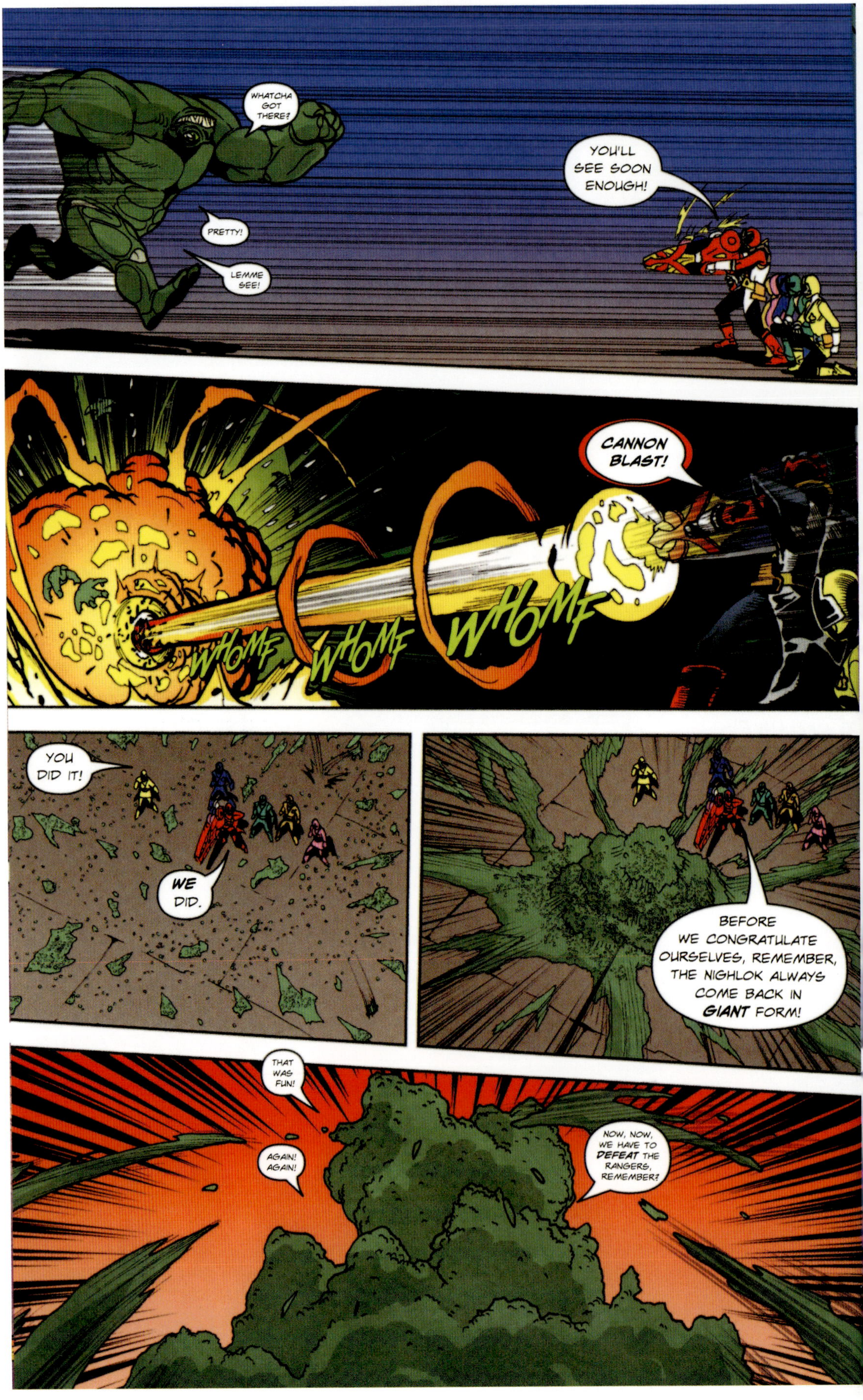
WHATCHA GOT THERE?
PRETTY!
LEMME SEE!
YOU'LL SEE SOON ENOUGH!
CANNON BLAST!
WHOMF
WHOMF
WHOMF
YOU DID IT!
WE DID.
BEFORE WE CONGRATULATE OURSELVES, REMEMBER, THE NIGHLOK ALWAYS COME BACK IN GIANT FORM!
THAT WAS FUN!
AGAIN! AGAIN!
NOW, NOW, WE HAVE TO DEFEAT THE RANGERS, REMEMBER?

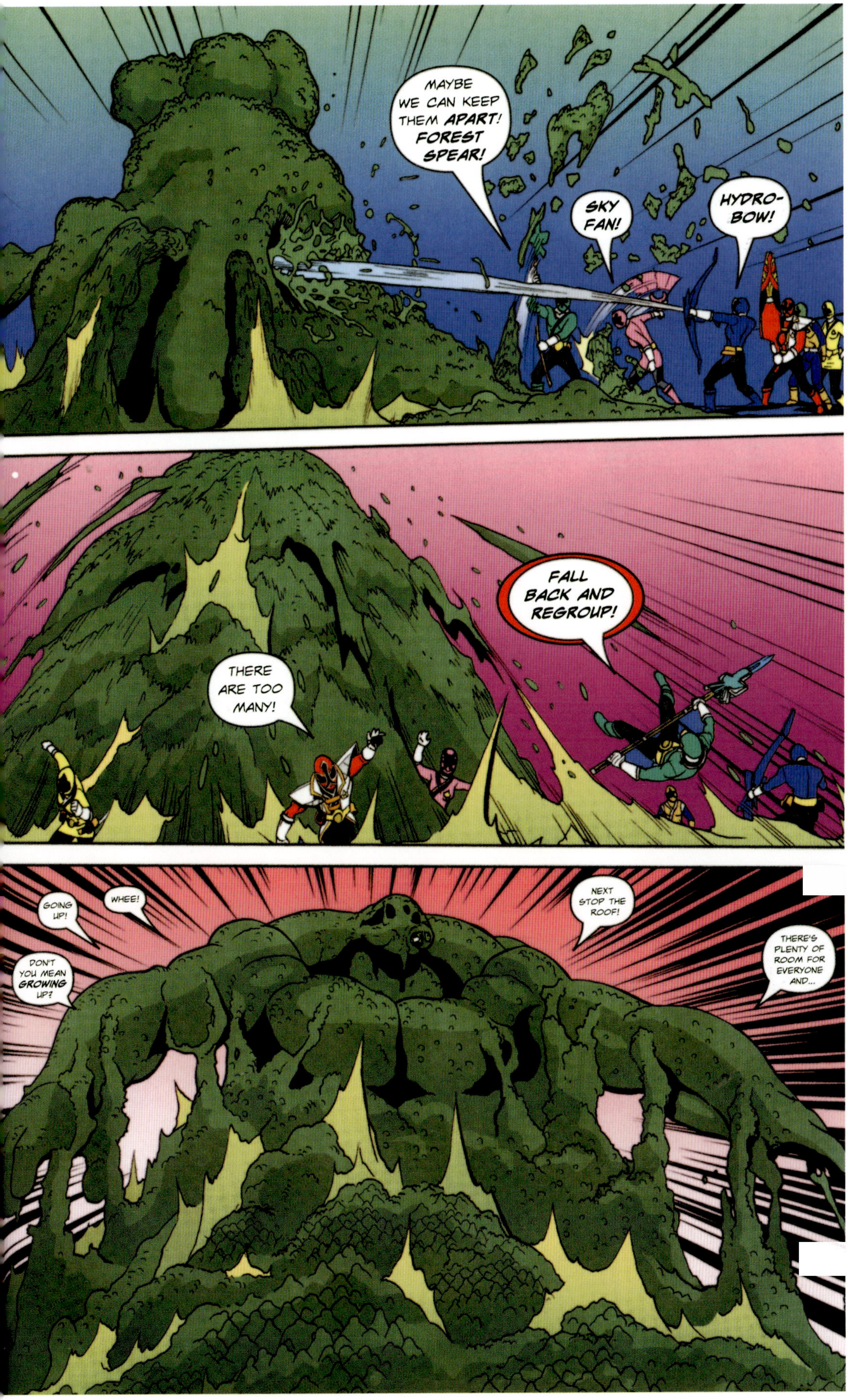
MAYBE WE CAN KEEP THEM APART! FOREST SPEAR!
SKY FAN!
HYDRO-BOW!
FALL BACK AND REGROUP!
THERE ARE TOO MANY!
GOING UP!
WHEE!
DON'T YOU MEAN GROWING UP?
NEXT STOP THE ROOF!
THERE'S PLENTY OF ROOM FOR EVERYONE AND...

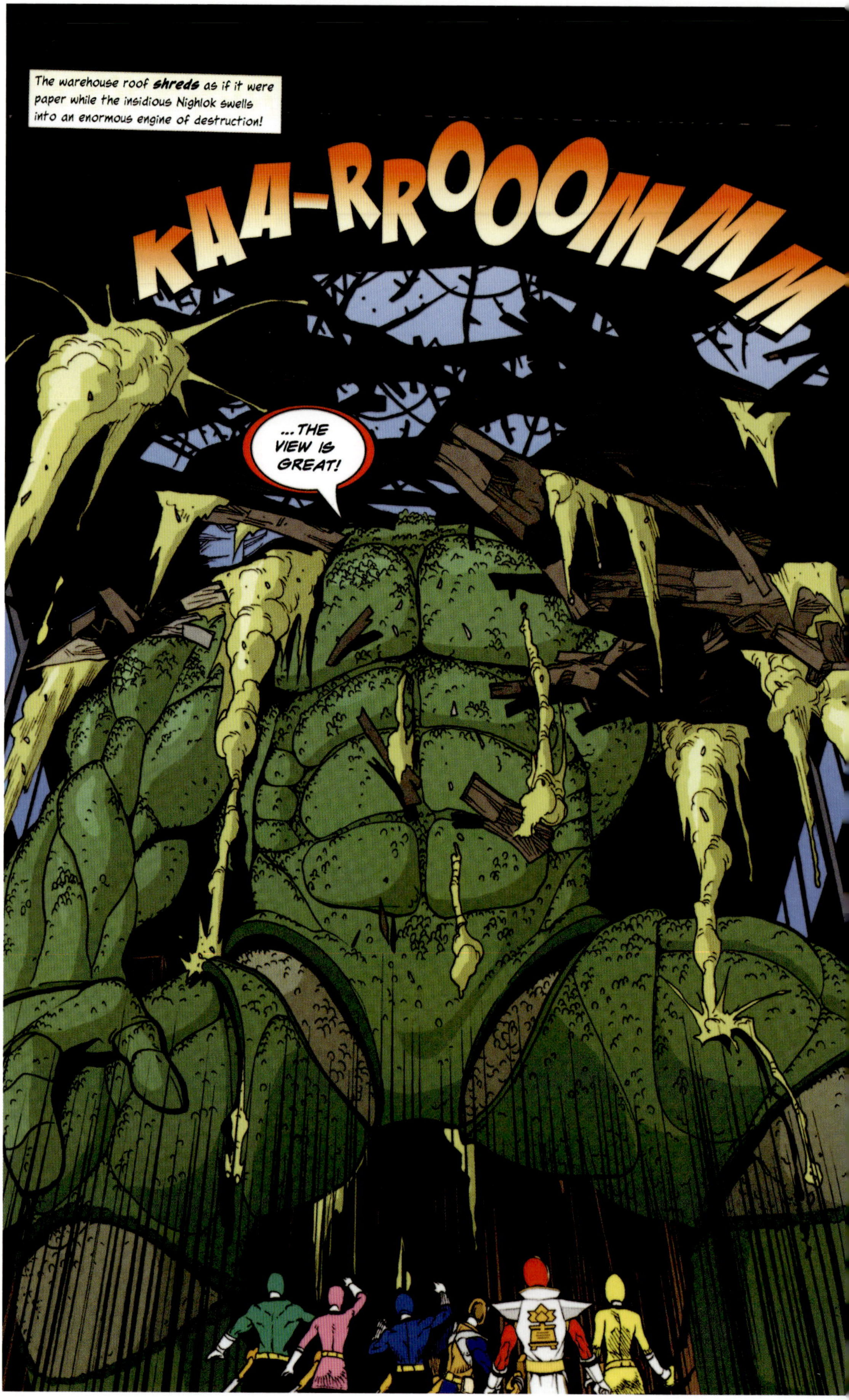

The warehouse roof **shreds** as if it were paper while the insidious Nighlok swells into an enormous engine of destruction!
KAA-RROOOOMMMM
...THE VIEW IS GREAT!

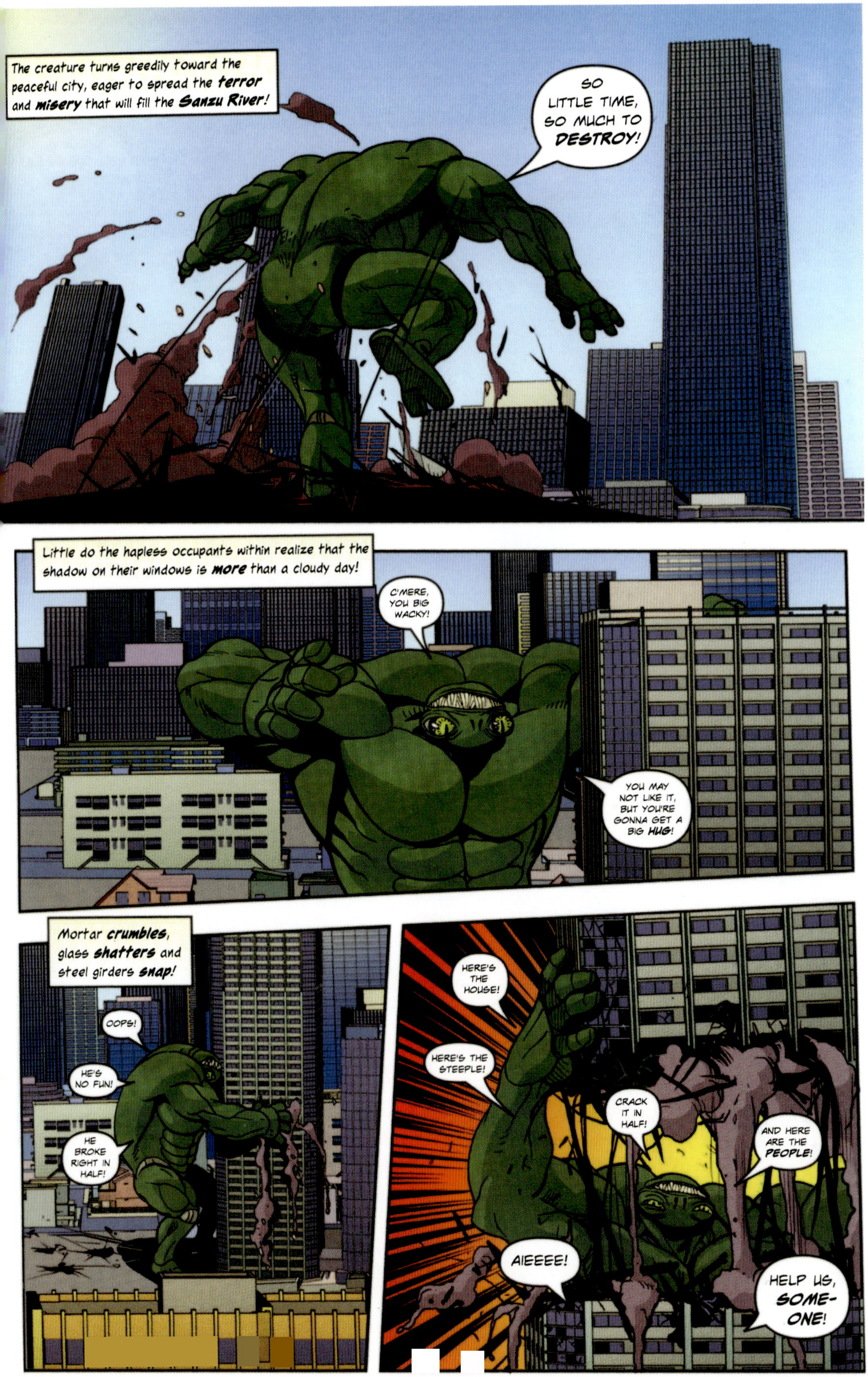
The creature turns greedily toward the peaceful city, eager to spread the *terror* and *misery* that will fill the *Sanzu River*!
SO LITTLE TIME, SO MUCH TO *DESTROY*!
Little do the hapless occupants within realize that the shadow on their windows is *more* than a cloudy day!
C'MERE, YOU BIG WACKY!
YOU MAY NOT LIKE IT, BUT YOU'RE GONNA GET A BIG *HUG*!
Mortar *crumbles*, glass *shatters* and steel girders *snap*!
OOPS!
HE'S NO FUN!
HE BROKE RIGHT IN HALF!
HERE'S THE HOUSE!
HERE'S THE STEEPLE!
CRACK IT IN HALF!
AND HERE ARE THE *PEOPLE*!
AIEEEE!
HELP US, *SOME-ONE*!

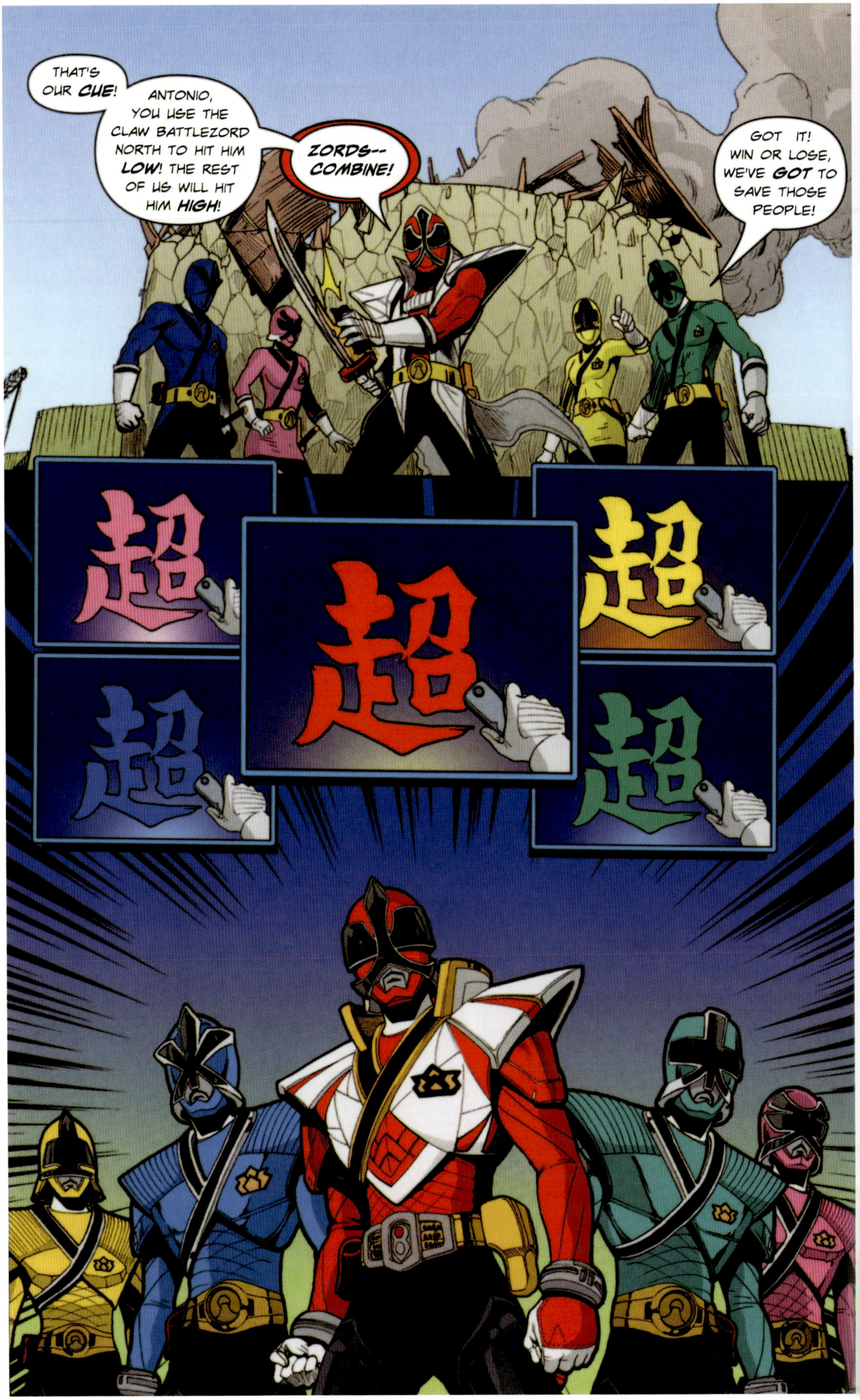
THAT'S OUR CUE!
ANTONIO, YOU USE THE CLAW BATTLEZORD NORTH TO HIT HIM LOW! THE REST OF US WILL HIT HIM HIGH!
ZORDS-- COMBINE!
GOT IT! WIN OR LOSE, WE'VE GOT TO SAVE THOSE PEOPLE!
超
超
超
超
超

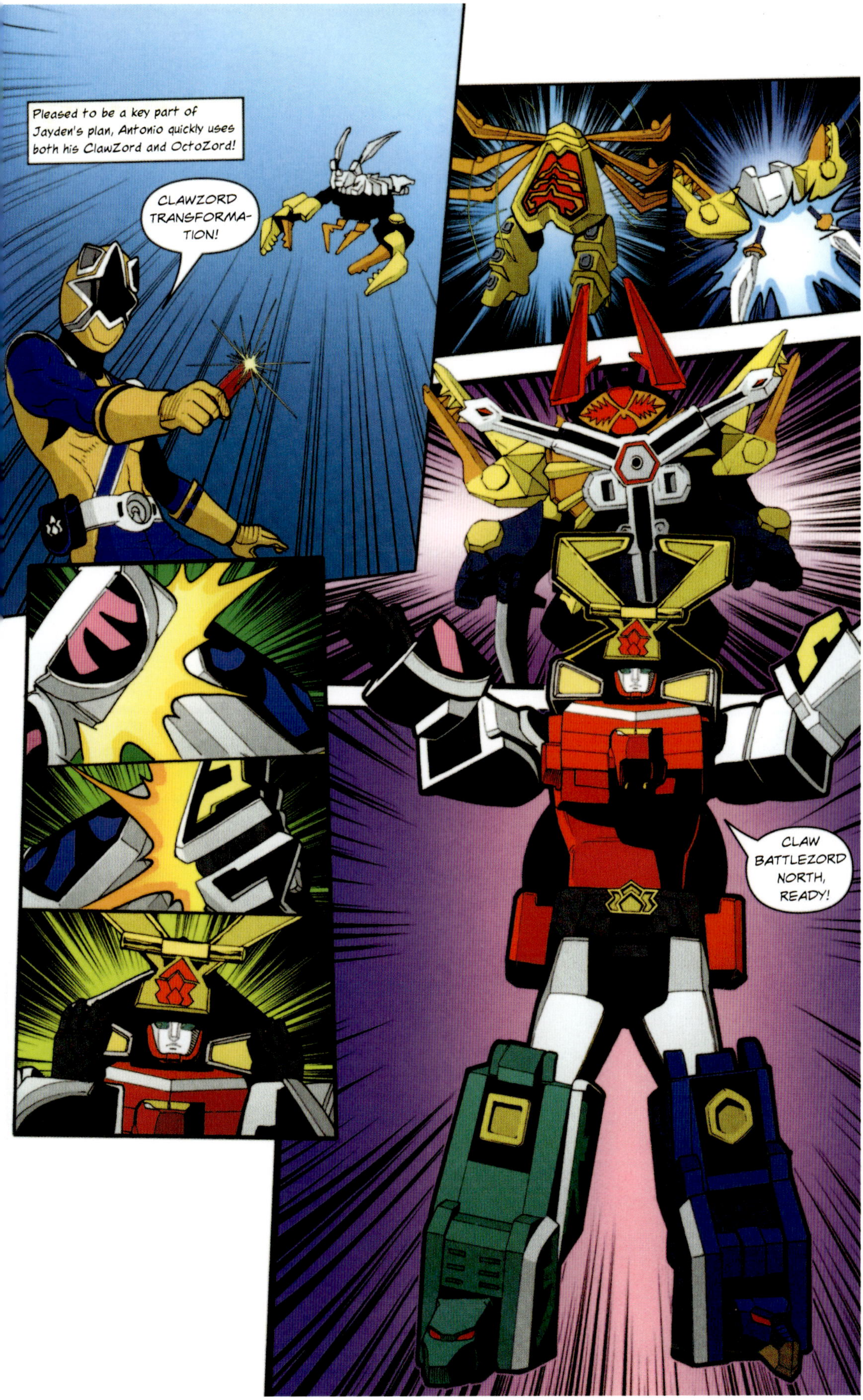

Pleased to be a key part of Jayden's plan, Antonio quickly uses both his ClawZord and OctoZord!
CLAWZORD TRANSFORMA-TION!
CLAW BATTLEZORD NORTH, READY!

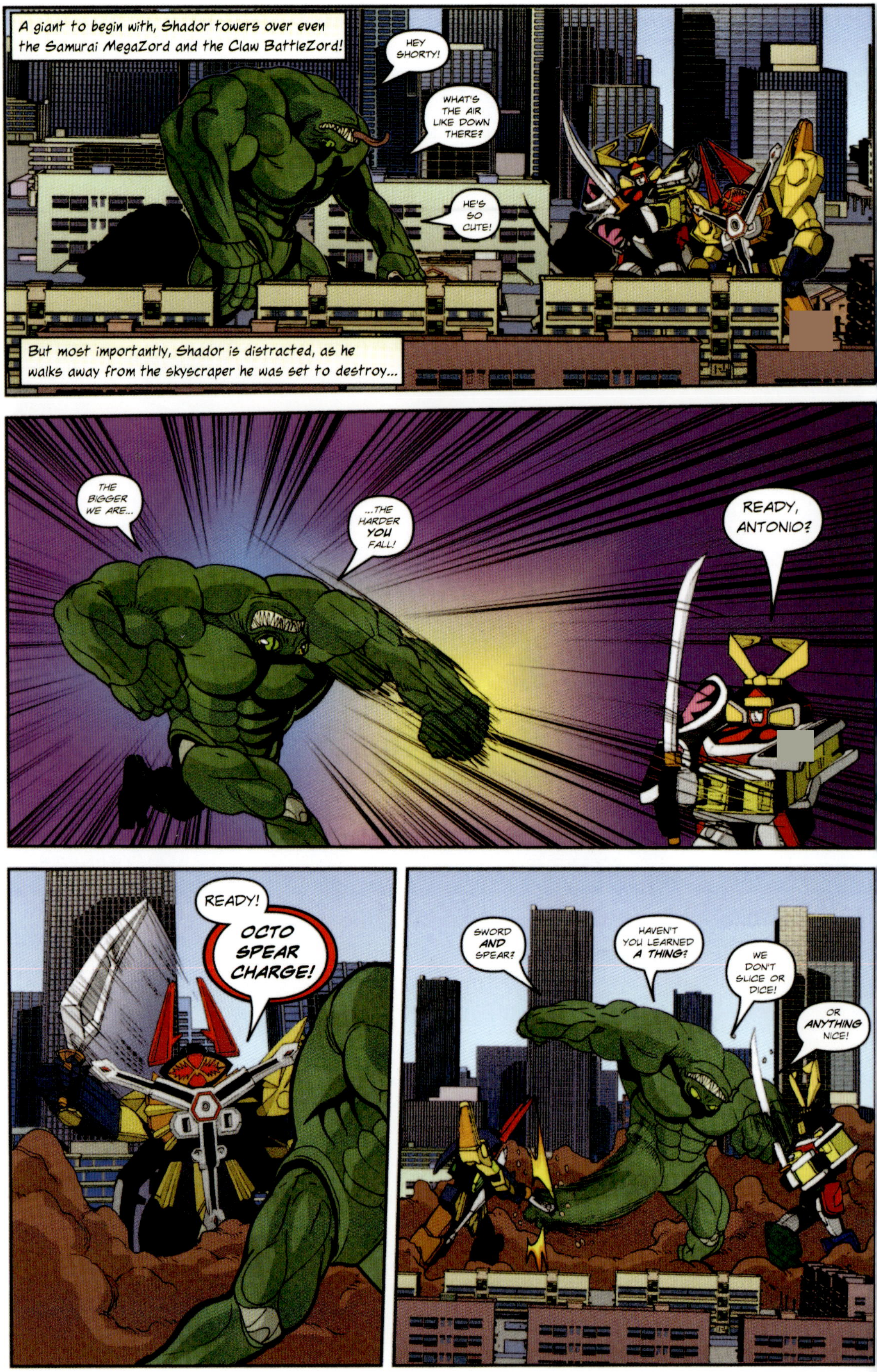
A giant to begin with, Shador towers over even the Samurai MegaZord and the Claw BattleZord!
HEY SHORTY!
WHAT'S THE AIR LIKE DOWN THERE?
HE'S SO CUTE!
But most importantly, Shador is distracted, as he walks away from the skyscraper he was set to destroy...
THE BIGGER WE ARE...
...THE HARDER YOU FALL!
READY, ANTONIO?
READY!
OCTO SPEAR CHARGE!
SWORD AND SPEAR?
HAVEN'T YOU LEARNED A THING?
WE DON'T SLICE OR DICE!
OR ANYTHING NICE!

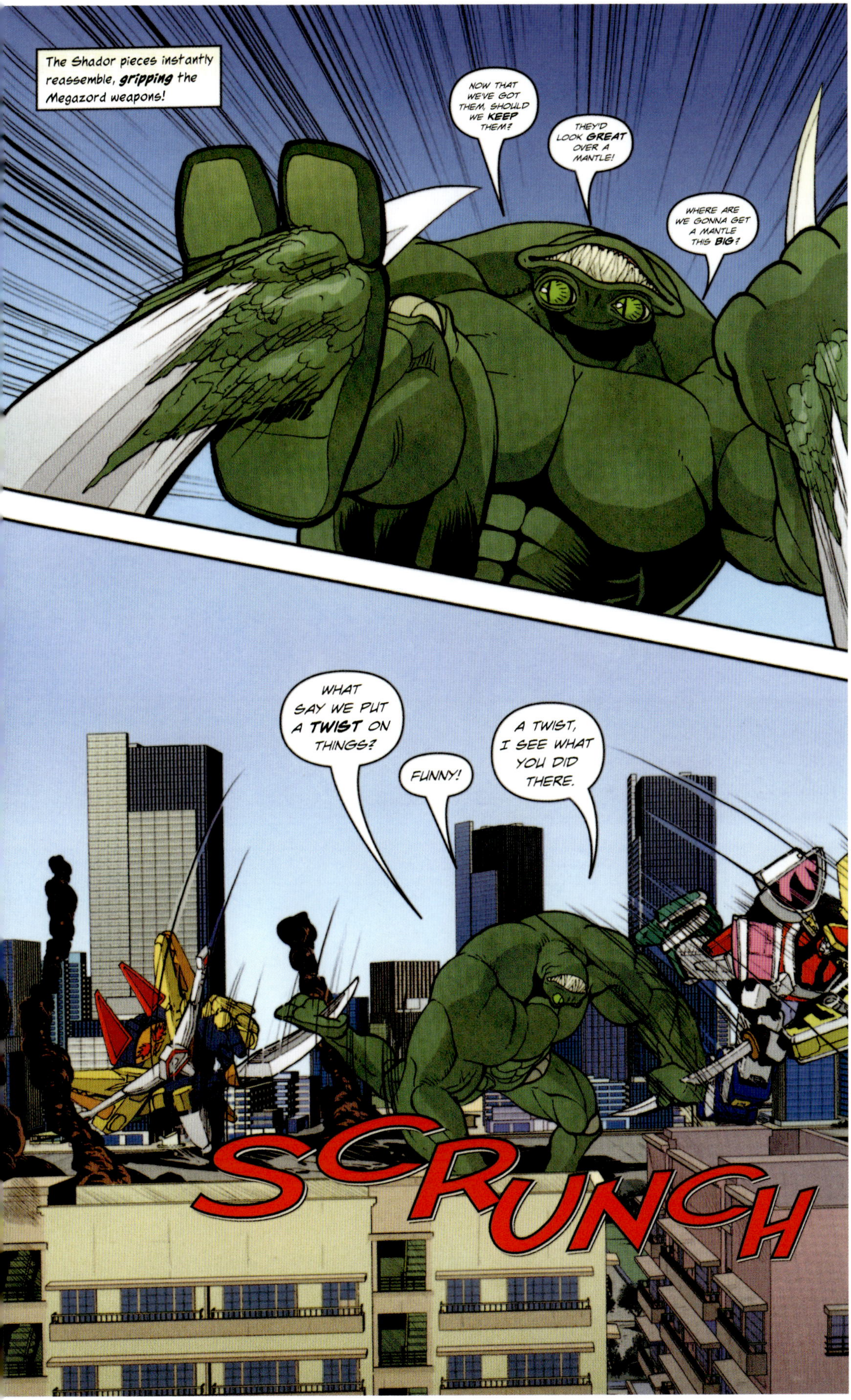
The Shador pieces instantly reassemble, **gripping** the Megazord weapons!
NOW THAT WE'VE GOT THEM, SHOULD WE **KEEP** THEM?
THEY'D LOOK **GREAT** OVER A MANTLE!
WHERE ARE WE GONNA GET A MANTLE THIS **BIG**?
WHAT SAY WE PUT A **TWIST** ON THINGS?
FUNNY!
A TWIST, I SEE WHAT YOU DID THERE.
SCRUNCH

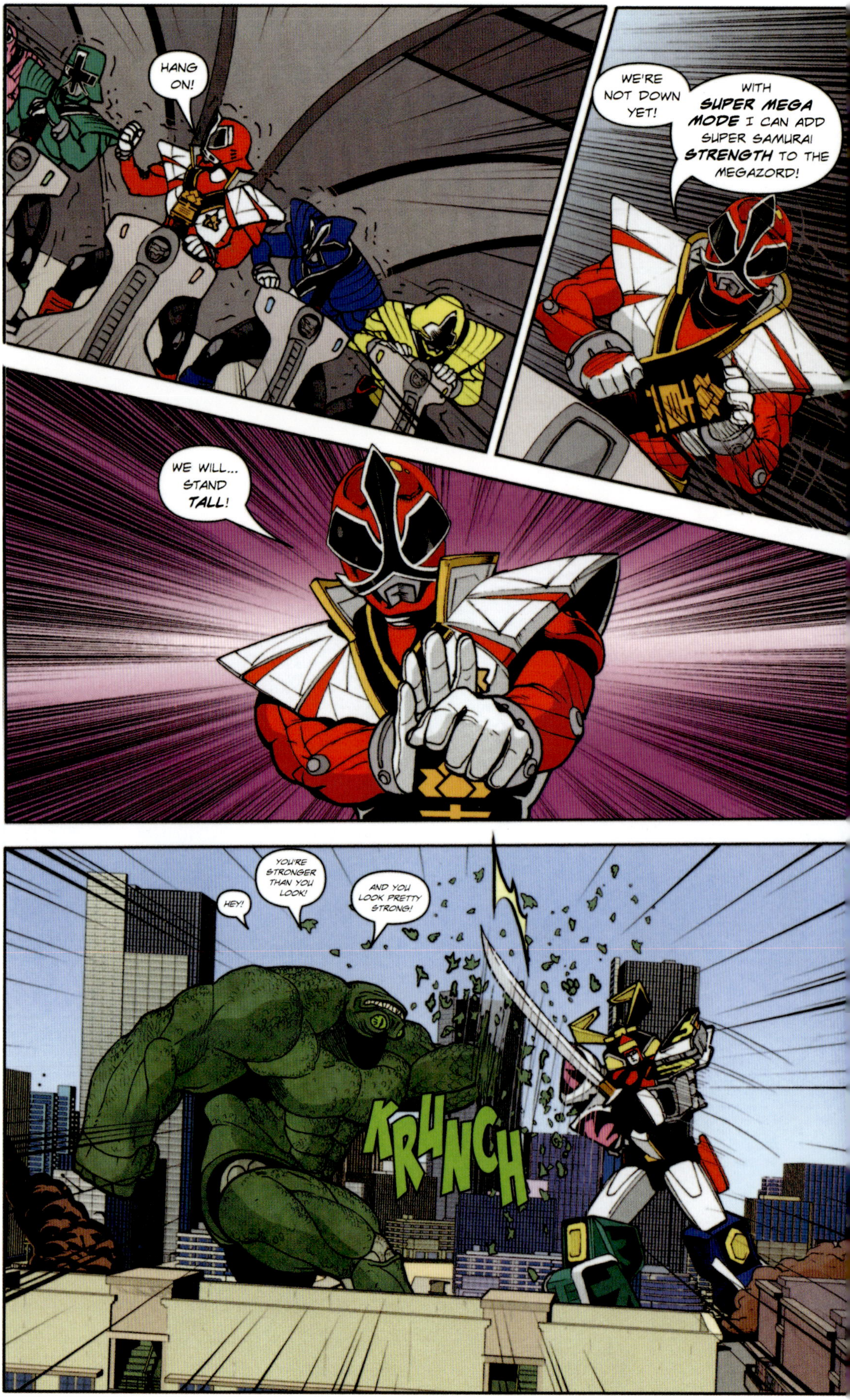
HANG ON!
WE'RE NOT DOWN YET!
WITH SUPER MEGA MODE I CAN ADD SUPER SAMURAI STRENGTH TO THE MEGAZORD!
WE WILL... STAND TALL!
HEY!
YOU'RE STRONGER THAN YOU LOOK!
AND YOU LOOK PRETTY STRONG!
KRUNCH

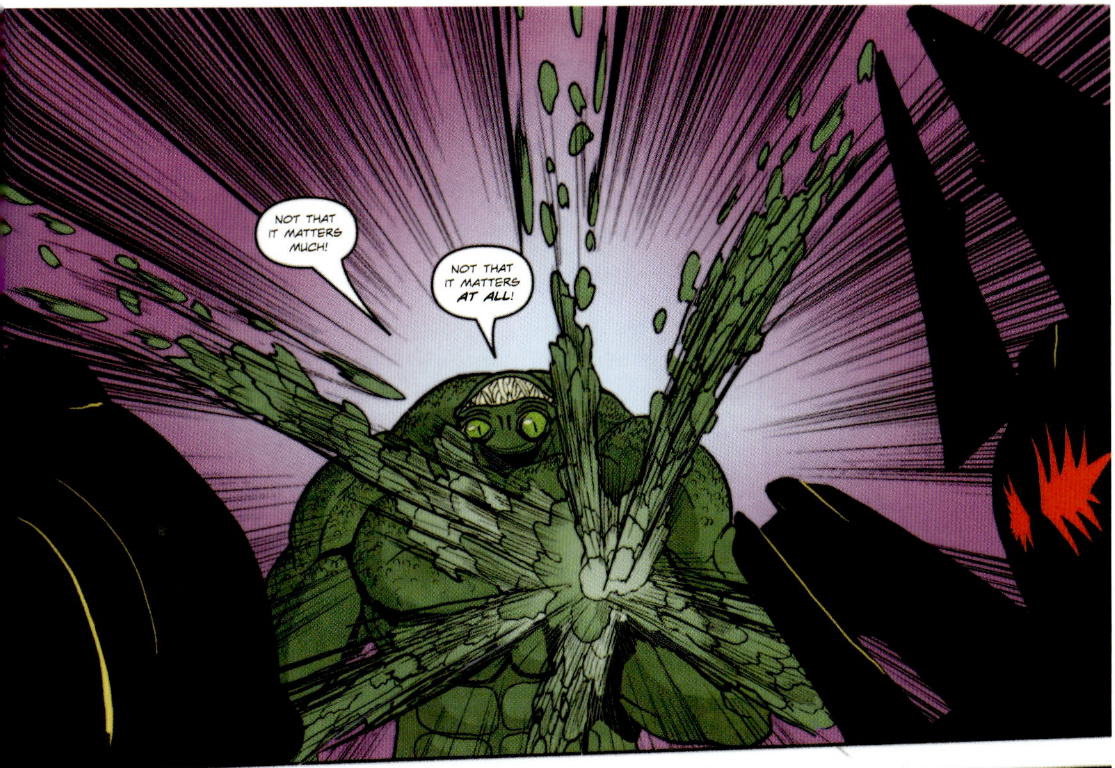
NOT THAT IT MATTERS MUCH!
NOT THAT IT MATTERS AT ALL!

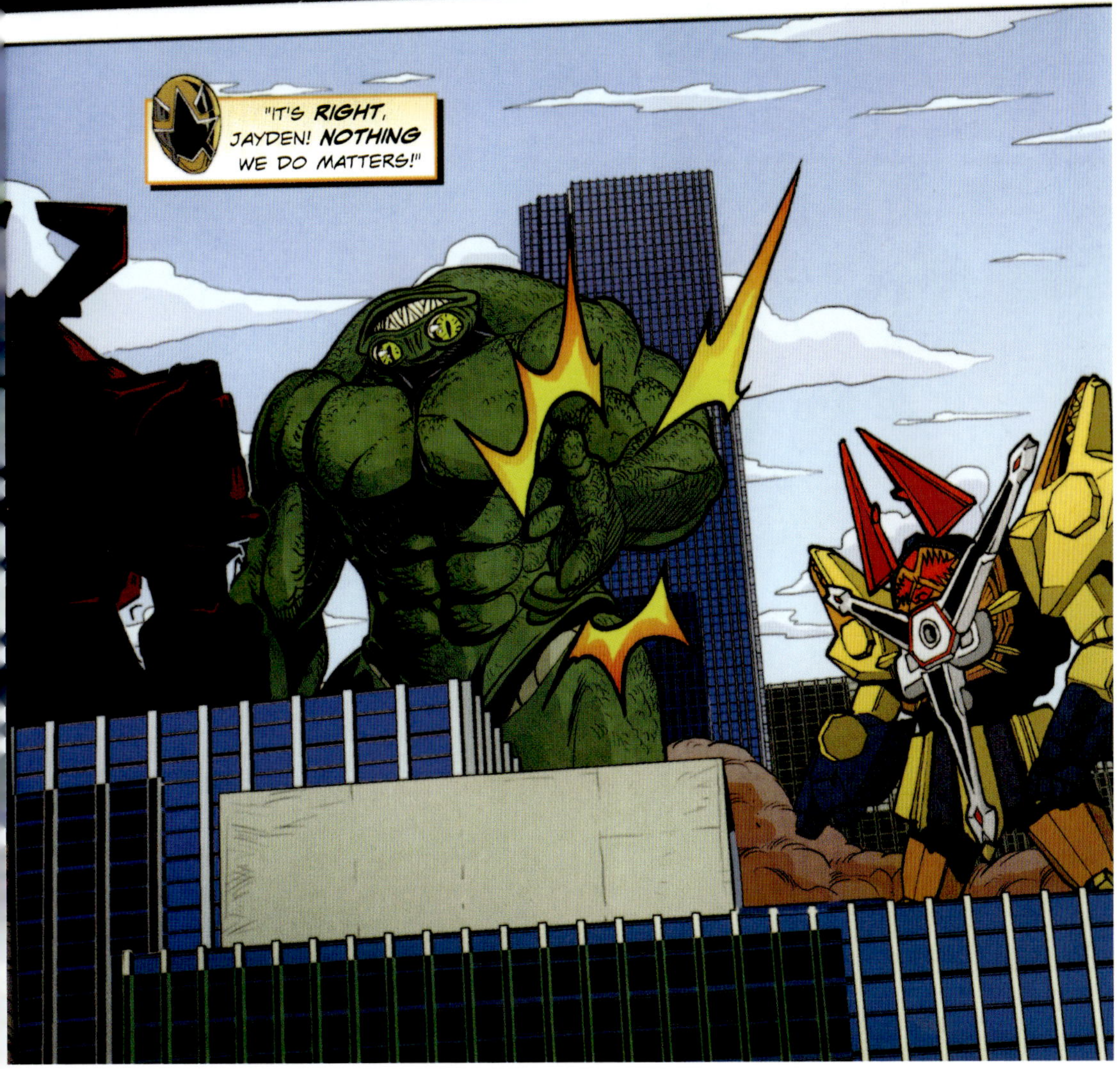
"IT'S RIGHT, JAYDEN! NOTHING WE DO MATTERS!"

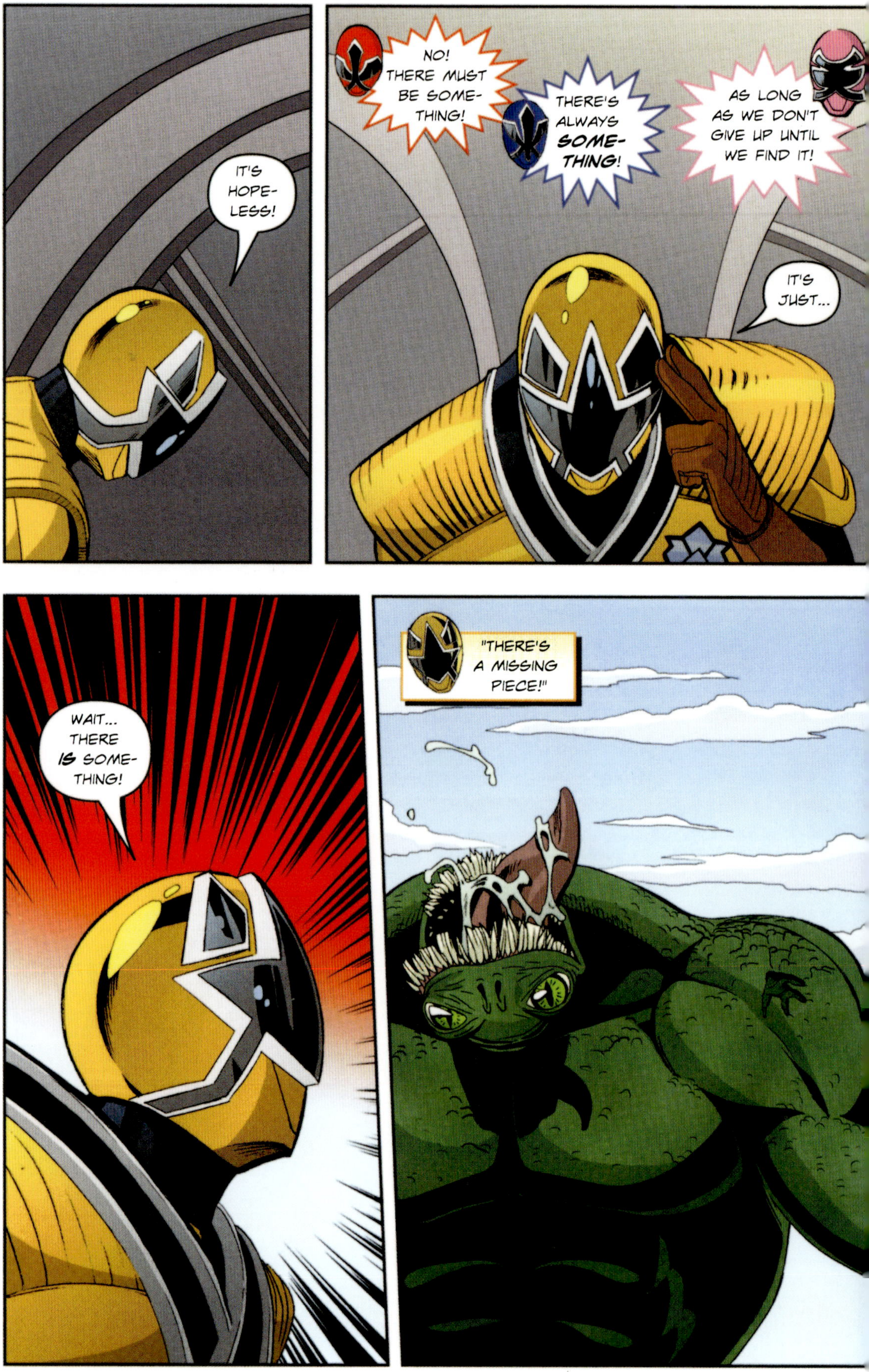
IT'S HOPE-LESS!
NO! THERE MUST BE SOME-THING!
THERE'S ALWAYS SOME-THING!
AS LONG AS WE DON'T GIVE UP UNTIL WE FIND IT!
IT'S JUST...
WAIT... THERE IS SOME-THING!
"THERE'S A MISSING PIECE!"

"AND IT'S GIVING ME AN *IDEA!*"

DON'T HOLD BACK, ANTONIO! WHAT'S THE IDEA?

WE'LL NEED MORE ENERGY TO GET IN CLOSE!

JAYDEN, USE THE BLACK BOX TO COMBINE US INTO THE *CLAW ARMOR MEGAZORD!*

WILL DO!

SUPER SAMURAI COMBINATION!

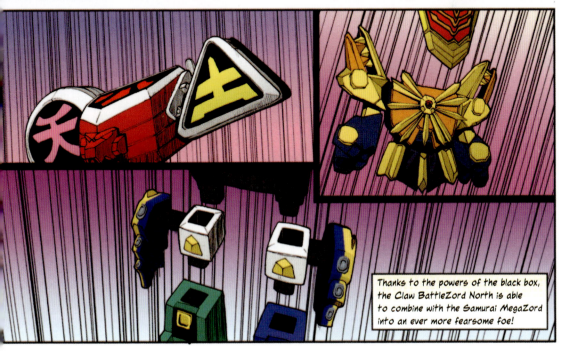

Thanks to the powers of the black box, the Claw BattleZord North is able to combine with the Samurai MegaZord into an ever more fearsome foe!

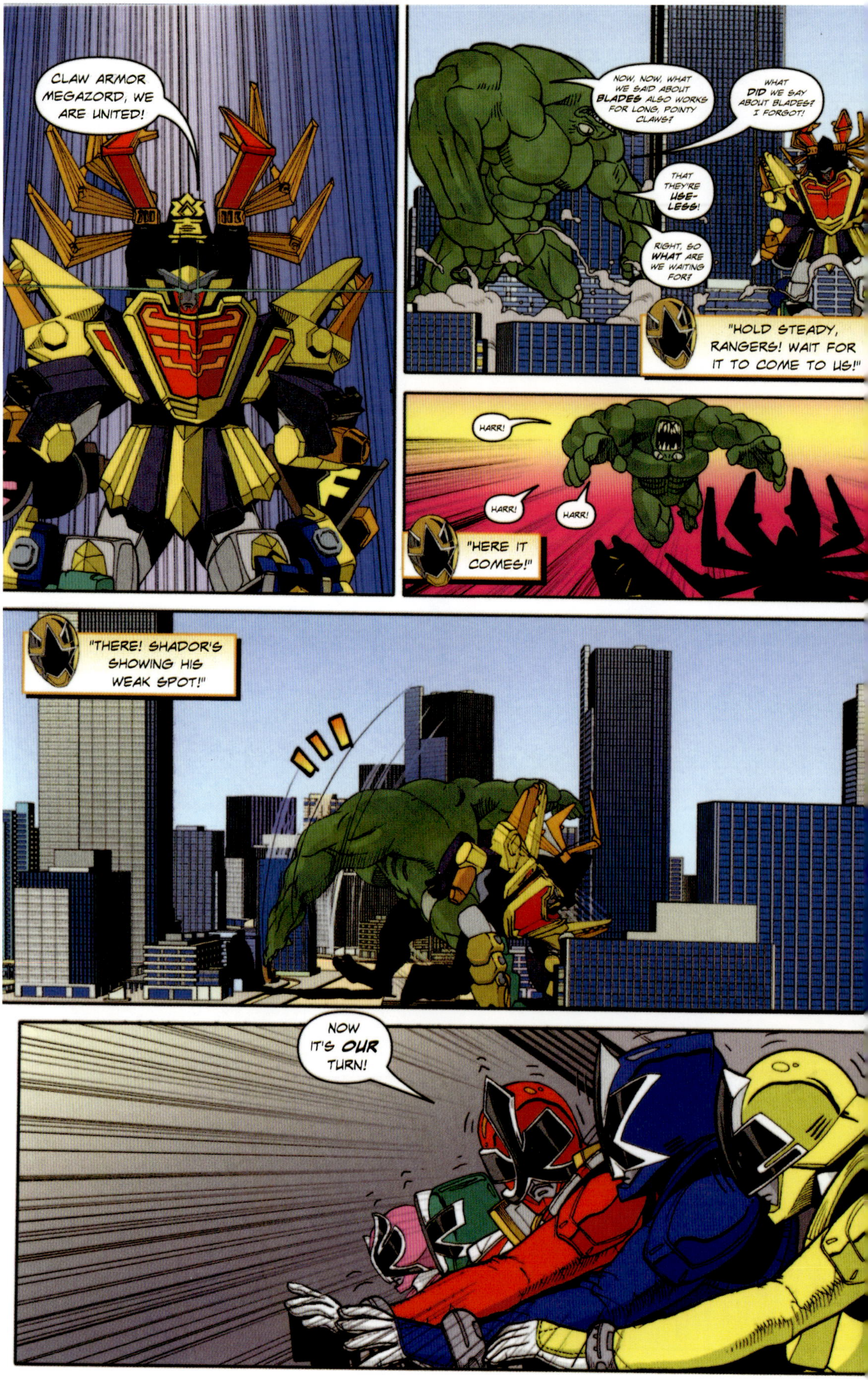

CLAW ARMOR MEGAZORD, WE ARE UNITED!
NOW, NOW, WHAT WE SAID ABOUT BLADES ALSO WORKS FOR LONG, POINTY CLAWS?
WHAT DID WE SAY ABOUT BLADES? I FORGOT!
THAT THEY'RE USE-LESS!
RIGHT, SO WHAT ARE WE WAITING FOR?
"HOLD STEADY, RANGERS! WAIT FOR IT TO COME TO US!"
HARR!
HARR!
HARR!
"HERE IT COMES!"
"THERE! SHADOR'S SHOWING HIS WEAK SPOT!"
NOW IT'S OUR TURN!

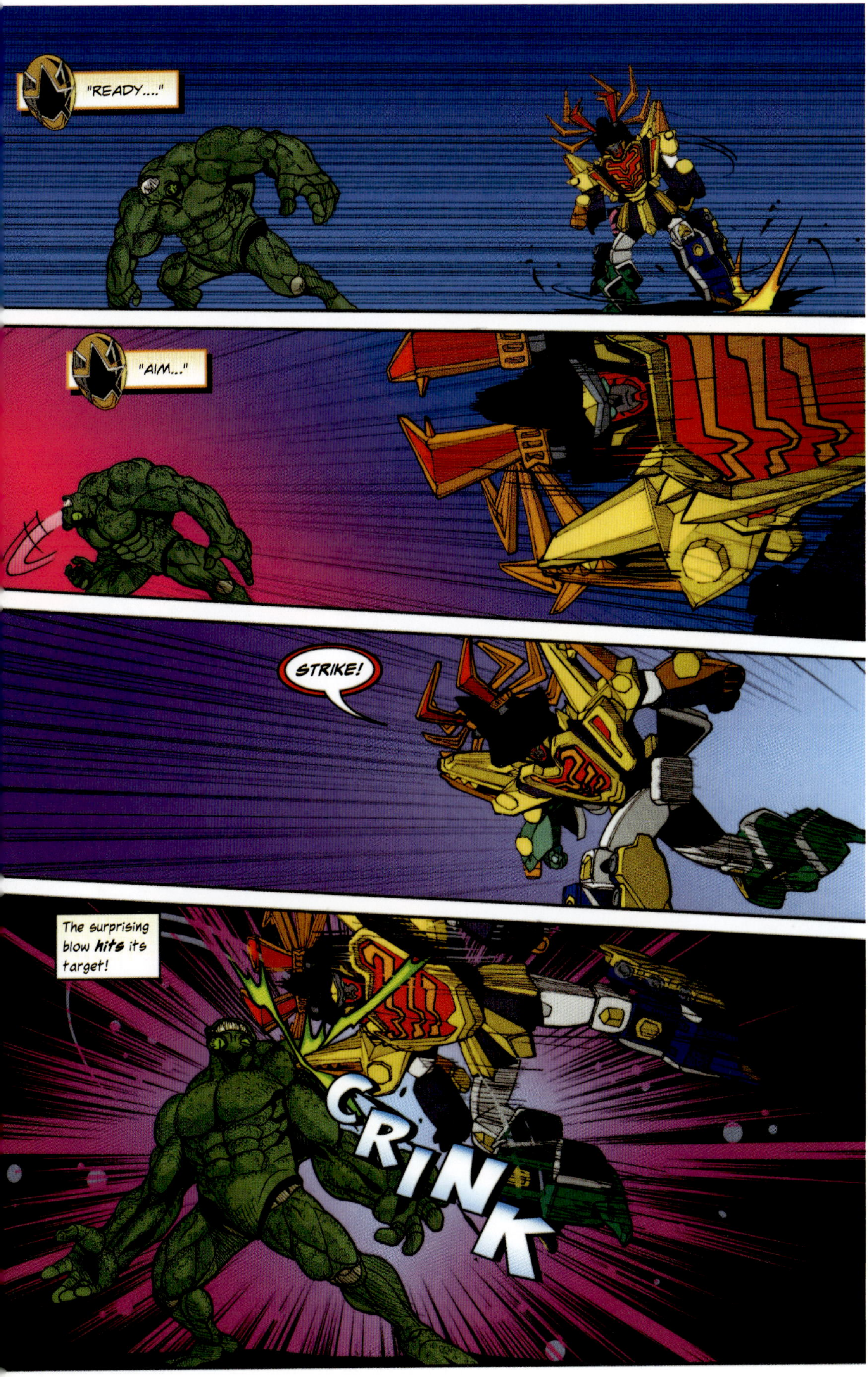
"READY...."
"AIM..."
STRIKE!
The surprising blow **hits** its target!
CRINK

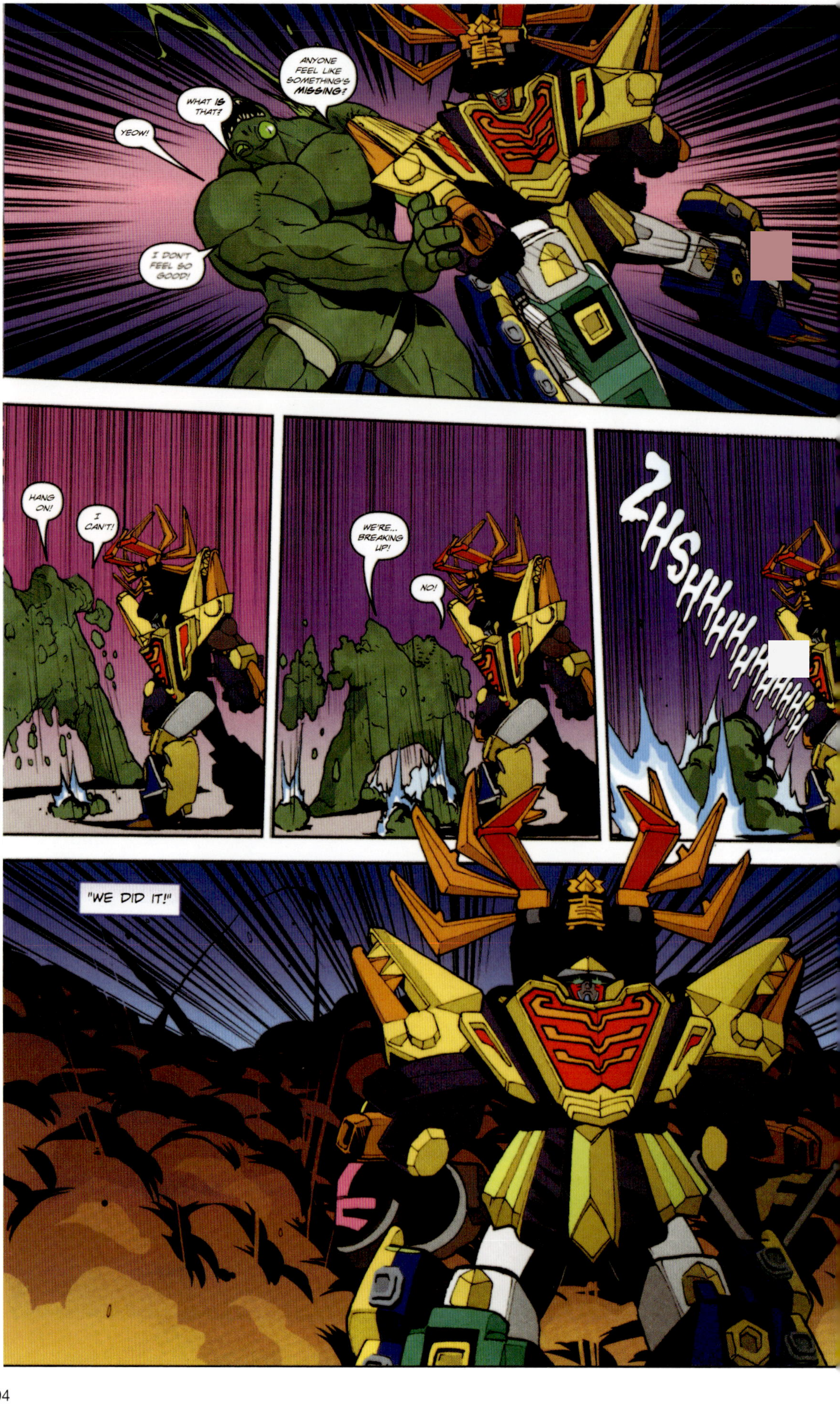
YEOW!
WHAT IS THAT?
ANYONE FEEL LIKE SOMETHING'S MISSING?
I DON'T FEEL SO GOOD!
HANG ON!
I CAN'T!
WE'RE... BREAKING UP!
NO!
ZHSHHHHHHHHHHH
"WE DID IT!"

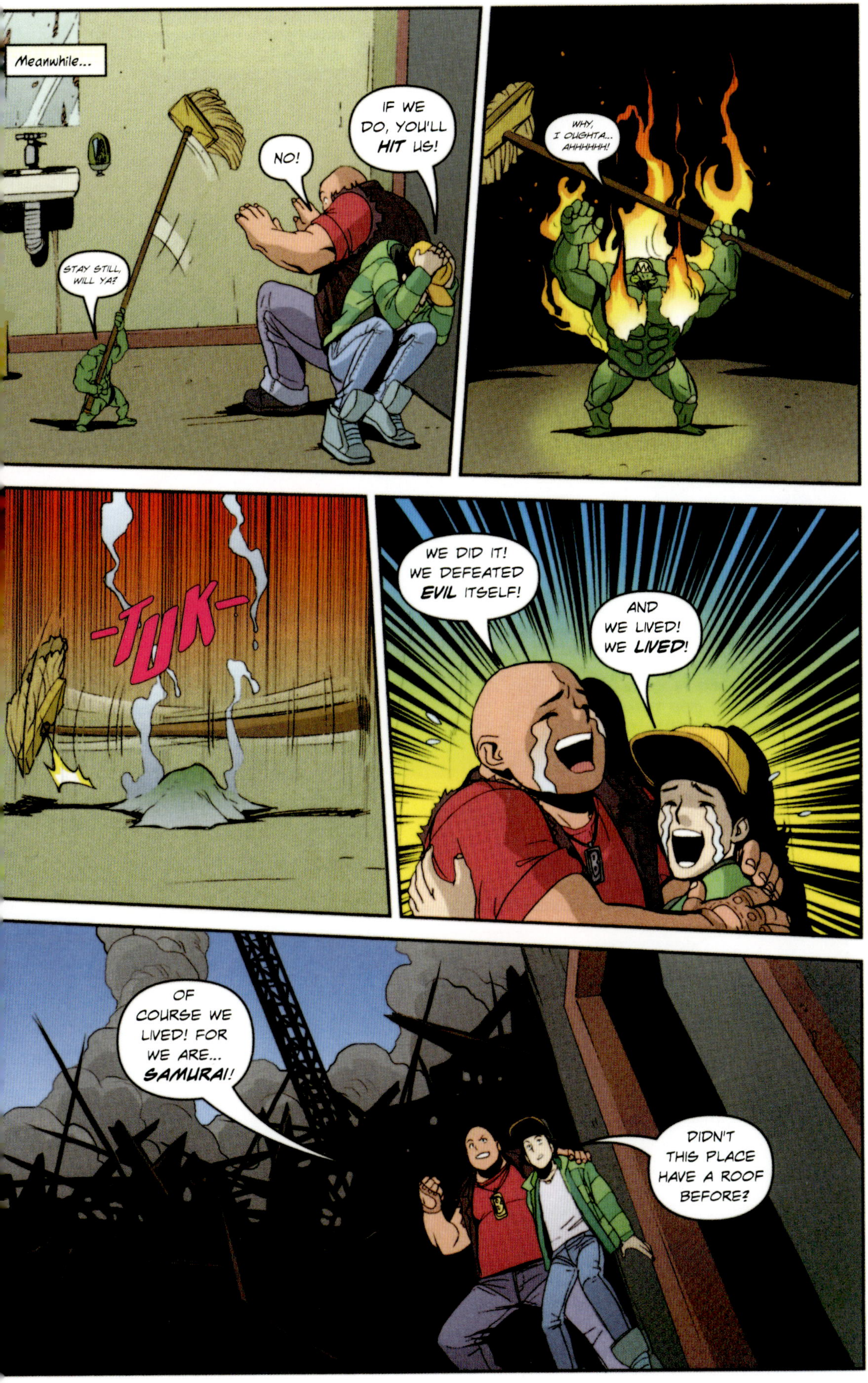

Meanwhile...
STAY STILL, WILL YA?
NO!
IF WE DO, YOU'LL HIT US!
WHY, I OUGHTA... AHHHHHH!
-TUK-
WE DID IT! WE DEFEATED EVIL ITSELF!
AND WE LIVED! WE LIVED!
OF COURSE WE LIVED! FOR WE ARE... SAMURAI!
DIDN'T THIS PLACE HAVE A ROOF BEFORE?

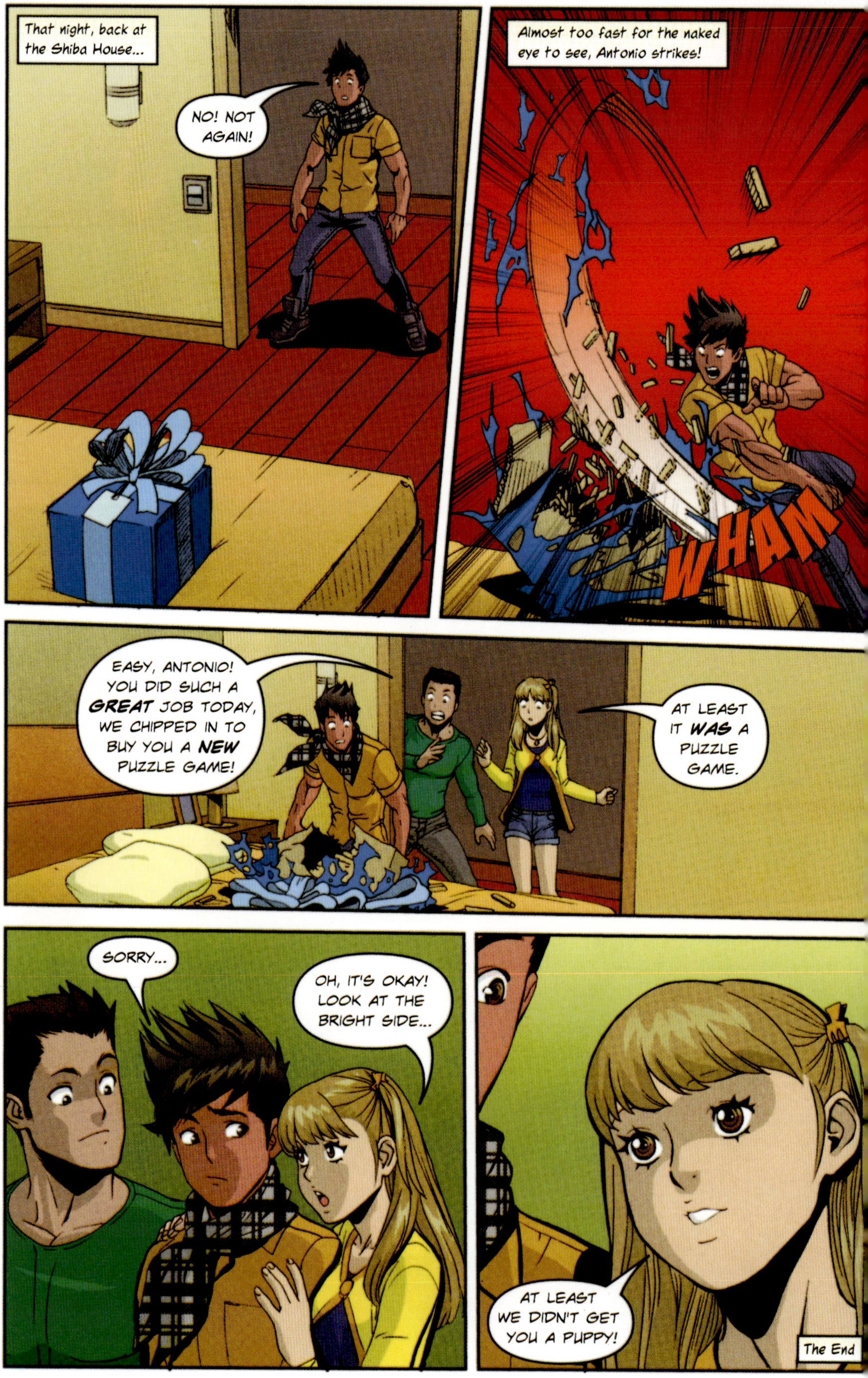
That night, back at the Shiba House...
NO! NOT AGAIN!
Almost too fast for the naked eye to see, Antonio strikes!
WHAM
EASY, ANTONIO! YOU DID SUCH A GREAT JOB TODAY, WE CHIPPED IN TO BUY YOU A NEW PUZZLE GAME!
AT LEAST IT WAS A PUZZLE GAME.
SORRY...
OH, IT'S OKAY! LOOK AT THE BRIGHT SIDE...
AT LEAST WE DIDN'T GET YOU A PUPPY!
The End

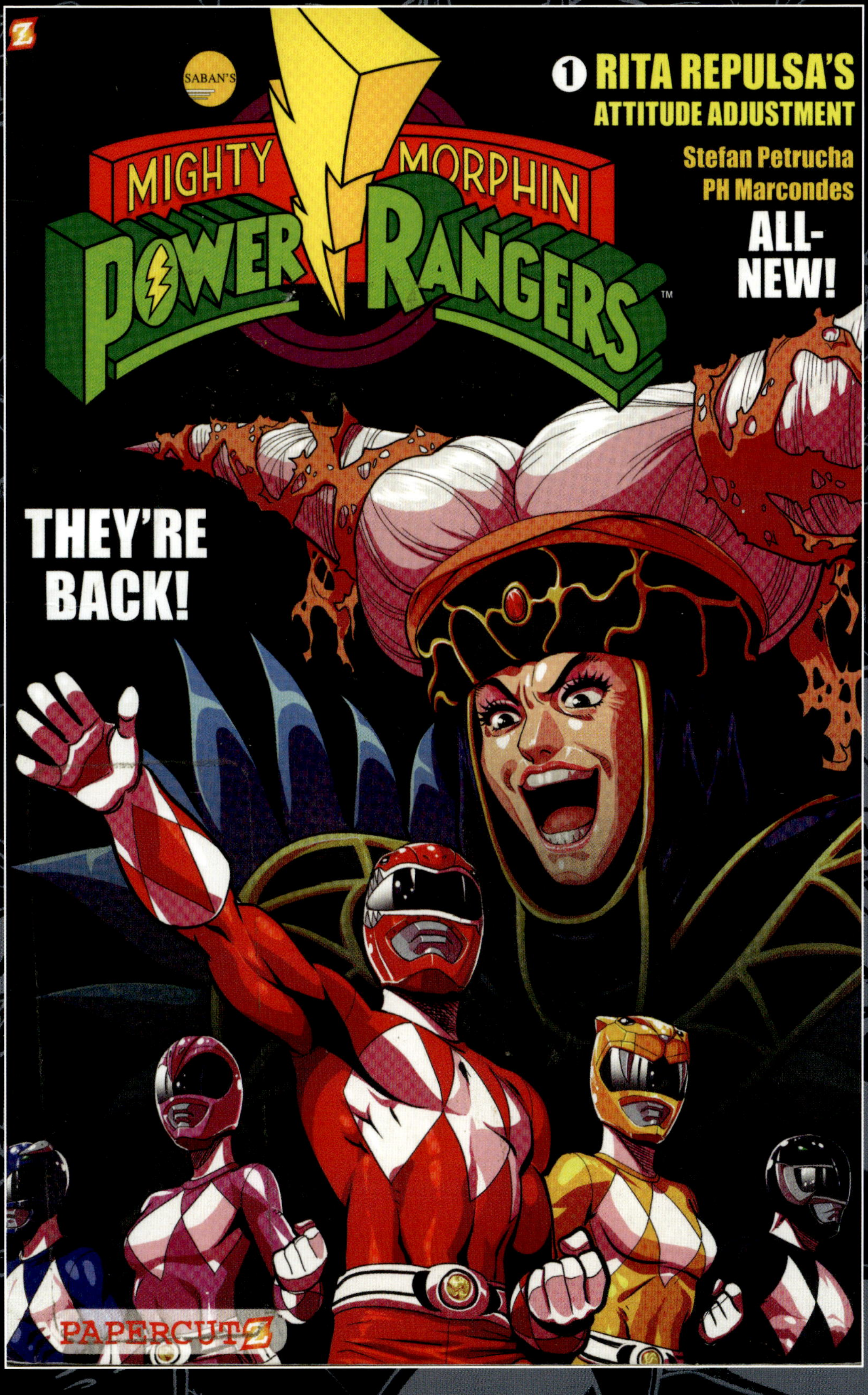
SABAN'S
MIGHTY MORPHIN
POWER RANGERS™
1 RITA REPULSA'S
ATTITUDE ADJUSTMENT
Stefan Petrucha
PH Marcondes
ALL-
NEW!
THEY'RE
BACK!
PAPERCUTZ

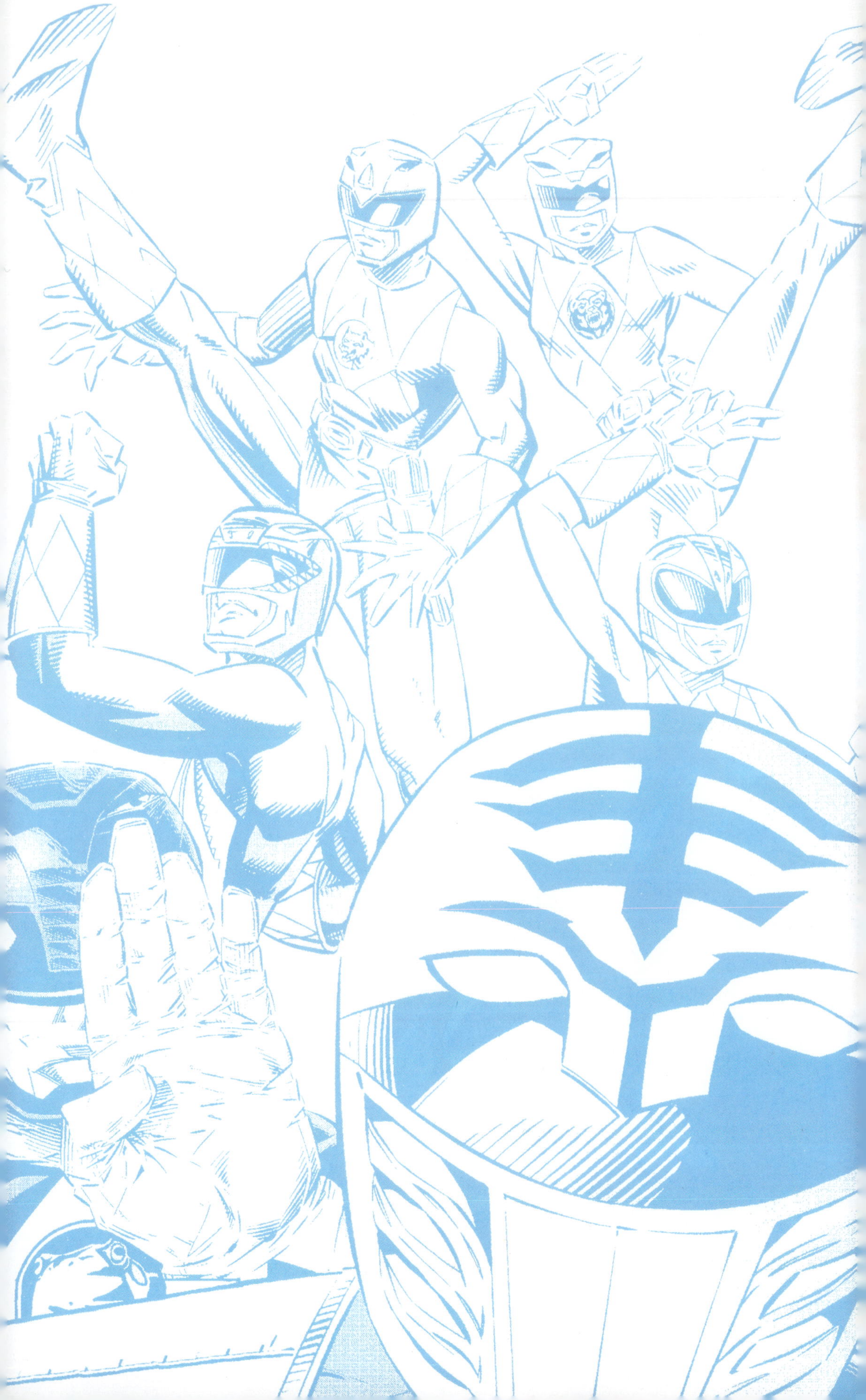

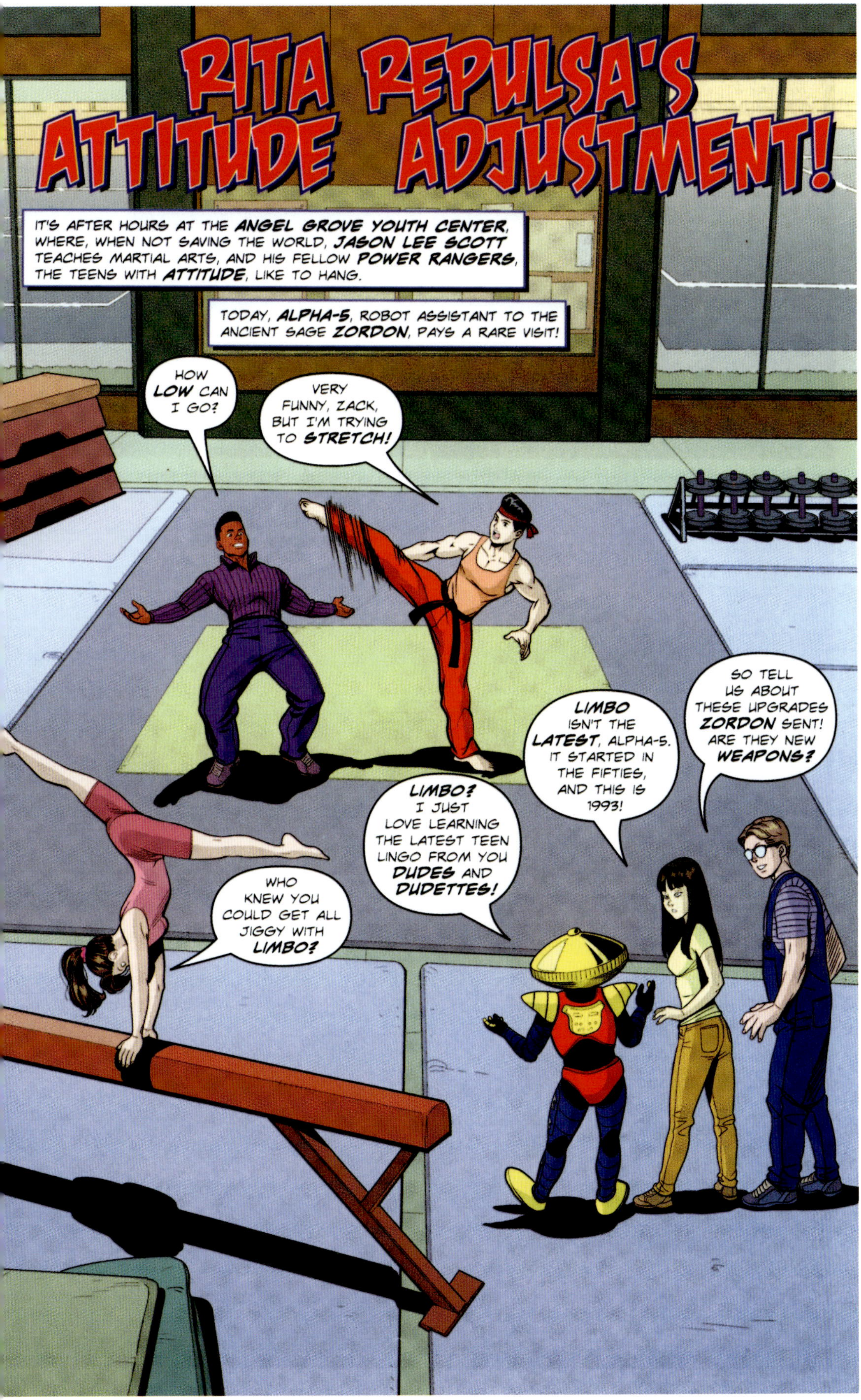
RITA REPULSA'S ATTITUDE ADJUSTMENT!
IT'S AFTER HOURS AT THE ANGEL GROVE YOUTH CENTER, WHERE, WHEN NOT SAVING THE WORLD, JASON LEE SCOTT TEACHES MARTIAL ARTS, AND HIS FELLOW POWER RANGERS, THE TEENS WITH ATTITUDE, LIKE TO HANG.
TODAY, ALPHA-5, ROBOT ASSISTANT TO THE ANCIENT SAGE ZORDON, PAYS A RARE VISIT!
HOW LOW CAN I GO?
VERY FUNNY, ZACK, BUT I'M TRYING TO STRETCH!
SO TELL US ABOUT THESE UPGRADES ZORDON SENT! ARE THEY NEW WEAPONS?
LIMBO ISN'T THE LATEST, ALPHA-5. IT STARTED IN THE FIFTIES, AND THIS IS 1993!
LIMBO? I JUST LOVE LEARNING THE LATEST TEEN LINGO FROM YOU DUDES AND DUDETTES!
WHO KNEW YOU COULD GET ALL JIGGY WITH LIMBO?

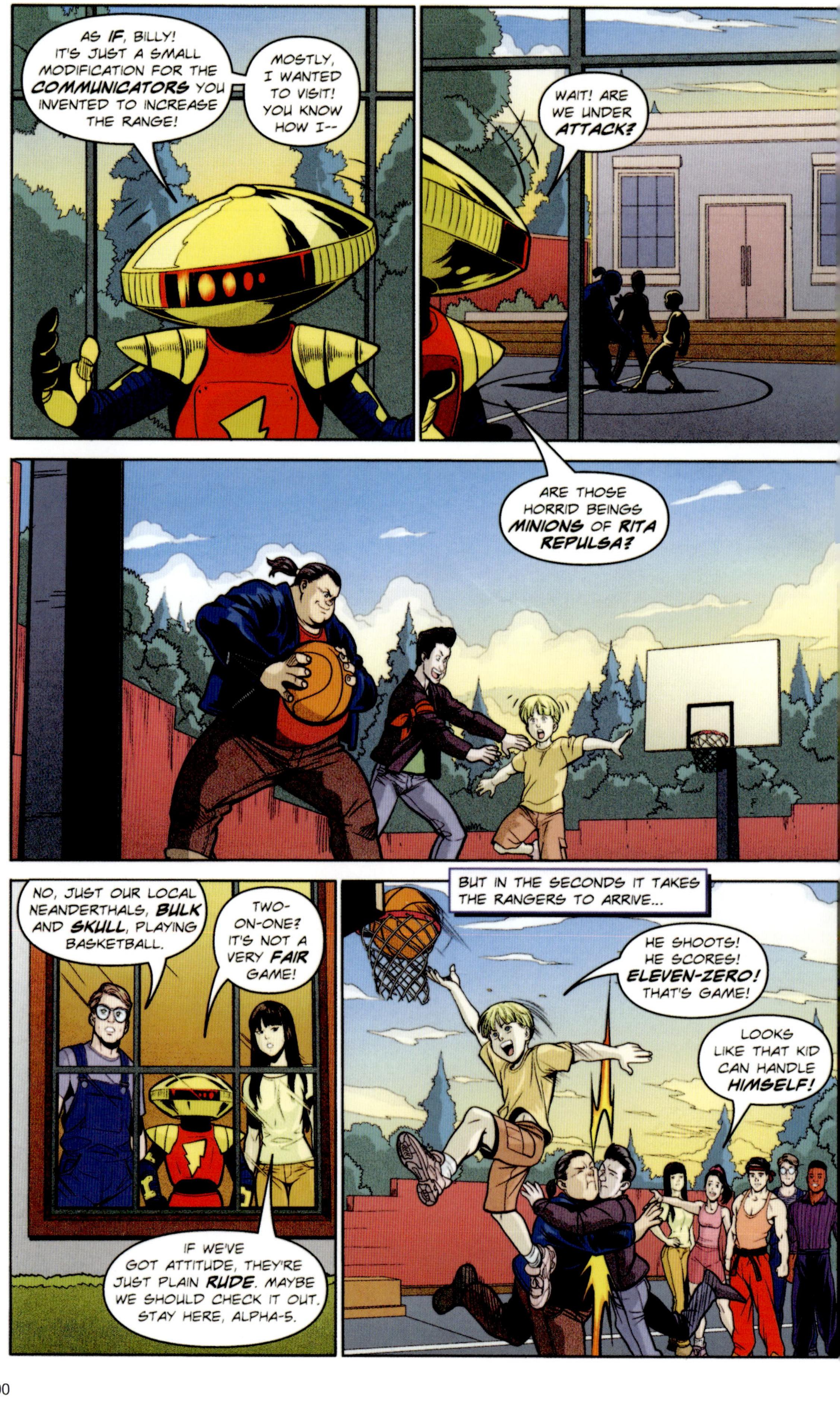
AS IF, BILLY! IT'S JUST A SMALL MODIFICATION FOR THE COMMUNICATORS YOU INVENTED TO INCREASE THE RANGE!
MOSTLY, I WANTED TO VISIT! YOU KNOW HOW I--
WAIT! ARE WE UNDER ATTACK?
ARE THOSE HORRID BEINGS MINIONS OF RITA REPULSA?
NO, JUST OUR LOCAL NEANDERTHALS, BULK AND SKULL, PLAYING BASKETBALL.
TWO-ON-ONE? IT'S NOT A VERY FAIR GAME!
IF WE'VE GOT ATTITUDE, THEY'RE JUST PLAIN RUDE. MAYBE WE SHOULD CHECK IT OUT. STAY HERE, ALPHA-5.
BUT IN THE SECONDS IT TAKES THE RANGERS TO ARRIVE...
HE SHOOTS! HE SCORES! ELEVEN-ZERO! THAT'S GAME!
LOOKS LIKE THAT KID CAN HANDLE HIMSELF!

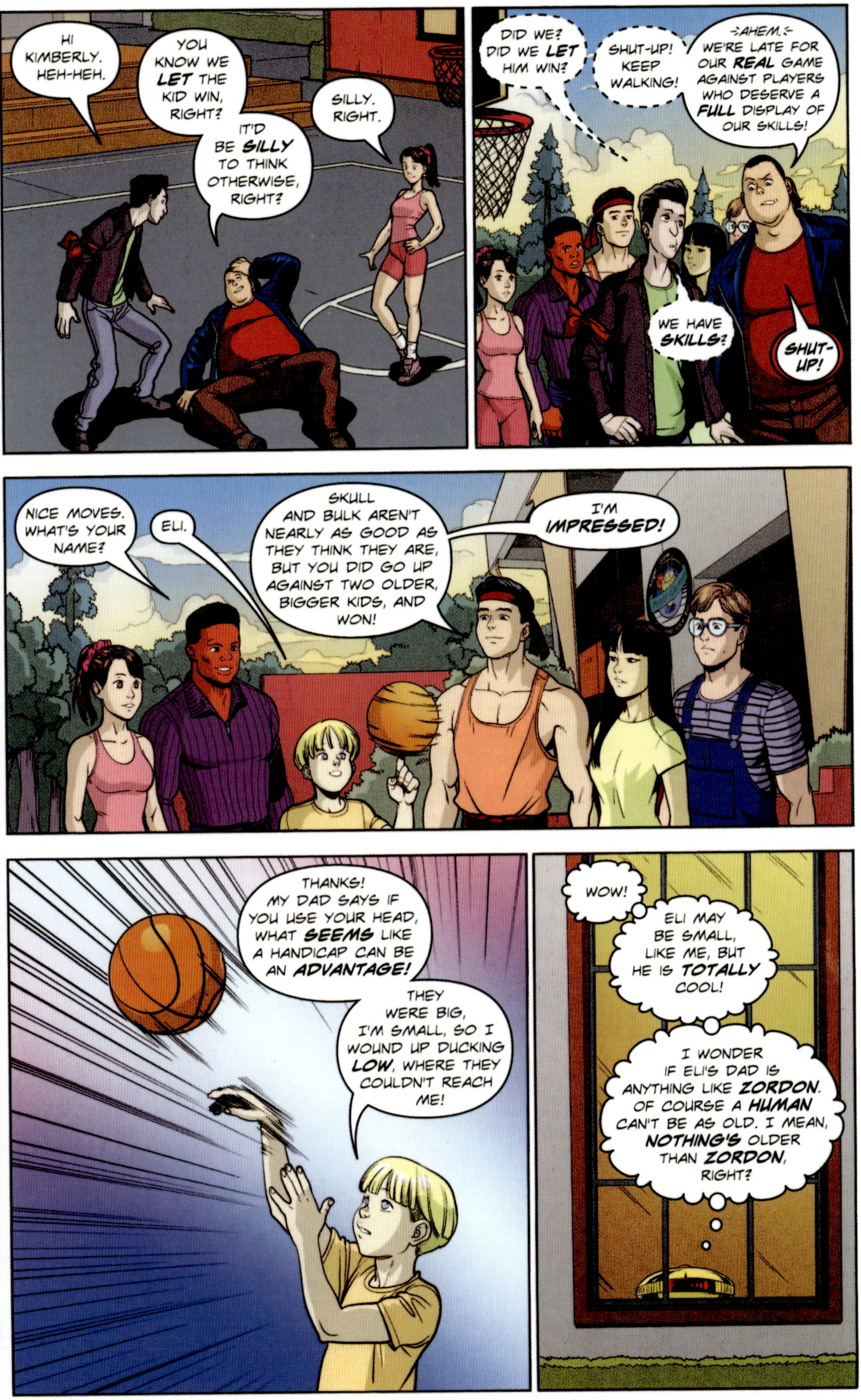

HI KIMBERLY. HEH-HEH.
YOU KNOW WE LET THE KID WIN, RIGHT?
IT'D BE SILLY TO THINK OTHERWISE, RIGHT?
SILLY. RIGHT.
DID WE? DID WE LET HIM WIN?
SHUT-UP! KEEP WALKING!
AHEM. WE'RE LATE FOR OUR REAL GAME AGAINST PLAYERS WHO DESERVE A FULL DISPLAY OF OUR SKILLS!
WE HAVE SKILLS?
SHUT-UP!
NICE MOVES. WHAT'S YOUR NAME?
ELI.
SKULL AND BULK AREN'T NEARLY AS GOOD AS THEY THINK THEY ARE, BUT YOU DID GO UP AGAINST TWO OLDER, BIGGER KIDS, AND WON!
I'M IMPRESSED!
THANKS! MY DAD SAYS IF YOU USE YOUR HEAD, WHAT SEEMS LIKE A HANDICAP CAN BE AN ADVANTAGE!
THEY WERE BIG, I'M SMALL, SO I WOUND UP DUCKING LOW, WHERE THEY COULDN'T REACH ME!
WOW!
ELI MAY BE SMALL, LIKE ME, BUT HE IS TOTALLY COOL!
I WONDER IF ELI'S DAD IS ANYTHING LIKE ZORDON. OF COURSE A HUMAN CAN'T BE AS OLD. I MEAN, NOTHING'S OLDER THAN ZORDON, RIGHT?

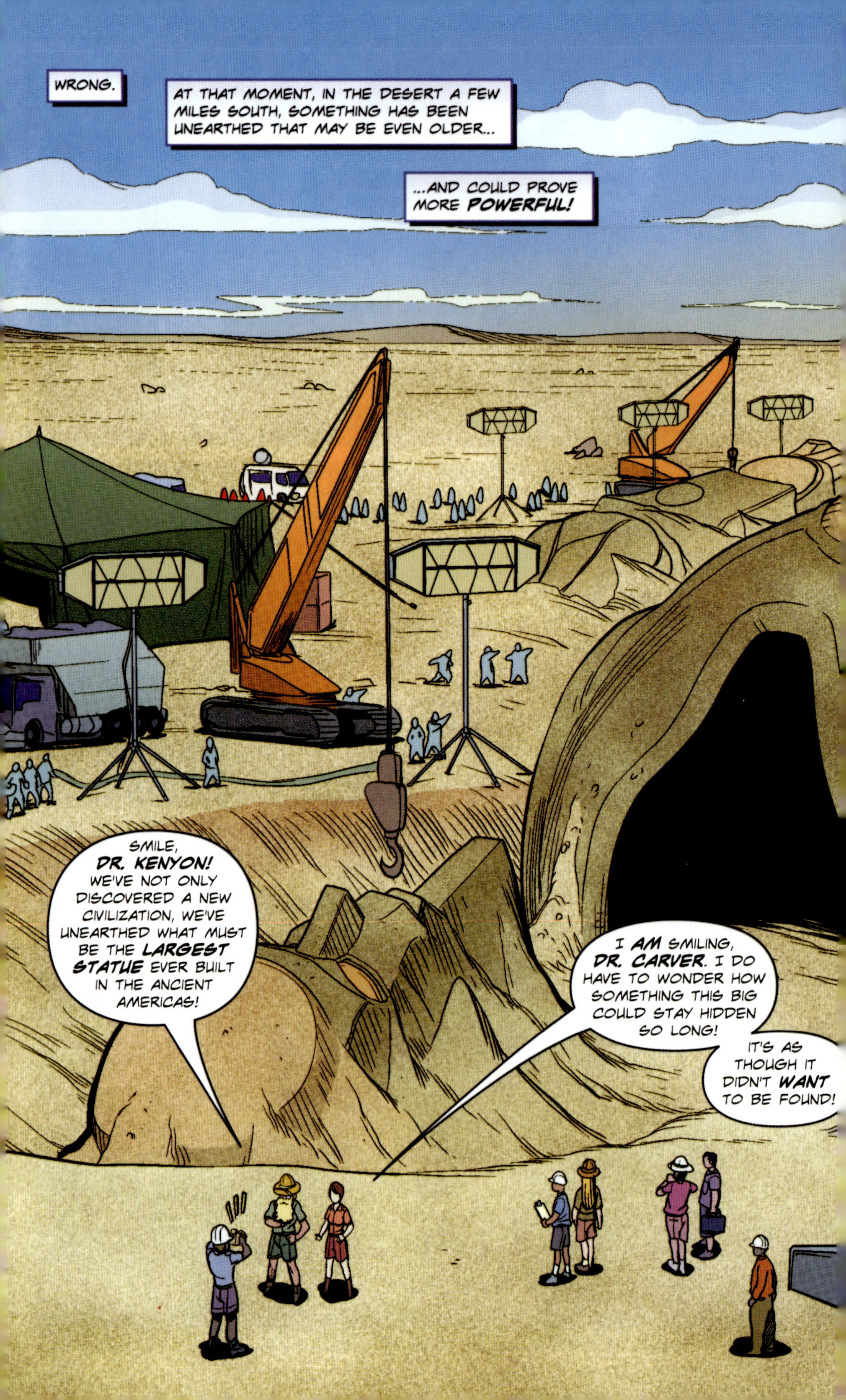
WRONG.
AT THAT MOMENT, IN THE DESERT A FEW MILES SOUTH, SOMETHING HAS BEEN UNEARTHED THAT MAY BE EVEN OLDER...
...AND COULD PROVE MORE POWERFUL!
SMILE, DR. KENYON! WE'VE NOT ONLY DISCOVERED A NEW CIVILIZATION, WE'VE UNEARTHED WHAT MUST BE THE LARGEST STATUE EVER BUILT IN THE ANCIENT AMERICAS!
I AM SMILING, DR. CARVER. I DO HAVE TO WONDER HOW SOMETHING THIS BIG COULD STAY HIDDEN SO LONG!
IT'S AS THOUGH IT DIDN'T WANT TO BE FOUND!

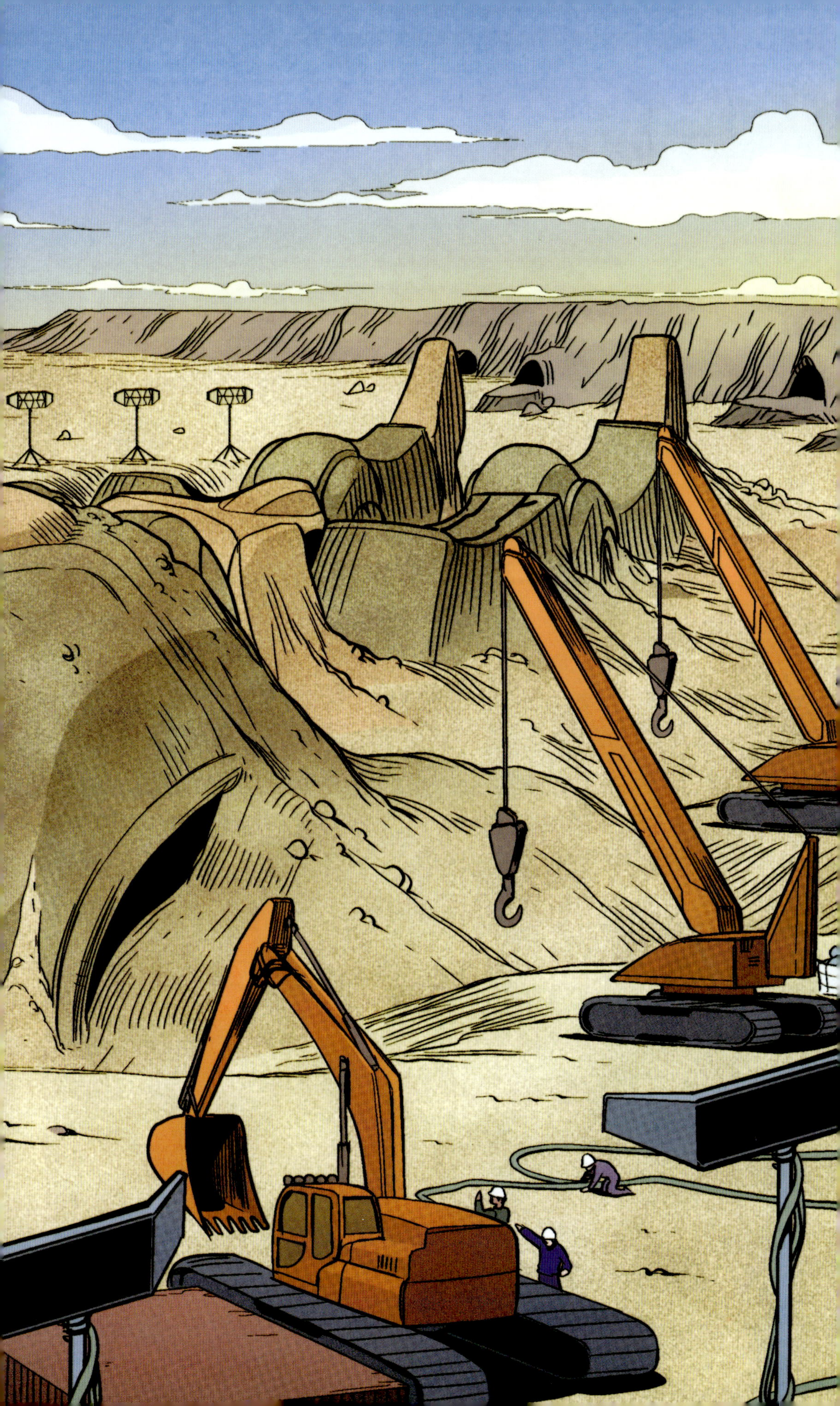

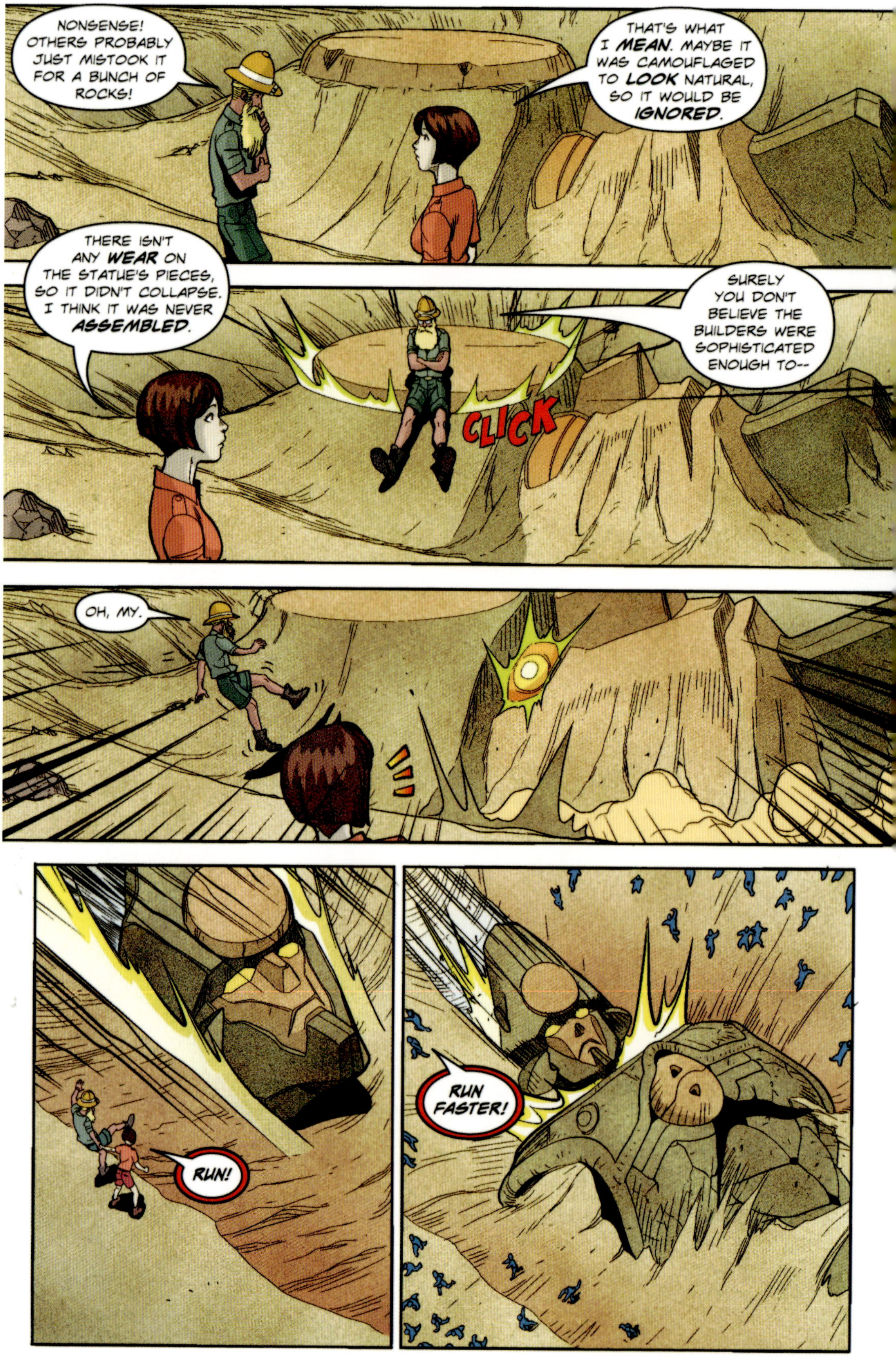

NONSENSE! OTHERS PROBABLY JUST MISTOOK IT FOR A BUNCH OF ROCKS!
THAT'S WHAT I MEAN. MAYBE IT WAS CAMOUFLAGED TO LOOK NATURAL, SO IT WOULD BE IGNORED.
THERE ISN'T ANY WEAR ON THE STATUE'S PIECES, SO IT DIDN'T COLLAPSE. I THINK IT WAS NEVER ASSEMBLED.
SURELY YOU DON'T BELIEVE THE BUILDERS WERE SOPHISTICATED ENOUGH TO--
CLICK
OH, MY.
RUN!
RUN FASTER!

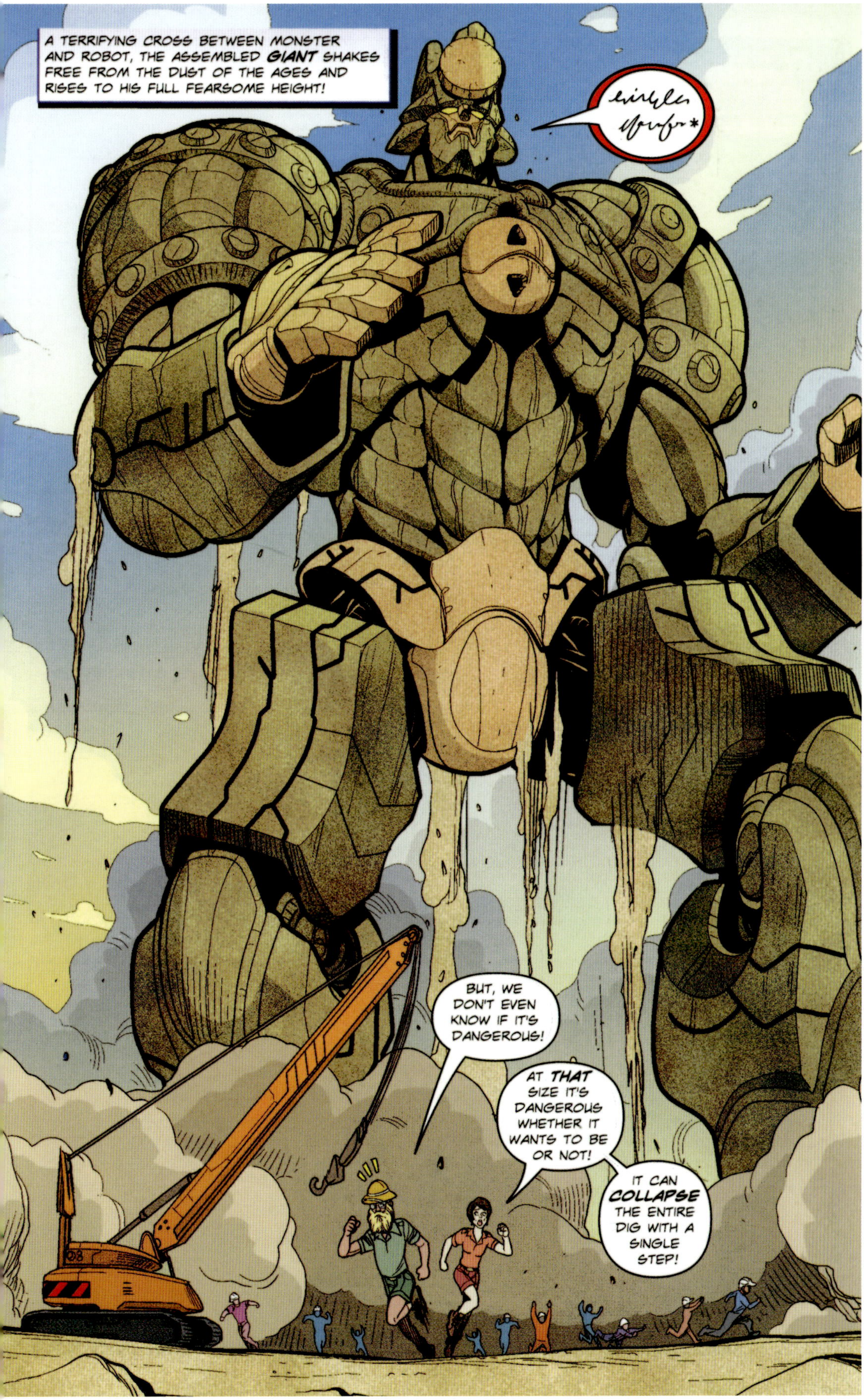
A TERRIFYING CROSS BETWEEN MONSTER AND ROBOT, THE ASSEMBLED **GIANT** SHAKES FREE FROM THE DUST OF THE AGES AND RISES TO HIS FULL FEARSOME HEIGHT!
BUT, WE DON'T EVEN KNOW IF IT'S DANGEROUS!
AT **THAT** SIZE IT'S DANGEROUS WHETHER IT WANTS TO BE OR NOT!
IT CAN **COLLAPSE** THE ENTIRE DIG WITH A SINGLE STEP!

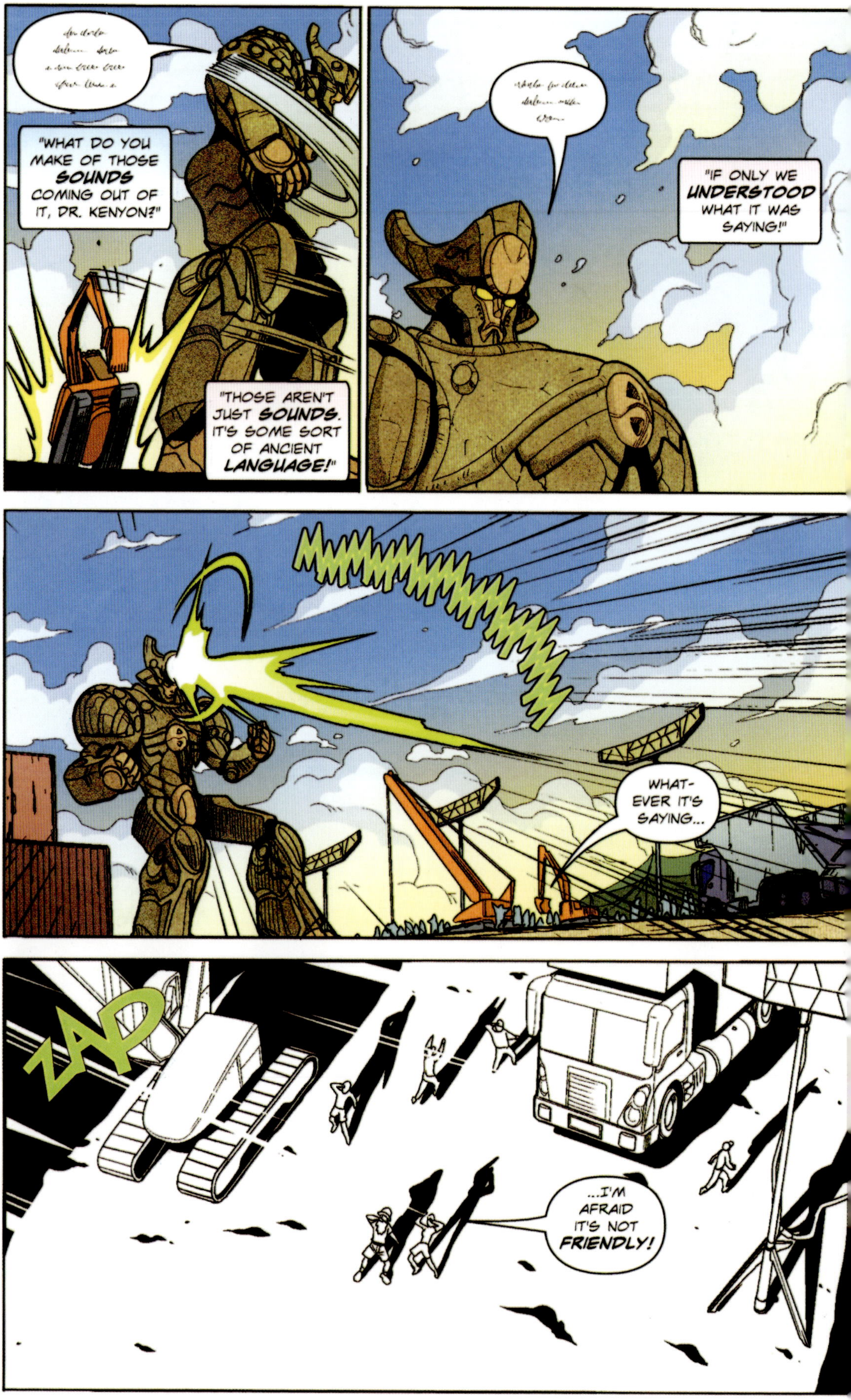
"WHAT DO YOU MAKE OF THOSE SOUNDS COMING OUT OF IT, DR. KENYON?"
"THOSE AREN'T JUST SOUNDS. IT'S SOME SORT OF ANCIENT LANGUAGE!"
"IF ONLY WE UNDERSTOOD WHAT IT WAS SAYING!"
MMMMMMMMMMMMM
WHAT-EVER IT'S SAYING...
ZAP
...I'M AFRAID IT'S NOT FRIENDLY!

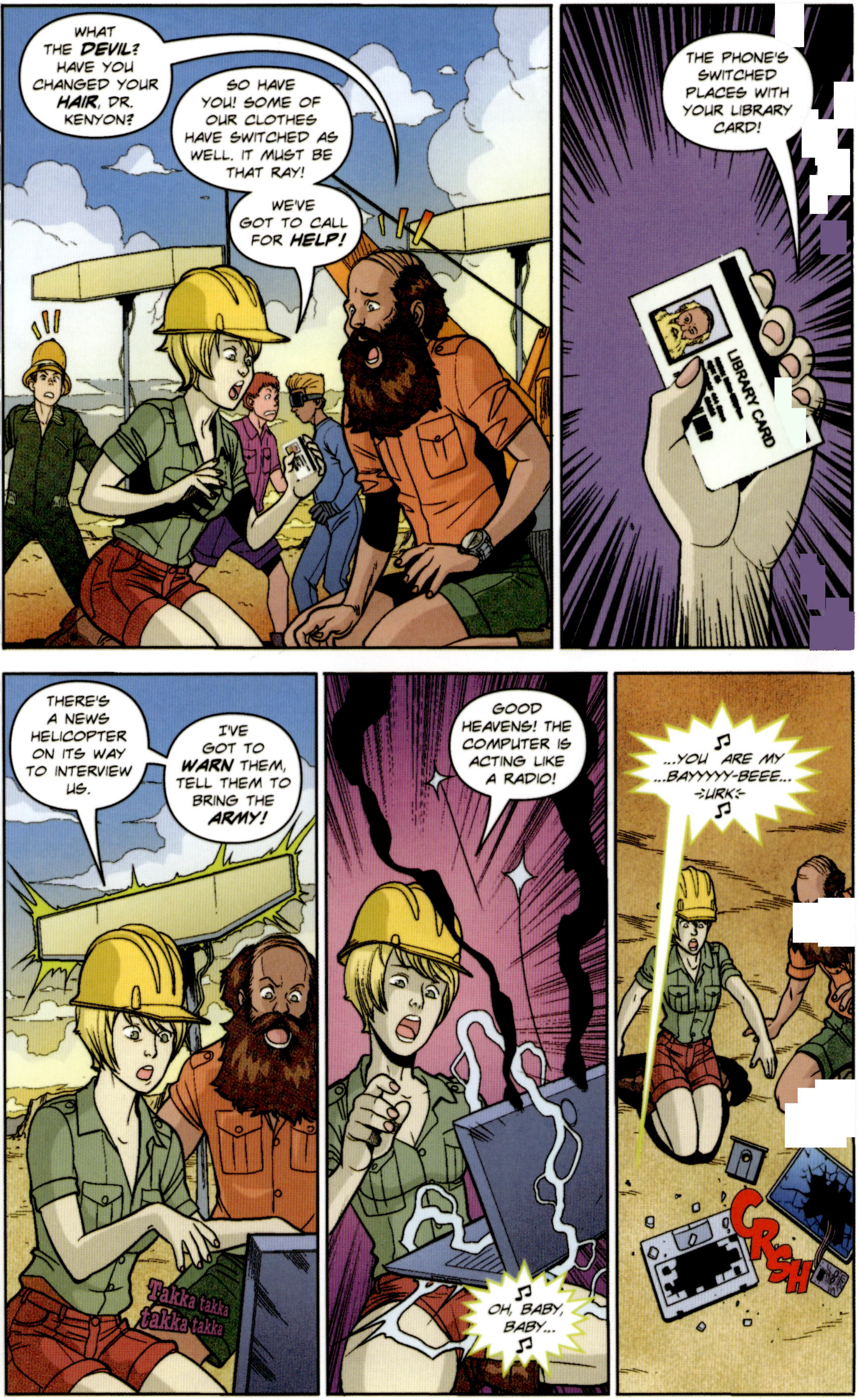
WHAT THE DEVIL? HAVE YOU CHANGED YOUR HAIR, DR. KENYON?
SO HAVE YOU! SOME OF OUR CLOTHES HAVE SWITCHED AS WELL. IT MUST BE THAT RAY!
WE'VE GOT TO CALL FOR HELP!
THE PHONE'S SWITCHED PLACES WITH YOUR LIBRARY CARD!
LIBRARY CARD
THERE'S A NEWS HELICOPTER ON ITS WAY TO INTERVIEW US.
I'VE GOT TO WARN THEM, TELL THEM TO BRING THE ARMY!
Takka takka takka takka
GOOD HEAVENS! THE COMPUTER IS ACTING LIKE A RADIO!
OH, BABY, BABY...
...YOU ARE MY ...BAYYYYY-BEEE... URK
CRSH

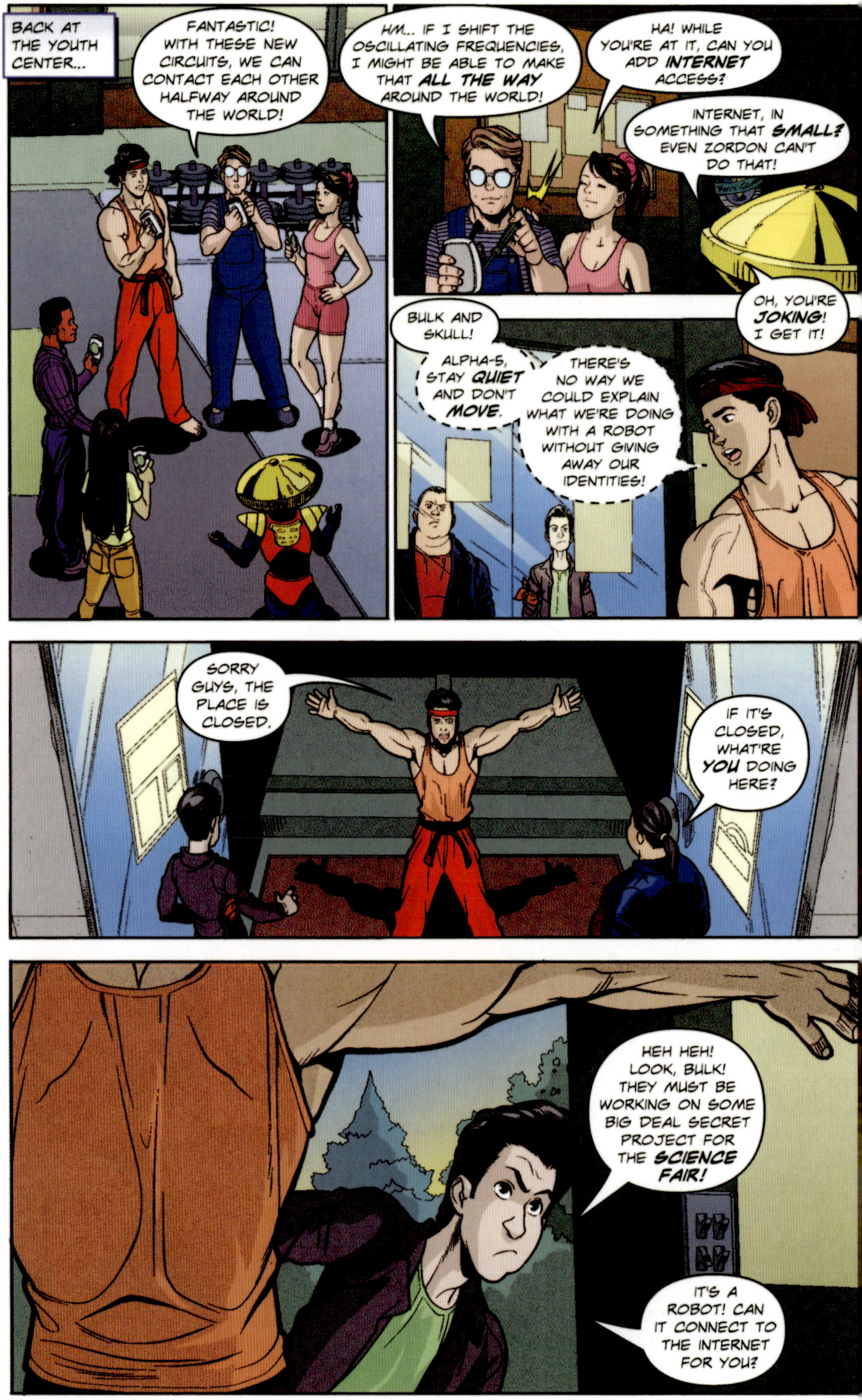
BACK AT THE YOUTH CENTER...
FANTASTIC! WITH THESE NEW CIRCUITS, WE CAN CONTACT EACH OTHER HALFWAY AROUND THE WORLD!
HM... IF I SHIFT THE OSCILLATING FREQUENCIES, I MIGHT BE ABLE TO MAKE THAT ALL THE WAY AROUND THE WORLD!
HA! WHILE YOU'RE AT IT, CAN YOU ADD INTERNET ACCESS?
INTERNET, IN SOMETHING THAT SMALL? EVEN ZORDON CAN'T DO THAT!
OH, YOU'RE JOKING! I GET IT!
BULK AND SKULL!
ALPHA-5, STAY QUIET AND DON'T MOVE.
THERE'S NO WAY WE COULD EXPLAIN WHAT WE'RE DOING WITH A ROBOT WITHOUT GIVING AWAY OUR IDENTITIES!
SORRY GUYS, THE PLACE IS CLOSED.
IF IT'S CLOSED, WHAT'RE YOU DOING HERE?
HEH HEH! LOOK, BULK! THEY MUST BE WORKING ON SOME BIG DEAL SECRET PROJECT FOR THE SCIENCE FAIR!
IT'S A ROBOT! CAN IT CONNECT TO THE INTERNET FOR YOU?

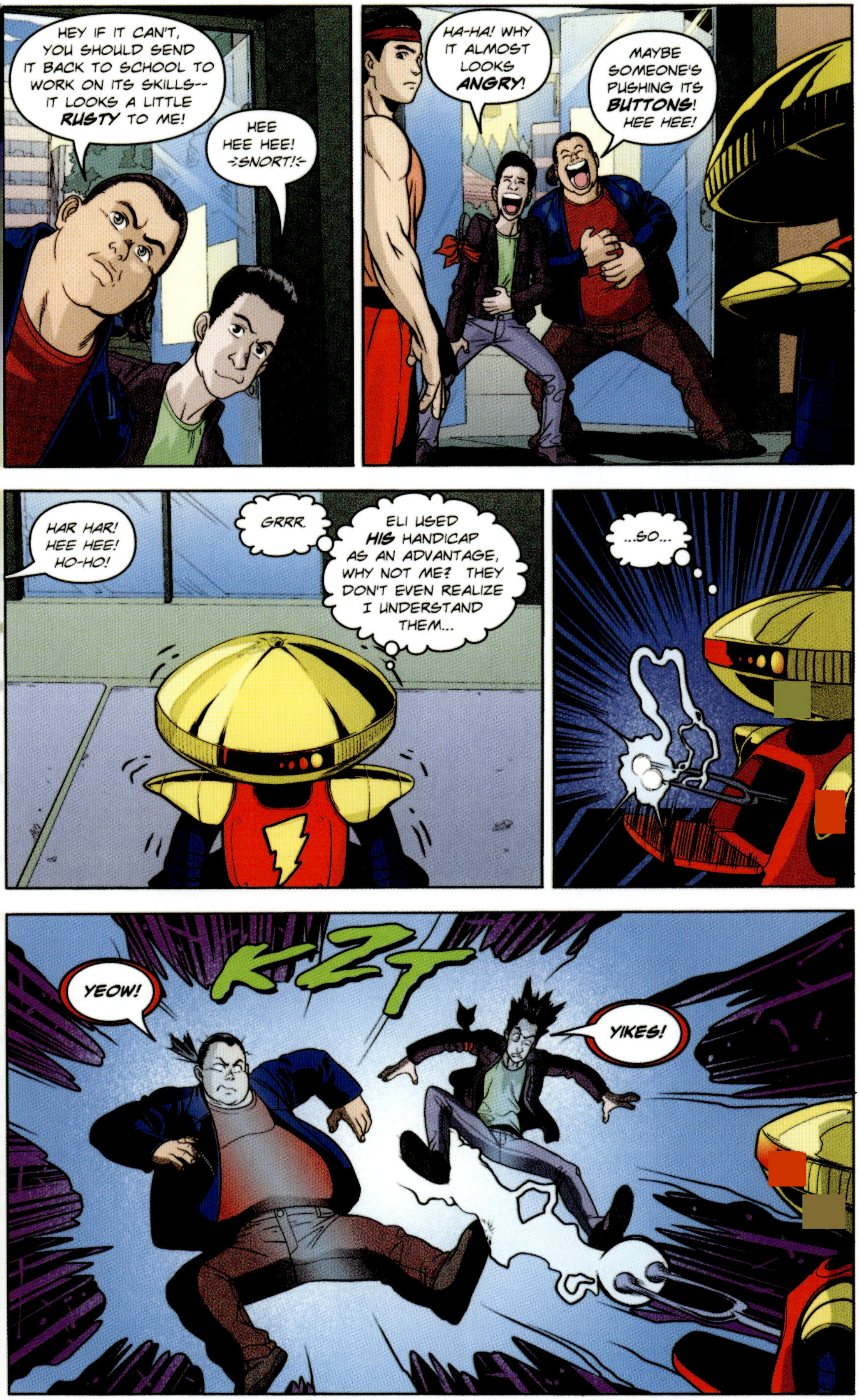

HEY IF IT CAN'T, YOU SHOULD SEND IT BACK TO SCHOOL TO WORK ON ITS SKILLS-- IT LOOKS A LITTLE RUSTY TO ME!
HEE HEE HEE! -SNORT!-
HA-HA! WHY IT ALMOST LOOKS ANGRY!
MAYBE SOMEONE'S PUSHING ITS BUTTONS! HEE HEE!
HAR HAR! HEE HEE! HO-HO!
GRRR.
ELI USED HIS HANDICAP AS AN ADVANTAGE, WHY NOT ME? THEY DON'T EVEN REALIZE I UNDERSTAND THEM...
...SO...
KZT
YEOW!
YIKES!

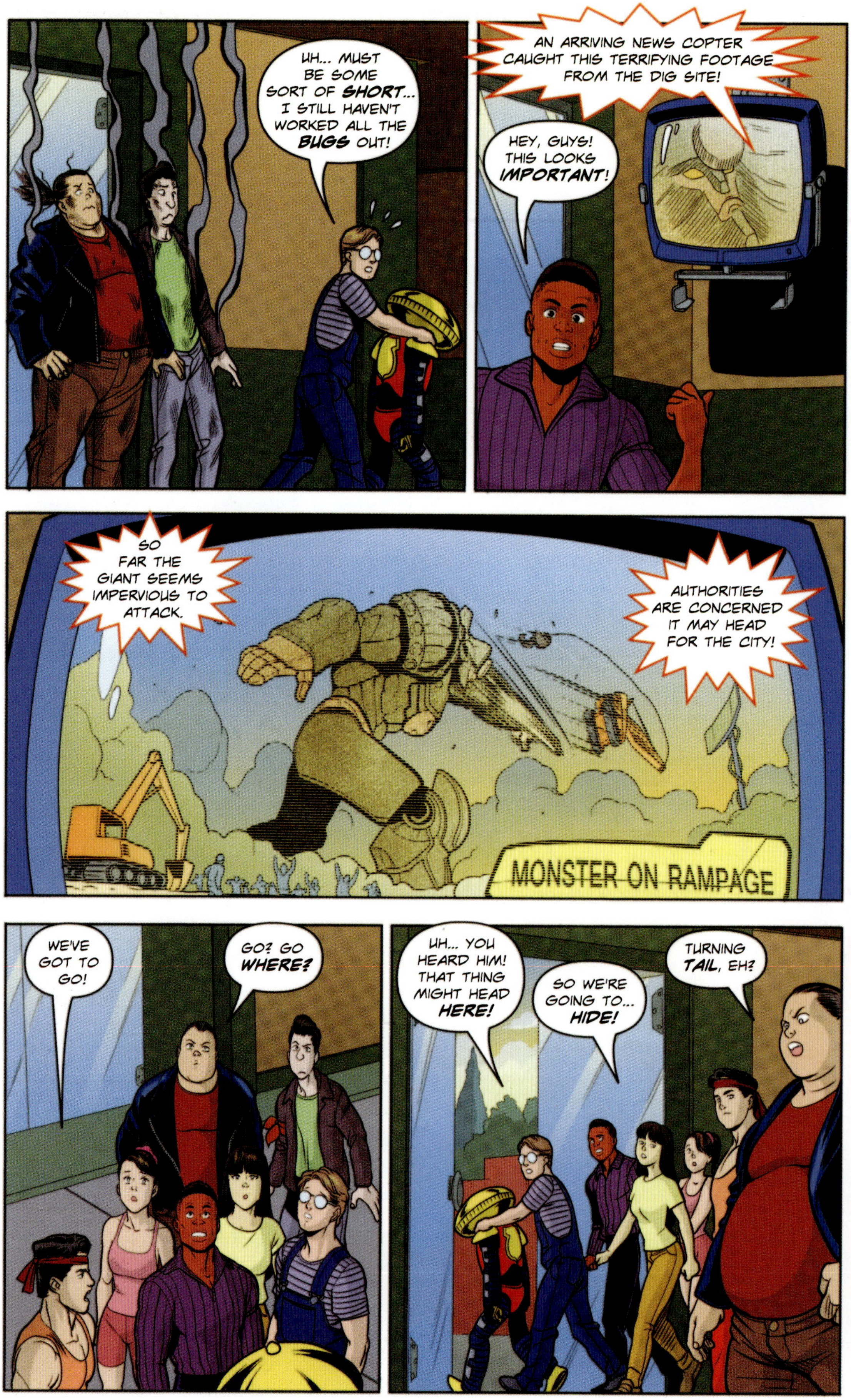
UH... MUST BE SOME SORT OF SHORT... I STILL HAVEN'T WORKED ALL THE BUGS OUT!
AN ARRIVING NEWS COPTER CAUGHT THIS TERRIFYING FOOTAGE FROM THE DIG SITE!
HEY, GUYS! THIS LOOKS IMPORTANT!
SO FAR THE GIANT SEEMS IMPERVIOUS TO ATTACK.
AUTHORITIES ARE CONCERNED IT MAY HEAD FOR THE CITY!
MONSTER ON RAMPAGE
WE'VE GOT TO GO!
GO? GO WHERE?
UH... YOU HEARD HIM! THAT THING MIGHT HEAD HERE!
SO WE'RE GOING TO... HIDE!
TURNING TAIL, EH?

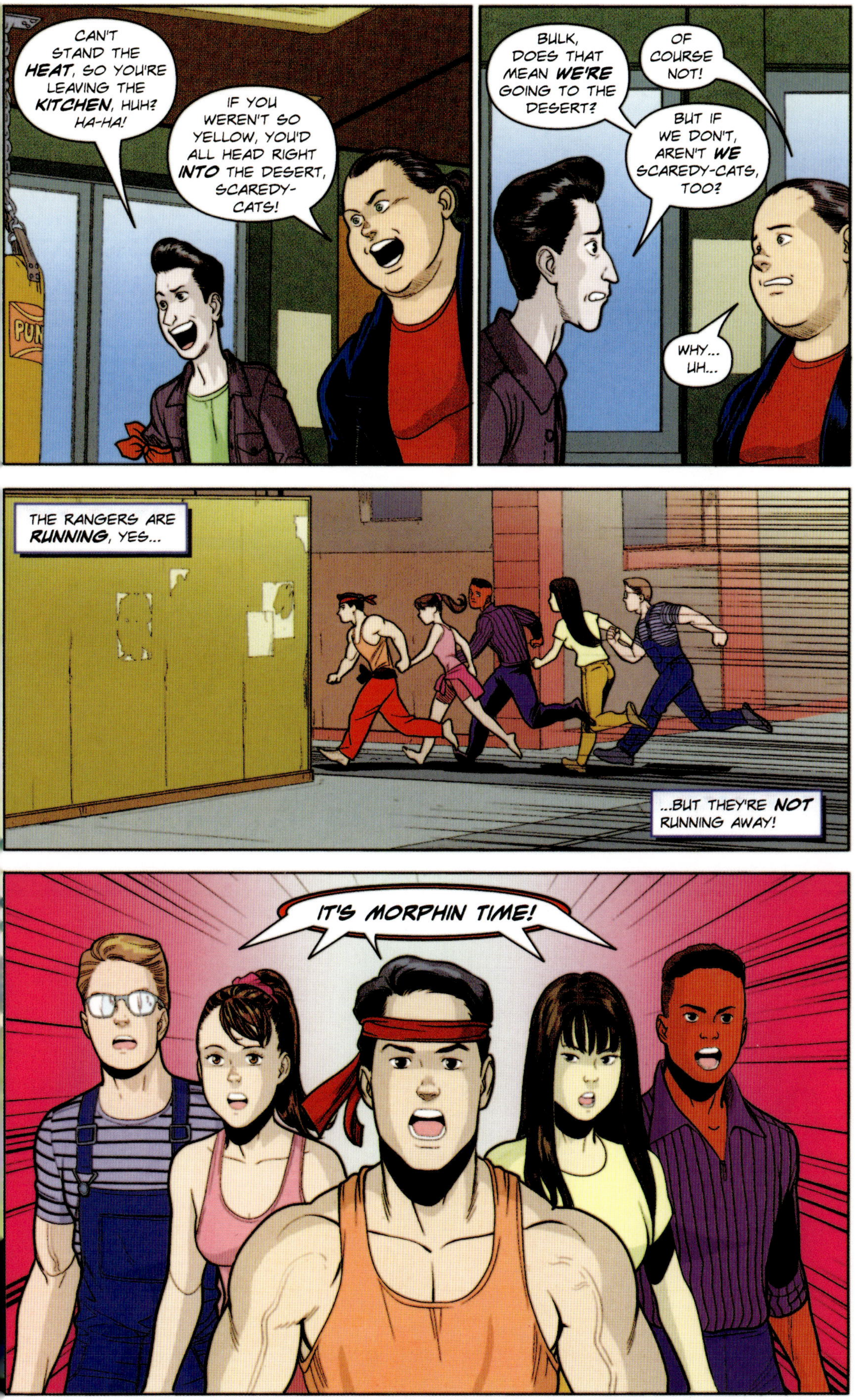
CAN'T STAND THE HEAT, SO YOU'RE LEAVING THE KITCHEN, HUH? HA-HA!
IF YOU WEREN'T SO YELLOW, YOU'D ALL HEAD RIGHT INTO THE DESERT, SCAREDY-CATS!
BULK, DOES THAT MEAN WE'RE GOING TO THE DESERT?
OF COURSE NOT!
BUT IF WE DON'T, AREN'T WE SCAREDY-CATS, TOO?
WHY... UH...
THE RANGERS ARE RUNNING, YES...
...BUT THEY'RE NOT RUNNING AWAY!
IT'S MORPHIN TIME!

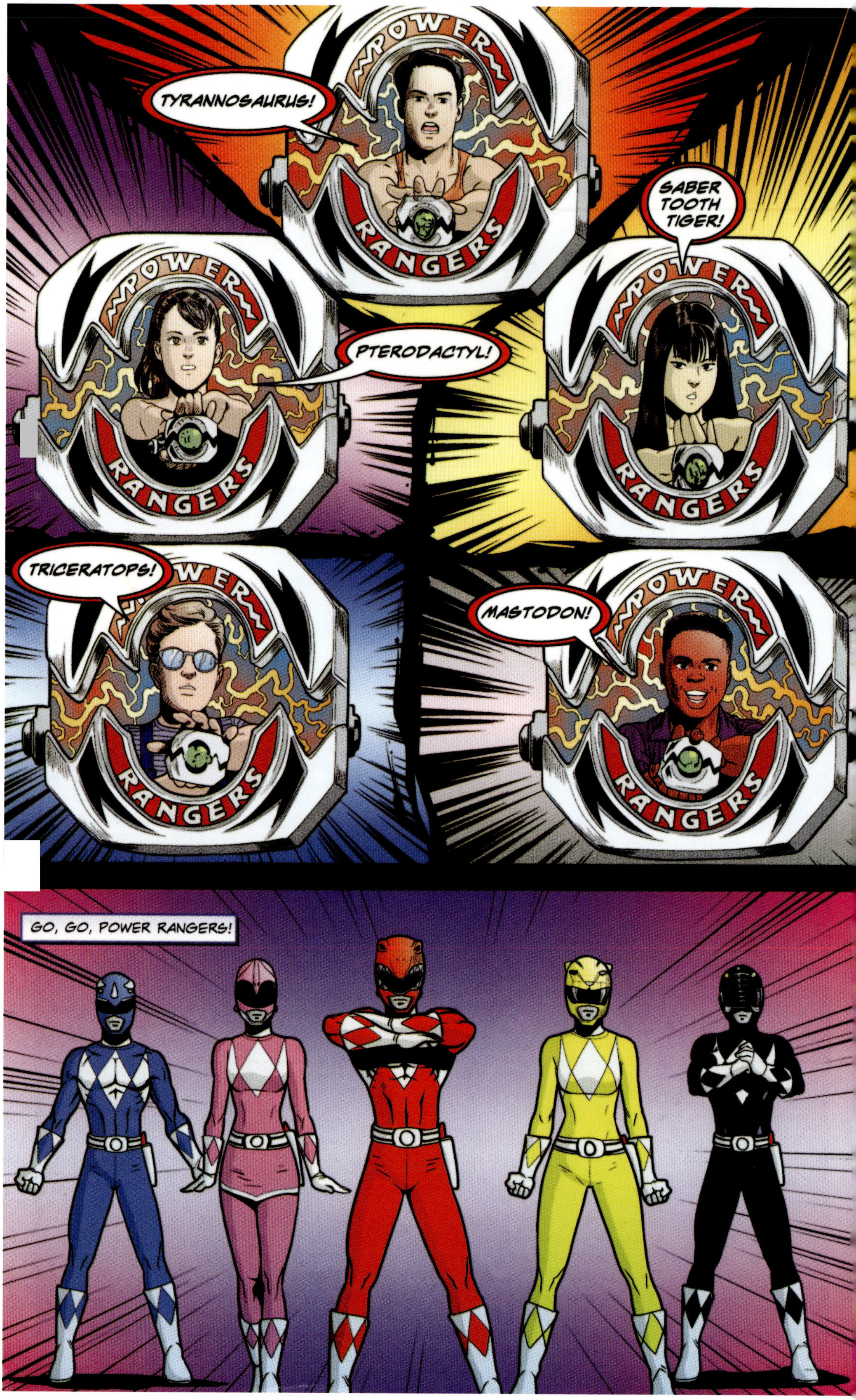
TYRANNOSAURUS!
POWER
RANGERS
SABER TOOTH TIGER!
PTERODACTYL!
TRICERATOPS!
MASTODON!
GO, GO, POWER RANGERS!

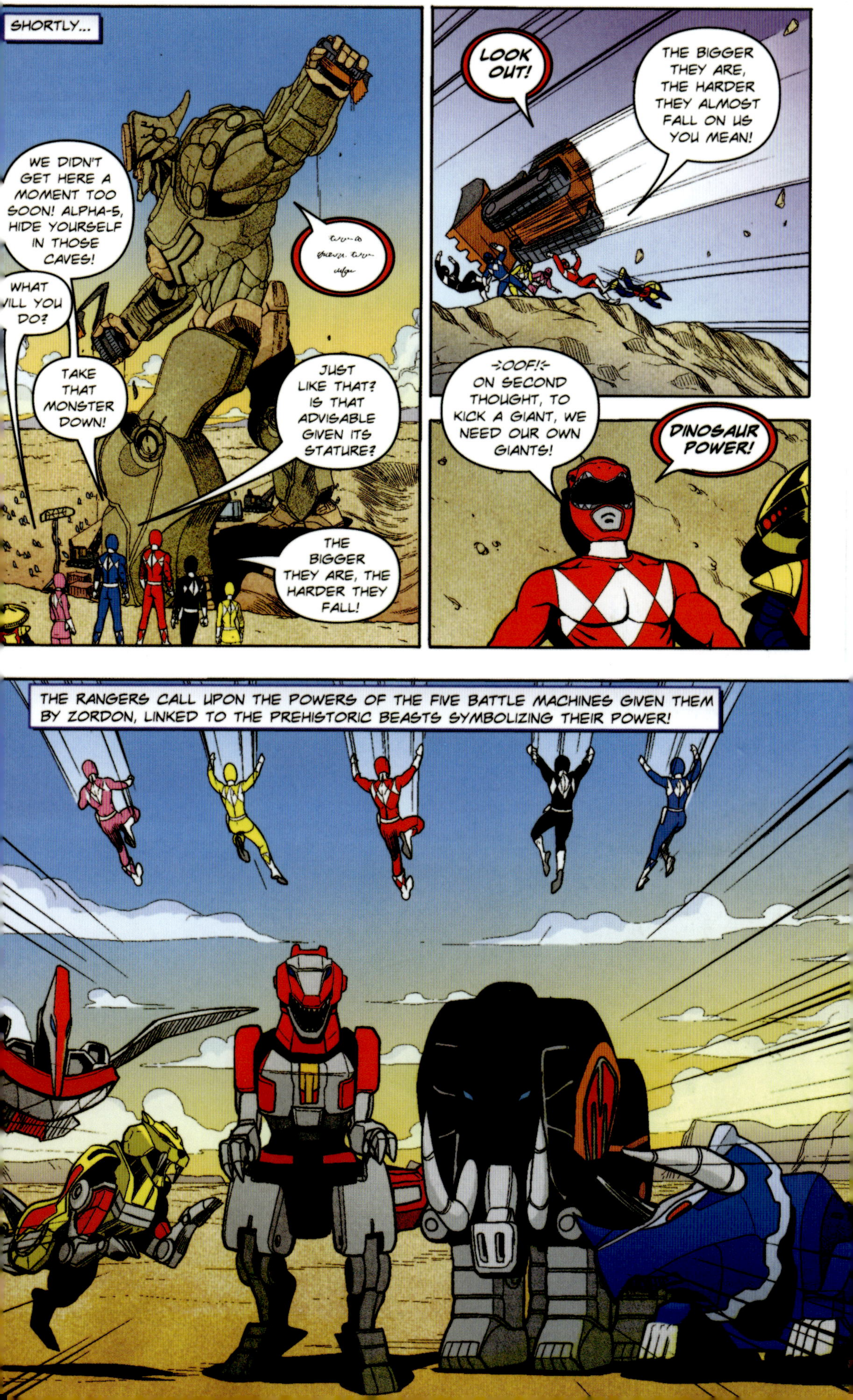

SHORTLY...
WE DIDN'T GET HERE A MOMENT TOO SOON! ALPHA-5, HIDE YOURSELF IN THOSE CAVES!
WHAT WILL YOU DO?
TAKE THAT MONSTER DOWN!
JUST LIKE THAT? IS THAT ADVISABLE GIVEN ITS STATURE?
THE BIGGER THEY ARE, THE HARDER THEY FALL!
LOOK OUT!
THE BIGGER THEY ARE, THE HARDER THEY ALMOST FALL ON US YOU MEAN!
OOF! ON SECOND THOUGHT, TO KICK A GIANT, WE NEED OUR OWN GIANTS!
DINOSAUR POWER!
THE RANGERS CALL UPON THE POWERS OF THE FIVE BATTLE MACHINES GIVEN THEM BY ZORDON, LINKED TO THE PREHISTORIC BEASTS SYMBOLIZING THEIR POWER!

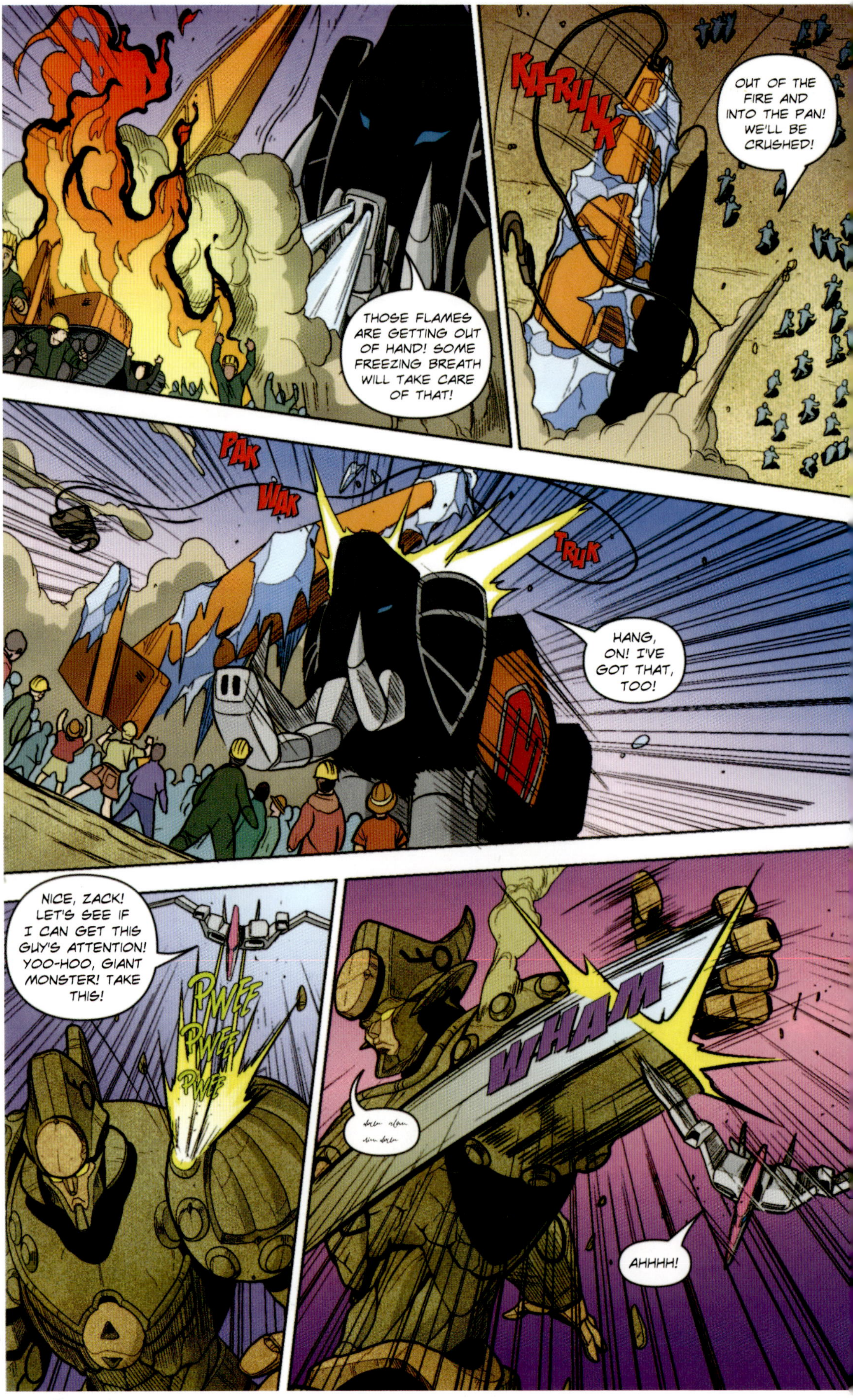
THOSE FLAMES ARE GETTING OUT OF HAND! SOME FREEZING BREATH WILL TAKE CARE OF THAT!
KA-RUNK
OUT OF THE FIRE AND INTO THE PAN! WE'LL BE CRUSHED!
PAK
WAK
TRUK
HANG, ON! I'VE GOT THAT, TOO!
NICE, ZACK! LET'S SEE IF I CAN GET THIS GUY'S ATTENTION! YOO-HOO, GIANT MONSTER! TAKE THIS!
PWEE
PWEE
PWEE
WHAM
AHHHH!

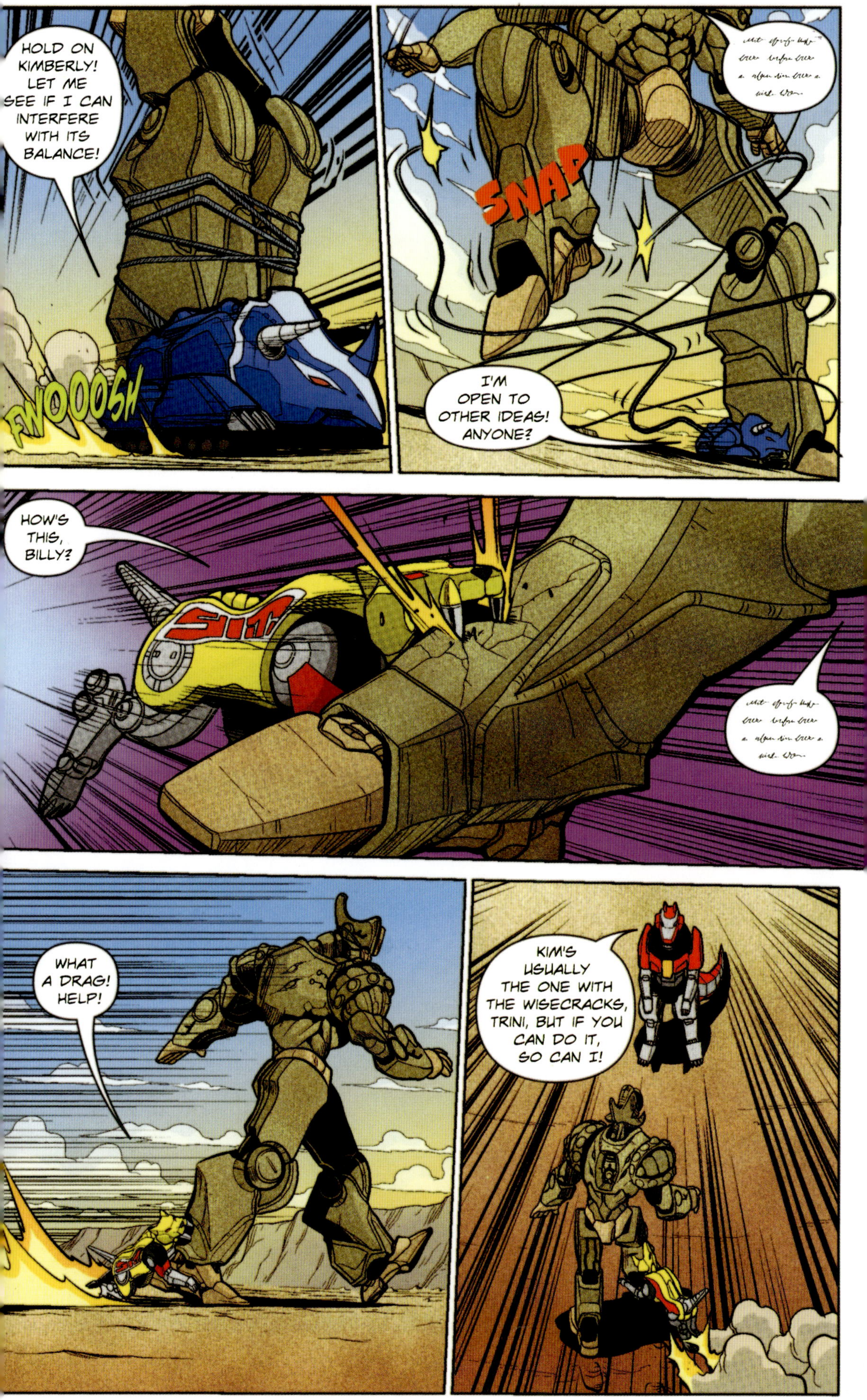

HOLD ON KIMBERLY! LET ME SEE IF I CAN INTERFERE WITH ITS BALANCE!
FWOOOSH
SNAP
I'M OPEN TO OTHER IDEAS! ANYONE?
HOW'S THIS, BILLY?
WHAT A DRAG! HELP!
KIM'S USUALLY THE ONE WITH THE WISECRACKS, TRINI, BUT IF YOU CAN DO IT, SO CAN I!

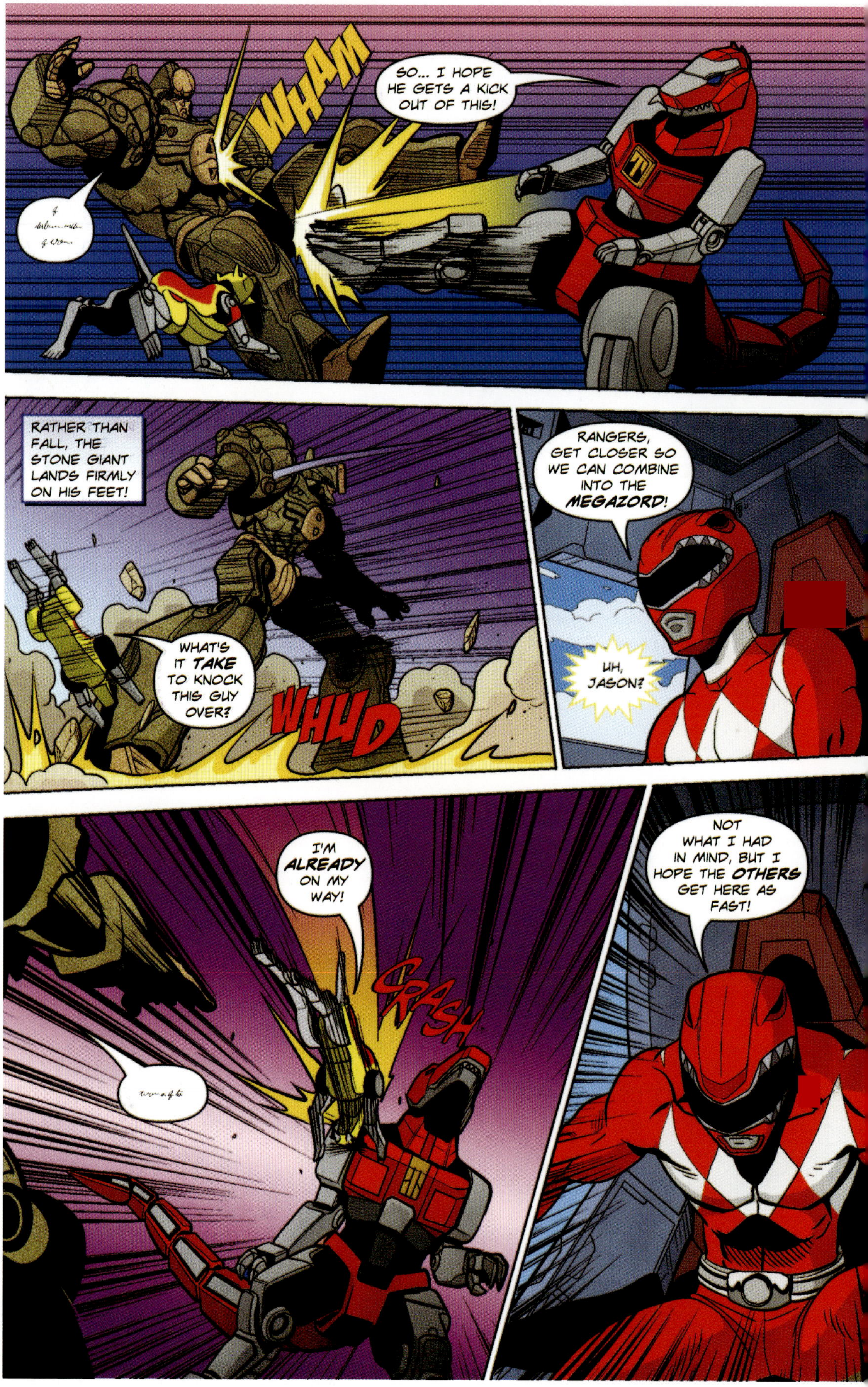
WHAM
SO... I HOPE HE GETS A KICK OUT OF THIS!
RATHER THAN FALL, THE STONE GIANT LANDS FIRMLY ON HIS FEET!
WHAT'S IT **TAKE** TO KNOCK THIS GUY OVER?
WHUD
RANGERS, GET CLOSER SO WE CAN COMBINE INTO THE ***MEGAZORD***!
UH, JASON?
I'M ***ALREADY*** ON MY WAY!
CRASH
NOT WHAT I HAD IN MIND, BUT I HOPE THE ***OTHERS*** GET HERE AS FAST!

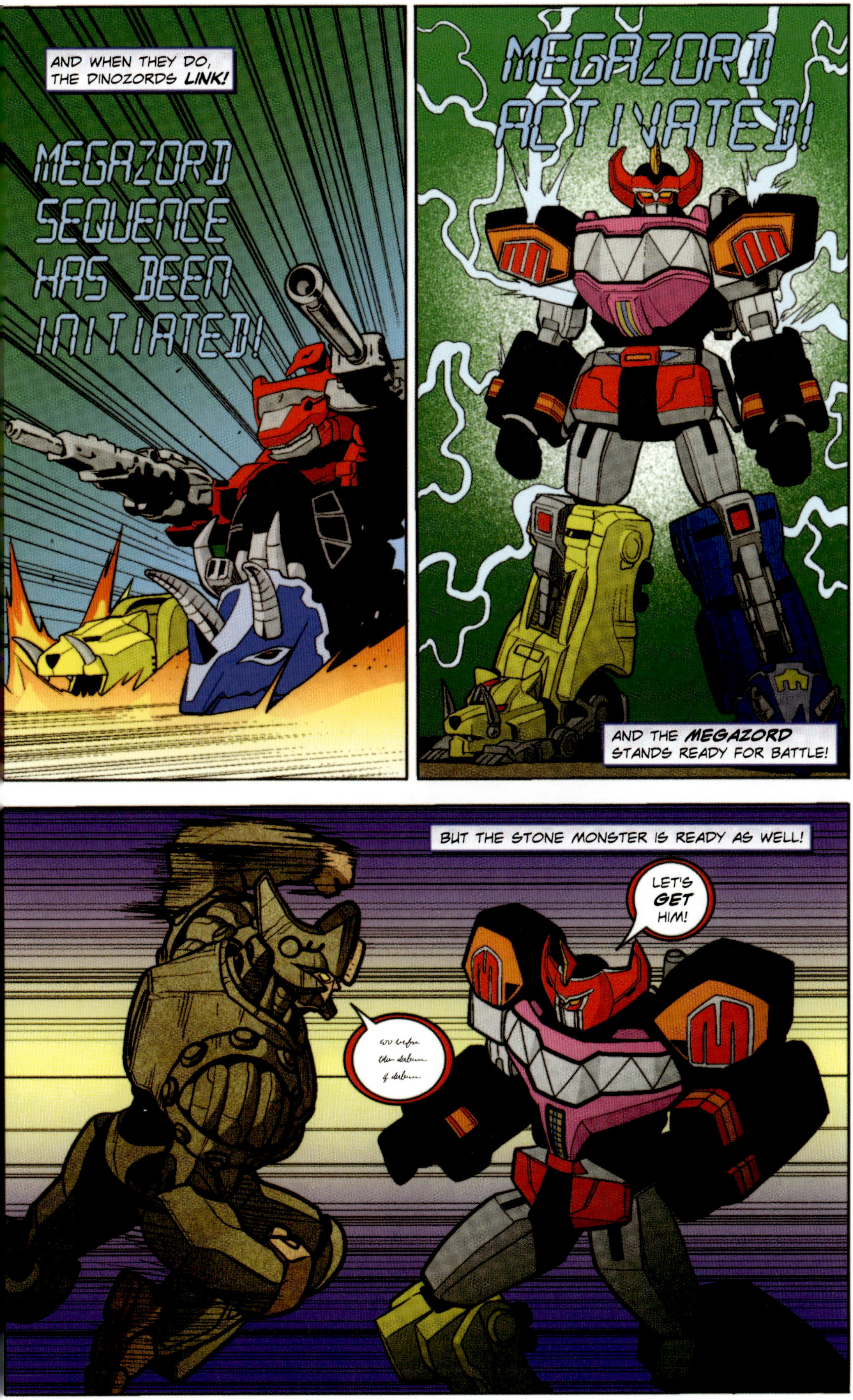
AND WHEN THEY DO, THE DINOZORDS LINK!
MEGAZORD SEQUENCE HAS BEEN INITIATED!
MEGAZORD ACTIVATED!
AND THE MEGAZORD STANDS READY FOR BATTLE!
BUT THE STONE MONSTER IS READY AS WELL!
LET'S GET HIM!

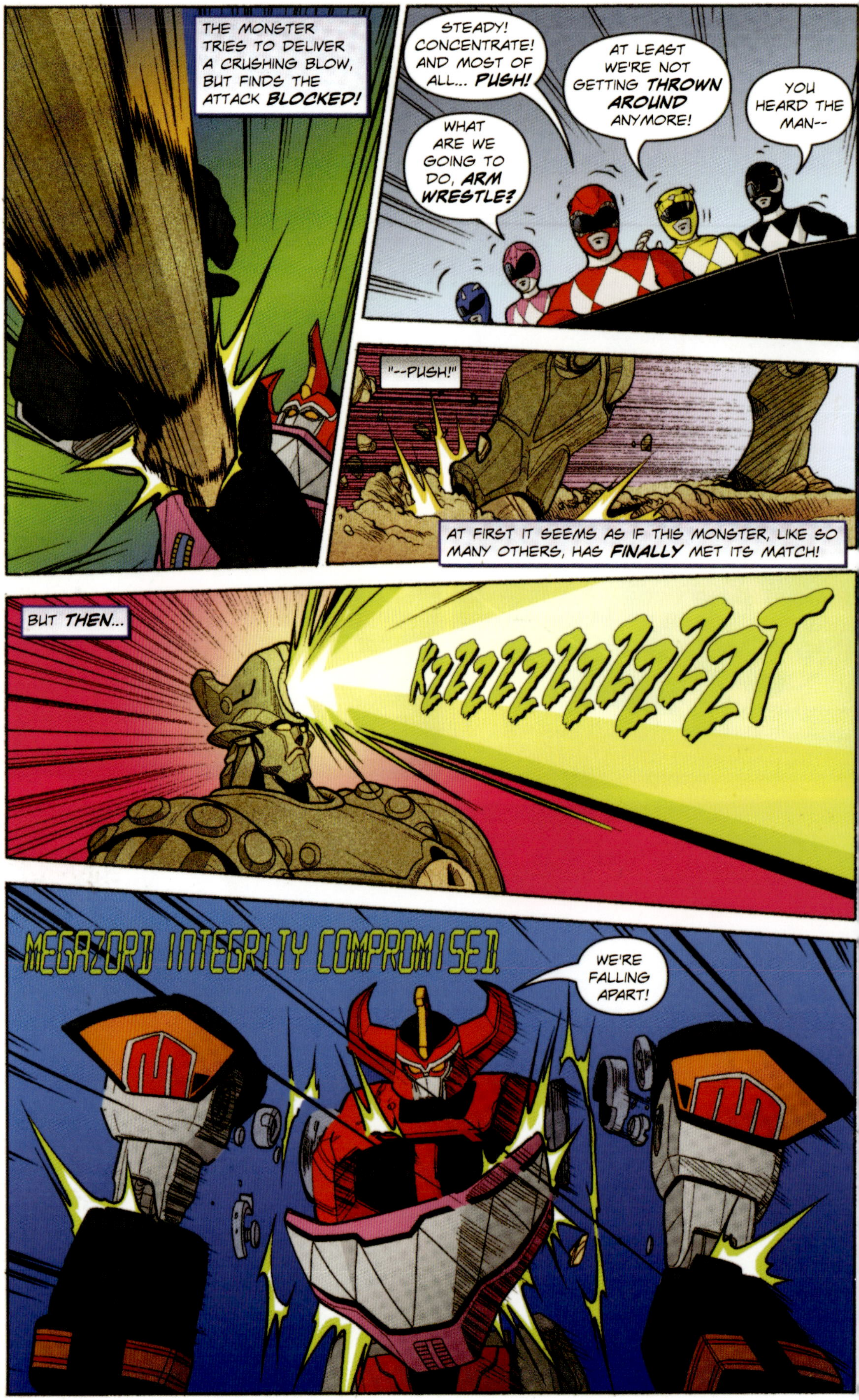
THE MONSTER TRIES TO DELIVER A CRUSHING BLOW, BUT FINDS THE ATTACK BLOCKED!
STEADY! CONCENTRATE! AND MOST OF ALL... PUSH!
WHAT ARE WE GOING TO DO, ARM WRESTLE?
AT LEAST WE'RE NOT GETTING THROWN AROUND ANYMORE!
YOU HEARD THE MAN--
"--PUSH!"
AT FIRST IT SEEMS AS IF THIS MONSTER, LIKE SO MANY OTHERS, HAS FINALLY MET ITS MATCH!
BUT THEN...
KZZZZZZZZZZZZT
MEGAZORD INTEGRITY COMPROMISED.
WE'RE FALLING APART!

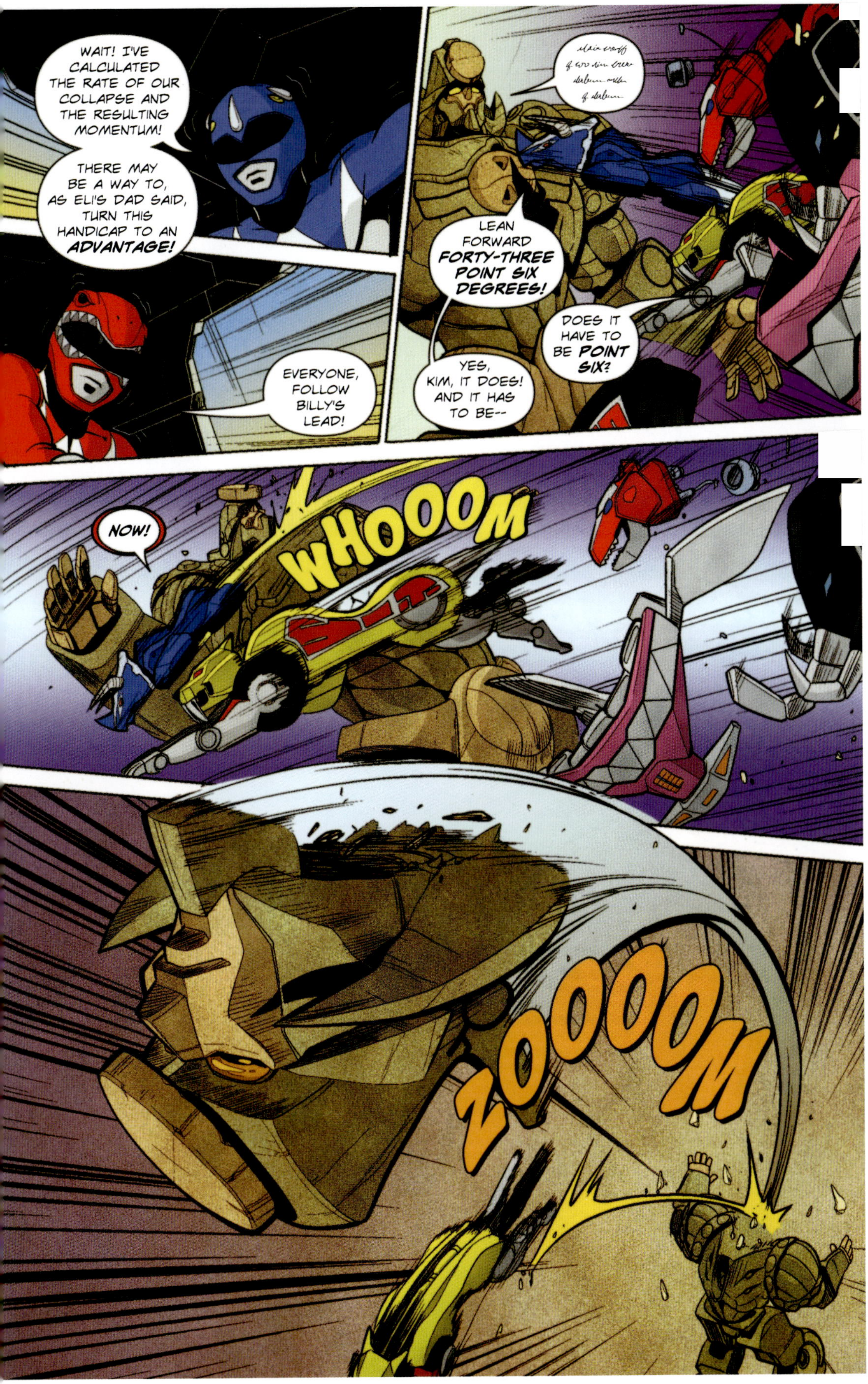
WAIT! I'VE CALCULATED THE RATE OF OUR COLLAPSE AND THE RESULTING MOMENTUM!
THERE MAY BE A WAY TO, AS ELI'S DAD SAID, TURN THIS HANDICAP TO AN ADVANTAGE!
EVERYONE, FOLLOW BILLY'S LEAD!
LEAN FORWARD FORTY-THREE POINT SIX DEGREES!
DOES IT HAVE TO BE POINT SIX?
YES, KIM, IT DOES! AND IT HAS TO BE--
NOW!
WHOOOM
ZOOOOM

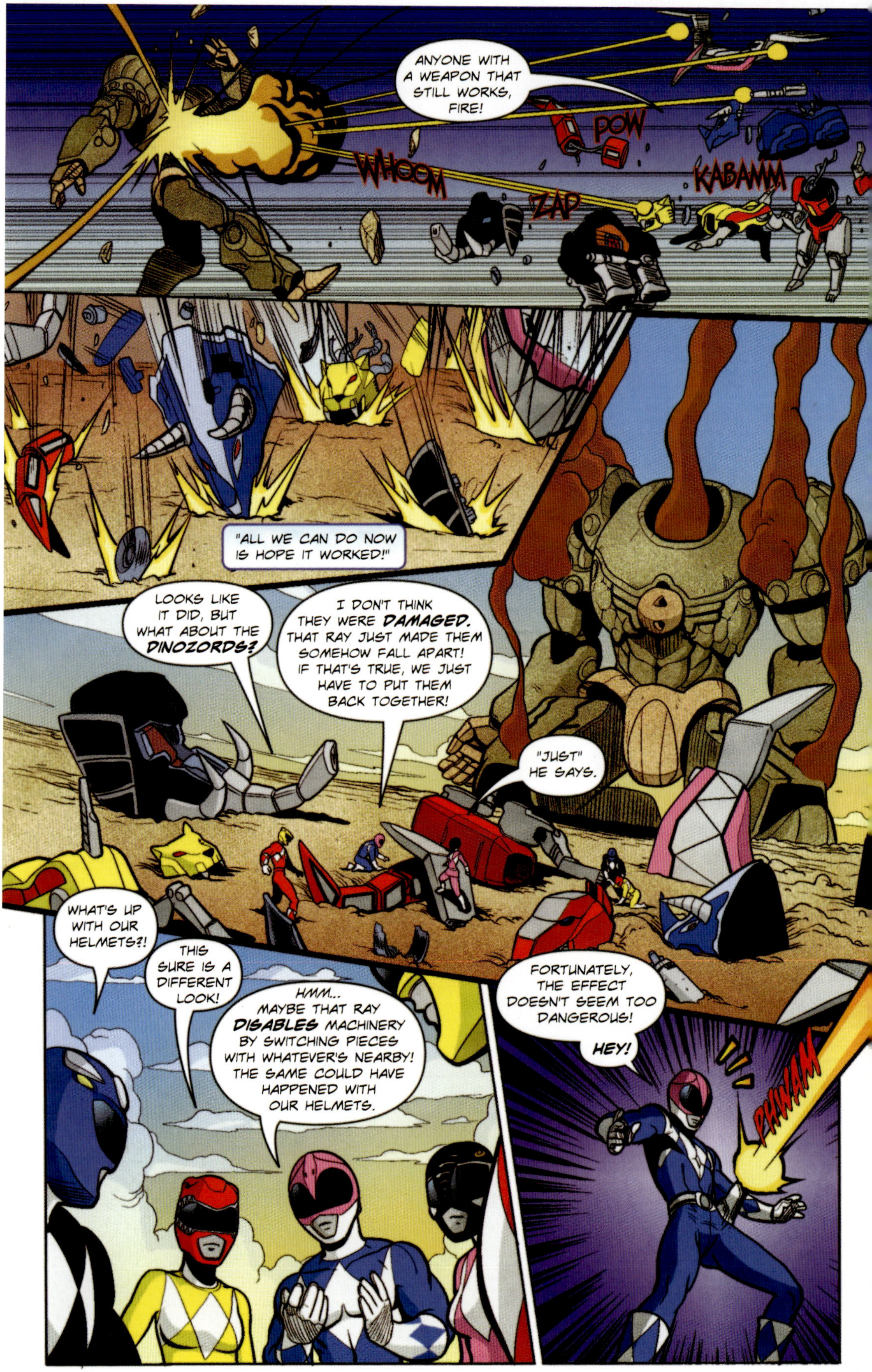
ANYONE WITH A WEAPON THAT STILL WORKS, FIRE!
POW
WHOOM
ZAP
KABAMM
"ALL WE CAN DO NOW IS HOPE IT WORKED!"
LOOKS LIKE IT DID, BUT WHAT ABOUT THE DINOZORDS?
I DON'T THINK THEY WERE DAMAGED. THAT RAY JUST MADE THEM SOMEHOW FALL APART! IF THAT'S TRUE, WE JUST HAVE TO PUT THEM BACK TOGETHER!
"JUST" HE SAYS.
WHAT'S UP WITH OUR HELMETS?!
THIS SURE IS A DIFFERENT LOOK!
HMM... MAYBE THAT RAY DISABLES MACHINERY BY SWITCHING PIECES WITH WHATEVER'S NEARBY! THE SAME COULD HAVE HAPPENED WITH OUR HELMETS.
FORTUNATELY, THE EFFECT DOESN'T SEEM TOO DANGEROUS!
HEY!
PHWAM

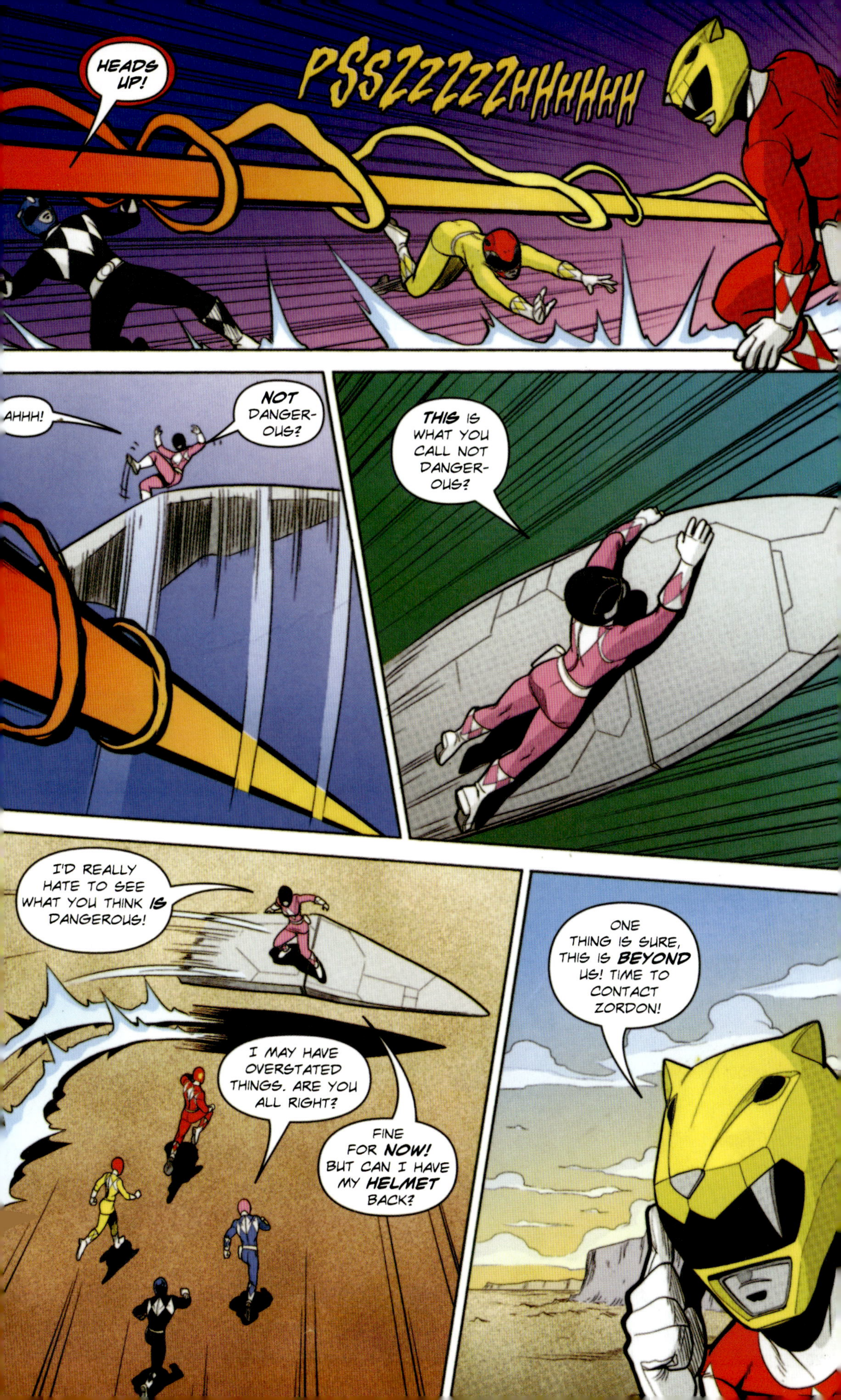
HEADS UP!
PSSZZZZZZHHHHHH
AHHH!
NOT DANGER-OUS?
THIS IS WHAT YOU CALL NOT DANGER-OUS?
I'D REALLY HATE TO SEE WHAT YOU THINK IS DANGEROUS!
I MAY HAVE OVERSTATED THINGS. ARE YOU ALL RIGHT?
FINE FOR NOW! BUT CAN I HAVE MY HELMET BACK?
ONE THING IS SURE, THIS IS BEYOND US! TIME TO CONTACT ZORDON!

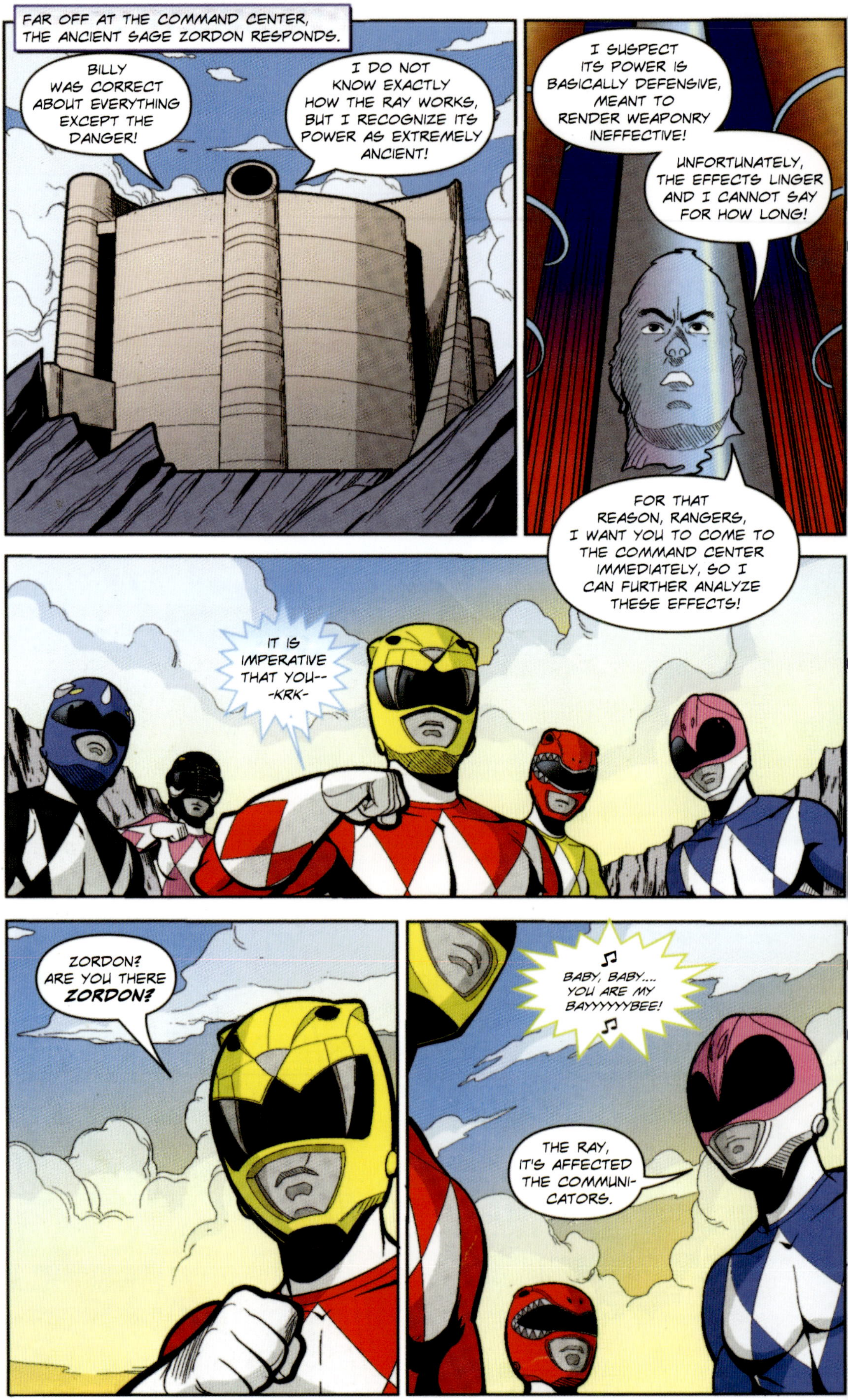
FAR OFF AT THE COMMAND CENTER, THE ANCIENT SAGE ZORDON RESPONDS.
BILLY WAS CORRECT ABOUT EVERYTHING EXCEPT THE DANGER!
I DO NOT KNOW EXACTLY HOW THE RAY WORKS, BUT I RECOGNIZE ITS POWER AS EXTREMELY ANCIENT!
I SUSPECT ITS POWER IS BASICALLY DEFENSIVE, MEANT TO RENDER WEAPONRY INEFFECTIVE!
UNFORTUNATELY, THE EFFECTS LINGER AND I CANNOT SAY FOR HOW LONG!
FOR THAT REASON, RANGERS, I WANT YOU TO COME TO THE COMMAND CENTER IMMEDIATELY, SO I CAN FURTHER ANALYZE THESE EFFECTS!
IT IS IMPERATIVE THAT YOU-- -KRK-
ZORDON? ARE YOU THERE ZORDON?
BABY, BABY.... YOU ARE MY BAYYYYYYBEE!
THE RAY, IT'S AFFECTED THE COMMUNI-CATORS.

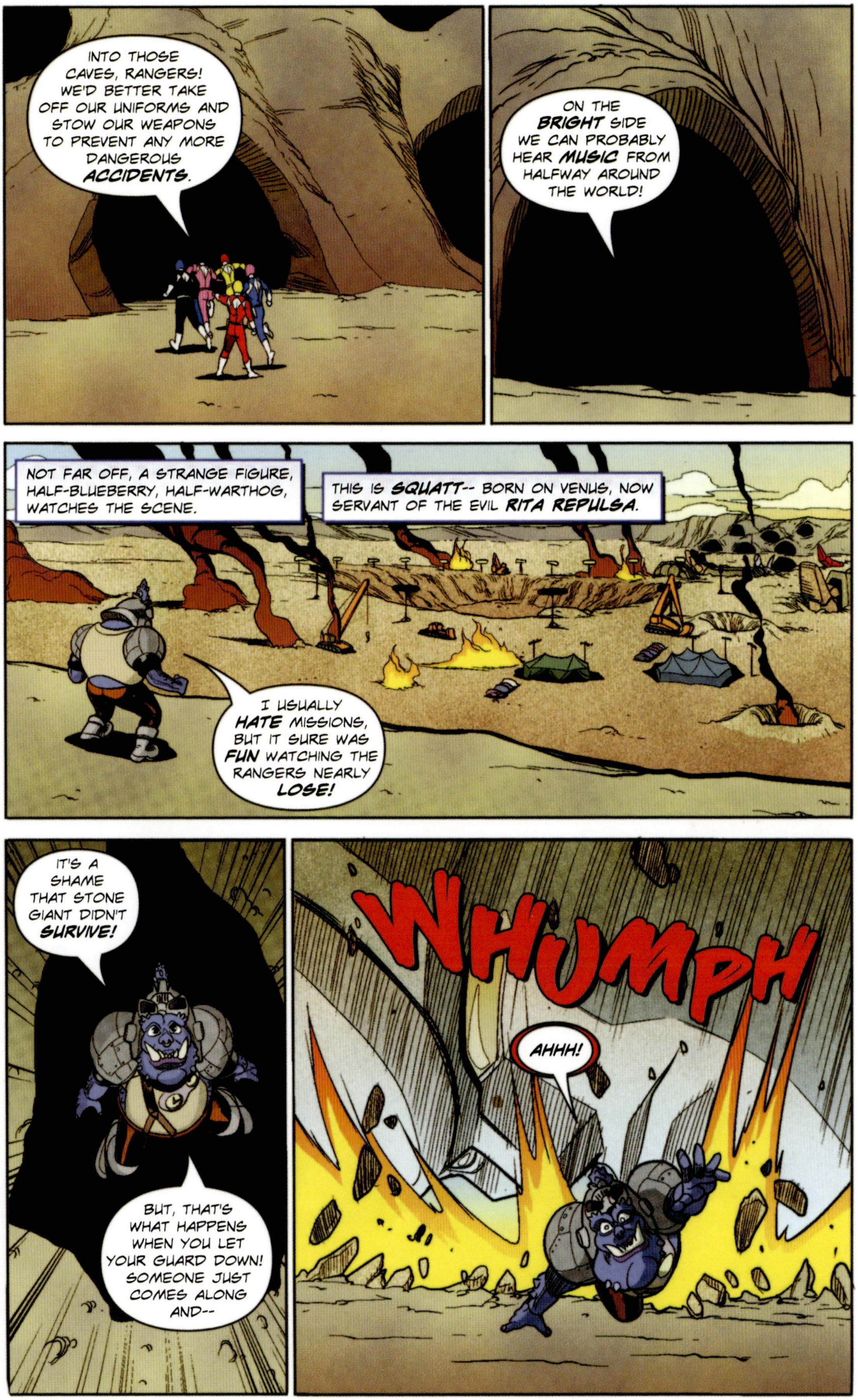
INTO THOSE CAVES, RANGERS! WE'D BETTER TAKE OFF OUR UNIFORMS AND STOW OUR WEAPONS TO PREVENT ANY MORE DANGEROUS ACCIDENTS.
ON THE BRIGHT SIDE WE CAN PROBABLY HEAR MUSIC FROM HALFWAY AROUND THE WORLD!
NOT FAR OFF, A STRANGE FIGURE, HALF-BLUEBERRY, HALF-WARTHOG, WATCHES THE SCENE.
THIS IS SQUATT-- BORN ON VENUS, NOW SERVANT OF THE EVIL RITA REPULSA.
I USUALLY HATE MISSIONS, BUT IT SURE WAS FUN WATCHING THE RANGERS NEARLY LOSE!
IT'S A SHAME THAT STONE GIANT DIDN'T SURVIVE!
BUT, THAT'S WHAT HAPPENS WHEN YOU LET YOUR GUARD DOWN! SOMEONE JUST COMES ALONG AND--
WHUMPH
AHHH!

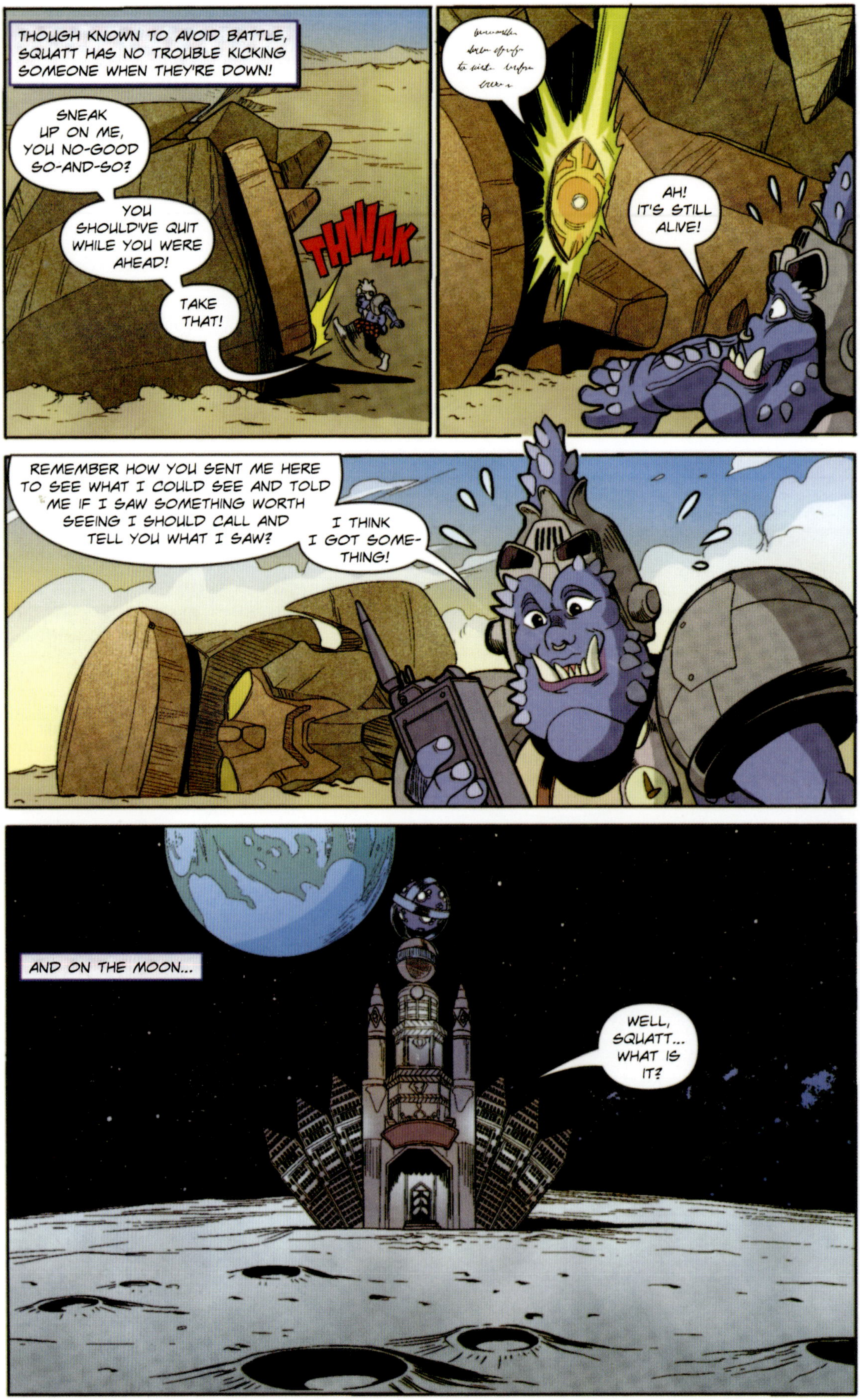

THOUGH KNOWN TO AVOID BATTLE, SQUATT HAS NO TROUBLE KICKING SOMEONE WHEN THEY'RE DOWN!
SNEAK UP ON ME, YOU NO-GOOD SO-AND-SO?
YOU SHOULD'VE QUIT WHILE YOU WERE AHEAD!
TAKE THAT!
THWAK
AH! IT'S STILL ALIVE!
REMEMBER HOW YOU SENT ME HERE TO SEE WHAT I COULD SEE AND TOLD ME IF I SAW SOMETHING WORTH SEEING I SHOULD CALL AND TELL YOU WHAT I SAW?
I THINK I GOT SOME-THING!
AND ON THE MOON...
WELL, SQUATT... WHAT IS IT?

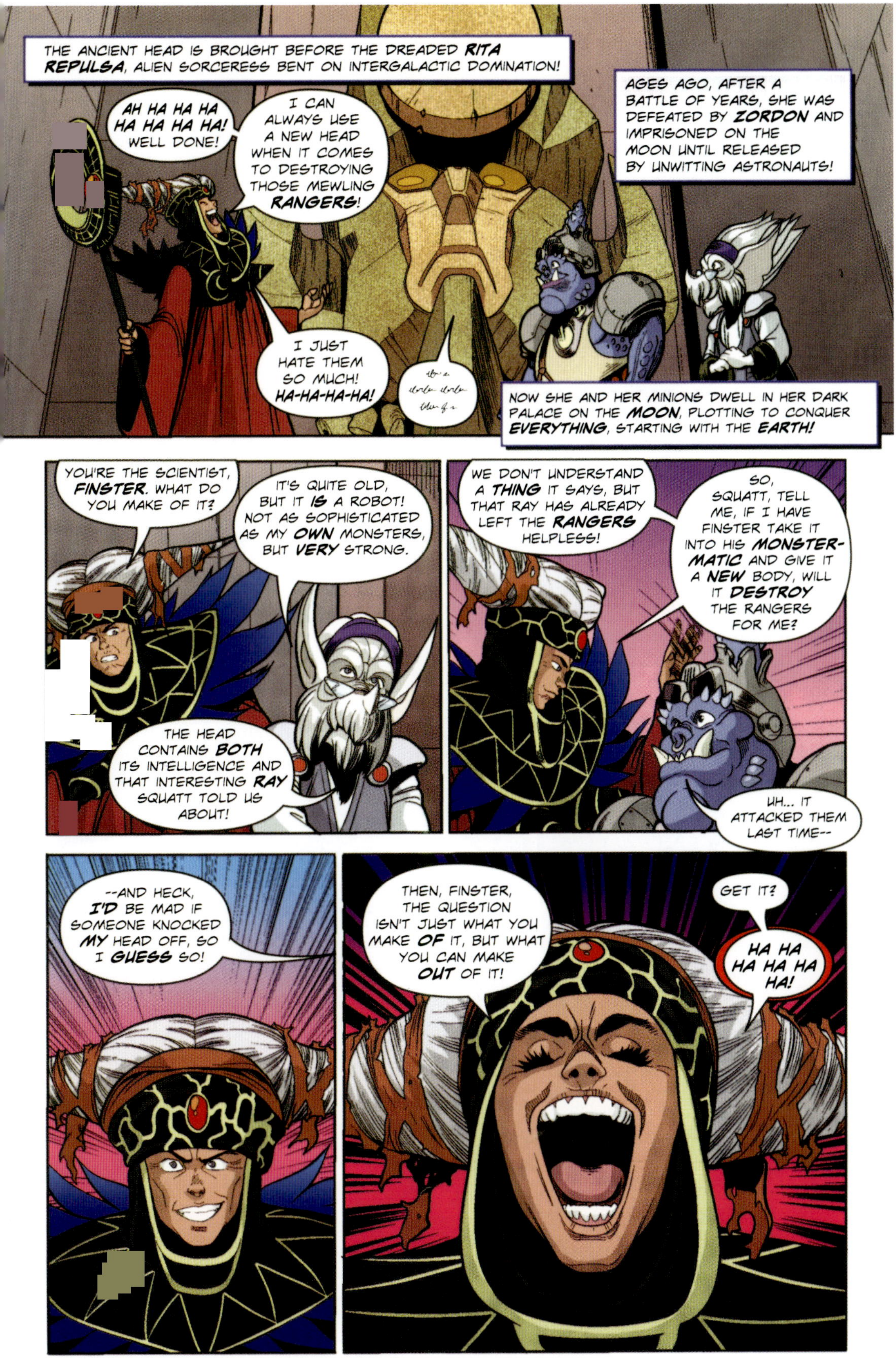
THE ANCIENT HEAD IS BROUGHT BEFORE THE DREADED RITA REPULSA, ALIEN SORCERESS BENT ON INTERGALACTIC DOMINATION!
AH HA HA HA HA HA HA HA! WELL DONE!
I CAN ALWAYS USE A NEW HEAD WHEN IT COMES TO DESTROYING THOSE MEWLING RANGERS!
I JUST HATE THEM SO MUCH! HA-HA-HA-HA!
AGES AGO, AFTER A BATTLE OF YEARS, SHE WAS DEFEATED BY ZORDON AND IMPRISONED ON THE MOON UNTIL RELEASED BY UNWITTING ASTRONAUTS!
NOW SHE AND HER MINIONS DWELL IN HER DARK PALACE ON THE MOON, PLOTTING TO CONQUER EVERYTHING, STARTING WITH THE EARTH!
YOU'RE THE SCIENTIST, FINSTER. WHAT DO YOU MAKE OF IT?
IT'S QUITE OLD, BUT IT IS A ROBOT! NOT AS SOPHISTICATED AS MY OWN MONSTERS, BUT VERY STRONG.
THE HEAD CONTAINS BOTH ITS INTELLIGENCE AND THAT INTERESTING RAY SQUATT TOLD US ABOUT!
WE DON'T UNDERSTAND A THING IT SAYS, BUT THAT RAY HAS ALREADY LEFT THE RANGERS HELPLESS!
SO, SQUATT, TELL ME, IF I HAVE FINSTER TAKE IT INTO HIS MONSTER-MATIC AND GIVE IT A NEW BODY, WILL IT DESTROY THE RANGERS FOR ME?
UH... IT ATTACKED THEM LAST TIME--
--AND HECK, I'D BE MAD IF SOMEONE KNOCKED MY HEAD OFF, SO I GUESS SO!
THEN, FINSTER, THE QUESTION ISN'T JUST WHAT YOU MAKE OF IT, BUT WHAT YOU CAN MAKE OUT OF IT!
GET IT?
HA HA HA HA HA HA!

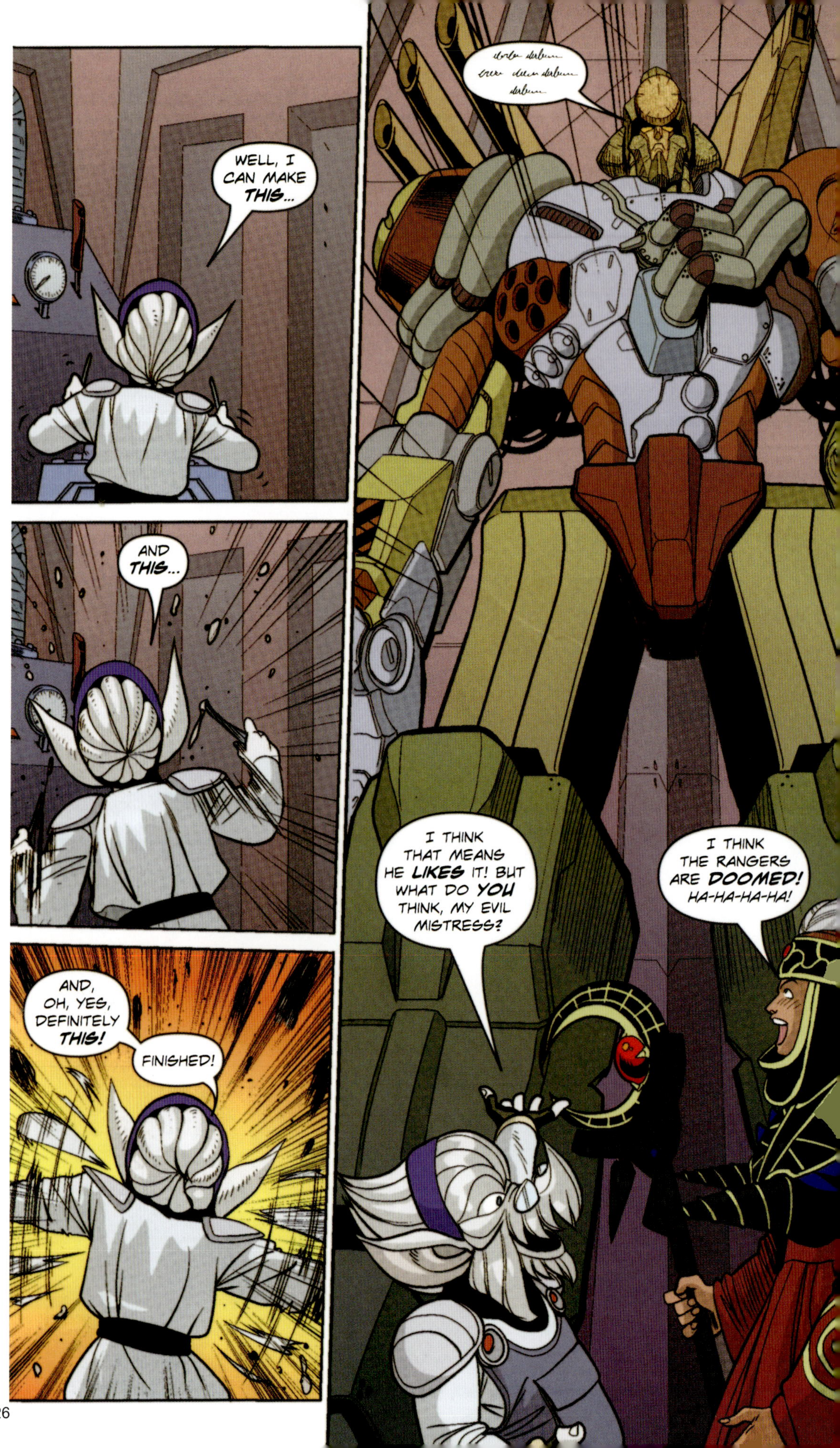
WELL, I CAN MAKE THIS...
AND THIS...
AND, OH, YES, DEFINITELY THIS!
FINISHED!
I THINK THAT MEANS HE LIKES IT! BUT WHAT DO YOU THINK, MY EVIL MISTRESS?
I THINK THE RANGERS ARE DOOMED! HA-HA-HA-HA!

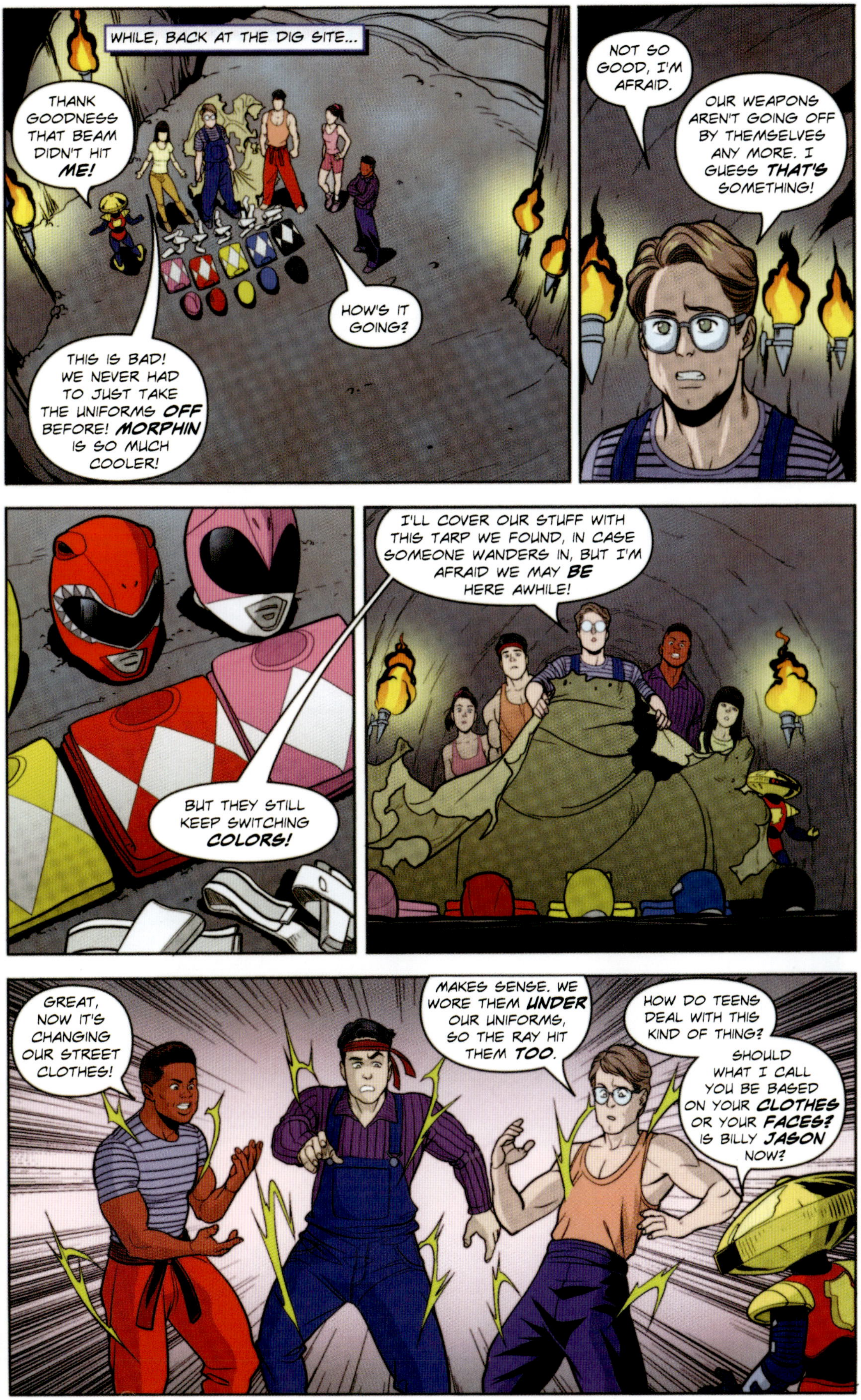

WHILE, BACK AT THE DIG SITE...
THANK GOODNESS THAT BEAM DIDN'T HIT ME!
THIS IS BAD! WE NEVER HAD TO JUST TAKE THE UNIFORMS OFF BEFORE! MORPHIN IS SO MUCH COOLER!
HOW'S IT GOING?
NOT SO GOOD, I'M AFRAID.
OUR WEAPONS AREN'T GOING OFF BY THEMSELVES ANY MORE. I GUESS THAT'S SOMETHING!
BUT THEY STILL KEEP SWITCHING COLORS!
I'LL COVER OUR STUFF WITH THIS TARP WE FOUND, IN CASE SOMEONE WANDERS IN, BUT I'M AFRAID WE MAY BE HERE AWHILE!
GREAT, NOW IT'S CHANGING OUR STREET CLOTHES!
MAKES SENSE. WE WORE THEM UNDER OUR UNIFORMS, SO THE RAY HIT THEM TOO.
HOW DO TEENS DEAL WITH THIS KIND OF THING?
SHOULD WHAT I CALL YOU BE BASED ON YOUR CLOTHES OR YOUR FACES? IS BILLY JASON NOW?

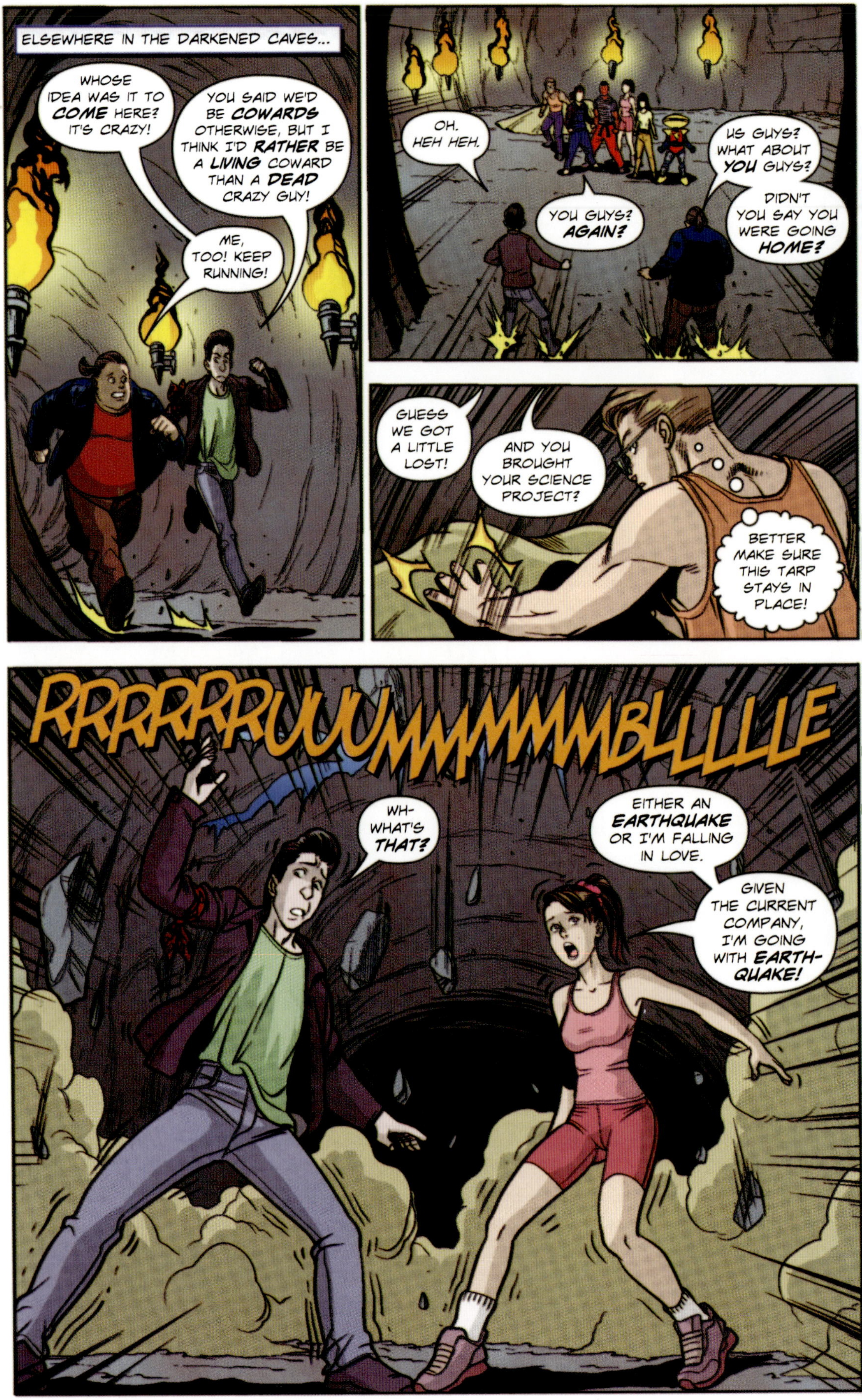

ELSEWHERE IN THE DARKENED CAVES...
WHOSE IDEA WAS IT TO COME HERE? IT'S CRAZY!
YOU SAID WE'D BE COWARDS OTHERWISE, BUT I THINK I'D RATHER BE A LIVING COWARD THAN A DEAD CRAZY GUY!
ME, TOO! KEEP RUNNING!
OH. HEH HEH.
YOU GUYS? AGAIN?
US GUYS? WHAT ABOUT YOU GUYS?
DIDN'T YOU SAY YOU WERE GOING HOME?
GUESS WE GOT A LITTLE LOST!
AND YOU BROUGHT YOUR SCIENCE PROJECT?
BETTER MAKE SURE THIS TARP STAYS IN PLACE!
RRRRRRUUUMMMMMBLLLLLE
WH-WHAT'S THAT?
EITHER AN EARTHQUAKE OR I'M FALLING IN LOVE.
GIVEN THE CURRENT COMPANY, I'M GOING WITH EARTHQUAKE!

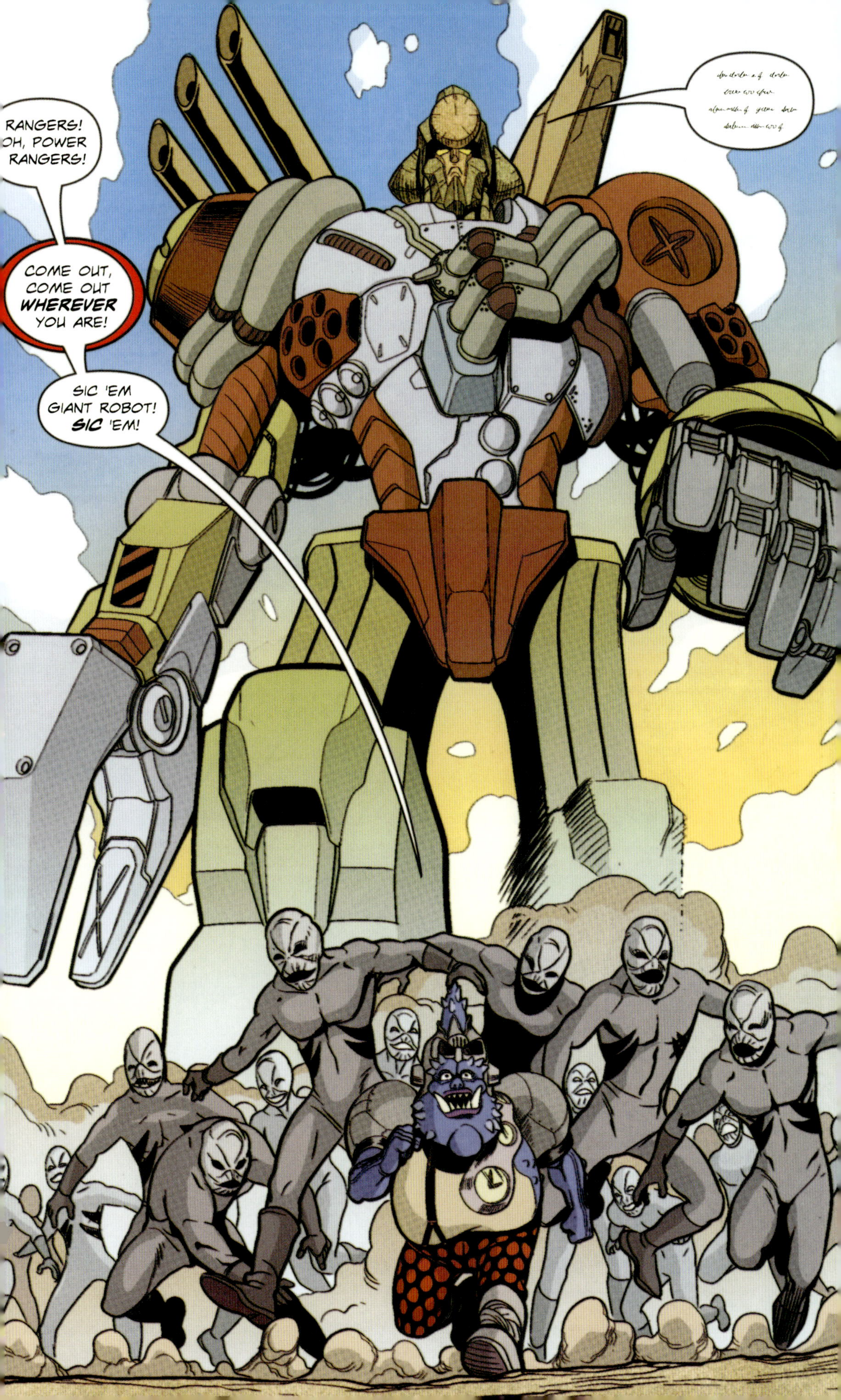
RANGERS! OH, POWER RANGERS!
COME OUT, COME OUT **WHEREVER** YOU ARE!
SIC 'EM GIANT ROBOT! **SIC** 'EM!

BOY, OH, BOY! GOTTA FIND 'EM, GOTTA FIND 'EM!

AFTER ALL, SINCE THE **BIG GUY** DOESN'T SPEAK OUR LANGUAGE, RITA PUT **ME** IN CHARGE.

DON'T WANT TO DISAPPOINT **HER!** NO, SIR!

DARN TEEN HEROES! WHAT'LL IT TAKE TO GET YOU TO SHOW?

WAIT... **HEROES.** HEROES LIKE TO **SAVE** PEOPLE, SO...

OH! I GOT IT! I **GOT** IT!

FIRST A GIANT ROBOT, NOW AND ALIEN INVASION! WHATEVER SHALL WE DO, DR. KENYON?

WE COULD START BY STAYING **QUIET,** DR. CARTER! THANK HEAVENS THEY HAVEN'T **HEARD** US YET!

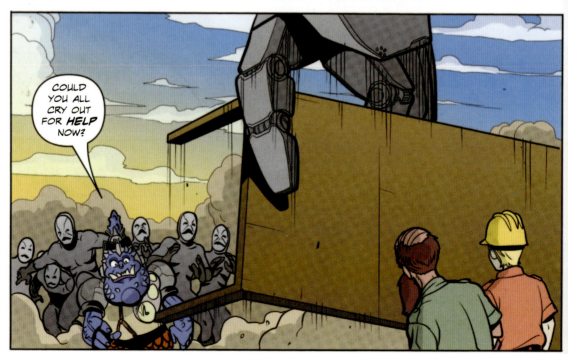

COULD YOU ALL CRY OUT FOR **HELP** NOW?

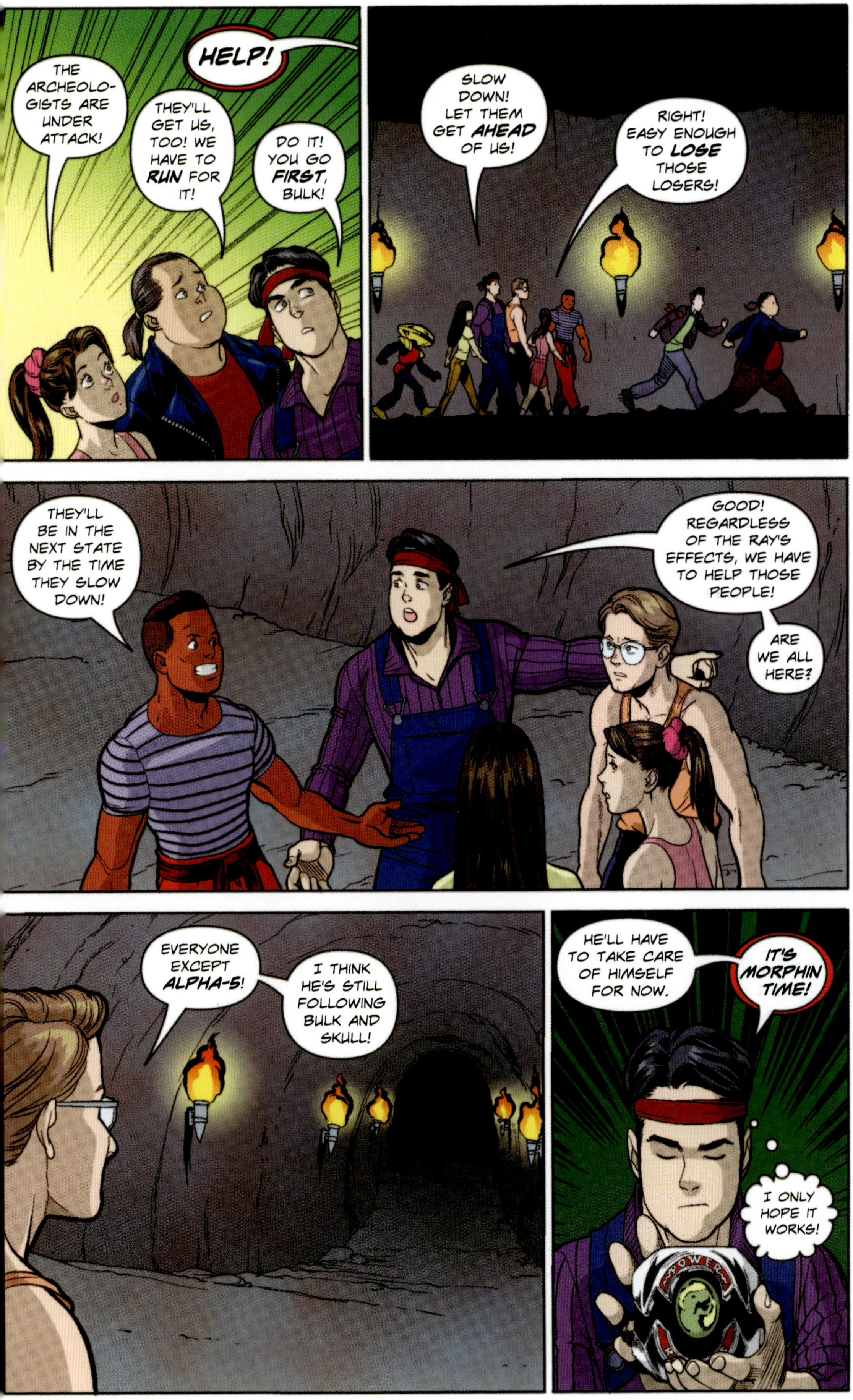

THE ARCHEOLOGISTS ARE UNDER ATTACK!
HELP!
THEY'LL GET US, TOO! WE HAVE TO RUN FOR IT!
DO IT! YOU GO FIRST, BULK!
SLOW DOWN! LET THEM GET AHEAD OF US!
RIGHT! EASY ENOUGH TO LOSE THOSE LOSERS!
THEY'LL BE IN THE NEXT STATE BY THE TIME THEY SLOW DOWN!
GOOD! REGARDLESS OF THE RAY'S EFFECTS, WE HAVE TO HELP THOSE PEOPLE!
ARE WE ALL HERE?
EVERYONE EXCEPT ALPHA-5!
I THINK HE'S STILL FOLLOWING BULK AND SKULL!
HE'LL HAVE TO TAKE CARE OF HIMSELF FOR NOW.
IT'S MORPHIN TIME!
I ONLY HOPE IT WORKS!
POWER

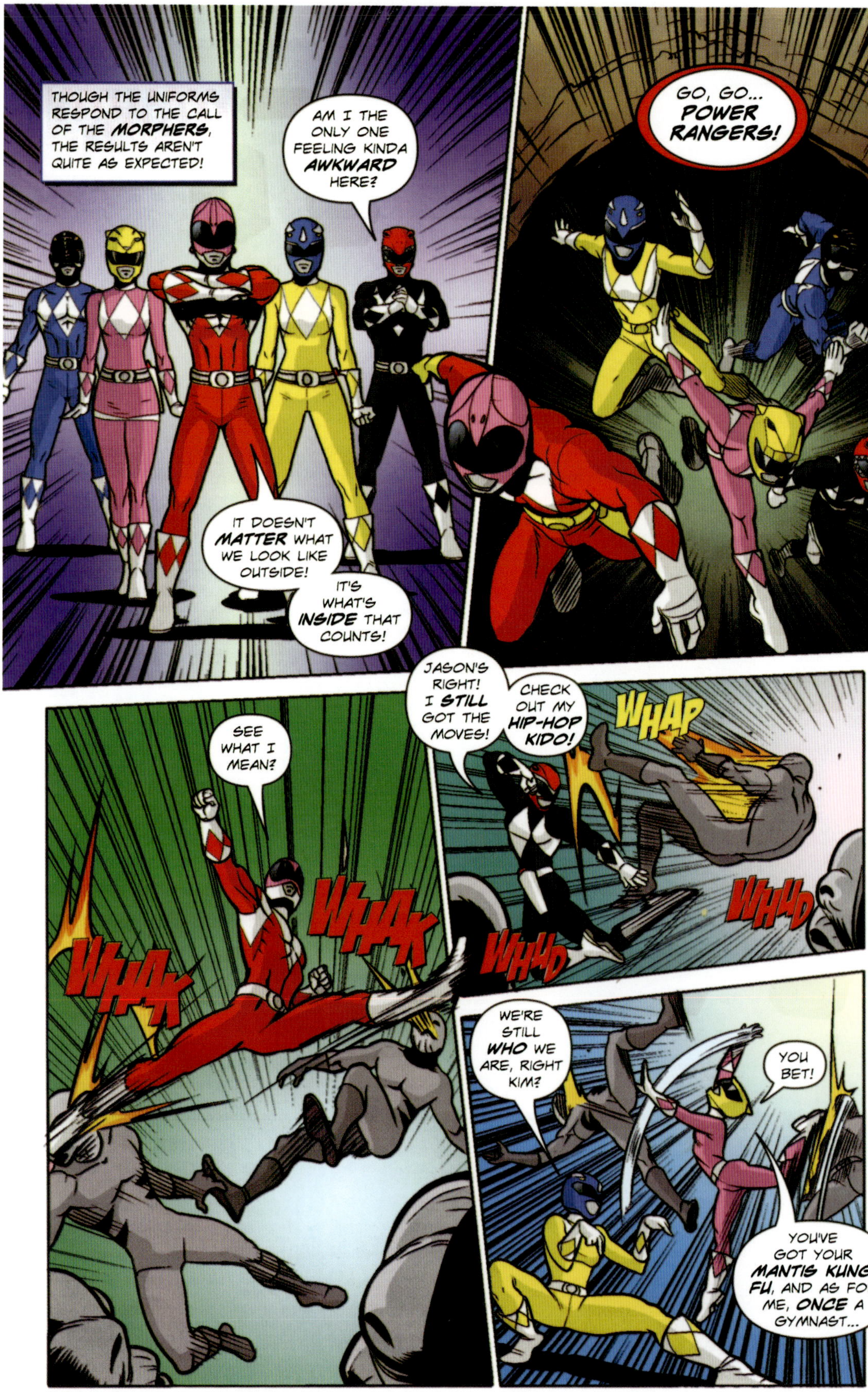
THOUGH THE UNIFORMS RESPOND TO THE CALL OF THE MORPHERS, THE RESULTS AREN'T QUITE AS EXPECTED!
AM I THE ONLY ONE FEELING KINDA AWKWARD HERE?
IT DOESN'T MATTER WHAT WE LOOK LIKE OUTSIDE!
IT'S WHAT'S INSIDE THAT COUNTS!
GO, GO... POWER RANGERS!
SEE WHAT I MEAN?
WHAK
WHAK
JASON'S RIGHT! I STILL GOT THE MOVES!
CHECK OUT MY HIP-HOP KIDO!
WHAP
WHUD
WHUD
WE'RE STILL WHO WE ARE, RIGHT KIM?
YOU BET!
YOU'VE GOT YOUR MANTIS KUNG FU, AND AS FOR ME, ONCE A GYMNAST...

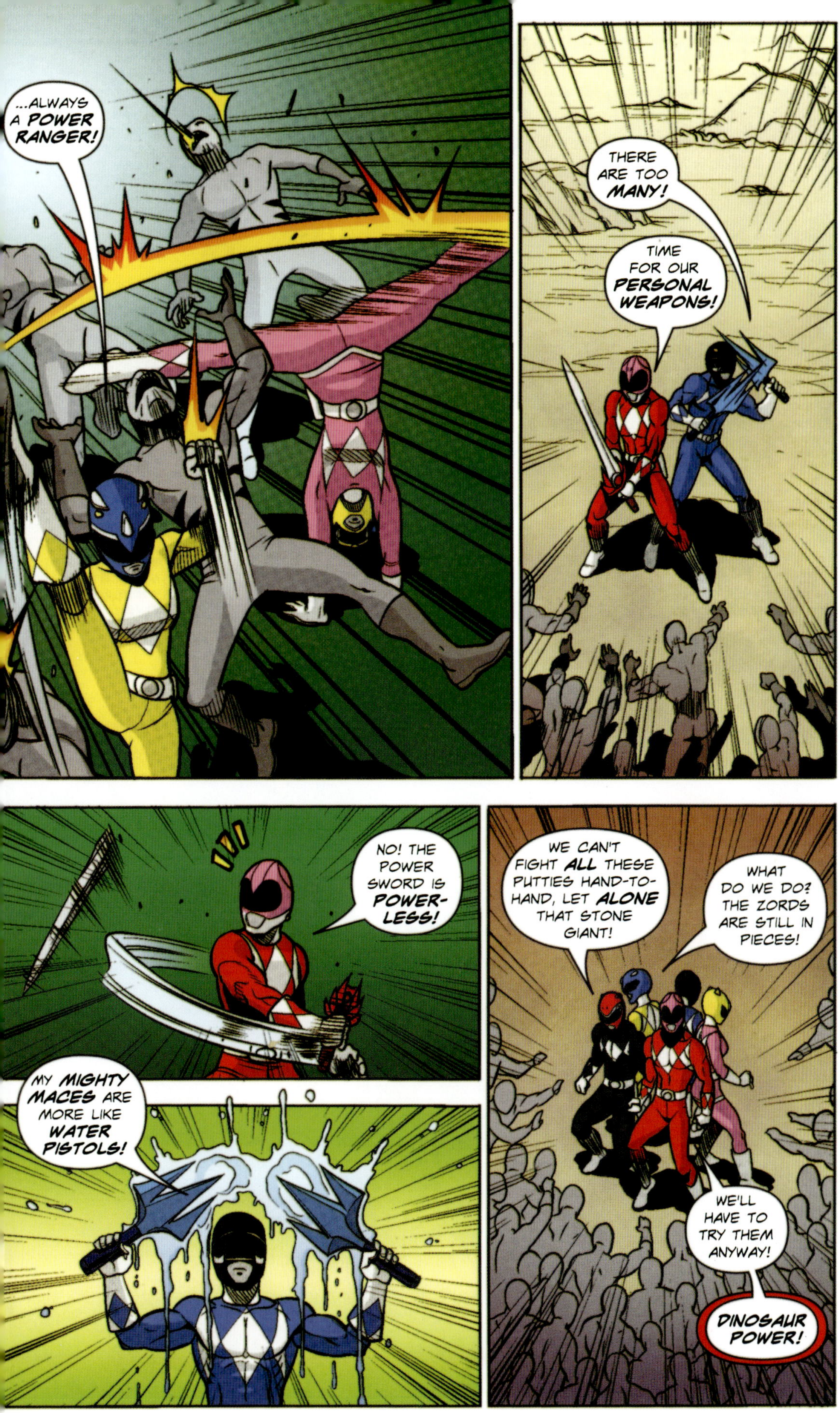
...ALWAYS A POWER RANGER!
THERE ARE TOO MANY!
TIME FOR OUR PERSONAL WEAPONS!
NO! THE POWER SWORD IS POWER-LESS!
MY MIGHTY MACES ARE MORE LIKE WATER PISTOLS!
WE CAN'T FIGHT ALL THESE PUTTIES HAND-TO-HAND, LET ALONE THAT STONE GIANT!
WHAT DO WE DO? THE ZORDS ARE STILL IN PIECES!
WE'LL HAVE TO TRY THEM ANYWAY!
DINOSAUR POWER!

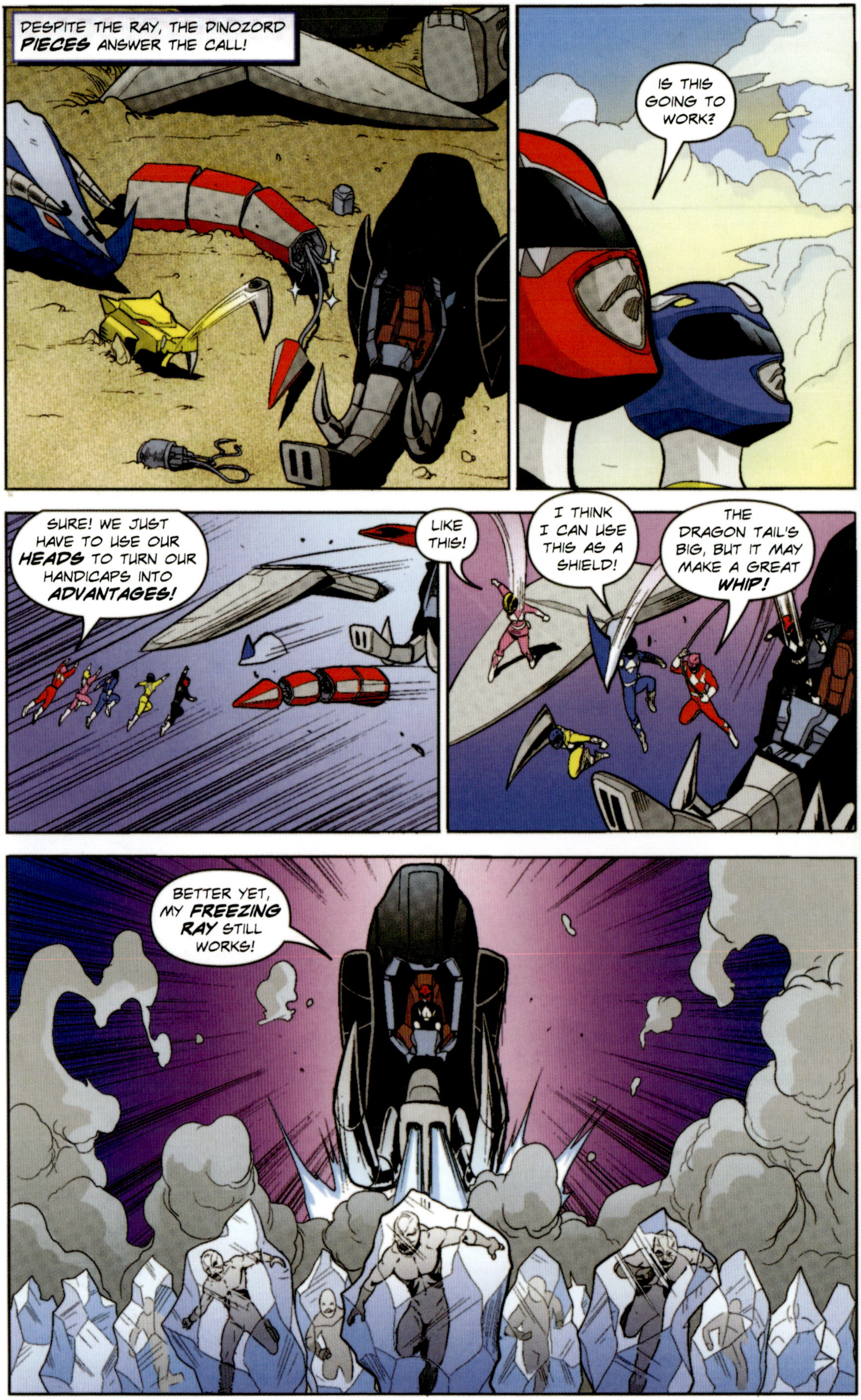

DESPITE THE RAY, THE DINOZORD **PIECES** ANSWER THE CALL!
IS THIS GOING TO WORK?
SURE! WE JUST HAVE TO USE OUR **HEADS** TO TURN OUR HANDICAPS INTO **ADVANTAGES!**
LIKE THIS!
I THINK I CAN USE THIS AS A SHIELD!
THE DRAGON TAIL'S BIG, BUT IT MAY MAKE A GREAT **WHIP!**
BETTER YET, MY **FREEZING RAY** STILL WORKS!

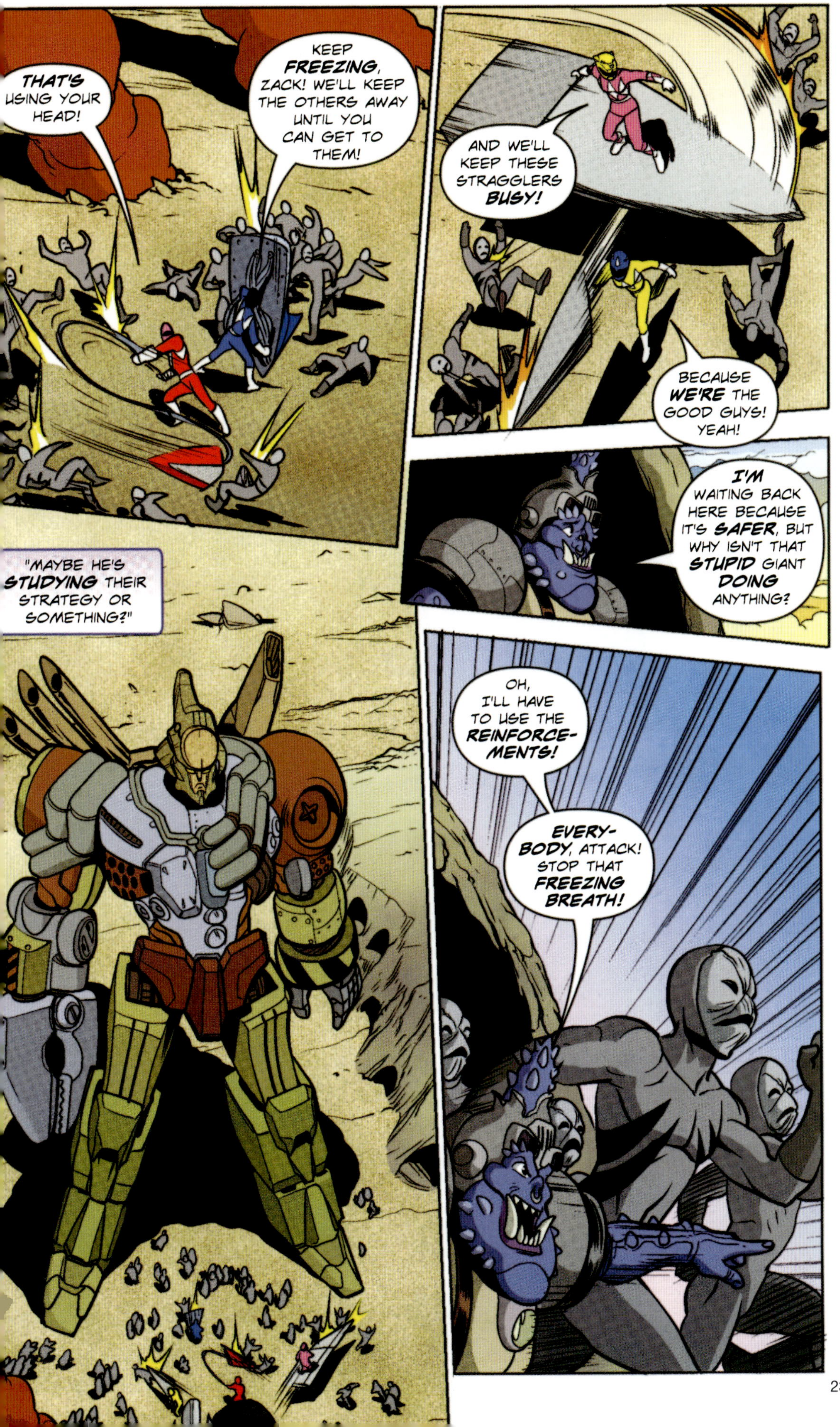
THAT'S USING YOUR HEAD!
KEEP FREEZING, ZACK! WE'LL KEEP THE OTHERS AWAY UNTIL YOU CAN GET TO THEM!
AND WE'LL KEEP THESE STRAGGLERS BUSY!
BECAUSE WE'RE THE GOOD GUYS! YEAH!
I'M WAITING BACK HERE BECAUSE IT'S SAFER, BUT WHY ISN'T THAT STUPID GIANT DOING ANYTHING?
"MAYBE HE'S STUDYING THEIR STRATEGY OR SOMETHING?"
OH, I'LL HAVE TO USE THE REINFORCE-MENTS!
EVERY-BODY, ATTACK! STOP THAT FREEZING BREATH!

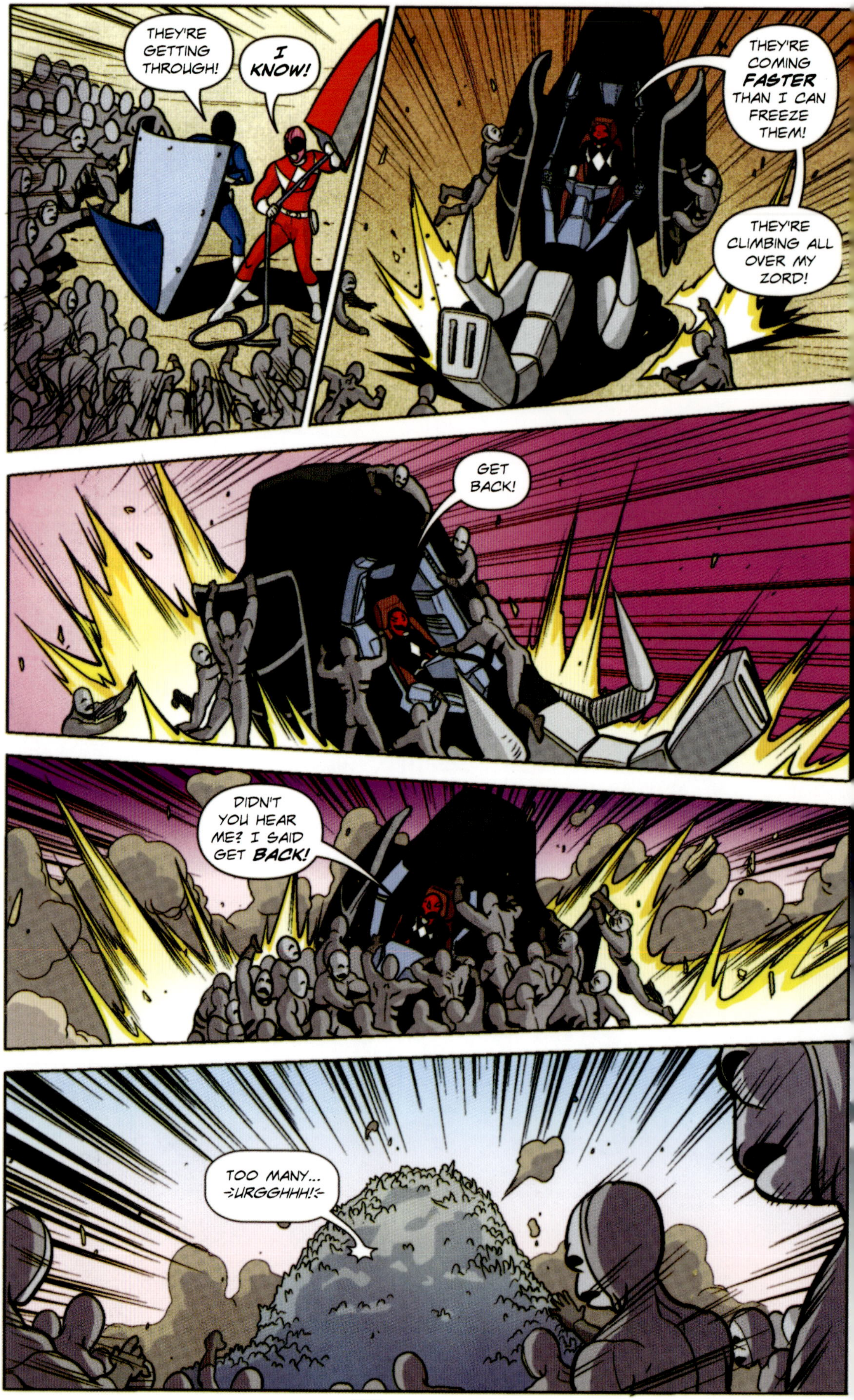
THEY'RE GETTING THROUGH!
I KNOW!
THEY'RE COMING FASTER THAN I CAN FREEZE THEM!
THEY'RE CLIMBING ALL OVER MY ZORD!
GET BACK!
DIDN'T YOU HEAR ME? I SAID GET BACK!
TOO MANY... URGGHHH!

WOWEE! ARE YOU SEEING THIS, MY QUEEN?

YOU **BET!**

HA HA HA HA HA HA HA!

HA HA HA HA!

HA HA HA HA HA HA!

YOU HEAR THAT **LAUGHING?** IT'S KIND OF **CATCHING!** HEH HEH!

NEVER MIND THAT! WHERE **IS** EVERYONE?

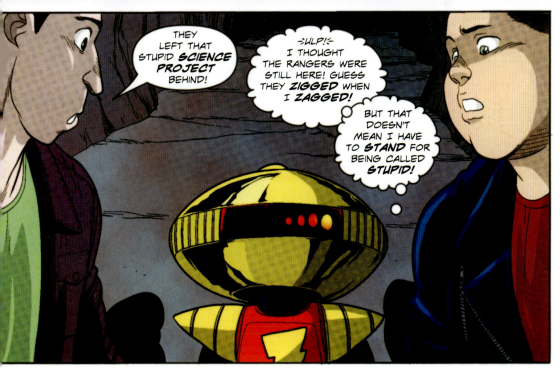

THEY LEFT THAT STUPID **SCIENCE PROJECT** BEHIND!

:ULP!: I THOUGHT THE RANGERS WERE STILL HERE! GUESS THEY **ZIGGED** WHEN I **ZAGGED!**

BUT THAT DOESN'T MEAN I HAVE TO **STAND** FOR BEING CALLED **STUPID!**

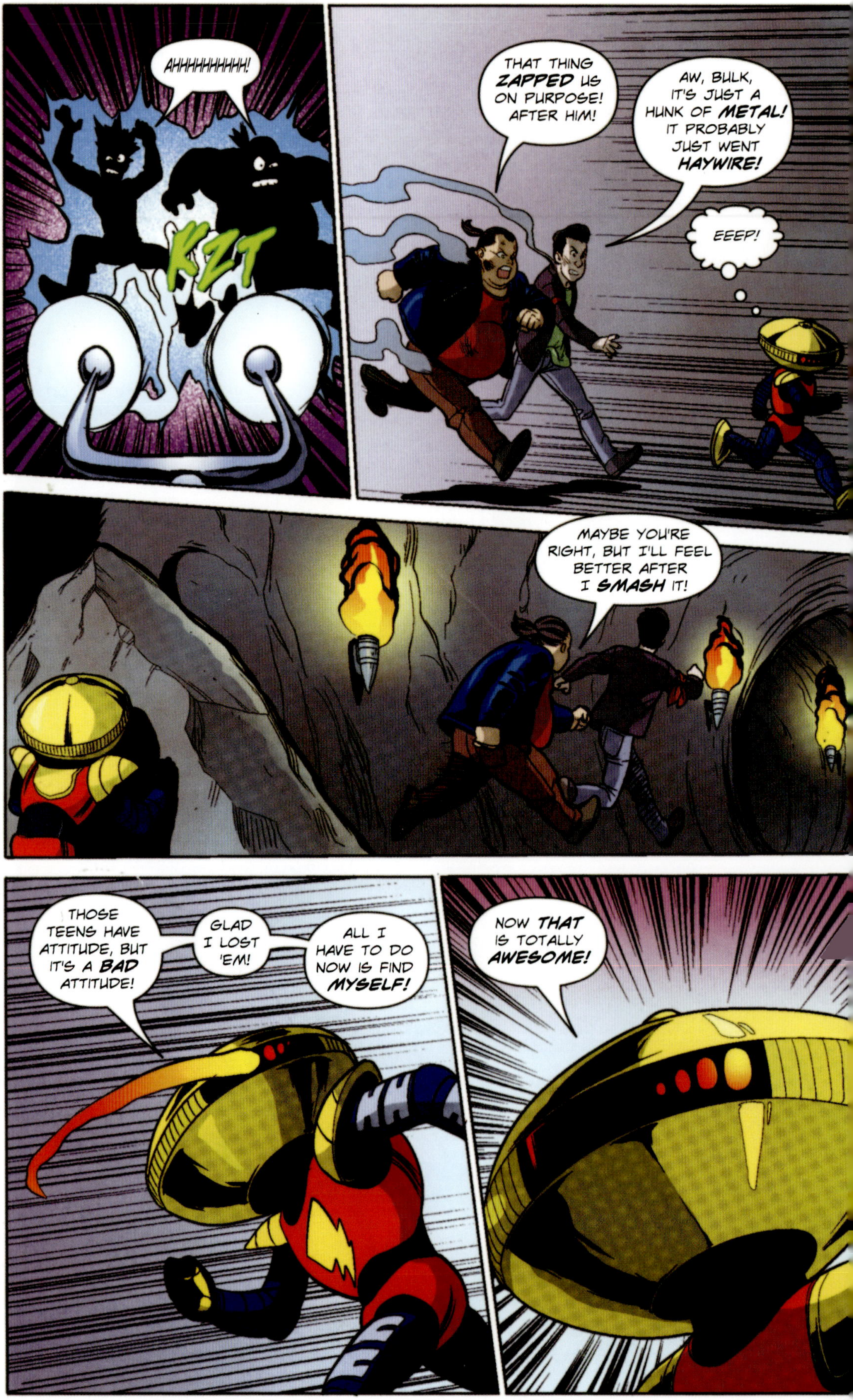
AHHHHHHHHHH!
KZT
THAT THING ZAPPED US ON PURPOSE! AFTER HIM!
AW, BULK, IT'S JUST A HUNK OF METAL! IT PROBABLY JUST WENT HAYWIRE!
EEEP!
MAYBE YOU'RE RIGHT, BUT I'LL FEEL BETTER AFTER I SMASH IT!
THOSE TEENS HAVE ATTITUDE, BUT IT'S A BAD ATTITUDE!
GLAD I LOST 'EM!
ALL I HAVE TO DO NOW IS FIND MYSELF!
NOW THAT IS TOTALLY AWESOME!

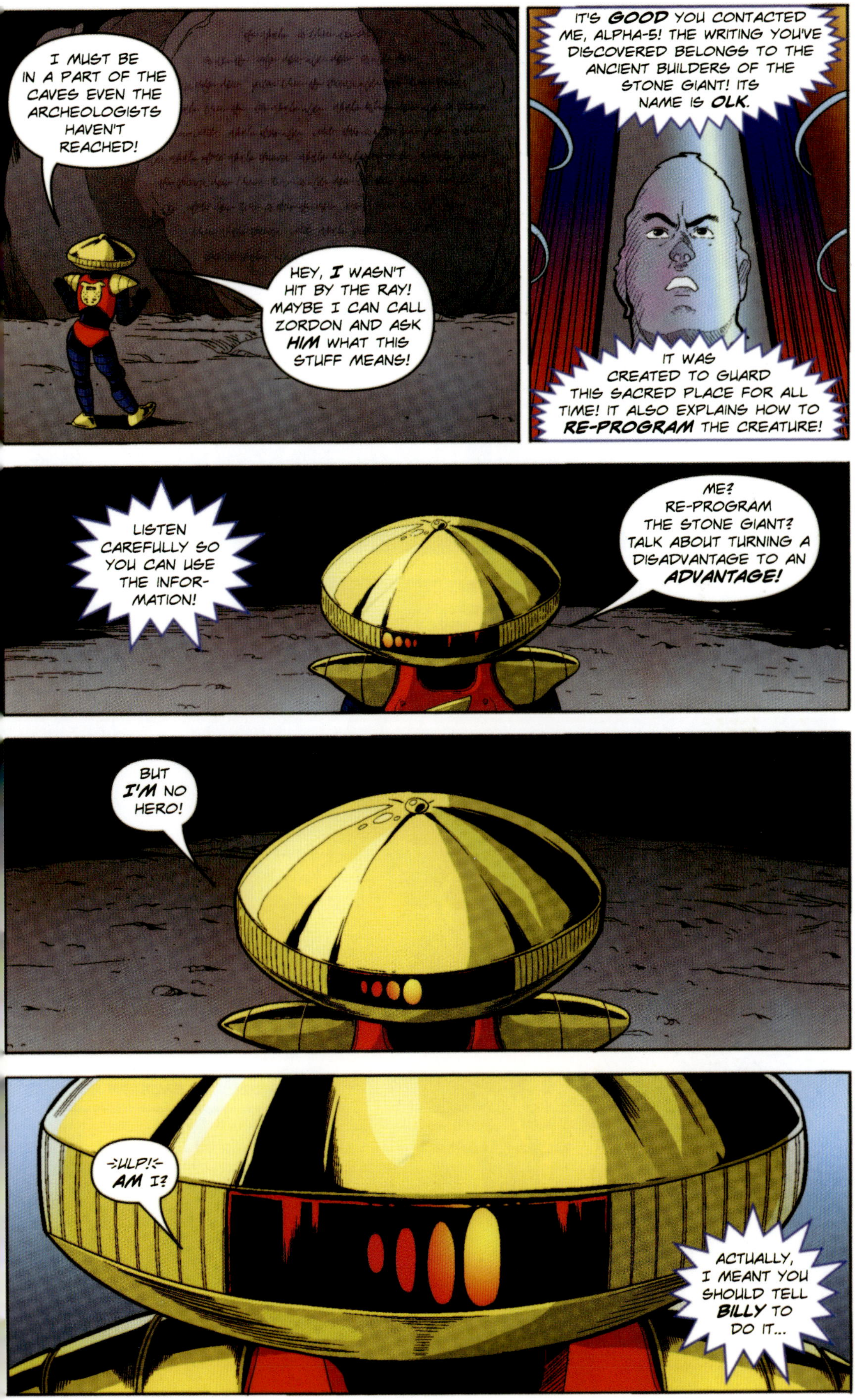
I MUST BE IN A PART OF THE CAVES EVEN THE ARCHEOLOGISTS HAVEN'T REACHED!
HEY, I WASN'T HIT BY THE RAY! MAYBE I CAN CALL ZORDON AND ASK HIM WHAT THIS STUFF MEANS!
IT'S GOOD YOU CONTACTED ME, ALPHA-5! THE WRITING YOU'VE DISCOVERED BELONGS TO THE ANCIENT BUILDERS OF THE STONE GIANT! ITS NAME IS OLK.
IT WAS CREATED TO GUARD THIS SACRED PLACE FOR ALL TIME! IT ALSO EXPLAINS HOW TO RE-PROGRAM THE CREATURE!
LISTEN CAREFULLY SO YOU CAN USE THE INFOR-MATION!
ME? RE-PROGRAM THE STONE GIANT? TALK ABOUT TURNING A DISADVANTAGE TO AN ADVANTAGE!
BUT I'M NO HERO!
ULP! AM I?
ACTUALLY, I MEANT YOU SHOULD TELL BILLY TO DO IT...

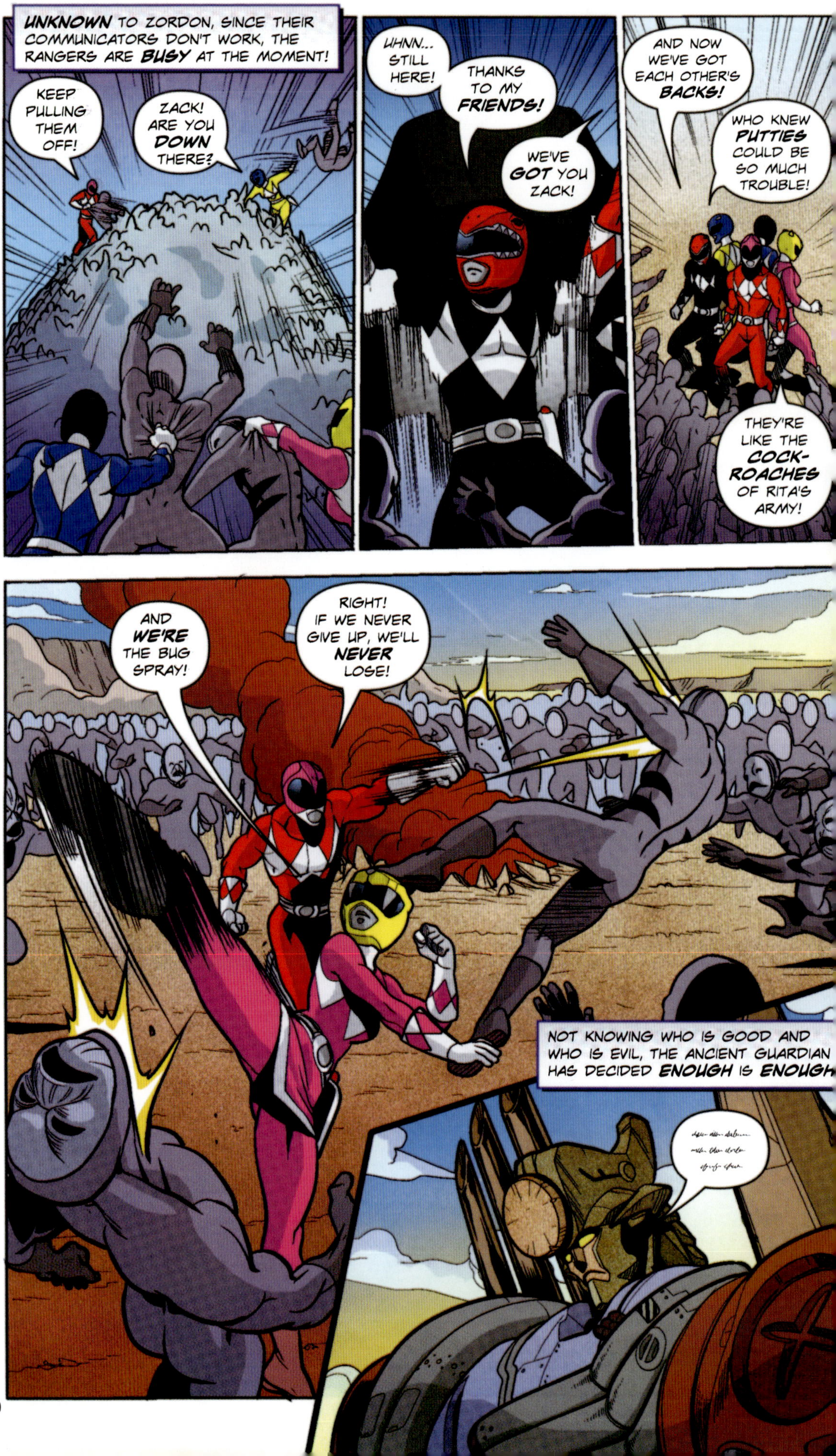
UNKNOWN TO ZORDON, SINCE THEIR COMMUNICATORS DON'T WORK, THE RANGERS ARE BUSY AT THE MOMENT!
KEEP PULLING THEM OFF!
ZACK! ARE YOU DOWN THERE?
UHNN... STILL HERE!
THANKS TO MY FRIENDS!
WE'VE GOT YOU ZACK!
AND NOW WE'VE GOT EACH OTHER'S BACKS!
WHO KNEW PUTTIES COULD BE SO MUCH TROUBLE!
THEY'RE LIKE THE COCK-ROACHES OF RITA'S ARMY!
AND WE'RE THE BUG SPRAY!
RIGHT! IF WE NEVER GIVE UP, WE'LL NEVER LOSE!
NOT KNOWING WHO IS GOOD AND WHO IS EVIL, THE ANCIENT GUARDIAN HAS DECIDED ENOUGH IS ENOUGH

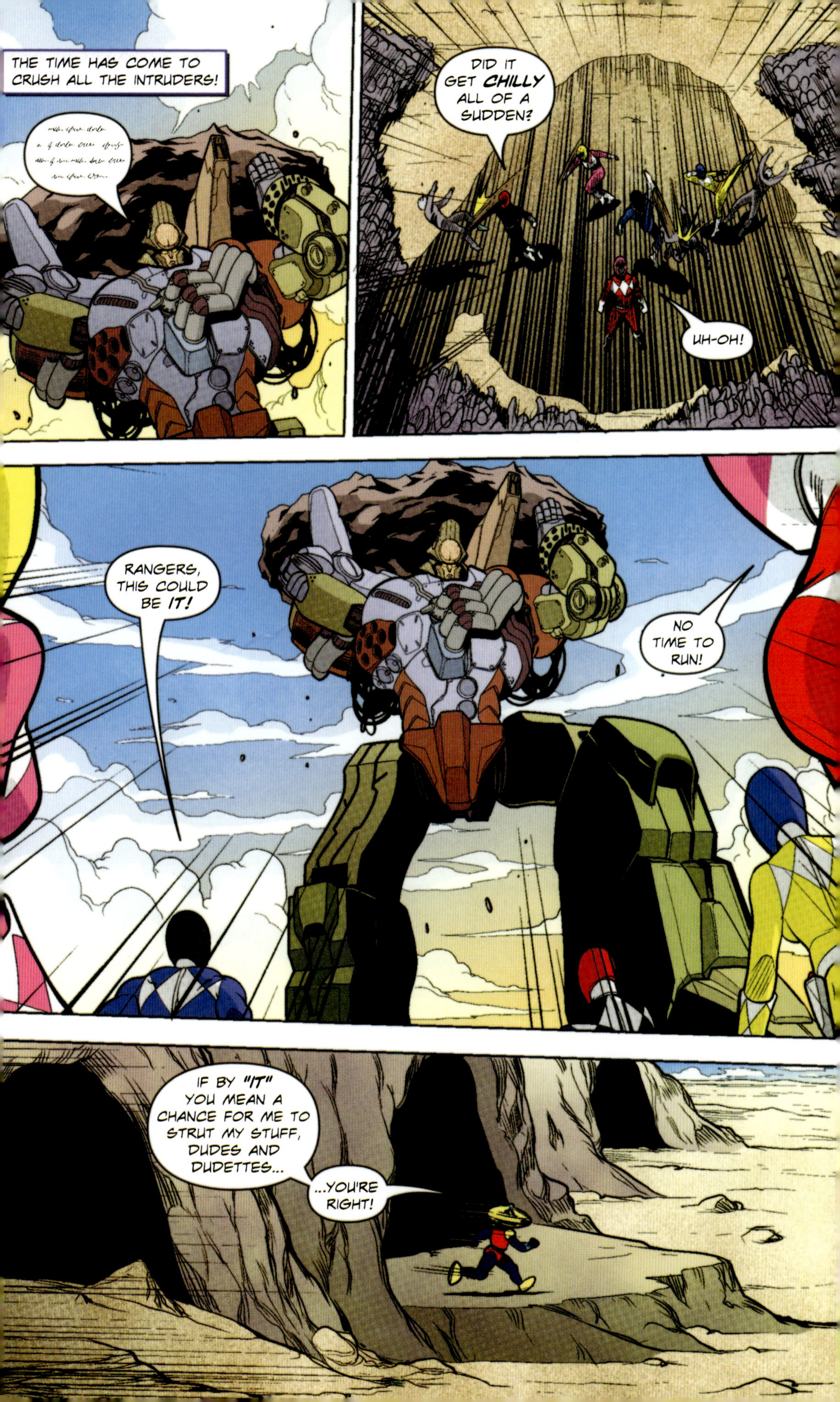
THE TIME HAS COME TO CRUSH ALL THE INTRUDERS!
DID IT GET CHILLY ALL OF A SUDDEN?
UH-OH!
RANGERS, THIS COULD BE IT!
NO TIME TO RUN!
IF BY "IT" YOU MEAN A CHANCE FOR ME TO STRUT MY STUFF, DUDES AND DUDETTES...
...YOU'RE RIGHT!

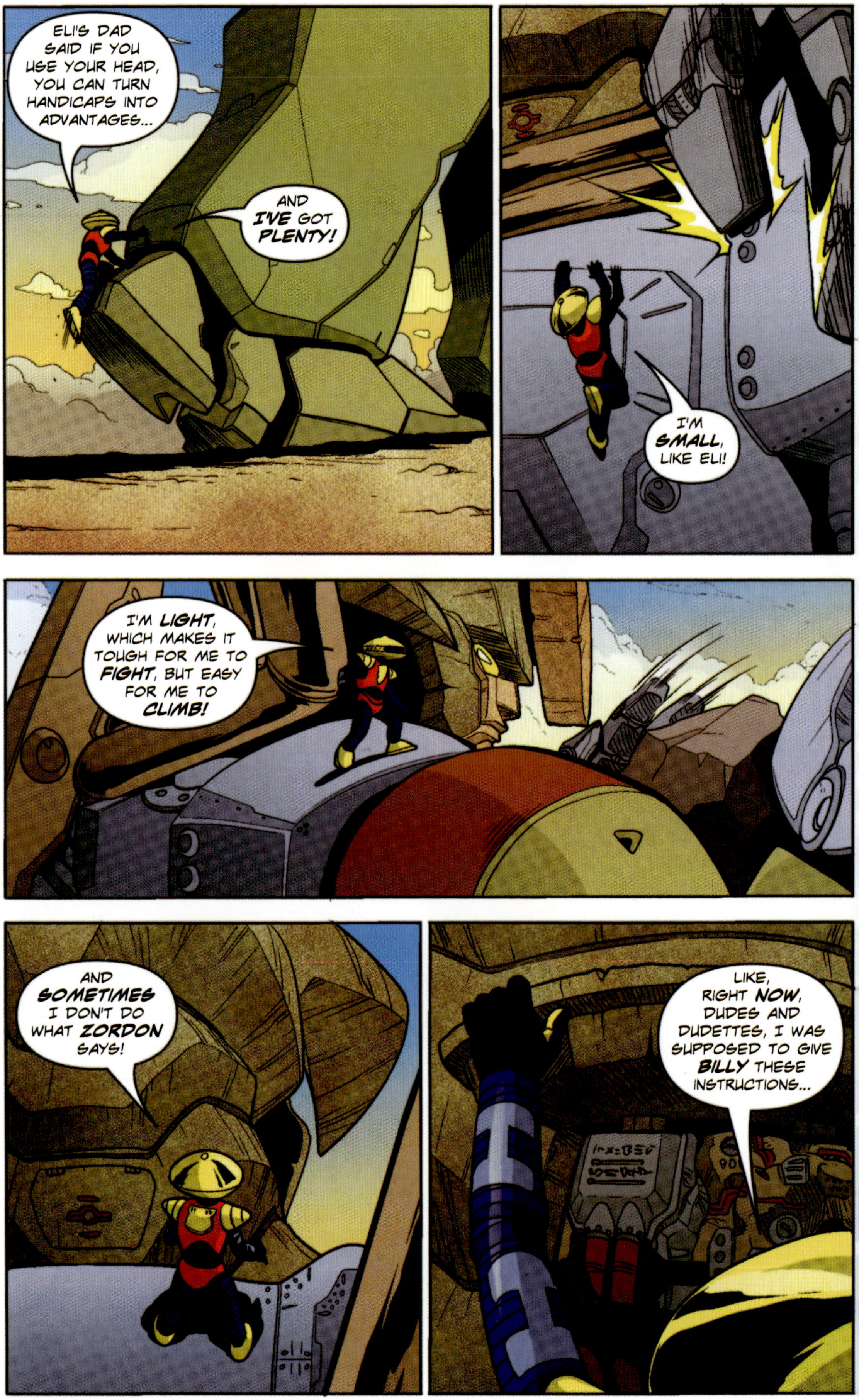
ELI'S DAD SAID IF YOU USE YOUR HEAD, YOU CAN TURN HANDICAPS INTO ADVANTAGES...
AND I'VE GOT PLENTY!
I'M SMALL, LIKE ELI!
I'M LIGHT, WHICH MAKES IT TOUGH FOR ME TO FIGHT, BUT EASY FOR ME TO CLIMB!
AND SOMETIMES I DON'T DO WHAT ZORDON SAYS!
LIKE, RIGHT NOW, DUDES AND DUDETTES, I WAS SUPPOSED TO GIVE BILLY THESE INSTRUCTIONS...

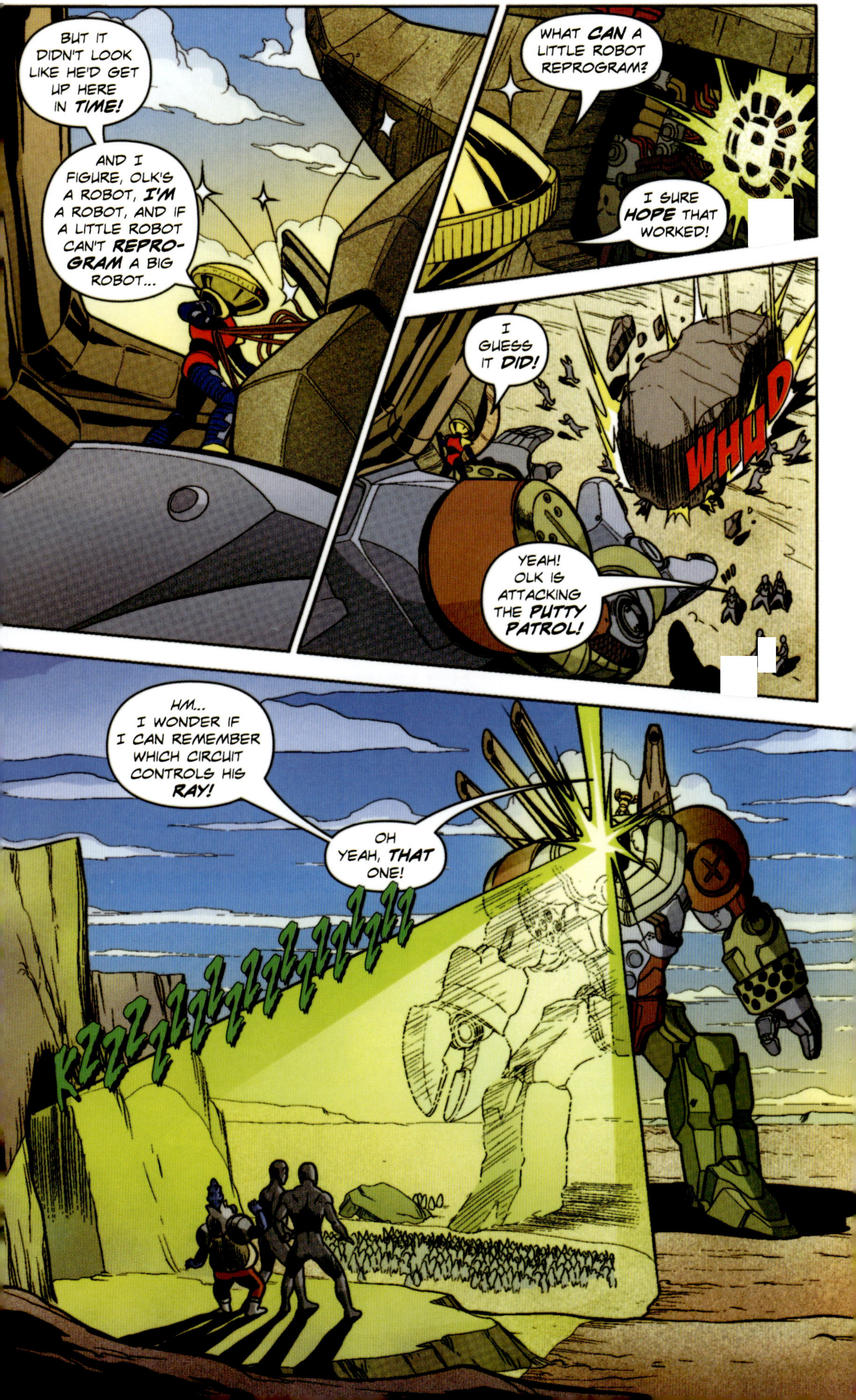
BUT IT DIDN'T LOOK LIKE HE'D GET UP HERE IN TIME!
AND I FIGURE, OLK'S A ROBOT, I'M A ROBOT, AND IF A LITTLE ROBOT CAN'T REPRO-GRAM A BIG ROBOT...
WHAT CAN A LITTLE ROBOT REPROGRAM?
I SURE HOPE THAT WORKED!
I GUESS IT DID!
WHUD
YEAH! OLK IS ATTACKING THE PUTTY PATROL!
HM... I WONDER IF I CAN REMEMBER WHICH CIRCUIT CONTROLS HIS RAY!
OH YEAH, THAT ONE!
KZZZZZZZZZZZZZZZZZZZZ

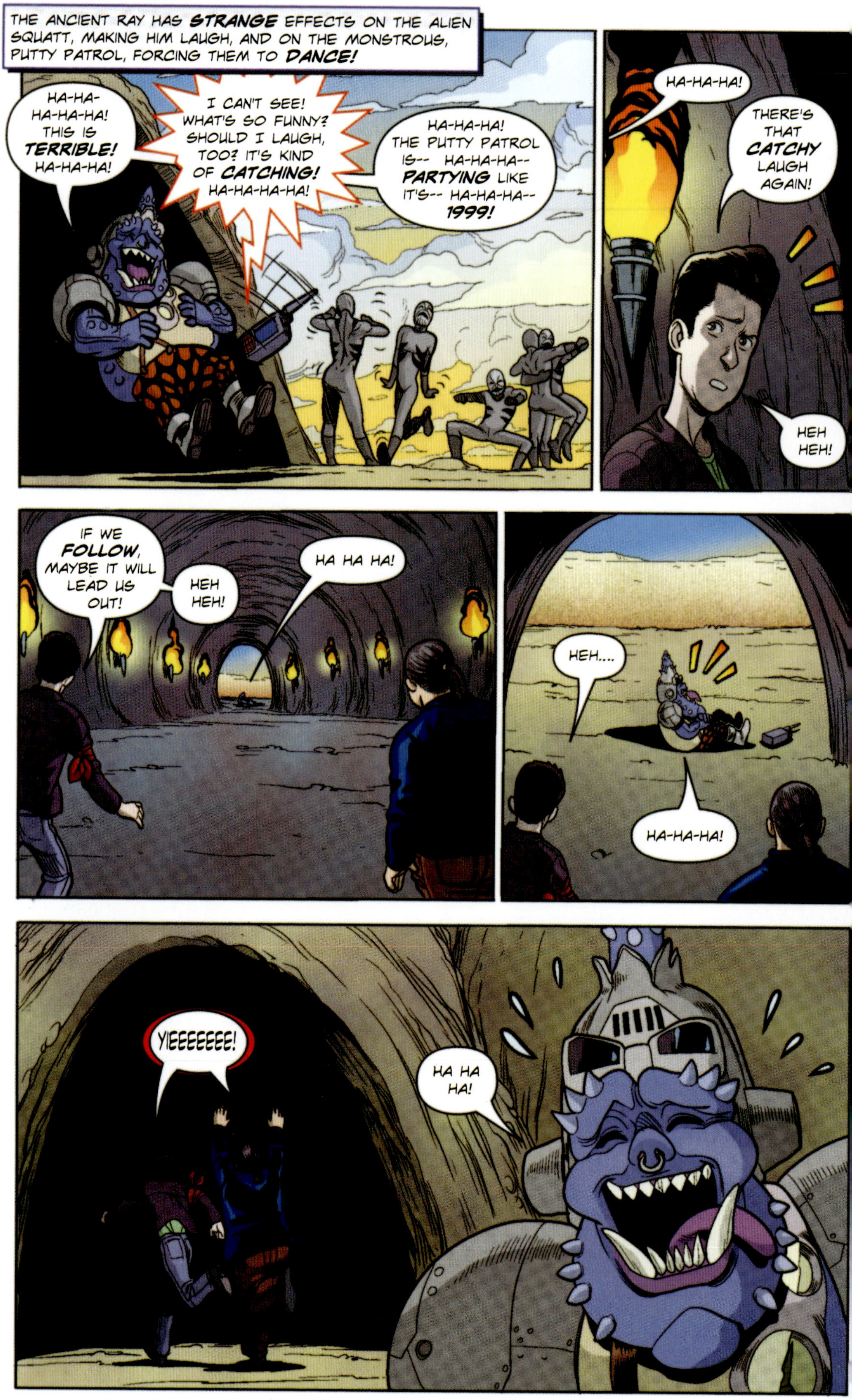
THE ANCIENT RAY HAS STRANGE EFFECTS ON THE ALIEN SQUATT, MAKING HIM LAUGH, AND ON THE MONSTROUS PUTTY PATROL, FORCING THEM TO DANCE!
HA-HA-HA-HA-HA! THIS IS TERRIBLE! HA-HA-HA!
I CAN'T SEE! WHAT'S SO FUNNY? SHOULD I LAUGH, TOO? IT'S KIND OF CATCHING! HA-HA-HA-HA!
HA-HA-HA! THE PUTTY PATROL IS-- HA-HA-HA-- PARTYING LIKE IT'S-- HA-HA-HA-- 1999!
HA-HA-HA!
THERE'S THAT CATCHY LAUGH AGAIN!
HEH HEH!
IF WE FOLLOW, MAYBE IT WILL LEAD US OUT!
HEH HEH!
HA HA HA!
HEH....
HA-HA-HA!
YIEEEEEEE!
HA HA HA!

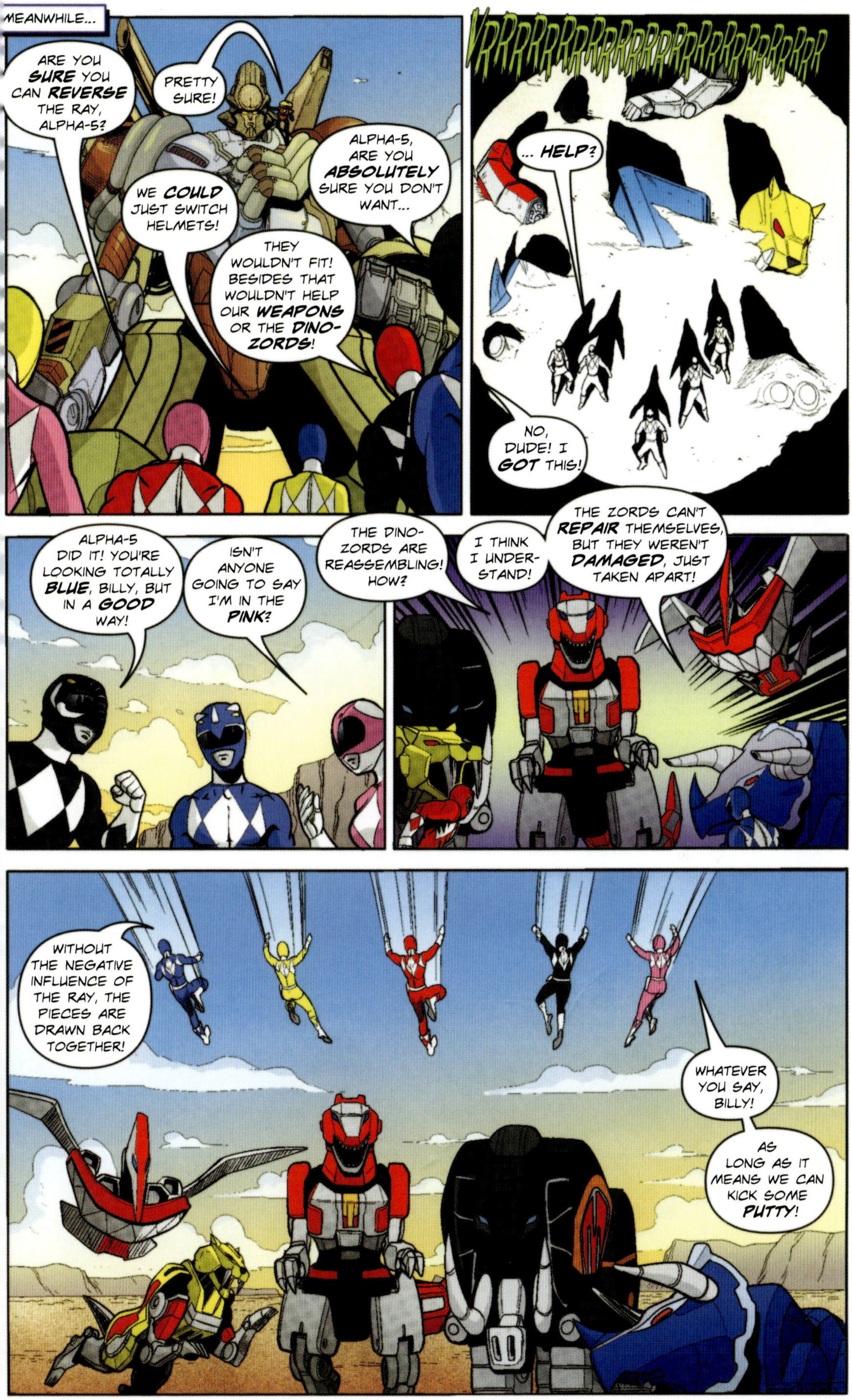
MEANWHILE...
ARE YOU SURE YOU CAN REVERSE THE RAY, ALPHA-5?
PRETTY SURE!
ALPHA-5, ARE YOU ABSOLUTELY SURE YOU DON'T WANT...
WE COULD JUST SWITCH HELMETS!
THEY WOULDN'T FIT! BESIDES THAT WOULDN'T HELP OUR WEAPONS OR THE DINO-ZORDS!
VRRRRRRRRRRRRRRRRRRRRRRRRRRRR
... HELP?
NO, DUDE! I GOT THIS!
ALPHA-5 DID IT! YOU'RE LOOKING TOTALLY BLUE, BILLY, BUT IN A GOOD WAY!
ISN'T ANYONE GOING TO SAY I'M IN THE PINK?
THE DINO-ZORDS ARE REASSEMBLING! HOW?
I THINK I UNDER-STAND!
THE ZORDS CAN'T REPAIR THEMSELVES, BUT THEY WEREN'T DAMAGED, JUST TAKEN APART!
WITHOUT THE NEGATIVE INFLUENCE OF THE RAY, THE PIECES ARE DRAWN BACK TOGETHER!
WHATEVER YOU SAY, BILLY!
AS LONG AS IT MEANS WE CAN KICK SOME PUTTY!

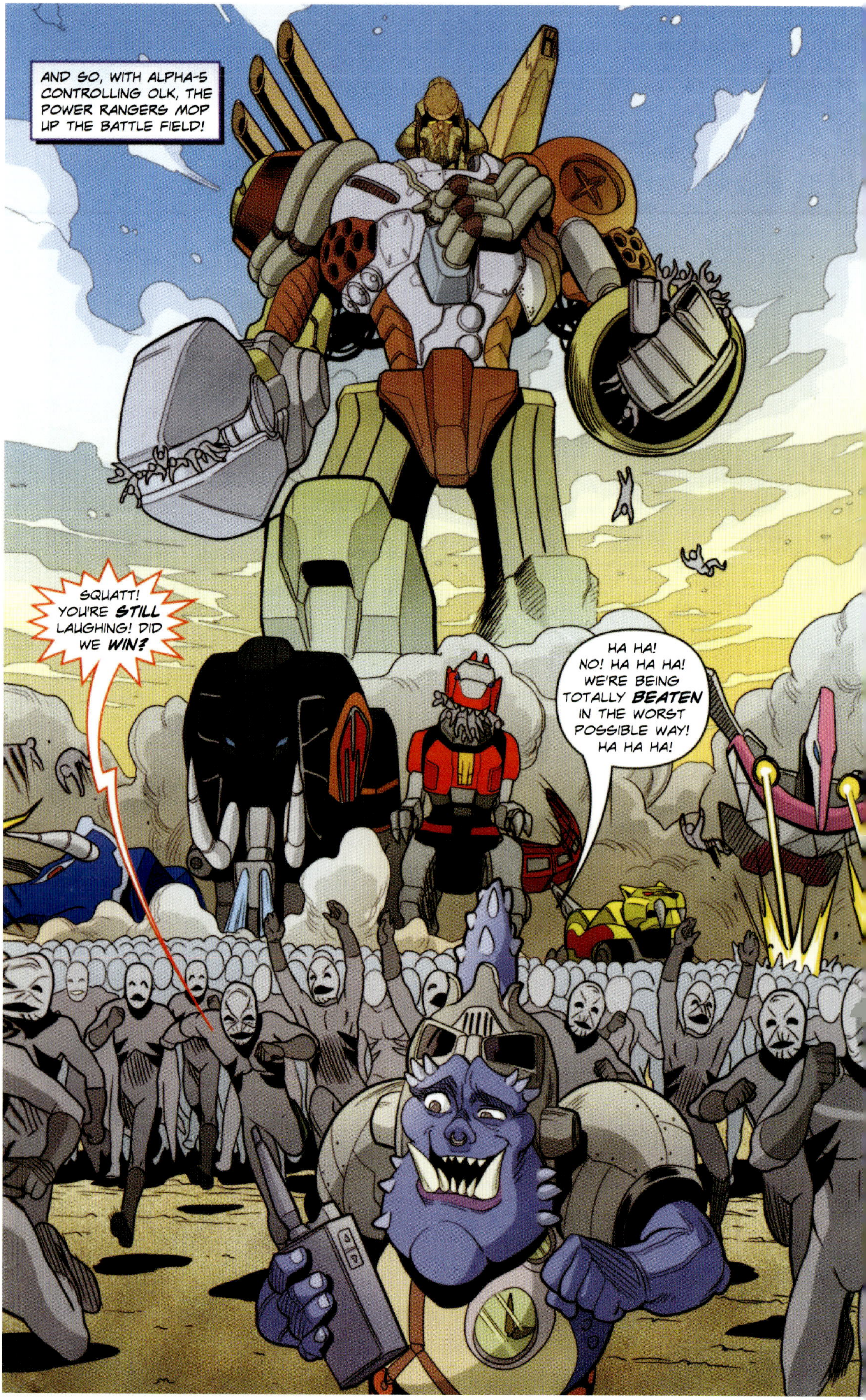
AND SO, WITH ALPHA-5 CONTROLLING OLK, THE POWER RANGERS MOP UP THE BATTLE FIELD!
SQUATT! YOU'RE **STILL** LAUGHING! DID WE **WIN?**
HA HA! NO! HA HA HA! WE'RE BEING TOTALLY **BEATEN** IN THE WORST POSSIBLE WAY! HA HA HA!

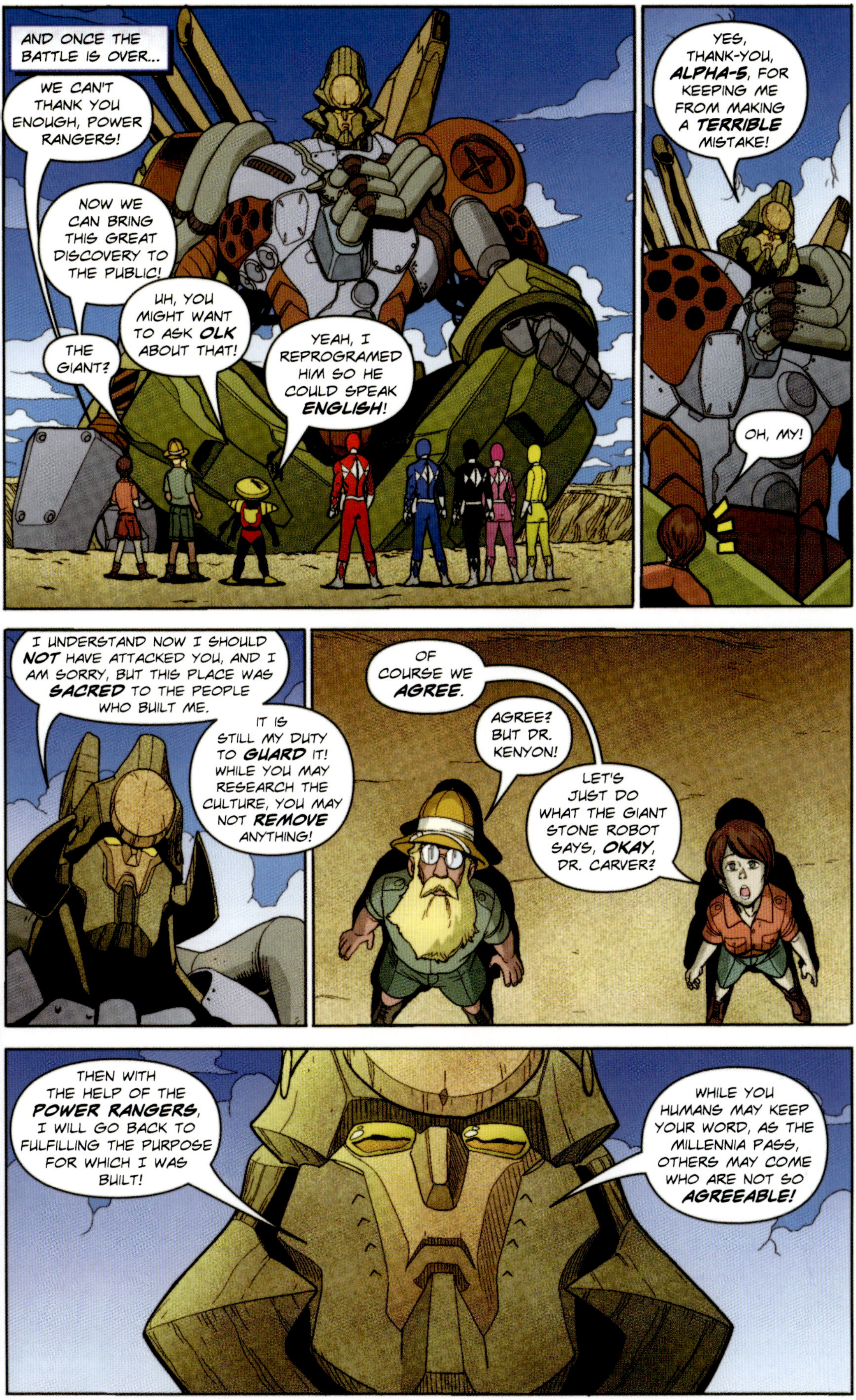
AND ONCE THE BATTLE IS OVER...
WE CAN'T THANK YOU ENOUGH, POWER RANGERS!
NOW WE CAN BRING THIS GREAT DISCOVERY TO THE PUBLIC!
THE GIANT?
UH, YOU MIGHT WANT TO ASK OLK ABOUT THAT!
YEAH, I REPROGRAMED HIM SO HE COULD SPEAK ENGLISH!
YES, THANK-YOU, ALPHA-5, FOR KEEPING ME FROM MAKING A TERRIBLE MISTAKE!
OH, MY!
I UNDERSTAND NOW I SHOULD NOT HAVE ATTACKED YOU, AND I AM SORRY, BUT THIS PLACE WAS SACRED TO THE PEOPLE WHO BUILT ME.
IT IS STILL MY DUTY TO GUARD IT! WHILE YOU MAY RESEARCH THE CULTURE, YOU MAY NOT REMOVE ANYTHING!
OF COURSE WE AGREE.
AGREE? BUT DR. KENYON!
LET'S JUST DO WHAT THE GIANT STONE ROBOT SAYS, OKAY, DR. CARVER?
THEN WITH THE HELP OF THE POWER RANGERS, I WILL GO BACK TO FULFILLING THE PURPOSE FOR WHICH I WAS BUILT!
WHILE YOU HUMANS MAY KEEP YOUR WORD, AS THE MILLENNIA PASS, OTHERS MAY COME WHO ARE NOT SO AGREEABLE!

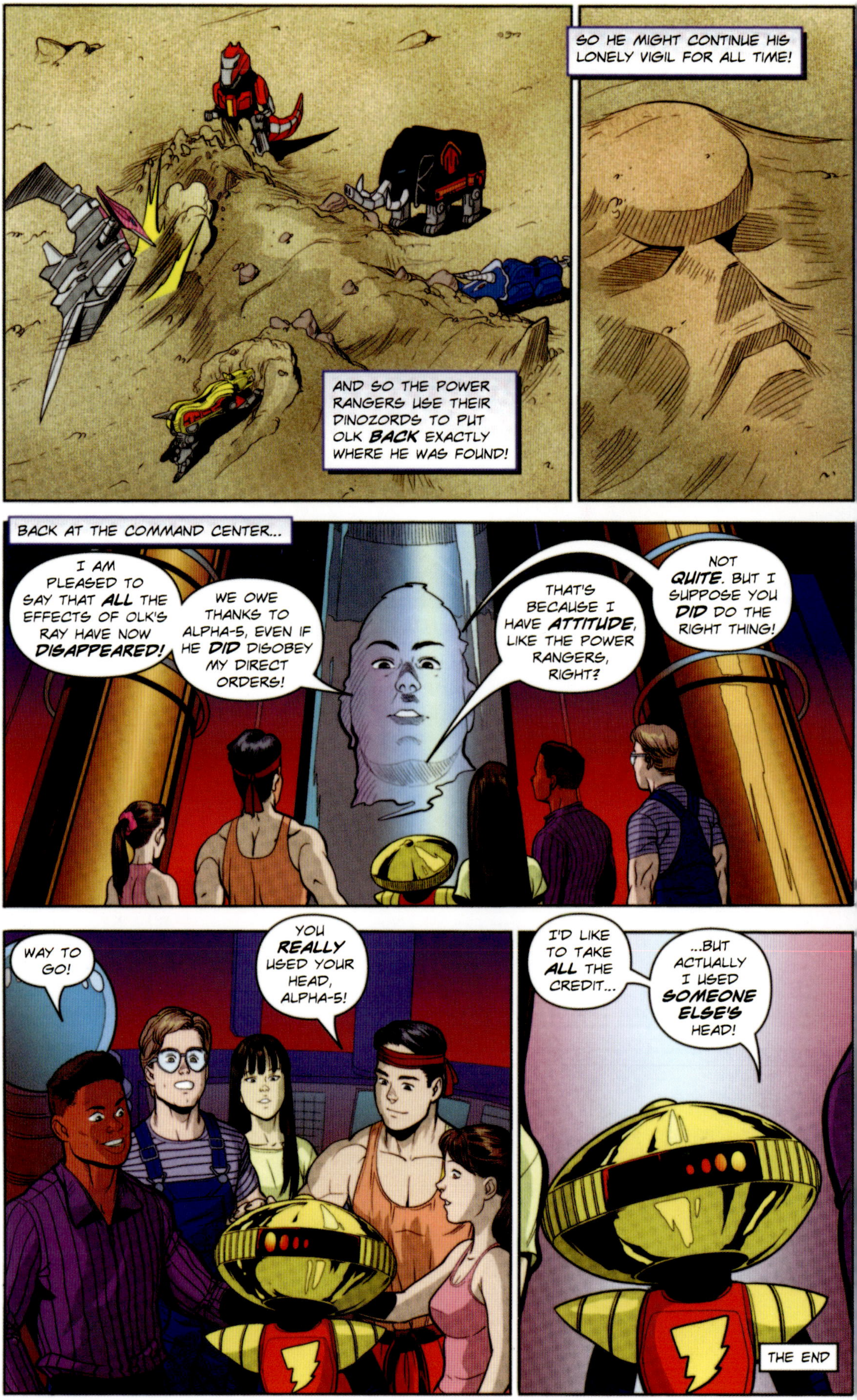
AND SO THE POWER RANGERS USE THEIR DINOZORDS TO PUT OLK BACK EXACTLY WHERE HE WAS FOUND!
SO HE MIGHT CONTINUE HIS LONELY VIGIL FOR ALL TIME!
BACK AT THE COMMAND CENTER...
I AM PLEASED TO SAY THAT ALL THE EFFECTS OF OLK'S RAY HAVE NOW DISAPPEARED!
WE OWE THANKS TO ALPHA-5, EVEN IF HE DID DISOBEY MY DIRECT ORDERS!
THAT'S BECAUSE I HAVE ATTITUDE, LIKE THE POWER RANGERS, RIGHT?
NOT QUITE. BUT I SUPPOSE YOU DID DO THE RIGHT THING!
WAY TO GO!
YOU REALLY USED YOUR HEAD, ALPHA-5!
I'D LIKE TO TAKE ALL THE CREDIT...
...BUT ACTUALLY I USED SOMEONE ELSE'S HEAD!
THE END

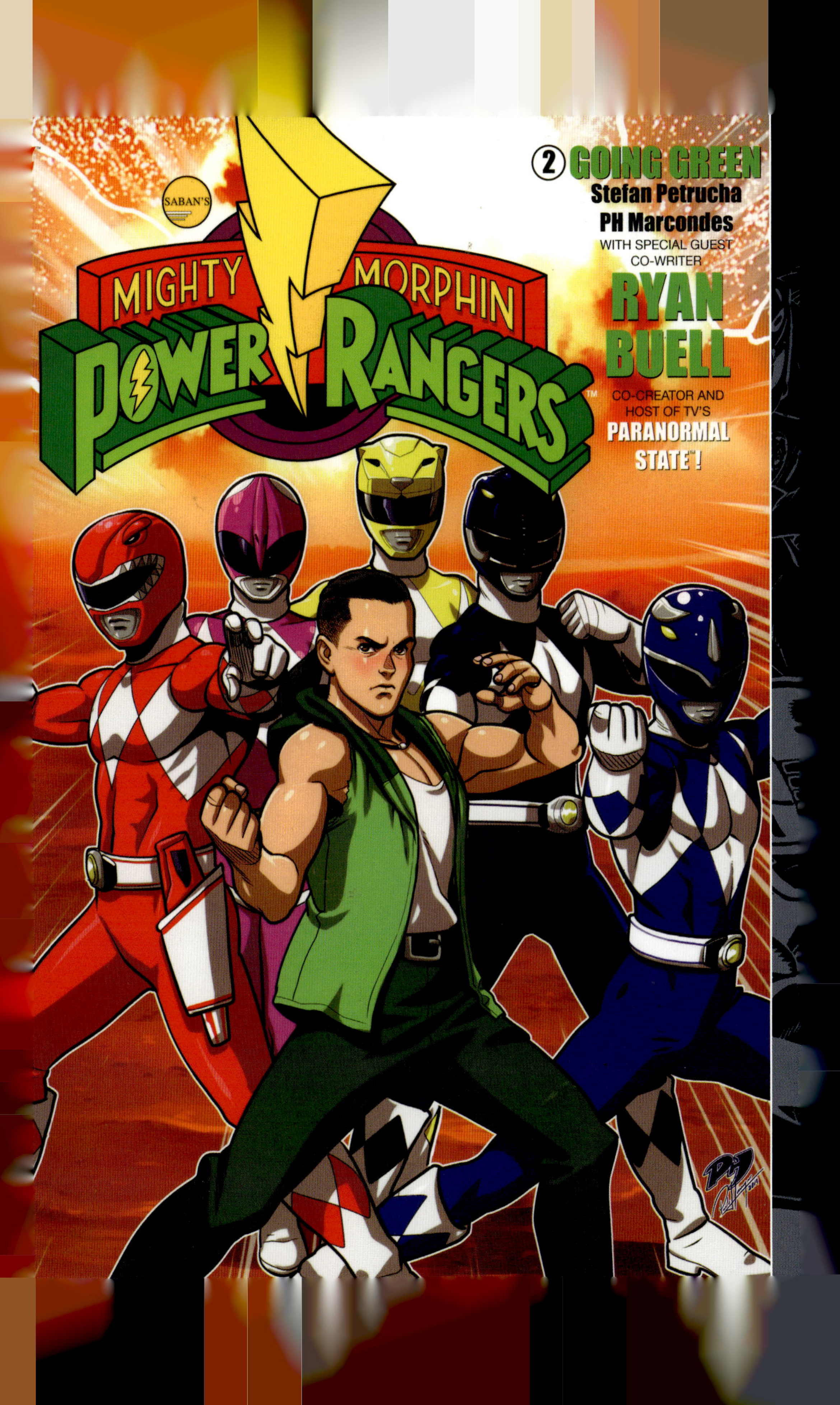

SABAN'S
MIGHTY MORPHIN
POWER RANGERS™
2 GOING GREEN
Stefan Petrucha
PH Marcondes
WITH SPECIAL GUEST CO-WRITER
RYAN BUELL
CO-CREATOR AND HOST OF TV'S
PARANORMAL STATE™!

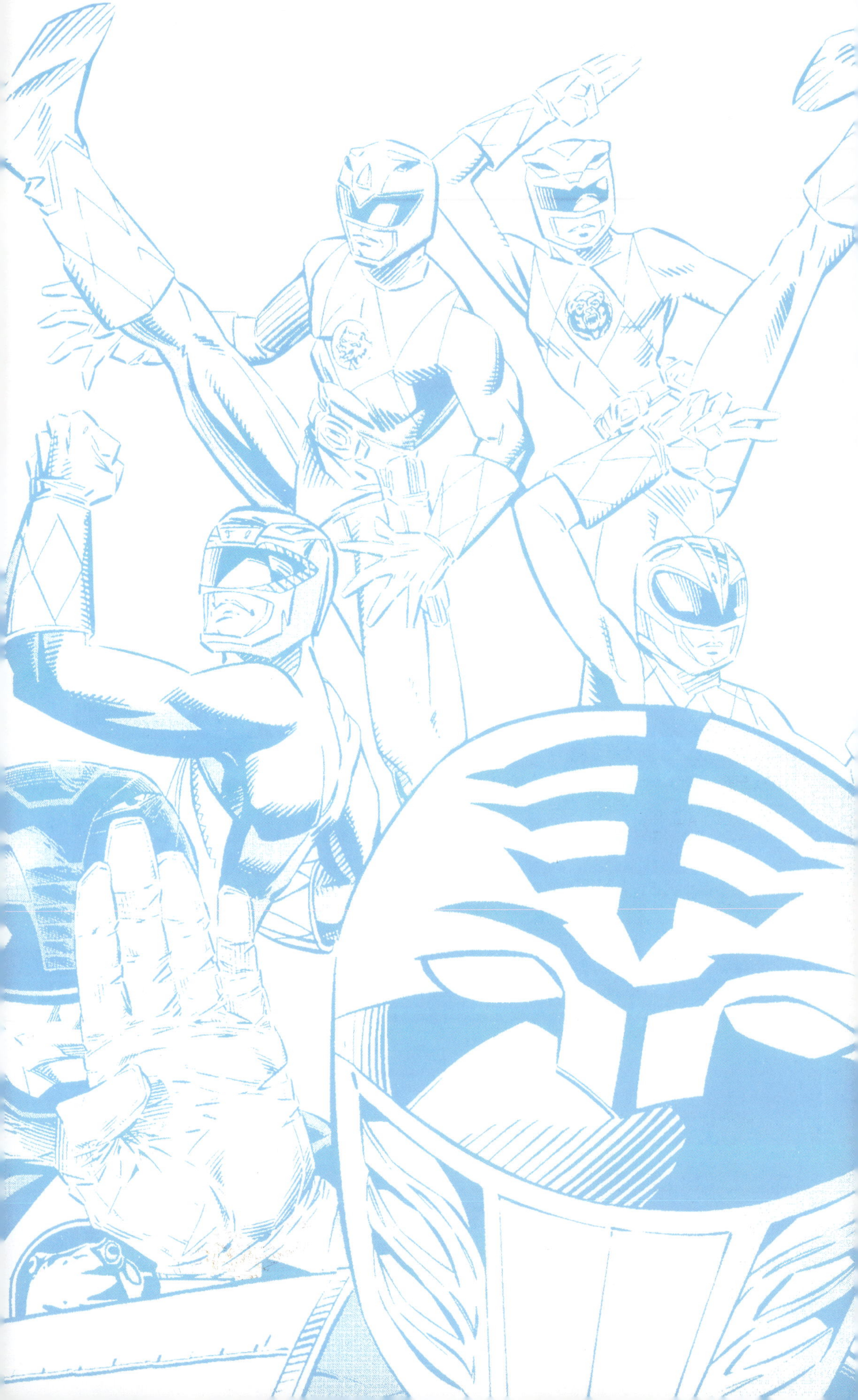

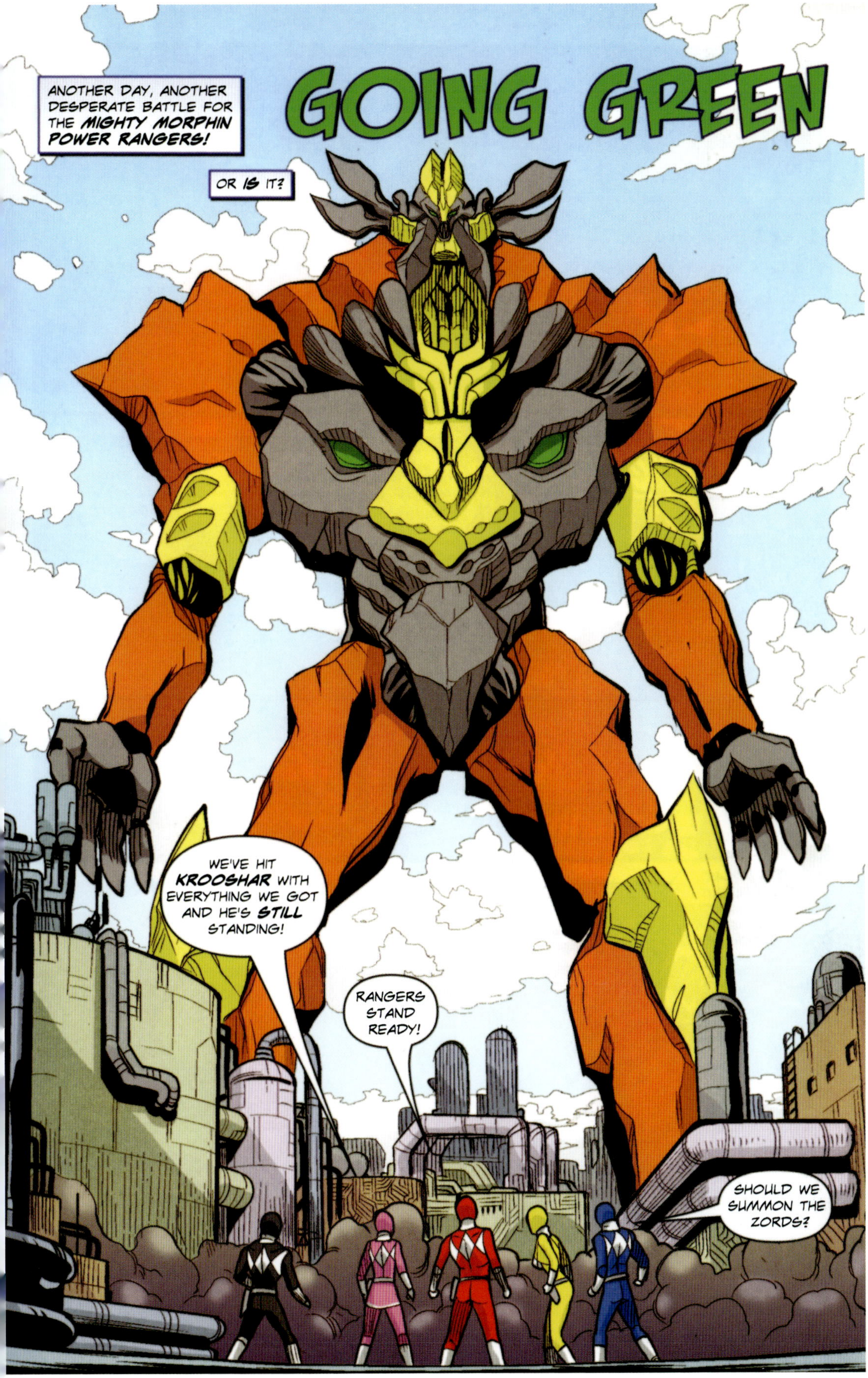
ANOTHER DAY, ANOTHER DESPERATE BATTLE FOR THE MIGHTY MORPHIN POWER RANGERS!
GOING GREEN
OR IS IT?
WE'VE HIT KROOSHAR WITH EVERYTHING WE GOT AND HE'S STILL STANDING!
RANGERS STAND READY!
SHOULD WE SUMMON THE ZORDS?

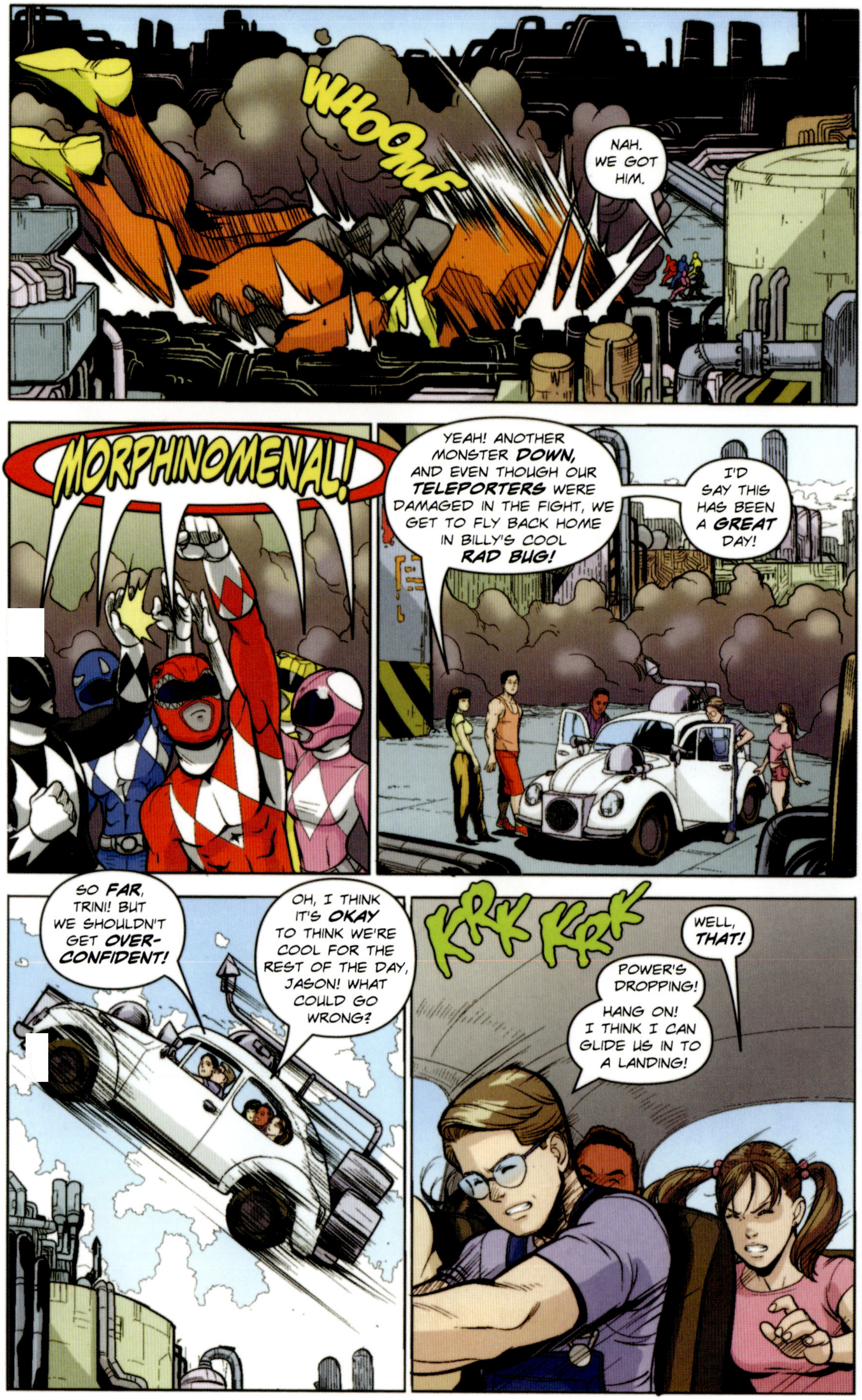
WHOOMF
NAH. WE GOT HIM.
MORPHINOMENAL!
YEAH! ANOTHER MONSTER DOWN, AND EVEN THOUGH OUR TELEPORTERS WERE DAMAGED IN THE FIGHT, WE GET TO FLY BACK HOME IN BILLY'S COOL RAD BUG!
I'D SAY THIS HAS BEEN A GREAT DAY!
SO FAR, TRINI! BUT WE SHOULDN'T GET OVER-CONFIDENT!
OH, I THINK IT'S OKAY TO THINK WE'RE COOL FOR THE REST OF THE DAY, JASON! WHAT COULD GO WRONG?
KRK KRK
WELL, THAT!
POWER'S DROPPING!
HANG ON! I THINK I CAN GLIDE US IN TO A LANDING!

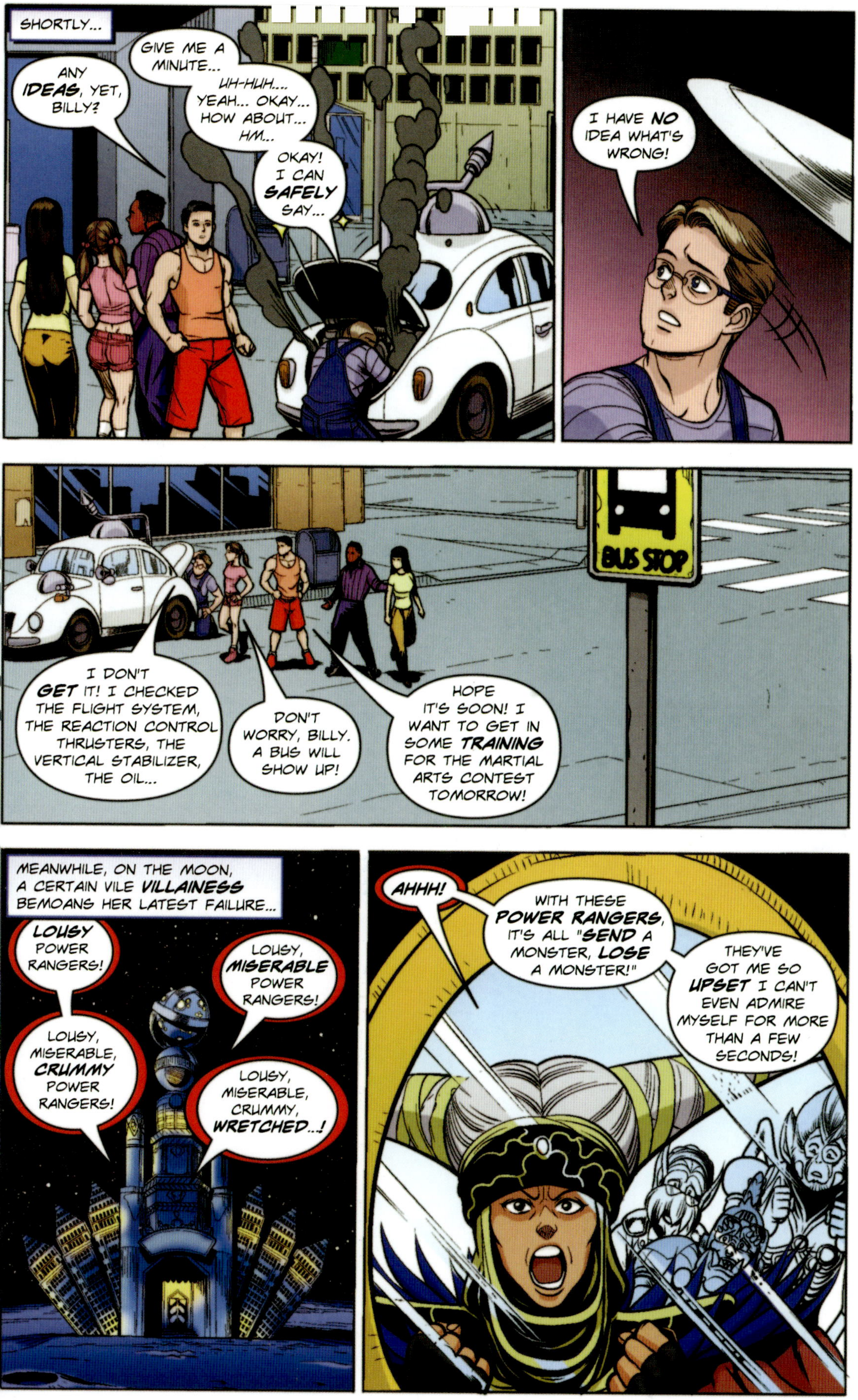
SHORTLY...
ANY IDEAS, YET, BILLY?
GIVE ME A MINUTE...
UH-HUH... YEAH... OKAY... HOW ABOUT... HM...
OKAY! I CAN SAFELY SAY...
I HAVE NO IDEA WHAT'S WRONG!
BUS STOP
I DON'T GET IT! I CHECKED THE FLIGHT SYSTEM, THE REACTION CONTROL THRUSTERS, THE VERTICAL STABILIZER, THE OIL...
DON'T WORRY, BILLY. A BUS WILL SHOW UP!
HOPE IT'S SOON! I WANT TO GET IN SOME TRAINING FOR THE MARTIAL ARTS CONTEST TOMORROW!
MEANWHILE, ON THE MOON, A CERTAIN VILE VILLAINESS BEMOANS HER LATEST FAILURE...
LOUSY POWER RANGERS!
LOUSY, MISERABLE POWER RANGERS!
LOUSY, MISERABLE, CRUMMY POWER RANGERS!
LOUSY, MISERABLE, CRUMMY, WRETCHED...!
AHHH!
WITH THESE POWER RANGERS, IT'S ALL "SEND A MONSTER, LOSE A MONSTER!"
THEY'VE GOT ME SO UPSET I CAN'T EVEN ADMIRE MYSELF FOR MORE THAN A FEW SECONDS!

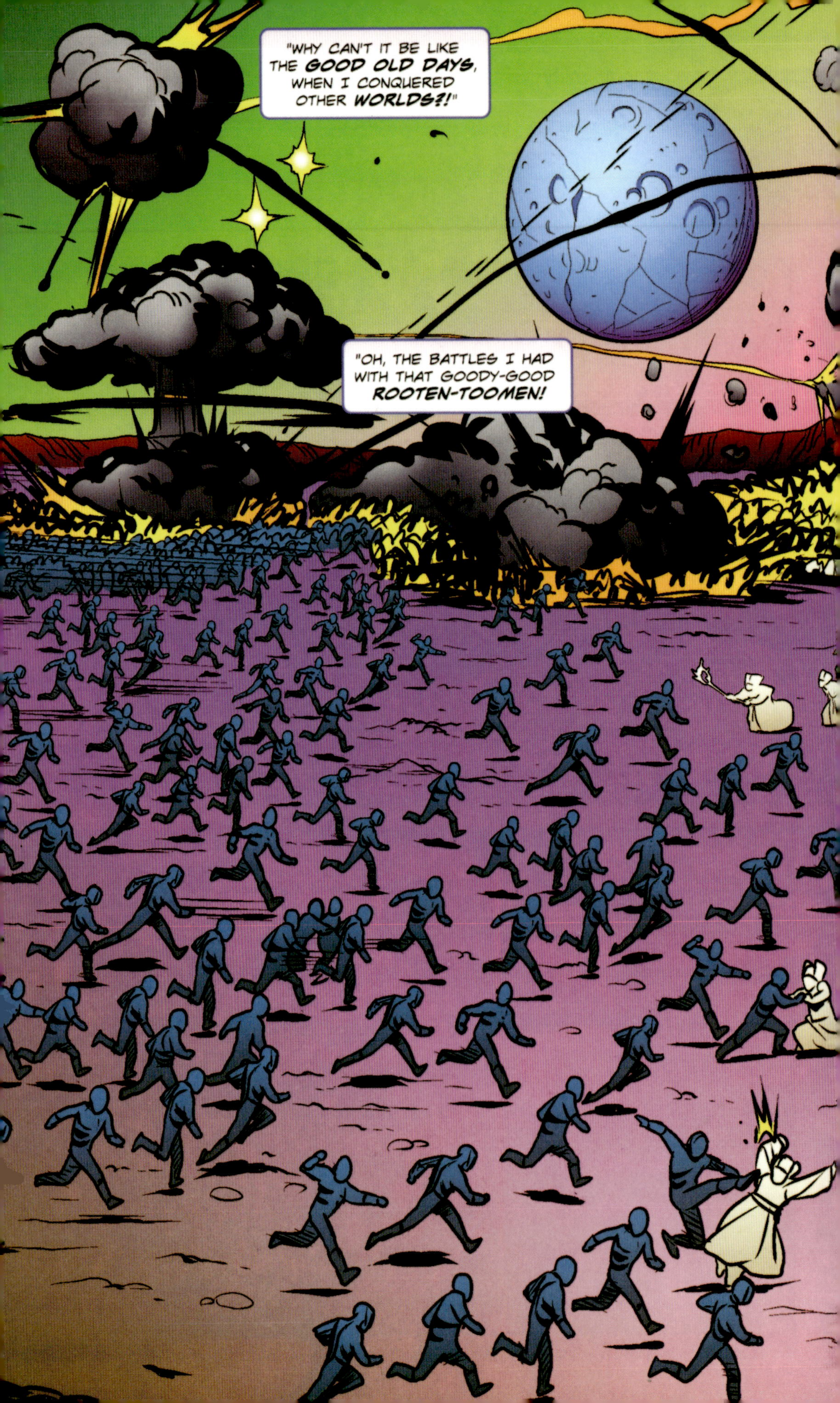
"WHY CAN'T IT BE LIKE THE GOOD OLD DAYS, WHEN I CONQUERED OTHER WORLDS?!"
"OH, THE BATTLES I HAD WITH THAT GOODY-GOOD ROOTEN-TOOMEN!

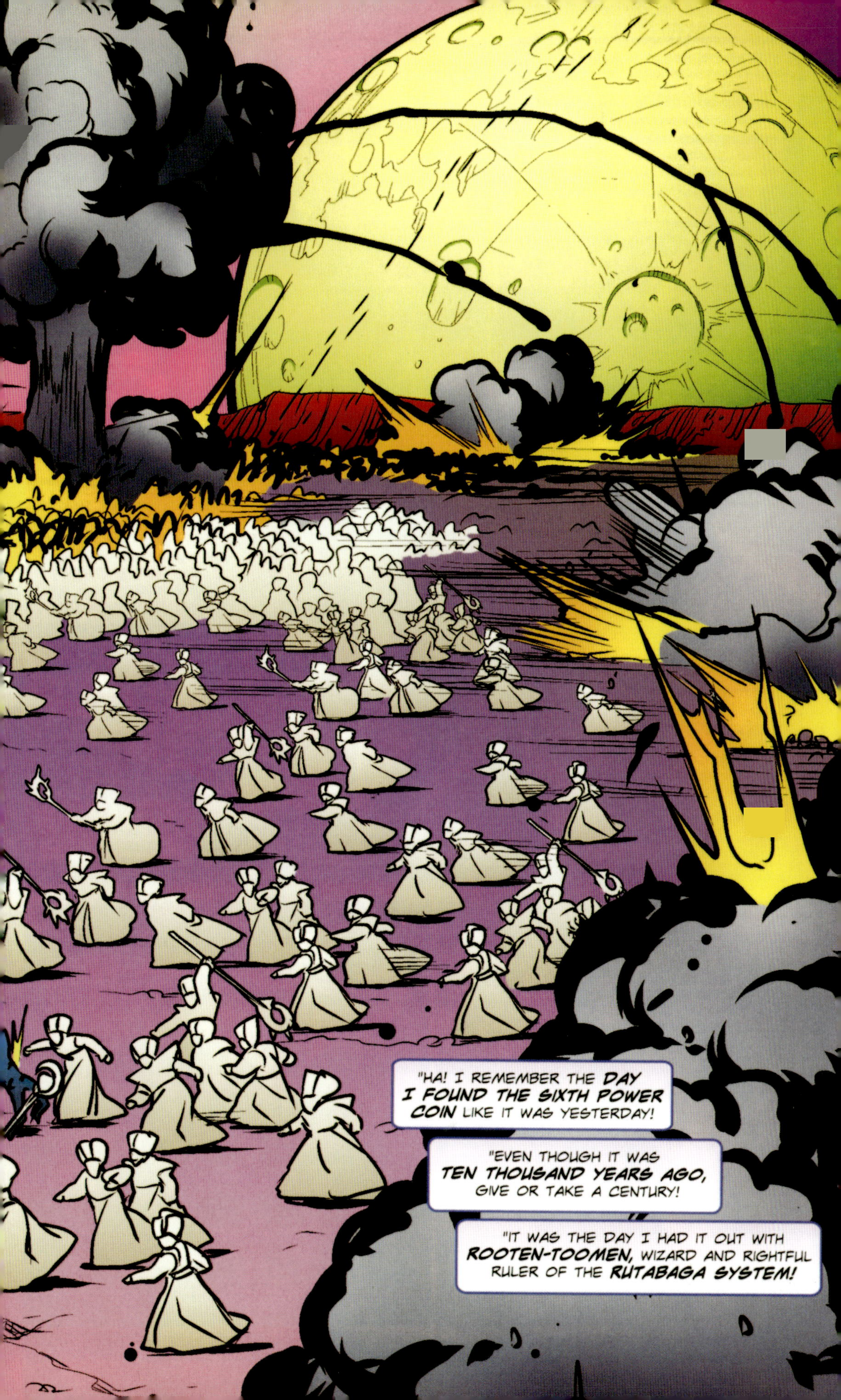
"HA! I REMEMBER THE DAY I FOUND THE SIXTH POWER COIN LIKE IT WAS YESTERDAY!
"EVEN THOUGH IT WAS TEN THOUSAND YEARS AGO, GIVE OR TAKE A CENTURY!
"IT WAS THE DAY I HAD IT OUT WITH ROOTEN-TOOMEN, WIZARD AND RIGHTFUL RULER OF THE RUTABAGA SYSTEM!

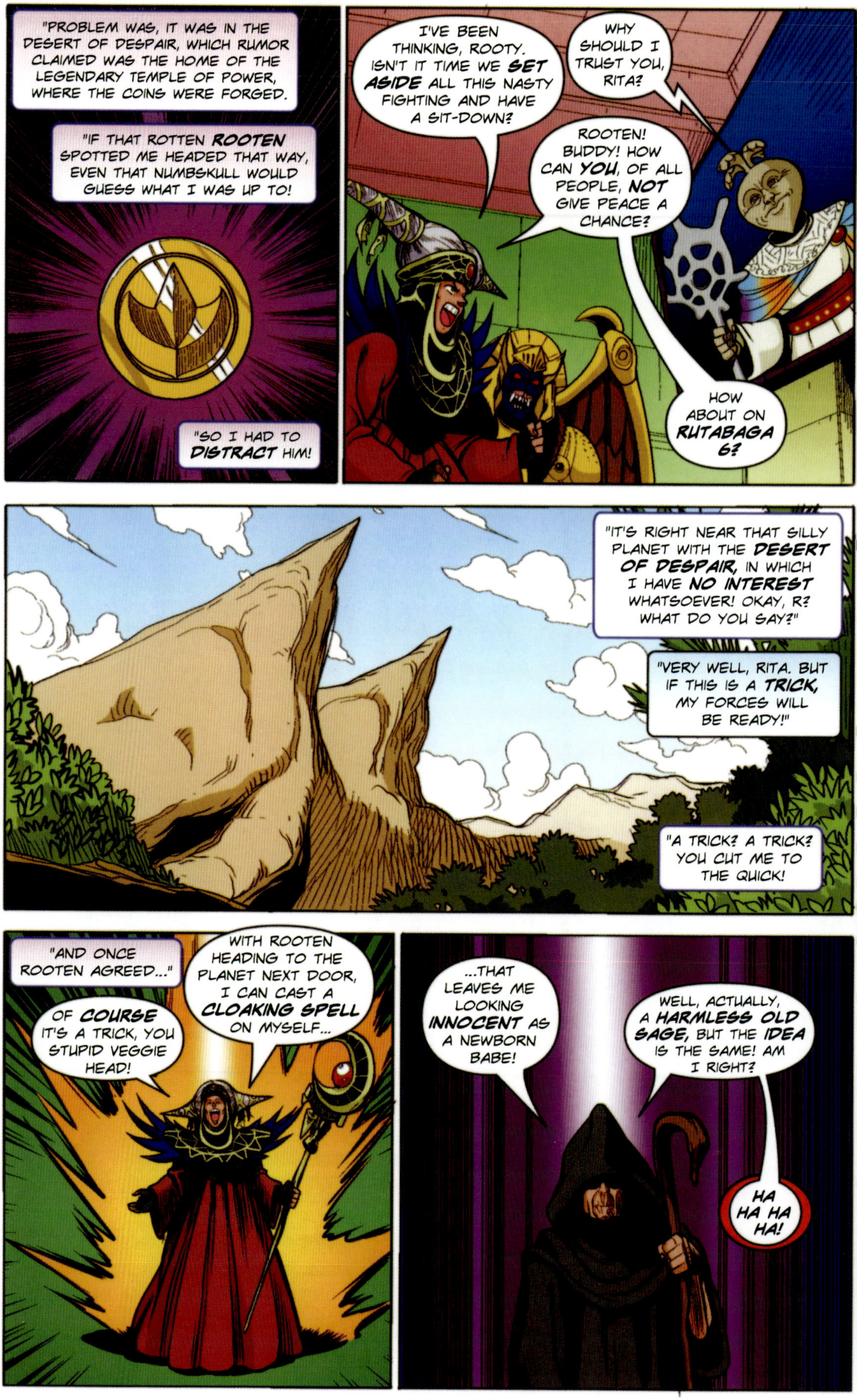
"PROBLEM WAS, IT WAS IN THE DESERT OF DESPAIR, WHICH RUMOR CLAIMED WAS THE HOME OF THE LEGENDARY TEMPLE OF POWER, WHERE THE COINS WERE FORGED.
"IF THAT ROTTEN ROOTEN SPOTTED ME HEADED THAT WAY, EVEN THAT NUMBSKULL WOULD GUESS WHAT I WAS UP TO!
"SO I HAD TO DISTRACT HIM!
I'VE BEEN THINKING, ROOTY. ISN'T IT TIME WE SET ASIDE ALL THIS NASTY FIGHTING AND HAVE A SIT-DOWN?
WHY SHOULD I TRUST YOU, RITA?
ROOTEN! BUDDY! HOW CAN YOU, OF ALL PEOPLE, NOT GIVE PEACE A CHANCE?
HOW ABOUT ON RUTABAGA 6?
"IT'S RIGHT NEAR THAT SILLY PLANET WITH THE DESERT OF DESPAIR, IN WHICH I HAVE NO INTEREST WHATSOEVER! OKAY, R? WHAT DO YOU SAY?"
"VERY WELL, RITA. BUT IF THIS IS A TRICK, MY FORCES WILL BE READY!"
"A TRICK? A TRICK? YOU CUT ME TO THE QUICK!
"AND ONCE ROOTEN AGREED..."
OF COURSE IT'S A TRICK, YOU STUPID VEGGIE HEAD!
WITH ROOTEN HEADING TO THE PLANET NEXT DOOR, I CAN CAST A CLOAKING SPELL ON MYSELF...
...THAT LEAVES ME LOOKING INNOCENT AS A NEWBORN BABE!
WELL, ACTUALLY, A HARMLESS OLD SAGE, BUT THE IDEA IS THE SAME! AM I RIGHT?
HA HA HA HA!

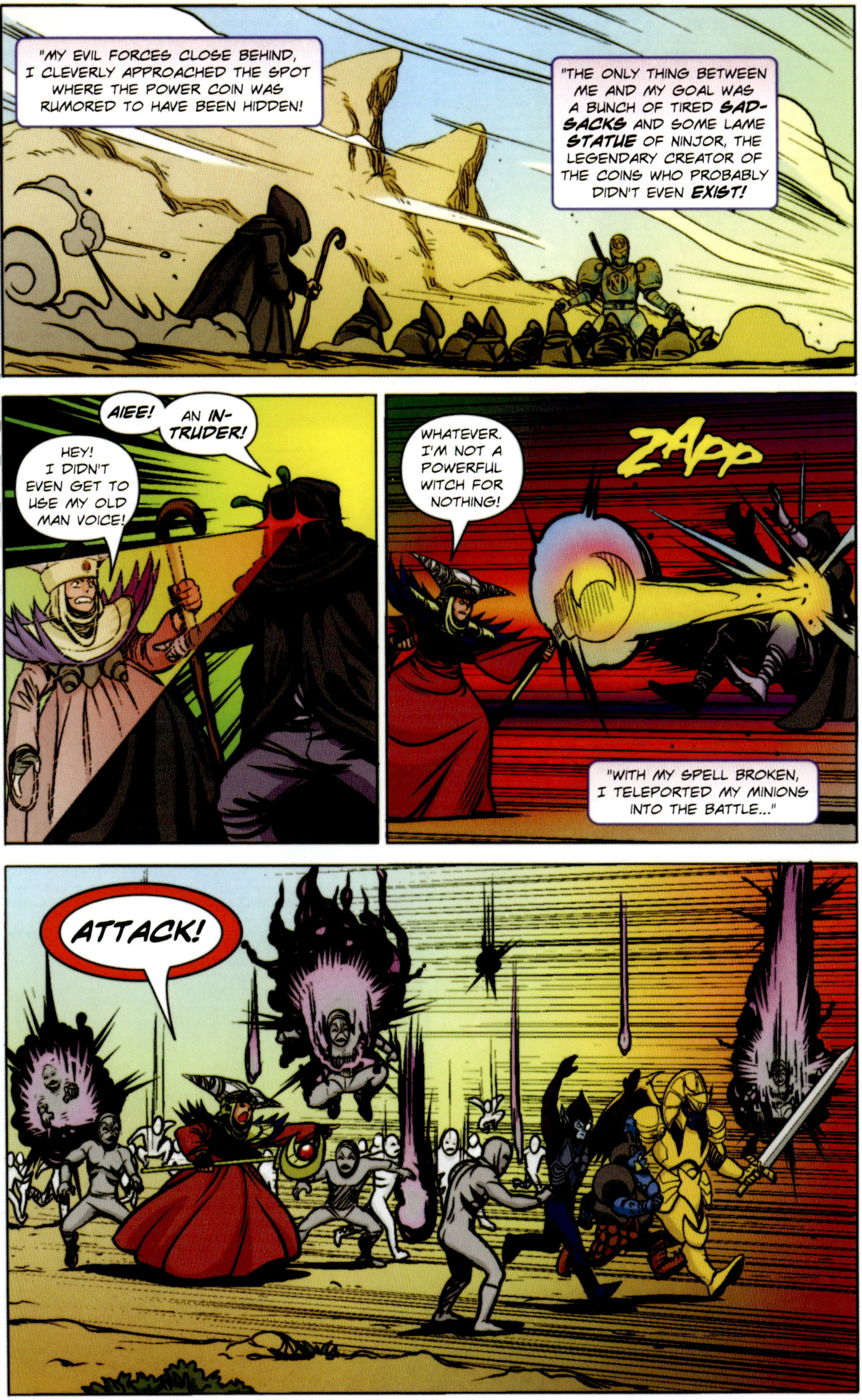
"MY EVIL FORCES CLOSE BEHIND, I CLEVERLY APPROACHED THE SPOT WHERE THE POWER COIN WAS RUMORED TO HAVE BEEN HIDDEN!
"THE ONLY THING BETWEEN ME AND MY GOAL WAS A BUNCH OF TIRED SAD-SACKS AND SOME LAME STATUE OF NINJOR, THE LEGENDARY CREATOR OF THE COINS WHO PROBABLY DIDN'T EVEN EXIST!
AIEE!
AN IN-TRUDER!
HEY! I DIDN'T EVEN GET TO USE MY OLD MAN VOICE!
WHATEVER. I'M NOT A POWERFUL WITCH FOR NOTHING!
ZAPP
"WITH MY SPELL BROKEN, I TELEPORTED MY MINIONS INTO THE BATTLE..."
ATTACK!

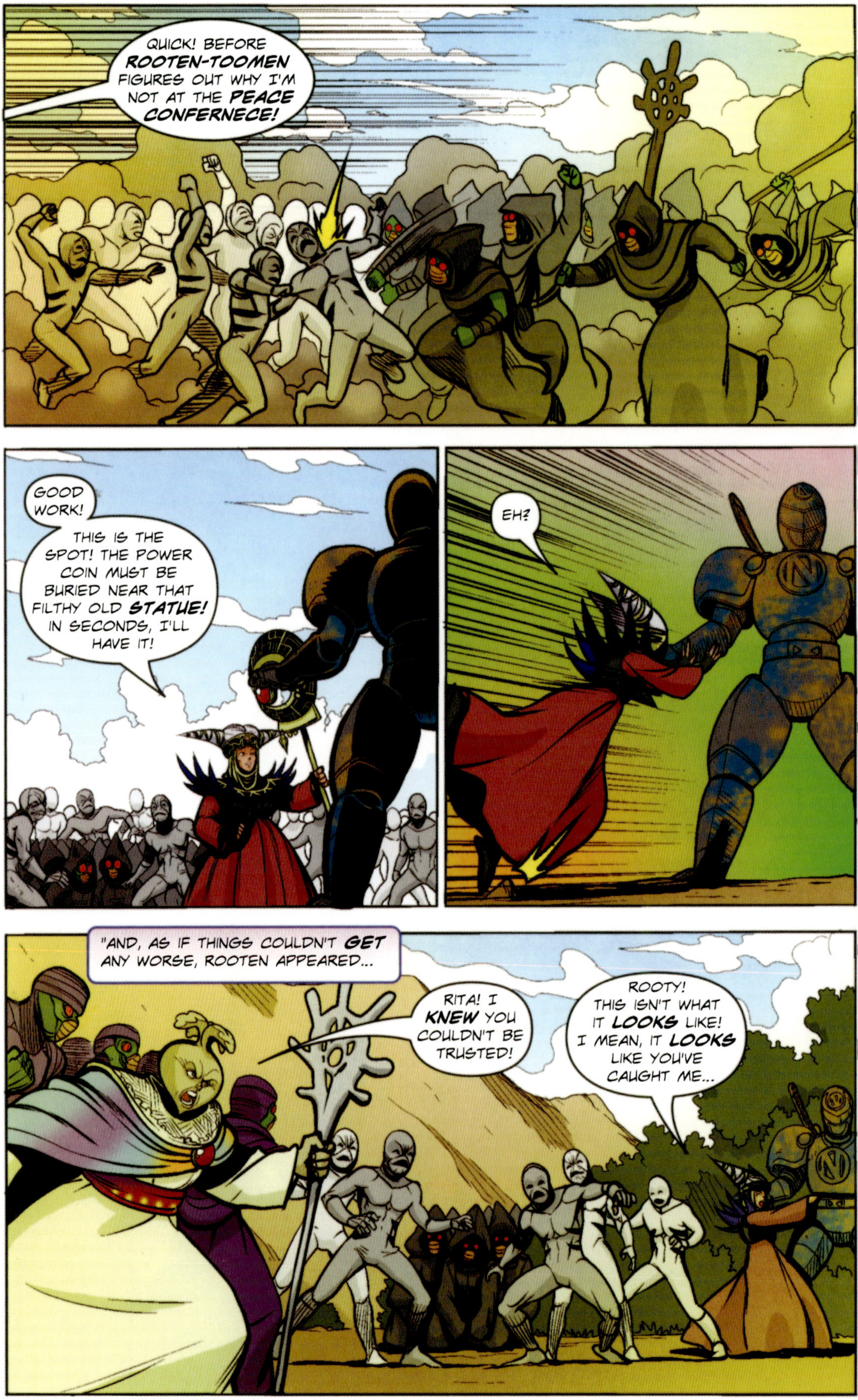
QUICK! BEFORE ROOTEN-TOOMEN FIGURES OUT WHY I'M NOT AT THE PEACE CONFERNECE!
GOOD WORK!
THIS IS THE SPOT! THE POWER COIN MUST BE BURIED NEAR THAT FILTHY OLD STATUE! IN SECONDS, I'LL HAVE IT!
EH?
"AND, AS IF THINGS COULDN'T GET ANY WORSE, ROOTEN APPEARED...
RITA! I KNEW YOU COULDN'T BE TRUSTED!
ROOTY! THIS ISN'T WHAT IT LOOKS LIKE! I MEAN, IT LOOKS LIKE YOU'VE CAUGHT ME...

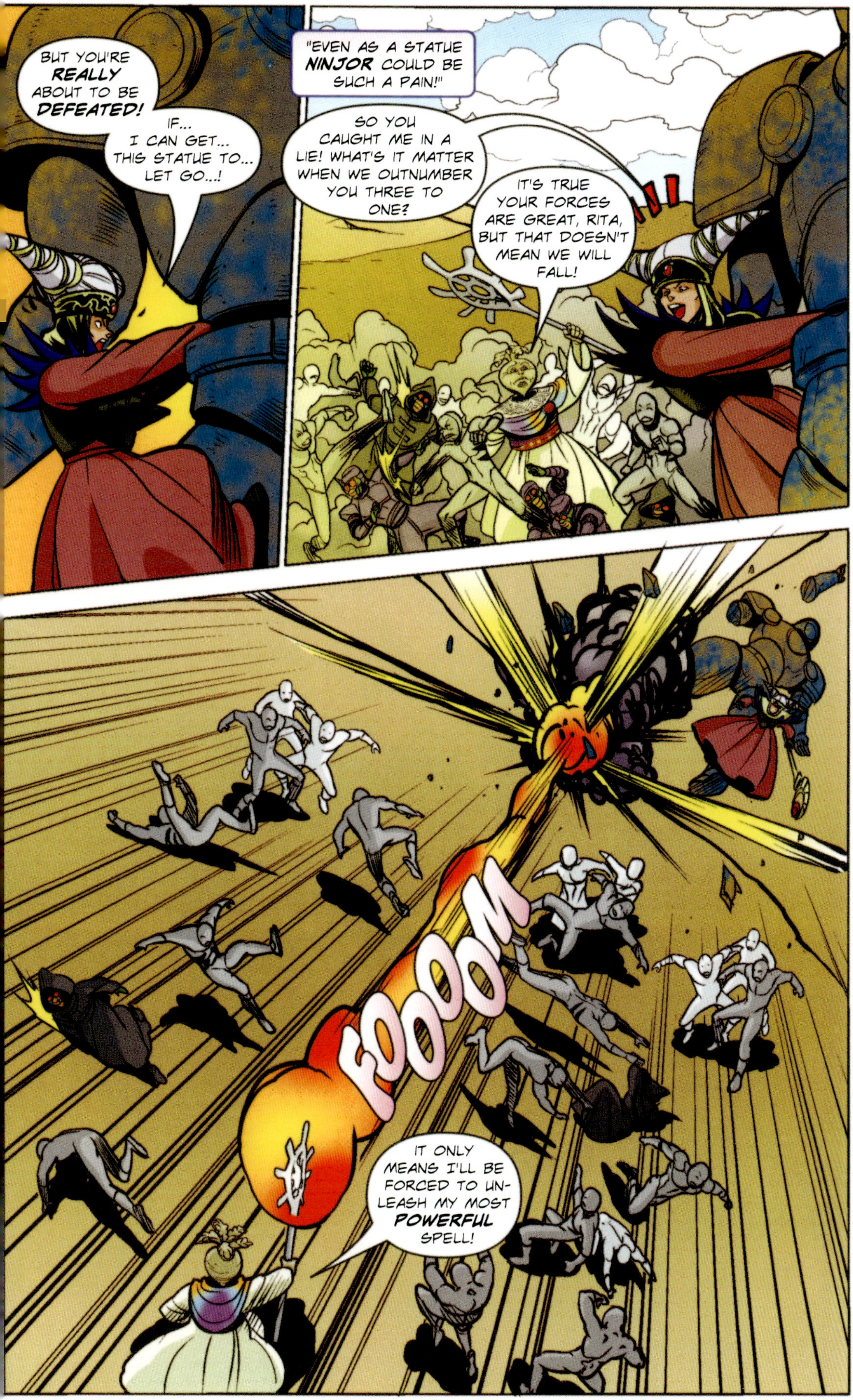

BUT YOU'RE **REALLY** ABOUT TO BE **DEFEATED!**
IF... I CAN GET... THIS STATUE TO... LET GO...!
"EVEN AS A STATUE **NINJOR** COULD BE SUCH A PAIN!"
SO YOU CAUGHT ME IN A LIE! WHAT'S IT MATTER WHEN WE OUTNUMBER YOU THREE TO ONE?
IT'S TRUE YOUR FORCES ARE GREAT, RITA, BUT THAT DOESN'T MEAN WE WILL FALL!
FOOOOM
IT ONLY MEANS I'LL BE FORCED TO UN-LEASH MY MOST **POWERFUL** SPELL!

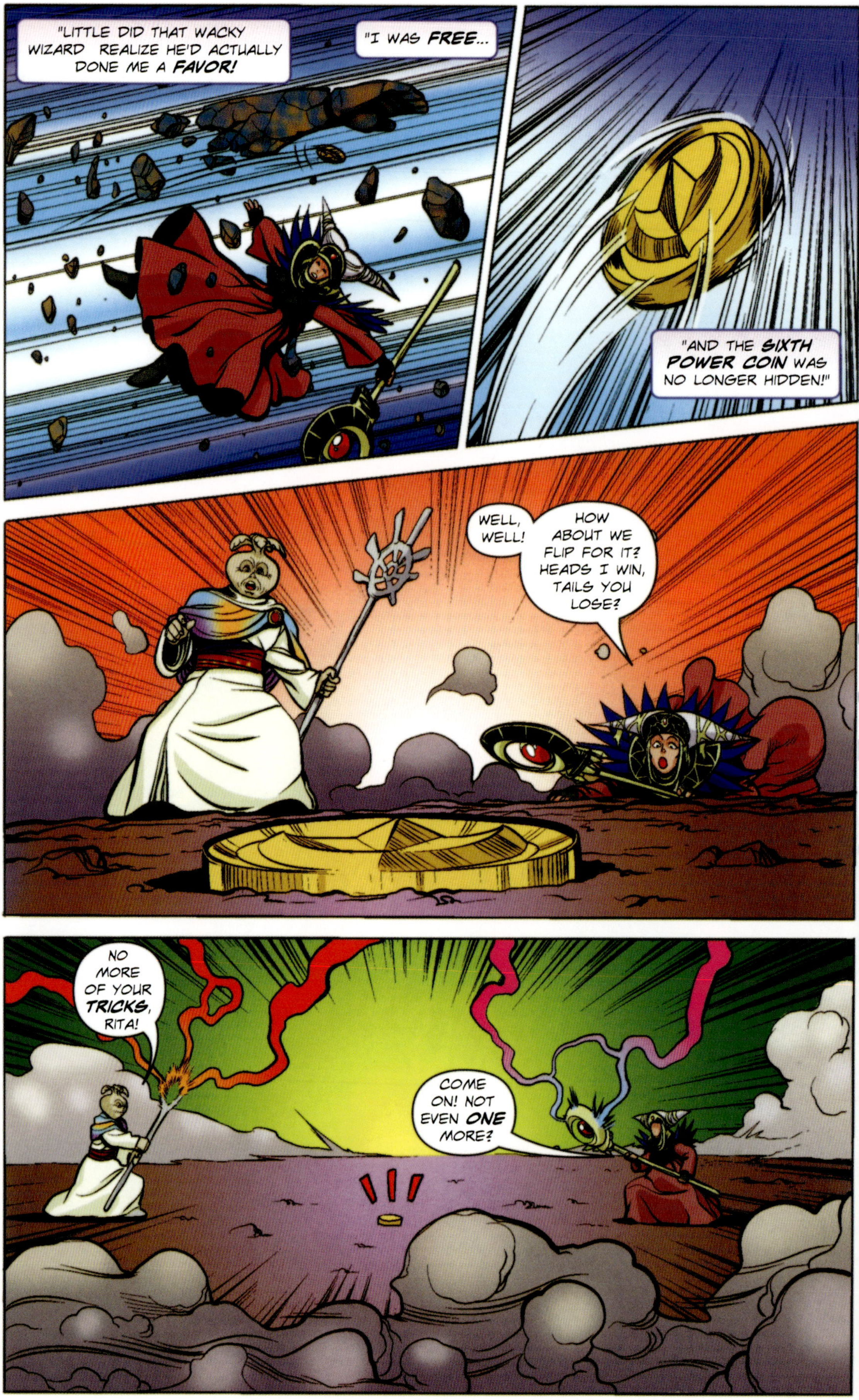
"LITTLE DID THAT WACKY WIZARD REALIZE HE'D ACTUALLY DONE ME A FAVOR!
"I WAS FREE...
"AND THE SIXTH POWER COIN WAS NO LONGER HIDDEN!"
WELL, WELL!
HOW ABOUT WE FLIP FOR IT? HEADS I WIN, TAILS YOU LOSE?
NO MORE OF YOUR TRICKS, RITA!
COME ON! NOT EVEN ONE MORE?
!!!

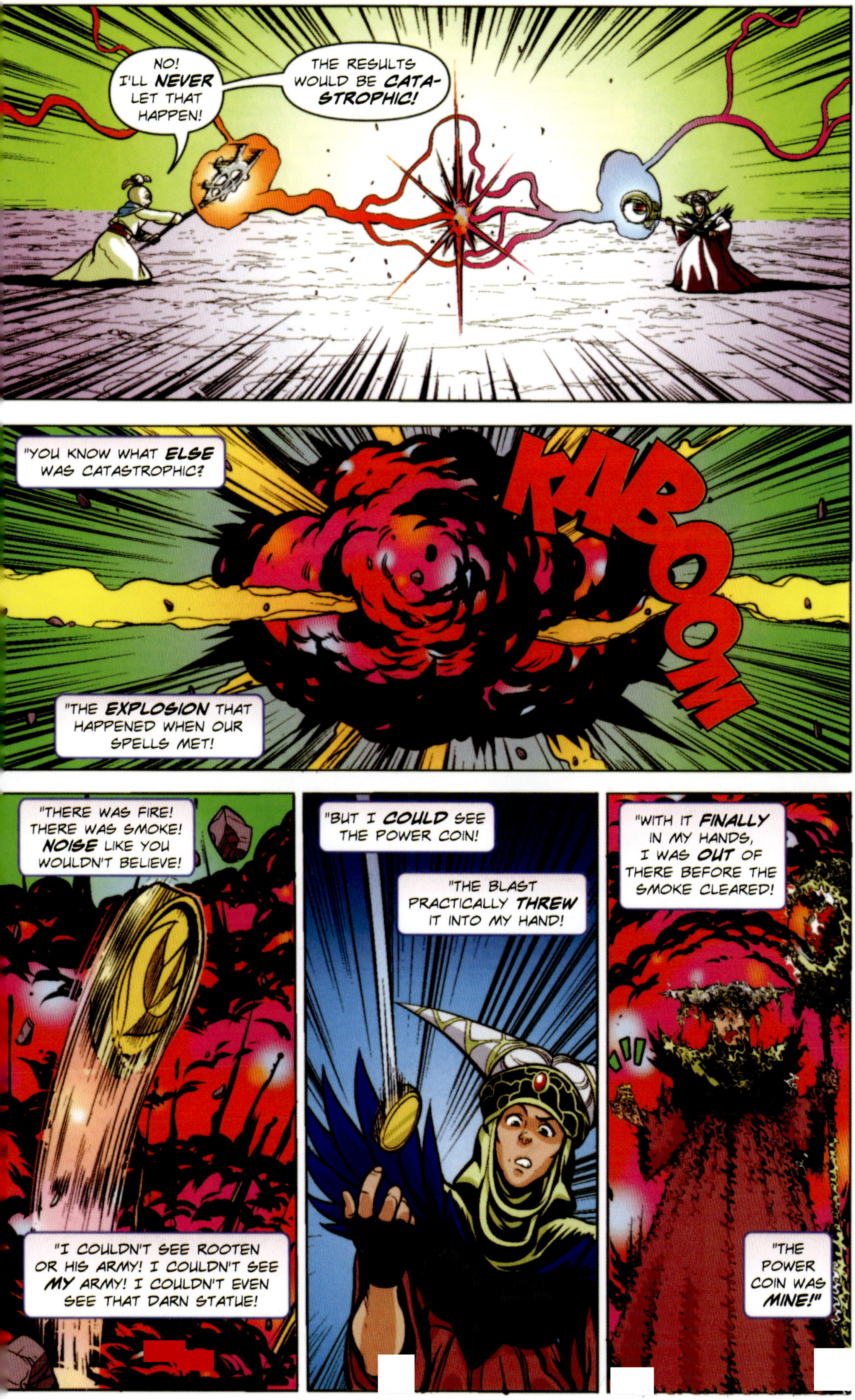
NO! I'LL NEVER LET THAT HAPPEN!
THE RESULTS WOULD BE CATA-STROPHIC!
"YOU KNOW WHAT ELSE WAS CATASTROPHIC?
KABOOM
"THE EXPLOSION THAT HAPPENED WHEN OUR SPELLS MET!
"THERE WAS FIRE! THERE WAS SMOKE! NOISE LIKE YOU WOULDN'T BELIEVE!
"I COULDN'T SEE ROOTEN OR HIS ARMY! I COULDN'T SEE MY ARMY! I COULDN'T EVEN SEE THAT DARN STATUE!
"BUT I COULD SEE THE POWER COIN!
"THE BLAST PRACTICALLY THREW IT INTO MY HAND!
"WITH IT FINALLY IN MY HANDS, I WAS OUT OF THERE BEFORE THE SMOKE CLEARED!
"THE POWER COIN WAS MINE!"

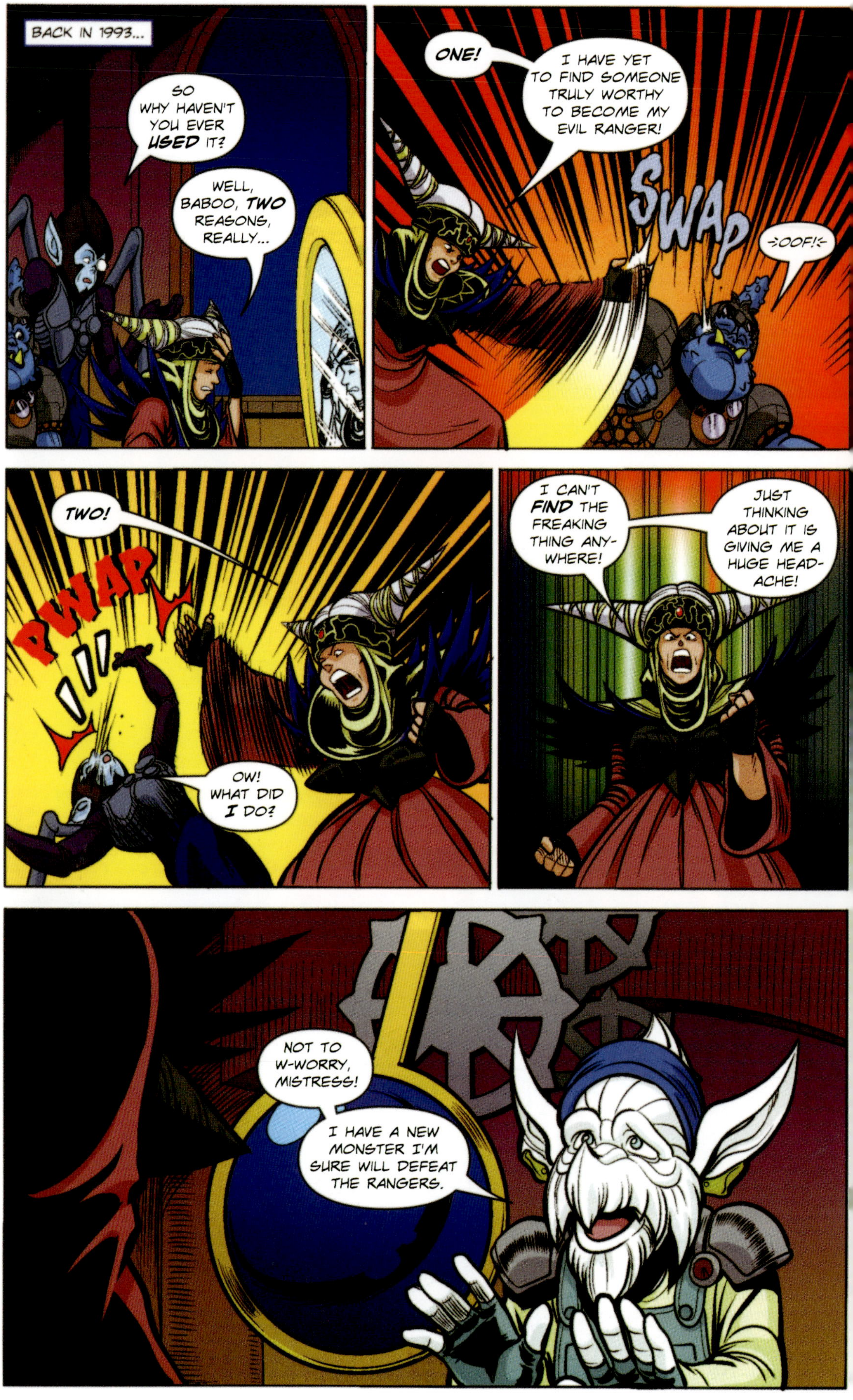
BACK IN 1993...
SO WHY HAVEN'T YOU EVER USED IT?
WELL, BABOO, TWO REASONS, REALLY...
ONE!
I HAVE YET TO FIND SOMEONE TRULY WORTHY TO BECOME MY EVIL RANGER!
SWAP
OOF!
TWO!
PWAP
OW! WHAT DID I DO?
I CAN'T FIND THE FREAKING THING ANY-WHERE!
JUST THINKING ABOUT IT IS GIVING ME A HUGE HEAD-ACHE!
NOT TO W-WORRY, MISTRESS!
I HAVE A NEW MONSTER I'M SURE WILL DEFEAT THE RANGERS.

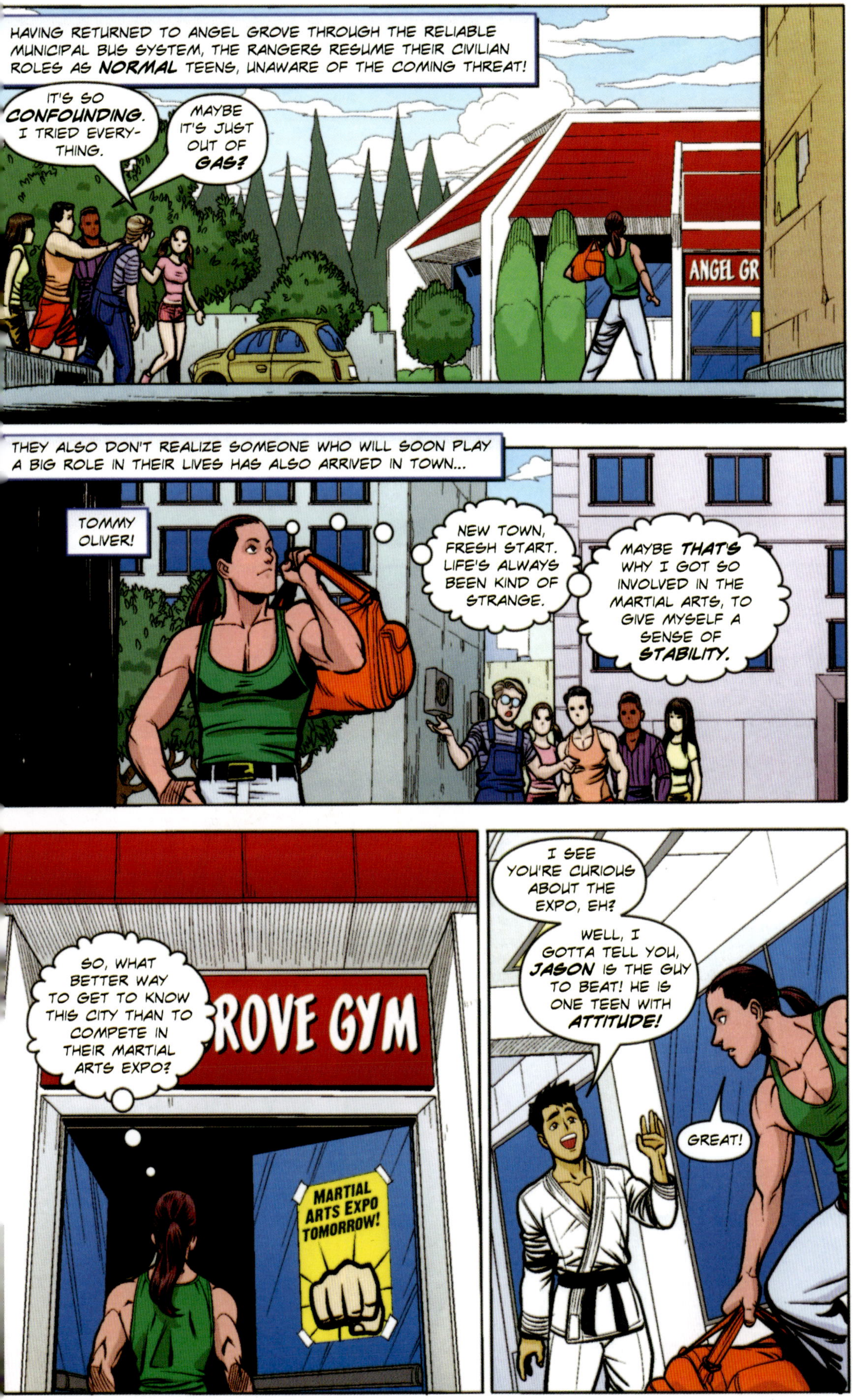
HAVING RETURNED TO ANGEL GROVE THROUGH THE RELIABLE MUNICIPAL BUS SYSTEM, THE RANGERS RESUME THEIR CIVILIAN ROLES AS NORMAL TEENS, UNAWARE OF THE COMING THREAT!
IT'S SO CONFOUNDING. I TRIED EVERY-THING.
MAYBE IT'S JUST OUT OF GAS?
ANGEL GR
THEY ALSO DON'T REALIZE SOMEONE WHO WILL SOON PLAY A BIG ROLE IN THEIR LIVES HAS ALSO ARRIVED IN TOWN...
TOMMY OLIVER!
NEW TOWN, FRESH START. LIFE'S ALWAYS BEEN KIND OF STRANGE.
MAYBE THAT'S WHY I GOT SO INVOLVED IN THE MARTIAL ARTS, TO GIVE MYSELF A SENSE OF STABILITY.
SO, WHAT BETTER WAY TO GET TO KNOW THIS CITY THAN TO COMPETE IN THEIR MARTIAL ARTS EXPO?
ROVE GYM
MARTIAL ARTS EXPO TOMORROW!
I SEE YOU'RE CURIOUS ABOUT THE EXPO, EH?
WELL, I GOTTA TELL YOU, JASON IS THE GUY TO BEAT! HE IS ONE TEEN WITH ATTITUDE!
GREAT!

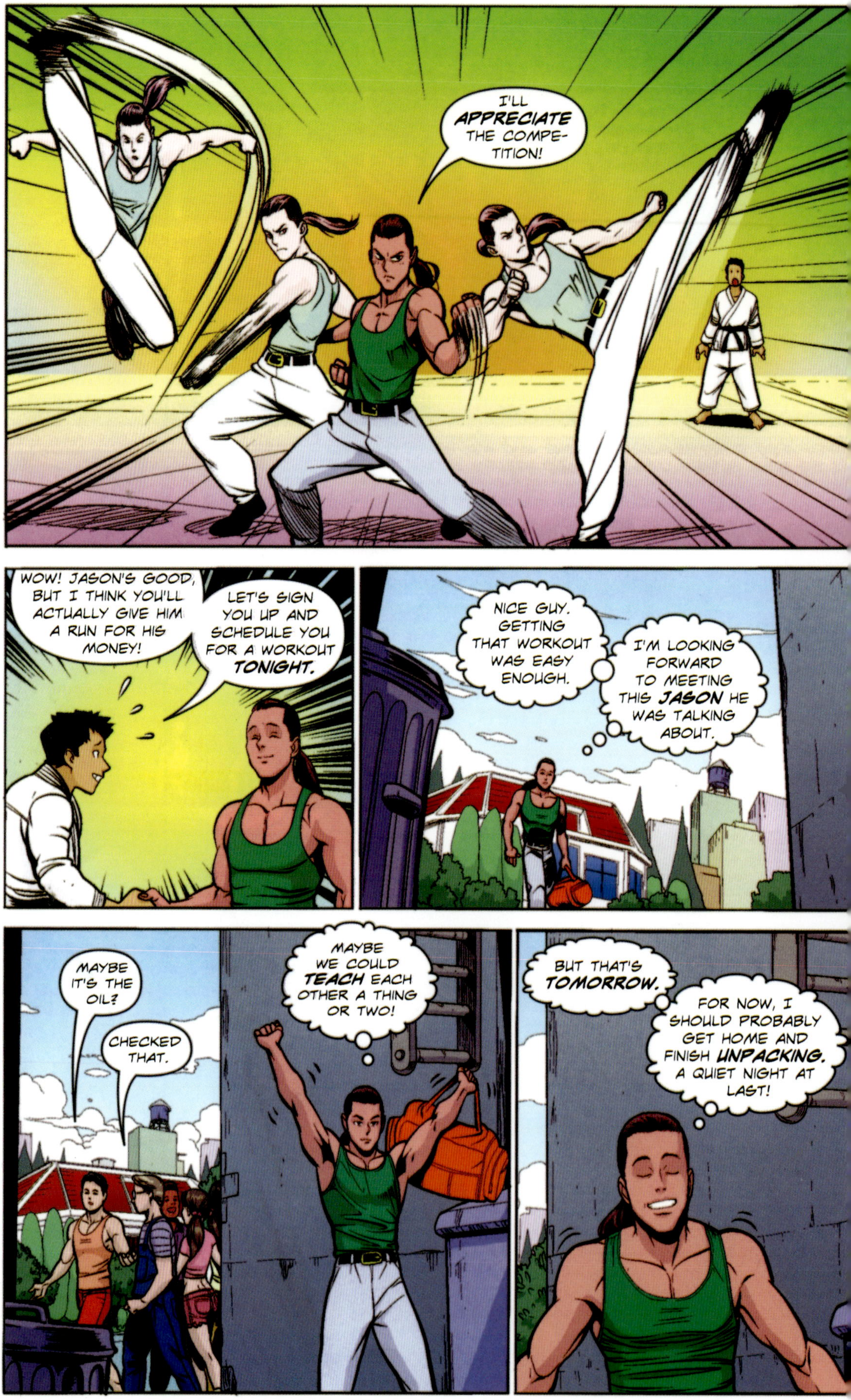

I'LL APPRECIATE THE COMPETITION!
WOW! JASON'S GOOD, BUT I THINK YOU'LL ACTUALLY GIVE HIM A RUN FOR HIS MONEY!
LET'S SIGN YOU UP AND SCHEDULE YOU FOR A WORKOUT TONIGHT.
NICE GUY. GETTING THAT WORKOUT WAS EASY ENOUGH.
I'M LOOKING FORWARD TO MEETING THIS JASON HE WAS TALKING ABOUT.
MAYBE IT'S THE OIL?
CHECKED THAT.
MAYBE WE COULD TEACH EACH OTHER A THING OR TWO!
BUT THAT'S TOMORROW.
FOR NOW, I SHOULD PROBABLY GET HOME AND FINISH UNPACKING. A QUIET NIGHT AT LAST!

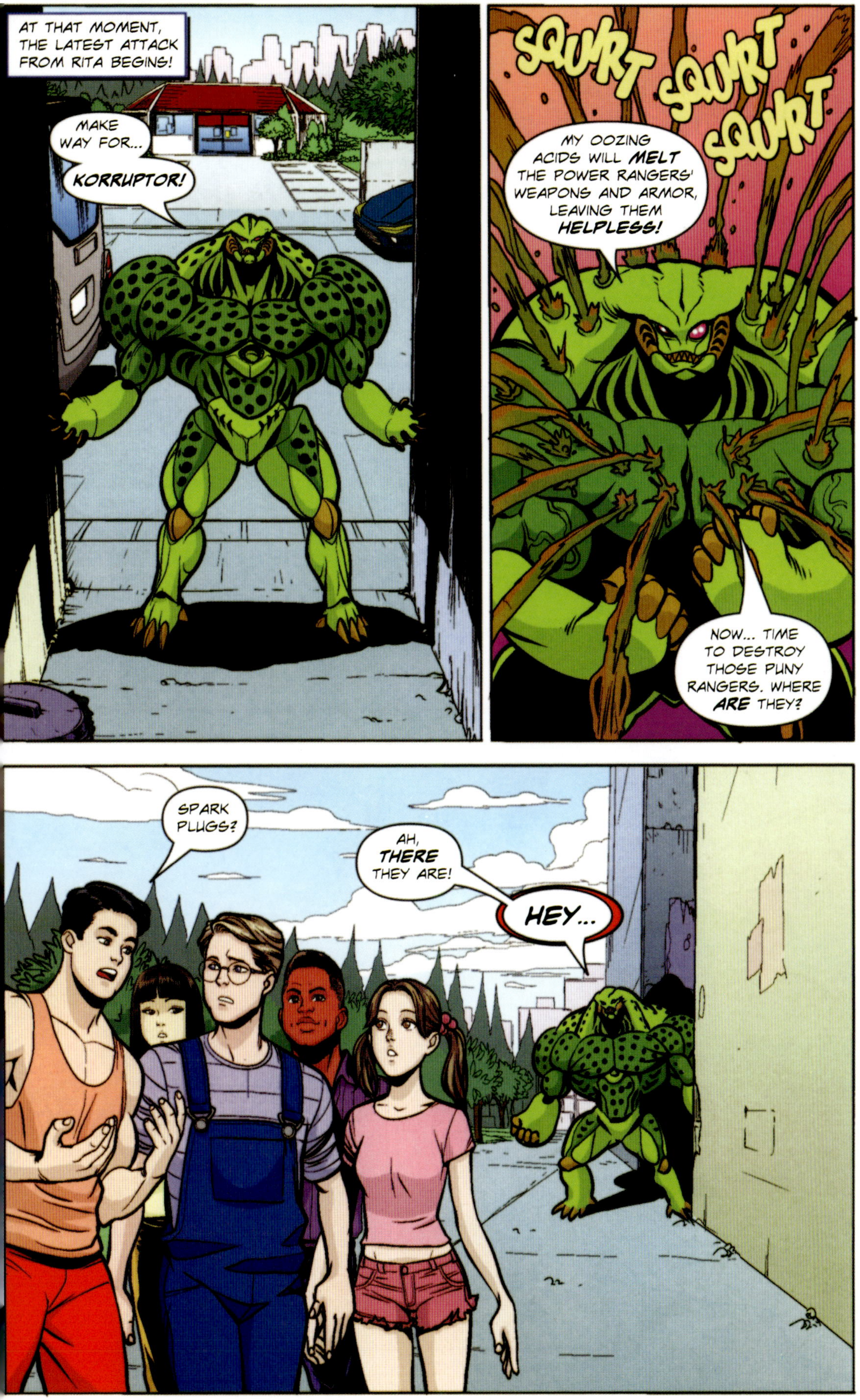
AT THAT MOMENT, THE LATEST ATTACK FROM RITA BEGINS!
MAKE WAY FOR...
KORRUPTOR!
SQUIRT SQUIRT SQUIRT
MY OOZING ACIDS WILL MELT THE POWER RANGERS' WEAPONS AND ARMOR, LEAVING THEM HELPLESS!
NOW... TIME TO DESTROY THOSE PUNY RANGERS. WHERE ARE THEY?
SPARK PLUGS?
AH, THERE THEY ARE!
HEY...

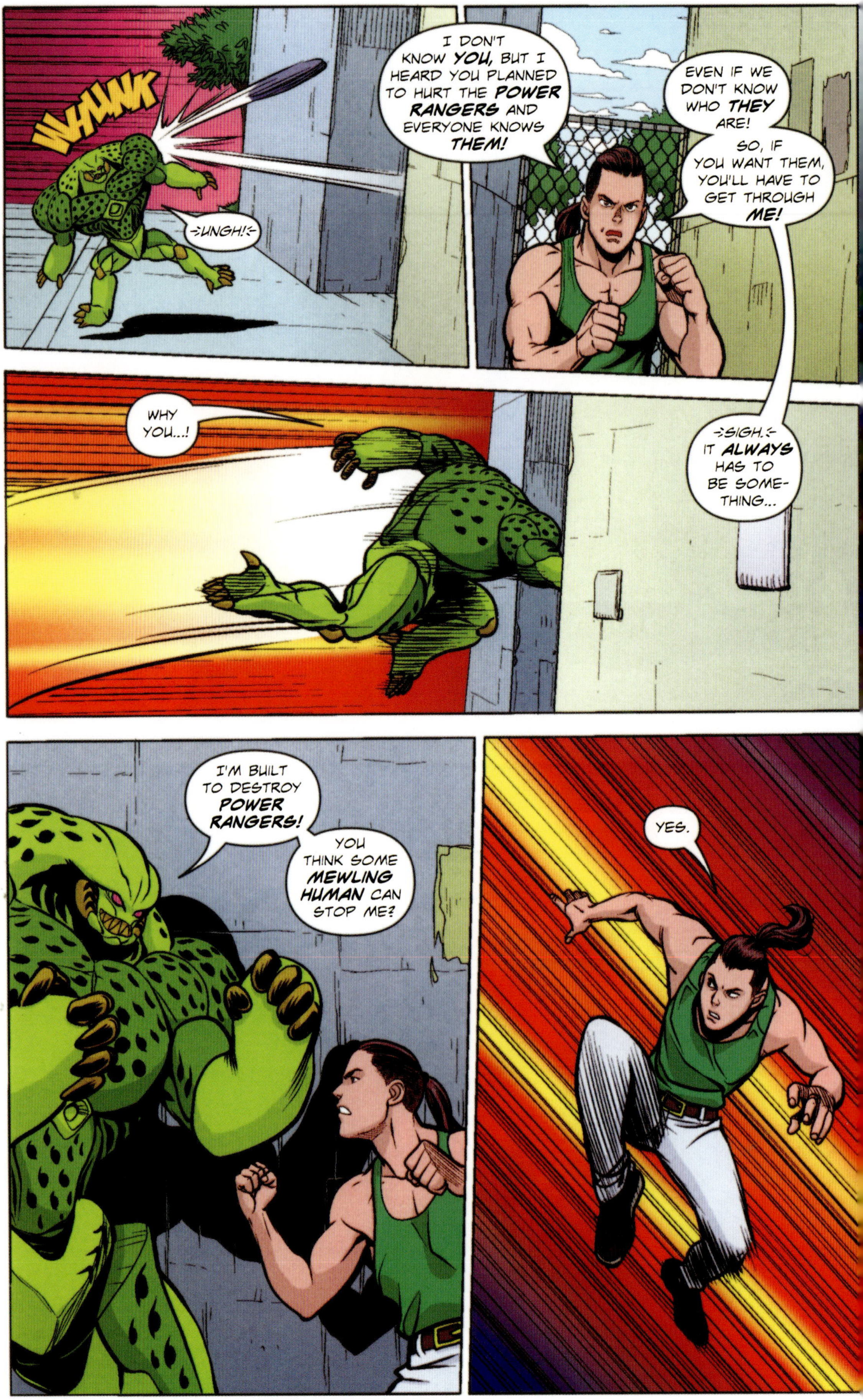
WHUNK
-UNGH!-
I DON'T KNOW YOU, BUT I HEARD YOU PLANNED TO HURT THE POWER RANGERS AND EVERYONE KNOWS THEM!
EVEN IF WE DON'T KNOW WHO THEY ARE!
SO, IF YOU WANT THEM, YOU'LL HAVE TO GET THROUGH ME!
WHY YOU...!
-SIGH.- IT ALWAYS HAS TO BE SOME-THING...
I'M BUILT TO DESTROY POWER RANGERS!
YOU THINK SOME MEWLING HUMAN CAN STOP ME?
YES.

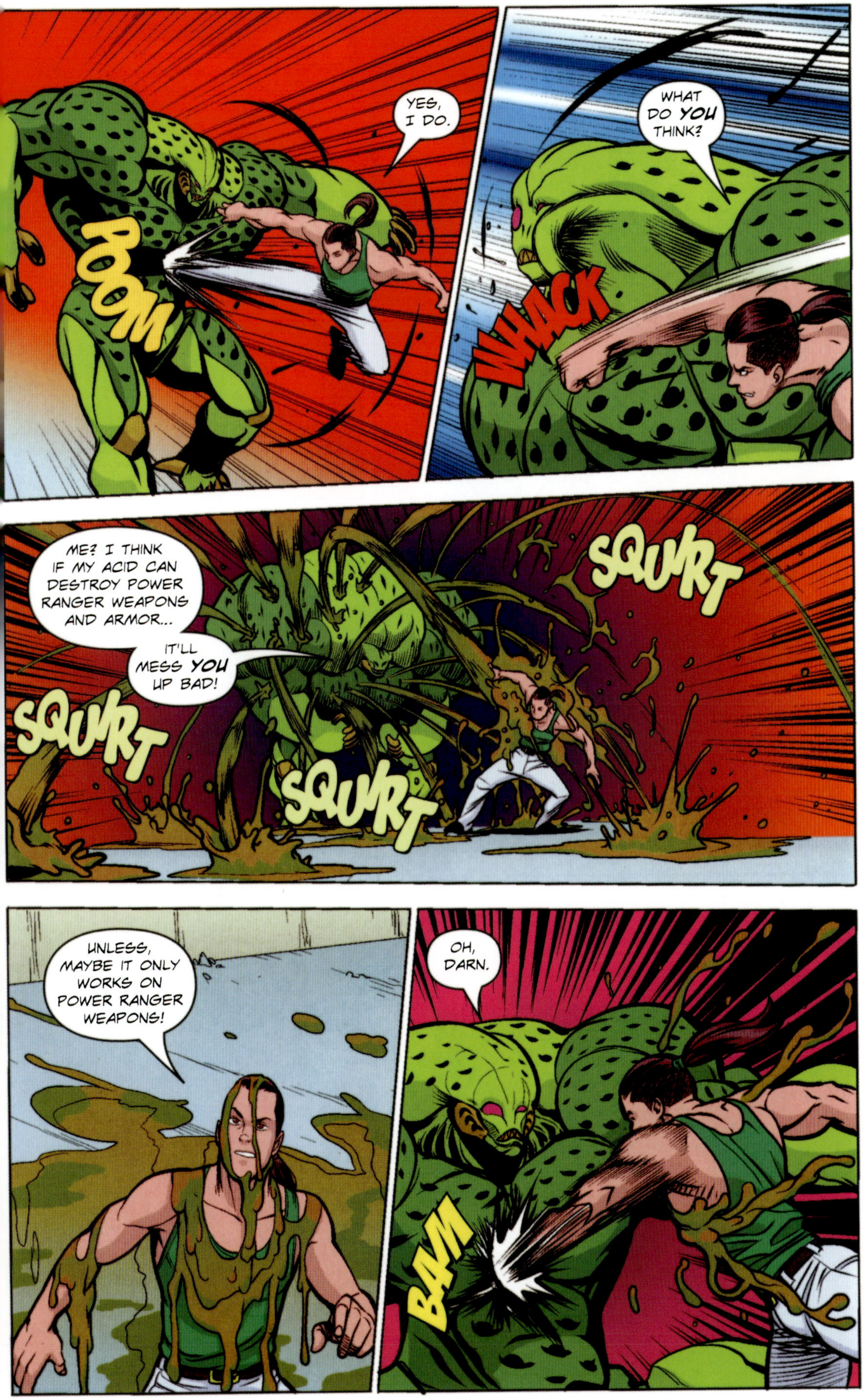

POOM
YES, I DO.
WHAT DO YOU THINK?
WHACK
ME? I THINK IF MY ACID CAN DESTROY POWER RANGER WEAPONS AND ARMOR...
IT'LL MESS YOU UP BAD!
SQUIRT
SQUIRT
SQUIRT
UNLESS, MAYBE IT ONLY WORKS ON POWER RANGER WEAPONS!
OH, DARN.
BAM

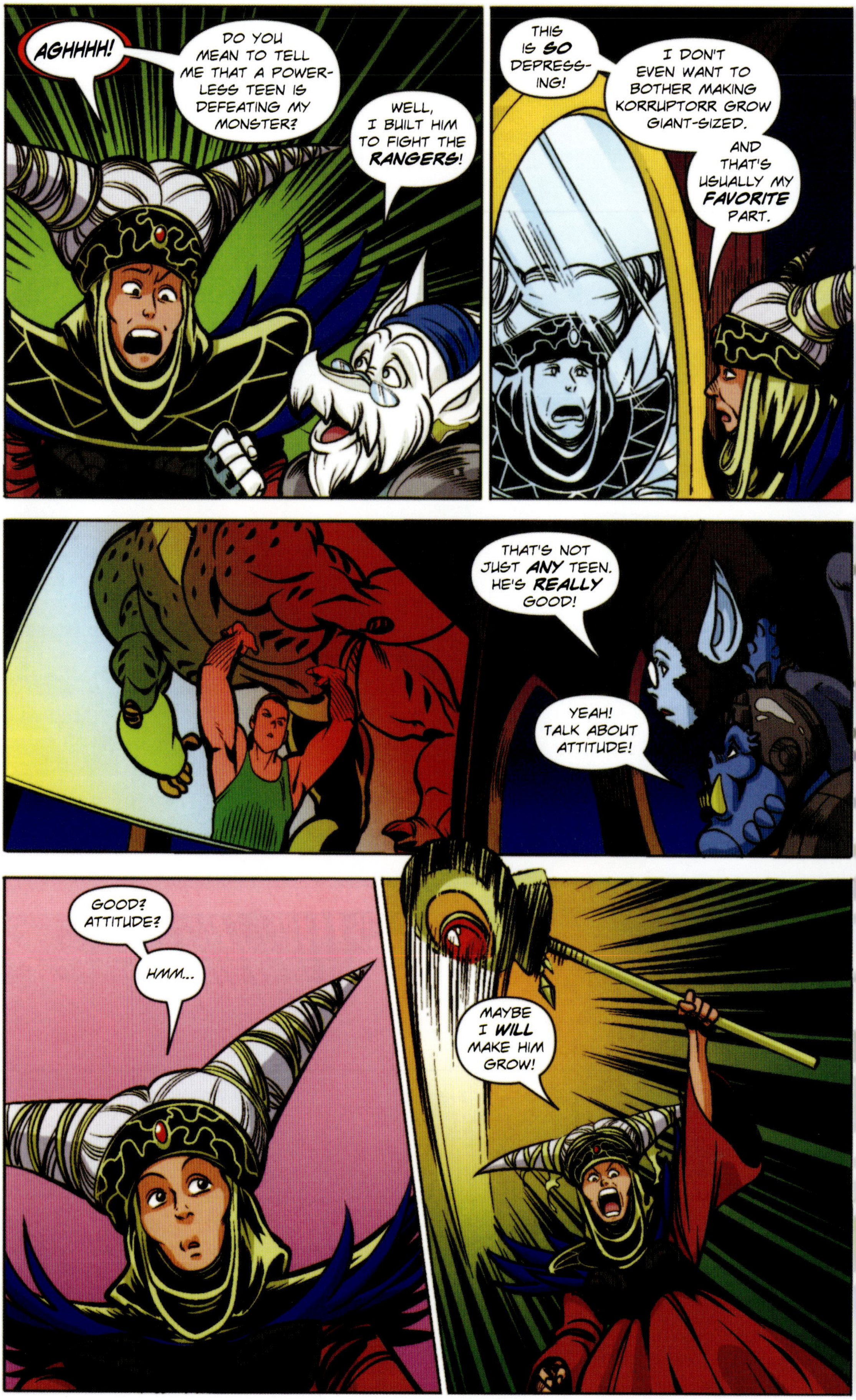
AGHHHH!
DO YOU MEAN TO TELL ME THAT A POWER-LESS TEEN IS DEFEATING MY MONSTER?
WELL, I BUILT HIM TO FIGHT THE RANGERS!
THIS IS SO DEPRESS-ING!
I DON'T EVEN WANT TO BOTHER MAKING KORRUPTORR GROW GIANT-SIZED.
AND THAT'S USUALLY MY FAVORITE PART.
THAT'S NOT JUST ANY TEEN. HE'S REALLY GOOD!
YEAH! TALK ABOUT ATTITUDE!
GOOD? ATTITUDE?
HMM...
MAYBE I WILL MAKE HIM GROW!

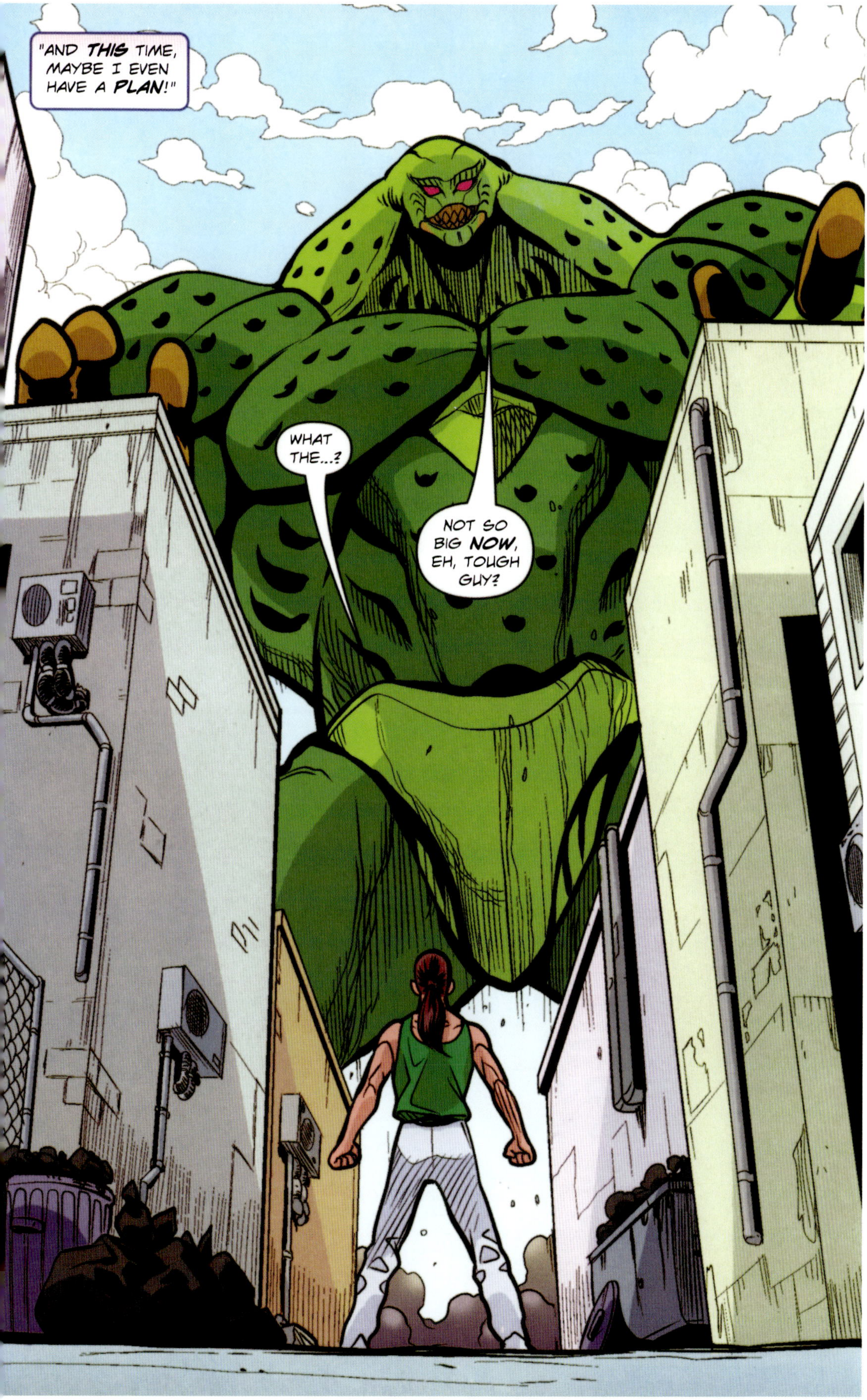
"AND THIS TIME, MAYBE I EVEN HAVE A PLAN!"
WHAT THE...?
NOT SO BIG NOW, EH, TOUGH GUY?

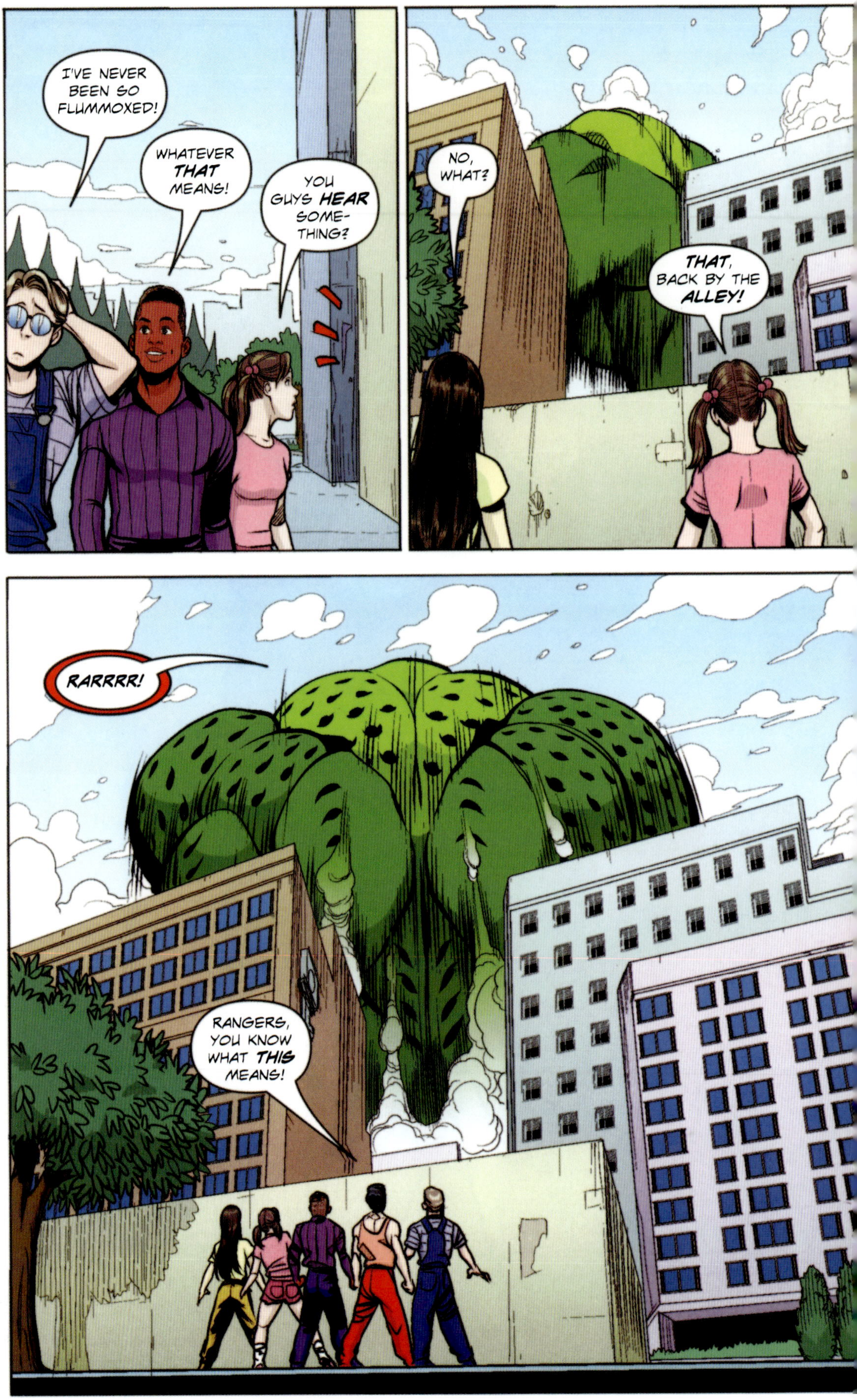
I'VE NEVER BEEN SO FLUMMOXED!
WHATEVER THAT MEANS!
YOU GUYS HEAR SOME-THING?
NO, WHAT?
THAT, BACK BY THE ALLEY!
RARRRR!
RANGERS, YOU KNOW WHAT THIS MEANS!

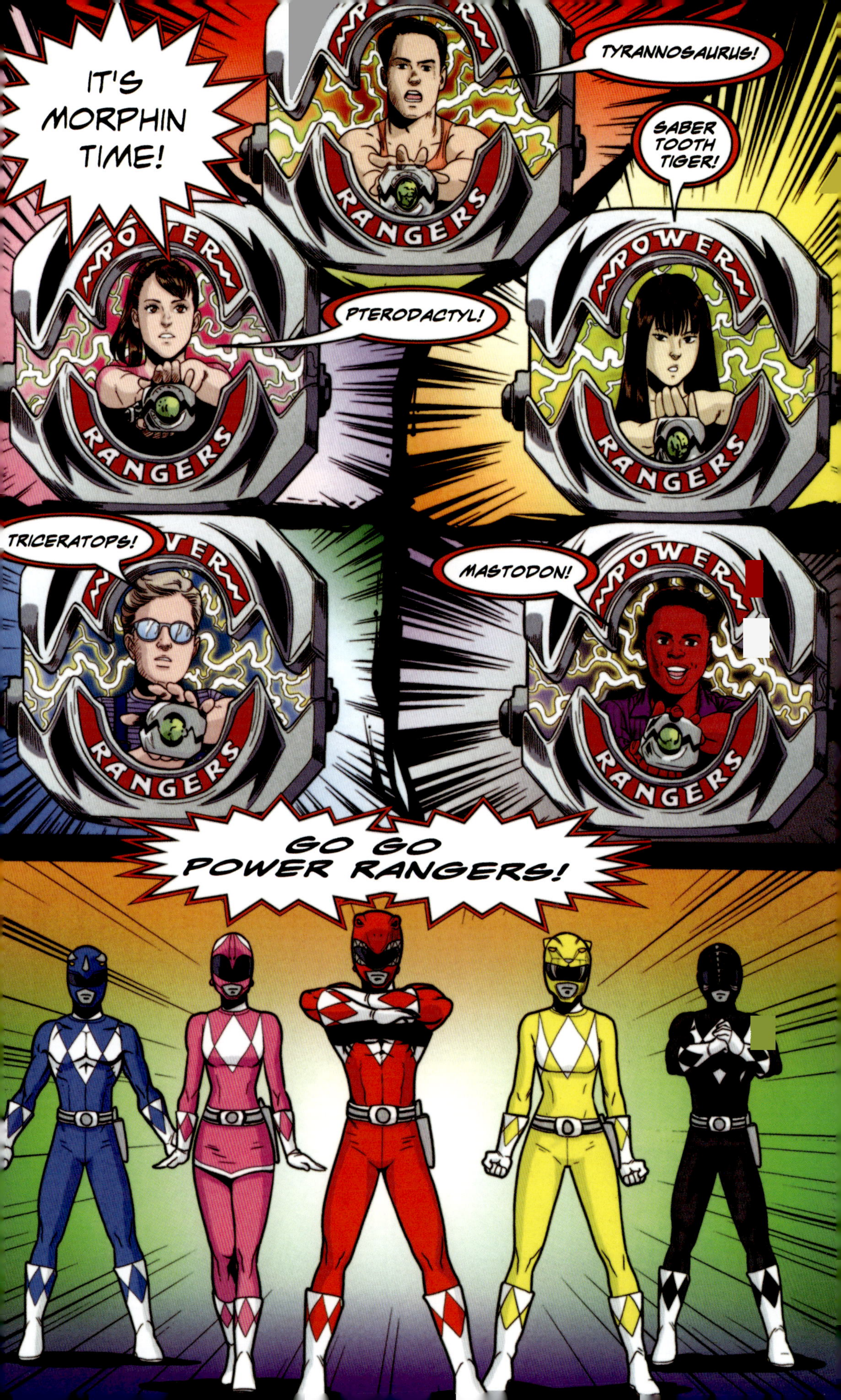
IT'S MORPHIN TIME!
TYRANNOSAURUS!
SABER TOOTH TIGER!
PTERODACTYL!
TRICERATOPS!
MASTODON!
GO GO POWER RANGERS!

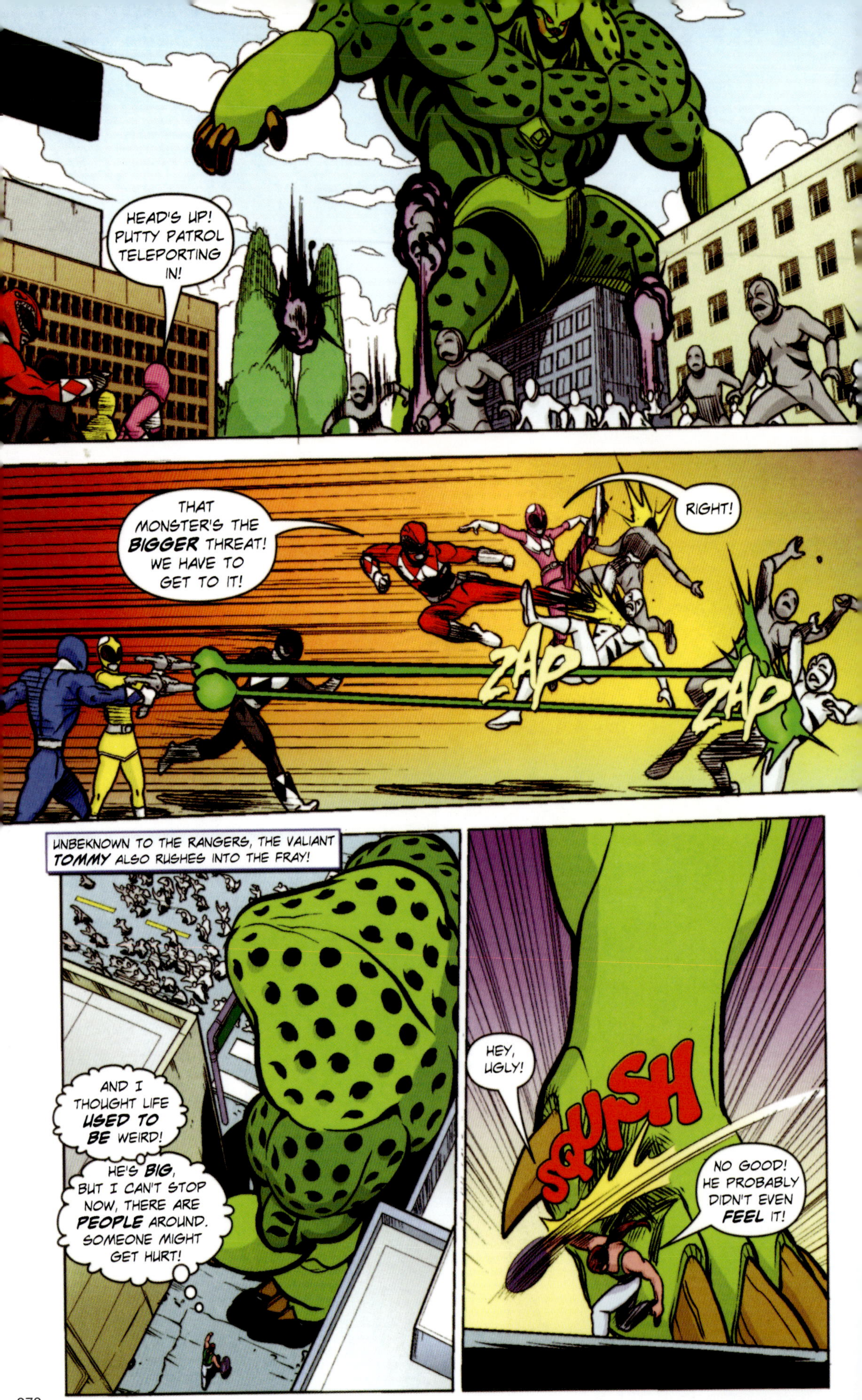
HEAD'S UP! PUTTY PATROL TELEPORTING IN!
THAT MONSTER'S THE BIGGER THREAT! WE HAVE TO GET TO IT!
RIGHT!
ZAP
ZAP
UNBEKNOWN TO THE RANGERS, THE VALIANT TOMMY ALSO RUSHES INTO THE FRAY!
AND I THOUGHT LIFE USED TO BE WEIRD!
HE'S BIG, BUT I CAN'T STOP NOW, THERE ARE PEOPLE AROUND. SOMEONE MIGHT GET HURT!
HEY, UGLY!
SQUISH
NO GOOD! HE PROBABLY DIDN'T EVEN FEEL IT!

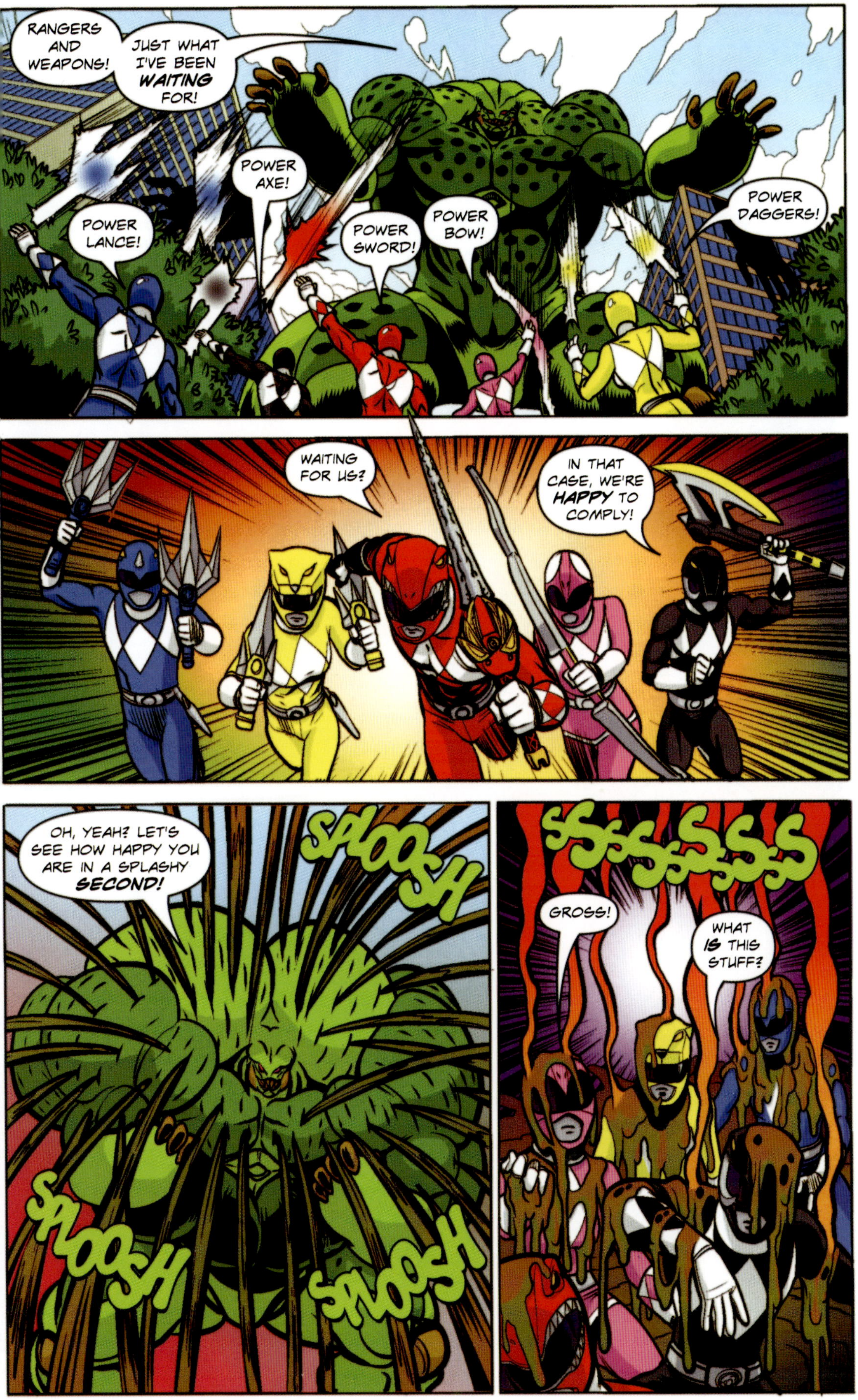
RANGERS AND WEAPONS!
JUST WHAT I'VE BEEN WAITING FOR!
POWER AXE!
POWER LANCE!
POWER SWORD!
POWER BOW!
POWER DAGGERS!
WAITING FOR US?
IN THAT CASE, WE'RE HAPPY TO COMPLY!
OH, YEAH? LET'S SEE HOW HAPPY YOU ARE IN A SPLASHY SECOND!
SPLOOSH
SPLOOSH
SPLOOSH
SSSSSSSSS
GROSS!
WHAT IS THIS STUFF?

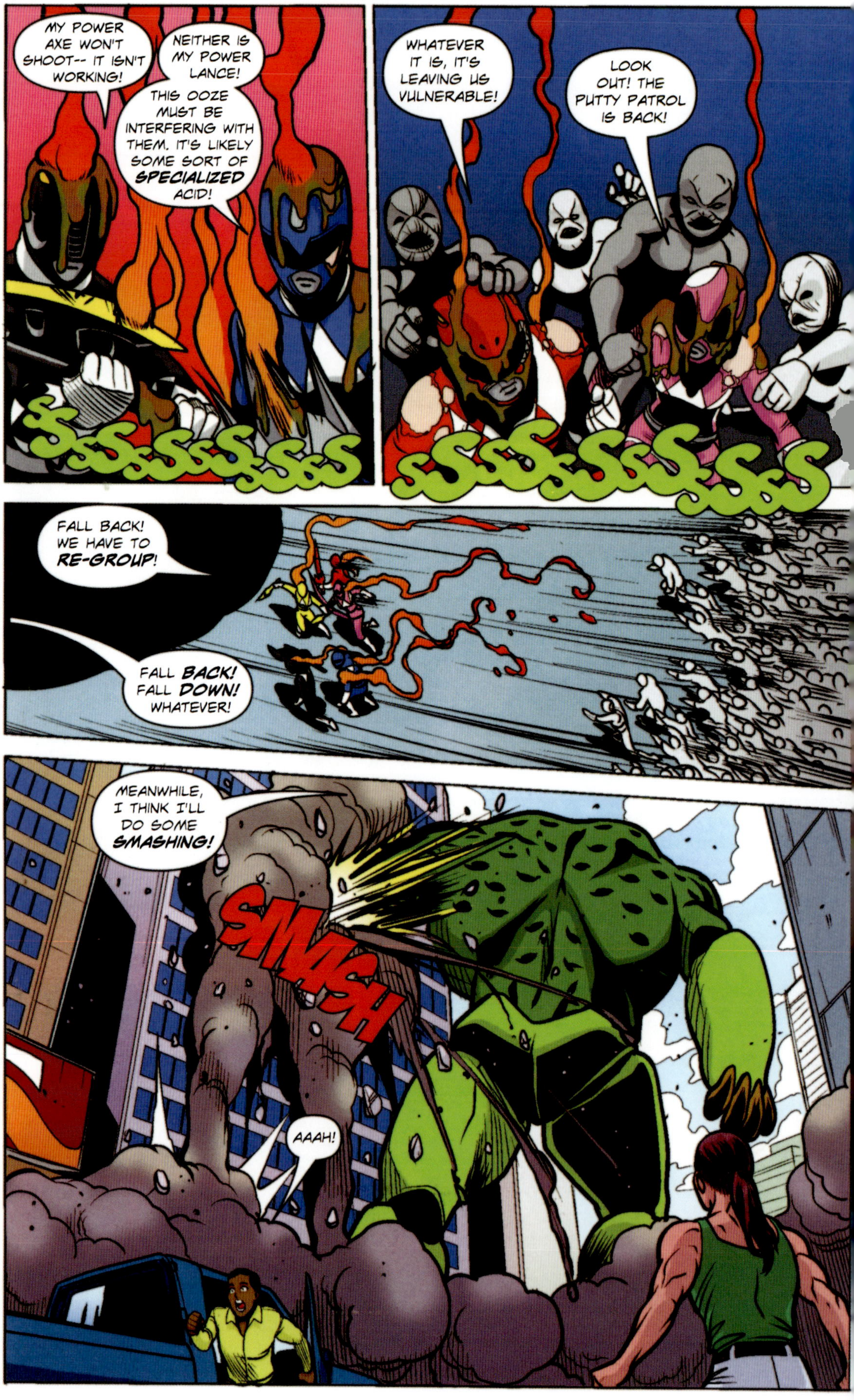
MY POWER AXE WON'T SHOOT-- IT ISN'T WORKING!
NEITHER IS MY POWER LANCE!
THIS OOZE MUST BE INTERFERING WITH THEM. IT'S LIKELY SOME SORT OF SPECIALIZED ACID!
SSSSSSSSSSS
WHATEVER IT IS, IT'S LEAVING US VULNERABLE!
LOOK OUT! THE PUTTY PATROL IS BACK!
SSSSSSSSSSSSSS
FALL BACK! WE HAVE TO RE-GROUP!
FALL BACK! FALL DOWN! WHATEVER!
MEANWHILE, I THINK I'LL DO SOME SMASHING!
SMASH
AAAH!

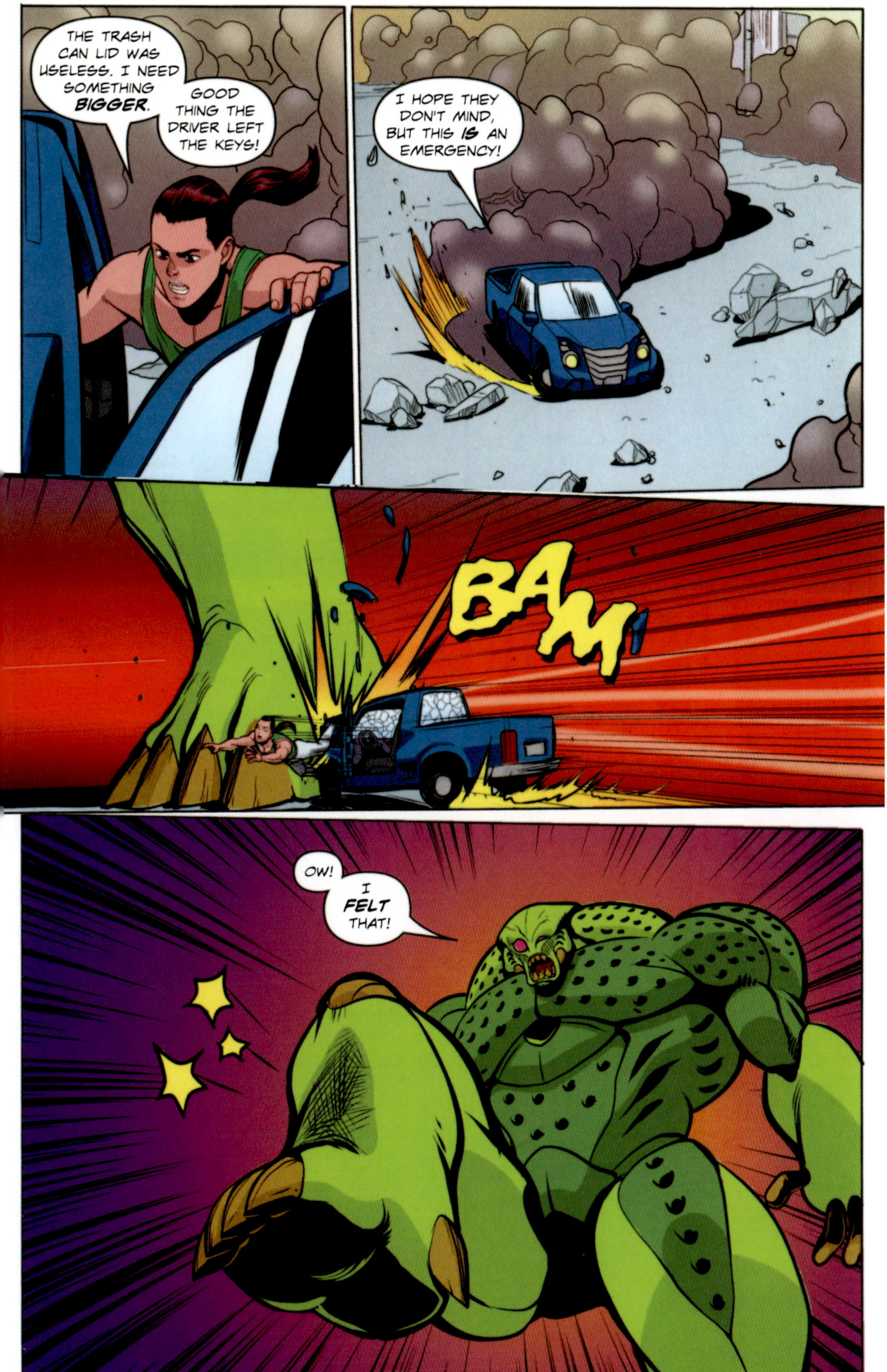
THE TRASH CAN LID WAS USELESS. I NEED SOMETHING **BIGGER**.
GOOD THING THE DRIVER LEFT THE KEYS!
I HOPE THEY DON'T MIND, BUT THIS **IS** AN EMERGENCY!
BAM
OW!
I **FELT** THAT!

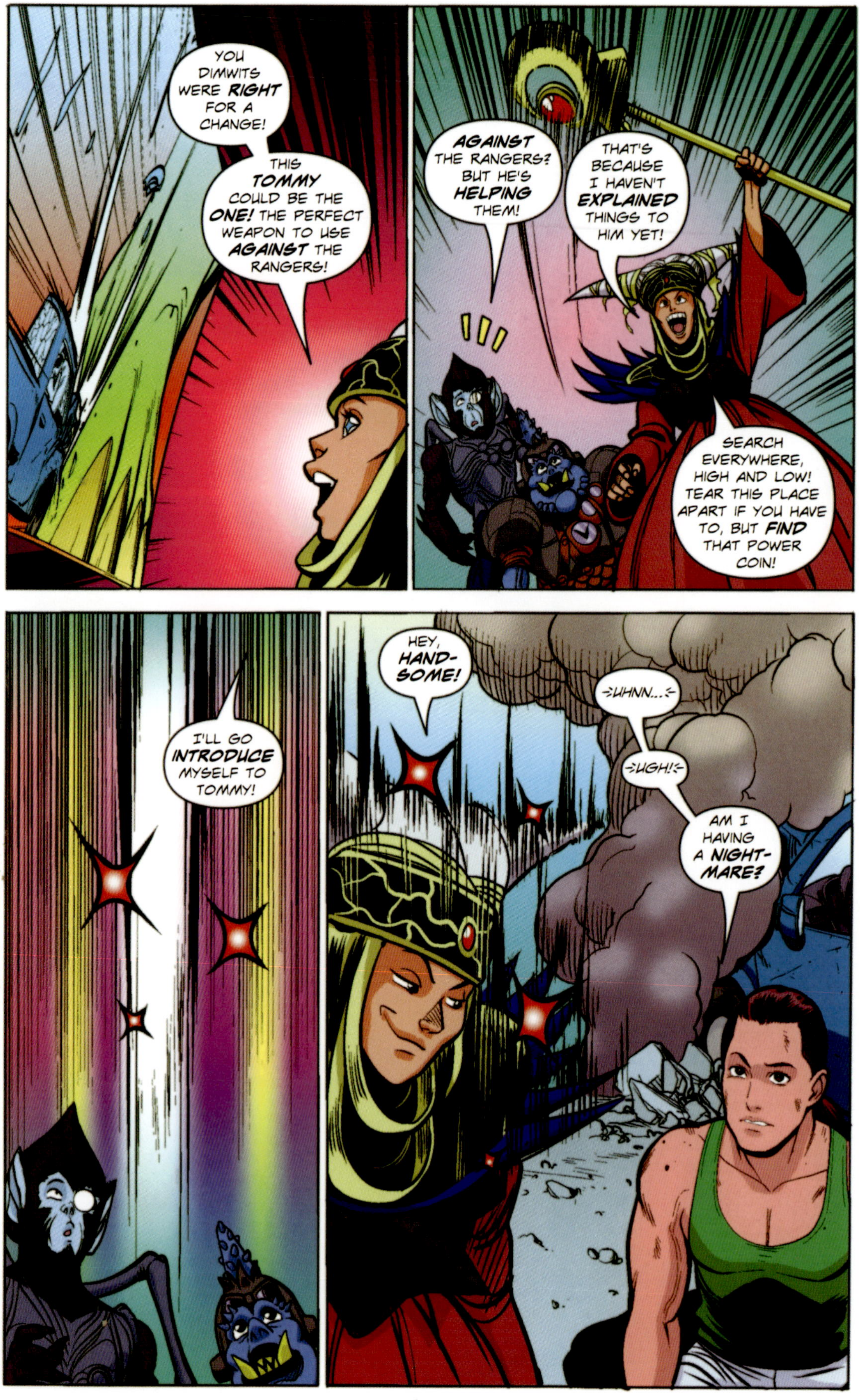
YOU DIMWITS WERE RIGHT FOR A CHANGE!
THIS TOMMY COULD BE THE ONE! THE PERFECT WEAPON TO USE AGAINST THE RANGERS!
AGAINST THE RANGERS? BUT HE'S HELPING THEM!
THAT'S BECAUSE I HAVEN'T EXPLAINED THINGS TO HIM YET!
SEARCH EVERYWHERE, HIGH AND LOW! TEAR THIS PLACE APART IF YOU HAVE TO, BUT FIND THAT POWER COIN!
I'LL GO INTRODUCE MYSELF TO TOMMY!
HEY, HAND-SOME!
UHNN...
UGH!
AM I HAVING A NIGHT-MARE?

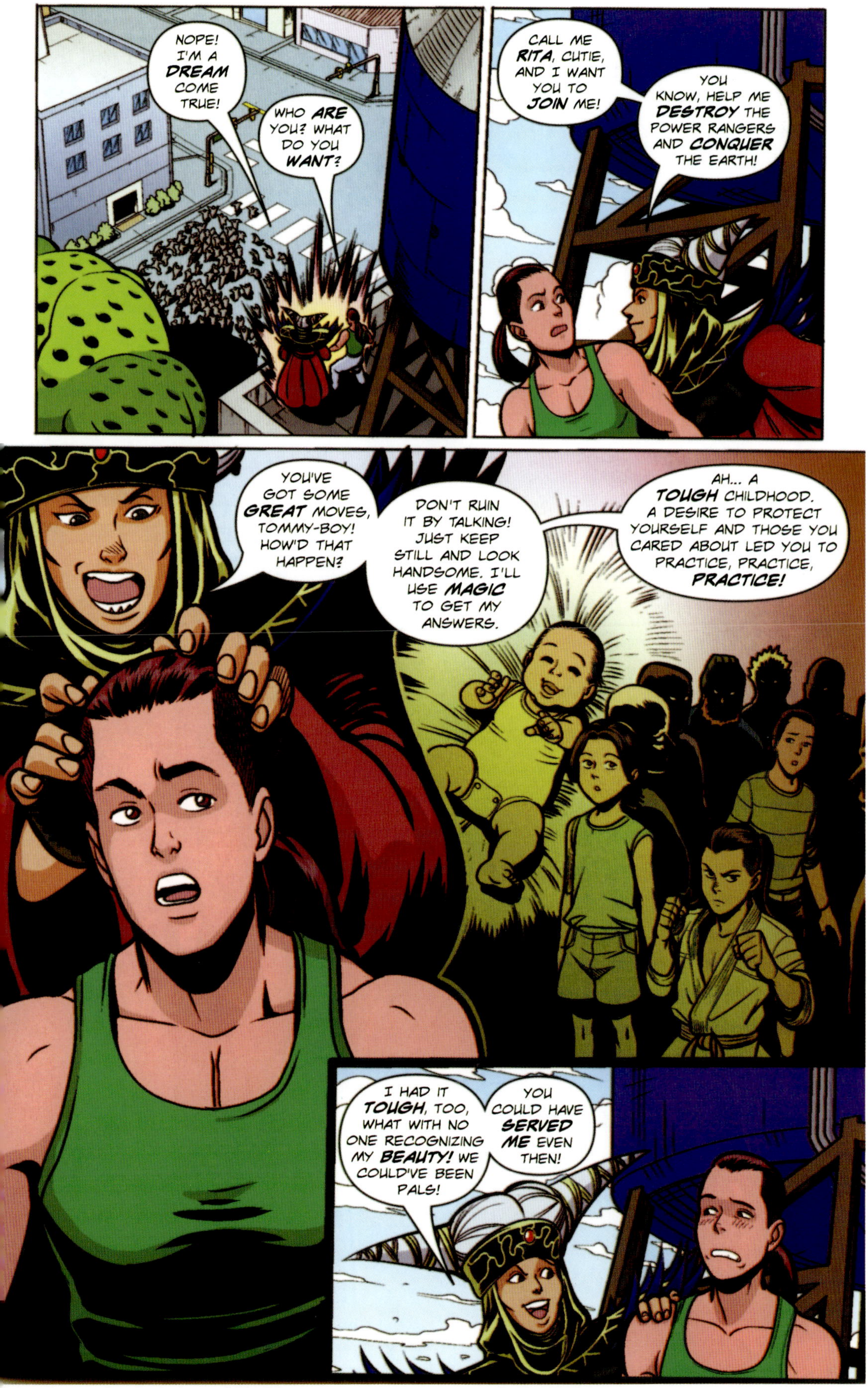
NOPE! I'M A DREAM COME TRUE!
WHO ARE YOU? WHAT DO YOU WANT?
CALL ME RITA, CUTIE, AND I WANT YOU TO JOIN ME!
YOU KNOW, HELP ME DESTROY THE POWER RANGERS AND CONQUER THE EARTH!
YOU'VE GOT SOME GREAT MOVES, TOMMY-BOY! HOW'D THAT HAPPEN?
DON'T RUIN IT BY TALKING! JUST KEEP STILL AND LOOK HANDSOME. I'LL USE MAGIC TO GET MY ANSWERS.
AH... A TOUGH CHILDHOOD. A DESIRE TO PROTECT YOURSELF AND THOSE YOU CARED ABOUT LED YOU TO PRACTICE, PRACTICE, PRACTICE!
I HAD IT TOUGH, TOO, WHAT WITH NO ONE RECOGNIZING MY BEAUTY! WE COULD'VE BEEN PALS!
YOU COULD HAVE SERVED ME EVEN THEN!

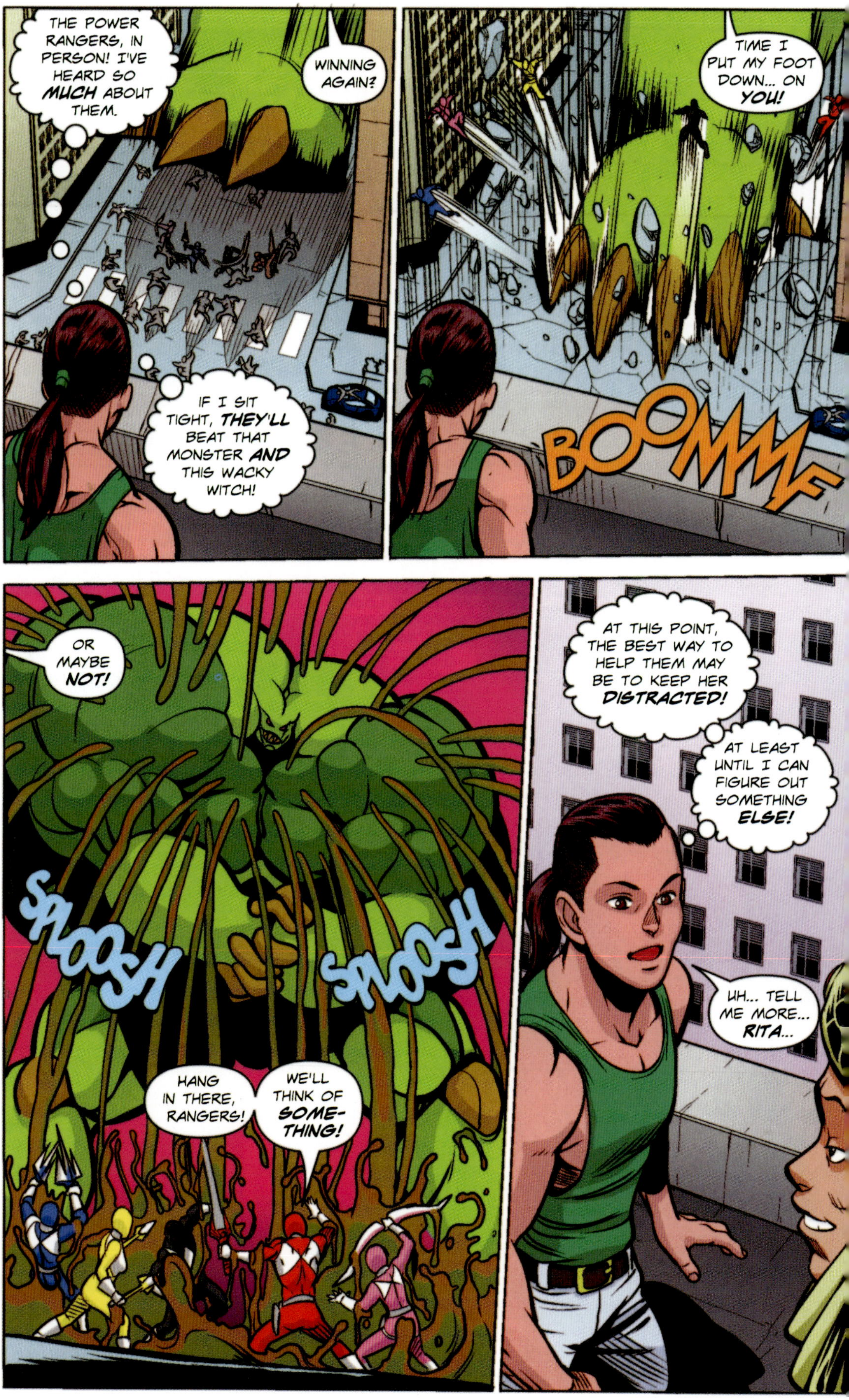
THE POWER RANGERS, IN PERSON! I'VE HEARD SO MUCH ABOUT THEM.
WINNING AGAIN?
IF I SIT TIGHT, THEY'LL BEAT THAT MONSTER AND THIS WACKY WITCH!
TIME I PUT MY FOOT DOWN... ON YOU!
BOOMMF
OR MAYBE NOT!
SPLOOSH
SPLOOSH
HANG IN THERE, RANGERS!
WE'LL THINK OF SOME-THING!
AT THIS POINT, THE BEST WAY TO HELP THEM MAY BE TO KEEP HER DISTRACTED!
AT LEAST UNTIL I CAN FIGURE OUT SOMETHING ELSE!
UH... TELL ME MORE... RITA...

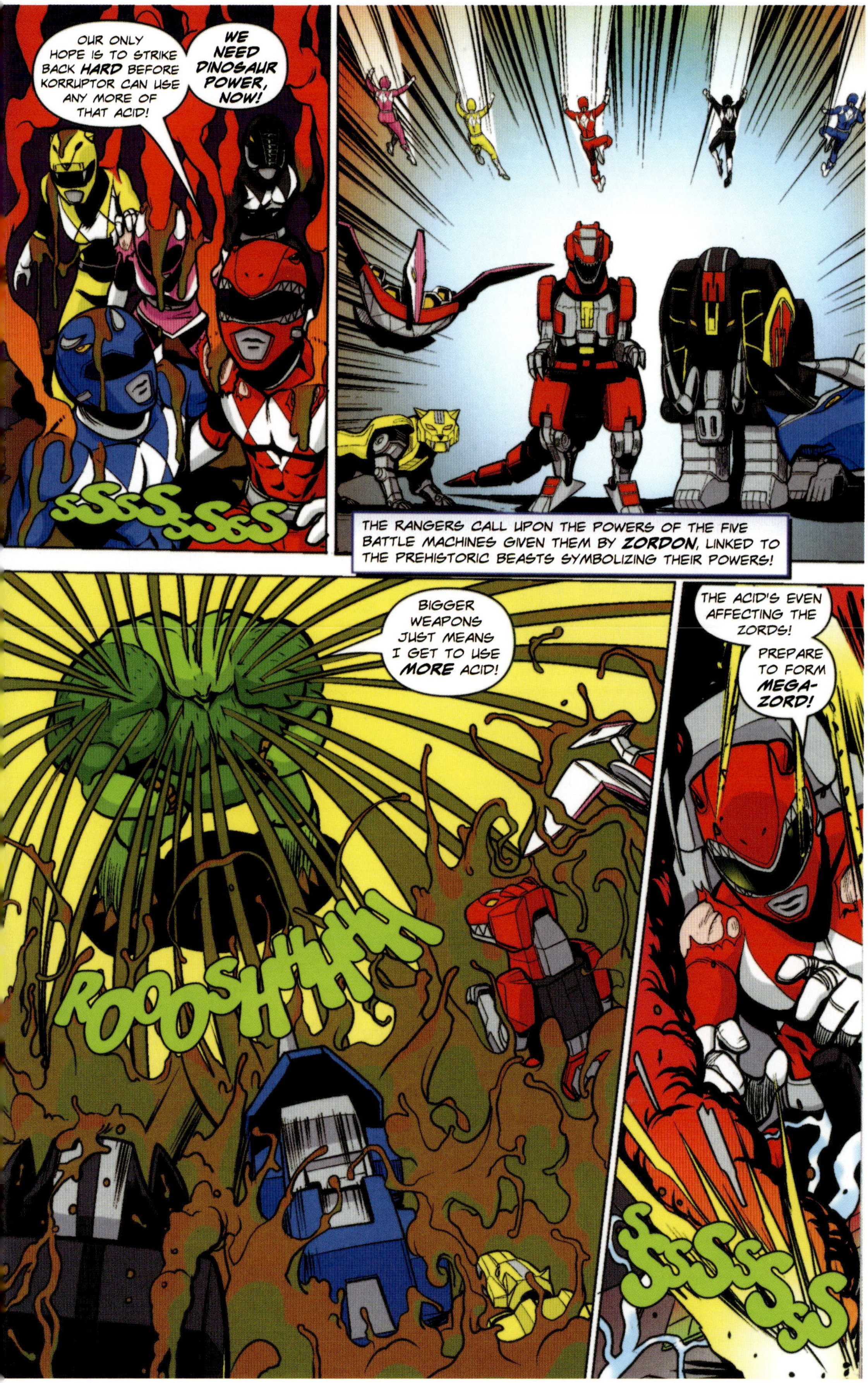

OUR ONLY HOPE IS TO STRIKE BACK **HARD** BEFORE KORRUPTOR CAN USE ANY MORE OF THAT ACID!
WE NEED DINOSAUR POWER, NOW!
sSsSsSsS
THE RANGERS CALL UPON THE POWERS OF THE FIVE BATTLE MACHINES GIVEN THEM BY ***ZORDON***, LINKED TO THE PREHISTORIC BEASTS SYMBOLIZING THEIR POWERS!
BIGGER WEAPONS JUST MEANS I GET TO USE ***MORE*** ACID!
ROOOSHHHH
THE ACID'S EVEN AFFECTING THE ZORDS!
PREPARE TO FORM ***MEGA-ZORD!***
SSSSSSS

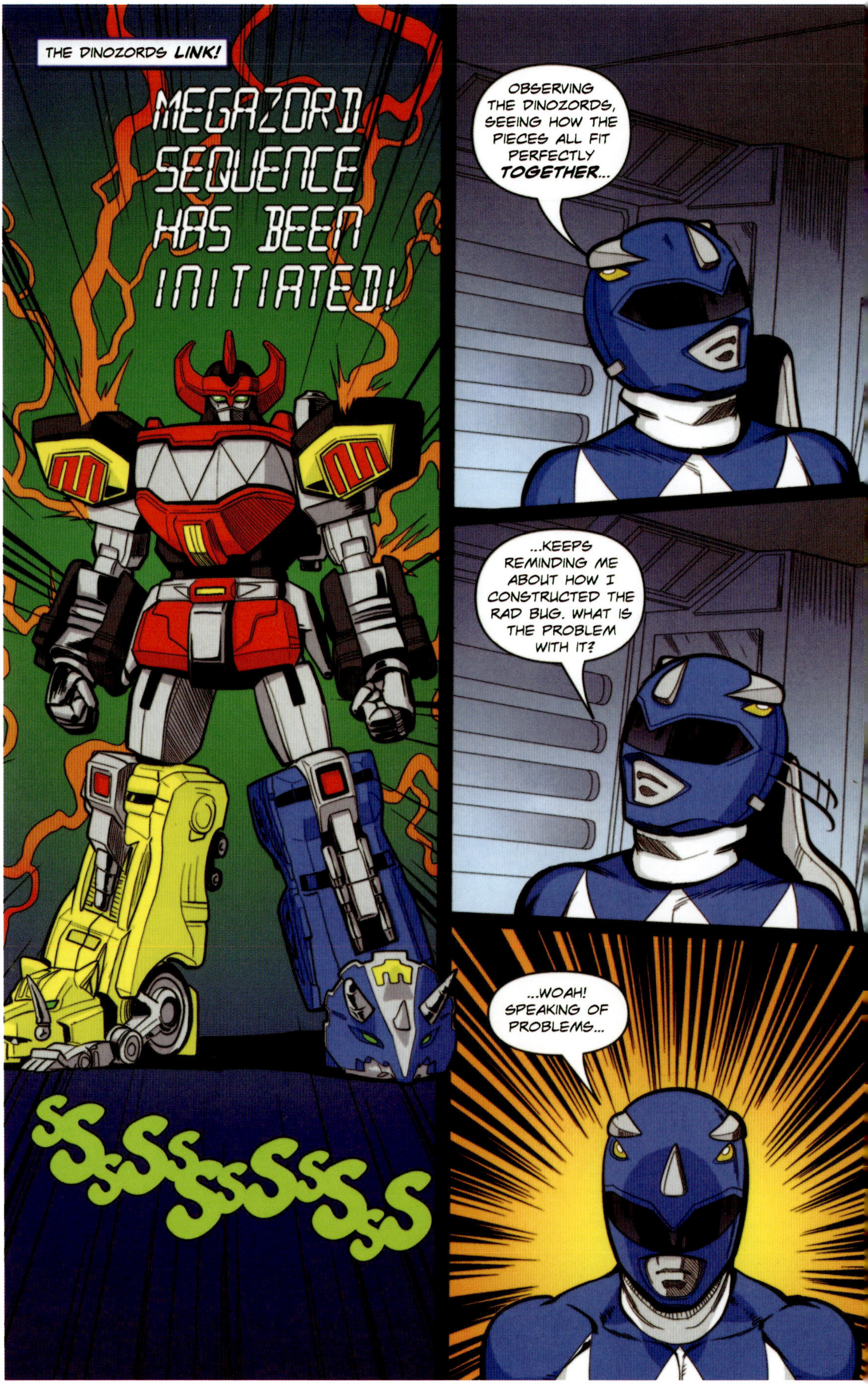
THE DINOZORDS LINK!
MEGAZORD SEQUENCE HAS BEEN INITIATED!
SSSSSSSSSSS
OBSERVING THE DINOZORDS, SEEING HOW THE PIECES ALL FIT PERFECTLY TOGETHER...
...KEEPS REMINDING ME ABOUT HOW I CONSTRUCTED THE RAD BUG. WHAT IS THE PROBLEM WITH IT?
...WOAH! SPEAKING OF PROBLEMS...

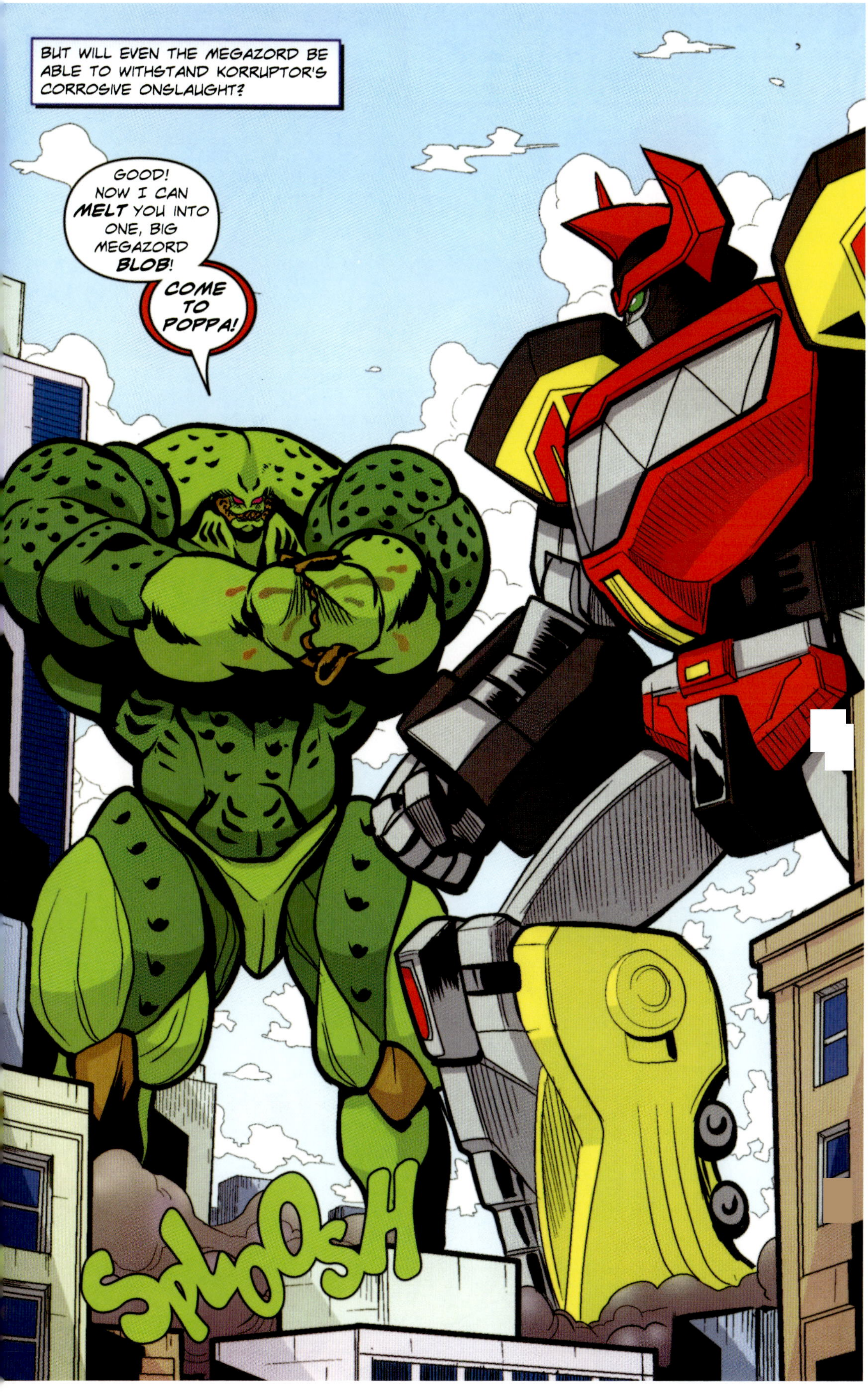

BUT WILL EVEN THE MEGAZORD BE ABLE TO WITHSTAND KORRUPTOR'S CORROSIVE ONSLAUGHT?
GOOD! NOW I CAN MELT YOU INTO ONE, BIG MEGAZORD BLOB!
COME TO POPPA!
SPLOOSH

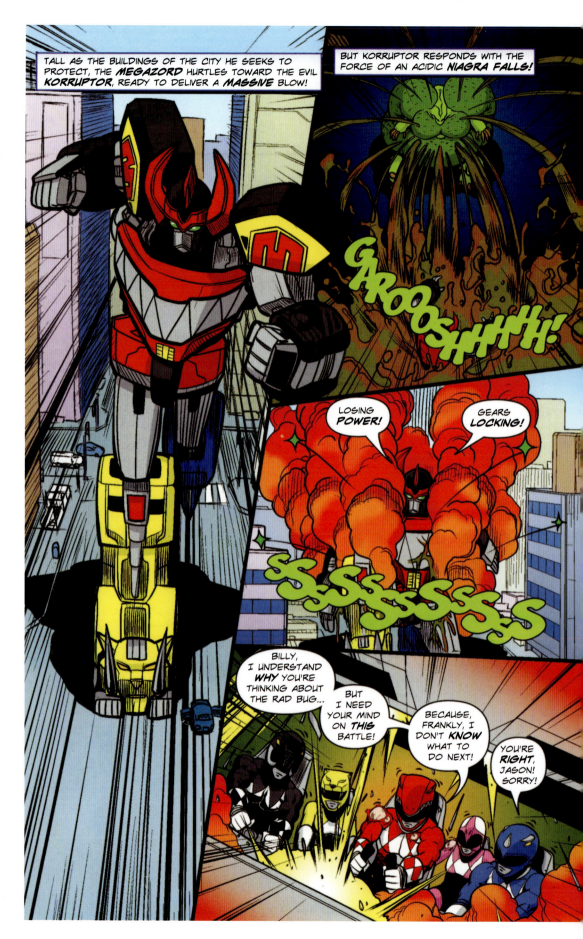

TALL AS THE BUILDINGS OF THE CITY HE SEEKS TO PROTECT, THE **MEGAZORD** HURTLES TOWARD THE EVIL **KORRUPTOR**, READY TO DELIVER A **MASSIVE** BLOW!

BUT KORRUPTOR RESPONDS WITH THE FORCE OF AN ACIDIC **NIAGRA FALLS!**

GAROOSHHHH!

SSSSSSSSS

LOSING **POWER!**

GEARS **LOCKING!**

BILLY, I UNDERSTAND **WHY** YOU'RE THINKING ABOUT THE RAD BUG...

BUT I NEED YOUR MIND ON **THIS** BATTLE!

BECAUSE, FRANKLY, I DON'T **KNOW** WHAT TO DO NEXT!

YOU'RE **RIGHT**, JASON! SORRY!

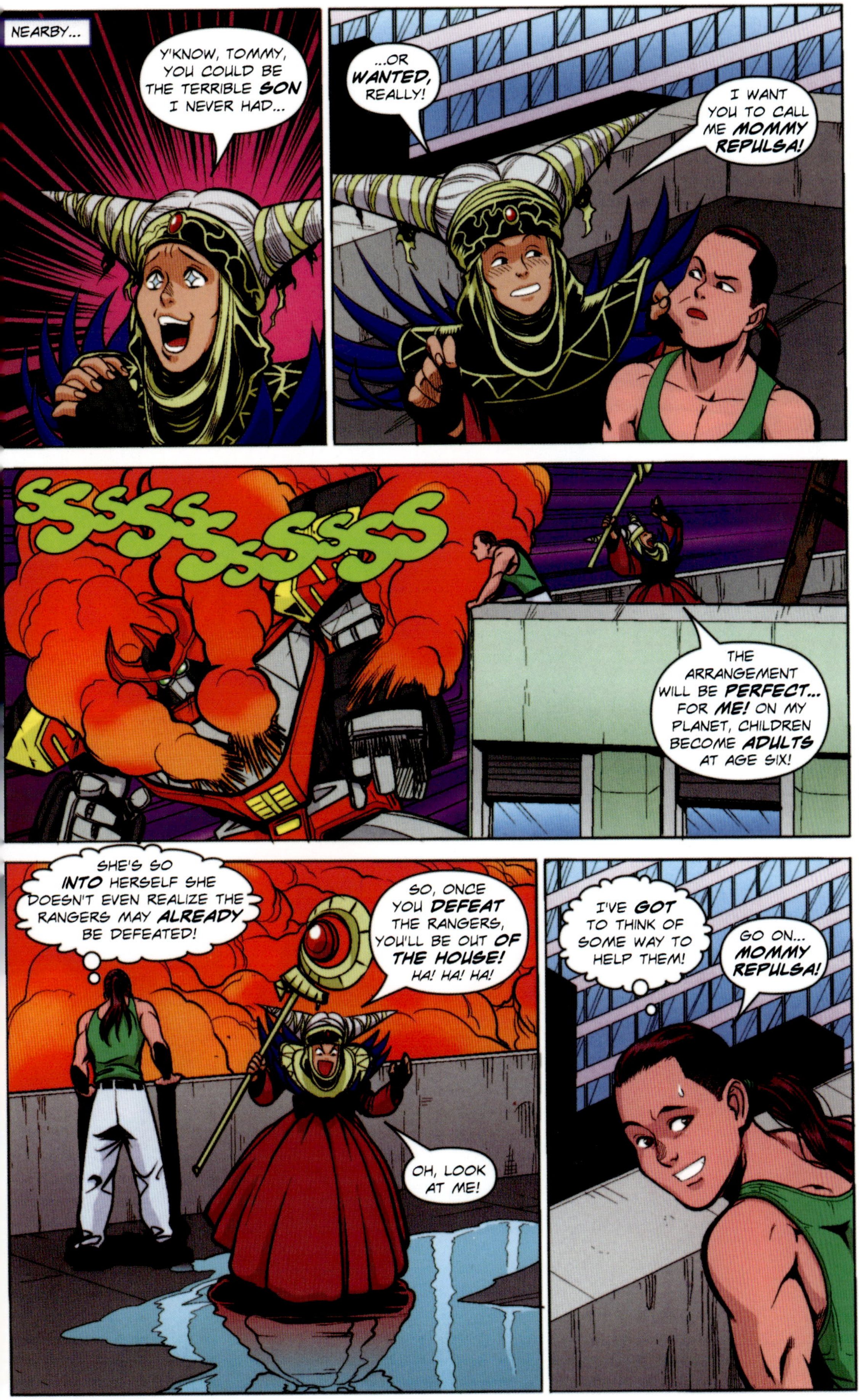
NEARBY...
Y'KNOW, TOMMY, YOU COULD BE THE TERRIBLE SON I NEVER HAD...
...OR WANTED, REALLY!
I WANT YOU TO CALL ME MOMMY REPULSA!
SSSSSSSSSSS
THE ARRANGEMENT WILL BE PERFECT... FOR ME! ON MY PLANET, CHILDREN BECOME ADULTS AT AGE SIX!
SHE'S SO INTO HERSELF SHE DOESN'T EVEN REALIZE THE RANGERS MAY ALREADY BE DEFEATED!
SO, ONCE YOU DEFEAT THE RANGERS, YOU'LL BE OUT OF THE HOUSE! HA! HA! HA!
OH, LOOK AT ME!
I'VE GOT TO THINK OF SOME WAY TO HELP THEM!
GO ON... MOMMY REPULSA!

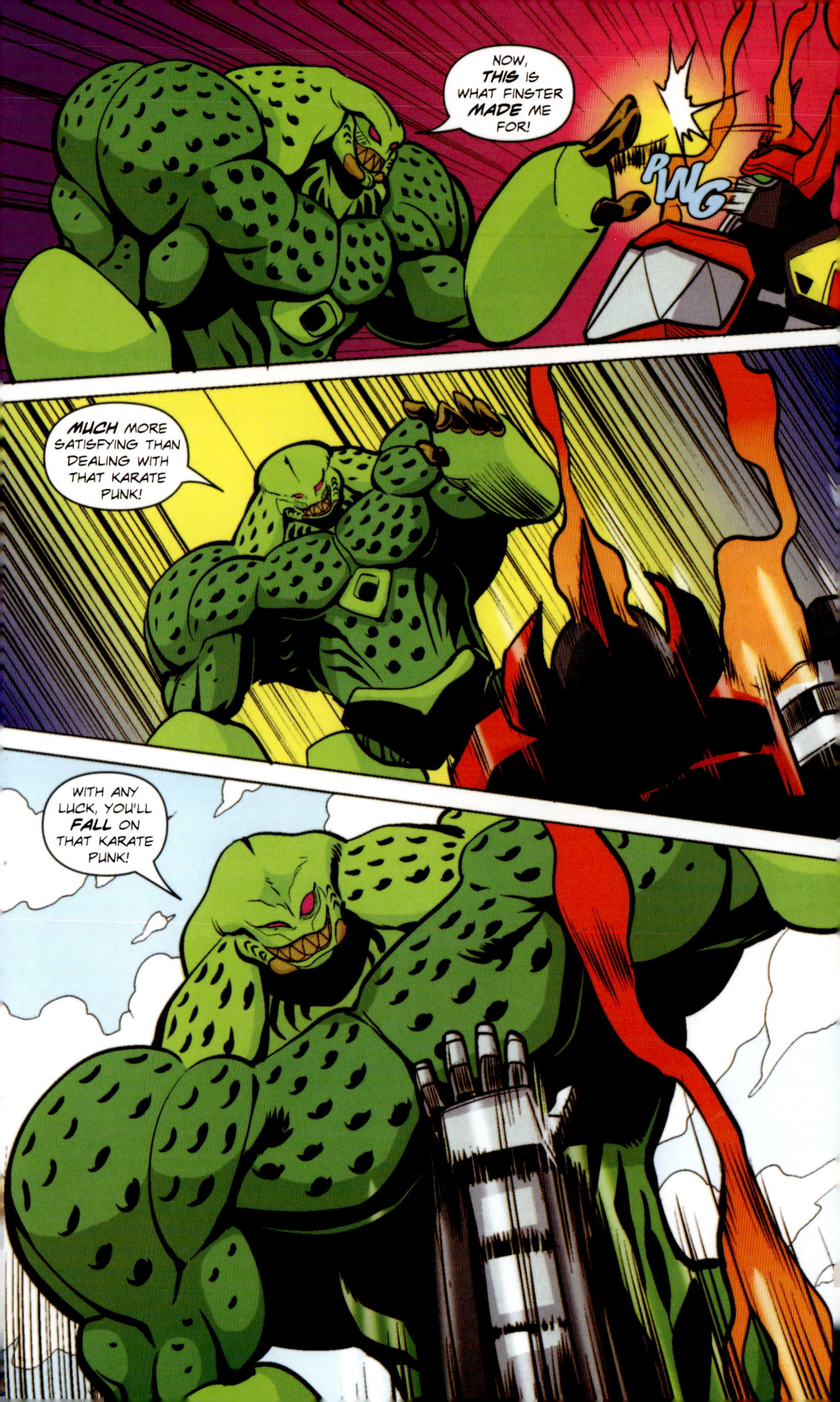
NOW, THIS IS WHAT FINSTER MADE ME FOR!
PING
MUCH MORE SATISFYING THAN DEALING WITH THAT KARATE PUNK!
WITH ANY LUCK, YOU'LL FALL ON THAT KARATE PUNK!

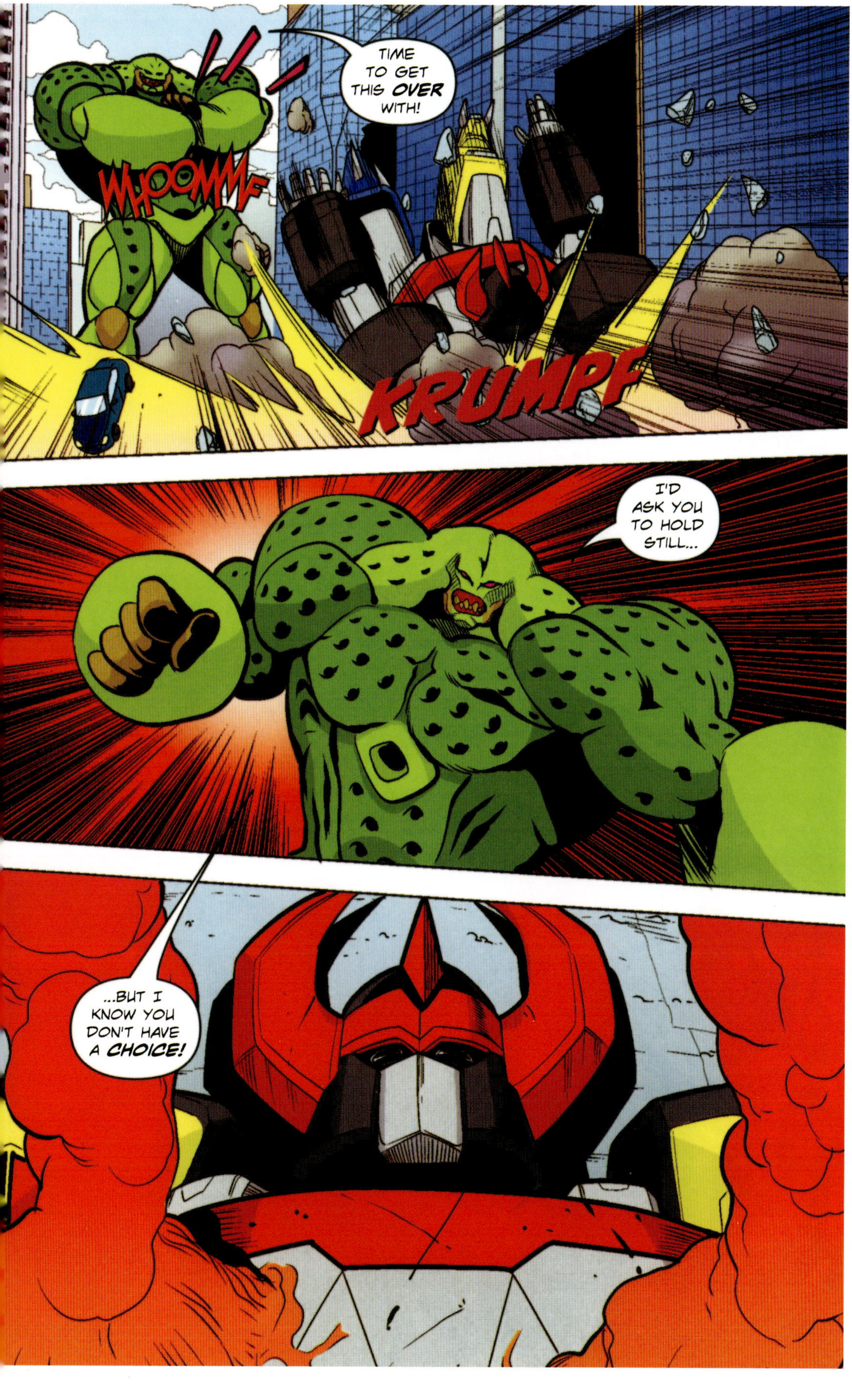
TIME TO GET THIS OVER WITH!
WHOOMMF
KRUMPF
I'D ASK YOU TO HOLD STILL...
...BUT I KNOW YOU DON'T HAVE A CHOICE!

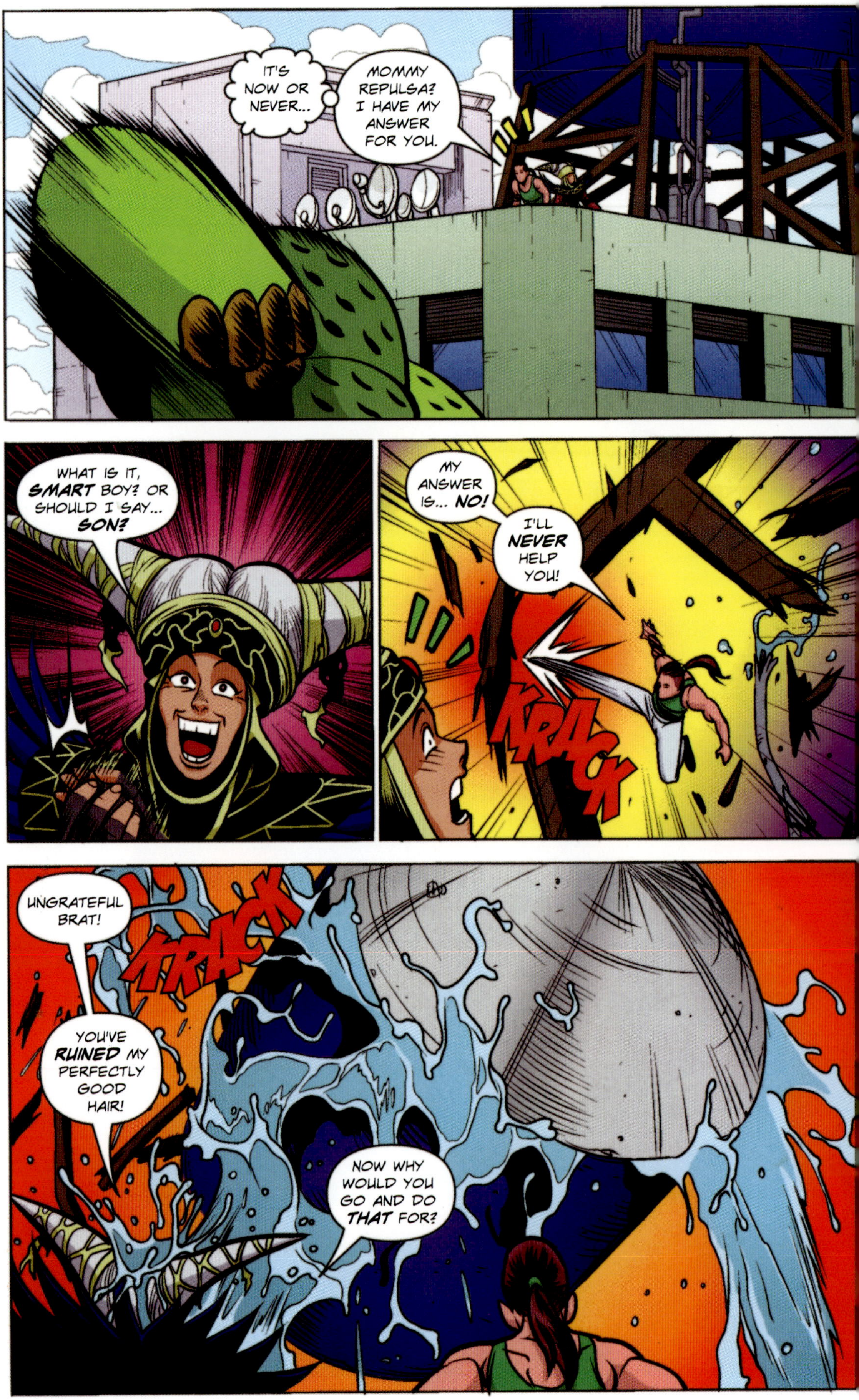
IT'S NOW OR NEVER...
MOMMY REPULSA? I HAVE MY ANSWER FOR YOU.
WHAT IS IT, SMART BOY? OR SHOULD I SAY... SON?
MY ANSWER IS... NO!
I'LL NEVER HELP YOU!
KRACK
UNGRATEFUL BRAT!
KRACK
YOU'VE RUINED MY PERFECTLY GOOD HAIR!
NOW WHY WOULD YOU GO AND DO THAT FOR?

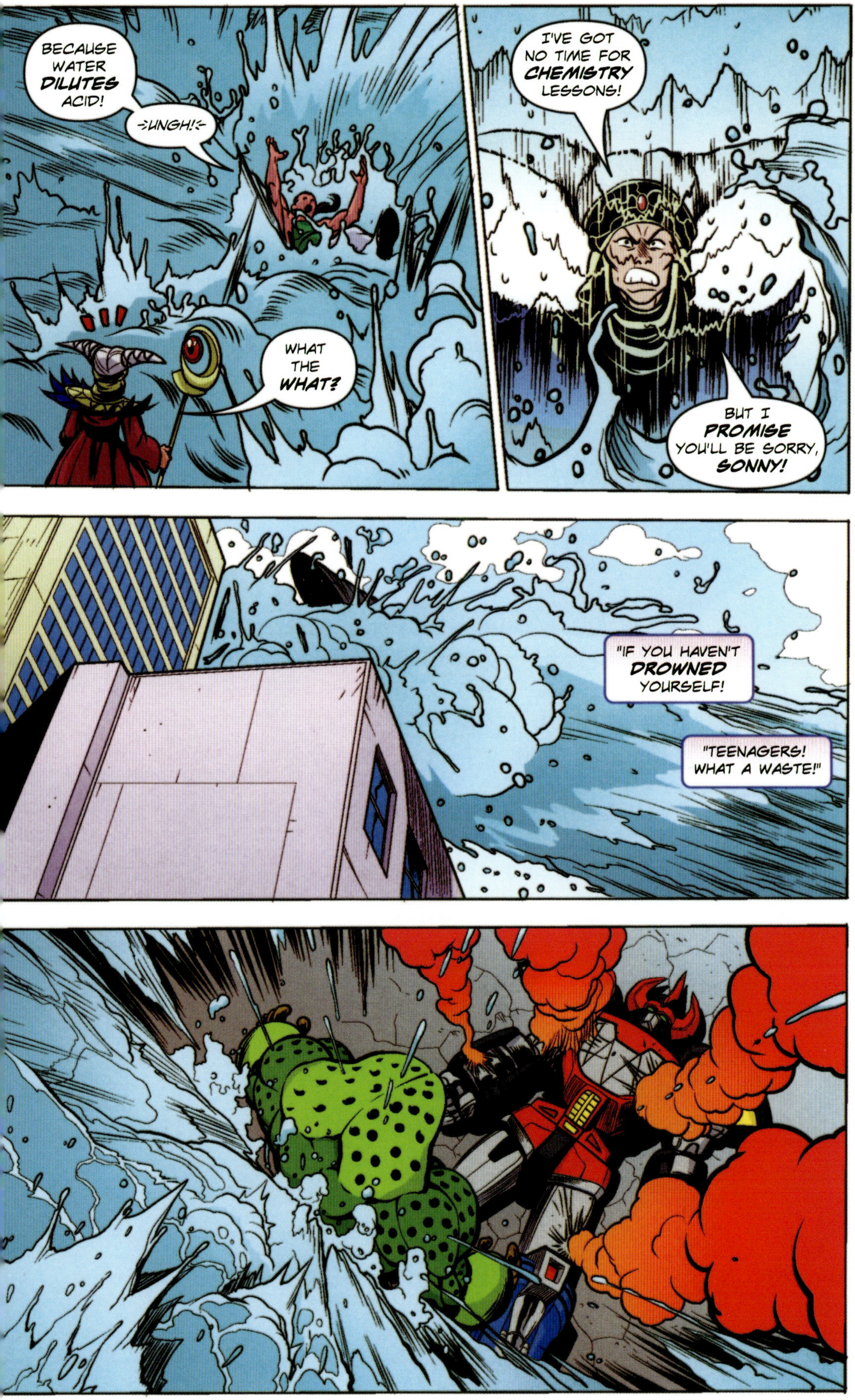
BECAUSE WATER DILUTES ACID!
UNGH!
WHAT THE WHAT?
I'VE GOT NO TIME FOR CHEMISTRY LESSONS!
BUT I PROMISE YOU'LL BE SORRY, SONNY!
"IF YOU HAVEN'T DROWNED YOURSELF!
"TEENAGERS! WHAT A WASTE!"

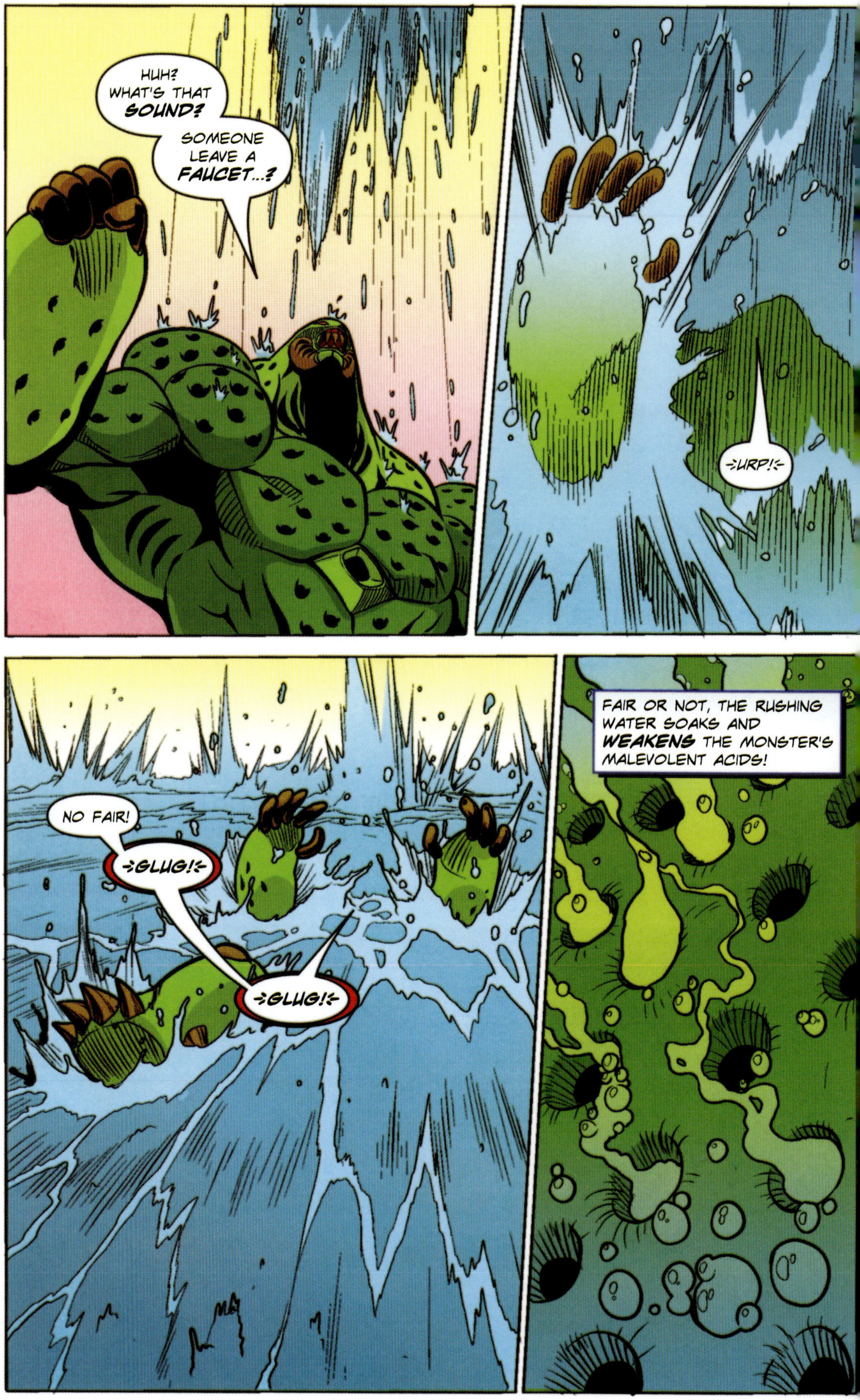
HUH? WHAT'S THAT SOUND?
SOMEONE LEAVE A FAUCET...?
-URP!-
NO FAIR!
-GLUG!-
-GLUG!-
FAIR OR NOT, THE RUSHING WATER SOAKS AND WEAKENS THE MONSTER'S MALEVOLENT ACIDS!

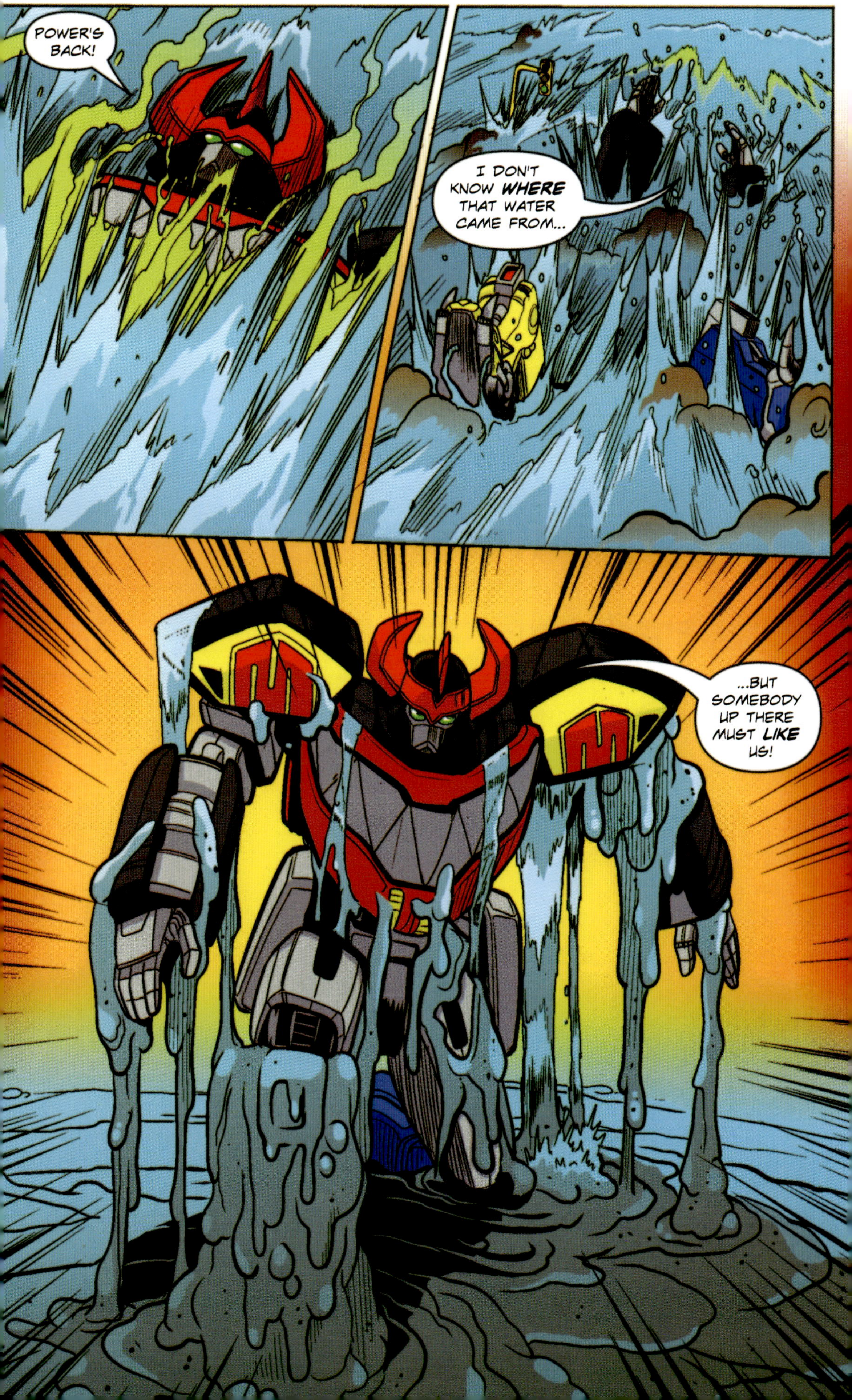
POWER'S BACK!
I DON'T KNOW WHERE THAT WATER CAME FROM...
...BUT SOMEBODY UP THERE MUST LIKE US!

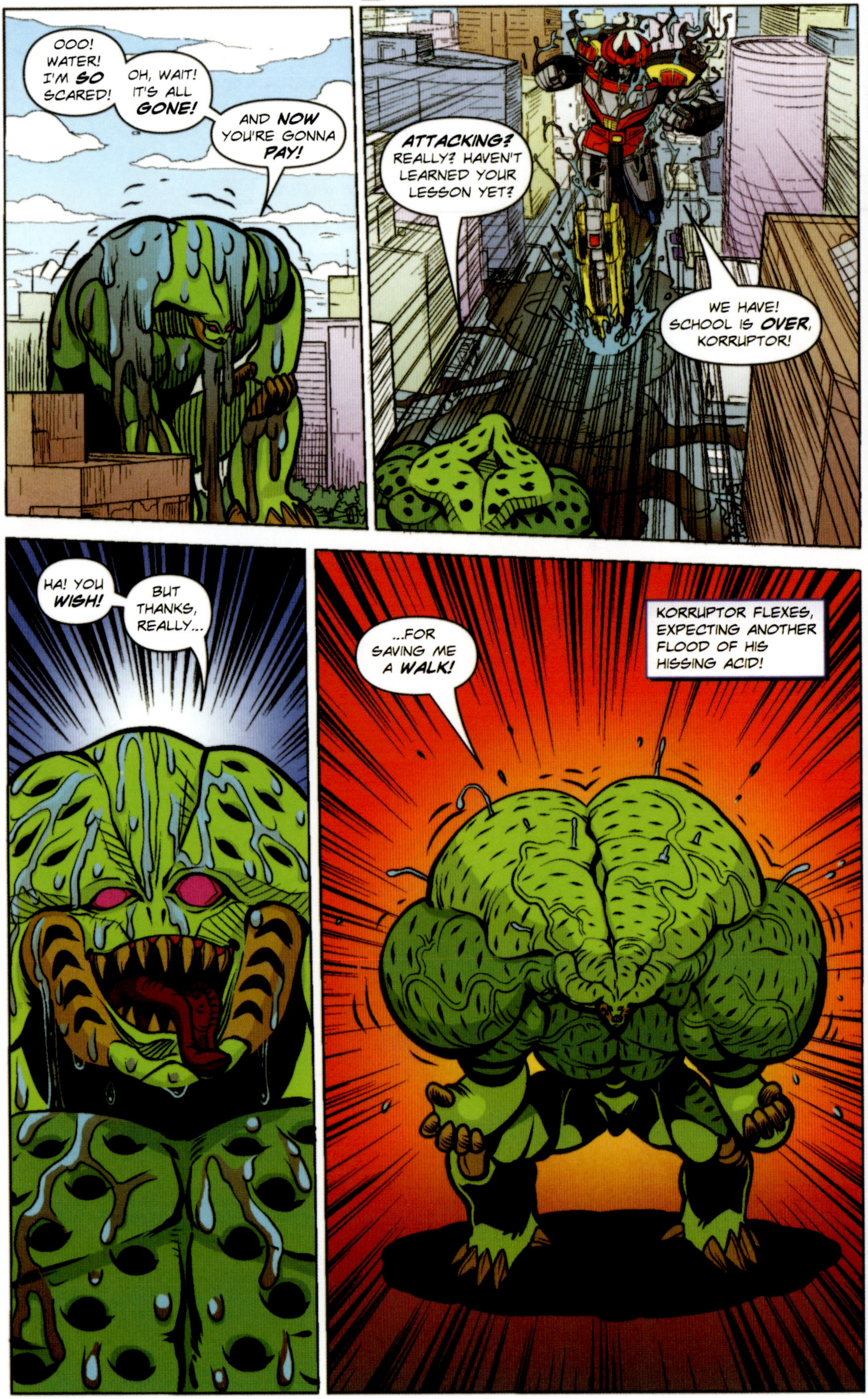

OOO! WATER! I'M SO SCARED!
OH, WAIT! IT'S ALL GONE!
AND NOW YOU'RE GONNA PAY!
ATTACKING? REALLY? HAVEN'T LEARNED YOUR LESSON YET?
WE HAVE! SCHOOL IS OVER, KORRUPTOR!
HA! YOU WISH!
BUT THANKS, REALLY...
...FOR SAVING ME A WALK!
KORRUPTOR FLEXES, EXPECTING ANOTHER FLOOD OF HIS HISSING ACID!

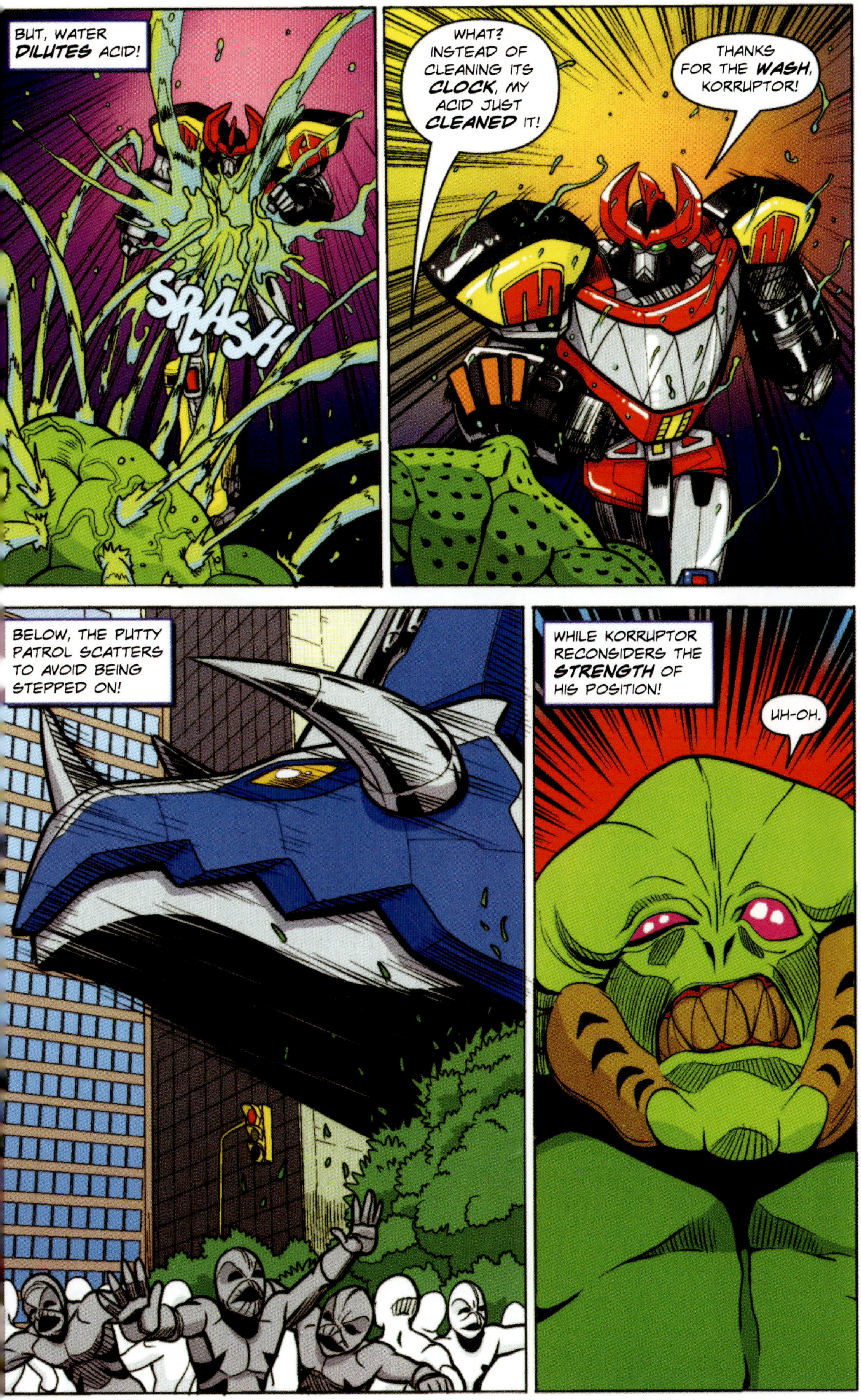

BUT, WATER **DILUTES** ACID!
SPLASH
WHAT? INSTEAD OF CLEANING ITS **CLOCK**, MY ACID JUST **CLEANED** IT!
THANKS FOR THE **WASH**, KORRUPTOR!
BELOW, THE PUTTY PATROL SCATTERS TO AVOID BEING STEPPED ON!
WHILE KORRUPTOR RECONSIDERS THE **STRENGTH** OF HIS POSITION!
UH-OH.

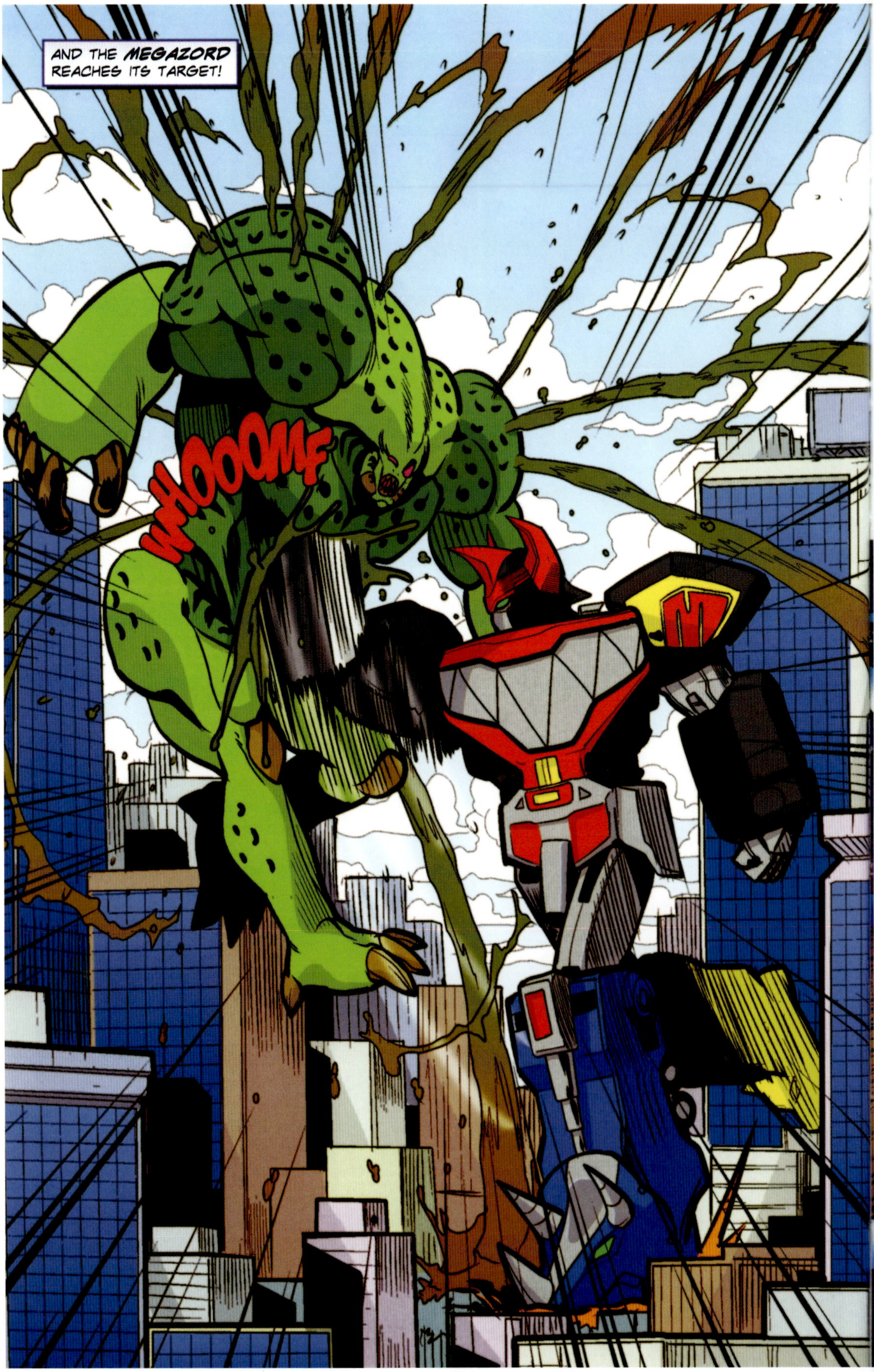
AND THE MEGAZORD REACHES ITS TARGET!
WHOOOMF

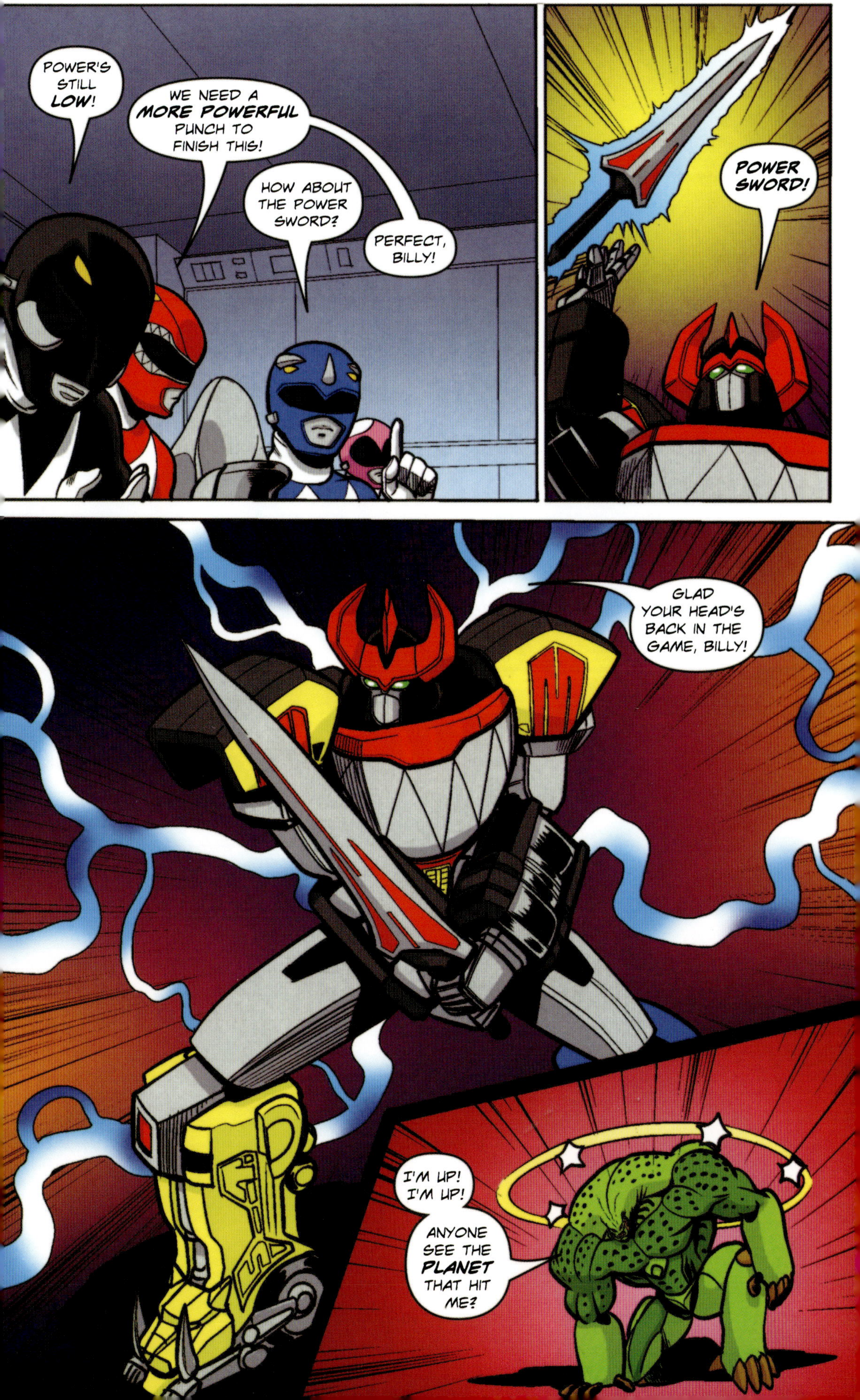
POWER'S STILL LOW!
WE NEED A MORE POWERFUL PUNCH TO FINISH THIS!
HOW ABOUT THE POWER SWORD?
PERFECT, BILLY!
POWER SWORD!
GLAD YOUR HEAD'S BACK IN THE GAME, BILLY!
I'M UP! I'M UP!
ANYONE SEE THE PLANET THAT HIT ME?

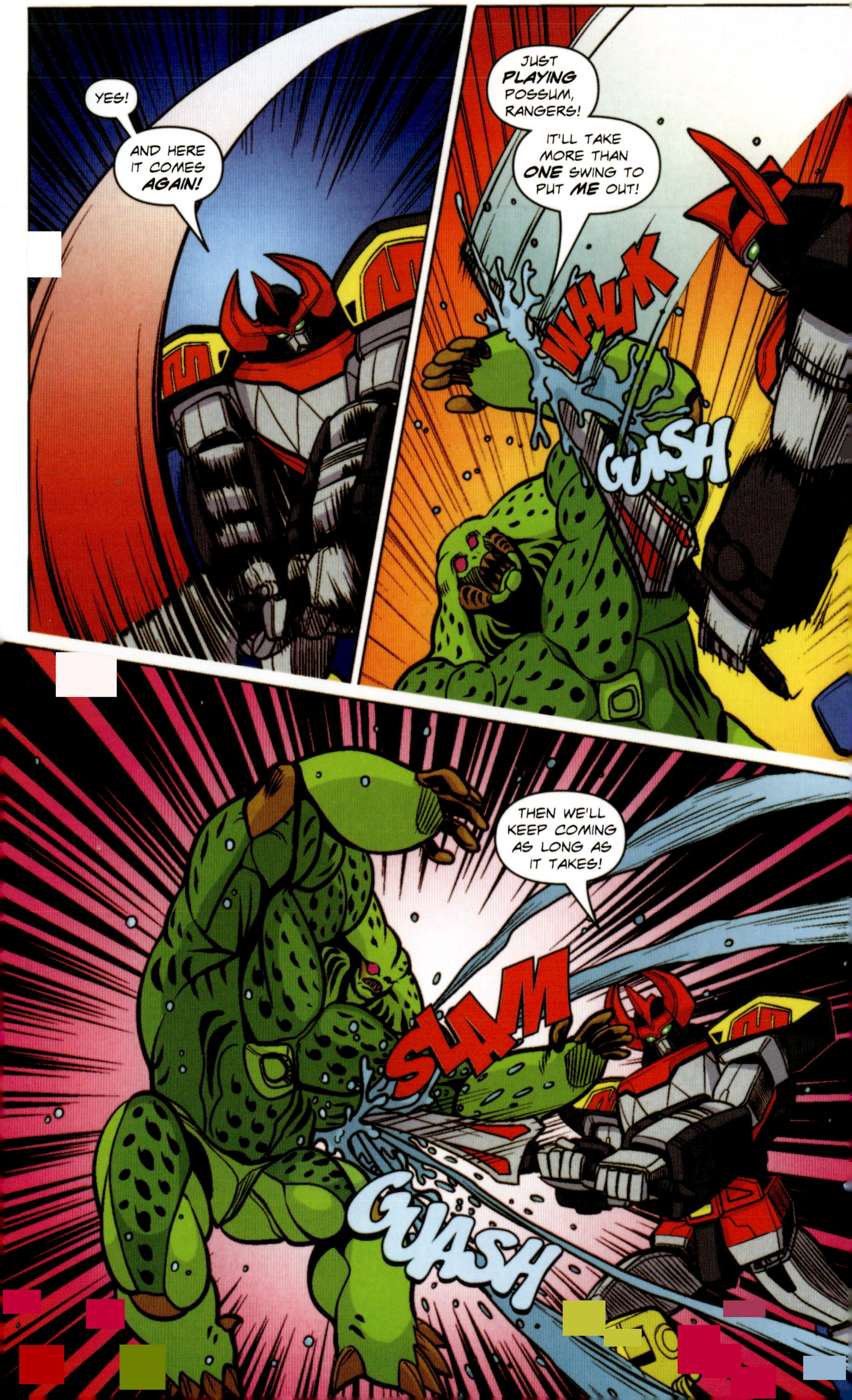

YES!
AND HERE IT COMES AGAIN!
JUST PLAYING POSSUM, RANGERS!
IT'LL TAKE MORE THAN ONE SWING TO PUT ME OUT!
WHUK
GUSH
THEN WE'LL KEEP COMING AS LONG AS IT TAKES!
SLAM
GUASH

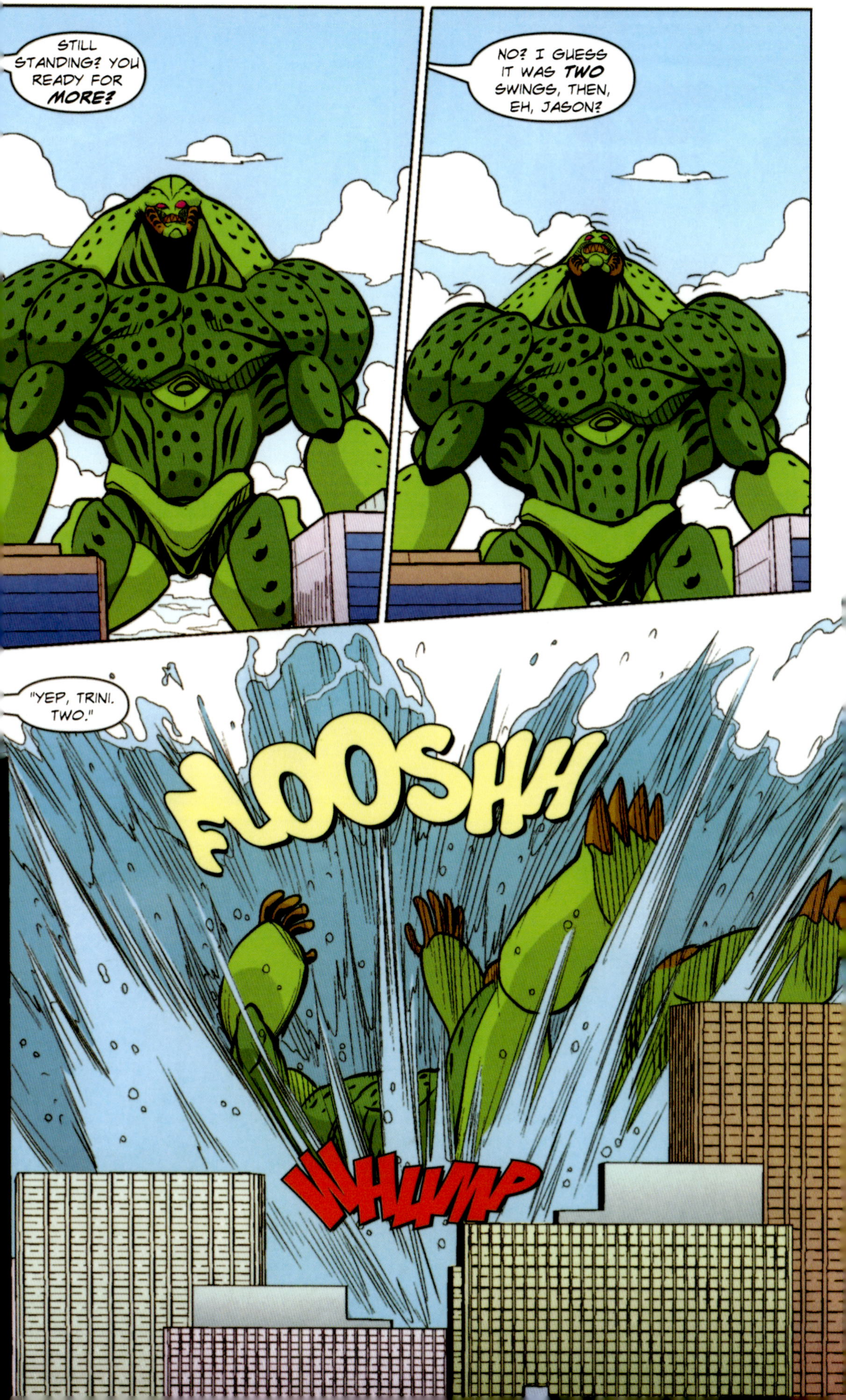
STILL STANDING? YOU READY FOR **MORE?**
NO? I GUESS IT WAS **TWO** SWINGS, THEN, EH, JASON?
"YEP, TRINI. TWO."
FLOOSHH
WHUMP

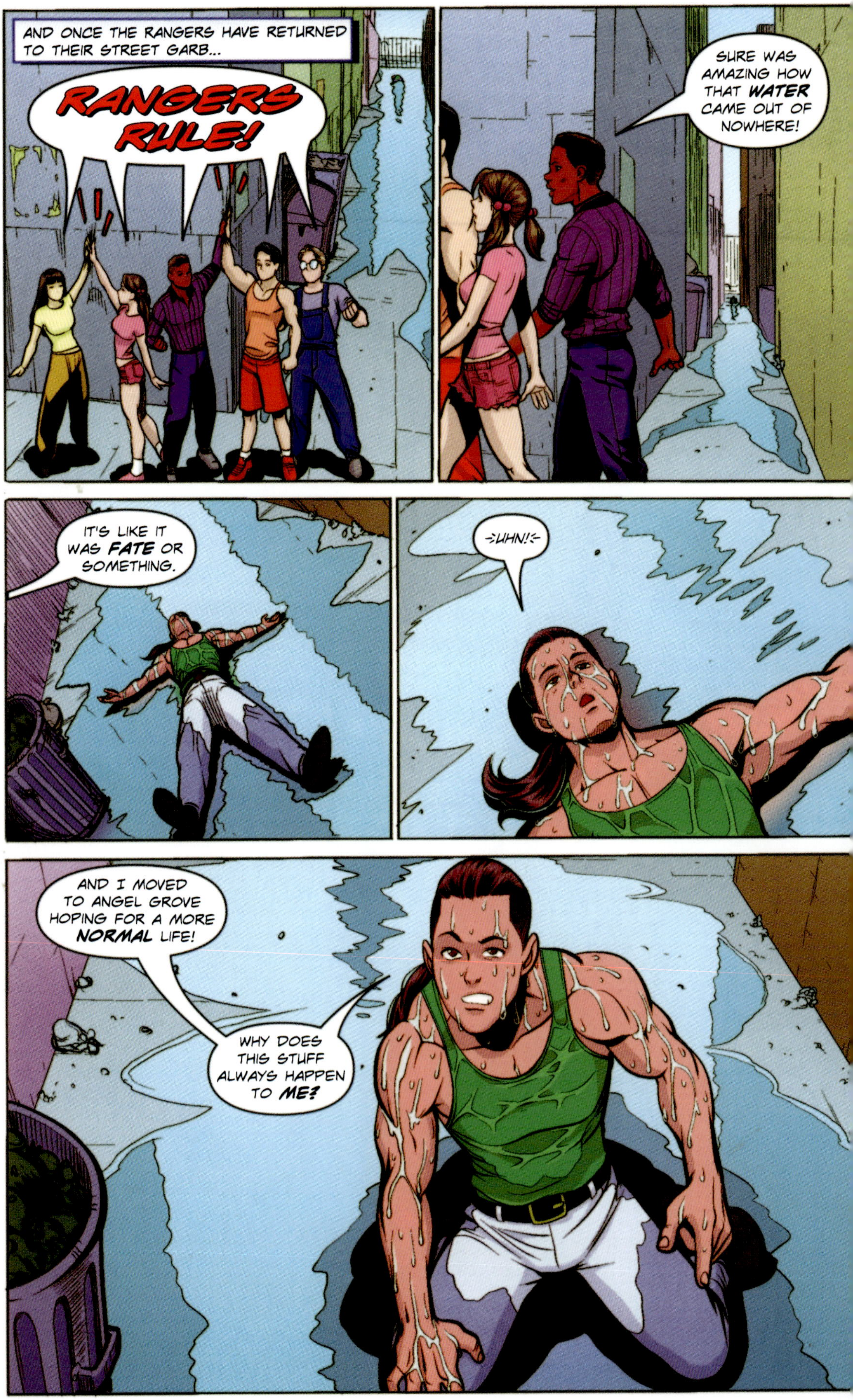
AND ONCE THE RANGERS HAVE RETURNED TO THEIR STREET GARB...
RANGERS RULE!
SURE WAS AMAZING HOW THAT WATER CAME OUT OF NOWHERE!
IT'S LIKE IT WAS FATE OR SOMETHING.
UHN!
AND I MOVED TO ANGEL GROVE HOPING FOR A MORE NORMAL LIFE!
WHY DOES THIS STUFF ALWAYS HAPPEN TO ME?

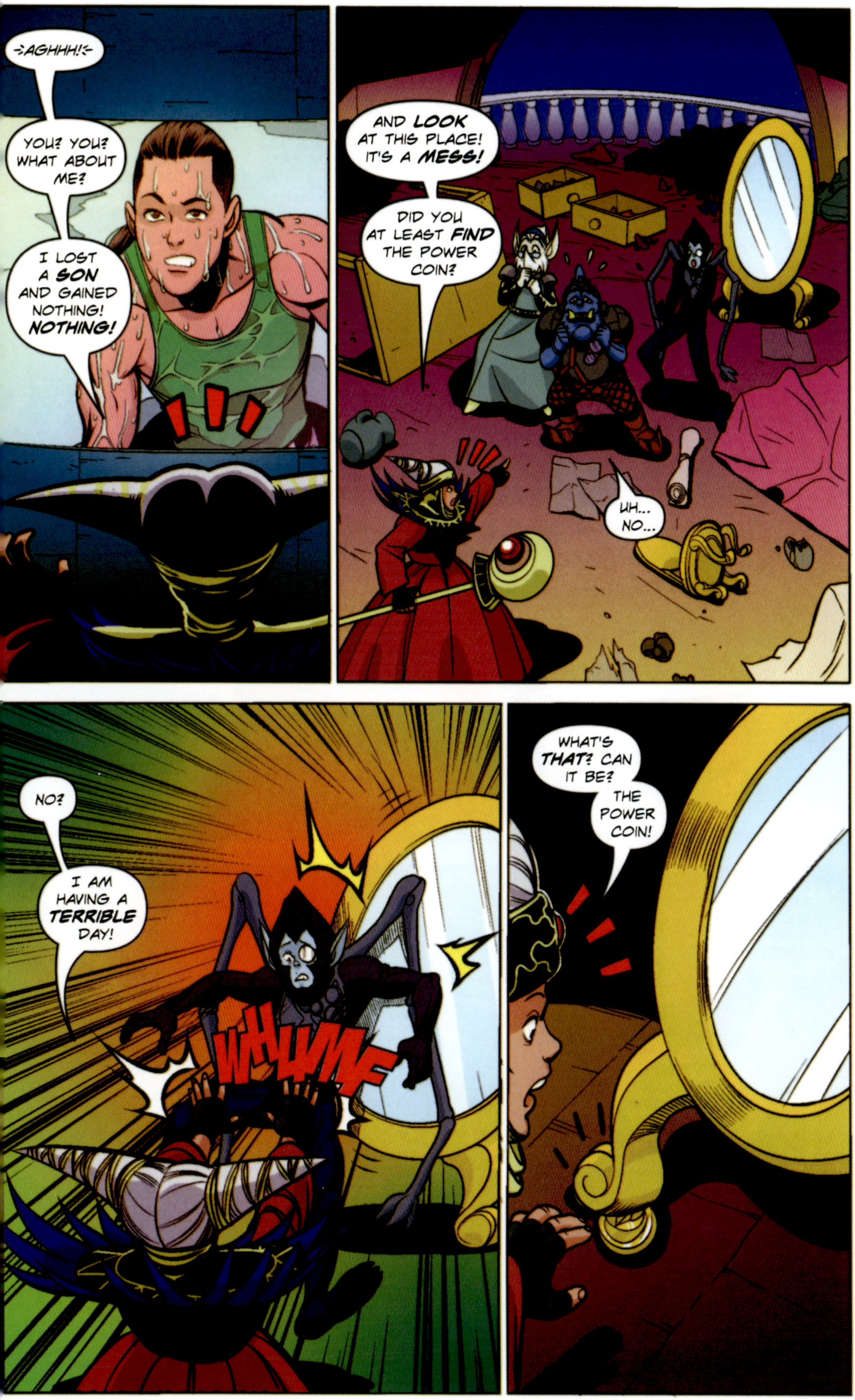
-AGHHH!-
YOU? YOU? WHAT ABOUT ME?
I LOST A SON AND GAINED NOTHING! NOTHING!
AND LOOK AT THIS PLACE! IT'S A MESS!
DID YOU AT LEAST FIND THE POWER COIN?
UH... NO...
NO?
I AM HAVING A TERRIBLE DAY!
WHUMF
WHAT'S THAT? CAN IT BE?
THE POWER COIN!

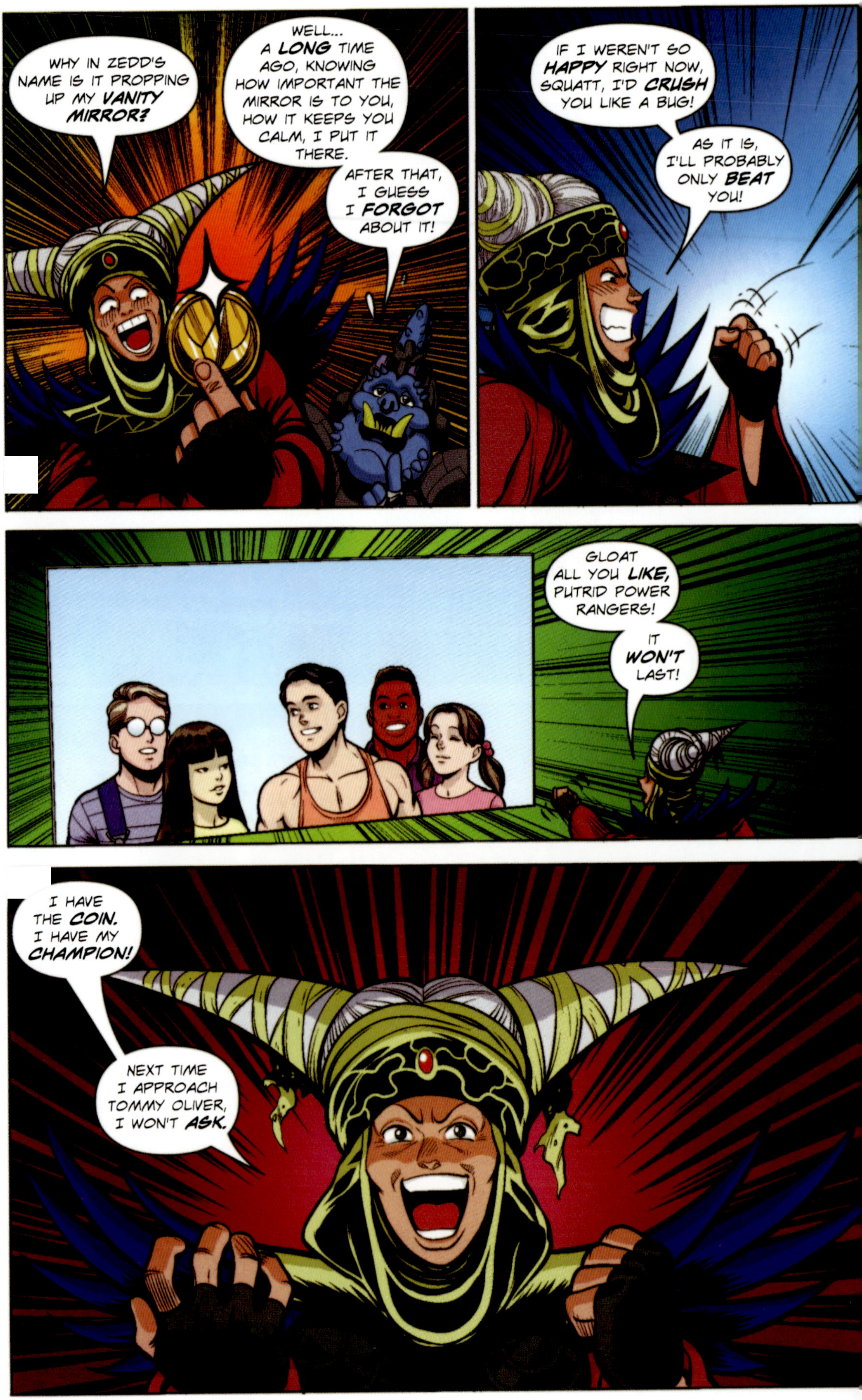

WHY IN ZEDD'S NAME IS IT PROPPING UP MY VANITY MIRROR?
WELL... A LONG TIME AGO, KNOWING HOW IMPORTANT THE MIRROR IS TO YOU, HOW IT KEEPS YOU CALM, I PUT IT THERE.
AFTER THAT, I GUESS I FORGOT ABOUT IT!
!
IF I WEREN'T SO HAPPY RIGHT NOW, SQUATT, I'D CRUSH YOU LIKE A BUG!
AS IT IS, I'LL PROBABLY ONLY BEAT YOU!
GLOAT ALL YOU LIKE, PUTRID POWER RANGERS!
IT WON'T LAST!
I HAVE THE COIN. I HAVE MY CHAMPION!
NEXT TIME I APPROACH TOMMY OLIVER, I WON'T ASK.

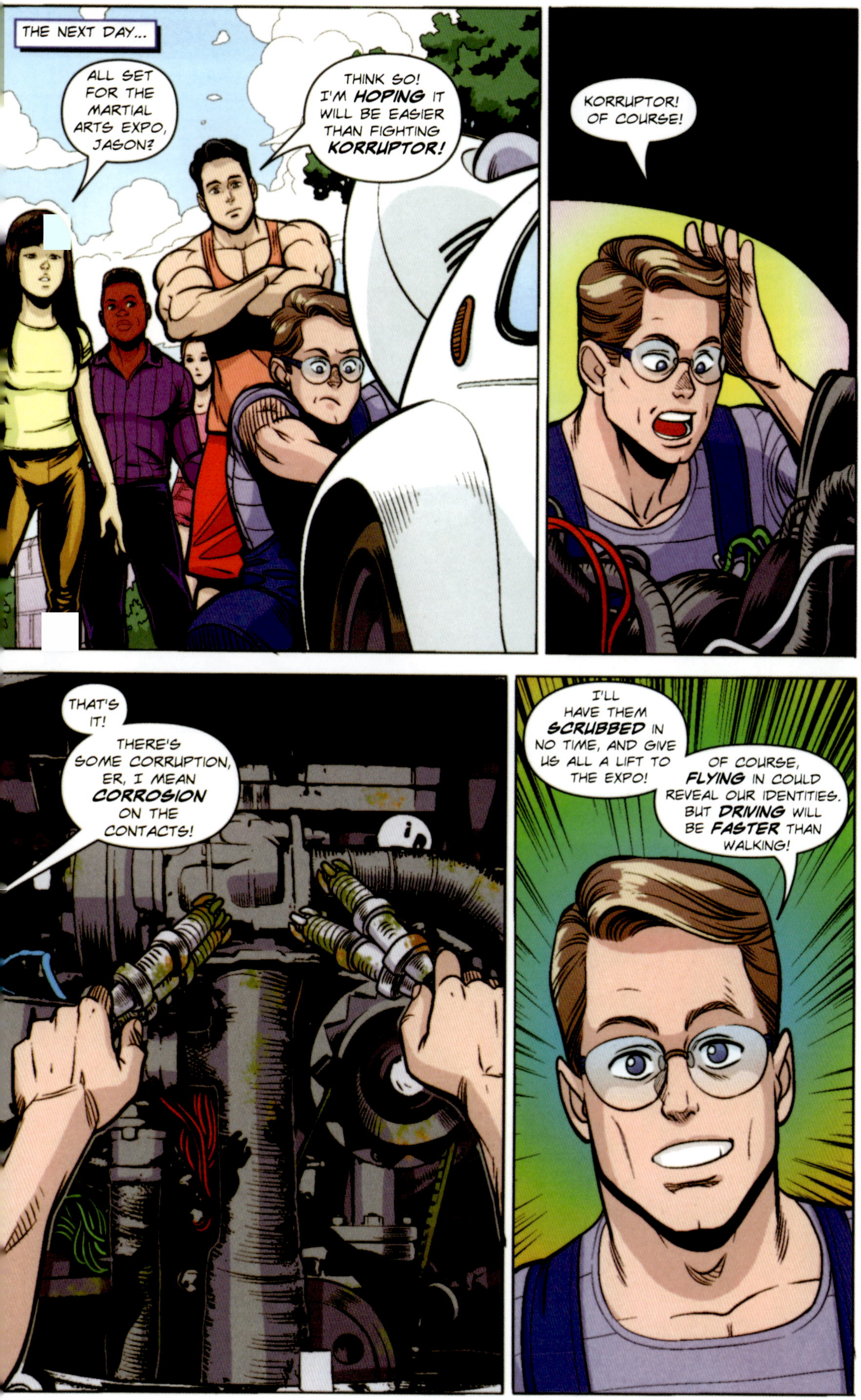
THE NEXT DAY...
ALL SET FOR THE MARTIAL ARTS EXPO, JASON?
THINK SO! I'M **HOPING** IT WILL BE EASIER THAN FIGHTING **KORRUPTOR!**
KORRUPTOR! OF COURSE!
THAT'S IT!
THERE'S SOME CORRUPTION, ER, I MEAN **CORROSION** ON THE CONTACTS!
I'LL HAVE THEM **SCRUBBED** IN NO TIME, AND GIVE US ALL A LIFT TO THE EXPO!
OF COURSE, **FLYING** IN COULD REVEAL OUR IDENTITIES. BUT **DRIVING** WILL BE **FASTER** THAN WALKING!

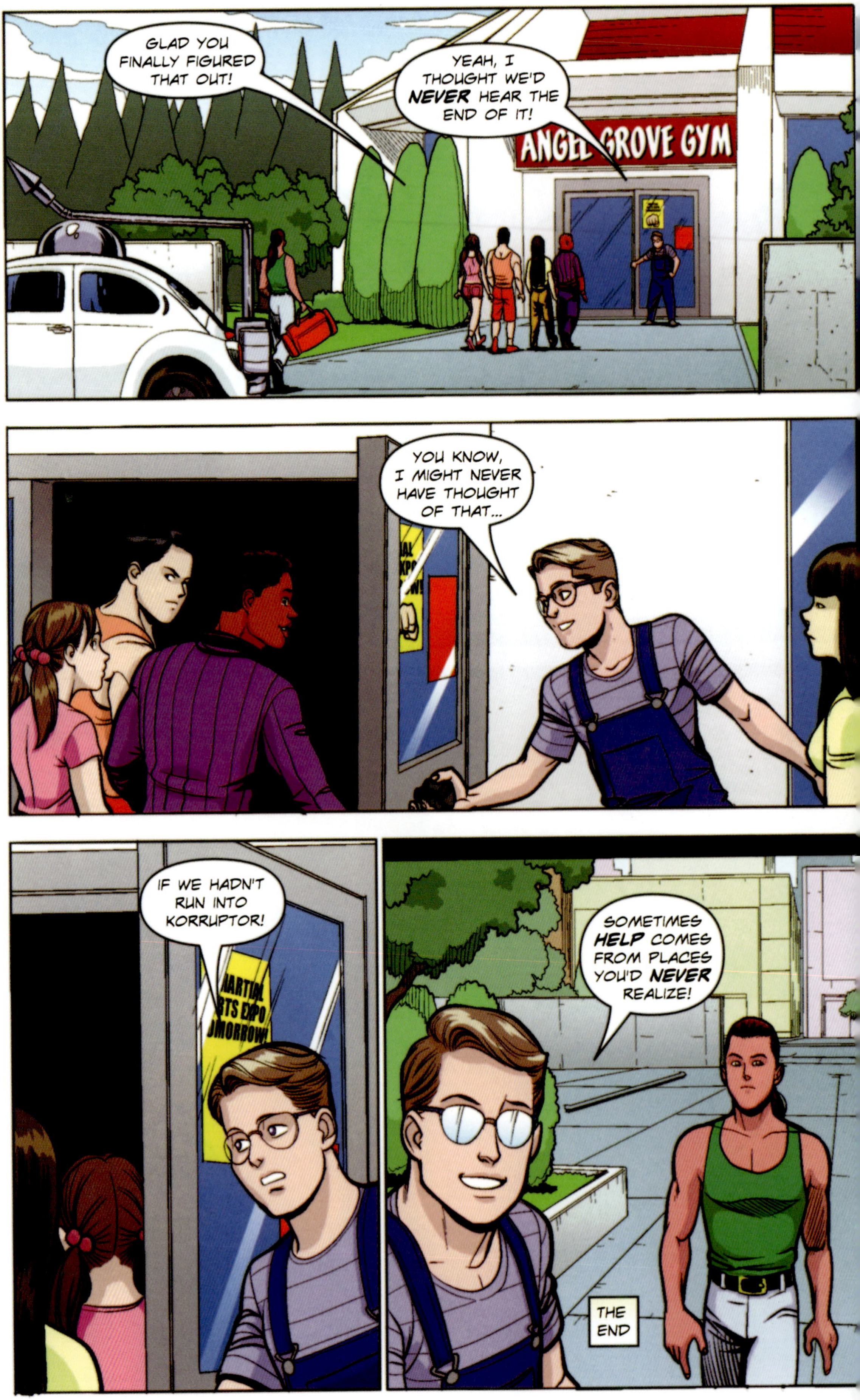
GLAD YOU FINALLY FIGURED THAT OUT!
YEAH, I THOUGHT WE'D **NEVER** HEAR THE END OF IT!
ANGEL GROVE GYM
YOU KNOW, I MIGHT NEVER HAVE THOUGHT OF THAT...
IF WE HADN'T RUN INTO KORRUPTOR!
SOMETIMES **HELP** COMES FROM PLACES YOU'D **NEVER** REALIZE!
THE END

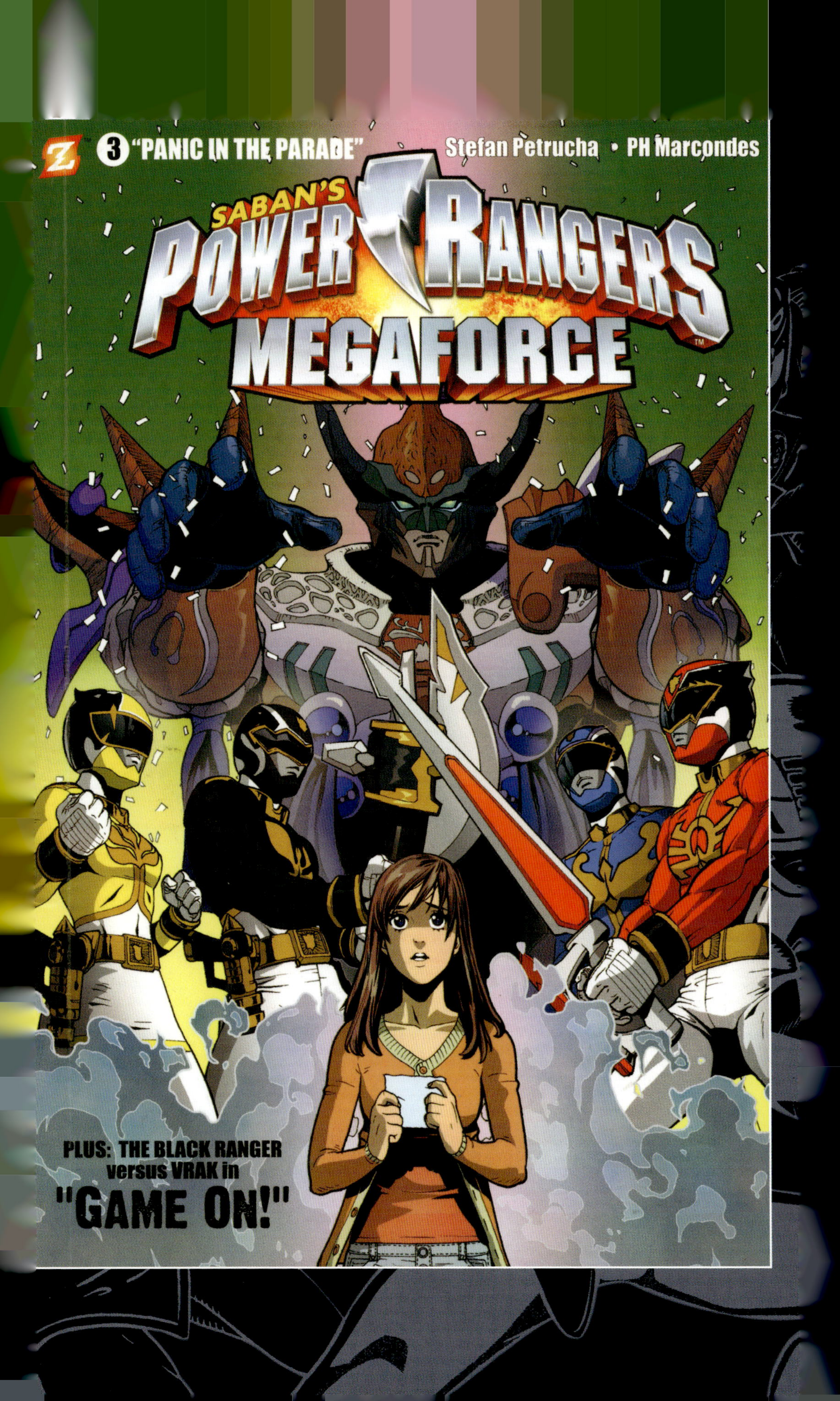

3 "PANIC IN THE PARADE"
Stefan Petrucha • PH Marcondes
SABAN'S POWER RANGERS MEGAFORCE
PLUS: THE BLACK RANGER versus VRAK in
"GAME ON!"

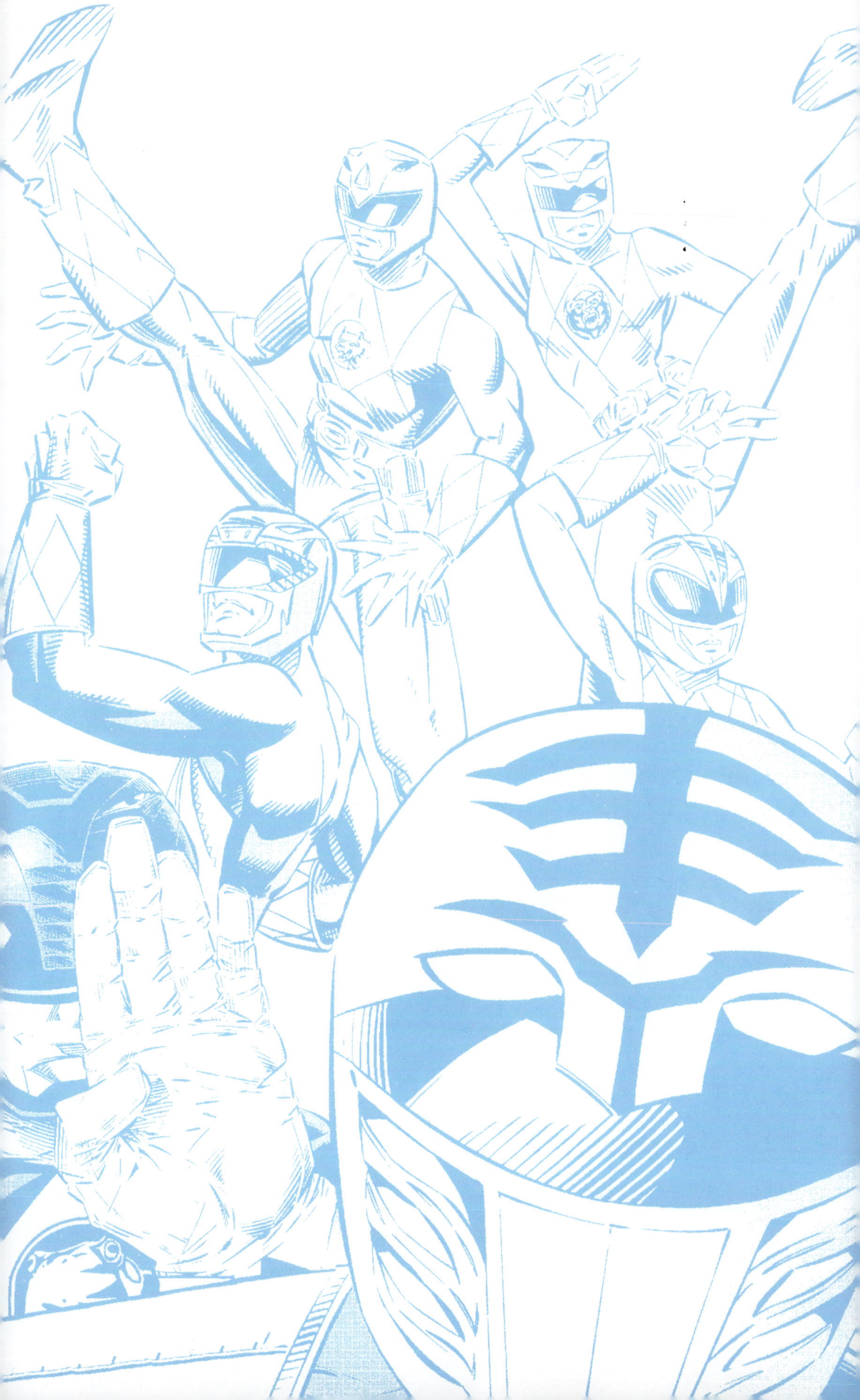

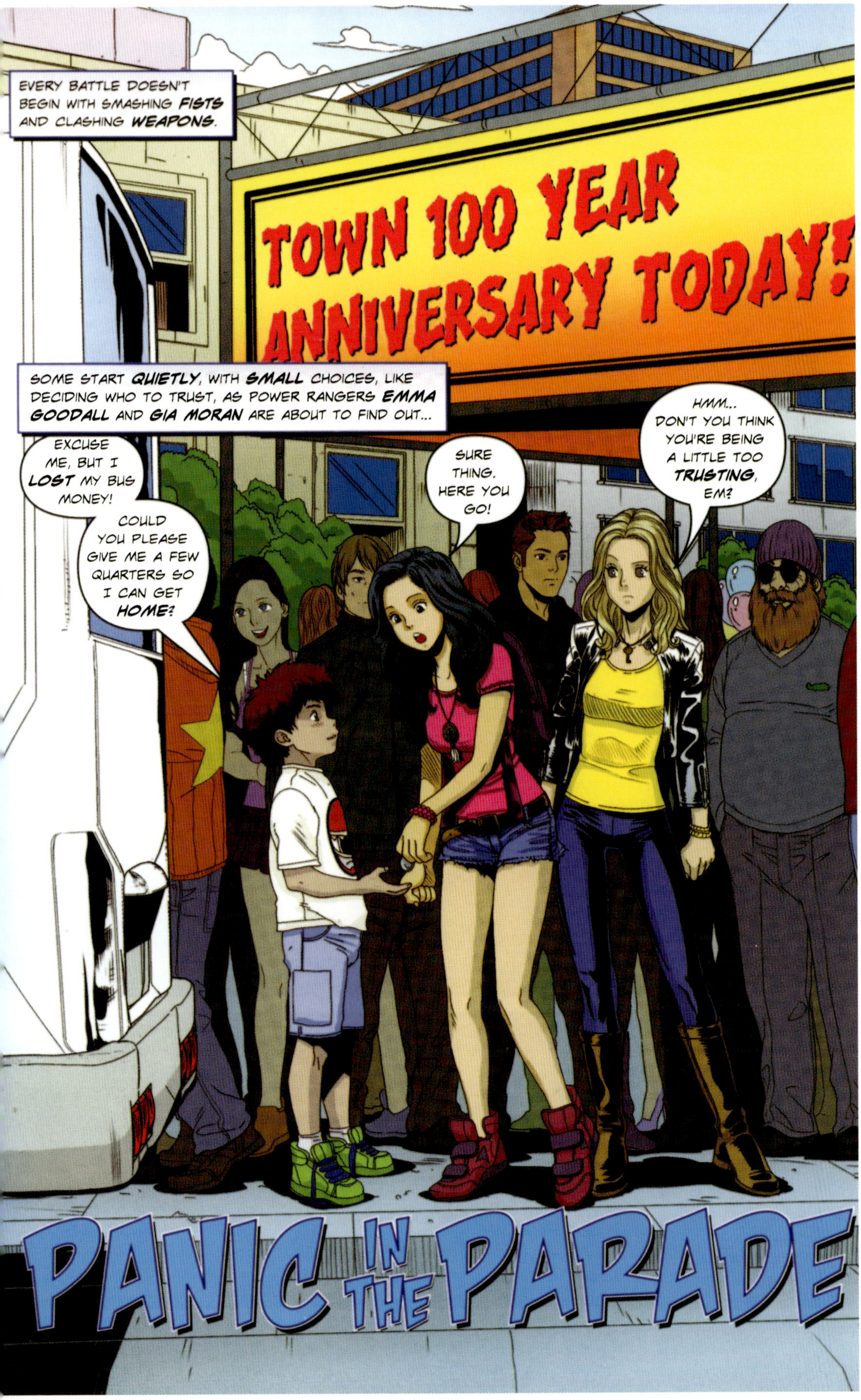
EVERY BATTLE DOESN'T BEGIN WITH SMASHING FISTS AND CLASHING WEAPONS.
TOWN 100 YEAR ANNIVERSARY TODAY!
SOME START QUIETLY, WITH SMALL CHOICES, LIKE DECIDING WHO TO TRUST, AS POWER RANGERS EMMA GOODALL AND GIA MORAN ARE ABOUT TO FIND OUT...
EXCUSE ME, BUT I LOST MY BUS MONEY!
COULD YOU PLEASE GIVE ME A FEW QUARTERS SO I CAN GET HOME?
SURE THING. HERE YOU GO!
HMM... DON'T YOU THINK YOU'RE BEING A LITTLE TOO TRUSTING, EM?
PANIC IN THE PARADE

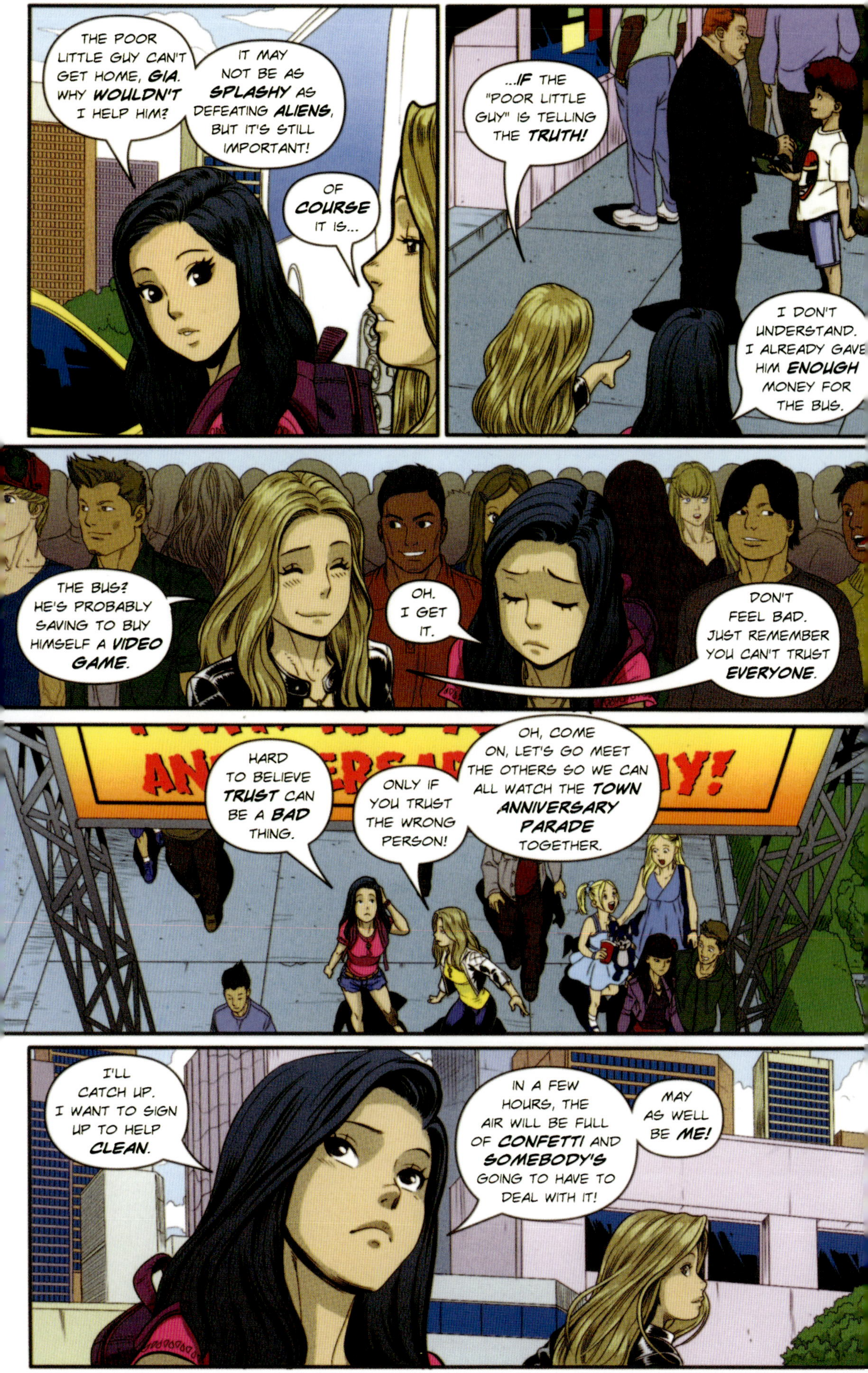
THE POOR LITTLE GUY CAN'T GET HOME, GIA. WHY WOULDN'T I HELP HIM?
IT MAY NOT BE AS SPLASHY AS DEFEATING ALIENS, BUT IT'S STILL IMPORTANT!
OF COURSE IT IS...
...IF THE "POOR LITTLE GUY" IS TELLING THE TRUTH!
I DON'T UNDERSTAND. I ALREADY GAVE HIM ENOUGH MONEY FOR THE BUS.
THE BUS? HE'S PROBABLY SAVING TO BUY HIMSELF A VIDEO GAME.
OH. I GET IT.
DON'T FEEL BAD. JUST REMEMBER YOU CAN'T TRUST EVERYONE.
HARD TO BELIEVE TRUST CAN BE A BAD THING.
ONLY IF YOU TRUST THE WRONG PERSON!
OH, COME ON, LET'S GO MEET THE OTHERS SO WE CAN ALL WATCH THE TOWN ANNIVERSARY PARADE TOGETHER.
I'LL CATCH UP. I WANT TO SIGN UP TO HELP CLEAN.
IN A FEW HOURS, THE AIR WILL BE FULL OF CONFETTI AND SOMEBODY'S GOING TO HAVE TO DEAL WITH IT!
MAY AS WELL BE ME!

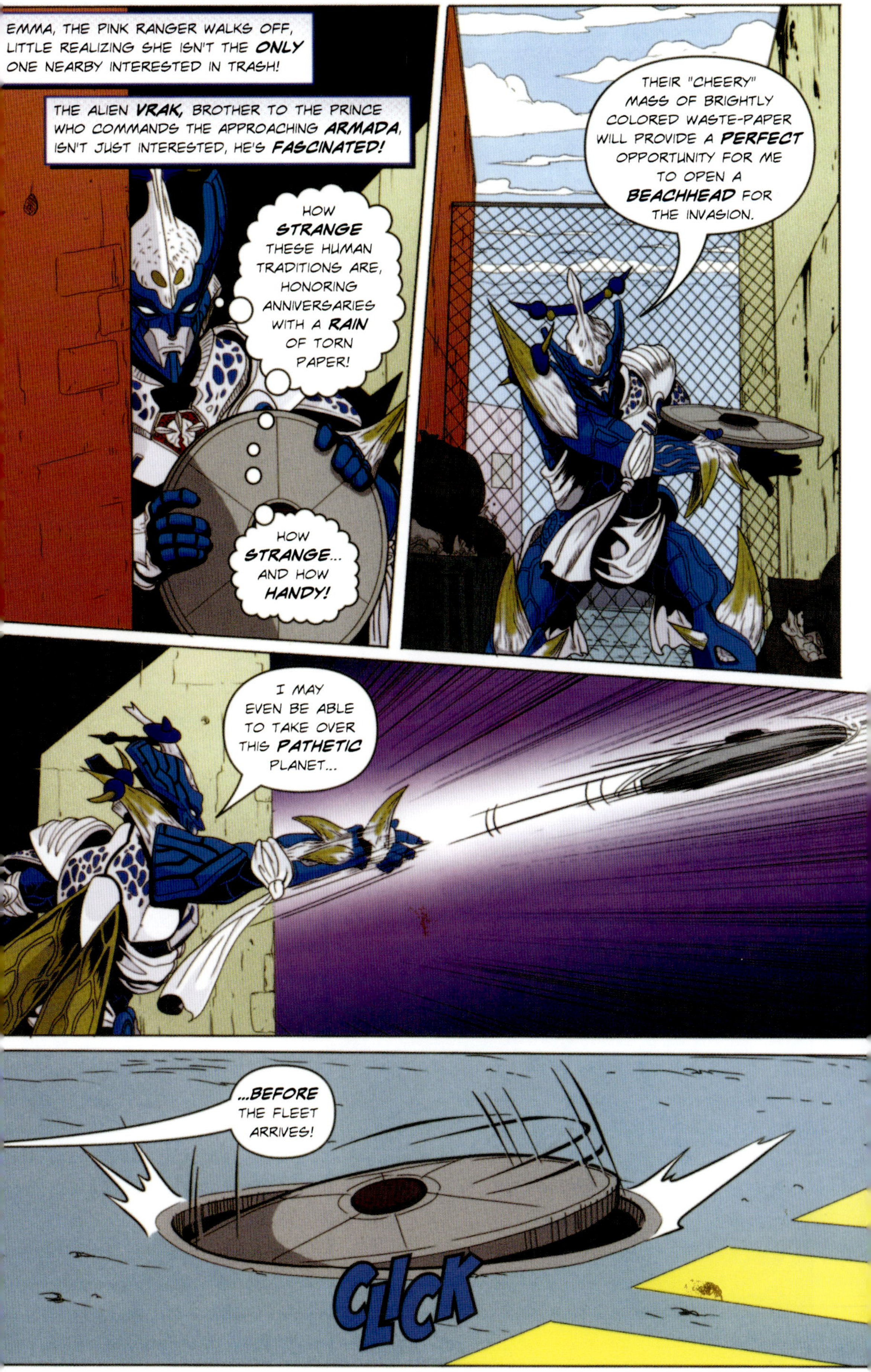
EMMA, THE PINK RANGER WALKS OFF, LITTLE REALIZING SHE ISN'T THE ONLY ONE NEARBY INTERESTED IN TRASH!
THE ALIEN VRAK, BROTHER TO THE PRINCE WHO COMMANDS THE APPROACHING ARMADA, ISN'T JUST INTERESTED, HE'S FASCINATED!
HOW STRANGE THESE HUMAN TRADITIONS ARE, HONORING ANNIVERSARIES WITH A RAIN OF TORN PAPER!
HOW STRANGE... AND HOW HANDY!
THEIR "CHEERY" MASS OF BRIGHTLY COLORED WASTE-PAPER WILL PROVIDE A PERFECT OPPORTUNITY FOR ME TO OPEN A BEACHHEAD FOR THE INVASION.
I MAY EVEN BE ABLE TO TAKE OVER THIS PATHETIC PLANET...
...BEFORE THE FLEET ARRIVES!
CLICK

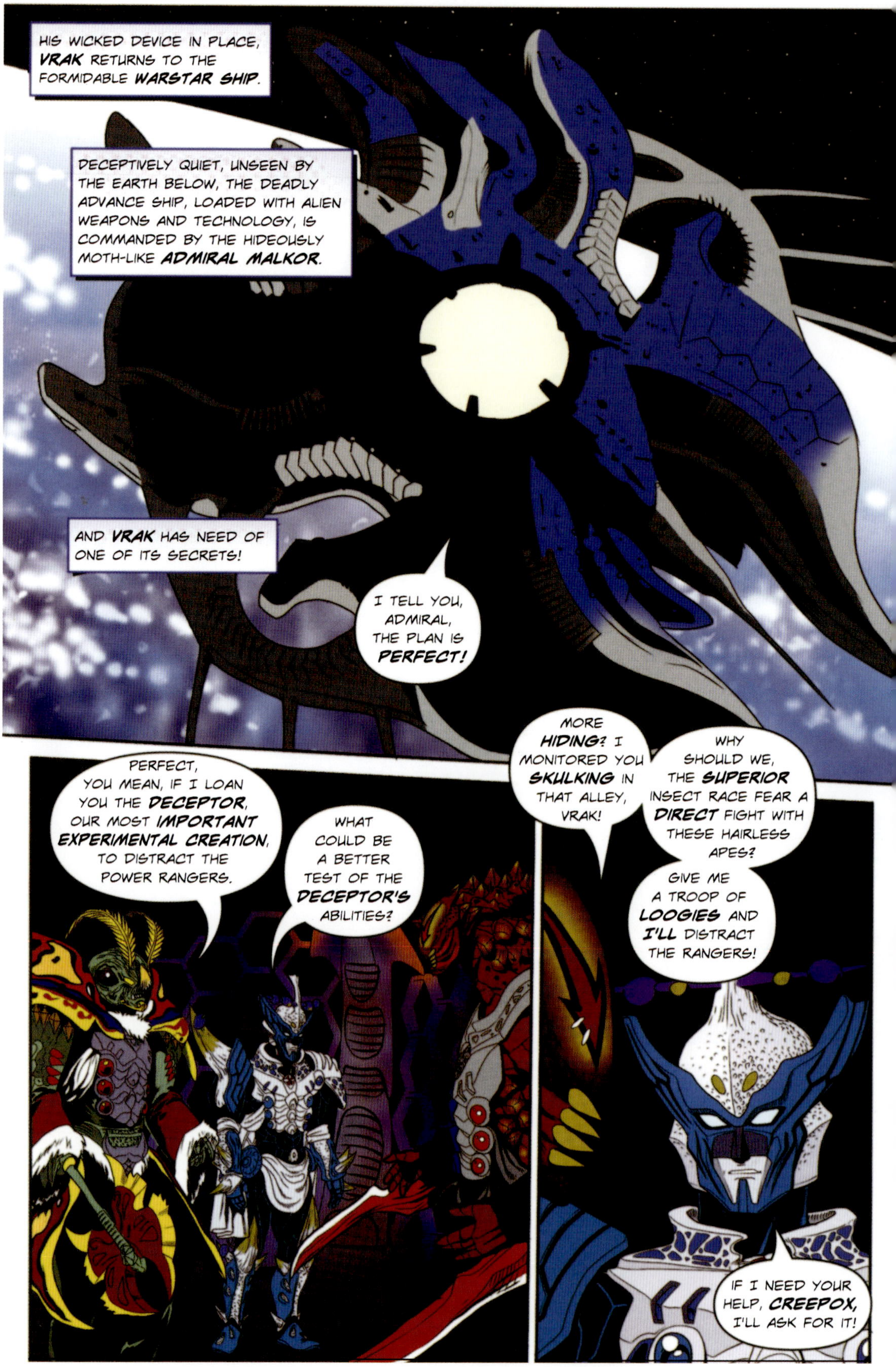

HIS WICKED DEVICE IN PLACE, VRAK RETURNS TO THE FORMIDABLE WARSTAR SHIP.
DECEPTIVELY QUIET, UNSEEN BY THE EARTH BELOW, THE DEADLY ADVANCE SHIP, LOADED WITH ALIEN WEAPONS AND TECHNOLOGY, IS COMMANDED BY THE HIDEOUSLY MOTH-LIKE ADMIRAL MALKOR.
AND VRAK HAS NEED OF ONE OF ITS SECRETS!
I TELL YOU, ADMIRAL, THE PLAN IS PERFECT!
PERFECT, YOU MEAN, IF I LOAN YOU THE DECEPTOR, OUR MOST IMPORTANT EXPERIMENTAL CREATION, TO DISTRACT THE POWER RANGERS.
WHAT COULD BE A BETTER TEST OF THE DECEPTOR'S ABILITIES?
MORE HIDING? I MONITORED YOU SKULKING IN THAT ALLEY, VRAK!
WHY SHOULD WE, THE SUPERIOR INSECT RACE FEAR A DIRECT FIGHT WITH THESE HAIRLESS APES?
GIVE ME A TROOP OF LOOGIES AND I'LL DISTRACT THE RANGERS!
IF I NEED YOUR HELP, CREEPOX, I'LL ASK FOR IT!

WE'LL USE **BOTH** PLANS. CREEPOX, ASSEMBLE YOUR TROOPS!

YES, ADMIRAL!

AND THE **DECEPTOR**, ADMIRAL?

YOU SHALL HAVE IT!

FLAGE!

YES, ADMIRAL MALKOR?

USE THE DECEPTOR ON VRAK AT ONCE.

⇒ULP!⇐ YOU MEAN... RIGHT **NOW?**

THAT **IS** WHAT **AT ONCE** MEANS. YES, **NOW!**

BUT IT'S **UNTESTED**... IT'S **EXPERIMENTAL**... IT'S...

YOU **HEARD** THE ADMIRAL!

NOW!

BVVVVVVT

AGHHHHHHHH!

OOPS!

IT MIGHT BE A LITTLE **UNCOMFORTABLE.**

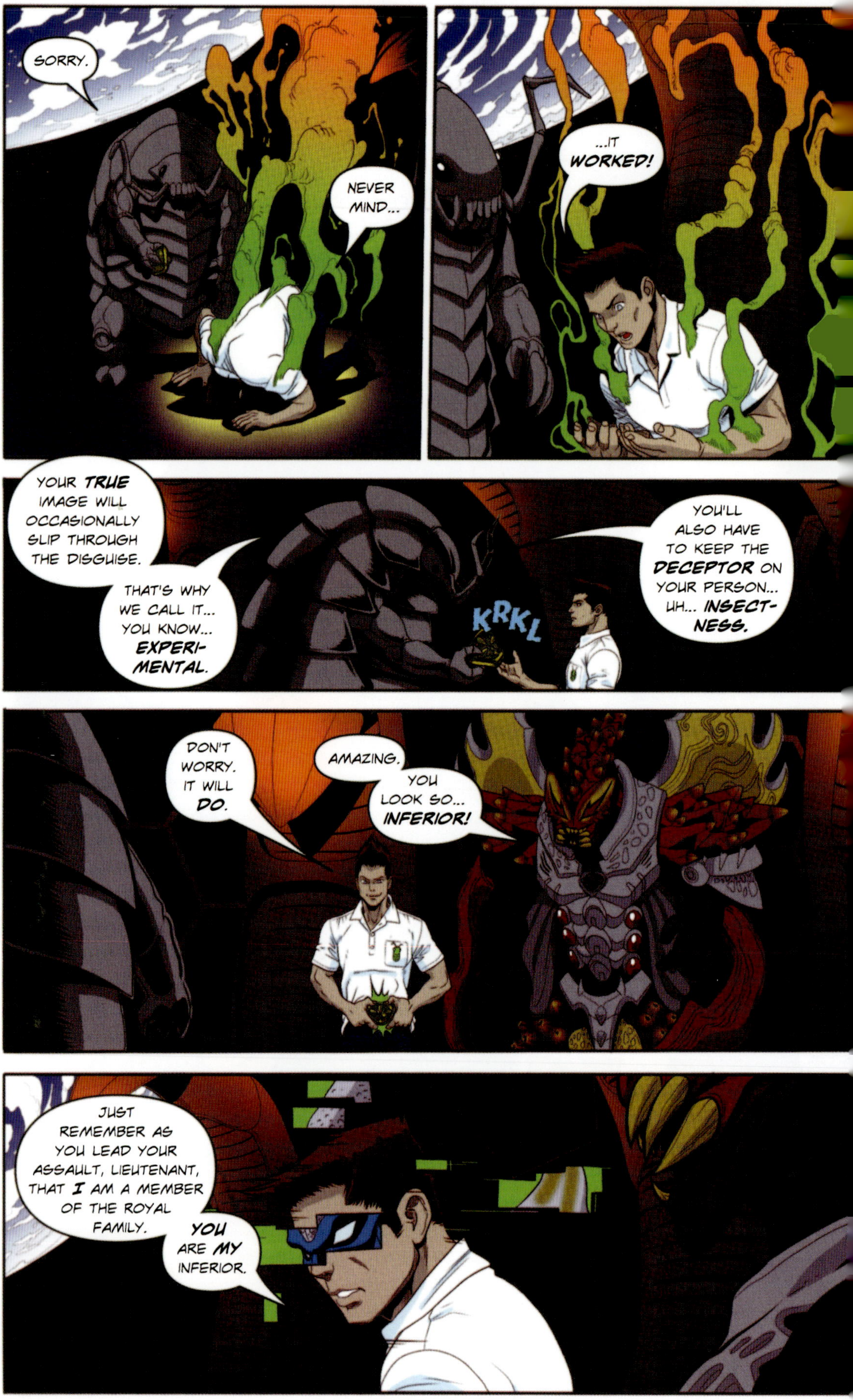
SORRY.
NEVER MIND...
...IT WORKED!
YOUR TRUE IMAGE WILL OCCASIONALLY SLIP THROUGH THE DISGUISE.
THAT'S WHY WE CALL IT... YOU KNOW... EXPERI-MENTAL.
KRKL
YOU'LL ALSO HAVE TO KEEP THE DECEPTOR ON YOUR PERSON... UH... INSECT-NESS.
DON'T WORRY. IT WILL DO.
AMAZING.
YOU LOOK SO... INFERIOR!
JUST REMEMBER AS YOU LEAD YOUR ASSAULT, LIEUTENANT, THAT I AM A MEMBER OF THE ROYAL FAMILY.
YOU ARE MY INFERIOR.

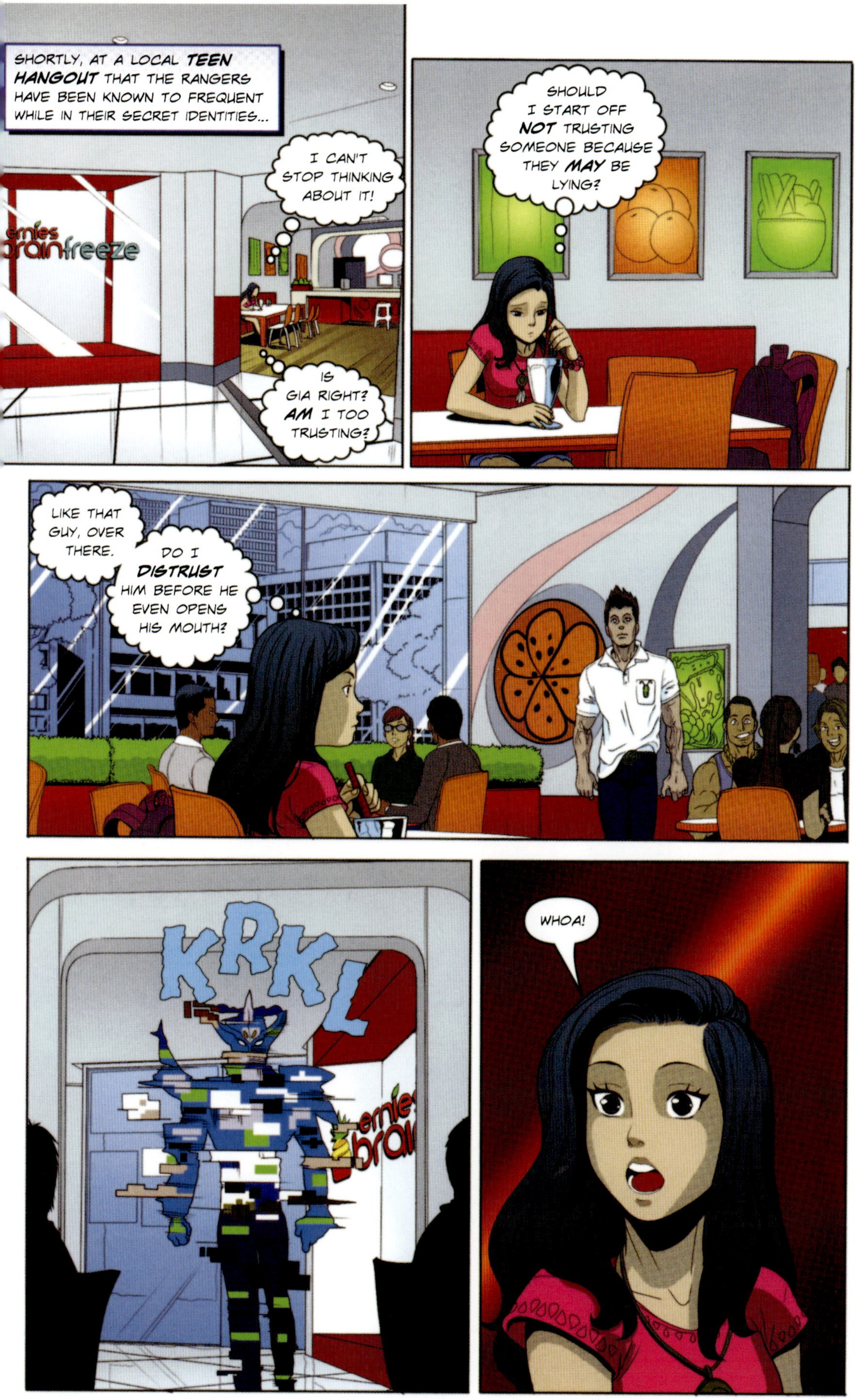
SHORTLY, AT A LOCAL TEEN HANGOUT THAT THE RANGERS HAVE BEEN KNOWN TO FREQUENT WHILE IN THEIR SECRET IDENTITIES...
I CAN'T STOP THINKING ABOUT IT!
ernies brainfreeze
IS GIA RIGHT? AM I TOO TRUSTING?
SHOULD I START OFF NOT TRUSTING SOMEONE BECAUSE THEY MAY BE LYING?
LIKE THAT GUY, OVER THERE.
DO I DISTRUST HIM BEFORE HE EVEN OPENS HIS MOUTH?
KRKL
WHOA!

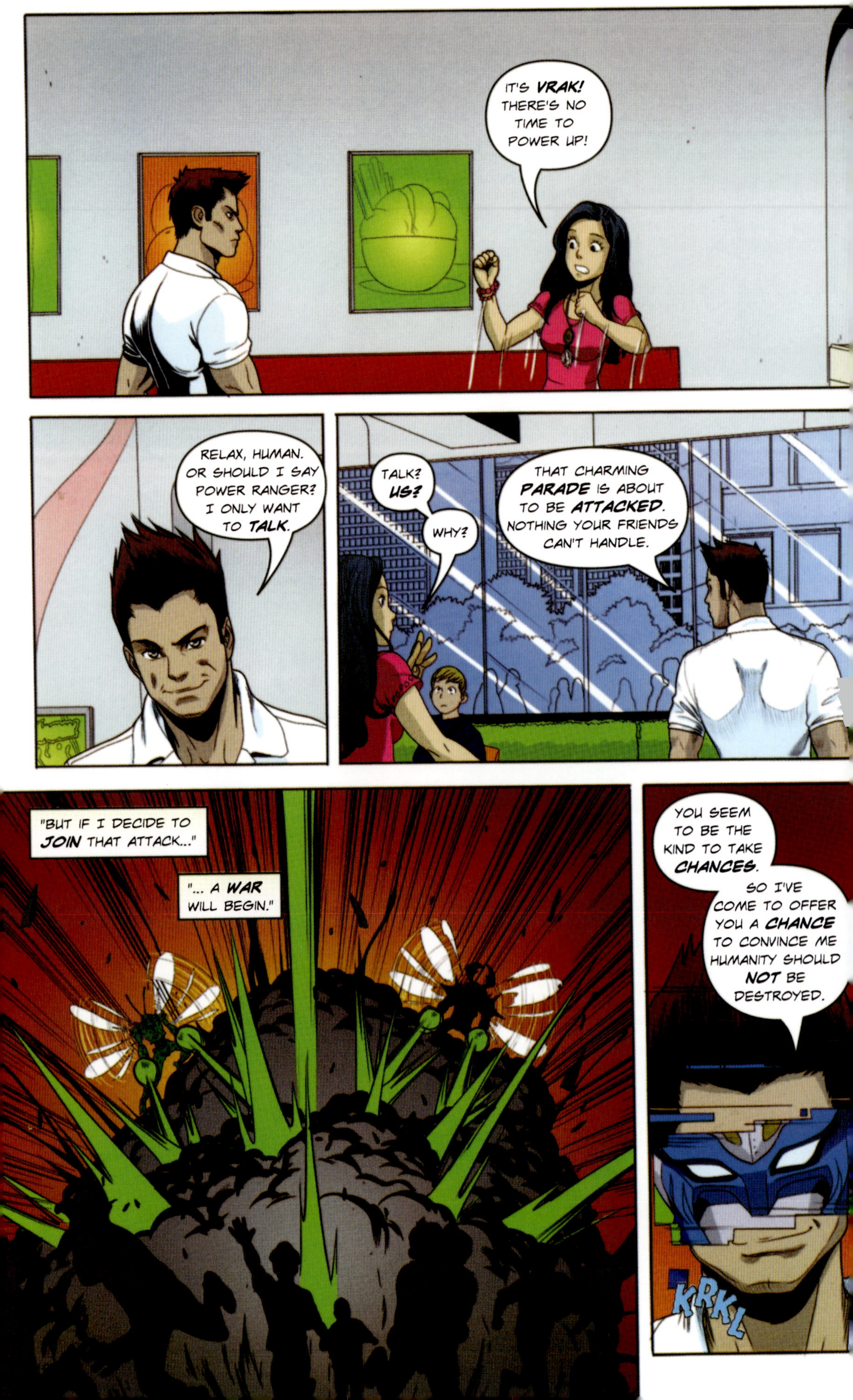
IT'S VRAK! THERE'S NO TIME TO POWER UP!
RELAX, HUMAN. OR SHOULD I SAY POWER RANGER? I ONLY WANT TO TALK.
TALK? US?
WHY?
THAT CHARMING PARADE IS ABOUT TO BE ATTACKED. NOTHING YOUR FRIENDS CAN'T HANDLE.
"BUT IF I DECIDE TO JOIN THAT ATTACK..."
"... A WAR WILL BEGIN."
YOU SEEM TO BE THE KIND TO TAKE CHANCES.
SO I'VE COME TO OFFER YOU A CHANCE TO CONVINCE ME HUMANITY SHOULD NOT BE DESTROYED.
KRKL

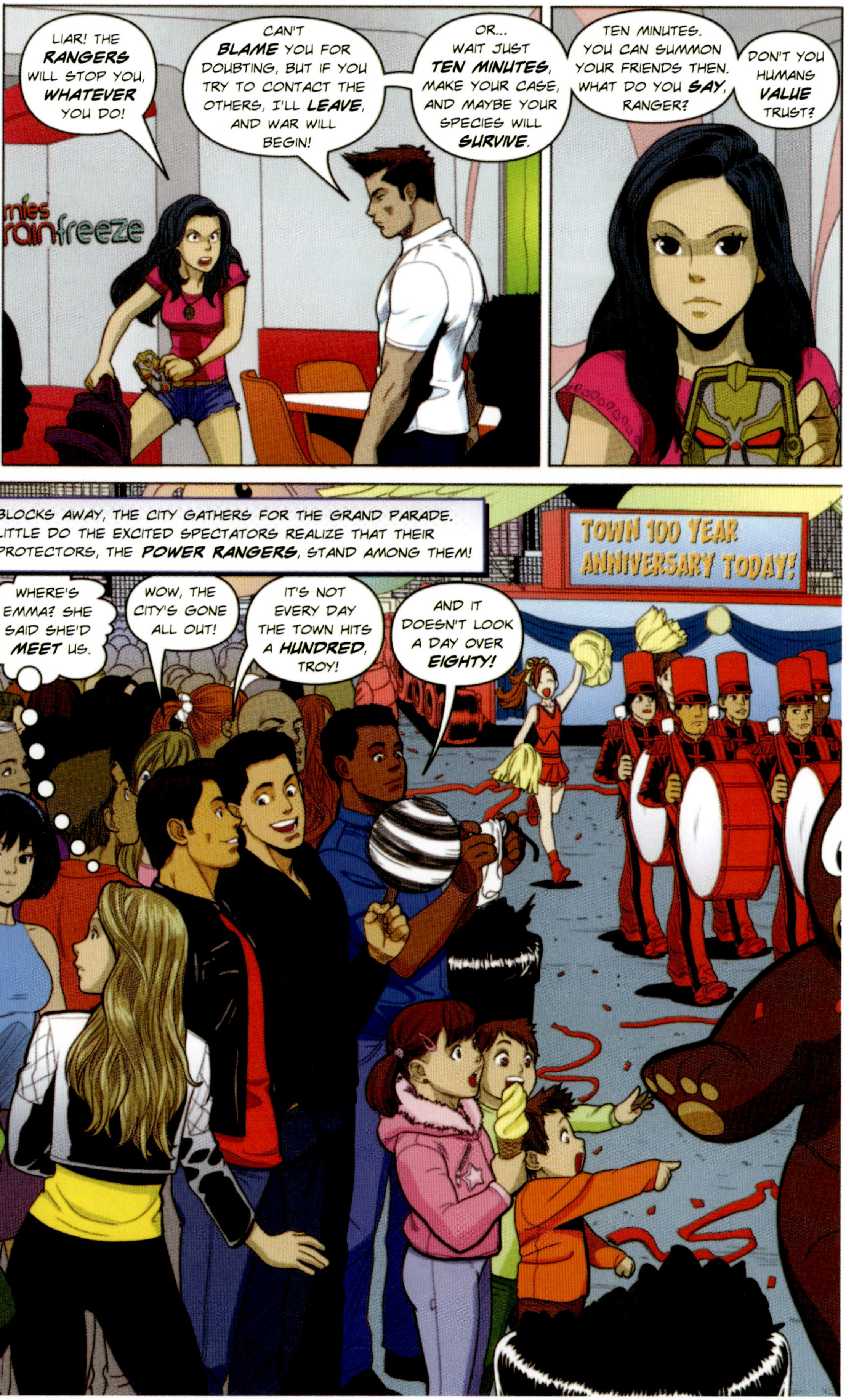

rnies
rainfreeze
LIAR! THE RANGERS WILL STOP YOU, WHATEVER YOU DO!
CAN'T BLAME YOU FOR DOUBTING, BUT IF YOU TRY TO CONTACT THE OTHERS, I'LL LEAVE, AND WAR WILL BEGIN!
OR... WAIT JUST TEN MINUTES, MAKE YOUR CASE, AND MAYBE YOUR SPECIES WILL SURVIVE.
TEN MINUTES. YOU CAN SUMMON YOUR FRIENDS THEN. WHAT DO YOU SAY, RANGER?
DON'T YOU HUMANS VALUE TRUST?
BLOCKS AWAY, THE CITY GATHERS FOR THE GRAND PARADE. LITTLE DO THE EXCITED SPECTATORS REALIZE THAT THEIR PROTECTORS, THE POWER RANGERS, STAND AMONG THEM!
TOWN 100 YEAR ANNIVERSARY TODAY!
WHERE'S EMMA? SHE SAID SHE'D MEET US.
WOW, THE CITY'S GONE ALL OUT!
IT'S NOT EVERY DAY THE TOWN HITS A HUNDRED, TROY!
AND IT DOESN'T LOOK A DAY OVER EIGHTY!

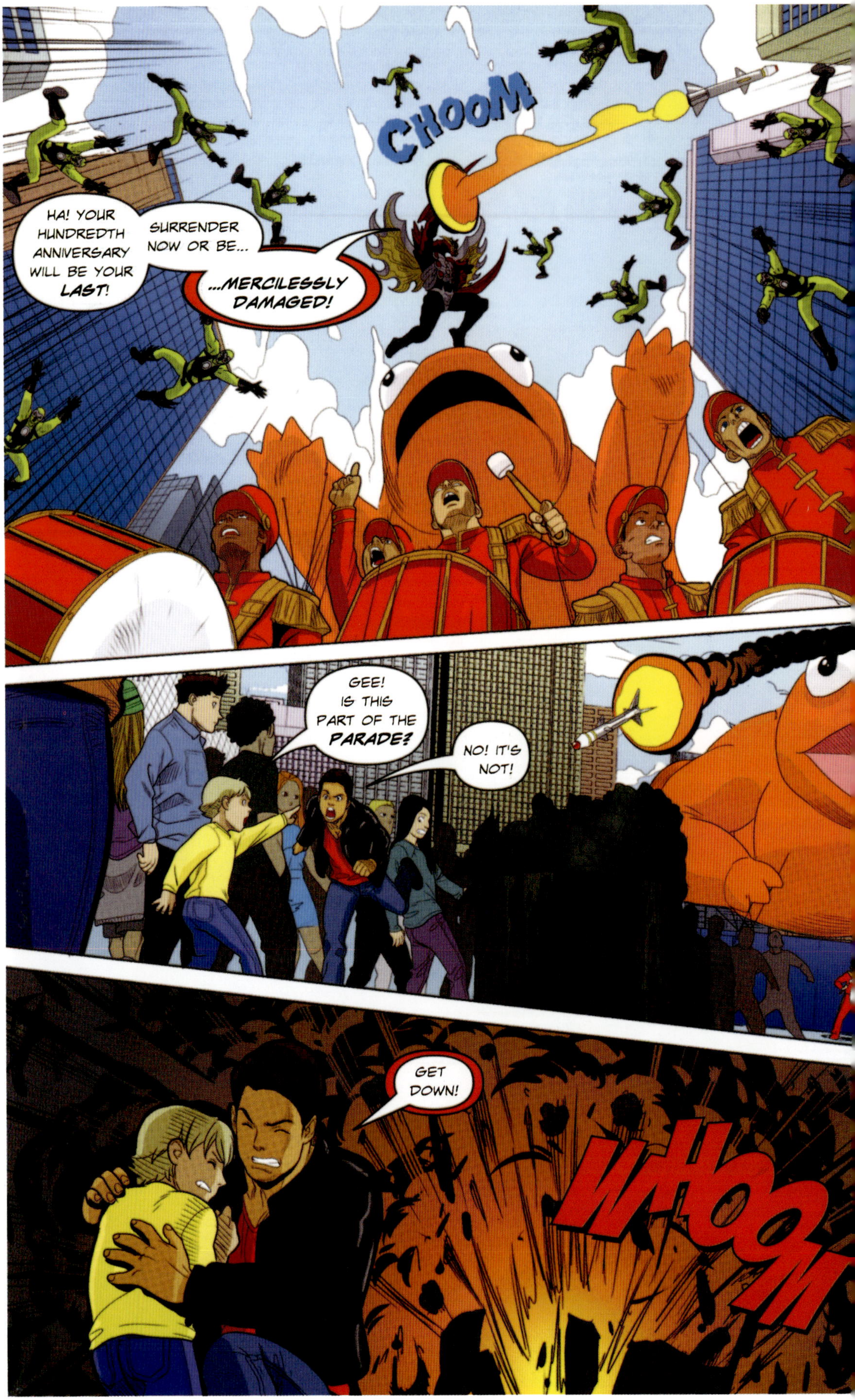
CHOOM
HA! YOUR HUNDREDTH ANNIVERSARY WILL BE YOUR LAST!
SURRENDER NOW OR BE...
...MERCILESSLY DAMAGED!
GEE! IS THIS PART OF THE PARADE?
NO! IT'S NOT!
GET DOWN!
WHOOM

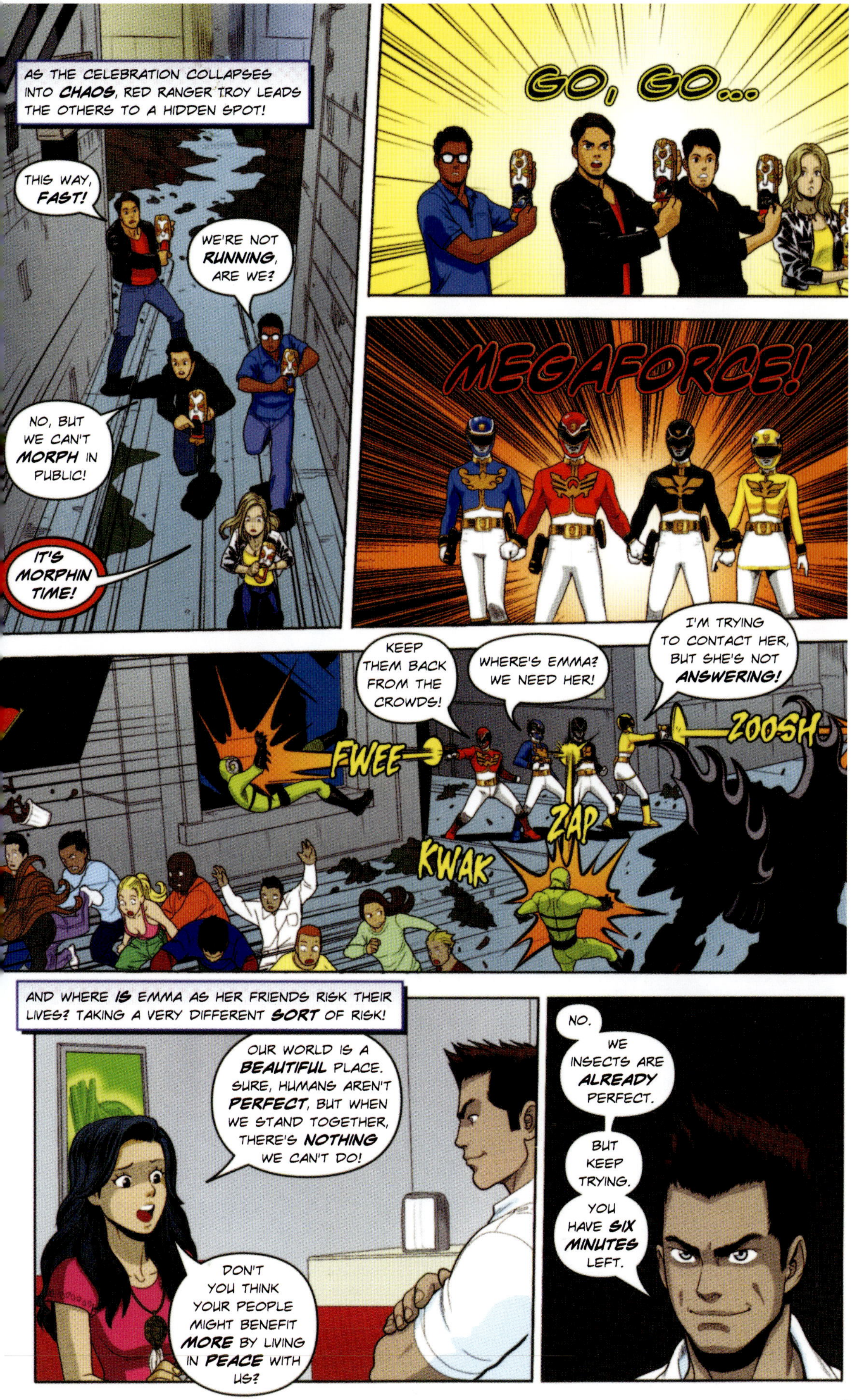
AS THE CELEBRATION COLLAPSES INTO CHAOS, RED RANGER TROY LEADS THE OTHERS TO A HIDDEN SPOT!
THIS WAY, FAST!
WE'RE NOT RUNNING, ARE WE?
NO, BUT WE CAN'T MORPH IN PUBLIC!
IT'S MORPHIN TIME!
GO, GO...
MEGAFORCE!
KEEP THEM BACK FROM THE CROWDS!
WHERE'S EMMA? WE NEED HER!
I'M TRYING TO CONTACT HER, BUT SHE'S NOT ANSWERING!
FWEE
ZOOSH
ZAP
KWAK
AND WHERE IS EMMA AS HER FRIENDS RISK THEIR LIVES? TAKING A VERY DIFFERENT SORT OF RISK!
OUR WORLD IS A BEAUTIFUL PLACE. SURE, HUMANS AREN'T PERFECT, BUT WHEN WE STAND TOGETHER, THERE'S NOTHING WE CAN'T DO!
DON'T YOU THINK YOUR PEOPLE MIGHT BENEFIT MORE BY LIVING IN PEACE WITH US?
NO.
WE INSECTS ARE ALREADY PERFECT.
BUT KEEP TRYING.
YOU HAVE SIX MINUTES LEFT.

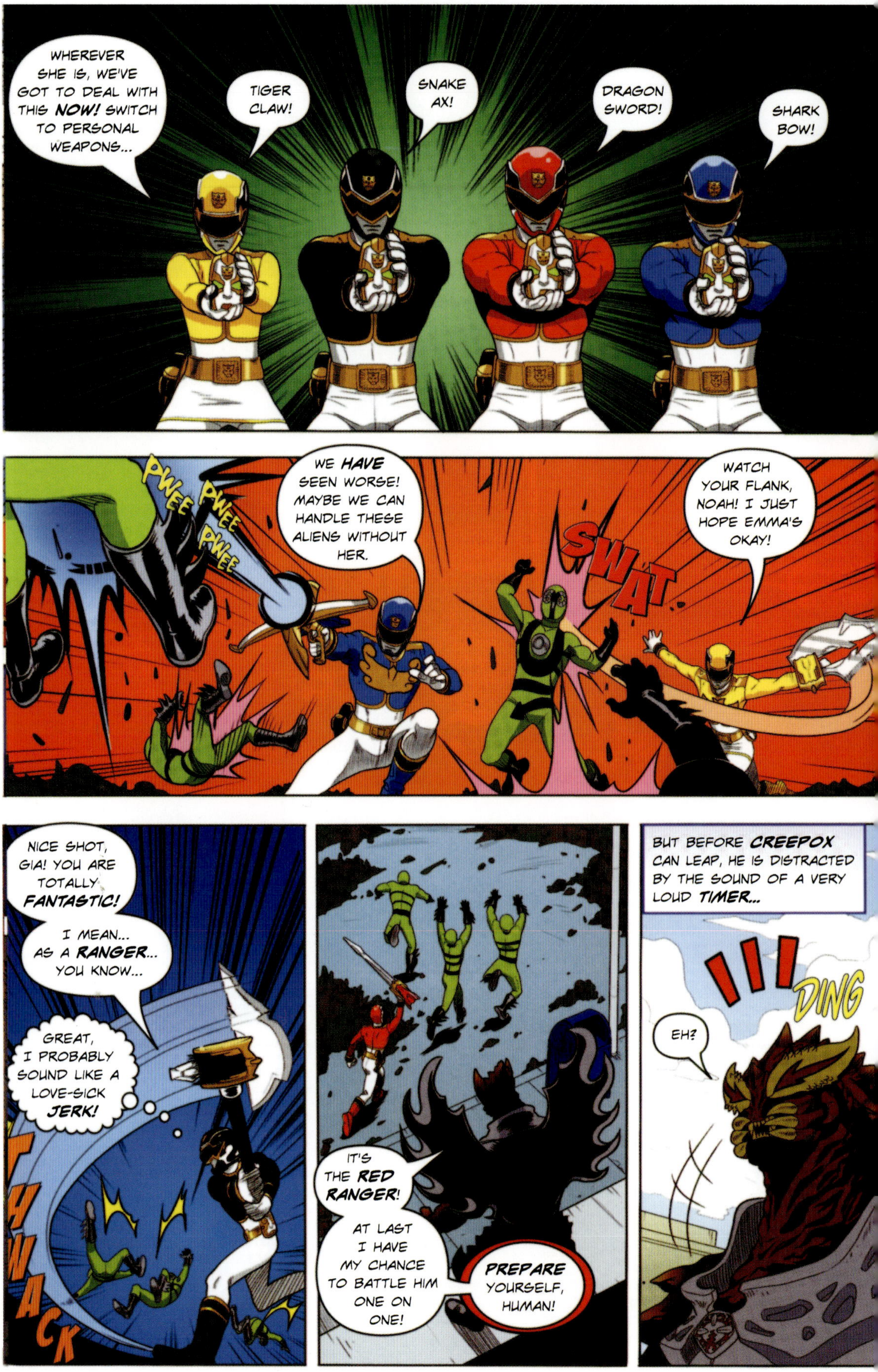
WHEREVER SHE IS, WE'VE GOT TO DEAL WITH THIS NOW! SWITCH TO PERSONAL WEAPONS...
TIGER CLAW!
SNAKE AX!
DRAGON SWORD!
SHARK BOW!
PWEE PWEE PWEE
WE HAVE SEEN WORSE! MAYBE WE CAN HANDLE THESE ALIENS WITHOUT HER.
SWAT
WATCH YOUR FLANK, NOAH! I JUST HOPE EMMA'S OKAY!
NICE SHOT, GIA! YOU ARE TOTALLY FANTASTIC!
I MEAN... AS A RANGER... YOU KNOW...
GREAT, I PROBABLY SOUND LIKE A LOVE-SICK JERK!
THWACK
IT'S THE RED RANGER!
AT LAST I HAVE MY CHANCE TO BATTLE HIM ONE ON ONE!
PREPARE YOURSELF, HUMAN!
BUT BEFORE CREEPOX CAN LEAP, HE IS DISTRACTED BY THE SOUND OF A VERY LOUD TIMER...
DING
EH?

BOOM

WHAT COWARDLY **TRICK** IS THIS?

NO TRICK! JUST **FOUR HUNDRED** CONFETTI-CANNONS TIMED TO GO OFF IN CELEBRATION OF THE **EXACT MOMENT** OUR CITY WAS FORMED!

IT'LL **STILL** BE GREAT, ONCE WE CLEAR THE STREETS OF THIS ALIEN TRASH!

IT WOULD'VE BEEN **GREAT** IF YOU HADN'T **RUINED** IT!

TOWN 100 YEAR ANNIVERSARY TODAY!

WHAT CREEPOX AND THE OTHERS DON'T REALIZE IS THAT THE **REAL** TRICK BELONGS TO VRAK, AS THE EVIL DEVICE HE PLANTED **ACTIVATES!**

BEEP.

RRHUUUUMMBBLLLE!

THE STREET! IT'S SHAKING LIKE A HUGE **TRUCK'S** PASSING!

NOT JUST A **TRUCK**, TROY!

WN 100 ANNIVERSA

IT'S AN **EARTH-QUAKE!**

RHUMMMMBBBBLLLLE

315

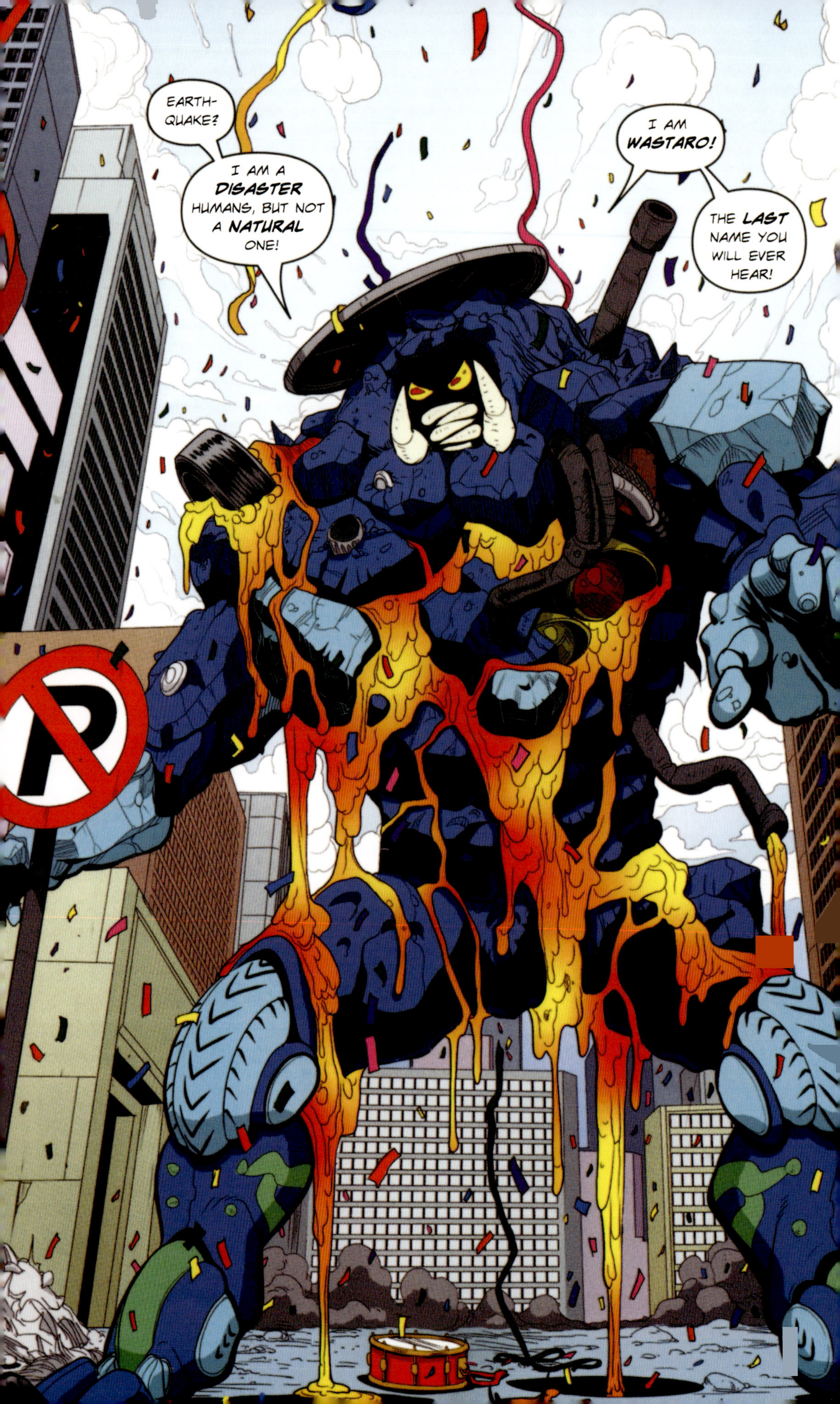
EARTH-QUAKE?
I AM A DISASTER HUMANS, BUT NOT A NATURAL ONE!
I AM WASTARO!
THE LAST NAME YOU WILL EVER HEAR!

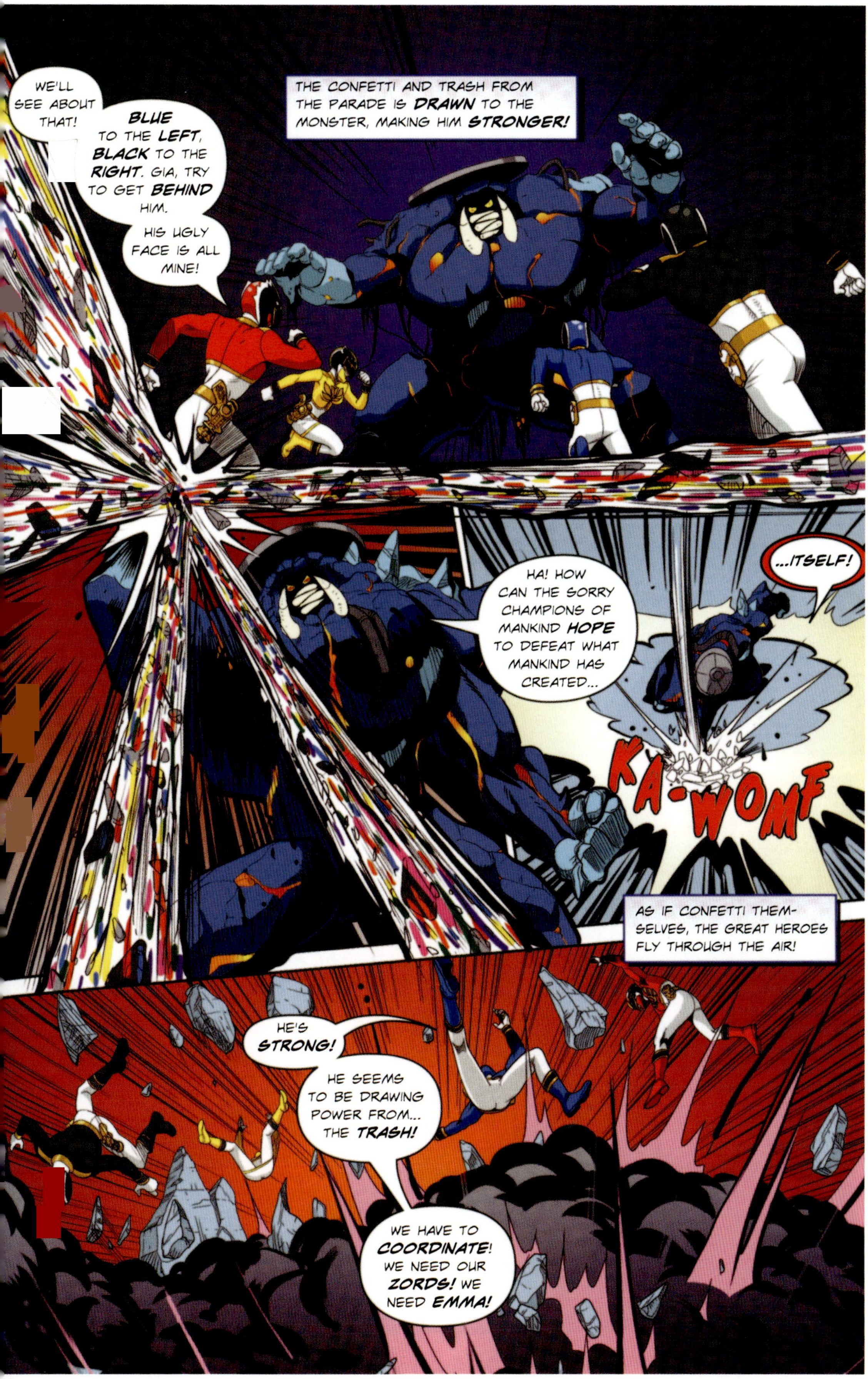
THE CONFETTI AND TRASH FROM THE PARADE IS DRAWN TO THE MONSTER, MAKING HIM STRONGER!
WE'LL SEE ABOUT THAT!
BLUE TO THE LEFT, BLACK TO THE RIGHT. GIA, TRY TO GET BEHIND HIM.
HIS UGLY FACE IS ALL MINE!
HA! HOW CAN THE SORRY CHAMPIONS OF MANKIND HOPE TO DEFEAT WHAT MANKIND HAS CREATED...
...ITSELF!
KA-WOMF
AS IF CONFETTI THEMSELVES, THE GREAT HEROES FLY THROUGH THE AIR!
HE'S STRONG!
HE SEEMS TO BE DRAWING POWER FROM... THE TRASH!
WE HAVE TO COORDINATE! WE NEED OUR ZORDS! WE NEED EMMA!

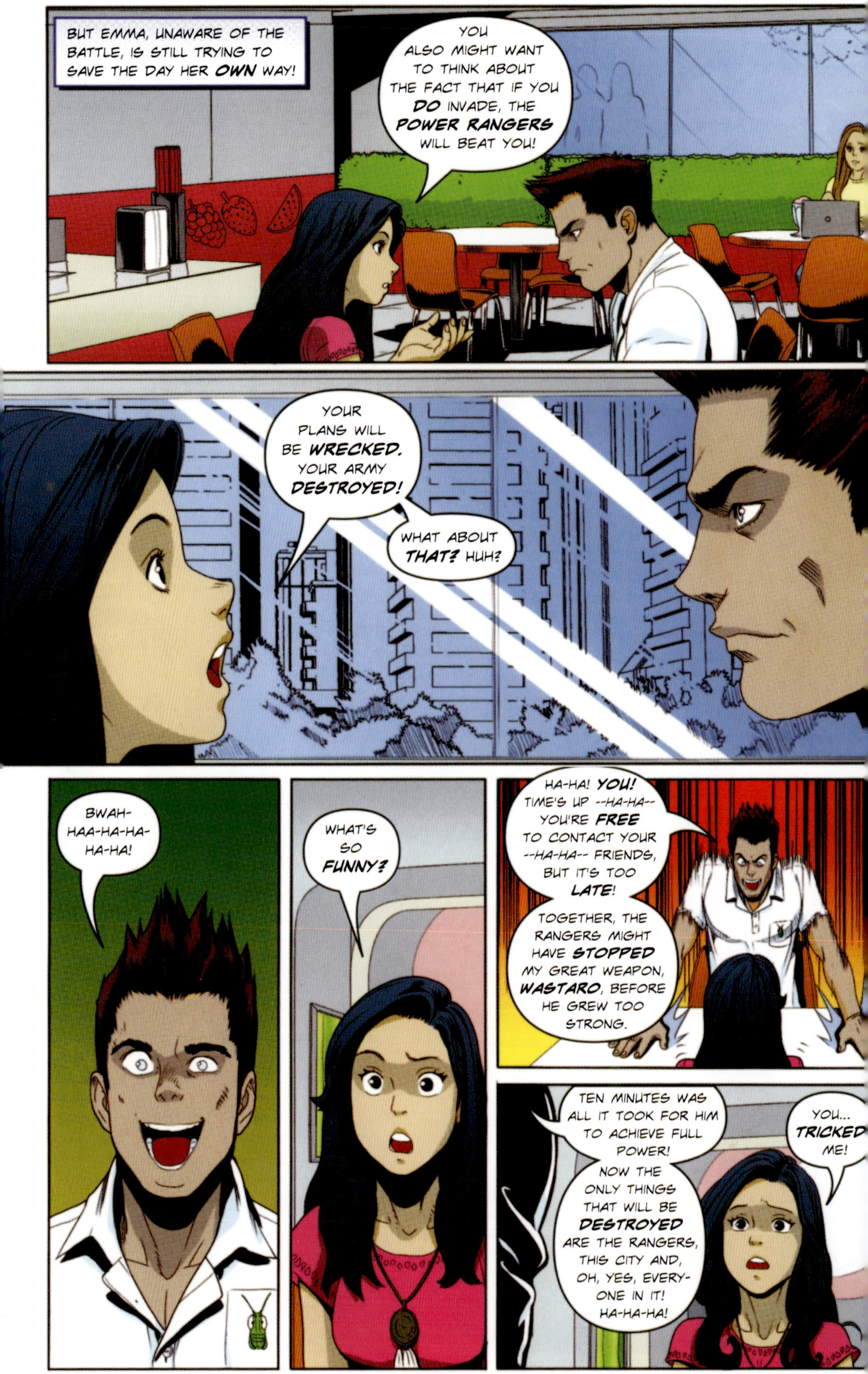
BUT EMMA, UNAWARE OF THE BATTLE, IS STILL TRYING TO SAVE THE DAY HER **OWN** WAY!
YOU ALSO MIGHT WANT TO THINK ABOUT THE FACT THAT IF YOU **DO** INVADE, THE **POWER RANGERS** WILL BEAT YOU!
YOUR PLANS WILL BE **WRECKED.** YOUR ARMY **DESTROYED!**
WHAT ABOUT **THAT?** HUH?
BWAH-HAA-HA-HA-HA-HA!
WHAT'S SO **FUNNY?**
HA-HA! **YOU!** TIME'S UP --HA-HA-- YOU'RE **FREE** TO CONTACT YOUR --HA-HA-- FRIENDS, BUT IT'S TOO **LATE**!
TOGETHER, THE RANGERS MIGHT HAVE **STOPPED** MY GREAT WEAPON, **WASTARO**, BEFORE HE GREW TOO STRONG.
TEN MINUTES WAS ALL IT TOOK FOR HIM TO ACHIEVE FULL POWER!
NOW THE ONLY THINGS THAT WILL BE **DESTROYED** ARE THE RANGERS, THIS CITY AND, OH, YES, EVERY-ONE IN IT! HA-HA-HA!
YOU... **TRICKED** ME!

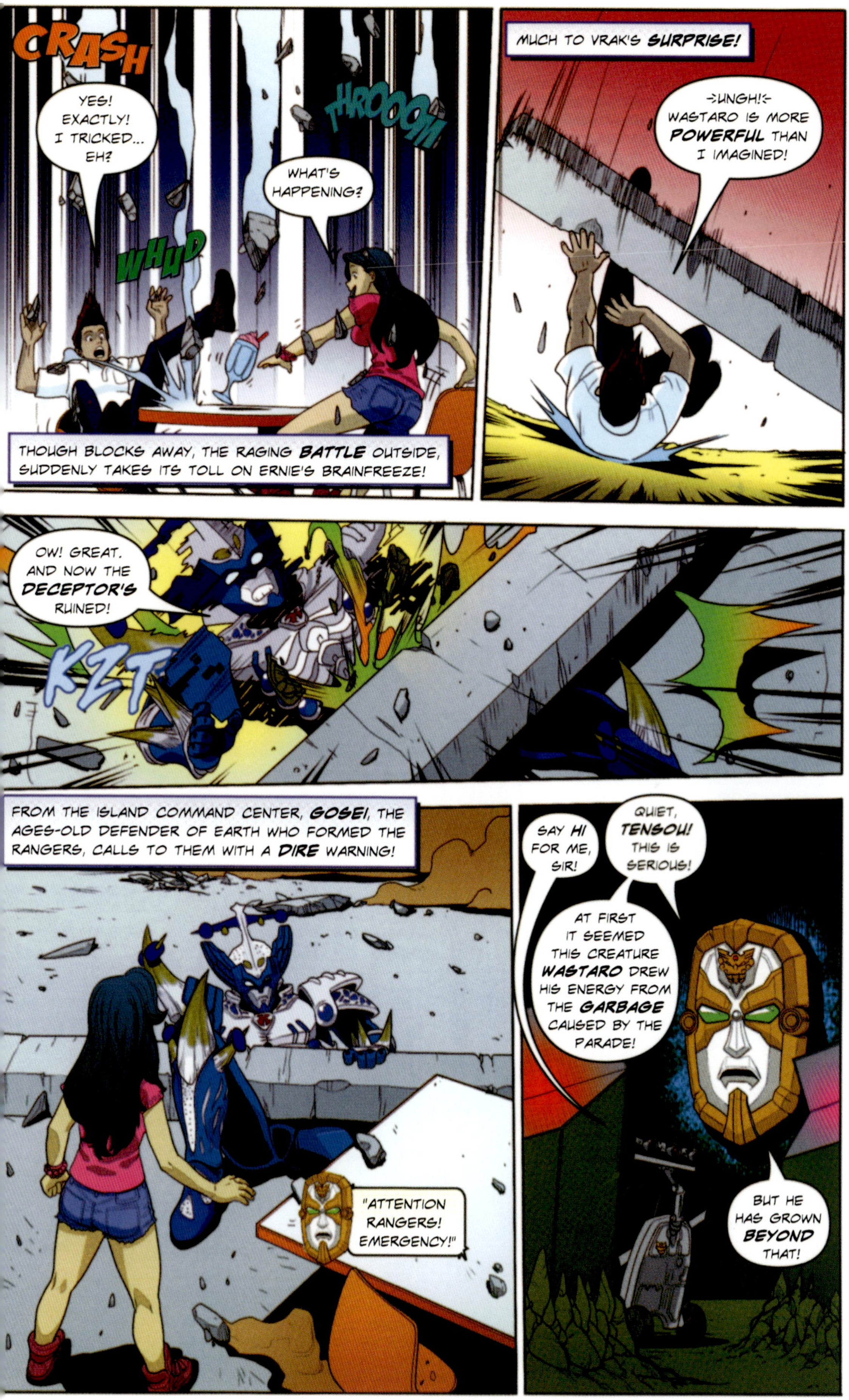
CRASH
YES! EXACTLY! I TRICKED... EH?
THROOOM
WHAT'S HAPPENING?
WHUD
THOUGH BLOCKS AWAY, THE RAGING BATTLE OUTSIDE, SUDDENLY TAKES ITS TOLL ON ERNIE'S BRAINFREEZE!
MUCH TO VRAK'S SURPRISE!
-UNGH!- WASTARO IS MORE POWERFUL THAN I IMAGINED!
OW! GREAT. AND NOW THE DECEPTOR'S RUINED!
KZT
FROM THE ISLAND COMMAND CENTER, GOSEI, THE AGES-OLD DEFENDER OF EARTH WHO FORMED THE RANGERS, CALLS TO THEM WITH A DIRE WARNING!
"ATTENTION RANGERS! EMERGENCY!"
SAY HI FOR ME, SIR!
QUIET, TENSOU! THIS IS SERIOUS!
AT FIRST IT SEEMED THIS CREATURE WASTARO DREW HIS ENERGY FROM THE GARBAGE CAUSED BY THE PARADE!
BUT HE HAS GROWN BEYOND THAT!

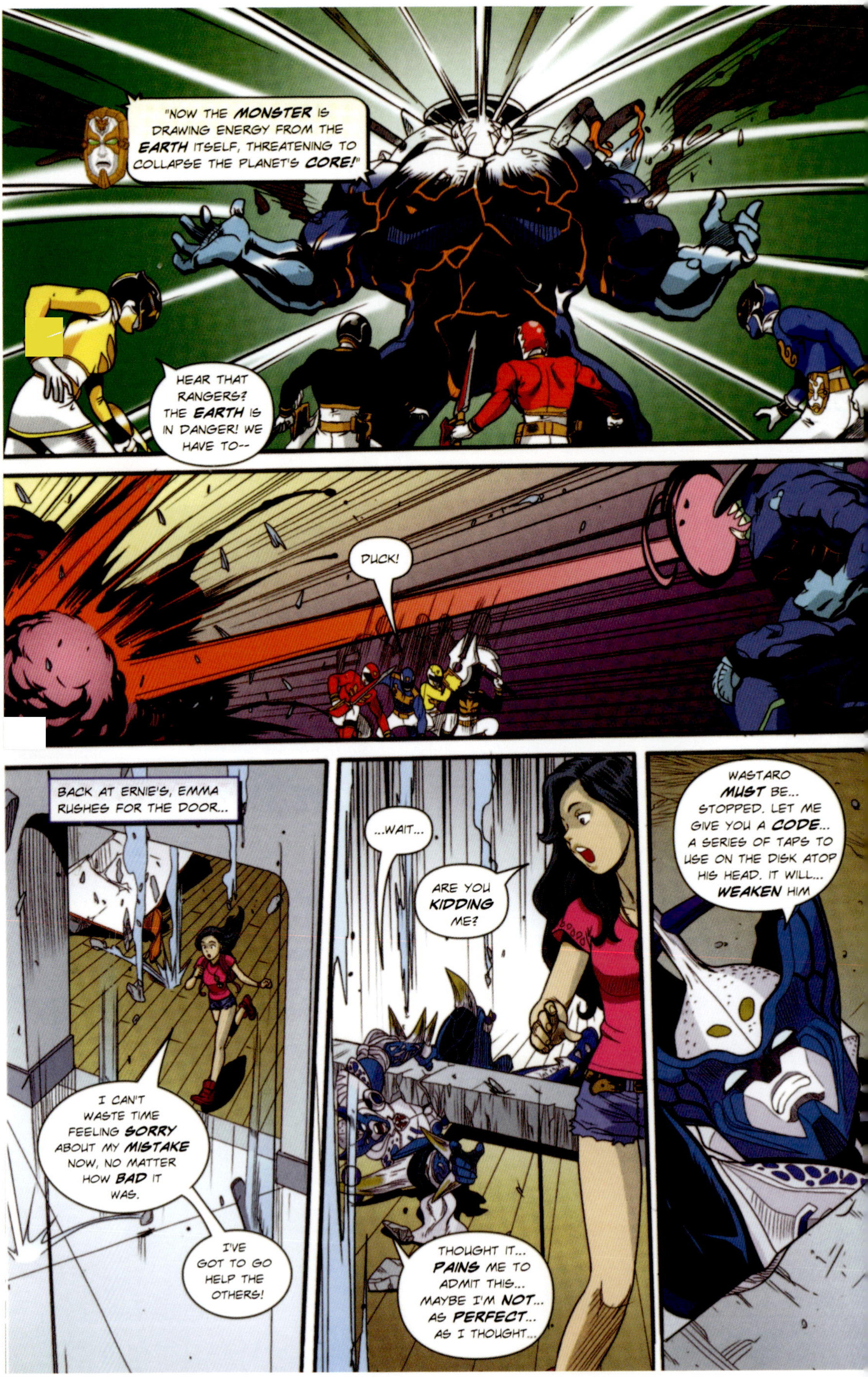
"NOW THE MONSTER IS DRAWING ENERGY FROM THE EARTH ITSELF, THREATENING TO COLLAPSE THE PLANET'S CORE!"
HEAR THAT RANGERS? THE EARTH IS IN DANGER! WE HAVE TO--
DUCK!
BACK AT ERNIE'S, EMMA RUSHES FOR THE DOOR...
I CAN'T WASTE TIME FEELING SORRY ABOUT MY MISTAKE NOW, NO MATTER HOW BAD IT WAS.
I'VE GOT TO GO HELP THE OTHERS!
...WAIT...
ARE YOU KIDDING ME?
THOUGHT IT... PAINS ME TO ADMIT THIS... MAYBE I'M NOT... AS PERFECT... AS I THOUGHT...
WASTARO MUST BE... STOPPED. LET ME GIVE YOU A CODE... A SERIES OF TAPS TO USE ON THE DISK ATOP HIS HEAD. IT WILL... WEAKEN HIM

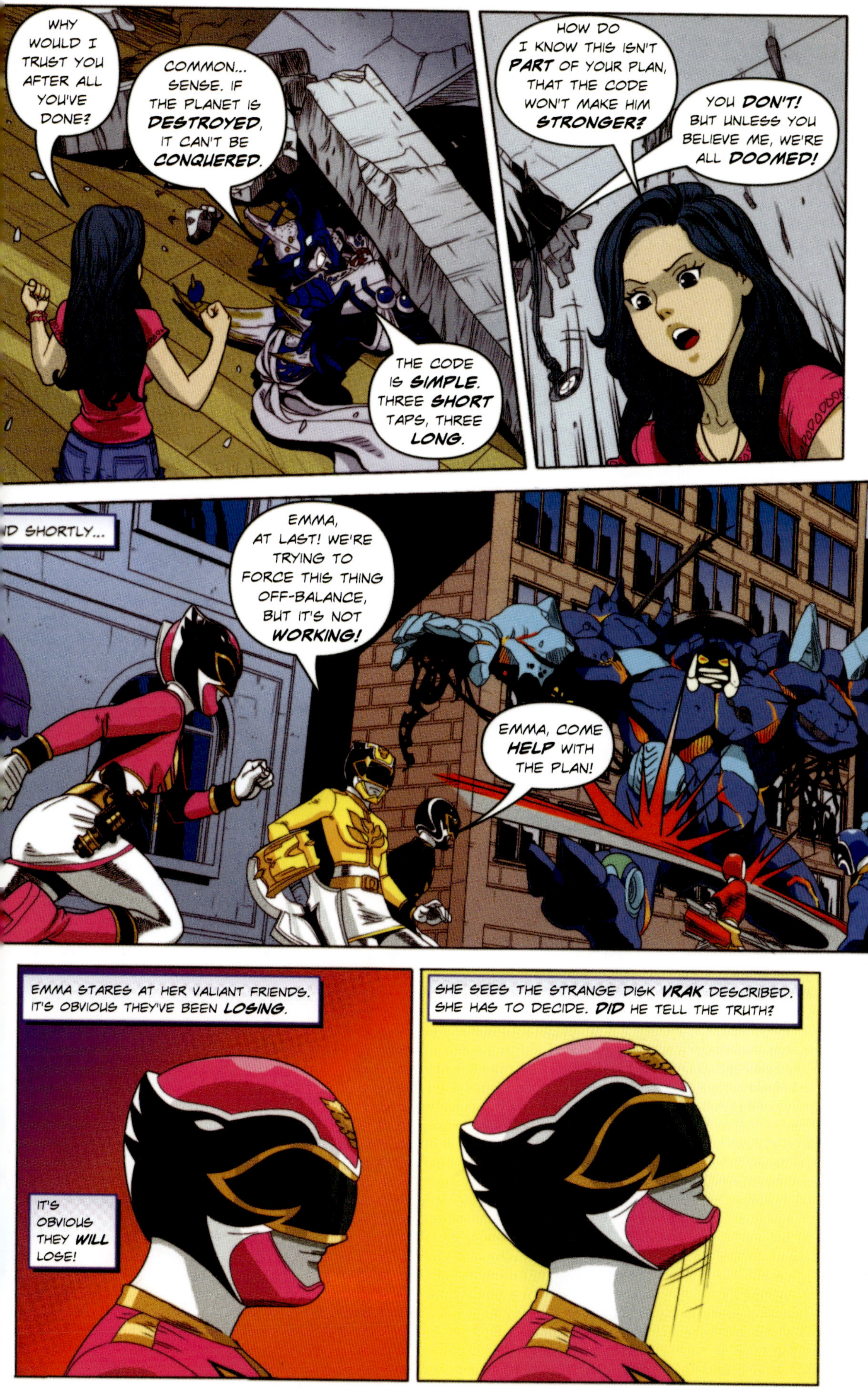
WHY WOULD I TRUST YOU AFTER ALL YOU'VE DONE?
COMMON... SENSE. IF THE PLANET IS DESTROYED, IT CAN'T BE CONQUERED.
THE CODE IS SIMPLE. THREE SHORT TAPS, THREE LONG.
HOW DO I KNOW THIS ISN'T PART OF YOUR PLAN, THAT THE CODE WON'T MAKE HIM STRONGER?
YOU DON'T! BUT UNLESS YOU BELIEVE ME, WE'RE ALL DOOMED!
D SHORTLY...
EMMA, AT LAST! WE'RE TRYING TO FORCE THIS THING OFF-BALANCE, BUT IT'S NOT WORKING!
EMMA, COME HELP WITH THE PLAN!
EMMA STARES AT HER VALIANT FRIENDS. IT'S OBVIOUS THEY'VE BEEN LOSING.
IT'S OBVIOUS THEY WILL LOSE!
SHE SEES THE STRANGE DISK VRAK DESCRIBED. SHE HAS TO DECIDE. DID HE TELL THE TRUTH?

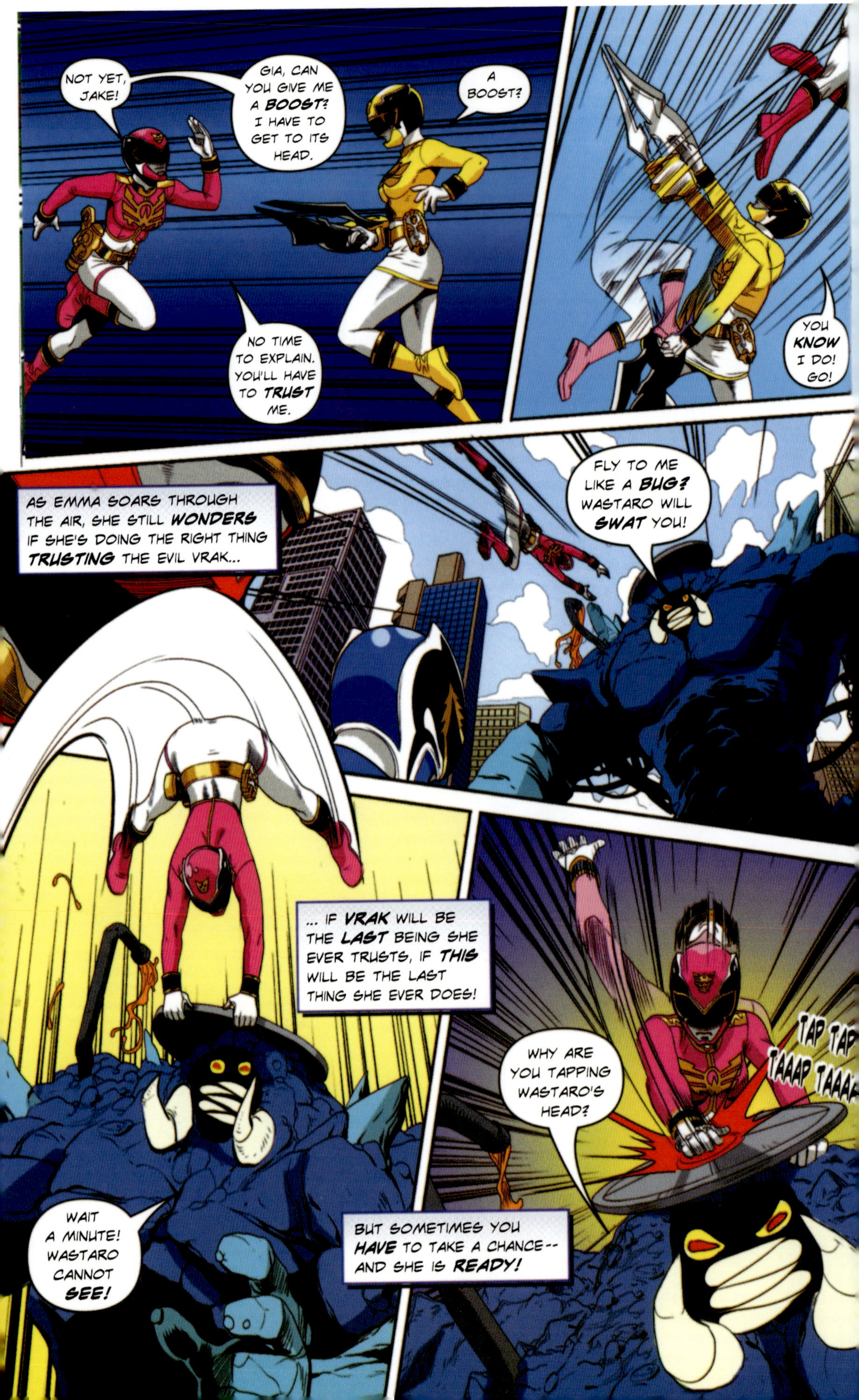
NOT YET, JAKE!
GIA, CAN YOU GIVE ME A BOOST? I HAVE TO GET TO ITS HEAD.
A BOOST?
NO TIME TO EXPLAIN. YOU'LL HAVE TO TRUST ME.
YOU KNOW I DO! GO!
AS EMMA SOARS THROUGH THE AIR, SHE STILL WONDERS IF SHE'S DOING THE RIGHT THING TRUSTING THE EVIL VRAK...
FLY TO ME LIKE A BUG? WASTARO WILL SWAT YOU!
... IF VRAK WILL BE THE LAST BEING SHE EVER TRUSTS, IF THIS WILL BE THE LAST THING SHE EVER DOES!
WAIT A MINUTE! WASTARO CANNOT SEE!
BUT SOMETIMES YOU HAVE TO TAKE A CHANCE-- AND SHE IS READY!
WHY ARE YOU TAPPING WASTARO'S HEAD?
TAP TAP TAAAP TAAA

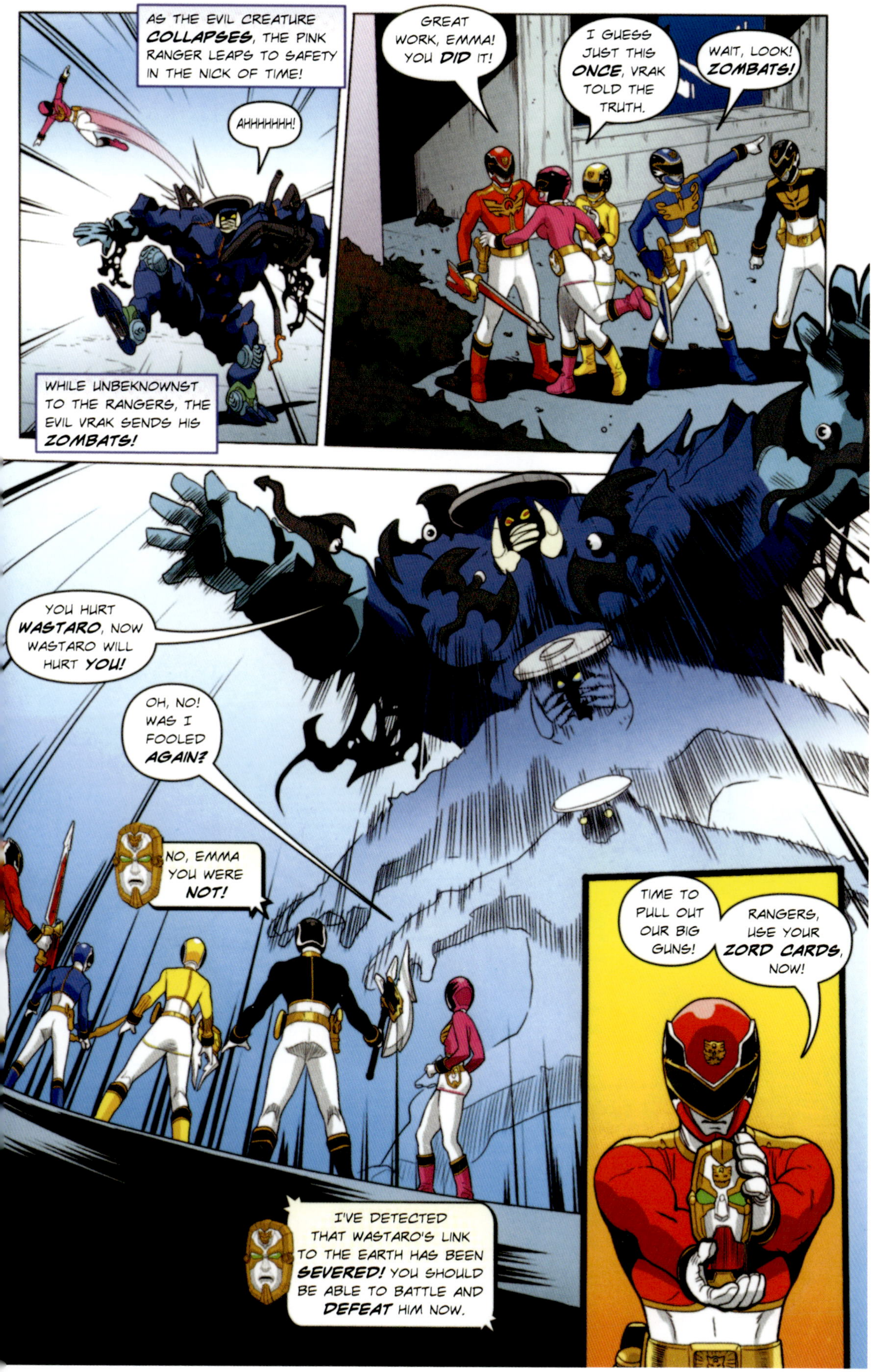
AS THE EVIL CREATURE COLLAPSES, THE PINK RANGER LEAPS TO SAFETY IN THE NICK OF TIME!
AHHHHHHH!
WHILE UNBEKNOWNST TO THE RANGERS, THE EVIL VRAK SENDS HIS ZOMBATS!
GREAT WORK, EMMA! YOU DID IT!
I GUESS JUST THIS ONCE, VRAK TOLD THE TRUTH.
WAIT, LOOK! ZOMBATS!
YOU HURT WASTARO, NOW WASTARO WILL HURT YOU!
OH, NO! WAS I FOOLED AGAIN?
NO, EMMA YOU WERE NOT!
I'VE DETECTED THAT WASTARO'S LINK TO THE EARTH HAS BEEN SEVERED! YOU SHOULD BE ABLE TO BATTLE AND DEFEAT HIM NOW.
TIME TO PULL OUT OUR BIG GUNS!
RANGERS, USE YOUR ZORD CARDS, NOW!

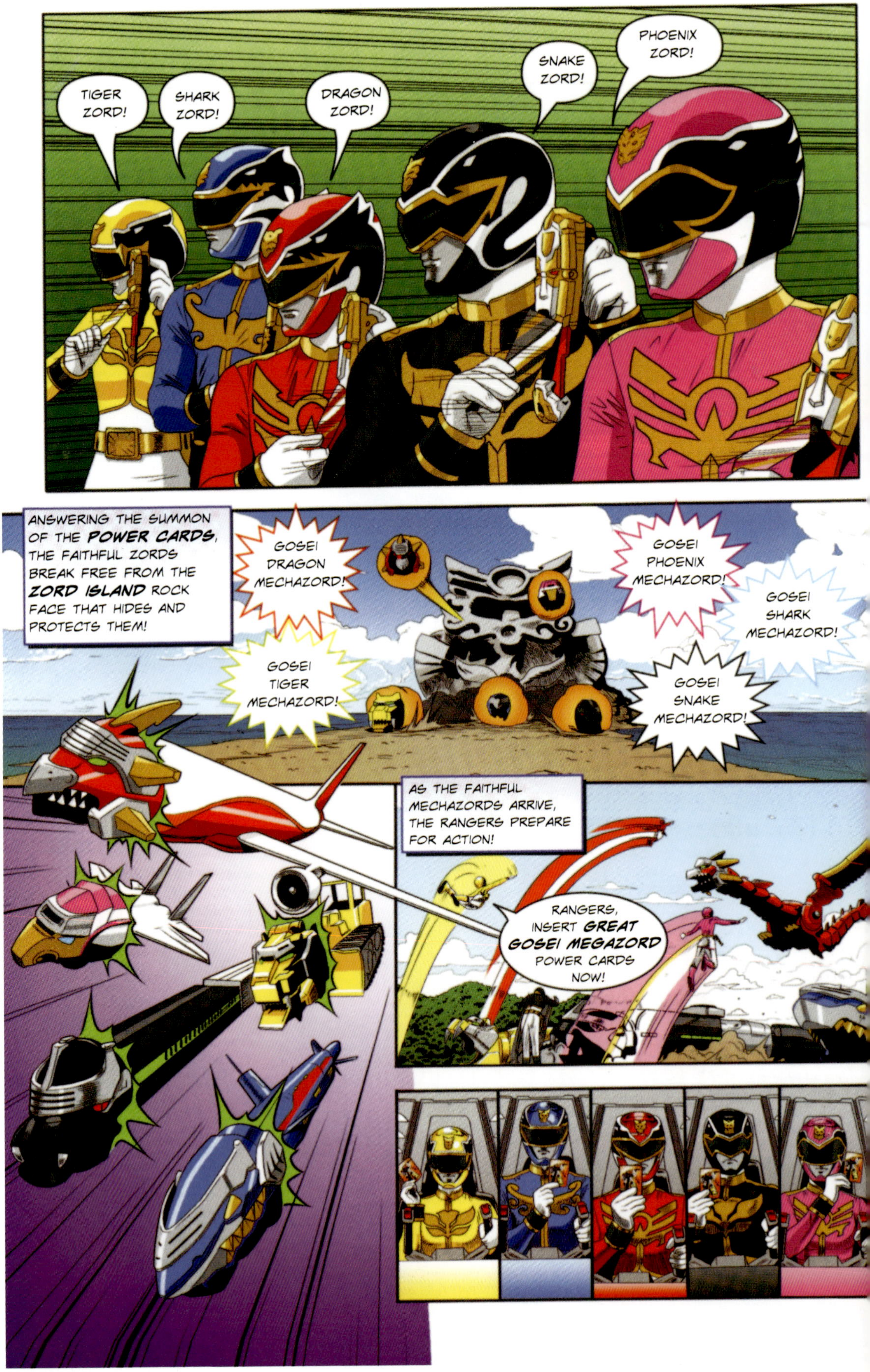
TIGER ZORD!
SHARK ZORD!
DRAGON ZORD!
SNAKE ZORD!
PHOENIX ZORD!
ANSWERING THE SUMMON OF THE **POWER CARDS**, THE FAITHFUL ZORDS BREAK FREE FROM THE **ZORD ISLAND** ROCK FACE THAT HIDES AND PROTECTS THEM!
GOSEI DRAGON MECHAZORD!
GOSEI TIGER MECHAZORD!
GOSEI PHOENIX MECHAZORD!
GOSEI SHARK MECHAZORD!
GOSEI SNAKE MECHAZORD!
AS THE FAITHFUL MECHAZORDS ARRIVE, THE RANGERS PREPARE FOR ACTION!
RANGERS, INSERT **GREAT GOSEI MEGAZORD** POWER CARDS NOW!

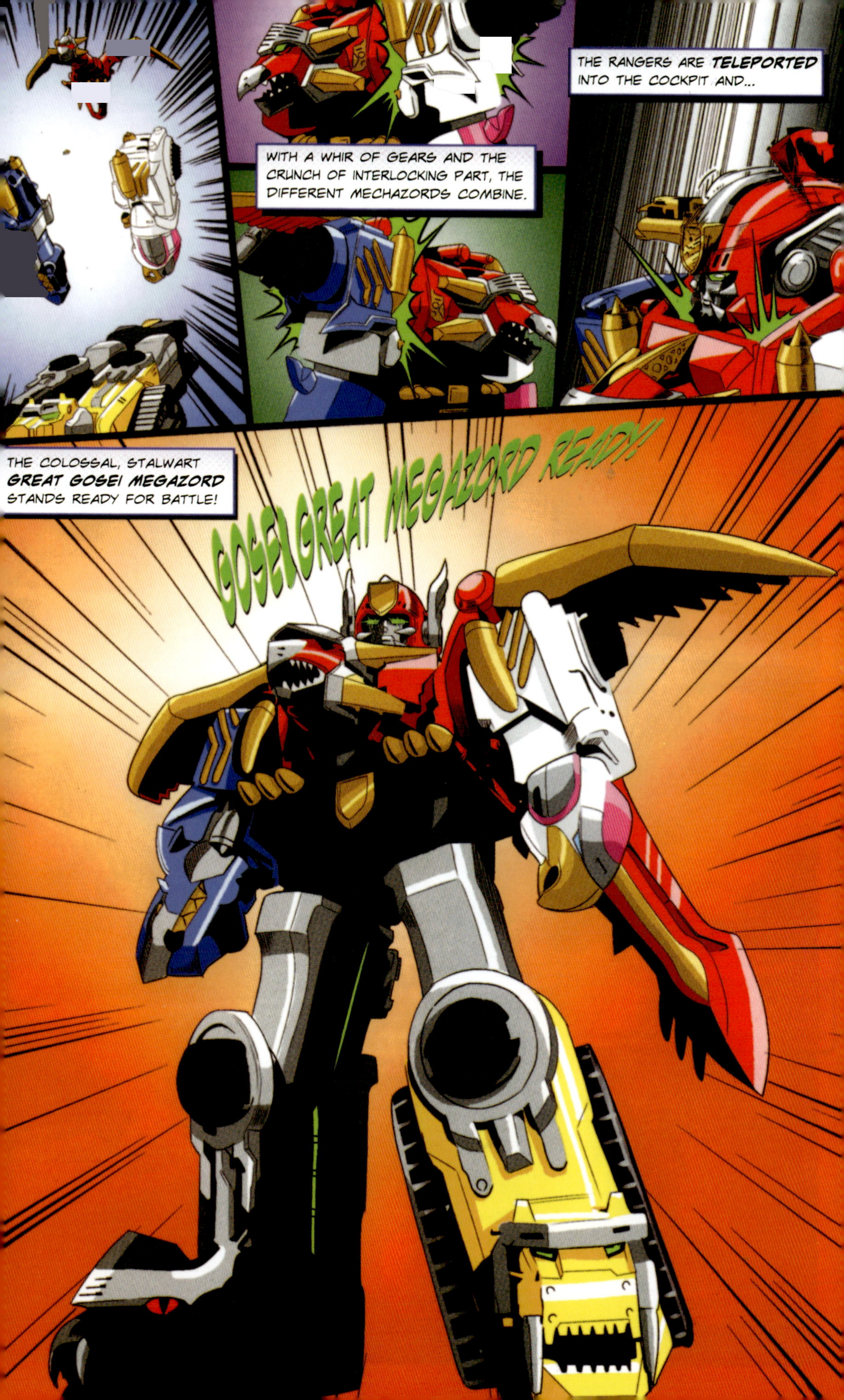
WITH A WHIR OF GEARS AND THE CRUNCH OF INTERLOCKING PART, THE DIFFERENT MECHAZORDS COMBINE.
THE RANGERS ARE TELEPORTED INTO THE COCKPIT AND...
THE COLOSSAL, STALWART GREAT GOSEI MEGAZORD STANDS READY FOR BATTLE!
GOSEI GREAT MEGAZORD READY!

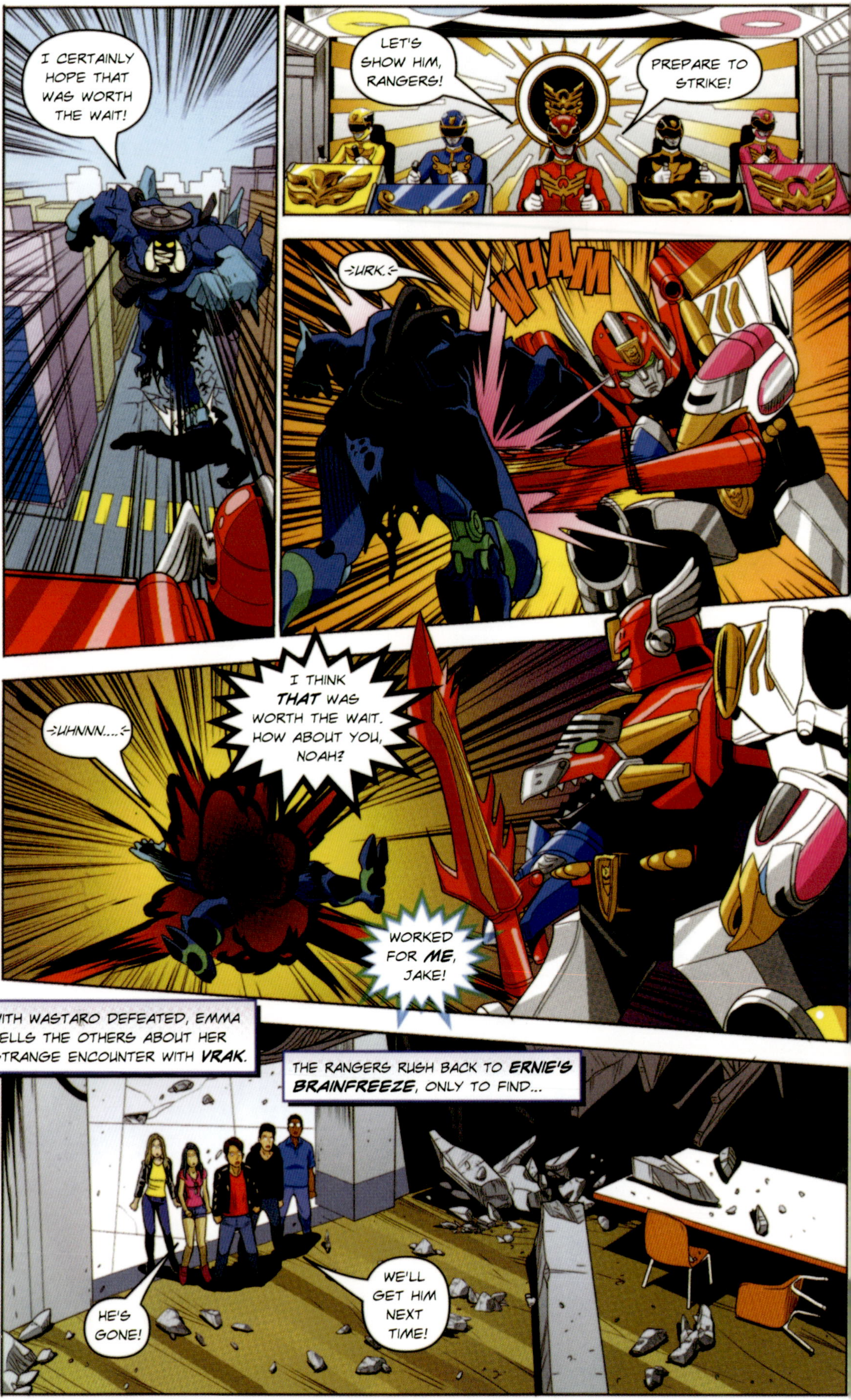
I CERTAINLY HOPE THAT WAS WORTH THE WAIT!
LET'S SHOW HIM, RANGERS!
PREPARE TO STRIKE!
URK.
WHAM
I THINK THAT WAS WORTH THE WAIT. HOW ABOUT YOU, NOAH?
UHNNN....
WORKED FOR ME, JAKE!
WITH WASTARO DEFEATED, EMMA TELLS THE OTHERS ABOUT HER STRANGE ENCOUNTER WITH VRAK.
THE RANGERS RUSH BACK TO ERNIE'S BRAINFREEZE, ONLY TO FIND...
HE'S GONE!
WE'LL GET HIM NEXT TIME!

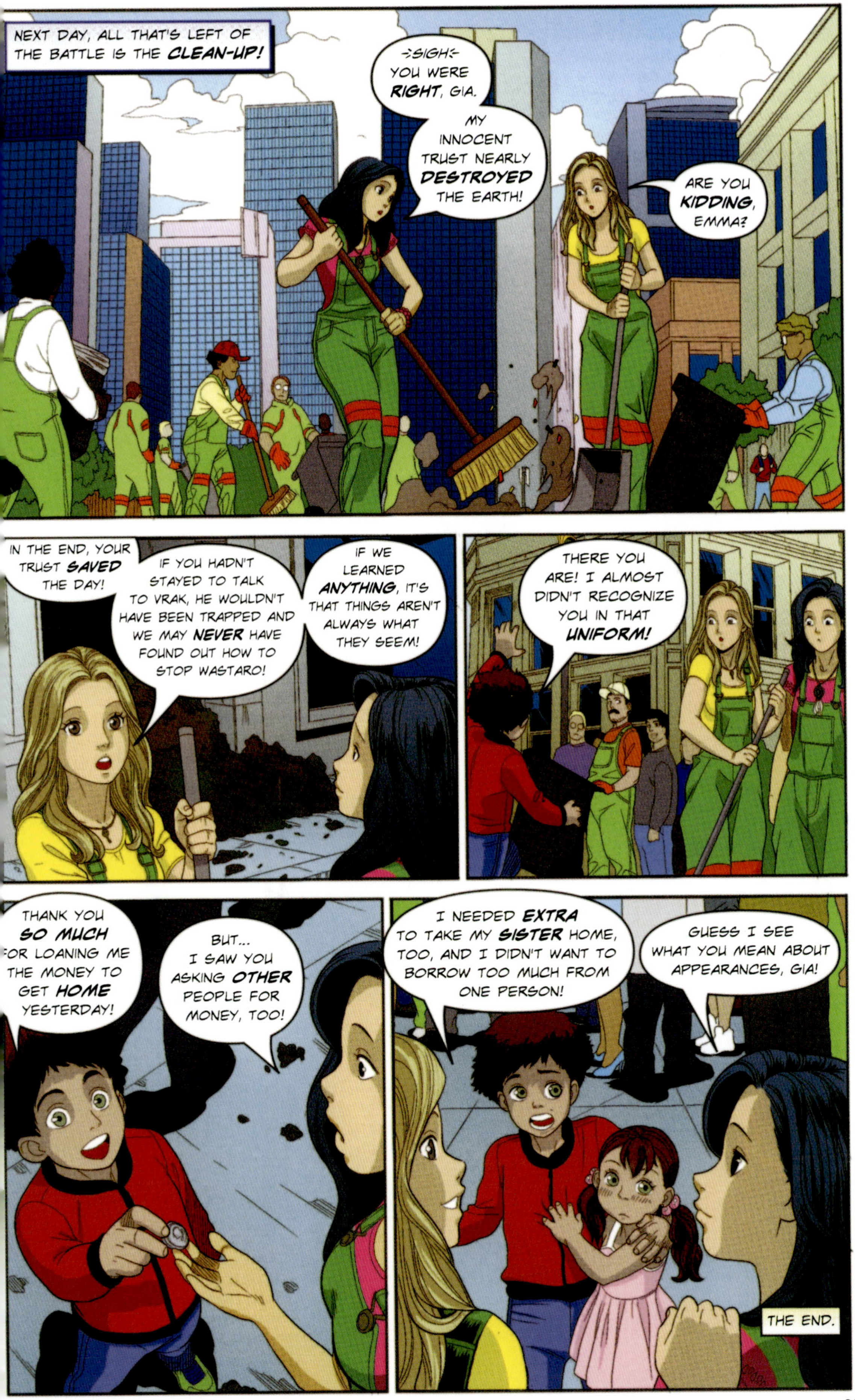
NEXT DAY, ALL THAT'S LEFT OF THE BATTLE IS THE CLEAN-UP!
>SIGH< YOU WERE RIGHT, GIA.
MY INNOCENT TRUST NEARLY DESTROYED THE EARTH!
ARE YOU KIDDING, EMMA?
IN THE END, YOUR TRUST SAVED THE DAY!
IF YOU HADN'T STAYED TO TALK TO VRAK, HE WOULDN'T HAVE BEEN TRAPPED AND WE MAY NEVER HAVE FOUND OUT HOW TO STOP WASTARO!
IF WE LEARNED ANYTHING, IT'S THAT THINGS AREN'T ALWAYS WHAT THEY SEEM!
THERE YOU ARE! I ALMOST DIDN'T RECOGNIZE YOU IN THAT UNIFORM!
THANK YOU SO MUCH FOR LOANING ME THE MONEY TO GET HOME YESTERDAY!
BUT... I SAW YOU ASKING OTHER PEOPLE FOR MONEY, TOO!
I NEEDED EXTRA TO TAKE MY SISTER HOME, TOO, AND I DIDN'T WANT TO BORROW TOO MUCH FROM ONE PERSON!
GUESS I SEE WHAT YOU MEAN ABOUT APPEARANCES, GIA!
THE END.

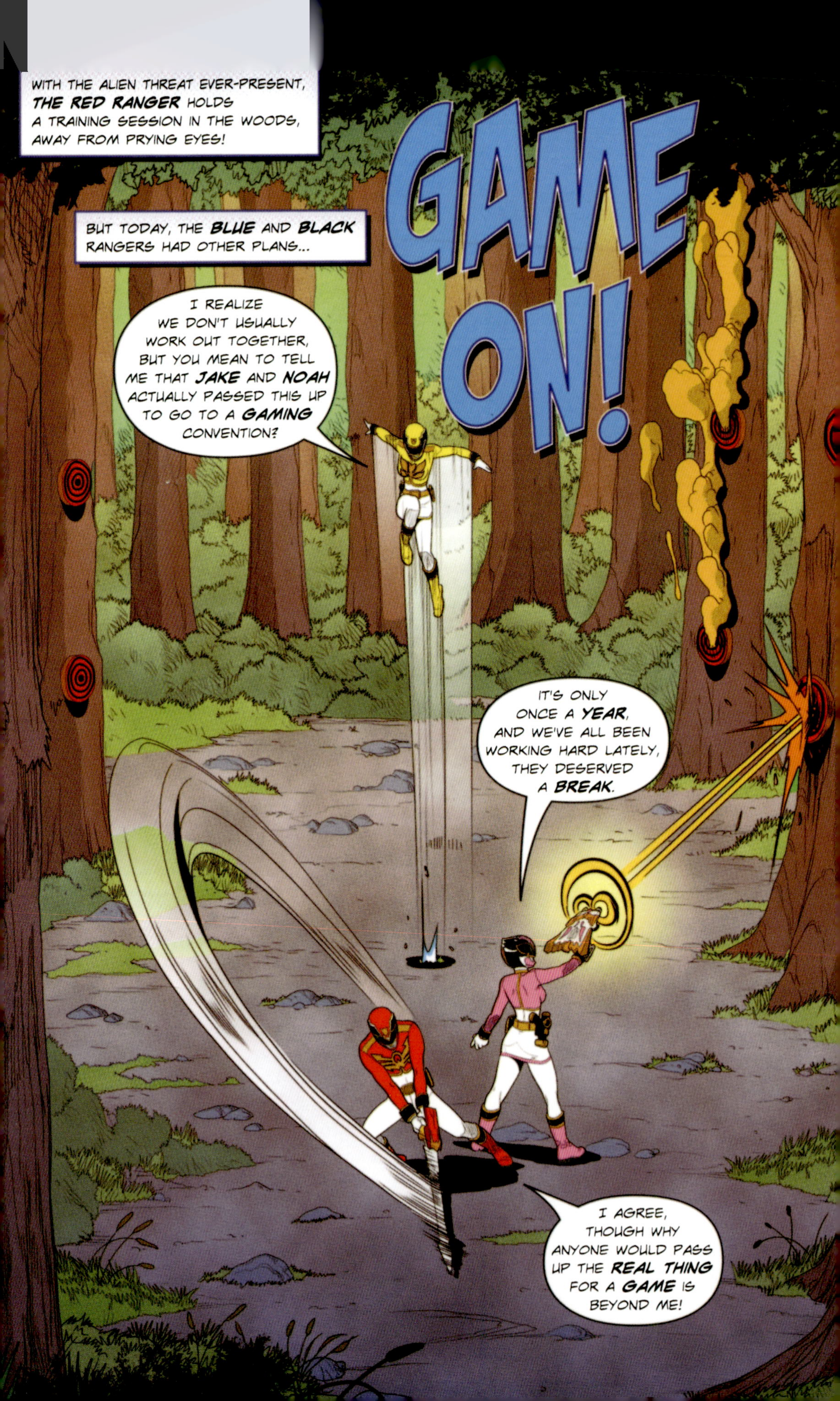

WITH THE ALIEN THREAT EVER-PRESENT, THE RED RANGER HOLDS A TRAINING SESSION IN THE WOODS, AWAY FROM PRYING EYES!
BUT TODAY, THE BLUE AND BLACK RANGERS HAD OTHER PLANS...
GAME ON!
I REALIZE WE DON'T USUALLY WORK OUT TOGETHER, BUT YOU MEAN TO TELL ME THAT JAKE AND NOAH ACTUALLY PASSED THIS UP TO GO TO A GAMING CONVENTION?
IT'S ONLY ONCE A YEAR, AND WE'VE ALL BEEN WORKING HARD LATELY, THEY DESERVED A BREAK.
I AGREE, THOUGH WHY ANYONE WOULD PASS UP THE REAL THING FOR A GAME IS BEYOND ME!

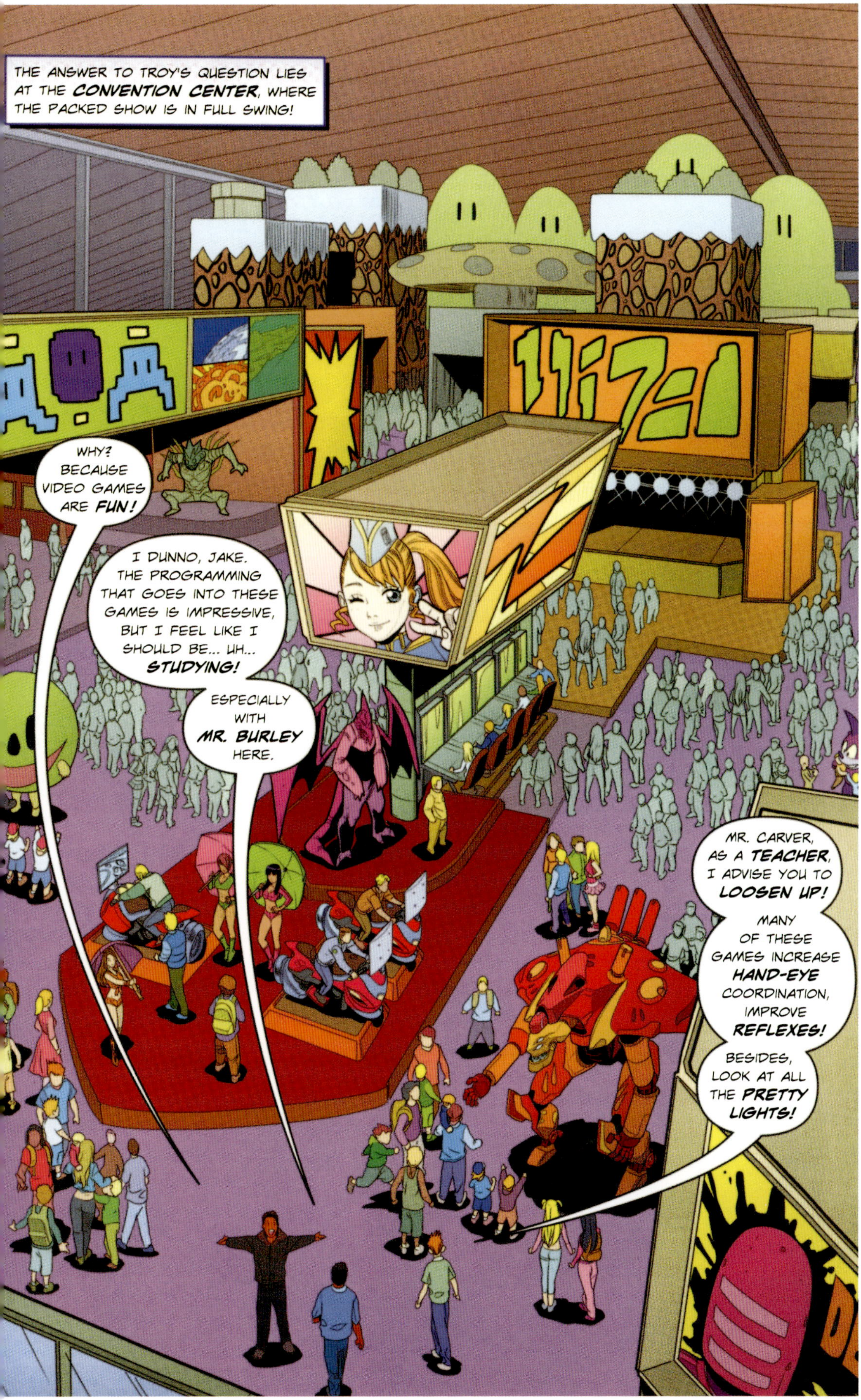

THE ANSWER TO TROY'S QUESTION LIES AT THE CONVENTION CENTER, WHERE THE PACKED SHOW IS IN FULL SWING!
WHY? BECAUSE VIDEO GAMES ARE FUN!
I DUNNO, JAKE. THE PROGRAMMING THAT GOES INTO THESE GAMES IS IMPRESSIVE, BUT I FEEL LIKE I SHOULD BE... UH... STUDYING!
ESPECIALLY WITH MR. BURLEY HERE.
MR. CARVER, AS A TEACHER, I ADVISE YOU TO LOOSEN UP!
MANY OF THESE GAMES INCREASE HAND-EYE COORDINATION, IMPROVE REFLEXES!
BESIDES, LOOK AT ALL THE PRETTY LIGHTS!

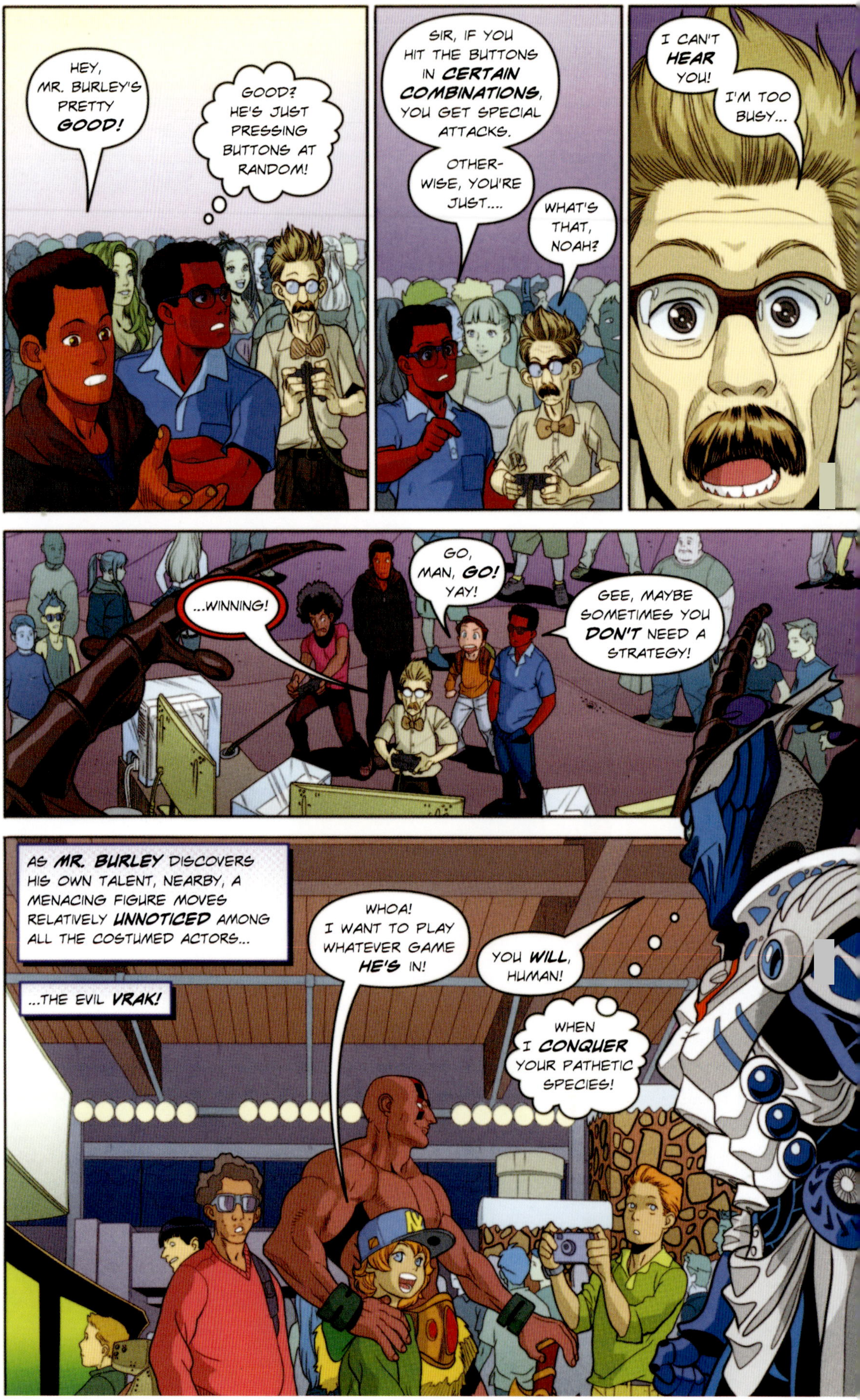
HEY, MR. BURLEY'S PRETTY GOOD!
GOOD? HE'S JUST PRESSING BUTTONS AT RANDOM!
SIR, IF YOU HIT THE BUTTONS IN CERTAIN COMBINATIONS, YOU GET SPECIAL ATTACKS.
OTHER-WISE, YOU'RE JUST....
WHAT'S THAT, NOAH?
I CAN'T HEAR YOU!
I'M TOO BUSY...
...WINNING!
GO, MAN, GO! YAY!
GEE, MAYBE SOMETIMES YOU DON'T NEED A STRATEGY!
AS MR. BURLEY DISCOVERS HIS OWN TALENT, NEARBY, A MENACING FIGURE MOVES RELATIVELY UNNOTICED AMONG ALL THE COSTUMED ACTORS...
...THE EVIL VRAK!
WHOA! I WANT TO PLAY WHATEVER GAME HE'S IN!
YOU WILL, HUMAN!
WHEN I CONQUER YOUR PATHETIC SPECIES!

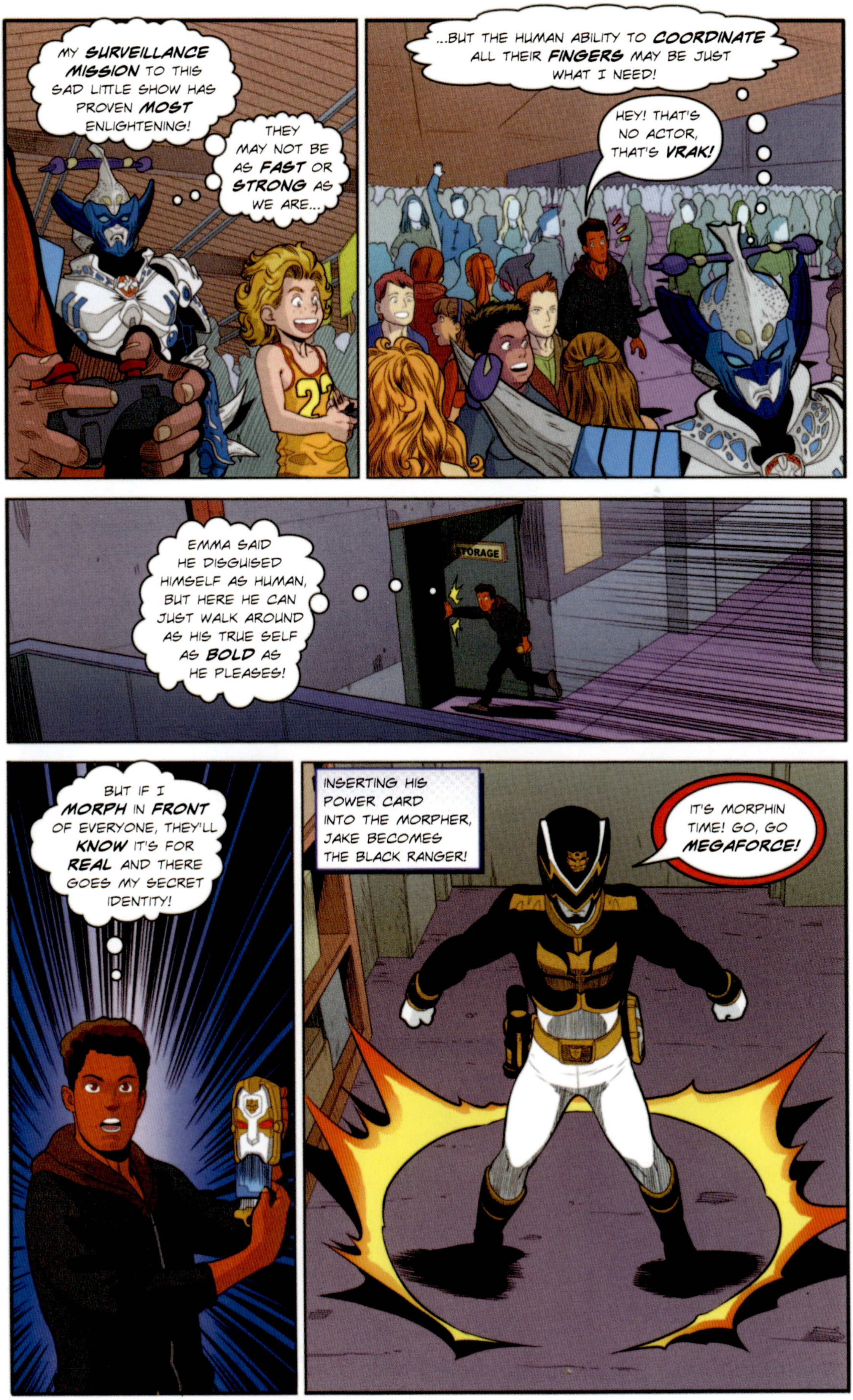
MY SURVEILLANCE MISSION TO THIS SAD LITTLE SHOW HAS PROVEN MOST ENLIGHTENING!
THEY MAY NOT BE AS FAST OR STRONG AS WE ARE...
...BUT THE HUMAN ABILITY TO COORDINATE ALL THEIR FINGERS MAY BE JUST WHAT I NEED!
HEY! THAT'S NO ACTOR, THAT'S VRAK!
STORAGE
EMMA SAID HE DISGUISED HIMSELF AS HUMAN, BUT HERE HE CAN JUST WALK AROUND AS HIS TRUE SELF AS BOLD AS HE PLEASES!
BUT IF I MORPH IN FRONT OF EVERYONE, THEY'LL KNOW IT'S FOR REAL AND THERE GOES MY SECRET IDENTITY!
INSERTING HIS POWER CARD INTO THE MORPHER, JAKE BECOMES THE BLACK RANGER!
IT'S MORPHIN TIME! GO, GO MEGAFORCE!

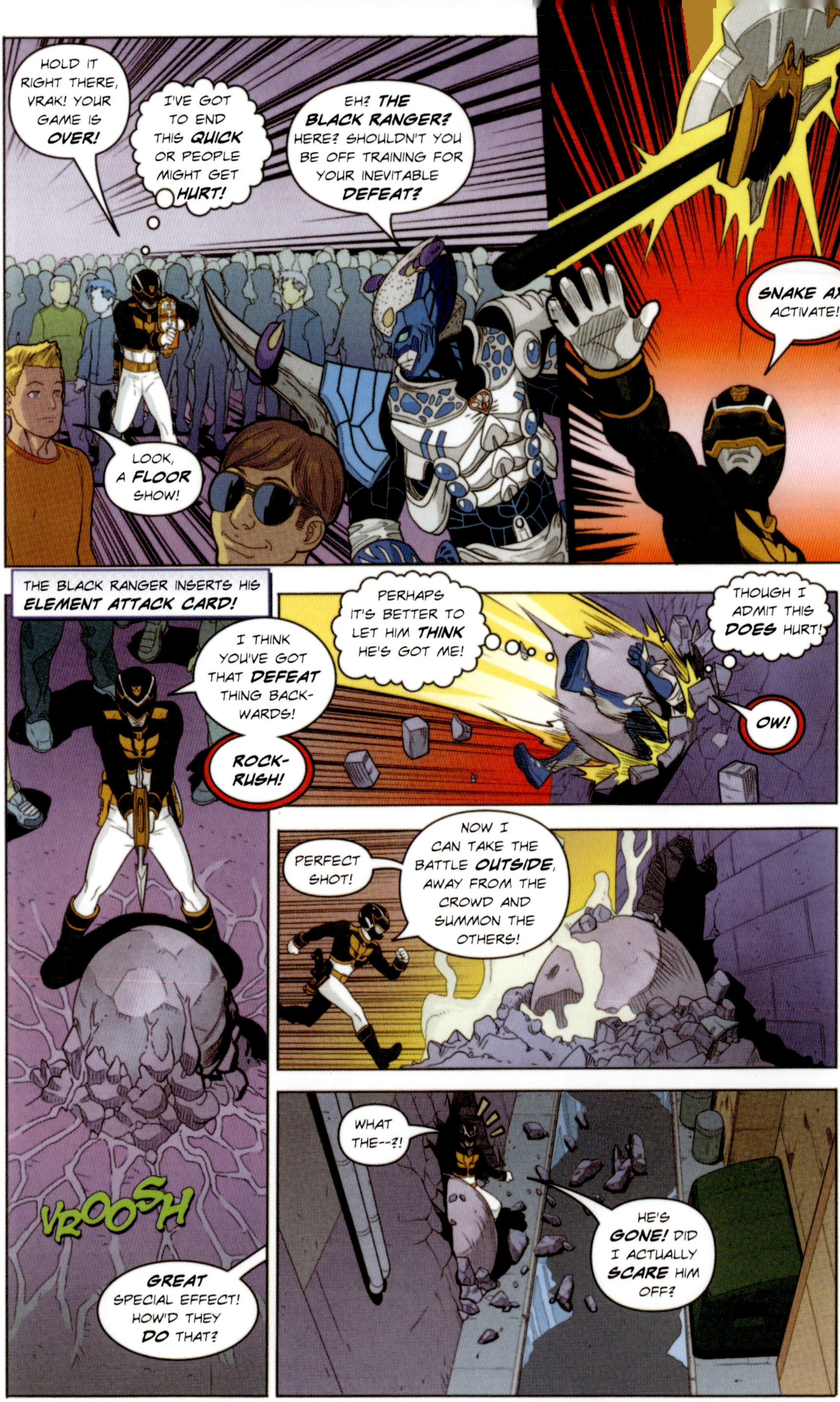

HOLD IT RIGHT THERE, VRAK! YOUR GAME IS OVER!
I'VE GOT TO END THIS QUICK OR PEOPLE MIGHT GET HURT!
EH? THE BLACK RANGER? HERE? SHOULDN'T YOU BE OFF TRAINING FOR YOUR INEVITABLE DEFEAT?
LOOK, A FLOOR SHOW!
SNAKE AX ACTIVATE!
THE BLACK RANGER INSERTS HIS ELEMENT ATTACK CARD!
I THINK YOU'VE GOT THAT DEFEAT THING BACK-WARDS!
ROCK-RUSH!
VROOSH
GREAT SPECIAL EFFECT! HOW'D THEY DO THAT?
PERHAPS IT'S BETTER TO LET HIM THINK HE'S GOT ME!
THOUGH I ADMIT THIS DOES HURT!
OW!
PERFECT SHOT!
NOW I CAN TAKE THE BATTLE OUTSIDE, AWAY FROM THE CROWD AND SUMMON THE OTHERS!
WHAT THE--?!
HE'S GONE! DID I ACTUALLY SCARE HIM OFF?

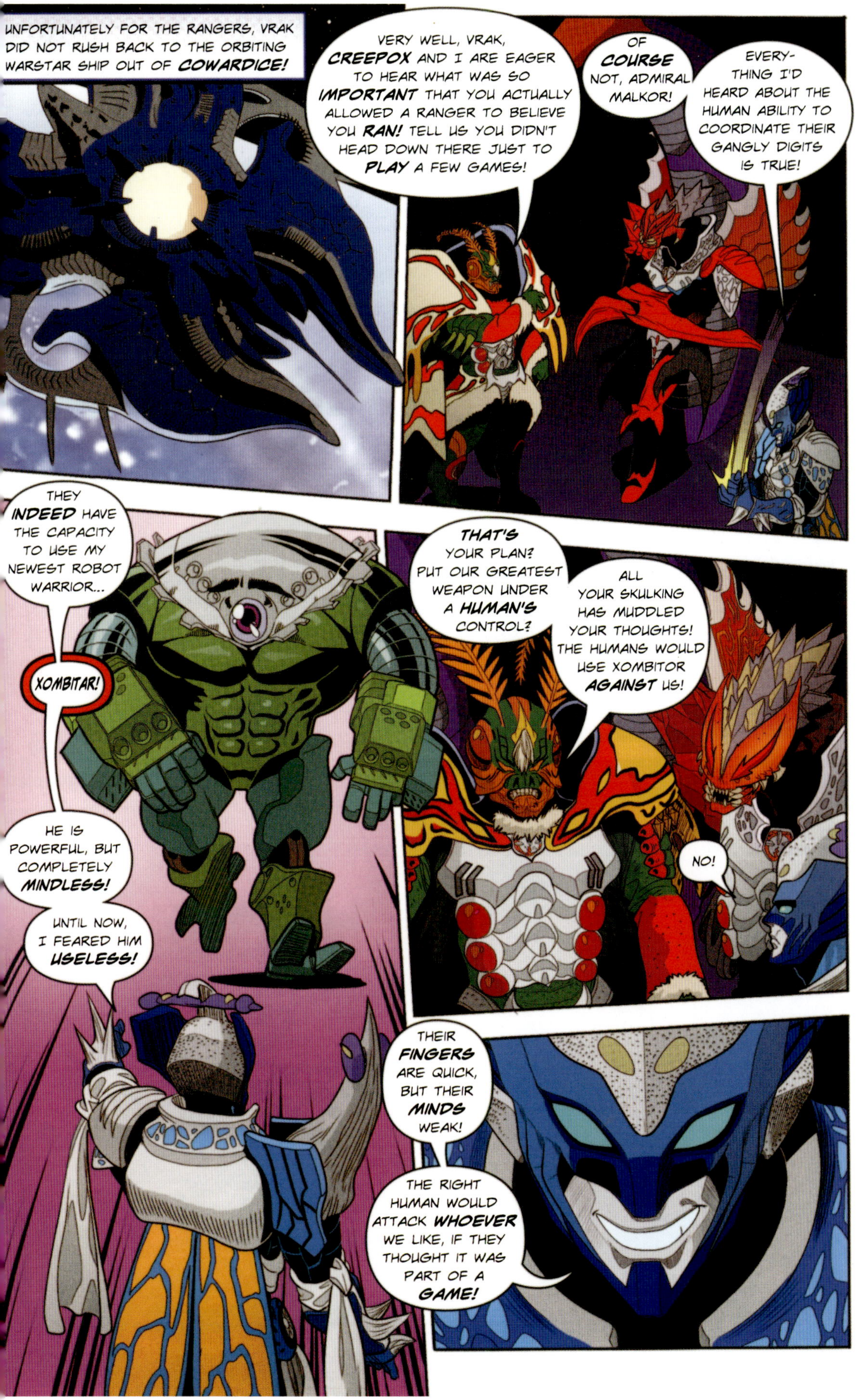
UNFORTUNATELY FOR THE RANGERS, VRAK DID NOT RUSH BACK TO THE ORBITING WARSTAR SHIP OUT OF COWARDICE!
VERY WELL, VRAK, CREEPOX AND I ARE EAGER TO HEAR WHAT WAS SO IMPORTANT THAT YOU ACTUALLY ALLOWED A RANGER TO BELIEVE YOU RAN! TELL US YOU DIDN'T HEAD DOWN THERE JUST TO PLAY A FEW GAMES!
OF COURSE NOT, ADMIRAL MALKOR!
EVERY-THING I'D HEARD ABOUT THE HUMAN ABILITY TO COORDINATE THEIR GANGLY DIGITS IS TRUE!
THEY INDEED HAVE THE CAPACITY TO USE MY NEWEST ROBOT WARRIOR...
XOMBITAR!
HE IS POWERFUL, BUT COMPLETELY MINDLESS!
UNTIL NOW, I FEARED HIM USELESS!
THAT'S YOUR PLAN? PUT OUR GREATEST WEAPON UNDER A HUMAN'S CONTROL?
ALL YOUR SKULKING HAS MUDDLED YOUR THOUGHTS! THE HUMANS WOULD USE XOMBITOR AGAINST US!
NO!
THEIR FINGERS ARE QUICK, BUT THEIR MINDS WEAK!
THE RIGHT HUMAN WOULD ATTACK WHOEVER WE LIKE, IF THEY THOUGHT IT WAS PART OF A GAME!

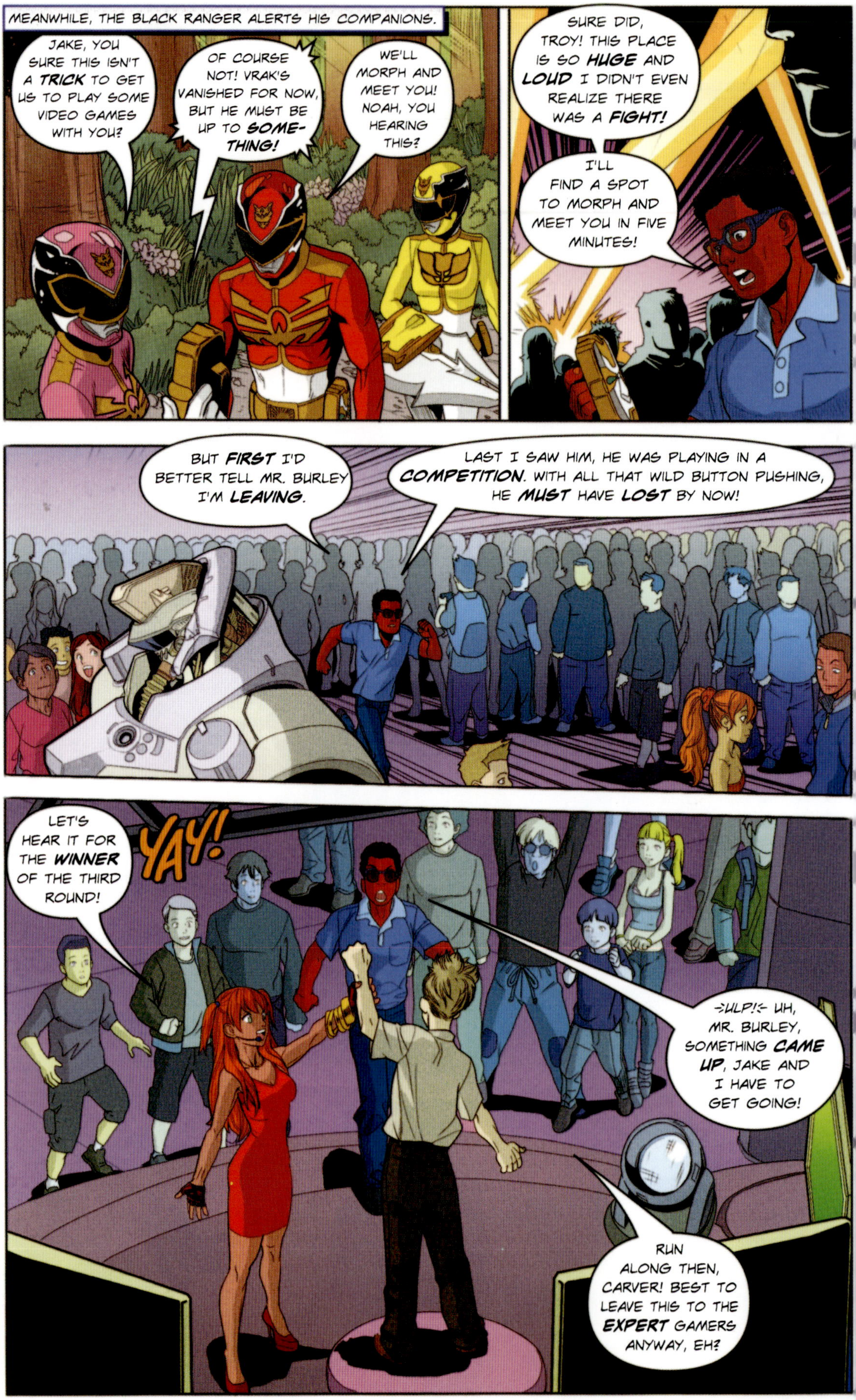
MEANWHILE, THE BLACK RANGER ALERTS HIS COMPANIONS.
JAKE, YOU SURE THIS ISN'T A TRICK TO GET US TO PLAY SOME VIDEO GAMES WITH YOU?
OF COURSE NOT! VRAK'S VANISHED FOR NOW, BUT HE MUST BE UP TO SOME-THING!
WE'LL MORPH AND MEET YOU! NOAH, YOU HEARING THIS?
SURE DID, TROY! THIS PLACE IS SO HUGE AND LOUD I DIDN'T EVEN REALIZE THERE WAS A FIGHT!
I'LL FIND A SPOT TO MORPH AND MEET YOU IN FIVE MINUTES!
BUT FIRST I'D BETTER TELL MR. BURLEY I'M LEAVING.
LAST I SAW HIM, HE WAS PLAYING IN A COMPETITION. WITH ALL THAT WILD BUTTON PUSHING, HE MUST HAVE LOST BY NOW!
LET'S HEAR IT FOR THE WINNER OF THE THIRD ROUND!
YAY!
>ULP!< UH, MR. BURLEY, SOMETHING CAME UP, JAKE AND I HAVE TO GET GOING!
RUN ALONG THEN, CARVER! BEST TO LEAVE THIS TO THE EXPERT GAMERS ANYWAY, EH?

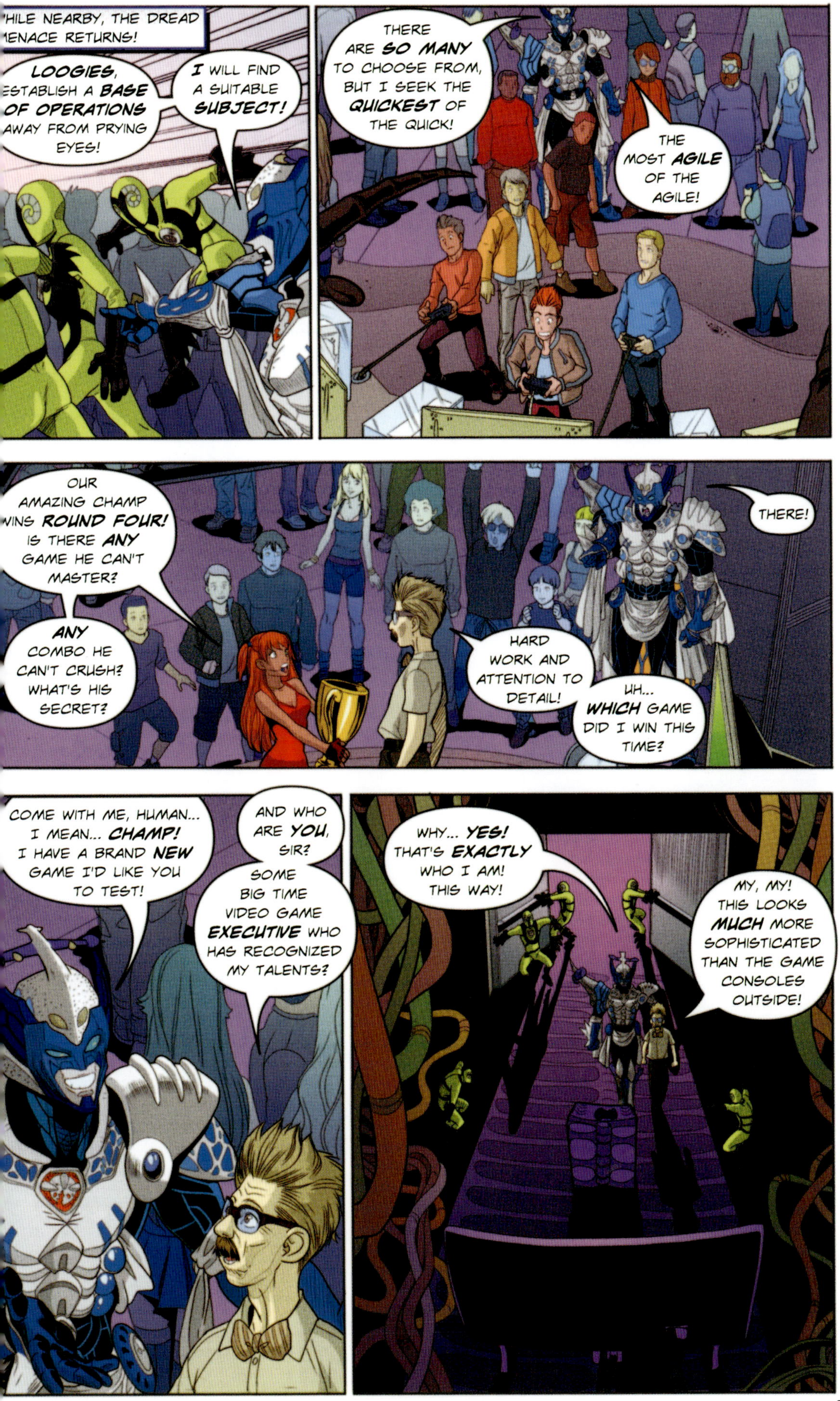

'HILE NEARBY, THE DREAD
IENACE RETURNS!
LOOGIES, ESTABLISH A BASE OF OPERATIONS AWAY FROM PRYING EYES!
I WILL FIND A SUITABLE SUBJECT!
THERE ARE SO MANY TO CHOOSE FROM, BUT I SEEK THE QUICKEST OF THE QUICK!
THE MOST AGILE OF THE AGILE!
OUR AMAZING CHAMP WINS ROUND FOUR! IS THERE ANY GAME HE CAN'T MASTER?
ANY COMBO HE CAN'T CRUSH? WHAT'S HIS SECRET?
HARD WORK AND ATTENTION TO DETAIL!
UH... WHICH GAME DID I WIN THIS TIME?
THERE!
COME WITH ME, HUMAN... I MEAN... CHAMP! I HAVE A BRAND NEW GAME I'D LIKE YOU TO TEST!
AND WHO ARE YOU, SIR?
SOME BIG TIME VIDEO GAME EXECUTIVE WHO HAS RECOGNIZED MY TALENTS?
WHY... YES! THAT'S EXACTLY WHO I AM! THIS WAY!
MY, MY! THIS LOOKS MUCH MORE SOPHISTICATED THAN THE GAME CONSOLES OUTSIDE!

OF **COURSE** IT IS! MY **COMMUNI-CONSOLE** ISN'T MEANT FOR THOSE **MEWLING** MASSES OF HUMANITY!

ER... THAT IS, UNTIL IT'S OFFICIAL RELEASE THIS EARTH-**HOLIDAY** SEASON!

TAKE THE **CONTROLLER**, MAMMAL, AND I WILL EXPLAIN!

IN THIS GAME, YOU CONTROL THE MIGHTY **XOMBITAR!** USING HIS MAGNIFICENT ROBOTIC WEAPONRY, YOU WILL **DECIMATE** THE **POWER RANGERS!**

AHEM. IN THE **"GAME,"** OF COURSE!

THAT LOOKS **JUST LIKE** THE CONVENTION FLOOR!

THANK-YOU! IN ALL THINGS WE STRIVE FOR... **REALISM!**

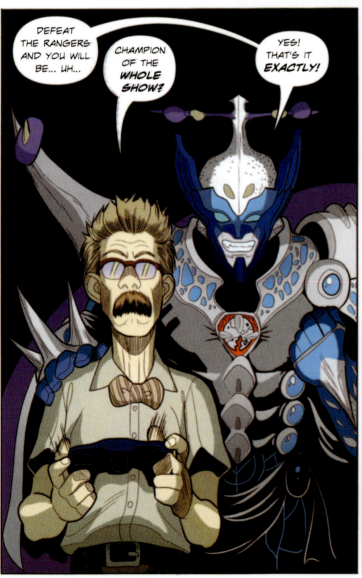

DEFEAT THE RANGERS AND YOU WILL BE... UH...

CHAMPION OF THE **WHOLE SHOW?**

YES! THAT'S IT **EXACTLY!**

THEN LET ME AT THOSE **BUTTONS!**

TIKKA TIKKA TIKKA

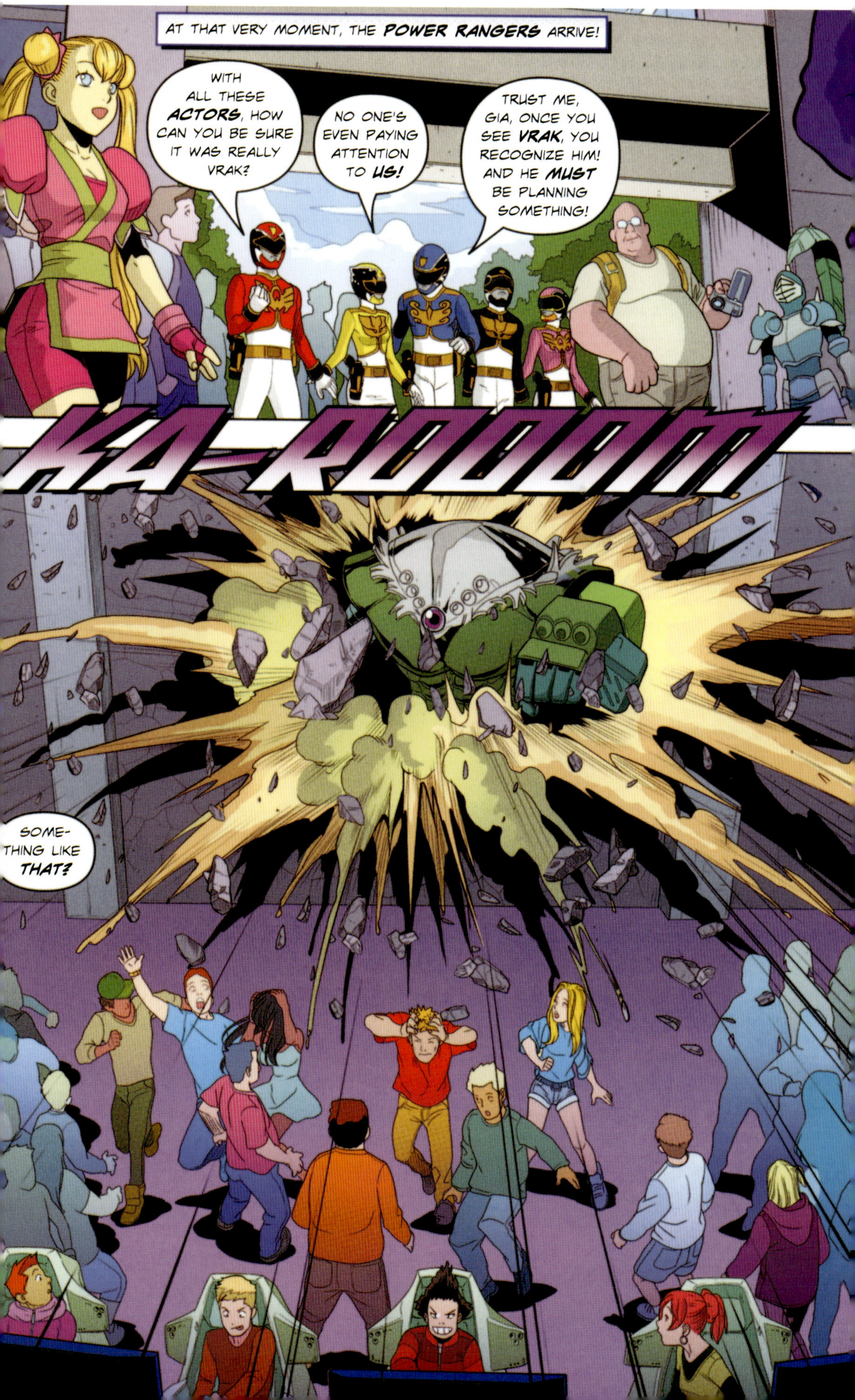
AT THAT VERY MOMENT, THE POWER RANGERS ARRIVE!
WITH ALL THESE ACTORS, HOW CAN YOU BE SURE IT WAS REALLY VRAK?
NO ONE'S EVEN PAYING ATTENTION TO US!
TRUST ME, GIA, ONCE YOU SEE VRAK, YOU RECOGNIZE HIM! AND HE MUST BE PLANNING SOMETHING!
KA-ROOOM
SOME-THING LIKE THAT?

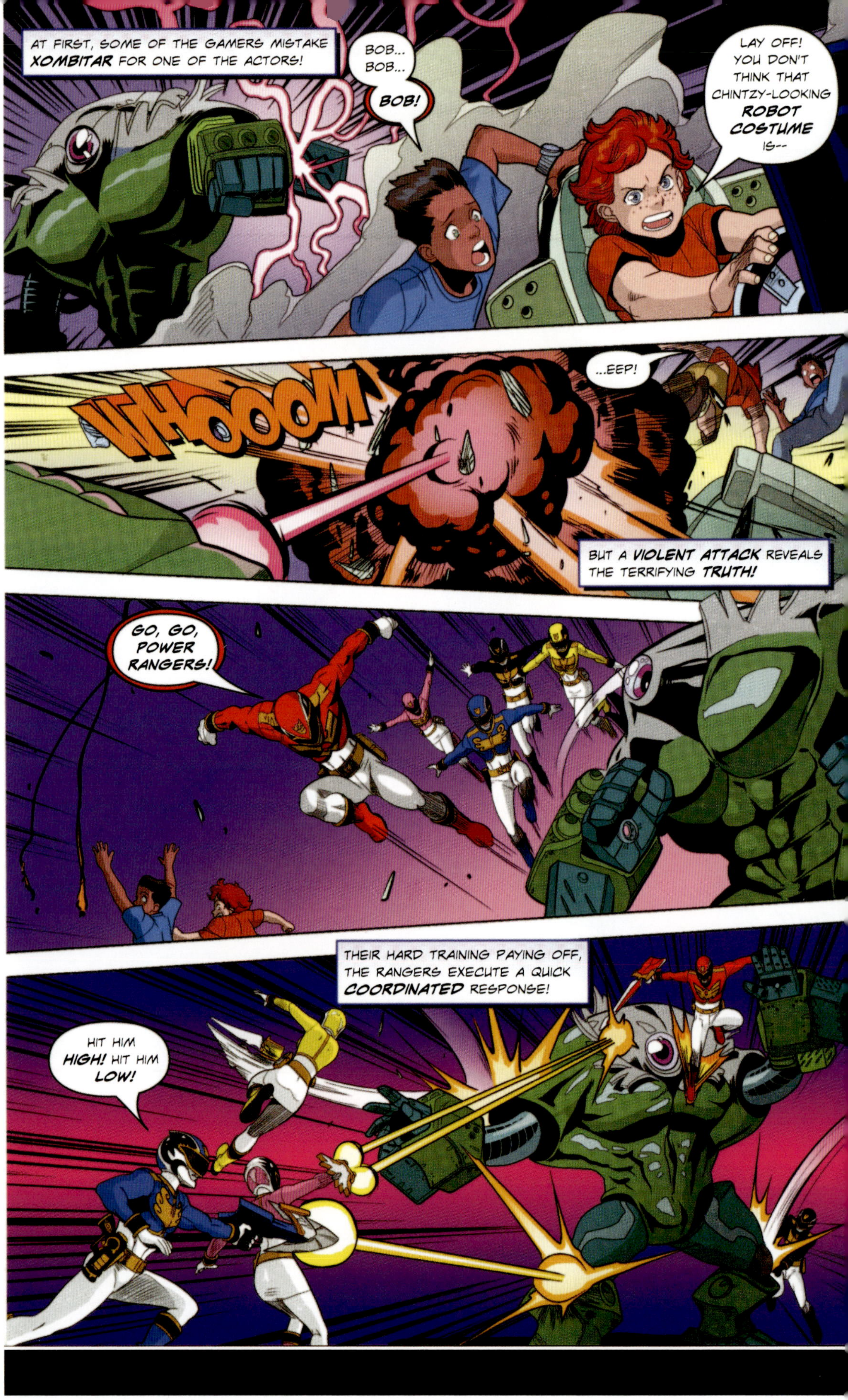
AT FIRST, SOME OF THE GAMERS MISTAKE XOMBITAR FOR ONE OF THE ACTORS!
BOB... BOB...
BOB!
LAY OFF! YOU DON'T THINK THAT CHINTZY-LOOKING ROBOT COSTUME IS--
WHOOOM
...EEP!
BUT A VIOLENT ATTACK REVEALS THE TERRIFYING TRUTH!
GO, GO, POWER RANGERS!
THEIR HARD TRAINING PAYING OFF, THE RANGERS EXECUTE A QUICK COORDINATED RESPONSE!
HIT HIM HIGH! HIT HIM LOW!

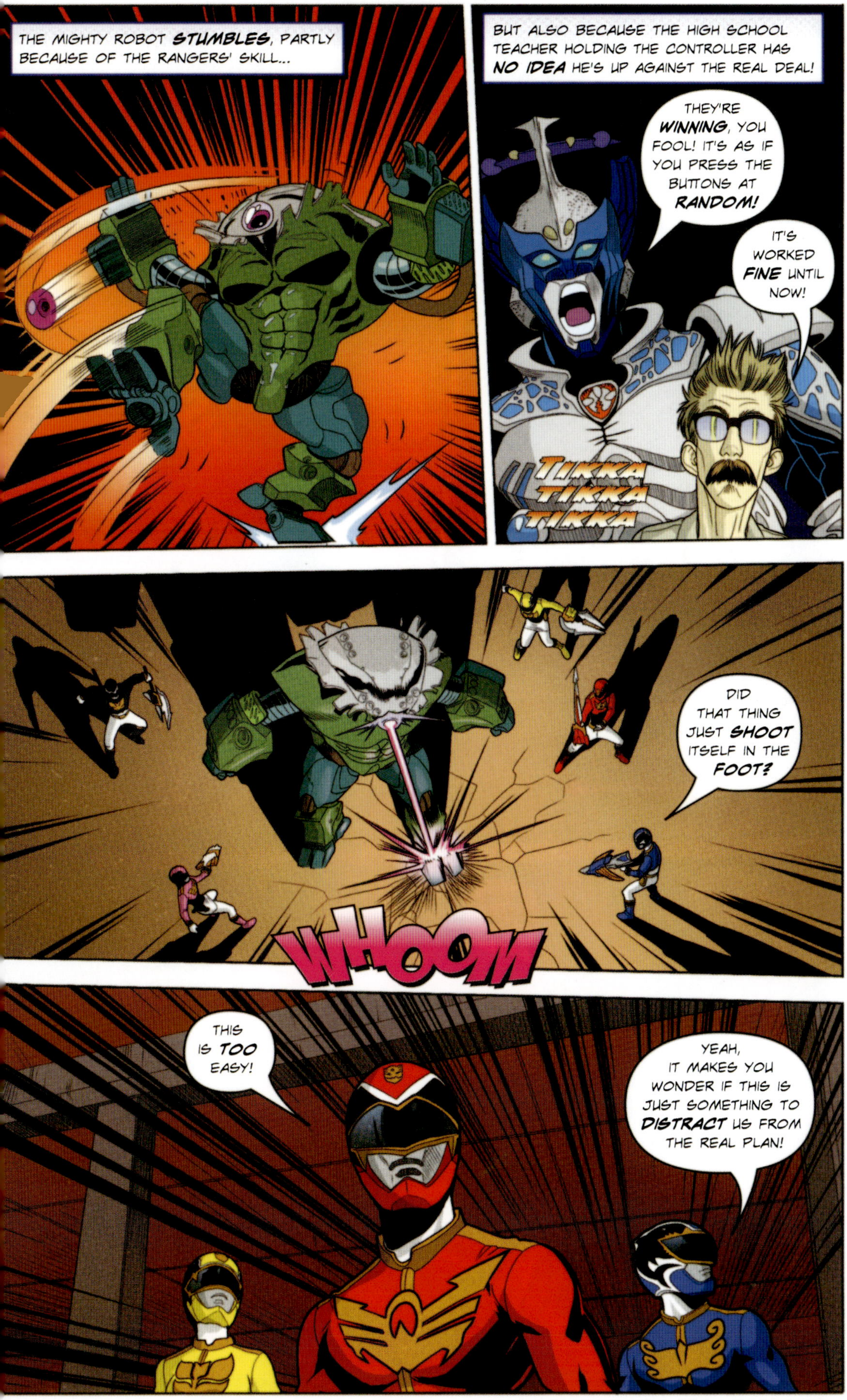
THE MIGHTY ROBOT STUMBLES, PARTLY BECAUSE OF THE RANGERS' SKILL...
BUT ALSO BECAUSE THE HIGH SCHOOL TEACHER HOLDING THE CONTROLLER HAS NO IDEA HE'S UP AGAINST THE REAL DEAL!
THEY'RE WINNING, YOU FOOL! IT'S AS IF YOU PRESS THE BUTTONS AT RANDOM!
IT'S WORKED FINE UNTIL NOW!
TIKKA TIKKA TIKKA
DID THAT THING JUST SHOOT ITSELF IN THE FOOT?
WHOOM
THIS IS TOO EASY!
YEAH, IT MAKES YOU WONDER IF THIS IS JUST SOMETHING TO DISTRACT US FROM THE REAL PLAN!

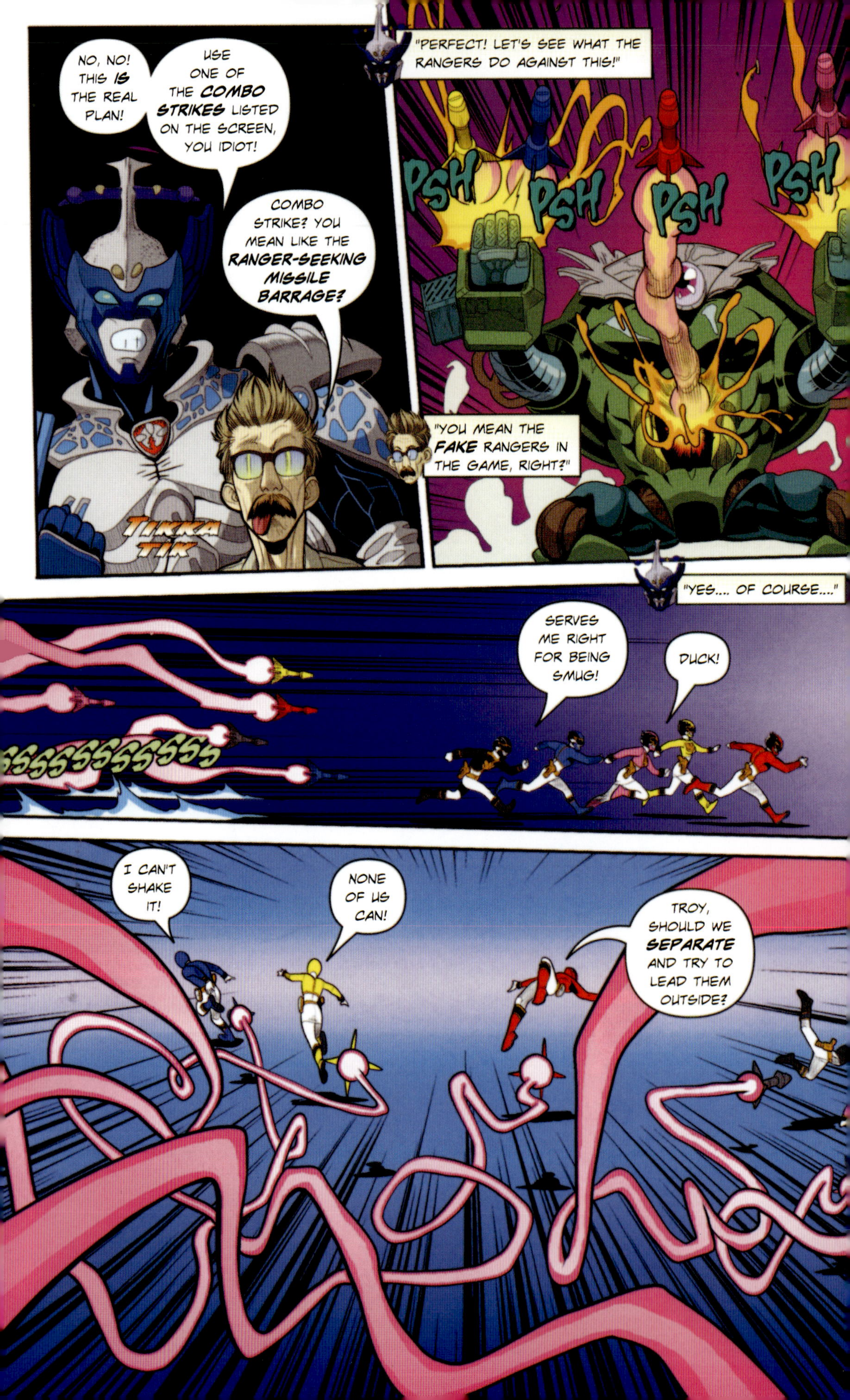
NO, NO! THIS IS THE REAL PLAN!
USE ONE OF THE COMBO STRIKES LISTED ON THE SCREEN, YOU IDIOT!
COMBO STRIKE? YOU MEAN LIKE THE RANGER-SEEKING MISSILE BARRAGE?
TIKKA TIK
"PERFECT! LET'S SEE WHAT THE RANGERS DO AGAINST THIS!"
PSH PSH PSH PSH
"YOU MEAN THE FAKE RANGERS IN THE GAME, RIGHT?"
"YES.... OF COURSE...."
SSSSSSSSSSSS
SERVES ME RIGHT FOR BEING SMUG!
DUCK!
I CAN'T SHAKE IT!
NONE OF US CAN!
TROY, SHOULD WE SEPARATE AND TRY TO LEAD THEM OUTSIDE?

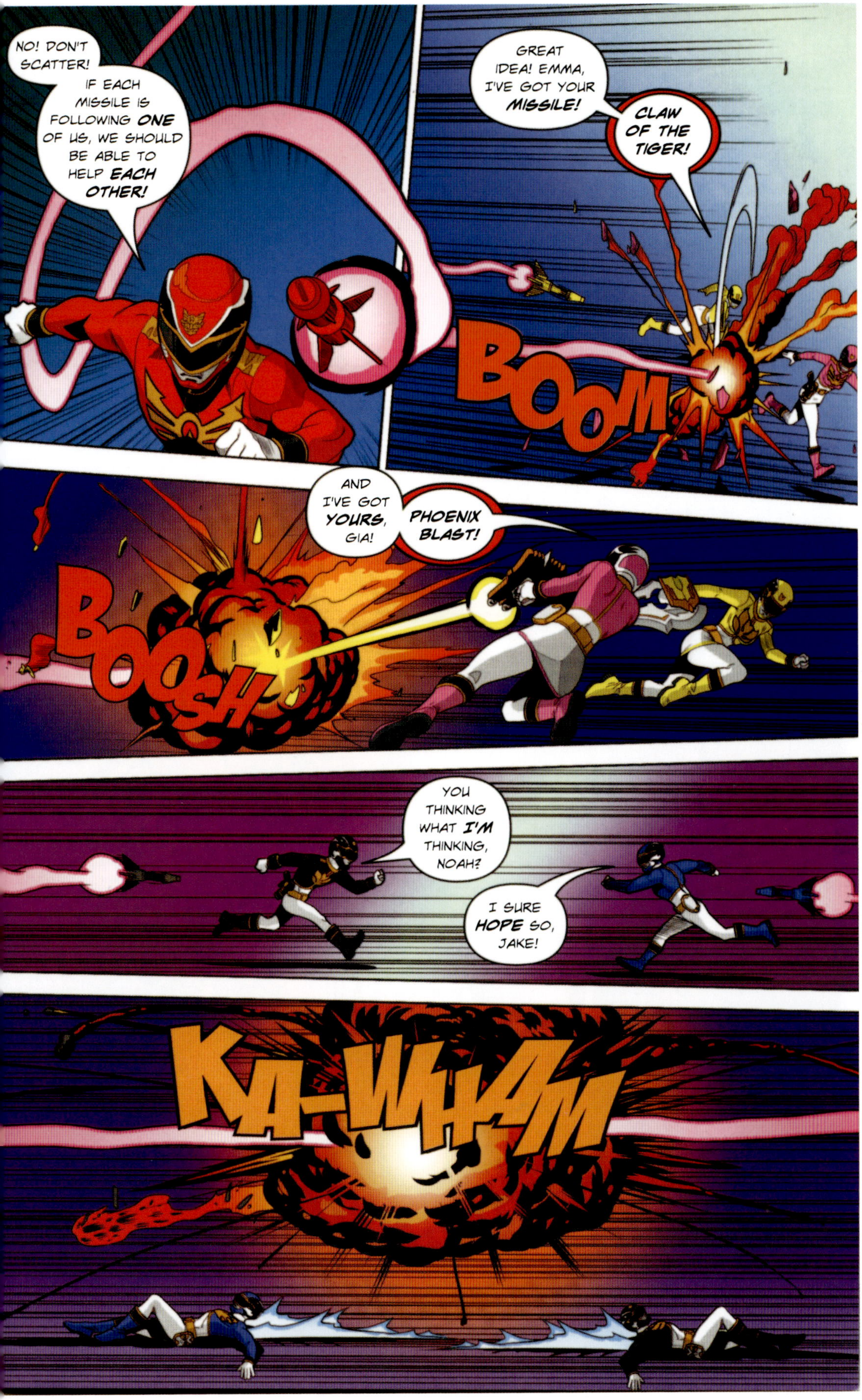

NO! DON'T SCATTER!
IF EACH MISSILE IS FOLLOWING ONE OF US, WE SHOULD BE ABLE TO HELP EACH OTHER!
GREAT IDEA! EMMA, I'VE GOT YOUR MISSILE!
CLAW OF THE TIGER!
BOOM
AND I'VE GOT YOURS, GIA!
PHOENIX BLAST!
BOOSH
YOU THINKING WHAT I'M THINKING, NOAH?
I SURE HOPE SO, JAKE!
KA-WHAM

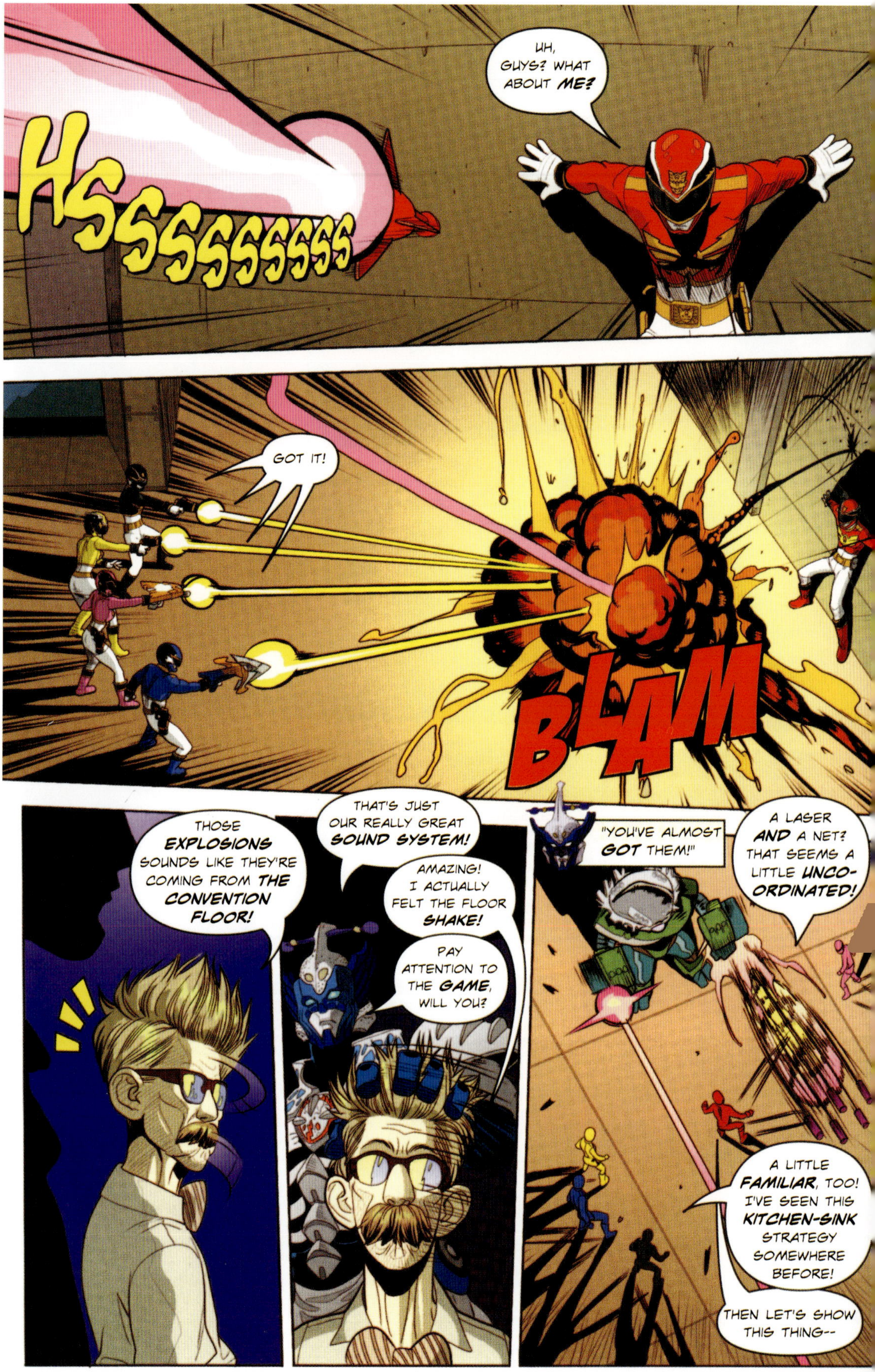
HSSSSSSSSS
UH, GUYS? WHAT ABOUT ME?
GOT IT!
BLAM
THOSE EXPLOSIONS SOUNDS LIKE THEY'RE COMING FROM THE CONVENTION FLOOR!
THAT'S JUST OUR REALLY GREAT SOUND SYSTEM!
AMAZING! I ACTUALLY FELT THE FLOOR SHAKE!
PAY ATTENTION TO THE GAME, WILL YOU?
"YOU'VE ALMOST GOT THEM!"
A LASER AND A NET? THAT SEEMS A LITTLE UNCO-ORDINATED!
A LITTLE FAMILIAR, TOO! I'VE SEEN THIS KITCHEN-SINK STRATEGY SOMEWHERE BEFORE!
THEN LET'S SHOW THIS THING--

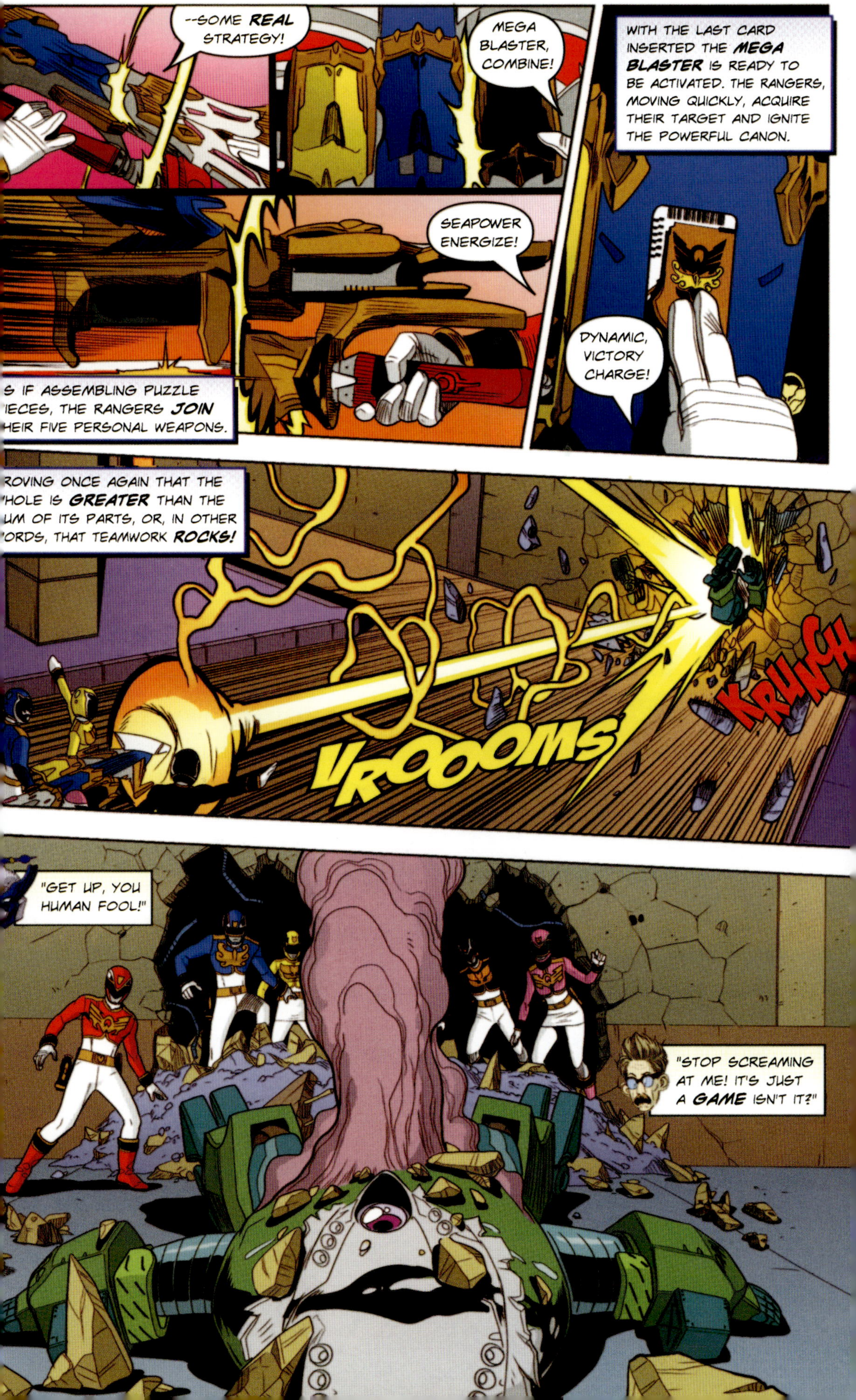
--SOME REAL STRATEGY!
MEGA BLASTER, COMBINE!
WITH THE LAST CARD INSERTED THE MEGA BLASTER IS READY TO BE ACTIVATED. THE RANGERS, MOVING QUICKLY, ACQUIRE THEIR TARGET AND IGNITE THE POWERFUL CANON.
SEAPOWER ENERGIZE!
S IF ASSEMBLING PUZZLE IECES, THE RANGERS JOIN HEIR FIVE PERSONAL WEAPONS.
DYNAMIC, VICTORY CHARGE!
ROVING ONCE AGAIN THAT THE 'HOLE IS GREATER THAN THE UM OF ITS PARTS, OR, IN OTHER 'ORDS, THAT TEAMWORK ROCKS!
VROOOMS
KRUNCH
"GET UP, YOU HUMAN FOOL!"
"STOP SCREAMING AT ME! IT'S JUST A GAME ISN'T IT?"

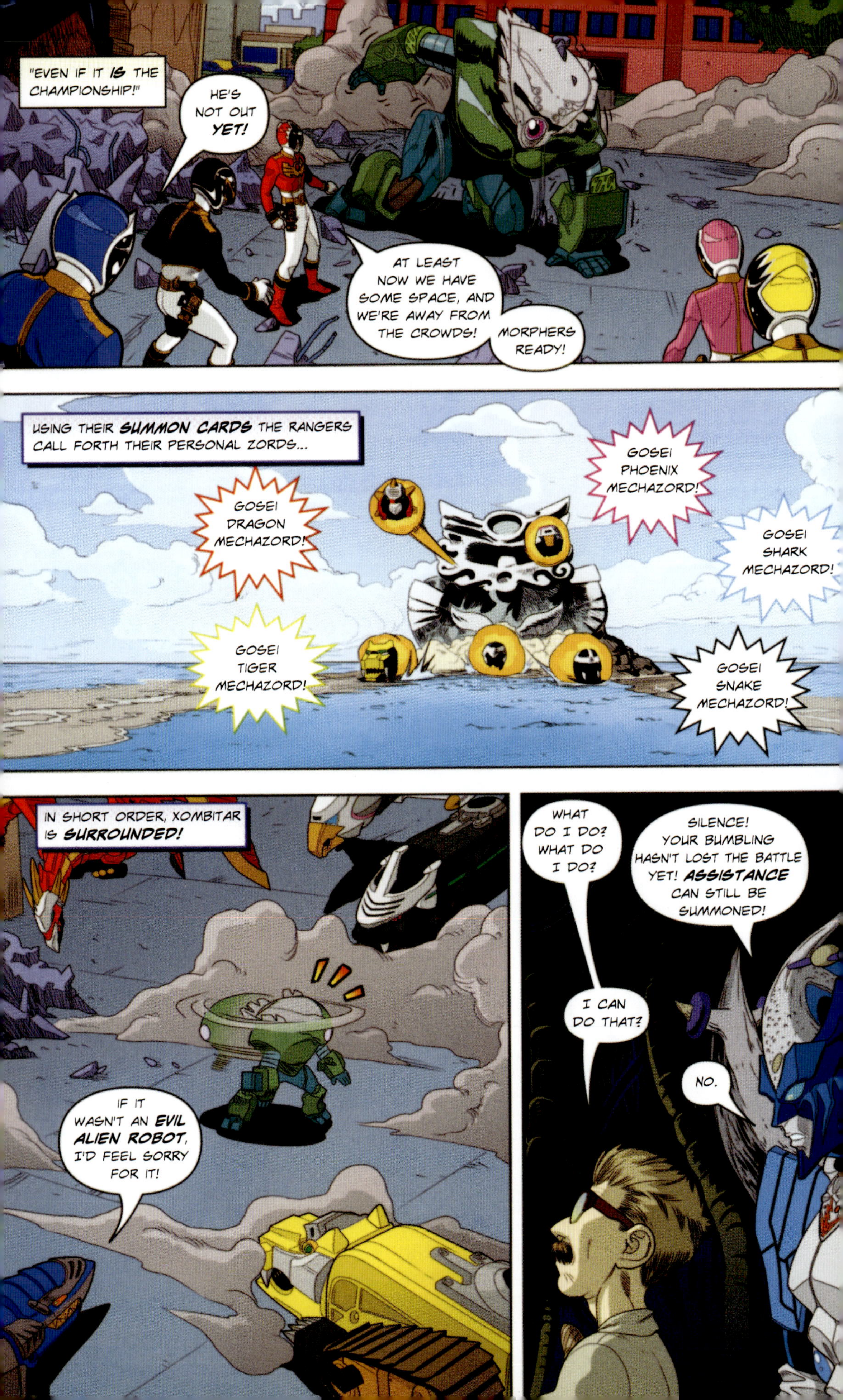
"EVEN IF IT IS THE CHAMPIONSHIP!"
HE'S NOT OUT YET!
AT LEAST NOW WE HAVE SOME SPACE, AND WE'RE AWAY FROM THE CROWDS!
MORPHERS READY!
USING THEIR SUMMON CARDS THE RANGERS CALL FORTH THEIR PERSONAL ZORDS...
GOSEI DRAGON MECHAZORD!
GOSEI PHOENIX MECHAZORD!
GOSEI SHARK MECHAZORD!
GOSEI TIGER MECHAZORD!
GOSEI SNAKE MECHAZORD!
IN SHORT ORDER, XOMBITAR IS SURROUNDED!
IF IT WASN'T AN EVIL ALIEN ROBOT, I'D FEEL SORRY FOR IT!
WHAT DO I DO? WHAT DO I DO?
SILENCE! YOUR BUMBLING HASN'T LOST THE BATTLE YET! ASSISTANCE CAN STILL BE SUMMONED!
I CAN DO THAT?
NO.

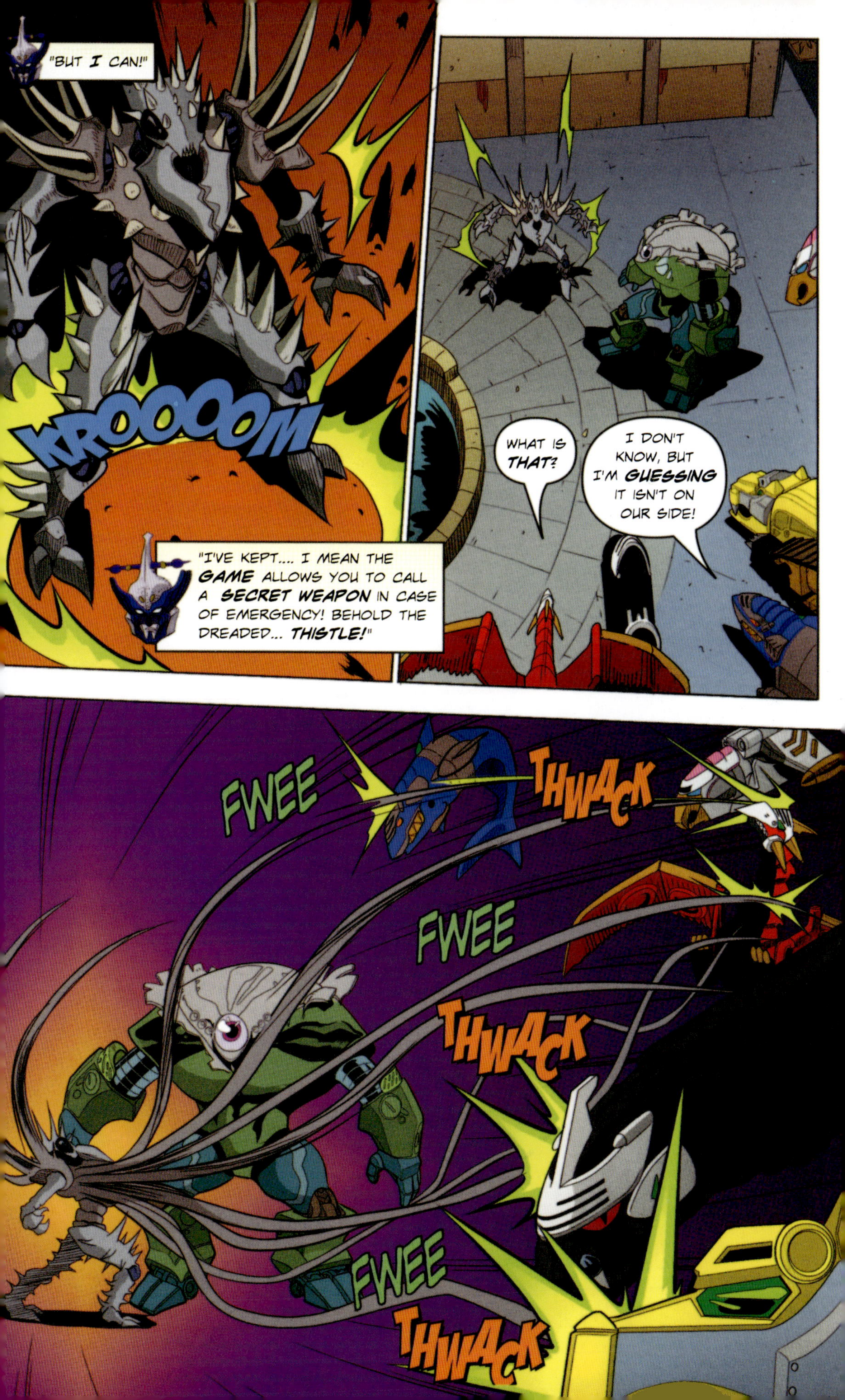
"BUT I CAN!"
KROOOOM
"I'VE KEPT.... I MEAN THE GAME ALLOWS YOU TO CALL A SECRET WEAPON IN CASE OF EMERGENCY! BEHOLD THE DREADED... THISTLE!"
WHAT IS THAT?
I DON'T KNOW, BUT I'M GUESSING IT ISN'T ON OUR SIDE!
FWEE
THWACK
FWEE
THWACK
FWEE
THWACK

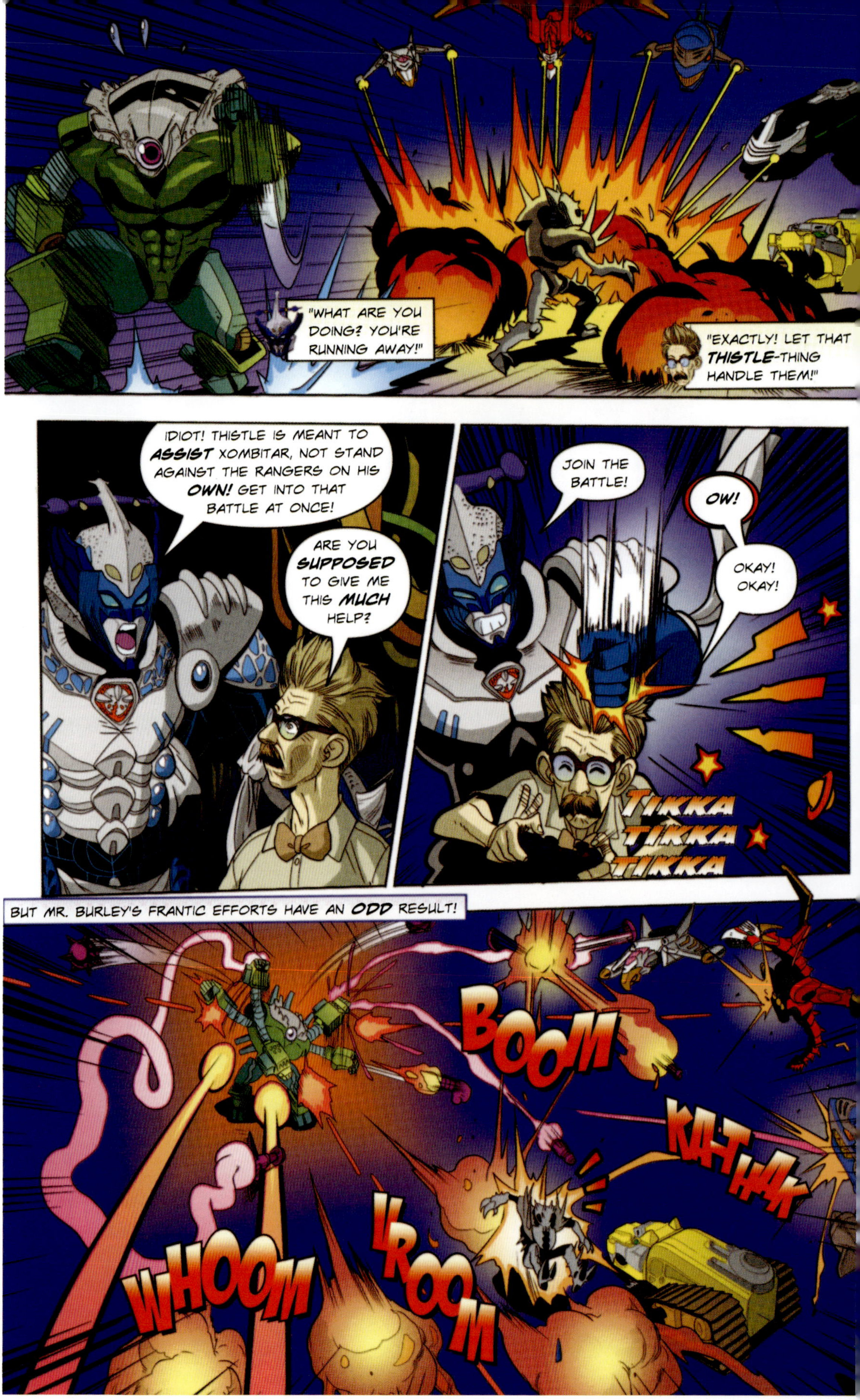
"WHAT ARE YOU DOING? YOU'RE RUNNING AWAY!"
"EXACTLY! LET THAT THISTLE-THING HANDLE THEM!"
IDIOT! THISTLE IS MEANT TO ASSIST XOMBITAR, NOT STAND AGAINST THE RANGERS ON HIS OWN! GET INTO THAT BATTLE AT ONCE!
ARE YOU SUPPOSED TO GIVE ME THIS MUCH HELP?
JOIN THE BATTLE!
OW!
OKAY! OKAY!
TIKKA TIKKA TIKKA
BUT MR. BURLEY'S FRANTIC EFFORTS HAVE AN ODD RESULT!
BOOM
KA-THAK
WHOOM
VROOM

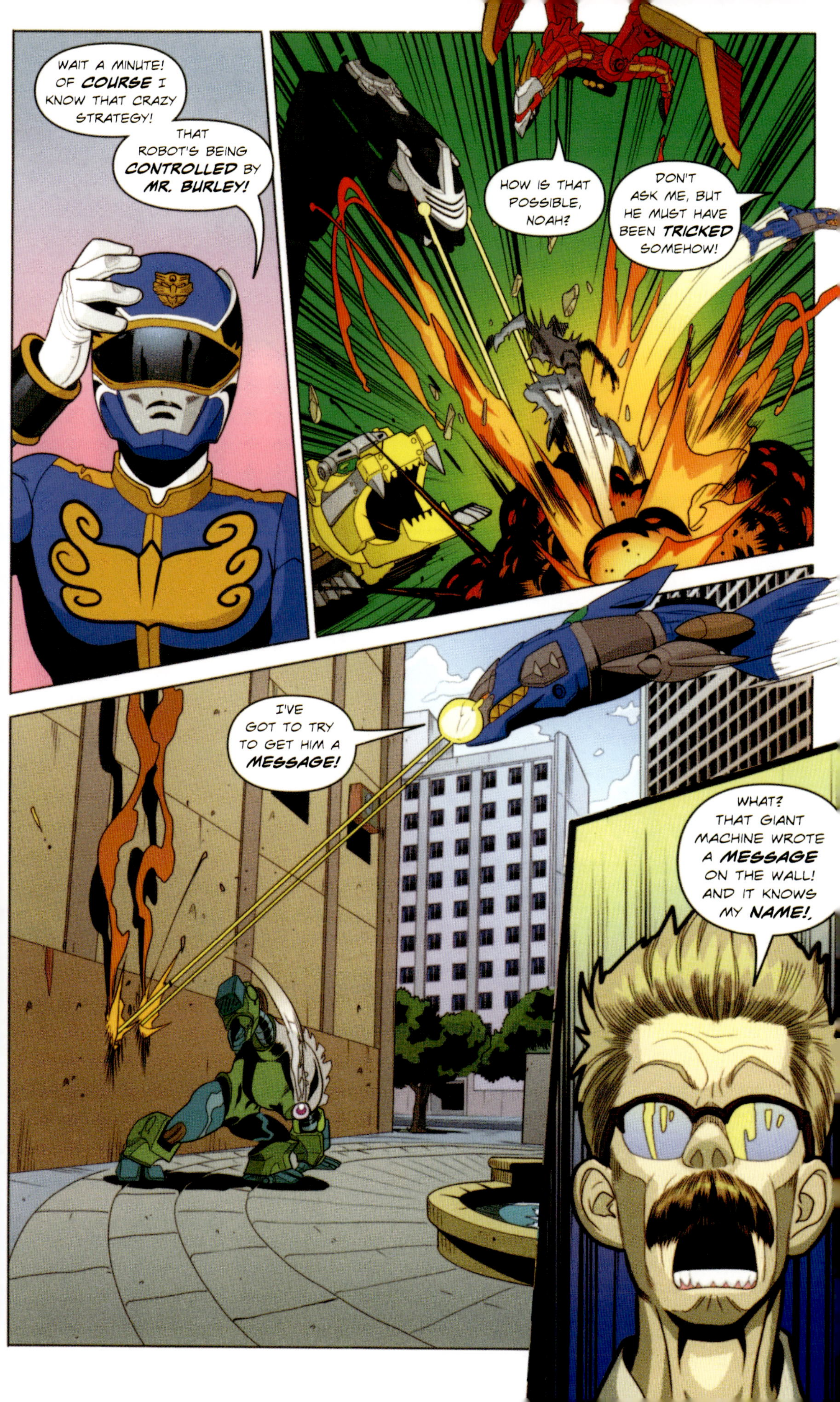
WAIT A MINUTE! OF COURSE I KNOW THAT CRAZY STRATEGY!
THAT ROBOT'S BEING CONTROLLED BY MR. BURLEY!
HOW IS THAT POSSIBLE, NOAH?
DON'T ASK ME, BUT HE MUST HAVE BEEN TRICKED SOMEHOW!
I'VE GOT TO TRY TO GET HIM A MESSAGE!
WHAT? THAT GIANT MACHINE WROTE A MESSAGE ON THE WALL! AND IT KNOWS MY NAME!.

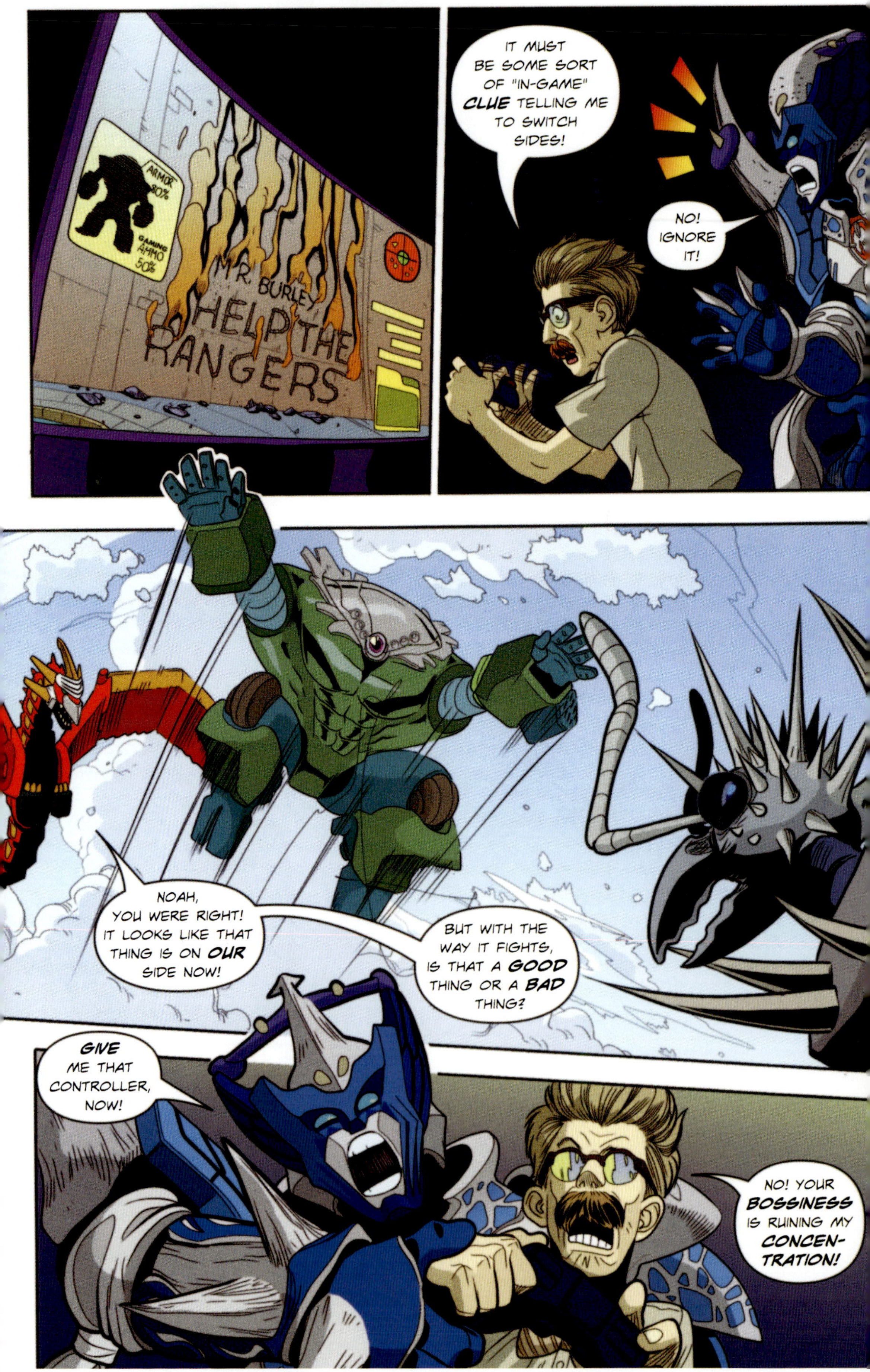
ARMOR 80%
GAMING AMMO 50%
MR. BURLEY HELP THE RANGERS
IT MUST BE SOME SORT OF "IN-GAME" CLUE TELLING ME TO SWITCH SIDES!
NO! IGNORE IT!
NOAH, YOU WERE RIGHT! IT LOOKS LIKE THAT THING IS ON OUR SIDE NOW!
BUT WITH THE WAY IT FIGHTS, IS THAT A GOOD THING OR A BAD THING?
GIVE ME THAT CONTROLLER, NOW!
NO! YOUR BOSSINESS IS RUINING MY CONCEN-TRATION!

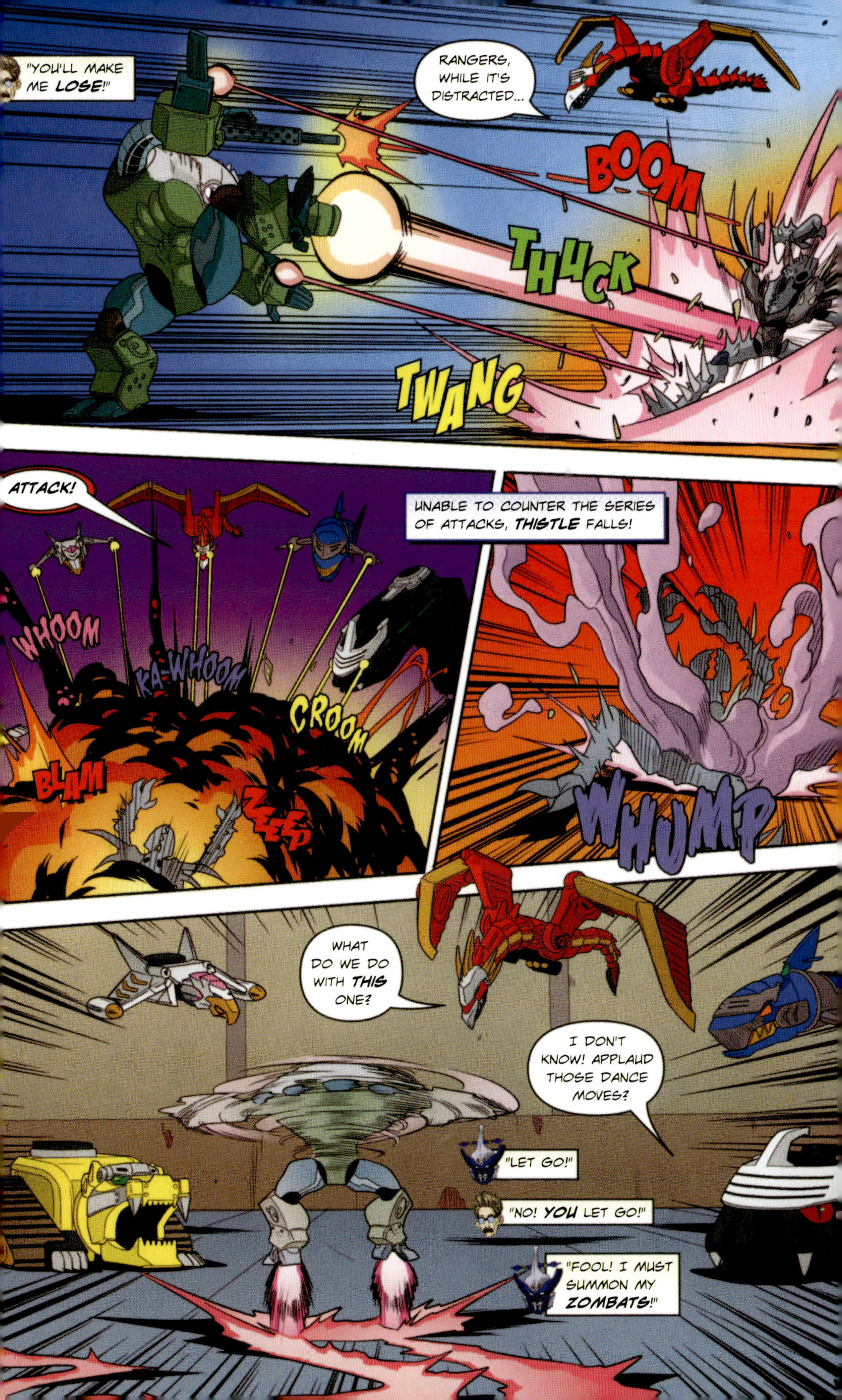
"YOU'LL MAKE ME LOSE!"
RANGERS, WHILE IT'S DISTRACTED...
BOOM
THUCK
TWANG
ATTACK!
WHOOM
KA-WHOOM
CROOM
BLAM
ZEEED
UNABLE TO COUNTER THE SERIES OF ATTACKS, THISTLE FALLS!
WHUMP
WHAT DO WE DO WITH THIS ONE?
I DON'T KNOW! APPLAUD THOSE DANCE MOVES?
"LET GO!"
"NO! YOU LET GO!"
"FOOL! I MUST SUMMON MY ZOMBATS!"

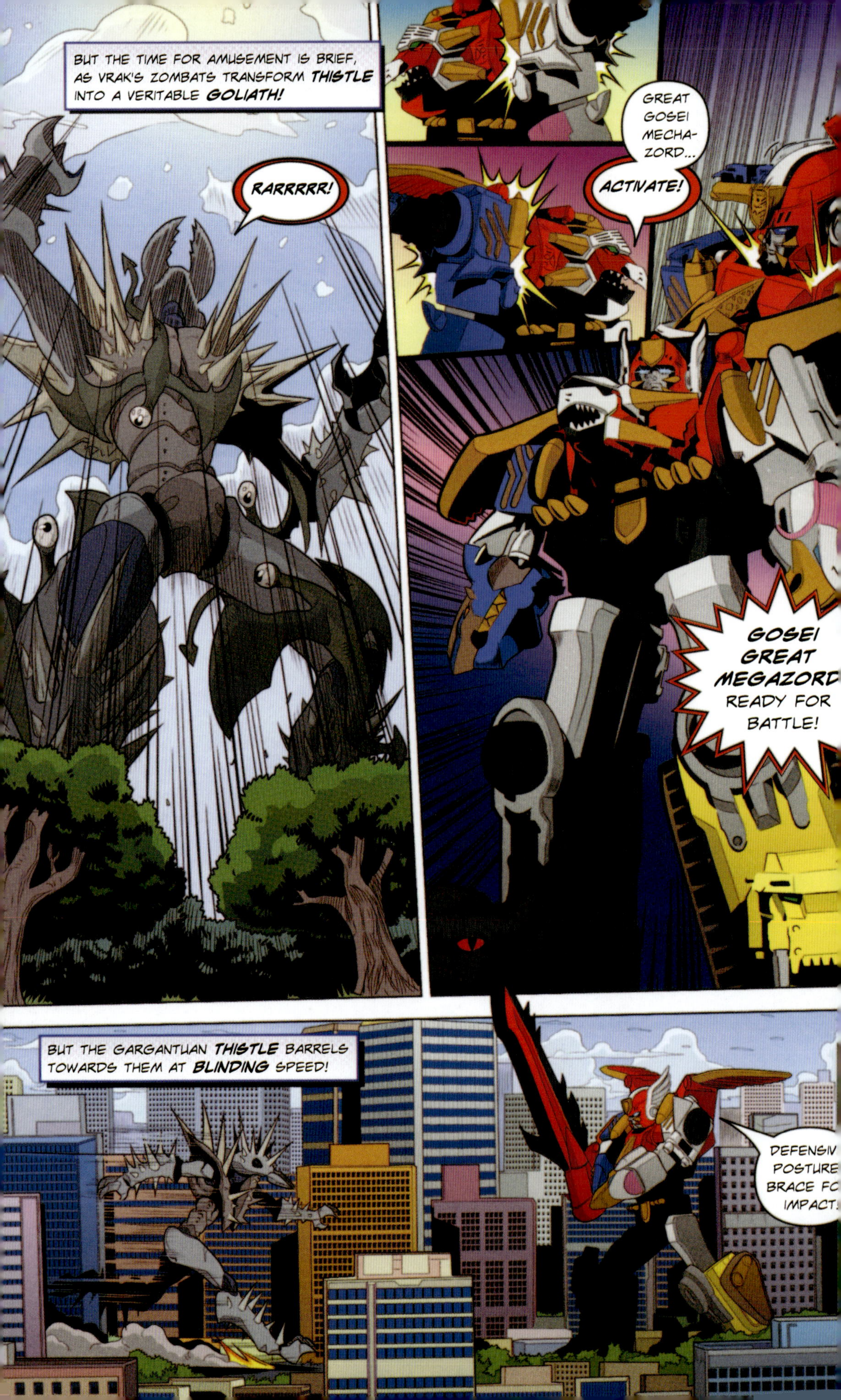
BUT THE TIME FOR AMUSEMENT IS BRIEF, AS VRAK'S ZOMBATS TRANSFORM THISTLE INTO A VERITABLE GOLIATH!
RARRRRR!
GREAT GOSEI MECHA-ZORD...
ACTIVATE!
GOSEI GREAT MEGAZORD READY FOR BATTLE!
BUT THE GARGANTUAN THISTLE BARRELS TOWARDS THEM AT BLINDING SPEED!
DEFENSIV POSTURE BRACE FO IMPACT.

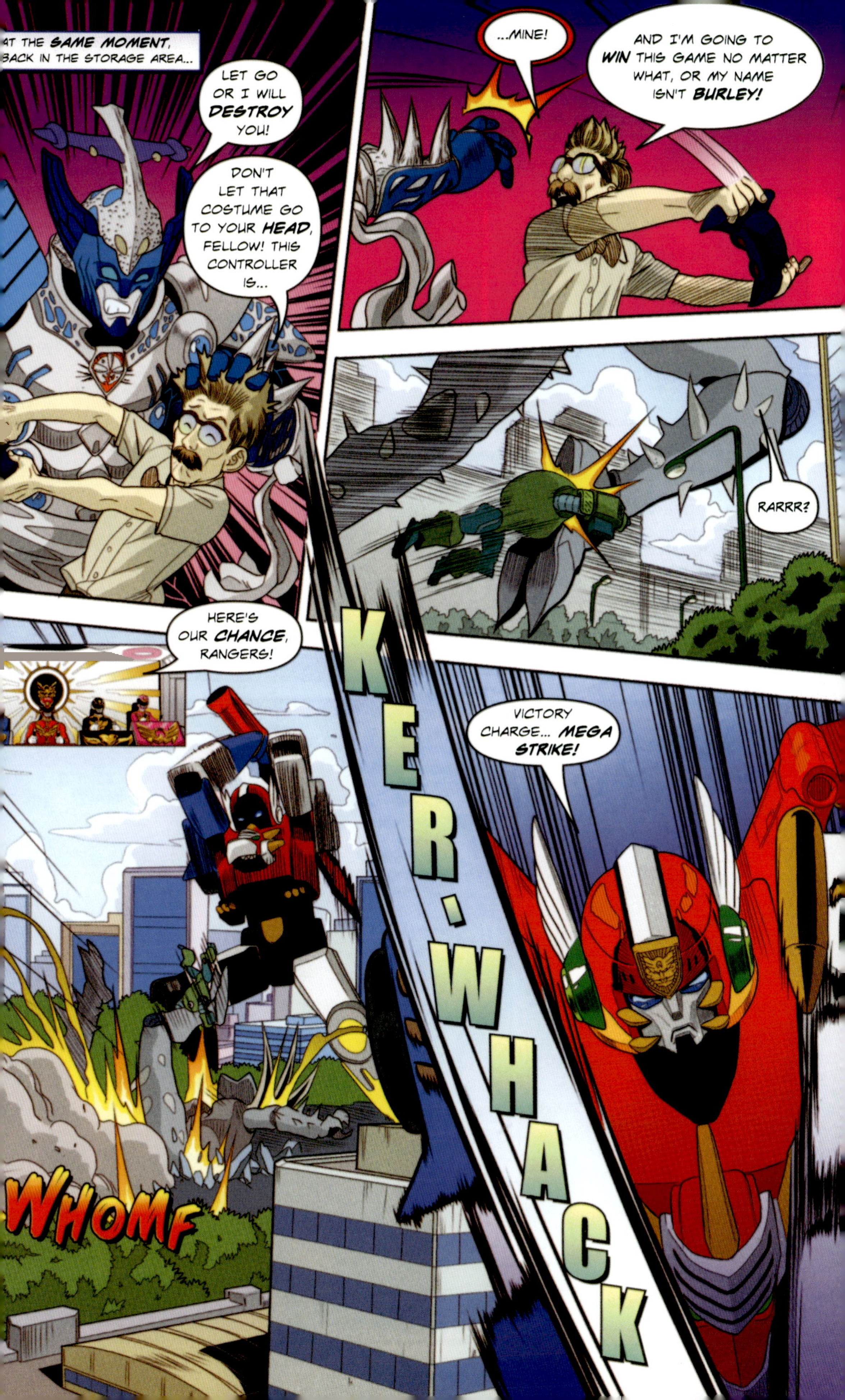
AT THE SAME MOMENT, BACK IN THE STORAGE AREA...
LET GO OR I WILL DESTROY YOU!
DON'T LET THAT COSTUME GO TO YOUR HEAD, FELLOW! THIS CONTROLLER IS...
...MINE!
AND I'M GOING TO WIN THIS GAME NO MATTER WHAT, OR MY NAME ISN'T BURLEY!
RARRR?
HERE'S OUR CHANCE, RANGERS!
VICTORY CHARGE... MEGA STRIKE!
KER-WHACK
WHOMF

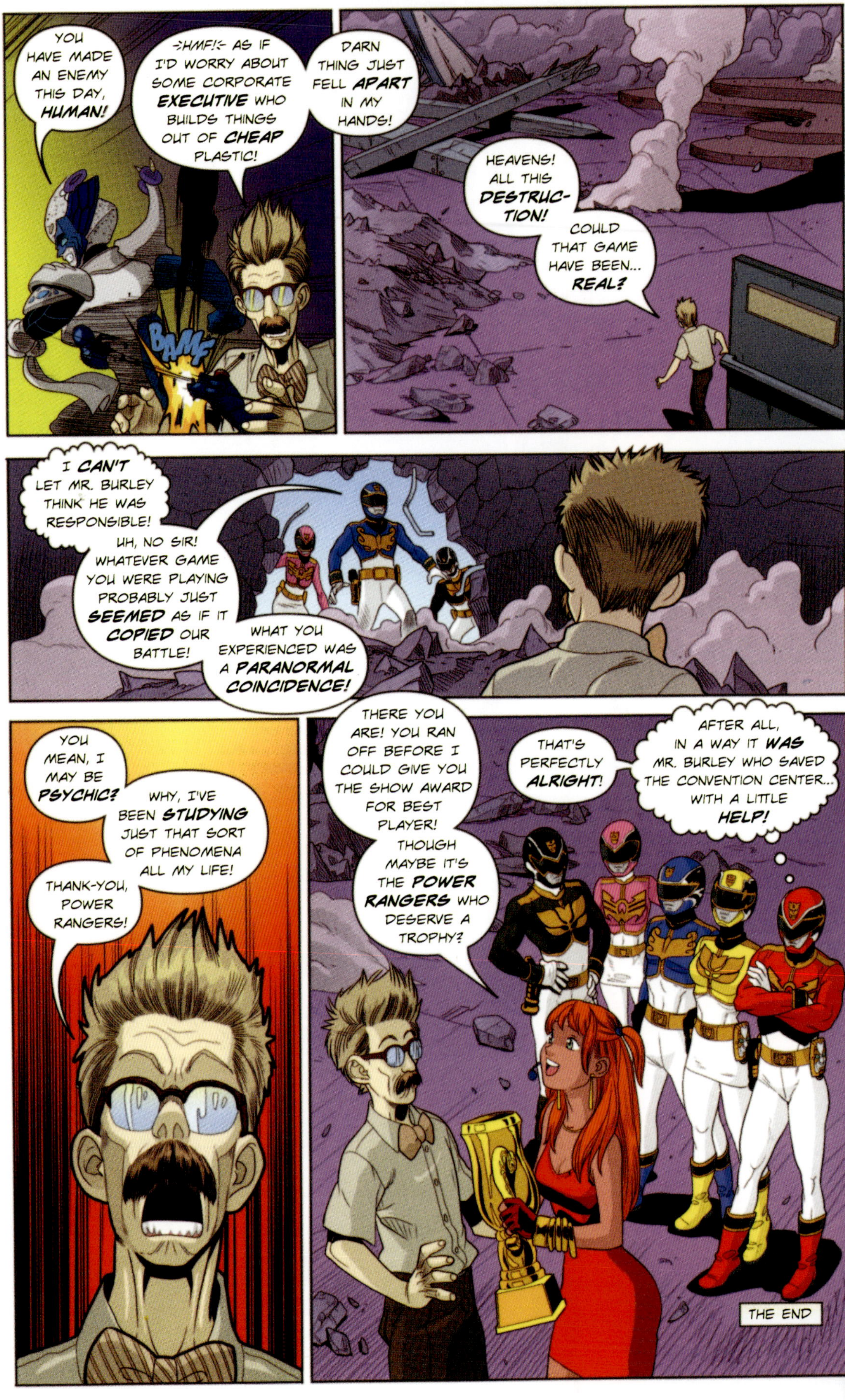
YOU HAVE MADE AN ENEMY THIS DAY, HUMAN!
-HMF!- AS IF I'D WORRY ABOUT SOME CORPORATE EXECUTIVE WHO BUILDS THINGS OUT OF CHEAP PLASTIC!
BAMF
DARN THING JUST FELL APART IN MY HANDS!
HEAVENS! ALL THIS DESTRUCTION!
COULD THAT GAME HAVE BEEN... REAL?
I CAN'T LET MR. BURLEY THINK HE WAS RESPONSIBLE!
UH, NO SIR! WHATEVER GAME YOU WERE PLAYING PROBABLY JUST SEEMED AS IF IT COPIED OUR BATTLE!
WHAT YOU EXPERIENCED WAS A PARANORMAL COINCIDENCE!
YOU MEAN, I MAY BE PSYCHIC?
WHY, I'VE BEEN STUDYING JUST THAT SORT OF PHENOMENA ALL MY LIFE!
THANK-YOU, POWER RANGERS!
THERE YOU ARE! YOU RAN OFF BEFORE I COULD GIVE YOU THE SHOW AWARD FOR BEST PLAYER!
THOUGH MAYBE IT'S THE POWER RANGERS WHO DESERVE A TROPHY?
THAT'S PERFECTLY ALRIGHT!
AFTER ALL, IN A WAY IT WAS MR. BURLEY WHO SAVED THE CONVENTION CENTER... WITH A LITTLE HELP!
THE END

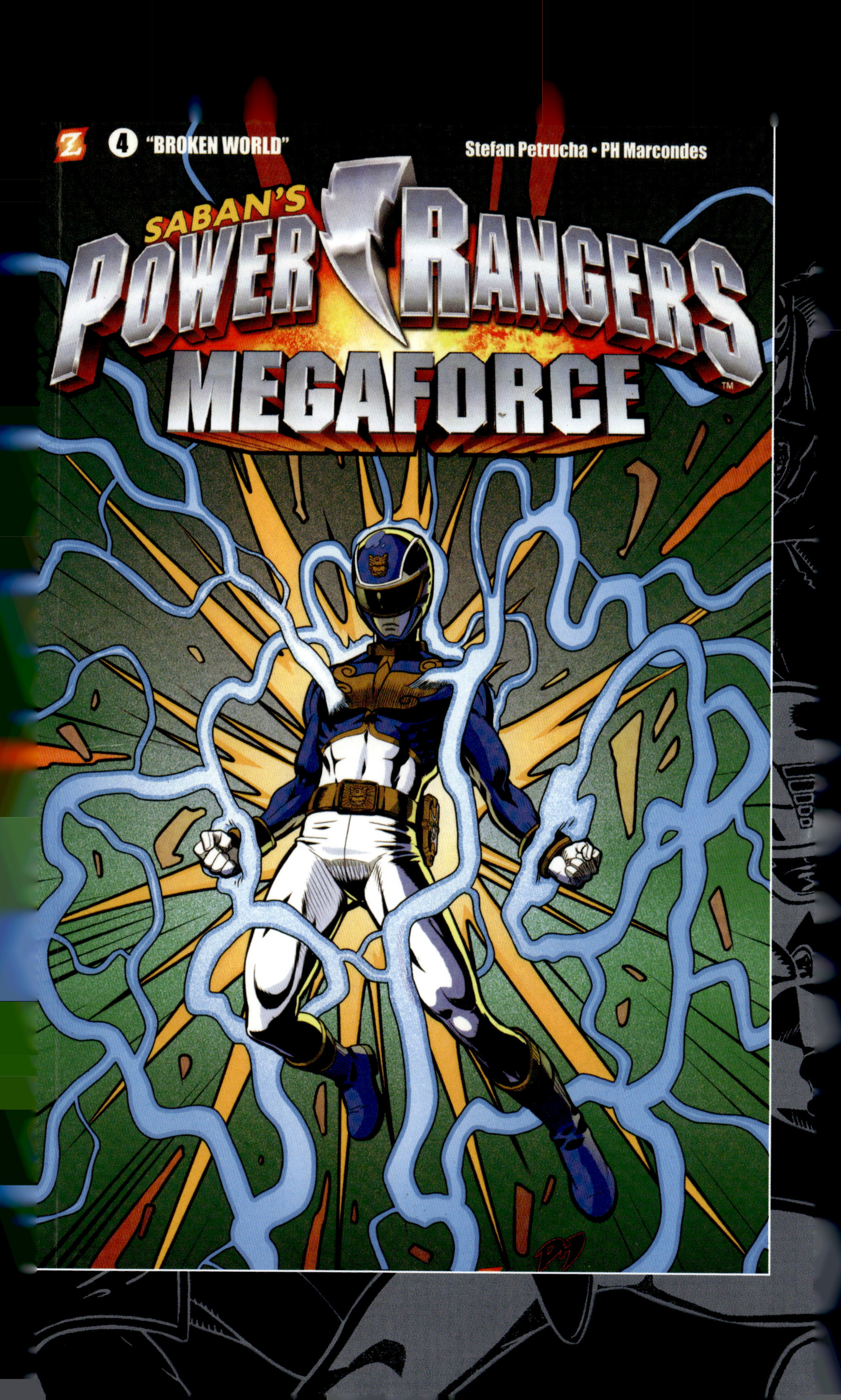
4 "BROKEN WORLD"
Stefan Petrucha • PH Marcondes
SABAN'S
POWER RANGERS
MEGAFORCE
TM

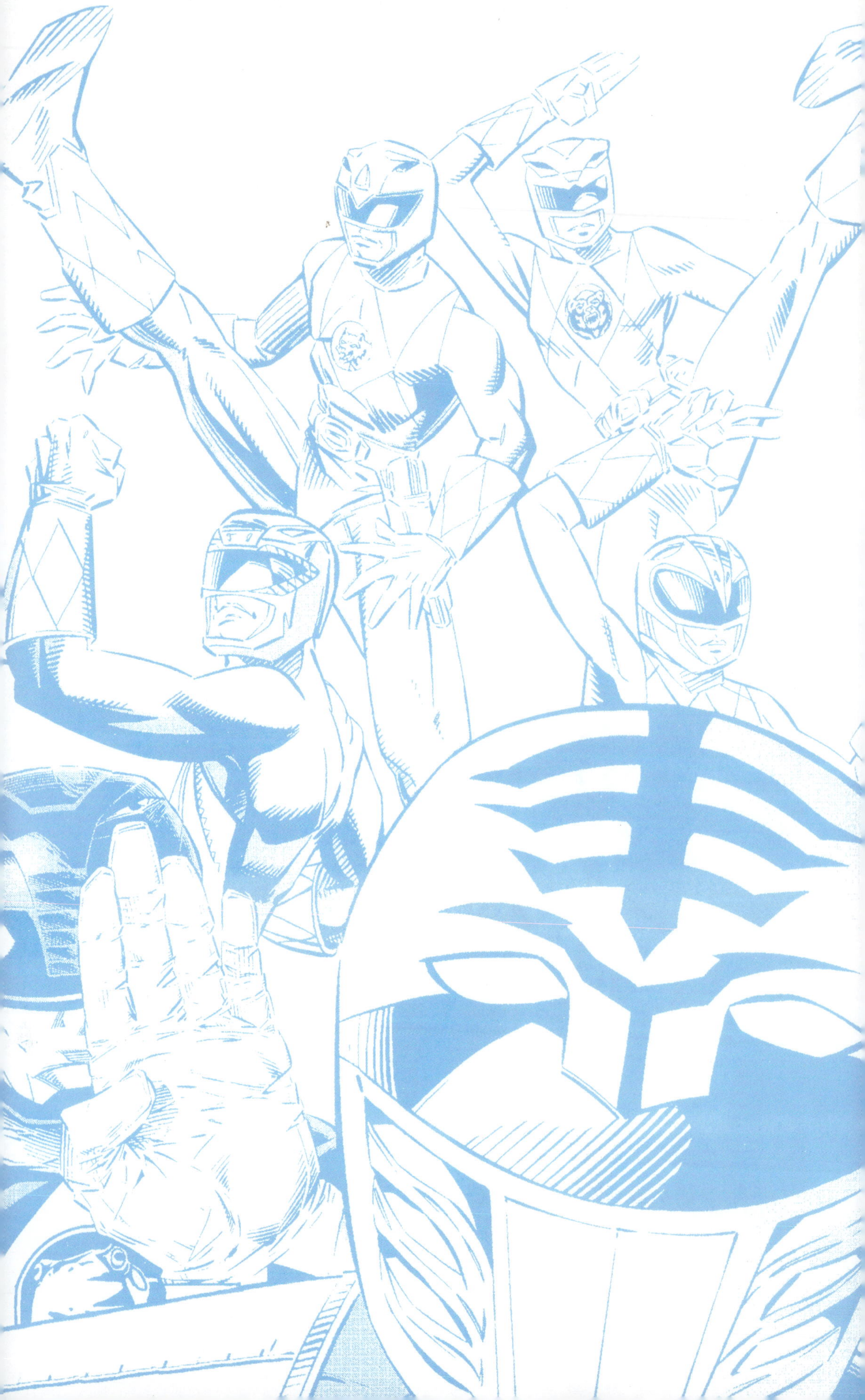

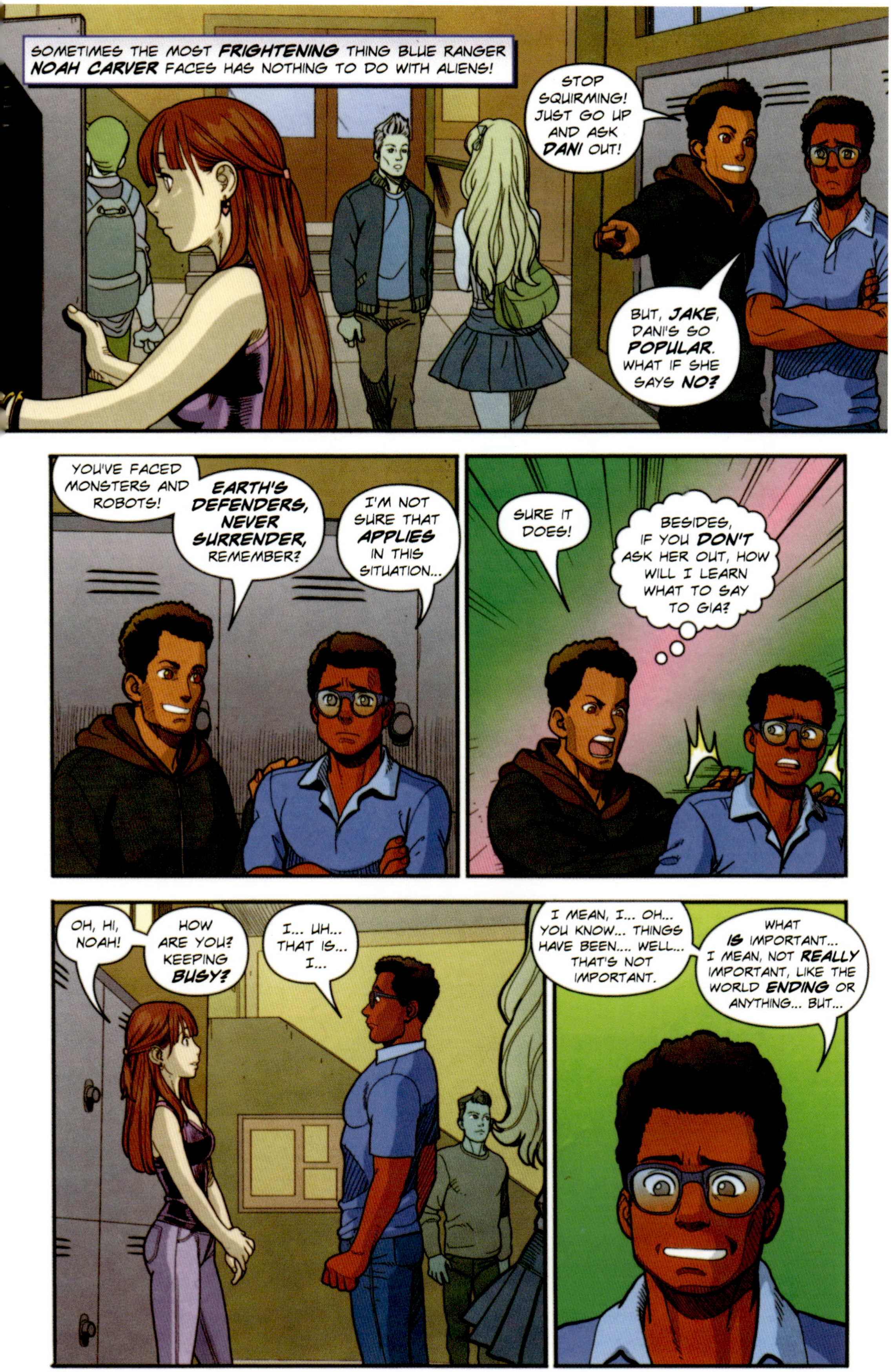
SOMETIMES THE MOST FRIGHTENING THING BLUE RANGER NOAH CARVER FACES HAS NOTHING TO DO WITH ALIENS!
STOP SQUIRMING! JUST GO UP AND ASK DANI OUT!
BUT, JAKE, DANI'S SO POPULAR. WHAT IF SHE SAYS NO?
YOU'VE FACED MONSTERS AND ROBOTS!
EARTH'S DEFENDERS, NEVER SURRENDER, REMEMBER?
I'M NOT SURE THAT APPLIES IN THIS SITUATION...
SURE IT DOES!
BESIDES, IF YOU DON'T ASK HER OUT, HOW WILL I LEARN WHAT TO SAY TO GIA?
OH, HI, NOAH!
HOW ARE YOU? KEEPING BUSY?
I... UH... THAT IS... I...
I MEAN, I... OH... YOU KNOW... THINGS HAVE BEEN.... WELL... THAT'S NOT IMPORTANT.
WHAT IS IMPORTANT... I MEAN, NOT REALLY IMPORTANT, LIKE THE WORLD ENDING OR ANYTHING... BUT...

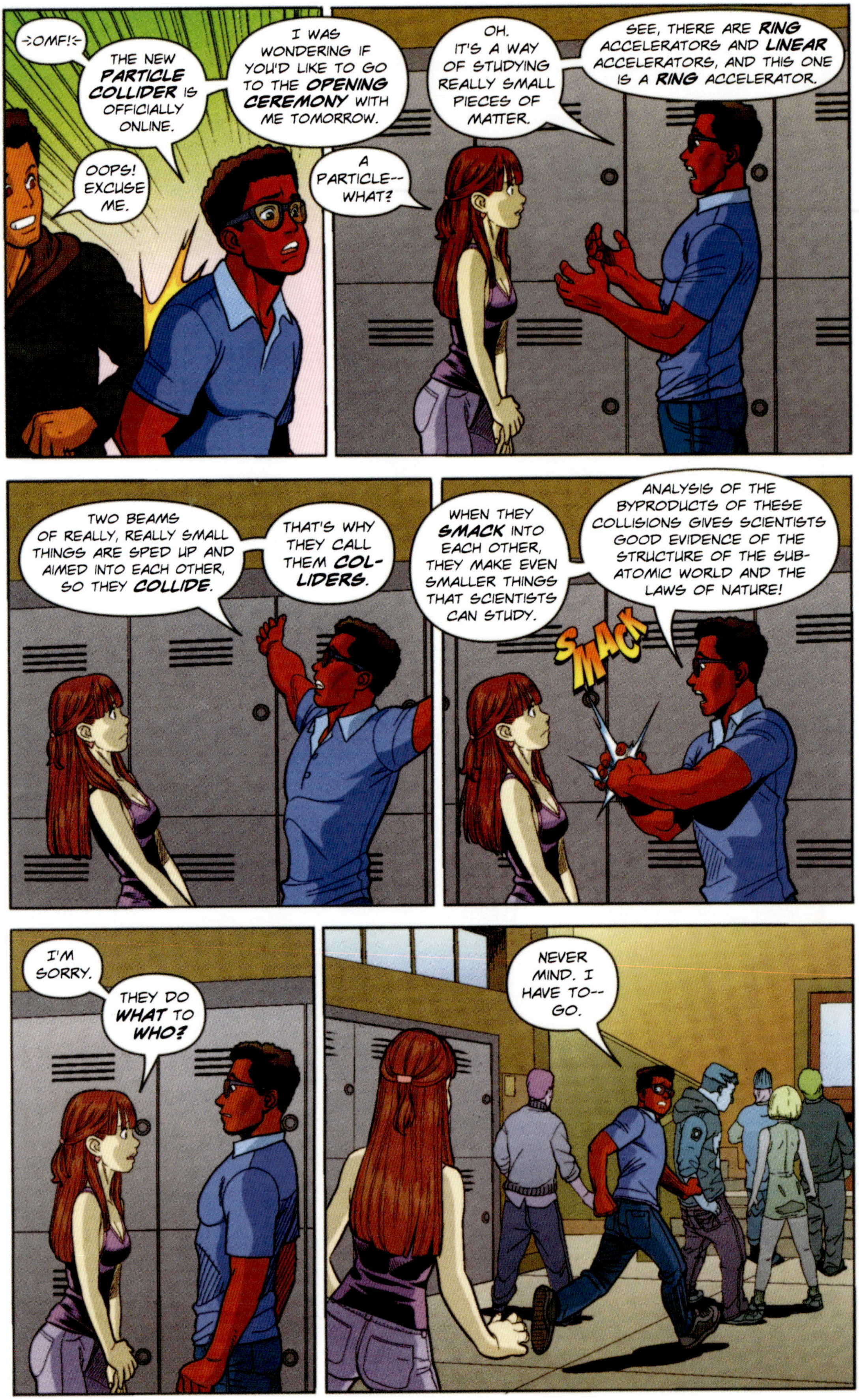
-OMF!-
THE NEW PARTICLE COLLIDER IS OFFICIALLY ONLINE.
OOPS! EXCUSE ME.
I WAS WONDERING IF YOU'D LIKE TO GO TO THE OPENING CEREMONY WITH ME TOMORROW.
A PARTICLE-- WHAT?
OH. IT'S A WAY OF STUDYING REALLY SMALL PIECES OF MATTER.
SEE, THERE ARE RING ACCELERATORS AND LINEAR ACCELERATORS, AND THIS ONE IS A RING ACCELERATOR.
TWO BEAMS OF REALLY, REALLY SMALL THINGS ARE SPED UP AND AIMED INTO EACH OTHER, SO THEY COLLIDE.
THAT'S WHY THEY CALL THEM COL-LIDERS.
WHEN THEY SMACK INTO EACH OTHER, THEY MAKE EVEN SMALLER THINGS THAT SCIENTISTS CAN STUDY.
SMACK
ANALYSIS OF THE BYPRODUCTS OF THESE COLLISIONS GIVES SCIENTISTS GOOD EVIDENCE OF THE STRUCTURE OF THE SUB-ATOMIC WORLD AND THE LAWS OF NATURE!
I'M SORRY.
THEY DO WHAT TO WHO?
NEVER MIND. I HAVE TO-- GO.

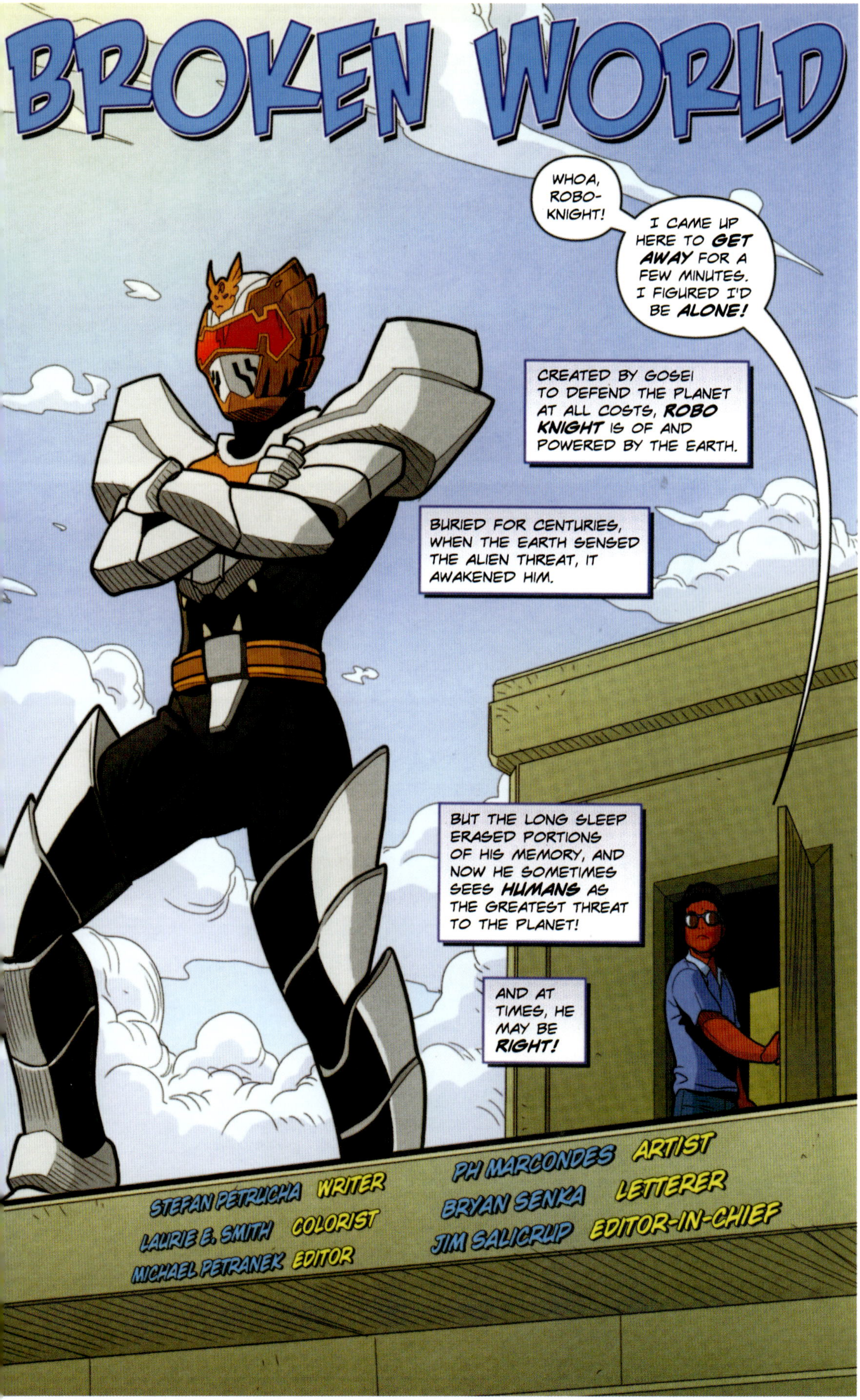
BROKEN WORLD
WHOA, ROBO-KNIGHT!
I CAME UP HERE TO GET AWAY FOR A FEW MINUTES. I FIGURED I'D BE ALONE!
CREATED BY GOSEI TO DEFEND THE PLANET AT ALL COSTS, ROBO KNIGHT IS OF AND POWERED BY THE EARTH.
BURIED FOR CENTURIES, WHEN THE EARTH SENSED THE ALIEN THREAT, IT AWAKENED HIM.
BUT THE LONG SLEEP ERASED PORTIONS OF HIS MEMORY, AND NOW HE SOMETIMES SEES HUMANS AS THE GREATEST THREAT TO THE PLANET!
AND AT TIMES, HE MAY BE RIGHT!
STEFAN PETRUCHA WRITER
LAURIE E. SMITH COLORIST
MICHAEL PETRANEK EDITOR
PH MARCONDES ARTIST
BRYAN SENKA LETTERER
JIM SALICRUP EDITOR-IN-CHIEF

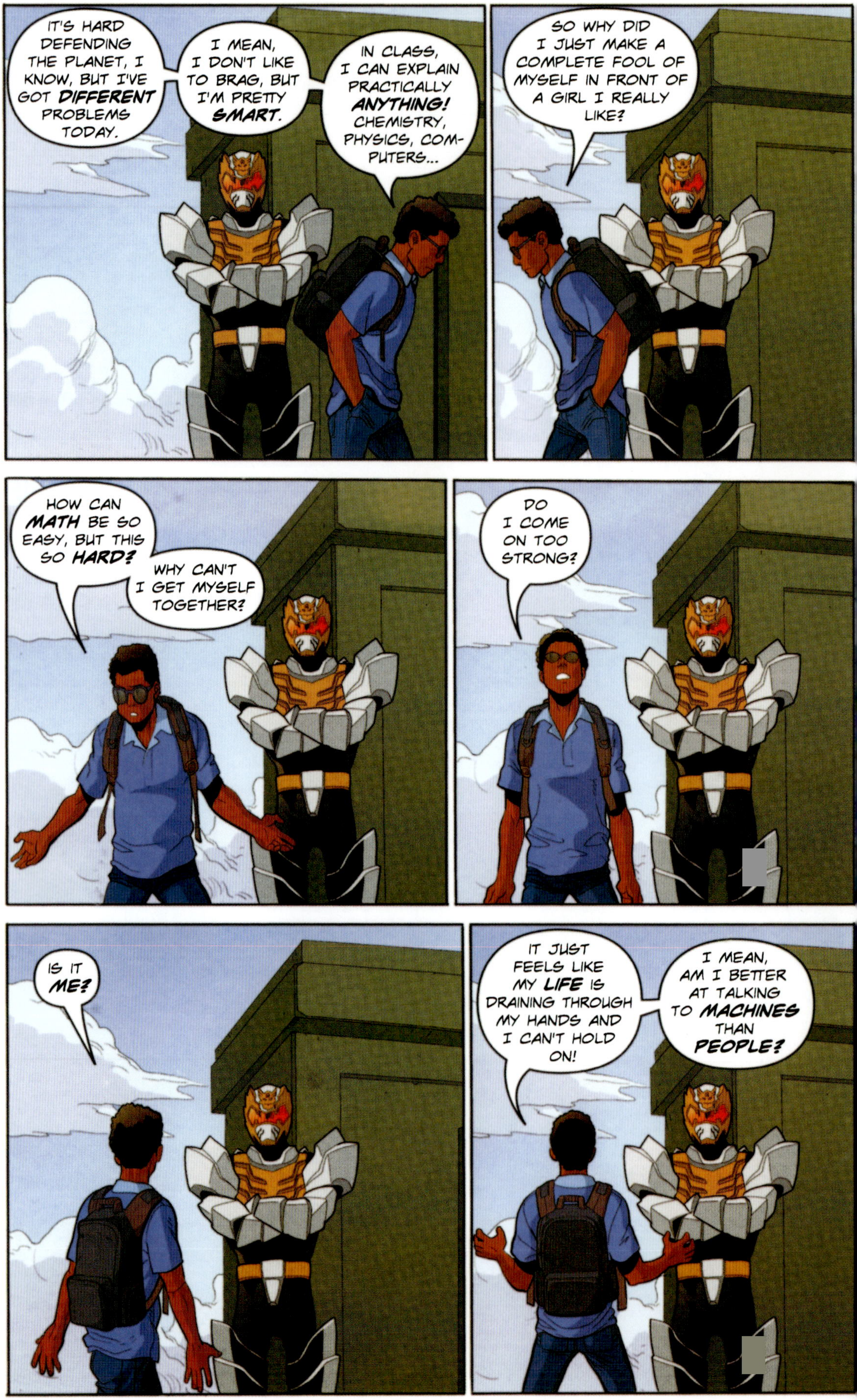

IT'S HARD DEFENDING THE PLANET, I KNOW, BUT I'VE GOT DIFFERENT PROBLEMS TODAY.
I MEAN, I DON'T LIKE TO BRAG, BUT I'M PRETTY SMART.
IN CLASS, I CAN EXPLAIN PRACTICALLY ANYTHING! CHEMISTRY, PHYSICS, COMPUTERS...
SO WHY DID I JUST MAKE A COMPLETE FOOL OF MYSELF IN FRONT OF A GIRL I REALLY LIKE?
HOW CAN MATH BE SO EASY, BUT THIS SO HARD?
WHY CAN'T I GET MYSELF TOGETHER?
DO I COME ON TOO STRONG?
IS IT ME?
IT JUST FEELS LIKE MY LIFE IS DRAINING THROUGH MY HANDS AND I CAN'T HOLD ON!
I MEAN, AM I BETTER AT TALKING TO MACHINES THAN PEOPLE?

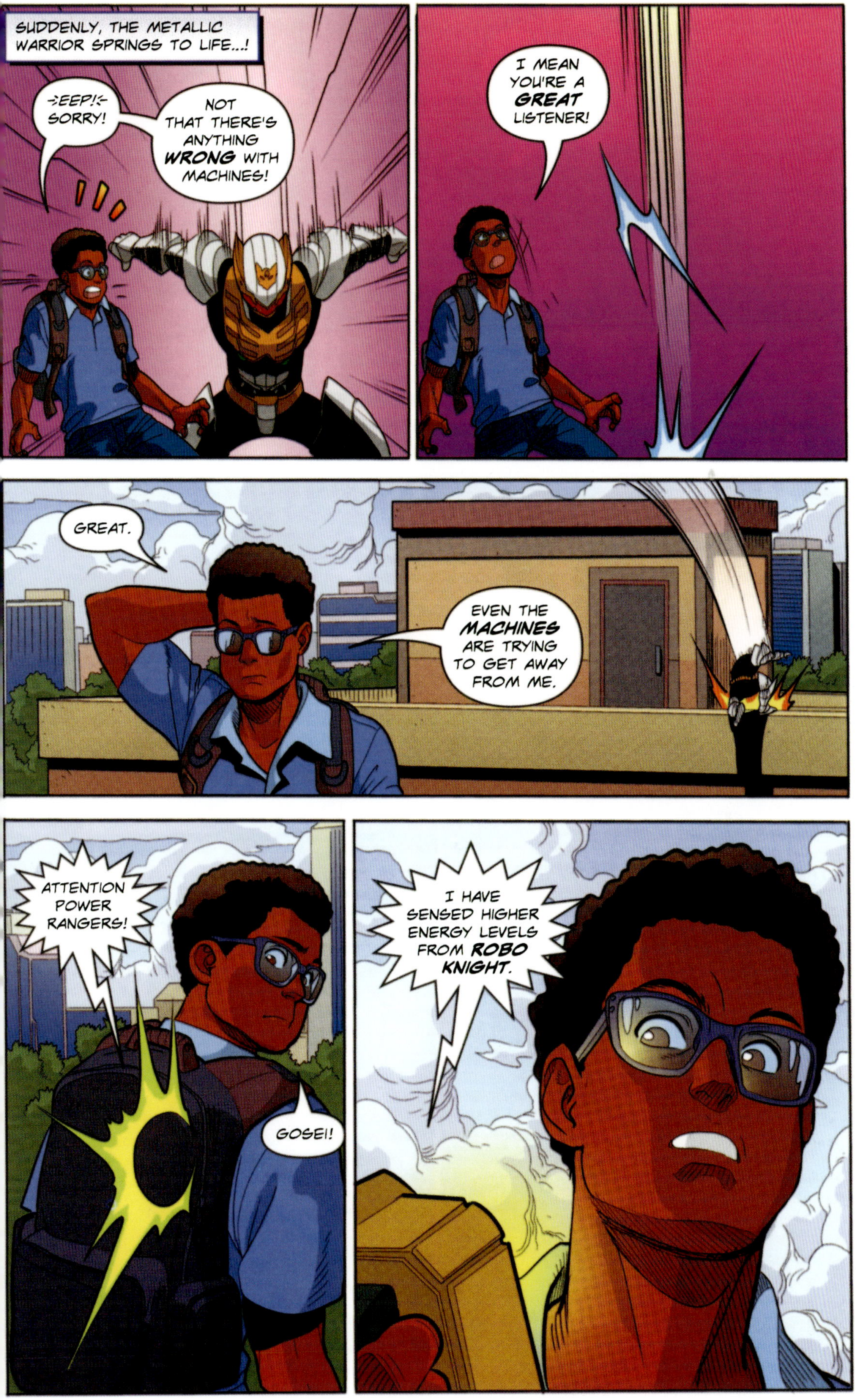
SUDDENLY, THE METALLIC WARRIOR SPRINGS TO LIFE...!
>EEP!< SORRY!
NOT THAT THERE'S ANYTHING WRONG WITH MACHINES!
I MEAN YOU'RE A GREAT LISTENER!
GREAT.
EVEN THE MACHINES ARE TRYING TO GET AWAY FROM ME.
ATTENTION POWER RANGERS!
GOSEI!
I HAVE SENSED HIGHER ENERGY LEVELS FROM ROBO KNIGHT.

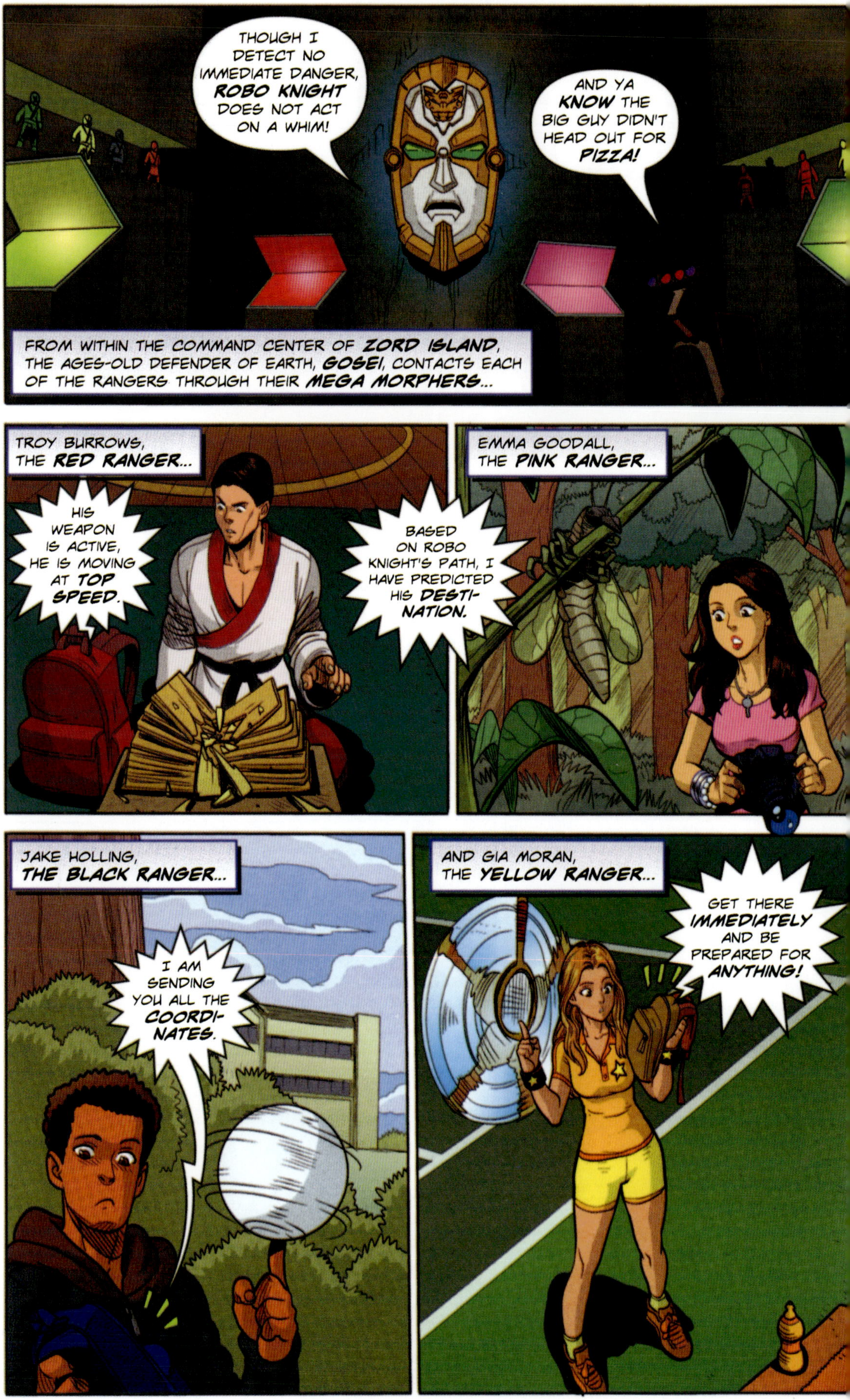

THOUGH I DETECT NO IMMEDIATE DANGER, ROBO KNIGHT DOES NOT ACT ON A WHIM!
AND YA KNOW THE BIG GUY DIDN'T HEAD OUT FOR PIZZA!
FROM WITHIN THE COMMAND CENTER OF ZORD ISLAND, THE AGES-OLD DEFENDER OF EARTH, GOSEI, CONTACTS EACH OF THE RANGERS THROUGH THEIR MEGA MORPHERS...
TROY BURROWS, THE RED RANGER...
HIS WEAPON IS ACTIVE, HE IS MOVING AT TOP SPEED.
BASED ON ROBO KNIGHT'S PATH, I HAVE PREDICTED HIS DESTI-NATION.
EMMA GOODALL, THE PINK RANGER...
JAKE HOLLING, THE BLACK RANGER...
I AM SENDING YOU ALL THE COORDI-NATES.
AND GIA MORAN, THE YELLOW RANGER...
GET THERE IMMEDIATELY AND BE PREPARED FOR ANYTHING!

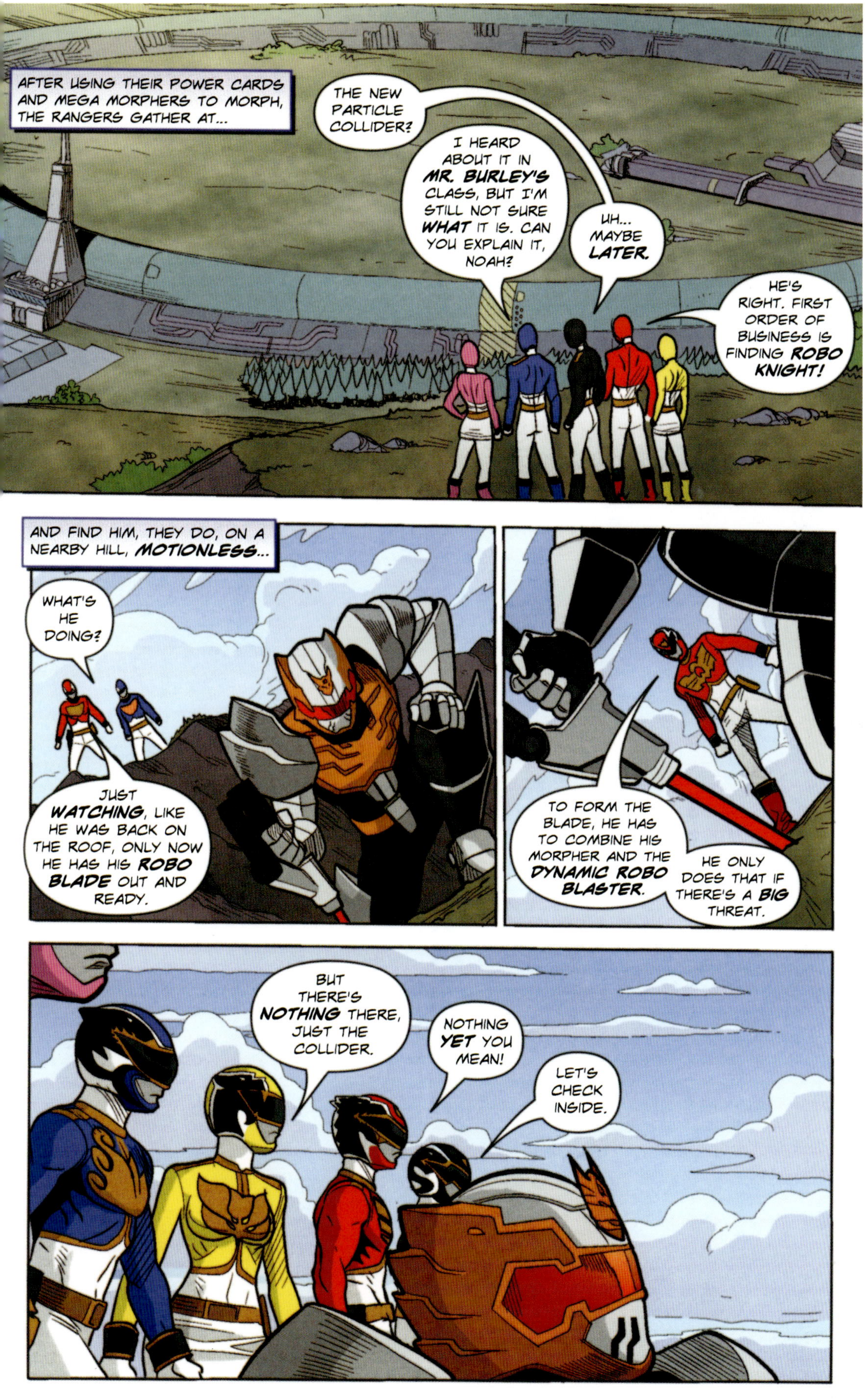

AFTER USING THEIR POWER CARDS AND MEGA MORPHERS TO MORPH, THE RANGERS GATHER AT...
THE NEW PARTICLE COLLIDER?
I HEARD ABOUT IT IN MR. BURLEY'S CLASS, BUT I'M STILL NOT SURE WHAT IT IS. CAN YOU EXPLAIN IT, NOAH?
UH... MAYBE LATER.
HE'S RIGHT. FIRST ORDER OF BUSINESS IS FINDING ROBO KNIGHT!
AND FIND HIM, THEY DO, ON A NEARBY HILL, MOTIONLESS...
WHAT'S HE DOING?
JUST WATCHING, LIKE HE WAS BACK ON THE ROOF, ONLY NOW HE HAS HIS ROBO BLADE OUT AND READY.
TO FORM THE BLADE, HE HAS TO COMBINE HIS MORPHER AND THE DYNAMIC ROBO BLASTER.
HE ONLY DOES THAT IF THERE'S A BIG THREAT.
BUT THERE'S NOTHING THERE, JUST THE COLLIDER.
NOTHING YET YOU MEAN!
LET'S CHECK INSIDE.

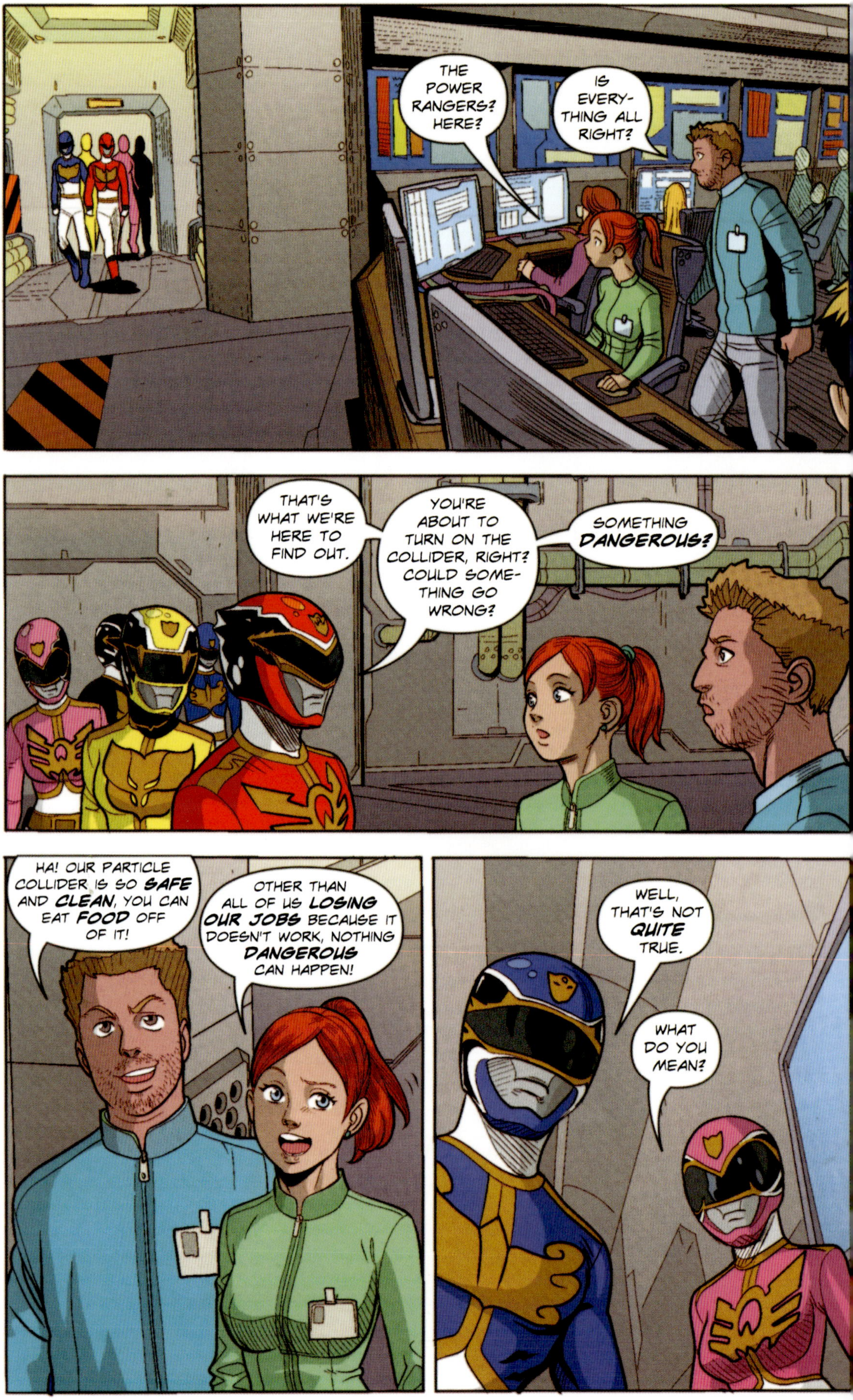
THE POWER RANGERS? HERE?
IS EVERY-THING ALL RIGHT?
THAT'S WHAT WE'RE HERE TO FIND OUT.
YOU'RE ABOUT TO TURN ON THE COLLIDER, RIGHT? COULD SOME-THING GO WRONG?
SOMETHING DANGEROUS?
HA! OUR PARTICLE COLLIDER IS SO SAFE AND CLEAN, YOU CAN EAT FOOD OFF OF IT!
OTHER THAN ALL OF US LOSING OUR JOBS BECAUSE IT DOESN'T WORK, NOTHING DANGEROUS CAN HAPPEN!
WELL, THAT'S NOT QUITE TRUE.
WHAT DO YOU MEAN?

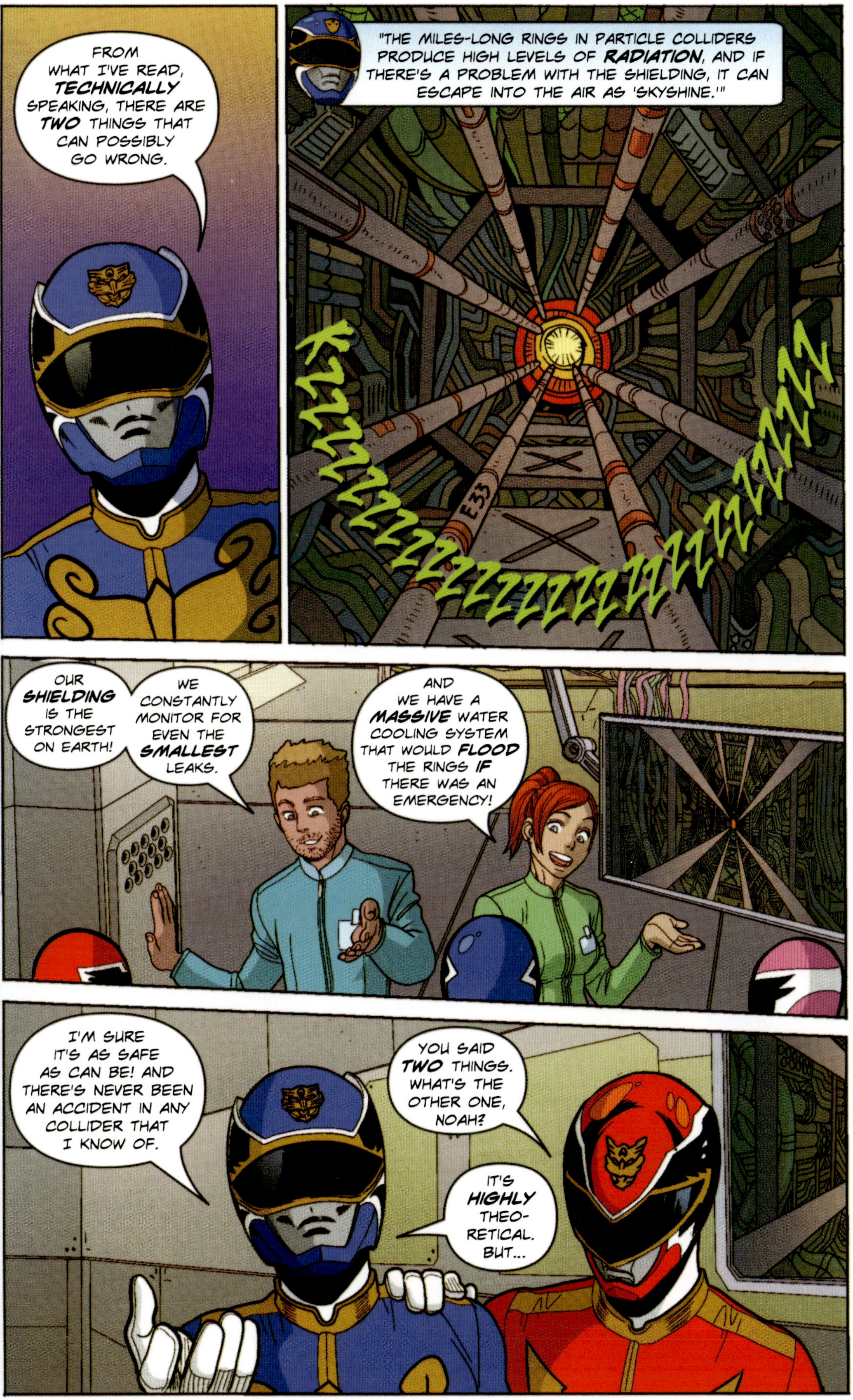
FROM WHAT I'VE READ, TECHNICALLY SPEAKING, THERE ARE TWO THINGS THAT CAN POSSIBLY GO WRONG.
"THE MILES-LONG RINGS IN PARTICLE COLLIDERS PRODUCE HIGH LEVELS OF RADIATION, AND IF THERE'S A PROBLEM WITH THE SHIELDING, IT CAN ESCAPE INTO THE AIR AS 'SKYSHINE.'"
KZZZZZZZZZZZZZZZZZZZZZZZZZZZ
E33
OUR SHIELDING IS THE STRONGEST ON EARTH!
WE CONSTANTLY MONITOR FOR EVEN THE SMALLEST LEAKS.
AND WE HAVE A MASSIVE WATER COOLING SYSTEM THAT WOULD FLOOD THE RINGS IF THERE WAS AN EMERGENCY!
I'M SURE IT'S AS SAFE AS CAN BE! AND THERE'S NEVER BEEN AN ACCIDENT IN ANY COLLIDER THAT I KNOW OF.
YOU SAID TWO THINGS. WHAT'S THE OTHER ONE, NOAH?
IT'S HIGHLY THEO-RETICAL. BUT...

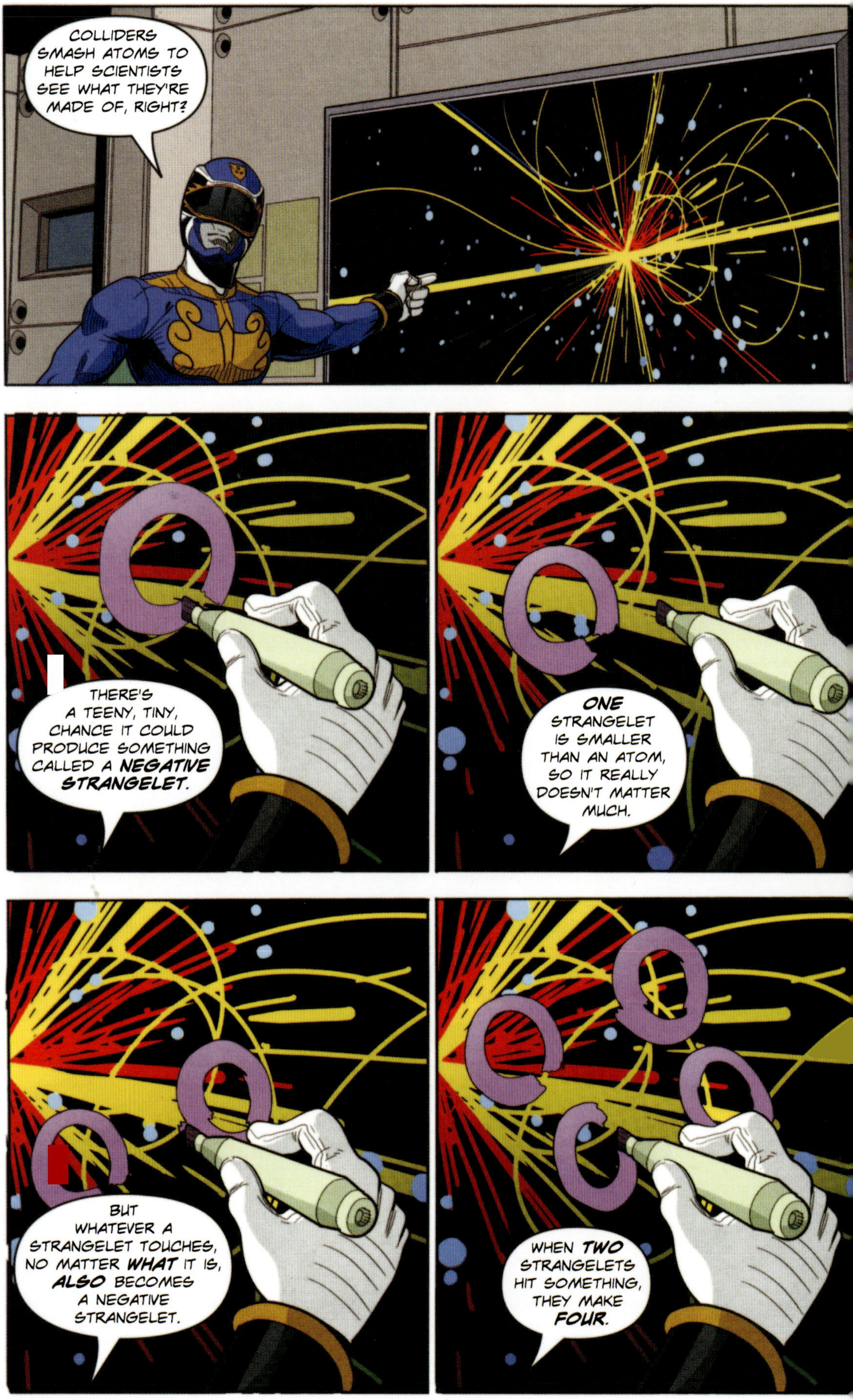
COLLIDERS SMASH ATOMS TO HELP SCIENTISTS SEE WHAT THEY'RE MADE OF, RIGHT?
THERE'S A TEENY, TINY, CHANCE IT COULD PRODUCE SOMETHING CALLED A **NEGATIVE STRANGELET**.
ONE STRANGELET IS SMALLER THAN AN ATOM, SO IT REALLY DOESN'T MATTER MUCH.
BUT WHATEVER A STRANGELET TOUCHES, NO MATTER **WHAT** IT IS, **ALSO** BECOMES A NEGATIVE STRANGELET.
WHEN **TWO** STRANGELETS HIT SOMETHING, THEY MAKE **FOUR**.

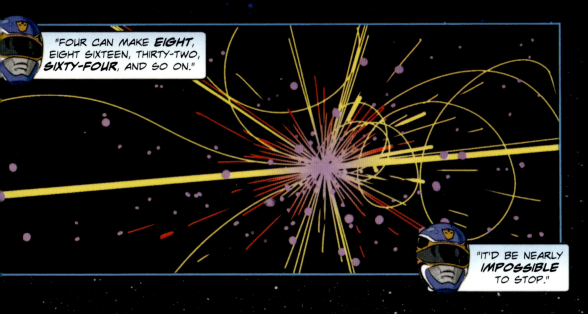

"FOUR CAN MAKE *EIGHT*, EIGHT SIXTEEN, THIRTY-TWO, *SIXTY-FOUR*, AND SO ON."

"IT'D BE NEARLY *IMPOSSIBLE* TO STOP."

"SO, EVEN IF YOU ONLY START WITH ONE, EVENTUALLY THE *ENTIRE PLANET* WOULD CHANGE INTO NEGATIVE STRANGELETS, *DESTROYING* WHATEVER WAS THERE BEFORE!"

"I WONDER: IS *THAT* THE THREAT *ROBO KNIGHT* IS WORRIED ABOUT?"

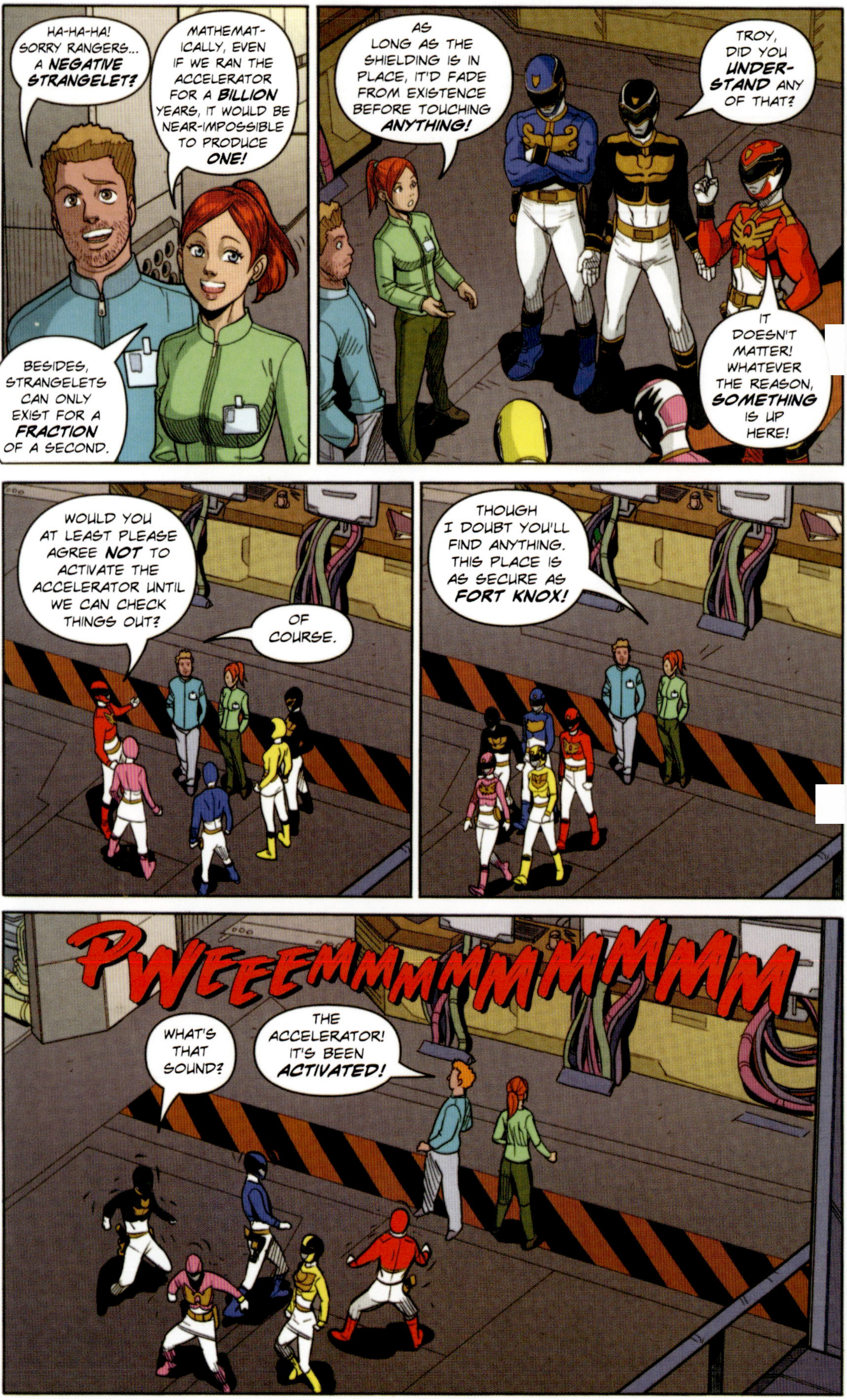
HA-HA-HA! SORRY RANGERS... A NEGATIVE STRANGELET?
MATHEMATICALLY, EVEN IF WE RAN THE ACCELERATOR FOR A BILLION YEARS, IT WOULD BE NEAR-IMPOSSIBLE TO PRODUCE ONE!
BESIDES, STRANGELETS CAN ONLY EXIST FOR A FRACTION OF A SECOND.
AS LONG AS THE SHIELDING IS IN PLACE, IT'D FADE FROM EXISTENCE BEFORE TOUCHING ANYTHING!
TROY, DID YOU UNDERSTAND ANY OF THAT?
IT DOESN'T MATTER! WHATEVER THE REASON, SOMETHING IS UP HERE!
WOULD YOU AT LEAST PLEASE AGREE NOT TO ACTIVATE THE ACCELERATOR UNTIL WE CAN CHECK THINGS OUT?
OF COURSE.
THOUGH I DOUBT YOU'LL FIND ANYTHING. THIS PLACE IS AS SECURE AS FORT KNOX!
PWEEEMMMMMMMMMM
WHAT'S THAT SOUND?
THE ACCELERATOR! IT'S BEEN ACTIVATED!

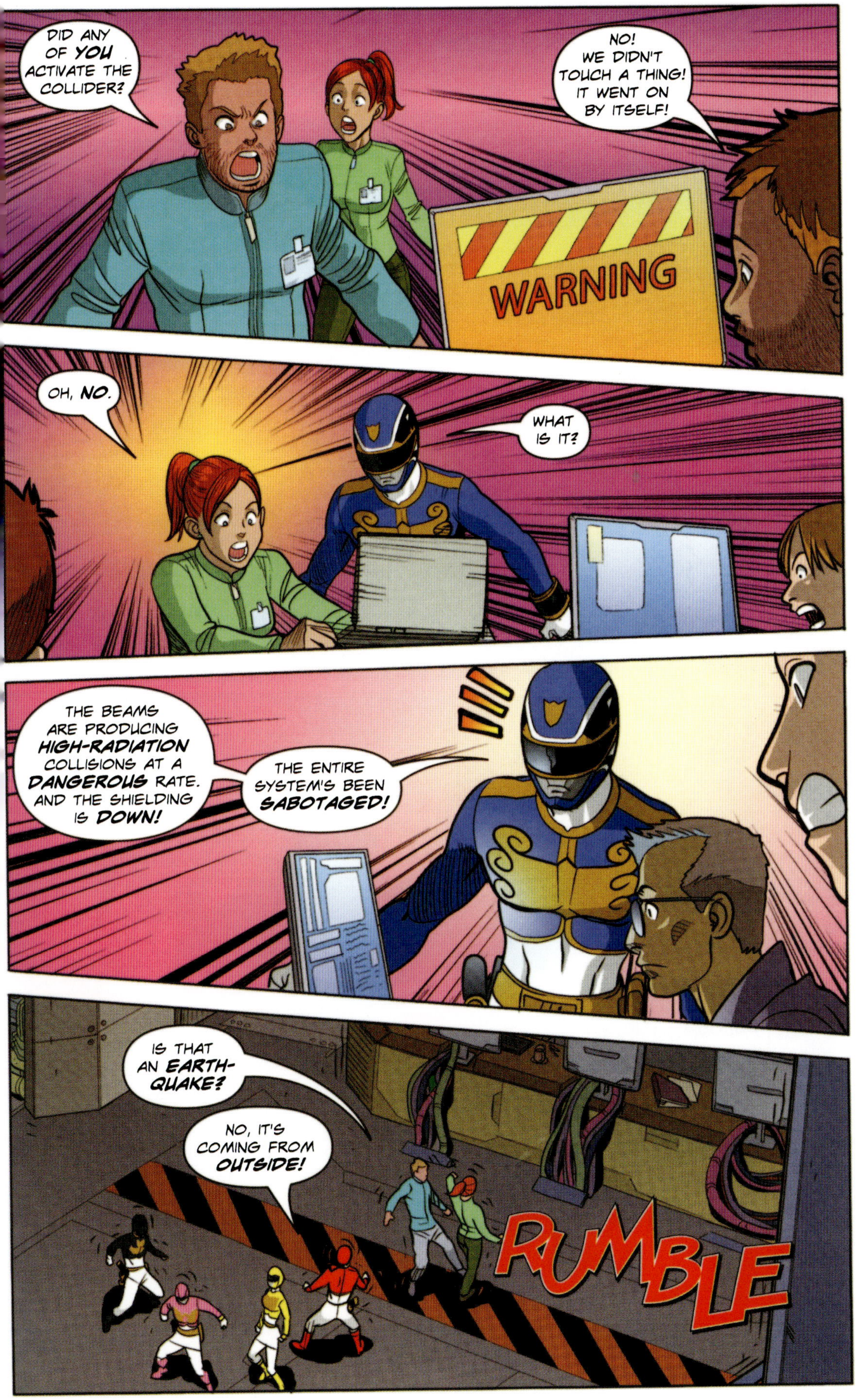
DID ANY OF YOU ACTIVATE THE COLLIDER?
NO! WE DIDN'T TOUCH A THING! IT WENT ON BY ITSELF!
WARNING
OH, NO.
WHAT IS IT?
THE BEAMS ARE PRODUCING HIGH-RADIATION COLLISIONS AT A DANGEROUS RATE. AND THE SHIELDING IS DOWN!
THE ENTIRE SYSTEM'S BEEN SABOTAGED!
IS THAT AN EARTH-QUAKE?
NO, IT'S COMING FROM OUTSIDE!
RUMBLE

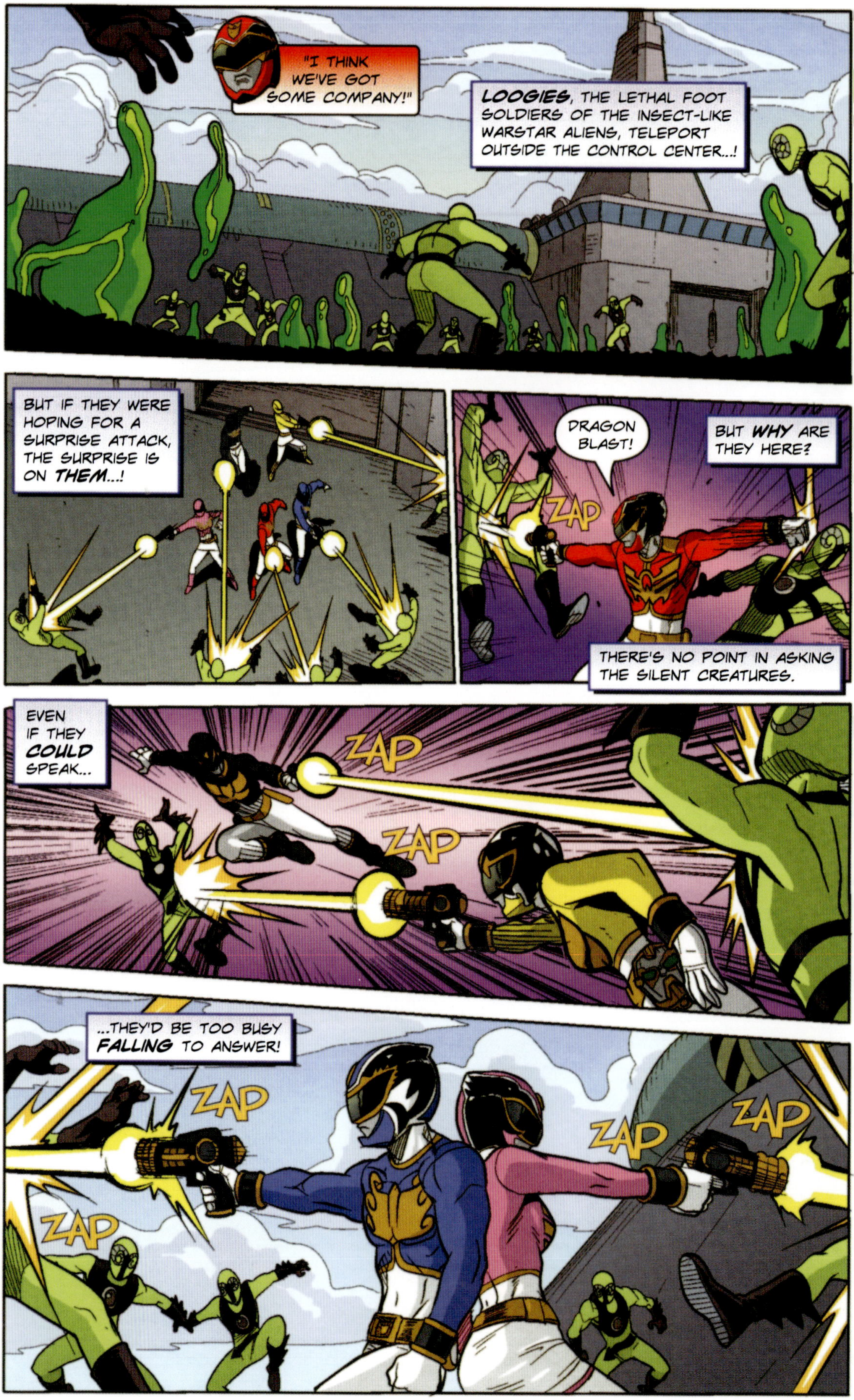

"I THINK WE'VE GOT SOME COMPANY!"
LOOGIES, THE LETHAL FOOT SOLDIERS OF THE INSECT-LIKE WARSTAR ALIENS, TELEPORT OUTSIDE THE CONTROL CENTER...!
BUT IF THEY WERE HOPING FOR A SURPRISE ATTACK, THE SURPRISE IS ON THEM...!
DRAGON BLAST!
BUT WHY ARE THEY HERE?
ZAP
THERE'S NO POINT IN ASKING THE SILENT CREATURES.
EVEN IF THEY COULD SPEAK...
ZAP
ZAP
...THEY'D BE TOO BUSY FALLING TO ANSWER!
ZAP
ZAP
ZAP
ZAP

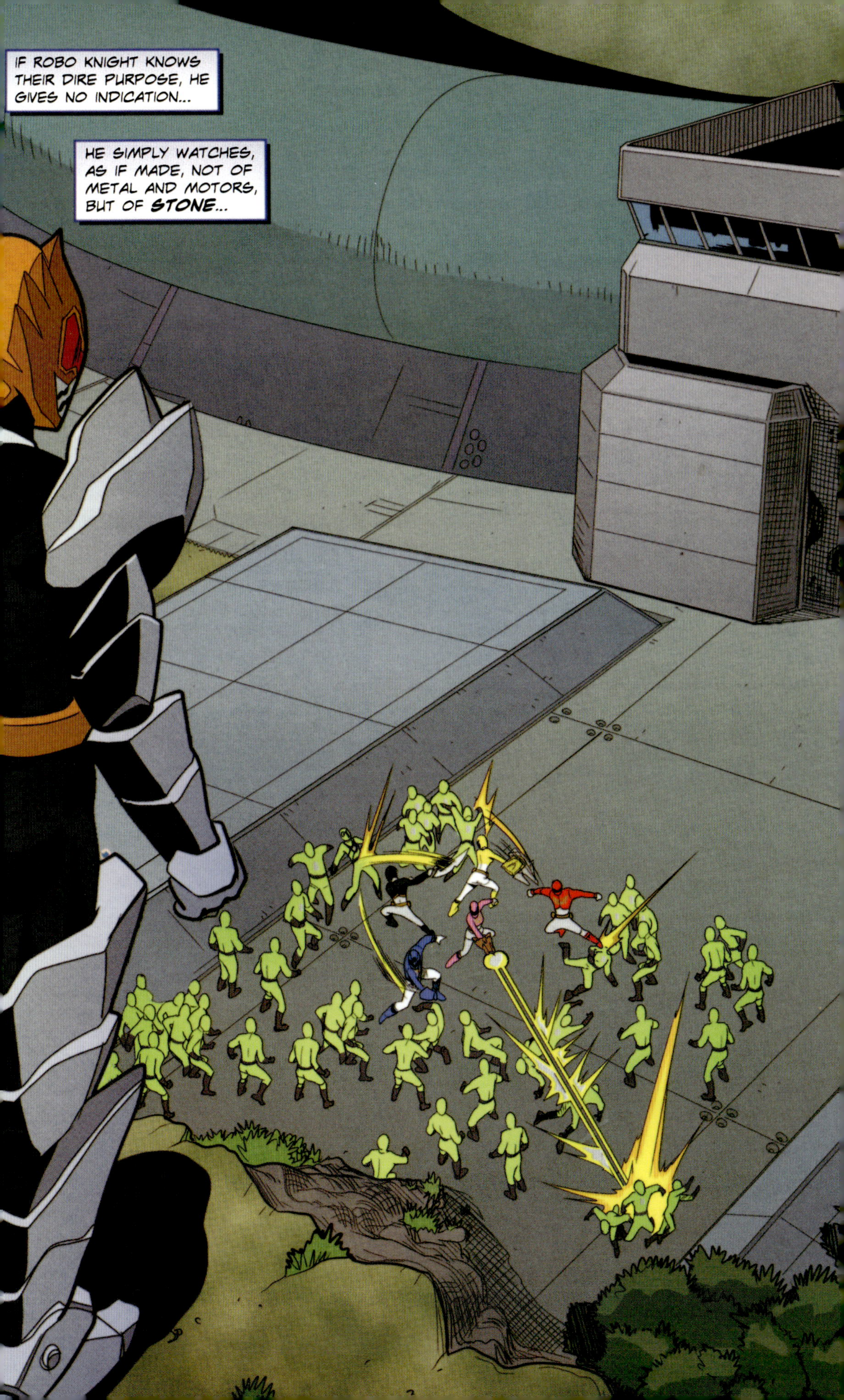
IF ROBO KNIGHT KNOWS THEIR DIRE PURPOSE, HE GIVES NO INDICATION...
HE SIMPLY WATCHES, AS IF MADE, NOT OF METAL AND MOTORS, BUT OF STONE...

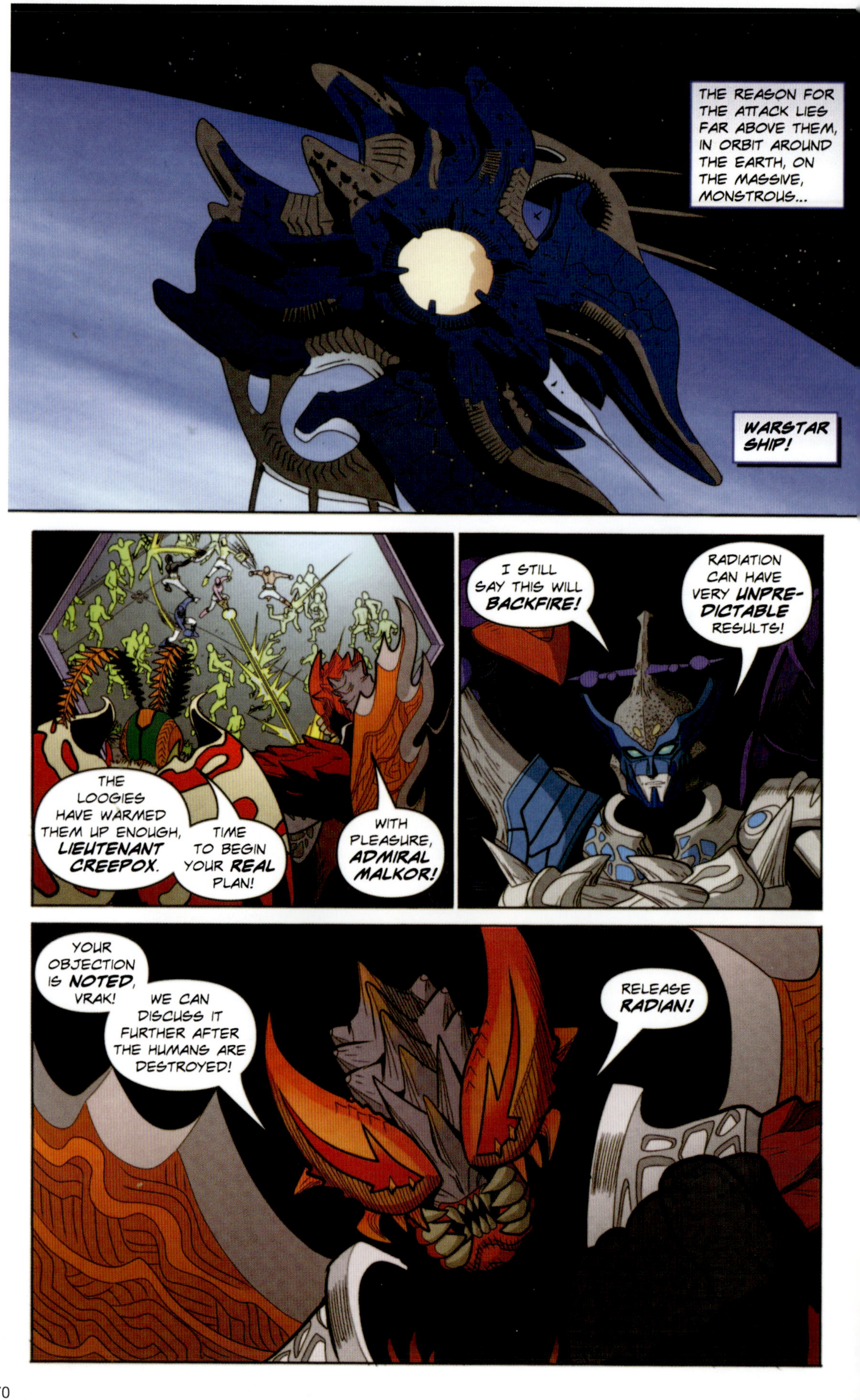
THE REASON FOR THE ATTACK LIES FAR ABOVE THEM, IN ORBIT AROUND THE EARTH, ON THE MASSIVE, MONSTROUS...
WARSTAR SHIP!
THE LOOGIES HAVE WARMED THEM UP ENOUGH, LIEUTENANT CREEPOX.
TIME TO BEGIN YOUR REAL PLAN!
WITH PLEASURE, ADMIRAL MALKOR!
I STILL SAY THIS WILL BACKFIRE!
RADIATION CAN HAVE VERY UNPREDICTABLE RESULTS!
YOUR OBJECTION IS NOTED, VRAK!
WE CAN DISCUSS IT FURTHER AFTER THE HUMANS ARE DESTROYED!
RELEASE RADIAN!

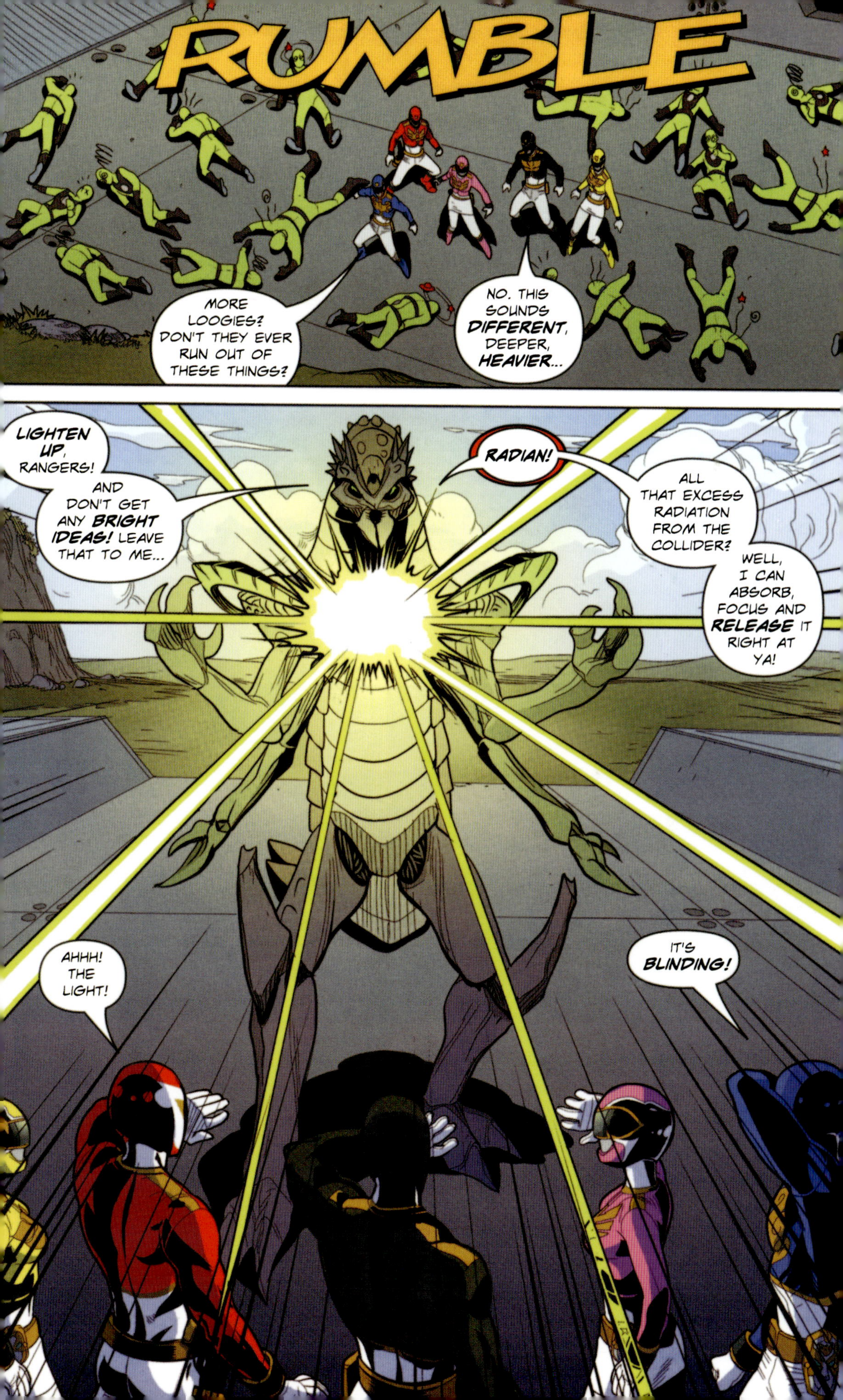
RUMBLE
MORE LOOGIES? DON'T THEY EVER RUN OUT OF THESE THINGS?
NO. THIS SOUNDS DIFFERENT, DEEPER, HEAVIER...
LIGHTEN UP, RANGERS!
AND DON'T GET ANY BRIGHT IDEAS! LEAVE THAT TO ME...
RADIAN!
ALL THAT EXCESS RADIATION FROM THE COLLIDER?
WELL, I CAN ABSORB, FOCUS AND RELEASE IT RIGHT AT YA!
AHHH! THE LIGHT!
IT'S BLINDING!

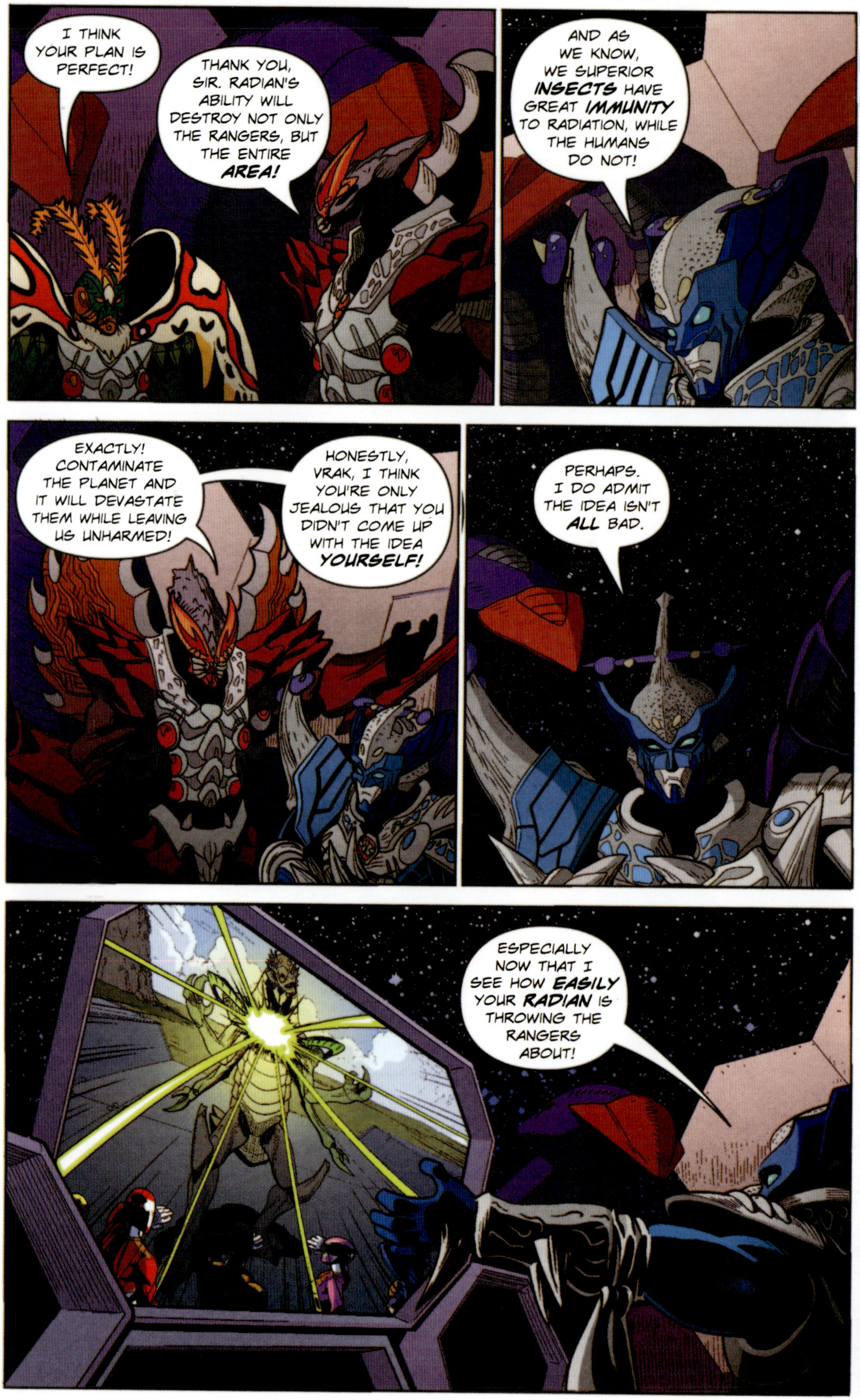
I THINK YOUR PLAN IS PERFECT!
THANK YOU, SIR. RADIAN'S ABILITY WILL DESTROY NOT ONLY THE RANGERS, BUT THE ENTIRE AREA!
AND AS WE KNOW, WE SUPERIOR INSECTS HAVE GREAT IMMUNITY TO RADIATION, WHILE THE HUMANS DO NOT!
EXACTLY! CONTAMINATE THE PLANET AND IT WILL DEVASTATE THEM WHILE LEAVING US UNHARMED!
HONESTLY, VRAK, I THINK YOU'RE ONLY JEALOUS THAT YOU DIDN'T COME UP WITH THE IDEA YOURSELF!
PERHAPS. I DO ADMIT THE IDEA ISN'T ALL BAD.
ESPECIALLY NOW THAT I SEE HOW EASILY YOUR RADIAN IS THROWING THE RANGERS ABOUT!

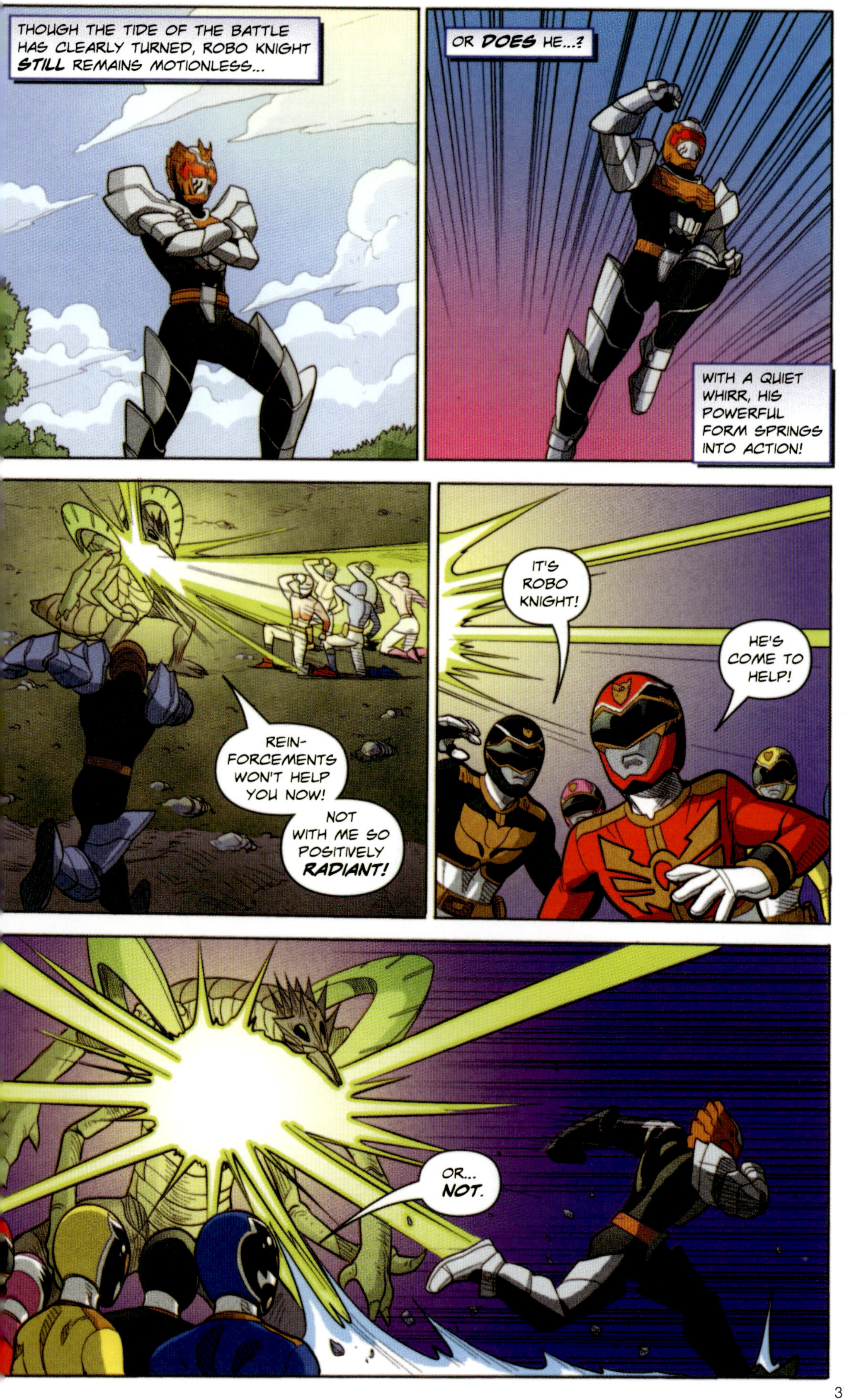
THOUGH THE TIDE OF THE BATTLE HAS CLEARLY TURNED, ROBO KNIGHT STILL REMAINS MOTIONLESS...
OR DOES HE...?
WITH A QUIET WHIRR, HIS POWERFUL FORM SPRINGS INTO ACTION!
REIN-FORCEMENTS WON'T HELP YOU NOW!
NOT WITH ME SO POSITIVELY RADIANT!
IT'S ROBO KNIGHT!
HE'S COME TO HELP!
OR... NOT.

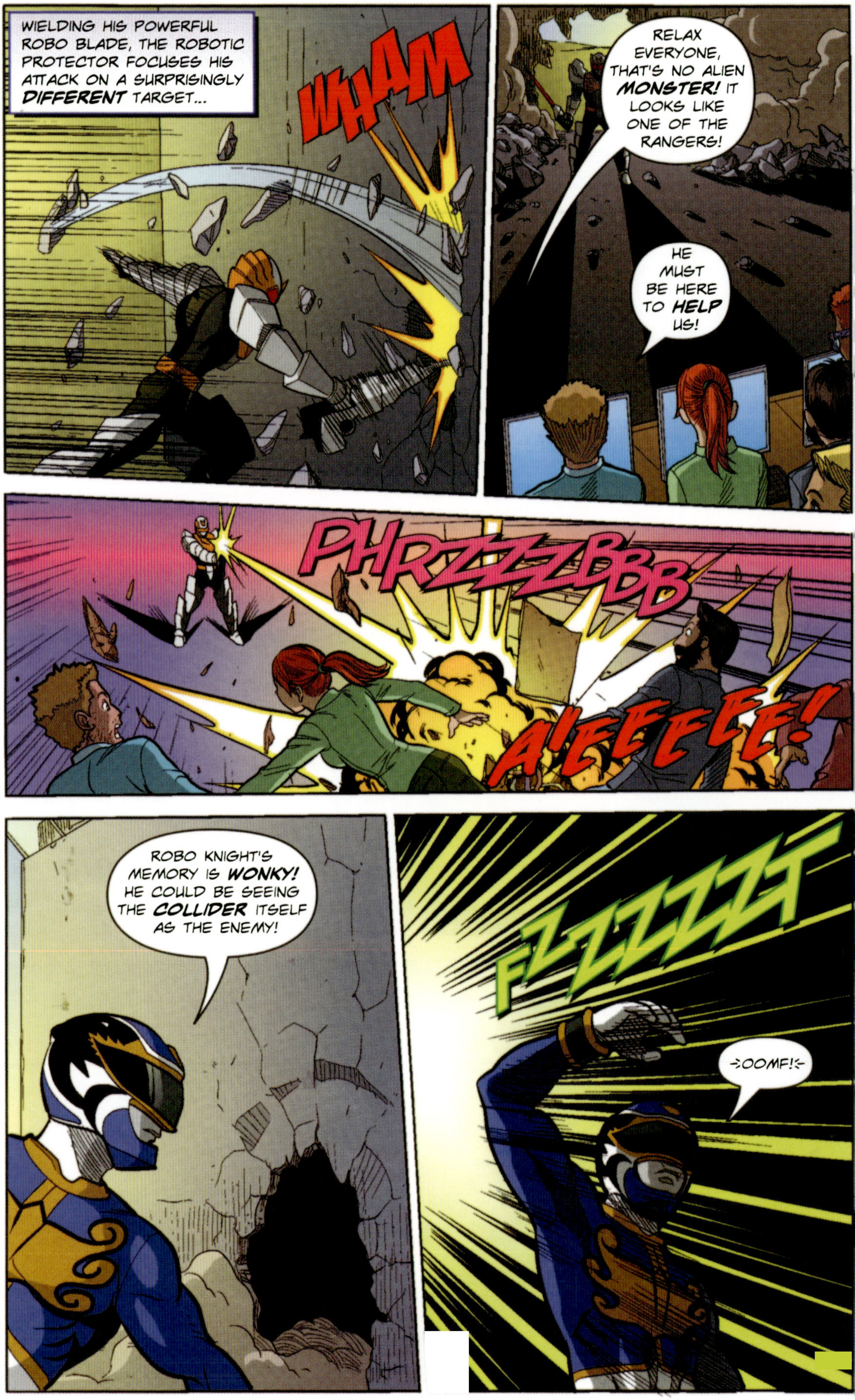
WIELDING HIS POWERFUL ROBO BLADE, THE ROBOTIC PROTECTOR FOCUSES HIS ATTACK ON A SURPRISINGLY DIFFERENT TARGET...
WHAM
RELAX EVERYONE, THAT'S NO ALIEN MONSTER! IT LOOKS LIKE ONE OF THE RANGERS!
HE MUST BE HERE TO HELP US!
PHRZZZZBBB
AIEEEEEE!
ROBO KNIGHT'S MEMORY IS WONKY! HE COULD BE SEEING THE COLLIDER ITSELF AS THE ENEMY!
FZZZZZT
OOMF!

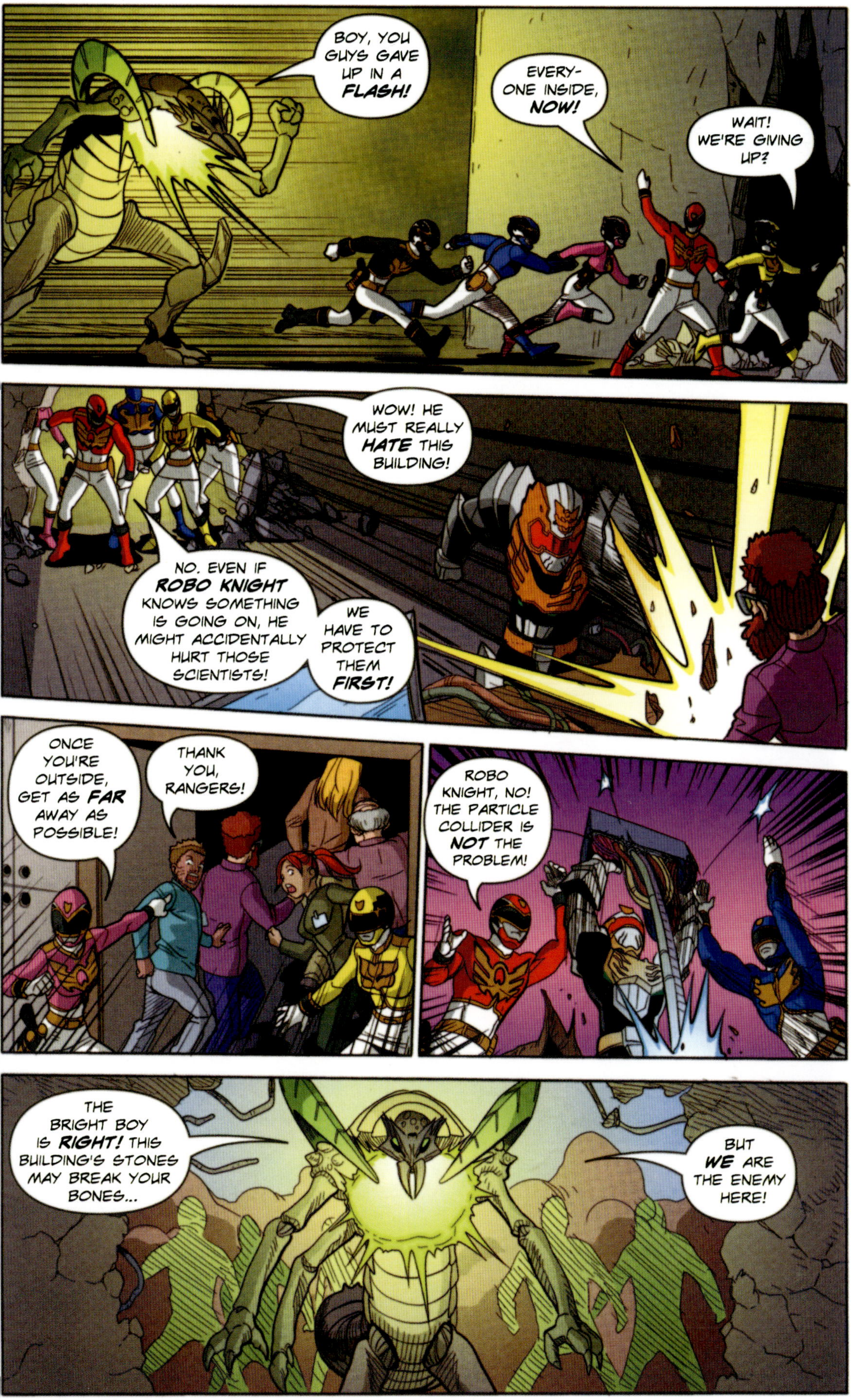
BOY, YOU GUYS GAVE UP IN A FLASH!
EVERY-ONE INSIDE, NOW!
WAIT! WE'RE GIVING UP?
WOW! HE MUST REALLY HATE THIS BUILDING!
NO. EVEN IF ROBO KNIGHT KNOWS SOMETHING IS GOING ON, HE MIGHT ACCIDENTALLY HURT THOSE SCIENTISTS!
WE HAVE TO PROTECT THEM FIRST!
ONCE YOU'RE OUTSIDE, GET AS FAR AWAY AS POSSIBLE!
THANK YOU, RANGERS!
ROBO KNIGHT, NO! THE PARTICLE COLLIDER IS NOT THE PROBLEM!
THE BRIGHT BOY IS RIGHT! THIS BUILDING'S STONES MAY BREAK YOUR BONES...
BUT WE ARE THE ENEMY HERE!

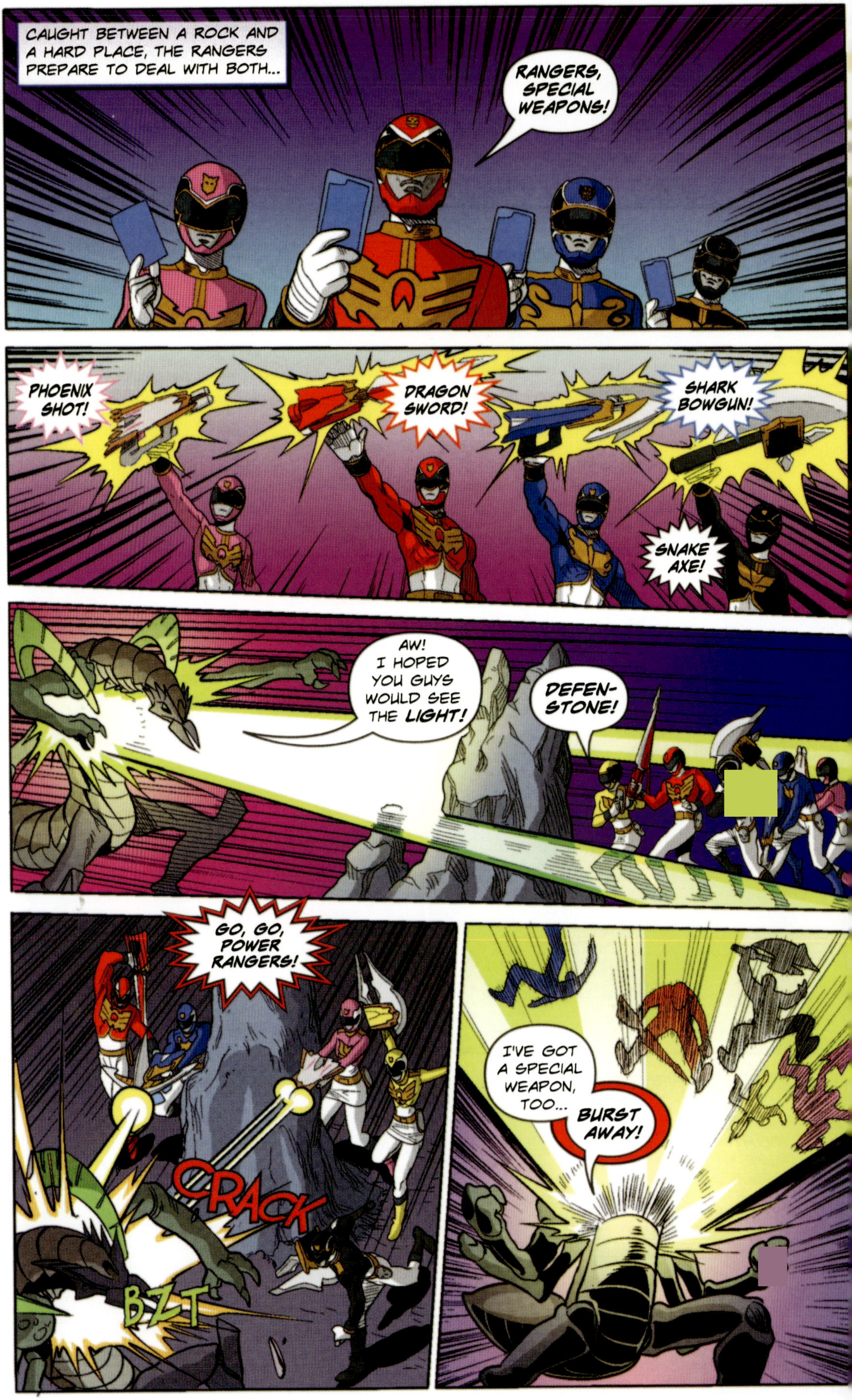
CAUGHT BETWEEN A ROCK AND A HARD PLACE, THE RANGERS PREPARE TO DEAL WITH BOTH...
RANGERS, SPECIAL WEAPONS!
PHOENIX SHOT!
DRAGON SWORD!
SHARK BOWGUN!
SNAKE AXE!
AW! I HOPED YOU GUYS WOULD SEE THE LIGHT!
DEFEN-STONE!
GO, GO, POWER RANGERS!
CRACK
BZZT
I'VE GOT A SPECIAL WEAPON, TOO...
BURST AWAY!

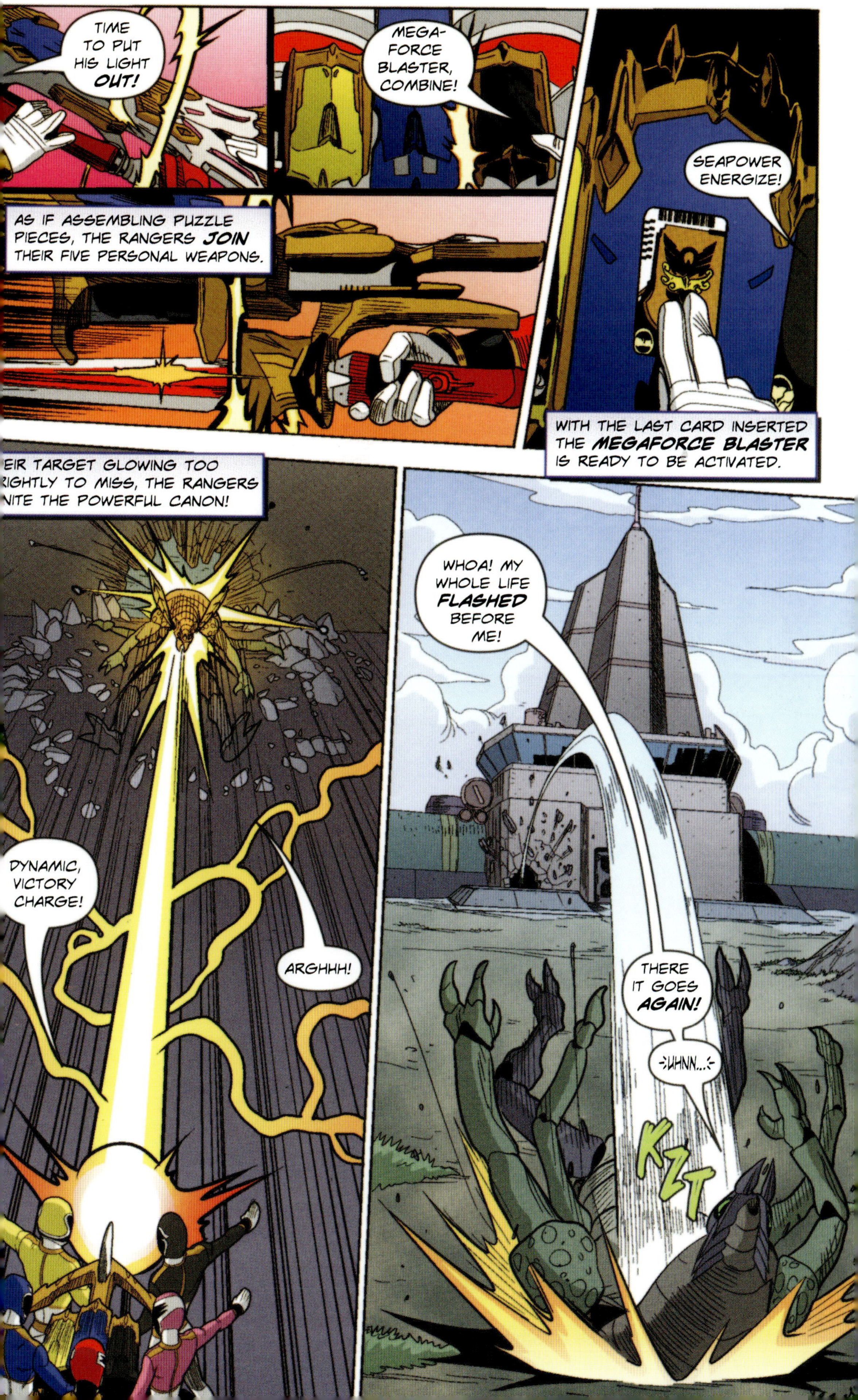
TIME TO PUT HIS LIGHT OUT!
MEGA-FORCE BLASTER, COMBINE!
SEAPOWER ENERGIZE!
AS IF ASSEMBLING PUZZLE PIECES, THE RANGERS JOIN THEIR FIVE PERSONAL WEAPONS.
WITH THE LAST CARD INSERTED THE MEGAFORCE BLASTER IS READY TO BE ACTIVATED.
EIR TARGET GLOWING TOO
RIGHTLY TO MISS, THE RANGERS
NITE THE POWERFUL CANON!
DYNAMIC, VICTORY CHARGE!
ARGHHH!
WHOA! MY WHOLE LIFE FLASHED BEFORE ME!
THERE IT GOES AGAIN!
UHNN...
KZT

NOW WE HAVE TO STOP ROBO KNIGHT!

I THINK I KNOW **WHY** HE'S ATTACKING THE COLLIDER.

THE SABOTAGE CAUSED AN OVERLOAD, AND BECAUSE OF THAT, THE COLLIDER **HAS** PRODUCED A **STRANGELET!**

"HE MUST HAVE SOMEHOW **SENSED** IT WOULD HAPPEN, DESPITE THE INCREDIBLE ODDS!"

"THE EMERGENCY COOLING IS FLOODING THE COLLIDER, BUT THE **REACTION** HAS ALREADY STARTED!"

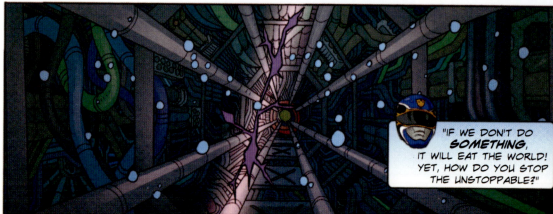

"IF WE DON'T DO **SOMETHING,** IT WILL EAT THE WORLD! YET, HOW DO YOU STOP THE UNSTOPPABLE?"

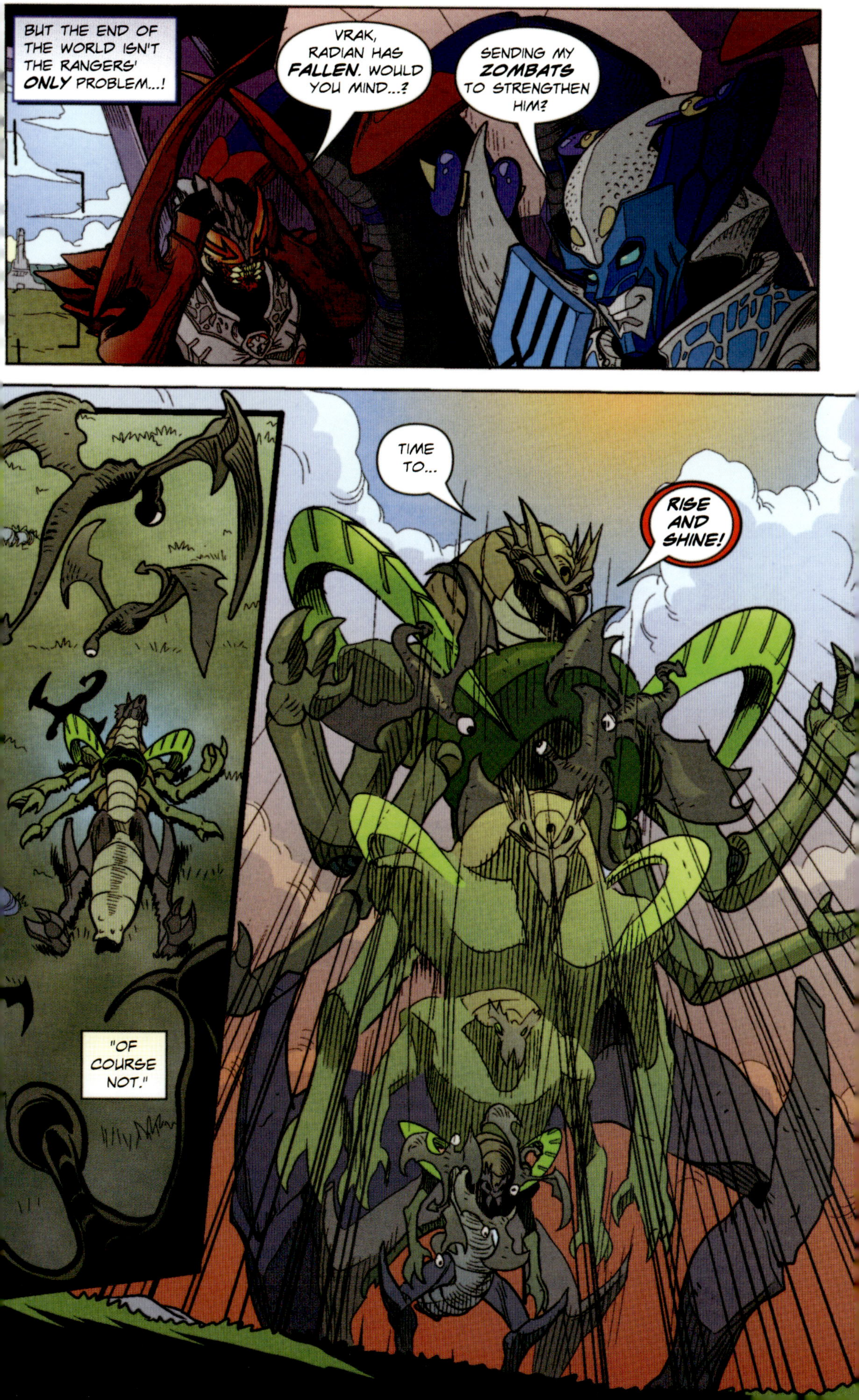
BUT THE END OF THE WORLD ISN'T THE RANGERS' ONLY PROBLEM...!
VRAK, RADIAN HAS FALLEN. WOULD YOU MIND...?
SENDING MY ZOMBATS TO STRENGTHEN HIM?
"OF COURSE NOT."
TIME TO...
RISE AND SHINE!

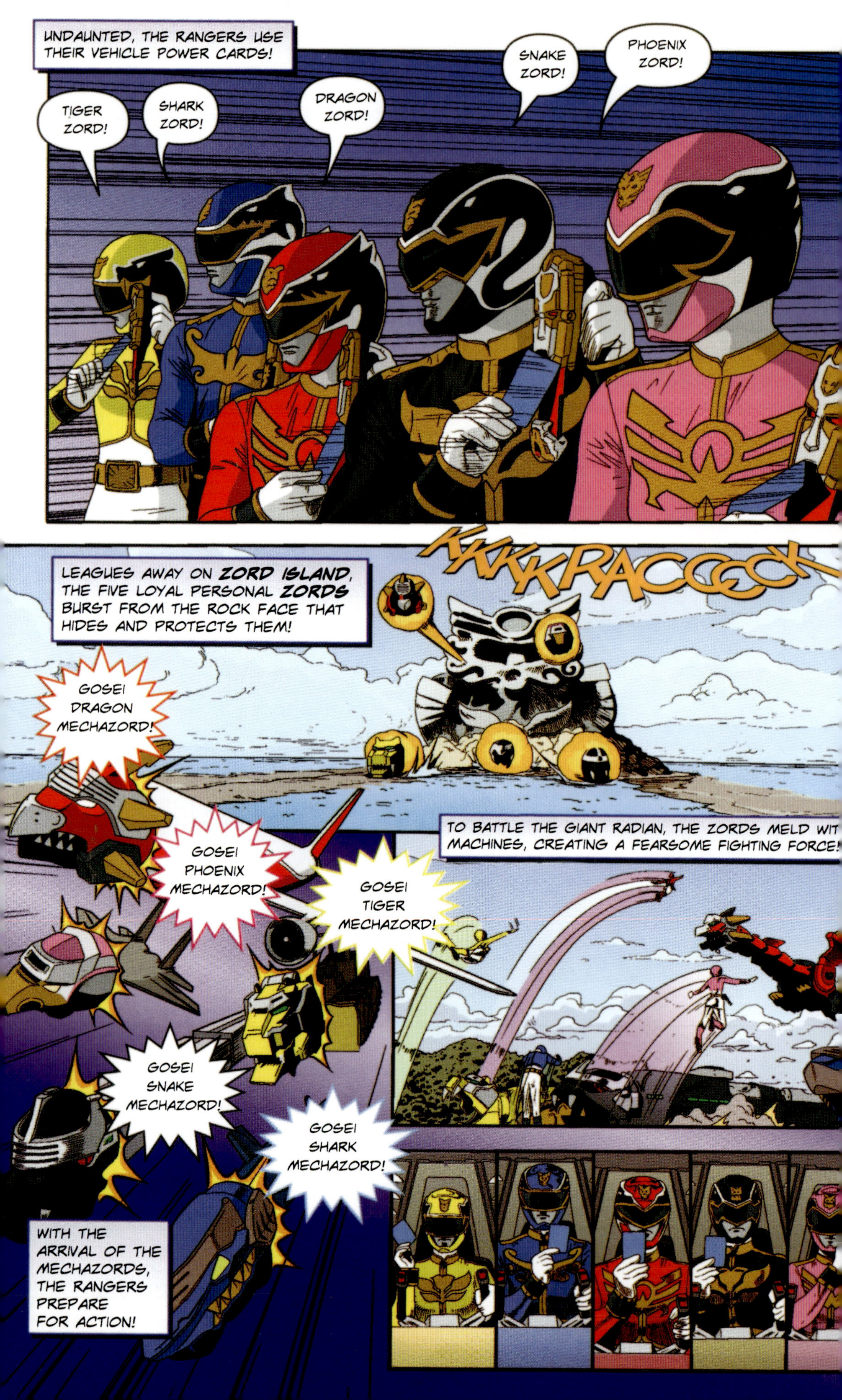
UNDAUNTED, THE RANGERS USE THEIR VEHICLE POWER CARDS!
TIGER ZORD!
SHARK ZORD!
DRAGON ZORD!
SNAKE ZORD!
PHOENIX ZORD!
KKKKRACCCCCK
LEAGUES AWAY ON ZORD ISLAND, THE FIVE LOYAL PERSONAL ZORDS BURST FROM THE ROCK FACE THAT HIDES AND PROTECTS THEM!
GOSEI DRAGON MECHAZORD!
GOSEI PHOENIX MECHAZORD!
GOSEI TIGER MECHAZORD!
GOSEI SNAKE MECHAZORD!
GOSEI SHARK MECHAZORD!
TO BATTLE THE GIANT RADIAN, THE ZORDS MELD WIT MACHINES, CREATING A FEARSOME FIGHTING FORCE!
WITH THE ARRIVAL OF THE MECHAZORDS, THE RANGERS PREPARE FOR ACTION!

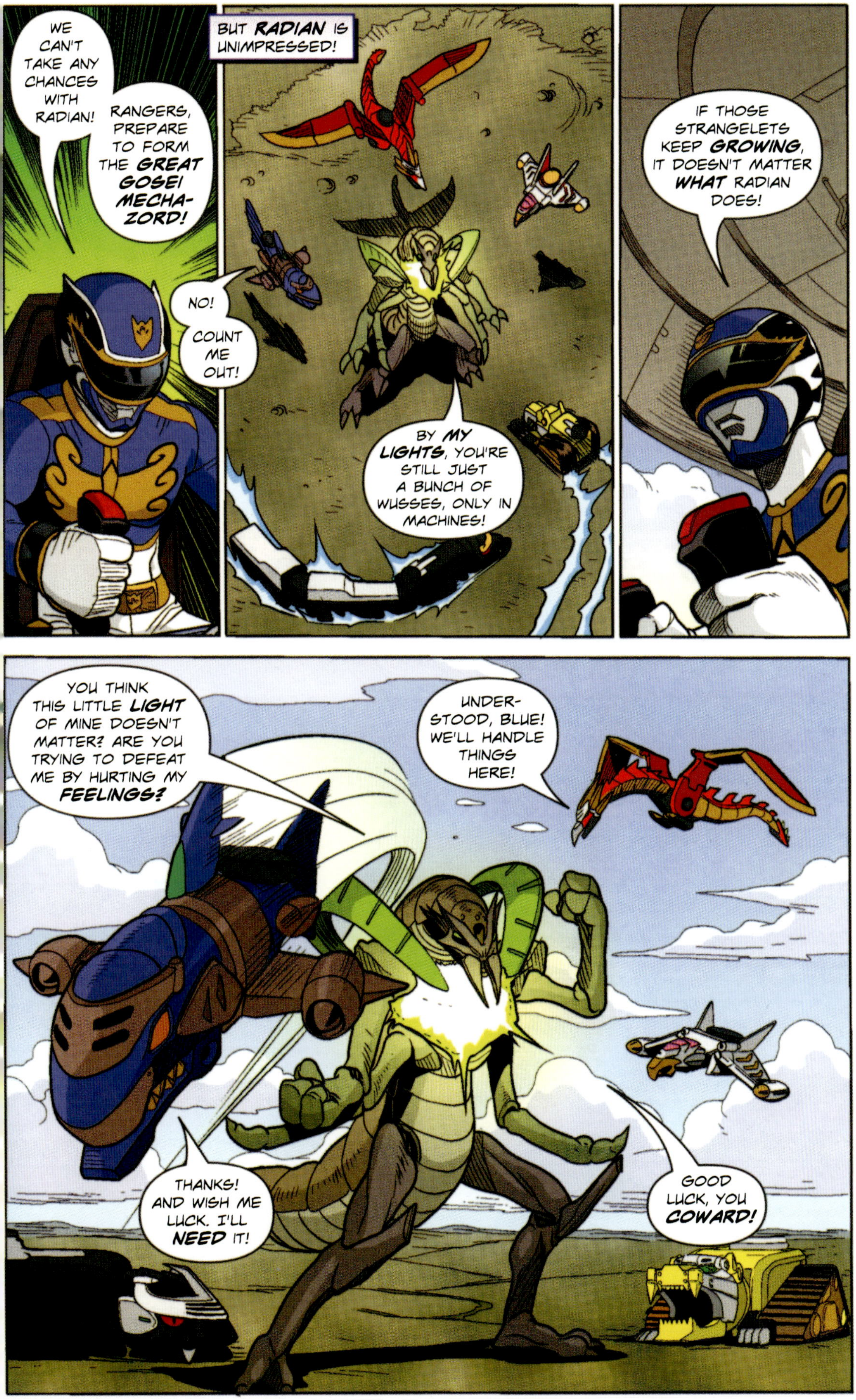

WE CAN'T TAKE ANY CHANCES WITH RADIAN!
RANGERS, PREPARE TO FORM THE GREAT GOSEI MECHA-ZORD!
BUT RADIAN IS UNIMPRESSED!
NO!
COUNT ME OUT!
BY MY LIGHTS, YOU'RE STILL JUST A BUNCH OF WUSSES, ONLY IN MACHINES!
IF THOSE STRANGELETS KEEP GROWING, IT DOESN'T MATTER WHAT RADIAN DOES!
YOU THINK THIS LITTLE LIGHT OF MINE DOESN'T MATTER? ARE YOU TRYING TO DEFEAT ME BY HURTING MY FEELINGS?
UNDER-STOOD, BLUE! WE'LL HANDLE THINGS HERE!
THANKS! AND WISH ME LUCK. I'LL NEED IT!
GOOD LUCK, YOU COWARD!

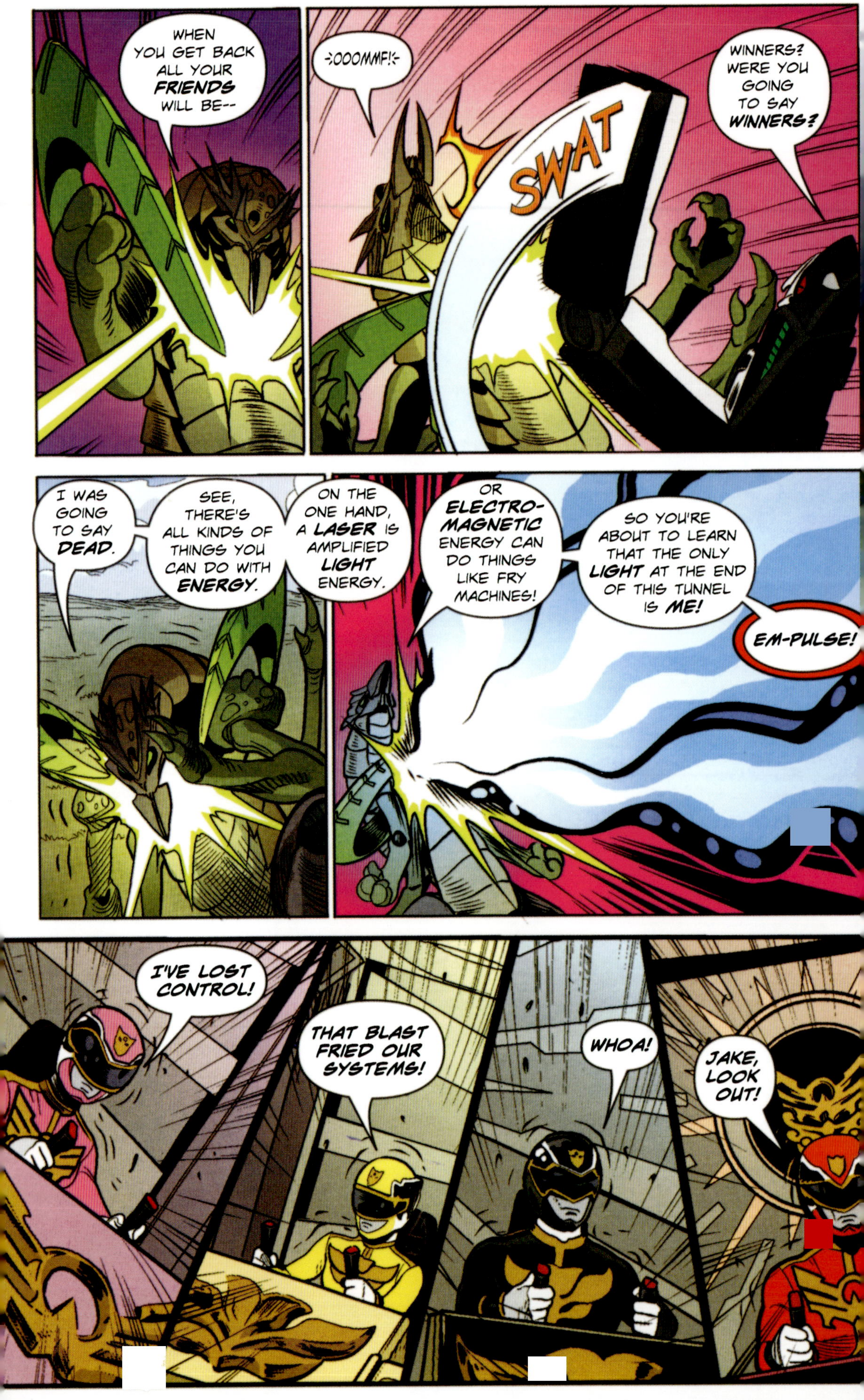
WHEN YOU GET BACK ALL YOUR **FRIENDS** WILL BE--
-:OOOMMF!:-
SWAT
WINNERS? WERE YOU GOING TO SAY **WINNERS?**
I WAS GOING TO SAY **DEAD**.
SEE, THERE'S ALL KINDS OF THINGS YOU CAN DO WITH **ENERGY**.
ON THE ONE HAND, A **LASER** IS AMPLIFIED **LIGHT** ENERGY.
OR **ELECTRO-MAGNETIC** ENERGY CAN DO THINGS LIKE FRY MACHINES!
SO YOU'RE ABOUT TO LEARN THAT THE ONLY **LIGHT** AT THE END OF THIS TUNNEL IS **ME!**
EM-PULSE!
I'VE LOST CONTROL!
THAT BLAST FRIED OUR SYSTEMS!
WHOA!
JAKE, LOOK OUT!

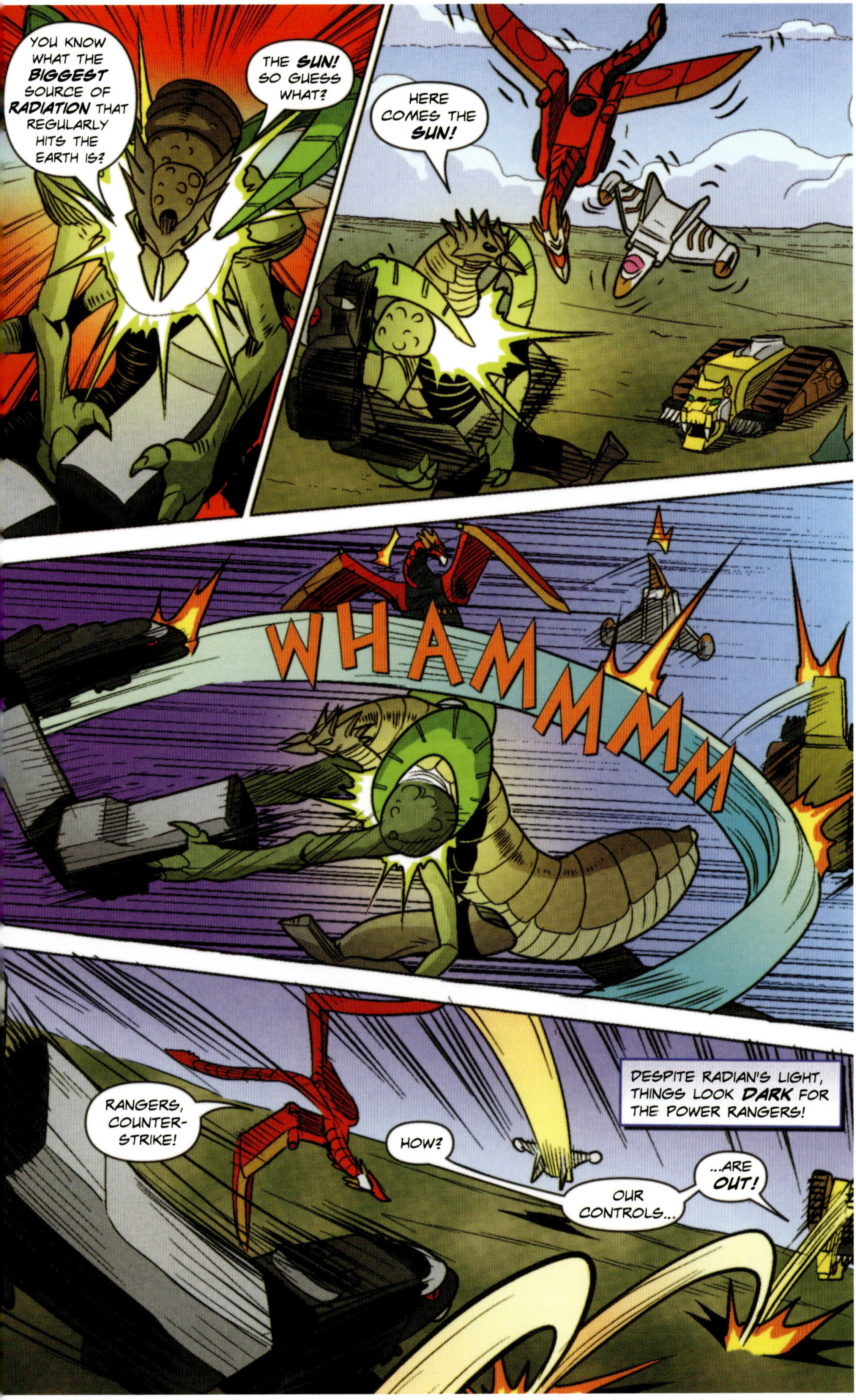
YOU KNOW WHAT THE BIGGEST SOURCE OF RADIATION THAT REGULARLY HITS THE EARTH IS?
THE SUN! SO GUESS WHAT?
HERE COMES THE SUN!
WHAMMMMM
RANGERS, COUNTER-STRIKE!
HOW?
OUR CONTROLS...
...ARE OUT!
DESPITE RADIAN'S LIGHT, THINGS LOOK DARK FOR THE POWER RANGERS!

BUT THEY'RE *DARKER STILL* FOR BLUE RANGER NOAH, AS HE STEERS THE SHARK MECHAZORD INTO THE COOLING WATERS THAT HAVE FLOODED THE COLLIDER RING!

THE POWER AUTOMATICALLY SHUT DOWN. I CAN BARELY SEE A THING.

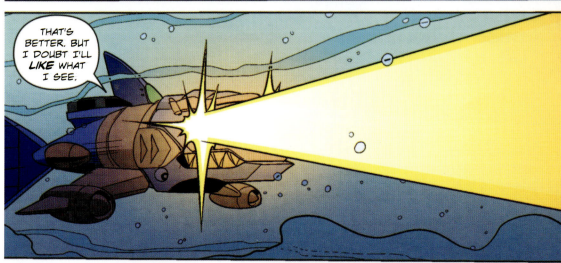

THAT'S BETTER. BUT I DOUBT I'LL *LIKE* WHAT I SEE.

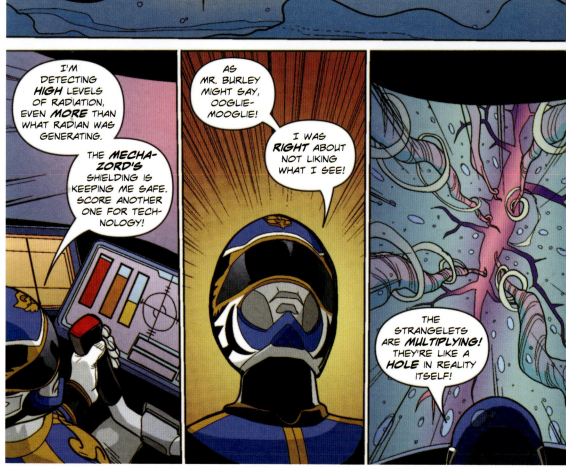

I'M DETECTING *HIGH* LEVELS OF RADIATION, EVEN *MORE* THAN WHAT RADIAN WAS GENERATING.

THE *MECHA-ZORD'S* SHIELDING IS KEEPING ME SAFE. SCORE ANOTHER ONE FOR TECH-NOLOGY!

AS MR. BURLEY MIGHT SAY, OOGLIE-MOOGLIE!

I WAS *RIGHT* ABOUT NOT LIKING WHAT I SEE!

THE STRANGELETS ARE *MULTIPLYING!* THEY'RE LIKE A *HOLE* IN REALITY ITSELF!

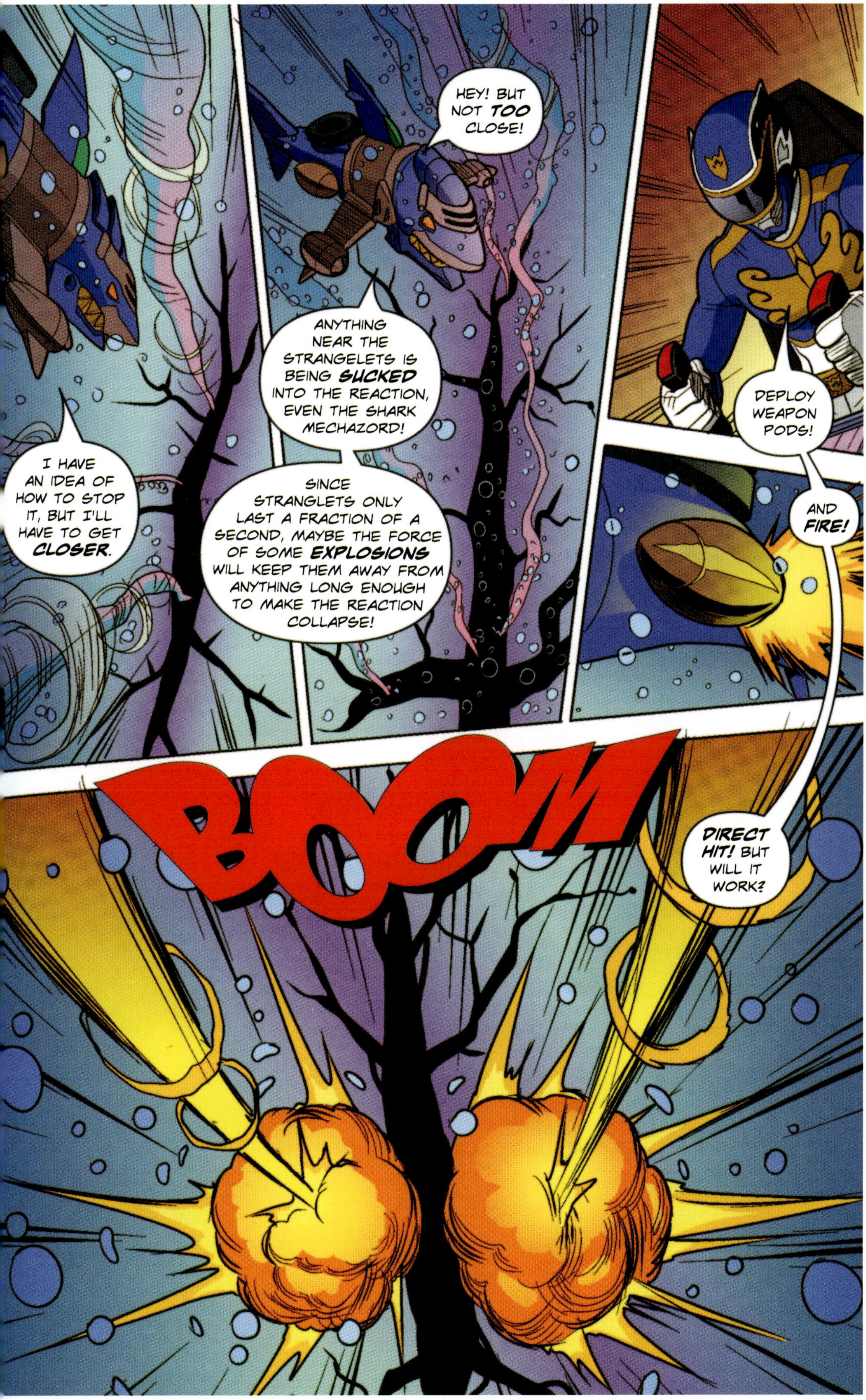
I HAVE AN IDEA OF HOW TO STOP IT, BUT I'LL HAVE TO GET CLOSER.
HEY! BUT NOT TOO CLOSE!
ANYTHING NEAR THE STRANGELETS IS BEING SUCKED INTO THE REACTION, EVEN THE SHARK MECHAZORD!
SINCE STRANGLETS ONLY LAST A FRACTION OF A SECOND, MAYBE THE FORCE OF SOME EXPLOSIONS WILL KEEP THEM AWAY FROM ANYTHING LONG ENOUGH TO MAKE THE REACTION COLLAPSE!
DEPLOY WEAPON PODS!
AND FIRE!
BOOM
DIRECT HIT! BUT WILL IT WORK?

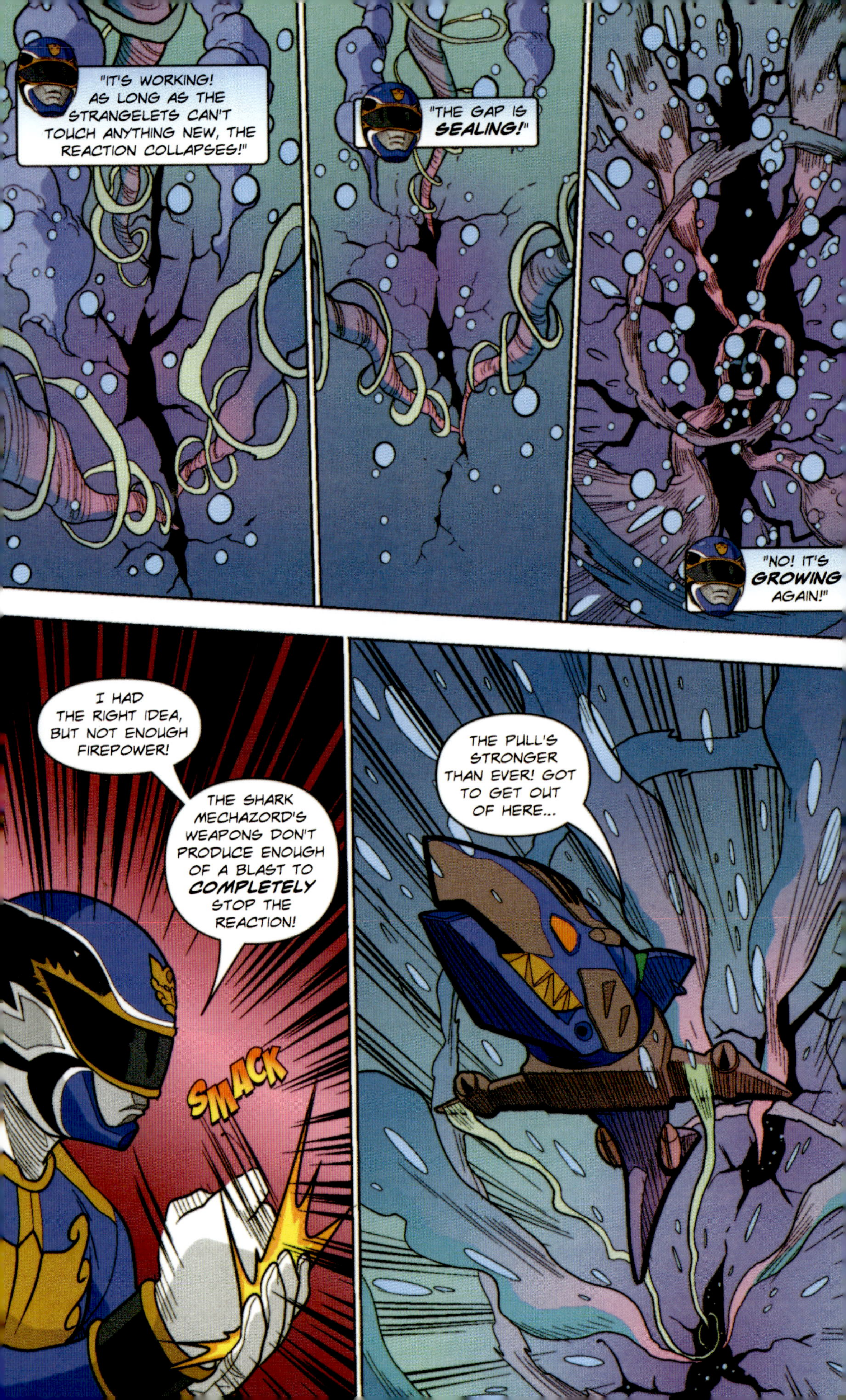
"IT'S WORKING! AS LONG AS THE STRANGELETS CAN'T TOUCH ANYTHING NEW, THE REACTION COLLAPSES!"
"THE GAP IS SEALING!"
"NO! IT'S GROWING AGAIN!"
I HAD THE RIGHT IDEA, BUT NOT ENOUGH FIREPOWER!
THE SHARK MECHAZORD'S WEAPONS DON'T PRODUCE ENOUGH OF A BLAST TO COMPLETELY STOP THE REACTION!
SMACK
THE PULL'S STRONGER THAN EVER! GOT TO GET OUT OF HERE...

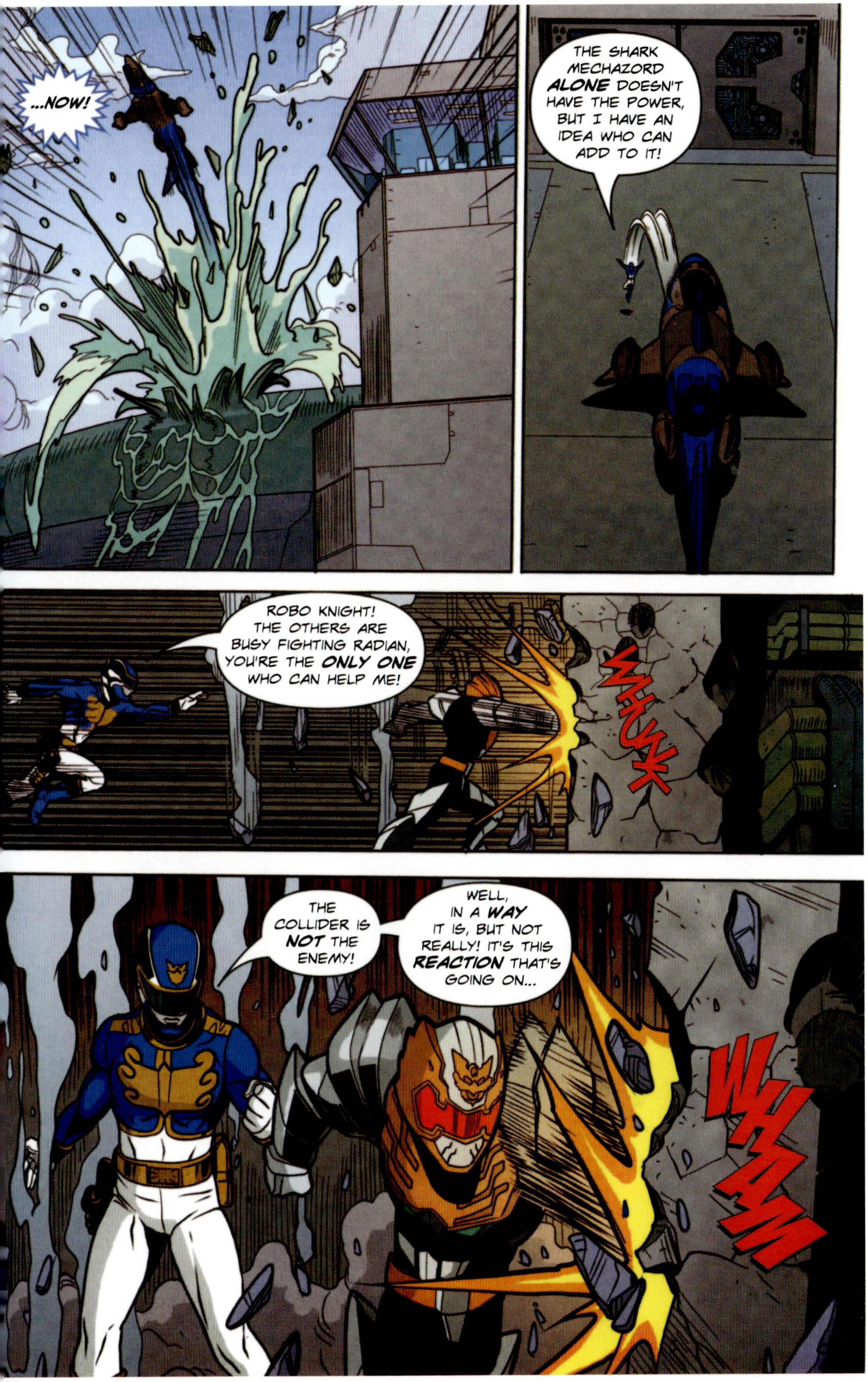

...NOW!
THE SHARK MECHAZORD ALONE DOESN'T HAVE THE POWER, BUT I HAVE AN IDEA WHO CAN ADD TO IT!
ROBO KNIGHT! THE OTHERS ARE BUSY FIGHTING RADIAN, YOU'RE THE ONLY ONE WHO CAN HELP ME!
WHUNK
THE COLLIDER IS NOT THE ENEMY!
WELL, IN A WAY IT IS, BUT NOT REALLY! IT'S THIS REACTION THAT'S GOING ON...
WHAM

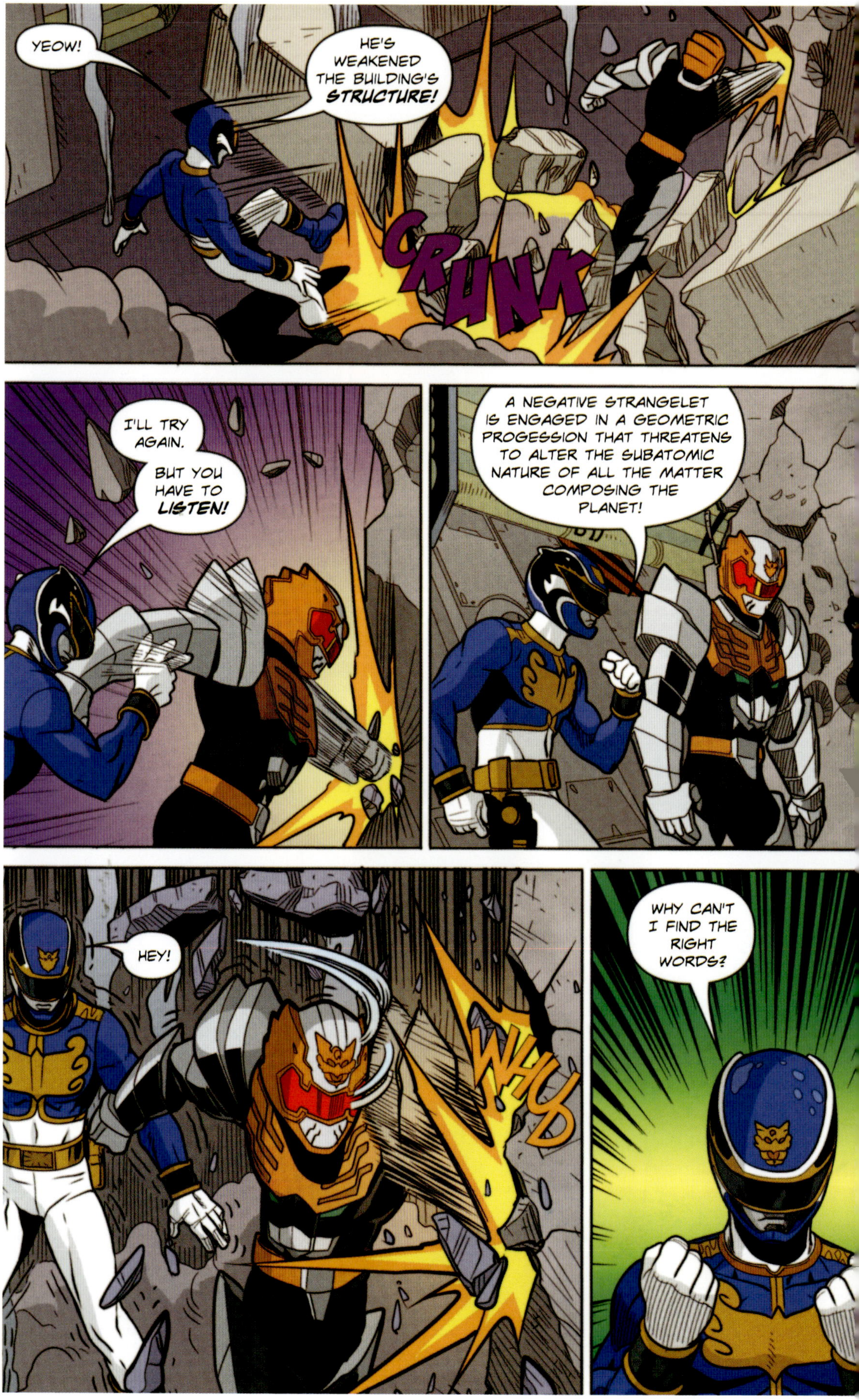
YEOW!
HE'S WEAKENED THE BUILDING'S STRUCTURE!
CRUNK
I'LL TRY AGAIN.
BUT YOU HAVE TO LISTEN!
A NEGATIVE STRANGELET IS ENGAGED IN A GEOMETRIC PROGESSION THAT THREATENS TO ALTER THE SUBATOMIC NATURE OF ALL THE MATTER COMPOSING THE PLANET!
HEY!
WHUD
WHY CAN'T I FIND THE RIGHT WORDS?

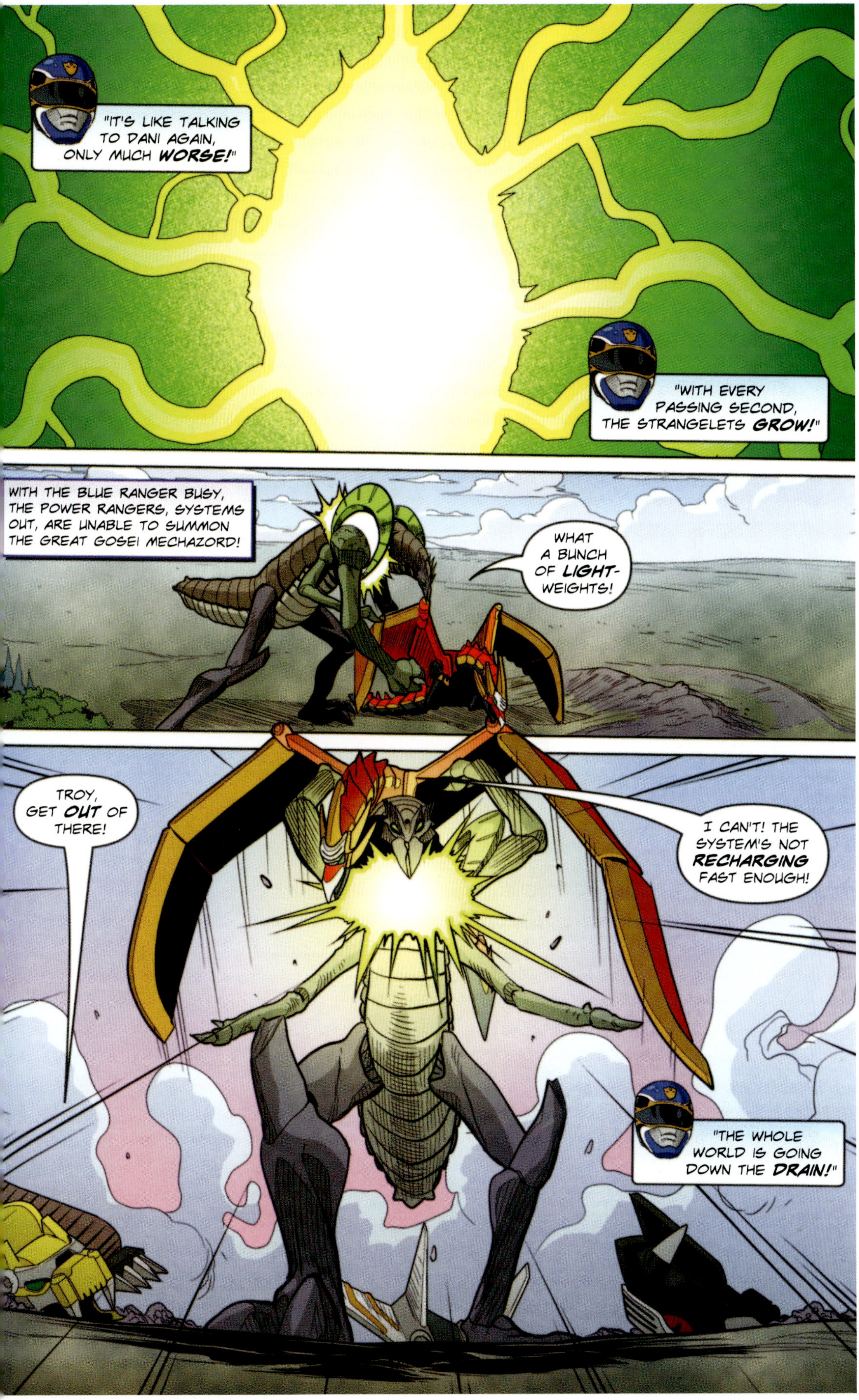
"IT'S LIKE TALKING TO DANI AGAIN, ONLY MUCH WORSE!"
"WITH EVERY PASSING SECOND, THE STRANGELETS GROW!"
WITH THE BLUE RANGER BUSY, THE POWER RANGERS, SYSTEMS OUT, ARE UNABLE TO SUMMON THE GREAT GOSEI MECHAZORD!
WHAT A BUNCH OF LIGHT-WEIGHTS!
TROY, GET OUT OF THERE!
I CAN'T! THE SYSTEM'S NOT RECHARGING FAST ENOUGH!
"THE WHOLE WORLD IS GOING DOWN THE DRAIN!"

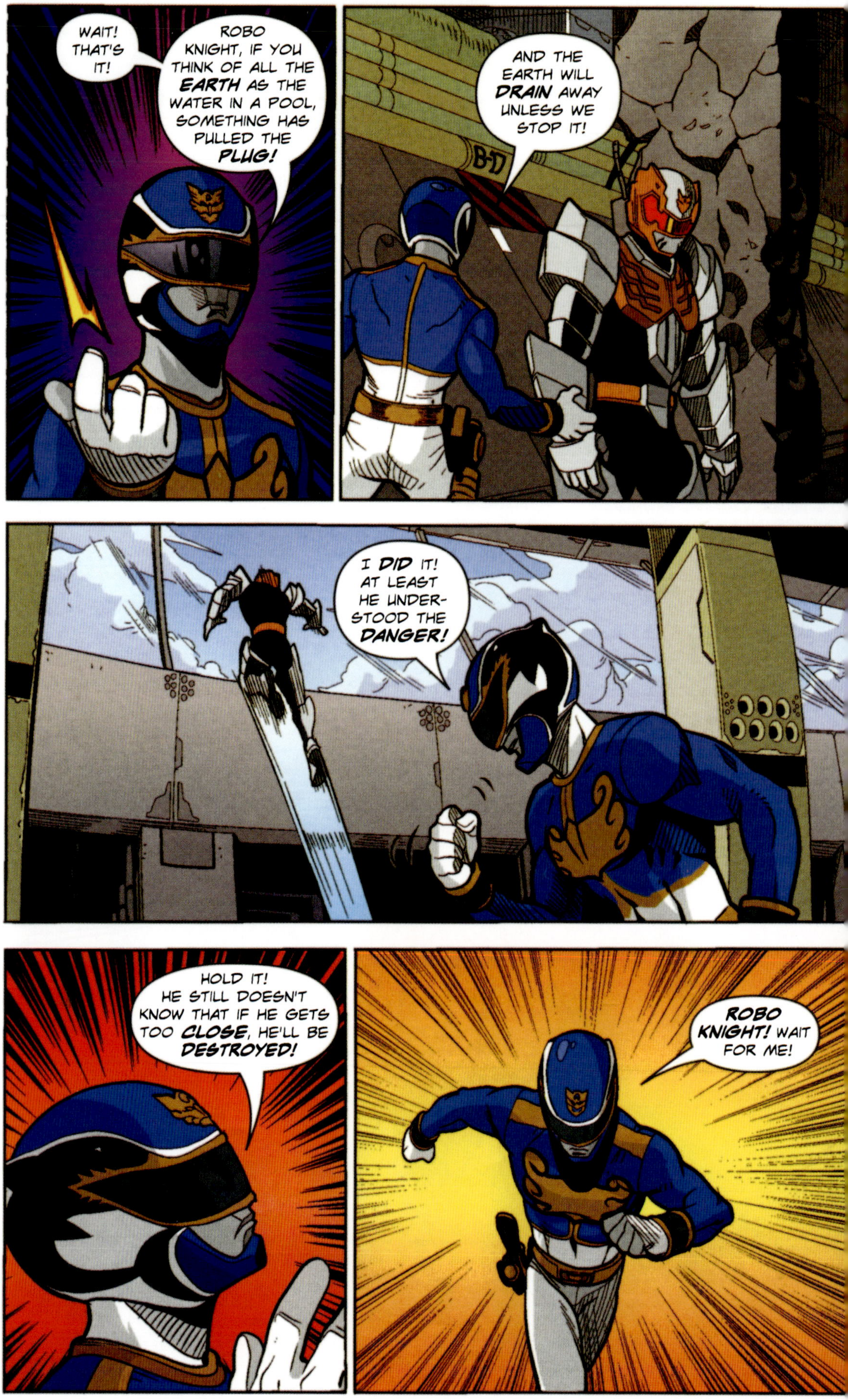
WAIT! THAT'S IT!
ROBO KNIGHT, IF YOU THINK OF ALL THE EARTH AS THE WATER IN A POOL, SOMETHING HAS PULLED THE PLUG!
AND THE EARTH WILL DRAIN AWAY UNLESS WE STOP IT!
B-D
I DID IT! AT LEAST HE UNDER-STOOD THE DANGER!
HOLD IT! HE STILL DOESN'T KNOW THAT IF HE GETS TOO CLOSE, HE'LL BE DESTROYED!
ROBO KNIGHT! WAIT FOR ME!

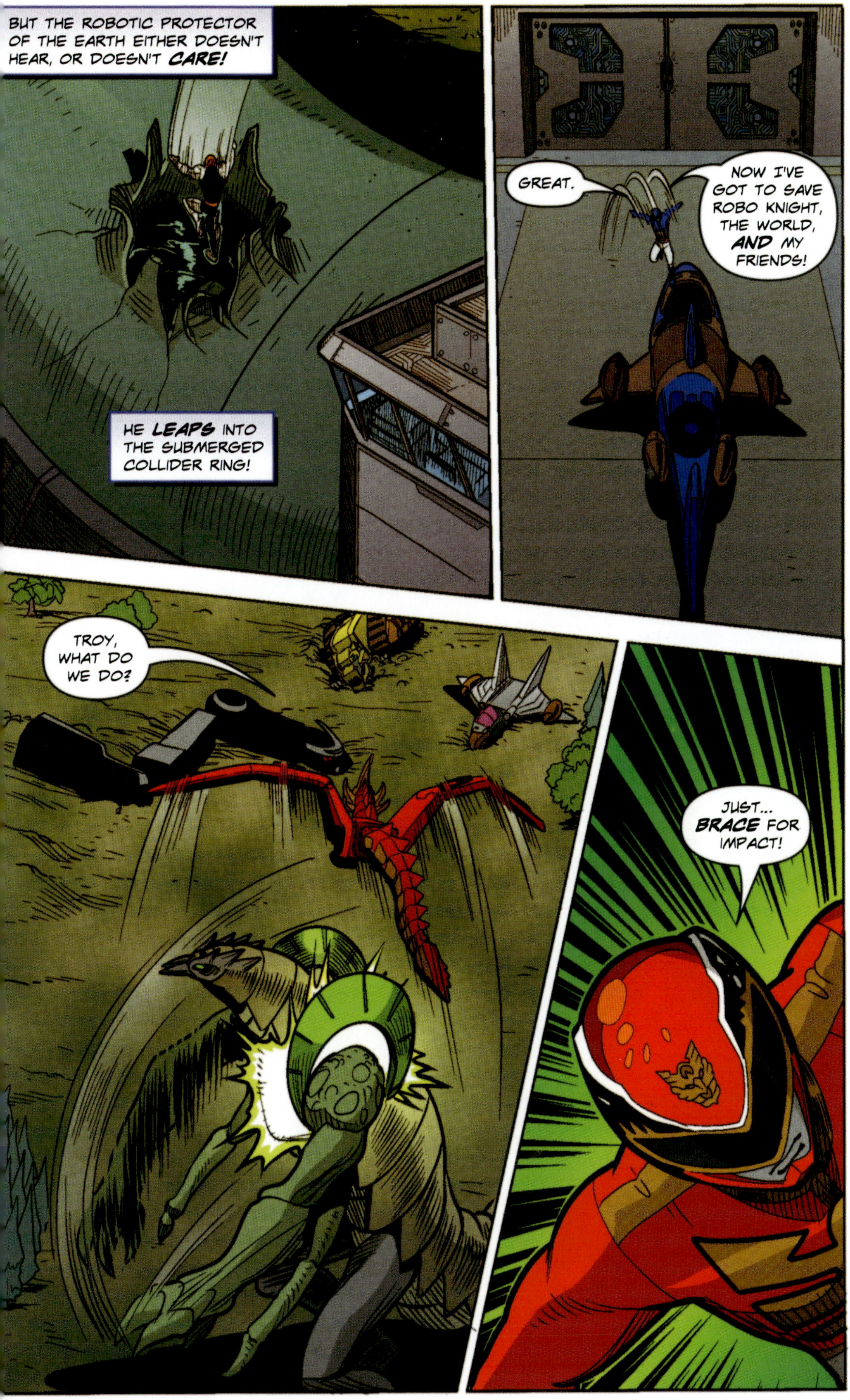
BUT THE ROBOTIC PROTECTOR OF THE EARTH EITHER DOESN'T HEAR, OR DOESN'T CARE!
HE LEAPS INTO THE SUBMERGED COLLIDER RING!
GREAT.
NOW I'VE GOT TO SAVE ROBO KNIGHT, THE WORLD, AND MY FRIENDS!
TROY, WHAT DO WE DO?
JUST... BRACE FOR IMPACT!

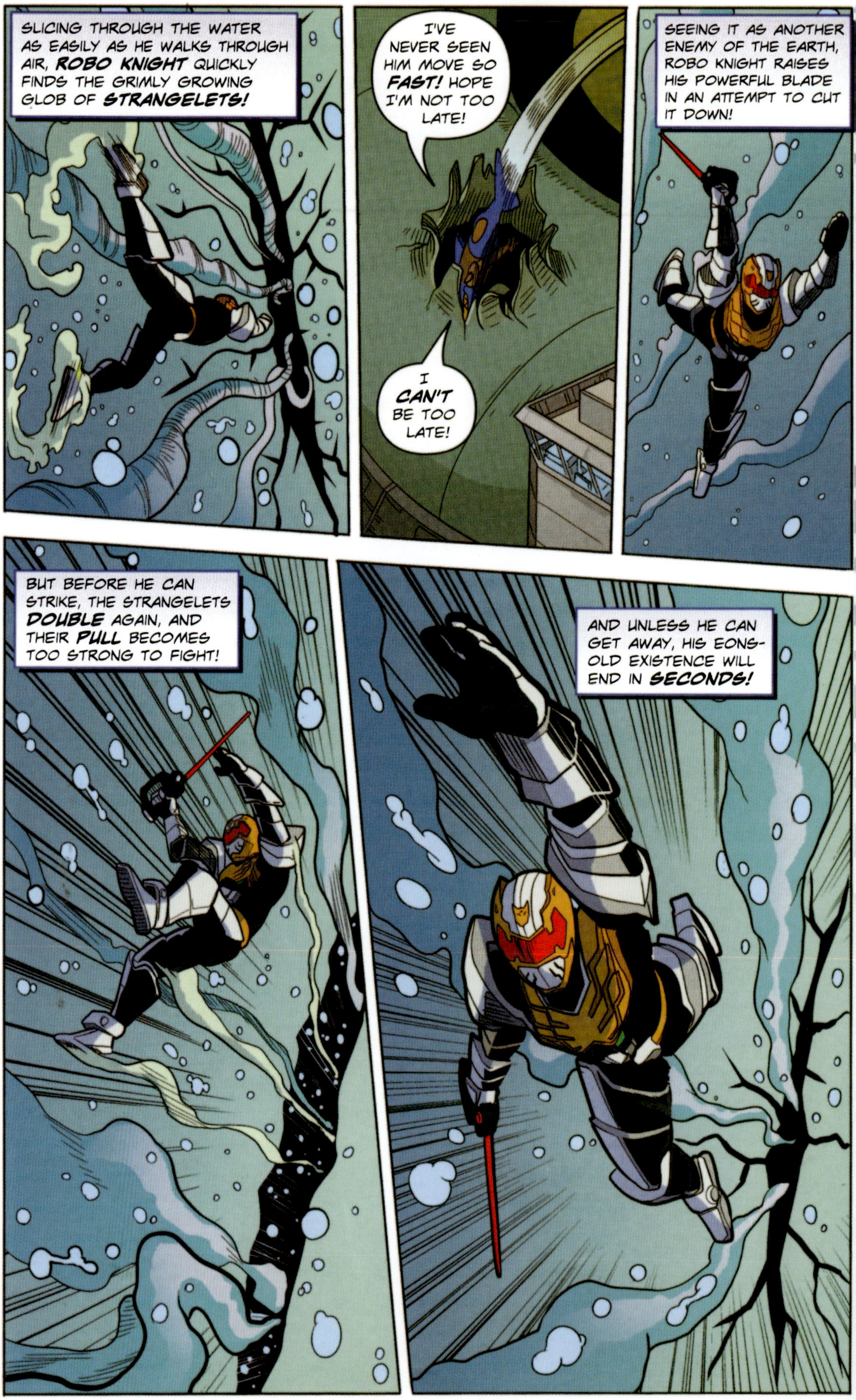

SLICING THROUGH THE WATER AS EASILY AS HE WALKS THROUGH AIR, ROBO KNIGHT QUICKLY FINDS THE GRIMLY GROWING GLOB OF STRANGELETS!
I'VE NEVER SEEN HIM MOVE SO FAST! HOPE I'M NOT TOO LATE!
I CAN'T BE TOO LATE!
SEEING IT AS ANOTHER ENEMY OF THE EARTH, ROBO KNIGHT RAISES HIS POWERFUL BLADE IN AN ATTEMPT TO CUT IT DOWN!
BUT BEFORE HE CAN STRIKE, THE STRANGELETS DOUBLE AGAIN, AND THEIR PULL BECOMES TOO STRONG TO FIGHT!
AND UNLESS HE CAN GET AWAY, HIS EONS-OLD EXISTENCE WILL END IN SECONDS!

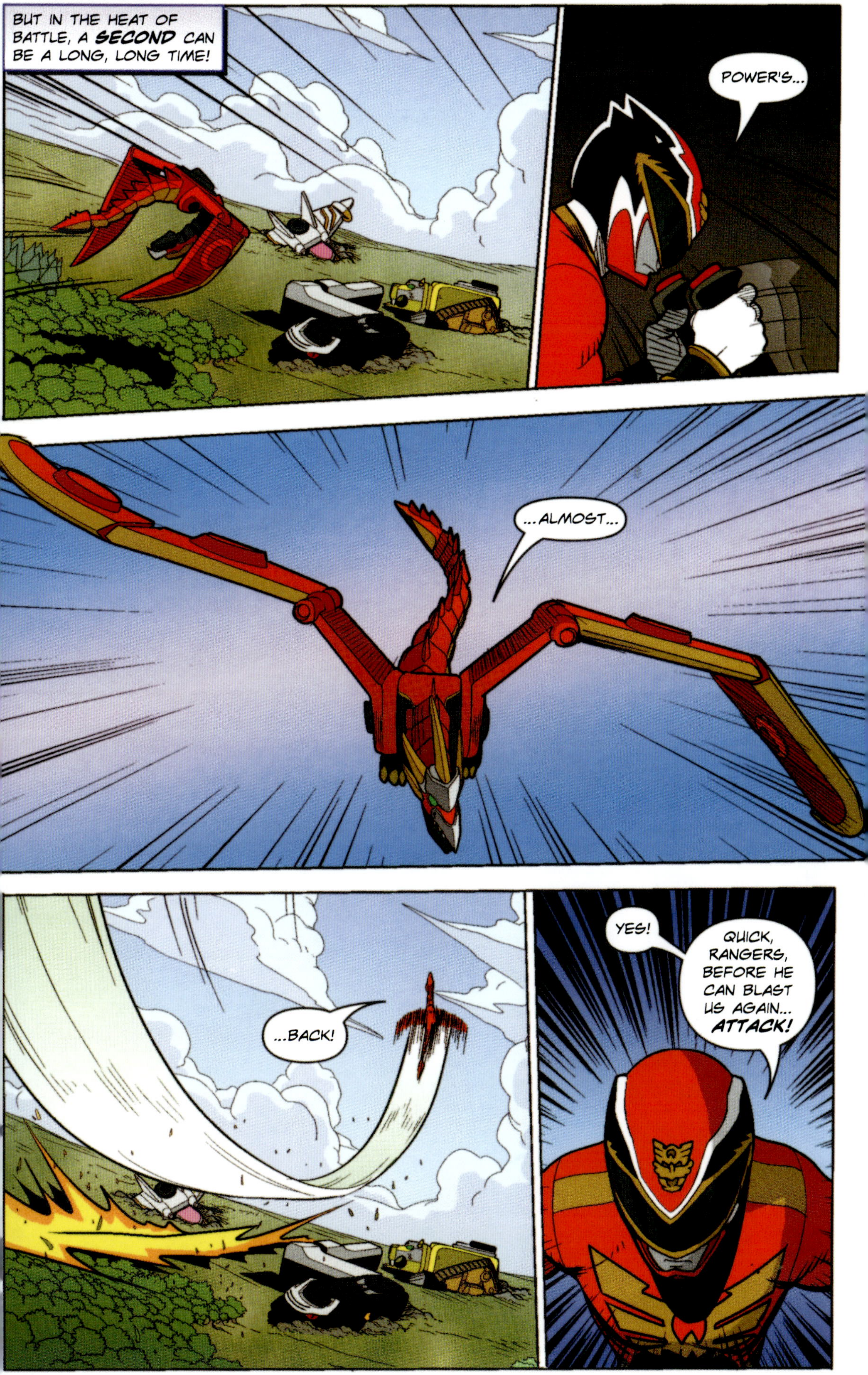
BUT IN THE HEAT OF BATTLE, A **SECOND** CAN BE A LONG, LONG TIME!
POWER'S...
...ALMOST...
...BACK!
YES!
QUICK, RANGERS, BEFORE HE CAN BLAST US AGAIN... **ATTACK!**

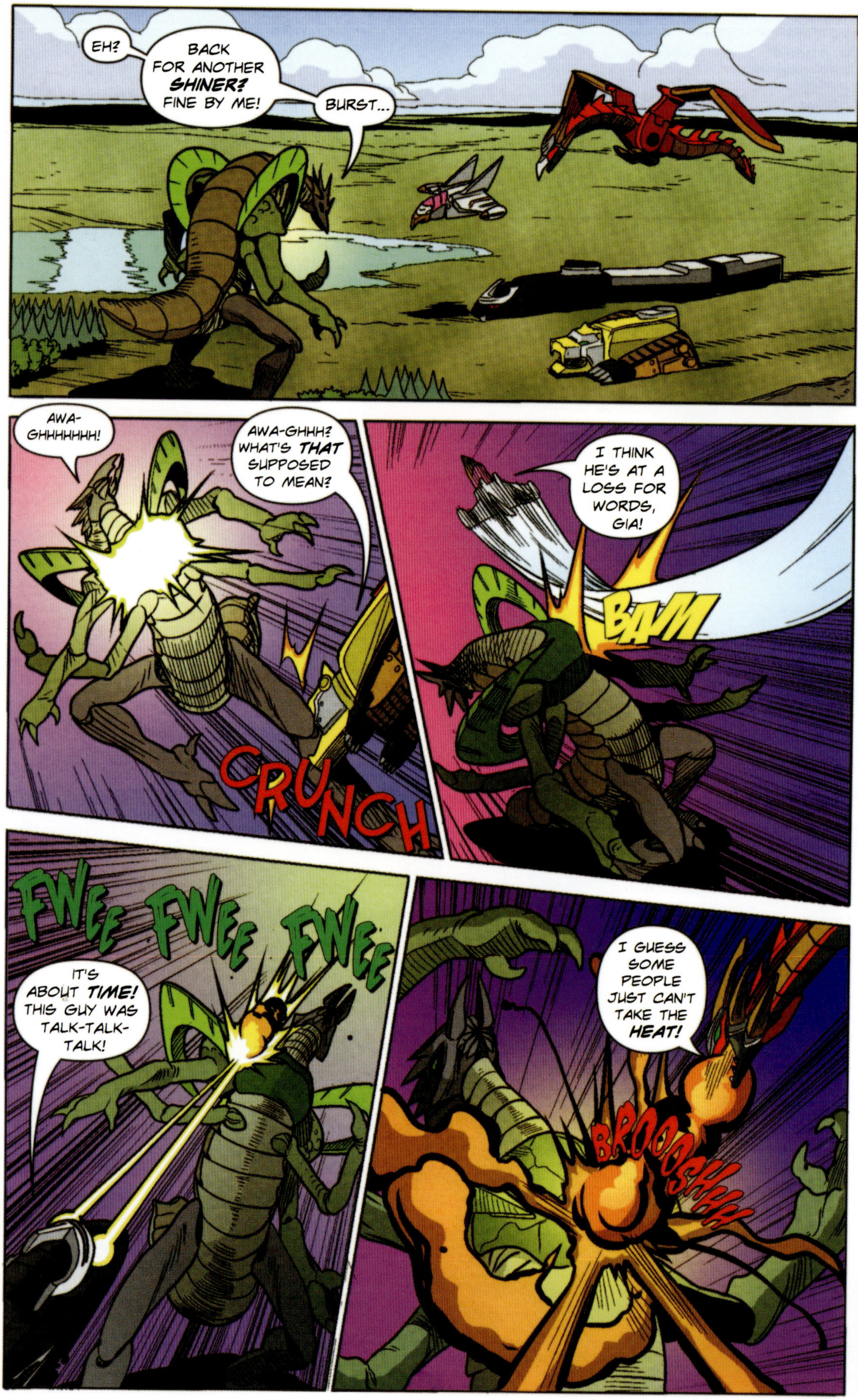
EH?
BACK FOR ANOTHER SHINER? FINE BY ME!
BURST...
AWA-GHHHHHHH!
AWA-GHHH? WHAT'S THAT SUPPOSED TO MEAN?
CRUNCH
I THINK HE'S AT A LOSS FOR WORDS, GIA!
BAM
FWEE FWEE FWEE
IT'S ABOUT TIME! THIS GUY WAS TALK-TALK-TALK!
I GUESS SOME PEOPLE JUST CAN'T TAKE THE HEAT!
BROOOSHHH

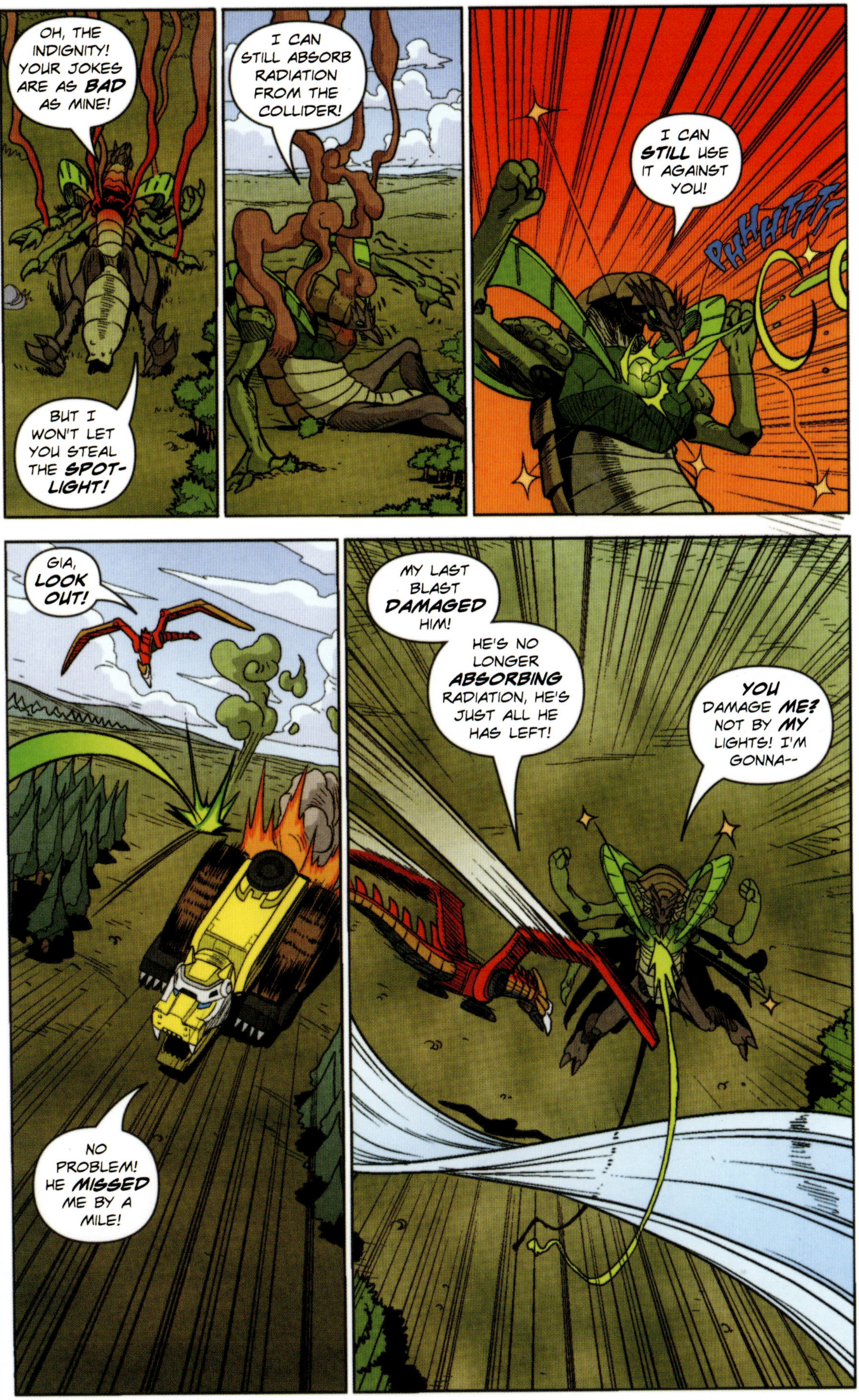

OH, THE INDIGNITY! YOUR JOKES ARE AS BAD AS MINE!
BUT I WON'T LET YOU STEAL THE SPOT-LIGHT!
I CAN STILL ABSORB RADIATION FROM THE COLLIDER!
I CAN STILL USE IT AGAINST YOU!
PHHHTTTT
GIA, LOOK OUT!
NO PROBLEM! HE MISSED ME BY A MILE!
MY LAST BLAST DAMAGED HIM!
HE'S NO LONGER ABSORBING RADIATION, HE'S JUST ALL HE HAS LEFT!
YOU DAMAGE ME? NOT BY MY LIGHTS! I'M GONNA--

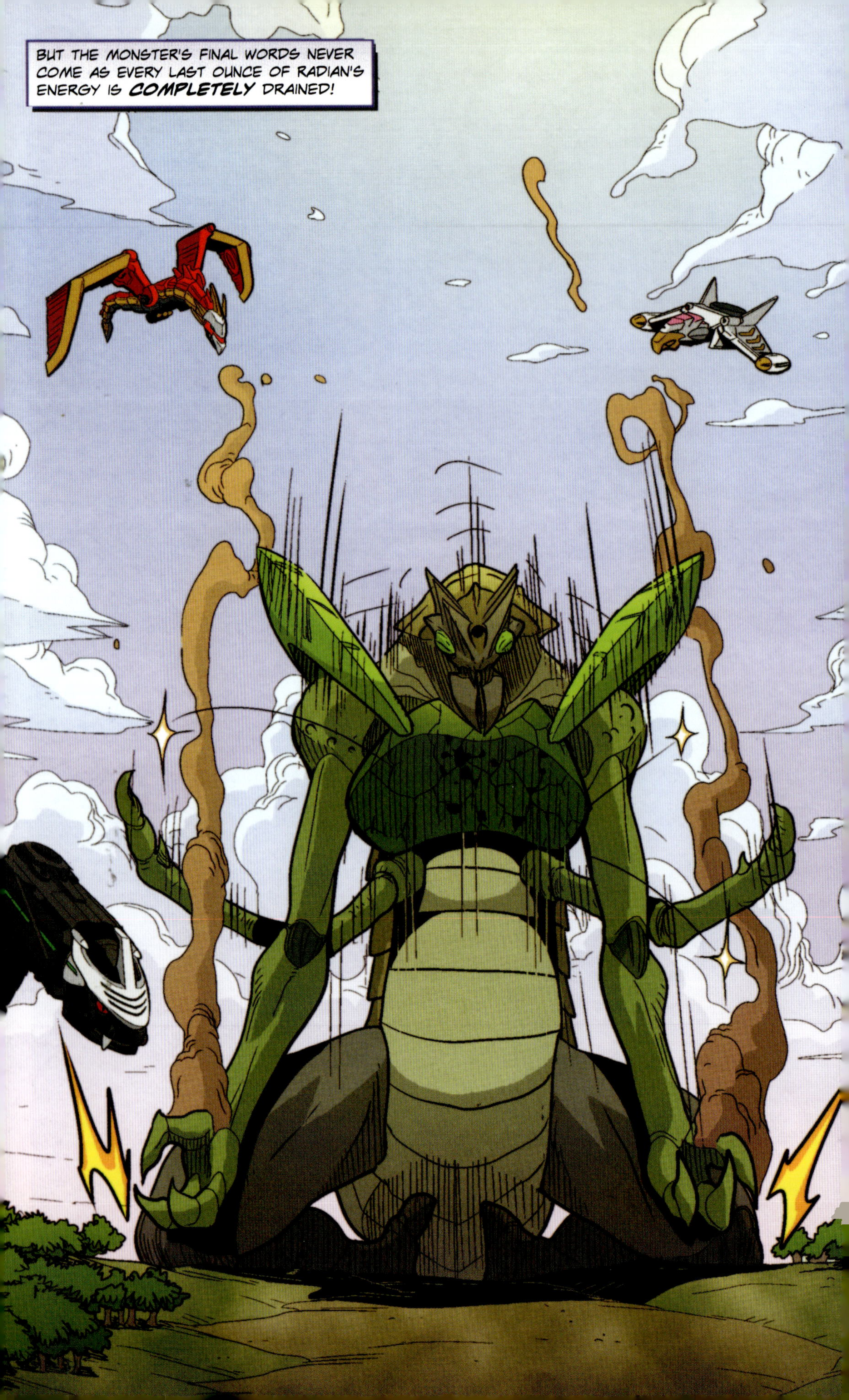
BUT THE MONSTER'S FINAL WORDS NEVER COME AS EVERY LAST OUNCE OF RADIAN'S ENERGY IS COMPLETELY DRAINED!

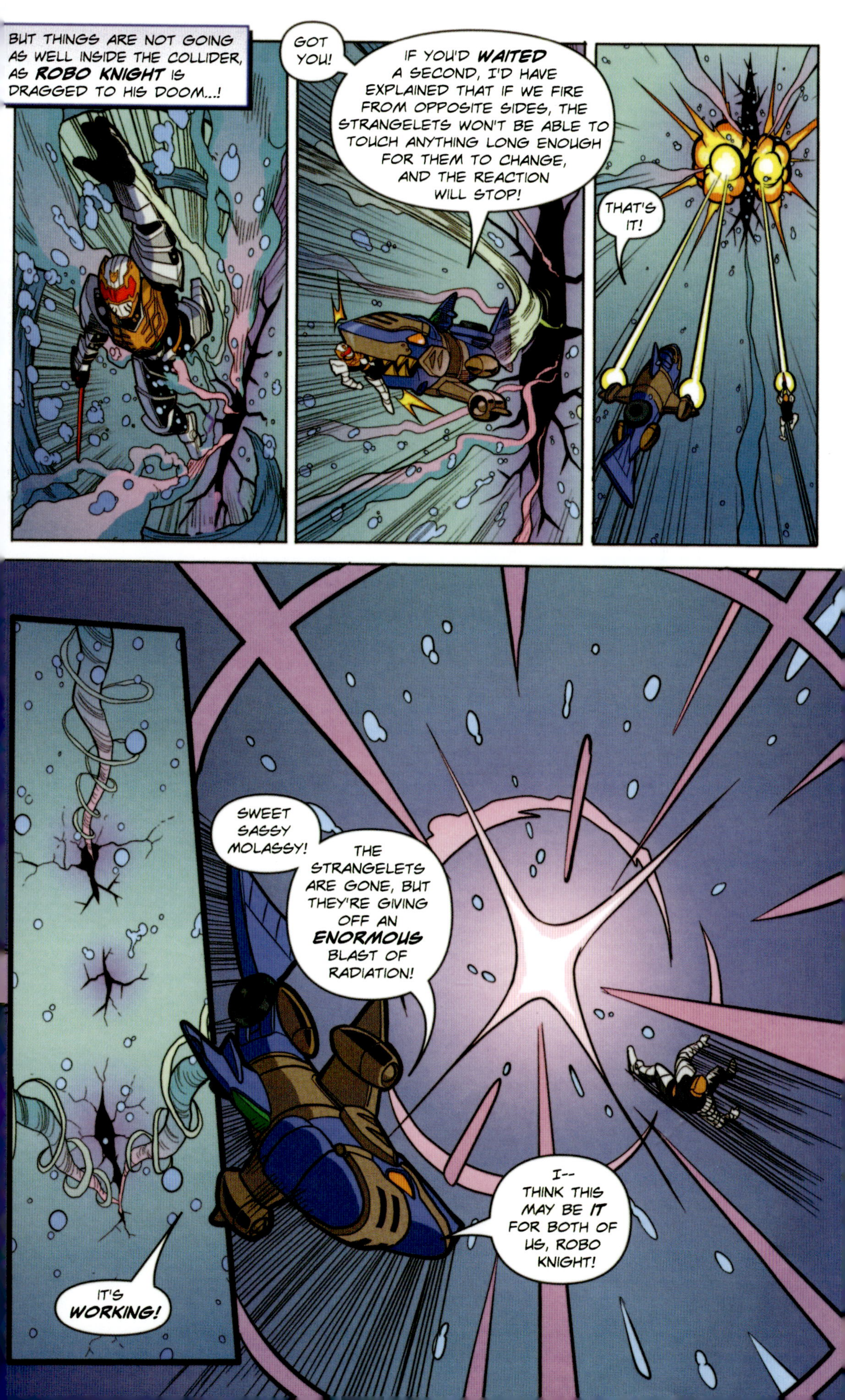
BUT THINGS ARE NOT GOING AS WELL INSIDE THE COLLIDER, AS ROBO KNIGHT IS DRAGGED TO HIS DOOM...!
GOT YOU!
IF YOU'D WAITED A SECOND, I'D HAVE EXPLAINED THAT IF WE FIRE FROM OPPOSITE SIDES, THE STRANGELETS WON'T BE ABLE TO TOUCH ANYTHING LONG ENOUGH FOR THEM TO CHANGE, AND THE REACTION WILL STOP!
THAT'S IT!
SWEET SASSY MOLASSY!
THE STRANGELETS ARE GONE, BUT THEY'RE GIVING OFF AN ENORMOUS BLAST OF RADIATION!
I-- THINK THIS MAY BE IT FOR BOTH OF US, ROBO KNIGHT!
IT'S WORKING!

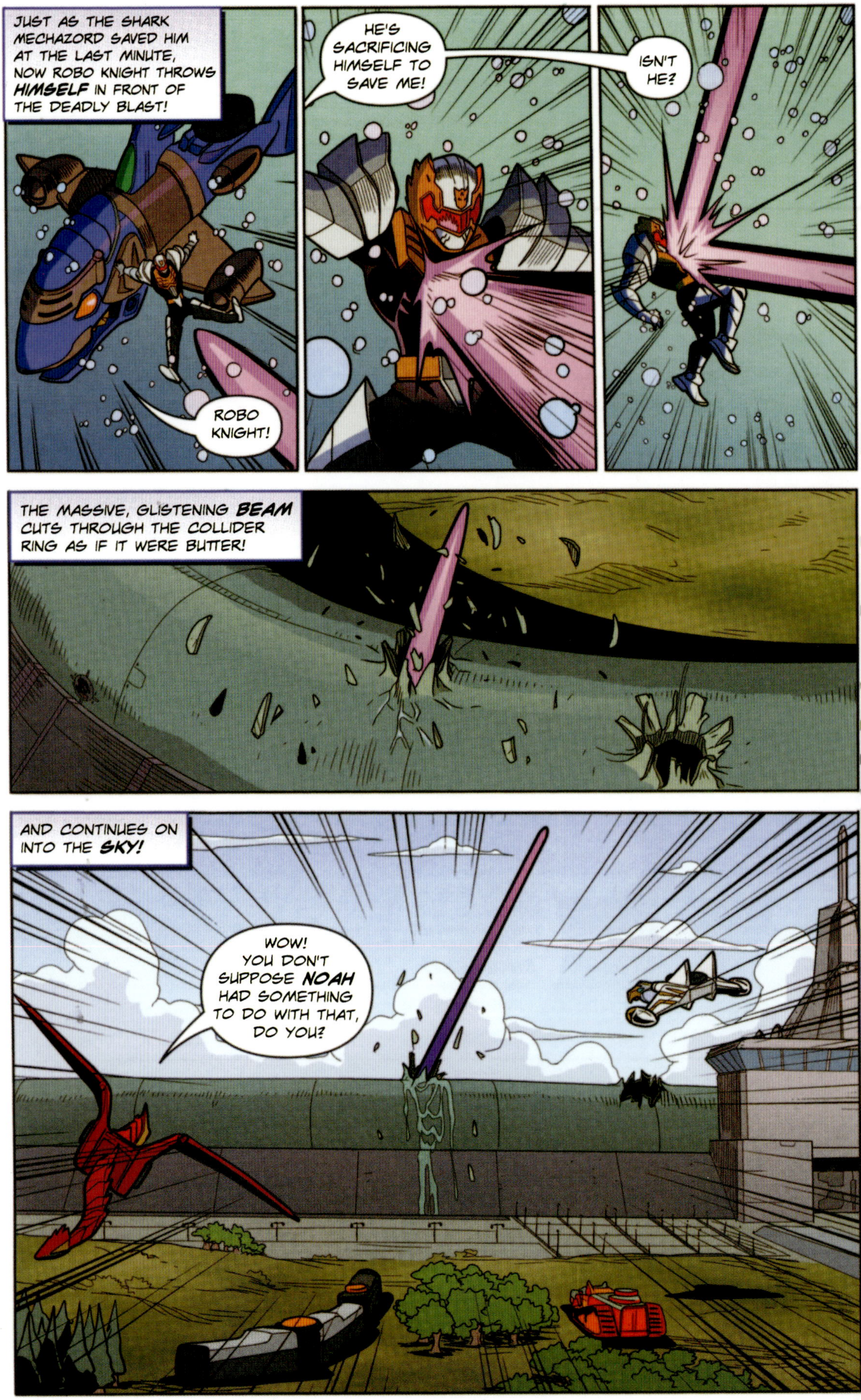

JUST AS THE SHARK MECHAZORD SAVED HIM AT THE LAST MINUTE, NOW ROBO KNIGHT THROWS HIMSELF IN FRONT OF THE DEADLY BLAST!
ROBO KNIGHT!
HE'S SACRIFICING HIMSELF TO SAVE ME!
ISN'T HE?
THE MASSIVE, GLISTENING BEAM CUTS THROUGH THE COLLIDER RING AS IF IT WERE BUTTER!
AND CONTINUES ON INTO THE SKY!
WOW! YOU DON'T SUPPOSE NOAH HAD SOMETHING TO DO WITH THAT, DO YOU?

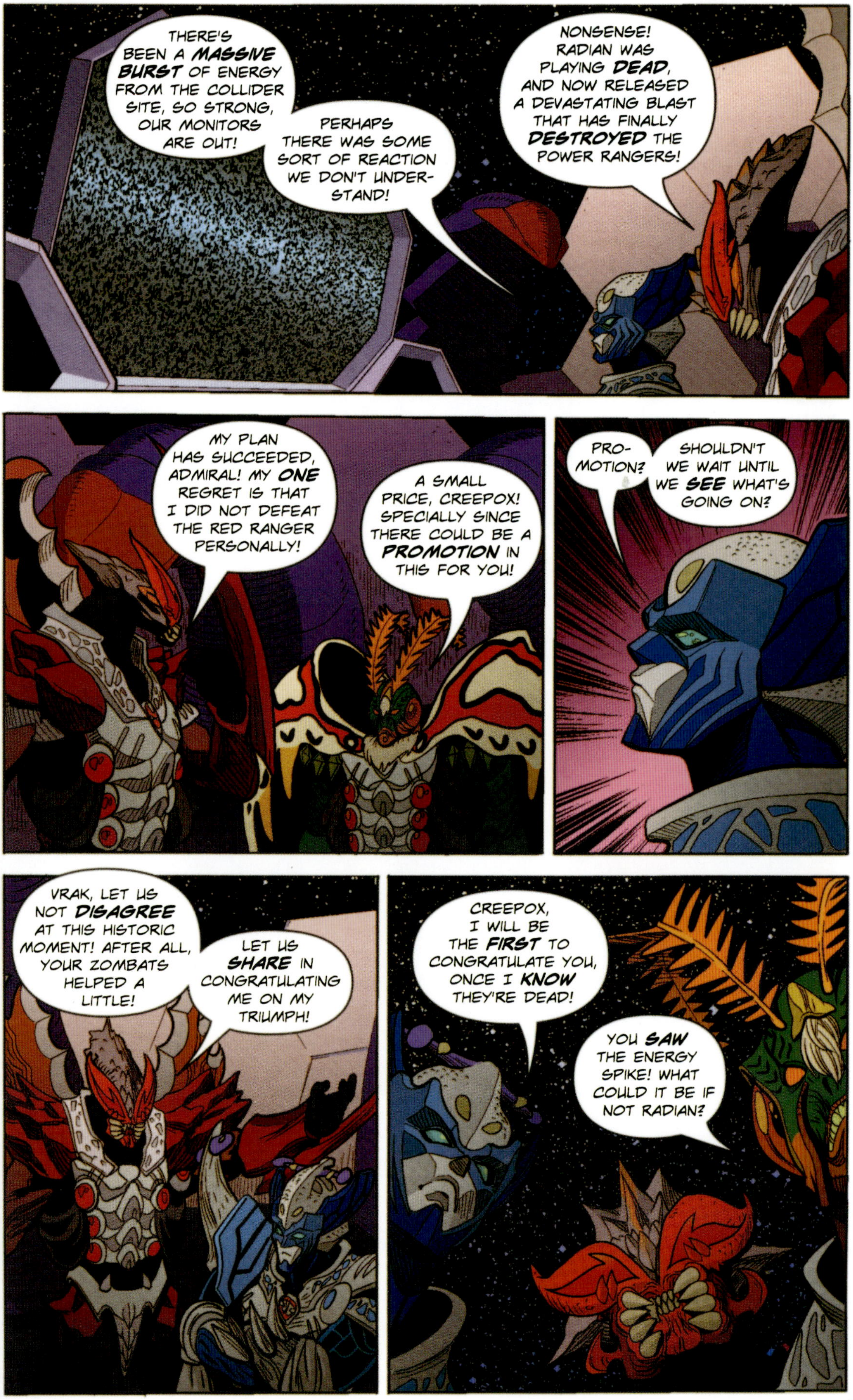
THERE'S BEEN A MASSIVE BURST OF ENERGY FROM THE COLLIDER SITE, SO STRONG, OUR MONITORS ARE OUT!
PERHAPS THERE WAS SOME SORT OF REACTION WE DON'T UNDER-STAND!
NONSENSE! RADIAN WAS PLAYING DEAD, AND NOW RELEASED A DEVASTATING BLAST THAT HAS FINALLY DESTROYED THE POWER RANGERS!
MY PLAN HAS SUCCEEDED, ADMIRAL! MY ONE REGRET IS THAT I DID NOT DEFEAT THE RED RANGER PERSONALLY!
A SMALL PRICE, CREEPOX! SPECIALLY SINCE THERE COULD BE A PROMOTION IN THIS FOR YOU!
PRO-MOTION?
SHOULDN'T WE WAIT UNTIL WE SEE WHAT'S GOING ON?
VRAK, LET US NOT DISAGREE AT THIS HISTORIC MOMENT! AFTER ALL, YOUR ZOMBATS HELPED A LITTLE!
LET US SHARE IN CONGRATULATING ME ON MY TRIUMPH!
CREEPOX, I WILL BE THE FIRST TO CONGRATULATE YOU, ONCE I KNOW THEY'RE DEAD!
YOU SAW THE ENERGY SPIKE! WHAT COULD IT BE IF NOT RADIAN?

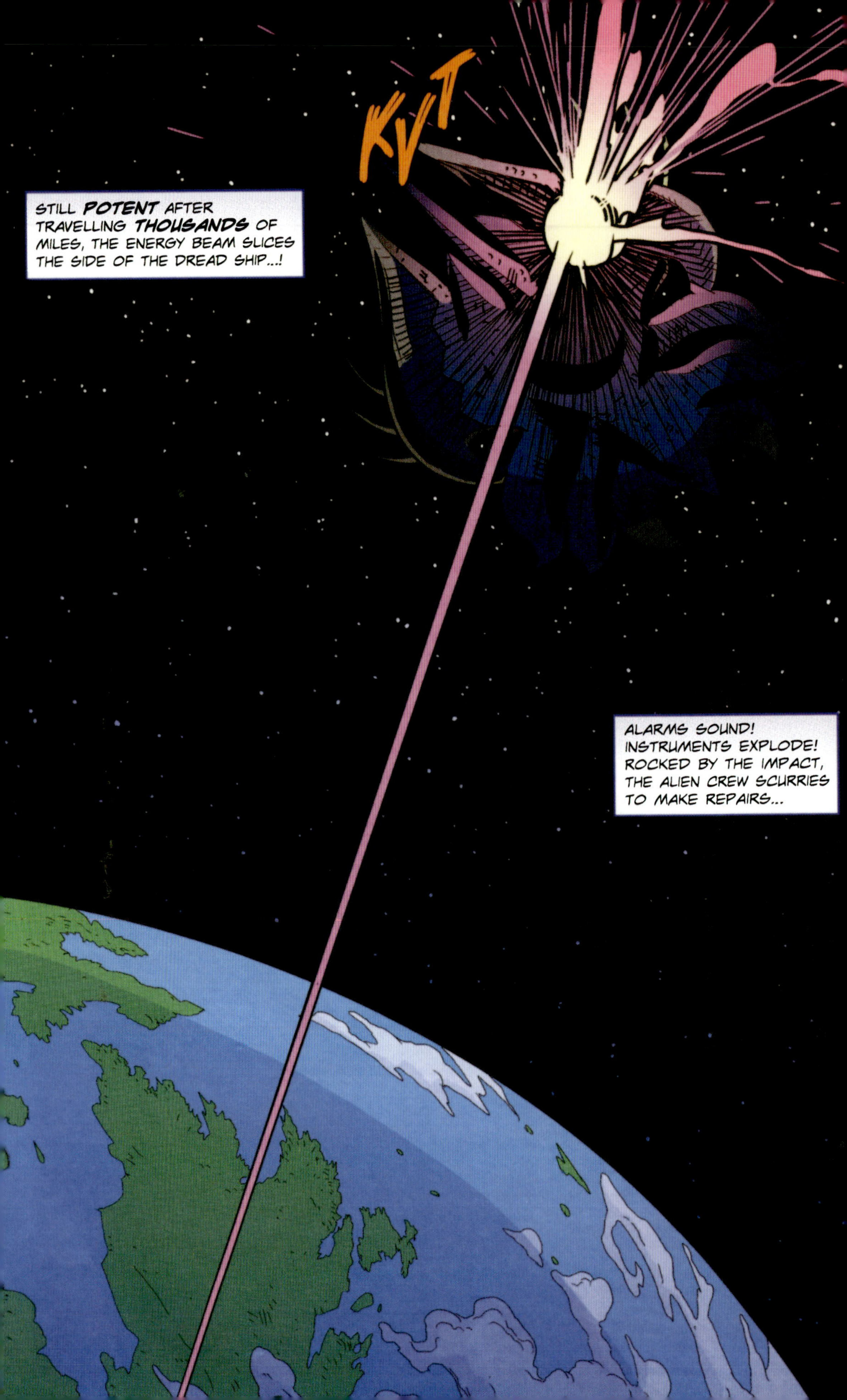
KVT
STILL POTENT AFTER TRAVELLING THOUSANDS OF MILES, THE ENERGY BEAM SLICES THE SIDE OF THE DREAD SHIP...!
ALARMS SOUND! INSTRUMENTS EXPLODE! ROCKED BY THE IMPACT, THE ALIEN CREW SCURRIES TO MAKE REPAIRS...

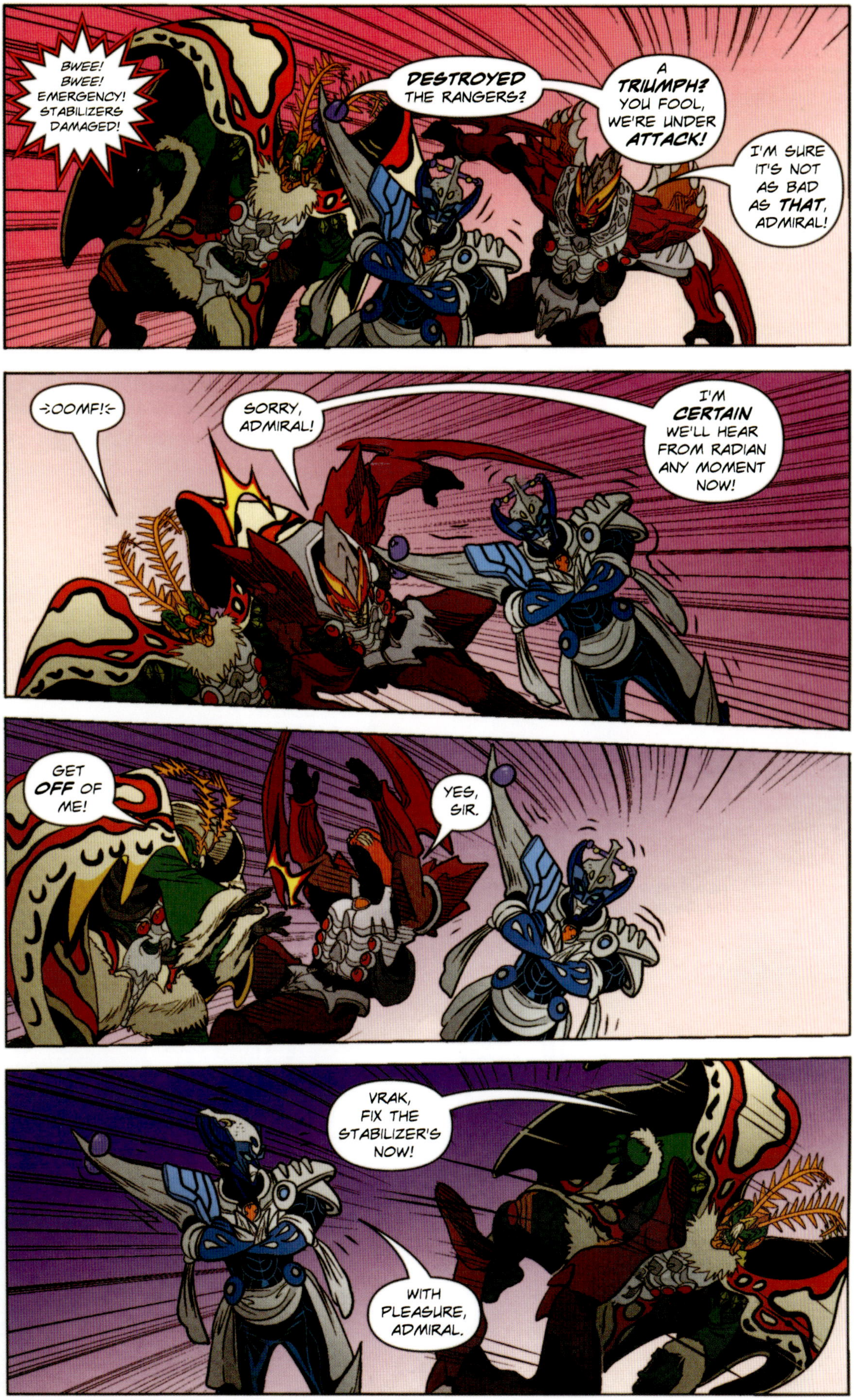
BWEE! BWEE! EMERGENCY! STABILIZERS DAMAGED!
DESTROYED THE RANGERS?
A TRIUMPH? YOU FOOL, WE'RE UNDER ATTACK!
I'M SURE IT'S NOT AS BAD AS THAT, ADMIRAL!
-:OOMF!:-
SORRY, ADMIRAL!
I'M CERTAIN WE'LL HEAR FROM RADIAN ANY MOMENT NOW!
GET OFF OF ME!
YES, SIR.
VRAK, FIX THE STABILIZER'S NOW!
WITH PLEASURE, ADMIRAL.

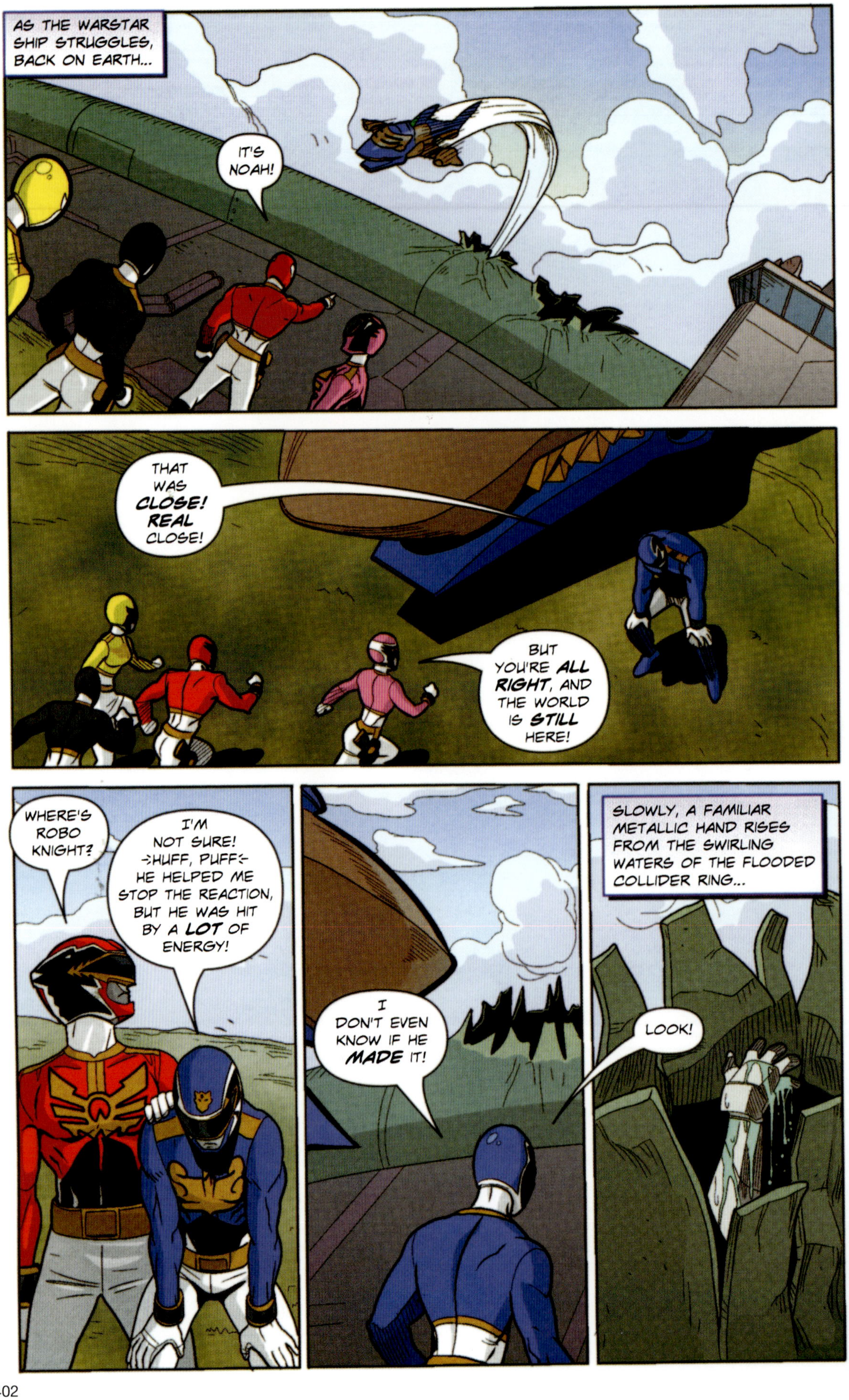
AS THE WARSTAR SHIP STRUGGLES, BACK ON EARTH...
IT'S NOAH!
THAT WAS CLOSE! REAL CLOSE!
BUT YOU'RE ALL RIGHT, AND THE WORLD IS STILL HERE!
WHERE'S ROBO KNIGHT?
I'M NOT SURE! *HUFF, PUFF* HE HELPED ME STOP THE REACTION, BUT HE WAS HIT BY A LOT OF ENERGY!
I DON'T EVEN KNOW IF HE MADE IT!
SLOWLY, A FAMILIAR METALLIC HAND RISES FROM THE SWIRLING WATERS OF THE FLOODED COLLIDER RING...
LOOK!

HE DOESN'T LOOK ANY WORSE FOR WEAR!

WHAT DO WE DO IF HE TRIES TO **DESTROY** THE COLLIDER AGAIN. **FIGHT** HIM?

BUT THE DANGER HAS PASSED, AND THE GUARDIAN OF EARTH RETURNS TO HIS VIGIL!

⇌PHEW!⇌ I HOPE THAT'S A QUESTION WE **NEVER** HAVE TO ANSWER, EMMA!

YOU GOT HIM TO **HELP** YOU!

WAY TO GO, NOAH!

OH, IT'S PROBABLY JUST FURTHER EVIDENCE THAT I GET ALONG BETTER WITH MACHINES THAN I DO WITH **PEOPLE!**

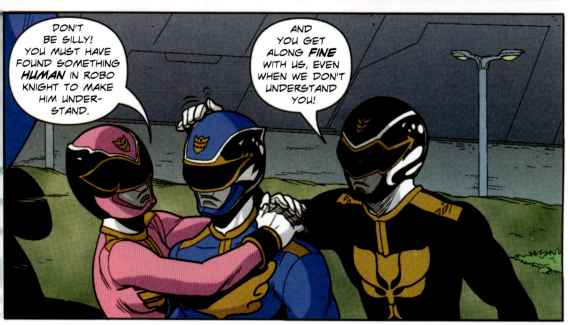

DON'T BE SILLY! YOU MUST HAVE FOUND SOMETHING **HUMAN** IN ROBO KNIGHT TO MAKE HIM UNDER-STAND.

AND YOU GET ALONG **FINE** WITH US, EVEN WHEN WE DON'T UNDERSTAND YOU!

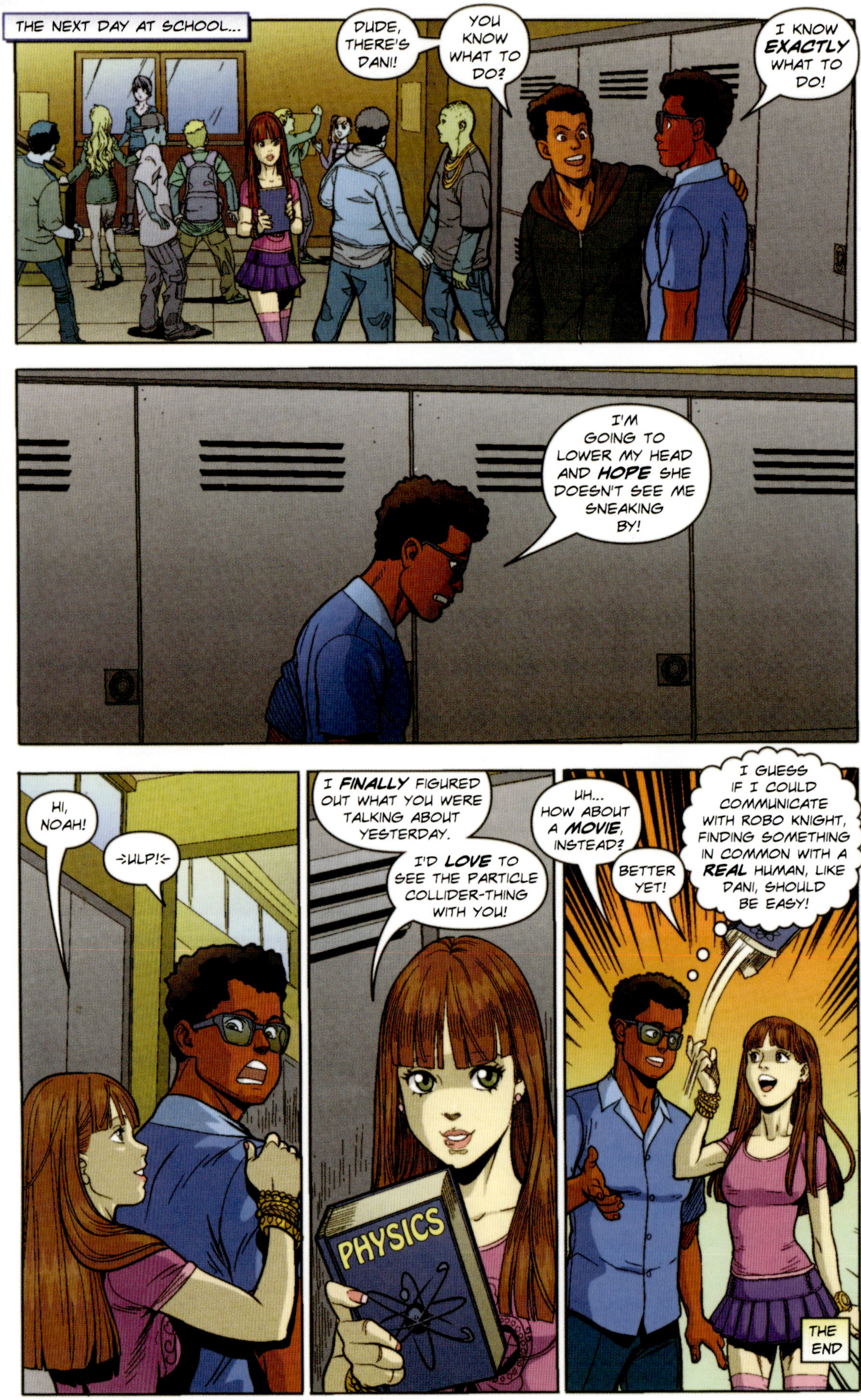
THE NEXT DAY AT SCHOOL...
DUDE, THERE'S DANI!
YOU KNOW WHAT TO DO?
I KNOW EXACTLY WHAT TO DO!
I'M GOING TO LOWER MY HEAD AND HOPE SHE DOESN'T SEE ME SNEAKING BY!
HI, NOAH!
GULP!
I FINALLY FIGURED OUT WHAT YOU WERE TALKING ABOUT YESTERDAY.
I'D LOVE TO SEE THE PARTICLE COLLIDER-THING WITH YOU!
PHYSICS
UH... HOW ABOUT A MOVIE, INSTEAD?
BETTER YET!
I GUESS IF I COULD COMMUNICATE WITH ROBO KNIGHT, FINDING SOMETHING IN COMMON WITH A REAL HUMAN, LIKE DANI, SHOULD BE EASY!
THE END

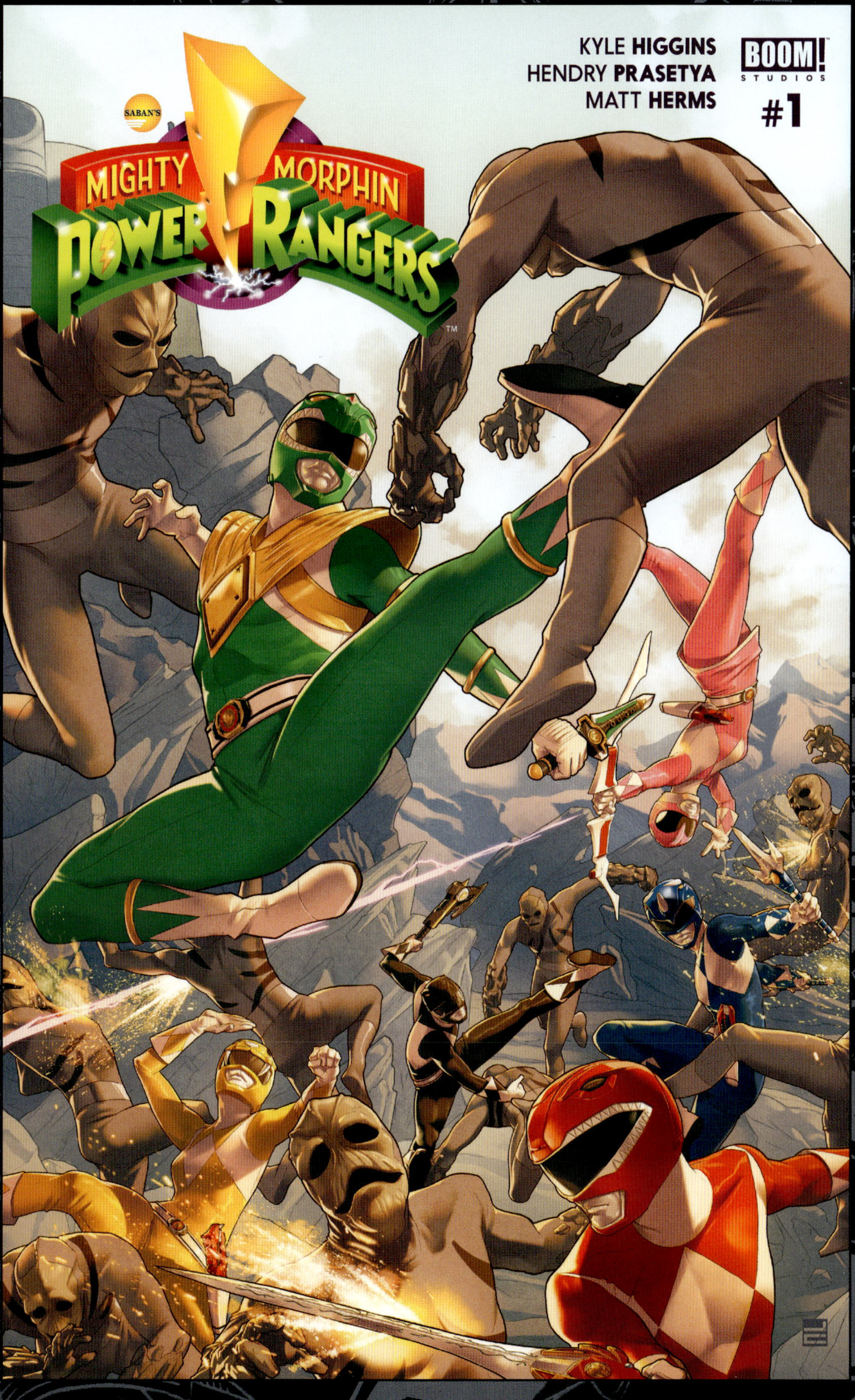
KYLE HIGGINS
HENDRY PRASETYA
MATT HERMS
BOOM! STUDIOS
#1
SABAN'S
MIGHTY MORPHIN
POWER RANGERS

SABAN'S MIGHTY MORPHIN POWER RANGERS™

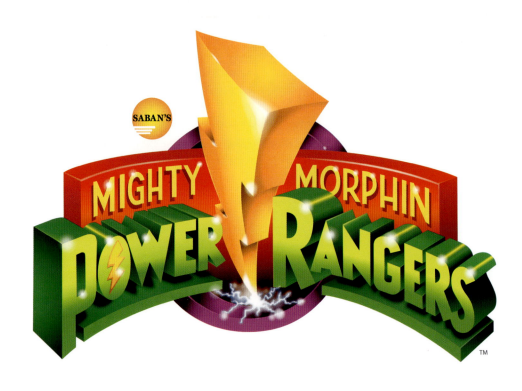

CHAPTER ONE

Written by
KYLE HIGGINS

Illustrated by
HENDRY PRASETYA

Colored by
MATT HERMS

Lettered by
ED DUKESHIRE

Cover by
JAMAL CAMPBELL

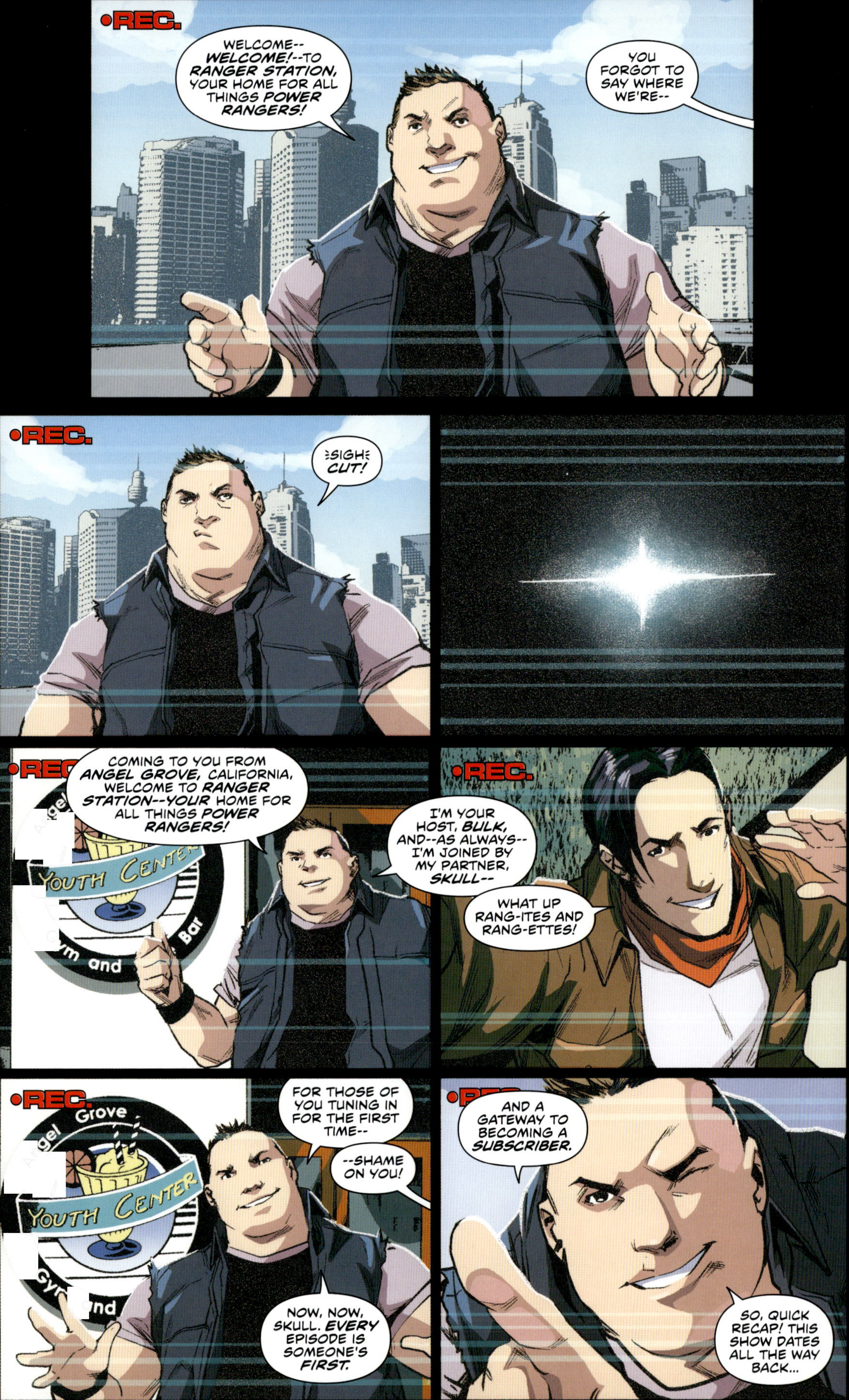

REC.
WELCOME-- WELCOME!--TO RANGER STATION, YOUR HOME FOR ALL THINGS POWER RANGERS!
YOU FORGOT TO SAY WHERE WE'RE--
REC.
SIGH CUT!
REC.
COMING TO YOU FROM ANGEL GROVE, CALIFORNIA, WELCOME TO RANGER STATION--YOUR HOME FOR ALL THINGS POWER RANGERS!
YOUTH CENTER
Bar
and
REC.
I'M YOUR HOST, BULK, AND--AS ALWAYS-- I'M JOINED BY MY PARTNER, SKULL--
WHAT UP RANG-ITES AND RANG-ETTES!
REC.
Angel Grove
YOUTH CENTER
FOR THOSE OF YOU TUNING IN FOR THE FIRST TIME--
--SHAME ON YOU!
NOW, NOW, SKULL. EVERY EPISODE IS SOMEONE'S FIRST.
AND A GATEWAY TO BECOMING A SUBSCRIBER.
SO, QUICK RECAP! THIS SHOW DATES ALL THE WAY BACK...

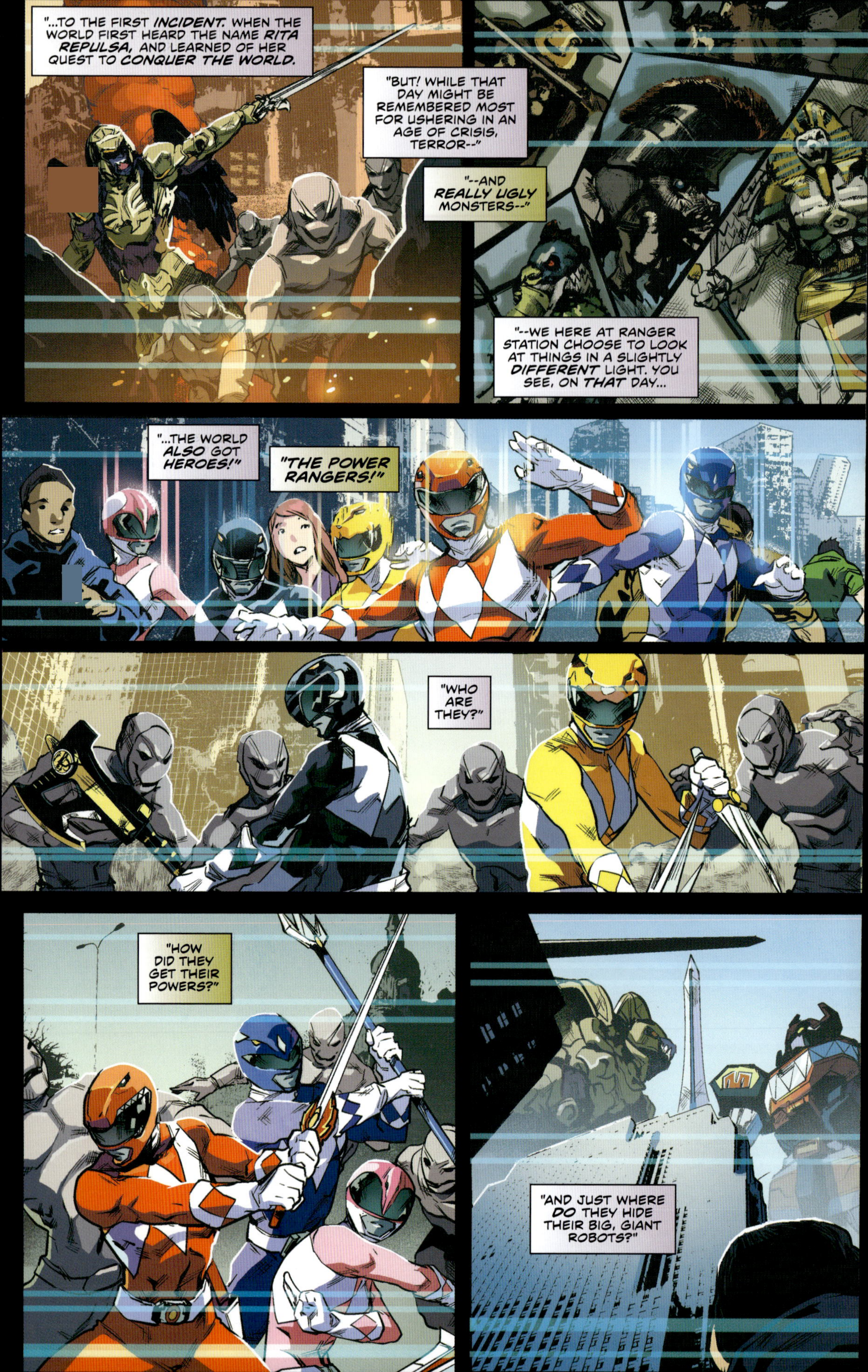
"...TO THE FIRST INCIDENT. WHEN THE WORLD FIRST HEARD THE NAME RITA REPULSA, AND LEARNED OF HER QUEST TO CONQUER THE WORLD.
"BUT! WHILE THAT DAY MIGHT BE REMEMBERED MOST FOR USHERING IN AN AGE OF CRISIS, TERROR--"
"--AND REALLY UGLY MONSTERS--"
"--WE HERE AT RANGER STATION CHOOSE TO LOOK AT THINGS IN A SLIGHTLY DIFFERENT LIGHT. YOU SEE, ON THAT DAY...
"...THE WORLD ALSO GOT HEROES!"
"THE POWER RANGERS!"
"WHO ARE THEY?"
"HOW DID THEY GET THEIR POWERS?"
"AND JUST WHERE DO THEY HIDE THEIR BIG, GIANT ROBOTS?"

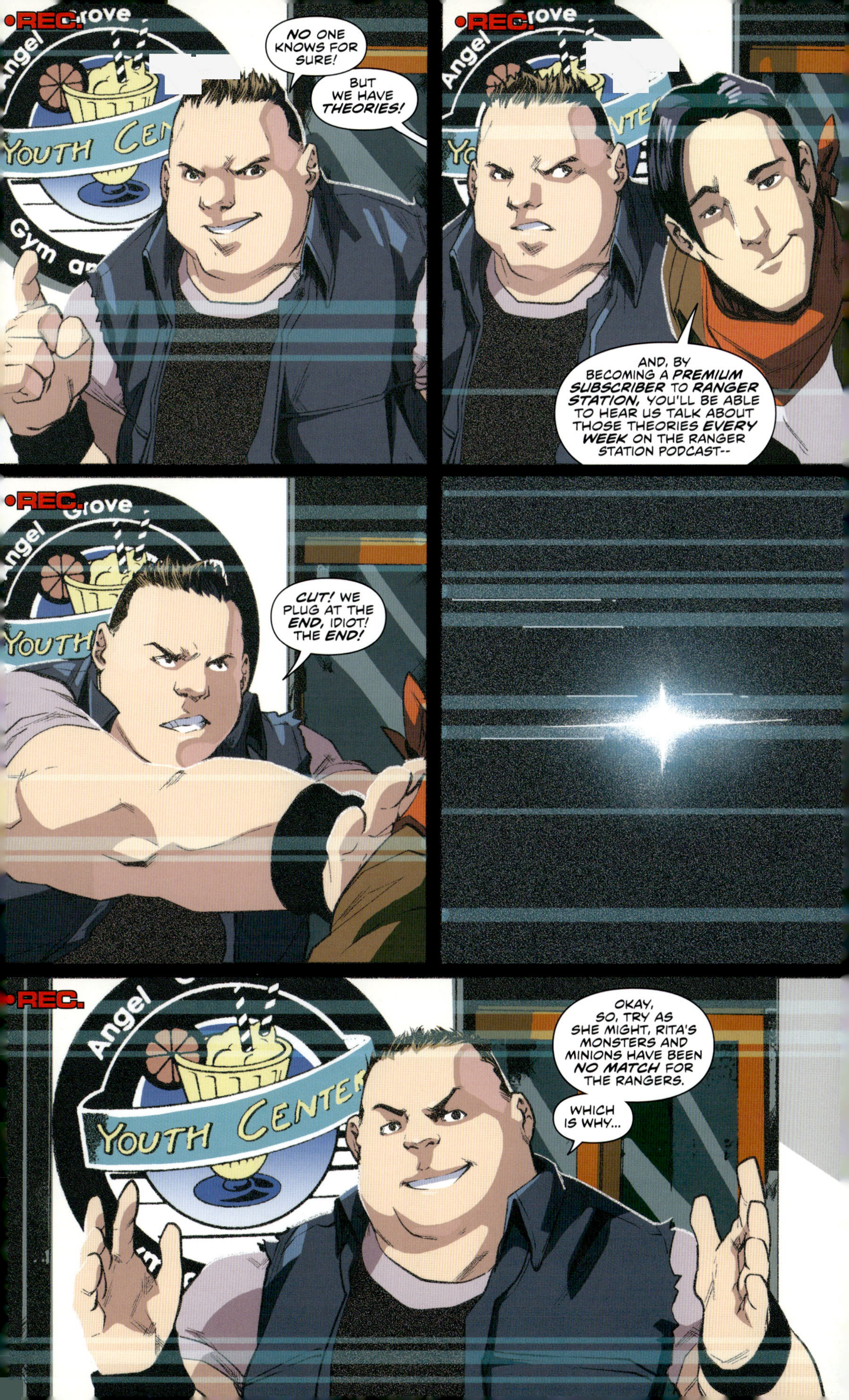

•REC.
Angel Grove
Youth Cen
Gym an
NO ONE KNOWS FOR SURE!
BUT WE HAVE THEORIES!
•REC.
Angel
AND, BY BECOMING A PREMIUM SUBSCRIBER TO RANGER STATION, YOU'LL BE ABLE TO HEAR US TALK ABOUT THOSE THEORIES EVERY WEEK ON THE RANGER STATION PODCAST--
•REC.
Grove
Youth
CUT! WE PLUG AT THE END, IDIOT! THE END!
•REC.
Angel
Youth Center
OKAY, SO, TRY AS SHE MIGHT, RITA'S MONSTERS AND MINIONS HAVE BEEN NO MATCH FOR THE RANGERS.
WHICH IS WHY...

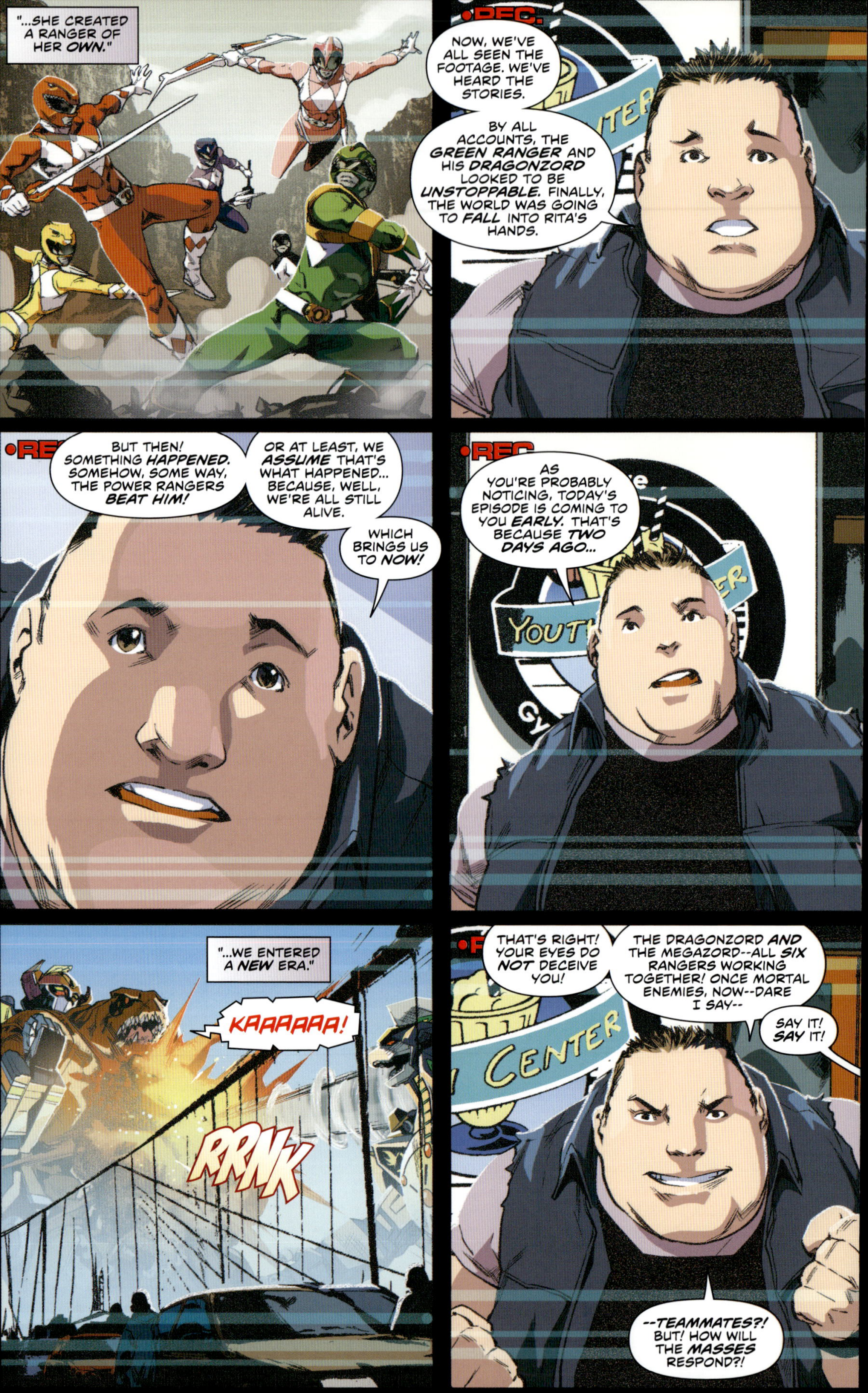
"...SHE CREATED A RANGER OF HER OWN."
•REC
NOW, WE'VE ALL SEEN THE FOOTAGE. WE'VE HEARD THE STORIES.
BY ALL ACCOUNTS, THE GREEN RANGER AND HIS DRAGONZORD LOOKED TO BE UNSTOPPABLE. FINALLY, THE WORLD WAS GOING TO FALL INTO RITA'S HANDS.
BUT THEN! SOMETHING HAPPENED. SOMEHOW, SOME WAY, THE POWER RANGERS BEAT HIM!
OR AT LEAST, WE ASSUME THAT'S WHAT HAPPENED... BECAUSE, WELL, WE'RE ALL STILL ALIVE.
WHICH BRINGS US TO NOW!
AS YOU'RE PROBABLY NOTICING, TODAY'S EPISODE IS COMING TO YOU EARLY. THAT'S BECAUSE TWO DAYS AGO...
"...WE ENTERED A NEW ERA."
KAAAAAA!
RRNK
THAT'S RIGHT! YOUR EYES DO NOT DECEIVE YOU!
THE DRAGONZORD AND THE MEGAZORD--ALL SIX RANGERS WORKING TOGETHER! ONCE MORTAL ENEMIES, NOW--DARE I SAY--
SAY IT! SAY IT!
--TEAMMATES?! BUT! HOW WILL THE MASSES RESPOND?!

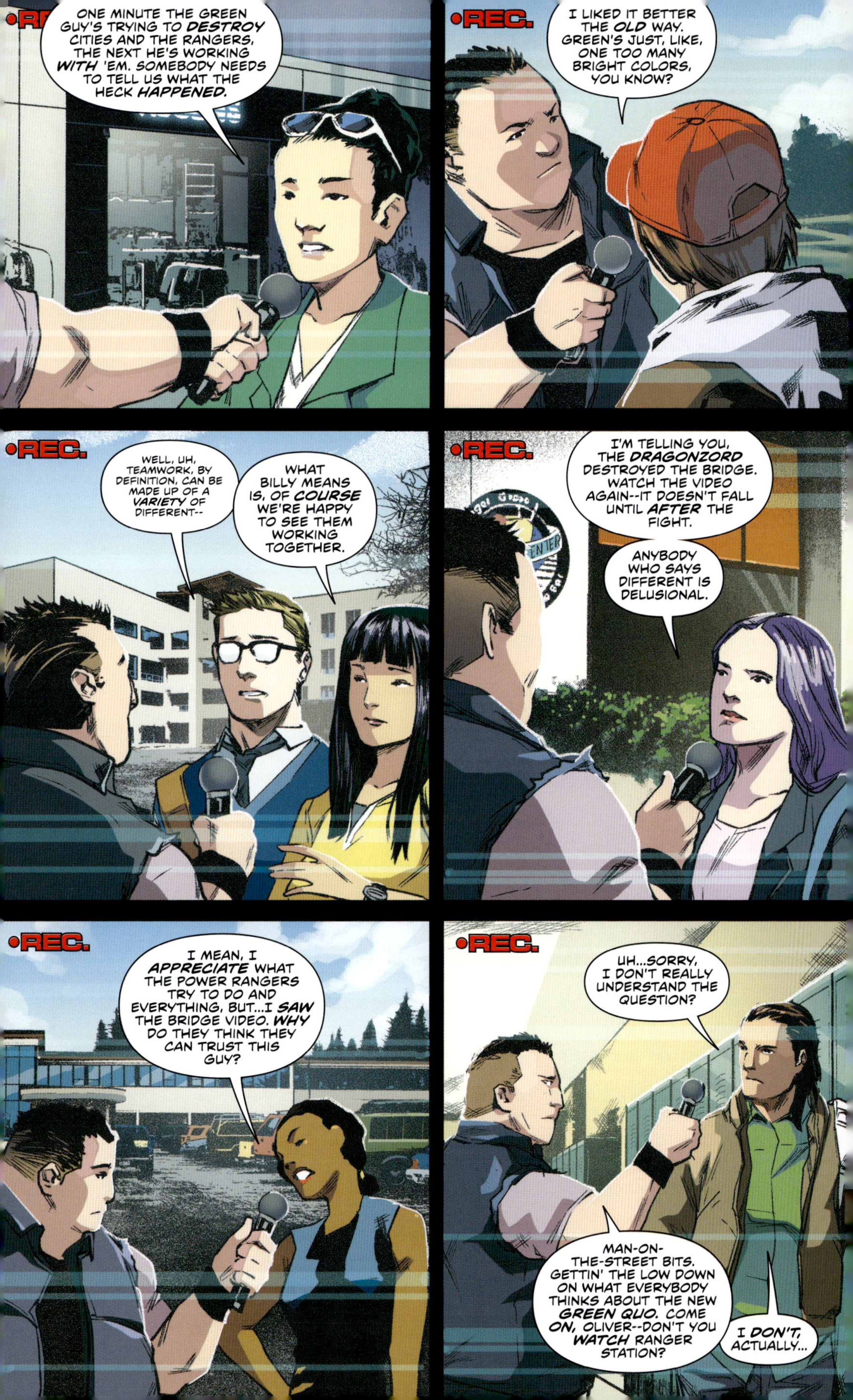
REC.
ONE MINUTE THE GREEN GUY'S TRYING TO DESTROY CITIES AND THE RANGERS, THE NEXT HE'S WORKING WITH 'EM. SOMEBODY NEEDS TO TELL US WHAT THE HECK HAPPENED.
REC.
I LIKED IT BETTER THE OLD WAY. GREEN'S JUST, LIKE, ONE TOO MANY BRIGHT COLORS, YOU KNOW?
REC.
WELL, UH, TEAMWORK, BY DEFINITION, CAN BE MADE UP OF A VARIETY OF DIFFERENT--
WHAT BILLY MEANS IS, OF COURSE WE'RE HAPPY TO SEE THEM WORKING TOGETHER.
REC.
I'M TELLING YOU, THE DRAGONZORD DESTROYED THE BRIDGE. WATCH THE VIDEO AGAIN--IT DOESN'T FALL UNTIL AFTER THE FIGHT.
ANYBODY WHO SAYS DIFFERENT IS DELUSIONAL.
REC.
I MEAN, I APPRECIATE WHAT THE POWER RANGERS TRY TO DO AND EVERYTHING, BUT...I SAW THE BRIDGE VIDEO. WHY DO THEY THINK THEY CAN TRUST THIS GUY?
REC.
UH...SORRY, I DON'T REALLY UNDERSTAND THE QUESTION?
MAN-ON-THE-STREET BITS. GETTIN' THE LOW DOWN ON WHAT EVERYBODY THINKS ABOUT THE NEW GREEN QUO. COME ON, OLIVER--DON'T YOU WATCH RANGER STATION?
I DON'T, ACTUALLY...

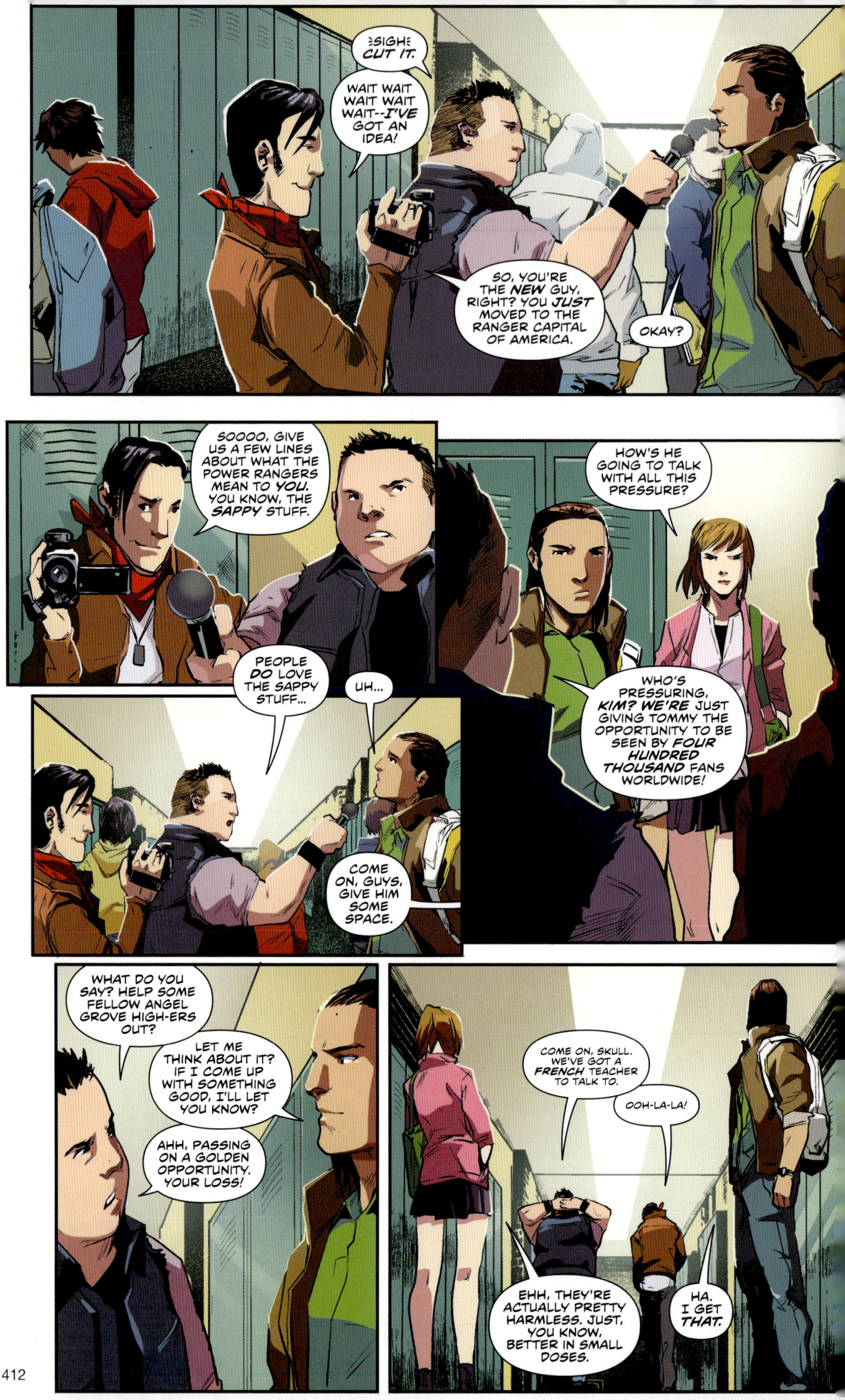
⁝SIGH⁝
CUT IT.
WAIT WAIT WAIT WAIT WAIT--I'VE GOT AN IDEA!
SO, YOU'RE THE NEW GUY, RIGHT? YOU JUST MOVED TO THE RANGER CAPITAL OF AMERICA.
OKAY?
SOOOO, GIVE US A FEW LINES ABOUT WHAT THE POWER RANGERS MEAN TO YOU. YOU KNOW, THE SAPPY STUFF.
HOW'S HE GOING TO TALK WITH ALL THIS PRESSURE?
WHO'S PRESSURING, KIM? WE'RE JUST GIVING TOMMY THE OPPORTUNITY TO BE SEEN BY FOUR HUNDRED THOUSAND FANS WORLDWIDE!
PEOPLE DO LOVE THE SAPPY STUFF...
UH...
COME ON, GUYS, GIVE HIM SOME SPACE.
WHAT DO YOU SAY? HELP SOME FELLOW ANGEL GROVE HIGH-ERS OUT?
LET ME THINK ABOUT IT? IF I COME UP WITH SOMETHING GOOD, I'LL LET YOU KNOW?
AHH, PASSING ON A GOLDEN OPPORTUNITY. YOUR LOSS!
COME ON, SKULL. WE'VE GOT A FRENCH TEACHER TO TALK TO.
OOH-LA-LA!
EHH, THEY'RE ACTUALLY PRETTY HARMLESS. JUST, YOU KNOW, BETTER IN SMALL DOSES.
HA. I GET THAT.

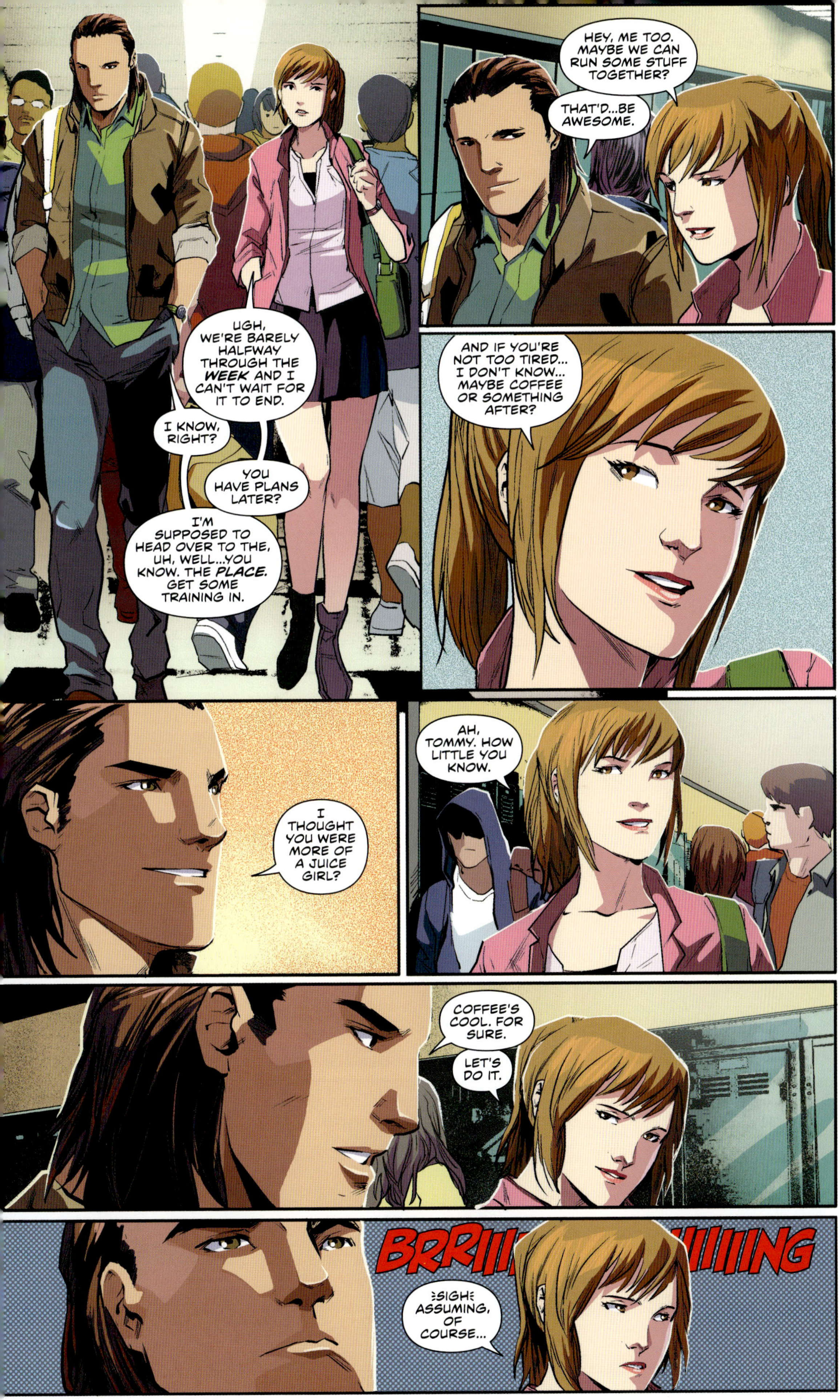
UGH, WE'RE BARELY HALFWAY THROUGH THE WEEK AND I CAN'T WAIT FOR IT TO END.
I KNOW, RIGHT?
YOU HAVE PLANS LATER?
I'M SUPPOSED TO HEAD OVER TO THE, UH, WELL...YOU KNOW. THE PLACE. GET SOME TRAINING IN.
HEY, ME TOO. MAYBE WE CAN RUN SOME STUFF TOGETHER?
THAT'D...BE AWESOME.
AND IF YOU'RE NOT TOO TIRED... I DON'T KNOW... MAYBE COFFEE OR SOMETHING AFTER?
I THOUGHT YOU WERE MORE OF A JUICE GIRL?
AH, TOMMY. HOW LITTLE YOU KNOW.
COFFEE'S COOL. FOR SURE.
LET'S DO IT.
BRRIIIIIIIIIIIIING
SIGH ASSUMING, OF COURSE...

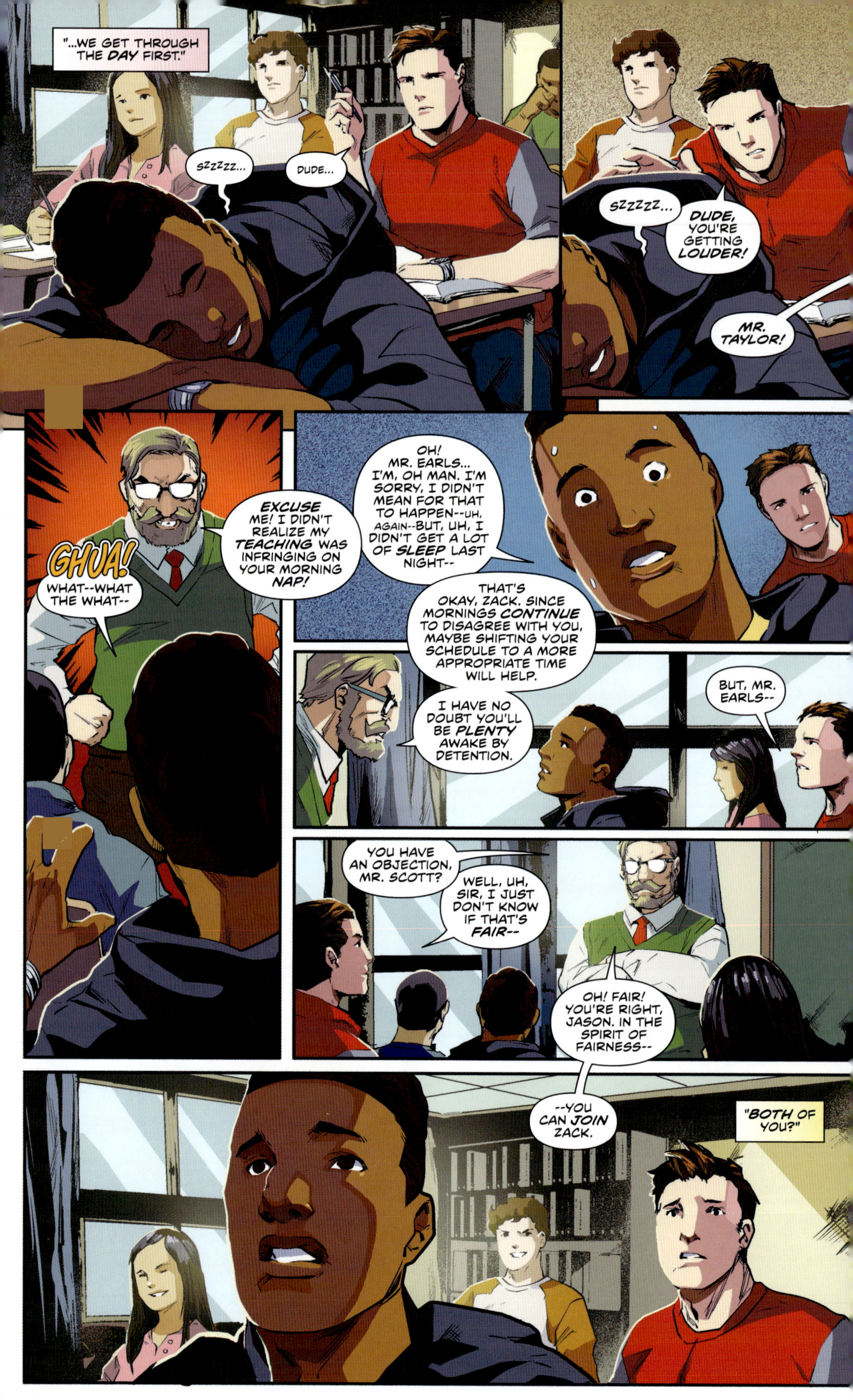
"...WE GET THROUGH THE DAY FIRST."
SZZZZZ...
DUDE...
SZZZZZ...
DUDE, YOU'RE GETTING LOUDER!
MR. TAYLOR!
GHUA!
WHAT--WHAT THE WHAT--
EXCUSE ME! I DIDN'T REALIZE MY TEACHING WAS INFRINGING ON YOUR MORNING NAP!
OH! MR. EARLS... I'M, OH MAN. I'M SORRY, I DIDN'T MEAN FOR THAT TO HAPPEN--UH, AGAIN--BUT, UH, I DIDN'T GET A LOT OF SLEEP LAST NIGHT--
THAT'S OKAY, ZACK. SINCE MORNINGS CONTINUE TO DISAGREE WITH YOU, MAYBE SHIFTING YOUR SCHEDULE TO A MORE APPROPRIATE TIME WILL HELP.
I HAVE NO DOUBT YOU'LL BE PLENTY AWAKE BY DETENTION.
BUT, MR. EARLS--
YOU HAVE AN OBJECTION, MR. SCOTT?
WELL, UH, SIR, I JUST DON'T KNOW IF THAT'S FAIR--
OH! FAIR! YOU'RE RIGHT, JASON. IN THE SPIRIT OF FAIRNESS--
--YOU CAN JOIN ZACK.
"BOTH OF YOU?"

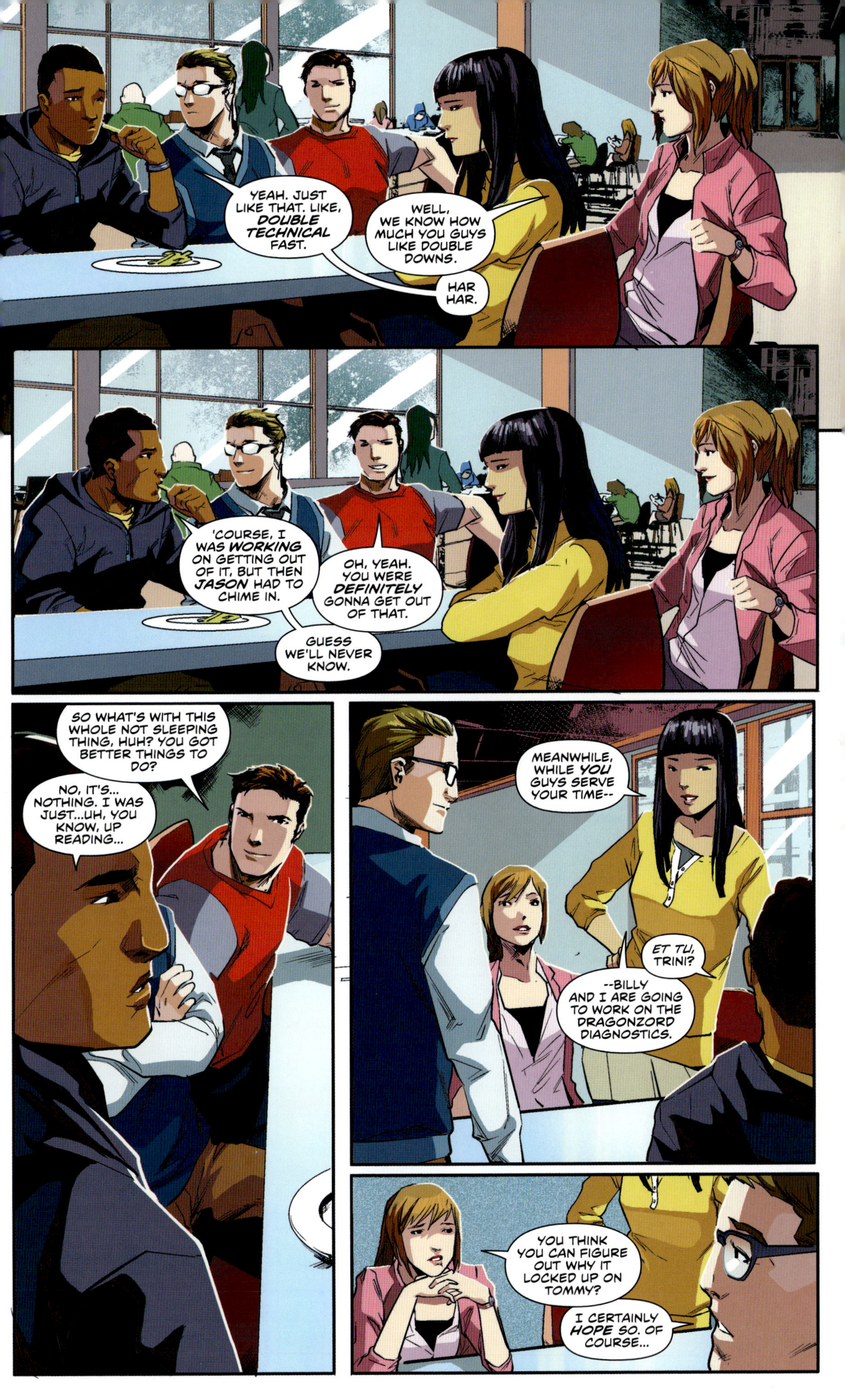
YEAH. JUST LIKE THAT. LIKE, **DOUBLE TECHNICAL** FAST.
WELL, WE KNOW HOW MUCH YOU GUYS LIKE DOUBLE DOWNS.
HAR HAR.
'COURSE, I WAS **WORKING** ON GETTING OUT OF IT, BUT THEN **JASON** HAD TO CHIME IN.
OH, YEAH. YOU WERE **DEFINITELY** GONNA GET OUT OF THAT.
GUESS WE'LL NEVER KNOW.
SO WHAT'S WITH THIS WHOLE NOT SLEEPING THING, HUH? YOU GOT BETTER THINGS TO DO?
NO, IT'S... NOTHING. I WAS JUST...UH, YOU KNOW, UP READING...
MEANWHILE, WHILE **YOU** GUYS SERVE YOUR TIME--
ET TU, TRINI?
--BILLY AND I ARE GOING TO WORK ON THE DRAGONZORD DIAGNOSTICS.
YOU THINK YOU CAN FIGURE OUT WHY IT LOCKED UP ON TOMMY?
I CERTAINLY **HOPE** SO. OF COURSE...

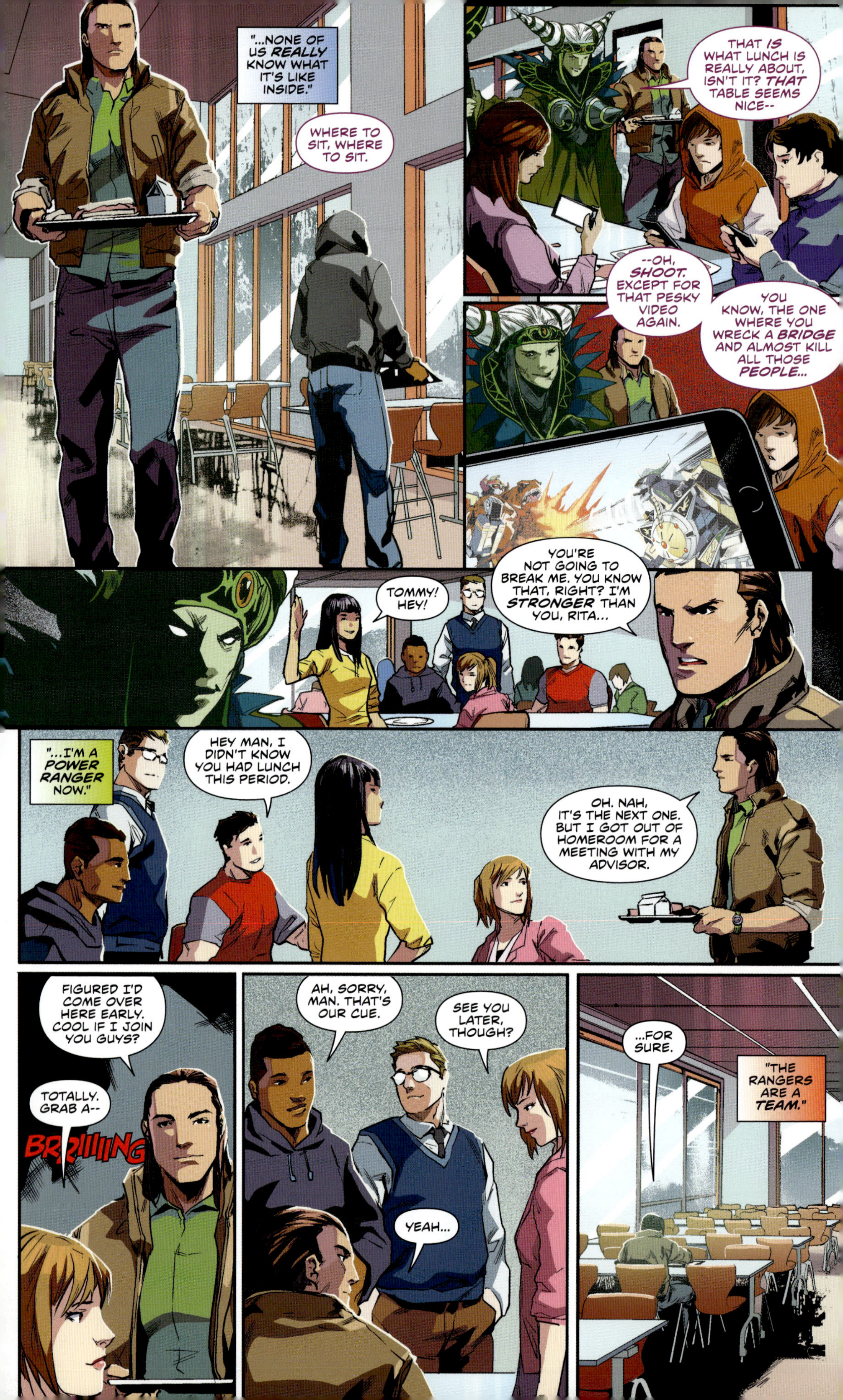
"...NONE OF US REALLY KNOW WHAT IT'S LIKE INSIDE."
WHERE TO SIT, WHERE TO SIT.
THAT IS WHAT LUNCH IS REALLY ABOUT, ISN'T IT? THAT TABLE SEEMS NICE--
--OH, SHOOT. EXCEPT FOR THAT PESKY VIDEO AGAIN.
YOU KNOW, THE ONE WHERE YOU WRECK A BRIDGE AND ALMOST KILL ALL THOSE PEOPLE...
TOMMY! HEY!
YOU'RE NOT GOING TO BREAK ME. YOU KNOW THAT, RIGHT? I'M STRONGER THAN YOU, RITA...
"...I'M A POWER RANGER NOW."
HEY MAN, I DIDN'T KNOW YOU HAD LUNCH THIS PERIOD.
OH. NAH, IT'S THE NEXT ONE. BUT I GOT OUT OF HOMEROOM FOR A MEETING WITH MY ADVISOR.
FIGURED I'D COME OVER HERE EARLY. COOL IF I JOIN YOU GUYS?
TOTALLY. GRAB A--
BRIIIIING
AH, SORRY, MAN. THAT'S OUR CUE.
SEE YOU LATER, THOUGH?
YEAH...
...FOR SURE.
"THE RANGERS ARE A TEAM."

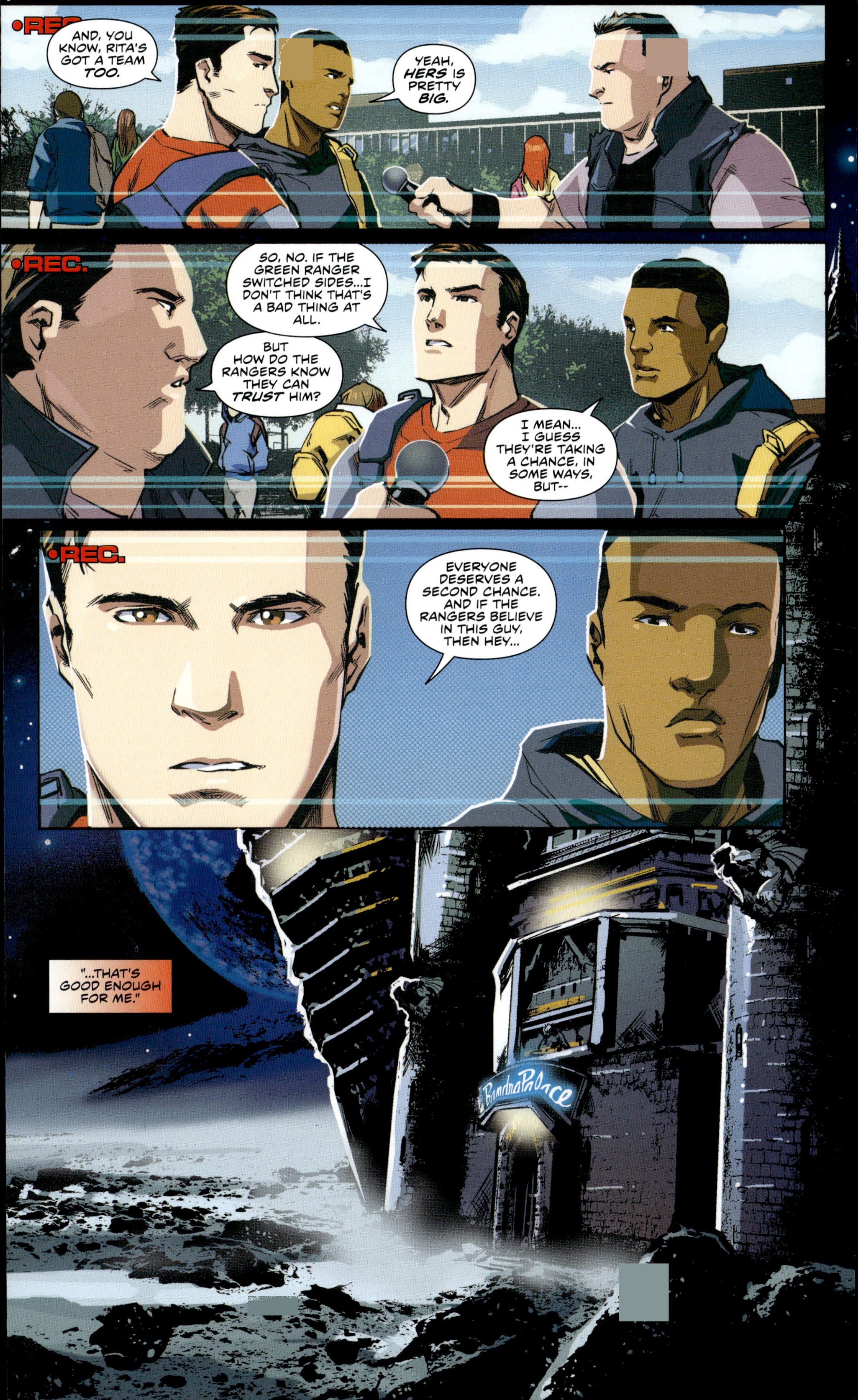
•REC.
AND, YOU KNOW, RITA'S GOT A TEAM TOO.
YEAH, HERS IS PRETTY BIG.
•REC.
SO, NO. IF THE GREEN RANGER SWITCHED SIDES...I DON'T THINK THAT'S A BAD THING AT ALL.
BUT HOW DO THE RANGERS KNOW THEY CAN TRUST HIM?
I MEAN... I GUESS THEY'RE TAKING A CHANCE, IN SOME WAYS, BUT--
•REC.
EVERYONE DESERVES A SECOND CHANCE. AND IF THE RANGERS BELIEVE IN THIS GUY, THEN HEY...
"...THAT'S GOOD ENOUGH FOR ME."
Bandora Palace

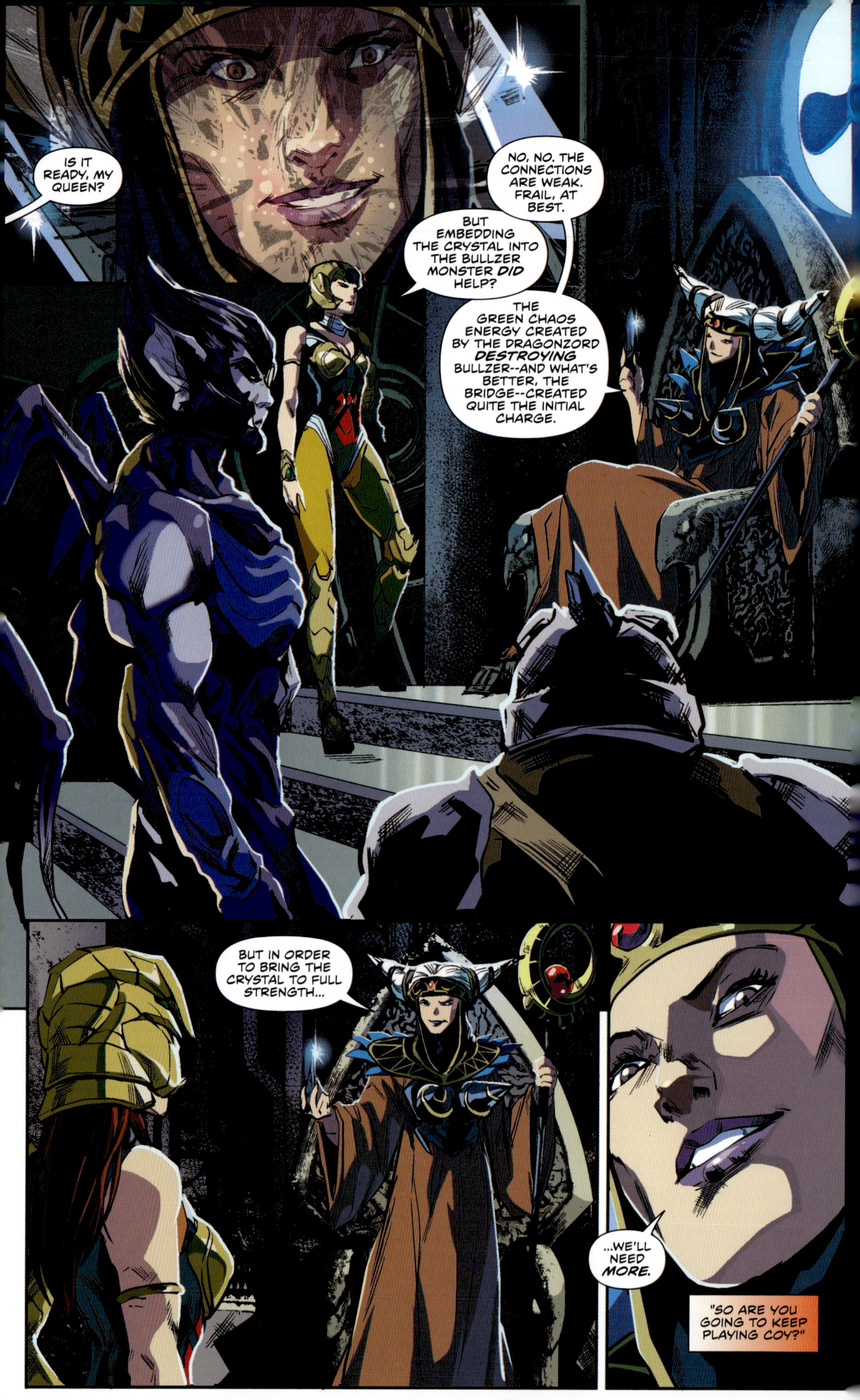
IS IT READY, MY QUEEN?
NO, NO. THE CONNECTIONS ARE WEAK. FRAIL, AT BEST.
BUT EMBEDDING THE CRYSTAL INTO THE BULLZER MONSTER DID HELP?
THE GREEN CHAOS ENERGY CREATED BY THE DRAGONZORD DESTROYING BULLZER--AND WHAT'S BETTER, THE BRIDGE--CREATED QUITE THE INITIAL CHARGE.
BUT IN ORDER TO BRING THE CRYSTAL TO FULL STRENGTH...
...WE'LL NEED MORE.
"SO ARE YOU GOING TO KEEP PLAYING COY?"

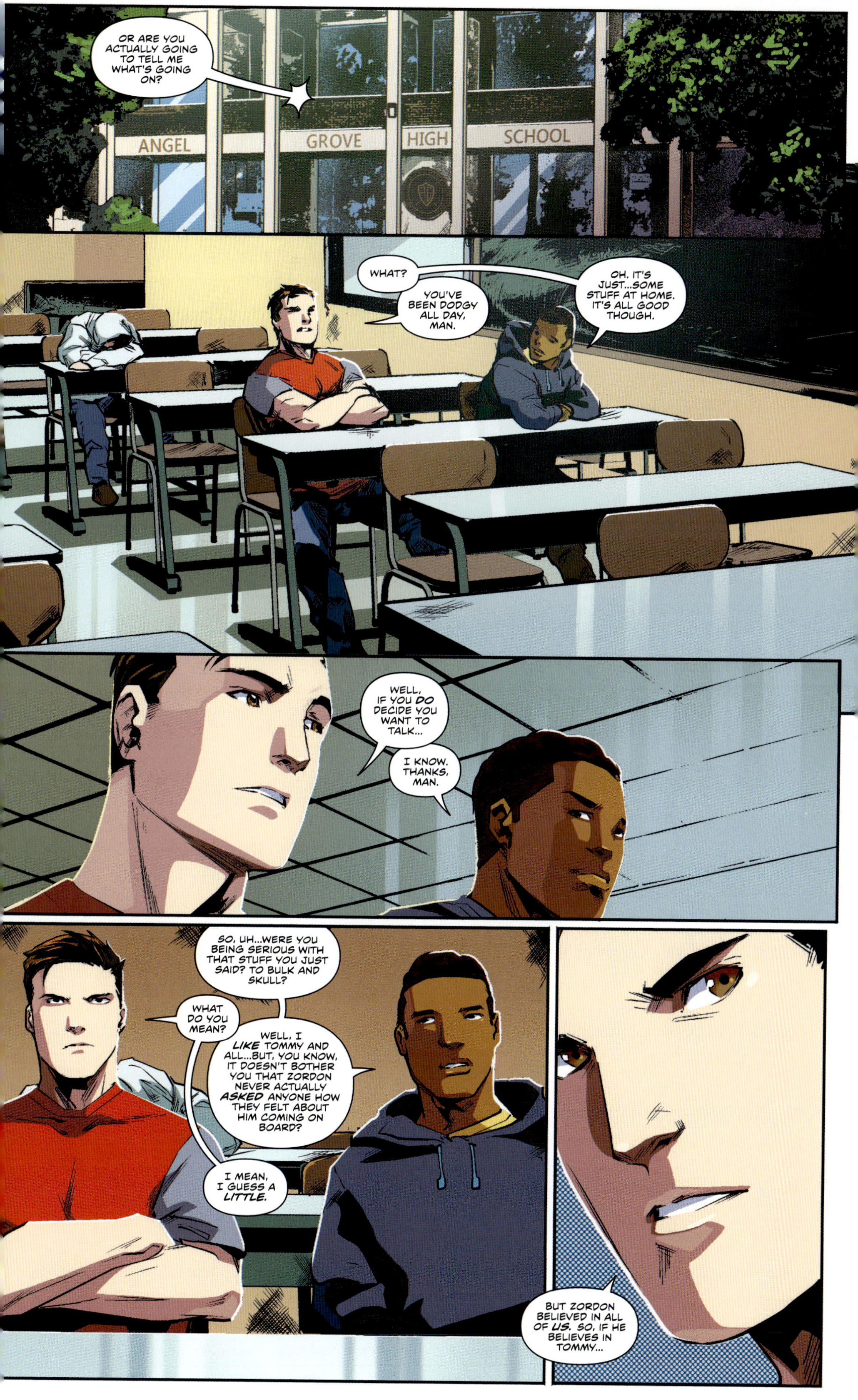
OR ARE YOU ACTUALLY GOING TO TELL ME WHAT'S GOING ON?
ANGEL GROVE HIGH SCHOOL
WHAT?
YOU'VE BEEN DODGY ALL DAY, MAN.
OH. IT'S JUST...SOME STUFF AT HOME. IT'S ALL GOOD THOUGH.
WELL, IF YOU DO DECIDE YOU WANT TO TALK...
I KNOW. THANKS, MAN.
SO, UH...WERE YOU BEING SERIOUS WITH THAT STUFF YOU JUST SAID? TO BULK AND SKULL?
WHAT DO YOU MEAN?
WELL, I LIKE TOMMY AND ALL...BUT, YOU KNOW, IT DOESN'T BOTHER YOU THAT ZORDON NEVER ACTUALLY ASKED ANYONE HOW THEY FELT ABOUT HIM COMING ON BOARD?
I MEAN, I GUESS A LITTLE.
BUT ZORDON BELIEVED IN ALL OF US. SO, IF HE BELIEVES IN TOMMY...

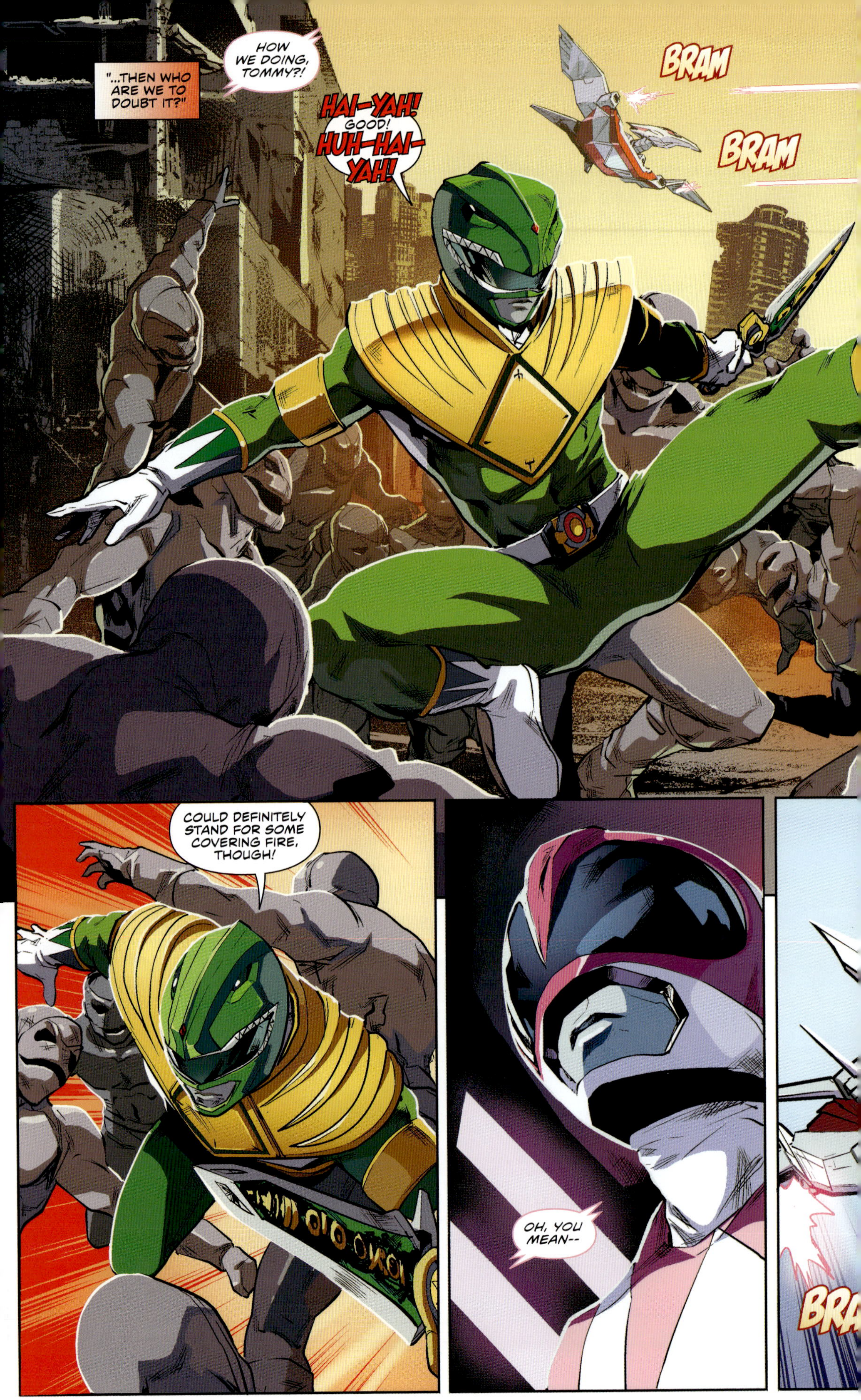
"...THEN WHO ARE WE TO DOUBT IT?"
HOW WE DOING, TOMMY?!
HAI-YAH! GOOD! HUH-HAI-YAH!
BRAM
BRAM
COULD DEFINITELY STAND FOR SOME COVERING FIRE, THOUGH!
OH, YOU MEAN--

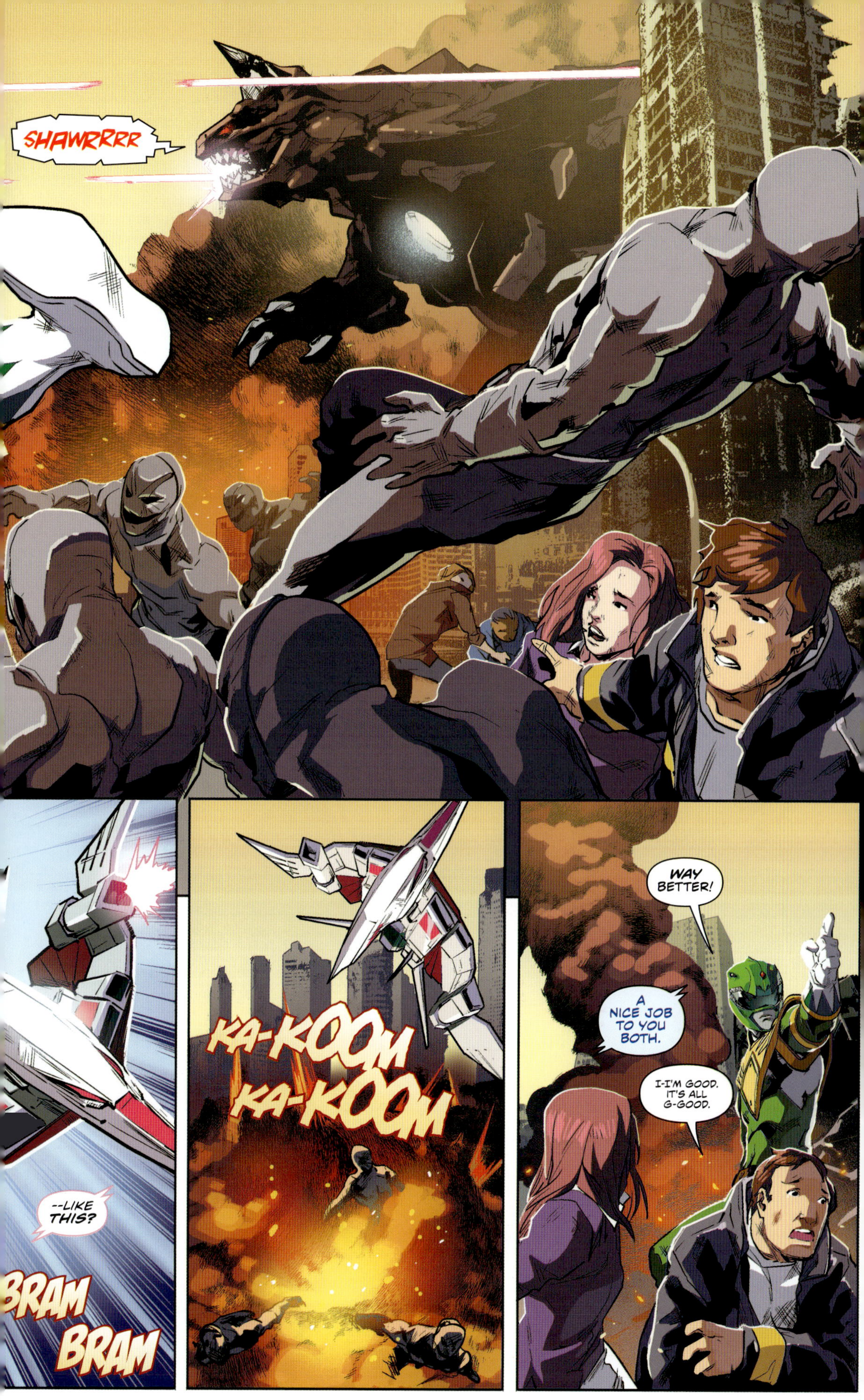
SHAWRRRR
--LIKE THIS?
BRAM
BRAM
KA-KOOM
KA-KOOM
WAY BETTER!
A NICE JOB TO YOU BOTH.
I-I'M GOOD. IT'S ALL G-GOOD.

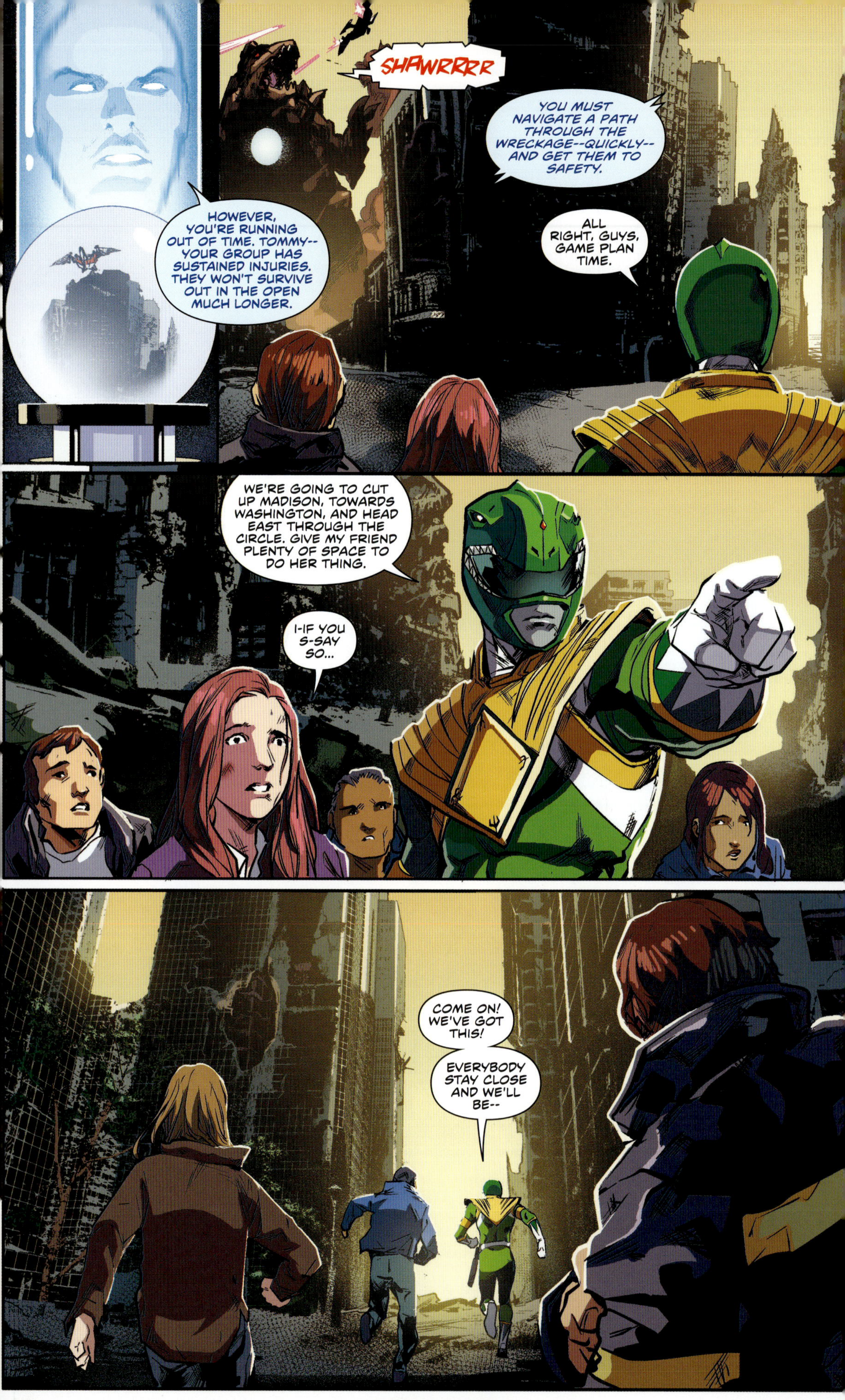
SHAWRRRR
YOU MUST NAVIGATE A PATH THROUGH THE WRECKAGE--QUICKLY--AND GET THEM TO SAFETY.
HOWEVER, YOU'RE RUNNING OUT OF TIME. TOMMY--YOUR GROUP HAS SUSTAINED INJURIES. THEY WON'T SURVIVE OUT IN THE OPEN MUCH LONGER.
ALL RIGHT, GUYS, GAME PLAN TIME.
WE'RE GOING TO CUT UP MADISON, TOWARDS WASHINGTON, AND HEAD EAST THROUGH THE CIRCLE. GIVE MY FRIEND PLENTY OF SPACE TO DO HER THING.
I-IF YOU S-SAY SO...
COME ON! WE'VE GOT THIS!
EVERYBODY STAY CLOSE AND WE'LL BE--

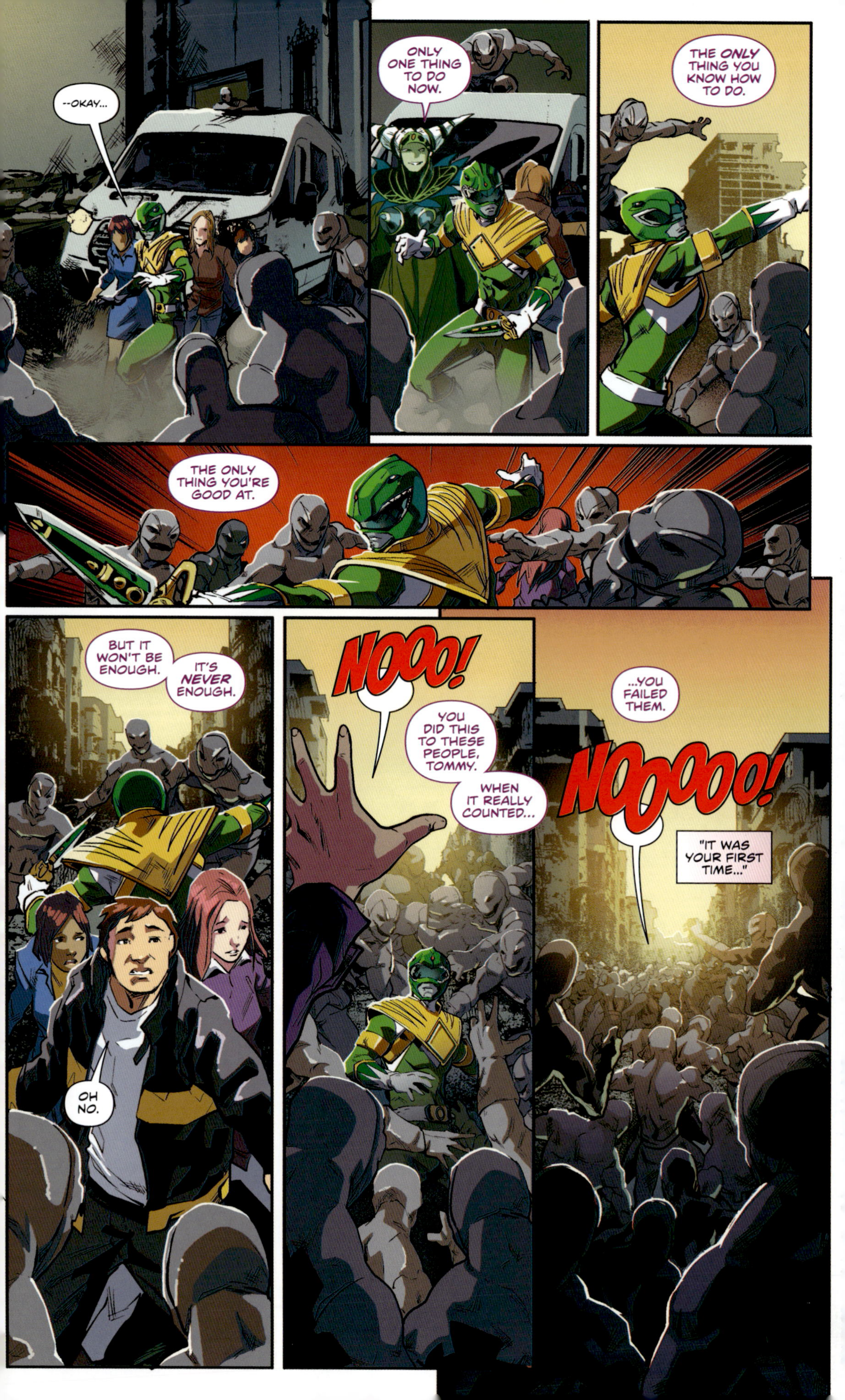
--OKAY...
ONLY ONE THING TO DO NOW.
THE ONLY THING YOU KNOW HOW TO DO.
THE ONLY THING YOU'RE GOOD AT.
BUT IT WON'T BE ENOUGH.
IT'S NEVER ENOUGH.
OH NO.
NOOO!
YOU DID THIS TO THESE PEOPLE, TOMMY.
WHEN IT REALLY COUNTED...
...YOU FAILED THEM.
NOOOOO!
"IT WAS YOUR FIRST TIME..."

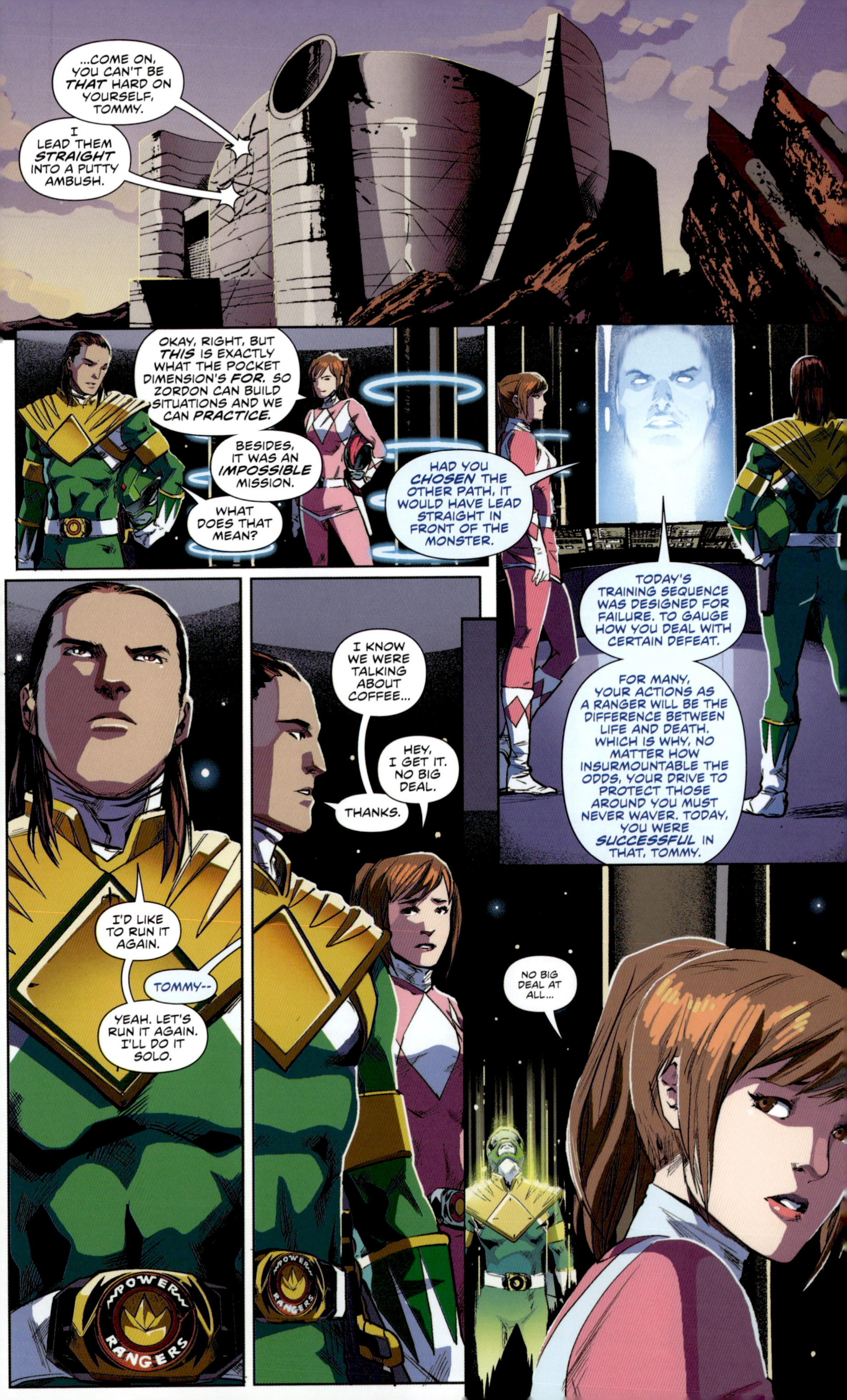
...COME ON, YOU CAN'T BE *THAT* HARD ON YOURSELF, TOMMY.
I LEAD THEM *STRAIGHT* INTO A PUTTY AMBUSH.
OKAY, RIGHT, BUT *THIS* IS EXACTLY WHAT THE POCKET DIMENSION'S *FOR.* SO ZORDON CAN BUILD SITUATIONS AND WE CAN *PRACTICE.*
BESIDES, IT WAS AN *IMPOSSIBLE* MISSION.
WHAT DOES THAT MEAN?
HAD YOU *CHOSEN* THE OTHER PATH, IT WOULD HAVE LEAD STRAIGHT IN FRONT OF THE MONSTER.
TODAY'S TRAINING SEQUENCE WAS DESIGNED FOR FAILURE. TO GAUGE HOW YOU DEAL WITH CERTAIN DEFEAT.
FOR MANY, YOUR ACTIONS AS A RANGER WILL BE THE DIFFERENCE BETWEEN LIFE AND DEATH. WHICH IS WHY, NO MATTER HOW INSURMOUNTABLE THE ODDS, YOUR DRIVE TO PROTECT THOSE AROUND YOU MUST NEVER WAVER. TODAY, YOU WERE *SUCCESSFUL* IN THAT, TOMMY.
I'D LIKE TO RUN IT AGAIN.
TOMMY--
YEAH. LET'S RUN IT AGAIN. I'LL DO IT SOLO.
I KNOW WE WERE TALKING ABOUT COFFEE...
THANKS.
HEY, I GET IT. NO BIG DEAL.
NO BIG DEAL AT ALL...
POWER RANGERS

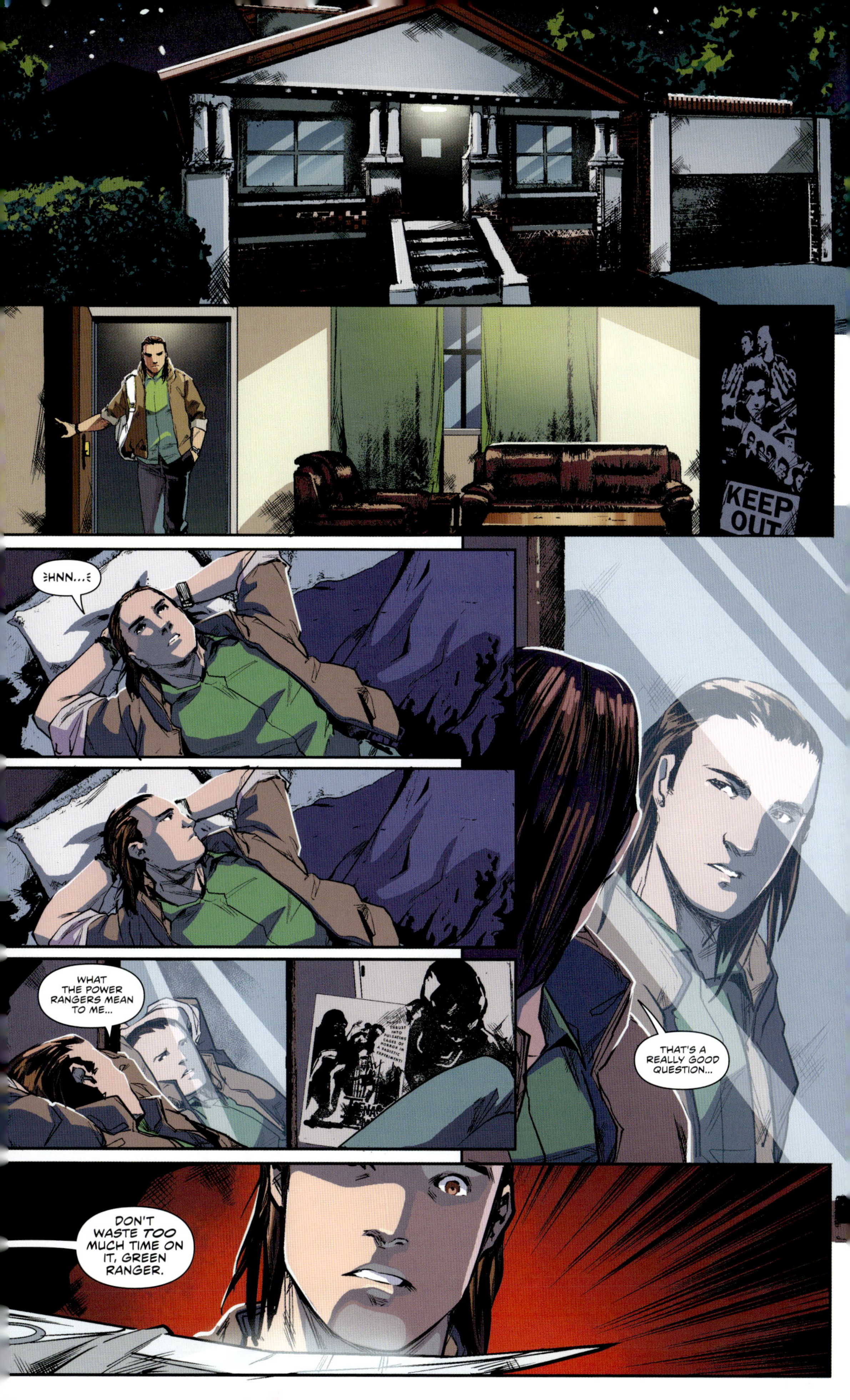
KEEP OUT
HNN...
WHAT THE POWER RANGERS MEAN TO ME...
THAT'S A REALLY GOOD QUESTION...
DON'T WASTE *TOO* MUCH TIME ON IT, GREEN RANGER.

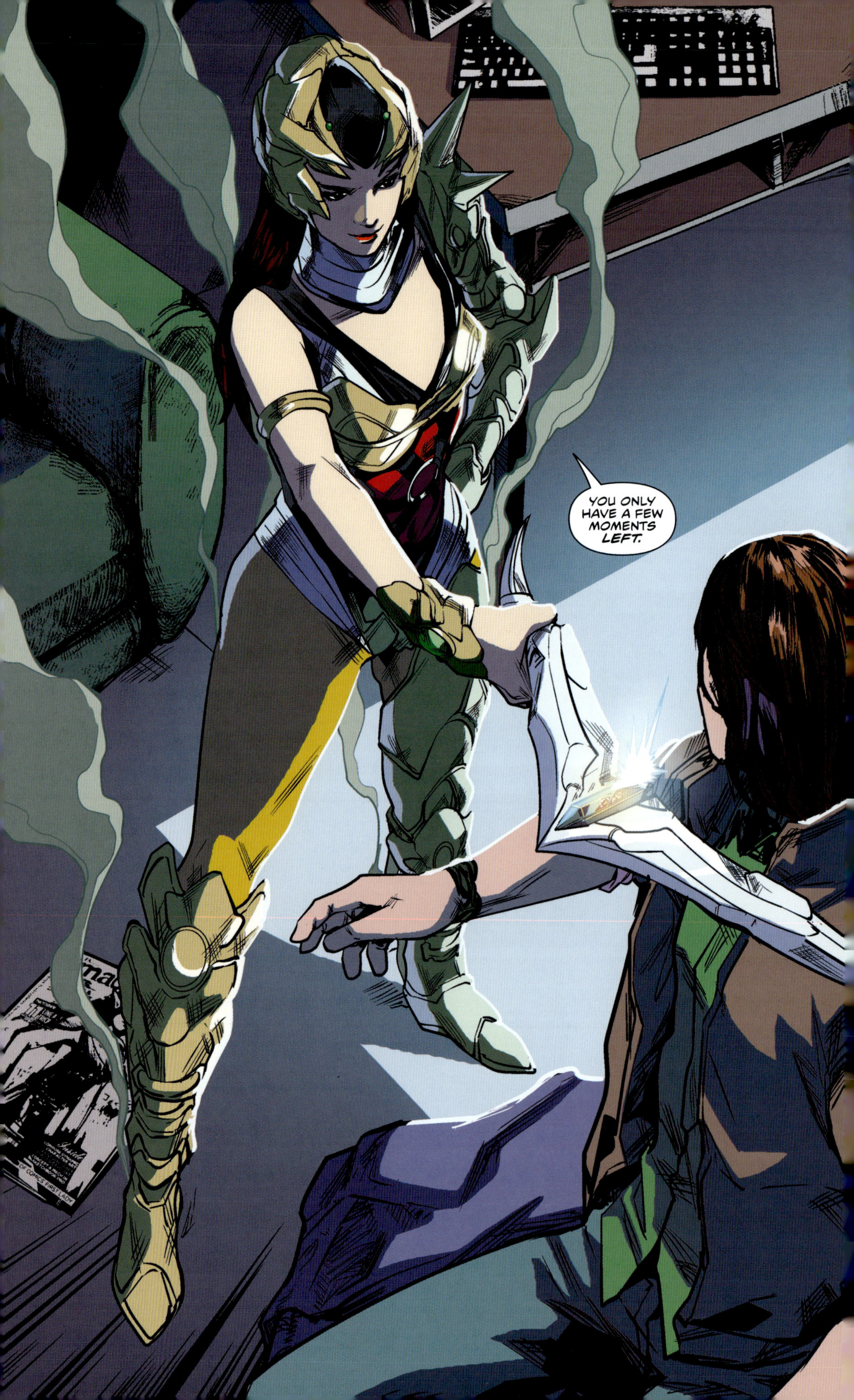
YOU ONLY HAVE A FEW MOMENTS LEFT.

SABAN'S

MIGHTY MORPHIN POWER RANGERS™

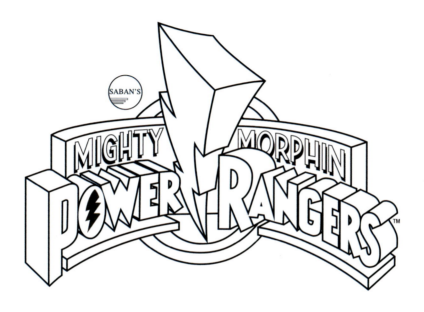

ACTIVITY PAGES

GO! GO! POWER RANGERS!

IT'S UP TO THE **POWER RANGERS** TO FREE **ALPHA 5** FROM THE CLUTCHES OF **LORD ZEDD**. BUT THE EVIL **ZEDD** HAS STATIONED HIS HENCHMEN TO GUARD THE WAY AND FOIL THE **RANGERS'** RESCUE. THEY NEED **YOUR** HELP! CAN YOU SHOW THEM THE RIGHT PATH TO TAKE?

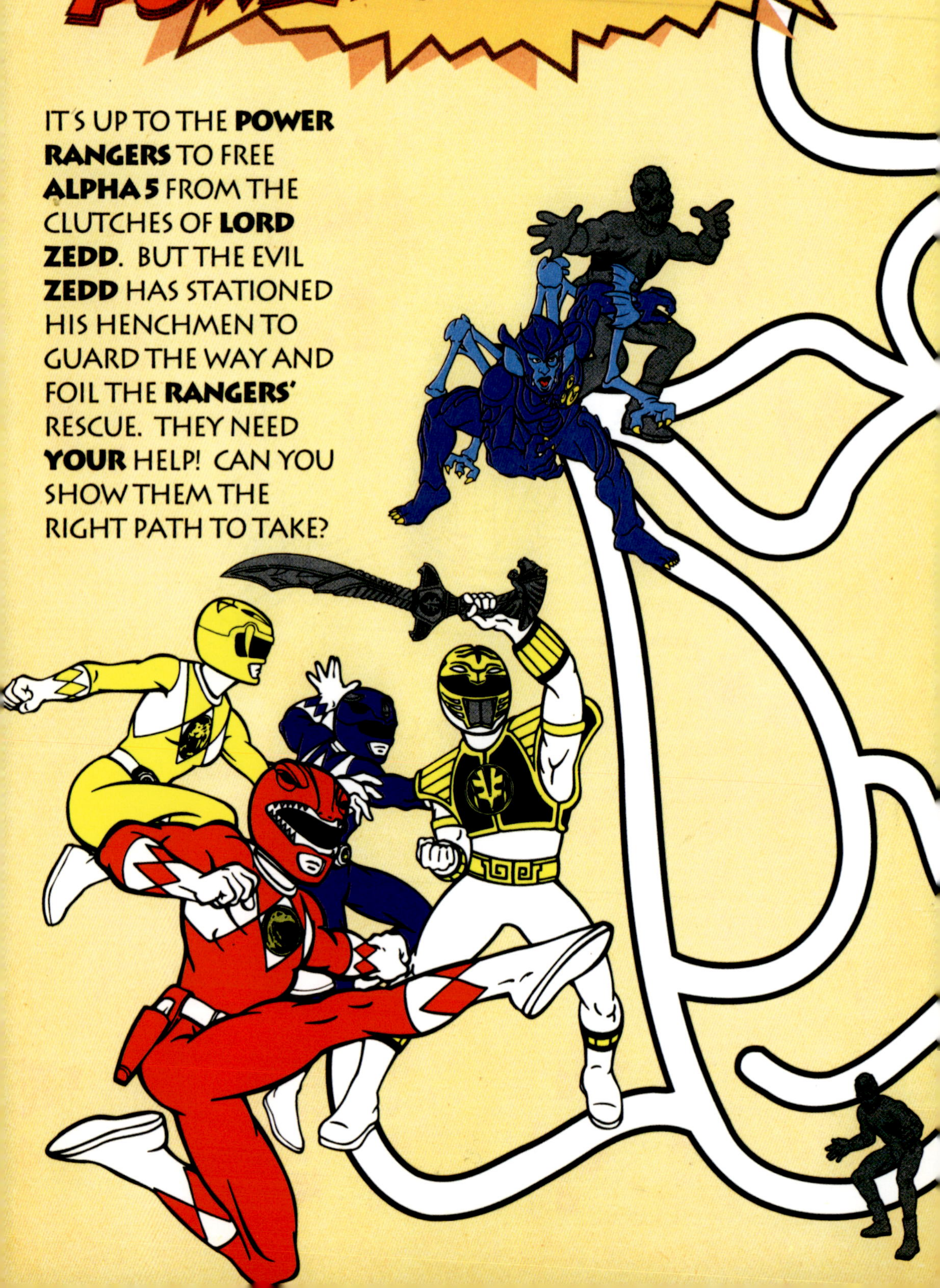

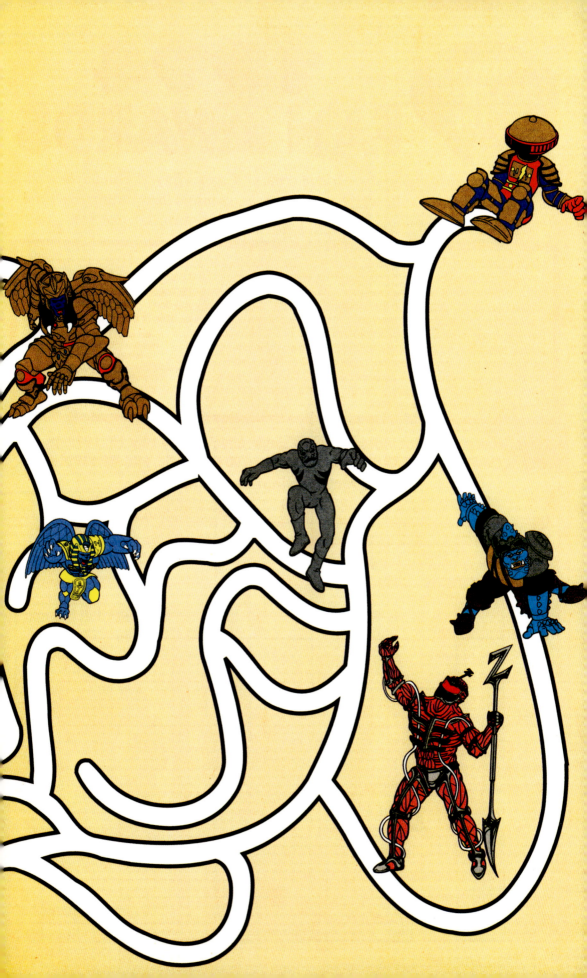

SABAN'S Mighty Morphin Power Rangers

PUZZLE PAGE

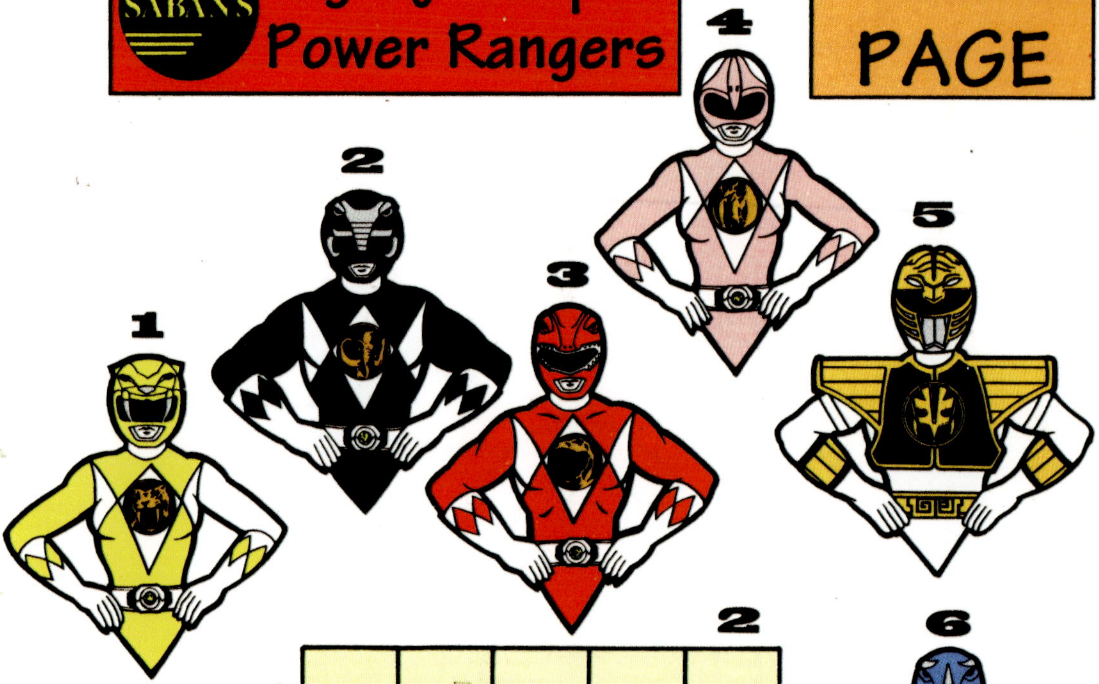

1
2
3
4
5

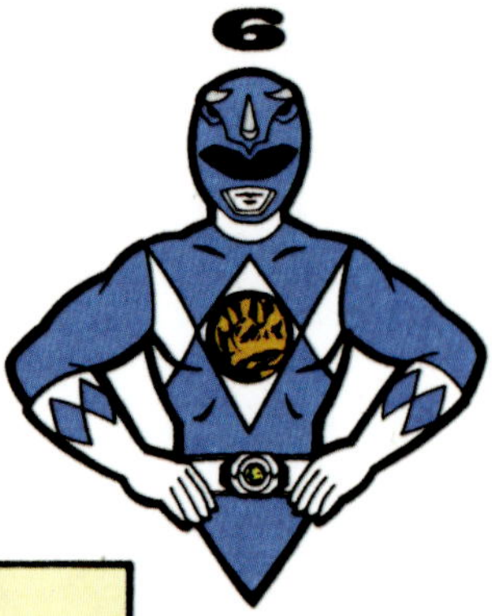

6

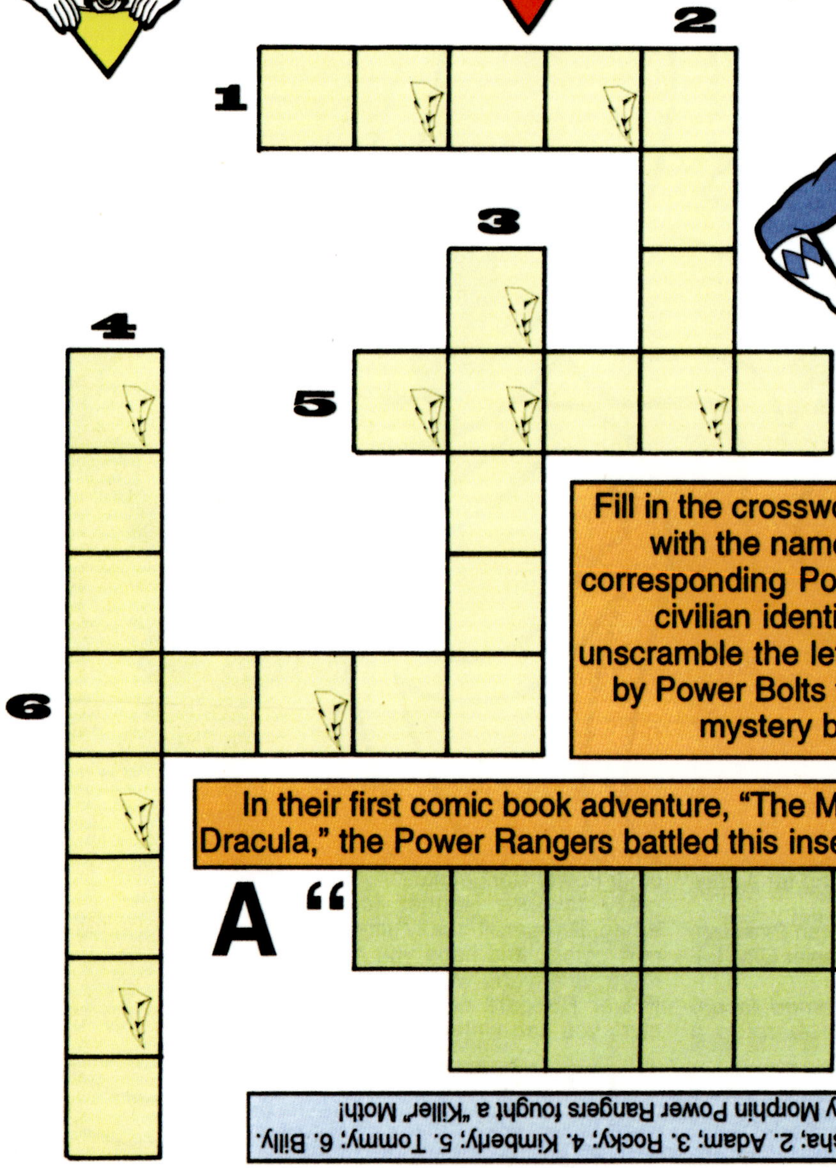

1
2
3
4
5
6

Fill in the crossword at the left with the name of each corresponding Power Ranger's civilian identity. Then unscramble the letters indicated by Power Bolts to solve the mystery below.

In their first comic book adventure, "The Menace of Dracula," the Power Rangers battled this insect monster:

A "_ _ _ _ _ _ _ _ _ _"

ANSWERS: 1. Aisha; 2. Adam; 3. Rocky; 4. Kimberly; 5. Tommy; 6. Billy. The Mighty Morphin Power Rangers fought a "Killer" Moth!

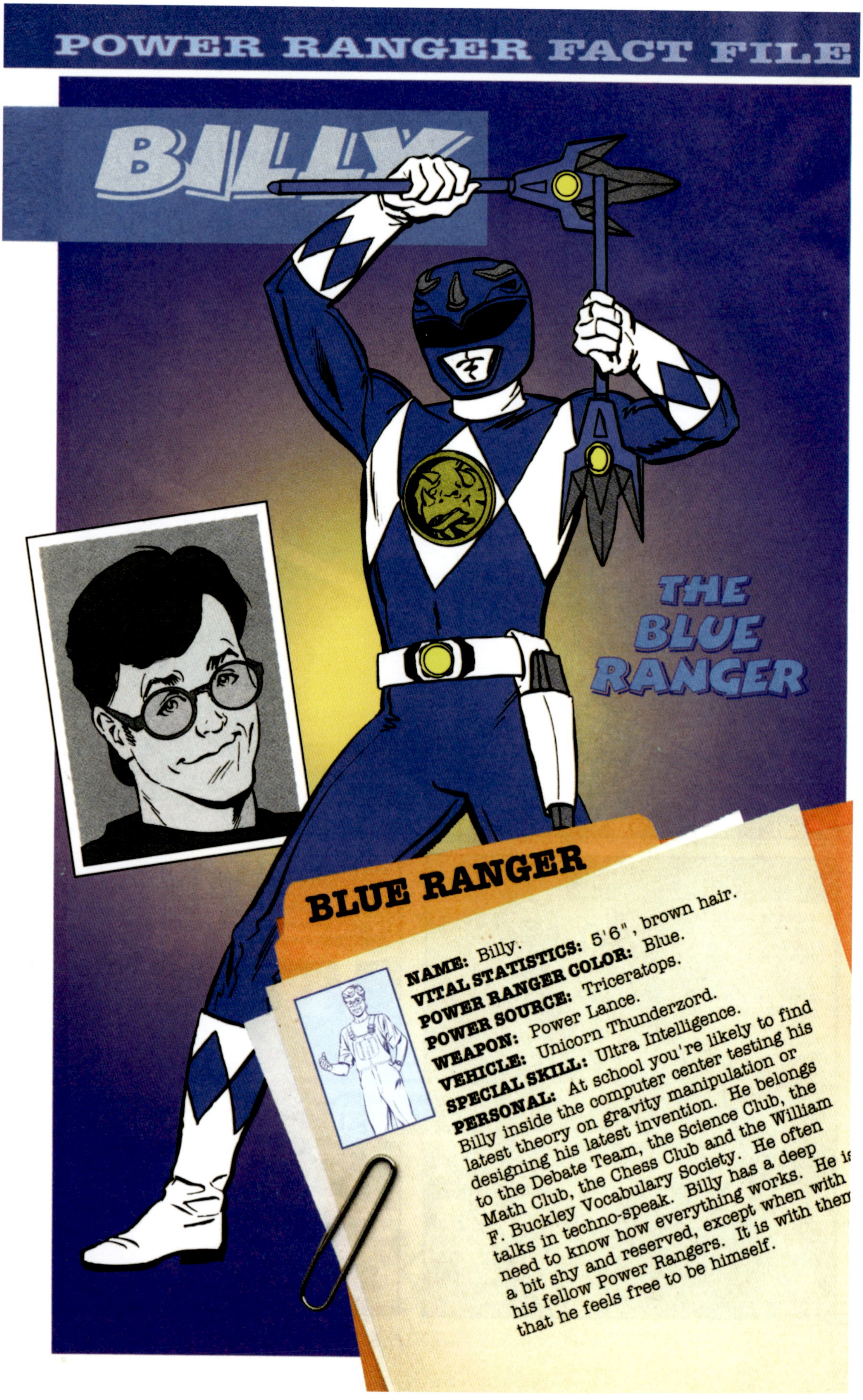
POWER RANGER FACT FILE
BILLY
THE BLUE RANGER
BLUE RANGER
NAME: Billy.
VITAL STATISTICS: 5'6", brown hair.
POWER RANGER COLOR: Blue.
POWER SOURCE: Triceratops.
WEAPON: Power Lance.
VEHICLE: Unicorn Thunderzord.
SPECIAL SKILL: Ultra Intelligence.
PERSONAL: At school you're likely to find Billy inside the computer center testing his latest theory on gravity manipulation or designing his latest invention. He belongs to the Debate Team, the Science Club, the Math Club, the Chess Club and the William F. Buckley Vocabulary Society. He often talks in techno-speak. Billy has a deep need to know how everything works. He is a bit shy and reserved, except when with his fellow Power Rangers. It is with them that he feels free to be himself.

POWER RANGER FACT FILE

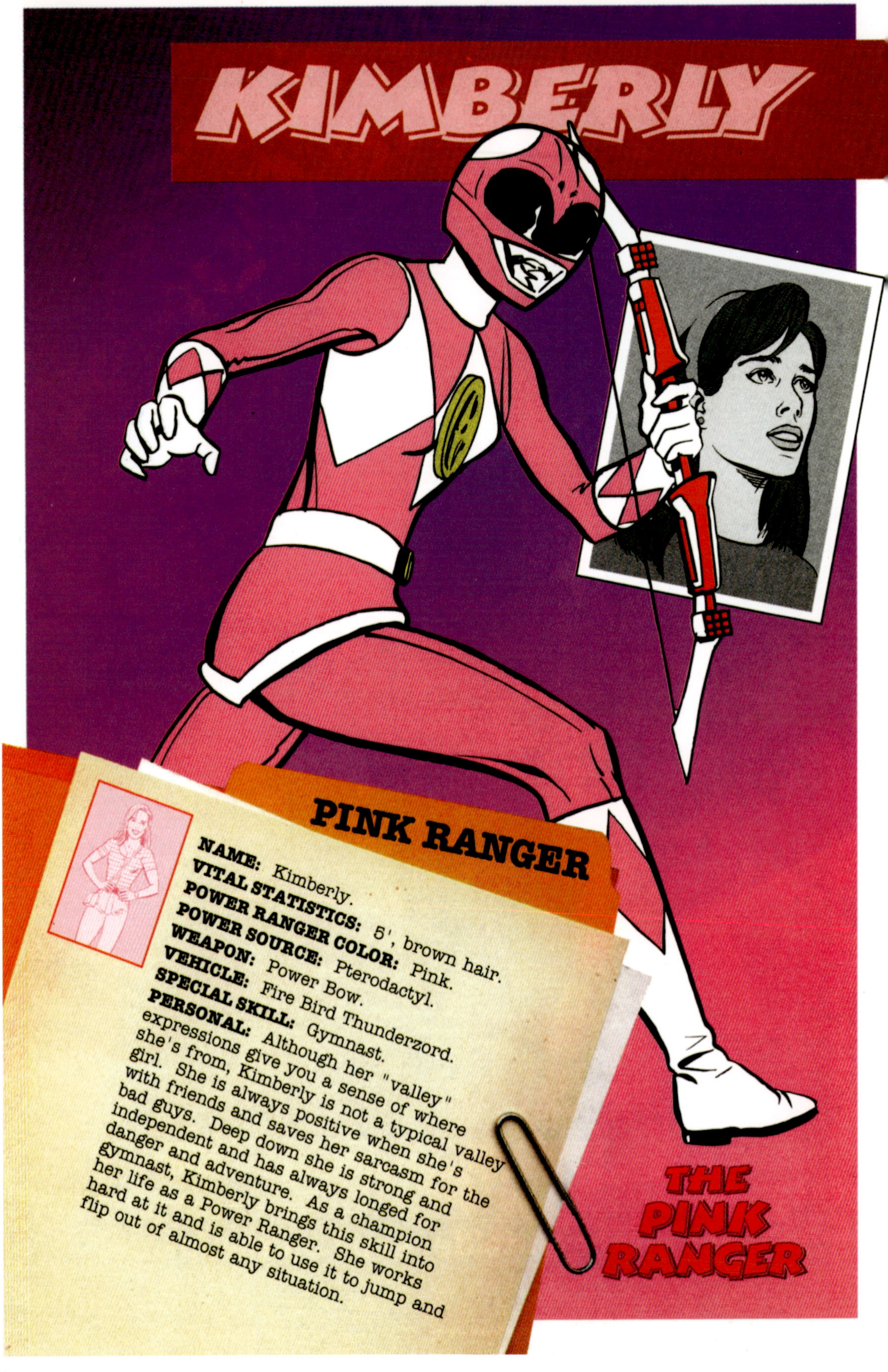
KIMBERLY
THE PINK RANGER

PINK RANGER

NAME: Kimberly.
VITAL STATISTICS: 5', brown hair.
POWER RANGER COLOR: Pink.
POWER SOURCE: Pterodactyl.
WEAPON: Power Bow.
VEHICLE: Fire Bird Thunderzord.
SPECIAL SKILL: Gymnast.
PERSONAL: Although her "valley" expressions give you a sense of where she's from, Kimberly is not a typical valley girl. She is always positive when she's with friends and saves her sarcasm for the bad guys. Deep down she is strong and independent and has always longed for danger and adventure. As a champion gymnast, Kimberly brings this skill into her life as a Power Ranger. She works hard at it and is able to use it to jump and flip out of almost any situation.

POWER RANGER FACT FILE

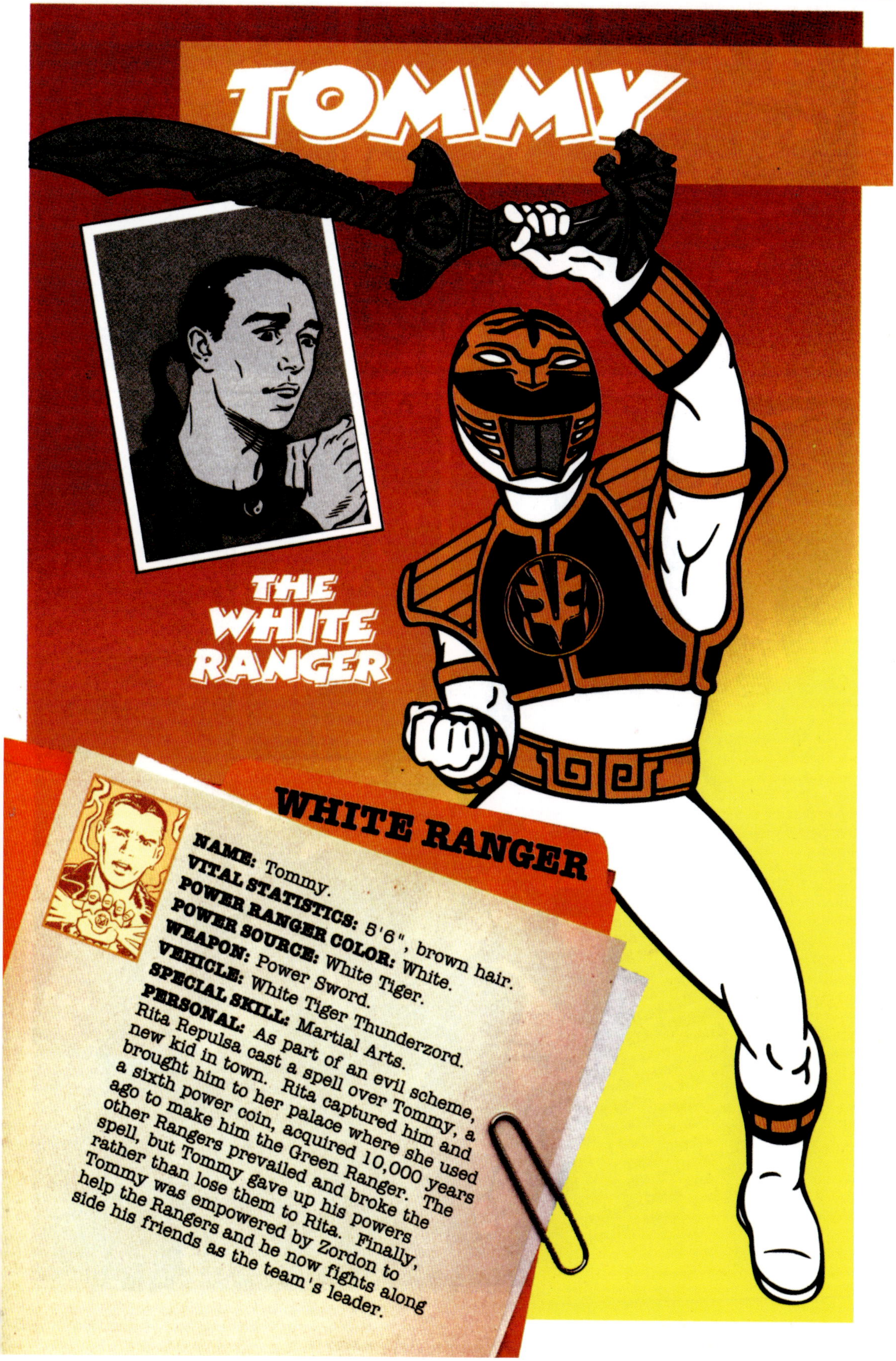
TOMMY
THE WHITE RANGER
WHITE RANGER
NAME: Tommy.
VITAL STATISTICS: 5'6", brown hair.
POWER RANGER COLOR: White.
POWER SOURCE: White Tiger.
WEAPON: Power Sword.
VEHICLE: White Tiger Thunderzord.
SPECIAL SKILL: Martial Arts.
PERSONAL: As part of an evil scheme, Rita Repulsa cast a spell over Tommy, a new kid in town. Rita captured him and brought him to her palace where she used a sixth power coin, acquired 10,000 years ago to make him the Green Ranger. The other Rangers prevailed and broke the spell, but Tommy gave up his powers rather than lose them to Rita. Finally, Tommy was empowered by Zordon to help the Rangers and he now fights along side his friends as the team's leader.

POWER RANGER FACT FILE

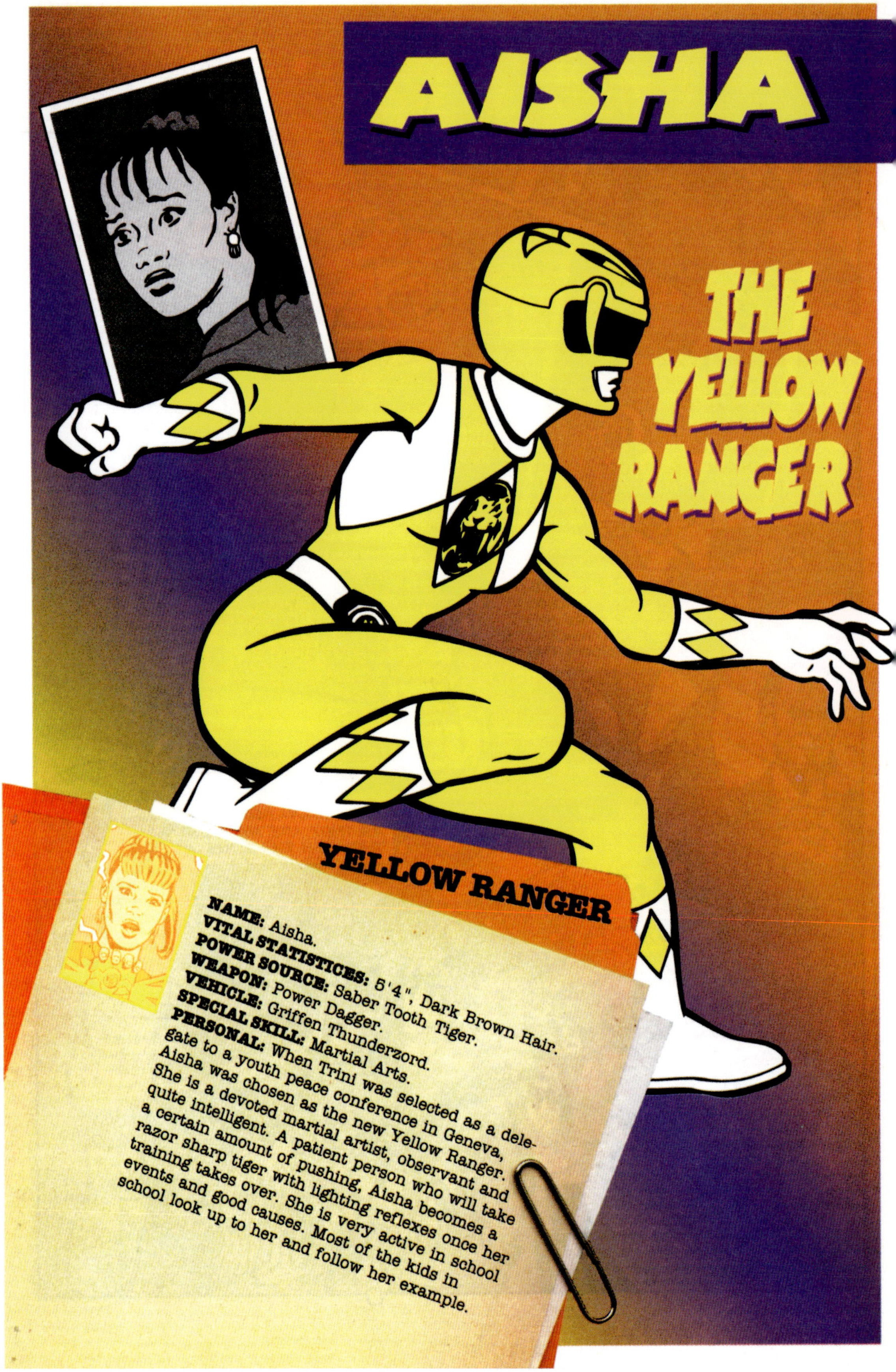
AISHA
THE YELLOW RANGER

YELLOW RANGER

NAME: Aisha.
VITAL STATISTICES: 5'4", Dark Brown Hair.
POWER SOURCE: Saber Tooth Tiger.
WEAPON: Power Dagger.
VEHICLE: Griffen Thunderzord.
SPECIAL SKILL: Martial Arts.
PERSONAL: When Trini was selected as a delegate to a youth peace conference in Geneva, Aisha was chosen as the new Yellow Ranger. She is a devoted martial artist, observant and quite intelligent. A patient person who will take a certain amount of pushing, Aisha becomes a razor sharp tiger with lighting reflexes once her training takes over. She is very active in school events and good causes. Most of the kids in school look up to her and follow her example.

POWER RANGER FACT FILE

ROCKY

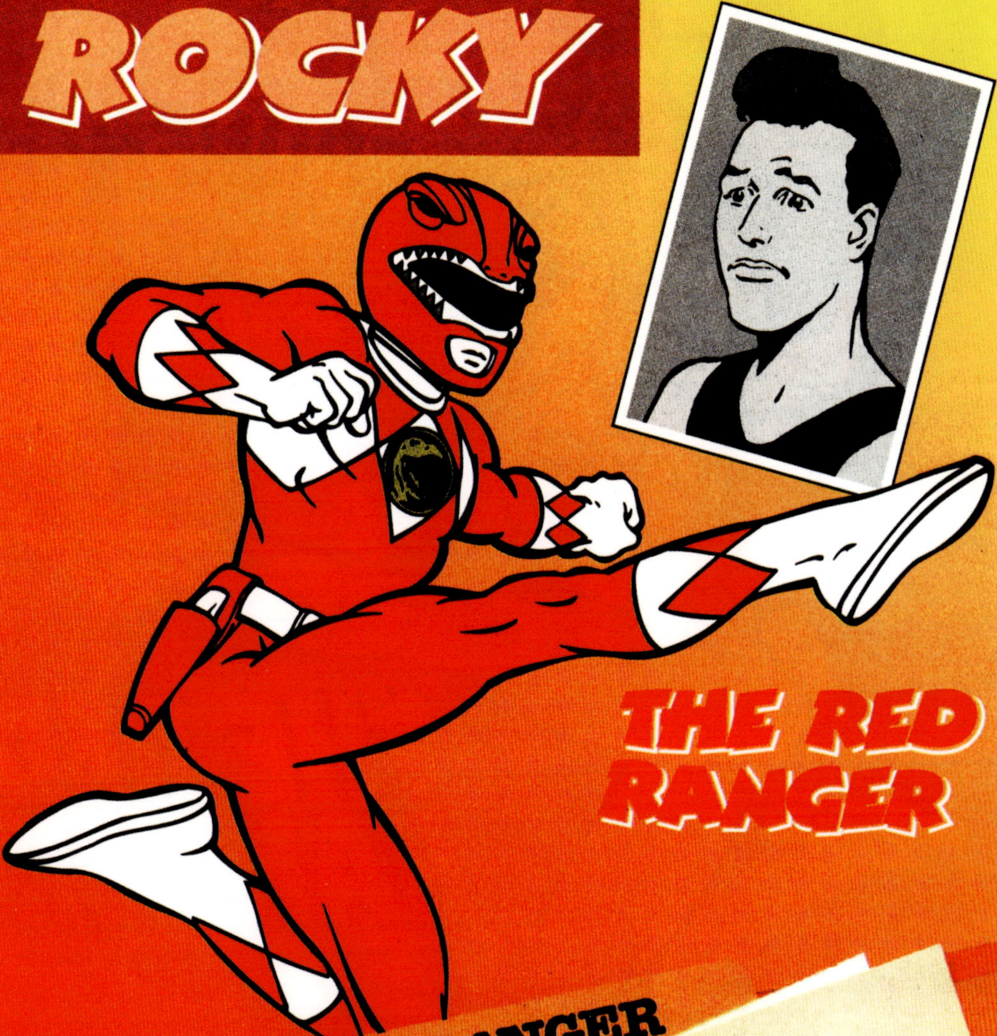

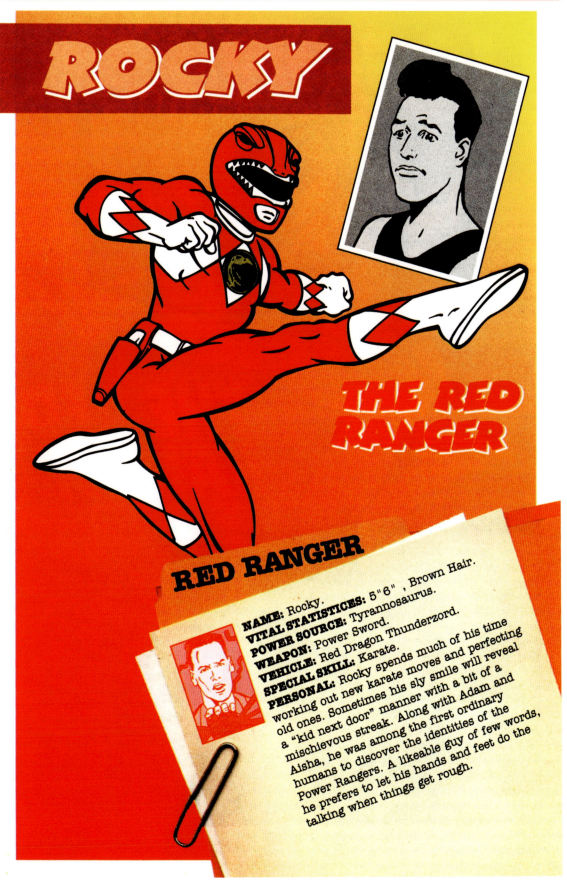

THE RED RANGER

RED RANGER

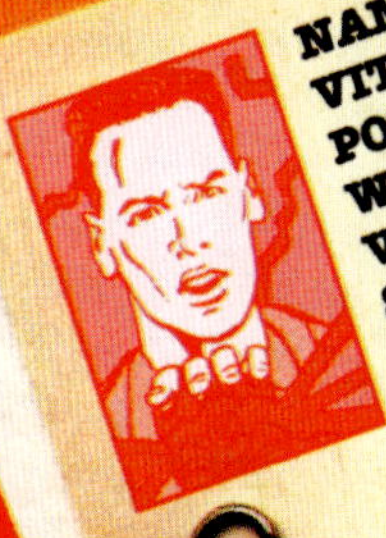

NAME: Rocky.
VITAL STATISTICES: 5"6" , Brown Hair.
POWER SOURCE: Tyrannosaurus.
WEAPON: Power Sword.
VEHICLE: Red Dragon Thunderzord.
SPECIAL SKILL: Karate.
PERSONAL: Rocky spends much of his time working out new karate moves and perfecting old ones. Sometimes his sly smile will reveal a "kid next door" manner with a bit of a mischievous streak. Along with Adam and Aisha, he was among the first ordinary humans to discover the identities of the Power Rangers. A likeable guy of few words, he prefers to let his hands and feet do the talking when things get rough.

POWER RANGER FACT FILE

JASON

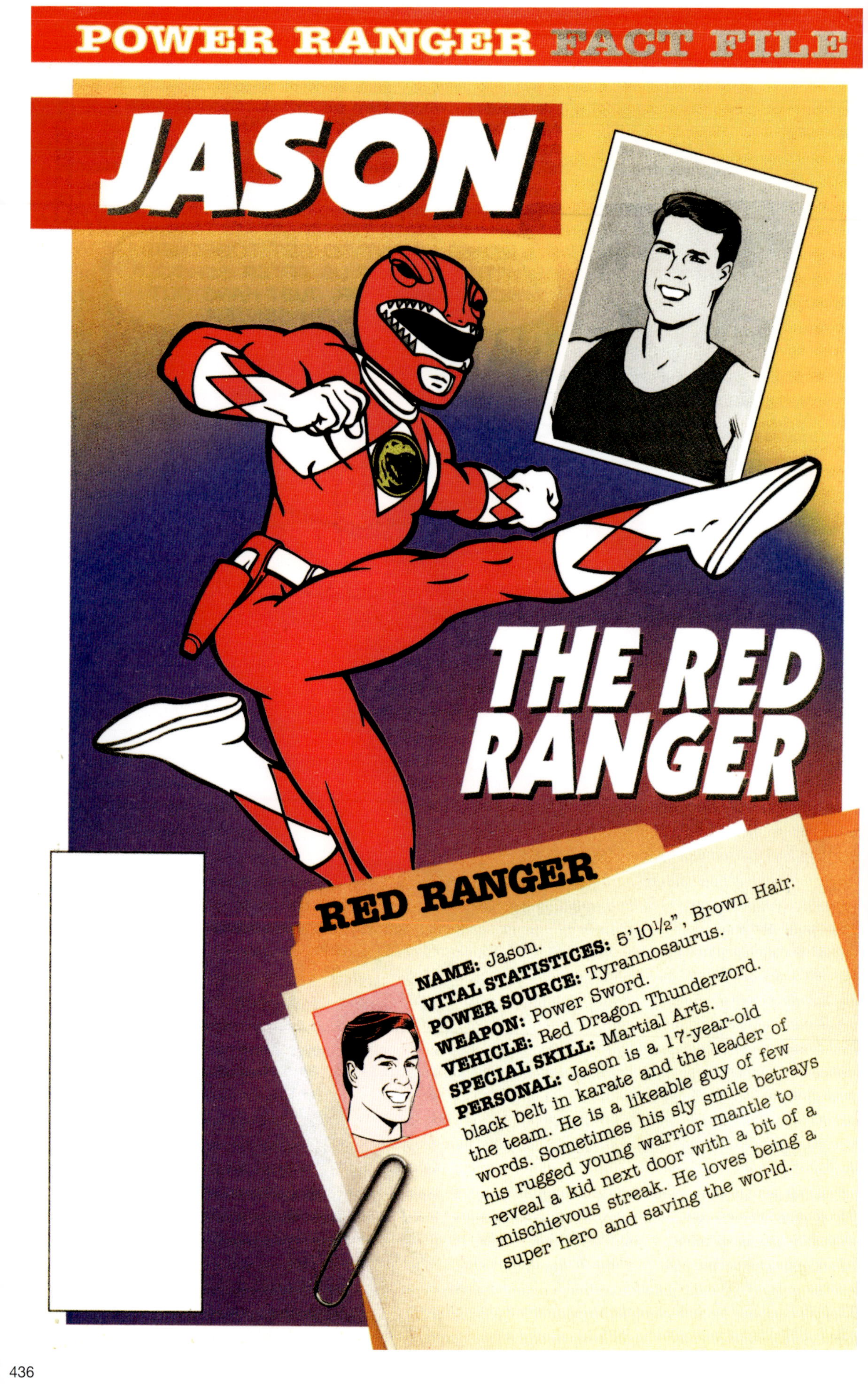

THE RED RANGER

RED RANGER

NAME: Jason.
VITAL STATISTICES: 5'10½", Brown Hair.
POWER SOURCE: Tyrannosaurus.
WEAPON: Power Sword.
VEHICLE: Red Dragon Thunderzord.
SPECIAL SKILL: Martial Arts.
PERSONAL: Jason is a 17-year-old black belt in karate and the leader of the team. He is a likeable guy of few words. Sometimes his sly smile betrays his rugged young warrior mantle to reveal a kid next door with a bit of a mischievous streak. He loves being a super hero and saving the world.

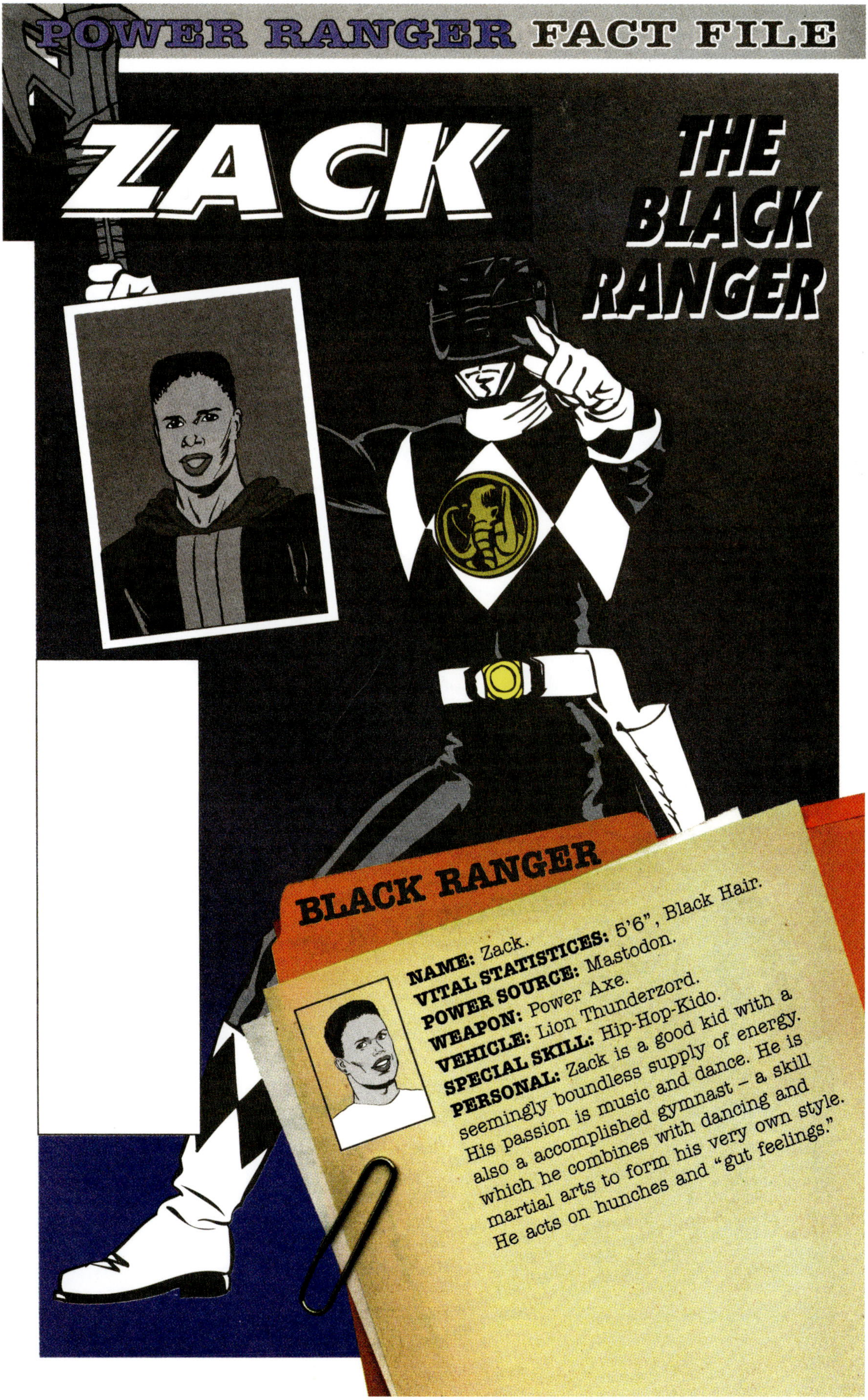
POWER RANGER FACT FILE
ZACK
THE BLACK RANGER
BLACK RANGER
NAME: Zack.
VITAL STATISTICES: 5'6", Black Hair.
POWER SOURCE: Mastodon.
WEAPON: Power Axe.
VEHICLE: Lion Thunderzord.
SPECIAL SKILL: Hip-Hop-Kido.
PERSONAL: Zack is a good kid with a seemingly boundless supply of energy. His passion is music and dance. He is also a accomplished gymnast – a skill which he combines with dancing and martial arts to form his very own style. He acts on hunches and "gut feelings."

POWER RANGER FACT FILE

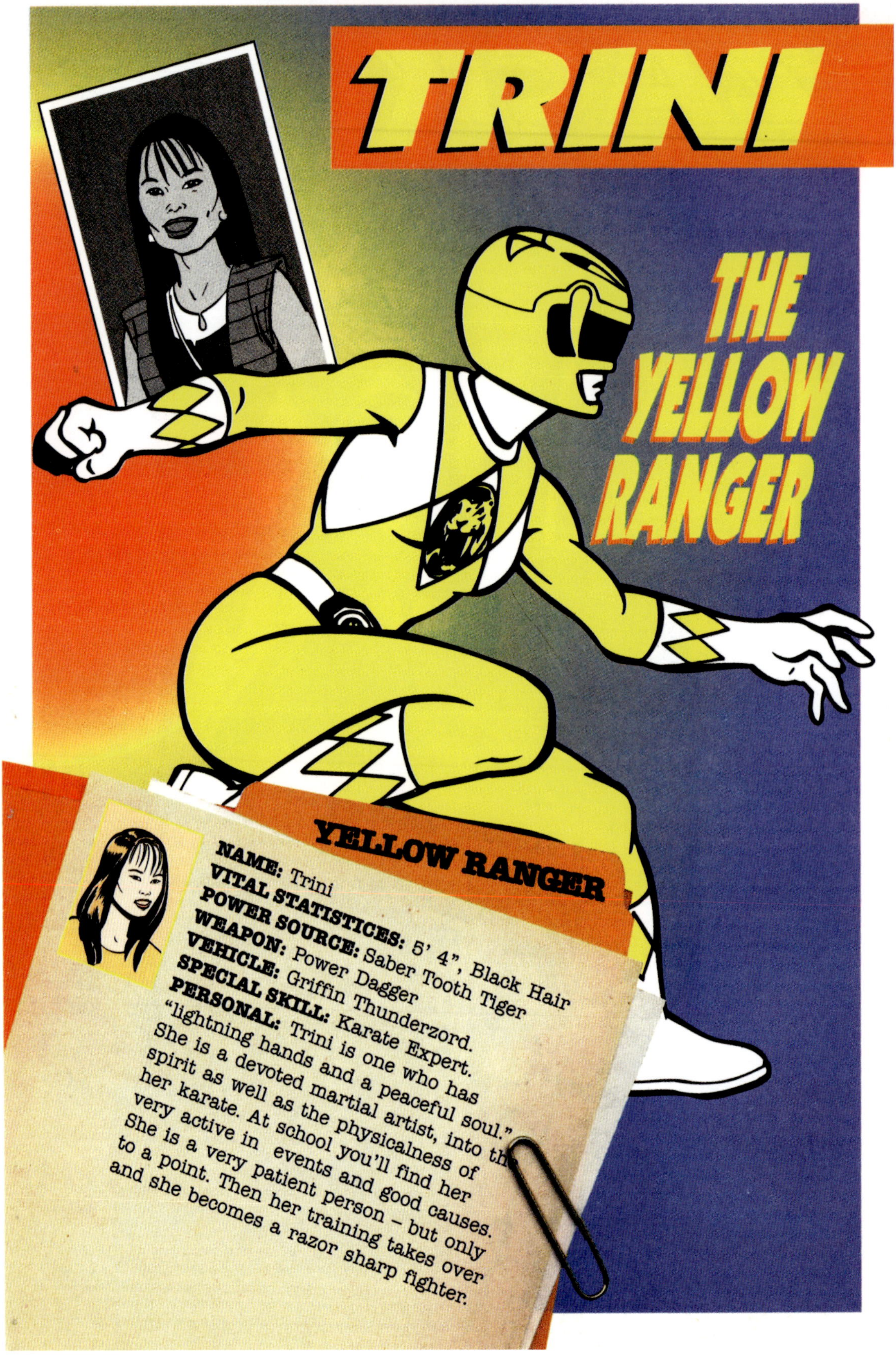
TRINI
THE YELLOW RANGER
YELLOW RANGER
NAME: Trini
VITAL STATISTICES: 5' 4", Black Hair
POWER SOURCE: Saber Tooth Tiger
WEAPON: Power Dagger
VEHICLE: Griffin Thunderzord.
SPECIAL SKILL: Karate Expert.
PERSONAL: Trini is one who has "lightning hands and a peaceful soul." She is a devoted martial artist, into the spirit as well as the physicalness of her karate. At school you'll find her very active in events and good causes. She is a very patient person – but only to a point. Then her training takes over and she becomes a razor sharp fighter.

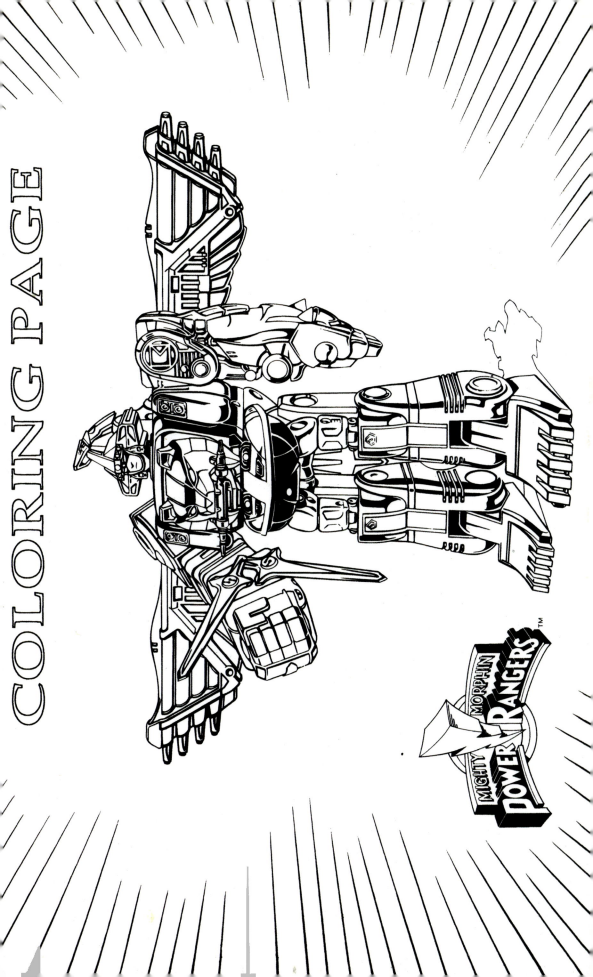

COLORING PAGE

MIGHTY MORPHIN POWER RANGERS™

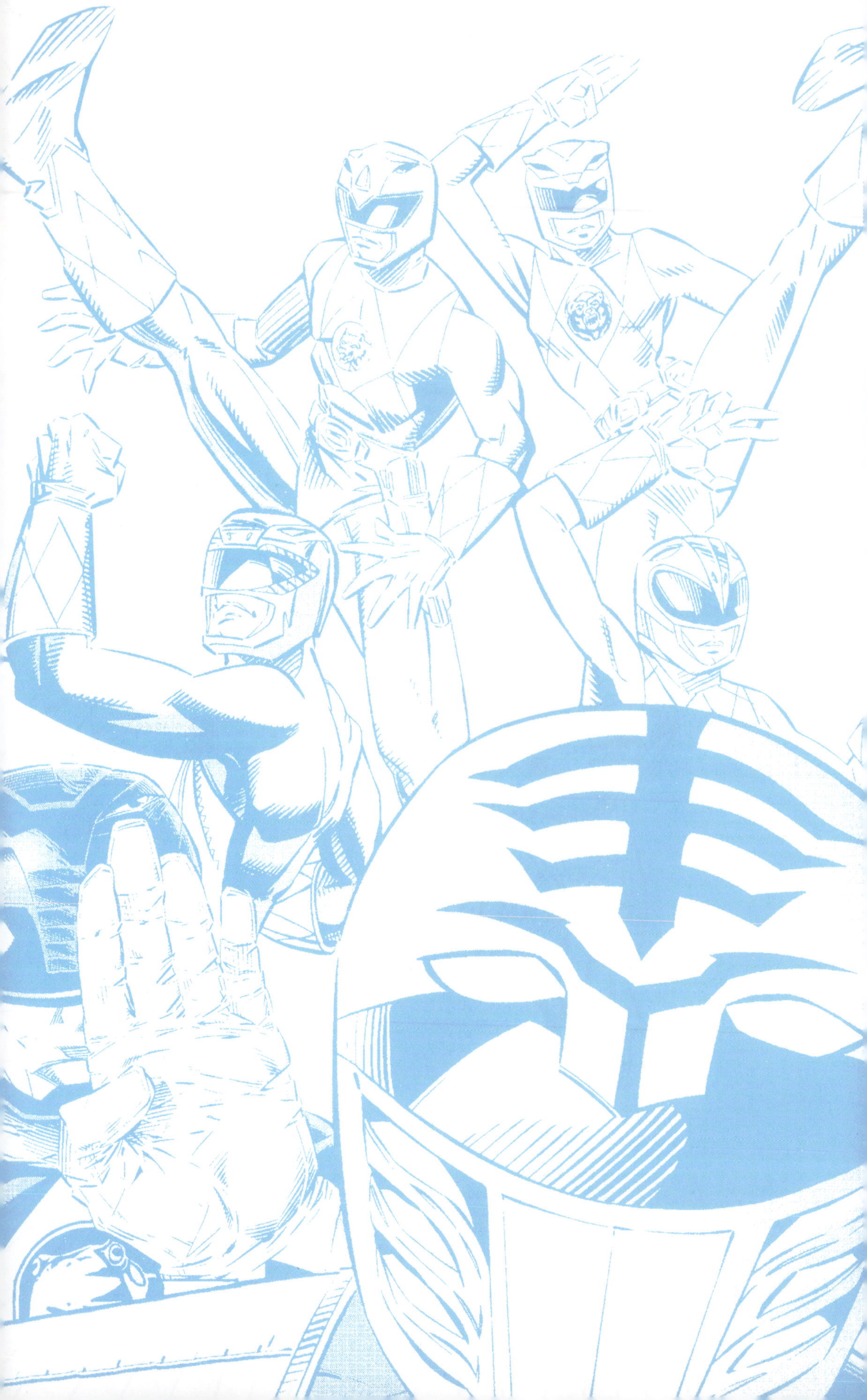

MORPHIN MAIL

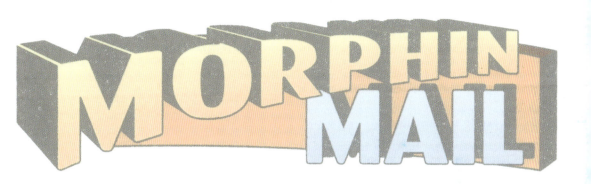

Morphin MAIL

Before we get to the letters, Hamilton Comics wishes to extend our sincerest apologies to the contributing creators on our first issue of **Mighty Morphin Power Rangers**. Through misadventures too embarrassingly complex to relate here, we left them entirely uncredited in the book. As some manner of recompense, we list them at the end of this letter column, along with the creators for the issue you now hold in your hand.

Dear Rangers,

Issue #1 of **Saban's Mighty Morphin Power Rangers** was very exciting. I was glad to see the original rangers there. Don't get me wrong, I like the newer Rangers also, it's just nice to see them in case you changed them around in the future. The Power Rangers TV show always has a good message for kids, and I think that your comic will have a good impact on little kids...and big kids like **me**! I hope that you decide to have a letters column. If you do, I'd like to suggest that you call it "Mighty Morphin Power Mail." It's a lot better than "Rita's Readers." Good luck with your comic book. I'll be along for the ride. Until next time!

Your Buddy,
Jeffrey Hamel
Lewiston, ME

We think your suggestion for a letter column title is a goodie, Jeffrey. Before we decide on a permanent one, however, we'd like to give the rest of our readers the chance to offer their suggestions.

Dear Folks,

I just finished reading **MMPR** #1 and it was great! I have been waiting for this book to come out, and it was well worth it. I am 24 years old and love the Power Rangers, especially Trini! This was my first experience with Hamilton Comics, and I was impressed. The art and writing were

Bruce Hamilton	President/Publisher
Richard Hinton	Associate Publisher
Helen Hamilton	Secretary/Treasurer
Leonard (John) Clark	Editor
Gary Leach	Editor/Art Director
Gary Gabner	Assistant Editor
Susan Daigle-Leach	Production Manager
Michael Myers	Production Assistant
Colleen Winkler	Production Liaison
Steve Calrow	Comptroller
Deborah Jones	Accounting
Janet Dvorak	Subscriptions
Charlene Palmer	Direct Sales
Mary Jane Cullumber	Mail Orders
Joseph R. Cigler	Shipping

excellent. I will continue to support your company. Keep up the good work!

Sincerely,
Mark "Troll" Trollinger
Smyrna, GA

Our inadvertently uncredited creators thank you for your kind words, Mark (or should we address you as "Troll"?).

Dear Hamilton Comics,

Your first issue of **Mighty Morphin Power Rangers** was awful! You don't have to make it just like the show! It's **your** comic, so make it more action packed, and use the new Rangers! Have them go over the world, or into outer space, or have a ranger lose his/her powers, or have Zordon killed off! No reason why you can't do this because...it's **your** comic!!! Take off the kid gloves. Do you think the **X-Men** got this popular by acting like kids? All I'm saying is toughen them up, have them explore their powers and make new enemies, friends and allies.

Watch every show, and I mean **watch them**! Because the way you're writing it now, it's just awful, and will be a flop!

Derek Mossman
Flushing, NY

There would seem to be a

somewhat mixed message here, Derek. Do you want us to make **MMPR** our comic, going beyond the TV show, yet stick to exactly what the TV show does?

Our aim is to bring both a new approach to the Power Rangers, yet keep things solidly grounded in the basics established by the TV show. This isn't always easy. For instance, the three new rangers introduced during this season—Rocky, Adam and Aisha—were made known to us well before their first appearance on TV, but too late to be incorporated into the storylines of our first two issues. (They'll make **their** comic book bow **next** issue.)

Last Issue's Credits

Written by
Donald D. Markstein
Drawn by
Gray Morrow
Colored by
Summer Hinton
Edited by
John Clark and **Gary Leach**
Lettered by
A. Machine
Creative Consultant
Cheryl Saban

This Issue's Credits

Written by
Donald D. Markstein
Drawn by
John Heebink
with Aaron McClellan
Colored by
Summer Hinton
Edited by
John Clark and **Gary Leach**
Lettered by
A. Machine
Creative Consultant
Cheryl Saban

NEXT ISSUE:

There's grime afoot when the Power Rangers clash with a monster of trash—and Kimberly desperately searches for her missing morpher—in "It's Not the End of the World," brought to you by writer Jack C. Harris and artist Al Bigley.

On Sale February 21st!

MORPHIN MAIL

*This issue reintroduces the team of writer Jack C. Harris and artist Al Bigley to the **Mighty Morphin Power Rangers** comic book. Why reintroduced? Well, Jack and Al did our **very first MMPR** comic book story back in the spring of last year–an 8-page tale in a mini-comic produced as a premium for Fruit-of-the-Loom. Though more of a novelty item than a part of our current Power Rangers series, that project demonstrated what Jack and Al could do with the feature, and this issue has given them the chance to really shine!*

*Important: Hamilton Comics welcomes any and all correspondence concerning the **Mighty Morphin Power Rangers** comic book. However, anyone wishing to write to the Power Rangers **TV show** should send their cards and letters to: **Saban's Mighty Morphin Power Rangers**, P.O. Box 10277, Van Nuys, CA 91410-0277.*

Bruce Hamilton	President/Publisher
Richard Hinton	Associate Publisher
Helen Hamilton	Secretary/Treasurer
Leonard (John) Clark	Editor
Gary Gabner	Assistant Editor
Gary Leach	Art Director
Susan Daigle-Leach	Production Manager
Jim Flanagan	Production Design
Michael Myers	Production Assistant
Colleen Winkler	Production Liaison
Steve Cairow	Comptroller
Deborah Jones	Accounting
Janet Dvorak	Subscriptions
Charlene Palmer	Direct Sales
Mary Jane Cullumber	Mail Orders
Joseph R. Cigler	Shipping

Dear People,
I am writing to let you know how much I enjoyed **Mighty Morphin Power Rangers** #1. The writing was great–the drawings and colors were the best. I can't wait till issue #2 comes out.
Could I suggest something? Could you please have a pen pal column in future issues? There are a lot of fans who could connect and be friends. If you do have a pen pal column, please list my name and address.
You have done a great job on issue #1 and I can't wait to see what future issues will be.
Best of luck.

Doug Marion
P.O. Box 1180
Marshall, NC 28753

I'm a 37-year-old guy who has never seen an episode of **MMPR** or bought a single action figure of any kind. Maybe I ordered **MMPR** #1 with hopes of its value multiplying hundreds-fold (*a la* **Teenage Mutant Ninja Turtles** #1), I don't know. All I know is after reading this issue, I am impressed with the artwork and the reading level portrayed therein. I hope the younger readers are holding their dictionaries nearby as they read the book—they'll need them.

Dear Editor,
I owed it to Gladstone/Hamilton to check out the debut of **Mighty Morphin Power Rangers**. Your Disney comics are among the best books on the market, and to get such a high-profile license like Power Rangers must mean you were doing something right. So I picked up #1.
Now, let me say this flat out: I detest the TV show. To me, it's labored by stiff acting, bad Japanese battle footage and simplistic writing. A "fad" show, in other words. Yet if I enjoyed the comic adaptation, it wouldn't be the first time. Both **Ren and Stimpy** and **Rocko's Modern Life** are cartoons I don't enjoy with comics which are, at times, rather good. And **The Simpsons**! Bongo puts out fantistic, solidly-done comics. And I can't stand the TV show, except on rare occasions. Enough about me, now something about you...
The story to #1 was the weakest part, relying heavily on clichés which may entertain younger readers, but are not to my taste: the dumb, "tuff" bully and the outrageous villains. But the latter can also work to an advantage: few comics today have the kind of old-fashioned, "all talk" kind of supervillains that were so prevalent in comics' Golden and Silver Ages. That kind of "fun" villain **was** present

here, so I won't complain too much. I would have liked to know a little more about the scaly creature and his minions. You can't assume that everybody willing to give Hamilton a try is a died-in-the-wool fan, any more than you can expect a new Disney reader to figure out the Duck Family Tree! (I've been reading Gladstones a good 7, 8 years and still haven't the foggiest!)
"The Menace of Dracula" read quickly, which was another reason I found it weak. I'm not asking for anything deep here—it would defeat the purpose of the comic—but a little more substance would be nice. I know what you're capable of, as well as what the superhero genre is capable of (even for a toy/TV tie-in!) and you can do better.
The artwork to #1, on the other hand, was astonishing. Under a cover by Bret Blevins and the incomparable Terry Austin, the interiors stole my breath away with realistic human expressions as well as lush drawings in the fight sequence. The artist and the colorist, who imbued the work with wonderfully vivid colors, deserve much credit.
Well, I will pick up Power Rangers again, not only for the great artwork, but for the hopes that you'll make sense out of this odd phenomenon for me. Grade B footage and colorful costumes do not make a TV show, but clever writing (on your way) and lively art (already there) do make a comic book. On that note, I'll see you in 30 days.

Joey Marchese
Clark, NJ

Dear Lord Zedd,
I hope you find the cover to your brains! My favorite part in issue #2 is when we see how you see through your laser beams.

Sincerly,
Yonah Fuchs (7 years old)
Monsey, NY

Dear Hamilton Comics,
I love the Power Rangers comic very much. I read #1 and #2 five times! What I want to see is the White Ranger in the comics because I think he's the best Ranger.

Andy Rawls
Jamesville, NC

White Ranger makes his comic book debut next issue, Andy!

Heads up Hamilton!
Thanks for **MMPR** #1. It was a great way to give the series a good start. **MMPR** #2 was a

Keep up the quality work and may I wish you success.

Jim Bacigalupo
Braidwood, IL

definite upgrade. It was faster, funnier & just had more fun about it. Seeing Ernie in action made me realize how underused he is on the show. Mauve & Puce Rangers? Yep, that's certified Bulk & Skull! When Ernie went into action as the Goatman & the Rangers (real & wannabes) came into the picture, it was a miracle I wasn't on the floor in stitches at the restaurant I was reading the book in!

Tommy's behavior in the book was in tune to his behavior on the show, including his change of heart thanks to Jason's reasoning with him.

MMPR #2 gets an A, but please, lighten up on Billy's extremely educated vocabulary. He's lightened up on the show & has even used the slang, "Yeah." Some folks may not like having to keep a dictionary handy to translate Billy's speech.

Thanks also for printing Mark "Troll" Trollinger's letter. It's good to know there's other 20-plus-year-old Ranger fans out there. I turned 22 in December.

I'd like to submit "Ranger Reading(s)" (singular or plural, your choice) as a letter column title.

Clint Christal
Trussville, AL

Dear Hamilton Comics,

Your first two issues of **Mighty Morphin Power Rangers** were excellent! I love the way you relate the comics and stories to the show, but also incorporate your own ideas. Your artists are great, the Rangers look just the same on TV except for a few pictures where they don't look anything like them. This is one comic that I'm really going to stick to! I want you to keep the old Rangers in the stories, though. I like the newer Rangers but Saban Entertainment should have not let the old ones go away. I hope they come back and show those wannabe Rangers what real power is! Other than this your comic is "Morphin-ominal!" Please, keep my favorite Rangers on and keep up the morphin work!

Christian Peña
Bronx, NY

I'm afraid that issue #2 marks the final appearance of the "old" Rangers, Christian, at least for the foreseeable future. Glad to know you still plan to stick with

us, though.

Dear Morphin Mail,

I just finished reading the second issue of **Mighty Morphin Power Rangers**, and I have to admit, I was impressed. The art was fantastic—Kimberly really looked like Kimberly! Also, I was able to see Tommy. The story line was also rather cute, much like the show itself. After a rocky start, you managed to pull together a respectable comic book, not just more endless Power Ranger memorabilia.

I'm not sure you realize the potential of this Power Rangers comic you've invented. You have the chance to develop characters that, unfortunately, were dropped from the program, such as Richie, Angela, and Curtis. You have the opportunity to further develop the relationship between Tommy and Kimberly, which has nearly been totally ignored by Saban. I mean, come on, Tommy only kissed her **once**!

I have a few suggestions: first, get Tommy into the picture. make him White Ranger so he can join in on the action with his teammates. Also, make sure to write fully developed stories, and let them span over a few issues. And finally, consider developing Tommy and Kimberly's relationship. They are my favorite Rangers, and they're perfect for each other. Besides, every comic book needs a little romance.

Keep up the good work!

R. Dawson
Hillsdale, NJ

Couldn't agree more about the romance, R.! As for whether something of that sort develops between Tommy and Kimberly, we'll have to see what Saban decides to do (or not do) in that department.

Dear Power Publishers,

MMPR #2 was, if not exactly a complete turnaround from #1, at least a powerful step in the **right** direction! The cover was a 1000% improvement, and Don Markstein's story showed him more relaxed and involved with the Power Rangers and their world. I especially enjoyed the twist on the "monster of the moment" motif, which made clever use of the otherwise inexplicable and unwieldy fact that the **villain** knows who the Power Rangers really are, but they can't

tell their friends and families?! (Somebody at Saban was not paying attention when they came up with that one!) As for John Heebink, he's finally been given a chance to showcase his abilities, which were only hinted at in his pencil work on Marvel's **Quasar**.

Keep improving like this, and you can definitely make mine **Morphin**!

Pamela Hartbauer
Kutztown, PA

Dear Mighty Morphin Editors,

Not only was your second issue of **MMPR** an exciting adventure with great art, but you had an appearance by my all-time favorite Ranger: the Green Ranger! Even though he didn't have his powers, Tommy was still a hero who deserved his moment in the spotlight! My only regret is that this probably means this is the last time we'll ever see the Green Ranger, right?

Another thing I liked was Bulk and Skull, and how they really aren't such bad guys. In fact, they want to be good guys, they just don't have a clue how to really go about it! They're such showoffs they don't realize what a serious business being a real hero is. Thank goodness they don't have any powers, or they'd really give the hero business a bad name!

Until Mr. Kaplan decides to get in on the action as the Scarlet-With-Purple-Accents Ranger, I'll sign myself...

"Morphin" Mike Swasey
Palo Alto, CA

That's all the letters we have space for this go-round. While we can't promise to print every letter that we receive, we read every one, so don't hesitate to drop us a line.

By the way, the nominating process for a title for this letter column is still underway. Any and all suggestions are welcome!

NEXT ISSUE:

The Power Rangers are eager champions of ecology, but they're soon mired in menace when Zedd conjures his "Swamp Man!" It's a full-length adventure brought to you by writer Donald D. Markstein and artist Sparky Moore.

On Sale March 21st!

MORPHIN MAIL

Many readers have been wondering when and if The White Ranger would be appearing in this comic. Now, if you've read this issue, you know. Tommy will also be working into the role of the team's new leader over the next two issues, taking over from Jason, the original Red Ranger. That will complete the six-issue run of our first mini-series. Our **next** mini-series will follow almost immediately, so keep a lookout for it.

Important: Hamilton Comics welcomes any and all correspondence concerning the **Mighty Morphin Power Rangers** comic book. However, anyone wishing to write to the Power Rangers **TV show** or about Power Rangers **toys** should send their cards and letters to: **Saban's Mighty Morphin Power Rangers**, P.O. Box 10277, Van Nuys, CA 91410-0277.

Bruce Hamilton	President/Publisher
Richard Hinton	Associate Publisher
Helen Hamilton	Secretary/Treasurer
Leonard (John) Clark	Editor
Geoffrey Blum	Associate Editor
Gary Gabner	Assistant Editor
Gary Leach	Art Director
Susan Daigle-Leach	Production Manager
Jim Flanagan	Production Design
Michael Myers	Production Assistant
Colleen Winkler	Production Liaison
Steve Cairow	Comptroller
Deborah Jones	Accounting
Janet Dvorak	Subscriptions
Mary Jane Cullumber	Mail Orders
Charlene Palmer	Direct Sales
Joseph R. Cigler	Shipping

Dear Hamilton Comics,

I think your Power Rangers comic book is great! I love the way it's just like the show! I was waiting for a comic book like this to come out. I just turned 13 and I still like the Power Rangers. I am also glad that you guys put in the new Zords so that way it makes the comic book more up-to-date. Also, who cares what other people think and who say your comic stinks because it really doesn't! This is the first time I read Hamilton Comics and they are so good I will buy this comic till you guys quit making it! I think you guys should put the new guys in and put the White Ranger in it so it can be even cooler!

P.S.: Did the Power Rangers ever copy the old cartoon series **Voltron** in the 1980's? Because I rented the tapes and it sure looks like it.

Your Best Buddy and fan,
Rene Encarnacion
Beverly Hills, CA

Mighty Morphin Power Rangers shares certain similar traits with **Voltron** in the same way **Wagon Train** shared certain traits with **Rawhide**, or any sitcom with any other sitcom. They work the same genres, doing their own variations. Copying—even the **appearance** of copying—is in no way part of their formulas (though appearances, as you make clear, aren't always easy to prevent).

Dear Rangers,

Your comics are the coolest. I read #1 and just finished reading #2, and I thought they were both great. Derek Mossman who wrote you and said #1 was awful is completely wrong. Both comics were great. I like Kimberly the best. I read that #3 is going to be about Kimberly. I can't wait to read it. Please don't put the new Rangers in, as I like Jason, Zack and Trini better.

Leighann Ross
Centereach, NY

Dear Morphin Mail,

I enjoyed **MMPR** #2. It was morphin! My favorite characters are Kimberly, Billy and Tommy. Is Tommy going to become the White Ranger? And will Rocky, Adam and Aisha appear in the comic book? I hope you have more than six comics, and I hope you keep on doing the great art! Will you show the Rangers calling their Thunderzords?

Well, thank you for listening. Keep on Morphing!

Your Ranger,
Sean Millhouse
Kansas City, KS

Dear Power Rangers,

I am a fan of the TV series and I also like the comic (too bad it's only a 6-issue series); anyway, remember when Tommy was the Green Ranger (on the TV series)? He had his own powerzord, the Dragonzord. I was hoping you all at Hamilton Comics could find a way to return the Dragonzord (to the Power Rangers, of course). I know that in the TV series Tommy is now the White Ranger and pilots the White Tigerzord, but I really liked and miss seeing the Dragonzord (the Green Dragonzord), I should say, since the Red Ranger has the Red Dragon Thunderzord). If you all do decide to bring back the Green Dragonzord, I think the book or book series should be titled "The Return of the Dragonzord," (what else would be appropriate?).

Until next time, "Go Go Power Rangers!"

James Means
Apple Valley, CA

Dear Hamilton Comics,

I enjoyed your first two issues of the Power Rangers. The colors and detail are great. This is the first time that a 22-year-old woman has ever written to people like you. Well, I love Power Rangers! In fact, I collect lots of PR items from cards to posters, I even tape the TV show. So keep up the good work and I'm looking forward to issue #3. And I'm also in the Fan Club (forgot to mention that).

Pauline Russ
Browns Mills, NJ
P.S.: One question: when will you have the White Ranger in your comics?

Yo Rangers!

Your first comic was okay, but your second rocked! Your Jason looked like he does in the shows. Why don't you have a monster that can freeze people by flashing a light at them? And please, don't only make 6 **MMPR** comics. They are real good and I'm a huge fan of the Power Rangers (I'm 10 years old). So don't stop your awesome comic after 6 issues.

I also have a few questions:
1. Is White Ranger going to appear?
2. Are Rocky, Adam, and Aisha going to be shown?
3. Are there going to be more comics of Power Rangers?

Well, I hope that you read this letter.

Mike Hollan
Succasunna, NJ

Dear **MMPR** editors,

I love your new comic book! I think the comic book will be a big success. But Lord Zedd, the bad guy, acts so much like Rita Repulssa. Lord Zedd doesn't ask

Finster to make his monsters. Plus, Lord Zedd doesn't use a telescope—he uses his eyes as a telescope. Once again, I enjoy your comic.

Respectfully,
Zane White
Lilburn, GA

Glad you enjoyed it, Zane. Your observations on Lord Zedd are on track, since our first MMPR stories were originally written with Rita Repulssa and Finster. When the change to Lord Zedd was made, our information on him was sketchy, so we incorporated him into the already existing stories as best we could. This was another reason we chose to go the mini-series route with our MMPR title: Zedd goes through something of a transition in these first six issues, just as the Power Rangers do.

Dear Hamilton Comics,

Issue #2 was terrific, but I found a few things that were "different" from the T.V. version. #1-Finster never made a monster for Lord Zedd; #2-The "morphing" order was wrong; #3-How would Bulk and Skull know to "morph" if they never saw the Rangers do it? #4-Lord Zedd uses a hand grenade type of device to make his monsters grow, not his staff; #5-They never showed the Rangers using the Power Crystals to activate the Thunder Megazord; #6-Why is one arm of the Thunder Megazord a different color from the other; #7-The Rangers on TV do not show their symbols on their chests. But don't get me wrong, I loved the comic book and I will continue to buy each issue. I would like to make a couple of suggestions: #1-If you put Adam, Aisha and Rocky into your comics, remember they never saw the Green Ranger, only the White Ranger, unless there will be some "time mess-ups" or Lord Zedd made a new Green Ranger; #2-At the end of each story I think you shold tell the "moral" of the story, like the moral of issue #2 was "Don't try to be someone that you're not." Please continue to make more of the Power Ranger comics, but for now I'm still out looking for a way to get Zordon home.

Deborah Pinksten
Bossier City, LA

It has always seemed to us, Deborah, that If the moral in a story must be spelled out, as you suggest, then the storyteller hasn't done his or her job. As for the symbols on the Rangers' chests, these are directed by Saban for two-dimensional representations of the characters, and Saban has the final say on such matters.

Dear Hamilton Comics,

While I'm more of an animation freak than a comic book reader, I really get a kick out of your **Mighty Morphin Power Rangers**! I watch the TV program pretty regularly (mostly on Saturday), and though I find it rather silly and derivative, it is...well, fun! And so is your comic.

One thing really bothers me, though (and you've probably got a lot of mail on this already), and that is the Power Rangers "secret identities." I know you're just following what the show does, but it really doesn't come across as very obvious on the show the way it does in your comic. What am I talking about? It's this: how is it possible for **Zedd** (and before him, Rita) to know who the Power Rangers really are? Rita would have just finished them off in their sleep and been done with it, never mind what Zedd would have done if he'd got first crack. In comic book terms, having Zordon pick you as a Power Ranger would be an automatic death sentence!

As I said, the show can get away with it, but with the comic, where you have the time to dwell on it, such a setup doesn't make sense. Am I expecting too much, or is there some way you can explain it for your comic book readers?

Good luck, and I hope you do another mini-series!

Wayman Mobley
Port Smith, VA

Dear Power Ranger fans,

(I'm writing this letter in case you have a letter page in the comic.) Sometimes I watch the Power Rangers show every day on TV. I have a Power Rangers poster, Power Rangers suit, a White Ranger beeper, and lots of other Power Ranger stuff.

My favorite Ranger is the White Ranger. I really like the new comic, and hope you make more. If anyone want to start a Power Rangers comic pen pal club, you can write to me. I'm 8 years old.

If there is already a pen pal club, could you please give me its address?

Matthew Alan Carmack
Poteau, OK

Dear sirs,

After reading issue #2 of Power Rangers and seeing that Goat Man was suggested by a reader, my 7-year-old son decided that he would like to design a monster.

When I was age 7, we had **Famous Monsters of Filmland** to send monsters in to. As I got older DC revived **Dial H for Hero** and asked for reader submissions. I hope Power Rangers will actively pursue reader submissions. Any time a book that a child enjoys encourages him or her to be creative, it may be helping to unleash the next Stan Lee, Jack Kirby, Steven Spielberg, Quincy Jones, Chuck Jones, or Haim Saban or Shuki Levy.

Thank you, and I hope you continue past the six-issue mini-series.

Garvis M. Reed II
South Charleston, WV

Dear Power Ranger Mail,

I like your issue #1 & 2. Your art is very well done. Why not have a Power Rangers vs. **X-Men** comic book? That would be way cool. Keep up the great work.

Sincerely,
Jesse Newcomb
Owls Head, ME

An intriguing idea, Jesse. Something like that may come about down the road, though there are no immediate plans in the works.

And so, another letters page draws to a close. It's always great hearing from you. Keep reading, and keep writing!

NEXT ISSUE:

The Power Rangers must come to terms with parental discipline when Kimberly is "Grounded," by Don Markstein and John Heebink. Then, Aisha skydives into a weird reality in "Stranger in Strange Town," by Nicola Cuti and Sparky Moore.

On Sale April 11th!

MORPHIN MAIL

Dear Power Rangers,

I love your comic books and am a very big fan of the TV show. Right now I have issues #1, #2, and #3. I think they get better every time. The drawings of ac-tions and people are fantastic. On a scale from one through ten I give it a ten or an A+. Thanks to your comics, some of my friends are encouraged to read and learn more about reading. My favorite Rangers are Tommy and Kimberly and I think they were drawn very good so far. I hope that Tommy will get to be the White Ranger and have the White Tigerzord. I also wish to see the new Ultrazord in the comics. Could I make a small suggestion. Some parents are complaining about violence on the Power Ranger TV shows. Maybe the shows and comics should be a little more educational, so parents will let their kids watch and buy your comics more. I am eleven years old and try to pick up smart ideas from the TV shows and the comics. In the third issue I liked it when you reminded people about recycling. My wish is to see the actors who are in Power Rangers and hope there will be a movie one day. My suggestion for the new mail section is called: "Mail of Power."

Sincerely,
Paul John Gale
Winnetka, CA

I just want to take the time to tell you some stuff you might know and might really care about, but some readers will probably pick out since I did:

1. Issue Number One: To start out with, the Power Rangers just don't have the little gold insignias on their chests depicting their dinosaurs. Watch the show sometime.

2. Numbero Dos: Zedd doesn't throw his staff to make the monster grow, nor does he have a headache. That's Rita's department. Watch the show sometime.

3. Threeish: It's called a Thunder Megazord, not a Megathunderzord. Watch the show sometime.

4. Four: Alpha doesn't call Zordon "Great Zordon," as he did in issue number three several

Bruce Hamilton	President/Publisher
Richard Hinton	Associate Publisher
Helen Hamilton	Secretary/Treasurer
Leonard (John) Clark	Editor
Geoffrey Blum	Associate Editor
Gary Gabner	Assistant Editor
Gary Leach	Art Director
Susan Daigle-Leach	Production Manager
Jim Flanagan	Production Design
Michael Myers	Production Assistant
Colleen Winkler	Production Liaison
Steve Calrow	Comptroller
Deborah Jones	Accounting
Janet Dvorak	Subscriptions
Mary Jane Cullumber	Mail Orders
Charlene Palmer	Direct Sales
Joseph R. Cigler	Shipping

times. I mean hey, watch the show sometime.

5. Big Five-Oh: Er, ah, well, that's pretty much it I think. But it's just these little discrepancies that really make a perfectionist's teeth grate. The only thing I can prescribe for your lack of detail is to spend a half hour of your weekday watching this nearly fine show.

I did, however, like the fact that in issue number three you did use the individual zords in battle against the trash monster. (Sorry: Garbagantrous. My apologies to Finster.) What I think would probably attract more enthusiasm in some of the hardcore readers is to perhaps have backgrounds of the various characters and maybe a behind-the-scenes look at the show. Let's try and find out whether Squatt is supposed to be a blueberry or a pineapple, and why he dresses so much like Bulk. Why does Baboo have a little bat on his arm? Why doesn't Goldar get any good lines? Why doesn't Zordon get a body? Why why why why why? Why do we call Goldar "bucket-head," "big gold monkey," and "Thomas Edison"? Can't Zedd really think of anything Rita didn't? Did Rita and Zedd go to college together with Grimlord? Can't Zedd and Grimlord collaborate to find a way to defeat either the VR Troopers or the Power Rangers? Yeah, people tell me I talk to much.

Angus, the Plaid Ranger
Northeast, TN

Dear Morphin Mail,

I have to be one of the biggest Power Ranger fans in the entire world. I have every single episode on tape, also every Ranger action figure there is, not to mention countless trading cards and other merchandise.

However, I was greatly disappointed by the lack of effort put into the first issue of the comics series. Issue #2 also left many things to be desired. I have an honest question for you: Do the writers really know the show that well? The Thunder Megazord never finishes monsters with a kick!!! In issue #3 the artwork is much more detailed with a very impressive cover, but again the fighting sequence was unclear and confusing...I didn't even see the "Garbagantrous" be destroyed.

Lord Zedd has no use for Finster...he's hardly ever on the show and, when it's time for a monster to grow, Zedd uses a potion bomb, not his staff. Zedd is not Rita!!!

If only you could straighten some of these misconceptions out, you would have an awesome comic.

Derik Roberts,
Brooklyn, NY

Dear Hamilton Comics,

I have the first three isues of **MMPR** comic books. They were excellent! I am an 11-year-old boy at Westampton Middle School. I love Power Rangers, especially Trini.

In **MMPR** #1, I like how it shows Billy and Kimberly tele-porting back to the command center from the Zarathustra Dimension.

I have a few questions I would like to ask you:

1. In **MMPR** #1, why does Lord Zedd look from a telescope and not from his eye beam?

2. Why does Lord Zedd throw his wand in **MMPR** #1? Rita does that.

3. In **MMPR** #1, why does Zack get out of the cocoon without his Ranger suit on?

4, In last issue's **Morphin Mail**, when Clint Cristal wrote that you should lighten up on Billy's vocabulary, why not have Rocky, Aisha, or Adam translate like Trini did?

Finally, a suggestion for a monster could be from a locket called the Locketness Monster?

So, until the Rangers join Lord Zedd, make mine Morphin.

Joel Young
Westampton, NJ

Dear Hamilton Comics,

I think you are doing a great

job on writing your comics. Except that I didn't understand that part when you mentioned the new Rangers. You didn't say how they got there. I saw on the show how they got there except I think you should put that down in your comics. And I saw that you didn't put Green Ranger in #3. The Green Ranger was in #2. I also noticed that on the **MMPR** show the Power Rangers don't have the symbols on their chests. Could you take the symbols off their chests in your comics, please? I noticed another thing is that Lord Zedd doesn't throw his stick on the show to make his monsters grow. And another thing is that Finster doesn't make the monsters. Lord Zedd makes the monsters big. Just watch the show. What I'm saying is that you should do the basics but do new adventures, like new weird monsters. Oh, what would the monsters from the powers of his stick. He finds an object from Earth and turns it into a monster. I still think you're doing a good job. Please try to do these things for me. I would appreciate it a lot. I am 9 years old. When will the White Ranger make his first appearance?

Blake Swanson
Greenville, TX

Dear **MMPR** writers and artists,
I am pleased with your first and second comics of the **Mighty Morphin Power Rangers**. But some things were missing. It's like you mixed the original show that had Rita Repulsa and the new season with Lord Zedd and the White Ranger (Tommy). Lord Zedd does not go to Finster for a monster, he makes them. He looks down on Earth for material like a book. One time he created a monster called Robo Goat, from a Greek mythology book, or the time he made the Buzz Beetle to suck up the Green Ranger's powers. (That was before Tommy became the White Ranger.) The Buzz Beetle was made from a poster. And to make the monsters grow he would use a ball the size of a fist and throw it down to Earth, the monster would catch it and like a grenade he would pull the pin and throw it on the ground and Boom!–super deluxe monster a la Zedd! Oh, and the putties, the way they're killed is by hitting them in the "Z" on their chests. I've included a picture of the ball Lord Zedd uses to make the monsters big. Just watch the show. What I'm saying is that you should do the basics but do new adventures, like new weird monsters. Oh, what would

you thing of putting in an art column? It would be cool. People could send in pictures of the Power Rangers and give you new ideas for enemies and friends like a Purple Ranger.
Keep up the good work, guys!
Demetrios Travlos
Glen Oaks, NY

*Many readers have been asking about the apparent inconsistencies between the **MMPR** TV show and the comic book. The main suggestion offered seems to be, "watch the show."*
*We do. Our writers do. We see the shows at the same time most of our readers do. Then we find out what's happening, then the writers can **start** writing, and then–five months later–the developments on the show finally show up in the comic. Meanwhile, our readers understandably wonder why the comics coming out right now don't reflect the way things are in the show right now.*
Of course, certain elements, such as the chest symbols on the Rangers in the comics, are required by Saban for printed matter, in spite of the fact that they are not part of the TV uniforms. These will remain on the comic book Power Rangers for that reason.
As for Finster, we kinda like the little fiend. Though he has been largely absent on the TV show lately, that doesn't mean he isn't around to create the odd monster for Zedd when Zedd's own inspiration languishes.

I think your Power Rangers comic is excellent. I have bought issues 1 & 3, but my newsagent cannot obtain a copy of issue 2. As you can see, I live in England. I wondered if it is possible to order issue 2. Your comic is better than any **MMPR** comics available in England.
yours sincerely,
Nik Gilbert
West Sussex, England

Sorry to hear you're having trouble getting #2, Nik, but I'm not sure what recourse you have other than checking back with your newsagent and having him or her check again with the supplier. Other than that, you might look into one of the various comic book mail order services, either based in your country or in the U.S.. Many of them will offer periodicals for cover price (and

some offer discounts!), though there are almost always shipping and handling fees involved.

I am crazy about **MMPR**! I like the show but on the comics you should have a new Ranger or have a zord get broken down or Zordon get killed. You should also have Goldar and Rita Repulsa.
Kyle Ballard
Comstock Park, MI

I bought your first three issues of **MMPR**, and they were great! I can't wait for #4 because it has my favorite Ranger, Tommy, the White Ranger!!! I am twelve years old and a big fan of both Saban's show and your comic book! Thanks for putting in Rocky, Adam and Aisha! If Christian Peña from the Bronx is reading, Rocky, Adam and Aisha are not wannabe Rangers because the Red, Black and Yellow Rangers' powers were officially transferred to them. Besides, the three old Rangers left the show because they wanted more money. And they're not coming back because they already blew it!!! Thanks, Hamilton, and see you next month.

Matt Soileau
Rayne, CA

I am a big fan of the Power Rangers. I just finished reading issue #3 and it was great! I am glad that you used the newer characters. I am glad that you are going to use the White Ranger in the next issue. Even though I like the new characters I also like the old. After watching the show I have discovered that there are a few zords missing from your comics, like Tor and Lord Zedd's zord Sepentara.
I would also like to have Rita Repulsa in the comics. But for now the comics are perfect!
Chad Brandt-Gentile
Thousand Oaks, CA

NEXT ISSUE:

Zedd unleashes a **big** monster with a **bigger**–and **deadlier**–secret in "Attack of the Gargantutron" by Jack C. Harris and Al Bigley. Zedd then invites Angel Grove to "Shop Till You Drop...Dead" by Nicola Cuti and Gray Morrow.

On Sale May 16th!

Dear Hamilton Comics,

I loved the first three comics you have made and hope the best for you in the future. You are doing fine so I have no suggestions. Please make lots more just like issues #1, #2, and #3. I can't wait for issue #4.

Wishing you the best
Justin Andrews
Newark, DE

I enjoy the Power Rangers comic book. I just finished reading #3. I would enjoy it even more if Rita was with Lord Zedd. I like the idea of making it like the show. But I also respect the idea of making the monsters different from the show's monsters. I also love the graphics and illustrations in the book. Keep up the good work!

Sincerely,
Zane G. White
Lilburn, GA

Dear Morphin Dudes,

Up front I've just got to say this is a great comic. I'm a diehard comic fan and I've liked the Rangers since the start (though at first I thought they were just a complete rip-off of Voltron). Issues #3 and #4 were pure and simple excellence, even with the new guys (Zack was my favorite). #3 had a great story and now I'm gonna clean my room when my mom says so! It had great art and Zedd looked like you could reach out and touch him (not that I'd want to!). Only one thing, why was Kimberly on the cover when she never fought without her Zord?

#4 was cool. It had a bit of drama when Tommy thought he didn't contribute. Though for this story it wouldn't have worked, I'd like to see Tommy more. The art (again) was beautiful with Tommy, Adam and the Zords looking so real. The monster was well thought out with a good power for more destruction. This was Bulk and Skull's best scam yet, too.

I hope you guys just keep rollin' out those issues, they're "Morphinomenal."

Matt Ealer
Bear, DE

I just finished reading issue #4. I thought it was awesome! #5

Bruce Hamilton	President/Publisher
Richard Hinton	Vice President/ Associate Publisher
Helen Hamilton	Secretary/Treasurer
Leonard (John) Clark	Editor
Gary Leach	Art Director/Editor
Gary Gabner	Assistant Editor
Susan Daigle-Leach	Production Manager
Jim Flanagan	Creative Development
Michael Myers	Production Artist
Colleen Winkler	Production Liaison
Steve Calrow	Comptroller
Deborah Jones	Accounting
Janet Dvorak	Subscriptions
Mary Jane Cullumber	Mail Orders
Susan Morse	Direct Sales

seems interesting. I can't wait until it comes out! By the way, my name is Laura and I go to third grade in St. Theresa School. Just one thing: if you want the Rangers to power up their crystals, use Megazord, Dragonzord, and Rita Repulsa.

Your fan,
Laura Alonso
Coral Gables, FL

I just bought the fourth issue of Power Rangers. I thought it was great with the White Ranger and White Tigerzord in it. I hope that in the next mini-series you will put the old zords in the first half and the new zords in the second half. I think if you have my idea you should call it Dinozords to Thunderzords, or what you would choose.

We'll see you next time, and I'm looking forward to getting the fifth issue.

Sincerely,
Paul Gale
Winnetka, CA

To Morphin Mail,

Does a 45-year-old collector appreciate your **Mighty Morphin Power Rangers** comics? Yes, for the artistic appreciation of your art work and the marketing of the comics. We own 500 copies of #1, 250 copies of #2, 300 copies of #3, and presently 100 copies of #4. As an antique art and print dealer, I can offer you my following opinions on the art work. Issue #1 I find perfectly designed for an introduction to the charac-

ters–not overly done–but a graphic statement that does succeed. I find #2 and #3 overly done; it was apparent that the artists had somewhat of a difficult time with drawing the perspective of the Rangers. Issue #4 is as good a statement of craftsmanship as #1.

What I do not understand is why your company does not advertise on the TV show as other companies do. Why not put your money where the image is–especially for the movie?

Now, for my historic reasoning of the Power Rangers: 1) I always felt that the character changes were evident–that came to pass; 2) I always felt that White (the purest color) would be added–that came to pass; 3) I always felt that a movie–if done with artistic merit–could only help your comic (I would strongly suggest that you mention the movie); 4) I always felt that packaging of licensed products with actual photographs of the actors was a mistake–for future marketing (for collectors it is great).

Now for the serious business side of me: how would I go about purchasing the original cover designs–in color–that were used for issues #1 and #4?

How about this for your letter column: Zeddoric News/Letters.

Sincerely,
Harvey Kornick
Vero Beach, FL

It would be nice to advertise on the TV show, Harvey, but it's more than just a matter of money. Last we checked, all ad spots on the program were booked solid for months!

Sorry to disappoint you on another matter, but we are unable to make comic book production materials, including original art, available for sale.

Dear Power Rangers,

The first, second, and third issues were okay, but the fourth one was the best. My favorite Rangers are Tommy and Kimberly. I'm ten years old. Here are some questions: 1) Will Thunder Ultrazord be in the comic books?; 2) Will Zedd stop acting like Rita?; 3) Will my favorite monsters be in the comics, like Pexter, Eyeguy, Robogoat and the Goo Fish?; 4) Please don't have only six comics.

Matthew Scarella
Valhalla, NY

Dear Morphin Mail,

I'm a good fan of MMPR in shows and comic books. I just picked up issue #5 and I see you guys made one little mistake. That was Tommy's morphin line—it's not "White Tiger," it's "Tigerzord." Hey, watch the show and I'm telling you that I'm right. But you guys did good on art and writing. Oh, by any chance are you having a last Ranger? If so, I've got a name for a Ranger and his/her own zord. I call it "Ultra-zord," for "Ultra Ranger." The color may be neon or ultraviolet. Thanks for reading my comments. Keep up the good work.

Greggie Hernandez
Miami Lakes, FL

Dear Sir,

I just read in your Power Rangers comic about a special Power Ranger mini-comic written by Jack C. Harris with Al Bigley as artist, done for Fruit of the Loom. I would realy like to have a copy of this publication. I have asked around and no one seems to have knowledge of this comic.

Can you tell me how I could go about getting this issue or put me in touch with someone who might have it? I have everything (toys, cards, magazines, articles) about Power Rangers and can't stand the thought of having missed something.

If there is anything else that you think I might have missed, please advise.

Thank you for your help. I really enjoy your comics. I am a "Power Ranger Grandma," and all my six grandchildren are P.R. fans.

Sincerely,
Lee Negri
Tobyhanna, PA

We're as much at a loss as how to find that mini-comic as you are, Lee. All distributable copies were purchased by and turned over to Fruit of the Loom, and that was the end of our involvement with them.

But this brings up a question that's nagged at us lately, too: who actually has seen this seemingly elusive item, and is it still available anywhere? Readers?

I have a new name for your letters page. Call it, "Power Lines."
Patsy Zukav
Rockville, MD

Dear Rangers,

I love Power Rangers, that is why I had my grandfather order the comic book series. It is the greatest comic book series in comic book history! Everything about them is perfect. But if I could make a suggestion: there is no romance between Tommy and Kimberly. There should be magic when they fight as Rangers. But when they are not fighting, they should be together doing something special. They are my favorite Rangers, so their "dates," if there are going to be any, should be good.

Joey Donovan
Putnam Station, NY

Bruce Hamilton Company,

Hi! My name is Pat Carpenter. I drew this picture of a new Power Ranger [below]. He has a Thunderzord, the orange Bengal Tiger. I was wondering if you could use this Ranger in your comics. This Power Ranger is a good guy!

Pat Carpenter
Cortland, OH

Thanks for the drawing, Pat. Your Power Ranger sure seems to have all the right ingredients.

Due to reader enthusiasm, we are initiating a section in our letter column featuring artwork contributions from our readers. We'll publish the best of the batch for that month, right here in full color!

There is also a possibility that a reader's contribution might wind up in one of our stories; if that is the case, the reader will get full

credit for his or her contribution right on the story, plus free contributor's copies of that issue. However, be advised that all rights—including trademarks and copyrights—pertaining to that contribution become the sole property of Saban Entertainment, Inc. and Saban International, N.V.

Speaking of credit, we missed an important one last issue. Kid Zippo, the Wild West monster featured in Don Markstein's story "Grounded," was based on a drawing by Ryan Reading, age 10, of Phoenix, Arizona. Good going, Ryan!

Dear Power Rangers,

I enjoy your comics very much. Please don't stop with six issues. If you do, please make a VR Troopers series. My last request is to put Tor the Shuttlezord in your comics for issue #6.
Daniel Frederick
N. Lauderdale, FL

NEXT ISSUE:

Baboo and Squatt try monster making in "While the Cat's Away," by Markstein and Heebink. Then the Rangers meet an "Unstoppable Force," by Gertler and Moore.

ON SALE JUNE 6th!

MORPHIN MAIL

Dear Hamilton Comics,

Nice to talk to you again! You recently published my letter in an earlier comic. I have just finished reading **Mighty Morphin Power Rangers** #5 and it's dope! "Stranger in a Strange Town" was a little confusing, but good. Continuing on, I read your mail column. Oh boy, was I surprised when I saw my name in a letter. Responding to Matt Soileau from California, I now realize how I made my mistake. You do have your own opinions about Power Rangers, but didn't you at first dislike the three new Rangers? I did. But, soon after I saw **Mighty Morphin Power Rangers Live**, I began to like Rocky, Adam, and Aisha. So to you, Matt, I know Thuy, Austin, and Walter wanted more money, but in my book Trini Kwan is still *numero uno*! Hamilton Comics, thank you for allowing me to speak my mind about Matt's remark. So, keep up the excellent work and please don't only make six issues, because I **love** your comics!

Another Morphin Reader,
Christian Peña
Bronx, NY

Dear Hamilton Comics,

Hi, my name is Joshua. I really like the Power Rangers comics. I have all of the issues that have come out. Is it really only six parts? I hope it lives longer than that. Power Rangers is my favorite show and my favorite comic. Keep on Morphin!

Sincerely,
Joshua King
Ventura, CA

We have not stopped with issue #6—at least, not exactly. If you look at the indicia at the bottom of this page, you'll see that this issue is #1 of a four-issue series—our second series, following on the heels of our first series, which ran six issues.

I've really enjoyed your past five issues. I hope you continue

Bruce Hamilton	President/Publisher
Richard Hinton	Vice President/Associate Publisher
Helen Hamilton	Secretary/Treasurer
Leonard (John) Clark	Editor
Gary Leach	Art Director/Editor
Gary Gabner	Assistant Editor
Susan Daigle-Leach	Production Manager
Jim Flanagan	Creative Development
Michael Myers	Production Artist
Colleen Winkler	Production Liaison
Steve Calrow	Comptroller
Deborah Jones	Accounting
Janet Dvorak	Subscriptions
Mary Jane Cullumber	Mail Orders
Susan Morse	Direct Sales
Joseph R. Cigler	Shipping

the comics. The **MMPR** movie is coming out on June 30th, '95, so I was wondering if in the next couple of issues you would put the 3rd set of zords, Ivan Ooze, the new armored outfits and the new command center.

I've also read how people are always trying to tell you to make up your own story because it's your comic. But I disagree; listen to Saban or you might get fired.

Teleporting out,
Jonathan Ledoux
Camarillo, CA

I'm ten years old, but I still like the Power Rangers. I think your comic is sweet!

I'll be honest. I've never read Hamilton Comics before this. The artwork belongs in a museum, and the plots are great. I like the fact you used the power weapons and ThunderZords separately. The show doesn't do that often. I also like you putting in the new White Ranger. I don't read comics much but I'm sticking with your comics.

Sincerely,
Scott Dixon
Mechanicsville, VA

I love **MMPR** #5 with the monster called Kid Zippo, and I love all the other Power Ranger comics. I would like to see Rita and Zedd get married in your comics. I would also like to see Billy and Trini repairing their Zords. They talk about it on the show but you don't see it.

A.J. Mako
Bricktowne, NJ

Dear Power Rangers,

I just bought your comic book and I love it. I am a big fan of yours, and I always watch your TV show. I am eight years old and my favorite rangers are Tommy and Kimberly. My wish is to see the Power Rangers in person and I am gonna see your movie in summer.

Yours truly,
Ron
Mississauga, Ontario, Canada

Dear **MMPR** staff,

I think your **MMPR** comic is awesome! Especially issue #5! I'm 24 years old, so I never outgrow those Power Rangers!

After reading issue #5's letter page where the readers pointed out errors and differences, here's mine:

1. When Tommy changes into the White Ranger, he doesn't say "White Tiger," he says "Tigerzord."

2. Wrong order of call of Power Rangers. It's this way: Tigerzord! Mastodon! Pterodactyl! Triceratops! Saber-Tooth Tiger! Tyrannosaurus!

3. When will the White Ranger's Tigerzord appear in the comic book as well as Tor the Turtlezord? And when will Rita Repulsa and Scorpina appear in the comic book series? (I noticed Rita and Lord Zedd got married on a recent **MMPR** TV episode.)

Until these are found out, Keep on Morphin!

Darryl Heine
Inverness, IL

We will, Darryl, we will!

NEXT ISSUE:

Lord Zedd decides to blow the Rangers out of sight and out of time in "The Yesterday Bomb," a book-length epic by writer Jack C. Harris and artists Al Bigley and Sparky Moore.

ON SALE JUNE 20th!

Dear Hamilton Comics,

I am a great fan of your comic books. I know just about everything there is to know about the Power Rangers. I'm a big fan of Tommy! I have pictures and posters of him and even his auto Morphin action figure. I collect the cards. I have a lot of them. And after issue six I'll have the whole series! I also want to give you an idea. I want to know if you would do a biography on Tommy? A whole comic book on Tommy's past and present. People tell me that the Power Rangers are for little kids and that I should act my age (14). But I just ignore it, I am a very loyal fan.

Justin Rivera
Guttenberg, NJ

You made my day! I was so excited when my letters got printed in your fifth and sixth issues. I was so ultrazordly out of this world happy! Here are some suggestions for your comic books. Try to use the Power Cannon, the Power Blast weapon, and have Rita and Lord Zedd married like on the show. Oh yeah, I also want to tell you, I saw an awesome advertisement for the Power Ranger's movie! It was so cool, their suits changed a lot, their command center changed, Zordon came out of the tube, and there is a new bad guy leader called Ooze! I was thinking that maybe you could have Ooze and his group of bad monster bird henchmen in the Power Ranger comic books. Maybe you could also have some scenes from the movies in your comic books or just have a new series just based on the movie. Also on the movie it was so cool how Tommy fought the bad guys. I think the Amy Jo Johnson is the best girl to be Kimberly, and the rest of the cast is fantastic for their parts, too! I wish I could at least be with the Power Rangers for a few minutes on the show or in the movie. Well, keep up the good work until next time.

Paul Gale
Winnetka, CA

Hello, my name is Stephan. I'm 11 years old and I read your first three Power Rangers comics and

Bruce Hamilton . . . . . . President/Publisher
Richard Hinton . . . . Vice President/
                                Associate Publisher
Helen Hamilton . . . . . Secretary/Treasurer
Leonard (John) Clark . . . . Editor
Gary Leach . . . . Art Director/Editor
Gary Gabner . . . . Assistant Editor
Susan Daigle-Leach . . Production Manager
Jim Flanagan . . . . . . Creative Development
Sarah Flanagan . . . . Production Artist
Colleen Winkler . . . . . . Production Liaison
Steve Calrow . . . . Comptroller
Deborah Jones . . . . Accounting
Janet Dvorak . . . . Subscriptions
Mary Jane Cullumber . . . . Mail Orders
Susan Morse . . . . Direct Sales
Joseph R. Cigler . . . . Shipping

I really like them. These comics were my friend's and I was wondering if you could help me get the first 4,5, or 6 issues because I liked the first 3 comics. I will pay your price if I could buy them if the price is suitable. I am also a friend of Bandai's and I gave them ideas for toys like that Power Ranger game for Sega. I was hoping if we become friends I'd let you in on some of my ideas.

Stephan Stryjewski
Philadelphia, PA

I love your comic! So far, I have the first five issues, I just finished the 5th issue. I loved the three old Rangers, especially Jason. I totally agree with Christian Peña from the Bronx. Rocky, Adam and Aisha are wannabes, and if Matt Soileau from Rayne, CA is reading, the three old Rangers did not want more money! And they may not be coming back, but it's not because they blew it! Matter of fact, I look forward to the reruns with the three original Rangers more than I look forward to the new episodes. Walter Jones, who played Zack, has been on an episode of **Step by Step**. Austin St. John, who played Jason, has been writing two books, traveling the country, and could be in two movies! My favorite Ranger is Kimberly, the Pink Ranger. By the way, at the bottom of 5's "Morphin Mail," I saw that it said: Power Rangers, no. 5 (of a six-issue series). Is the next issue going to be the last? I really hope not! I'd miss it a lot! I'm 15 years old. I

also watch VR troopers. For the Pink Ranger's other fans, Amy Jo Johnson, or Kimberly, is supposed to have a starring role in the upcoming movie: Suzie Q. Also in 5's "Morphin Mail," someone said they'd like to see a movie of the Rangers. Well, the Mighty Morphin Power Rangers Movie is coming June 30th. I know I'll be the first one there! When is the Power Ranger's Graphic Novel coming out? I can't wait to see Jason again!

Carol Dapson
Oswego, NY

You have an awesome comic. Almost everything I was gonna ask or suggest has been said already. But well, anyway, here it goes:

Suggestions:

1. I agree with Kyle Ballard, why not have a zord get broken down? Like the Rangers destroy Serpantera with the Power Cannon. Use the Tigerzord and Tor, please. Also, use the new Power Cannon.

2. Have Lord Zedd make a monster. Maybe a fly monster called "Fly Guy."

3. Have Zedd create a new Ranger. Have the Rangers turn him good, after about three appearances, have Lord Zedd drain his powers with his staff.

4. Use Ricky, Angelia, Curtis and Marge, (Billy's girlfriend) in your comics.

5. Use Rita as Zedd's wife.

6. "Letters from the command center" could be the letter column title.

Questions:

I can't find issue 4 anywhere. Could I buy it from your company? Thanks for printing Doug Marion's letter. Now I have a new pal. I'm available, too, for all you that did or didn't write to Doug Marion. Have more putties. Make your comic have more putty fights and action. But your comic is still good without it. But I still like even more action. Could you have Ooze, the villain in the Ranger movie or in your next comic? I am including my address for the people who would like a penpal.

Jesse Basham
Rt. 1, Box 223
Tenaha, TX 75974

Hey, my name is Laura Whitefield. I really love Power Rangers. They're cool! I love Tommy, the White Ranger. I like him when he's White. The other Power Rangers are cool also. I think you should have Kimberly and Tommy go on a date or something. I love to read your

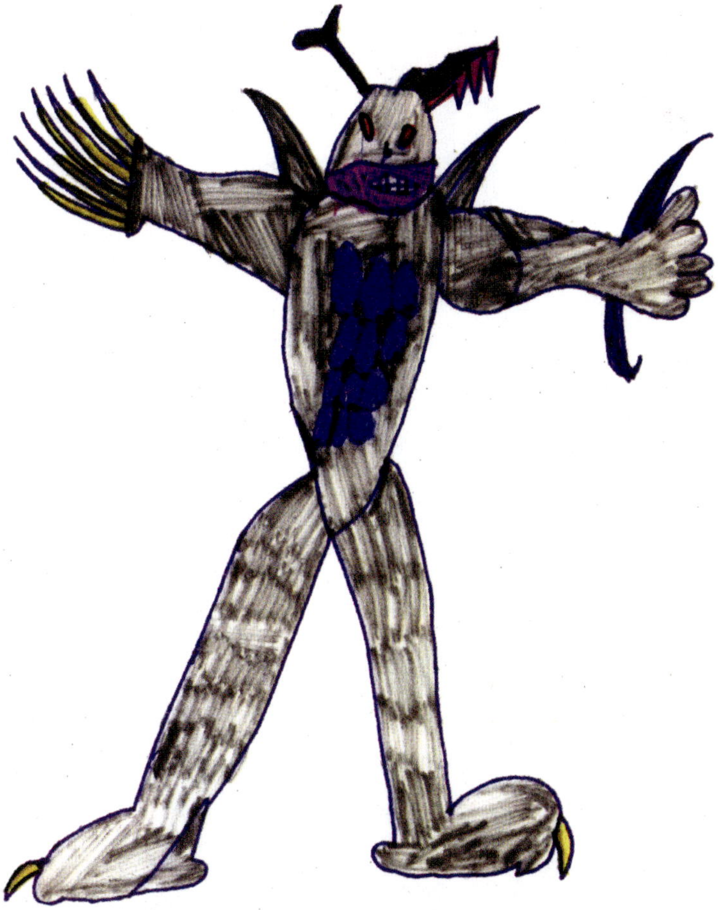

ıagazines. The comments are ool. I watch Power Rangers very weekday at 4:30 on Fox 40 .ids Club, and Saturdays at 7:30 n Fox also. Will the Power langer novel be sold in stores ke Wal-Mart or not? Because ıere's no comic stores around.

Laura Whitefield
Crystal Springs, MS

I love your Power Rangers omic book, especially issue 5. At rst, when I found out about the ower Rangers, I didn't think that ıey were interesting. But one ay my little brother was watching and wouldn't watch anything lse. I decided to watch it instead f sitting around doing nothing. hen I thought that maybe they re more interesting than I ought. I hope to one day meet e actors that play the Pink and /hite Rangers. They are great ctors. Anyway, I sent in a suggestion for a monster. I call him Channels the Television monter." I was thinking that Zedd ould create him from a new TV set. Along with a picture of this monster I sent a picture of his main weapon, his remote control. The picture also describes certain functions on the remote control. I also have a question. In the TV show, Zedd and Rita are now married. Will Rita ever show up in the comic books? I'm also wondering if you know the original red, black and yellow Rangers will ever return? I hope they will. Well, I'm glad that the pink and white Rangers didn't leave. Not only do I think that they are good actors, but they are my most favorite Rangers. Well, keep up the good work!

Matthew Zabarkes
Pottsville, PA

I think your Power Ranger comic book is excellent! I am anxiously awaiting the arrival of the Power Rangers comic at the book store. I'm 13 years old and I love the Power Ranger's show. I never miss it. I collect the toys, posters games, etc. When I bought the first issue I couldn't put it down, it was so exciting. I was sad to hear it was a six-issue series. I read all the issue two or three times. Because they are so entertaining, I hope you guys will make an ongoing series. Keep up the great work! Please print my address, I love to get Penpals!

Michael Martinez
6041 S California Avenue
Chicago, IL 60629

Dear Rangers,

I think your comics are great.

I've made this monster (*pictured at left*) for your comics.

His name is "Dogotron." His powers are shooting spears out of his eyes and shooting his claws at the Rangers. His strength comes from a special kind of metal from an asteroid.

Sean Pott
Turtle Creek, PA
Age 8

That's it for this month. Before we go, we want to mention that next month marks the debut of our second Power Rangers title, ***Saga of the Mighty Morphin Power Rangers****! This series will recount the early days of the Power Rangers, starting from the day Rita Repulsa was first set free from her space dumpster! For our readers who have yearned to see the* ***original*** *Rangers in action in our comics again (and, judging by the mail, you are legion!), this is the book you* ***won't*** *want to miss!*

The first issue of ***Saga of the Mighty Morphin Power Rangers*** *is written by Power Rangers veteran Don D. Markstein, and features the artwork of John Heebink (with an able assist from Sparky Moore and Aaron McClellan). It goes on sale August 1st, so be sure to reserve your copies with your favorite retailer as soon as possible!*

NEXT ISSUE:

The Rangers suddenly acquire "Bad Attitudes," by Michael T. Gilbert, then deal with a most peculiar threat under "Grey Skies," by Nat Gertler. Both stories are drawn by ace Power Rangers artist Sparky Moore.

ON SALE AUGUST 8th!

MORPHIN MAIL

Important: Hamilton Comics welcomes any and all correspondence concerning the **Mighty Morphin Power Rangers** comic book. However, anyone wishing to write to the Power Rangers **TV show** (or the Power Rangers Movie, which is being released to theaters even as this letter column is being written) should send cards and letters to **Saban's Mighty Morphin Power Rangers**, P.O. Box 10277, Van Nuys, CA 91410-0277. Thanks!

We are 16-year-olds who actually watch the Power Rangers, but you've got to admit the guys are hot! It's not the fact that we have absolutely nothing to do in this little town, but we've really grown attached to the Rangers, especially Rocky, Aisha and of course, Billy, the beautifully built Blue Ranger. We were really excited that you put Rocky, Aisha and Adam in the comic book; as far as we're concerned, Trini, Jason and Zach do not deserve the pleasure of being seen in a comic book! We noticed in issue 5 you got a lot of suggestions, including the creation of a Purple Ranger. A Purple Ranger would rock! We think you all are doing a great job and we hope there are more comics to come! Also, if there are more comics, are you going to have Rita and Lord Zedd getting married? And would Rita be Rita Zedd or still Rita Repulsa, or even Rita Repulsa-Zedd? Hope to find out!

Shelly Weiss
and Shannon Phillips
Miamisburg, OH

Your Ranger comics are great! I just got **Mighty Morphin Power Rangers** 5 and it was great! But there were some things I didn't understand. Why did Tommy get into the MegaThunderzord and not call for the Tigerzord? Because on the TV show he doesn't! Why don't the Rangers ever morph in order like the show? (Tommy, Adam, Kimberly, Billy, Aisha and Rocky?) Why did Billy say, "Shouldn't that be zounds! No I suppose Zords would be more appropriate in this case?"

Why did Aisha say "We're not Rangers" to Zedd pretending to be Rocky when Adam was morphed? Please answer my questions. I suggest "Mighty Morphin Mail" for the letter page. And I suggest a monster frog called the "Bog Frog."

Tyler Smoot
Winchester, IN

Hi, my name is Dana Rivera. I think your show is great! So are your comics. But there are a few mistakes that were not mentioned.

In issue 5 when you see Alpha his eyes are separated from his head (helmet). But in the show he doesn't have eyes, he has a thick red ring around his helmet.

In battle, the Power Rangers don't call each other White Ranger, Red Ranger and so on. They call them by their names, Tommy, Rocky, etc.

Kimberly's stepfather doesn't look anything like his illustration in issue 5. He has brown hair and a beard and mustache. He is also not chubby and doesn't have gray hair.

When all of the Power Rangers morph, it goes; Tiger Zord, Mastodon, Pterodactyl, Triceratops, Saber-tooth Tiger, Tyrannosaurus. Not White Tiger, Pterodactyl, Tyrannosaurus, Triceratops, Saber-tooth Tiger, Mastodon.

The Power Rangers jump into their zords before they are fully assembled, not when the Thunder Megazord is finished.

When they call out their Thunder Zords on the show they say their names like for example: Pterodactyl Firebird Thunderzord Power. They just don't say "We need Thunder Megazord power now!"

The White Ranger doesn't jump into the Thunder Megazord with the other Rangers. The only zords that he is in are; Tiger Zord, Mega Tiger Zord, and Thunder Ultra Zord.

I also wanted to say to Demetrious Travlos who wrote in issue 5 that the monster that Zedd made from a poster to suck up the Green Ranger's (Tommy) power, was not called the "Buzz Beetle" but, the "Stag Beetle." There was never any monster named the Buzz Beetle. I also have a few suggestions for the story line in the comic book. Rita and Zedd should be married in some of them. You should make a comic based on the TV episodes.

I also have a few questions: In issue 5, the second story was called "A Stranger in a Strange Town," you had the characters Billy, Adam, Aisha, Kimberly and Rocky, but not Tommy. Where was he all the time? And how come you are located in Prescott, Arizona, and not in L.A. California with Saban and the **MMPR**?

Dana Rivera
Long Island City, NY

I like your comics, your show and your pogs. But I like your comics the best. My favorite Ranger is Tommy. And my brother's favorite is Jason. We have issue 5. It has Tommy the White Ranger. I want to see Tommy's parents. And I want to see the Mighty Morphin Power Rangers movie.

In **Power Rangers** issue 5, why did Kid Zippo just use a thumb to fight? I want Tommy to marry Kimberly. I wish I was Tommy and the White Ranger.

Matthew
San Antonio, TX

I hope you come out with another series of Power Ranger comics after Series 2. Can you make another series of "Power Rangers The Movie"? I'd like to see Ivan Ooze and stuff from the movie, like the Falcon Ninjazord, the Crane Ninjazord, and all the new Ninjazords.

Never stop making Power Rangers comics. Even my mom reads them. We both like Tommy. Morph On!!

Patrick Siebe
Myrtle Beach, SC

I'd like to start out by letting you know I love your **MMPR** comic books, especially issue 5. But there are some things that are not on the TV show.

The White Ranger does not jump into the Thunder Megazord with the other Rangers. **MMPR** do not have their symbols on their chests. Only Tommy has his symbol on his chest. To make a monster grow, Zedd does not throw his wand like Rita Repulsa, he throws a bomb.

If you can fix up these minor problems, kids will have a "Morphin" comic book to look at!

Marshall Riley
Siloam Springs, AR

I am writing to compliment you on your Power Rangers comics and also to show you some mistakes in comic 1. (Oh yes, no offense, I didn't think the art was good at all in 3.) The mistakes are: Jason is too fat, Bulk and Skull don't look like them, (plus Skull says "Why get your hopes up? You know when you've met your match!" and then Bulk says "Yeah! Met your match!" That is Skull's line.) Zedd looks through a telescope, not his eyes, which it's supposed to be. The putties don't explode. When the caterpillar wraps up Zack, Trini and Jason and they get them back, Zack does not have his costume on but the others do. Zedd throws his stuff down to make the monster grow, and not the bomb. In the end Zedd says "Arrgh! I have a headache" and the Rangers have their emblems on their chests. I'm not telling you to stop the comics, but the artwork should be good like in issue 2.

John Darcy
Rockport, MA

How long did it take to make the Power Ranger Movie? Saban, I've heard that the reason the 3 Rangers left was because they wanted more money. Is this true? If it isn't, then why did they leave? One more question: why are you adding these new zords? I'm not meaning to be rude, just please answer my questions.

Wayne Cato Jr.
La Grange, GA

Although we've explained in other letter columns why there are inconsistencies between what readers see on the TV show and what appears in the comic book, the information bears repeating.

We and our writers see the shows at the same time most of our readers do. That's when we find out what's happening, and then, after the several months it takes to write, draw, letter, approve, color, have film made and sent to the printer, where the comic is printed and sent out to distributors who then send it around to newsstands and the like, **then** *the developments on the show finally appear in the comic. By that time, of course, other changes have occurred on the show.*

*Certain elements, such as the chest symbols, are required by Saban for all printed matter showing the Rangers, in spite of the fact that they are **not** part of the TV uniforms. These will remain on the comic book Power Rangers for that reason.*

I think it would be neat if you would make a comic book where the Rangers are teleported by one of Lord Zedd's monsters to a planet of robots. In your second series will the Power Rangers travel back in time?

Jeff Zagoudis
Palatine, IL

Power Rangers are fun to read in comics. The issue I have is my very first. It's the one with the Gargantutron and when the Rangers go to a mall which is Zedd's trap, I like it when they call on the Thunderzords.

The Rangers in the comics look the same as in the show. Looks like you got some great art skills.

Aaron Jeon
Seatac, WA

I really like your comic books and hope to see them as a permanent series. I just finished reading the first comic of your second series. This is the first time I've admitted outside of my family that I like the Power Rangers, because I'm twelve years old and my friends hate **MMPR**.

I have three questions to ask:

Is there going to be a third miniseries?

Are you going to change the zords to match the movie's new zords?

Is Tommy really 5'6"? (If so I'm taller than him; I'm a girl in the sixth grade who happens to be 5'7".)

Again, I love your comic books!

Aubrey Bowling
Leasburg, VA

Congratulations on a great comic book! It's absolutely morphinominal! I am the proud owner of issues 1-6. I know a lot of people have written to you to complain that the comic doesn't follow the show. I have almost every episode on tape, and even I have a little trouble keeping up with some of the changes. Besides, your stories are getting better and better all the time. You seem to have captured the spirit of the show. My only regret is that there is no permanent artist. I know you would have a hard time choosing one, as Billy would note, every single one of them is prestigious. But there are some who stand out above the rest. These are John Heebink and Al Bigley. I would like to see Bigley's version of the White Ranger, who hasn't made an appearance yet. I think the best way to solve this little artist problem would be to mix Bigley's fight scenes with Heebink's teenager scenes.

When is Tor the Shuttlezord going to make his comic book debut? Also give Saba some lines. This character is underused on the show and deserves his chance in the spotlight.

You are doing a great job! Keep up the good work! So, until Lord Zedd gets scared back into his skin, make mine morphin!

Andrew Pierre Kowtow
Oxford, Al

Thanks for the interest and kind words, readers! We can't answer letters personally, but we read every one, and print as many as we can.

NEXT ISSUE:

"The Lost Ranger," by Jack C. Harris, and "Footloose," by Michael T. Gilbert. Both stories are drawn by ace Power Rangers artist Gray Morrow.

**ON SALE
SEPTEMBER 19th!**

MORPHIN MAIL

I am 18 years old and am not ashamed to admit that I have been one of the biggest Power Ranger fans since the beginning. The show is great and your comic is just as great, if not better.

I just finished issue #2 of the second series and I must say it was one very cool story. I like that you gave Adam a sense of humor instead of his usual shy personality. My favorite Rangers are Tommy and Kimberly (but, aren't they everyone's favorite.) And I agree with the rest of the fans when I say "have more issues with the two of them together." I mean even the show has started to do more with them.

I have seen the Power Rangers movie twice already and I really loved it. I was wondering if Hamilton comics was going to make a movie adaption comic of it? I know you guys would do an excellent job with it.

Well gang keep making great comics and I'll keep spending my hard earned buck-ninety-five a month on **Saban's Mighty Morphin Power Rangers** the comic. (As long as **you** keep making the comic, I mean.)

Freddy Aguirre
Levelland, TX

I picked up #2 yesterday and it was fantastic! I also agree with Michael Martinez about wanting a permanent series. Please print my address because I like having penpals.

Brian Miller
4875 Hyde Rd
Springfield, TN 37172

Just finished issue #2 of Series II and got a glimpse of the **MMPR** movie to be released on June 30th—well consider yourselves lucky, because over here we have to wait until September 14, but then again, the movie was filmed out here. Some people over here think that because I'm 24 years old I am childish, but I don't care, they don't know what they are missing, do they?

Could you please print my address?

Luke "Logan" Howell
8 Reddington Ave
St Clair NSW
Australia 2759

Bruce Hamilton . . . . . . President/Publisher
Richard Hinton . . . . Vice President/
                                Associate Publisher
Helen Hamilton . . . . . . Secretary/Treasurer
Leonard (John) Clark . . . . Editor
Gary Leach. . . . . Art Director/Editor
Gary Gabner. . . . . Assistant Editor
Susan Daigle-Leach . . Production Manager
Jim Flanagan . . . . . . Creative Development
Sarah Flanagan . . . . Production Artist
Colleen Winkler . . . . Production Liaison
Steve Calrow . . . . Comptroller
Janet Dvorak . . . . Subscriptions
Mary Jane Cullumber . . . . Mail Orders
Susan Morse. . . . . Lithograph Manager
Sandy Hulquist . . . Direct Sales/Accounting
Joseph R. Cigler. . . . . Shipping

My seven-year-old niece accompanied me to my local comic shop today, and in addition to my more "mature" selection, she had me buy **MMPR** #3 (series II). When we got home, naturally I had to read it to her, and it was as much fun for me as it was for her!

As a man of 31, I don't **purposely** ever watch the Power Rangers on television, but with her living here, I can't help but be exposed to it. Therefore, it was enjoyable to read your stories in #3, because I knew what was going on. My niece knows **everything** about them!

There were some inconsistencies in your stories, but I see that a number of them have been mentioned in your letters columns by the "experts," so I'll only bug you about one. And that is, the way Zordon treated the "bad-attitude" Rangers. It's not the first time the Rangers have had evil personality changes due to machinations of Zedd or even Rita, but Zordon always knew about it and gave the Rangers the benefit of the doubt. Then he worked to find a cure for what he knew was an evil influence beyond their control.

In your first story in #3, he didn't even give them a chance! If Alpha had not discovered the 'Tude Tick' in their uniforms, the Rangers would still be evil today, unknowing victims of Zedd's villainy, and separated for good from their mentor, Zordon. The personality traits of the cast are pretty solid, so I just couldn't let this one slip

by without bringing it up.

In the second tale, however, Nat Gertler did a good job for the most part with the individuals, especially Billy, who sounded as technical and "brainy" as he does on the show. It was a kick to read this story to my niece! I, for one, want to see Gray Morrow's version of this series!

Now her comments: Squatt had a very good idea about the bad attitude tick! He was also funny in the story, especially when he broke his arm and hurt his head at the end! Also, Zedd and Rita should be married in your comics. In the second story, I liked the part when the bats scared the elephants. That was sure smart of Billy to think of that idea! In the first story, why did some of the Rangers take their helmets off? Now, Angel Grove people know who they really are underneath! That's not right! (She's the expert!)

Chris Khalaf (uncle)
Amber Cannady (niece)
Houston, TX

I'm not really into comic books, because I can't comprehend them. But amazingly, I can the Power Rangers. It may be that I am interested in what the Power Rangers say. Some cartoons/comics make no sense and have bad effects on what kids do. The Power Rangers are a good & positive thing to children, as decent role models are supposed to be. I like each one of the Power Rangers in a special way. I hope one day I can meet them.

Raven Tollett
DeQueen, AR

After the up & down quality of the previous books, **MMPR** #3's story, "Bad Attitudes" was the much needed antidote to a really lousy day.

Squatt contributing largely to the mayhem was a good idea since he and Baboo are all but gone from the show. My favorite moment in the story was when Aisha had Bulk by the collar ('Bout bloody time in my opinion!) You also made Zordon someone we can all respect when he stripped the bad attitude Rangers of their power. Thanks for easing up on Billy's educated vocabulary & oh yeah, the story would've been better if you'd shown Zordon working some magic to make the good citizens of Angel Grove forget the faces of the unmasked Rangers. Still, you receive an A from me.

Clint Christa
Trussville, AL

You guys have made a very respectable comic book out of Power Rangers and I don't think anyone could do it better. Just remember:

1. Make Mighty Morphin Power Rangers permanent!
2. Make "Power Ranger Classic" series.
3. Publish comic adaption of "Power Rangers" movie.
4. Give John Heebink a permanent job!

In Series II, #1, you listed the statistics of Tommy, the White Ranger. There is one discrepancy: Tommy is not 5'6"! Jason Frank, the actor who plays Tommy on the TV show, is 6 feet tall! My ten year old brother is 5'6". Just keep that in mind.

So long as you keep this comic as good as it is right now, you'll always get my $1.95!

Rachel
Hillsdale, NJ

I say that Hamilton Comics is a success hit in America. I don't know how many times I read **MMPR** #3, even though it's the only one I have. I'm impressed with the artwork and the writing. I wish I could draw like that! Do you remember the show "Voltron?" The Rangers remind me of them, but the Rangers are better, and the show is more exciting, and the comics are cooler!

I congratulate your writers and artists on the "morphinmind" work they have done. Keep up the good work!

Don Frenchwood, Jr.
Brownwood, TX

Are you going to make a comic of the **Mighty Morphin Power Ranger** movie? If so, could you please have it drawn by John Heebink! Also, please don't stop with four issues of the second series!

Andrew Pinder
Marne, MI

I find it interesting that the Power Rangers have found their way into the comic realm for all to enjoy, and nobody in my family enjoys comics as much as I do. However, I am pretty disappointed in the treatment of this series by an unfamiliar comics publisher.

Already people have written in to complain about the little things like how Lord Zedd takes on the mannerisms of Rita Repulsa, why Finster still exists in the comic and not in the show, that the morphing sequence is out of order, (First it's the Tigerzord, then it's Mastodon, Pterodactyl, Triceratops, Sabertooth Tiger and Tyrannosaurus! Get it right!!) why the Rangers have their Power Morpher insignias on their costumes, why the layouts aren't as impressive as Marvel or DC, why the dialogue balloon pointers aren't jagged when they communicate from their zords . . . okay, I made up those last two myself, but these are little things that annoy more-than-obsessed fans. My problem as a serious comic book collector, is that Mighty Morphin Power Rangers the comic book is a limited series (yes, I read the indicia).

I don't want to complain, but comic books cost money, and I don't feel like wasting it on a series that won't last beyond 6 issues. Especially since I'm an unemployed, full-time college student and art major seeking a career in animation and/or comics illustration that's never going to happen in real life. And it's not just me either. Remember those more-than-obsessed fans that I mentioned earlier? If you discontinue this series, these "freaks" as I call them are going to be very angry at you. What's the problem anyway? Are Saban's royalties too expensive for you or something?

Peter Fay
Brooklyn, NY

I just wanted to drop a line to say how much I enjoy your Power Rangers comic. I had never picked up a Hamilton comic before, and I had never even heard of Hamilton Comics until the Power Rangers comic appeared. I am 14 years old and I enjoy the action-adventure Power Rangers Saga. I must say that Hamilton Comics makes a very good comic. So far, I have every issue of the series, and I plan to continue my collection. I am not going to make it a priority to see the movie–perhaps I will rent it or possibly purchase it when it arrives on video. I hope that you, or some other comic company will adapt the movie into a comic, and then I will buy that. I have heard about your six-issue mini-series on the Power Rangers' beginnings. Although I do enjoy the new stories you have every month, especially with the White Ranger, I am fascinated by the original stories of the Power Rangers with my favorite Ranger–the Green Ranger. I look forward to this upcoming mini-series. After that, you can look for me to stay with Hamilton Comics for years of the Power Rangers. Please keep up the great work that you have already accomplished.

Brian Husvar
Newton, CT

Hamilton Comics wishes to extend our sincerest appreciation to all of you who have written to our ***Mighty Morphin Power Rangers*** *comic book. This letter column simply could not have happened without you!*

While we'd like to respond more fully to many of the things brought up in the letters printed this issue, we must forego it because…

This is Hamilton Comics' final issue of ***Mighty Morphin Power Rangers****. It's been quite a ride, and while we have been sometimes bemused by the questions, complaints and requests you, the readers, have sent us concerning our treatment of the Power Rangers, we've noticed that you have also been very supportive of what we actually accomplished. That it why it is our pleasure to announce (though this may already be old news to many of you) that, starting next month,* ***MIghty Morphin Power Rangers*** *will continue their comic book adventures under the Marvel banner! Saban and Marvel have a great deal of enthusiasm for this new arrangement, so the results should be…if you'll permit one last hurrah…MORPHINOMENAL!*

Be sure to check out ***Mighty Morphin Power Rangers Saga*** *#3, featuring the* ***concluding chapter*** *of the* ***origin*** *of Earth's mightiest protectors!*

ON SALE OCTOBER 3rd!

"THE MENACE FROM WITHIN"

by **Don Markstein**

As I look over the script for this issue, the expression "This one has it all!" comes to mind. It isn't quite true, but look at what this issue does have.

It has Rita. It has Zedd. It has the original Rangers. It has the current Rangers. It has the original Zords. It has the first replacement Zords. Tommy appears as both the Green Ranger and the White Ranger. It doesn't have Ivan Ooze or the third-season Zords, but hey–is there any other single story, in any medium, that has as many separate Power Rangers elements as this one comic book? •

What you don't see in this issue, you would have seen in future issues of **Mighty Morphin Power Rangers Saga**, but for one unfortunate circumstance–there aren't any. It was planned as a six-issue series, but a variety of factors–including several very complex behind-the-scenes re-shufflings within the comic book industry–dictated that it be cut off at three.

Needless to say, I'm disappointed. Not just because I don't get a chance to bring the Saga right up to the present (or as close to present as our lead time will allow), but also because I was telling a story of my own in this series, and now, it's never going to have a chance to be told.

A story of my own? Look back over these three issues. They're just about chock-full of the primary story I was dealing with–the history of the Power Rangers, as told in key episodes of the TV show (dubbed for me by David Crowe, who also supplied an episode guide). And what a mass of story that is!

I not only wrote more panels per page, on average, than is usually considered desirable in a superhero comic book–I also had more than one thing happening in many of the panels. There were separate actions going on in foreground and background…panels in which key story elements appeared on TV screens or the Viewing Globe…insets, divided panels, crowd scenes on postage stamps…

I'm sure everyone who had a hand in drawing any of this grew to hate me.

And yet, I found a tiny bit of room here and there to start developing a story of my own.

Y'know that running gag that's been going these past three issues? The one about the poor, helpless restaurant supplier who keeps being wiped out by monsters? Well, he has a name–Jim–and next issue, he was going to have his first speaking part (unless you count that inarticulate cry of terror back on page 8). That would have marked his promotion from running gag to full-fledged subplot.

The next issue was to open with the kids talking among themselves at the Youth Center, continuing what Zordon and Alpha had started–recounting the history of the Power Rangers. Jim, one of Ernie's regular suppliers, comes by to make a delivery, and the kids overhear a conversation between the two. Jim is understandably very upset with the way things have gone recently, and says so in no uncertain terms.

Not so understandably, he blames the Power Rangers for attracting all the monsters.

Naturally, this point of view doesn't get much support from Ernie. But the kids wonder if perhaps there isn't some truth in what he says. After all–if Zordon had chosen teens in some other community as his Power Rangers, Angel Grove would have been spared the brunt of Rita Repulsa's and then Lord Zedd's wrath.

Of course, equally innocent citizens of some other community would have been in that position. And Angel Grove would have been at least indirectly threatened anyway, because wherever his actual attack is made, Zedd's goal is to conquer all of Earth.

But the light of reason offers little warmth when it shines on a case like Jim's.

A few days later, in the park, the kids are again reminiscing about the group's history, their uncertain feelings at least partly forgotten. They are reminded when Bulk and Skull come by and ask them to sign a petition demanding that the Power Rangers leave Angel Grove.

It seems Jim's frequently-expressed opinion has gained converts–two, at least–who, with their usual fuzzy-brained reasoning, figure this petition drive will put them in a position to find out who the Power Rangers really are.

The popularity of the petition can be seen in the responses of passers-by, which range from shaken fists to inarticulate growls. The scene ends with Bulk being kicked in the shin by an indignant 3-year-old.

The only ones who take it seriously are the kids themselves. They know very well Jim's troubles aren't their fault–but they can't help feeling bad about it anyway, just because that's the kind of guys they are.

They share their misgivings with Zordon, who (in one last set of flashbacks, bringing the back-story completely up-to-date) reminds them of all the good they've done. They feel a little better about themselves as they leave. But not completely good, and not for long, because Zedd and Rita have now noticed their self-doubt and are starting to nurture it by magical means.

It is at this point–right at the end of #5, for a nice cliffhanger–that the former running gag is promoted once again, to become the main plot of the final issue.

Bulk and Skull step up their petition drive. They have somehow managed to find a couple of children whose family has suffered financially from property damage caused by Power Ranger battles. But even with thrift-store rags making the children look extra-pitiful, all they receive for their efforts is a series of amusing and sometimes messy insults.

Zedd and Rita send down a monster called Whirly Willy, who has gigantic fans where his head and hands should be, capable of whipping up hurricane winds. The Power Rangers, under intense psychic attack, can fight only half-heartedly. Billy, in fact, can't help comparing this foe with Don Quixote's windmill.

They retreat to the Command Center.

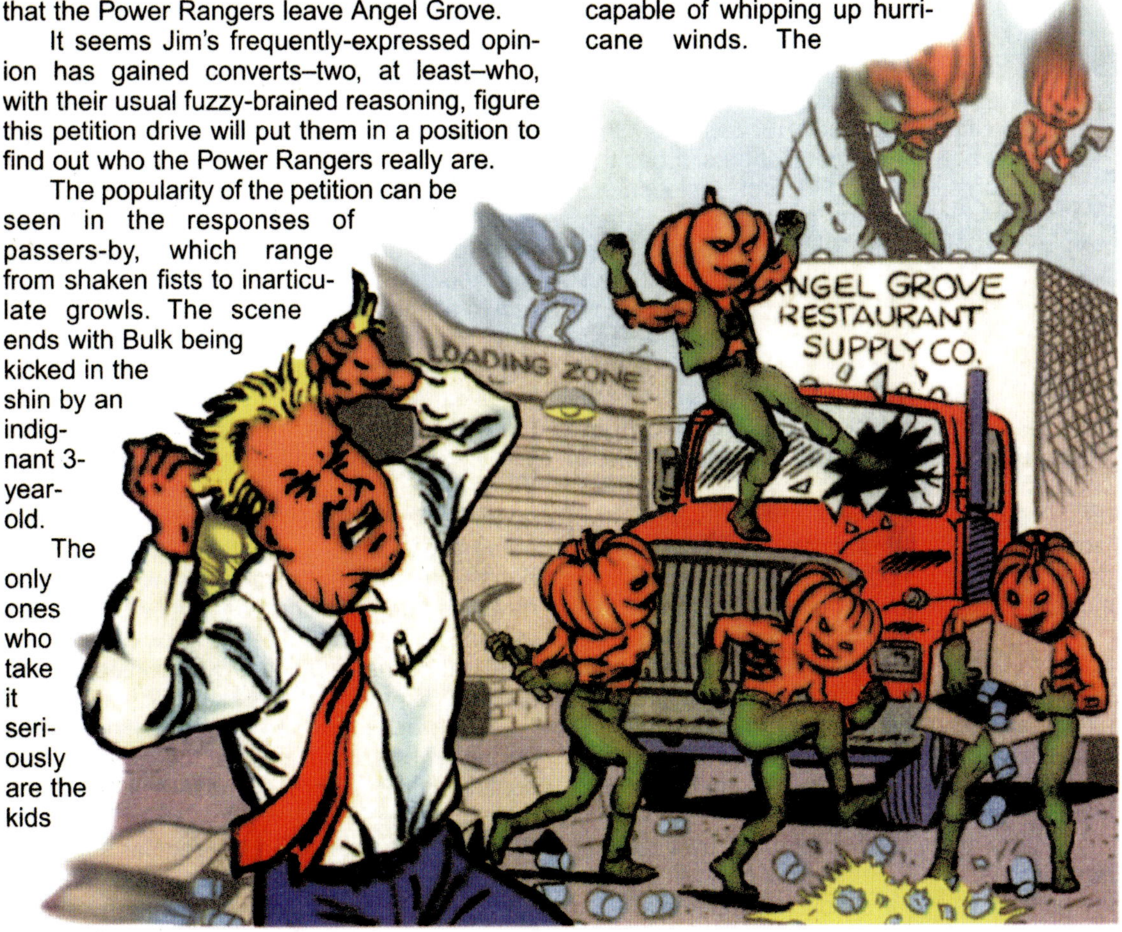
LOADING ZONE
ANGEL GROVE
RESTAURANT
SUPPLY CO.

Zordon gives them a stepped-up pep talk, using the Viewing Globe to show what Earth would have been like already, if the Power Rangers hadn't protected it. Horrifying scenes of worldwide destruction and unspeakable cruelty help strengthen the Rangers' will to fight–but Rita and Zedd are still able to prevent them summoning their full resolve.

As they teleport back into battle, Alpha expresses his usual frantic dismay. But Zordon says he's certain they'll find the strength they need despite every effort to prevent it.

At the downtown battle site, the usual evacuation procedures have been followed, leaving only one small party of stragglers: Bulk and Skull (the only ones stupid enough to stay because they thought it would somehow further their goals), and the innocent children in their care.

The Rangers' self-doubt is forgotten–at least for the duration of this battle–as they suddenly become aware that lives depend on their actions. To quote a phrase I like to use in my plot submissions, they then proceed to pound the monster into a smoking ruin. Rita and Zedd, however, see this as only a minor setback, because there is still plenty of self-doubt for them to work with.

The defeated Whirly Willy falls straight toward Bulk, Skull and the children, threatening to crush them to death. Summoning the very last of their strenth, the Power Rangers manage to deflect the monstrous carcass so instead of crushing people, it merely crushes a single small building.

Jim's building.

And there's Jim–with his face contorted almost beyond recognition! Shouting and waving his arms! Running toward them!

The Rangers' bad feelings return stronger than ever, as they brace themselves for attack from a foe they can not defeat–a foe against whom they can not so much as raise their hands, even in self-defense.

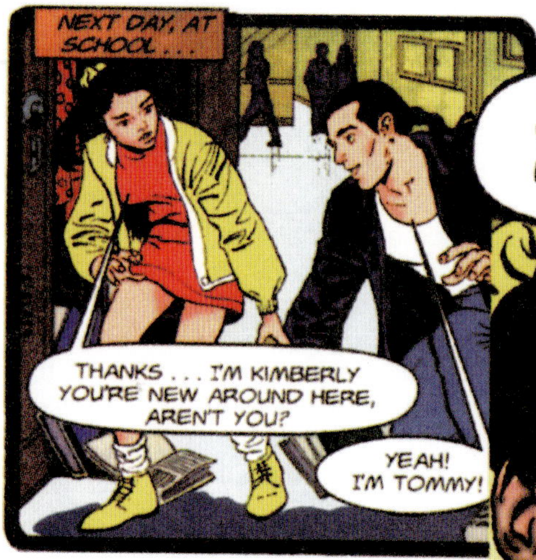
NEXT DAY, AT SCHOOL . . .
THANKS . . . I'M KIMBERLY YOU'RE NEW AROUND HERE, AREN'T YOU?
YEAH! I'M TOMMY!

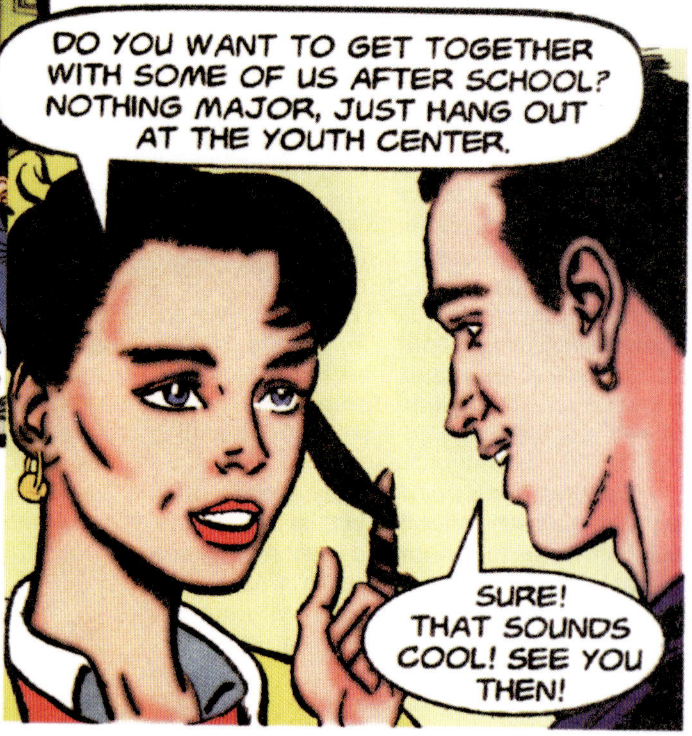
DO YOU WANT TO GET TOGETHER WITH SOME OF US AFTER SCHOOL? NOTHING MAJOR, JUST HANG OUT AT THE YOUTH CENTER.
SURE! THAT SOUNDS COOL! SEE YOU THEN!

To their amazement, however, Jim runs past them. Instead of venting his frustration futilely against the Power Rangers, he embraces the children.

His children.

Jim shrugs off the ruined building, saying he now realizes what's important. Bulk and Skull slink away as inconspicuously as they can. Zedd and Rita blame each other for the debacle.

And the Power Rangers overcome all self-doubt. The end.

Anyway–that's the story I was going to write.◊◊◊

And so Hamilton Comics concludes our tenure with ***Mighty Morphin Power Rangers****. As of this very month, Marvel will be taking over all Power Rangers comic book projects, and we wish them every success.*

One point, before we go: many, many readers wrote in asking–sometimes beseeching–us to pursue a romance between Kimberly and Tommy. As the two panels above indicate, we were beginning to look into that (if only, at the moment, in flashback). Our direction with this will, of course, go unrealized, but perhaps Marvel will give it a go.

–The Editors

SABAN'S

MIGHTY MORPHIN POWER RANGERS™

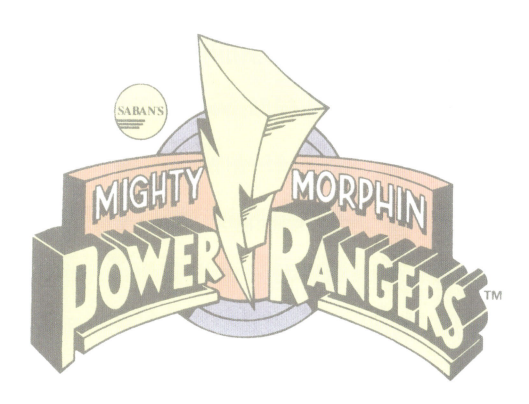

LETTERS PAGE

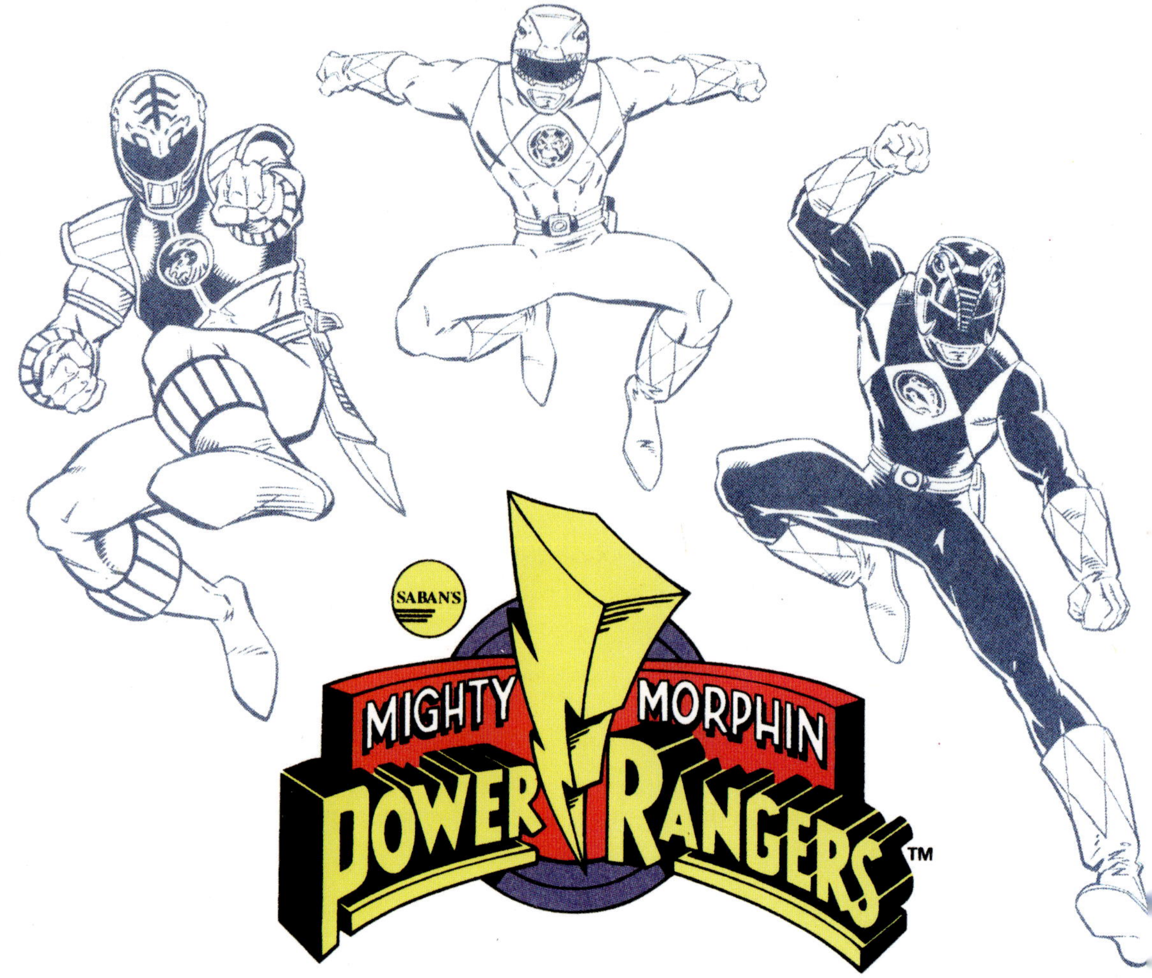
SABAN'S
MIGHTY MORPHIN
POWER RANGERS™

LETTERS PAGE

Welcome to MARVEL COMICS' official MIGHTY MORPHIN POWER RANGERS LETTERS PAGE. The Power is on, and so is the new MIGHTY MORPHIN POWER RANGERS comic book. The entire creative team for this new series is very proud of this book and we hope you enjoy it as much as we do.

Who is your favorite POWER RANGER? Who is your favorite villain? We would love to hear from you, our loyal fans!

Just to keep things interesting when you write in, give us a suggestion for the title of this letters page. We will review the suggestions and print the best one as the official title. The lucky winner will receive a mint copy of this issue signed by talented X-MEN writers SCOTT LOBDELL and FABIAN NICIEZA (listed in alphabetical order to protect their fragile egos) who wrote the two thrilling MIGHTY MORPHIN POWER RANGERS tales you've just read! As an added bonus we'll even get the rest of the creative team to autograph the comic!

You can send us mail at the address below. We will list the best entries and the winner by issue #5!!

GOOD LUCK!

MARIANO

MARVEL COMICS
POWER RANGERS LETTERS PAGE
Mariano Nicieza Editor/ Nancy Poletti Assistant Editor
387 Park Ave. South, New York, NY 10016
Please include your name and address, though we will gladly withhold that information upon request.

NEXT MONTH!

DOUBLE THE ACTION! DOUBLE THE EXCITEMENT!!
SABAN'S MIGHTY MORPHIN POWER RANGERS #2!
SABAN'S MIGHTY MORPHIN POWER RANGERS– NINJA RANGERS #1!!
CATCH'EM AT YOUR LOCAL COMICS SHOP!!

MIGHTY MORPHIN POWER RANGERS™

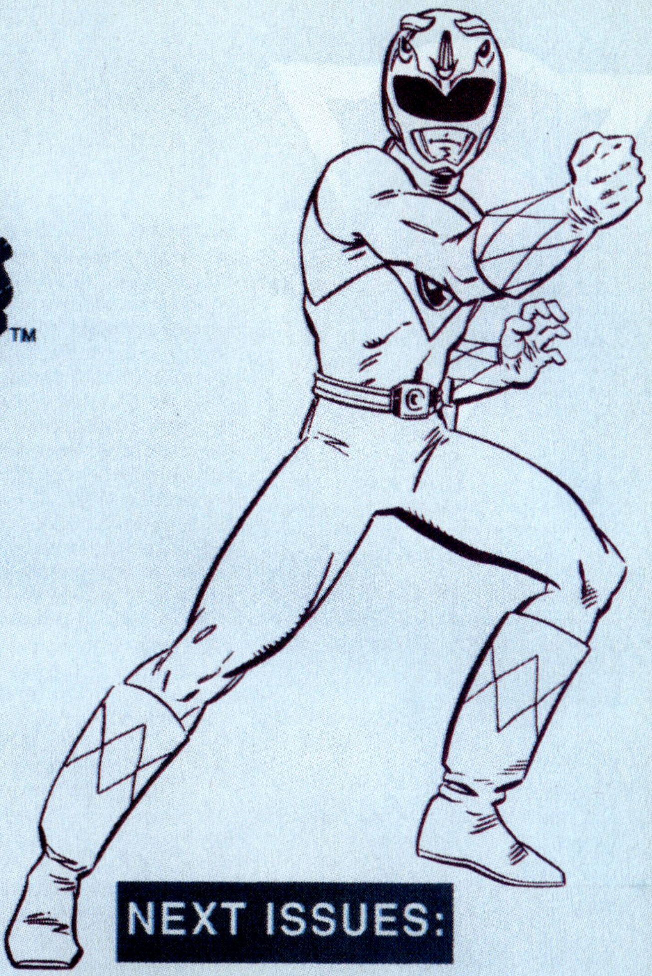

Welcome to the second issue of the **MIGHTY MORPHIN POWER RANGERS**-We hope you've enjoyed this issue's stories, crafted by some of the hottest talent in the comic's industry.

Your thoughts and comments are very important to us. We want to hear from you...so get your letter writing pen ready, 'cause we're about to announce a fantastic letter writing contest! That's right...the official MARVEL **"name the letters page contest"**. Remember, the theme is Power Rangers!

Send us a letter or postcard with your entry to win! "Win what?" you ask? We're glad you did...Each winner will receive a mint condition copy of this very issue, signed by as many creators as we can fit on one cover! We're just as excited about this new comic book as you are, so write in and let us know what you think of it.

And while you're at it, let us know what you think of the MASKED RIDER! Should MARVEL do a comic based on this hot new hero!?

As always, you, the readers are in charge. We'll print your votes and comments in future letter pages!

Check out the sneak preview of next issue's cover!!

MARVEL COMICS
POWER RANGERS LETTER PAGE
Mariano Nicieza-editor/Nancy Poletti-ass't. editor
387 Park Ave. South
New York, N.Y. 10016

NEXT ISSUES:

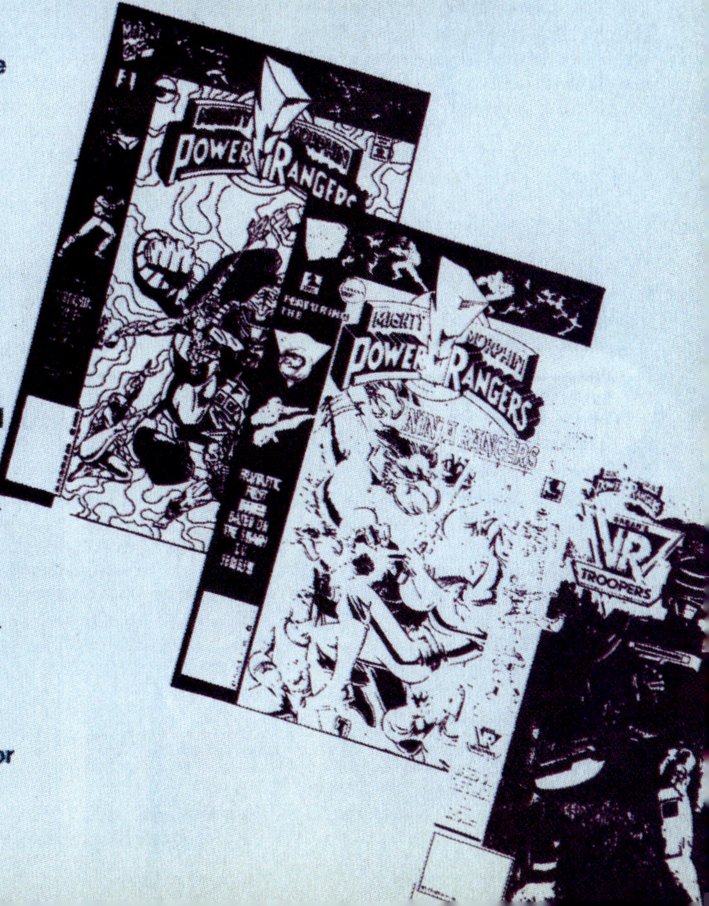
MIGHTY MORPHIN POWER RANGERS
MIGHTY MORPHIN POWER RANGERS
NINJA RANGERS
VR TROOPERS

THE MAIL HAS STARTED TO POUR IN! WE'VE EDITED YOUR LETTERS TO MAKE ROOM TO PRINT AS MANY AS POSSIBLE. THANK YOU ALL FOR YOUR SUPPORT AND COMMENTS! EVERY PIECE OF MAIL IS READ AND CONSIDERED, SO IF YOUR LETTER WASN'T PRINTED THIS TIME, AT LEAST YOU KNOW WE LISTENED TO WHAT YOU HAD TO SAY! WITH-OUT ANY FURTHER ADO, LET'S GET INTO IT!!

Dear Power Ranger Comic Writer Guys,

Great idea! I love your Power Rangers comic! I got the first issue, and it's great!

Your loyal fan,

David Hoang
Folcroft, PA

Dear M. comics,

I just read M.M.P.R. issue #1 two times! I think it's pretty cool!!

Sincerely,

Kevin Scott
Sunny Hills, FL

Dear Marvel Comics,

Thank you for putting out the Mighty Morphin Power Rangers comic book series!!!! And thank you very much for using the Ninjazords from the movie!!! Keep up the good work!!!

Matt Soileau
Rayne, Lousiana

Okay, okay!! Enough already!! We get the message loud and clear!! You love us!! You really, really love us!!

Dear writers of the Mighty Morphin Power Rangers from Marvel Comics,

I think it would be cool if you were to make a comic of the new season starting with the adventure with the Masked Rider guest-starring in it. I think I'm not alone when I say every comic should take advice from readers once in a while...I have a few suggestions to make:

1) On the show Rita has married Lord Zedd. Why don't you do that?

2) Have an issue with the Green Ranger like Hamilton Comics did.

3) Don't make limited series, make series that have more than 200 issues.

Your now loyal M.M.P.R. freak,

Jeffrey L. Daniel,
The Wanna Be Ranger
Ft. Worth, TX

Well Jeffrey Wanna Be, here at Marvel our readers are the true bosses! We always listen to advice, especially when it's as good as yours! We debated long and hard about adapting T.V. episodes, but in the end, isn't it better to get ALL NEW stories? So far our plans for both Mighty Morphin Power Rangers and its sister book, Mighty Morphin Power Rangers-Ninja Rangers include only new material.But...you're the bosses! Would any of you like to see adapted T.V. episodes? And by the way, if you want to see a Masked Rider comic, let us know! We'll see what we can do!!

As for your questions, in order: 1) What ever made you think they weren't in the comic?!! 2) First of all, we've heard of the Green Ranger, but who's this Hamilton guy? Second of all, you'll love our plans for Mighty Morphin Power Rangers-Ninja Rangers #3 coming out in December. That issue will feature the return of the Dark Rangers!! Aren't five evil Rangers better than one?!! 3) A Marvel Power Rangers series that goes for over 200 issues? You got it pal. Both Marvel Power Ranger books are monthly, unlimited and here to stay! Stick around for the ride!!!

Dear Marvel Comics,

I like your Power Ranger comics. My favorite Ranger is the White Ranger. I have noticed a few mistakes: Zedd looks at a crystal ball, the Ninja MegaFalconZord has a sword unlike the show...I think Rito Revolto is cool. Hope to hear from you!

Your biggest fan,

George Green
Pocano Lake, PA

Hey George, you're not related to that Green-Ranger-Hamilton guy from that last letter are you? Nevermind! For the record, we never make myys-takkes! To answer some of your questions, Lord Zedd has many evil devices that he keeps in his base on the Moon, a crystal ball is only one of the ones we'll be showing you! Sorry, but the other Ninja MegaFalconZord sword was at the cleaners that issue! If you like Rita, then you must have enjoyed Mighty Morphin Power Rangers — issue #2!!

Dear Mariano,

I just got finished reading the first issue of the Power Rangers comic book...done by the fabulous Ron Lim. I have been enjoying his penciling work since his days on the Silver Surfer... if anyone can make the conversion from T.V. to comics it will be Mr. Lim.

Sincerely,

Kevin D. Brown

We couldn't agree more, Kevin! Not only did we get the talented pencils of Ron Lim, but we also got the considerable talents of Scott Lobdell and Fabian Nicieza! As a special note to long-time fans, a very young Ron Lim and Fabian Nicieza were teamed up at the beginning of their careers on a Marvel book titled "Psi-Force". These two titanic talents have wanted to work together again ever since, and now they've got their chance!!

To whom it may concern,

I was hoping your company could tell me the name and address I could write to, of the Editor of the Mighty Morphin Power Rangers regular comic. I hope you will be able to help me.

Thank you,

Cristal Moser
Springfield, OH

Cristal, Cristal, Cristal... we told you no letter was left unread! Below is the answer to your question, and since there is a "Power Rangers Magazine" at Marvel, please be sure to write "Comic Book" large and bold along with the rest of the address info!!

THAT'S ALL WE HAVE ROOM FOR RIGHT NOW!

TWO MAJOR ANNOUNCEMENTS: 1) CONGRATULATIONS TO OUR VERY OWN NANCY POLETTI WHO WAS RECENTLY PROMOTED FROM ASSISTANT EDITOR TO ASSOCIATE EDITOR! CHECK OUT HER WORK ON OTHER MARVEL TITLES AND PRESS POSTERS...AND WELCOME ANITA SHARPE, OUR TALENTED NEW ASSISTANT EDITOR!! WE WISH THEM THE BEST OF LUCK IN THEIR NEW POSITIONS!

THAT'S ALL FOR NOW, KEEP THOSE LETTERS COMING!! THE CONTEST IS STILL GOING FULL FORCE!!

POWER RANGERS LETTER PAGE
387 Park Ave. South
New York, N.Y. 10016

MIGHTY MORPHIN POWER RANGERS

LETTERS

THE MAIL HAS STARTED TO POUR IN! WE'VE EDITED YOUR LETTERS TO MAKE ROOM TO PRINT AS MANY AS POSSIBLE. THANK YOU ALL FOR YOUR SUPPORT AND COMMENTS! EVERY PIECE OF MAIL IS READ AND CONSIDERED, SO IF YOUR LETTER WASN'T PRINTED THIS TIME, AT LEAST YOU KNOW WE LISTENED TO WHAT YOU HAD TO SAY! WITHOUT ANY FURTHER ADO, LET'S GET INTO IT!!

Dear Marvel Comics,

I really love your Power Rangers comic... and I love the drawings. I have about half the toys. I'm sending you a picture of Kim, Tommy and Adam, and my favorite Rangers are the White and Red. And in one of your issues you should put Rita's brother Rito. Well that's all I have to say for now.

Sincerely,
Jordan Costilla
Clyde, OH
Age 9

RITO appeared last issue, Jordan! See, we do read and listen to requests!! We also loved the art!

Dear Marvel Comics,

Hi. My name is Chris Dowd. I love your Power Rangers comics...

Your fan,
Chris Dowd
Wayne, NJ

Let's see...first Jordan, now you, Chris. You love us... you really, really love us!! We're blushing!!

MIGHTY MORPHIN POWER RANGERS

Dear Marvel's Mighty Morphin Power Rangers,

My name is Fernando Marchan and I'm one of the Power Rangers' greatest fans. I love the show and the comic book is even better! I recently bought your Mighty Morphin Power Rangers #1 and I thought it was great! ...My favorite Power Ranger is Rocky the Red Ranger because he makes me laugh. Also my favorite villain is Rita Repulsa, you know "It's very good to be very bad." Well it was fun writing in to you guys and keep the comics coming.

Your friend,
Fernando Marchan
P.S. The power is on!

Thanks for the letter, Fernando, and thanks for the praise, but we love the T.V. show just as much as the comic...where would we be without it?! Keep the Power on!!

NAME THE LETTERS PAGE CONTEST

ALL YOU HAVE TO DO TO ENTER IS SEND US A LETTER WITH YOUR NAME AND ADDRESS AND YOUR SUGGESTION FOR A COOL NAME FOR THIS PAGE! WE WILL REVIEW ALL SUBMISSIONS AND A PANEL OF TENGA WARRIORS WILL PICK A WINNER! THE WINNER WILL RECEIVE ONE MINT COPY OF ISSUE #1 SIGNED BY THE ENTIRE CREATIVE TEAM!!!

GOOD LUCK - MARIANO

MARVEL COMICS
POWER RANGERS LETTER PAGE
Mariano Nicieza-editor/Nancy Poletti-ass't. editor
387 Park Ave. South
New York, N.Y. 10016

THAT'S ALL WE HAVE ROOM FOR RIGHT NOW! BELOW, CHECK OUT SHOTS OF OUR NEXT TWO ISSUES ON SALE IN JUST A FEW SHORT WEEKS!! ALSO ON SALE IS THE SUPER, FULL COLOR, PHOTO-FILLED, MIGHTY MORPHIN POWER RANGERS: THE MOVIE ADAPTATION! IF YOU LIKED THE MOVIE, YOU'LL LOVE THE PHOTO COMIC, IT'S ALL BRAND NEW!!!

THE "NAME THE LETTERS PAGE" CONTEST IS STILL GOING FULL FORCE!! GET YOUR ENTRIES IN BEFORE JANUARY 30, 1996! SEE YOU SOON!

NEXT ISSUES:

MIGHTY MORPHIN POWER RANGERS

LETTERS

WE'VE EDITED YOUR LETTERS TO MAKE ROOM TO PRINT AS MANY AS POSSIBLE. THANK YOU ALL FOR YOUR SUPPORT AND COMMENTS! EVERY PIECE OF MAIL IS READ AND CONSIDERED, SO IF YOUR LETTER WASN'T PRINTED THIS TIME, KEEP TRYING! IT'S LETTER TIME!!

Dear Marvel Comics,

I just want to say your storyline and drawings are amazing! You give your drawings that magic touch, which makes it look real. I just want to compliment on your comic. Everything's cool, but when are you going to show the command center, the fortress, and RITA and RITO and the rest? And will you make the MOVIE COMIC?

Your biggest fan,

Bill Rasoul
Whittier, CA

Thanks for the praise, Bill! Ron and the rest of our artists in the Mighty Marvel Bullpen love to hear positive reviews on their art! As for some of those other things you asked for, check out some upcoming issues of both POWER RANGERS and POWER RANGERS-NINJA RANGERS/ VR TROOPERS FLIP BOOK! If you hurry to your local comics shop, you can still catch both the COMIC BOOK version and the PHOTO version of the POWER RANGERS MOVIE!!

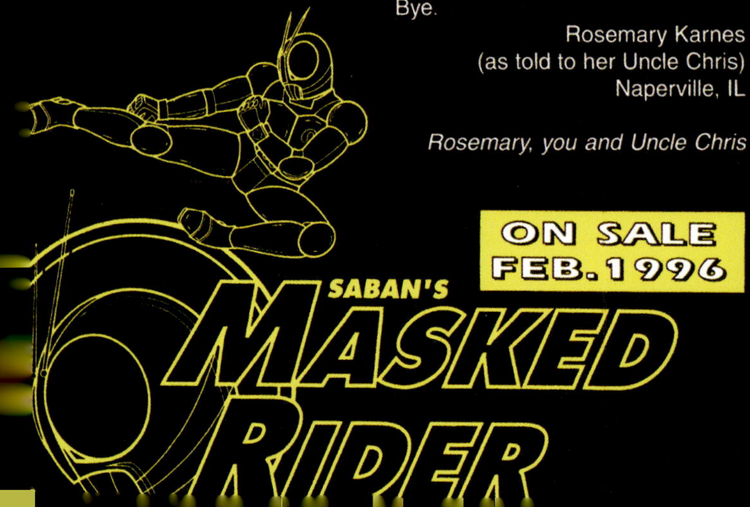

ON SALE FEB. 1996
SABAN'S
MASKED RIDER

Dear Sirs,

I am a 26-year-old father of two young children who really like the POWER RANGERS. I hope you have the RANGERS speak to kids about the dangers of drug and alcohol abuse as well as some of the other things of the world. About the comic, good interior art, story and cover art. Good job on a great book. This is the first letter I have been compelled to write to a book so please give my letter consideration for print...Will the RANGERS team up with other MARVEL characters?

Thank You,
Bobby Bright
Bristol, VA

You've raised some great points for a first-time letter writer, Bobby! What do the rest of you out there think about the RANGERS facing some decidedly more "down to Earth" evils? And what about a meeting with MARVEL characters? If you want it, folks, write in and let us know; we'll ask our friends at SABAN ENT., the producers of the MIGHTY MORPHIN POWER RANGERS T.V. show and see what we can do!! In the meantime, stay tuned for a special announcement real soon, regarding everyone's favorite MASKED RIDER!!!

Dear Mariano and Anita,

Hi! my name is Rosemary. I am three years old. Lord Zedd is my favorite bad guy. I love Tommy. He's my favorite Ranger. I want Spider-Man to meet the Power Rangers. Bye.

Rosemary Karnes
(as told to her Uncle Chris)
Naperville, IL

Rosemary, you and Uncle Chris should get together with Bobby Bright and start a letter writing campaign! I think you guys might have something here!

NAME THE LETTERS PAGE CONTEST

ALL YOU HAVE TO DO TO ENTER IS SEND US A LETTER WITH YOUR NAME AND ADDRESS WITH YOUR SUGGESTION FOR A COOL NAME TO THIS PAGE! WE WILL REVIEW ALL SUBMISSIONS AND A PANEL OF TENGA WARRIORS WILL PICK A WINNER! THE WINNER WILL RECEIVE ONE MINT COPY OF ISSUE #1 SIGNED BY THE ENTIRE CREATIVE TEAM!!! GOOD LUCK — *MARIANO*

Dear writers of the Power Rangers comic,

Even though I'm an eleven-year old, I'm still a loyal fan of the RANGERS. My favorite RANGER is the WHITE RANGER. My favorite villain has got to be LORD ZEDD. I love the entire book!

Sincerely,
Michael Ziege
Mishawaka, IN

Michael, look at this entire letters page. We've heard from age 3 all the way up to age 26 (we won't tell you how old our blushing Editorial staff is) and we all love the POWER RANGERS!! Age doesn't matter, as long as you're having fun! Great picture, by the way!

THAT'S ALL WE HAVE ROOM FOR RIGHT NOW! BELOW, CHECK OUT OUR NEW COMIC, MASKED RIDER, SHIPPING IN FEBRUARY! OUR NEXT TWO ISSUES, MIGHTY MORPHIN POWER RANGERS #6 AND MIGHTY MORPHIN POWER RANGERS-NINJA RANGERS/ VR TROOPERS FLIP BOOK #5 ARE ON SALE IN JUST A FEW SHORT WEEKS!!

THIS IS THE LAST MONTH FOR THE "NAME THE LETTERS PAGE" CONTEST ENTRIES. HURRY AND GET YOURS IN!

SABAN'S

POWER RANGERS

ZEO

FACT FILES

SABAN'S POWER RANGERS ZEO

FACT FILES

Zeo Ranger I (Pink)
Katherine

Australian-born Katherine is a natural-born leader. Sophisticated and assertive, she can take control of any situation. Katherine is a champion diver, a promising student of ballet and an accomplished singer. Her upbringing on a ranch "down under" has taught Katherine to regard the land and all its plants and animals as sacred.

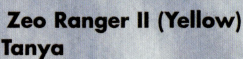

Zeo Ranger II (Yellow)
Tanya

Tanya is a whirlwind of upbeat energy who doesn't let any obstacle stand in her way. She loves music and sports and is a star pitcher for the Angel Grove High baseball team.

Zeo Ranger III (Blue)
Rocky

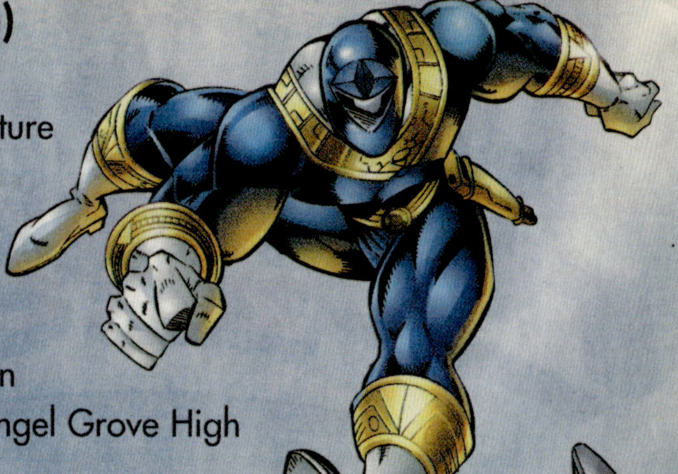

When a Zeo Ranger adventure starts getting a little too intense, Rocky keeps things light with his jovial attitude and lively sense of humor. Adventurous Rocky is also an enthusiastic participant in Angel Grove High athletics and other extra-curricular activities.

Zeo Ranger IV (Green)
Adam

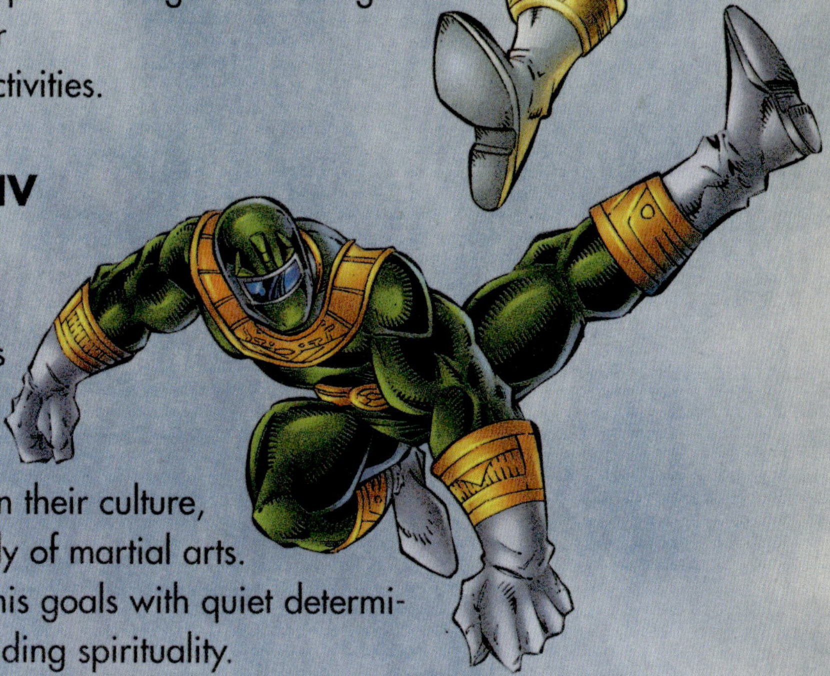

Adam's forebears come from the Far East and he's centered his life on their culture, especially the study of martial arts. Thus, he pursues his goals with quiet determination and an abiding spirituality.

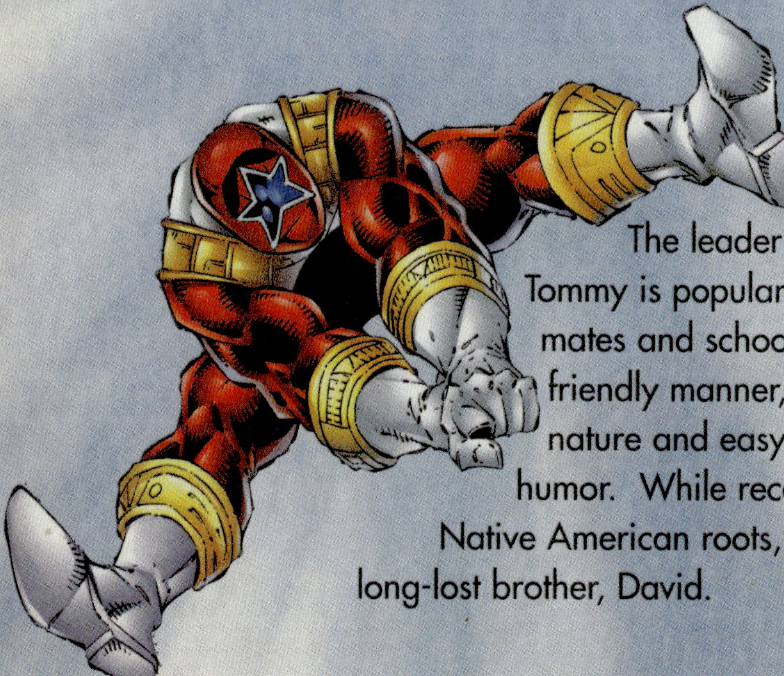

Zeo Ranger V (Red)
Tommy

The leader of the Zeo Rangers, Tommy is popular among both team-mates and school mates thanks to his friendly manner, down-to-Earth nature and easy-going sense of humor. While recently exploring his Native American roots, Tommy discovered a long-lost brother, David.

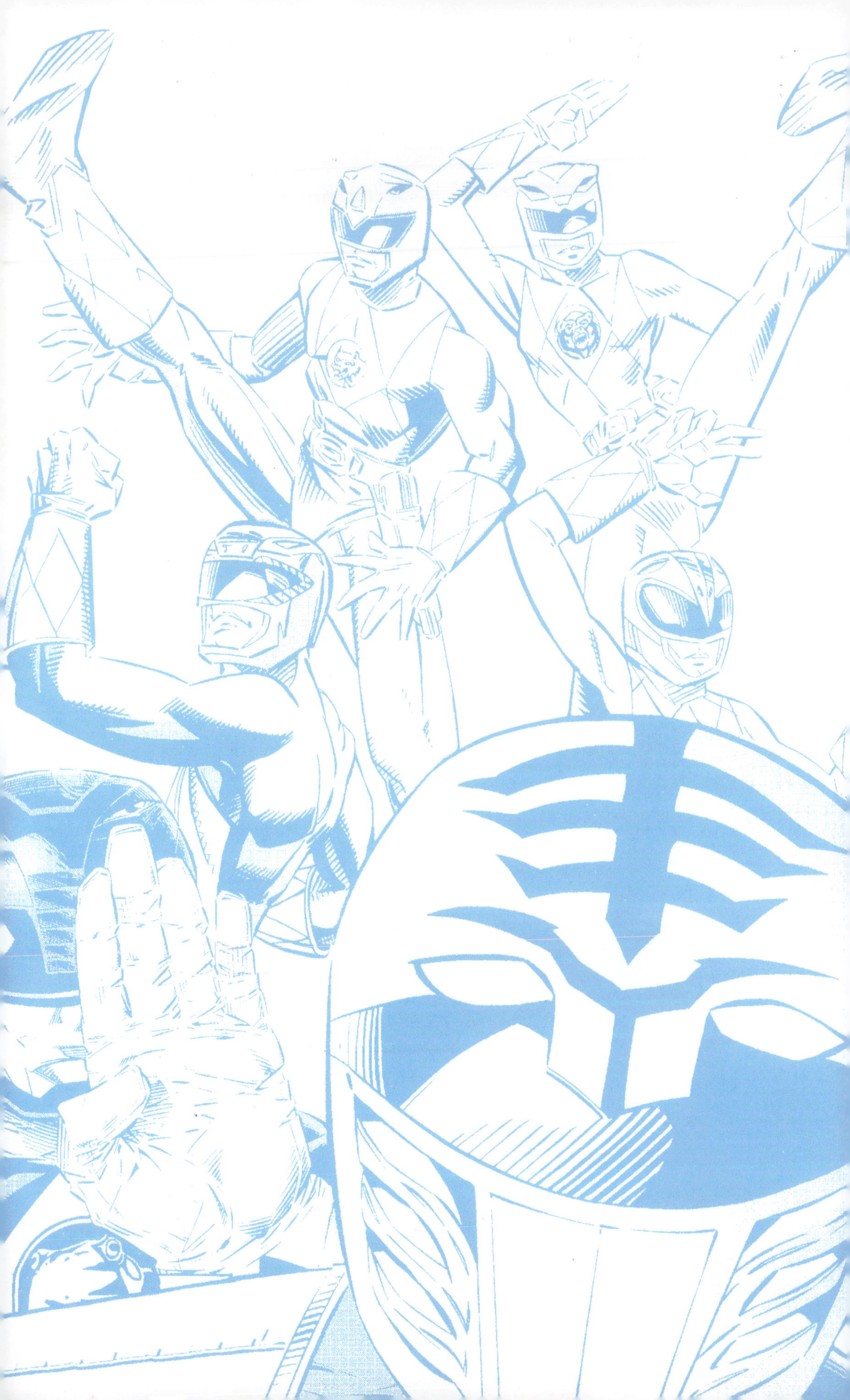

WATCH OUT FOR PAPERCUT**Z**

Welcome to the pulse-pounding premiere of the SABAN'S POWER RANGERS SUPER SAMURAI graphic novel series from Papercutz. I'm Jim Salicrup, the Editor-in-Chief of Papercutz. Papercutz publisher Terry Nantier and I thought the time was right to bring the longest-running TV super-heroes to graphic novels, and fortunately our friends at Saban Brands agreed. To make sure this debut was worthy of the POWER RANGERS we went directly to our top-talents to find the very best writer and artist team—Stefan Petrucha and Paulo Henrique. Here's a brief biography of my ol' pal, Stefan Petrucha…

Born in the Bronx, Stefan Petrucha spent his formative years moving between the big city and the suburbs, both of which made him prefer escapism. A fan of comicbooks, science fiction and horror since learning to read, in high school and college he added a love for all sorts of literary work, eventually learning that the very best fiction always brings you back to reality, so, really, there's no way out.

An obsessive compulsion to create his own stories began at age ten and has since taken many forms, including novels, comics and video productions. At times, the need to pay the bills made him a tech writer, an educational writer, a public relations writer and an editor for trade journals, but fiction, in all its forms, has always been his passion. Every year he's made a living at that, he counts a lucky one. Fortunately, there've been many.

Over the years, I've been fortunate to have the very talented Mr. Petrucha write many comics that I edited; titles such as WEB OF SPIDER-MAN (at Marvel Comics), DUCKMAN, THE X-FILES (at Topps Comics), NANCY DREW, PAPERCUTZ SLICES, and THE THREE STOOGES (at Papercutz). But that's just the tip of the literary iceberg. Stefan's written many other comics, such as MICKEY MOUSE, META-4, SQUALOR, and many more, as well as such prose novels as Ripper (Pholomel), Dead Mann Walking (Ace Books), Blood Prophecy (Grand Central Publishing), Paranormal State: My Journey Into the Unknown (with Ryan Buell; Harper Collins), and many others. Despite knowing Stefan, and being familiar with his work since we were both kids back in the Bronx, he continues to surprise and delight me with every word he writes.

I'm sure there will be lots of surprises, as well as lots of exciting action, and a short biography of Paulo Henrique (who prefers to be known as "PH") in SABAN'S POWER RANGERS SUPER SAMURAI #2 "Terrible Toys" coming soon. Oh, and don't forget to tell us what you thought of this premiere Papercutz POWER RANGERS graphic novel by Papercutz! Send your comments to me at: Jim Salicrup, Papercutz, 160 Broadway, East Wing, New York, NY 10038 or email me at salicrup@papercutz.com. We know there are many loyal POWER RANGERS fans out there, and we"ll be eagerly waiting to hear your feedback.

Until then, be sure to check out www.papercutz.com for all the latest news and information on the POWER RANGERS graphic novels, as well as the many other great graphic novels created for all-ages published by Papercutz. And remember, if Master Xandred, Octoroo, or Dayu happen to invite you to a party of any kind, simply say "no," and contact the POWER RANGERS immediately!

Thanks,

JIM

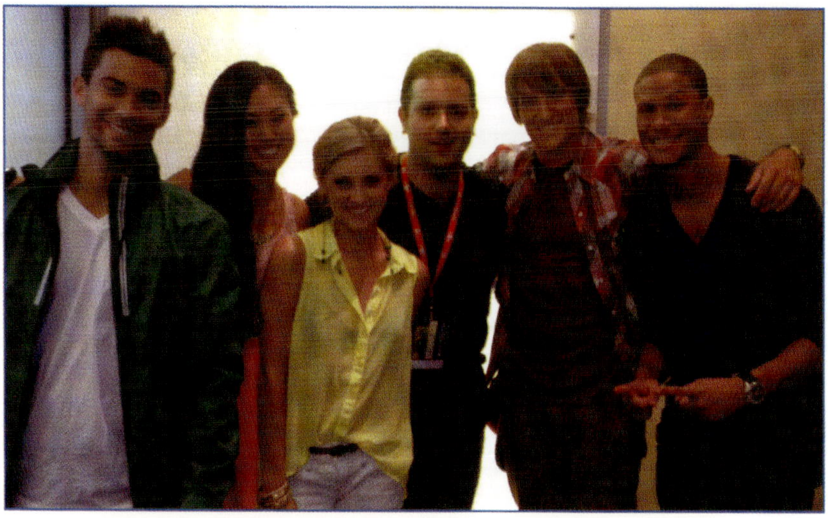

Associate Editor Michael Petranek (third from the right) with the cast of SABAN'S POWER RANGERS SUPER SAMURAI

Recently, Papercutz Associate Editor Michael Petranek attended POWER MORPHICON, a convention just for POWER RANGERS fans, and filed this mini-report:

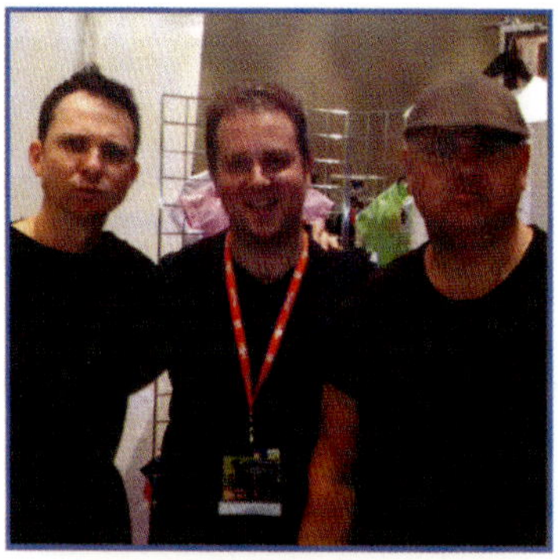

Michael with Jason A. Narvy and Paul Schrier

I had a great time in Pasadena, California attending the third annual Power Morphicon! I brought 1,000 exclusive to-the-show POWER RANGERS mini comics and a few hundred posters, and they were all gone by the first day! I met several past and current cast members including Jason A. Narvy and Paul Schrier (Skull and Bulk), along with the cast of POWER RANGERS SUPER SAMURAI. It was a lot of fun to show the actors how Paulo depicts them in the comics, and I found then all to be very warm and friendly. It was very hard keeping a straight face next to Paul – he had me laughing nonstop! The actors enjoyed seeing themselves in comics, and I enjoyed my time with all of them. It was a great show!

I want to thank Umesh Patel at Ranger Crew for introducing me to so many fans, and Saban, without which none of this would have been possible! Thanks to everyone who attended.

As you can tell we're all excited about the POWER RANGERS, and like you, we can't wait till our next POWER RANGERS graphic novel coming soon! Be sure not to miss it!

Thanks,

Jim

STAY IN TOUCH!

EMAIL:	papercutz@papercutz.com
WEB:	www.papercutz.com
TWITTER:	@papercutzgn
FACEBOOK:	PAPERCUTZGRAPHICNOVELS
REGULAR MAIL:	Papercutz, 160 Broadway, Suite 700, East Wing, New York, NY 10038

WATCH OUT FOR PAPERCUTZ™

Editor-in-Chief Jim Salicrup is ready to go into action with the POWER RANGERS at the San Diego Comic-Con!

Welcome to the smashing second SABAN'S POWER RANGERS SUPER SAMURAI graphic novel series from Papercutz. I'm Jim Salicrup, the bleary-eyed EditorZord-in-Chief of Papercutz, the folks dedicated to creating great graphic novels for all ages. As promised last time, in our premiere POWER RANGERS SUPER SAMURAI graphic novel, here's a short bio of super-star artist Paulo Henrique...

Paulo Henrique

Paulo truly is an amazingly talented artist, and we're all thrilled to be working with him at Papercutz! Born in Sao Paolo, Brazil in 1979, he started his professional career drawing MEGAMAN comics for Brazilian publisher Magnum. Later, Paulo drew MYTH WARRIORS for Top Cow Productions, and illustrated volumes 6-20 of THE HARDY BOYS and volumes 1 and 2 of THE HARDY BOYS: THE NEW CASE FILES for Papercutz. Paulo drew volumes 1 and 2 of LEGO® NINJAGO both of which were runaway hits. When approached to draw the POWER RANGERS series, he said it was a "dream job" for him. He lives in Brazil where he is also a musician, and loves watching THE SIMPSONS.

WATCH OUT FOR PAPERCUTZ™

Welcome to the first MIGHTY MORPHIN POWER RANGERS graphic novel, by Stefan Petrucha and PH Marcondes, from Papercutz, the perpetually-morphing comics company dedicated to publishing great graphic novels for all ages. I'm Jim Salicrup, the Editor-in-Chief, and I'm here to take you behind-the-scenes to explain exactly how this graphic novel came to be.

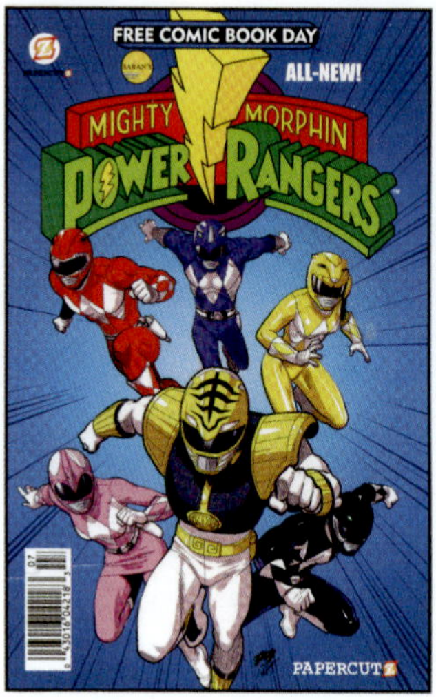

FREE COMIC BOOK DAY
ALL-NEW!
MIGHTY MORPHIN
POWER RANGERS
PAPERCUTZ

But first, I have to go into my rant. Once upon a time, comics (there really weren't any "graphic novels" back then) in North America were essentially for everyone. While generally considered kids' stuff, anyone could and would enjoy comics, no matter how old they were, or whether they were male or female. There was a comicbook for him or her. Now, things are a little different. Many comics and graphic novels are created for adults. Some, of course, are created just for children. But, if a comic or graphic novel declares itself suitable for all ages—well, folks think that just means kids. Which brings us to the MIGHTY MORPHIN POWER RANGERS.

Clearly, the original *Mighty Morphin Power Rangers* TV series was created for children. But those children who were fans of the original series are now adults, and many are into comics and graphic novels. When Papercutz first announced that we were launching a new series of POWER RANGERS graphic novels, the one question I got repeatedly was, "Which Power Rangers?" As PR fans all know, there have many incarnations of the Power Rangers over the past twenty years, the show keeps morphin into new series for new generations of fans. And whenever I answered an adult fan, and said we were publishing POWER RANGERS SUPER SAMURAI, they seemed to instantly lose interest, because that wasn't "their" Power Rangers. Always eager to please, I had to ask who were their Power Rangers, and the answer came back loud and clear—the MIGHTY MORPHIN POWER RANGERS! Countless fans would ask, and often demand, that we bring them back. And obviously, we did just that.

But as an Editor-in-Chief of a comics company, one of the things you wind up doing a lot is worry. In general, one of the biggest worries (and heartbreaks) is the fear of producing a wonderful graphic novel, with brilliant writing and awesome artwork, and no one finds out about it. And that was my concern with MIGHTY MORPHIN POWER RANGERS. Turns out, when we announced that we were bringing back MMPR at the San Diego Comic-Con, people paid attention! The Internet was suddenly all abuzz about the return of these classic super-heroes! Yet as we get closer and closer to our publication date, I'm still worried.

I'm worried that the fans that are most interested in this graphic novel, won't find us. If you're one of those fans, and you found us, I can't tell you how happy I am! I'm worried that this graphic novel will be shelved in the Children's Books sections in bookstores and the Kids Comics section in comicbook shops. Now, many people can't understand why that would worry me, after all, isn't MIGHTY MORPHIN POWER RANGERS a children's show? Well, yeah, over twenty years ago! Unless the original fans now have children of their own, how will they find us? One way we hope to direct comics fans to MIGHTY MORPHIN POWER RANGERS is by publishing a Free Comic Book Day comic featuring an all-new story, by our stellar creative team of Petrucha and Marcondes. (If you missed that, don't worry—we'll be collecting that story soon in an upcoming graphic novel!) Another way to bring attention to this series will be bringing on best-selling author, star of the TV series *Paranormal State*, and major MMPR fan Ryan Buell to co-write the next graphic novel along with Stefan.

Will it all work? Will the Mighty Morphin Power Ranger fans find us and enjoy what Stefan and PH (not to mention colorist, Laurie E. Smith, letterer, Bryan Senka, and Editor, Michael Petranek) created here? You tell us! Contact us through the means listed below, and let us know what you think! After all, if you didn't tell us you wanted the MIGHTY MORPHIN POWER RANGERS, this graphic novel simply wouldn't exist!

Go, go, POWER RANGERS!

Thanks,

Jim

STAY IN TOUCH!

EMAIL:	salicrup@papercutz.com
WEB:	www.papercutz.com
TWITTER:	@papercutzgn
FACEBOOK:	PAPERCUTZGRAPHICNOVELS
SNAIL MAIL:	Papercutz, 160 Broadway, Suite 700, East Wing, New York, NY 10038

WATCH OUT FOR PAPERCUTZ™

Welcome to the super-powered second MIGHTY MORPHIN POWER RANGERS graphic novel, by Stefan Petrucha and PH Marcondes, from Papercutz, the slightly amorphous comics company dedicated to publishing great graphic novels for all ages. I'm Jim Salicrup, the Editor-in-Chief, AKA the Prematurely Gray Ranger, and I'm here with all sorts of thrilling announcements and behind-the-scenes fun…

Perhaps the biggest, most exciting news for any MIGHTY MORPHIN POWER RANGERS fan was recently announced in *Variety*, and other Hollywood trade news magazines—coming July 22, 2016, at a theater near you—an all-new POWER RANGERS motion picture! Saban Brands and Lionsgate have announced Roberto Orci as executive producer for the first original live action Power Rangers feature film. Orci will develop the story along with writers Ashley Miller and Zach Stentz. Orci's writing credits include *The Amazing Spider-Man 2*, *Star Trek*, *Transformers* and *Mission: Impossible III*. Miller and Stentz have previously written screenplays for *X-Men: First Class* and *Thor*. That's got to be the biggest news regarding MMPR since Papercutz announced last year at the San Diego Comic-Con that we'd be publishing MIGHTY MORPHIN POWER RANGERS graphic novels!

But don't for one second think we've run out of surprises! Take this very graphic novel, for example. When writer Stefan Petrucha suggested that he'd bring on a special co-writer, I was curious who he had

Ryan Buell

in mind. He told me that it was a celebrity who was a big fan of the Power Rangers— but that can be so many people! Finally he revealed it was **Ryan Buell**, co-creator and host of TV's *Paranormal State*. Stefan had previously worked with Ryan co-writing *Paranormal State: My Journey into the Unknown* and even appearing on a couple of episodes of *Paranormal State* the TV series (I've always known Stefan was interested in such things, which is why he was the perfect choice to write THE X-FILES comics back in the early 90s.). We can't tell you how thrilled we were to have Ryan contribute to this very special story and hope you enjoy it as much as we do!

Photo by Cherie Tierie
Jim with the Power Rangers

But the best is yet to come! In MIGHTY MORPHIN POWER RANGERS #3 "By Bug, Betrayed!" we'll be featuring two big stories starring The Mighty Morphin Power Rangers, plus a report from the 2014 Power Morphicon from Editor Michael Petranek. Trust me, you don't want to miss this one! If nothing else, it'll give you something to do while waiting for a certain movie to premiere on July 22, 2016!

Go, go, POWER RANGERS!

Thanks,

Jim

STAY IN TOUCH!

EMAIL: salicrup@papercutz.com
WEB: papercutz.com
TWITTER: @papercutzgn
FACEBOOK: PAPERCUTZGRAPHICNOVELS
SNAIL MAIL: Papercutz, 160 Broadway, Suite 700, East Wing, New York, NY 10038

WATCH OUT FOR PAPERCUTZ

SABAN'S POWER RANGERS MEGAFORCE

THE GRAY RANGER (JIM SALICRUP)

Jim, the Gray Ranger, is the Editor-in-Chief of Papercutz, the group dedicated to creating great graphic novels for all ages. He works closely the SABAN'S POWER RANGERS MEGAFORCE creative team of Stefan Petrucha, writer; PH Marcondes (AKA Paulo Henrique), artist; Laurie E. Smith, colorist; Indy Mindy, guest colorist; Bryan Senka, letterer; and Michael Petranek, Editor, to create the best POWER RANGERS comics ever!

His elemental power is hot air, and his Zord is mightier than the pen.

NINJAGO

Email:
Papercutz@papercutz.com

Web:
www.papercutz.com

Facebook:
PAPERCUTZGRAPHICNOVELS

Mail:
Papercutz, 160 Broadway
Suite 700, East Wing
New York, NY 10038

WATCH OUT FOR PAPERCUTZ

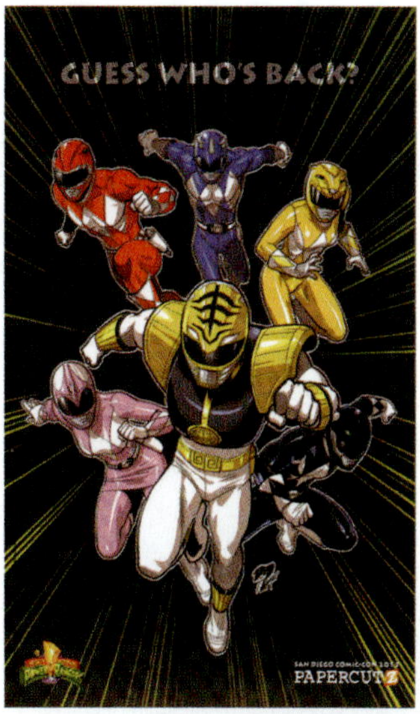
GUESS WHO'S BACK?
PAPERCUTZ

Welcome to the fantastic, fact-filled fourth SABAN'S POWER RANGERS MEGAFORCE graphic novel from Papercutz. Though technically, this is actually the second MEGAFORCE graphic novel, as the first two POWER RANGERS graphic novels were devoted to the SUPER SAMURAI team. In any case, they were all from Papercutz, the friendly folks dedicated to publishing great graphic novels for all-ages. I'm Jim Salicrup, the positive strangelet who happens to be the Gosei-like Editor-in-Chief of Papercutz, here with a few news items you may enjoy...

As we morphed from a series of POWER RANGERS SUPER SAMURAI graphic novels into a series of POWER RANGERS MEGAFORCE graphic novels, there was also a subtle change amongst our creative crew. Specifically, Paulo Henrique, the artist on the first series, was replaced by someone who draws remarkably like him, named PH Marcondes. Well, the reason for the startling similar art style is that Paulo Henrique and PH Marcondes are actually one and the same! Paulo simply prefers to be known as PH, and we're willing to do almost anything to keep such a super-talented artist as happy as possible (especially when it doesn't cost us anything extra.)!

Now, if you're a POWER RANGERS fan who follows all the POWER RANGERS news and developments online, then you're probably already aware of our next bit of really BIG NEWS. This year, at the COMIC-CON® INTERNATIONAL: SAN DIEGO, we announced that in honor of the 20th Anniversary of the POWER RANGERS we would be bringing back to comics the original MIGHTY MORPHIN POWER RANGERS! That's right, due to popular demand, we'll be presenting an all-new, never before seen tale of THE MIGHTY MORPHIN POWER RANGERS! No sooner did we drop that little bombshell on an unsuspecting public, the Internet was abuzz—spreading the word far and wide that Papercutz was actually listening to the thousands of fans that suggested that we do just that! Hey, we'd be crazy not to! That's why we run that little "Stay In Touch" box on all these "Watch Out for Papercutz" pages—so that we can hear from you! You tell us what you want, and we'll do everything we possibly can to give it to you! Or in this case, Stefan Petrucha, PH (or who knows what his name will be next?) Marcondes, Laurie E. Smith, Bryan Senka, and Michael Petranek—the creative team supreme will do it!

We actually had another major announcement at Comic-Con—that we'll be publishing all-new comics based on the WWE, written by 3-time WWE Champion and New York Times bestselling author Mick Foley—but we're sure you know all about it, if you're keeping your eye on our wacky website!

Whew! That's enough exciting announcements for now. Let's just all agree to pick up this conversation in SABAN'S MIGHTY MORPHIN POWER RANGERS #1, shall we? Until then, don't ever forget those immortal words of many a great hero—"Go, go, Power Rangers!"

Thanks,

Jim

STAY IN TOUCH!

EMAIL:	salicrup@papercutz.com
WEB:	www.papercutz.com
TWITTER:	@papercutzgn
FACEBOOK:	PAPERCUTZGRAPHICNOVELS
SNAIL MAIL:	Papercutz, 160 Broadway, Suite 700, East Wing, New York, NY 10038

SABAN'S

MIGHTY MORPHIN

POWER RANGERS™

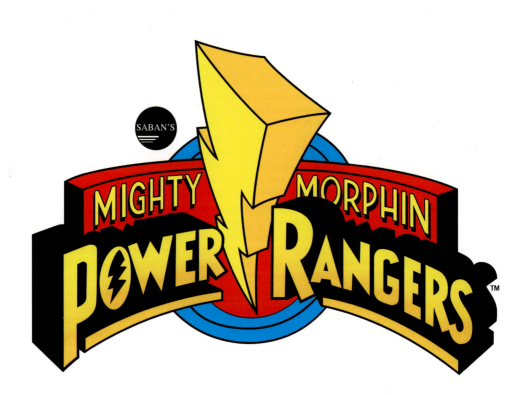

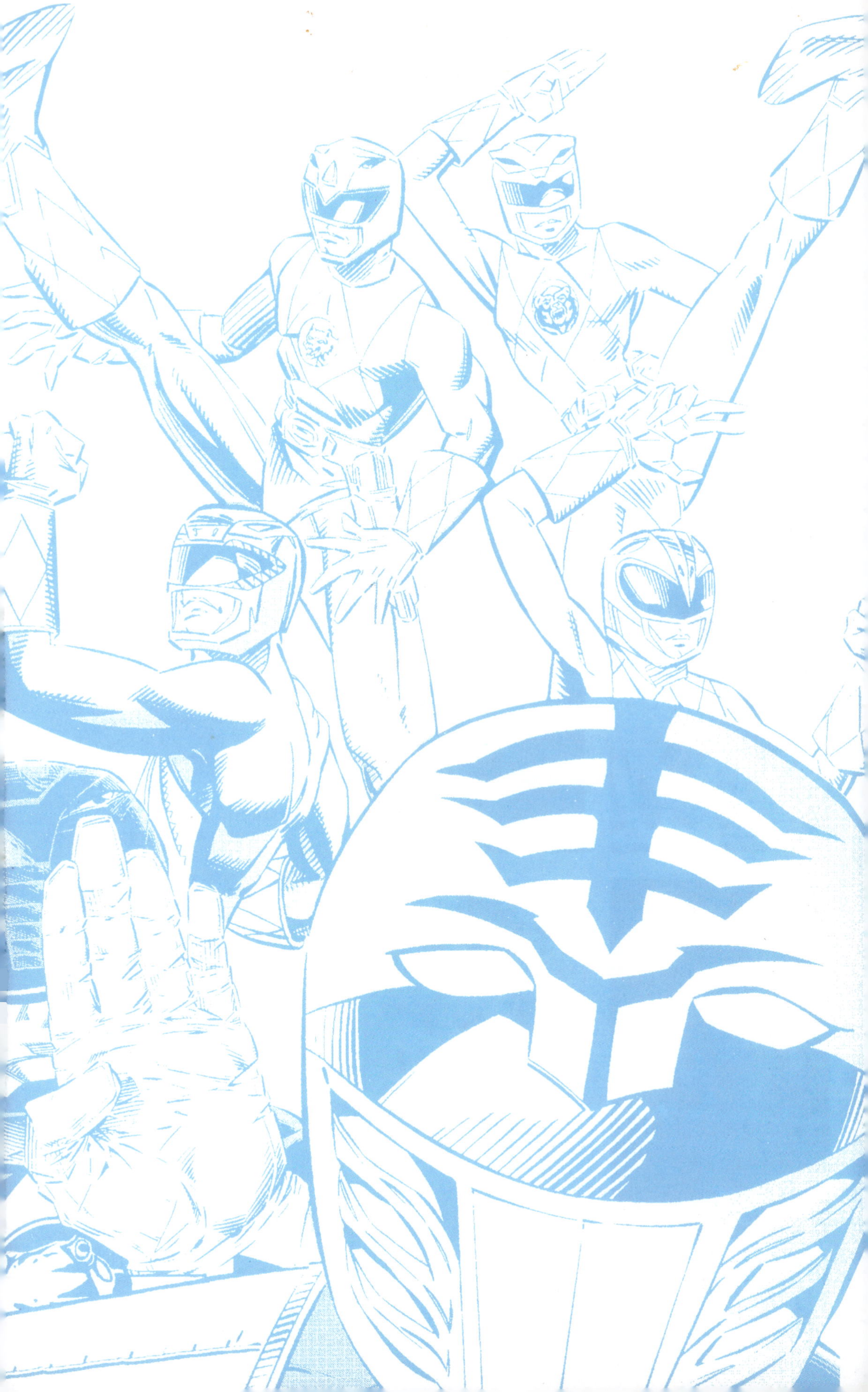

DISCOVER
MORE POWER RANGERS!

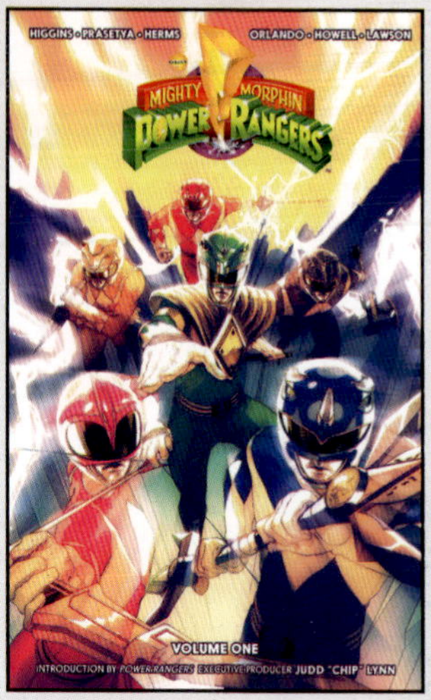
HIGGINS • PRASETYA • HERMS
ORLANDO • HOWELL • LAWSON
MIGHTY MORPHIN POWER RANGERS
VOLUME ONE
INTRODUCTION BY POWER RANGERS EXECUTIVE PRODUCER JUDD "CHIP" LYNN

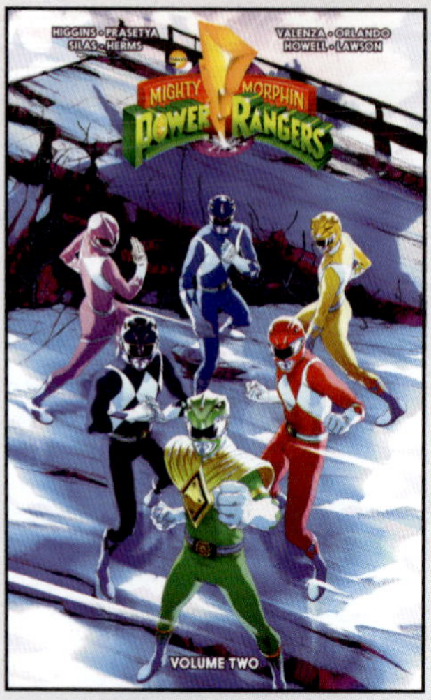
HIGGINS • PRASETYA SILAS • HERMS
VALENZA • ORLANDO HOWELL • LAWSON
MIGHTY MORPHIN POWER RANGERS
VOLUME TWO

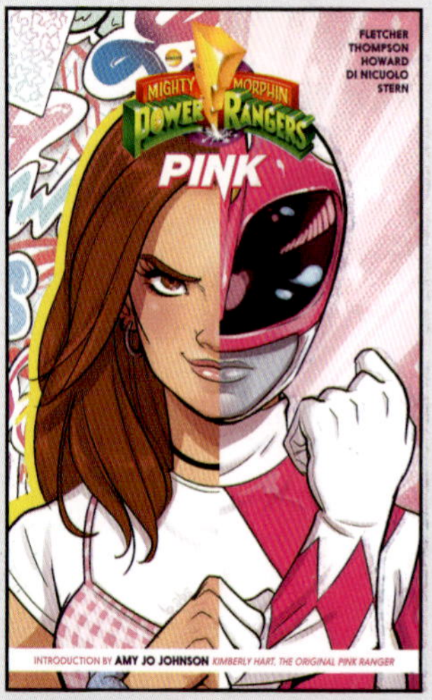
FLETCHER
THOMPSON
HOWARD
DI NICUOLO
STERN
MIGHTY MORPHIN POWER RANGERS
PINK
INTRODUCTION BY AMY JO JOHNSON KIMBERLY HART, THE ORIGINAL PINK RANGER

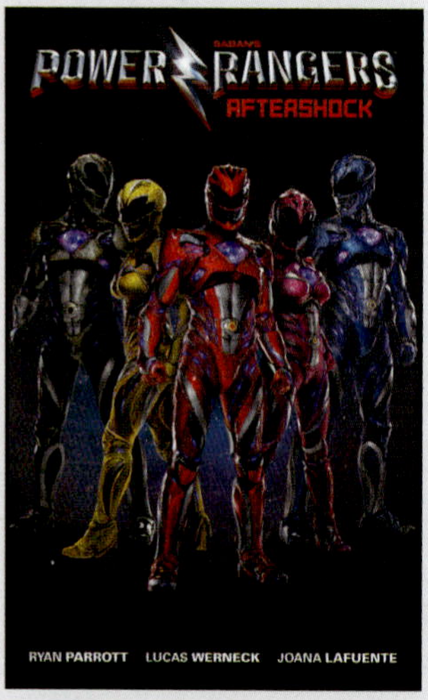
POWER RANGERS
AFTERSHOCK
RYAN PARROTT LUCAS WERNECK JOANA LAFUENTE

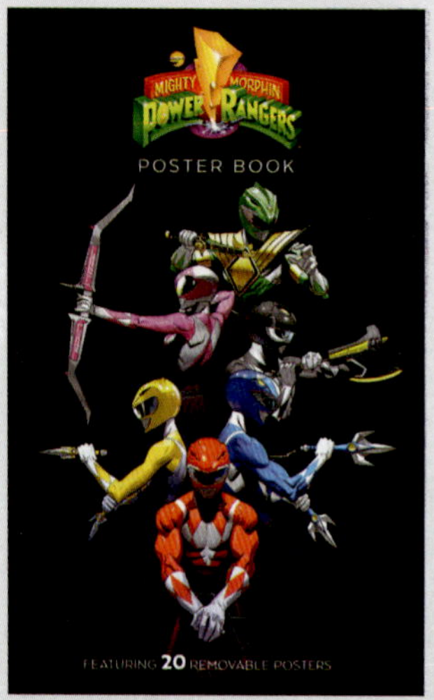
MIGHTY MORPHIN POWER RANGERS
POSTER BOOK
FEATURING 20 REMOVABLE POSTERS

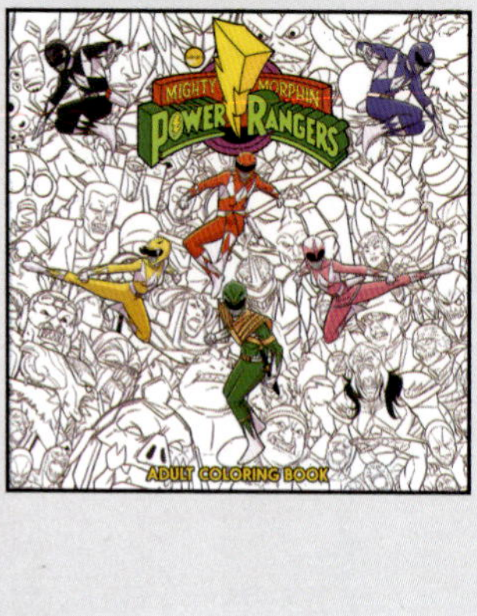
MIGHTY MORPHIN POWER RANGERS
ADULT COLORING BOOK

Mighty Morphin Power Rangers
Kyle Higgins, Hendry Prasetya, Matt Herms
Volume 1
ISBN: 978-1-60886-893-3 | $19.99
Volume 2
ISBN: 978-1-60886-942-8 | $16.99
Volume 3
ISBN: 978-1-60886-977-0 | $16.99
Volume 4
ISBN: 978-1-68415-031-1 | $16.99

Mighty Morphin Power Rangers: Pink
Kelly Thompson, Brenden Fletcher, Tini Howard, Daniele Di Nicuolo
ISBN: 978-1-60886-952-7 | $19.99

Saban's Power Rangers: Aftershock
Ryan Parrott, Lucas Werneck
ISBN: 978-1-60886-937-4 | $14.99

Mighty Morphin Power Rangers Poster Book
Goñi Montes, Jamal Campbell, Joe Quinones
ISBN: 978-1-60886-966-4 | $19.99

Mighty Morphin Power Rangers Adult Coloring Book
Goni Montes, Jamal Campbell, Hendry Prasetya
ISBN: 978-1-60886-955-8 | $16.99

Mighty Morphin Power Rangers Year One: Deluxe HC
Kyle Higgins, Hendry Prasetya, Steve Orlando
ISBN: 978-1-68415-012-0 | $75.00

BOOM! STUDIOS

AVAILABLE AT YOUR LOCAL COMICS SHOP AND BOOKSTORE
Find a comic shop near you at www.comicshoplocator.com
WWW.**BOOM-STUDIOS**.COM

Licensed by: Hasbro